ANNUAL REVIEW OF PSYCHOLOGY

VOLUME 54, 2003

SUSAN T. FISKE, *Editor*
Princeton University

DANIEL L. SCHACTER, *Associate Editor*
Harvard University

CAROLYN ZAHN-WAXLER, *Associate Editor*
National Institute of Mental Health

www.annualreviews.org   science@annualreviews.org   650-493-4400

ANNUAL REVIEWS
4139 El Camino Way • P.O. Box 10139 • Palo Alto, California 94303-0139

ANNUAL REVIEWS
Palo Alto, California, USA

International Standard Serial Number: 0066-4308
International Standard Book Number: 0-8243-0254-0
Library of Congress Catalog Card Number: 50-13143

TYPESET BY TECHBOOKS, FAIRFAX, VA
PRINTED AND BOUND BY MALLOY INCORPORATED, ANN ARBOR, MI

PREFACE

Enlightened schools and colleges all tout a lifelong love of learning as their central goal. By graduate school, love of learning somehow loses salience as a goal, perhaps because getting to that educational level is such a challenge that motivation to learn is presumed. But love of learning is under-appreciated. Scientists, teachers, and professionals (as well as those on their way to those careers) read the *Annual Reviews* precisely as a form of continuing education. Certainly serving on the editorial committee and editing the manuscripts provides the regular experience of new knowledge, thanks to the high-level job our authors do.

How would we measure our effectiveness at encouraging lifelong learning? The *Annual Review of Psychology*'s citation count is high, and we are not complaining. For example, the Institute for Scientific Information's Journal Citation Reports (both Science and Social Science Editions) measures impact, immediacy, and half-life of citations. In impact ratings, the *Annual Review* regularly ranks #2–4, along with *American Psychologist, Psychological Review*, and *Psychological Bulletin*. (The impact factor is total citations in one year to articles published in the two prior years, divided by the number of articles published in those two years; you might think of it as the number of recent citations of the average recent *Annual Review of Psychology* article.) On the cutting-edge dimension, our immediacy factor (cites to this volume's articles this year) is the highest or second highest in the two Journal Citation Reports editions. The cited half-life is about eight years; the average article receives 50% of its citations by eight years after publication. Editors can know we are picking the right authors and topics. And authors can verify that their articles are having high impact. Of course articles cited are but a fraction of articles read. Our PDF downloads of articles average over a thousand per month. And our completed requests are over 15,000 per week. Of course, articles accessed are not articles read, but perhaps the articles accessed and articles cited form the boundaries of the estimated usage by students, lecturers, autodidacts, and colleagues catching up, not to mention those writing and citing for other scientific publications. And all for the love of learning.

Susan T. Fiske, Princeton
Daniel L. Schacter, Cambridge
Carolyn Zahn-Waxler, Madison

Annual Review of Psychology
Volume 54, 2003

CONTENTS

QUALITATIVE METHODS

INDEXES

ERRATA

An online log of corrections to *Annual Review of Psychology* chapters
may be found at http://psych.annualreviews.org/errata.shtml

RELATED ARTICLES

Jerome Kagan

Annu. Rev. Psychol. 2003. 54:1–23
doi: 10.1146/annurev.psych.54.101601.145240
First published online as a Review in Advance on August 14, 2002

BIOLOGY, CONTEXT, AND DEVELOPMENTAL INQUIRY

Jerome Kagan

*Department of Psychology, Harvard University, Cambridge,
Massachusetts 02138; e-mail: jk@wjh.harvard.edu*

Key Words   maturation, temperament, infancy, psychological structures, personality

■ **Abstract**   This chapter summarizes some of the conceptual changes in developmental research over the last half-century. These advances include an acknowledgment of the role of maturation; also recognized have been the need for positing distinct psychological structures, the influence of temperament, the malleability of the infant, the role of the local context, and the dynamic nature of the categories describing human psychological types.

CONTENTS

0066-4308/03/0203-0001$14.00

INTRODUCTION

Scholarship in developmental psychology during the last half-century, the era that brackets my graduate years and this moment, has reformulated old questions and rejected premises that failed empirical challenge. Four obvious changes are evident in a comparison of papers in the journal *Child Development* during the 1950s with last year's titles. Most of the early work ignored the contributions of biology, the specificity and variety of cognitive processes, and the cumulative effects of identification with ethnic and social class groups because the discipline was shackled by a commitment to the exclusive power of external rewards to shape habit. In the 1950s Yale's department faculty was confident that a satisfying, essentially behavioristic explanation of behavior, both the ontogeny of universal qualities as well as individual variation, was attainable. John Dollard and Neal Miller declared in *Personality and Psychotherapy* that most human qualities were learned responses to drive conditions. "Human behavior is learned; precisely that behavior which is widely felt to characterize man as a rational being" (1950, p. 25). Although contemporary investigators acknowledge the relevance of conditioning mechanisms to certain domains, they appreciate that the spontaneous reorganization of concepts, rules, and beliefs that accompany brain growth and new experiences are of equal (and for some human qualities, of far greater) potency.

Although developmental psychologists, then and now, celebrate rational, pragmatic, material, and experimental analyses of functional components, only the current cohort legitimizes the symbolic representations, combined in emotions, identifications, and intentions, that need not have an obvious referent in action. Psychologists of the 1950s were constrained by the demands of operational theory, absence of measurements of brain function, and a habit of quantifying limited samples of behavior in austere laboratory settings. As a result, the evidence revealed surface phenomena rather than a deeper psychological architecture. For example, the phenomena of object permanence and stranger anxiety, which usually appear at 7–10 months of age, were treated as independent events. When psychologists learned that the brain growth that occurs at this age is accompanied by an enhanced ability to retrieve the immediate past and to compare it with the present, they recognized that both phenomena were derivatives of changes in brain function in infants living with people and objects to manipulate. The advantages of new methods enable the current cohort of investigators to peer beyond the behavioral display to infer more fundamental processes, as the student of musical composition perceives the theme hiding in the surface improvisations.

Two premises remain unchallenged. The first holds that psychological freedom is the hidden telos in development. This belief, explicit in the writings of Locke and Watson, is implicit in research reports on play, independence, and autonomy. The supposition that all children should grow toward freedom from external restraints on the perfection of self is a derivative of a political philosophy that enjoys special favor in the West, but, unfortunately, has a weak foundation in historical scholarship or ethnographies. Social scientists have permitted their ethical preferences to influence their theories.

The second favored premise that resists critique is that parental love, especially the affection from the biological mother, is necessary if children are to attain the prize of psychological freedom. The observed signs of this resource a half-century earlier were adult actions that regularly relieved the infant drive states of hunger, thirst, cold, and pain. The contemporary referents are not a well-defined set of adult behaviors but the vaguer notion of continued sensitivity to the young child's need to feel secure. Parental sensitivity and security are harder to infer than hunger or pain.

Although these two premises still penetrate much research, a number of conceptual advances have accompanied the replacement of conditioned responses with cognitive and affective processes. Six such advances are recognition of (*a*) the influence of brain maturation, (*b*) distinct psychological structures, (*c*) the role of temperament, (*d*) flaws in the assumption of infant determinism, (*e*) the importance of the contexts in which agents act, and (*f*) the dynamic nature of the categories for psychological types.

THE CONTRIBUTION OF BIOLOGICAL MATURATION

Most contemporary investigators accept the fact that brain maturation sets constraints on behavior, feeling, and cognition in the opening years. As noted earlier, the appearance of object permanence and stranger and separation fear requires an enhanced ability to retrieve schemata related to the present and to hold both structures in working memory while trying to assimilate the new event. This competence is made possible by predictable changes in brain organization. The second half of the first year is marked by accelerated growth and differentiation of pyramidal neurons, especially lengthening of dendritic terminal segments and dendritic bifurcations in layers III and V of the cortex (Koenderink et al. 1994), and sharp increases in the number of spines and extra large excrescences on the proximal dendrites of pyramidal cells in the CA3 region of Ammons horn (Seress & Mrzljak 1992). These anatomical changes are accompanied by increased glucose uptake in the lateral frontal cortex at 6–8 months, and in the dorso-lateral prefrontal cortex at 8–12 months (Chugani et al. 1987). All of these classes of growth permit retrieval of past events and a comparison of the retrieved representations with the present (KA Pelphrey, JS Reznick, B Goldman, N Sasson, J Morrow, unpublished). Hence, 8-month-old infants living in a typical social environment will cry in response to strangers and separation and will search for a toy hidden under a cover by an adult several seconds earlier. Piaget would have written a different theory to account for his acute observations if he had been born a century later. I blush as I recall telling my first undergraduate class in 1954 that a rejecting mother could create an autistic child.

The quartet of talents that emerges in the second year includes initial understanding of, and the ability to express, language; an appreciation that some actions are punishable; the capacity to infer some intentions and feelings in others; and an early form of awareness of self's feelings, intentions, and abilities. The actualization of these competences is aided by a different set of maturational events.

The accelerated elongation of the dendrites on pyramidal neurons in layer III of Wernicke's area should help the child understand spoken language, and because the axons of these neurons connect the right and left hemispheres this growth should aid not only language but other functions as well (Goldman-Rakic & Porrino 1986, Jacobson & Trojamowski 1977). Children should now show more efficient coordination of lexical categories (stored primarily in the left hemisphere) with schematic structures (stored primarily in the right) and as a result, begin to describe an event that has alerted them.

The coordination of schemata for bodily feelings with the initial corpus of semantic categories should make empathy possible, for the semantic labeling of another as "in pain" will be integrated with the retrieval of the representations that were created when the child had been distressed in the past. The coordination of representations of uncertainty or fear with semantic categories for punishable acts should cause the child to suppress behaviors that violate the family's standards. Finally, the coordination of the representations of bodily feelings with the new semantic categories for self should make consciousness possible. The fact that the number of neurons per unit volume decreases rapidly until birth and slows toward the middle of the second year led one scientist to assert that the period between 15 and 24 months was a significant moment in brain growth, when almost all layers of the cortex reached, for the first time, a similar state of maturation (Rabinowicz 1979). It is likely that equally specific anatomical and chemical changes to be discovered in the coming decades will help to explain the victories of concrete and formal operations.

THE NEED FOR VARIED PSYCHOLOGICAL FORMS

The diverse categories of behavior, cognition, and emotion require positing distinctly different psychological structures. Biologists appreciate that form is the fundamental riddle in nature, where form—or structure—is defined as a pattern of relations among a set of constituent features. Every mature natural science combines an understanding of each of its many forms with their correlated functions. Psychologists have been slower to recognize this truth because they typically study functions—actions, memories, feelings, and perceptions—and have been less interested in the psychological structures that permit those functions to be actualized. Unfortunately, function does not reveal form. It is not possible to infer the anatomy of the retina from the adult's perception of a soaring hawk, nor the form of the psychological structures that permit a two-year-old to ask about the name of an unfamiliar animal.

Although discovery of the patterns of activated neuronal ensembles that accompany a psychological reaction may illuminate the nature of the relevant psychological forms, the biological knowledge cannot be a substitute for a description of the psychological structures. The latter are an emergent property of the entire system of brain activity. The concept of robustness in systems biology provides an analogy. The ability to cope with an intrusion is a property of the entire system of biological networks and is not a property of any single constituent. That is, melancholy is a property of a mind, not of the neuronal circuits that participate in that emotional state. Although the psychological processes, and the psychological structures on which they rest, emerge from brain activity, the former cannot be reduced to or explained by a description of the latter. This means that the words used to describe the psychological events cannot be replaced with sentences that contain only biological words. Roald Hoffmann, an eminent chemist, used the example of the oxidative state of a molecule to remind us that the same conclusion holds for chemistry: "The life giving ideas of chemistry are not reducible to physics . . . . If one tries to reduce them, they wilt at the edges, lose not only their meaning, but their interest too" (Hoffmann 2001, p. 311).

Thus, the social scientist who acknowledges that thought, feeling, and action arise from cascades of brain events, but insists, nonetheless, that these events must be described in a language different from the one that describes the underlying neural processes, is not a metaphysical dualist. All of nature cannot be described with one vocabulary.

Below I discuss three distinct psychological forms: schemata, sensory motor structures, and semantic networks.

Schemata

A schema is a representation of an event, often combined with features of the context, which retains to varying degrees the patterned features of the original event (Gibson 1969, Paivio 1986, Vernon 1954). The representation of a friend's face is a prototypic example. There are at least two different schematic forms. Visceral schemata, which originate in the activity of sensory receptors in body organs, including skin, nose, tongue, muscles, and inner ear, represent states of the body. A visceral schema is activated when a person retrieves the pain of a stomach cramp or the sweetness of ice cream.

Perceptual schemata, on the other hand, are representations of external events. Infants can create some schemata with minimal experience because they are biologically prepared to perceive whole objects and do not have to connect separate features to create a representation of a face, cup, or hand. Newborns, for example, can discriminate between recordings of their own cry and the cry of another infant; two-week-olds can discriminate the breast odor of a nursing woman from many other odors (Morrongiello et al. 1998, Dondi et al. 1999, Makin & Porter 1989). Young infants attend longer to circular over linear patterns, moving over stationary objects, and contoured over homogeneous fields (Haith 1980). It is not surprising, therefore, that they quickly create schemata for human faces, which are circular, often in motion, and contain contour at the hair line, sclera, and mouth (de Haan & Nelson 1999).

Infants also create prototypic schemata that are psychological averages of a number of similar events. This phenomenon is clearest for the schemata that represent the phonemes of the child's local language (Doupe & Kuhl 1999) and for familiar objects like toy animals (Arterberry & Bornstein 2001). Infants can also construct schematic concepts for temporal patterns of meaningless vocal sounds. In a test of this idea, 7-month-olds first heard a 2-minute speech sample containing 3 representations of each of 16 different 3-syllable utterances of the form a-b-a. For example, on the first trial the infant might hear "ga-ti-ga," on the second trial, "li-no-li," and on the third trial, "bo-gu-bo." The feature shared by all utterances was that the first and third syllables were identical. After being familiarized with this pattern they heard on test trials either an utterance of the same form—a-b-a—or a new set of syllables with a new form; for example, a-b-b, as in "wo-fe-fe." The infants displayed greater attention to the unfamiliar a-b-b pattern, indicating they had created a schematic concept for the a-b-a pattern of sounds (Marcus et al. 1999).

The representations of features shared by events in two different modalities, called cross-modal processing, are also schematic concepts. Three-year-olds will point to a sad over a happy face after listening to a 20-second excerpt from a Mozart symphony in a minor key but will point to the happy face after listening to a segment in a major key (Droller 2000). Three-year-olds usually select the color red, rather than brown, as most fitting a smiling face (Zentner 2001). The ability to create cross-modal representations matures in a major way after six months, in part because the prefrontal cortex links symbolic information from different modalities, and anatomical links among sensory association areas and medial-temporal and prefrontal cortex are immature during the first six months. Cross-modal schemata are possible, but very fragile, during the first half-year.

Perceptual schemata of external events differ from visceral schemata in three important ways. First, perceptual schemata are more easily retrieved from memory. Most individuals can retrieve a rich visual representation of the Statue of Liberty visited 20 years ago but have difficulty recreating the taste of yesterday's chocolate mousse. Second, the ability to attend to, or ignore, most external events is seriously compromised for bodily sensations. Finally, visceral schemata have a weaker link to semantic structures because information from the body synapses primarily on the corticomedial and central areas of the amygdala, while visual and auditory stimuli synapse first on the lateral area. Reciprocal connections with cortical association areas are richer for the lateral than the corticomedial and central areas. One reason why questionnaires and interviews are relatively insensitive indexes of human emotional states, and why scientists code changes in face, posture, and physiology to aid inferences about an individual's emotions, is that language has a limited number of words to describe the visceral representations of bodily sensations that are the essential components of every emotion.

Sensory Motor Schemes

Representations of coordinated motor sequences permit the skilled performances of violinists and athletes, as well as implementation of each morning's automatic routines. The behaviors of seven-month-old infants illustrate the ease with which sensory motor representations are implemented. Infants first saw either a small or a large hoop while simultaneously hearing a distinctive sound accompanying each hoop. After a number of familiarization trials, the room was darkened and the infants heard one of the two sounds but could not see whether the hoop was small or large. Remarkably, the infants adjusted their hands and arms to fit the sound, for they reached with both hands to the sound that had accompanied the large hoop, but with one hand to the sound that had accompanied the small object (Clifton et al. 1991). Presumably, the schema for each hoop evoked a distinct sensory motor scheme when its particular sound was heard.

Semantic Networks

Semantic representations combine the representations of words, called lexical structures, with schemata and sensory motor structures to form networks that are logically constrained, occasionally hierarchical, and exploited to communicate information and to facilitate thought (Bickerton 1995). The distinction between schemata and semantic structures is critical. The relations among the features of my schema for a terrier who barks early in the morning (the color, size, gait, sound of bark, and spatial relations among head, ears, eyes, limbs, and tail) are different from the relations among my semantic representations of this animal, which include links among the semantic concepts dog, pet, mammal, domesticated, and annoying.

The distinctive qualities of schemata, sensory motor structures, and semantic networks have implications for current discussions of consciousness, especially whether minds experience a number of qualitatively different conscious states on the one hand, or one unified state with different features on the other (Searle 2000). Humans can be conscious of very different events, including sensations, thoughts, intentions, and symbolic categories for self. Imagining a pink cloud at dusk can be mediated by schemata with minimal contributions from semantic or motor structures. Recalling the taste of chocolate, the feeling of ice on the skin, or the pain of a cut finger differs in both brain profile and subjective state from the awareness that accompanies remembering one's childhood home, deciding whether to have a second glass of wine, brooding about one's ethnic category, or trying to solve a difficult mathematical problem. We celebrate Marcel Proust's rich descriptions of the childhood visceral schemata he retrieved when he tasted a madeleine cookie he had dipped into his tea. Most writers have been less able to capture as evocatively the feelings of a child who wakes up to find no one at home or the visceral schemata that pierce consciousness on a Christmas morning with fresh snow on the lawn and cinnamon biscuits in the oven.

TEMPERAMENT

The ancient concept of human temperaments, ignored by almost all investigators during the first half of the twentieth century, was reintroduced to psychology by Alexander Thomas and Stella Chess (1977) and gained acceptability because neuroscientists provided an empirical scaffolding for explanations of consistency in certain behaviors. Most psychologists regard this term as referring to stable profiles of mood and behavior with a biological foundation that emerge early in development, although not always in the opening weeks or months. Each temperamental category implies the possession of a particular physiology and an envelope of potential behavioral phenotypes whose final form depends on the rearing environment. A child with a temperament that protects him from excessive fear or anxiety over challenge or reprimand is likely to become a popular, accomplished ten-year-old if reared in an economically secure home with consistent socialization of aggressive behavior, but he is more likely to become a delinquent if raised by economically disadvantaged parents who are inconsistent in punishing disobedience and aggression. The varied forms that condensed water vapor can assume supply an analogy for, depending upon circumstances, the vapor can be a distinct cloud, a mackerel sky, or a dense fog. Although the cloud and fog are distinctly different in appearance, the constituents of both are identical.

Current discussions of temperament refer primarily to behavioral features because psychologists do not yet understand the relation between the inherited physiological profiles and the behavioral phenotypes. In the future, however, temperamental categories will include biological measures as part of their definition. Research on voles (a small rodent resembling a mouse) provides an example. Prairie voles pair-bond but montane voles do not. Insel and colleagues have discovered that this dramatic behavioral difference is due, in part, to a small segment of DNA in the promoter region of the gene responsible for the distribution of receptors for vasopressin (Insel & Hulihan 1995, Insel & Winslow 1999). Some human temperament types—extremely irritable infants, for example—may result in part from another genetic profile.

Mary Rothbart's synthetic writings appropriately dominate discussions of infant temperament (Rothbart 1989). Temperament, for Rothbart, refers to constitutionally based differences in reactivity and self-regulation. "Constitution" refers to relatively enduring biological processes influenced in part by heredity and in part by experience. "Reactivity" refers to the ease of arousal of motor, affective, autonomic, and endocrine responses. "Self-regulation" refers to processes that modulate reactivity, including attention, approach, withdrawal, attack, inhibition, and self-soothing.

Most investigators agree that stable displays of high or low degrees of irritability, smiling, and activity, as well as distinct profiles of attention are likely to have a temperamental contribution. Two temperamental categories, observed in the second year in response to unfamiliar events, are excessive shyness/sociability and timidity/boldness. Nancy Snidman and I, along with Mark McManis, Susan Woodward, Doreen Arcus, and many others, believe there is a relationship between these two categories and two infant profiles observable at four months of age.

Reactivity in Infants

Healthy middle-class Caucasian four-month-old infants who show vigorous motor activity and distress in response to unfamiliar visual, auditory, and olfactory stimuli are called high-reactive and comprise about 20% of similar samples. High-reactive infants tend to become shy, timid, and fearful in response to unfamiliar events in the second year (Kagan 1994). One third of the high-reactive infants become very fearful and are called inhibited. By contrast, infants who display low levels of motor activity and minimal irritability in response to the same stimuli (about 40% of most samples and called low-reactive) are biased to become sociable, relatively fearless children. One third of the low-reactive infants become minimally fearful and are called uninhibited. We believe that each temperamental type inherits a distinct neurochemistry that affects the excitability of the amygdala and/or the bed nucleus of the stria terminalis and their projections. The neurochemical profiles might involve variation in the concentration of, or distribution of receptors for, dopamine, norepinephrine, corticotropin-releasing hormone, opioids, or gamma-amino butyric acid (GABA). The potential role of the latter molecule is seen in a collaborative, and as yet unpublished, study with Kevin Nugent which revealed that the small number of newborn infants who displayed great difficulty controlling excessive distress during an examination were likely to be categorized as high-reactive when they were four months old. Because one function of GABA is to inhibit neural activation, newborns who cannot regulate their distress may possess compromised GABA function.

Longitudinal evaluations of children through age 11, from these two temperamental categories, indicate that although the specific behavioral reactions to unfamiliar events change with age—11-year-olds do not cry in response to adult strangers—a larger proportion of high- than of low-reactive children remained shy and subdued in the face of unfamiliarity, while a larger proportion of low-than of high-reactive children were sociable and affectively spontaneous in the same unfamiliar situations.

Because not all high-reactive infants become avoidant, and not all low-reactives become bold, we confront the question of how to classify high-reactive infants who did not become timid and low-reactive infants who did not become sociable. We have two choices, and which one is favored depends on the scientist's theoretical interests. On the one hand, we can emphasize the infant's temperament and continue to place sociable, spontaneous children who had been high-reactive infants in the same category with high-reactives who became inhibited. However, it is reasonable to acknowledge the obvious changes in behavioral phenotype and to classify the children in accord with both their infant temperamental category and their current behavior.

The 11-year-olds who had been classified as high- or low-reactive at 4 months were administered a 3-hour battery that included measurements of autonomic and brain functions. The pre-adolescents who had been classified as high-reactive infants showed greater electroencephalogram (EEG) activation (loss of alpha band power) on the right than on the left parietal area (McManis et al. 2002), and, if classified as fearful in the second year, greater activation in the right frontal area (see Fox 1991). The high-reactives also showed larger brain stem-evoked potentials from the inferior colliculus in response to a series of clicks (Woodward et al. 2001), and a larger negative wave form between 400 and 1000 msec in the event-related potential in response to discrepant visual stimuli. The possession of a more excitable amygdala among the high-reactives could desynchronize alpha frequencies in the cortex, potentiate the evoked potential from the inferior colliculus, and contribute to an enhanced event-related potential to unfamiliar events. However, a small number of 11-year-olds who had been high-reactives and in addition displayed this biological profile were not especially shy or subdued—that is, the biology presumed to be the foundation of the infant category was preserved to some degree, even though the behavioral phenotype of these children had changed over time. Thus, in some theoretical contexts it is useful to distinguish, within a group of high-reactives, the shy children from the sociable ones. However, on other occasions, it is theoretically more fruitful to distinguish between children who had been high- or low-reactive at four months and to ignore their current social behavior.

The genes that contribute to high and low reactivity may be pleiotropic and contribute to body size and eye color as well. One of every four 11-year-olds who had been a high-reactive infant was small in size and had blue eyes, compared with only one of 20 low-reactive infants. The tame silver foxes that were the product of 20 generations of interbreeding tame with tame animals on a Siberian farm showed more flexible ears and tails and a unique distribution of melanin in the fur than the less tame foxes. These facts suggest that the genes contributing to the tame behavior may influence physical features that, on the surface, seem unrelated to the behavioral phenotype (Trut 1999).

The Ambiguity of Measures

Many scientists assume that the relationships among variables presumed to reflect a psychological or biological process are essentially the same across all individuals, especially if the sample consists of volunteers free of pathology. A typical report notes the age and gender distribution of the sample and occasionally mentions social class, but rarely do authors describe some biological features of their subjects. Psychologists are reluctant to acknowledge that individuals with different physiological profiles might display different relations among the same set of variables. For example, investigators will report correlations between biological and psychological measures in a volunteer sample but fail to parse the sample into those who are high or low on some other relevant biological variable, like body size or sympathetic reactivity in the cardiovascular system. Psychological and biological processes occur together within a person, and the individual's particular biology often affects the nature of the relations among the variables of interest.

Our research on temperament is illustrative. About 5% of our large sample of Caucasian children showed a combination of high reactivity at four months, high levels of fear in response to unfamiliar events in the second year, and extreme shyness with strangers during the school years. If we add to the above three features a small body size, blue eyes, right hemisphere activation in the EEG, and a large evoked potential from the inferior colliculus, this category represents about 3% of middle-class Caucasian children. This small group is a meaningful psychological category. That is, rather than regard small size and blue eyes as correlates of a high reactivity, it might be theoretically useful for some arguments to claim that 3% of middle-class Caucasian children combine high reactivity in infancy, high fear in the second year, childhood shyness, a small body size, and blue eyes.

A second illustration involves several variables quantified on our 11-year-old longitudinal subjects: a stable profile of shy or sociable behavior at both 7 and 11 years, lateral asymmetry of alpha power in the EEG, and resting heart rate. Boys who were low-reactive as infants and who had right frontal activation in the EEG at age 11 were sociable and spontaneous; high-reactive boys with right frontal activation were not sociable. High-reactive girls who were shy had high resting heart rates; low-reactive girls who were shy did not. Finally, the relation between the number of comments the child made to the examiner and resting heart rate was low across all 237 children ($r = 0.03$). But high-reactive boys showed a significant positive correlation between spontaneous comments and heart rate. Thus, the relations among behavioral and biological variables can vary with temperament and gender. These facts imply that the meaning of a behavioral or biological variable can be ambiguous until additional qualities of the subjects are specified.

DOUBTS ABOUT INFANT DETERMINISM

The attractiveness of human development to college seniors planning graduate study is based, in part, on the popular assumption that early experiences create psychological structures that persist for an indefinite time. The two beliefs hiding in this Platonic conception are, first, that the dispositions established in early childhood persist and, second, that they will be actualized in different contexts because, like skin color, they are stable features that belong to the child. These assumptions form the basis for the belief held by many European and American commentators that some habits wrought by the events of infancy cannot be abrogated. This premise has deep historical roots. One commentator wrote nearly 80 years ago, "the powerful significance of the intellectual processes—perception, fantasy, thinking, and their social results in science, art, and philosophy in the human being—have their first roots in the specifically human mental structures of the three month old child . . . Historically, all phenomena of adult mental life must be traceable to birth" (Bernfeld 1929).

Why have many social scientists been persuaded of the permanent power of the early years, especially when evolutionary biologists have demonstrated that the persistence of a feature over generations depends on its adaptive value in a particular ecological niche? One clue lies with the social conditions in eighteenth-century Europe. A growing number of wives of merchants and skilled artisans, freed of the responsibility of gathering wood, tending animals, and weeding vegetable plots, were assigned the task of socializing their infants. A well-nurtured child who married the proper partner and mastered the skills that led to positions of prestige in the community would enhance the family's status. As the children of the bourgeoisie lost their economic value, they became investments in the family's future pride, and middle-class parents began to view them as objects of sentiment and pleasure rather than as a source of labor needed for family survival.

Second, because eighteenth-century European society had become socially more mobile, it was possible for the son of a blacksmith to rise in the social hierarchy and for the son of a squire to fall. Change in social class position became simultaneously a hope and a fear and, therefore, a source of uncertainty for families located in the middle, most vulnerable, rungs of the class ladder. When a source of uncertainty permeates the consciousness of a large segment of a society, an explanation will be invented that is reasonable and, more important, implies actions that, if taken, will reduce the number of sleepless nights filled with worry. The suggestion that certain maternal behaviors guarantee the development of character traits necessary for a successful future and, as a result, protect the family against a descent in status, rationalized ritual practices that swept some of the anxiety away. But if mothers did not nurture their infants properly, their children would become vulnerable to a dull mind, a wild spirit, and a downward spiral.

It has proven difficult, however, to demonstrate that experiences of the infant years determine profiles during childhood or adolescence. The orphans produced by World War II and the Korean conflict, who had fragile bonds to any caretaker, developed reasonably well after adoption by nurturing foster parents (Rathbun et al. 1958; Winick et al. 1975). One group of frightened, quiet two- to four-year-olds, who had been raised in an overcrowded institution with few caretakers, were subsequently enrolled in regular play sessions with adults and children. The restrained affect apparently caused by the indifference of caretakers lifted after less than two years and the emotional vitality seen in most four-year-olds emerged (Flint 1966).

The Influence of Social Class

A longitudinal study of children born and reared on the Hawaiian isle of Kauai revealed that about 15% had serious academic or conduct problems during adolescence. The best predictor of these problems was the social class of the family. Over 80% of those with problems came from the poorest segment of the sample; only one upper-middle-class child developed a psychological problem. But the conditions that define social class have a continuing influence on the child; they are not limited to the first year or two of life (Werner & Smith 1982). Social class also has a far more profound influence on children's development than the fact of surrogate care. Regular attendance in a day-care center, or in another form of surrogate care, does not produce children who are very different from those raised at home, as long as the children come from the same social class and ethnic background (NICHD Early Child Care Research Network 2001).

No scientist has been able to demonstrate that a particular set of experiences during the first two years in children growing up in typical American or European homes produces a particular adolescent or adult outcome in even one-tenth of those exposed to those experiences. An extreme level of deprivation, such as existed in the Romanian day-care centers a decade ago, does produce an undesirable outcome (O'Connor et al. 2000). But this degree of deprivation is rare in most families, even poor ones; and, as noted above, some of the severely deprived children become resilient after adoption by nurturing parents.

One reason why long-term preservation of early qualities, and of the representations on which they are based, is unlikely is that the brain is immature during the first two years. The frontal lobes, which evaluate information from the environment and the body, are not fully connected to the rest of the brain during the first year. As a result, emotional experiences are not evaluated, and it is likely that many early memories are lost. Few adults can remember episodes that occurred before their third birthday.

The most important argument against the doctrine of infant determinism flows from the hypothesis that infants, like adults, are influenced primarily by events that are discrepant from their usual experience, rather than by a particular experience qua experience. The most formative discrepancies are those that violate the child's symbolic interpretations, and children do not regularly interpret experience symbolically until their third birthday. These symbolic constructions are more critical determinants of future anxiety, depression, apathy, or anger than the events of the first year. Palestinian youths throw stones at Israeli soldiers because they believe that the Israeli government has unjustly oppressed their ethnic group. Their violent behavior is not traceable to the parental treatment they received as infants. No smiling African-American infant knows of the history of oppression of blacks or the remaining pockets of racism in American society. The realization that there is prejudice will not form until these children are five or six years old.

The psychological products created by the first two years will be preserved only if the environment sustains them. Infants living in poverty have more frequent colds and bouts of diarrhea than those in affluent homes; adults raised in poverty are more likely to have strokes, heart attacks, and sexually transmitted diseases than those raised in affluence. But the higher rates of morbidity among poor adults are not the result of having more colds and diarrhea in the first two years of life. They are due to the continuity, over years, of a poorer diet, greater life stress, and less adequate medical care. The advocates of infant determinism fail to award sufficient power to the experiences of later childhood, many of which are correlated with social class.

Other Conditions of Influence

The child's birth order, profile of identifications, cultural context, and historical era also critically influence development, but these factors are not operative during the infant years. For example, first-, compared with later-born, children from middle-class American homes attain better grades in schools, are more often valedictorians of their high school class, and are more often listed in *Who's Who in America* (Altus 1966, Sampson & Hancock 1967, Sulloway 1996).

Identifications with class and ethnic categories affect certain aspects of development. Children, like adults, feel pride (or shame) when they learn about the experiences of another person (or group) with whom they believe they share essential features. The ethical values of most adolescents are more similar to those of their parents and other relatives whom they respect than to those of randomly selected individuals. Because identification with a family in poverty can generate shame, guilt, or anger in societies where many live in affluence, poverty can create a physiological state that contributes to the poorer physical and psychological health among those who are disadvantaged. The divergent patterns of development in children from different social classes are analogous to the developmental fates of young embryonic cells, which are determined by their spatial position. Whether a cell becomes part of the retina or a pigment cell in the skin is a function of where it is in the young embryo. Analogously, the psychological profiles of adolescents are determined in a major way by their family's place in the social class hierarchy of their society. However, identification with a class category does not emerge until after the fifth birthday.

Finally, the historical era during which the adolescent years are spent often has a profound effect on adult values. The new cognitive capacities of adolescents motivate them to probe their assumptions about self and society in an attempt to remove inconsistencies between their childhood ideas and their understanding of the present. Adolescents are unusually receptive to historical events that challenge existing premises as they synthesize the assumptions they will rely on for the rest of their lives. Youth in Kosovo have witnessed cruelties that will make deep skeptics of their generation even if they had caring parents during the first year. Samuel Beckett probably exploited his adolescent memory of the anarchy that tore through Ireland in the early decades of the last century when he had one of the tramps in *Waiting for Godot* say, "This is becoming really insignificant" and had the other tramp reply, "Not enough." The consequences of sibling order, identification, and historical era, which can produce sharp discontinuities in development, have little relevance during the first two years. As William Greenough wrote, "To focus upon the first three years and to downplay the later years is not warranted, by either human behavioral or neuroscience research" (Greenough 1997, p. 19).

CONTEXTS AND SOURCES OF EVIDENCE

The willingness to attribute power to the context of observation—i.e., to acknowledge that many conclusions must be restricted to the specific behavior displayed in a particular situation—is a fruitful product of the last few decades. Hala & Russell

(2001) provide a stunning example of the significance of the context of observation. A three-year-old watches an examiner place a piece of candy in one of two boxes. An accomplice of the examiner then enters the room and the examiner tells the child to point to the box where the piece of candy is hidden. The child had been told earlier that if the child showed the accomplice the correct box, the adult would get the treat and the child would not. But if the child pointed to the box not containing the candy, the child would enjoy the sweet. If the child is told to use his finger to point to the box, he is "honest" and points to the box containing the candy. But the child given a mechanical pointer is more likely to point to the box that does not contain the candy. That is, simply changing the way the child indicates which box contains the prize affects behavior in a serious way (Hala & Russell 2001).

The assumption that a particular behavior, or biological reaction, maintains the same meaning across different incentives and contexts is retarding theoretical progress. Consider the following two assumptions regarding a rat that has experienced several light-followed-by-shock trials: 1. that the duration of bodily immobility ("freezing") or the magnitude of potentiated startle in response to the light means that the rat is in a state of "fear"; and 2. that absence of freezing or potentiation of startle implies absence of (or minimal) "fear." The second assumption is inconsistent with the fact that a conditioned startle reaction is muted if the shock used in training is very intense. Although a rat with a lesioned amygdala shows minimal freezing, implying low fear, the same animal will defecate in the place where it was shocked, implying some form of fear state (Antoniadis & McDonald 2000). Thus, the meaning of "freezing" or startle depends on the specific context and "response in a context" should be the proper construct.

Put differently, the brain structures that must be intact in order for Pavlovian conditioning of a particular response to occur depend on the specific response. If the response is an eye blink to a puff of air applied to the cornea the cerebellum is necessary. If the response is bodily freezing the amygdala and central grey area are necessary. The assumption that an animal is in a state of fear when a stimulus produces conditioned freezing may be unwarranted. Investigators who apply an air puff to the cornea do not ascribe a fear state if the subject blinks in response to a conditioned stimulus that precedes the air puff.

Too many psychological concepts are indifferent to the species, response, and particular situation in which a behavior occurs. As a result, words like fear and aggression are often used to describe an animal's state. The authors of a recent essay in the journal *Trends in Neuroscience* on the molecular basis of aggression in animals never defined aggression; they simply assumed that a mouse biting an intruder belongs to the same psychological category as an adolescent bullying a peer (Nelson & Chiavegatto 2001). However, an intention to harm another, which is absent in mice, is an essential feature of all human acts we call aggressive. These authors would probably not regard termite destruction of a house as an instance of aggressive insect behavior; they should display the same caution when describing mice.

The problem lies with the borrowing of predicates intended to apply to human behavior and attributing the same meaning to these words when applying them to animals. This practice tends to occur because there is a smaller number of distinct verbs than nouns for different living forms. A relatively accurate inference regarding an object is less dependent on the attached predicate. This fact is an instance of the more general principle that there are fewer functions, mathematical or empirical, than there are entities participating in those functions (e.g., physical and biological objects display curvilinear functions). The predicate "fall" can apply to a child, rock, leaf, building, or meteor. The psychological meaning of "bit" in the sentence "The boy bit his brother" is not the same as its meaning in "The mouse bit the intruder." Unfortunately, English does not have a word other than "bit" to describe the animal's behavior. Thus the behavioral biologist selects this word but assumes, incorrectly, that the act is aggressive in intent whether it occurs in humans or animals. Because the meaning of a predicate often varies with the agent—that is why the ancient Romans used different words for the act of kissing when the actor was a mother or a lover—neurobiologists should be careful when they apply to animals verbs that are intended to describe human behavior (Magnusson 2000).

Sources of Evidence

Scientists should recognize the wisdom in Bohr's insistence that the meaning of a scientific construct cannot be separated from the source of its evidence. Fear has one meaning when the referent is a rat freezing in response to a conditioned stimulus that had been paired with electric shock, but a different meaning when a child says that she is afraid of failing an examination. Similarly, "possession of a number concept" has one meaning if the evidence comes from infants looking longer at six dots after being familiarized with two dots, but a different meaning when an adolescent correctly divides 1362 by 18.5.

Consider a third example of the importance of the source of evidence. Four-month-olds facing an adult who is playing peek-a-boo with them first saw a happy face on the adult for three successive trials. On the fourth trial, some infants saw the adult display a fear face, some saw an angry face, and a third group saw a sad face. The infants looked longer at the first two expressions but did not devote longer attention to the sad face. That fact does not mean that they did not discriminate the sad from the happy face for the infants showed distinct changes in facial expression in response to the sad demeanor (Montague & Walker-Andrews 2001). Absence of increased attention does not always mean a failure of discrimination; presence of increased attention does not always mean that a child is surprised by a discrepant event.

Failure to appreciate that changing the source of evidence can alter the meaning of a construct poses a problem because contemporary students of development belong to distinct groups that are defined, in part, by method. Investigators concerned with pathology or social problems find it hard to obtain relevant information by bringing children into a laboratory and are forced to ask informants, or the child, about behaviors and moods. These scientists assume that a parent's or a teacher's verbal descriptions of a child's aggression, restlessness, or fearfulness is almost as good as observing the child directly. This assumption is overly optimistic (Baillargeon et al. 2001).

A Critique of Self-Report

The distinction noted above between schemata and semantic structures is relevant here because the most popular personality and temperamental dimensions are based on the semantic structures activated when children or adults answer questionnaires. However, different personality and temperamental types would be inferred if the thousands of people who filled out these questionnaires had been filmed for 10 hours a month over a six-month period in different contexts and those observations had been factor-analyzed. Answers to questionnaires represent a particular type of evidence.

Several problems trail the use of questionnaires and interviews as the sole basis for inferring psychological qualities. First, each semantic representation of a trait is related to other semantic categories. A mother who affirms on a questionnaire that her child likes meeting new children is biased to respond affirmatively to all questions semantically related to that statement in order to maintain semantic consistency. Terms like sociable and shy are antonyms; the features linked to each word are inversely correlated in the semantic networks of most respondents. Because most parents treat the semantic concepts happy and sad as antonyms, parents who say their infants laugh frequently will resist describing them as irritable, even though films of infants reveal a large group who both laugh and cry frequently.

Second, if a psychological trait does not have a popular name and therefore is not part of a semantic network, questionnaires do not include relevant items. Variation in the degree of ambivalence over one's motives, energy level, intensity and quality of sexual arousal, and degree of virtue assigned to self—four qualities that influence life choices—are not easily measured with questionnaires.

Of equal importance is the fact that children and adults vary in the biological activity that contributes to conscious feelings and chronic moods. However, few individuals have conscious access to these bodily events and, therefore, children and adults cannot be asked about them on questionnaires. Two parents could report equivalent irritation with their child but differ in the degree of noradrenergic activity that occurs when the child disobeys.

Further, children described similarly by a parent can be very different biologically. For example, the mothers of our longitudinal subjects ranked 28 statements descriptive of their child. A group of boys described as having "high energy" contained two very different types of children. The low-reactive boys with this description were low in beta power in the EEG and showed greater left than right activation in the frontal and parietal areas. The high-reactive boys assigned the same trait by their parent did not display these two biological features. A second illustration comes from the children in this sample who described themselves as "happy most of the time." The boys who described themselves this way, who had been low-reactive infants, showed left frontal activation in the EEG. The other children who described themselves as equally happy did not display this property. This fact suggests that the low-reactive boys may have based their judgment on internal feeling tone, while most of the other children used their life conditions. Even if this interpretation is incorrect, the evidence indicates that different categories of children can provide the same self-descriptions.

On some occasions, questionnaire evidence leads to conclusions that violate both biology and common sense. One team interviewed 794 pairs of adult female twins about their physical health and emotional states. The replies to the questions posed by a stranger revealed, surprisingly, that self-esteem was as heritable as physical health (Kendler et al. 2000). Had the evidence consisted of a physical examination, with blood and urine tests and direct observations of behavior, I suspect the results would have been very different. For these reasons, conclusions about a child's psychological features based only on questionnaires or interviews have a meaning that is as limited as Ptolemy's conclusions about the cosmos based on the reports of observers staring at the night sky without telescopes.

CLASSIFICATION OF TEMPERAMENT
AND PERSONALITY

Recent essays critical of the concept of biological species may have useful implications for conceptions of temperamental and personality types (Hey 2001, Schilthuizen 2001). The new theorists argue that species are not natural objects defined by a small number of fixed features but constructs invented to serve the human addiction to categorizing experience. Animal groups vary over time on a correlated number of dimensions and features. The conditions that exist during a particular era create correlational patterns among features that include (a) genes, (b) anatomical, physiological, and behavioral properties, some derivative of the genome, and (c) the local ecology. Each cluster of related features can be treated as a category, but a new category may be theoretically fruitful when one or more features change. Pet beagles in American represent one cluster; wild dogs in Zaire represent another. Should the beagle and wild dog mate, the offspring belong to a new cluster.

The relevant features that define personality types include: (a) the individual's temperament, derivative in part from the genome, (b) current physiological profile, (c) psychological properties created by past experience, and (d) contexts of action. Imagine a hypothetical cluster consisting of a high-reactive infant with a low density of GABA receptors in the medulla and the limbic system, socialization by a middle-class family that promotes conformity and anxiety over error, and residence in a large metropolitan area in the United States. This cluster defines a psychological type. However, if we change the residence to an isolated village in

New Guinea but keep everything else the same, a different category is warranted. If we change only the biology, so that the child has a high density of GABA receptors, another psychological category is actualized. And if we change the historical era to second-century Gaul as the Roman empire was collapsing, still another type would be proper.

Psychiatric categories of mental illness emphasize self-descriptions of feeling and behavior and ignore the patient's biology, contexts, and historical era. Hysterical paralyses, which were prevalent in 1900, are rare today, while attention deficit disorder has become a more frequent diagnosis than it was a century earlier. John Cheever and Alice James, born only a century apart, appear to have inherited a similar temperamental bias for depression. But they differed in the interpretation of their states and in their coping strategies because they were born in different historical eras. Danish citizens who live in Copenhagen are at twice the risk for schizophrenia as Danes who live in the rural areas of Denmark (Pedersen & Mortensen 2001). A 50-year-old man in New York City who insists that he talks to God regularly would be classified as psychotic. But few psychiatrists would apply the same diagnosis to a Muslim who blows himself up in a suicide attack because he is certain that the action permits him entrance to paradise. A restless seven-year-old American child doing poorly in school who possesses a neurochemistry characterized by dopamine deficiency in the frontal lobes would be classified as having attention deficit hyperactivity disorder (ADHD), but a child with exactly the same biology would not belong to this category if he lived with a family who raised goats in an isolated Tibetan village without any school.

Ordinary citizens in their daily interactions acknowledge the significance of the context of a person's statement. Most adults would interpret the declaration "I wish I were dead" in different ways depending upon their knowledge of the speaker's mood and past events. This declaration from a friend who had committed a minor faux pas would be ignored; the same statement from a friend who has been suffering from cancer for two years would be taken seriously. I do not suggest that every context invites the invention of a new category; only that investigators should not automatically assume that the central feature of a psychological category is a particular behavior or verbal description of motive, feeling, or action free of any contextual constraints.

For many contemporary psychologists, psychological types resemble biological species as traditionally defined. That is, a psychological category is defined by a set of fundamental features (for example, a depressed mood). This position regards the context in which the individual acts as irrelevant. A reform position holds that when the context of action affects the relations among the defining features it should be included in the definition of the category. Thus, a salesman living in suburban Chicago with a spouse and two children who meets the criteria for extraversion would have to be reclassified if he lost his family in a motor vehicle accident and took a job as a forest ranger in a remote village in rural Manitoba. The earlier reference to the products of water vapor is appropriate.

The air in most locations contains some condensed water vapor, but whether that vapor is classified as fog, cloud, or neither depends on the local context. The products of a gene depend on its location in the body. Similarly, every contemporary category in personality and pathology requires specifying the contexts of its actualization.

CONCLUSIONS

The scholarship of the last 50 years invites a skeptical posture toward the simple, aesthetically pleasing perspectives that dominated psychology in the middle of the twentieth century. Contemporary scientists are more receptive to the suggestion that the meaning of most behavioral and biological reactions depends on the context; brain profiles and behavior are not always closely yoked; schemata, sensory motor structures, and semantic representations represent distinct psychological forms; and maturation of the central nervous system modulates development.

Because personal history affects each person's reactions to an event, developmental evidence should be a component in a great deal of psychological research. An agent's history is as significant for her contemporary thought, feeling, and action as the evolutionary history of a species is for its form and physiology. The challenge for psychologists is to invent methods that might reveal the early consequences of that history; the challenge for neuroscientists is to devise machines and analytic programs that can detect in brain patterns the psychological structures that originated years earlier in interpretations of childhood encounters. I am not certain that either victory is possible. That is, it is not obvious that the evidence produced by the most sophisticated examination of the brain of the writer Frank Kermode could ever reveal a childhood identification with a poor family—an identification that became a critical feature of his behaviors and moods. If this claim proves valid, prediction of the psychological reaction to an incentive from contemporary evidence alone must remain imperfect.

The deep disappointment among twentieth-century mathematicians was Gödel's formal proof that incompleteness, and therefore lack of certainty, was an inherent feature of every set of axioms. Scholars vary in the strength of their conviction that a creative mind, sitting alone in a quiet room manipulating propositions, linguistic or mathematical, can discover deep truths about nature. Biologists are more skeptical of this assumption than physicists. But the intellectual heroes celebrated in college lecture halls in Europe and America are more often Einstein, Heisenberg, Shrödinger, and Dirac than Sherrington, Cushing, Cajal, or Yalow, because formal arguments generate greater aesthetic satisfaction among members of our culture than empirical discoveries whose beauty is tainted by lists of exceptions. There is a fable of a king who asked his wisest advisors to reduce to one word the knowledge contained in all of the volumes in the palace's library. After years of work, the scholars brought the king a piece of paper on which was written the single word "maybe."

ACKNOWLEDGMENTS

I thank Nancy Snidman, Mark McManis, Susan Woodward, Robin Schacht, Eric Peterson, Melissa Lewis, Tracey Shissler, Rosa Arriaga, Steven Reznick, Vali Kahn, and many other students for their contributions to the longitudinal research on temperament supported by the John D. and Catherine T. MacArthur Foundation, W.T. Grant Foundation, Bial Foundation, and NIMH.

The *Annual Review of Psychology* is online at http://psych.annualreviews.org

LITERATURE CITED

Altus WD. 1966. Birth order and its sequelae. *Science* 151:44–49

Antoniadis EA, McDonald RJ. 2000. Amygdala, hippocampus, and discriminative conditioning to context. *Behav. Brain Res.* 108:1–9

Arterberry ME, Bornstein MH. 2001. Three month old infants' categorization of animals and vehicles based on static and dynamic attributes. *J. Exp. Child Psychol.* 80:333–46

Baillargeon RH, Boulerice B, Tremblay RE, Joccolillo M, Vitaro F, Kohen DE. 2001. Modeling inter-informant agreement in the absence of a gold standard. *J. Child Psychol. Psychiatry Allied Discipl.* 42:463–73

Bernfeld S. 1929. *The Psychology of the Infant.* New York: Brentanos

Bickerton D. 1995. *Language and Human Behavior.* Seattle: Univ. Wash. Press

Chugani HT, Phelps ME, Mazziotta JC. 1987. Positron emission tomography study of human brain functional development. *Ann. Neurol.* 22:487–97

Clifton RK, Rochat P, Litovsky RY, Perris EE. 1991. Object representation guides infants reaching in the dark. *J. Exp. Psychol.: Hum. Percept. Perform.* 17:323–29

de Haan M, Nelson CA. 1999. Brain activity differentiates face and object processing in six-month-old infants. *Dev. Psychol.* 35:1113–21

Dollard J, Miller NE. 1950. *Personality and Psychotherapy.* New York: McGraw-Hill

Dondi M, Simion F, Caltran G. 1999. Can newborns discriminate between their own cry and the cry of another newborn infant? *Dev. Psychol.* 35:418–26

Doupe AJ, Kuhl PK. 1999. Bird song and human speech. *Annu. Rev. Neurosci.* 22:567–631

Droller ME. 2000. *The modality of music and its effects on childrens' perceptions.* Honors thesis. Harvard Univ.

Flint BM. 1966. *The Child in the Institution.* Toronto: Univ. Toronto Press

Fox NA. 1991. If it's not left, it's right. *Am. Psychol.* 46:863–72

Gibson EJ. 1969. *Principles of Perceptual Learning and Development.* New York: Appleton Century Crofts

Goldman-Rakic P, Porrino LJ. 1986. The primate mediodorsal (MD) nucleus and its projections to the frontal lobe. *J. Comp. Neurol.* 242:535–60

Greenough WJ. 1997. We can't focus just on ages zero to three. *Monitor* 28:19

Haith MM. 1980. *Rules That Babies Look By.* Hillsdale, NJ: Erlbaum

Hala S, Russell J. 2001. Executive control within strategic deception: a window on early cognitive development. *J. Exp. Child Psychol.* 80:112–41

Hey J. 2001. *Categories and Species.* New York: Oxford Univ. Press

Hoffmann R. 2001. Hi O Silver. *Am. Sci.* 89:311–13

Insel TR, Hulihan TJ. 1995. A gender specific mechanism for pair bonding. *Behav. Neurosci.* 109:782–89

Insel TR, Winslow JT. 1999. The neurobiology of social attachment. In *Neurobiology of*

Mental Illness, ed. DS Charney, EJ Nestler, BS Bunney, pp. 880–90. New York: Oxford

Jacobson S, Trojamowski JQ. 1977. Prefrontal granular cortex of the rhesus monkey. *Brain Res.* 132:235–46

Kagan J. 1994. *Galen's Prophecy*. New York: Basic Books

Kendler KS, Myers JM, Neale MC. 2000. A multi-dimensional twin study of mental health in women. *Am. J. Psychiatry* 157:506–17

Koenderink MJJ, Uylings HBM, Mrzljak L. 1994. Postnatal maturation of the layer III pyramidal neurons in the human prefrontal cortex. *Brain Res.* 653:173–82

Magnusson D. 2000. The individual as the organizing principle in psychological inquiry. In *Developmental Sciences and the Holistic Approach*, ed. LR Bergman, RB Cairns, LG Nilsson, L Nystedt, pp. 33–47. Mahwah, NJ: Erlbaum

Makin JW, Porter RH. 1989. Attractiveness of lactating females' breast odors to neonates. *Child Dev.* 60:803–10

Marcus GF, Vijayan S, Rao S, Bandi L, Vishton PM. 1999. Rule learning by seven month old infants. *Science* 283:77–80

McManis MH, Kagan J, Snidman NC, Woodward SA. 2002. EEG asymmetry, power, and temperament in children. *Dev. Psychobiol.* In press

Montague DPF, Walker-Andrews AS. 2001. Peek-a-boo: a new look at infants' perception of emotion expressions. *Dev. Psychol.* 37:826–38

Morrongiello BA, Fenwick KD, Chance G. 1998. Cross-modal learning in newborn infants. *Infant Behav. Dev.* 21:543–54

Nelson RJ, Chiavegatto S. 2001. Molecular basis of aggression. *Trends Neurosci.* 24:713–18

NICHD Early Child Care Res. Network. 2001. Nonmaternal care and family factors in early development. *Appl. Dev. Psychol.* 22:457–92

O'Connor TG, Rutter M, Beckett C, Keaveney L, Kreppner JM. 2000. The effects of global severe privation on cognitive competence. *Child Dev.* 71:376–90

Paivio A. 1986. *Mental Representations*. New York: Oxford

Pedersen CB, Mortensen PB. 2001. Evidence of a dose response relationship between urbanicity during upbringing and schizophrenia risk. *Arch. Gen. Psychiatry* 58:1039–46

Pelphrey KA, Reznick JS, Goldman B, Sasson N, Morrow J, et al. The development of working memory. Unpublished

Rabinowicz T. 1979. The differentiated maturation of the human cerebral cortex. In *Human Growth*, ed. F Falkner, JM Tanner, 3:97–123. New York: Plenum

Rathbun C, DiVirgilio L, Waldfogel S. 1958. A restitutive process in children following radical separation from family and culture. *Am. J. Orthopsychiatry* 28:408–15

Rothbart MK. 1989. Temperament in childhood. In *Temperament in Childhood*, ed. GA Kohnstamn, JE Bates, MK Rothbart, pp. 59–73. New York: Wiley

Sampson EE, Hancock FT. 1967. An examination of the relationship between ordinal position, personality and conformity. *J. Personal. Soc. Psychol.* 5:398–407

Schilthuizen M. 2001. *Frogs, Flies, and Dandelions*. Oxford: Oxford Univ. Press

Searle J. 2000. Consciousness. *Annu. Rev. Neurosci.* 23:557–78

Seress L, Mrzljak L. 1992. Postnatal development of mossy cells in the human dentate gyrus. *Hippocampus* 2:127–42

Sulloway F. 1996. *Born to Rebel*. New York: Pantheon

Thomas A, Chess S. 1977. *Temperament and Development*. New York: Brunner-Mazel

Trut LN. 1999. Early canid domestication: the farm-fox experiment. *Am. Sci.* 87:162–71

Vernon MD. 1954. *A Further Study of Perception*. Cambridge: Cambridge Univ. Press

Werner EE, Smith RS. 1982. *Vulnerable but Invincible*. New York: McGraw-Hill

Winick M, Meyer KK, Harris RC. 1975. Malnutrition and environmental enrichment by early adoption. *Science* 190:1173–75

Woodward SA, McManis MH, Kagan J, Deldin P, Snidman N, et al. 2001. Infant temperament and the brain stem auditory evoked response in later childhood. *Dev. Psychol.* 37:533–38

Zentner MR. 2001. Preferences for colors and color-emotion combinations in early childhood. *Dev. Sci.* 4:389–98

Annu. Rev. Psychol. 2003. 54:25–53
doi: 10.1146/annurev.psych.54.101601.145237
Copyright © 2003 by Annual Reviews. All rights reserved
First published online as a Review in Advance on August 14, 2002

ADDICTION

Terry E. Robinson and Kent C. Berridge
*Department of Psychology (Biopsychology Program), University of Michigan, Ann Arbor,
Michigan 48109-1109; e-mail: ter@umich.edu, berridge@umich.edu*

Key Words   sensitization, learning, nucleus accumbens, dopamine, drug abuse

■ **Abstract**   The development of addiction involves a transition from casual to compulsive patterns of drug use. This transition to addiction is accompanied by many drug-induced changes in the brain and associated changes in psychological functions. In this article we present a critical analysis of the major theoretical explanations of how drug-induced alterations in psychological function might cause a transition to addiction. These include: (*a*) the traditional hedonic view that drug pleasure and subsequent unpleasant withdrawal symptoms are the chief causes of addiction; (*b*) the view that addiction is due to aberrant learning, especially the development of strong stimulus-response habits; (*c*) our incentive-sensitization view, which suggests that sensitization of a neural system that attributes incentive salience causes compulsive motivation or "wanting" to take addictive drugs; and (*d*) the idea that dysfunction of frontal cortical systems, which normally regulate decision making and inhibitory control over behavior, leads to impaired judgment and impulsivity in addicts.

CONTENTS

                                                                    25

INTRODUCTION

Many people experiment with potentially addictive drugs. About 60% of Americans sample an illicit drug at least once in their lifetime, and even after excluding marijuana, the lifetime prevalence for illicit drug use is about 32% (Johnston et al. 2001). If alcohol is included, the percentage of Americans exposed to a potentially addictive drug rises to over 90%, but few of these people become addicts. Even for a very addictive drug like cocaine, only 15–16% of people become addicted within 10 years of first use (Wagner & Anthony 2002). Substantial numbers of people do become addicts, of course, but the fact remains that drug use does not inevitably lead to addiction. Addiction is more than mere drug use. It is defined specifically as a compulsive pattern of drug-seeking and drug-taking behavior that takes place at the expense of most other activities. The key questions in addiction, therefore, are why do some susceptible individuals undergo a transition from casual drug use to compulsive patterns of drug use, and why do addicts find it so difficult to stop using drugs (Edwards 1981)?

To address these questions requires some consideration of how drugs affect the brain. Thus, much research on the transition to addiction has aimed at identifying and characterizing brain systems that mediate the rewarding effects of potentially addictive drugs and how these brain systems are changed by drug use. It is now well accepted that addictive drugs usurp neural circuitry normally involved in pleasure, incentive motivation, and learning (Wise 1989, Robbins & Everitt 1996, Berridge & Robinson 1998, Di Chiara 1999, Kelley 1999, Hyman & Malenka 2001, Kelley & Berridge 2002). These brain reward circuits include dopamine projections from the ventral tegmental area and substantia nigra to the nucleus accumbens (NAcc) and striatum, as well as glutamate inputs from the prefrontal cortex, amygdala and hippocampus, and other key parts of this network that we refer to as *NAcc-related circuitry*. This circuitry did not evolve to mediate the effects of drugs, of course, but to endow stimuli beneficial for survival, such as nutrients, water, sexual partners, and safety, with psychological reward properties. Thus, NAcc-related circuitry is critical for natural rewards to acquire and exert motivational control over behavior (Kelley & Berridge 2002). However, addictive drugs not only engage these brain reward systems, often more potently than natural rewards, but they can also change them. Persistent drug-induced neuroadaptations in NAcc-related circuitry have been found at molecular, cellular, and neural system levels (Nestler et al. 1993; Robinson & Berridge 1993, 2000; Vanderschuren & Kalivas 2000; Hyman & Malenka 2001; Everitt & Wolf 2002; De Vries & Shippenberg 2002). These drug-induced neuroadaptations are thought by many to be critical in the transition to addiction. It is not well understood, however, what psychological functions are changed as a consequence of these drug-induced neuroadaptations, or how those changes cause addiction. That is the topic of this chapter.

The major theoretical explanations for the transition to addiction all incorporate the idea that drugs change the brain and thereby change some psychological function. They differ in terms of which psychological changes are thought to carry the weight of explanatory burden. We first discuss a traditional view that emphasizes tolerance and associated decreases in pleasurable drug effects and the corresponding growth of unpleasant withdrawal symptoms (Wikler 1948, Koob et al. 1997, Koob & Le Moal 1997). Second, we discuss the idea that drug-taking habits are caused by aberrant learning, because drugs subvert neuronal mechanisms involved in normal learning and memory (Tiffany 1990, O'Brien et al. 1992, Berke & Hyman 2000, Everitt et al. 2001). Third, we present our incentive-sensitization theory, first proposed in 1993, which suggests that drug-induced sensitization of brain systems that mediate a specific incentive-motivational function (incentive salience) causes drugs to become compulsively and enduringly "wanted," independent of drug pleasure, withdrawal, habits, or memories (Robinson & Berridge 1993, 2000; Berridge & Robinson 1995). Finally, we discuss the notion that drug-induced dysfunction of frontocortical systems may impair normal cognition and inhibitory control over behavior, further leading to impaired judgment and promoting impulsivity (Jentsch & Taylor 1999, Robbins & Everitt 1999b).

PLEASURE, WITHDRAWAL, AND OPPONENT PROCESSES

The most intuitive explanation for addiction is the traditional view that drugs are taken first because they are pleasant, but with repeated drug use homeostatic neuroadaptations lead to tolerance and dependence, such that unpleasant withdrawal symptoms ensue upon the cessation of use. Compulsive drug taking is maintained, by this view, to avoid unpleasant withdrawal symptoms. This two-sided hedonic hypothesis has gone by many different names: pleasure-pain, positive-negative reinforcement, opponent processes, hedonic homeostasis, hedonic dysregulation, reward allostasis, etc. (Wikler 1948; Solomon 1977; Koob et al. 1997; Koob & Le Moal 1997, 2001). No matter what the name, these hypotheses posit the same basic explanatory logic: Addictive drugs are taken initially simply to achieve pleasant drug "highs," and after addiction, to escape withdrawal "lows."

Opponent Process Theory of Addiction

The most elegant psychological version of the pleasure/withdrawal view of addiction is the opponent process theory of Solomon and colleagues (Solomon & Corbit 1973, Solomon 1977). The opponent process theory makes testable predictions and describes the underlying positive and negative affective processes of addiction in graphic ways that allow the transition to addiction to be visualized (Figure 1).

The opponent process theory posits that pleasant doses of a drug activate a dose-dependent a-process in brain reward circuits, which in turn triggers activation of a negative or opponent b-process. Usually the b-process serves to help restore homeostasis and bring brain states back to normal. The summation of the a- and b-processes creates the final subjectively experienced state felt by the person. The resulting experience is called the A-state when the summed effect is

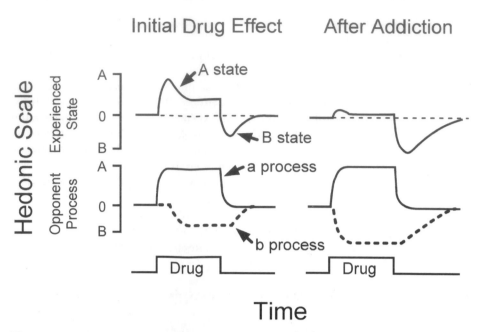

Figure 1 Opponent process model of addiction. According to the opponent process theory the affective (hedonic or emotional) response to a stimulus (a drug in this case) is the underlying a-process, which in turn elicits the opponent b-process (*bottom*). The underlying processes add together to cause the initial pleasant A-state, which is actually experienced, followed by an opponent unpleasant B-state. Initially the pleasant A-state is large, followed by a small B-state. With repeated drug use and in addiction, however, the opponent b-process increases in magnitude and duration, leading to an experience dominated by the unpleasant symptoms associated with withdrawal. (Adapted from Solomon 1977 and Solomon & Corbit 1973.)

pleasantly drug-like (a-process > b-process) and the B-state when it is unpleasantly drug-opposite (b-process > a-process). The euphoric high of the drug A-state is directly caused by the a-process. The b-process is manifest first as mild decay of the drug's high after the initial peak (A-state decay). Later if the drug is taken again the b-process is strengthened and manifest as tolerance to drug euphoria (reduced A-state). Finally, unpleasant withdrawal is caused when drug effects wear off because the sluggish b-process is posited to last longer than the a-process (B-state) [similar to a neural opponent process involved in visual color processing (Hurvich 1981)]. Further, only the b-process is posited to change with repeated drug taking: It grows both in magnitude and in duration (Figure 1). Once the b-process is strengthened, even a small drug dose can instate it and thereby trigger withdrawal again. Conversely, prolonged abstinence from the drug would decay the b-process, and the ability to reactivate it would return to normal. Once the b-process returns back to normal, the person would no longer be addicted.

Neural versions of the opponent process theory have been offered, most notably by Koob and colleagues (Koob et al. 1997; Koob & Le Moal 1997, 2001). For example, Koob & Le Moal (1997) suggest the positive a-process is caused by activation of mesolimbic dopamine projections to the nucleus accumbens and amygdala that mediate "the acute reinforcing effects" of drugs. Repeated drug use, they suggest, induces tolerance or downregulation in the mesolimbic dopamine system, decreasing the drug A-state. Sudden cessation of drug use causes dopamine (and serotonin) neurotransmission to further drop below normal levels, at least for several days, resulting in a dysphoric B-state of withdrawal. Finally, they suggest that repeated drug use also activates an additional b-process via the hypothalamic-pituitary axis stress system, causing release of corticotropin releasing factor (CRF) in the amygdala, as well as other stress responses (Koob et al. 1997, Koob & Le Moal 1997). As a result, addicts who originally take drugs to gain a positive hedonic state are spiraled into a predominantly negative hedonic state, which according to Koob and colleagues causes the transition to addiction.

An implication of hedonic/withdrawal views of addiction, whether couched in psychological or neural terms, is that they tend to interpret all aspects of addiction in terms of affective processes. Even drug-induced changes that render NAcc-related circuitry hypersensitive, such as sensitization of dopamine neurotransmission (see below), may be considered as hedonic or pleasurable in nature by such theorists. For example, Koob & Le Moal (1997) depict neural sensitization as magnifying the positive hedonic a-process caused by drugs (Figure 2). The conclusion that with repeated use addicts derive more pleasure from drugs may seem counterintuitive, and we know of little evidence for this. However, true or false, the claim becomes more understandable when viewed as a conclusion forced by a pure hedonic or opponent process framework.

Limitations of Pleasure-Withdrawal Opponent Process Explanations

Everyone agrees that addicts sometimes take drugs chiefly for pleasure and sometimes chiefly to escape withdrawal or other dysphoric states (e.g., life stresses). However, there are several major problems with hedonic/withdrawal theories as full explanations of drug addiction. One of the most striking is that drug withdrawal actually may be much less powerful at motivating drug-taking behavior than people generally think. Relative to positive incentive processes caused directly by drugs themselves, or stress, withdrawal states are not especially potent in motivating drug-seeking behavior (Stewart & Wise 1992). For example, in animal studies Stewart and colleagues have examined what causes rats to "relapse" into drug-seeking behavior if they previously were dependent on cocaine or heroin but have been drug-free for some time (for reviews see Shaham et al. 2000, Stewart 2000, Shalev et al. 2002). Stewart, Shaham, and colleagues measured lever pressing to obtain drug infusions under extinction conditions after activating either an a-process or b-process. To activate the a-process the rats were simply given a

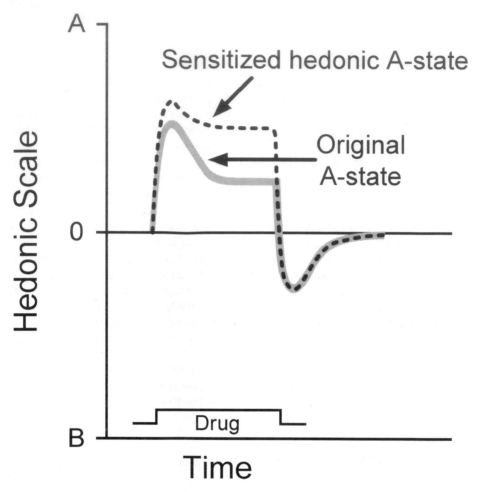

Figure 2 Adaptation of Figure 4 (panel B) in Koob & Le Moal (1997, p. 56), in which they depict sensitization as amplifying the hedonic a-process. They state that this panel shows an "affective stimulus in an individual with an intermittent history of drug use that may result in sensitized response. The shaded line illustrates . . . the initial experience. The dotted line represents the sensitized response" (p. 56). Note that sensitization is hypothesized to increase the hedonic A-state by this view, which would be experienced as enhanced drug pleasure.

small injection of their old drug prior to the test (called a priming injection). To activate the b-process rats received naltrexone, an opioid antagonist drug that blocks opioid receptors in the brain and can induce "precipitated withdrawal" symptoms in individuals who are heroin dependent. Precipitated withdrawal is clearly a B-state and thus would be expected by any withdrawal-based hypothesis of addiction to be the most powerful cause for reactivating drug-seeking behavior. However, a priming drug injection (or a stressor; see below) turns out to be far more effective at reinstating drug-seeking than naltrexone administration (Stewart & Wise 1992,

Shalev et al. 2002). Thus, activation of an a-process appears to be far more effective than the b-process at motivating drug pursuit. Furthermore, withdrawal symptoms are maximal within 1–2 days after the cessation of drug use, but the susceptibility to reinstatement continues to grow for weeks to months (Grimm et al. 2001, Shalev et al. 2001).

The finding that drug withdrawal can be relatively weak at motivating drug-seeking is counterintuitive to many and is a direct contradiction of the opponent process prediction. However, it fits with the reports of some human addicts who say that their sick feelings of withdrawal are quite different from their most intense feelings of drug craving. As one heroin addict explained to a researcher studying craving, "No doc, craving is when you want it—want it so bad you can almost taste it...but you ain't sick...sick is, well sick" (Childress et al. 1988).

Another major problem for withdrawal theories is explaining why addicts so often relapse into drug-taking again even after they are free from withdrawal. After long periods of drug abstinence, the b-process should decay away. Yet elimination of withdrawal symptoms does not protect against future relapse, as the many recidivist graduates of detoxification programs can attest. One explanation for this is suggested by conditioned opponent theories, namely, that associative conditioning causes predictive drug cues to elicit conditioned tolerance and conditioned withdrawal essentially as conditioned b-processes (Wikler 1948, Schull 1979, Ramsay & Woods 1997, Siegel & Allan 1998). Conditioned withdrawal effects have been found in studies of human drug addicts as well as in animal studies and in principle could prompt relapse long after unconditioned withdrawal symptoms have subsided. However, many human addicts report that cues often fail to elicit conditioned withdrawal. Plus, drug cues often elicit quite different effects, such as conditioned feelings of a drug high (a-process), or feelings of drug craving by themselves (O'Brien et al. 1988). Indeed, McAuliffe (1982) found that only 27.5% of heroin addicts experienced conditioned withdrawal, and of these, only 5% indicated this was a reason for relapse.

In conclusion, conditioned feelings of withdrawal do not seem to be sufficiently strong or reliable to serve as the principal explanation for relapse. These and other considerations have prompted many researchers to explore other explanations for the transition to addiction and for relapse (for more on limitations of hedonic reinforcement/withdrawal theories, see Wise & Bozarth 1987; Robinson & Berridge 1993, 2000).

ABERRANT LEARNING

Recently considerable attention has been paid to the role of learning in the transition to addiction, prompted in part by the realization that NAcc-related circuitry is involved in reward learning (for reviews see White 1996, Kelley 1999, Schultz 2000). For example, cues that predict the availability of rewards can powerfully activate NAcc-related circuitry in both animals and humans (Schultz 1998, Childress et al. 1999, Knutson et al. 2001), sometimes even better than the reward itself

(Schultz 1998). Further, repeated exposure to drugs of abuse facilitates some forms of learning (Harmer & Phillips 1998, 1999) and triggers some of the same types of neuroadaptations in reward-related neurons as seen in learning (Hyman & Malenka 2001). Several researchers have hypothesized, therefore, that the transition to addiction results from the ability of drugs to promote *aberrant learning* (Tiffany 1990, O'Brien et al. 1992, White 1996, Robbins & Everitt 1999a, Di Chiara 1999, Berke & Hyman 2000, Everitt et al. 2001, Hyman & Malenka 2001).

Most aberrant learning hypotheses of addiction have focused at the level of neuronal systems. Few have provided a psychological step-by-step account of how abnormal learning could actually produce addiction. Nevertheless, most suggest that drugs produce abnormally strong or aberrant associations involved in reward learning, more powerful than natural reward associations. In principle, these associations could be any of several types [e.g., act-outcome (A-O: cognitive, explicit recognition of the causal relationship between an act and its outcome), stimulus-response (S-R: a habitual link between a specific stimulus and a specific response), stimulus-stimulus (S-S: associations among two or more stimuli)] (see below) and could be either explicit (declarative, conscious) or implicit (procedural, unconscious).

Explicit Learning?

The first possibility is that abnormally strong declarative (explicit) learning could contribute to addiction. This is the most straightforward version of the hypothesis that drugs promote aberrant learning. When people take drugs they learn at a declarative conscious level about causal relationships between their actions and an outcome, such as a drug effect (A-O cognition). They also learn declarative predictive relationships between certain cues in the environment and ensuing rewards (explicit S-S learning). That is, people (and presumably many animals) have declarative, conscious expectations about rewards (Balleine & Dickinson 1998, Cardinal et al. 2002). Abnormally strong explicit learning might distort declarative memories or expectations in two ways. (*a*) Conscious memories of the hedonic drug experience might be especially vivid and/or abnormally intrusive. (*b*) Drugs could exaggerate or distort declarative memories such that memory-based cognitive expectations about drugs become excessively optimistic. Such memories or expectations would be both false and dangerous because they make inaccurate predictions about the consequences of taking drugs.

Can vivid declarative memories, even excessively optimistic or inaccurate memories, explain the transition to addiction? Probably not. When distilled to its essence this explanation suggests that the fundamental problem in addiction is that cognitively accessible memories of drug pleasure are exaggerated or otherwise altered. That idea seems strained when compared with what addicts typically say about their lives. Most addicts do not seem to have rose-colored delusions of reward implied by a hypothesis of exaggerated declarative memories or expectations of drug pleasure. Instead, they accurately predict drug pleasure and often agree their drug use is not justified by the pleasure they get.

Implicit Learning?

S-R HABIT LEARNING   What about the idea that drugs cause pathologically strong implicit learning (unconscious S-R or S-S learning processes), which is not necessarily conscious or accessible to cognitive declaration (Tiffany 1990, Robbins & Everitt 1999a, Berke & Hyman 2000, Everitt et al. 2001)? The most prominent implicit learning view of addiction is the automatic S-R habit hypothesis. This proposes that the transition to addiction involves a transition from behavior originally controlled by explicit and cognitively guided expectations about A-O relationships (i.e., the memory of drug pleasure) to more automatic behavior consisting primarily of S-R habits. Implicit S-R habits occur without explicit cognitive expectations of a given outcome (i.e., "automatically"). Like the procedural memory of how to tie your shoe, once started they simply play out automatically. In an excellent and illuminating formulation Everitt, Dickinson, & Robbins (2001, p. 134) propose neural bases for this "progression from action to habit." They suggest, "drug-seeking actions, mediated by the A-O (act-outcome) process, eventually consolidate habitual S-R drug-seeking through the engagement of corticostriatal loops operating through the dorsal striatum" (also see Robbins & Everitt 1999a, White 1996, Everitt & Wolf 2002). Similarly, Berke & Hyman (2000) suggest that "the engagement of these striatal 'habit'-learning mechanisms by addictive drugs could promote a tendency for drug-related cues and contexts to provoke specific behaviors, such as drug self-administration" (p. 523). These ideas are similar (although not identical) to the earlier suggestion by Tiffany (1990) that "with sufficient practice, performance on any task...can become automatic..." and "drug-use behavior in the addict represent one such activity, controlled largely by automatic processes" (p. 152). So how do these hypotheses explain addiction? Basically they suggest that over-learned habits become so automatic that they essentially become compulsive.

Habit (S-R) learning formulations are attractive because they are conceptually simple and straightforward. They also fit well with operant studies of drug-taking behavior in rats, in which the same lever is pressed again and again, a situation that strongly promotes the formation of S-R habits. Furthermore, the phrase "drug habits" captures the ritualized automatic habits addicts sometimes display when taking drugs. But can extra-strong S-R learning explain a pathological desire to take drugs, or explain the varied and complex behavior often necessary to obtain drugs?

We suggest that habit learning theories do not explain the compulsive nature of addiction for several reasons. First, habit learning theories mistake automatic performance for motivational compulsion. However, habits are not intrinsically compulsive in any motivational sense, no matter how automatic they are. For example, tying your shoe, brushing your teeth, and many other habits in daily life are highly automatic and may be executed without need of cognitive attention.

However, none of these behaviors are performed compulsively (except perhaps in obsessive-compulsive disorder, which requires a separate explanation). You probably have no overwhelming motivational urgency to tie your shoe, and you can stop brushing your teeth midway without distress at leaving the habit unfinished. You would not sacrifice your home, your job, your friends, and all that is dear in your life to engage in a shoe-tying habit, even though it is strongly learned and quite automatic. Its practiced automaticity does not compel you to perform it. No matter how strong implicit S-R associations, no matter how over-learned or pharmacologically boosted, there is no reason to believe that automatic S-R associations per se can confer compulsive qualities.

Further, as mentioned above, many aspects of addictive drug pursuit are flexible and not habitual. Human addicts face a situation different from rats that merely lever-press for drugs. We suspect that if animals were required to forage freely in a complex environment for drugs the picture seen in animal neuroscience might look more like the situation in human addiction, and automatic habit hypotheses would be less tempting. An addict who steals, another who scams, another who has the money and simply must negotiate a drug purchase—all face new and unique challenges with each new victim or negotiation. Instrumental ingenuity and variation are central to addictive drug pursuit in real life. When an addict's drug-taking ritual is interrupted, for example, by lack of available drugs, flexible and compulsive pursuit is brought to the fore (Tiffany 1990). The strongest S-R habit in the world does not explain the frantic behavior that ensues. Thus, the formation of S-R habits may explain the rituals addicts display in consuming drugs, but they do not account for the flexible and deliberate behaviors involved in obtaining drugs. We believe the flexible and compulsive nature of drug-seeking behavior in the addict requires an additional motivational explanation, separate from habit learning (see Figure 3 for a graphic representation of the critical change in addiction posited by the S-R habit learning hypothesis versus the incentive-motivational explanation described below).

S-S LEARNING   Finally, it is possible that addictive drugs cause over-learning of implicit S-S associations among reward-related stimuli. For example, drugs might distort "the process by which the drug abuser connects a specific cue such as a particular place with drug-induced states" (Robbins & Everitt 1999a, p. 569). Similarly, Schultz (2000) suggests that "drugs of abuse that mimic or boost the phasic dopamine reward prediction error might generate a powerful teaching signal and might even produce lasting behavioral changes through synaptic modifications" (p. 205). Although we regard implicit S-S associations as very important in addiction (see below), no aberrant learning hypothesis of this sort has clearly described the psychological mechanism by which implicit over-prediction could cause addiction. Conceivably strong S-S learning might exaggerate implicit Pavlovian conditioned highs (in which the associative learning can be implicit even though the final product is conscious euphoria) or strengthen conditioned reinforcement (e.g., when a Pavlovian cue increases any response it follows by strengthening

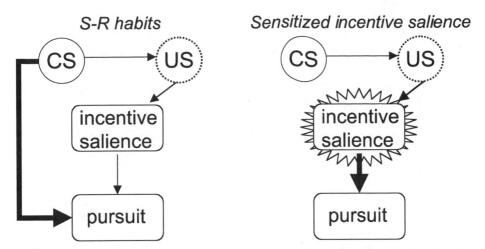

Figure 3 Comparison of the critical change in addiction leading to compulsive drug pursuit according the stimulus-response (S-R) habit learning hypothesis (*left*) and the incentive-sensitization hypothesis (*right*). According to the S-R habit learning model addiction (compulsive drug pursuit) is primarily due to the development of very strong S-R habits [indicated by the thick arrow from a drug cue (CS) to a response (drug pursuit)]. According to the incentive-sensitization view the critical change is in the ability of representations of drug cues (the dashed US evoked by a drug cue) to engage a sensitized motivational response of incentive salience (as indicated by the starburst). This enhanced motivational response is primarily responsible for compulsive drug pursuit (*thick arrow*) in addiction according to our view.

S-R associations). However, conditioned highs are usually weak, and conditioned reinforcement explanations, if taken literally, would require presentation of the reinforcer immediately after emission of the action to be reinforced, but cues are often encountered first, and the cue causes the action to follow (relapse). This is not explicable by conditioned reinforcement in its technical sense.

Despite our criticisms of learning hypotheses of addiction, we hasten to emphasize that we agree that implicit S-S associations are very important in addiction, as described below. However, we believe the problem is not because the S-S associations themselves are aberrant or pathologically strong. The problem is not in learning per se but in the motivational impact of drug-associated cues, that is, in their ability to engage brain motivational systems. The relationship between cues and drug effects are learned, and this learning is important, but by itself it will not generate compulsive behavior. We suggest that most implicit S-S associations may actually remain normal in addicts. What is aberrant in addiction is the response of brain motivational systems to Pavlovian-conditioned drug cues (see Figure 3).

In summary, we suggest the transition to addiction may not be reducible to aberrant learning per se, just as it is not reducible to withdrawal. Knowledge, in any implicit or explicit form of association, no matter how strong, does not necessarily compel the pursuit of drugs. The critical question is, what goads addicts to action? We believe the answer lies in understanding how learning and incentive-motivational processes are joined in the transition to addiction. We take up this topic next.

INCENTIVE SENSITIZATION

The incentive-sensitization theory of addiction focuses on how drug cues trigger excessive incentive motivation for drugs, leading to compulsive drug seeking, drug taking, and relapse (Robinson & Berridge 1993, 2000). The central idea is that addictive drugs enduringly alter NAcc-related brain systems that mediate a basic incentive-motivational function, the attribution of incentive salience. As a consequence, these neural circuits may become enduringly hypersensitive (or "sensitized") to specific drug effects and to drug-associated stimuli (via activation by S-S associations). The drug-induced brain change is called neural sensitization. We proposed that this leads psychologically to excessive attribution of incentive salience to drug-related representations, causing pathological "wanting" to take drugs. (The term "wanting" in quotation marks is used as a shorthand to refer to activation of incentive-salience processes; for a detailed discussion see Berridge & Robinson 1998).

The activation of a sensitized system that attributes incentive salience to drug-associated stimuli and their representations can sometimes be manifest implicitly in drug-seeking behavior. If the "wanting" system is activated implicitly it can instigate and guide behavior without a person necessarily having conscious emotion, desire, or a declarative goal. For example, in normal people the brief subliminal presentation of faces expressing positive emotions (backward masked and so brief they do not cause any conscious feeling of emotion at the time they are presented) can activate implicit "wanting," increasing subsequent consumption of a beverage (Berridge & Winkielman 2002). In addicts, doses of drugs that are too low to produce any conscious experience of pleasure can activate implicit "wanting," as indicated by an increase in drug-seeking behavior (Lamb et al. 1991, Fischman & Foltin 1992). Implicit "wanting" is similar to implicit memory and to unconscious perception (e.g., blindsight), which can occur and influence behavior without conscious awareness (Schacter 1996, Weiskrantz 1997). At other times incentive-sensitization can be manifest explicitly, when cognitive elaboration translates incentive salience attributions into the level of conscious awareness of the corresponding representations. In those cases, the initial activation of an implicit "wanting" system contributes to the explicit subjective experience of a conscious desire for drugs, in the ordinary sense of wanting. Finally, the sensitized neural systems responsible for excessive incentive salience can be dissociated from neural systems that mediate the hedonic effects of drugs, how much they are "liked." In other words, "wanting" is not "liking." Hedonic "liking" is a different psychological process that has its own neural substrates (e.g., NAcc opioid neurotransmission; Berridge 2002). Neural sensitization by drugs increases only "wanting." We suggest that this incentive-sensitization process is the fundamental problem in the transition to addiction and in relapse (Robinson & Berridge 1993, 2000; Berridge & Robinson 1995).

What is Sensitization?

Pharmacologists use the term sensitization to refer to an increase in a drug effect with repeated drug administration. In other words, the change in drug effect is in the opposite direction as seen with the development of tolerance (a decrease in a drug effect with repeated administration). When drugs are given repeatedly some effects undergo tolerance, some effects undergo sensitization, and yet other effects do not change. This is because the biological systems that mediate different drug effects adapt in different ways to repeated drug exposure. There are two major classes of drug effects that are sensitized by addictive drugs: psychomotor activating effects and incentive motivational effects. Both of these classes of drug effects are mediated at least in part by NAcc-related circuitry, and therefore sensitization of these behaviors is thought to reflect reorganization and sensitization of this neural system (Robinson & Becker 1986, Robinson & Berridge 1993).

Psychomotor Sensitization

In humans and animals many potentially addictive drugs can increase arousal, attention, and motor behavior, producing heightened locomotion, exploration, and approach. At higher doses psychomotor effects can also include intense repetitive stereotyped movements (Wise & Bozarth 1987). These psychomotor-activating effects are easy to measure and are mediated by brain systems that overlap with those involved in reward (involving NAcc dopamine, etc.) (Wise & Bozarth 1987), and therefore they provide an excellent means for studying neurobehavioral sensitization. The study of psychomotor sensitization has provided a great deal of information about factors that influence both the induction and expression of neurobehavioral sensitization, including genetic, hormonal, and experiential determinants of individual differences in susceptibility to sensitization, the roles of pharmacological factors such as drug dose, and of psychological factors such as learning, stress, etc. (Robinson & Becker 1986, Robinson 1988, Stewart & Badiani 1993, Robinson et al. 1998). For example, they have shown that sensitization is produced by many different drugs of abuse, including amphetamines, cocaine, opiates, methylphenidate, ethanol (alcohol), and nicotine. Sensitization is strongest when high or escalating doses are given, especially when the drug is administered rapidly (Samaha et al. 2002) and intermittently (continuous infusions are relatively ineffective). Psychomotor sensitization has also revealed one of the most important features of sensitization for addiction, namely, its remarkable persistence. In animals psychomotor sensitization can persist for months to years after drug treatment is discontinued (Paulson et al. 1991, Castner & Goldman-Rakic 1999). Psychomotor sensitization has also been described in humans (Strakowski et al. 1996, Strakowski & Sax 1998), and if in humans the neural adaptations responsible for sensitization last a proportional length of time as in rats, it could amount to most of a lifetime.

Another important feature of sensitization for addiction concerns individual differences in susceptibility to sensitization. Some individuals sensitize readily, whereas others are more resistant. That may help explain why only some drug users become addicts. Susceptibility to sensitization is determined by a host of factors, including genes, sex hormones, stress hormones, past trauma, etc., in addition to individualized patterns of drug exposure (Robinson 1988). Further, once sensitized, most individuals show cross-sensitization, which means that sensitization to one drug can cause sensitized effects for other drugs as well. Even more intriguing, cross-sensitization can occur between drugs and nondrug stress. Animals previously exposed to stress may become sensitized to some potentially addictive drugs. Conversely, animals sensitized by drugs may become hypersensitive to stress (Antelman et al. 1980, Antelman & Chiodo 1983, Robinson 1988). Stress-drug cross-sensitization might be especially important in influencing stress-precipitated relapse, as well as initial susceptibility to addiction (Piazza et al. 1991, Shaham et al. 2000). (Also see Miczek & Pilotte, eds., *Psychopharmacology*, Vol. 158(4), 2001 for a special issue on "Stress and Drug Abuse.")

Neurobiology of Sensitization

What changes in the brain are involved in drug sensitization? We now know that neural sensitization involves many long-lasting changes in NAcc-related reward circuitry. For example, behavioral sensitization is accompanied by an increase in the ability of a number of drugs to promote dopamine efflux in the NAcc (Robinson & Berridge 2000). In addition, dopamine D1 receptors on neurons in the NAcc become hypersensitive after sensitization, presumably further potentiating the mesolimbic dopamine signal (White & Kalivas 1998). However, more than dopamine is involved in reward and sensitization. Glutamate is also released in the NAcc by neurons from the neocortex, amygdala, and hippocampus, and recent studies of neural sensitization have found distinct changes in glutamate neurotransmission in sensitized animals (Wolf 1998, Vanderschuren & Kalivas 2000, Hyman & Malenka 2001, Everitt & Wolf 2002). In fact, sensitization-related changes have been described in many neurotransmitter systems that are integral to the function of NAcc-related reward circuits including serotonin, norepinephrine, acetylcholine, opioid, and GABA systems (as well as changes in a number of intracellular signaling pathways that are activated by these neurotransmitters). Thus, sensitization globally alters the neurochemistry of NAcc-related reward circuitry (Robinson & Berridge 2000).

Consistent with circuit-level alterations (Pierce & Kalivas 1997, Everitt & Wolf 2002), sensitization is also associated with persistent changes in the physical structure of neurons themselves (Robinson & Kolb 1997, 1999a,b). For example, cells in the NAcc and prefrontal cortex show changes in the length of dendrites and the extent to which dendrites are branched. At an even finer level changes also occur in the density and types of dendritic spines, which are the primary site of

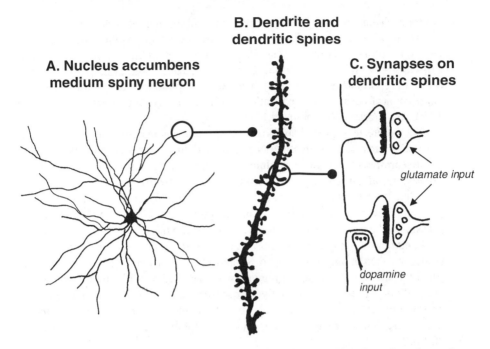

Figure 4 Graphic representation of the sites on neurons at which drugs have been shown to produce morphological changes. (*A*) The most common type of neuron in the nucleus accumbens, a medium spiny neuron. Past experience with amphetamine, cocaine, or morphine has been shown to alter the number of dendritic branches seen radiating away from the cell body. (*B*) Magnified view of a dendrite that is studded with many dendritic spines. As indicated by the schematic drawing in (*C*), dendritic spines are the site of synapses, and spines on the distal dendrites on medium spiny neurons receive both glutamate and dopamine inputs. Treatment with amphetamine, cocaine, or morphine also produces persistent changes in the number of dendritic spines on these neurons and therefore presumably in the number of synapses (Robinson & Kolb 1997, 1999a,b; Robinson et al. 2001). Camera lucida drawings (*A* and *B*) courtesy of Grazyna Gorny.

excitatory glutamate synapses (see Figure 4). These sensitization-related changes in dendritic structure may reflect changes in patterns of synaptic connectivity within these brain regions and therefore may alter information processing within NAcc-related circuitry. Although many questions concerning causal relationships remain to be addressed, it is now well accepted that sensitization is accompanied by a major reorganization of brain reward systems (Pierce & Kalivas 1997, Wolf 1998, Robinson & Berridge 2000, Hyman & Malenka 2001, Everitt & Wolf 2002, Vanderschuren & Kalivas 2000).

ROLE OF LEARNING AND CONTEXT   Neural sensitization itself appears to be a non-associative process, but learning powerfully modulates both the expression and the induction of behavioral sensitization, and contextual learning about where drugs are taken seems to be especially important (Robinson et al. 1998). For example, if rats are given repeated drug treatments in one distinct environment and they develop robust psychomotor sensitization in that environment, they often fail to express behavioral sensitization if they are later tested with a drug challenge in a different environment, where they have never experienced drug. In this case the expression of behavioral sensitization is said to be "context specific" (Pert et al. 1990, Anagnostaras & Robinson 1996).

The failure to express behavioral sensitization when context is shifted does not occur because drug treatments failed to induce neural sensitization but because learning about context modulates whether neural sensitization is expressed in behavior at any given place or time. There are two ways learning appears to modulate the behavioral expression of sensitization. (*a*) An inhibitory associative process (Stewart & Vezina 1991, Anagnostaras et al. 2002) can prevent the expression of behavioral sensitization in contexts in which the drug is not expected. (*b*) Excitatory Pavlovian associations can increase the drug-induced psychomotor response when animals are placed in environments where the drug is expected [the opposite of conditioned opponent-processes and conditioned tolerance (Pert et al. 1990)]. These two associative processes may combine to modulate the expression of sensitization, which may be why contextual factors are so important in drug craving and relapse (Anagnostaras & Robinson 1996, Anagnostaras et al. 2002).

In addition to expression, the *induction* of sensitization—that is, whether drugs change the brain in the first place—also is modulated by the context in which drugs are administered (Robinson et al. 1998). For example, when amphetamine, cocaine, or morphine are given to rats in a distinct and relatively novel environment they induce much more robust sensitization than when they are given in the home cage (Badiani et al. 1995a,b, 2000). This does not appear to be due simply to the ability of a distinct environment to act as a drug predictive cue, thereby facilitating an associative learning process (Crombag et al. 2001, 2000). Instead, environmental factors also directly modulate the neurobiological impact of drugs. For example, drugs such as amphetamine or cocaine cause some neurons to express immediate early genes, including c-*fos* and *arc*, which can be visualized and used as an indicator of what circuitry is engaged by drugs. In many brain regions the intensity of c-*fos* and *arc* expression is greater if drugs are given in a novel environment than if they are given at home (Badiani et al. 1998, Klebaur et al. 2002). This novelty-dependent increase in immediate early gene expression is not just due to increased expression within the same neurons but also involves recruitment of additional populations of neurons when drugs are given in a novel environment. For example, when given at home, amphetamine or cocaine induce c-*fos* mRNA in only one subpopulation of neurons in the striatum, neurons that project to the substantia nigra and contain mRNA for the opioid neurotransmitter, dynorphin. However, when given in a novel environment, amphetamine and cocaine also induce c-*fos* mRNA in a different subpopulation of neurons, one that projects to the globus pallidus and contains mRNA for enkephalin (Badiani et al. 1999, Uslaner et al. 2001). Therefore, something about a novel environment determines which neuronal populations in the striatum are engaged by sensitizing drugs and enhances susceptibility to sensitization. Although again many causal relationships remain to be determined, these studies highlight the extent to which the neurobiological impact of drugs, and their ability to sensitize the brain, is modulated by environmental and psychological factors.

Sensitization of Drug Reward Pursuit

More direct evidence for our hypothesis that neural sensitization increases the "wanting" for drug rewards comes from studies that quantify the pursuit of drugs and other rewards. For example, many studies using operant techniques have shown that sensitization decreases the threshold dose necessary for rats to learn to self-administer drugs and facilitates how quickly they learn (Piazza et al. 1989, 1990; Horger et al. 1990, 1992; Valadez & Schenk 1994; Pierre & Vezina 1998). Sensitized rats also show an increase in "breakpoint" when tested using progressive ratio schedules, indicating that they will work harder than normal to gain drug reward (Mendrek et al. 1998, Lorrain et al. 2000). Sensitization also increases rats' learning of a conditioned place preference for a location paired with a drug reward (Lett 1989, Shippenberg & Heidbreder 1995, Shippenberg et al. 1996) and increases their motivation to obtain a cocaine reward in a runway, reflected by running speed for that reward (Deroche et al. 1999). Furthermore, in an animal model of relapse, sensitization is associated with the ability of a priming drug injection to reinstate drug-seeking responses after extinction of the behavior (De Vries et al. 1998, 2002). Finally, sensitization can also increase the incentive value of other rewards, such as sugar, food, a sexually receptive female (for male rats), and conditioned stimuli for such rewards (Fiorino & Phillips 1999a,b; Taylor & Horger 1999; Wyvell & Berridge 2001; Nocjar & Panksepp 2002).

In addicts, of course, the primary excessive motivation is for drugs in particular, although evidence suggests some cocaine addicts are hypersexual (Washton & Stone-Washton 1993) and some substance-dependent individuals may even be hyper-responsive to money rewards (Bechara et al. 2002), raising the possibility of a degree of motivation spillover to nondrug rewards. A major question that is only beginning to be addressed is how the focus of sensitized reward value becomes directed to one particular target, such as taking drugs. Associative learning about the temporal relationships between reward-related cues and sensitizing stimuli, as well as nonassociative individual factors, may be involved (Robinson & Berridge 1993, Nocjar & Panksepp 2002). In any case it is clear that motivation for rewards can be enhanced as a consequence of sensitization caused by addictive drugs.

Incentive-Sensitization

The evidence for sensitization of drug reward pursuit described above is compatible with the incentive-sensitization view of addiction, but it is not conclusive, because it could be alternatively explained by changes in a number of other components of reward or learning (Wyvell & Berridge 2000, Cardinal et al. 2002). Our hypothesis is quite specific regarding the nature of the psychological process that is sensitized in addiction. We hypothesize that it is specifically sensitization of incentive salience attribution to representations of drug cues and drug-taking that causes the compulsive pursuit of drugs and persisting vulnerability to relapse in addiction. Incentive salience attribution is hypothesized to transform the neural representations of otherwise neutral stimuli into salient incentives, able to "grab" attention, and makes them attractive and "wanted." Individuals are guided to incentive stimuli by the influence of Pavlovian stimulus-stimulus (S-S) associations on motivational systems, which is psychologically separable from the symbolic cognitive systems that mediate conscious desire, declarative expectancies of reward, and act-outcome representations (Berridge 1999, Dickinson et al. 2000, Robinson & Berridge 2000). Indeed, different brain systems appear to mediate cognitive versus incentive salience forms of motivation. Prefrontal and other cortical areas primarily mediate cognitive forms of desire and act-outcome representations, whereas NAcc-related circuitry (especially dopamine-related systems) play a more important role in Pavlovian-guided attributions of incentive salience (Balleine & Dickinson 1998, 2000; Berridge & Robinson 1998; Dickinson et al. 2000; De Borchgrave et al. 2002).

In order to test whether sensitization can specifically enhance incentive salience or "wanting" triggered by reward cues (S-S associations), it is necessary to design experiments to exclude alternative explanations. A true test for a sensitized "wanting" process requires a rigorous experimental design that prevents results from being influenced by changes in other components of reward or learning, such as "liking" or hedonic impact of the pleasant reward, cognitive predictive expectancies about it, the formation of S-S associations during learning trials, automatic stimulus-response (S-R) habits triggered by cues toward rewards, and conditioned reinforcement of reward-seeking responses by subsequent contingent cues among other alternative explanations.

Wyvell provided such evidence as part of her dissertation studies at the University of Michigan (Wyvell & Berridge 2000, 2001). She showed that both sensitization (by prior drug administration) and direct stimulation of dopamine neurotransmission in the NAcc (by amphetamine microinjection) specifically increased incentive salience attributed to a cue for sugar reward, causing that cue to elicit exaggerated "wanting" for the reward. To separate incentive salience from the other potential explanations above, Wyvell used a pure conditioned incentive paradigm based on a more general learning procedure known as a Pavlovian-instrumental transfer task (in which Pavlovian predictive cues for food, shock, etc. alter ongoing instrumental performance) (Rescorla & Solomon 1967, Dickinson & Balleine 1994). The conditioned incentive effect refers to the observation that brief presentation of a Pavlovian-conditioned cue (such as a light or a distinct sound) that has been paired with a reward can enhance instrumental responding (such as lever pressing) for that reward—even under conditions that exclude contributions from changes in hedonic "liking," S-R habits, conditioned reinforcement of instrumental responses, etc. In a conditioned incentive experiment the cue is presented under extinction conditions, which excludes contributions from any change in "liking," hedonic impact, or primary reinforcement. Predictive S-S associations about the Pavlovian-conditioned cue are learned in separate sessions from the instrumental training sessions to exclude contributions from automatic S-R habits and from operant discriminative stimulus signals that a response will be rewarded. Finally, the cue is never presented contingent upon lever pressing during the extinction test, so it cannot act by strengthening a preceding response, excluding conditioned-reinforcement explanations for an increase in instrumental responding. Under these restricted conditions, the only plausible explanation for why a Pavlovian-conditioned cue would suddenly intensify pursuit of a reward is that incentive salience is attributed to the Pavlovian cue and its associated reward, causing cue-triggered "wanting."

Dopamine neurotransmission in the NAcc is increased by amphetamine, and if the drug is placed directly into NAcc by microinjection, it increases dopamine release there. In order to test whether amphetamine-induced dopamine release in the NAcc increases incentive salience, as hypothesized, amphetamine was microinjected into the NAcc immediately before testing using the conditioned-incentive paradigm (Wyvell & Berridge 2000). "Intra-accumbens amphetamine increased the ability of a sucrose cue to spur performance for a sucrose reward, even under extinction conditions" (p. 8129). The excessive "wanting" for reward after amphetamine microinjections was strongly under the control of the sugar cue, returning each time the cue was presented and decaying within minutes after it was removed. In parallel studies the effect of intra-NAcc amphetamine on "liking" was measured, based on affective facial reactions to the taste of sugar that are homologous to the affective facial expressions that sweet tastes elicit from human infants (Berridge 2000). It was found that microinjections of amphetamine into the NAcc did not increase the hedonic impact or "liking" for sugar, even though they had increased "wanting" for the sugar. These studies show, therefore, that intra-accumbens amphetamine, and presumably an increase in dopamine neurotransmission in the NAcc, can magnify "wanting" without changing "liking." They show, as we have suggested, that the primary role of learning in this situation is to guide incentive salience attributions so that cues trigger "wanting" as a *conditioned motivational response*. This conclusion is consistent with that of a converse experiment by Dickinson et al. (2000), who found that dopamine antagonists selectively suppress the Pavlovian-instrumental transfer effect (and further excluded an alternative explanation that dopamine changes the cognitive declarative expectation regarding act-outcome relations).

Most important to our incentive-sensitization hypothesis of addiction, Wyvell & Berridge (2001) also examined the effect of sensitization on cue-triggered "wanting" for a sugar reward. In this experiment rats were first sensitized by several injections of amphetamine. Then, after being drug free for about 2 weeks, they were tested using the conditioned-incentive paradigm described above. In sensitized rats the Pavlovian-conditioned sugar cue produced a greater wanting for sugar than in nonsensitized rats. Thus, sensitized rats attributed excessive cue-elicited incentive salience to their reward at a time when they had received no drug at all for many days—and under conditions that exclude the alternative hypotheses above. This situation seems to model that of the drug-abstinent and "recovered" addict who suddenly relapses again after encountering drug cues. Wyvell's results suggest that relapse in human addicts after attempts to quit might also be caused by persisting sensitization in brain systems that mediate incentive salience. Upon encountering drug cues, the addict might suddenly "want" to take drugs again—to an excessive and compulsive degree—regardless of cognitive expectancies about "liking," declarative goals, absence of withdrawal, etc.

Of course, human addiction is far more complex than rats "wanting" a sugar reward. Nevertheless, these results have important implications for understanding what sensitization does to brain systems that generate motivated behavior. Sensitization enhances the ability of drug-associated cues to trigger irrational bursts of "wanting" for their reward, and in human addicts, who may have many years of drug experience with all the attendant opportunity for sensitization and learning, this may lead to the compulsive pursuit of drugs. In this view an optimal future medication for addiction would be one that reduces or prevents the expression of sensitized attributions of excessive incentive salience to drug cues and representations, thereby reducing compulsive "wanting" to take drugs (unfortunately such a medication has not yet been identified).

In summary, we suggest that at its heart, addiction is a disorder of aberrant incentive motivation due to drug-induced sensitization of neural systems that attribute salience to particular stimuli. It can be triggered by drug cues as a *learned motivational response* of the brain, but it is not a disorder of aberrant learning per se (see Figure 3). Once it exists, sensitized "wanting" may compel drug pursuit whether or not an addict has any withdrawal symptoms at all. And because incentive salience is distinct from pleasure or "liking" processes, sensitization gives impulsive drug "wanting" an enduring life of its own.

DECISION-MAKING AND LOSS OF INHIBITORY CONTROL

In addicts the excessive incentive salience posited by the incentive-sensitization theory can not only lead to the pathological pursuit of drugs (drug "wanting") but to apparently irrational choices to take drugs. The irrationality of the sensitized pursuit of drugs arises from several features of incentive sensitization. For example, even if a person knows cognitively that the drug will not give much pleasure (e.g., if the dose is low or quality is poor), sensitized implicit "wanting" can overcome low expectations of "liking." The distinction between "wanting" and "liking" can sometimes result in strange dissociations in addicts, in which goal-directed drug-seeking behavior occurs in the absence of conscious awareness that pursuit is underway, and is dissociated from the ability of drugs to produce pleasure; that is, addicts will pursue drugs they do not like, as well as those they like (Lamb et al. 1991, Fischman & Foltin 1992). Second, irrationality could arise from the temporary reversibility of cue-triggered "wanting," which momentarily overrides more rational and stable life priorities (Elster 1999). Even if a person's explicit declarative goal is abstinence, implicit incentive salience attributions can undermine these explicit goals. And even if a person has a stable rational resolution to abstain from taking drugs, an encounter with drug cues may trigger "wanting" that competes with, and may momentarily surpass, rational intentions, precipitating a binge of relapse.

For some addicts and some drugs, additional alterations in the function of neocortical systems may further weaken the "rational brake" of cognitive regulatory processes that normally inhibit strong motivational impulses. Although prefrontal cortical systems may engage NAcc-related incentive processes (Kelley 1999, Park et al. 2002), frontocortical systems are also involved in executive processes such as decision-making and the ability to make judgments about the future consequences of one's actions (Balleine & Dickinson 1998, Smith & Jonides 1999, Bechara et al. 2000). Frontostriatal projections may be especially important in regulating emotions and providing inhibitory control over behavior (Davidson et al. 2000). In an excellent paper Jentsch & Taylor (1999) review evidence that chronic exposure to some drugs can depress neural processing in frontal regions and distort functions of the prefrontal cortex. For example, persistent changes in frontocortical blood flow and glucose utilization have been described in amphetamine and cocaine addicts (Volkow et al. 1991, 1992; Biggins et al. 1997; Bolla et al. 1998), and in polysubstance abusers there is even a decrease in the volume of the prefrontal cortex (Liu et al. 1998). In rats structural anomalies in the dendrites of pyramidal neurons in the prefrontal cortex have been found after extended cocaine self-administration (Robinson et al. 2001). This neurobiological evidence is augmented by reports that some addicts show a variety of neuropsychological deficits shared with patients who have frontal dysfunction (Bolla et al. 1998, Jentsch & Taylor 1999, Robbins & Everitt 1999b, Rogers et al. 1999, Bechara & Damasio 2002, Bechara et al. 2002). For example, Rogers et al. (1999) studied psychological function in chronic amphetamine or opiate users and found deficits in decision making "indicative of difficulties in resolving competing choices" similar to those of patients with lesions of the orbital frontal cortex (p. 325). Jentsch & Taylor (1999) have argued that dysfunction in frontostriatal systems involved in cognitive inhibitory control over behavior leads to behavior unduly dominated by "pre-potent tendencies," resulting "in a condition associated with profound impulsivity that may contribute to compulsive drug-seeking and drug-taking behavior" (p. 374).

Thus, drug-induced impairments in frontocortical function may contribute in important ways to the suboptimal choices and decisions addicts make concerning drug use. In addition, decreased activity in the prefrontal cortex may increase activity in subcortical dopamine systems (Carlsson et al. 2001, Jackson et al. 2001, Meyer-Lindenberg et al. 2002). This raises the interesting possibility that frontocortical dysfunction may not only lead to poor decision-making and judgment, but it could further exacerbate incentive-sensitization. A loss of inhibitory control over behavior and poor judgment, combined with sensitization of addicts' motivational impulses to obtain and take drugs, makes for a potentially disastrous combination.

OTHER ADDICTIONS?

Are any of the factors we have discussed involved in other so-called addictions, such as addictions to food, sex, gambling, etc.? It is difficult to see how factors such as opponent withdrawal states or drug-induced cortical dysfunction would be involved in these other addictions. The activation of NAcc-related circuitry and incentive-salience systems might more plausibly play a role in food binging, sexual compulsions, etc., but it is simply unknown whether such compulsive motivations involve any brain features at all similar to those associated with drug sensitization. Alternatively, these kinds of compulsions might only involve the activation of NAcc-related circuitry within normal limits, with other psychological factors playing more primary causal roles. Although the question clearly is of interest, in the absence of data anything we might say further would be too wildly speculative.

SUMMARY

In contrast to hedonic/withdrawal views of addiction, we suggest that drug pleasure becomes less and less important during the transition to addiction. Even relief from withdrawal symptoms does not account for the compulsive character of drug-seeking and drug-taking behavior in addicts or for their vulnerability to relapse after detoxification (especially upon encountering drug cues and contexts). In contrast to aberrant learning theories, we suggest that no abnormality of associative learning explains the compulsive yet flexible behaviors addicts employ in their pursuit of drugs (even if abnormal associations contribute to rigid drug-taking rituals). The transition to addiction instead is due, we suggest, to the incentive-motivational consequences of drug-induced alterations in NAcc-related circuitry that mediates incentive salience. This circuitry is activated by implicit S-S associations, but the S-S associations themselves may remain quite normal, even in addicts. It is the response of the neural system that generates incentive salience that is abnormal: It results in pathological wanting. This is directed especially to drug-associated cues because excessive incentive salience is attributed chiefly to these cues, making drug-related cues into effective triggers of relapse (Figure 3).

This excessive implicit "wanting" may be compounded further in some addicts by drug-induced dysfunction in prefrontal cortical systems normally involved in decision-making, judgment, emotional regulation and inhibitory control over behavior. Cognitive deficits in the ability to inhibit or properly assess the future consequences of one's actions due to prefrontal dysfunction, combined with excessive incentive salience due to sensitization of NAcc-related circuitry, leads to the compulsive pursuit of drugs out of proportion to the pleasure drugs provide and in the face of negative consequences for all those concerned.

DEDICATION

This paper is dedicated to the memory of Dr. Cindy L. Wyvell, who died in December 2001 shortly after completing the dissertation studies described here and after years of struggle against cancer. Throughout, Cindy evinced a degree of courage and dedication that we can only describe as heroic. Her premature death was a loss to psychology as well as to those who knew her.

ACKNOWLEDGMENTS

We thank Anthony Dickinson, Daniel Schacter, Yavin Shaham, and Frederick Toates for helpful comments on this manuscript. The research by the authors described here was supported by grants from the National Institute on Drug Abuse and the National Science Foundation.

The *Annual Review of Psychology* is online at http://psych.annualreviews.org

LITERATURE CITED

Anagnostaras SG, Robinson TE. 1996. Sensitization to the psychomotor stimulant effects of amphetamine: modulation by associative learning. *Behav. Neurosci.* 110:1397–414

Anagnostaras SG, Schallert TJ, Robinson TE. 2002. Memory process governing amphetamine-induced psychomotor sensitization. *Neuropsychopharmacology* 26:703–15

Antelman SM, Chiodo LA. 1983. Amphetamine as a stressor. In *Stimulants: Neurochemical, Behavioral and Clinical Perspectives*, ed. I Creese, pp. 269–99. New York: Raven

Antelman SM, Eichler AJ, Black CA, Kocan D. 1980. Interchangeability of stress and amphetamine in sensitization. *Science* 207:329–31

Badiani A, Anagnostaras SG, Robinson TE. 1995a. The development of sensitization to the psychomotor stimulant effects of amphetamine is enhanced in a novel environment. *Psychopharmacol.* 117:443–52

Badiani A, Browman KE, Robinson TE. 1995b. Influence of novel versus home environments on sensitization to the psychomotor stimulant effects of cocaine and amphetamine. *Brain Res.* 674:291–98

Badiani A, Oates MM, Day HEW, Watson SJ, Akil H, Robinson TE. 1998. Amphetamine-induced behavior, dopamine release, and c-fos mRNA expression: modulation by environmental novelty. *J. Neurosci.* 18:10579–93

Badiani A, Oates MM, Day HEW, Watson SJ, Akil H, Robinson TE. 1999. Environmental modulation of amphetamine-induced c-fos expression in D1 versus D2 striatal neurons. *Behav. Brain Res.* 103:203–9

Badiani A, Oates MM, Robinson TE. 2000. Modulation of morphine sensitization in the rat by contextual stimuli. *Psychopharmacol.* 151:273–82

Balleine BW, Dickinson A. 1998. Goal-directed instrumental action: contingency and incentive learning and their cortical substrates. *Neuropharmacology* 37:407–19

Balleine BW, Dickinson A. 2000. The effect of lesions of the insular cortex on instrumental conditioning: evidence for a role in incentive memory. *J. Neurosci.* 20:8954–64

Bechara A, Damasio H. 2002. Decision-making and addiction. Part I. Impaired activation of somatic states in substance dependent individuals when pondering decisions with negative future consequences. *Neuropsychologia* 40:1675–89

Bechara A, Damasio H, Damasio AR. 2000. Emotion, decision making and the orbitofrontal cortex. *Cereb. Cortex* 10:295–307

Bechara A, Dolan S, Hindes A. 2002. Decision-making and addiction. Part II. Myopia for the future or hypersensitivity to reward? *Neuropsychologia* 40:1690–705

Berke JD, Hyman SE. 2000. Addiction, dopamine, and the molecular mechanisms of memory. *Neuron* 25:515–32

Berridge KC. 1999. Pleasure, pain, desire and dread: hidden core processes of emotion. In *Well Being: The Foundations of Hedonic Psychology*, ed. D Kahneman, E Diener, N Schwarz, pp. 527–59. New York: Sage Found.

Berridge KC. 2000. Measuring hedonic impact in animals and infants: microstructure of affective taste reactivity patterns. *Neurosci. Biobehav. Rev.* 24:173–98

Berridge KC. 2002. Pleasures of the brain. *Brain Cogn.* In press

Berridge KC, Robinson TE. 1995. The mind of an addicted brain: neural sensitization of wanting versus liking. *Curr. Dir. Psychol. Sci.* 4:71–76

Berridge KC, Robinson TE. 1998. What is the role of dopamine in reward: hedonic impact, reward learning, or incentive salience? *Brain Res. Rev.* 28:309–69

Berridge KC, Winkielman P. 2002. What is an unconscious emotion? (The case for unconscious 'liking'.) *Cogn. Emot.* In press

Biggins CA, MacKay S, Clark W, Fein G. 1997. Event-related potential evidence for frontal cortex effects of chronic cocaine dependence. *Biol. Psychiatry* 42:472–85

Bolla KI, Cadet JL, London ED. 1998. The neuropsychiatry of chronic cocaine abuse. *J. Neuropsychiatry Clin. Neurosci.* 10:280–89

Cardinal RN, Parkinson JA, Hall J, Everitt BJ. 2002. Emotion and motivation: the role of the amygdala, ventral striatum, and prefrontal cortex. *Neurosci. Biobehav. Rev.* 26:321–52

Carlsson A, Waters N, Holm-Waters S, Tedroff J, Nilsson M, Carlsson ML. 2001. Interactions between monoamines, glutamate, and GABA in schizophrenia: new evidence. *Annu. Rev. Pharmacol. Toxicol.* 41:237–60

Castner SA, Goldman-Rakic PS. 1999. Long-lasting psychotomimetic consequences of repeated low-dose amphetamine exposure in rhesus monkeys. *Neuropsychopharmacology* 20:10–28

Childress AR, McLellan AT, Ehrman R, O'Brien CP. 1988. Classically conditioned responses in opioid and cocaine dependence: a role in relapse? *Natl. Inst. Drug Abuse Res. Monogr.* 84:25–43

Childress AR, Mozley PD, McElgin W, Fitzgerald J, Reivich M, O'Brien CP. 1999. Limbic activation during cue-induced cocaine craving. *Am. J. Psychiatry* 156:11–18

Crombag HS, Badiani A, Chan J, Dell'Orco J, Dineen SP, Robinson TE. 2001. The ability of environmental context to facilitate psychomotor sensitization to amphetamine can be dissociated from its effect on acute drug responsiveness and on conditioned responding. *Neuropsychopharmacology* 24:680–90

Crombag HS, Badiani A, Maren S, Robinson TE. 2000. The role of contextual versus discrete drug-associated cues in promoting the induction of psychomotor sensitization to intravenous amphetamine. *Behav. Brain Res.* 116:1–22

Davidson RJ, Jackson DC, Kalin NH. 2000. Emotion, plasticity, context, and regulation: perspectives from affective neuroscience. *Psychol. Bull.* 126:890–909

De Borchgrave R, Rawlins JNP, Dickinson A, Balleine BW. 2002. Effects of cytotoxic nucleus accumbens lesions on instrumental conditioning in rats. *Exp. Brain Res.* 144:50–68

Deroche V, Le Moal M, Piazza PV. 1999. Cocaine self-administration increases the incentive motivational properties of the drug in rats. *Eur. J. Neurosci.* 11:2731–36

De Vries TJ, Schoffelmeer AN, Binnekade R, Mulder AH, Vanderschuren LJ. 1998. Drug-induced reinstatement of heroin- and cocaine-seeking behaviour following long-term extinction is associated with expression of behavioural sensitization. *Eur. J. Neurosci.* 10:3565–71

De Vries TJ, Schoffelmeer AN, Binnekade R, Raaso H, Vanderschuren LJ. 2002. Relapse to cocaine- and heroin-seeking behavior mediated by dopamine D2 receptors is time-dependent and associated with behavioral sensitization. *Neuropsychopharmacology* 26:18–26

De Vries TJ, Shippenberg TS. 2002. Neural systems underlying opiate addiction. *J. Neurosci.* 22:3321–25

Di Chiara G. 1999. Drug addiction as dopamine-dependent associative learning disorder. *Eur. J. Pharmacol.* 375:13–30

Dickinson A, Balleine B. 1994. Motivational control of goal-directed action. *Anim. Learn. Behav.* 22:1–18

Dickinson A, Smith J, Mirenowicz J. 2000. Dissociation of Pavlovian and instrumental incentive learning under dopamine antagonists. *Behav. Neurosci.* 114:468–83

Edwards G. 1981. Nomenclature and classification of drug- and alcohol-related problems: a WHO memorandum. *Bull. WHO* 59:225–42

Elster J. 1999. *Strong Feelings: Emotion, Addiction, and Human Behavior.* Cambridge, MA: MIT Press

Everitt BJ, Dickinson A, Robbins TW. 2001. The neuropsychological basis of addictive behaviour. *Brain Res. Rev.* 36:129–38

Everitt BJ, Wolf ME. 2002. Psychomotor stimulant addiction: a neural systems perspective. *J. Neurosci.* 22:3312–20

Fiorino DF, Phillips AG. 1999a. Facilitation of sexual behavior and enhanced dopamine efflux in the nucleus accumbens of male rats after D-amphetamine-induced behavioral sensitization. *J. Neurosci.* 19:456–63

Fiorino DF, Phillips AG. 1999b. Facilitation of sexual behavior in male rats following d-amphetamine-induced behavioral sensitization. *Psychopharmacol.* 142:200–8

Fischman MW, Foltin RW. 1992. Self-administration of cocaine by humans: a laboratory perspective. In *Cocaine: Scientific and Social Dimensions. CIBA Found. Symp. 166*, ed. GR Bock, J Whelan, pp. 165–80. Chichester, UK: Wiley

Grimm JW, Hope BT, Wise RA, Shaham Y. 2001. Incubation of cocaine craving after withdrawal. *Nature* 412:141–42

Harmer CJ, Phillips GD. 1998. Enhanced appetitive conditioning following repeated pretreatment with d-amphetamine. *Behav. Pharmacol.* 9:299–308

Harmer CJ, Phillips GD. 1999. Enhanced conditioned inhibition following repeated pretreatment with d-amphetamine. *Psychopharmacol.* 142:120–31

Horger BA, Giles MK, Schenk S. 1992. Preexposure to amphetamine and nicotine predisposes rats to self-administer a low dose of cocaine. *Psychopharmacol.* 107:271–76

Horger BA, Shelton K, Schenk S. 1990. Preexposure sensitizes rats to the rewarding effects of cocaine. *Pharmacol. Biochem. Behav.* 37:707–11

Hurvich LM. 1981. *Color Vision.* Sunderland, MA: Sinauer

Hyman SE, Malenka RC. 2001. Addiction and the brain: the neurobiology of compulsion and its persistence. *Nat. Rev. Neurosci.* 2:695–703

Jackson ME, Frost AS, Moghaddam B. 2001. Stimulation of prefrontal cortex at physiologically relevant frequencies inhibits dopamine release in the nucleus accumbens. *J. Neurochem.* 78:920–23

Jentsch JD, Taylor JR. 1999. Impulsivity resulting from frontostriatal dysfunction in drug abuse: implications for the control of behavior by reward-related stimuli. *Psychopharmacol.* 146:373–90

Johnston LD, O'Malley PM, Bachman JG.

2001. *Monitoring the Future National Survey Results on Drug Use, 1975–2000,* Vol. II. *College Students and Adults Ages 19–40.* Bethesda, MD: Natl. Inst. Drug Abuse: NIH Publ. No. 01-4925

Kelley AE. 1999. Neural integrative activities of nucleus accumbens subregions in relation to learning and motivation. *Psychobiology* 27:198–213

Kelley AE, Berridge KC. 2002. The neuroscience of natural rewards: relevance to addictive drugs. *J. Neurosci.* 22:3306–11

Klebaur JE, Ostrander MM, Norton CS, Watson SJ, Akil H, Robinson TE. 2002. The ability of amphetamine to evoke arc (Arg 3.1) mRNA expression in the caudate, nucleus accumbens and neocortex is modulated by environmental context. *Brain Res.* 930:30–36

Knutson B, Adams CM, Fong GW, Hommer D. 2001. Anticipation of increasing monetary reward selectively recruits nucleus accumbens. *J. Neurosci.* 21:RC159

Koob GF, Caine SB, Parsons L, Markou A, Weiss F. 1997. Opponent process model and psychostimulant addiction. *Pharmacol. Biochem. Behav.* 57:513–21

Koob GF, Le Moal M. 1997. Drug abuse: hedonic homeostatic dysregulation. *Science* 278:52–58

Koob GF, Le Moal M. 2001. Drug addiction, dysregulation of reward, and allostasis. *Neuropsychopharmacology* 24:97–129

Lamb RJ, Preston KL, Schindler CW, Meisch RA, Davis F, et al. 1991. The reinforcing and subjective effects of morphine in postaddicts: a dose-response study. *J. Pharmacol. Exp. Ther.* 259:1165–73

Lett BT. 1989. Repeated exposures intensify rather than diminish the rewarding effects of amphetamine, morphine, and cocaine. *Psychopharmacol.* 98:357–62

Liu X, Matochik JA, Cadet JL, London ED. 1998. Smaller volume of prefrontal lobe in polysubstance abusers: a magnetic resonance imaging study. *Neuropsychopharmacology* 18:243–52

Lorrain DS, Arnold GM, Vezina P. 2000.

Previous exposure to amphetamine increases incentive to obtain the drug: long-lasting effects revealed by the progressive ratio schedule. *Behav. Brain Res.* 107:9–19

McAuliffe WE. 1982. A test of Wikler's theory of relapse: the frequency of relapse due to conditioned withdrawal sickness. *Int. J. Addict.* 17:19–33

Mendrek A, Blaha CD, Phillips AG. 1998. Pre-exposure of rats to amphetamine sensitizes self-administration of this drug under a progressive ratio schedule. *Psychopharmacol.* 135:416–22

Meyer-Lindenberg A, Miletich RS, Kohn PD, Esposito G, Carson RE, et al. 2002. Reduced prefrontal activity predicts exaggerated striatal dopaminergic function in schizophrenia. *Nat. Neurosci.* 5:267–71

Miczek KA, Pilotte N, eds. 2001. Special issue on stress and drug abuse. *Psychopharmacol.* 158:331–99

Nestler EJ, Hope BT, Widnell KL. 1993. Drug addiction: a model for the molecular basis of neural plasticity. *Neuron* 11:995–1006

Nocjar C, Panksepp J. 2002. Chronic intermittent amphetamine pretreatment enhances future appetitive behavior for drug- and natural-reward: interaction with environmental variables. *Behav. Brain Res.* 128:189–203

O'Brien CP, Childress AR, McLellan AT, Ehrman R. 1992. A learning model of addiction. In *Addictive States,* ed. CP O'Brien, JH Jaffe, pp. 157–77. New York: Raven

O'Brien CP, Childress AR, McLellan AT, Ehrman R, Ternes JW. 1988. Types of conditioning found in drug-dependent humans. *NIDA Res. Monogr.* 84:44–61

Park WK, Bari AA, Jey AR, Anderson SM, Spealman RD, et al. 2002. Cocaine administered into the medial prefrontal cortex reinstates cocaine-seeking behavior by increasing AMPA receptor-mediated glutamate transmission in the nucleus accumbens. *J. Neurosci.* 22:2916–25

Paulson PE, Camp DM, Robinson TE. 1991. The time course of transient behavioral depression and persistent behavioral sensitization in relation to regional brain monoamine concentrations during amphetamine withdrawal in rats. *Psychopharmacol.* 103:480–92

Pert A, Post R, Weiss SR. 1990. Conditioning as a critical determinant of sensitization induced by psychomotor stimulants. *NIDA Res. Monogr.* 97:208–41

Piazza PV, Deminière JM, Le Moal M, Simon H. 1989. Factors that predict individual vulnerability to amphetamine self-administration. *Science* 245:1511–13

Piazza PV, Deminière JM, Le Moal M, Simon H. 1990. Stress- and pharmacologically-induced behavioral sensitization increases vulnerability to acquisition of amphetamine self-administration. *Brain Res.* 514:22–26

Piazza PV, Deminière J-M, Maccari S, Le Moal M, Mormède P, Simon H. 1991. Individual vulnerability to drug self-administration: action of corticosterone on dopaminergic systems as a possible pathophysiological mechanism. In *The Mesolimbic Dopamine System: From Motivation to Action*, ed. P Willner, J Scheel-Krüger, pp. 473–95. New York: Wiley & Sons

Pierce RC, Kalivas PW. 1997. A circuitry model of the expression of behavioral sensitization to amphetamine-like psychostimulants. *Brain Res. Rev.* 25:192–216

Pierre PJ, Vezina P. 1998. D1 dopamine receptor blockade prevents the facilitation of amphetamine self-administration induced by prior exposure to the drug. *Psychopharmacol.* 138:159–66

Ramsay DS, Woods SC. 1997. Biological consequences of drug administration: implications for acute and chronic tolerance. *Psychol. Rev.* 104:170–93

Rescorla RA, Solomon RL. 1967. Two-process learning theory: relationships between Pavlovian conditioning and instrumental learning. *Psychol. Rev.* 74:151–82

Robbins TW, Everitt BJ. 1996. Neurobehavioural mechanisms of reward and motivation. *Curr. Opin. Neurobiol.* 6:228–36

Robbins TW, Everitt BJ. 1999a. Drug addiction: Bad habits add up. *Nature* 398:567–70

Robbins TW, Everitt BJ. 1999b. Interaction of the dopaminergic system with mechanisms of associative learning and cognition: implications for drug abuse. *Psychol. Sci.* 10:199–202

Robinson TE. 1988. Stimulant drugs and stress: factors influencing individual differences in the susceptibility to sensitization. In *Sensitization of the Nervous System*, ed. PW Kalivas, C Barnes, pp. 145–73. Caldwell, NJ: Telford

Robinson TE, Becker JB. 1986. Enduring changes in brain and behavior produced by chronic amphetamine administration: a review and evaluation of animal models of amphetamine psychosis. *Brain Res. Rev.* 11:157–98

Robinson TE, Berridge KC. 1993. The neural basis of drug craving: an incentive-sensitization theory of addiction. *Brain Res. Rev.* 18:247–91

Robinson TE, Berridge KC. 2000. The psychology and neurobiology of addiction: an incentive-sensitization view. *Addiction* 95(Suppl. 2):S91–117

Robinson TE, Browman KE, Crombag HS, Badiani A. 1998. Modulation of the induction or expression of psychostimulant sensitization by the circumstances surrounding drug administration. *Neurosci. Biobehav. Rev.* 22:347–54

Robinson TE, Gorny G, Mitton E, Kolb B. 2001. Cocaine self-administration alters the morphology of dendrites and dendritic spines in the nucleus accumbens and neocortex. *Synapse* 39:257–66

Robinson TE, Kolb B. 1997. Persistent structural modifications in nucleus accumbens and prefrontal cortex neurons produced by previous experience with amphetamine. *J. Neurosci.* 17:8491–97

Robinson TE, Kolb B. 1999a. Alterations in the morphology of dendrites and dendritic spines in the nucleus accumbens and prefrontal cortex following repeated treatment with amphetamine or cocaine. *Eur. J. Neurosci.* 11:1598–604

Robinson TE, Kolb B. 1999b. Morphine

alters the structure of neurons in the nucleus accumbens and neocortex of rats. *Synapse* 33:60–62

Rogers RD, Everitt BJ, Baldacchino A, Blackshaw AJ, Swainson R, et al. 1999. Dissociable deficits in the decision-making cognition of chronic amphetamine abusers, opiate abusers, patients with focal damage to prefrontal cortex, and tryptophan-depleted normal volunteers: evidence for monoaminergic mechanisms. *Neuropsychopharmacology* 20:322–39

Samaha A-N, Li Y, Robinson TE. 2002. The rate of intravenous cocaine administration determines susceptibility to sensitization. *J. Neurosci.* 22:3244–50

Schacter DL. 1996. *Searching for Memory: The Brain, The Mind, and The Past.* New York: Basic Books

Schull J. 1979. A conditioned opponent theory of Pavlovian conditioning and habituation. In *The Psychology of Learning and Motivation*, ed. GH Bower, pp. 57–90. New York: Academic

Schultz W. 1998. Predictive reward signal of dopamine neurons. *J. Neurophysiol.* 80:1–27

Schultz W. 2000. Multiple reward signals in the brain. *Nat. Rev. Neurosci.* 1:199–207

Shaham Y, Erb S, Stewart J. 2000. Stress-induced relapse to heroin and cocaine seeking in rats: a review. *Brain Res. Rev.* 33:13–33

Shalev U, Grimm JW, Shaham Y. 2002. Neurobiology of relapse to heroin and cocaine seeking: a review. *Pharmacol. Rev.* 54:1–42

Shalev U, Morales M, Hope B, Yap J, Shaham Y. 2001. Time-dependent changes in extinction behavior and stress-induced reinstatement of drug seeking following withdrawal from heroin in rats. *Psychopharmacol.* 156:98–107

Shippenberg TS, Heidbreder C. 1995. Sensitization to the conditioned rewarding effects of cocaine: pharmacological and temporal characteristics. *J. Pharmacol. Exp. Ther.* 273:808–15

Shippenberg TS, Heidbreder C, Lefevour A. 1996. Sensitization to the conditioned rewarding effects of morphine: pharmacology and temporal characteristics. *Eur. J. Pharmacol.* 299:33–39

Siegel S, Allan LG. 1998. Learning and homeostasis: drug addiction and the McCollough effect. *Psychol. Bull.* 124:230–39

Smith EE, Jonides J. 1999. Storage and executive processes in the frontal lobes. *Science* 283:1657–61

Solomon RL. 1977. Addiction: an opponent-process theory of acquired motivation: the affective dynamics of addiction. In *Psychopathology: Experimental Models*, ed. JD Maser, pp. 66–103. San Francisco: Freeman

Solomon RL, Corbit JD. 1973. An opponent-process theory of motivation. II. Cigarette addiction. *J. Abnorm. Psychol.* 81:158–71

Stewart J. 2000. Pathways to relapse: the neurobiology of drug- and stress-induced relapse to drug-taking. *J. Psychiatry Neurosci.* 25:125–36

Stewart J, Badiani A. 1993. Tolerance and sensitization to the behavioral effects of drugs. *Behav. Pharmacol.* 4:289–312

Stewart J, Vezina P. 1991. Extinction procedures abolish conditioned stimulus control but spare sensitized responding to amphetamine. *Behav. Pharmacol.* 2:65–71

Stewart J, Wise RA. 1992. Reinstatement of heroin self-administration habits: morphine prompts and naltrexone discourages renewed responding after extinction. *Psychopharmacol.* 108:79–84

Strakowski SM, Sax KW. 1998. Progressive behavioral response to repeated d-amphetamine challenge: further evidence for sensitization in humans. *Biol. Psychiatry* 44:1171–77

Strakowski SM, Sax KW, Setters MJ, Keck PE Jr. 1996. Enhanced response to repeated d-amphetamine challenge: evidence for behavioral sensitization in humans. *Biol. Psychiatry* 40:872–80

Taylor JR, Horger BA. 1999. Enhanced responding for conditioned reward produced by intra-accumbens amphetamine is potentiated after cocaine sensitization. *Psychopharmacol.* 142:31–40

Tiffany ST. 1990. A cognitive model of drug urges and drug-use behavior: role of automatic and nonautomatic processes. *Psychol. Rev.* 97:147–68

Uslaner J, Badiani A, Norton C, Day HEW, Watson SJ, et al. 2001. Amphetamine and cocaine induce different patterns of c-fos mRNA expression in the striatum and subthalamic nucleus depending on environmental context. *Eur. J. Neurosci.* 13:1977–83

Valadez A, Schenk S. 1994. Persistence of the ability of amphetamine preexposure to facilitate acquisition of cocaine self-administration. *Pharmacol. Biochem. Behav.* 47:203–5

Vanderschuren LJ, Kalivas PW. 2000. Alterations in dopaminergic and glutamatergic transmission in the induction and expression of behavioral sensitization: a critical review of preclinical studies. *Psychopharmacology* 151:99–120

Volkow ND, Fowler JS, Wolf AP, Hitzemann R, Dewey S, et al. 1991. Changes in brain glucose metabolism in cocaine dependence and withdrawal. *Am. J. Psychiatry* 148:621–26

Volkow ND, Hitzemann R, Wang GJ, Fowler JS, Wolf AP, et al. 1992. Long-term frontal brain metabolic changes in cocaine abusers. *Synapse* 11:184–90

Wagner FA, Anthony JC. 2002. From first drug use to drug dependence: developmental periods of risk for dependence upon marijuana, cocaine, and alcohol. *Neuropsychopharmacology* 26:479–88

Washton AM, Stone-Washton N. 1993. Outpatient treatment of cocaine and crack addiction: a clinical perspective. *NIDA Res. Monogr.* 135:15–30

Weiskrantz L. 1997. *Consciousness Lost and Found: A Neuropsychological Exploration.* New York: Oxford Univ. Press

White FJ, Kalivas PW. 1998. Neuroadaptations involved in amphetamine and cocaine addiction. *Drug Alcohol Depend.* 51:141–53

White NM. 1996. Addictive drugs as reinforcers: multiple partial actions on memory systems. *Addiction* 91:921–49; discussion 51–65

Wikler A. 1948. Recent progress in research on the neurophysiological basis of morphine addiction. *Am. J. Psychiatry* 105:329–38

Wise RA. 1989. The brain and reward. In *The Neuropharmacological Basis of Reward*, ed. JM Liebman, SJ Cooper, pp. 377–424. New York: Oxford Univ. Press

Wise RA, Bozarth MA. 1987. A psychomotor stimulant theory of addiction. *Psychol. Rev.* 94:469–92

Wolf ME. 1998. The role of excitatory amino acids in behavioral sensitization to psychomotor stimulants. *Prog. Neurobiol.* 54:679–720

Wyvell CL, Berridge KC. 2000. Intraaccumbens amphetamine increases the conditioned incentive salience of sucrose reward: enhancement of reward "wanting" without enhanced "liking" or response reinforcement. *J. Neurosci.* 20:8122–30

Wyvell CL, Berridge KC. 2001. Incentive sensitization by previous amphetamine exposure: increased cue-triggered "wanting" for sucrose reward. *J. Neurosci.* 21:7831–40

Annu. Rev. Psychol. 2003. 54:55–89
doi: 10.1146/annurev.psych.54.101601.145201
First published online as a Review in Advance on September 17, 2002

LANGUAGE PROCESSING: Functional Organization and Neuroanatomical Basis

Randi C. Martin

Psychology Department, Rice University, Houston, Texas 77251-1892;
e-mail: rmartin@rice.edu

Key Words aphasia, neuropsychology, word processing, sentence processing, neuroimaging

■ **Abstract** Earlier formulations of the relation of language and the brain provided oversimplified accounts of the nature of language disorders, classifying patients into syndromes characterized by the disruption of sensory or motor word representations or by the disruption of syntax or semantics. More recent neuropsychological findings, drawn mainly from case studies, provide evidence regarding the various levels of representations and processes involved in single-word and sentence processing. Lesion data and neuroimaging findings are converging to some extent in providing localization of these components of language processing, particularly at the single-word level. Much work remains to be done in developing precise theoretical accounts of sentence processing that can accommodate the observed patterns of breakdown. Such theoretical developments may provide a means of accommodating the seemingly contradictory findings regarding the neural organization of sentence processing.

CONTENTS

0066-4308/03/0203-0055$14.00

55

INTRODUCTION

The traditional view of language and the brain, instantiated in the Wernicke-Lichtheim model (Wernicke 1874, Lichtheim 1885), held that auditory word representations were localized in a posterior temporal brain region, now known as Wernicke's area, and motor word representations were localized in a frontal region, now known as Broca's area (see also Geschwind 1970). Damage to the motor word representations in Broca's area would result in a disruption of language production with a sparing of comprehension. Damage to sensory word images in Wernicke's area would impair comprehension but would not produce the mirror image syndrome to Broca's aphasia, as production would also be affected. That is, Wernicke argued that input from sensory word images was needed to select the appropriate motor word representations.

The description above is oversimplified, but even in a more elaborated form, the Wernicke-Lichtheim model falls far short of explaining the complexities of language processing (see Caplan 1987, Dronkers & Larsen 2001). The model does capture a striking difference between patients who have anterior damage and those who do not in that those with anterior damage produce nonfluent speech characterized by slow, labored articulation, whereas those with posterior damage typically produce fluent, rapidly articulated speech (though marked by phonological, grammatical, and semantic errors). (See Table 1, examples 1 and 2.) One salient limitation of this theory is that it is a theory of single-word processing and thus says nothing about the means by which words are combined into sentences. Patients who produce nonfluent speech tend to produce speech that is "agrammatic," that is, having reduced syntactic complexity and an absence of function words (e.g., prepositions and auxiliary verbs) and inflectional markers (e.g., plural markers on nouns and past tense markers on verbs). This agrammatism is not obviously accounted for by a disruption to motor word representations (but see Lenneberg 1973).

Studies during the 1970s and early 1980s uncovered surprising findings that challenged the traditional model. These findings demonstrated that although Broca's aphasics seemed to have good comprehension on clinical assessment, they showed poor comprehension when comprehension depended on understanding the syntactic information in a sentence (e.g., Caramazza & Zurif 1976, Schwartz et al. 1980). For example, when asked to match a sentence such as "The dog was chased by the cat" to a picture, these patients had difficulty choosing between a correct picture and one that reversed the roles of agent and object (i.e., a picture of a dog chasing a cat). They did well, however, if the incorrect picture substituted a different noun or verb. Berndt & Caramazza (1980) argued that the syndrome of Broca's aphasia should be redefined as reflecting a disruption of syntax, which was the underlying cause of agrammatic speech and the sentence comprehension deficit. The labored articulation of the Broca's aphasics was thought to be a co-occurring deficit resulting from damage to motor areas for speech adjacent to Broca's area. Caramazza & Berndt (1978) presented evidence that aphasic patients with posterior damage had

TABLE 1   Examples of aphasic language production

1. Nonfluent aphasics telling Cinderella story
   a. Severely nonfluent (left frontal/parietal/temporal CVA)
      JS: girl . . . three . . . bad . . . wish . . . pump . . . poor girl . . .
   b. Moderately nonfluent (left frontal parietal CVA)
      ML: Always working . . . Doesn't do . . . Sunrise and sunset, work, work, work . . .
      Three ladies will attend . . . uh . . . All the fineries and . . . uh . . . all the . . .
2. Fluent aphasic conversation with speech therapist (left temporal parietal CVA)
   Therapist: What did you have (to eat)?
   PH: Today I haven't touched a /maiwa/ /dˀ/ David. He had beastly tomorrow.
   Therapist: Was the food good?
   PH: Yes, it was fine.
3. Anomic aphasic attempting to name a picture of a vest (herpes encephalitis,
   predominantly left temporal damage)
   MS: This is something that . . . depends on what it looks like. Sometimes women wear it,
   sometimes men wear it. And you put underneath before you . . . You put a shirt on. Then
   you put this on. Then you put a coat on . . .

a disruption of semantic representations, which again affected both comprehension and production. They cited findings from Blumstein et al. (1977) as indicating that these patients' word comprehension deficits could not be attributed to difficulty perceiving phonological information. Thus, according to these authors, the theoretical distinction between Broca's and Wernicke's aphasia was more appropriately thought of as damage to syntax versus semantics, respectively, rather than damage to motor versus sensory word representations.

In the past 25 years neuroanatomical and behavioral findings have caused difficulties for this more modern synthesis as well as the traditional approach. Mohr et al. (1978) concluded that a circumscribed lesion to Broca's area gave rise to only temporary disruptions of motor speech and other language functions, with the deficits lasting only a few days to a few months. Agrammatism was not a feature of the acute or chronic state for these patients. In order for permanent disruptions of language output and agrammatism to occur, a larger lesion was required involving the insula and other areas of the frontal and parietal opercula (with such lesions often extending well posteriorly, sometimes including the supramarginal gyrus). More recently, in a study of lesion overlap, Dronkers (1996) concluded that the insula was the critical region involved in apraxia of speech, that is, in a disruption of speech motor planning.

Similar problematic findings have been uncovered with regard to the functional role of Wernicke's area. One difficulty is that the definition of Wernicke's area is not so agreed upon as Broca's area (see Wise et al. 2001 for discussion). Assuming the most common definition—the posterior third of the superior temporal gyrus (Damasio 1998)—there is evidence that a lesion restricted to this area does not give rise to the long-lasting symptom complex termed Wernicke's aphasia and that a wider lesion is needed (Selnes et al. 1983). Also, patients have been reported who have lesions outside of Wernicke's area yet who show the symptoms of Wernicke's aphasia (e.g., Murdoch et al. 1986, Dronkers et al. 2000).

Both the traditional and more recent syndrome-based approaches suffer from the heterogeneity of the deficits exhibited by patients assigned to one of the clinical classifications. For example, the poor comprehension of patients classified as Wernicke's aphasics may arise from a disruption of phoneme identification, a disruption of phonological word forms, or a disruption of semantics (see Howard & Franklin 1988 for discussion). Among Broca's aphasics with agrammatic speech, a substantial proportion does not show syntactic comprehension deficits (Berndt et al. 1996). Group studies that average results across members of the group and contrast these averages across clinical groups or with normal subjects are thus unlikely to provide a solid basis for determining the functional components of language and their organization in the brain. What is needed is a more fine-grained, theory-based analysis of the nature of the language deficits in individual cases (Caramazza & McCloskey 1988, McCloskey 1993). With such a functional analysis, one is in a much better position to determine whether consistent brain/language relationships can be identified.

Consequently, the discussion of neuropsychological data in this chapter focuses on individual case studies in which the precise nature of the patients' deficit has been identified. Lesion localization from a series of cases with the same deficits provides better information than group studies concerning the relation between language function and brain areas. Of course, we now have other sources of information regarding the localization of language function in the brain from neuroimaging studies carried out with intact normal subjects. Results from these studies may provide much more precise information than lesion studies, given the accidental nature of the size and extent of lesions in humans. It remains quite difficult, however, to design imaging studies to isolate specific cognitive functions (see Norris & Wise 2000 for discussion in the domain of speech perception). Patient data provide crucial corroborating evidence regarding the necessity of a given brain region for a particular cognitive function. In some cases unexpected results from neuroimaging have led to studies of patients with lesions to the activated region that have confirmed the localization that had not previously been uncovered in lesion studies (Thompson-Schill et al. 1997, 1998).

WORD PROCESSING

Data from normal subjects and brain-damaged patients have led to the overall model of word processing shown in Figure 1. (The model includes the processes involved in picture naming, as this task is often used to test word production.) The model assumes a separation between the lexical forms involved in spoken and written word processing, but a single semantic system that is accessed from

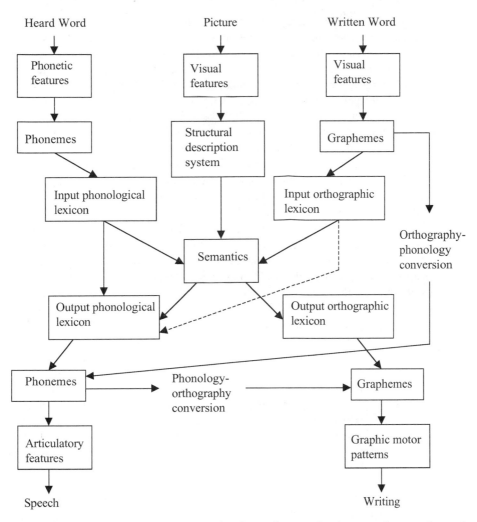

Figure 1   Model of single-word processing for auditory and written word perception and production. Also included are processes involved in picture naming.

both modalities. On both the input and output sides there are peripheral processing components involved in auditory and visual perception and the motor control of speaking and writing. The discussion focuses on the more central aspects of word processing, concentrating mainly on spoken language.

Spoken Word Recognition

NEUROPSYCHOLOGICAL STUDIES   As shown in the model, phonetic, phonemic, lexical-phonological, and semantic representations are assumed to be involved in word recognition, and disruptions at any of these levels should lead to deficits in word comprehension. Disruptions of semantic representations are discussed separately; this section concentrates on phonological aspects of word recognition.

Patients labeled as "pure word deaf" would seem to provide evidence that different systems are involved in speech and nonspeech auditory perception, as they have difficulty perceiving speech but do better with music or environmental sounds. (See Griffiths et al. 1999, Poeppel 2001 for recent reviews). Several researchers have presented evidence that, contrary to the word deaf label, these patients' deficit is not at a lexical or even phonemic level, but rather at the level of extracting the acoustic cues to speech. That is, they have difficulty perceiving rapid changes in complex pitch patterns, which affect the perception of speech more than other common sounds. Consistent with this view, these patients have difficulty discriminating nonspeech sounds that depend on perceiving rapid temporal changes (e.g., Albert & Bear 1957, Auerbach et al. 1982, Tanaka et al. 1987, Wang et al. 2000).

Pure word deaf patients typically have bilateral lesions of the superior temporal lobe, though some have unilateral lesions that, in all but one case, have been localized to the left hemisphere (Griffiths et al. 1999, Poeppel 2001). The bilateral lesions suggest that both hemispheres are involved in extracting phonetic cues to speech (Praamstra et al. 1991). The unilateral lesions have also been argued to be consistent with bilateral processing as these lesions typically include deep subcortical structures and thus could damage both phonetic processing on the left and disconnect the results of such processing on the right from lexical phonological representations on the left (Geschwind 1965, Takahasi et al. 1992, Poeppel 2001).

According to the model in Figure 1, phonetic cues are mapped onto phonemes. Some researchers have argued, however, that phonetic features are mapped directly onto lexical representations, and thus a phonemic level is not needed (Marslen-Wilson & Warren 1994). In fact, it appears that no cases have been reported that show the pattern predicted from a deficit to the phonemic level, that is, impaired vowel and consonant perception but preserved perception of nonspeech stimuli with acoustic features similar to those in speech. In contrast to the lack of evidence for a phonemic level, there is evidence supporting a lexical phonological level separate from semantics. That is, some patients have been reported who show preserved phoneme discrimination and identification but impaired performance on spoken word recognition tasks tapping lexical and semantic levels such as auditory lexical decision and synonymy judgments (Howard & Franklin 1988, Martin & Saffran 1992, Hillis et al. 1999). As with the pure word deaf patients, these patients show much better semantic processing for written words, again ruling out a semantic deficit per se. All of these cases have had unilateral left hemisphere damage. For all, the damage included temporal or parietal regions, but for two the damage was quite widespread and included other left hemisphere regions (Howard & Franklin 1988, Hillis et al. 1999).

Other patients show a preservation of lexical phonological information but disrupted access from this information to semantics. Hall & Riddoch (1997) reported a particularly striking example of this pattern. Their patient, KW, with a left parietal lesion, performed well on auditory and written lexical decisions. On semantic tasks he performed very poorly with auditory presentation but was within the normal range with written presentation. Franklin et al. (1994, 1996) and Kohn & Friedman (1986) have reported similar cases. Two of these (Franklin et al. 1994, 1996) were reported to have left middle cerebral artery infarcts, which could implicate frontal, parietal, and temporal regions. The case of Kohn & Friedman had damage to Wernicke's area.

In sum, patients with damage either to lexical phonological representations or to the connections between these representations and semantics all have left hemisphere damage, with temporal or parietal regions most often involved. Thus, whereas phonetic feature extraction may be carried out bilaterally, the results of this feature analysis appear to be mapped onto lexical phonological representations in the posterior left hemisphere, which then provide access to semantic representations. Consistent with this conclusion are findings from a study by Hillis et al. (2001), which examined the effects of reperfusion of the left superior temporal lobe in six stroke patients who had word comprehension difficulties and showed hypoperfusion of this region. Using a pharmacological agent to increase blood pressure they demonstrated increases in word comprehension that were directly related to the extent of reperfusion of this region as measured through magnetic resonance perfusion weighted imaging.

Contrary to the tenets of the traditional Wernicke-Lichtheim model, some findings from lesion studies suggest a role for the frontal lobes, specifically Broca's area, in speech perception (Blumstein 1998, 2001; Martin et al. 1999a). Blumstein (1998) reviewed studies showing that aphasic patients of all clinical categories, including Broca's aphasics, have speech perception deficits when tested on phoneme and word discrimination and identification. Functional neuroimaging of neurally intact individuals have also implicated a role for frontal regions in speech perception (see neuroimaging section for discussion).

NEUROIMAGING STUDIES   The findings from neuorimaging studies are consistent with the lesion data with regard to bilateral temporal lobe involvement in the extraction of phonetic cues from speech. When passive listening to speech sounds has been compared with rest or listening to simple auditory signals like tones, bilateral superior-temporal lobe activation has been obtained (e.g., Petersen et al. 1988; Zatorre et al. 1992; Binder et al. 1994, 1996, 1997; see Cabeza & Nyberg 2000 for an overview).

Left-lateralized activation would be predicted for phonological processing beyond the level of phonetic feature extraction. In order to reveal such processing, speech stimuli need to be compared to a control condition (or conditions) that employs stimuli with acoustic features like those in speech. The results of such studies have varied depending on the nature of the control condition and the subjects' task. Some studies have contrasted an active speech task, such as phoneme monitoring, with passive listening to speech (Zatorre et al. 1992, Poeppel et al. 1996). Others have contrasted two active listening conditions in which attention is directed either towards phonological or semantic properties of speech stimuli (Démonet et al. 1992, 1994). More left-lateralized activation is obtained in active conditions. The interpretation of such findings is open to debate, however, as some argue that passive listening or performing a semantic task automatically activates all regions normally engaged in speech processing, and thus, such subtractions would have eliminated relevant cortical areas (Norris & Wise 2000), leaving only task- or strategy-specific activation. Others argue, however, that performing an active task simply boosts activation in the most critical regions because attention is directed to speech-specific processing (Fiez et al. 1995).

Other studies have compared passive listening to speech to passive listening to stimuli with speech-like features (e.g., Binder et al. 2000, Howard et al. 1992). Binder et al. (2000) contrasted the activation resulting from passive listening to words, pseudowords (e.g., splin), reversed words (i.e., recorded speech played backwards), tones, and noise. No areas were found to be more activated in the word condition than the pseudoword or reversed word conditions. All three stimuli produced greater activation bilaterally in the mid–superior temporal gyrus and adjacent superior temporal sulcus than the nonspeech stimuli. There was only weak evidence of more extensive activation in the left than right hemisphere for the speech stimuli.

Wise and colleagues (Scott et al. 2000, Wise et al. 2001), however, have suggested that considerable lexical activation may arise from processing pseudowords (see Gaskell & Marslen-Wilson 1997, McClelland & Elman 1986) or even reversed words, as subjects consistently identify a fairly large proportion of phonemes in reversed speech (Binder et al. 2000). Scott et al. (2000) used as stimuli spoken sentences and altered versions of these sentences that varied in intelligibility and the presence of phonetic features. They reported a region of the left superior temporal sulcus that responded more to the conditions with phonetic information (whether or not they were intelligible) and also found that an anterior portion of this sulcus responded only to intelligible speech. The interpretation of the role of this more anterior region is unclear, however, as the intelligible sentences engaged sentential semantic and syntactic processes in addition to lexical processes.

Activation in frontal regions has also been uncovered in neuroimaging studies of speech perception. Price et al. (1996) reported a complex relation between task factors and inferior frontal activation [Brodmann's area (BA) 45] during speech perception (e.g., the activation was greater for slower rates of presentation of the words). Frontal areas are routinely activated, however, when the neuroimaging study employs a speech perception task that involves active manipulation of phonological information such as phoneme monitoring or phoneme discrimination (e.g., Démonet et al. 1992, 1994; Zatorre et al. 1992). Burton et al. (2000) showed that in two closely matched syllable discrimination tasks, inferior frontal activation was obtained only when the task required segmentation of the initial phoneme from the remainder of the syllable. As Norris & Wise (2000) have pointed out, tasks that require phonemic segmentation cannot be performed by illiterate individuals, yet these individuals have no difficulty perceiving speech. The process of learning letter-sound correspondences during reading acquisition may foster an awareness of sublexical phonological representations typically involved in speech output (rather than speech perception). Using a task in a neuroimaging study that requires attention to sublexical units may tap these output representations that have a frontal localization.

Spoken Word Production

NEUROPSYCHOLOGICAL STUDIES   As with word recognition, deficits in spoken word production could arise from several sources, depending on the affected stage of processing (see Figure 1). The types of errors patients produce in naming (e.g., picture naming or naming to definition) or other speech production tasks (oral reading, repetition) have been used as one source of data for identifying the locus of damage. In naming, patients may produce predominantly semantically related words (e.g., "parsley" for "carrot") (e.g., Hodges et al. 1992), predominantly phonologically related words (e.g., "golf" for "glove") (Blanken 1990), or predominantly phonologically related nonwords (e.g., "brind" for "bread") (e.g., Caplan et al. 1986), which might suggest disruptions at the semantic, lexical phonological, and sublexical phonological levels, respectively.

Even though a certain type of error may predominate, most patients produce a mixture of error types. Dell et al. (1997) attempted to account for the different relative proportions of correct responses and different error types for fluent aphasic patients in terms of disruptions to all levels of an interactive activation model of word production initially derived to account for normal production (Dell & O'Seaghdha 1992). As shown in Figure 2, the model includes semantic, lexical, and phonological levels and feedforward and feedback connections between levels.

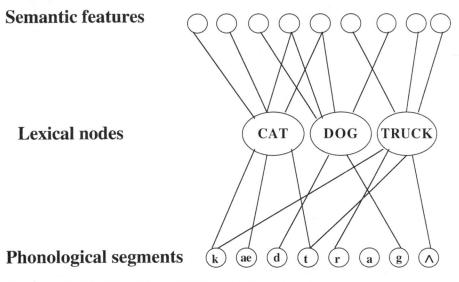

Semantic features

Lexical nodes

Phonological segments

Figure 2   Dell & O'Seaghdha's (1992) model of word production.

In the first version of the model to be applied to patient data (Dell et al. 1997), global "lesions" were made that consisted of reducing connection strengths between all levels and increasing the decay rate at all levels (with changes in the two relevant parameters adjusted to fit individual patient data). Although this approach provided a relatively good fit to the error patterns of their patients, it did not account for patients who produce virtually all semantic errors (Caramazza & Hillis 1990, Cuetos et al. 2000) nor those who produce virtually all phonological errors (Caplan et al. 1986, Caramazza et al. 2000). Foygel & Dell (2000) proposed a revised model in which the globality assumption was abandoned and lesions were made separately to the connections between the semantic and lexical and between the lexical and phonemic levels. Although this approach provided a better fit to a response pattern of predominantly phonological errors and to word repetition data, the interactivity in the model still made it unable to fit a pattern of predominantly semantic errors (Rapp & Goldrick 2000) or one in which phonologically related nonword errors greatly outnumber phonologically related word errors (Caramazza et al. 2000). Thus, the data strongly suggest that selective deficits can occur to different levels in the production process, but the details of models to account for such errors are debated with regard to the degree of interactivity between levels (Ruml et al. 2000, Rapp & Goldrick 2000).

The approach of Dell and colleagues (Dell et al. 1997, Foygel & Dell 2000) used the proportion of different error types in naming to identify the functional locus of damage. Clearly, other data may be brought to bear. Among patients producing predominantly semantic errors, some show a disruption of semantic knowledge on comprehension tests (e.g., Howard & Orchard-Lisle 1984, Hillis et al. 1990, Hodges et al. 1992), whereas others do not (e.g., Caramazza & Hillis 1990, Cuetos et al. 2000). Thus, the former appear to have damage at the semantic level per se, whereas the latter have damage beyond the semantic level, that is, in accessing phonological representations from semantic representations. Another relevant factor in determining the locus of damage is the patients' ability to repeat words and nonwords. Some patients with preserved semantics but difficulty in accessing lexical phonology show preserved word and nonword repetition (e.g., Caramazza & Hillis 1990, Martin et al. 1999b), indicating that their deficit is not at the level of producing sublexical phonological segments. Patients who make phonologically related word or nonword errors in naming typically have difficulty with repetition as well (e.g., Caramazza et al. 1986, Caplan et al. 1986, Bub et al. 1987, Shallice et al. 2000). These cases have sometimes been claimed to have a deficit in a phonological output buffer, that is, a short-term storage system for maintaining phonological information while articulatory programs are derived.

Lesion localization for word production deficits has been addressed most often with respect to the clinical category of "anomic aphasia," which is characterized by pervasive word-finding impairments in spontaneous speech and naming in conjunction with intact repetition and fluent, grammatically correct speech (see Table 1, example 3). Damasio & Damasio (1989, Damasio et al. 1996) have reported that the lesions in anomic aphasia are outside the peri-sylvian region in anterior or inferior temporal regions. Semantic abilities in comprehension have not typically been extensively assessed for these patients, however, and thus it is difficult to know whether the word-finding difficulties derive from a semantic disruption or from a disruption of lexical phonological retrieval. Some evidence suggests that a left posterior temporal region (BA 37) is crucial for the retrieval of phonological word forms in speech production, as patients with damage to this region have naming deficits even though they show preserved semantic knowledge (Raymer et al. 1997, Foundas et al. 1998, Hillis et al. 2001).

Less attention has been devoted to the issue of lesion localization with regard to sublexical phonological deficits. All but one of the cases described above that were claimed to have deficits to the output phonological buffer had left hemisphere lesions affecting a number of temporal-parietal regions, including cortical and underlying white matter; the remaining case had a similar lesion on the right. Thus, the evidence suggests posterior rather than anterior regions are involved in maintaining sublexical phonological representations.

NEUROIMAGING STUDIES   Indefrey and Levelt (2000) reviewed 58 neuroimaging studies that used a variety of tasks involving speech production (e.g., picture naming, word reading, nonword repetition). Based on these data, they argued that the left posterior middle and superior temporal gyri are involved in phonological word-form retrieval, as this area was more activated in tasks involving word than nonword production. For sublexical phonological coding, no region strictly met their criterion for proportion of studies showing significant activation, but the regions coming closest were the left posterior inferior frontal gyrus and the left mid-superior temporal gyrus.

Indefrey & Levelt (2000) identified regions that were active in overt speech tasks compared with silent controls and not active in covert speech tasks as areas involved in articulatory coding and execution. The areas satisfying this criterion were bilateral pre- and postcentral gyri. Also, typically more active in overt than covert tasks were the left anterior superior temporal gyrus, the right supplementary motor area, and the left and medial cerebellum. A recent study by Wise et al. (2001), however, identified an area of the temporo-parietal junction that showed greater activation with overt than covert articulation of a phrase (see also Buchsbaum et al. 2001).

Independent or Common Lexical Phonological Representations?

NEUROPSYCHOLOGICAL STUDIES   The model shown in Figure 1 has separate input and output lexical phonological representations. The Wernicke-Lichtheim model assumed separate sensory and motor representations for words, though access to the sensory representation was needed to insure access to the correct motor representation. There is currently considerable debate regarding whether independent input and output lexical representations are needed (Nickels et al. 1997, Martin et al. 1999b) or whether a single lexical phonological representation will suffice

(Hillis et al. 1999, Martin & Saffran 2002). Shallice (1988) argued that the semantic errors in single-word repetition (e.g., repeating "woman" as "lady") that define the syndrome of "deep dysphasia" provide strong support for the independent-lexicons view. These semantic errors indicate that the word has been perceived, so their deficit cannot be in accessing a lexical phonological form on the input side. This phonological form should be the basis of repetition if the form is the same for perception and production. In terms of a two-lexicon model, this pattern can be accounted for by a disruption in direct connections between input and output phonological forms, with the result that translation between input and output involves access to a semantic representation. Martin & Saffran (1992) have argued, however, that this deep dysphasic pattern can be accounted for with a single lexicon model by assuming that, even though the correct phonological form is initially activated, the activation decays very rapidly and the patient has to use whatever semantic information has been activated to reconstruct the phonological form for output (see Howard & Franklin 1990 for evidence counter to the rapid decay account).

NEUROIMAGING STUDIES   Although an early positron emission tomography study showed no activation of left posterior temporal areas in word production (Petersen et al. 1989), more recent studies have uncovered similar temporal regions involved in speech perception and production (Indefrey & Levelt 2000). One might question whether exactly the same areas are involved. Anderson et al. (1999) found that intra-cranial cortical stimulation of the left superior temporal lobe caused significant phonological errors in production but did not impair the patient's auditory word comprehension. However, Wise et al. (2001) found in a positron emission tomography imaging study that a region in the left posterior superior temporal sulcus that responded to words in perception was also activated during word production.

It is possible that, in line with Wernicke's original hypothesis, there is a (input) phonological representation involved in both perception and production and a separate output lexical representation involved only in production. According to such a view, it should be possible to find patients with normal word perception but impaired output (Romani 1992, Howard 1995, Martin et al. 1999b), but those showing impairments of lexical phonology on the input side should also show impaired output (Hillis et al. 1999).

Semantic Representations of Words

Recent overviews by Shelton & Caramazza (1999, 2001) have summarized neuropsychological findings on the organization of semantic representations. They have dealt extensively with the nature of category-specific deficits (e.g., semantic deficits for living but not nonliving things), concerning their underlying cause and possible neuroanatomical basis, but these are not dealt with here (see also Devlin et al. 2002). Considerable lesion data suggest that regions of the middle and inferior temporal lobe are involved in the representation of semantic knowledge (Dronkers et al. 1995). Semantic dementia cases (i.e., patients whose primary symptom is a progressively severe disruption of semantic knowledge) have damage to the left middle and inferior temporal lobes that begins at the temporal pole and proceeds posteriorly as the condition progresses (Mummery et al. 2000). Mummery et al. also found that the degree of temporal damage predicted the degree of semantic disruption. Neuroimaging studies have also uncovered left middle and inferior temporal lobe activations during semantic processing (e.g., Vandenberghe et al. 1996, Binder et al. 1997). The extent of right hemisphere involvement is unclear. Mummery et al. (2000) noted atrophy in the right temporal pole in most of their semantic dementia cases and suggested that bilateral damage was necessary for the most severe semantic deficits.

A surprising outcome of neuroimaging studies has been that robust activations appear in left inferior frontal regions (BA 45 and 47) across numerous tasks such as categorization, semantic generation, concrete/abstract judgments, and judgments of semantic similarity (see Poldrack et al. 1999 for a review) that can be differentiated from the more posterior frontal activations observed during phonological processing tasks such as phoneme monitoring or rhyme judgments (Poldrack et al. 1999, Roskies et al. 2001, McDermott et al. 2002). These frontal activations are surprising in that patients with damage to these regions do not typically show severe semantic deficits, at least on single-word processing tasks. The explanation offered for these findings is that whereas semantic knowledge may be stored posteriorly, these frontal areas serve as a semantic executive system involved in retrieving, storing, and manipulating these semantic representations (Roskies et al. 2001). Consistent with this claim are findings from patients with inferior frontal damage who show good semantic processing of single words but a short-term memory deficit specific to the retention of semantic information (Romani & Martin 1999, Freedman & Martin 2001).

Grammatical Representations of Words

WORD-CLASS EFFECTS   Words contain grammatical information as well as semantic and phonological information. For example, word-class information (noun, verb) is needed in sentence comprehension and production for syntactic information to be understood or produced correctly. Many studies have reported double dissociations in the production of different word classes [e.g., function words versus content words (Goodglass 1993), nouns versus verbs (e.g., Miceli et al. 1984; Zingeser & Berndt 1988, 1990)] (see Druks 2002 for a review). For some patients these apparent word-class effects may have a semantic basis. For example, better production of nouns than verbs and better production of verbs than function words may occur because the patient is better able to produce more concrete words (e.g., Bird et al. 2002). For some patients, however, it appears that word-class effects cannot be reduced to a semantic basis (Berndt et al. 2002, Rapp & Caramazza 2002). Consequently, these deficits suggest that at some level in the production system words are distinguished neurally with regard to the grammatical role they play in a sentence.

Some models of word production assume two levels of lexical representations: a semantic/syntactic representation (termed the lemma) and a phonological representation (termed the lexeme), with the lemma necessarily accessed prior to the lexeme (Garrett 1993, Levelt et al. 1999). Taken as support for these two levels are findings from patients who in picture naming could correctly judge the grammatical gender of a target word (Badecker et al. 1995) or whether the word fits into count or mass phrasal contexts (Vigliocco et al. 1999), even though they were unable to retrieve any of the phonemes in the word. Others researchers have argued that these findings can be accommodated in a model assuming a single lexical representation that is phonological and that connects to general syntactic properties for words (Caramazza & Miozzo 1997). The two positions appear difficult to distinguish on the basis of the available data (Nickels 2001).

MORPHOLOGICAL PROCESSING   Researchers have debated whether morphologically complex words (e.g., "worked," "teacher," "undecided") are broken down into their separate morphemes in language production and comprehension (e.g., Allen & Badecker 1999) or whether they are treated as unitary words (e.g., Bybee 1988). Many aphasic patients produce inflectional errors in speech and oral reading (e.g., producing "welds" for "welding" or "teaching" for "teacher"), which would appear to support a decompositional view of morphological processing (Allen & Badecker 1999). Such apparently inflectional or derivational errors might be attributed, however, to whole-word confusions based on phonological and semantic similarity (see Funnell 1987). Some findings argue against such an interpretation (Badecker & Caramazza 1991, Shapiro et al. 2000, Tsapkini et al. 2002). For instance, some of these patients make morphological errors only on words of one word class, that is, either nouns (Shapiro et al. 2000) or verbs (Tsapkini et al. 2000), which would not be expected if the errors were due solely to semantic and phonological similarity of the error to the target.

An issue that has recently attracted a great deal of debate is whether one or two systems are involved in computing past tense forms for regular versus irregular verbs. According to standard linguistic formulations, regular past tense forms in English (e.g., talked, gazed, needed) are computed by a rule that adds a past tense marker /d/ to verbs, with the pronunciation depending on the final phoneme of the verb. Irregular past tense forms must be retrieved from memory, as the pronunciations are not predictable from the present tense forms (e.g., "is, was"; "run, ran"). Because novel words (i.e., pseudowords such as "plag" or "spuff") have no representation in memory, the regular rule should apply to these as well. In opposition to the dual systems view, some have argued that a single connectionist system supports computation of the past tense for regular and irregular forms and for novel forms (e.g., Rumelhart & McClelland 1986).

Ullman et al. (1997) presented evidence supporting the dual systems approach. Patient groups with posterior damage (posterior aphasia, Alzheimer's disease) had difficulty producing irregular but not regular past tense forms for real words and novel words, whereas patients with frontal or basal ganglia damage (i.e., anterior aphasics or Parkinson's patients) showed the reverse pattern. Ullman et al. argued that these results were due to general properties of posterior versus frontal systems in which posterior regions support declarative memory-based representations, whereas frontal/basal ganglia regions support procedural or rule-based knowledge. On the other side of the issue, Joanisse & Seidenberg (1999) and Patterson et al. (2001) have provided computational and empirical evidence for a single system approach. They argue that the observed double dissociation in the patient data derives from other factors, specifically, semantic deficits in patients with posterior damage (Patterson et al. 2001) and phonological deficits in patients with frontal damage (Patterson 2002). Tyler et al. (2002) argued, however, that a phonological deficit cannot account for anterior aphasics' difficulty with regular forms, as the anterior aphasics they tested who showed worse performance on regular than irregular verb inflection performed quite well on various phoneme discrimination tasks.

It should be noted that the plausibility of the claim that frontal brain regions support rule-based grammatical processing hinges in part on claims that anterior aphasics have difficulty with such processes in comprehension. As discussed in the next section, it is far from clear that this is the case.

SENTENCE PROCESSING

Sentence Comprehension

DISSOCIATIONS AMONG SYNTACTIC ABILITIES   As mentioned in the introduction, proposals from the 1970s and 1980s about a general syntactic deficit in Broca's aphasia were undermined by several lines of evidence: for one, the not infrequent co-occurrence of agrammatic speech and preserved syntactic comprehension (Berndt et al. 1996). In addition, several studies demonstrated that many patients who showed asyntactic comprehension on sentence-picture matching did well on judging the grammatical acceptability of sentences (Linebarger et al. 1983, Shankweiler et al. 1989, Wulfeck 1988). Included among the types of errors the patients could detect were the omission or substitution of function words and inflections—the elements most affected in their speech. Linebarger and colleagues (Linebarger et al. 1983, Linebarger 1990, Saffran & Schwartz 1988) argued that these findings demonstrated a dissociation between two aspects of sentence-level processing: determining the grammatical structure of the sentence and the mapping between grammatical and thematic roles, with only the latter being affected in these patients. That is, for example, these patients would be able to determine that "The truck that the car splashed was green" is a grammatical sentence and that "car" is the grammatical subject and "truck" the grammatical object of "splashed." They would be unable to determine, however, that "car" should be mapped as the agent of "splashed" and "truck" as the theme (i.e., the entity acted upon). Thus, they would fail on all tasks requiring the interpretation of sentence meaning, such as sentence-picture matching, enactment (acting out the action with toy objects), or sentence anomaly judgments (e.g., determining that "The quarterback that the football threw was old" was a nonsensical sentence). They would succeed if the task tapped only the determination of acceptable structure, even for sentences with complex structures, such as judging as ungrammatical a sentence like "The cake that the boy ate the pie was delicious" (Linebarger 1990).

INDEPENDENCE OF SEMANTIC AND SYNTACTIC REPRESENTATIONS   Whereas   in general agrammatic speakers do not provide the clearest evidence of a dissociation between the processing of syntax and semantics in comprehension, some patients do provide such evidence. Ostrin & Tyler (1995) reported a patient (JG) who performed poorly on sentence-picture matching when the distractor picture depicted a reversal of role relations but performed well when the distractor included a lexical substitution. Unlike the patients reported by Linebarger et al. (1983), however, this patient performed poorly on grammaticality judgment tasks and showed no sensitivity to violations of grammatical structure in a word-detection task. JG performed well on comprehension tests for single words and showed normal semantic priming. Although classified behaviorally as a Broca's aphasic, JG's lesion was left temporo-parietal.

Some patients with Alzheimer's dementia demonstrate the opposite dissociation of very impaired knowledge of word meanings but preserved grammatical knowledge. For example, they might be unable to realize that a phrase such as "The jeeps walked" is nonsensical but yet be able to detect the grammatical error in a phrase like "The jeeps goes" (Hodges et al. 1994). Two semantic dementia patients have been reported who showed a remarkable ability to understand grammatical structure and appropriately assign thematic roles such as agent or theme to complex constructions like "It was the tiger that the lion bit" even though they could not distinguish the meaning of the nouns in the sentence (Schwartz & Chawluk 1990, Breedin & Saffran 1999). Semantic dementia cases such as these typically have diffuse frontal and temporal damage, and their temporal lobe damage presumably underlies their inability to comprehend the nouns in the sentences (Mummery et al. 2000). It is difficult, though, to speculate about which preserved brain areas subserve their spared grammatical processing.

Although the neuropsychological findings indicate that semantic and syntactic knowledge may be independently represented, findings from normal subjects indicate that during sentence processing the two sources of knowledge interact in determining sentence interpretation (Boland 1997, Trueswell et al. 1994). Some patient data are consistent with this conclusion. Saffran et al. (1998) showed that some patients may use the grammatical structure of sentences during comprehension when there are weak semantic constraints (e.g., understanding that "boy" is the agent of "pushed" in "The boy that the girl pushed ..."), but fail to use the grammatical structure when there are strong semantic constraints (e.g., mistakenly interpreting the "woman" as the agent of "spanked" in "The woman that the child spanked ...") (see also Tyler 1989).

WORKING MEMORY AND SENTENCE COMPREHENSION   Theories of comprehension often assume a role for a short-term or working memory system that is used to hold partial results of comprehension processes while the rest of a sentence is processed and integrated with earlier parts (e.g., Just & Carpenter 1992). Aphasic patients often have very restricted short-term memory spans, typically being able to recall only two or three words from a list, compared with normal subjects' five or six words (de Renzi & Nichelli 1975). Studies with normal subjects indicate that comprehension becomes more difficult when the working memory demands of sentence processing increase (Just & Carpenter 1992, Gibson 1998). Thus, one might hypothesize that patients' restricted memory span is the source of observed sentence comprehension difficulties. However, a number of studies have shown that patients with very restricted memory spans may show excellent sentence comprehension even for sentences with complex syntactic structures (Butterworth et al. 1986, Caplan & Waters 1999, Hanten & Martin 2001, Waters et al. 1991).

Caplan & Waters (1999; see also Caplan & Hildebrandt 1988) have interpreted such findings to indicate that there is a working memory capacity specific to sentence processing that is different from that tapped by span tasks. They divide the procedures involved in sentence processing into interpretive and post-interpretive processes. Interpretive processes include all on-line syntactic and semantic processes, including those involved in semantic interpretation based on the ongoing discourse. Post-interpretive processes involve using the products of interpretive processing to carry out some task, such as sentence-picture matching or enactment of the action in the sentence. Based on a large number of findings with normal and brain-damaged subjects, Caplan & Waters argue that interpretive processing draws on the capacity specific to sentence processing, whereas post-interpretive processing draws on the capacity tapped by span tasks.

Martin and colleagues (Hanten & Martin 2000; Martin et al. 1994, 1999b; Martin & Romani 1994) have provided a different view on the relation between the capacities involved in span tasks and sentence processing. They argue that span tasks tap both phonological and semantic retention (see also Martin & Saffran 1997). The phonological component of span tasks is independent of the capacity involved in sentence processing, as patients with difficulty retaining phonological information may show preserved sentence comprehension. However, the semantic component does play a role in sentence comprehension in the maintenance of word meanings prior to their integration with other word meanings. Specifically, patients with a semantic retention deficit had difficulty detecting the semantic anomaly in sentences with several adjectives preceding a noun (e.g., "The rusty old red swimsuit") or with several nouns preceding a verb (e.g., "Rocks, trees, and shrubs grew in the back yard") but did better when the adjectives followed the noun or the nouns followed the verb. Martin and colleagues agree with Caplan & Waters (1999) to some extent, as they argue that the retention of specifically syntactic structural information is independent of both phonological and semantic capacities (Martin & Romani 1994).

NEUROANATOMICAL BASIS OF SENTENCE COMPREHENSION

Lesion studies   Although many studies investigating syntactic comprehension deficits have focused on Broca's aphasics, several studies have demonstrated a similar pattern of increasing comprehension difficulty with increasing syntactic complexity for patients falling into other syndrome categories or having lesions restricted to posterior regions (Naeser et al. 1987, Caplan & Hildebrandt 1988, Caplan et al. 1996). Dronkers et al. (1994) found that among Broca's aphasics, those who had lesions affecting a portion of the left anterior temporal lobe had difficulty computing sentence meaning based on syntactic information, whereas those with a lesion restricted to Broca's area did not. Dronkers & Larsen (2001) state, however, that lesions restricted to this temporal lobe region did not result in this comprehension deficit. Moreover, some of the patients in the Caplan et al. (1996) study who had syntactic comprehension deficits did not have lesions affecting this region. Several researchers have suggested that a complex system of brain regions underlies syntactic aspects of comprehension (Caplan et al. 1996, Dronkers & Larsen 2001, Dick et al. 2001) and that the degree of damage to the overall system predicts the degree of comprehension deficit. Although this may be the case, there are many aspects to syntactic processing (e.g., the assignment of hierarchical structure, the assignment of thematic roles, the processing of long-distance relations, the maintenance of working memory representations), and the failure of any of these could lead to difficulty with more complex constructions (Martin 1995). Individual cases need to be studied in enough detail to specify the nature of the deficit in order to determine if subcomponents of syntactic processing map onto more precise brain regions.

Neuroimaging studies   As with the lesion data, there is no clear-cut conclusion emerging from neuroimaging studies regarding the brain regions underlying syntactic processing. The patient data imply that different brain regions are involved in determining syntactic structure and using that structure to assign thematic roles. Neuroimaging studies have typically employed tasks that emphasize one or the other, but without consideration of the implications of these methodological differences. Another methodological variation is the use of passive listening versus active tasks, with the attendant concerns, as in the word-comprehension literature, of whether the passive tasks do not sufficiently engage the subject to reveal activation of all critical brain regions and whether the active tasks introduce activation specific to task demands.

One approach to isolating syntactic from semantic processing has been to use sentence materials in which content words have been replaced with pseudowords (e.g., "The blives semble on the plim") or, less often, with semantically anomalous words (e.g., "The kitchens march on the clouds"). In a passive listening study, Mazoyer et al. (1993) found that the temporal poles were activated bilaterally in their normal prose and syntactic conditions (which employed both of these manipulations) but not in their word-list condition. Two recent studies involving active processing of sentences with pseudowords required judgments of whether the stimuli had syntactic structure (Friederici et al. 2000) or were grammatically acceptable (Moro et al. 2001). Both studies found deep inferior frontal activation bilaterally for the pseudoword relative to control conditions. Importantly, however, Friederici et al. did not find such frontal activation when subjects made the same judgment about normal sentences. It is possible that the frontal activations with pseudoword stimuli derived from the difficulty in maintaining these stimuli in short-term memory long enough to extract grammatical information.

Another approach to isolating syntactic processing has been to use sentences with semantically appropriate words and active tasks that stress either syntactic processing (e.g., grammaticality judgments) or semantic processing (e.g., semantic acceptability). Two studies taking this approach failed to find regions that were selectively activated by their syntactic conditions (Ni et al. 2000, Kuperberg et al. 2000), though both found regions selectively activated by their semantic conditions. Of course, one might argue that the semantic conditions necessarily engage syntactic processing, and thus subtracting the semantic from the syntactic conditions takes out activation owing to syntactic processing. Dapretto & Bookheimer (1999) took a somewhat similar approach and found greater activation in Broca's area (left BA 44) for their syntactic condition and greater activation in a more anterior frontal region (left BA 47) in their semantic condition. This study, unlike the other two, required the determination of sentence meaning in the syntactic condition (e.g., determining that "The teacher was outsmarted by the student" meant the same as "The student outsmarted the teacher").

A third approach has been to determine the brain regions that show greater activation with increasing syntactic complexity of the stimuli. In a passive listening study, Stowe et al. (1998) found that the left posterior and middle temporal gyrus showed increasing activation with more complex structures. Their study did not, however, control for the specific words in the sentences and sentence length in the different conditions. Other studies have used active tasks in which subjects judge semantic acceptability or answer comprehension questions for different sentence types that are closely matched in length and content words but vary in syntactic complexity. Structures such as the following have been compared:

1. Center-embedded subject relative: The child that spilled the juice stained the rug.
2. Center-embedded object relative: The juice that the child spilled stained the rug.

Numerous studies with normal subjects have demonstrated that the object-relative structure is more difficult than the subject-relative structure and that a contributing factor is the memory demand in the object-relative form involved in reactivating the head noun following the embedded clause verb (e.g., "juice" following "spilled") after having processed the embedded clause subject (e.g., "child") (see Gibson 1998 for discussion).

Taking this approach, Just et al. (1996) found that activation increased with increasing sentence difficulty in the left inferior frontal gyrus and the left middle- and superior temporal gyri. Homologous areas on the right also showed increasing activation, but the overall level of activation was smaller. In contrast, Stromswold et al. (1996) found that only a region within Broca's area was more active for their more complex structure. Caplan et al. (1998) replicated this finding of greater activation in (or near) Broca's area but also showed greater activation for the more complex structures in a left medial frontal area and in the cingulate. More recently, Caplan (2001) reported some additional replications but also some failures to replicate activation in Broca's area in studies using similar sentence contrasts. In one study using elderly subjects and another using young subjects matched in education to the elderly subjects, activation was obtained in parietal and superior frontal areas, though the exact locations were different for the two groups. In an event-related design using young subjects Caplan et al. (2001) uncovered activation in the angular gyrus and a superior temporal region. Caplan et al. have suggested that one possible source of this variation across studies is the varying syntactic proficiencies of their subjects and the varying difficulty of the tasks assigned the subjects (i.e., whole sentence reading versus word-by-word reading).

It is perhaps premature to draw general conclusions about the brain regions underlying syntactic processing until a better understanding has been obtained about the effects of different tasks, different types of materials, different presentation modes, and different subject groups. It is the case, however, that inferior frontal activation has been observed in Brodmann's areas (BAs) 44 and 45 across several studies (though not all) that have required subjects to compute a meaning representation for complex structures. To interpret this activation one has to keep in mind that patients with damage to this region do not typically have difficulty with grammaticality judgments. Thus, this region should not be interpreted as one involved in assigning syntactic structure to a sentence. Instead, this region may be involved in semantic working-memory functions such as those related to reactivating a semantic representation for an earlier occurring noun that has to be linked to a later occurring position in a sentence (as in the object-relative constructions) (see Caplan et al. 1998, Stowe et al. 1998 for related discussion). Such an effect related to semantic retrieval and manipulation would be consistent with findings showing activation in this region for various types of semantic processing tasks (Poldrack et al. 1999).

SENTENCE PRODUCTION

Patterns of Sentence Production Deficits in Aphasia: Challenges to Traditional Claims

Sentence production deficits have also been a focus of research in aphasia, although in this domain much of the work originated from a syndrome-based approach, concentrating on Broca's aphasics who produce agrammatic speech, that is, speech marked by simplified grammatical form and the omission of function words and inflections. Fluent speakers are said to produce "paragrammatic speech," which is characterized by the substitution of inappropriate function words and inflectional morphemes rather than their omission. Some researchers attributed these differences to a syntactic deficit in Broca's aphasics and a word retrieval deficit in fluent speakers that affects both content and function words (see Berndt 2001 for discusssion). As in the study of comprehension, more recent findings have challenged these claims concerning the differences between nonfluent and fluent speakers. Cross-linguistic studies of aphasia suggest that Broca's aphasics tend to produce a default form of a verb, which in English tends to be an infinitive form (i.e., without inflection), whereas in other languages this will be an inflected form (Menn 2001). Wernicke's aphasics also tend to over-produce verb forms that occur frequently in their native language but produce a wider range of options. Both omissions and substitutions of function words have been documented in detailed analyses of agrammatic (Miceli et al. 1989) and paragrammatic (Butterworth & Howard 1987) speech (see also Haarmann & Kolk 1992). Both nonfluent and fluent speakers show reduced structural complexity, with the deficit taking similar forms across the two groups (Bird & Franklin 1996).

Moreover, sentence-structure and function-word difficulties have been found to dissociate, arguing against the claim that both derive from the same syntactic deficit. Some patients demonstrate reduced sentence complexity but accurate production of function words and inflections (Bird & Franklin 1995/1996, Saffran et al. 1989), whereas others show the reverse (Miceli et al. 1983, Kolk et al. 1985, Nespoulous et al. 1988, Nadeau & Rothi 1992). A patient reported by Thompson et al. (2002) showed a particularly striking dissociation in this regard, as she produced complex syntactic structures as often as normal subjects but made many errors in the production of inflectional morphemes, though she was able to produce function words appropriately. As this indicates, the relative proportion of function words versus inflectional errors can vary substantially across patients, as can other properties of these errors such as the proportion of omissions versus substitutions and the relative difficulty with different kinds of function words (e.g., determiners versus auxiliary verbs) (Miceli et al. 1989).

THEORETICAL ACCOUNTS OF SENTENCE-PRODUCTION DISORDERS   These similarities in grammatical deficits across syndromes and variations within syndromes imply that, as in the study of comprehension, a more fruitful approach than group comparisons would be the study of individual cases with respect to their implications for theory. Figure 3 shows a standard model of language production. The model was presented by Bock & Levelt (1994) and represents a somewhat modified version of a theory initially proposed by Garrett (1980). At the top level is a nonlinguistic representation of the message to be expressed. At the next level lexical-semantic forms are accessed and the functional relations among them are spelled out (e.g., grammatical roles of nouns with respect to verb, modification relations between adjectives and nouns). At the next level syntactic

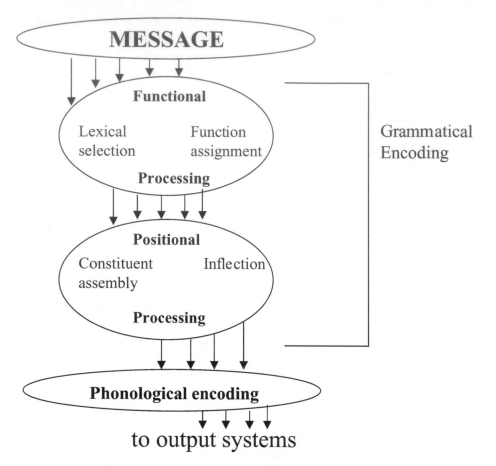

Figure 3   Bock & Levelt's (1994) model of sentence production.

frames are chosen to express the functional relations, and lexical phonological forms are inserted into the frame. At this point a linear ordering of the words is developed, and function words and grammatical markers are inserted at appropriate points. At the next stage the phonetic representation of the utterance is specified.

As the model postulates two levels of grammatical representation (the functional and positional levels), one might hypothesize that patients with grammatical deficits in production could have selective damage to one of these two components. At each level, however, there are various representations and processes involved, and thus, different types of deficits might appear from damage to the same level. At the functional level one major component involves mapping of the relations between the verbs and nouns that play thematic roles with respect to the verb (Bock & Levelt 1994). The specific verb to be used dictates what grammatical role a noun with a specific thematic role will play (e.g., the recipient will be the subject of an active sentence using the verb "receive" but the indirect object of an active sentence using "give"). A deficit in knowledge of the relations of thematic and grammatical roles entailed by verbs could potentially lead to an incomplete specification at the functional level and a reduction in sentence structure, such as the failure to produce a required indirect object (Saffran et al. 1980). Berndt et al. (1997) found some support for this notion in a study of 10 patients who varied in their relative ability to produce nouns and verbs in single-word tasks. They found a strong relation between greater difficulty with verbs than nouns and impairments on structural measures of spontaneous speech such as mean sentence length, sentence elaboration with content words, and proportion of words in sentences. Two of the five verb-impaired patients showed a much greater proportion of grammatically acceptable sentences and greater production of the object noun when asked to generate a sentence using an experimenter-provided verb compared with a noun.

Another type of production deficit has also been attributed to a disruption at the functional level. Martin & Blossom-Stach (1986) and Caramazza & Miceli (1991) reported case studies of patients who produced appropriate nouns and verbs but often reversed the roles of the nouns with respect to the verb (e.g., saying "The boy was pushed by the girl" for a picture of a boy pushing a girl). They argued that these patients had difficulty with the mapping between thematic roles and grammatical roles at the functional level (i.e., they had a mapping deficit on the production side). Interestingly, these patients produced otherwise grammatically correct utterances, indicating that the other stages in the production process were executed appropriately. Also, both patients showed similar mapping deficits in comprehension, suggesting that a central process subserves the mapping between grammatical and thematic roles in both production and comprehension. Whereas these patients showed a general mapping deficit, other patients have demonstrated difficulties that appear limited to certain verbs, specifically those for which there exists a closely related verb with different mapping relations (e.g., give-take, buy-sell) (Breedin & Martin 1996, Byng 1988).

A disruption at the positional level could also take different forms. Difficulty with accessing syntactic frames could be another possible locus of reduced structural complexity (Goodglass et al. 1994), as patients might be able to access only the simplest, most frequent structural frames (Stemberger 1984). Also, Garrett (1980) claimed that function words and inflectional markers are part of the syntactic frame. If so, difficulty with accessing frames would lead to errors involving such elements. Caramazza & Hillis (1989) endorsed Garrett's approach in their interpretation of findings from a patient who omitted function words and inflections on sentence production tasks but who had no difficulty with functions words on single-word tasks. They pointed out, however, that Garrett's model is under-specified with regard to accounting for aspects of their patient's behavior (e.g., the greater proportion of omissions of function words than inflections) and the variation in substitutions versus omissions of function words across different patients.

Other theorists have argued that grammatical elements are retrieved in the same fashion as content words (Bock 1989). If so, some other means of explaining disorders of function words and inflectional markers would have to be proposed. Various hypotheses have been advocated: (a) a disruption of function words and grammatical markers per se, which constitute a specialized word class (Bradley et al. 1980); (b) a syntactic deficit that prevents determination of the correct function word or inflection to express grammatical relations (Thompson et al. 2002); (c) a deficit in accessing all low imageability words (Bird et al. 2002); (d) a phonological disturbance that affects late stages of the production process, during which the phonological forms of function words and inflections are determined (Saffran et al. 1980). Of course, these hypotheses would not have to be mutually exclusive; that is, the different patterns of function-word deficits for different patients may have different underlying causes.

WORKING MEMORY DEFICITS IN PRODUCTION   Although the role of working memory in comprehension has been studied extensively, relatively little attention has been paid to its role in production. A model like that in Figure 3 would imply that working memory capacities of various types are involved, as the representations for several words would have to be activated and maintained simultaneously at different stages in the process. This maintenance would have to persist long enough for the processes at the next stage to be carried out.

Kolk (1995) has hypothesized that aphasic language production patterns derive from a disruption of temporal coordination during syntactic planning. He proposes that at the positional level both content words and function words are inserted into a syntactic frame. Difficulties arise owing to slow activation or overly rapid decay of some elements that should be expressed in the same syntactic unit. The more complex the syntactic structure, the more elements to be realized and the more likely some temporal mismatch will occur between elements. Patients can adapt to this deficit by either using simpler structures or sticking with more complex structures but omitting some elements. In support of this view, Kolk and his colleagues have shown that patients' production patterns can appear quite different under different task demands (Kolk & Heeschen 1992, Hofstede & Kolk 1994).

Martin & Freedman (2001) presented evidence that a semantic short-term memory limitation can affect patients' productions. Patients with a semantic retention deficit (but not those with a phonological retention deficit) had difficulty producing adjective-noun phrases (e.g., "small leaf," or "short dark hair"), although they were able to produce the individual adjectives and nouns in isolation. They argued that subjects plan speech in a phrase-by-phrase fashion, planning the head noun and all the preceding content words in the phrase at a lexical-semantic level prior to initiating phonological retrieval. These patients' lexical-semantic retention deficits prevented them from simultaneously maintaining such representations for several words. In support of this argument Martin & Freedman showed that these patients did better producing the same content in a sentence form (e.g., "The leaf is small" or "The hair is short and dark"), as these sentence forms allowed them to produce fewer content words in an individual phrase (see also Linebarger et al. 2000 for findings supporting a capacity limitation as a factor in at least the structural limitations of agrammatic speech).

NEUROANATOMICAL BASIS OF SENTENCE PRODUCTION

Lesion studies   As discussed earlier, Mohr et al. (1978) found that patients with a lesion restricted to Broca's area did not produce agrammatic speech. Larger lesions of the frontal and parietal opercula and the insula were required. The patient reported by Caramazza & Hillis (1989), who omitted a large proportion of function words, was left-handed and had a right frontal-parietal lesion. At least some types of grammatical deficits in production appear to derive from posterior lesions. The patients who had relatively preserved structural abilities in production but impaired production of function words (Miceli et al. 1983, Kolk et al. 1985, Nespoulous et al. 1988, Nadeau & Rothi 1992) had temporal or parietal lesions. The two patients reported above who showed a disruption in the assignment of thematic roles but preserved production and comprehension of grammatical morphemes had parietal (Caramazza & Miceli 1991) and temporo-parietal (Martin & Blossom-Stach 1986) lesions.

With regard to working memory deficits, the three cases reported by Martin & Freedman (2001) with lexical-semantic short-term memory deficits and disrupted production of adjective-noun phrases had lesions that overlapped in the left posterior inferior frontal gyrus and adjacent anterior parietal region, though one had an extensive lesion affecting temporal regions as well.

Neuroimaging studies   So far, only two neuroimaging studies have assessed production beyond the single word. In one of these, subjects described Rorschach inkblots in a spontaneous fashion while being scanned (Kircher et al. 2000). The rate of word production per 20-second interval was measured. Speech rate was positively correlated with the degree of signal change in the left superior temporal lobe and supramarginal gyrus. The authors attributed this activation to lexical retrieval, though the degree of syntactic, prosodic, and phonological planning would also vary with speech rate.

Indefrey et al. (2001) used a more controlled production task to determine the regions involved in syntactic processing during production. Subjects saw animated scenes involving the movement of simple colored objects and described them in a prespecified fashion using either full sentences (e.g., "The red square launches the blue ellipse"), a sequence of phrases with local but not sentence-level syntactic structure (e.g., "red square" "blue ellipse" "launch"), or a sequence of words without syntactic structure (e.g., "square" "red" "ellipse" "blue" "launch"). A frontal region that overlapped Broca's area (BA 44) to some extent but was mainly posterior to Broca's area (most likely in BA 6) was found to be most activated in the sentence condition, next most active in the phrase condition and least in the word condition. Although the degree of prosodic planning and the amount of phonological material produced were not equated across conditions, the authors concluded that this activation reflected syntactic planning, as a faster rate of stimulus presentation did not produce greater activation in this region. It should be noted, however, that according to the hypotheses of Martin & Freedman (2001), the demands on semantic short-term memory would also vary across conditions and could be the source of the frontal activation.

CONCLUSIONS

Since Wernicke's time, a great deal has been learned from neuropsychological studies about the functional organization of the language system. The study of word processing has moved from a consideration of only sensory and motor representations to the development of models containing levels of phonological, grammatical, and semantic representations. Studies of sentence comprehension have uncovered different components of grammatical processing and semantic integration. Progress in the study of sentence production has also been made, though here much more specific theoretical proposals are needed, as observed deficits can often be attributed to several different potential sources, and many details remain without explanation.

With regard to the neural systems underlying these complex processes, some progress has been made, though clearly much remains to be done. Some claims are well supported by both neuroimaging and lesion data: (*a*) Bilateral superior temporal lobes are involved in extracting the phonetic features of speech; (*b*) lexical phonological representations are represented in left posterior regions, most likely in the superior temporal lobe or sulcus; (*c*) semantic representations are localized in the left middle and inferior temporal gyri, with evidence that similar structures on the right may also be involved. Other claims have some support but need further verification, such as: (*a*) A left posterior temporal region (BA 37) is involved in linking semantic and phonological representations in word production; (*b*) left inferior frontal areas are involved in phoneme segmentation; (*c*) more anterior left inferior frontal regions are involved in semantic manipulation and retention. The localization of sentence-level processes seems much less clear based on both lesion and imaging data. Although some researchers seem committed to the notion that Broca's area is involved in syntactic processes in production and comprehension, there is much evidence indicating that syntactic deficits may derive from posterior lesions, and a number of neuroimaging studies show posterior activation related to syntactic processes.

One commonality across the several domains of language processing covered in this review is that frontal activation in neuroimaging studies is more likely to occur for phonological, semantic, and syntactic tasks that require active processing on the part of the subject. It is possible that, as has been hypothesized for semantic processing (Roskies et al. 2001), these frontal activations result from executive processes involved in manipulating or maintaining different types of representations—with different frontal regions specialized for maintaining different types of information (phonological, semantic, syntactic) or for carrying out different types of functions (retention, selection). More routinized functions may be carried out in temporal/parietal regions. Such claims are clearly speculative at this point but may provide a basis for further investigation.

ACKNOWLEDGMENTS

This preparation of this manuscript was supported in part by NIH Grant DC-00218 to Rice University. The author acknowledges Frank Tamborello's assistance with technical aspects of this chapter.

The *Annual Review of Psychology* is online at http://psych.annualreviews.org

LITERATURE CITED

Albert ML, Bear D. 1957. Time to understand: a case study of word deafness with reference to the role of time in auditory comprehension. *Brain* 97:373–84

Allen M, Badecker W. 1999. Stem homograph and stem allomorphy: representing and processing inflected forms in a multilevel lexical system. *J. Mem. Lang.* 41:105–23

Anderson JM, Gilmore R, Roper S, Crosson B, Bauer RM, et al. 1999. Conduction aphasia and the arcuate fasciculus: a reexamination of the Wernicke-Geschwind model. *Brain Lang.* 70:1–12

Auerbach SH, Allard T, Naeser M, Alexander MP, Albert ML. 1982. Pure word deafness: analysis of a case with bilateral lesions and a defect at the prephonemic level. *Brain* 105:271–300

Badecker W, Caramazza A. 1991. Morphological composition in the lexical output system. *Cogn. Neuropsychol.* 8:335–67

Badecker W, Miozzo M, Zanuttini R. 1995. The two-stage model of lexical retrieval: evidence from a case of anomia with selective preservation of grammatical gender. *Cognition* 57:193–216

Berndt RS, ed. 2001. *Handbook of Neuropsychology: Language and Aphasia.* Amsterdam: Elsevier. 2nd ed.

Berndt RS. 2001. Sentence production. See Rapp 2001, pp. 375–96

Berndt RS, Caramazza A. 1980. A redefinition of the syndrome of Broca's aphasia: impli-

cations for a neuropsychological model of language. *Appl. Psycholinguist.* 1:225–78

Berndt RS, Haendiges AN, Burton MW, Mitchum CC. 2002. Grammatical class and imageability in aphasic word production: their effects are independent. *J. Neurolinguist.* 15:353–71

Berndt RS, Haendiges AN, Mitchum CC, Sandson J. 1997. Verb retrieval in aphasia. 2. Relationship to sentence processing. *Brain Lang.* 56:107–37

Berndt RS, Mitchum C, Haendiges A. 1996. Comprehension of reversible sentences in "agrammatism": a meta-analysis. *Cognition* 58:289–308

Binder JR, Frost JA, Hammeke TA, Bellgowan PSF, Springer JA, et al. 2000. Human temporal lobe activation by speech and nonspeech sounds. *Cerebr. Cortex* 10:512–28

Binder JR, Frost JA, Hammeke TA, Cox RW, Rao SM, Prieto T. 1997. Human brain language areas identified by functional magnetic resonance imaging. *J. Neurosci.* 17:353–62

Binder JR, Frost JA, Hammeke TA, Rao SM, Cox RW. 1996. Function of the left planum temporale in auditory and linguistic processing. *Brain* 119:1239–47

Binder JR, Rao SM, Hammeke TA, Yetkin YZ, Jesmanowicz A, et al. 1994. Functional magnetic resonance imaging of human auditory cortex. *Ann. Neurol.* 35: 662–72

Bird H, Franklin S. 1995/1996. Cinderella revisited: a comparison of fluent and non-fluent aphasic speech. *J. Neurolinguist.* 9:187–206

Bird H, Franklin S, Howard D. 2002. 'Little words'—not really: function and content words in normal and aphasic speech. *J. Neurolinguist.* 15:209–37

Blanken G. 1990. Formal paraphasias: a single case study. *Brain Lang.* 38:534–54

Blumstein SE. 1998. Phonological aspects of aphasia. See Sarno 1998, pp. 157–85

Blumstein SE. 2001. Deficits of speech production and speech perception in aphasia. See Boller et al. 2001, pp. 95–113

Blumstein SE, Baker E, Goodglass H. 1977. Phonological factors in auditory comprehension in aphasia. *Neuropsychologia* 15:19–30

Bock K. 1989. Closed-class immanence in sentence production. *Cognition* 31:163–86

Bock K, Levelt W. 1994. Language production: grammatical encoding. In *Handbook of Psycholinguistics*, ed. MA Gernsbacher, pp. 945–84. San Diego, CA: Academic

Boland J. 1997. The relationship between syntactic and semantic processes in sentence comprehension. *Lang. Cogn. Process.* 12: 423–84

Bradley DC, Garrett MF, Zurif EB. 1980. Syntactic deficits in Broca's aphasia. In *Biological Studies of Mental Proceses*, ed. D Caplan, pp. 269–86. Cambridge, MA: MIT Press

Breedin S, Martin RC. 1996. Patterns of verb deficits in aphasia. An analysis of four cases. *Cogn. Neuropsychol.* 13:51–91

Breedin S, Saffran E. 1999. Sentence processing in the face of semantic loss: a case study. *J. Exp. Psychol.: Gen.* 128:547–62

Bub D, Black S, Howell J, Kertesz A. 1987. Speech output processes and reading. In *The Cognitive Neuropsychology of Language*, ed. M Coltheart, G. Sartori, R Job, pp. 79–110. Hillsdale, NJ: Erlbaum

Buchsbaum BR, Hickok G, Humphries C. 2001. Role of left posterior superior temporal gyrus in phonological processing for speech perception and production. *Cogn. Sci.* 25:663–78

Burton M, Small S, Blumstein S. 2000. The role of segmentation in phonological processing: an fMRI investigation. *J. Cogn. Neurosci.* 12:679–90

Butterworth B, ed. 1980. *Language Production*, Vol. 1. London: Academic

Butterworth B, Campbell R, Howard D. 1986. The uses of short-term memory: a case study. *Q. J. Exp. Psychol.* 38A:705–37

Butterworth B, Howard D. 1987. Paragrammatisms. *Cognition* 26:1–37

Bybee JL. 1988. Morphology as lexical organization. In *Theoretical Morphology: Approaches in Modern Linguistics*, ed. M Hammond, M Noonan, pp. 119–41. San Diego, CA: Academic

Byng S. 1988. Sentence processing deficits: theory and therapy. *Cogn. Neuropsychol.* 5:629–76

Cabeza R, Nyberg L. 2000. Imaging cognition. II. An empirical review of 275 PET and fMRI studies. *J. Cogn. Neurosci.* 12:1–47

Caplan D. 1987. *Neurolinguistics and Linguistic Aphasiology: An Introduction.* New York: Cambridge Univ. Press

Caplan D. 2001. Functional neuroimaging studies of syntactic processing. *J. Psycholinguist. Res.* 30:297–320

Caplan D, Alpert N, Waters G. 1998. Effects of syntactic structure and propositional number on patterns of regional cerebral blood flow. *J. Cogn. Neurosci.* 10:541–52

Caplan D, Hildebrandt N. 1988. *Disorders of Syntactic Comprehension.* Cambridge, MA: MIT Press

Caplan D, Hildebrandt N, Makris N. 1996. Location of lesions in stroke patients with deficits in syntactic processing in sentence comprehension. *Brain* 119:933–49

Caplan D, Vanier M, Baker C. 1986. A case study of reproduction conduction aphasia. 1. Word production. *Cogn. Neuropsychol.* 3:99–128

Caplan D, Vijayan S, Kuperberg G, West C, Waters G, et al. 2001. Vascular responses to syntactic processing: event-related fMRI study of relative clauses. *Hum. Brain Mapp.* 15:26–38

Caplan D, Waters G. 1999. Verbal working

memory and sentence comprehension. *Behav. Brain Sci.* 22:77–126

Caramazza A, Berndt RS. 1978. Semantic and syntactic processes in aphasia: a review of the literature. *Psychol. Bull.* 85:898–918

Caramazza A, Hillis AE. 1989. The disruption of sentence production: some dissociations. *Brain Lang.* 36:625–50

Caramazza A, Hillis AE. 1990. Where do semantic errors come from? *Cortex* 26:95–122

Caramazza A, McCloskey M. 1988. The case for single patient studies. *Cogn. Neuropsychol.* 5:517–28

Caramazza A, Miceli G. 1991. Selective impairment of thematic role assignment in sentence processing. *Brain Lang.* 41:402–36

Caramazza A, Miceli G, Villa G. 1986. The role of the (output) phonological buffer in reading, writing, and repetition. *Cogn. Neuropsychol.* 3:37–76

Caramazza A, Miozzo M. 1997. The relation between syntactic and phonological knowledge in lexical access: evidence from the "tip-of-the-tongue" phenomenon. *Cognition* 64:309–43

Caramazza A, Papagno C, Ruml W. 2000. The selective impairment of phonological processing in speech production. *Brain Lang.* 75:428–50

Caramazza A, Zurif EB. 1976. Dissociation of algorithmic and heuristic processes in language comprehension: evidence from aphasia. *Brain Lang.* 3:572–82

Cuetos F, Aguado G, Caramazza A. 2000. Dissociation of semantic and phonological errors in naming. *Brain Lang.* 75:451–60

Damasio H. 1998. Neuroanatomical correlates of the aphasias. See Sarno 1998, pp. 43–70

Damasio H, Damasio AR. 1989. *Lesion Analysis in Neuropsychology.* New York: Oxford Univ. Press

Damasio H, Grabowski T, Tranel D, Hichwa R, Damasio A. 1996. A neural basis for lexical retrieval. *Nature* 380:499–505

Dapretto M, Bookheimer SY. 1999. Form and content: dissociating syntax and semantics in sentence comprehension. *Neuron* 24:427–32

Dell G, O'Seaghdha P. 1992. Stages of lexical access in language production. *Cognition* 42:287–314

Dell G, Schwartz M, Martin N, Saffran E, Gagnon D. 1997. Lexical access in aphasic and nonaphasic speakers. *Psychol. Rev.* 104:801–38

Démonet J-F, Chollet F, Ramsay S, Cardebat D, Nespoulous J-L, et al. 1992. The anatomy of phonological and semantic processing in normal subjects. *Brain* 115:1753–68

Démonet J-F, Price C, Wise R, Frackowiak RSJ. 1994. Differential activation of right and left posterior sylvian regions by semantic and phonological tasks: a positron emission tomography study in normal human subjects. *Neurosci. Lett.* 182:25–28

de Renzi E, Nichelli P. 1975. Verbal and nonverbal short-term memory impairment following hemispheric damage. *Cortex* 11:341–54

Devlin J, Russell R, Davis M, Price C, Moss H, et al. 2002. Is there an anatomical basis for category-specificity? Semantic memory studies in PET and fMRI. *Neuropsychologia* 40:54–75

Dick F, Bates E, Wulfeck B, Utman JA, Dronkers N, Gernsbacher MA. 2001. Language deficits, localization, and grammar: evidence for a distributive model of language breakdown in aphasic patients and neurologically intact individuals. *Psychol. Rev.* 108:759–88

Dronkers NF. 1996. A new brain region for coordinating speech articulation. *Nature* 384:159–61

Dronkers NF, Larsen J. 2001. Neuroanatomy of the classical syndromes of aphasia. See Boller et al. 2001, pp. 19–30

Dronkers NF, Redfern BB, Knight RT. 2000. The neural architecture of language disorders. See Gazzaniga 2000, pp. 949–61

Dronkers NF, Redfern BB, Ludy CA. 1995. Lesion localization in chronic Wernicke's aphasia. *Brain Lang.* 51:62–65

Dronkers NF, Wilkins DP, Van Valin RD, Redfern BB, Jaeger JJ. 1994. A reconsideration of the brain areas involved in the disruption of morphosyntactic comprehension. *Brain Lang.* 47:461–63

Druks J. 2002. Verbs and nouns: a review of the literature. *J. Neurolinguist.* 15:289–315

Fiez JA, Raichle ME, Miezin FM, Petersen SE, Tallal P, Katz WF. 1995. PET studies of auditory and phonological processing: effects of stimulus characteristics and task demands. *J. Cogn. Neurosci.* 7:357–75

Foundas AL, Daniels SK, Vasterling JJ. 1998. Anomia: case studies with lesion localization. *Neurocase* 4:35–43

Foygel D, Dell GS. 2000. Models of impaired lexical access in speech production. *J. Mem. Lang.* 43:182–216

Franklin S, Howard D, Patterson K. 1994. Abstract word meaning deafness. *Cogn. Neuropsychol.* 11:1–34

Franklin S, Turner J, Ralph MAL, Morris J, Bailey PJ. 1996. A distinctive case of word meaning deafness? *Neuropsychology* 13:1139–62

Freedman ML, Martin RC. 2001. Dissociable components of short-term memory and their relation to long-term learning. *Cogn. Neuropsychol.* 18:193–226

Friederici AD, Meyer M, von Cramon DY. 2000. Auditory language comprehension: an event-related fMRI study on the processing of syntactic and lexical information. *Brain Lang.* 74:289–300

Funnell E. 1987. Morphological errors in acquired dyslexia: a case of mistaken identity. *Q. J. Exp. Psychol.* 39:497–539

Garrett MF. 1980. Levels of processing in sentence production. See Butterworth 1980, pp. 177–220

Garrett MF. 1993. Errors and their relevance for models of language production. In *Linguistic Disorders and Pathologies*, ed. G Blanken, J Dittman, H Grim, J Marshall, C Wallesch, pp. 69–96. Berlin: de Gruyter

Gaskell MG, Marslen-Wilson WD. 1997. Integrating form and meaning: a distributed model of speech perception. *Lang. Cogn. Process.* 12:613–56

Gazzaniga MS, ed. 2000. *The New Cognitive Neurosciences*. Cambridge, MA: MIT Press. 2nd ed.

Geschwind N. 1965. Disconnexion syndromes in animals and man. *Brain* 88:237–94, 585–644

Geschwind N. 1970. The organization of brain and language. *Science* 170:940–44

Gibson E. 1998. Linguistic complexity: locality of syntactic dependencies. *Cognition* 68:1–76

Goodglass H. 1993. *Understanding Aphasia*. San Diego, CA: Academic

Goodglass H, Christiansen JA, Gallagher RE. 1994. Syntactic constructions used by agrammatic speakers: comparison with conduction aphasics and normals. *Neuropsychology* 8:598–613

Griffiths TD, Rees A, Green GGR. 1999. Disorders of human complex sound processing. *Neurocase* 5:365–78

Haarmann HJ, Kolk HH. 1992. The production of grammatical morphology in Broca's and Wernicke's aphasics: speed and accuracy factors. *Cortex* 28:97–112

Hall DA, Riddoch MJ. 1997. Word meaning deafness: spelling words that are not understood. *Cogn. Neuropsychol.* 14:1131–64

Hanten G, Martin RC. 2000. Contributions of phonological and semantic short-term memory to sentence processing: Evidence from two cases of closed head injury in children. *J. Mem. Lang.* 43:335–61

Hanten G, Martin RC. 2001. A developmental phonological short-term memory deficit: a case study. *Brain Cogn.* 45:164–88

Hillis AE, Boatman D, Hart J, Gordon B. 1999. Making sense out of jargon: a neurolinguistic and computational account of jargon aphasia. *Neurology* 53:1813–24

Hillis AE, Rapp B, Romani C, Caramazza A. 1990. Selective impairment in semantics in lexical processing. *Cogn. Neuropsychol.* 7:191–243

Hillis AE, Kane A, Tuffiash E, Ulatowski JA, Barker PB, et al. 2001. Reperfusion of specific brain regions by raising blood pressure restores selective language functions in subacute stroke. *Brain Lang.* 79:495–510

Hodges JR, Patterson K, Tyler L. 1994. Loss of semantic memory: implications for the modularity of mind. *Cogn. Neuropsychol.* 11:505–42

Hodges JR, Patterson K, Oxbury S, Funnell E. 1992. Semantic dementia: progressive fluent aphasia with temporal lobe atrophy. *Brain* 115:1783–86

Hofstede B, Kolk H. 1994. The effects of task variation on the production of grammatical morphology in Broca's aphasia: a multiple case study. *Brain Lang.* 46:278–328

Howard D. 1995. Lexical anomia: or the case of the missing lexical entries. *Q. J. Exp. Psychol.* 48A:999–1023

Howard D, Franklin S. 1988. *Missing the Meaning: A Cognitive Neuropsychological Study of Processing of Words by an Aphasic Patient*. Cambridge, MA: MIT Press

Howard D, Franklin S. 1990. Memory without rehearsal. In *Neuropsychological Impairments of Short-Term Memory*, ed. G Vallar, T Shallice, pp. 287–318. Cambridge, UK: Cambridge Univ. Press

Howard D, Orchard-Lisle V. 1984. On the origin of semantic errors in naming: evidence from the case of a global aphasic. *Cogn. Neuropsychol.* 1:163–90

Howard D, Patterson K, Wise R, Brown WD, Friston K, et al. 1992. The cortical localization of the lexicons. *Brain* 115:1769–82

Indefrey P, Brown CM, Hellwig F, Amunts K, Herzog H, et al. 2001. A neural correlate of syntactic encoding during speech production. *Proc. Natl. Acad. Sci. USA* 98:5933–36

Indefrey P, Levelt W. 2000. The neural correlates of language production. See Gazzaniga 2000, pp. 845–65

Joanisse MF, Seidenberg MS. 1999. Impairments in verb morphology after brain injury: a connectionist model. *Proc. Natl. Acad. Sci. USA* 96:7592–97

Just M, Carpenter P. 1992. A capacity theory of comprehension: individual differences in working memory. *Psychol. Rev.* 99:122–49

Just MA, Carpenter PA, Keller TA, Eddy WF, Thulborn KR. 1996. Brain activation modulated by sentence comprehension. *Science* 274:114–16

Kircher TTJ, Brammer MJ, Williams SCR,

McGuire PK. 2000. Lexical retrieval during fluent speech production: an fMRI study. *NeuroReport* 11:4093–96

Kohn SE, Friedman RB. 1986. Word-meaning deafness: a phonological-semantic dissociation. *Cogn. Neuropsychol.* 3:291–308

Kolk H. 1995. A time-based approach to agrammatic production. *Brain Lang.* 50:282–303

Kolk H, Heeschen C. 1992. Agrammatism, paragrammatism, and the management of language. *Lang. Cogn. Process.* 7:89–129

Kolk HHJ, Van Grunsven MJF, Keyser A. 1985. On parallelism between production and comprehension in agrammatism. In *Agrammatism*, ed. ML Kean, pp. 165–206. Orlando, FL: Academic

Kuperberg GR, McGuire PK, Bullmore ET, Brammer MJ, Rabe-Hesketh S, et al. 2000. Common and distinct neural substrates for pragmatic, semantic, and syntactic processing of spoken sentences: an fMRI study. *J. Cogn. Neurosci.* 12:321–41

Lenneberg EH. 1973. The neurology of language. *Daedalus* 102:115–33

Levelt WJM, Roelofs A, Meyer AS. 1999. A theory of lexical access in speech production. *Behav. Brain Sci.* 22:1–75

Lichtheim L. 1885. On aphasia. *Brain* 7:433–84

Linebarger MC. 1990. Neuropsychology of sentence parsing. In *Cognitive Neuropsychology and Neurolinguistics: Advances in Models of Cognitive Function and Impairment*, ed. A Caramazza, pp. 55–122. Hillsdale, NJ: Erlbaum

Linebarger MC, Schwartz M, Saffran E. 1983. Sensitivity to grammatical structure in so-called agrammatic aphasics. *Cognition* 13:361–92

Linebarger MC, Schwartz MF, Romania JR, Kohn SE, Stephens DL. 2000. Grammatical encoding in aphasia: evidence from a "processing prosthesis." *Brain Lang.* 75:416–27

Marslen-Wilson W, Warren P. 1994. Levels of perceptual representation and process in lexical access: words, phonemes, and features. *Psychol. Rev.* 4:653–75

Martin N, Saffran EM. 1992. A computational

account of deep dysphasia: evidence from a single case study. *Brain Lang.* 43:240–74

Martin N, Saffran EM. 1997. Language and auditory-verbal short-term memory impairments: evidence for common underlying processes. *Cogn. Neuropsychol.* 14:641–82

Martin N, Saffran EM. 2002. The relationship of input and output phonological processing: an evaluation of models and evidence to support them. *Aphasiology* 16:107–50

Martin RC. 1995. Working memory doesn't work: a critique of Miyake et al.'s capacity theory of aphasic comprehension deficits. *Cogn. Neuropsychol.* 12:623–36

Martin RC, Blossom-Stach C. 1986. Evidence of syntactic deficits in a fluent aphasic. *Brain Lang.* 28:196–234

Martin RC, Breedin SD, Damian MF. 1999a. The relation of phoneme discrimination, lexical access, and short-term memory: a case study and interactive activation account. *Brain Lang.* 70:437–82

Martin RC, Freedman ML. 2001. Short-term retention of lexical-semantic representations: implications for speech production. *Memory* 9:261–80

Martin RC, Lesch MF, Bartha MC. 1999b. Independence of input and output phonology in word processing and short-term memory. *J. Mem. Lang.* 41:3–29

Martin RC, Romani C. 1994. Verbal working memory and sentence comprehension: a multiple-components view. *Neuropsychology* 8:506–23

Martin RC, Shelton JR, Yaffee LS. 1994. Language processing and working memory: neuropsychological evidence for separate phonological and semantic capacities. *J. Mem. Lang.* 33:83–111

Mazoyer BM, Tzourio N, Frak V, Syrota A, Murayama N, et al. 1993. The cortical representation of speech. *J. Cogn. Neurosci.* 5:467–79

McClelland JL, Elman JL. 1986. The TRACE model of speech perception. *Cogn. Psychol.* 18:1–86

McCloskey M. 1993. Theory and evidence in cognitive neuropsychology: a "radical" response to Robertson, Knight, Rafal, and Shimamura. *J. Exp. Psychol.: Learn. Mem. Cogn.* 19:718–34

McDermott K, Petersen S, Watson J, Ojemann J. 2002. A method for identifying regions selectively activated by semantic and phonological processing using functional magnetic resonance imaging. *Neuropsychologia.* In press

Menn L. 2001. Comparative aphasiology: cross-language studies of aphasia. See Boller et al. 2001, pp. 51–68

Miceli G, Mazzucchi A, Menn L, Goodglass H. 1983. Contrasting cases of Italian agrammatic aphasia without comprehension disorder. *Brain Lang.* 19:65–97

Miceli G, Silveri MC, Romani C, Caramazza A. 1989. Variation in the pattern of omissions and substitutions of grammatical morphemes in the spontaneous speech of so-called agrammatic patients. *Brain Lang.* 36:447–92

Miceli G, Silveri MC, Villa G, Caramazza A. 1984. On the basis for the agrammatics' difficulty in producing main verbs. *Cortex* 20:207–20

Mohr JP, Pessin MS, Finkelstein S, Funkenstein HH, Duncan GW, Davis KR. 1978. Broca aphasia: pathologic and clinical. *Neurology* 28:311–24

Moro A, Tettamanti M, Perani D, Donati C, Cappa SF, Fazio F. 2001. Syntax and the brain: disentangling grammar by selective anomalies. *NeuroImage* 13:110–18

Mummery CJ, Patterson K, Price CJ, Ashburner J, Frackowiak RSJ, Hodges JR. 2000. A voxel-based morphometry study of semantic dementia: relationship between temporal lobe atrophy and semantic memory. *Ann. Neurol.* 47:36–45

Murdoch BE, Afford RJ, Ling AR, Ganguley, B. 1986. Acute computerized tomographic scans: their value in the localization of lesions and as prognostic indicators in aphasia. *J. Commun. Disord.* 19:311–45

Nadeau SE, Rothi LJG. 1992. Morphologic agrammatism following a right hemisphere stroke in a dextral patient. *Brain Lang.* 43:642–67

Annu. Rev. Psychol. 2003. 54:91–114
doi: 10.1146/annurev.psych.54.101601.145128
Copyright © 2003 by Annual Reviews. All rights reserved
First published online as a Review in Advance on September 17, 2002

NEUROIMAGING STUDIES OF LANGUAGE PRODUCTION AND COMPREHENSION

Morton Ann Gernsbacher and Michael P. Kaschak

University of Wisconsin-Madison, Department of Psychology, Madison, Wisconsin 53706;
e-mail: magernsb@facstaff.wisc.edu, mpkaschak@students.wisc.edu

Key Words sentence processing, discourse processing, psycholinguistics, phonological processing, fMRI, PET

■ **Abstract** The 1990s were dubbed the "Decade of the Brain." During this time there was a marked increase in the amount of neuroimaging work observing how the brain accomplishes many tasks, including the processing of language. In this chapter we review the past 15 years of neuroimaging research on language production and comprehension. The findings of these studies indicate that the processing involved in language use occurs in diffuse brain regions. These regions include Broca's and Wernicke's areas, primary auditory and visual cortex, and frontal regions in the left hemisphere, as well as in the right hemisphere homologues to these regions. We conclude the chapter by discussing the future of neuroimaging research into language production and comprehension.

CONTENTS

INTRODUCTION

For cognitive neuroscientists the Holy Grail of research is to ascertain how the brain accomplishes its work. Throughout the history of psycholinguistics this goal could only be had through indirect means: Hints about the brain regions involved in language production and comprehension were provided by the vast and growing neuropsychological literature, documenting the task performance of patients who had suffered lesions to particular brain regions (e.g., Zurif & Swinney 1994, Obler & Gjerlow 1999).

In the decades following World War II, however, technology was developed that allowed researchers to exploit the changes in blood flow that accompany neural activity to study the brain at work. Use of this neuroimaging technology was in its infancy in 1994, when the first *Handbook of Psycholinguistics* appeared in print. Whereas a few pioneering neuroimaging studies had been performed incorporating language tasks (e.g., Petersen et al. 1988, 1989, 1990), research of this sort was scant. Indeed, there is hardly a reference to neuroimaging work in the pages of the *Handbook*, though there were chapters on neuropsychology. In the decade since then the situation has changed. There now exists a small but growing literature exploring the means by which the working brain of healthy individuals processes language, covering most of the major areas of psycholinguistics.

In this chapter we review the past 15 years of neuroimaging work on language processing. We take the term "neuroimaging" to refer to research using functional magnetic resonance imaging (fMRI) and positron emissions tomography (PET) methods. We do not attempt to distinguish between these imaging modalities with respect to the findings generated within each, given that both imaging methods will yield similar patterns of activation when participants engage in similar experimental tasks (e.g., Xiong et al. 1998). Additionally, our exclusion of event related potentials (ERP) studies (and studies using similar methodologies) reflects not a belief that these are not "true" imaging techniques, but rather a desire to focus on a body of literature developed using a limited set of techniques. First, however, we briefly review the logic and mechanics of neuroimaging studies.

The Logic of Neuroimaging Studies

PET and fMRI methodologies are based on the notion that increases in the neural activity in one particular brain region are accompanied by increases of the blood flow to that region (for a detailed technical explanation of how MRI works, see Turner & Jezzard 1994 and Cohen et al. 1993; the latter also explains the technical details of PET techniques). The increase in blood flow is delayed a few seconds from the initial increase in neural activity. Because of this delay, and because of the relatively slow rise and fall of the change in blood flow, the temporal resolution of neuroimaging studies is somewhat limited. A typical neuroimaging study relates stimulus- and task-related changes to changes in neural activity in an attempt to discern what brain regions underlie a particular type of processing and how those regions go about their work.

For example, suppose a researcher is interested in studying the detection of syntactic anomalies in sentences. One means of doing this would be to present participants with a set of sentences that contained anomalies and a set that did not. The researcher could then look at the task-related changes in blood flow (i.e., those changes that correlate with a particular event in the experiment) to determine which (if any) brain regions appear to be particularly active when anomalies are detected and which regions are not active at this time. These task-related changes have been examined using two primary techniques. First, one can compare the activity present in one task (e.g., normal sentence processing) with activity in another task (e.g., processing of sentences with anomalies). From this method, called the *subtraction* method, one can infer which brain regions are particularly important for detection of anomalies by noting the brain regions that show activity when processing sentences with anomalies that is over and above the activity shown in the same regions when processing normal sentences. To do this, the researcher subtracts the activation present in the "anomaly" condition from the activation present in the "normal" condition. Any regions that show activation following the subtraction are taken to be specifically involved in the processing of the anomalous sentences.

A second means of correlating brain activity with task performance is the *event-related* approach to neuroimaging. Similar to the use of ERPs, the event-related approach operates by correlating particular components of the changes in blood flow observed during the experiment with particular task-related events (e.g., the presentation of a syntactic anomaly in a sentence). By time-locking task-related and neural events, the researcher can determine which brain regions were particularly active in the processing associated with any given task component. The examples presented here obviously oversimplify the complexity of experimental design that is required to perform an interpretable neuroimaging study; for a more complete discussion, see Postle et al. (2000) and Sarter et al. (1996).

Imaging Studies of Language Processing

This review covers the results of neuroimaging studies on different aspects of language processing: sub–word-level processing, word processing, sentence-level processing, discourse processing, and issues of the neural architecture of language processing that have been addressed using imaging techniques. These findings complement and extend the traditional neuropsychological model of language (discussed in Caplan 1994, Zurif & Swinney 1994): Wernicke's area is involved in semantic processing, Broca's area is involved in syntax and production, and other distributed (mainly) left-hemisphere regions process language components such as phonology or orthography. To avoid presenting a confusing jumble of brain regions and Broadmann's areas (BA), we report the findings in this section using general descriptors (e.g., "inferior frontal gyrus") to locate brain activity. In the summary we incorporate Broadmann's areas to be more exact with regard to where the activity is occurring.

Processing Below the Word: Phonology and Orthography

Low-level linguistic processing involves a number of components, some of which are perceptual prerequisites for linguistic processing (e.g., primitive auditory and visual analysis of language forms) and some of which are language specific (e.g., phonological processing).

Speech processing begins bilaterally in the superior temporal gyrus, which includes the primary and secondary auditory processing regions. Imaging studies have demonstrated activation of this region in the processing of both linguistic and nonlinguistic sounds (Alavi et al. 1981; Petersen et al. 1988, 1989; Frith et al. 1991; Mazoyer et al. 1993). Many of these studies involve a subtraction between auditory stimulation and a passive resting state. Mazoyer et al. (1993) report that this region was the only active cortical region during the processing of speech sounds both from a familiar language (in this case French), and a language unfamiliar to the participants (Tamil). These authors also report that activation was greater in the left hemisphere than the right when the participants were processing their native language. In the same study it was observed that phonological processing was specific to the left middle-temporal gyrus.

These findings have been corroborated in a number of studies showing superior and middle temporal activation in phonological processing, as well as activation in the planum temporale (Binder et al. 1996a, Binder 1997). Additionally, the right temporal region (particularly the anterior regions) has been implicated in the processing of prosodic aspects of the speech signal (Buchanan et al. 2000). Other research involving the maintenance of phonological information (e.g., for deciding if two words rhyme or for a memory task) has implicated the inferior frontal gyrus and adjacent areas in phonological processing (Petersen & Fiez 1993, Shaywitz et al. 1995, Gabrieli et al. 1998, Wagner et al. 2001, Xu et al. 2001). Posterior temporal regions, including Wernicke's area and the supramarginal gyrus (Petersen et al. 1989, Demonet et al. 1994, Zatorre et al. 1996) have also been implicated in phonological processing. These regions may underlie the translation of orthographic symbols to phonemic representations (e.g., Xu et al. 2001), but there is evidence that they play a role in phonological processing that is independent of this translation process (e.g., Demonet et al. 1994).

The role of frontal regions in phonological processing has been debated. Evidence from rhyme judgment or generation tasks (Cuenod et al. 1995, Xu et al. 2001) indicates that the inferior frontal gyrus is involved in processing that is phonological in nature, although it appears that this processing is secondary to the initial temporal lobe processing of phonological information from the speech signal. Thus, the processing of phonological information in frontal regions may reflect a maintenance function (the phonemic information is maintained while the experimental task is performed). In addition, neighboring cortical regions (e.g., Broca's area) likely play a role in the production of speech sounds (Cuenod et al. 1995), and neighboring premotor areas may play a role in processing that is phonology dependent (e.g., Price et al. 1994). Buchanan et al. (2000) have suggested that the inferior frontal region in the right hemisphere is involved in detecting the emotional content of prosody. When participants in this experiment were asked to discriminate words based on their sounds, left prefrontal regions were active; however, when participants were asked to discriminate words based on the emotional tone conveyed by the prosody of the speaker, right frontal regions showed activation.

The processing of visual linguistic stimuli is slightly more involved than speech processing, owing to the translation between orthography and phonology believed to occur (Pugh et al. 1996, Xu et al. 2001). In Pugh et al.'s experiment participants performed four tasks for which they made same/different judgments, two of which are important for low-level word processing: (*a*) a line judgment task (same pattern of orientations in two sets of lines?) and (*b*) a letter case judgment task (same pattern of case alternation in two sets of consonant strings?). Consistent with lesion studies (Henderson 1986) and previous PET studies (e.g. Petersen et al. 1989), lateral extrastriate regions were activated during orthographic processing. In addition, Fujimaki et al. (1999) have shown that complex visual forms such as letters and pseudocharacters activate the occipital-temporal sulcus and the posterior inferior-temporal region bilaterally. These regions thus play a role in the early processing of visual linguistic stimuli.

Beyond orthographic processing, it has been proposed that visual linguistic input is translated into phonological form (e.g., Xu et al. 2001 and references therein). Regions in and around Wernicke's area, including the supramarginal gyrus and the angular gyrus, have been implicated in this process, both with regard to being "word-form centers" (especially regions in and near the angular gyrus; Small et al. 1996) and/or being responsible for the actual translation process. There remains some debate on the former issue. A series of conflicting studies of visual word processing (Petersen et al. 1990, Price et al. 1994, Pugh et al. 1996), suggest that whereas the brain regions involved in processing particular aspects of the linguistic stimulus have been identified, there does not yet appear to be any evidence of a specific word-form processing region. More recently, however, Polk & Farah (2002) conducted an experiment in which participants read alternating case words and pseudowords. These stimuli produced similar patterns of activation in the left-ventral visual cortex, suggesting the presence of a word form area that pays attention to abstract orthographic patterns rather than strictly perceptual components of visually presented language.

Xu et al. (2001) performed a PET study showing that whereas phonological processing of words and pseudowords shared regions of common cortical activation, processing pseudowords (but not words) activated the supramarginal gyrus and neighboring regions. This suggests that lexical items and pseudowords (and perhaps low-frequency lexical items) may undergo different routes in the visual-to-phonological translation, with the word forms of lexical items directly accessing phonological representations, and pseudowords needing to have a phonological code assembled in a more brute-force fashion, performed in the surpramarginal gyrus and neighboring regions. If it turns out that low-frequency lexical items are processed in a manner similar to that of pseudowords, the presence of frequency effects in a variety of cognitive tasks could be (at least in part) a function of the additional time required to access the phonological code of the low-frequency words.

As discussed in the next section, there appears to be a good deal of overlap between many aspects of auditory and visual word processing. The preliminary processes, however, differ across modalities. Initial speech processing appears to occur in the bilateral temporal lobes, with left lateralized processing occurring with higher levels of processing (i.e., phonological processing). Visual language processing begins in the occipital cortex and involves several regions near the boundary of the occipital and temporal lobes (e.g., left angular gyrus, bilateral fusiform gyrus, posterior inferior-temporal regions, occipital temporal sulcus, supramarginal gyrus, Wernicke's area). The putative function of these regions is to identify orthographic forms and to translate these forms into a phonological representation.

Word-Level Processing

The earliest imaging studies of language processing centered around the processing of words (e.g., Petersen et al. 1988). The authors of these early studies reported some degree of surprise at finding activation in brain regions not traditionally believed to be implicated in language processing (such as inferior frontal regions; Raichle 1996). Since then, these findings have been replicated and extended in a number of studies, identifying a wide range of regions of activation during word processing.

One set of tasks used to investigate word processing requires the participant to make a semantic judgment. In some cases this judgment is relatively simple: Is the word abstract or concrete (e.g., Demb et al. 1995, Desmond et al. 1995, Gabrieli et al. 1996)? In other cases (e.g., Frost et al. 1999) the judgment is more challenging: Is this an animal that lives in the United States and is used by humans? One such study (Gabrieli et al. 1996) involved comparing the abstract/concrete task with a perceptual judgment (are the letters in the words in upper or lower case?). The critical subtraction (semantic task–perceptual task) revealed activation in several left hemisphere regions: the inferior frontal gyrus, the cingulate cortex, and the superior frontal region.

These findings have been replicated with similar experimental tasks and with paradigms using slightly different subtractions (Desmond et al. 1995, Binder 1995, Binder et al. 1996b). For instance, Demb et al. (1995) have shown left inferior-frontal activation when the abstract/concrete task is contrasted to both easy non-semantic tasks (upper- versus lower-case judgments) and more difficult tasks (are the letters in the sequences ascending or descending alphabetically?). An interesting component of this study was the inclusion of a repeat condition, in which the stimulus materials were presented to the participants twice. In the repetition phase of the study a decrease in activation was noted in the inferior frontal regions. A similar decrease in activation was noted in the abstract/concrete-hard nonsemantic task subtraction, relative to the same subtraction using the easy nonsemantic task. This suggests that the frontal activation observed in studies of word processing may be the result of both semantic processing of some sort and the increased task difficulty of the semantic judgments relative to the baseline tasks.

Another task used to explore word processing is the word generation task. Participants are asked to generate words, aloud or silently, given a particular cue. A popular variant of this methodology is the verbal fluency task, in which participants generate words that start with a letter provided by the experimenter (e.g., generate words that start with "F") (e.g., Cuenod et al. 1995, Phelps et al. 1997, Schlosser et al. 1998). When compared to a baseline condition of rest (Cuenod et al. 1995), this task produces left inferior-frontal activity as well as activation in and around Wernicke's area and the superior temporal gyrus. In comparison to other baseline tasks (such as word repetition), the verbal fluency task has also produced activation in the superior frontal regions and the right cerebellum (Phelps et al. 1997, Schlosser et al. 1998). Similar results have been obtained in experiments in which participants are asked to generate nouns and/or verbs, although verb generation typically results in stronger activation in and around Broca's area (e.g., Weiller et al. 1995).

Other generation experiments involve sequence production (e.g., de Zubicaray et al. 1998, Wildgruber et al. 1999) and word stem completion (e.g., Desmond et al. 1998). Wildgruber et al. (1999) asked participants to silently recite the months of the year either forward or in reverse order. Subtracting forward recitation from reverse, one sees activation in bilateral middle and inferior frontal regions, in the parietal cortex, and in the anterior cingulate in the left hemisphere. Widespread activation was associated with purposeful recitation (i.e., reciting the months in reverse order) (similar results were found by de Zubicaray et al. 1998) as opposed to rote production (forward recitation). Word stem completion (given the stem "mat–", generate the first word that comes to mind) also shows inferior frontal activation, as well as activation in the supplementary motor area and the right cerebellum (Ojemann et al. 1998, Desmond et al. 1998, Chee et al. 1999b).

From the aforementioned studies there appears to be some regularity in the areas in which word-level information is accessed and processed, mostly centering around the inferior frontal region and posterior temporal regions near Wernicke's area, depending on the task demands and subtractions employed. Other studies have looked for finer distinctions in the ways particular types of words are processed. Kiehl et al. (1999) have explored the processing of abstract and concrete words. Comparing word processing to the processing of pseudowords, they found activation in superior parietal regions, anterior cingulate, left inferior-frontal regions, the left middle temporal gyrus, and the right superior temporal gyrus. Compared with concrete words, abstract words produced more activation in right temporal and frontal regions. These findings are consistent with literature that implicates the right hemisphere in abstract language processing (Bottini et al. 1994, Beauregard et al. 1997).

Chee et al. (1999a) have looked for differences in the processing of verbally and visually presented words. Participants engaged in an abstract/concrete task for words in both modalities. As a baseline task for visual words they performed a case judgment task (upper versus lower case); for spoken words they responded to whether the stimulus word had one or many syllables. Predictably, initial processing of visual and verbal stimuli involved different brain regions. As found in other studies (Pugh et al. 1996, Petersen et al. 1989), auditory language processing activated mainly left temporal regions, whereas visual word processing involved the posterior left superior–temporal gyrus, the left supramarginal gyrus, and the cerebellum. Nonetheless, a similar pattern of activation was observed for the semantic task performed in both modalities. This common pattern of activation involved the inferior frontal region, the anterior prefrontal region (bilaterally), the left premotor region, and the cerebellum.

These findings are consistent with studies that argue for a common semantic system across modalities. Similarities have been noted in the semantic processing of verbal and visual words (Chee et al. 1999a), words and pictures (Vandenberghe et al. 1996, Federmeier & Kutas 2001), and between faces and proper names (Gorno-Tempini et al. 1997). Whereas the specific modality and task demands associated with these individual comparisons can lead to variation in the exact regions of brain activation observed, the fact that verbal and visual language processing overlap so greatly may be due to the fact visually presented language is translated into phonological form at an early stage of processing (see Xu et al. 2001 for a discussion).

The distinction between regular verbs (those whose past tense is created by adding "-ed" to the verb stem: kill, killed) and irregular verbs (those whose past tense is formed by an irregular pattern: make, made; take, took) has also been explored (Marlsen-Wilson & Tyler 1997, Pinker 1997). Neuropsychological case studies (Marlsen-Wilson & Tyler 1997, Ullman et al. 1997) and neuroimaging experiments (Jaeger et al. 1996, Indefrey et al. 1997) have shown that irregular and regular verbs activate different cortical regions during processing. Jaeger et al. (1996) report that producing the past tense of regular verbs activates inferior frontal regions, whereas producing the past tense of irregular verbs activates middle temporal regions. The inferior frontal activation is argued to arise from the assembly of regular past tense forms by combining a verb stem (kill) and a morphological inflection (-ed). Irregular verbs activate temporal regions because they need to be recalled verbatim from the lexicon. Pinker (1997) concludes that this is evidence for the "words-and-rules" theory of lexical structure. Without a finer understanding of the processing that occurs in these cortical regions, however, it may be premature to rule out alternative theories.

Price et al. (1994) manipulated the duration with which words were displayed to participants. They report that many word processing regions were suppressed (i.e., showed decreased activation) once the word form had been processed (as evidenced by changes in activation in short versus long stimulus display times). This suggests an attentional component (or some other type of control component) in cognitive processing, which prevents the processing of redundant information in circumstances such as this (i.e., the word is not processed repeatedly while it is still displayed). This issue will require further investigation, and it appears that temporal factors need to be examined closely as research on lexical processing proceeds.

An interesting addendum to this literature is provided by Pulvermuller (1999). He presented a theory of word structure in the brain in which it is asserted that words are Hebbian cell assemblies that link orthographic, phonological, and meaning-specific information. For instance, Pulvermuller proposes that "vision words" have distributed representations that include temporal regions (phonological word-form representation) as well as areas in the occipital lobe (semantic information), whereas motor words (such as verbs) have representations that span temporal regions as well as frontal areas in and around the motor cortices. Evidence from ERP studies, neuropsychological case studies, and behavioral studies are cited in support of this hypothesis (e.g., Preissl et al. 1995, Pulvermuller 1996). In the main, activity associated with the semantics of particular words or word classes was absent from the studies reported here. Whereas some verb generation studies did show activation in and around Broca's area and the supplementary motor region (Weiller et al. 1995), this activation may have been the result of the language production demands of the experiment, not the firing of cell assemblies.

Across many studies, a general map of word processing has been generated. The left inferior-frontal gyrus and adjacent supplementary- and pre-motor areas are involved in semantic processing, phonological processing, and perhaps word-form access and production. Middle, superior, and anterior frontal regions have been associated with semantic processing. These regions are also implicated in the processing of semantic memory (see Cabeza & Nyberg 2000 for a review of some of this evidence). It is likely that frontal activation in word processing is due to some combination of several factors: short-term storage of phonological information, lexical access, semantic processing, and task difficulty. Similar right hemisphere regions appear to be active during the processing of abstract nouns. In addition, the superior temporal regions of both hemispheres have shown activation related to the processing of the semantics related to word forms.

Posterior temporal regions (in and around Wernicke's area) have been implicated in word-form access and production, semantic processing, and in some phonological tasks. Small et al. (1996) argue that regions near or in the left angular gyrus may serve as a word-form center, though there is debate on this issue (Price et al. 1992, Howard et al. 1992, Fujimaki et al. 1999). Other regions believed to be involved in word processing are the fusiform gyrus (bilaterally) and the left supramarginal gyrus. Finally, studies of word-level processing have revealed the surprising role of the cerebellum in cognitive tasks.

The cerebellum has long been thought to underlie motor-coordination functions. It was not until whole-brain scans of cognitive tasks were performed that it was discovered that the cerebellum was activated during higher-level tasks. Desmond et al. (1998) performed an experiment in which participants were asked to complete word stems that were either easy (many possible completions) or difficult (few possible completions). In other experiments of this sort it had been noted that there was a correlation between left frontal activation and right cerebellar activation (e.g., Ojemann et al. 1998), where left frontal activation appeared to be associated with right cerebellar activity. Desmond et al. (1998) qualified this relationship by noting a dissociation between activity in the frontal and cerebellar regions. Whereas frontal activation was associated with task performance when there were many possible stem completions, cerebellar activation was associated with performance when there were few possible stem completions. Desmond et al. (1998) hypothesize that the cerebellum may play a role in maintaining effortful cognitive activity, though the mechanism through which this is done remains obscure (see Leiner et al. 1995 for a discussion of the role of the cerebellum in cognitive processing).

Sentence Processing

Whereas many studies have explored issues related to word-level and sublexical processing, fewer studies have explored sentence processing. Indeed, most of the studies reported here treat sentence processing as a relatively monolithic construct and do not make an effort to tease apart the activation associated with specific components of the task.

The studies that have been performed reveal that sentence processing involves brain regions known as the "classical language areas" (e.g., Broca's and Wernicke's areas) and surrounding regions. Bavelier et al. (1997) report a sentence-reading study in which participants either read short, declarative sentences or viewed consonant strings in the experimental condition, and in the control condition viewed sentences or nonlinguistic strings in American Sign Language (ASL), a language that was unfamiliar to all of the participants. Activation unique to sentence processing was seen in and around both Broca's and Wernicke's areas (including the supramarginal gyrus), in the superior and middle temporal gyri in the left hemisphere, in the superior temporal gyrus in the right hemisphere, in the left inferior-frontal gyrus, and in the angular gyrus.

The activation in the angular gyrus is likely due to word processing, consistent with the neuropsychological literature (Bavelier et al. 1997). Activation in Broca's area suggests that this region plays a role in syntactic processing (e.g., Zurif & Swinney 1994, Ni et al. 2000). Wernicke's area activation is most likely the result of phonological processing (translating written language to a phonological code) or word-form processing (Demonet et al. 1992, Mazoyer et al. 1993). Hypotheses concerning the superior temporal gyrus and the inferior frontal gyrus are less clear. Both of these regions have been implicated in the maintenance of verbal information (see Milner 1971, Frisk & Milner 1990 for evidence based on lesion data) and in the processing of speech sounds. Additionally, the frontal regions have been associated with word-level processing, whereas the superior temporal regions have been associated with syntactic and semantic processing, as well as lexical processing (Damasio & Damasio 1992).

Similar patterns of activation have been observed in other studies in which sentence-level processing has been isolated (e.g., Robertson et al. 2000). These findings suggest that the temporal lobe is more active in sentence processing than had been assumed by neuropsychological models. Nonetheless, the temporal resolution of fMRI techniques makes it difficult to tease apart the components of sentence processing, given that most psycholinguistic research assumes that the processes of interest, to the degree that they are able to be differentiated, operate on the order of milliseconds, rather than seconds.

Ni et al. (2000) made a noteworthy attempt to separate the processes involved in comprehending sentences. In two experiments the researchers attempted to localize functions associated with syntactic and semantic processing. Unlike Bavelier et al.'s (1997) study, Ni et al.'s stimuli were presented verbally. In the first experiment participants engaged in an anomaly detection task. They heard blocks of (*a*) nonanomalous, syntactically anomalous sentences (e.g., "trees can grew"), (*b*) nonanomalous, semantically anomalous sentences (e.g., "trees can eat"), and (*c*) tone pairs that were the same or different in pitch. Relative to tone discrimination, the sentence judgment task activated regions in the inferior, middle, and superior frontal cortex bilaterally, as well as the superior and middle temporal gyri bilaterally. These regions of activation match closely with those reported by Bavelier et al. (1997), although this experiment featured much more frontal activation and a much more significant degree of bilateral activation. This may be due to the attentional or strategic components of the task, or to the use of auditory (as opposed to visual) stimuli (see Gabrieli et al. 1996, de Zubicaray et al. 1998 for examples in which frontal activation in both hemispheres accompanies increases in task difficulty).

In the second experiment participants heard the sentences from Experiment 1 but were not asked to detect anomalies. Rather, they were asked to determine if the sentence contained an animate being or not. The question of interest is what regions would show changes in activation to the syntactic and semantic anomalies. The event-related design allowed for the observation of changes in three time windows relative to the presentation of the anomaly (called early, middle, and late). Syntactically anomalous sentences produced no changes in early activation but caused activation in the left inferior and middle frontal regions in the middle and late periods. In the early period semantic anomalies caused activation in bilateral frontal regions (superior and middle frontal gyri). These regions remained active through the middle and late periods and were accompanied by activation in the left superior and middle temporal gyri. Thus, syntactic anomalies produced strongly lateralized activation in the inferior frontal regions in and around Broca's area, whereas semantic anomalies produced bilateral activation in frontal areas and in the left posterior temporal lobe.

These results suggest that there are separable regions that attempt to deal with sentence anomalies of different sorts. Given the role that "world knowledge" is assumed to play in semantics, it is perhaps not surprising that semantic anomalies produce widespread activation. This may represent efforts to recruit appropriate information to make a sentence like "Trees can eat" acceptable (e.g., information that would allow a figurative interpretation of the sentence), as well as the increased difficulty of processing such sentences. It is not as clear what activation associated with the syntactic anomalies represents, given that these sentences do not seem to require reanalysis to recover from errors. Since many of the sentences that occur in natural language use are ungrammatical in some way, the activation may represent an attempt to normalize the sentence for further processing. The Broca's area activation associated with syntactic anomalies may reflect the detection of sequencing anomalies. Similar regions were activated in a study in which participants heard a harmonic progression that ended with an anomalous (i.e., chromatic) chord (Maess et al. 2001). A more detailed understanding of what the language processing system attempts to do when it encounters this kind of syntactic anomaly is needed to investigate this matter further.

Studies have also assessed how changes in syntactic complexity alter brain activity. Stromswald et al. (1996) conducted a PET study in which participants read center-embedded sentences ("The car that the officer drove crashed into the wall") versus right-branching sentences ("The officer drove the car that crashed into the wall"). They found that the more difficult center-embedded sentences produced activation in inferior frontal regions. Their results were inconclusive, however, given the lack of a nonlinguistic baseline task and the lack of appropriate controls for sentence difficulty, memory demands, and the like, all of which can influence sentence processing (Just & Carpenter 1992, MacDonald et al. 1994).

A related study by Just et al. (1996) compared reading of simple conjoined sentences ("The reporter attacked the senator and admitted the error"), subject-relative sentences ("The reporter that attacked the senator admitted the error") and object-relative sentences ("The reporter that the senator attacked admitted the error"). Sentence reading was compared with a control task of reading consonant strings. They reported left hemisphere activation comparable to the studies discussed above for the sentence reading task. In addition, they found that activation in the right hemisphere homologues to these regions increased as sentence difficulty increased. Just et al. attributed this increased activation to the more resource-intensive nature of the processing of the object-relative and subject-relative sentences, in keeping with their capacity-based theory of language processing (Just & Carpenter 1992). Nonetheless, the increased activation need not signify only the recruitment of working memory resources. Bader (1998) argued that garden-path effects arise from sentences whose reanalysis requires particular types of changes in the prosodic contour of the sentence. Given the role of the right hemisphere in prosodic processing (Buchanan et al. 2000), the increased right hemisphere activation might reflect (in part) increased access to prosodic information rather than an increase in processing capacity per se. The activation may also reflect a lexical ambiguity resolution process (cf. MacDonald et al. 1994).

The processing of sentences thus involves Wernicke's area (word/phonological processing), superior and middle temporal regions (phonology/lexical/semantic processing), Broca's area (production/syntactic analysis), inferior frontal gyrus (phonological/syntactic/semantic processes), middle and superior frontal regions (semantics), and the right hemisphere homologues to these regions. The degree of right hemisphere activation found in studies of sentence processing varies with the nature of the task and the controls used in subtraction. The right hemisphere appears to be involved in lexical (e.g., Damasio & Damasio 1992) and prosodic processing, and activation in these regions may also reflect the recruitment of resources for task performance.

Discourse Processing

Studies of discourse processing have been of two types. The first type is concerned with the general processing that goes into comprehending connected discourse (e.g., St. George et al. 1994, 1999; Robertson et al. 2000). The second type is concerned with the processing of specific aspects of discourse, such as apprehending the moral or theme of a text (e.g., Nichelli et al. 1995). Each is discussed in turn.

Tzourio et al. (1998) had participants passively listen to stories. The listening task was contrasted with a resting condition. Story listening activated the temporal poles bilaterally, the superior temporal gyrus bilaterally, and the left middle temporal gyrus. The lack of a tight control task (i.e., a control task that matches the experimental task on several processing components, allowing one to determine more exactly which brain regions underlie specific subcomponents of the main task being performed) is due to the fact that the researchers were primarily interested in exploring the relationship between particular anatomical features of the brain and language lateralization. This design thus does not allow a detailed analysis of the circuitry associated with story processing.

Gernsbacher, Robertson, and colleagues (Robertson et al. 2000) have explored discourse processing in a series of experiments. In one experiment participants read sentences connected to a discourse and unrelated sentences and viewed non-alphabetic character strings. The creation of the "discourse" and "disconnected sentences" conditions was achieved by using the definite article "the" in one set of sentences and indefinite articles ("a" or "an") in another set. This manipulation produced no change in left hemisphere activation, but activation specific to connected sentences was found in middle and superior frontal regions of the right hemisphere.

Another narrative processing experiment from the same laboratory (Robertson 2000) showed that narrative processing increases in right hemisphere activation in more distributed regions: the precuneus, cuneus, posterior cingulate, parieto-temporo-occipital regions (bilaterally), the frontal poles, and a stretch of cortex extending along the right superior temporal sulcus to the right temporal pole. Interestingly, many of these same areas are activated when participants are asked to process picture stories in which a succession of pictures is presented such that a simple narrative like those used in the reading task is constructed. This suggests that these regions of activation are not specialized language centers but represent more general processes involved in story comprehension (e.g., a memory retrieval process).

St. George et al. (1999) asked participants to read both titled and untitled stories. They found patterns of activation nearly identical to those reported by Robertson et al. (2000). However, the right hemisphere activation was found to be stronger when the stories were untitled. This may indicate a greater degree of effort being expended to create a coherent episode out of the untitled stories relative to the titled stories.

Interestingly, Mazoyer et al. (1993) report a study in which participants listened passively to stories, and none of the right frontal regions reported by Robertson et al. (2000) or St. George et al. (1999) showed activation. The lack of right frontal activation was also observed by Tzourio et al. (1998). This suggests that the right hemisphere activation may only arise when the participant is building a story representation, rather than passively processing speech sounds.

The general finding that discourse processing involves extensive right hemisphere regions is in keeping with other studies noting the role of the right hemisphere in different aspects of language processing: processing prosody (Buchanan et al. 2000), comprehending irony and metaphor (Bottini et al. 1994), and processing words (Damasio & Damasio 1992), particularly abstract words (Kiehl et al. 1999). What we should make of this activation is not entirely clear. Studies indicate that increasing task difficulty can lead to the activation of more diffuse brain regions, and Just et al. (1996), among others, have noted that processing difficult sentences can involve the right hemisphere. That the right hemisphere activation noted in relation to sentence or lexical processing represents the same thing as the activation observed in the studies reported here is unlikely, given the subtractions that were performed (discourse–unrelated sentences). Indeed, the activation of the temporal poles during discourse comprehension appears to be unique to this task (relative to other language tasks), indicating that there are specific processes above and beyond those required for sentence processing involved in discourse processing. These findings argue that the right hemisphere activation observed in these experiments is not simply the recruitment of more processing resources. The activation noted in the precuneus (a region with extensive links to other cortical regions and implicated in memory processes) suggests that the right frontal activation associated with discourse processing might be the result of particular memory processes needed to create a coherent story representation.

Studies into more specific aspects of discourse processing have also been done. Nichelli et al. (1995) performed a PET study in which participants were presented with selections from Aesop's fables. When activation associated with a "semantic" task (e.g., answering whether or not the fable had a character with a particular characteristic) was subtracted from activation associated with a "moral" task (e.g., answering whether the fable contained a given moral), activation was observed in the right inferior-frontal gyrus and the right middle temporal gyrus.

Fletcher et al. (1995) asked participants to read three types of texts: theory-of-mind stories (which require the reader to make inferences about the internal mental states of the characters), physical stories (which are about physical events and do not require reasoning about the mental processes of the characters in the story), and collections of unrelated sentences (see Happe et al. 1996 for a similar study). Here again, story processing produced bilateral activation of the temporal poles, as well as in the left superior-temporal gyrus and the posterior cingulate cortex. Relative to the physical stories, theory-of-mind stories activated the posterior cingulate and the left middle-frontal gyrus. The posterior cingulate has connections throughout the cortex, including prefrontal and middle temporal regions. This region has been associated with the encoding of episodic memory (Grasby et al. 1993). Its activation may reflect the fact that the theory-of-mind stories are processed into a coherent episode, although this does not explain the difference in activation seen between the physical stories and theory-of-mind stories.

Brockway (1999, Brockway et al. 1998) noted that hippocampal structures are important to the role of memory in story processing and storage. In a study of patients with temporal lobe epilepsy, they demonstrated that damage to the left hippocampus impaired long-term memory for connected discourse ($\sim$35 min separated reading of the texts and recall). Based on the results of this and other memory tests, the authors concluded that the left temporal region (particularly, but perhaps not exclusively, the hippocampus) is of critical importance for maintaining the coherence of incoming information such as that presented by discourse.

The processing of discourse therefore appears to involve a distributed network of brain regions. These include the areas involved in lower levels of language processing (words, sentences, etc.), as well as areas specific to discourse: right temporal and frontal regions (important for the integrative aspects of discourse processing), as well as both temporal poles. The exact function of these regions is not yet known. A current hypothesis is that the discourse-specific activation seen in these studies is a function of memory processes that maintain the coherence of the discourse across sentences.

Particularly intriguing in this area of research is the activity of the temporal poles. This is a cortical region about which relatively little is known. The poles have been implicated in discourse processing (see above), and it is believed that they may serve an integrative function, sharing connections with the temporal and frontal lobes. Damasio et al. (1996) have also demonstrated (using patients with lesions in and around the temporal poles and controls with intact temporal regions) that the temporal poles are involved in lexical retrieval. Because so little is known about the temporal poles, the role of this region in language processing marks an important direction for future exploration.

Neuroimaging and Language Organization

In addition to exploring issues of where particular aspects of language are processed in the brain, neuroimaging experiments have been performed to explore issues related to the differences in language organization across different populations (e.g., males versus females, different categories of bilinguals).

Shaywitz et al. (1995) reported an experiment that looked for differences in activation for males and females in letter recognition, rhyme, and semantic tasks. Differences were found in the activation associated with the rhyme task (subtracting the letter processing task from the rhyme task): Whereas males showed activation that was strongly left lateralized in the inferior frontal region, females showed bilateral activation in this region.

Contrary to these findings, Frost et al. (1999) argued that there are no substantive differences in the organization of language in males and females. In this experiment participants alternated between a tone monitoring task (respond to sequences containing two "high" tones) and a semantic classification task ("Is this animal found in the United States and used by humans?"). As in the Shaywitz et al. (1995) study, no difference was found in the semantic processing of males and females. The authors assert that gender differences in processing may exist at the level of the microstructure of the brain but are absent from the macrostructure: For both sexes, language is strongly left lateralized. However, they did not replicate the phonological processing task of Shaywitz et al. (1995), leaving open the possibility that there is a genuine contrast between males and females with regard to that type of processing.

A similar debate over language organization has centered around bilinguals. The question is whether the native language of the bilingual (L1) and the second language (L2) share the same cortical space or whether they occupy different space. In a number of studies differences in where L1 and L2 are localized (Kim et al. 1997) and processed (Perani et al. 1996) were noted.

Chee et al. (1999b) conducted a word processing study with bilingual speakers of Mandarin and English. They collected data from bilinguals who were exposed to both languages before age 6 and bilinguals who learned Mandarin at an early age but were not exposed to English until after age 12. Participants were given word-stem completion tasks in both languages. The results of the study suggested no differences in the cortical organization or processing of language in this task, comparing across both L1 and L2, and across early and late acquisition of L2. This is in contrast to the findings of earlier studies suggesting differences in organization between L1 and L2. For example, Dehaene et al. (1997) report differences in sentence processing between L1 and L2 English-French bilinguals, with L2 processing requiring significantly more right hemisphere activation.

A possible way to reconcile the data observed in exploring L1-L2 differences is to note that in certain cases participants may use different strategies to perform the experimental task with L1 and L2. For instance, bilinguals may need to use a different strategy when processing L2 sentences than when they are processing L1 sentences. Or, in keeping with Just et al. (1996), it may be that task performance with L2 requires more processing resources. One way to clarify this issue is to design studies in which strategies or processing difficulty are controlled and can be ruled out as causal factors.

Another strategy might be to explore monolingual processing in each language as a preliminary step in the research process. In the case of visual processing of language, languages might differ in the complexity of the characters in the alphabet or in the degree to which particular letters can be translated into phonological forms (e.g., Japanese character systems, in which one system of characters have phonological counterparts and the other system has only semantic counterparts) (Kamada et al. 1998). To illustrate, it has been shown that American Sign Language (ASL) has a different cortical organization than English, involving a more widely distributed network of structures in both the right and left hemisphere (Neville et al. 1998). This is presumably due to the greater extent to which spatial and motor information is required to both produce and comprehend utterances in ASL. The pattern of activation on a given task in monolinguals can be an important baseline against which to judge activation in bilinguals. If the two languages have different processing requirements (like English and ASL), one might expect to see different areas of the cortex occupied with L1 and L2 in bilinguals regardless of whether L1 and L2 actually require different cortical space. However, if the processing requirements of the languages are similar, then one might propose, a priori, that there ought to be no substantial differences in the organization of L1 and L2 unless something about the acquisition of a second language requires this to be the case. In these circumstances, and to the degree that strategies, etc. can be ruled out as causal factors, one can interpret language-related differences in cortical activation of bilinguals more strongly.

Summary

Across the studies reviewed above the following conclusions about neural activation in language production and comprehension can be drawn:

FRONTAL REGIONS   The *inferior frontal regions*, including parts of Broadmann's areas (BA's) 45, 46, and 47, show activation during tasks involving phonological processing, semantic decision tasks, and sentence- and discourse-level processing. These regions are also believed to be involved in short-term memory storage and/or maintenance. The *middle and superior frontal regions* show activation mainly during semantic decision tasks (BA 6, 8, 9) and have also been implicated in semantic memory tasks. These regions also showed activation in tasks that required the processing of theory of mind information within a story. The *supplementary motor area* (BA 6, 44) and *Broca's area* (BA 6, 44) have been implicated in producing verbal and nonverbal motor responses to tasks, in the maintenance of phonological representations, and in the production of subvocalizations (Hinke et al. 1993). Broca's area has also shown activation during syntactic processing, as well as during music perception tasks (Maess et al. 2001).

Similar regions of activation occur in the right hemisphere. The *inferior frontal region* is active during processing of abstract words, sentence processing, discourse processing, detection of emotional content in speech, and phonological processing in limited cases. The middle and superior frontal regions have shown activation during semantic decision tasks and have been implicated in the integrative aspects of discourse processing.

TEMPORAL AND POSTERIOR REGIONS   The *superior temporal region* (BA 22) has shown activation during auditory processing of speech sounds, during semantic processing, and during syntactic processing (mostly in anterior regions). The *middle temporal region* (BA 21) has been implicated in both phonological and semantic processing. The *temporal pole* (BA 38) has been implicated in discourse-level processing. *Wernicke's area* (BA 40) as well as the *supramarginal gyrus* (BA 40) have been suggested to play a role in semantic processing and certain aspects of phonological processing, such as translating written words into phonological representations. *Posterior inferior-temporal regions*, as well as the *occipito-temporal sulcus* (BA 42, 37) have been implicated in the early visual processing of words, as have the *angular gyrus* (BA 39/40), the *fusiform gyrus* (BA 37), and the *lateral extrastriate regions* (BA 18/19). *Superior parietal regions* (BA 7, 19) have shown activation in the processing of discourse. The *cerebellum* has shown activation during cognitive search, decision tasks, and naming tasks.

In the right hemisphere many of these same regions show activation. The superior parietal regions show activation during discourse processing, as does the temporal pole. Superior temporal regions in the right hemisphere show activation during early speech processing, processing of difficult sentences, and discourse processing. Many of the visual processing regions are activated bilaterally in the early stages of word processing. Right temporal regions are also associated with the processing of prosody.

Two things need to be kept in mind when faced with this many-to-many mapping of structure and function. First, the labels attached to these tasks (e.g., "semantic decision") are probably best considered a convenient means of categorization. The labels are often so broad as to be next to useless in making generalizations across experiments. Second, the activation displayed in imaging studies is observed across trials and across participants. Thus, what is shown as active in a particular experiment is what is common to task performance across the experiment. This issue was discussed above when we considered word processing. A semantic decision task may activate frontal regions, but that does not preclude the possibility that these regions are accessing information from other regions of the cortex to actually perform the task. This additional activation for individual trials may not necessarily register as activity associated with the task. This failure to register might be because (*a*) the additional information is located in diffuse cortical regions and these cancel out across trials or (*b*) the circuitry involved in accessing this information does not produce a sufficiently strong signal (relative to baseline) to show up as significant activation.

THE FUTURE OF NEUROIMAGING WORK ON LANGUAGE PRODUCTION AND COMPREHENSION

The work presented in this review constitutes a groundbreaking effort by physicists, neuroscientists, radiologists, and psychologists to harness neuroimaging techniques in an attempt to observe the brain at work. In many ways the rules of the game are still being developed. Statistical analysis, experimental methodology, and imaging technology are rapidly advancing to allow more precise and veridical information about neural processes to be obtained. Indeed, studies using magnetoencephalography (MEG), an imaging technology with better spatial and temporal resolution than fMRI, have already appeared (e.g., Kamada et al. 1998, Patel & Balaban 2000).

The previous section summarized the state of the art regarding what is known from imaging studies about the neural circuitry that underlies language processing. This literature mainly focuses on answering the "where" question of neural processing. Across the body of studies reviewed, one can get a reasonable sense of the cortical regions that process language: The left hemisphere, superior, middle, and inferior temporal regions, as well as the temporal poles and superior, middle, and inferior frontal regions are implicated. In the right hemisphere, superior temporal regions, frontal regions, and homologues to left hemisphere language areas are implicated. Of course, many of these findings need to be replicated across a wider range of experimental paradigms before more stock is placed in them.

As we become more certain about the "where" questions in language processing, we must begin to consider the important question of "how?" As the temporal and spatial quality of imaging techniques improves, we can begin to look at the microstructure of the cortex to ascertain exactly how processing of a given type is carried out. The mapping work been done to this point will be an invaluable guide in this respect. Having some sense of where to look for a given type of process will greatly simplify the quest for the fine details of how the brain works. There is no guarantee that more precise observation of the brain will yield valuable information, but there is every hope that more precise observation, in combination with clear thinking about how the methods developed can best be applied to the task at hand, will shed light on the neural processing underlying language.

That said, there are a number of realms of psycholinguistics that have yet to be explored in any detail in neuroimaging studies. The processing of pragmatic information in language comprehension, as well as conversational aspects of language use, are an example of such an area of research that needs to be addressed (but see e.g., Caplan et al. 2000). Investigation can also be done to ascertain if there are any anatomical properties of "language areas" that cause linguistic processing to localize there regularly across the population (in keeping with the proposal of Jacobs's 1997 "mixture of experts" theory). As we noted in the previous section, the accessing of particular "semantic" information in task performance has not been adequately addressed and may be explored as described in that section. Exploration of all of these areas of language use may reveal important information about the neural processing the brain carries out.

None of this will be easy. An obstacle to understanding neural processing may arise from the field's co-opting of cognitive psychological methods and metaphors. The information-processing model of cognition, which underlies much work in psycholinguistics, arose at a time when the neural operations involved in cognition could mainly be discussed metaphorically. This framework has proven useful in yielding experimental paradigms and task analyses of the participants' performance in different experimental settings. Nonetheless, there is reason to suspect that nature has not cooperated by designing the brain to match our information processing intuitions. This likely explains why we observe the many-to-many mapping of structures and putative processes across imaging studies.

As Kosslyn (1999) argues, the results of neuroimaging studies are of interest only to the degree that they are theoretically informative; scanning participants while they perform tasks and interpreting the areas of activation post hoc is not in and of itself an interesting research enterprise. Cognitive theories allow the neuroscientist to avoid this by developing tasks and hypotheses that are potentially informative. Nonetheless, it may be that making fundamental progress in understanding how the brain processes language will require the exploration of neural processing in a way that does not rely as heavily on the theoretical baggage of cognitive psychology.

Three years into the new millennium, we can reflect on the Decade of the Brain (as the 1990s were dubbed) as an important time in cognitive neuroscience. Technological developments merged with an expansion of researcher interest to help the field of neuroimaging blossom into a viable young science. Whereas much work remains to be done in the quest for cognitive neuroscience's Holy Grail, the research described herein constitutes a good start along the path.

The *Annual Review of Psychology* is online at http://psych.annualreviews.org

LITERATURE CITED

Alavi A, Reivich M, Greenberg J, Rosenquist A, Hand P, et al. 1981. Mapping of functional activity in brain with 18F-fluoro-deoxyglucose. *Semin. Nucl. Med.* 11:24–31

Bader M. 1998. Prosodic influences on reading syntactically ambiguous sentences. In *Reanalysis in Sentence Processing*, ed. JD Fodor, F Ferreira, pp. 1–46. Boston: Kluwer Acad.

Bavelier D, Corina D, Jezzard P, Padmanabhan S, Clark VP, et al. 1997. Sentence reading: a functional MRI study at 4 Tesla. *J. Cogn. Neurosci.* 9:664–86

Beauregard M, Chertkow H, Bub D, Murtha S, Dixon R, Evans A. 1997. The neural substrate for concrete, abstract, and emotional word lexica: a positron emission tomography study. *J. Cogn. Neurosci.* 9:441–61

Binder JR. 1997. Neuroanatomy of language processing studied with functional MRI. *Clin. Neurosci.* 4:87–94

Binder JR, Frost JA, Hammeke TA, Rao SM, Cox RW. 1996a. Function of the left planum temporale in auditory and linguistic processing. *Brain* 119:1239–47

Binder JR, Rao SM, Hammeke TA, Frost JA, Bandettini PA, et al. 1995. Lateralized human brain language systems demonstrated by task subtraction functional magnetic resonance imaging. *Arch. Neurol.* 52:593–601

Binder JR, Swanson SJ, Hammeke TA, Morris GL, Mueller WM, et al. 1996b. Determination of language dominance using functional MRI: a comparison with the Wada test. *Neurology* 46:978–84

Bottini G, Corcoran R, Sterzi R, Paulesu E, Schenone P, et al. 1994. The role of the right hemisphere in the interpretation of figurative aspects of language. A positron emission tomography activation study. *Brain* 117:1241–53

Brockway JP. 1999. Deep language structures: memory for connected discourse produced unilateral (L) hippocampal activation observed by functional magnetic resonance imaging. *Brain Cogn.* 40:57–60

Brockway JP, Follmer RL, Preuss LA, Prioleau CE, Burrows GS, et al. 1998. Memory, simple and complex language, and the temporal lobe. *Brain Lang.* 61:1–29

Buchanan TW, Lutz K, Mirzazade S, Specht K, Shah NJ, et al. 2000. Recognition of emotional prosody and verbal components of spoken language: an fMRI study. *Cogn. Brain Res.* 9:227–38

Cabeza R, Nyberg L. 2000. Imaging cognition. II. An empirical review of 275 PET and fMRI studies. *J. Cogn. Neurosci.* 12:1–47

Caplan D. 1994. Language and the brain. See Gernsbacher 1994, pp. 1023–54

Caplan R, Dapretto M, Mazziotta JC. 2000. An fMRI study of discourse coherence. *NeuroImage* 11:S96

Chee MW, O'Craven KM, Bergida R, Rosen BR, Savoy RL. 1999a. Auditory and visual word processing studied with fMRI. *Hum. Brain Mapp.* 7:15–28

Chee MW, Tan EW, Thiel T. 1999b. Mandarin and English single word processing studied with functional magnetic resonance imaging. *J. Neurosci.* 19:3050–56

Cohen JD, Noll DC, Schneider W. 1993. Functional magnetic resonance imaging: overview and methods for psychological research. *Behav. Res. Methods Instrum. Comput.* 25:101–13

Cuenod CA, Bookheimer SY, Hertz-Pannier L, Zeffiro TA, Theodore WH, Le Bihan D. 1995. Functional MRI during word generation, using conventional equipment: a potential tool for language localization in the clinical environment. *Neurology* 45:1821–27

Damasio AR, Damasio H. 1992. Brain and language. *Sci. Am.* 267:88–95

Damasio H, Grabowski TJ, Tranel D, Hichwa RD, Damasio AR. 1996. A neural basis for lexical retrieval. *Nature* 380:499–505

Dehaene S, Dupoux E, Mehler J, Cohen L, Paulesu E, et al. 1997. Anatomical variability in the cortical representation of first and second language. *NeuroReport* 8:3809–15

Demb JB, Desmond JE, Wagner AD, Vaidya CJ, Glover GH, Gabrieli JD. 1995. Semantic encoding and retrieval in the left inferior prefrontal cortex: a functional MRI study of task difficulty and process specificity. *J. Neurosci.* 15:5870–78

Demonet JF, Chollet F, Ramsay S, Cardebat D, Nespoulous JL, et al. 1992. The anatomy of phonological and semantic processing in normal subjects. *Brain* 115:1753–68

Demonet JF, Price C, Wise R, Frackowiak RS. 1994. Differential activation of right and left posterior sylvian regions by semantic and phonological tasks: a positron-emission tomography study in normal human subjects. *Neurosci. Lett.* 182:25–28

Desmond JE, Gabrieli JD, Glover GH. 1998. Dissociation of frontal and cerebellar activity in a cognitive task: evidence for a distinction between selection and search. *NeuroImage* 7:368–76

Desmond JE, Sum JM, Wagner AD, Demb JB, Shear PK, et al. 1995. Functional MRI measurement of language lateralization in Wada-tested patients. *Brain* 118:155–78

de Zubicaray GI, Williams SCR, Wilson SJ, Rose SE, Brammer MJ, et al. 1998. Prefrontal cortex involvement in selective letter generation: a functional magnetic resonance imaging study. *Cortex* 34:389–401

Federmeier KD, Kutas M. 2001. Meaning and modality: influences of context, semantic memory organization, and perceptual predictability on picture processing. *J. Exp. Psychol.: Learn. Mem. Cogn.* 27:202–24

Fletcher PC, Happe F, Frith U, Baker SC, Dolan RJ, et al. 1995. Other minds in the brain: a functional imaging study of "theory of mind" in story comprehension. *Cognition* 57:109–28

Frisk V, Milner B. 1990. The relationship of working memory to the immediate recall of stories following unilateral temporal or frontal lobectomy. *Neuropsychologia* 28: 121–35

Frith CD, Friston K, Liddle PF, Frackowiak RS. 1991. A PET study of word finding. *Neuropsychologia* 29:1137–48

Frost JA, Binder JR, Springer JA, Hammeke TA, Bellgowan PS, et al. 1999. Language processing is strongly left lateralized in both sexes. Evidence from functional MRI. *Brain* 122:199–208

Fujimaki N, Miyauchi S, Putz B, Sasaki Y, Takino R, et al. 1999. Functional magnetic resonance imaging of neural activity related to orthographic, phonological, and lexico-semantic judgments of visually presented characters and words. *Hum. Brain Mapp.* 8:44–59

Gabrieli JDE, Demb JB, Stone MV, Desmond JE, Wagner HD, et al. 1996. Functional magnetic resonance imaging of semantic memory processes in the frontal lobes. *Psychol. Sci.* 7:278–83

Gabrieli JDE, Poldrack RA, Desmond JE. 1998. The role of left prefrontal cortex in language and memory. *Proc. Natl. Acad. Sci. USA* 95:906–13

Gernsbacher MA, ed. 1994. *Handbook of Psycholinguistics.* San Diego, CA: Academic

Gorno-Tempini ML, Price CJ, Josephs O, Vandenberghe R, Cappa SF, et al. 1998. The neural systems sustaining face and proper-name processing. *Brain* 121:2103–18

Grasby PM, Frith CD, Friston KJ, Beach CF, Frackowiak RSJ, Dolan RJ. 1993. Functional mapping of brain areas implicated in auditory-verbal memory function. *Brain* 116:1–20

Happe F, Ehlers S, Fletcher P, Frith U, Johansson M, et al. 1996. 'Theory of mind' in the brain. Evidence from a PET scan study of Asperger syndrome. *NeuroReport* 8:197–201

Henderson VW. 1986. Anatomy of posterior pathways in reading: a reassessment. *Brain Lang.* 29:119–33

Hinke RM, Hu X, Stillman AE, Kim SG, Merkle H, et al. 1993. Functional magnetic resonance imaging of Broca's area during internal speech. *NeuroReport* 4:675–78

Howard D, Patterson K, Wise R, Brown WD, Firston K, et al. 1992. The cortical localization of the lexicons. *Brain* 115:1769–82

Indefrey P, Brown C, Hagoort P, Herzog H, Sach M, Seits RJ. 1997. A PET study of cerebral activation patterns induced by verb inflection. *NeuroImage* 5:S548

Jacobs RA. 1997. Nature, nurture and the development of functional specializations: a computational approach. *Psychonom. Bull. Rev.* 4:299–309

Jaeger JJ, Lockwood AH, Kemmerer DL, van Valin RD, Murphy BW, Khalak HG. 1996. A positron emission tomography study or regular and irregular verb morphology in English. *Language* 72:451–97

Just MA, Carpenter PA. 1992. A capacity theory of comprehension: individual differences in working memory. *Psychol. Rev.* 99:122–49

Just MA, Carpenter PA, Keller TA, Eddy WF, Thulborn KR. 1996. Brain activation modulated by sentence comprehension. *Science* 274:114–16

Kamada K, Kober H, Saguer M, Moller M, Kaltenhauser M, Vieth J. 1998. Responses to silent *Kanji* reading of the native Japanese and German in task subtraction magnetoencephalography. *Cogn. Brain Res.* 7:89–98

Kiehl KA, Liddle PF, Smith AM, Mendrek A, Forster BB, Hare RD. 1999. Neural pathways involved in the processing of concrete and abstract words. *Hum. Brain Mapp.* 7:225–33

Kim KHS, Relkin NR, Lee KM, Hirsch J. 1997. Distinct cortical areas associated with native and second languages. *Nature* 388:171–74

Kosslyn SM. 1999. If neuroimaging is the answer, what is the question? *Philos. Trans. R. Soc. London Ser. B* 354:1283–94

Leiner HC, Leiner AL, Dow RS. 1995. The underestimated cerebellum. *Hum. Brain Mapp.* 2:244–54

MacDonald MC, Pearlmutter NJ, Seidenberg MS. 1994. Lexical nature of syntactic ambiguity resolution. *Psychol. Rev.* 101:676–703

Maess B, Koelsch S, Gunter TC, Frederici AD. 2001. Musical syntax is processed in Broca's area: an MEG study. *Nat. Neurosci.* 4:540–45

Marlsen-Wilson W, Tyler LK. 1997. Dissociating types of mental computation. *Nature* 387:592–94

Mazoyer BM, Tzourio N, Frak V, Syrota A, Murayama N, et al. 1993. The cortical representation of speech. *J. Cogn. Neurosci.* 5:467–79

Milner B. 1971. Disorders of learning and memory after temporal lobe lesions in man. *Clin. Neurosurg.* 19:421–46

Neville HJ, Bavelier D, Corina D, Rauschecker J, Karni A, et al. 1998. Cerebral organization for language in deaf and hearing subjects: biological constraints and effects of experience. *Proc. Natl. Acad. Sci. USA* 95:922–29

Ni W, Constable RT, Mencl WE, Pugh KR, Fulbright RK, et al. 2000. An event-related neuroimaging study distinguishing form and content in sentence processing. *J. Cogn. Neurosci.* 12:120–33

Nichelli P, Grafman J, Pietrini P, Clark K, Lee KY, Miletich R. 1995. Where the brain appreciates the moral of a story. *NeuroReport* 6:2309–13

Obler LK, Gjerlow K. 1999. *Language and the Brain.* New York: Cambridge Univ. Press

Ojemann JG, Buckner RL, Akbudak E, Snyder AZ, Ollinger JM, et al. 1998. Functional MRI studies of word-stem completion: reliability across laboratories and comparison to blood flow imaging with PET. *Hum. Brain Mapp.* 6:203–15

Patel AD, Balaban E. 2000. Temporal pattern of human cortical activity reflect tone sequence structure. *Nature* 404:80–84

Perani D, Dehaene S, Grassi F, Cohen L, Cappa SF, et al. 1996. Brain processing of native and foreign languages. *NeuroReport* 6:1637–41

Petersen SE, Fiez JA. 1993. The processing of single words studied with positron emission tomography. *Annu. Rev. Neurosci.* 16:509–30

Petersen SE, Fox PT, Posner MI, Mintun M, Raichle ME. 1988. Positron emission tomography studies of the cortical anatomy of single-word processing. *Nature* 331:585–89

Petersen SE, Fox PT, Posner MI, Mintun M, Raichle ME. 1989. Positron emission tomo-

graphic studies of the processing of single words. *J. Cogn. Neurosci.* 1:153–70

Petersen SE, Fox PT, Snyder AZ, Raichle ME. 1990. Activation of extrastriate and frontal cortical areas by visual words and word-like stimuli. *Science* 249:1041–44

Phelps EA, Hyder F, Blamire AM, Shulman RG. 1997. fMRI of the prefrontal cortex during overt verbal fluency. *NeuroReport* 8:561–65

Pinker S. 1997. Words and rules in the human brain. *Nature* 387:547–48

Polk TA, Farah MJ. 2002. Functional MRI evidence for an abstract, not perceptual, word-form area. *J. Exp. Psychol.: Gen.* 131:65–72

Postle BR, Zarahn E, D'Esposito M. 2000. Using event-related fMRI to assess delay-period activity during performance of spatial and nonspatial working memory tasks. *Brain Res. Protoc.* 5:57–66

Preissl H, Pulvermuller F, Lutzenberger W, Birbaumer N. 1995. Evoked potentials distinguish nouns from verbs. *Neurosci. Lett.* 197:81–83

Price C, Wise R, Ramsay S, Friston K, Howard D, et al. 1992. Regional response differences within the human auditory cortex when listening to words. *Neurosci. Lett.* 146:179–82

Price CJ, Wise RJ, Watson JD, Patterson K, Howard D, Frackowiak RS. 1994. Brain activity during reading. The effects of exposure duration and task. *Brain* 117:1255–69

Pugh KR, Shaywitz BA, Shaywitz SE, Constable RT, Skudlarski P, et al. 1996. Cerebral organization of component processes in reading. *Brain* 119:1221–38

Pulvermuller F. 1996. Hebb's concept of cell assemblies and the psychophysiology of word processing. *Psychophysiology* 33:317–33

Pulvermuller F. 1999. Words in the brain's language. *Behav. Brain Sci.* 22:253–336

Raichle ME. 1996. What words are telling us about the brain. *Cold Springs Harbor Symp. Quant. Biol.* 61:9–14

Robertson DA. 2000. *Functional neuroanatomy of language comprehension.* PhD diss., Univ. Wis., Madison

Robertson DA, Gernsbacher MA, Guidotti S, Robertson R, Irwin W, et al. 2000. Functional neuroanatomy of the cognitive process of mapping during discourse comprehension. *Psychol. Sci.* 11:255–60

Sarter M, Berntson GG, Cacioppo JT. 1996. Brain imaging and cognitive neuroscience. Toward strong inference in attributing function to structure. *Am. Psychol.* 51:13–21

Schlosser R, Hutchinson M, Joseffer S, Rusinek H, Saarimaki A, et al. 1998. Functional magnetic resonance imaging of human brain activity in a verbal fluency task. *J. Neurol. Neurosurg. Psychiatry* 64:492–98

Shaywitz BA, Shaywitz SE, Pugh KR, Constable RT, Skudlarski P, et al. 1995. Sex differences in the functional organization of the brain for language. *Nature* 373:607–9

Small SL, Noll DC, Perfetti CA, Hlustik P, Wellington R, Schneider W. 1996. Localizing the lexicon for reading aloud: replication of a PET study using fMRI. *NeuroReport* 7:961–65

St. George M, Kutas M, Martinez A, Sereno MI. 1999. Semantic integration in reading: engagement of the right hemisphere during discourse processing. *Brain* 122:1317–25

St. George M, Mannes S, Hoffman JE. 1994. Global semantic expectancy and language comprehension. *J. Cogn. Neurosci.* 6:70–83

Stromswold K, Caplan D, Alpert N, Rauch S. 1996. Localization of syntactic comprehension by positron emissions tomography. *Brain Lang.* 52:452–73

Turner R, Jezzard P. 1994. Magnetic resonance studies of brain functional activation using echo-planar imaging. In *Functional Neuroimaging*, ed. RWH Thatcher, M Zaffiro, ER John, M Heerta, pp. 69–78. San Diego, CA: Academic

Tzourio N, Nkanga-Ngila B, Mazoyer B. 1998. Left planum temporale surface correlates with functional dominance during story listening. *NeuroReport* 9:829–33

Ullman MT, Corkin S, Coppola M, Hickok G, Growdon JH, et al. 1997. A neural dissociation within language: evidence that the mental dictionary is part of declarative memory, and that grammatical rules are processed by the procedural system. *J. Cogn. Neurosci.* 9:266–76

Vandenberghe R, Price C, Wise R, Josephs O, Frackowiak RS. 1996. Functional anatomy of a common semantic system for words and pictures. *Nature* 383:254–56

Wagner AD, Maril A, Bjork RA, Schacter DL. 2001. Prefrontal contributions to executive control: fMRI evidence for functional distinctions within lateral prefrontal cortex. *NeuroImage* 14:1337–47

Weiller C, Isensee C, Rijntjes M, Huber W, Muller S, et al. 1995. Recovery from Wernicke's aphasia: a positron emission tomographic study. *Ann. Neurol.* 37:723–32

Wildgruber D, Kischka U, Ackermann H, Klose U, Grodd W. 1999. Dynamic pattern of brain activation during sequencing of word strings evaluated by fMRI. *Cogn. Brain Res.* 7:285–94

Xiong J, Shobini R, Gao J, Woldorff M, Fox PT. 1998. Evaluation of hemispheric dominance for language using functional MRI: a comparison with positron emission tomography. *Hum. Brain Mapp.* 6:42–58

Xu B, Grafman J, Gaillard WD, Ishii K, Vega-Bermudez F, et al. 2001. Conjoint and extended neural networks for the computation of speech codes: the neural basis of selective impairment in reading words and pseudowords. *Cereb. Cortex* 11:267–77

Zatorre RJ, Meyer E, Gjedde A, Evans AC. 1996. PET studies of phonetic processing of speech: review, replication, and reanalysis. *Cereb. Cortex* 6:21–30

Zurif E, Swinney D. 1994. The neuropsychology of language. See Gernsbacher 1994, pp. 1055–74

Annu. Rev. Psychol. 2003. 54:115–44
doi: 10.1146/annurev.psych.54.101601.145124
First published online as a Review in Advance on October 4, 2002

OPERANT CONDITIONING

J. E. R. Staddon and D. T. Cerutti

Department of Psychological and Brain Sciences, Duke University,
Durham, North Carolina 27708-0086; e-mail: staddon@psych.duke.edu,
cerutti@psych.duke.edu

Key Words   interval timing, choice, concurrent schedules, matching law, self-control

■ **Abstract**   Operant behavior is behavior "controlled" by its consequences. In practice, operant conditioning is the study of reversible behavior maintained by reinforcement schedules. We review empirical studies and theoretical approaches to two large classes of operant behavior: interval timing and choice. We discuss cognitive versus behavioral approaches to timing, the "gap" experiment and its implications, proportional timing and Weber's law, temporal dynamics and linear waiting, and the problem of simple chain-interval schedules. We review the long history of research on operant choice: the matching law, its extensions and problems, concurrent chain schedules, and self-control. We point out how linear waiting may be involved in timing, choice, and reinforcement schedules generally. There are prospects for a unified approach to all these areas.

CONTENTS

0066-4308/03/0203-0115$14.00   **115**

INTRODUCTION

The term *operant conditioning*[1] was coined by B. F. Skinner in 1937 in the context of reflex physiology, to differentiate what he was interested in—behavior that affects the environment—from the reflex-related subject matter of the Pavlovians. The term was novel, but its referent was not entirely new. *Operant behavior*, though defined by Skinner as behavior "controlled by its consequences" is in practice little different from what had previously been termed "instrumental learning" and what most people would call habit. Any well-trained "operant" is in effect a habit. What was truly new was Skinner's method of automated training with intermittent reinforcement and the subject matter of *reinforcement schedules* to which it led. Skinner and his colleagues and students discovered in the ensuing decades a completely unsuspected range of powerful and orderly schedule effects that provided new tools for understanding learning processes and new phenomena to challenge theory.

A reinforcement schedule is any procedure that delivers a *reinforcer* to an organism according to some well-defined rule. The usual reinforcer is food for a hungry rat or pigeon; the usual schedule is one that delivers the reinforcer for a switch closure caused by a peck or lever press. Reinforcement schedules have also been used with human subjects, and the results are broadly similar to the results with animals. However, for ethical and practical reasons, relatively weak reinforcers must be used—and the range of behavioral strategies people can adopt is of course greater than in the case of animals. This review is restricted to work with animals.

Two types of reinforcement schedule have excited the most interest. Most popular are time-based schedules such as fixed and variable interval, in which the reinforcer is delivered after a fixed or variable time period after a *time marker* (usually the preceding reinforcer). *Ratio* schedules require a fixed or variable number of responses before a reinforcer is delivered.

Trial-by-trial versions of all these *free-operant* procedures exist. For example, a version of the fixed-interval schedule specifically adapted to the study of interval timing is the peak-interval procedure, which adds to the fixed interval an intertrial interval (ITI) preceding each trial and a percentage of extra-long "empty" trials in which no food is given.

For theoretical reasons, Skinner believed that operant behavior ought to involve a response that can easily be repeated, such as pressing a lever, for rats, or pecking

---

[1]The first and only previous *Annual Review* contribution on this topic was as part of a 1965 article, "Learning, Operant Conditioning and Verbal Learning" by Blough & Millward. Since then there have been (by our estimate) seven articles on learning or learning theory in animals, six on the neurobiology of learning, and three on human learning and memory, but this is the first full *Annual Review* article on operant conditioning. We therefore include rather more old citations than is customary (for more on the history and philosophy of Skinnerian behaviorism, both pro and con, see Baum 1994, Rachlin 1991, Sidman 1960, Staddon 2001b, and Zuriff 1985).

an illuminated disk (key) for pigeons. The rate of such behavior was thought to be important as a measure of response strength (Skinner 1938, 1966, 1986; Killeen & Hall 2001). The current status of this assumption is one of the topics of this review. True or not, the emphasis on response rate has resulted in a dearth of experimental work by operant conditioners on nonrecurrent behavior such as movement in space.

Operant conditioning differs from other kinds of learning research in one important respect. The focus has been almost exclusively on what is called *reversible* behavior, that is, behavior in which the steady-state pattern under a given schedule is stable, meaning that in a sequence of conditions, XAXBXC. . ., where each condition is maintained for enough days that the pattern of behavior is locally stable, behavior under schedule X shows a pattern after one or two repetitions of X that is always the same. For example, the first time an animal is exposed to a fixed-interval schedule, after several daily sessions most animals show a "scalloped" pattern of responding (call it pattern A): a pause after each food delivery—also called *wait time* or *latency*—followed by responding at an accelerated rate until the next food delivery. However, some animals show negligible wait time and a steady rate (pattern B). If all are now trained on some other procedure—a variable-interval schedule, for example—and then after several sessions are returned to the fixed-interval schedule, almost all the animals will revert to pattern A. Thus, pattern A is the stable pattern. Pattern B, which may persist under unchanging conditions but does not recur after one or more intervening conditions, is sometimes termed *metastable* (Staddon 1965). The vast majority of published studies in operant conditioning are on behavior that is stable in this sense.

Although the theoretical issue is not a difficult one, there has been some confusion about what the idea of stability (reversibility) in behavior means. It should be obvious that the animal that shows pattern A after the second exposure to procedure X is not the same animal as when it showed pattern A on the first exposure. Its experimental history is different after the second exposure than after the first. If the animal has any kind of memory, therefore, its internal state[2] following the second exposure is likely to be different than after the first exposure, even though the observed behavior is the same. The behavior is reversible; the organism's internal state in general is not. The problems involved in studying nonreversible phenomena in individual organisms have been spelled out elsewhere (e.g., Staddon 2001a, Ch. 1); this review is mainly concerned with the reversible aspects of behavior.

Once the microscope was invented, microorganisms became a new field of investigation. Once automated operant conditioning was invented, reinforcement schedules became an independent subject of inquiry. In addition to being of great interest in their own right, schedules have also been used to study topics defined in more abstract ways such as timing and choice. These two areas constitute the majority of experimental papers in operant conditioning with animal subjects during

---

[2]By "internal" we mean not "physiological" but "hidden." The idea is simply that the organism's future behavior depends on variables not all of which are revealed in its current behavior (cf. Staddon 2001b, Ch. 7).

the past two decades. Great progress has been made in understanding free-operant choice behavior and interval timing. Yet several theories of choice still compete for consensus, and much the same is true of interval timing. In this review we attempt to summarize the current state of knowledge in these two areas, to suggest how common principles may apply in both, and to show how these principles may also apply to reinforcement schedule behavior considered as a topic in its own right.

INTERVAL TIMING

Interval timing is defined in several ways. The simplest is to define it as covariation between a dependent measure such as wait time and an independent measure such as interreinforcement interval (on fixed interval) or trial time-to-reinforcement (on the peak procedure). When interreinforcement interval is doubled, then after a learning period wait time also approximately doubles (*proportional timing*). This is an example of what is sometimes called a *time production* procedure: The organism produces an approximation to the to-be-timed interval. There are also explicit *time discrimination* procedures in which on each trial the subject is exposed to a stimulus and is then required to respond differentially depending on its absolute (Church & Deluty 1977, Stubbs 1968) or even relative (Fetterman et al. 1989) duration. For example, in *temporal bisection*, the subject (e.g., a rat) experiences either a 10-s or a 2-s stimulus, L or S. After the stimulus goes off, the subject is confronted with two choices. If the stimulus was L, a press on the left lever yields food; if S, a right press gives food; errors produce a brief time-out. Once the animal has learned, stimuli of intermediate duration are presented in lieu of S and L on test trials. The question is, how will the subject distribute its responses? In particular, at what intermediate duration will it be indifferent between the two choices? [Answer: typically in the vicinity of the geometric mean, i.e., $\sqrt{(L.S)} - 4.47$ for 2 and 10.]

Wait time is a latency; hence (it might be objected) it may vary on time-production procedures like fixed interval because of factors other than timing— such as degree of hunger (food deprivation). Using a time-discrimination procedure avoids this problem. It can also be mitigated by using the peak procedure and looking at performance during "empty" trials. "Filled" trials terminate with food reinforcement after (say) T s. "Empty" trials, typically $3T$ s long, contain no food and end with the onset of the ITI. During empty trials the animal therefore learns to wait, then respond, then stop (more or less) until the end of the trial (Catania 1970). The mean of the distribution of response rates averaged over empty trials (*peak time*) is then perhaps a better measure of timing than wait time because motivational variables are assumed to affect only the height and spread of the response-rate distribution, not its mean. This assumption is only partially true (Grace & Nevin 2000, MacEwen & Killeen 1991, Plowright et al. 2000).

There is still some debate about the actual pattern of behavior on the peak procedure in each individual trial. Is it just wait, respond at a constant rate, then wait again? Or is there some residual responding after the "stop" [yes, usually (e.g.,

Church et al. 1991)]? Is the response rate between start and stop really constant or are there two or more identifiable rates (Cheng & Westwood 1993, Meck et al. 1984)? Nevertheless, the method is still widely used, particularly by researchers in the cognitive/psychophysical tradition. The idea behind this approach is that interval timing is akin to sensory processes such as the perception of sound intensity (loudness) or luminance (brightness). As there is an ear for hearing and an eye for seeing, so (it is assumed) there must be a (real, physiological) clock for timing. Treisman (1963) proposed the idea of an internal pacemaker-driven clock in the context of human psychophysics. Gibbon (1977) further developed the approach and applied it to animal interval-timing experiments.

WEBER'S LAW, PROPORTIONAL TIMING AND TIMESCALE INVARIANCE

The major similarity between acknowledged sensory processes, such as brightness perception, and interval timing is *Weber's law*. Peak time on the peak procedure is not only proportional to time-to-food (T), its coefficient of variation (standard deviation divided by mean) is approximately constant, a result similar to Weber's law obeyed by most sensory dimensions. This property has been called *scalar timing* (Gibbon 1977). Most recently, Gallistel & Gibbon (2000) have proposed a grand principle of *timescale invariance*, the idea that the frequency distribution of any given temporal measure (the idea is assumed to apply generally, though in fact most experimental tests have used peak time) scales with the to-be-timed-interval. Thus, given the normalized peak-time distribution for $T = 60$ s, say; if the x-axis is divided by 2, it will match the distribution for $T = 30$ s. In other words, the frequency distribution for the temporal dependent variable, normalized on both axes, is asserted to be invariant.

Timescale invariance is in effect a combination of Weber's law and proportional timing. Like those principles, it is only approximately true. There are three kinds of evidence that limit its generality. The simplest is the steady-state pattern of responding (key-pecking or lever-pressing) observed on fixed-interval reinforcement schedules. This pattern should be the same at all fixed-interval values, but it is not. Gallistel & Gibbon wrote, "When responding on such a schedule, animals pause after each reinforcement and then resume responding after some interval has elapsed. It was generally supposed that the animals' rate of responding accelerated throughout the remainder of the interval leading up to reinforcement. In fact, however, conditioned responding in this paradigm ... is a two-state variable (slow, sporadic pecking vs. rapid, steady pecking), with one transition per interreinforcement interval (Schneider 1969)" (p. 293).

This conclusion over-generalizes Schneider's result. Reacting to reports of "break-and-run" fixed-interval performance under some conditions, Schneider sought to characterize this feature more objectively than the simple inspection of cumulative records. He found a way to identify the point of maximum acceleration in the fixed-interval "scallop" by using an iterative technique analogous to attaching an elastic band to the beginning of an interval and the end point of the cumulative record, then pushing a pin, representing the break point, against the middle of the band until the two resulting straight-line segments best fit the cumulative record (there are other ways to achieve the same result that do not fix the end points of the two line-segments). The postreinforcement time (x-coordinate) of the pin then gives the break point for that interval. Schneider showed that the break point is an orderly dependent measure: Break point is roughly 0.67 of interval duration, with standard deviation proportional to the mean (the Weber-law or scalar property).

This finding is by no means the same as the idea that the fixed-interval scallop is "a two-state variable" (Hanson & Killeen 1981). Schneider showed that a two-state model is an adequate approximation; he did not show that it is the best or truest approximation. A three- or four-line approximation (i.e., two or more pins) might well have fit significantly better than the two-line version. To show that the process is two-state, Schneider would have had to show that adding additional segments produced negligibly better fit to the data.

The frequent assertion that the fixed-interval scallop is always an artifact of averaging flies in the face of raw cumulative-record data—the many nonaveraged individual fixed-interval cumulative records in Ferster & Skinner (1957, e.g., pp. 159, 160, 162), which show clear curvature, particularly at longer fixed-interval values ($> \sim 2$ min). The issue for timescale invariance, therefore, is whether the shape, or relative frequency of different-shaped records, is the same at different absolute intervals.

The evidence is that there is more, and more frequent, curvature at longer intervals. Schneider's data show this effect. In Schneider's Figure 3, for example, the time to shift from low to high rate is clearly longer at longer intervals than shorter ones. On fixed-interval schedules, apparently, absolute duration does affect the pattern of responding. (A possible reason for this dependence of the scallop on fixed-interval value is described in Staddon 2001a, p. 317. The basic idea is that greater curvature at longer fixed-interval values follows from two things: a linear increase in response probability across the interval, combined with a nonlinear, negatively accelerated, relation between overall response rate and reinforcement rate.) If there is a reliable difference in the shape, or distribution of shapes, of cumulative records at long and short fixed-interval values, the timescale-invariance principle is violated.

A second dataset that does not agree with timescale invariance is an extensive set of studies on the peak procedure by Zeiler & Powell (1994; see also Hanson & Killeen 1981), who looked explicitly at the effect of interval duration on various measures of interval timing. They conclude, "Quantitative properties of temporal control depended on whether the aspect of behavior considered was initial pause duration, the point of maximum acceleration in responding [break point], the point of maximum deceleration, the point at which responding stopped, or several different statistical derivations of a point of maximum responding . . . . Existing theory does not explain why Weber's law [the scalar property] so rarely fit the results . . ."

(p. 1; see also Lowe et al. 1979, Wearden 1985 for other exceptions to proportionality between temporal measures of behavior and interval duration). Like Schneider (1969) and Hanson & Killeen (1981), Zeiler & Powell found that the break point measure was proportional to interval duration, with scalar variance (constant coefficient of variation), and thus consistent with timescale invariance, but no other measure fit the rule.

Moreover, the fit of the breakpoint measure is problematic because it is not a direct measure of behavior but is itself the result of a statistical fitting procedure. It is possible, therefore, that the fit of breakpoint to timescale invariance owes as much to the statistical method used to arrive at it as to the intrinsic properties of temporal control. Even if this caveat turns out to be false, the fact that every other measure studied by Zeiler & Powell failed to conform to timescale invariance surely rules it out as a general principle of interval timing.

The third and most direct test of the timescale invariance idea is an extensive series of time-discrimination experiments carried out by Dreyfus et al. (1988) and Stubbs et al. (1994). The usual procedure in these experiments was for pigeons to peck a center response key to produce a red light of one duration that is followed immediately by a green light of another duration. When the green center-key light goes off, two yellow side-keys light up. The animals are reinforced with food for pecking the left side-key if the red light was longer, the right side-key if the green light was longer.

The experimental question is, how does discrimination accuracy depend on relative and absolute duration of the two stimuli? Timescale invariance predicts that accuracy depends only on the ratio of red and green durations: For example, accuracy should be the same following the sequence red:10, green:20 as the sequence red:30, green:60, but it is not. Pigeons are better able to discriminate between the two short durations than the two long ones, even though their ratio is the same. Dreyfus et al. and Stubbs et al. present a plethora of quantitative data of the same sort, all showing that time discrimination depends on absolute as well as relative duration.

Timescale invariance is empirically indistinguishable from Weber's law as it applies to time, combined with the idea of proportional timing: The mean of a temporal dependent variable is proportional to the temporal independent variable. But Weber's law and proportional timing are dissociable—it is possible to have proportional timing without conforming to Weber's law and vice versa (cf. Hanson & Killeen 1981, Zeiler & Powell 1994), and in any case both are only approximately true. Timescale invariance therefore does not qualify as a principle in its own right.

Cognitive and Behavioral Approaches to Timing

The cognitive approach to timing dates from the late 1970s. It emphasizes the psychophysical properties of the timing process and the use of temporal dependent variables as measures of (for example) drug effects and the effects of physiological interventions. It de-emphasizes proximal environmental causes. Yet when timing (then called temporal control; see Zeiler 1977 for an early review) was first discovered by operant conditioners (Pavlov had studied essentially the same phenomenon—*delay conditioning*—many years earlier), the focus was on the *time marker*, the stimulus that triggered the temporally correlated behavior. (That is one virtue of the term *control*: It emphasizes the fact that interval timing behavior is usually not free-running. It must be cued by some aspect of the environment.) On so-called spaced-responding schedules, for example, the response is the time marker: The subject must learn to space its responses more than T s apart to get food. On fixed-interval schedules the time marker is reinforcer delivery; on the peak procedure it is the stimulus events associated with trial onset. This dependence on a time marker is especially obvious on time-production procedures, but on time-discrimination procedures the subject's choice behavior must also be under the control of stimuli associated with the onset and offset of the sample duration.

Not all stimuli are equally effective as time markers. For example, an early study by Staddon & Innis (1966a; see also 1969) showed that if, on alternate fixed intervals, 50% of reinforcers (F) are omitted and replaced by a neutral stimulus (N) of the same duration, wait time following N is much shorter than after F (the *reinforcement-omission effect*). Moreover, this difference persists indefinitely. Despite the fact that F and N have the same temporal relationship to the reinforcer, F is much more effective as a time marker than N. No exactly comparable experiment has been done using the peak procedure, partly because the time marker there involves ITI offset/trial onset rather than the reinforcer delivery, so that there is no simple manipulation equivalent to reinforcement omission.

These effects do not depend on the type of behavior controlled by the time marker. On fixed-interval schedules the time marker is in effect inhibitory: Responding is suppressed during the wait time and then occurs at an accelerating rate. Other experiments (Staddon 1970, 1972), however, showed that given the appropriate schedule, the time marker can control a burst of responding (rather than a wait) of a duration proportional to the schedule parameters (*temporal go–no-go* schedules) and later experiments have shown that the place of responding can be controlled by time since trial onset in the so-called tri-peak procedure (Matell & Meck 1999).

A theoretical review (Staddon 1974) concluded, "Temporal control by a given time marker depends on the properties of recall and attention, that is, on the same variables that affect attention to compound stimuli and recall in memory experiments such as delayed matching-to-sample." By far the most important variable seems to be "the *value* of the time-marker stimulus—Stimuli of high value . . . are more salient . . ." (p. 389), although the full range of properties that determine time-marker effectiveness is yet to be explored.

Reinforcement omission experiments are *transfer tests*, that is, tests to identify the effective stimulus. They pinpoint the stimulus property controlling interval timing—the effective time marker—by selectively eliminating candidate properties. For example, in a definitive experiment, Kello (1972) showed that on fixed interval the wait time is longest following standard reinforcer delivery (food hopper activated with food, hopper light on, house light off, etc.). Omission of any of those elements caused the wait time to decrease, a result consistent with the hypothesis that reinforcer delivery acquires inhibitory temporal control over the wait time. The only thing that makes this situation different from the usual generalization experiment is that the effects of reinforcement omission are relatively permanent. In the usual generalization experiment, delivery of the reinforcer according to the same schedule in the presence of both the training stimulus and the test stimuli would soon lead all to be responded to in the same way. Not so with temporal control: As we just saw, even though N and F events have the same temporal relationship to the next food delivery, animals never learn to respond similarly after both. The only exception is when the fixed-interval is relatively short, on the order of 20 s or less (Starr & Staddon 1974). Under these conditions pigeons are able to use a brief neutral stimulus as a time marker on fixed interval.

The Gap Experiment

The closest equivalent to fixed-interval reinforcement–omission using the peak procedure is the so-called gap experiment (Roberts 1981). In the standard gap paradigm the sequence of stimuli in a training trial (no gap stimulus) consists of three successive stimuli: the intertrial interval stimulus (ITI), the fixed-duration trial stimulus (S), and food reinforcement (F), which ends each training trial. The sequence is thus ITI, S, F, ITI. Training trials are typically interspersed with empty probe trials that last longer than reinforced trials but end with an ITI only and no reinforcement. The stimulus sequence on such trials is ITI, S, ITI, but the S is two or three times longer than on training trials. After performance has stabilized, gap trials are introduced into some or all of the probe trials. On gap trials the ITI stimulus reappears for a while in the middle of the trial stimulus. The sequence on gap trials is therefore ITI, S, ITI, S, ITI. Gap trials do not end in reinforcement.

What is the effective time marker (i.e., the stimulus that exerts temporal control) in such an experiment? ITI offset/trial onset is the best temporal predictor of reinforcement: Its time to food is shorter and less variable than any other experimental event. Most but not all ITIs follow reinforcement, and the ITI itself is often variable in duration and relatively long. So reinforcer delivery is a poor temporal predictor. The time marker therefore has something to do with the transition between ITI and trial onset, between ITI and S. Gap trials also involve presentation of the ITI stimulus, albeit with a different duration and within-trial location than the usual ITI, but the similarities to a regular trial are obvious. The gap experiment is therefore a sort of generalization (of temporal control) experiment. Buhusi & Meck (2000) presented gap stimuli more or less similar to the ITI stimulus during probe trials and found results resembling generalization decrement, in agreement with this analysis.

However, the gap procedure was not originally thought of as a generalization test, nor is it particularly well designed for that purpose. The gap procedure arose directly from the cognitive idea that interval timing behavior is driven by an internal clock (Church 1978). From this point of view it is perfectly natural to inquire about the conditions under which the clock can be started or stopped. If the to-be-timed interval is interrupted—a gap—will the clock restart when the trial stimulus returns (reset)? Will it continue running during the gap and afterwards? Or will it stop and then restart (stop)?

"Reset" corresponds to the maximum rightward shift (from trial onset) of the response-rate peak from its usual position t s after trial onset to $t + G_E$, where G_E is the offset time (end) of the gap stimulus. Conversely, no effect (clock keeps running) leaves the peak unchanged at t, and "stop and restart" is an intermediate result, a peak shift to $G_E - G_B + t$, where G_B is the time of onset (beginning) of the gap stimulus.

Both gap duration and placement within a trial have been varied. The results that have been obtained so far are rather complex (cf. Buhusi & Meck 2000, Cabeza de Vaca et al. 1994, Matell & Meck 1999). In general, the longer the gap and the later it appears in the trial, the greater the rightward peak shift. All these effects can be interpreted in clock terms, but the clock view provides no real explanation for them, because it does not specify which one will occur under a given set of conditions. The results of gap experiments can be understood in a qualitative way in terms of the similarity of the gap presentation to events associated with trial onset; the more similar, the closer the effect will be to reset, i.e., the onset of a new trial. Another resemblance between gap results and the results of reinforcement-omission experiments is that the effects of the gap are also permanent: Behavior on later trials usually does not differ from behavior on the first few (Roberts 1981). These effects have been successfully simulated quantitatively by a neural network timing model (Hopson 1999, 2002) that includes the assumption that the effects of time-marker presentation decay with time (Cabeza de Vaca et al. 1994).

The original temporal control studies were strictly empirical but tacitly accepted something like the psychophysical view of timing. Time was assumed to be a sensory modality like any other, so the experimental task was simply to explore the different kinds of effect, excitatory, inhibitory, discriminatory, that could come under temporal control. The psychophysical view was formalized by Gibbon (1977) in the context of animal studies, and this led to a static information-processing model, *scalar expectancy theory* (SET: Gibbon & Church 1984, Meck 1983, Roberts 1983), which comprised a pacemaker-driven clock, working and reference memories, a comparator, and various thresholds. A later dynamic version added memory for individual trials (see Gallistel 1990 for a review). This approach led to a long series of experimental studies exploring the clocklike properties of interval timing (see Gallistel & Gibbon 2000, Staddon & Higa 1999 for reviews), but none of these studies attempted to test the assumptions of the SET approach in a direct way.

SET was for many years the dominant theoretical approach to interval timing. In recent years, however, its limitations, of parsimony and predictive range, have become apparent and there are now a number of competitors such as the behavioral theory of timing (Killeen & Fetterman 1988, MacEwen & Killeen 1991, Machado 1997), spectral timing theory (Grossberg & Schmajuk 1989), neural network models (Church & Broadbent 1990, Hopson 1999, Dragoi et al. 2002), and the habituation-based multiple time scale theory (MTS: Staddon & Higa 1999, Staddon et al. 2002). There is as yet no consensus on the best theory.

Temporal Dynamics: Linear Waiting

A separate series of experiments in the temporal-control tradition, beginning in the late 1980s, studied the real-time dynamics of interval timing (e.g., Higa et al. 1991, Lejeune et al. 1997, Wynne & Staddon 1988; see Staddon 2001a for a review). These experiments have led to a simple empirical principle that may have wide application. Most of these experiments used the simplest possible timing schedule, a response-initiated delay (RID) schedule[3]. In this schedule the animal (e.g., a pigeon) can respond at any time, t, after food. The response changes the key color and food is delivered after a further T s. Time t is under the control of the animal; time T is determined by the experimenter. These experiments have shown that wait time on these and similar schedules (such as fixed interval) is strongly determined by the duration of the previous interfood interval (IFI). For example, wait time will track a cyclic sequence of IFIs, intercalated at a random point in a sequence of fixed ($t + T =$ constant) intervals, with a lag of one interval; a single short IFI is followed by a short wait time in the next interval (the effect of a single long interval is smaller), and so on (see Staddon et al. 2002 for a review and other examples of temporal tracking). To a first approximation, these results are consistent with a linear relation between wait time in IFI $N + 1$ and the duration of IFI N:

$$t(N + 1) = a[T(N) + t(N)] + b = aI(N) + b, \qquad (1)$$

where I is the IFI, a is a constant less than one, and b is usually negligible. This relation has been termed *linear waiting* (Wynne & Staddon 1988). The principle is an approximation: an expanded model, incorporating the multiple time scale theory, allows the principle to account for the slower effects of increases as opposed to decreases in IFI (see Staddon et al. 2002).

Most importantly for this discussion, the linear waiting principle appears to be obligatory. That is, organisms seem to follow the linear waiting rule even if they delay or even prevent reinforcer delivery by doing so. The simplest example is the RID schedule itself. Wynne & Staddon (1988) showed that it makes no difference whether the experimenter holds delay time T constant or the sum of $t +$ T constant ($t + T = K$): Equation 1 holds in both cases, even though the optimal (reinforcement-rate-maximizing) strategy in the first case is for the animal to set

---

[3]When there is no response-produced stimulus change, this procedure is also called a conjunctive fixed-ratio fixed-time schedule (Shull 1970).

t equal to zero, whereas in the second case reinforcement rate is maximized so long as $t < K$. Using a version of RID in which T in interval $N + 1$ depended on the value of *t* in the preceding interval, Wynne & Staddon also demonstrated two kinds of instability predicted by linear waiting.

The fact that linear waiting is obligatory allows us to look for its effects on schedules other than the simple RID schedule. The most obvious application is to ratio schedules. The time to emit a fixed number of responses is approximately constant; hence the delay to food after the first response in each interval is also approximately constant on fixed ratio (FR), as on fixed-*T* RID (Powell 1968). Thus, the optimal strategy on FR, as on fixed-*T* RID, is to respond immediately after food. However, in both cases animals wait before responding and, as one might expect based on the assumption of a roughly constant interresponse time on all ratio schedules, the duration of the wait on FR is proportional to the ratio requirement (Powell 1968), although longer than on a comparable chain-type schedule with the same interreinforcement time (Crossman et al. 1974). The phenomenon of *ratio strain*—the appearance of long pauses and even extinction on high ratio schedules (Ferster & Skinner 1957)—may also have something to do with obligatory linear waiting.

Chain Schedules

A *chain schedule* is one in which a stimulus change, rather than primary reinforcement, is scheduled. Thus, a chain fixed-interval–fixed-interval schedule is one in which, for example, food reinforcement is followed by the onset of a red key light in the presence of which, after a fixed interval, a response produces a change to green. In the presence of green, food delivery is scheduled according to another fixed interval. RID schedules resemble two-link chain schedules. The first link is time *t*, before the animal responds; the second link is time *T*, after a response. We may expect, therefore, that waiting time in the first link of a two-link schedule will depend on the duration of the second link. We describe two results consistent with this conjecture and then discuss some exceptions.

Davison (1974) studied a two-link chain fixed-interval–fixed-interval schedule. Each cycle of the schedule began with a red key. Responding was reinforced, on fixed-interval I_1 s, by a change in key color from red to white. In the presence of white, food reinforcement was delivered according to fixed-interval I_2 s, followed by reappearance of the red key. Davison varied I_1 and I_2 and collected steady-state rate, pause, and link-duration data. He reported that when programmed second-link duration was long in relation to the first-link duration, pause in the first link sometimes exceeded the programmed link duration. The linear waiting predictions for this procedure can therefore be most easily derived for those conditions where the second link is held constant and the first link duration is varied (because under these conditions, the first-link pause was always less than the programmed first-link duration). The prediction for the terminal link is

$$t_2 = aI_2, \tag{2}$$

where a is the proportionality constant, I_2 is the duration of the terminal-link fixed-interval, and t_2 is the pause in the terminal link. Because I_2 is constant in this phase, t_2 is also constant. The pause in the initial link is given by

$$t_1 = a(I_1 + I_2) = aI_1 + aI_2, \tag{3}$$

where I_1 is the duration of the first link. Because I_2 is constant, Equation 3 is a straight line with slope a and positive y-intercept aI_2.

Linear waiting theory can be tested with Davison's data by plotting, for every condition, t_1 and t_2 versus time-to-reinforcement (TTR); that is, plot pause in each link against TTR for that link in every condition. Linear waiting makes a straightforward prediction: All the data points for both links should lie on the same straight line through the origin (assuming that $b \to 0$). We show this plot in Figure 1. There is some variability, because the data points are individual subjects, not averages, but points from first and second links fit the same line, and the deviations do not seem to be systematic.

A study by Innis et al. (1993) provides a dynamic test of the linear waiting hypothesis as applied to chain schedules. Innis et al. studied two-link chain schedules with one link of fixed duration and the other varying from reinforcer to reinforcer

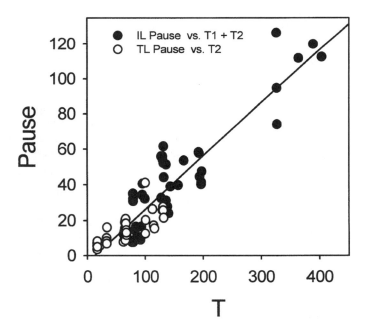

Figure 1   Steady-state pause duration plotted against actual time to reinforcement in the first and second links of a two-link chain schedule. Each data point is from a single pigeon in one experimental condition (three data points from an incomplete condition are omitted). (From Davison 1974, Table 1)

according to a triangular cycle. The dependent measure was pause in each link. Their Figure 3, for example, shows the programmed and actual values of the second link of the *constant-cycle* procedure (i.e., the first link was a constant 20 s; the second link varied from 5 to 35 s according to the triangular cycle) as well as the average pause, which clearly tracks the change in second-link duration with a lag of one interval. They found similar results for the reverse procedure, *cycle-constant*, in which the first link varied cyclically and the second link was constant. The tracking was a little better in the first procedure than in the second, but in both cases first-link pause was determined primarily by TTR.

There are some data suggesting that linear waiting is not the only factor that determines responding on simple chain schedules. In the four conditions of Davison's experiment in which the programmed durations of the first and second links added to a constant (120 s)—which implies a constant first-link pause according to linear waiting—pause in the first link covaried with first-link duration, although the data are noisy.

The alternative to the linear waiting account of responding on chain schedules is an account in terms of *conditioned reinforcement* (also called secondary reinforcement)—the idea that a stimulus paired with a primary reinforcer acquires some independent reinforcing power. This idea is also the organizing principle behind most theories of free-operant choice. There are some data that seem to imply a response-strengthening effect quite apart from the linear waiting effect, but they do not always hold up under closer inspection. Catania et al. (1980) reported that "higher rates of pecking were maintained by pigeons in the middle component of three-component chained fixed-interval schedules than in that component of the corresponding multiple schedule (two extinction components followed by a fixed-interval component)" (p. 213), but the effect was surprisingly small, given that no responding at all was required in the first two components. Moreover, results of a more critical control condition, chain versus tandem (rather than multiple) schedule, were the opposite: Rate was generally higher in the middle tandem component than in the second link of the chain. (A tandem schedule is one with the same response contingencies as a chain but with the same stimulus present throughout.)

Royalty et al. (1987) introduced a delay into the peck-stimulus-change contingency of a three-link variable-interval chain schedule and found large decreases in response rate [wait time (WT) was not reported] in both first and second links. They concluded that "because the effect of delaying stimulus change was comparable to the effect of delaying primary reinforcement in a simple variable-interval schedule . . . the results provide strong evidence for the concept of conditioned reinforcement" (p. 41). The implications of the Royalty et al. data for linear waiting are unclear, however, (*a*) because the linear waiting hypothesis does not deal with the assignment-of-credit problem, that is, the selection of the appropriate response by the schedule. Linear waiting makes predictions about response timing—when the operant response occurs—but not about which response will occur. Response-reinforcer contiguity may be essential for the selection of the operant response in each chain link (as it clearly is during "shaping"), and diminishing contiguity may reduce response rate, but contiguity may play little or no role in the timing of the response. The idea of conditioned reinforcement may well apply to the first function but not to the second. (*b*) Moreover, Royalty et al. did not report *obtained time-to-reinforcement* data; the effect of the imposed delay may therefore have been via an increase in component duration rather than directly on response rate.

Williams & Royalty (1990) explicitly compared conditioned reinforcement and time to reinforcement as explanations for chain schedule performance in three-link chains and concluded "that time to reinforcement itself accounts for little if any variance in initial-link responding" (p. 381) but not timing, which was not measured. However, these data are from chain schedules with both variable-interval and fixed-interval links, rather than fixed-interval only, and with respect to response rate rather than pause measures. In a later paper Williams qualified this claim: "The effects of stimuli in a chain schedule are due partly to the time to food correlated with the stimuli and partly to the time to the next conditioned reinforcer in the sequence" (1997, p. 145).

The conclusion seems to be that linear waiting plays a relatively major, and conditioned reinforcement (however defined) a relatively minor, role in the determination of response timing on chain fixed-interval schedules. Linear waiting also provides the best available account of a striking, unsolved problem with chain schedules: the fact that in chains with several links, pigeon subjects may respond at a low level or even quit completely in early links (Catania 1979, Gollub 1977). On fixed-interval chain schedules with five or more links, responding in the early links begins to extinguish and the overall reinforcement rate falls well below the maximum possible—even if the programmed interreinforcement interval is relatively short (e.g., $6 \times 15 = 90$ s). If the same stimulus is present in all links (tandem schedule), or if the six different stimuli are presented in random order (scrambled-stimuli chains), performance is maintained in all links and the overall reinforcement rate is close to the maximum possible ($6I$, where I is the interval length). Other studies have reported very weak responding in early components of a simple chain fixed-interval schedule (e.g., Catania et al. 1980, Davison 1974, Williams 1994; review in Kelleher & Gollub 1962). These studies found that chains with as few as three fixed-interval 60-s links (Kelleher & Fry 1962) occasionally produce extreme pausing in the first link. No formal theory of the kind that has proliferated to explain behavior on concurrent chain schedules (discussed below) has been offered to account for these strange results, even though they have been well known for many years.

The informal suggestion is that the low or zero response rates maintained by early components of a multi-link chain are a consequence of the same discrimination process that leads to extinction in the absence of primary reinforcement. Conversely, the stimulus at the end of the chain that is actually paired with primary reinforcement is assumed to be a conditioned reinforcer; stimuli in the middle sustain responding because they lead to production of a conditioned reinforcer

(Catania et al. 1980, Kelleher & Gollub 1962). Pairing also explains why behavior is maintained on tandem and scrambled-stimuli chains (Kelleher & Fry 1962). In both cases the stimuli early in the chain are either invariably (tandem) or occasionally (scrambled-stimulus) paired with primary reinforcement.

There are problems with the conditioned-reinforcement approach, however. It can explain responding in link two of a three-link chain but not in link one, which should be an extinction stimulus. The explanatory problem gets worse when more links are added. There is no well-defined principle to tell us when a stimulus changes from being a conditioned reinforcer, to a stimulus in whose presence responding is maintained by a conditioned reinforcer, to an extinction stimulus. What determines the stimulus property? Is it stimulus number, stimulus duration or the durations of stimuli later in the chain? Perhaps there is some balance between contrast/extinction, which depresses responding in early links, and conditioned reinforcement, which is supposed to (but sometimes does not) elevate responding in later links? No well-defined compound theory has been offered, even though there are several quantitative theories for multiple-schedule contrast (e.g., Herrnstein 1970, Nevin 1974, Staddon 1982; see review in Williams 1988). There are also data that cast doubt even on the idea that late-link stimuli have a rate-enhancing effect. In the Catania et al. (1980) study, for example, four of five pigeons responded faster in the middle link of a three-link tandem schedule than the comparable chain.

The lack of formal theories for performance on simple chains is matched by a dearth of data. Some pause data are presented in the study by Davison (1974) on pigeons in a two-link fixed-interval chain. The paper attempted to fit Herrnstein's (1970) matching law between response rates and link duration. The match was poor: The pigeon's rates fell more than predicted when the terminal links (contiguous with primary reinforcement) of the chain were long, but Davison did find that "the terminal link schedule clearly changes the pause in the initial link, longer terminal-link intervals giving longer initial-link pauses" (1974, p. 326). Davison's abstract concludes, "Data on pauses during the interval schedules showed that, in most conditions, the pause duration was a linear function of the interval length, and greater in the initial link than in the terminal link" (p. 323). In short, the pause (time-to-first-response) data were more lawful than response-rate data.

Linear waiting provides a simple explanation for excessive pausing on multi-link chain fixed-interval schedules. Suppose the chief function of the link stimuli on chain schedules is simply to signal changing times to primary reinforcement[4].

---

[4]This idea surfaced very early in the history of research on equal-link chain fixed-interval schedules, but because of the presumed importance of conditioned reinforcement, it was the time to reinforcement from link stimulus offset, rather than onset that was thought to be important. Thus, Gollub (1977), echoing his 1958 Ph.D. dissertation in the subsequent Kelleher & Gollub (1962) review, wrote, "In chained schedules with more than two components . . . the extent to which responding is sustained in the initial components . . . depends on the time that elapses from the end of the components to food reinforcement" (p. 291).

Thus, in a three-link fixed-interval chain, with link duration I, the TTR signaled by the end of reinforcement (or by the onset of the first link) is $3I$. The onset of the next link signals a TTR of $2I$ and the terminal, third, link signals a TTR of I. The assumptions of linear waiting as applied to this situation are that pausing (time to first response) in each link is determined entirely by TTR and that the wait time in interval $N+1$ is a linear function of the TTR in the preceding interval.

To see the implications of this process, consider again a three-link chain schedule with $I=1$ (arbitrary time units). The performance to be expected depends entirely on the value of the proportionality constant, a, that sets the fraction of time-to-primary-reinforcement that the animal waits (for simplicity we can neglect b; the logic of the argument is unaffected). All is well so long as a is less than one-third. If a is exactly 0.333, then for unit link duration the pause in the third link is 0.33, in the second link 0.67, and in the first link 1.0 However, if a is larger, for instance 0.5, the three pauses become 0.5, 1.0, and 1.5; that is, the pause in the first link is now longer than the programmed interval, which means the TTR in the first link will be longer than 3 the next time around, so the pause will increase further, and so on until the process stabilizes (which it always does: First-link pause never goes to ∞).

The steady-state wait times in each link predicted for a five-link chain, with unit-duration links, for two values of a are shown in Figure 2. In both cases wait times in the early links are very much longer than the programmed link duration. Clearly, this process has the potential to produce very large pauses in the early links of multilink-chain fixed-interval schedules and so may account for the data Catania (1979) and others have reported.

Gollub in his dissertation research (1958) noticed the additivity of this sequential pausing. Kelleher & Gollub (1962) in their subsequent review wrote, "No two pauses in [simple fixed interval] can both postpone food-delivery; however, pauses in different components of [a] five-component chain will postpone food-delivery additively" (p. 566). However, this additivity was only one of a number of processes suggested to account for the long pauses in early chain fixed-interval links, and its quantitative implications were never explored.

Note that the linear waiting hypothesis also accounts for the relative stability of tandem schedules and chain schedules with scrambled components. In the tandem schedule, reinforcement constitutes the only available time marker. Given that responding after the pause continues at a relatively high rate until the next time marker, Equation 1 (with b assumed negligible) and a little algebra shows that the steady-state postreinforcement pause for a tandem schedule with unit links will be

$$t = \frac{a(N-1)}{1-a}, \qquad \text{if } t \geq 1, \qquad (4)$$

where N is the number of links and a is the pause fraction. In the absence of any time markers, pauses in links after the first are necessarily short, so the experienced link duration equals the programmed duration. Thus, the total interfood-reinforcement

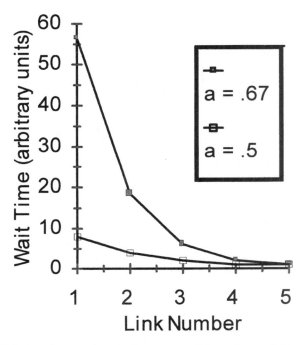

Figure 2   Wait time (pause, time to first response) in each equal-duration link of a five-link chain schedule (as a multiple of the programmed link duration) as predicted by the linear-waiting hypothesis. The two curves are for two values of parameter a in Equation 1 ($b = 0$). Note the very long pauses predicted in early links—almost two orders of magnitude greater than the programmed interval in the first link for $a = 0.67$. (From Mazur 2001)

interval will be $t + N - 1$ ($t \geq 1$): the pause in the first link (which will be longer than the programmed link duration for $N > 1/a$) plus the programmed durations of the succeeding links. For the case of $a = 0.67$ and unit link duration, which yielded a steady-state interfood interval (IFI) of 84 for the five-link chain schedule, the tandem yields 12. For $a = 0.5$, the two values are approximately 16 and 8.

The long waits in early links shown in Figure 2 depend critically on the value of a. If, as experience suggests (there has been no formal study), a tends to increase slowly with training, we might expect the long pausing in initial links to take some time to develop, which apparently it does (Gollub 1958).

On the scrambled-stimuli chain each stimulus occasionally ends in reinforcement, so each signals a time-to-reinforcement (TTR)[5] of I, and pause in each link should be less than the link duration—yielding a total IFI of approximately N,

---

[5]Interpreted as time to the first reinforcement opportunity.

i.e., 5 for the example in the figure. These predictions yield the order IFI in the chain > tandem > scrambled, but parametric data are not available for precise comparison. We do not know whether an N-link scrambled schedule typically stabilizes at a shorter IFI than the comparable tandem schedule, for example. Nor do we know whether steady-state pause in successive links of a multilink chain falls off in the exponential fashion shown in Figure 2.

In the final section we explore the implications of linear waiting for studies of free-operant choice behavior.

CHOICE

Although we can devote only limited space to it, choice is one of the major research topics in operant conditioning (see Mazur 2001, p. 96 for recent statistics). Choice is not something that can be directly observed. The subject does this or that and, in consequence, is said to choose. The term has unfortunate overtones of conscious deliberation and weighing of alternatives for which the behavior itself—response A or response B—provides no direct evidence. One result has been the assumption that the proper framework for all so-called choice studies is in terms of response strength and the value of the choice alternatives. Another is the assumption that procedures that are very different are nevertheless studying the same thing.

For example, in a classic series of experiments, Kahneman & Tversky (e.g., 1979) asked a number of human subjects to make a single choice of the following sort: between $400 for sure and a 50% chance of $1000. Most went for the sure thing, even though the expected value of the gamble is higher. This is termed *risk aversion*, and the same term has been applied to free-operant "choice" experiments. In one such experiment an animal subject must choose repeatedly between a response leading to a fixed amount of food and one leading equiprobably to either a large or a small amount with the same average value. Here the animals tend to be either indifferent or risk averse, preferring the fixed alternative (Staddon & Innis 1966b, Bateson & Kacelnik 1995, Kacelnik & Bateson 1996).

In a second example pigeons responded repeatedly to two keys associated with equal variable-interval schedules. A successful response on the left key, for example, is reinforced by a change in the color of the pecked key (the other key light goes off). In the presence of this second stimulus, food is delivered according to a fixed-interval schedule (fixed-interval X). The first stimulus, which is usually the same on both keys, is termed the *initial link*; the second stimulus is the *terminal link*. Pecks on the right key lead in the same way to food reinforcement on variable-interval X. (This is termed a *concurrent-chain* schedule.) In this case subjects overwhelmingly prefer the initial-link choice leading to the variable-interval terminal link; that is, they are apparently risk seeking rather than risk averse (Killeen 1968).

The fact that these three experiments (Kahneman & Tversky and the two free-operant studies) all produce different results is sometimes thought to pose a serious research problem, but, we contend, the problem is only in the use of the term *choice* for all three. The procedures (not to mention the subjects) are in fact very different, and in operant conditioning the devil is very much in the details. Apparently trivial procedural differences can sometimes lead to wildly different behavioral outcomes. Use of the term *choice* as if it denoted a unitary subject matter is therefore highly misleading. We also question the idea that the results of choice experiments are always best explained in terms of response strength and stimulus value.

Concurrent Schedules

Bearing these caveats in mind, let's look briefly at the extensive history of free-operant choice research. In Herrnstein's seminal experiment (1961; see Davison & McCarthy 1988, Williams 1988 for reviews; for collected papers see Rachlin & Laibson 1997) hungry pigeons pecked at two side-by-side response keys, one associated with variable-interval v_1 s and the other with variable-interval v_2 s (*concurrent variable-interval–variable-interval* schedule). After several experimental sessions and a range of v_1 and v_2 values chosen so that the overall programmed reinforcement rate was constant ($1/v_1 + 1/v_2 =$ constant), the result was matching between steady-state relative response rates and relative *obtained* reinforcement rates:

$$\frac{x}{y} = \frac{R(x)}{R(y)}, \tag{5}$$

where x and y are the response rates on the two alternatives and $R(x)$ and $R(y)$ are the rates of obtained reinforcement for them. This relation has become known as Herrnstein's matching law. Although the obtained reinforcement rates are dependent on the response rates that produce them, the matching relation is not forced, because x and y can vary over quite a wide range without much effect on $R(x)$ and $R(y)$.

Because of the negative feedback relation intrinsic to variable-interval schedules (the less you respond, the higher the probability of payoff), the matching law on concurrent variable-interval–variable-interval is consistent with reinforcement maximization (Staddon & Motheral 1978), although the maximum of the function relating overall payoff, $R(x) + R(y)$, to relative responding, $x/(x+y)$, is pretty flat. However, little else on these schedules fits the maximization idea. As noted above, even responding on simple fixed-T response-initiated delay (RID) schedules violates maximization. Matching is also highly overdetermined, in the sense that almost any learning rule consistent with the law of effect—an increase in reinforcement probability causes an increase in response probability—will yield either simple matching (Equation 5) or its power-law generalization (Baum 1974, Hinson & Staddon 1983, Lander & Irwin 1968, Staddon 1968). Matching by itself therefore reveals relatively little about the dynamic processes operating in the responding subject (but see Davison & Baum 2000). Despite this limitation, the strikingly regular functional relations characteristic of free-operant choice studies have attracted a great deal of experimental and theoretical attention.

Herrnstein (1970) proposed that Equation 5 can be derived from the function relating steady-state response rate, x, and reinforcement rate, $R(x)$, to each response key considered separately. This function is negatively accelerated and well approximated by a hyperbola:

$$x = \frac{kR(x)}{R(x) + R_0},\qquad(6)$$

where k is a constant and R_0 represents the effects of all other reinforcers in the situation. The denominator and parameter k cancel in the ratio x/y, yielding Equation 5 for the choice situation.

There are numerous empirical details that are not accounted for by this formulation: systematic deviations from matching [undermatching and overmatching (Baum 1974)] as a function of different types of variable-interval schedules, dependence of simple matching on use of a *changeover delay*, extensions to concurrent-chain schedules, and so on. For example, if animals are pretrained with two alternatives presented separately, so that they do not learn to switch between them, when given the opportunity to respond to both, they fixate on the richer one rather than matching [extreme overmatching (Donahoe & Palmer 1994, pp. 112–113; Gallistel & Gibbon 2000, pp. 321–322)]. (Fixation—extreme overmatching—is, trivially, matching, of course but if only fixation were observed, the idea of matching would never have arisen. Matching implies partial, not exclusive, preference.) Conversely, in the absence of a changeover delay, pigeons will often just alternate between two unequal variable-interval choices [extreme undermatching (Shull & Pliskoff 1967)]. In short, matching requires exactly the right amount of switching. Nevertheless, Herrnstein's idea of deriving behavior in choice experiments from the laws that govern responding to the choice alternatives in isolation is clearly worth pursuing.

In any event, Herrnstein's approach—molar data, predominantly variable-interval schedules, rate measures—set the basic pattern for subsequent operant choice research. It fits the basic presuppositions of the field: that choice is about *response strength*, that response strength is equivalent to response probability, and that response rate is a valid proxy for probability (e.g., Skinner 1938, 1966, 1986; Killeen & Hall 2001). (For typical studies in this tradition see, e.g., Fantino 1981; Grace 1994; Herrnstein 1961, 1964, 1970; Rachlin et al. 1976; see also Shimp 1969, 2001.)

We can also look at concurrent schedules in terms of linear waiting. Although published evidence is skimpy, recent unpublished data (Cerutti & Staddon 2002) show that even on variable-interval schedules (which necessarily always contain a few very short interfood intervals), postfood wait time and changeover time covary with mean interfood time. It has also long been known that Equation 6 can be derived from two time-based assumptions: that the number of responses emitted is proportional to the number of reinforcers received multiplied by the available time and that available time is limited by the time taken up by each response (Staddon 1977, Equations 23–25). Moreover, if we define mean interresponse time as the reciprocal of mean response rate,[6] x, and mean interfood interval is the reciprocal of obtained reinforcement rate, $R(x)$, then linear waiting yields

$$1/x = a/R(x) + b,$$

where a and b are linear waiting constants. Rearranging yields

$$x = \frac{\frac{1}{b}R(x)}{\frac{a}{b} + R(x)}, \tag{7}$$

where $1/b = k$ and $a/b = R_0$ in Equation 6. Both these derivations of the hyperbola in Equation 6 from a linear relation in the time domain imply a correlation between parameters k and R_0 in Equation 6 under parametric experimental variation of parameter b by (for example) varying response effort or, possibly, hunger motivation. Such covariation has been occasionally but not universally reported (Dallery et al. 2000, Heyman & Monaghan 1987, McDowell & Dallery 1999).

Concurrent-Chain Schedules

Organisms can be trained to choose between sources of primary reinforcement (concurrent schedules) or between stimuli that signal the occurrence of primary reinforcement (*conditioned reinforcement*: concurrent chain schedules). Many experimental and theoretical papers on conditioned reinforcement in pigeons and rats have been published since the early 1960s using some version of the concurrent chains procedure of Autor (1960, 1969). These studies have demonstrated a number of functional relations between rate measures and have led to several closely related theoretical proposals such as a version of the matching law, incentive theory, delay-reduction theory, and hyperbolic value-addition (e.g., Fantino 1969a,b; Grace 1994; Herrnstein 1964; Killeen 1982; Killeen & Fantino 1990; Mazur 1997, 2001; Williams 1988, 1994, 1997). Nevertheless, there is as yet no theoretical consensus on how best to describe choice between sources of conditioned reinforcement, and no one has proposed an integrated theoretical account of simple chain and concurrent chain schedules.

Molar response rate does not capture the essential feature of behavior on fixed-interval schedules: the systematic pattern of rate-change in each interfood interval, the "scallop." Hence, the emphasis on molar response rate as a dependent variable has meant that work on concurrent schedules has emphasized variable or random intervals over fixed intervals. We lack any theoretical account of concurrent fixed-interval–fixed-interval and fixed-interval–variable-interval schedules. However, a recent study by Shull et al. (2001; see also Shull 1979) suggests that response rate may not capture what is going on even on simple variable-interval schedules, where the time to initiate bouts of relatively fixed-rate responding seems to be a

---

[6]It is not of course: The reciprocal of the mean IRT is the harmonic mean rate. In practice, "mean response rate" usually means arithmetic mean, but note that harmonic mean rate usually works better for choice data than the arithmetic mean (cf. Killeen 1968).

more sensitive dependent measure than overall response rate. More attention to the role of temporal variables in choice is called for.

We conclude with a brief account of how linear waiting may be involved in several well-established phenomena of concurrent-chain schedules: preference for variable-interval versus fixed-interval terminal links, effect of initial-link duration, and finally, so-called self-control experiments.

PREFERENCE FOR VARIABLE-INTERVAL VERSUS FIXED-INTERVAL TERMINAL LINKS   On concurrent-chain schedules with equal variable-interval initial links, animals show a strong preference for the initial link leading to a variable-interval terminal link over the terminal-link alternative with an equal arithmetic-mean fixed interval. This result is usually interpreted as a manifestation of nonarithmetic (e.g., harmonic) reinforcement-rate averaging (Killeen 1968), but it can also be interpreted as linear waiting. Minimum TTR is necessarily much less on the variable-interval than on the fixed-interval side, because some variable intervals are short. If wait time is determined by minimum TTR—hence shorter wait times on the variable-interval side—and ratios of wait times and overall response rates are (inversely) correlated (Cerutti & Staddon 2002), the result will be an apparent bias in favor of the variable-interval choice.

EFFECT OF INITIAL-LINK DURATION   Preference for a given pair of terminal-link schedules depends on initial link duration. For example, pigeons may approximately match initial-link relative response rates to terminal-link relative reinforcement rates when the initial links are 60 s and the terminal links range from 15 to 45 s (Herrnstein 1964), but they will undermatch when the initial-link schedule is increased to, for example, 180 s. This effect is what led to Fantino's delay-reduction modification of Herrnstein's matching law (see Fantino et al. 1993 for a review). However, the same qualitative prediction follows from linear waiting: Increasing initial-link duration reduces the proportional TTR difference between the two choices. Hence the ratio of WTs or of initial-link response rates for the two choices should also approach unity, which is undermatching. Several other well-studied theories of concurrent choice, such as delay reduction and hyperbolic value addition, also explain these results.

Self-Control

The prototypical self-control experiment has a subject choosing between two outcomes: not-so-good cookie now or a good cookie after some delay (Rachlin & Green 1972; see Logue 1988 for a review; Mischel et al. 1989 reviewed human studies). Typically, the subject chooses the immediate, small reward, but if both delays are increased by the same amount, D, he will learn to choose the larger reward, providing D is long enough. Why? The standard answer is derived from Herrnstein's matching analysis (Herrnstein 1981) and is called *hyperbolic discounting* (see Mazur 2001 for a review and Ainslie 1992 and Rachlin 2000 for longer accounts). The idea is that the expected value of each reward is inversely related to the time at which it is expected according to a hyperbolic function:

$$V_i = \frac{A_i}{1 + kD_i}, \tag{8}$$

where A_i is the *undiscounted value* of the reward, D_i is the delay until reward is received, i denotes the large or small reward, and k is a fitted constant.

Now suppose we set D_L and D_S to values such that the animal shows a preference for the shorter, sooner reward. This would be the case ($k = 1$) if $A_L = 6$, $A_S = 2$, $D_L = 6$ s, and $D_S = 1$ s: $V_L = 0.86$ and $V_S = 1$—preference for the small, less-delayed reward. If 10 s is added to both delays, so that $D_L = 16$ s and $D_S = 11$ s, the values are $V_L = 0.35$ and $V_S = 0.17$—preference for the larger reward. Thus, Equation 8 predicts that added delay—sometimes awkwardly termed *pre-commitment*—should enhance self-control, which it does.

The most dramatic prediction from this analysis was made and confirmed by Mazur (1987, 2001) in an experiment that used an *adjusting-delay* procedure (also termed *titration*). "A response on the center key started each trial, and then a pigeon chose either a standard alternative (by pecking the red key) or an adjusting alternative (by pecking the green key) . . . the standard alternative delivered 2 s of access to grain after a 10-s delay, and the adjusting alternative delivered 6 s of access to grain after an adjusting delay" (2001, p. 97). The adjusting delay increased (on the next trial) when it was chosen and decreased when the standard alternative was chosen. (See Mazur 2001 for other procedural details.) The relevant independent variable is TTR. The discounted value of each choice is given by Equation 8. When the subject is indifferent does not discriminate between the two choices, $V_L = V_S$. Equating Equation 8 for the large and small choices yields

$$D_L = \frac{A_L}{A_S} \cdot D_S + \frac{A_L - A_S}{kA_S}; \tag{9}$$

that is, an *indifference curve* that is a linear function relating D_L and D_S, with slope $A_L/A_S > 1$ and a positive intercept. The data (Mazur 1987; 2001, Figure 2) are consistent with this prediction, but the intercept is small.

It is also possible to look at this situation in terms of linear waiting. One assumption is necessary: that the waiting fraction, a, in Equation 1 is smaller when the upcoming reinforcer is large than when it is small (Powell 1969 and Perone & Courtney 1992 showed this for fixed-ratio schedules; Howerton & Meltzer 1983, for fixed-interval). Given this assumption, the linear waiting analysis is even simpler than hyperbolic discounting. The idea is that the subject will appear to be indifferent when the wait times to the two alternatives are equal. According to linear waiting, the wait time for the small alternative is given by

$$t_S = a_S D_S + b_S, \tag{10}$$

where b_S is a small positive intercept and $a_S > a_L$. Equating the wait times for small and large alternatives yields

$$D_L = \frac{a_S}{a_L} \cdot D_S + \frac{b_S - b_L}{a_L}, \tag{11}$$

which is also a linear function with slope >1 and a small positive intercept.

Equations 9 and 11 are identical in form. Thus, the linear waiting and hyperbolic discounting models are almost indistinguishable in terms of these data. However, the linear waiting approach has three potential advantages: Parameters a and b can be independently measured by making appropriate measurements in a control study that retains the reinforcement-delay properties of the self-control experiments without the choice contingency; the linear waiting approach lacks the fitted parameter k in Equation 9; and linear waiting also applies to a wide range of time-production experiments not covered by the hyperbolic discounting approach.

CONCLUSION

Temporal control may be involved in unsuspected ways in a wide variety of operant conditioning procedures. A renewed emphasis on the causal factors operating in reinforcement schedules may help to unify research that has hitherto been defined in terms of more abstract topics like timing and choice.

ACKNOWLEDGMENTS

We thank Catalin Buhusi and Jim Mazur for comments on an earlier version and the NIMH for research support over many years.

The *Annual Review of Psychology* is online at http://psych.annualreviews.org

LITERATURE CITED

Ainslie G. 1992. *Picoeconomics: The Strategic Interaction of Successive Motivational States Within the Person.* Cambridge, MA: Harvard Univ. Press

Autor SM. 1960. *The strength of conditioned reinforcers as a function of frequency and probability of reinforcement.* PhD thesis. Harvard Univ., Cambridge, MA

Autor SM. 1969. The strength of conditioned reinforcers and a function of frequency and probability of reinforcement. In *Conditioned Reinforcement*, ed. DP Hendry, pp. 127–62. Homewood, IL: Dorsey

Bateson M, Kacelnik A. 1995. Preferences for fixed and variable food sources: variability in amount and delay. *J. Exp. Anal. Behav.* 63:313–29

Baum WM. 1974. On two types of deviation from the matching law: bias and undermatching. *J. Exp. Anal. Behav.* 22:231–42

Baum WM. 1994. *Understanding Behaviorism: Science, Behavior and Culture.* New York: HarperCollins

Blough DS, Millward RB. 1965. Learning: operant conditioning and verbal learning. *Annu. Rev. Psychol.* 17:63–94

Buhusi CV, Meck WH. 2000. Timing for the absence of the stimulus: the gap paradigm reversed. *J. Exp. Psychol.: Anim. Behav. Process.* 26:305–22

Cabeza de Vaca S, Brown BL, Hemmes NS. 1994. Internal clock and memory processes in animal timing. *J. Exp. Psychol.: Anim. Behav. Process.* 20:184–98

Catania AC. 1970. Reinforcement schedules and psychophysical judgments: a study of some temporal properties of behavior. In *The Theory of Reinforcement Schedules*, ed. WN Schoenfeld, pp. 1–42. New York: Appleton-Century-Crofts

Catania AC. 1979. *Learning.* Englewood Cliffs, NJ: Prentice-Hall

Catania AC, Yohalem R, Silverman PJ. 1980. Contingency and stimulus change in chained schedules of reinforcement. *J. Exp. Anal. Behav.* 5:167–73

Cerutti DT, Staddon JER. 2002. The temporal dynamics of choice: concurrent and concurrent-chain interval schedules. Submitted

Cheng K, Westwood R. 1993. Analysis of single trials in pigeons' timing performance. *J. Exp. Psychol.: Anim. Behav. Process.* 19:56–67

Church RM. 1978. The internal clock. In *Cognitive Processes in Animal Behavior,* ed. SH Hulse, H Fowler, WK Honig, pp. 277–310. Hillsdale, NJ: Erlbaum

Church RM, Broadbent HA. 1990. Alternative representations of time, number and rate. *Cognition* 37:55–81

Church RM, Deluty MZ. 1977. Bisection of temporal intervals. *J. Exp. Psychol.: Anim. Behav. Process.* 3:216–28

Church RM, Miller KD, Meck WH. 1991. Symmetrical and asymmetrical sources of variance in temporal generalization. *Anim. Learn. Behav.* 19:135–55

Crossman EK, Heaps RS, Nunes DL, Alferink LA. 1974. The effects of number of responses on pause length with temporal variables controlled. *J. Exp. Anal. Behav.* 22:115–20

Dallery J, McDowell JJ, Lancaster JS. 2000. Falsification of matching theory's account of single-alternative responding: Herrnstein's K varies with sucrose concentration. *J. Exp. Anal. Behav.* 73:23–43

Davison M. 1974. A functional analysis of chained fixed-interval schedule performance. *J. Exp. Anal. Behav.* 21:323–30

Davison M, Baum W. 2000. Choice in a variable environment: Every reinforcer counts. *J. Exp. Anal. Behav.* 74:1–24

Davison M, McCarthy D. 1988. *The Matching Law: A Research Review.* Hillsdale, NJ: Erlbaum

Donahoe JW, Palmer DC. 1994. *Learning and Complex Behavior.* Boston: Allyn & Bacon

Dragoi V, Staddon JER, Palmer RG, Buhusi VC. 2002. Interval timing as an emergent learning property. *Psychol. Rev.* In press

Dreyfus LR, Fetterman JG, Smith LD, Stubbs DA. 1988. Discrimination of temporal relations by pigeons. *J. Exp. Psychol.: Anim. Behav. Process.* 14:349–67

Fantino E. 1969a. Choice and rate of reinforcement. *J. Exp. Anal. Behav.* 12:723–30

Fantino E. 1969b. Conditioned reinforcement, choice, and the psychological distance to reward. In *Conditioned Reinforcement*, ed. DP Hendry, pp. 163–91. Homewood, IL: Dorsey

Fantino E. 1981. Contiguity, response strength, and the delay-reduction hypothesis. In *Advances in Analysis of Behavior: Predictability, Correlation, and Contiguity*, ed. P Harzem, M Zeiler, 2:169–201. Chichester, UK: Wiley

Fantino E, Preston RA, Dunn R. 1993. Delay reduction: current status. *J. Exp. Anal. Behav.* 60:159–69

Ferster CB, Skinner BF. 1957. *Schedules of Reinforcement.* New York: Appleton-Century-Crofts

Fetterman JG, Dreyfus LR, Stubbs DA. 1989. Discrimination of duration ratios. *J. Exp. Psychol.: Anim. Behav. Process.* 15:253–63

Gallistel CR. 1990. *The Organization of Learning.* Cambridge, MA: MIT/Bradford

Gallistel CR, Gibbon J. 2000. Time, rate, and conditioning. *Psychol. Rev.* 107:289–344

Gibbon J. 1977. Scalar expectancy theory and Weber's law in animal timing. *Psychol. Rev.* 84:279–325

Gibbon J, Church RM. 1984. Sources of variance in an information processing theory of timing. In *Animal Cognition*, ed. HL Roitblat, TG Bever, HS Terrace. Hillsdale, NJ: Erlbaum.

Gollub LR. 1958. *The chaining of fixed-interval schedules.* Unpublished doctoral dissertation, Harvard Univ.

Gollub L. 1977. Conditioned reinforcement: schedule effects. See Honig & Staddon 1977, pp. 288–312

Grace RC. 1994. A contextual choice model of concurrent-chains choice. *J. Exp. Anal. Behav.* 61:113–29

Grace RC, Nevin JA. 2000. Response strength and temporal control in fixed-interval schedules. *Anim. Learn. Behav.* 28:313–31

Grossberg S, Schmajuk NA. 1989. Neural dyamics of adaptive timing and temporal discrimination during associative learning. *Neural. Netw.* 2:79–102

Hanson SJ, Killeen PR. 1981. Measurement and modeling of behavior under fixed-interval schedules of reinforcement. *J. Exp. Psychol.: Anim. Behav. Process.* 7:129–39

Herrnstein RJ. 1961. Relative and absolute strength of response as a function of frequency of reinforcement. *J. Exp. Anal. Behav.* 4:267–72

Herrnstein RJ. 1964. Secondary reinforcement and rate of primary reinforcement. *J. Exp. Anal. Behav.* 7:27–36

Herrnstein RJ. 1970. On the law of effect. *J. Exp. Anal. Behav.* 13:243–66

Herrnstein RJ. 1981. Self control as response strength. In *Recent Developments in the Quantification of Steady-State Operant Behavior,* ed. CM Bradshaw, CP Lowe, F Szabadi, pp. 3–20. Amsterdam: Elsevier/North-Holland

Heyman GM, Monaghan MM. 1987. Effects of changes in response requirements and deprivation on the parameters of the matching law equation: new data and review. *J. Exp. Psychol.: Anim. Behav. Process.* 13:384–94

Higa JJ, Wynne CDL, Staddon JER. 1991. Dynamics of time discrimination. *J. Exp. Psychol.: Anim. Behav. Process.* 17:281–91

Hinson JM, Staddon JER. 1983. Matching,

maximizing and hill climbing. *J. Exp. Anal. Behav.* 40:321–31

Honig WK, Staddon JER, eds. 1977. *Handbook of Operant Behavior.* Englewood Cliffs, NJ: Prentice-Hall

Hopson JW. 1999. Gap timing and the spectral timing model. *Behav. Process.* 45:23–31

Hopson JW. 2002. *Timing without a clock: learning models as interval timing models.* PhD thesis. Duke Univ., Durham, NC

Howerton L, Meltzer D. 1983. Pigeons' FI behavior following signaled reinforcement duration. *Bull. Psychon. Soc.* 21:161–63

Innis NK, Mitchell S, Staddon JER. 1993. Temporal control on interval schedules: What determines the postreinforcement pause? *J. Exp. Anal. Behav.* 60:293–311

Kacelnik A, Bateson M. 1996. Risky theories—the effects of variance on foraging decisions. *Am. Zool.* 36:402–34

Kahneman D, Tversky A. 1979. Prospect theory: an analysis of decision under risk. *Econometrika* 47:263–91

Kelleher RT, Fry WT. 1962. Stimulus functions in chained and fixed-interval schedules. *J. Exp. Anal. Behav.* 5:167–73

Kelleher RT, Gollub LR. 1962. A review of positive conditioned reinforcement. *J. Exp. Anal. Behav.* 5:541–97

Kello JE. 1972. The reinforcement-omission effect on fixed-interval schedules: frustration or inhibition? *Learn. Motiv.* 3:138–47

Killeen PR. 1968. On the measurement of reinforcement frequency in the study of preference. *J. Exp. Anal. Behav.* 11:263–69

Killeen PR. 1982. Incentive theory: II. Models for choice. *J. Exp. Anal. Behav.* 38:217–32

Killeen PR, Fantino E. 1990. Unification of models for choice between delayed reinforcers. *J. Exp. Anal. Behav.* 53:189–200

Killeen PR, Fetterman JG. 1988. A behavioral theory of timing. *Psychol. Rev.* 95:274–95

Killeen PR, Hall SS. 2001. The principal components of response strength. *J. Exp. Anal. Behav.* 75:111–34

Lander DG, Irwin RJ. 1968. Multiple schedules: effects of the distribution of reinforcements between components on the distribution of responses between components. *J. Exp. Anal. Behav.* 11:517–24

Lejeune H, Ferrara A, Simons F, Wearden JH. 1997. Adjusting to changes in the time of reinforcement: peak-interval transitions in rats. *J. Exp. Psychol.: Anim. Behav. Process.* 23:211–321

Logue AW. 1988. Research on self-control: an integrating framework. *Behav. Brain Sci.* 11:665–709

Lowe CF, Harzem P, Spencer PT. 1979. Temporal control of behavior and the power law. *J. Exp. Anal. Behav.* 31:333–43

MacEwen D, Killeen P. 1991. The effects of rate and amount on the speed of the pacemaker in pigeons' timing behavior. *Anim. Learn. Behav.* 19:164–70

Machado A. 1997. Learning the temporal dynamics of behavior. *Psychol. Rev.* 104:241–65

Matell MS, Meck WH. 1999. Reinforcement-induced within-trial resetting of an internal clock. *Behav. Process.* 45:159–71

Mazur JE. 1987. An adjusting procedure for studying delayed reinforcement. In *Quantitative Analyses of Behavior, Vol. 5. The Effects of Delay and Intervening Events on Reinforcement Value*, ed. ML Commons, JE Mazur, JA Nevin, H Rachlin, pp. 55–73. Mahwah, NJ: Erlbaum

Mazur JE. 1997. Choice, delay, probability, and conditioned reinforcement. *Anim. Learn. Behav.* 25:131–47

Mazur JE. 2001. Hyperbolic value addition and general models of animal choice. *Psychol. Rev.* 108:96–112

McDowell JJ, Dallery J. 1999. Falsification of matching theory: changes in the asymptote of Herrnstein's hyperbola as a function of water deprivation. *J. Exp. Anal. Behav.* 72:251–68

Meck WH. 1983. Selective adjustment of the speed of an internal clock and memory processes. *J. Exp. Psychol.: Anim. Behav. Process.* 9:171–201

Meck WH, Komeily-Zadeh FN, Church RM. 1984. Two-step acquisition: modification of an internal clock's criterion. *J. Exp. Psychol.: Anim. Behav. Process.* 10:297–306

Mischel W, Shoda Y, Rodriguez M. 1989. Delay of gratification for children. *Science* 244:933–38

Nevin JA. 1974. Response strength in multiple schedules. *J. Exp. Anal. Behav.* 21:389–408

Perone M, Courtney K. 1992. Fixed-ratio pausing: joint effects of past reinforcer magnitude and stimuli correlated with upcoming magnitude. *J. Exp. Anal. Behav.* 57:33–46

Plowright CMS, Church D, Behnke P, Silverman A. 2000. Time estimation by pigeons on a fixed interval: the effect of pre-feeding. *Behav. Process.* 52:43–48

Powell RW. 1968. The effect of small sequential changes in fixed-ratio size upon the post-reinforcement pause. *J. Exp. Anal. Behav.* 11:589–93

Powell RW. 1969. The effect of reinforcement magnitude upon responding under fixed-ratio schedules. *J. Exp. Anal. Behav.* 12:605–8

Rachlin H. 1991. *Introduction to Modern Behaviorism*. New York: Freeman

Rachlin H. 2000. *The Science of Self-Control.* Cambridge, MA: Harvard Univ. Press

Rachlin H, Green L. 1972. Commitment, choice and self-control. *J. Exp. Anal. Behav.* 17:15–22

Rachlin H, Green L, Kagel JH, Battalio RC. 1976. Economic demand theory and psychological studies of choice. In *The Psychology of Learning and Motivation*, ed. GH Bower, 10:129–54. New York: Academic

Rachlin H, Laibson DI, eds. 1997. *The Matching Law: Papers in Psychology and Economics.* Cambridge, MA: Harvard Univ. Press

Roberts S. 1981. Isolation of an internal clock. *J. Exp. Psychol.: Anim. Behav. Process.* 7: 242–68

Roberts S. 1983. Properties and function of an internal clock. In *Animal Cognition and Behavior*, ed. R Melgren, pp. 345–97. Amsterdam: North-Holland

Royalty P, Williams B, Fantino E. 1987. Effects of delayed reinforcement in chain schedules. *J. Exp. Anal. Behav.* 47:41–56

Schneider BA. 1969. A two-state analysis of fixed-interval responding in pigeons. *J. Exp. Anal. Behav.* 12:677–87

Shimp CP. 1969. The concurrent reinforcement of two interresponse times: the relative frequency of an interresponse time equals its relative harmonic length. *J. Exp. Anal. Behav.* 1:403–11

Shimp CP. 2001. Behavior as a social construction. *Behav. Process.* 54:11–32

Shull RL. 1970. The response-reinforcement dependency in fixed-interval schedules of reinforcement. *J. Exp. Anal. Behav.* 14:55–60

Shull RL. 1979. The postreinforcement pause: some implications for the correlational law of effect. In *Reinforcement and the Organization of Behavior*, ed. MD Zeiler, P Harzem, pp. 193–221. New York: Academic

Shull RL, Gaynor ST, Grimes JA. 2001. Response rate viewed as engagement bouts: effects of relative reinforcement and schedule type. *J. Exp. Anal. Behav.* 75:247–74

Shull RL, Pliskoff SS. 1967. Changeover delay and concurrent schedules: some effects on relative performance measures. *J. Exp. Anal. Behav.* 10:517–27

Sidman M. 1960. *Tactics of Scientific Research: Evaluating Experimental Data in Psychology.* New York: Basic Books

Skinner BF. 1937. Two types of conditioned reflex: a reply to Konorski and Miller. *J. Gen. Psychol.* 16:272–79

Skinner BF. 1938. *The Behavior of Organisms.* New York: Appleton-Century

Skinner BF. 1966. Operant behavior. In *Operant Behavior: Areas of Research and Application*, ed. WK Honig, pp. 12–32. New York: Appleton-Century-Crofts

Skinner BF. 1986. Some thoughts about the future. *J. Exp. Anal. Behav.* 45:229–35

Staddon JER. 1965. Some properties of spaced responding in pigeons. *J. Exp. Anal. Behav.* 8:19–27

Staddon JER. 1968. Spaced responding and choice: a preliminary analysis. *J. Exp. Anal. Behav.* 11:669–82

Staddon JER. 1970. Temporal effects of reinforcement: a negative "frustration" effect. *Learn. Motiv.* 1:227–47

Staddon JER. 1972. Reinforcement omission on temporal go–no-go schedules. *J. Exp. Anal. Behav.* 18:223–29

Staddon JER. 1974. Temporal control, attention and memory. *Psychol. Rev.* 81:375–91

Staddon JER. 1977. On Herrnstein's equation and related forms. *J. Exp. Anal. Behav.* 28:163–70

Staddon JER. 1982. Behavioral competition, contrast, and matching. In *Quantitative Analyses of Behavior*, Vol. 2. *Quantitative Analyses of Operant Behavior: Matching and Maximizing Accounts,* ed. ML Commons, RJ Herrnstein, H Rachlin, pp. 243–61. Cambridge, MA: Ballinger. 5 Vols.

Staddon JER. 2001a. *Adaptive Dynamics: The Theoretical Analysis of Behavior.* Cambridge, MA: MIT/Bradford. 423 pp.

Staddon JER. 2001b. *The New Behaviorism: Mind, Mechanism and Society.* Philadelphia: Psychol. Press. 211 pp.

Staddon JER, Chelaru IM, Higa JJ. 2002. A tuned-trace theory of interval-timing dynamics. *J. Exp. Anal. Behav.* 77:105–24

Staddon JER, Higa JJ. 1999. Time and memory: towards a pacemaker-free theory of interval timing. *J. Exp. Anal. Behav.* 71:215–51

Staddon JER, Innis NK. 1966a. An effect analogous to "frustration" on interval reinforcement schedules. *Psychon. Sci.* 4:287–88

Staddon JER, Innis NK. 1966b. Preference for fixed vs. variable amounts of reward. *Psychon. Sci.* 4:193–94

Staddon JER, Innis NK. 1969. Reinforcement omission on fixed-interval schedules. *J. Exp. Anal. Behav.* 12:689–700

Staddon JER, Motheral S. 1978. On matching and maximizing in operant choice experiments. *Psychol. Rev.* 85:436–44

Starr B, Staddon JER. 1974. Temporal control on fixed-interval schedules: signal properties of reinforcement and blackout. *J. Exp. Anal. Behav.* 22:535–45

Stubbs A. 1968. The discrimination of stimulus duration by pigeons. *J. Exp. Anal. Behav.* 11:223–38

Stubbs DA, Dreyfus LR, Fetterman JG, Boynton DM, Locklin N, Smith LD. 1994. Duration comparison: relative stimulus differences, stimulus age and stimulus predictiveness. *J. Exp. Anal. Behav.* 62:15–32

Treisman M. 1963. Temporal discrimination and the indifference interval: implications for a model of the "internal clock." *Psychol. Monogr.* 77(756): entire issue

Wearden JH. 1985. The power law and Weber's law in fixed-interval post-reinforcement pausing. *Q. J. Exp. Psychol. B* 37:191–211

Williams BA. 1988. Reinforcement, choice, and response strength. In *Stevens' Handbook of Experimental Psychology*, ed. RC Atkinson, RJ Herrnstein, G Lindzey, RD Luce, pp. 167–244. New York: Wiley. 2nd ed.

Williams BA. 1994. Conditioned reinforcement: neglected or outmoded explanatory construct? *Psychon. Bull. Rev.* 1:457–75

Williams BA. 1997. Conditioned reinforcement dynamics in three-link chained schedules. *J. Exp. Anal. Behav.* 67:145–59

Williams BA, Royalty P. 1990. Conditioned reinforcement versus time to primary reinforcement in chain schedules. *J. Exp. Anal. Behav.* 53:381–93

Wynne CDL, Staddon JER. 1988. Typical delay determines waiting time on periodic-food schedules: static and dynamic tests. *J. Exp. Anal. Behav.* 50:197–210

Zeiler MD. 1977. Schedules of reinforcement: the controlling variables. See Honig & Staddon 1977, pp. 201–32

Zeiler MD, Powell DG. 1994. Temporal control in fixed-interval schedules. *J. Exp. Anal. Behav.* 61:1–9

Zuriff G. 1985. *Behaviorism: A Conceptual Reconstruction.* New York: Columbia Univ. Press

Annu. Rev. Psychol. 2003. 54:145–73
doi: 10.1146/annurev.psych.54.101601.145121
First published online as a Review in Advance on September 17, 2002

SIGNALERS AND RECEIVERS IN ANIMAL COMMUNICATION

Robert M. Seyfarth[1] and Dorothy L. Cheney[2]
*Departments of Psychology[1] and Biology[2], University of Pennsylvania, Philadelphia,
Pennsylvania 19104; e-mail: seyfarth@psych.upenn.edu, cheney@psych.upenn.edu*

Key Words vocalizations, animal social behavior, evolution, language

■ **Abstract** In animal communication natural selection favors callers who vocalize to affect the behavior of listeners and listeners who acquire information from vocalizations, using this information to represent their environment. The acquisition of information in the wild is similar to the learning that occurs in laboratory conditioning experiments. It also has some parallels with language. The dichotomous view that animal signals must be either referential or emotional is false, because they can easily be both: The mechanisms that cause a signaler to vocalize do not limit a listener's ability to extract information from the call. The inability of most animals to recognize the mental states of others distinguishes animal communication most clearly from human language. Whereas signalers may vocalize to change a listener's behavior, they do not call to inform others. Listeners acquire information from signalers who do not, in the human sense, intend to provide it.

CONTENTS

0066-4308/03/0203-0145$14.00

INTRODUCTION

On a warm spring evening at the edge of a small pool of water in Panama, a male frog (*Physalaemus pustulosus*) gives his advertising call, onomatopoetically described as a "whine" followed by a "chuck" (Ryan 1985). Almost immediately several things happen. In the mud nearby a smaller male of the same species, who has been calling with a whine alone, adds a chuck to his call (Rand & Ryan 1981). Simultaneously, a nearby female who had ignored the male giving a whine alone now becomes active. The female orients toward and then approaches the male giving the lower-pitched chuck (Ryan 1980, 1985). Ten feet overhead, a bat (*Trachops cirrhosus*) that has been circling the pond hears the frogs calling and dives down, flying directly at one of the calling males.

The evolution of calling in Physalaemus is now well understood. Male calls have been favored by natural selection to repel rivals and to attract females, while simultaneously minimizing the frogs' susceptibility to predation by bats. The strongest frequency of a male Physalemus' whine-plus-chuck falls neatly within the range of the best hearing frequencies of males and females of the same species (Capranica 1977). The male's call seems to have evolved to match the auditory system of its intended listeners (Ryan et al. 2001). Male Physalemus are more likely to begin vocalizing if they hear a neighboring male give a whine-plus-chuck than if they hear a whine alone, and more likely to vocalize if the calling male is closer than if he is farther away. Males also give more acoustically complex calls as the number of calling males nearby increases (Ryan 1985). Females are attracted to the calls of males, and given the choice will approach whine-plus-chucks in preference to whines alone, and lower-pitched chucks in preference to higher-pitched chucks (Ryan 1985).

Calling by male Physalemus is costly because it reveals the frog's location to predatory bats. Presumably in response to predation pressure, natural selection has shaped the acoustic properties of whines so that they are difficult to locate (Ryan et al. 1982). Frogs add chucks to their whine because the chucks make them more attractive to females (Ryan 1980), but adding chucks also makes the frogs easier for bats to locate (Rand & Ryan 1981). Over evolutionary time, hard-to-find frogs and super-sensitive bats have engaged in an evolutionary arms race, and despite the frog's best ventriloqual efforts some bats nonetheless manage to find their prey.

In functional terms, calling by male Physalaemus seems to have evolved with the goal of communicating as much as possible about the male's size and condition to potential rivals and mates, while communicating as little as possible to bats. Note, however, that whereas this functional explanation provides a plausible scenario for the evolution of calling behavior in frogs, it reveals little about the proximate mechanisms that underlie a caller's behavior and his listeners' responses. Does the frog's call produce its adaptive outcome because the caller "wants" to repel rivals or attract mates? When we describe the caller's behavior as "goal directed," do we really mean callers have a plan and monitor the outcome of their actions? Does the frog's call achieve its result because nearby individuals assess and compare the information conveyed by different calls, or are the responses of listeners reflexive, unthinking reactions to different stimuli?

The case of the bat is particularly instructive because the evolutionary tradeoffs are clear but the proximate mechanisms are not, and there is a striking difference between the interests of caller and recipient. From the frog's perspective, communication with bats is simply an unintended consequence of behavior that has evolved to deter rivals and attract mates. Although the frog has no goal of communicating to the bat, communication occurs nonetheless, as bats take advantage of a lucky accident and extract useful information from a signal that evolved for entirely different reasons. But does this mean that, when a bat hears a whine-plus-chuck it "thinks," or "conjures up images of," a frog even before it sees its prey? Or should we conclude more cautiously that the bat responds simply because it has, in the past, been reinforced for seeking food whenever it hears a particular sound?

In this chapter we discuss some recent research on the mechanisms that underlie vocal communication in animals. Our review is not meant to be exhaustive, either conceptually or taxonomically (for recent reviews see Hauser 1996, Bradbury & Vehrencamp 1998). Instead, we focus on several issues that allow us to make direct comparisons between animal communication and human language and between animal and human cognition.

EVOLUTION

The example above illustrates two important themes of this review. First, communication is first and foremost a social event, designed to influence the behavior of listeners. Second, despite the social nature of communicative signals, the meaning and function of signals from the listener's perspective may be fundamentally different from that of the signaler's (Marler 1961).

The social function of communication is made clear by the fact that signalers rarely call except when in the presence of a potential audience. For example, in a modern modification on Tinbergen's classic (1951) experiment, Marler and colleagues presented male jungle fowl (*Gallus gallus*) with a silhouette of a hawk that "flew" over the birds' cage on a wire. The roosters gave alarm calls at high rates whenever they were in the presence of a male or female of their own species but almost no alarm calls when they were alone (Gyger et al. 1986, Karakashian et al. 1988). Even if calls emerge as involuntary expressions of the signaler's emotions, therefore, their production depends strongly on the proximity of listeners. At the same time, selection has also acted on listeners' ability to extract as much information as possible from both the signal itself and the context in which it is given. In some cases, like that of the bat described above, the information extracted by listeners comes at a significant cost to the signaler.

In aggressive interactions, in which signaler and recipient have largely competing interests, natural selection appears to have favored signals with acoustic properties that make the signals aversive to opponents (Owren & Rendall 2001), or that accurately signal large size (Ryan 1985, Ryan & Brenowitz 1985) and a willingness to fight (Enquist 1985; reviewed in Bradbury & Vehrencamp 1998, p. 702). By signaling truthfully, large, dominant signalers can defeat opponents— and smaller, subordinate signalers can retreat—with minimal risk of injury. In some cases selection may have favored "deceptive" signals, uncorrelated with actual size or fighting ability, that succeed in driving away opponents as long as they are used only rarely (reviewed in Johnstone 1997). In all of these circumstances, selection appears to have favored signalers who can exploit the sensory abilities of their opponents, who accurately signal competitive skill when it is to their advantage to do so, and who bluff when doing so allows them to win with minimal cost. Simultaneously, selection appears to have favored recipients who are skilled in distinguishing those signals that genuinely reflect their opponents' competitive ability from those that do not.

In more cooperative contexts, in which the evolutionary interests of signaler and recipient overlap to a greater degree, selection appears to have favored recipients who are skilled in extracting information and signalers whose behavior makes it easy for them to do so. The production and perception of alarm calls offers a good example. Producing alarm calls is potentially costly because calls may reveal the location of both the signaler and the signaler's group to predators (e.g., Sherman 1977, 1980; Zuberbuhler et al. 1997). Despite this cost, alarm calls appear to have evolved both because they alert kin to the presence of danger (e.g., Sherman 1977, 1985) and because in some cases they also signal to predators that they have been detected (e.g., Zuberbuhler et al. 1999b). The number of acoustically distinct alarm calls in a given species' vocal repertoire also appears to be under strong selective pressure. As we discuss below, species that are hunted by predators whose hunting techniques demand qualitatively different escape strategies give more acoustically different alarm calls than species that use similar escape strategies for all predators. Simultaneously, selection has favored listeners who can rapidly decode these signals and respond appropriately to them.

In both competitive and cooperative interactions, different cognitive mechanisms may underlie signal production and perception [for a similar perspective applied to the communication of human emotions, see Russell et al. 2003 (this volume)]. In many species call production appears to be a reflexive, affective reaction to a particular stimulus. By contrast, the mechanisms underlying call perception may be very different. The close link between eliciting stimulus and call type in signalers allows listeners to extract subtle information from vocalizations, and perhaps also to form a mental representation of a call's meaning that affects the listener's subsequent behavior. In many species the information that listeners extract from vocalizations can be studied using experiments that offer insights into the selective value and evolution of some of the cognitive mechanisms underlying communication.

While the asymmetry between signaler and recipient is one major theme of this review, a second concerns the cognitive limitations that affect both signaler and recipient and that constitute a fundamental difference between animal communication and human language. The limitations arise, we argue, because most animals—with the possible exception of chimpanzees (*Pan troglodytes*; see below)—cannot attribute mental states to others (Cheney & Seyfarth 1990a, 1998; Seyfarth & Cheney 1997). As a result, whereas signalers call in response to many stimuli, including the overt expression of emotion in others, they seem not to produce calls in response to the perception of another animal's mental state such as knowledge or ignorance, which may not have any overt manifestation. And whereas listeners extract subtle information from vocalizations, they seem not to recognize that signals are reflections of the signaler's knowledge.

COMMUNICATION FROM THE SIGNALER'S PERSPECTIVE

The Stimuli that Elicit Vocalizations

What causes an individual to produce a vocalization? A number of different possibilities come to mind. Calls might be elicited by the sight of a particular stimulus, such as a predator, or by a particular sound, such as the call of a conspecific. In many species calls of a particular type are given only in distinct social or ecological circumstances, for example when interacting with a particular individual or foraging in dense vegetation. To gain a complete understanding of the mechanisms that underlie call production, we need to conduct experiments in which eliciting stimuli are manipulated and the production of a particular vocalization is the dependent variable. Such tests have been rare, however, largely because it is difficult to duplicate the complex social and ecological conditions that elicit vocalizations under natural conditions.

Some animal vocalizations are elicited by a broad array of stimuli, whereas others are highly stimulus specific. For example, both suricates (*Suricata suricatta*, a South African mongoose), and female diana monkeys (*Cercopithecus diana*) give "alert" calls to a large variety of stimuli, including mammalian and avian predators, large nonpredatory animals, falling trees, and social disturbances within the group (Gautier & Gautier 1977, Zuberbuhler et al. 1997, Manser 1998). These general alerting signals stand in marked contrast to the more acoustically distinct calls that individuals of the same species give to specific types of predator. Suricates, for example, give one alarm call type to mammalian predators, primarily jackals (*Canis mesomelas*), a second alarm call type to avian predators, primarily the martial eagle (*Polemaetus bellicosus*), and a third alarm call type to snakes such as the Cape cobra (*Naja nivea*) and to fecal, urine, or hair samples of predators and foreign suricates (Manser 2001). Diana monkeys give acoustically distinct alarm calls to mammalian predators such as leopards (*Panthera pardus*) and to avian predators such as the crowned eagle (*Stephanoetus coronatus*) (Zuberbuhler et al. 1997, 1999a).

In some species with predator-specific alarm calls, variation in predator type is the primary stimulus that determines which alarm call is given. Variation in other aspects of the social and ecological context are relatively unimportant. In vervet monkeys (*Cercopithecus aethiops*) and diana monkeys, for example, the sight or sound of a leopard or eagle elicits the appropriate alarm call, and the close link between eliciting stimulus and alarm call type is largely unaffected by variation in predator numbers, distance, elevation, or the immediacy of attack (Seyfarth et al. 1980, Zuberbuhler 2000).

In other cases the relation between eliciting stimulus and alarm call type is more complex. In suricates, for example, signalers also vary the acoustic properties of each alarm call type to signal levels of urgency (Manser 2001). Thus, for example, a low-urgency mammalian predator alarm call is not only acoustically different from a low-urgency avian predator alarm call but also from a high-urgency mammalian predator alarm call. Listeners respond in qualitatively different ways to different alarm call types and, within each alarm call category, in different ways to calls correlated with different levels of urgency (Manser et al. 2001). The eliciting stimuli for suricate alarms, therefore, include both predator type and some features of the immediate context that seem to be correlated with the caller's perception of urgency (Manser et al. 2002). Evans et al. (1993) discuss the necessary and sufficient cues for the elicitation of alarm calls in chickens. Fischer et al. (1995) provide other examples of calls that simultaneously encode information about specific external stimuli and urgency.

In California ground squirrels (*Spermophilus beecheyi*) and marmots (*Marmota flaviventris*), ecological context overrides predator type as an eliciting stimulus. If a predator arrives suddenly and there is little time to escape, California ground squirrels give "whistle" alarms regardless of whether the predator is a terrestrial mammal or a raptor. When a predator is spotted at a distance, squirrels give "chatter-chat" alarms, again regardless of predator type (Leger et al. 1980, Owings & Hennessy 1984; see also Blumstein & Armitage 1997 for similar data on marmots).

Studies of the "audience effect" in animal vocalizations demonstrate further how call production can depend on a combination of certain narrowly defined stimulus features (such as the predator) and other, equally specific contextual cues. As noted earlier, roosters give more alarm calls when paired with a member of their own species than when either alone or paired with a member of another species (Marler et al. 1990). Similarly, in ground squirrels alarm call production is strongly influenced by the presence or absence of kin (Sherman 1977; see also Cheney & Seyfarth 1990a for similar data on vervet monkeys).

Like predator alarm calls, most vocalizations given by animals during social interactions are elicited by a complex combination of stimuli. For example, the most common vocalization given by free-ranging baboons (*Papio cynocephalus ursinus*) is a low amplitude tonal grunt, which is produced in a variety of social contexts. One, the move grunt, is typically given when the group is about to initiate a move into a new area of its range. Move grunts are given in bouts of 1–2 calls and often elicit answering move grunts from others nearby. By contrast, infant grunts are given during friendly social interactions, for example, as the caller approaches a mother with an infant and attempts to touch or handle the baby. Infant grunts are given in bouts of 5–10 calls and seldom elicit answering grunts (Cheney et al. 1995a, Owren et al. 1997). Both call types are individually distinctive (Owren et al. 1997). Moreover, although grunts are acoustically graded, typical move grunts show subtle acoustic differences from typical infant grunts. Playback experiments conducted by Rendall et al. (1999) examined the stimuli that elicited vocal answers to move grunts and found an effect of both call type (vocal responses were more likely when the playback stimulus was a move grunt than when it was an infant grunt) and social context (grunt responses were more likely in the move than in the rest context). There was also an interaction between grunt type and context, with the majority of answers elicited by move grunts presented in a move context.

In many cases the elicitation of a vocalization or other communicative signal depends on both the immediate features of the social environment and the history of interactions between the individuals involved. Adult female squirrel monkeys (*Saimiri sciureus*) give "chuck" calls to one another when grooming, but only if the two females involved have a long-term, stable grooming relationship (Smith et al. 1982). Dominant female baboons occasionally grunt to a subordinate after an aggressive interaction, and such grunts seem to function as reconciliatory signals that restore the individuals' relationship to baseline levels of tolerance (Cheney et al. 1995a, Silk et al. 1996, Cheney & Seyfarth 1997). In the competitive displays of many species, opponents' signals are influenced both by their own motivation to attack and the responses elicited by their previous signals (e.g., Waas 1991).

THE SPECIFICITY OF CALL PRODUCTION   When a vocalization with specific acoustic features is elicited only by a narrow range of stimuli and is relatively uninfluenced by other contextual factors, the call has the potential to provide listeners with very specific information. For example, the eagle alarm calls of vervet monkeys are elicited almost exclusively by raptors (Seyfarth et al. 1980). They are rarely given to stimuli other than raptors, and these species rarely elicit any vocalizations other than eagle alarm calls. Under these circumstances, eagle alarm calls have the potential to provide reliable information about the presence of a specific predator type. Through processes that may be similar to those that produce associative conditioning in the laboratory, listeners who have learned the predictable relation between eliciting stimulus and alarm call type can recognize immediately upon hearing an eagle alarm call that a raptor has been spotted, even if they have no other supporting, contextual cues. (Cheney & Seyfarth 1990a, Seyfarth & Cheney 1997; see also Owren & Rendall 1997).

Two factors determine the extent to which a vocalization can provide listeners with specific information. First is the call's informative value. If call type A is elicited by eagles and eagles rarely appear without eliciting call type A, then the call has the potential to provide listeners with reliable information about the presence of an eagle. In the terms of associative, or Pavlovian, conditioning, the call is a conditioned stimulus (CS) and the eagle is an unconditioned stimulus (US). The informative value of the CS lies in the extent to which it accurately predicts the US. To be predictive, simple contiguity between call and predator is neither necessary nor sufficient (Rescorla 1988). Instead, prediction and information depend upon the difference between the probability of a US when the CS is present and the probability of the US when the CS is absent (Gleitman 1991, p. 127). In suricates, the probability of an eagle being present when listeners hear an eagle alarm is very high; the corresponding probability when listeners hear no eagle alarm is very low. Eagle alarms are thus highly informative about the presence of an eagle.

The second important variable is the breadth of stimuli that elicit a given call type, defined as the call's referential specificity. Suricate eagle alarms are predictive (and thus informative) not only about the presence of an eagle but about the presence of specific species of eagle, because suricates give eagle alarms to only three species: martial eagles, tawny eagles (*Aquila rapax*), and (rarely) pale chanting goshawks (*Melierax canorus*) (Manser 2001). The suricates' eagle alarm is therefore a CS that is potentially informative about a very narrow range of USs. By contrast, the suricates' mammalian predator alarm is equally informative in Pavlovian terms but not as referentially specific, because mammalian predator alarms are given to a wider variety of stimuli, including jackals, hyenas, African wild cats, lions, and dogs (Manser 1998). A suricate eagle alarm potentially informs listeners that one of three species has been detected; a suricate mammalian predator alarm potentially informs listeners that one of at least five predators is present. Still less precise is the suricates' alert call (see above), which provides listeners with information that is rather vague. The alert call is a CS for which the associated US is a wide variety of predators, other suricate groups, large nonpredatory animals, and within-group social disturbances. The CS-US link between alert call and eliciting stimuli may well be as strong as it is between eagle alarm and eagle, but the variety of stimuli for which this rule holds is extremely broad.

Like alarm calls, the vocalizations given during foraging or social interactions vary in their informative value and referential specificity. Baboon move grunts, for example, are individually distinctive and produced only when the group is moving, about to move, or has just begun a move from one location to another (R. Seyfarth & D. Cheney, personal observation; Rendall et al. 1999). Move grunts are particularly likely to be given in three circumstances: in the last few minutes of a rest period when the group is about to move and some individuals have already begun to do so; in the first few minutes after all individuals have begun to move; and as an answering call in the seconds immediately after another individual has produced a move grunt. A group's transition from resting to moving seldom occurs without at least one move grunt (R. Seyfarth & D. Cheney, personal observation). Move grunts are, therefore, highly informative because they accurately predict the onset of a group move and referentially specific because the breadth of stimuli that elicit them is relatively narrow.

By comparison, the infant grunts of baboons have a lower informative value than move grunts for two reasons. First, when infant grunts are heard (CS), the probability of infant handling (US) may be high, but infant handling also occurs in the absence of grunts (Cheney et al. 1995a). Second, infant grunts are elicited in many contexts that may not involve infant handling; for example, during friendly interactions between females without infants or as reconciliatory signals after aggression (Cheney et al. 1995a, Silk et al. 1996). Compared with move grunts, then, infant grunts are less informative because they are less predictive of infant handling and less referentially specific because the range of stimuli that elicit them is relatively broad. Infant grunts potentially provide listeners with information that a friendly social interaction is occurring, but they do not specify the precise type of social interaction.

In sum, the strength of association between call and eliciting stimulus (informative value) plus the breadth of eliciting stimuli involved (referential specificity) interact to determine the specificity of call production: the extent to which a call has the potential to convey precise information to listeners. Because they are strongly associated with a very narrow range of eliciting stimuli, some calls are highly specific and thus have the potential to transmit very precise information. Other calls are less contextually specific, and therefore have the potential to transmit less precise information, either because the association between call and eliciting stimulus is strong but the array of stimuli for which the association holds is relatively broad, or because the association between call and eliciting stimulus is weak. Finally, the specificity of call production says nothing about whether the vocalization actually does convey specific information to listeners; it simply describes the call's potential for doing so.

Referential Versus Affective Communication: Apples and Oranges

Vocal communication in animals is generally thought to differ from human language largely because the former is an "affective" system based on emotion, whereas the latter is a "referential" system based on the relation between words and the objects or events they represent. Over the years, much ink has been spilled—by ourselves and others—debating whether animal vocalizations could ever have a referential component and, if so, how referential and affective signaling might interact (Seyfarth et al. 1980, Cheney & Seyfarth 1990a, Marler et al. 1992, Hauser 1996, Macedonia & Evans 1993, Evans 1997, Owren & Rendall 1997, Owings & Morton 1998, Fischer & Hammerschmidt 2001). Often the debate has been cast as an either/or opposition between affective and referential signaling. Such a dichotomy, however, is logically false.

A call's potential to serve as a referential signal depends on the specificity of call production, as discussed above. The mechanisms that underlie this specificity are irrelevant. A tone that informs a rat about the imminence of a shock, an alarm call that informs a vervet about the presence of a leopard, or a scream that informs a baboon that her offspring is involved in a fight all have the potential to provide a listener with precise information because of their predictable association with a narrow range of events. The widely different mechanisms that lead to this association have no effect on the signal's potential to inform.

Put slightly differently, there is no obligatory relation between referential and affective signaling. Knowing that a call is referential (that is, has the potential to convey highly specific information) tells us nothing about whether its underlying cause is affective or not. Conversely, knowing that a call's production is due entirely to the caller's affect tells us nothing about the call's potential to serve as a referential signal. As Premack (1972) argued, a shout that is entirely based upon affect—e.g., a cry of delight at the sight of strawberries—can serve just as referential a function as the word "strawberries" as long as the shout is predictably elicited by strawberries and no other stimuli.

It is therefore wrong, on theoretical grounds, to treat animal signals as either referential or affective, because the two properties of a communicative event are logically distinct and independent dimensions. The first concerns a signal's relation to features of the environment, whereas the second concerns the underlying mechanisms by which that relation arises. Highly referential signals could, in principle, be caused entirely by a signaler's emotions, or their production could be relatively independent of measures of arousal. Highly affective signals could be elicited by very specific stimuli and thus function as referential calls or they could be elicited by so many different stimuli that they provide listeners with only general information. In principle, any combination of results is possible.

The affective and referential properties of signals are also logically distinct, at least in animal communication, because the former depends on mechanisms of call production in the signaler, whereas the latter depends on the listener's ability to extract information from events in its environment. Signalers and recipients, though linked in a communicative event, are nonetheless separate and distinct, because the mechanisms that cause a signaler to vocalize do not in any way constrain a listener's ability to extract information from the call, a point highlighted by the bat's eavesdropping on the frog.

Baboon grunts offer a good example. In a recent study, Rendall (2003) used behavioral data to code a social interaction involving move or infant grunts as having high or low arousal. He then examined calls given in these two circumstances and found that in each context certain acoustic features or modes of delivery were correlated with apparent arousal. Bouts of grunting given when arousal was apparently high had more calls, a higher rate of calling, and calls with a higher fundamental frequency than bouts given when arousal was apparently low. Further analysis revealed significant variation between contexts in the same three acoustic features that varied within context. By all three measures (call number, call rate, and fundamental frequency), infant grunts were correlated with higher arousal than were move grunts. Infant grunts also exhibited greater pitch modulation and more vocal "jitter," a measure of vocal instability (Rendall 2003). In human speech, variation in pitch, tempo, vocal modulation, and jitter are known to provide listeners with cues about the speaker's affect, or arousal (e.g., Scherer 1989, Bachorowski & Owren 1995).

It is, of course, difficult to obtain independent measures of a caller's arousal in the field. However, similarities between human and nonhuman primates in the mechanisms of phonation (Schon Ybarra 1995, Fitch & Hauser 1995, Fitch et al. 2002) support Rendall's (2003) conclusion that different levels of arousal play an important role in causing baboons to give acoustically different grunts in the infant and move contexts. This view, however, says nothing about the grunts' potential to act as referential signals that inform nearby listeners about social or ecological events taking place at the time. As noted above, move grunts have the potential to convey quite specific information to listeners, and infant grunts less so.

Baboons also produce loud barks that vary acoustically from tonal, harmonically rich calls given at high rates when an individual is at risk of becoming separated from the group (contact barks), to noisy, harsh calls given when a predator has been seen (alarm barks; Fischer et al. 2001a). The gradation in acoustic features from clear (or tonal) to noisy suggests that barks reflect a gradation in the signaler's emotion (e.g., Morton 1977, Owren & Rendall 2001). Field playback experiments demonstrate that infant baboons respond differently, and with increasing intensity, to typical contact barks, intermediate barks, and typical alarm barks (Fischer et al. 2000), but adults show a distinctive response only to alarm barks. Apparently, adult responses to contact and intermediate barks are determined largely by context (Fischer et al. 2001b). These results suggest that, whereas different levels of arousal may indeed play an important role in causing baboons to give acoustically different barks in different contexts, certain barks nonetheless can provide listeners with specific information. Because they are given rarely and are limited to particular ecological contexts, alarm barks have a greater informative value and a higher referential specificity than contact barks. As a result, alarm barks elicit responses from listeners that are more consistent and less dependent upon context.

Taking a somewhat different approach, Manser (2001) coded interactions between suricates and their predators as either high- or low-urgency depending on the distance between predator and prey. As noted above, she found that the acoustic features of alarm calls varied depending on both predator type and apparent level of urgency. Moreover, the acoustic measures that accounted for variation across alarm call types were, for all but one measure, different from the acoustic measures that accounted for variation across levels of urgency. Calls given to different predators did not follow any apparent acoustic "rule": The acoustic features that distinguished mammalian predator, avian predator, and snake alarm calls followed no consistent pattern. By contrast, in all three call types low-urgency calls tended to be clearer and more harmonic, whereas high-urgency calls were harsher and noisier (Manser et al. 2001, 2002).

The production of suricate alarm calls may depend entirely upon the caller's state of arousal. High- and low-urgency calls are certainly correlated with acoustic features known to be associated with fear or anxiety in both animal vocalizations (Morton 1977, Hauser 1993, Owren & Rendall 1997) and human speech (Scherer 1989). In a similar manner, future research may ultimately show that the suricates' different alarm call types also reflect different levels of arousal, with one predator type eliciting the most fear, another the least, and the third intermediate. It may also turn out that suricates' alarms for different predators do not map easily onto acoustic correlates of arousal. Whatever the outcome, the affective basis of call production is entirely separate from the calls' ability to convey specific information to others.

Acoustic variation of this sort, along two, largely uncorrelated dimensions, suggests that natural selection has acted simultaneously to favor calls that are correlated with urgency and calls that are correlated with predator type—just as selection has favored, in Physalaemus frogs, calls that simultaneously attract females and are as cryptic as possible to bats, and as selection has favored, in humans, speech that simultaneously provides listeners with referential information and information about the speaker's state of arousal. In all of these cases, questions about the emotions (or affect, or arousal) underlying call production are both empirically and theoretically separate from questions about a call's potential to convey referential information to listeners. We discuss this further below in "Communication from the Recipient's Perspective."

Communication and Classification

When a specific call type is elicited by only a narrow range of stimuli, observers have the opportunity to study the mechanisms by which animals classify the elements that make up their environment. Many nonhuman primates appear to classify stimuli into groups that cannot be defined solely on the basis of shared physical features. Female diana monkeys, for example, respond to a male diana monkey's leopard alarm call and a leopard's growl with the same response: by giving their own, acoustically distinct, leopard alarm call. Similarly, females respond to a male diana's eagle alarm call and the sound of an eagle's shriek by giving their own eagle alarm call (Zuberbuhler et al. 1997). In habituation-dishabituation experiments, diana monkey females who first heard a male's leopard alarm call and responded to it with calls of their own were then tested, five minutes later, with the growl of a leopard coming from the same area. Under these conditions they no longer responded to the growl. They did respond, however, if they were tested with the shriek of an eagle (they gave eagle alarms). Similarly, females who first heard a male diana's eagle alarm call did not respond, five minutes later, to the shriek of an eagle but did respond with leopard alarms if they heard the growl of a leopard (Zuberbuhler et al. 1999a). Diana monkey leopard alarms and the growls of a leopard are very different acoustically, as are diana monkey eagle alarms and the shriek of an eagle. Nonetheless, the monkeys treat the two leopard-associated noises, and the two eagle-associated noises, as if they provide the same information.

One interpretation of these results argues that the mechanisms underlying call production include the formation of some internal representation about the eliciting stimulus, and this information determines whether or not a call will be produced. Upon hearing a male's leopard alarm, for example, a female diana monkey stores the information that a leopard is present, and this information causes her to give her own leopard-specific vocalization. Five minutes later, when she hears a leopard's growl coming from the same location, she compares this new information with what she already knows. Because the new information is redundant, the female does not respond to the growl as she normally would, by giving an alarm call. Instead, she remains silent. Had the growl been an eagle's shriek, however, the female would have responded by giving her own eagle-specific vocalization.

The use of terms like "mental representation" and "information" in this account is similar to the use of a term like "memory" in other explanations of behavior. Upon hearing an auditory stimulus, a monkey is believed to store information that is specific to the stimulus. Later this information is retrieved and exerts a causal effect on behavior. Although we cannot at present specify the neural instantiation of this stored information, we use the terms mental representation and information as hypothetical, descriptive variables that may guide further research. For example, in this interpretation of the mechanisms underlying call production, there are parallels between the processing of calls by monkeys and the processing of words by humans. Just as humans respond to words by noting both their acoustic properties (auditory processing) and their meaning (semantic processing), monkeys process calls at two levels and can, in some circumstances, treat calls with different acoustic features as providing similar information (Cheney & Seyfarth 1990a, Zuberbuhler et al. 1999a).

The preceding interpretation finds parallels in modern animal learning theory (Dickinson 1980). If a rat learns that a light signals the imminence of shock, the rat begins to show fear and avoidance whenever the light comes on. In Rescorla's (1988) terms, the light provides the rat with "information" about the shock. Further, if a rat first learns that a tone is associated with the light and then learns that the light is associated with shock, it exhibits fear and avoidance behavior not only when the light comes on but also when the tone is heard, even though tone and shock have never been associated directly [Rizley & Rescorla 1972; see also Brogden (1939), who first described this phenomenon as "sensory preconditioning"]. Dickinson's (1980, p. 5) interpretation is that "during the first stage, exposure to the tone-light pairings set up some internal representation of this relationship [and] when the light subsequently acquired significance by being paired with the shock, the internal structure representing the tone as a predictor of the light resulted in the tone also becoming fear inducing." Though the light and the tone are qualitatively very different sorts of stimuli, and are processed by different sensory mechanisms, they have—like the leopard's growl and the diana monkey's leopard alarm call—come to elicit the same response because they provide the rat with similar information. Conditioning has led to "the learning of relations among events so as to allow the organism to represent its environment" (Rescorla 1988, p. 151).

Other explanations drawn from animal learning theory avoid terms like "information" and "internal representation." For example, Thompson (1995) suggests that, in experiments like those with diana monkeys described above, animals categorize conspecific leopard alarms and leopard growls as similar because the two calls have become associated with the same response and are therefore functionally equivalent (see also Heyes 1994, Schusterman & Kastak 1998). In this formulation there is no need to assume that an animal has acquired information or that there is any internal representation of the relation between a call and some feature of the environment. Selective call production can be explained without any reference to mental events as causal agents.

At present there are no experiments that distinguish clearly between an explanation of call production based on information or internal representations and an explanation of call production based on association with a shared behavioral response. Below we consider the same issue as it applies to listeners (see "Communication from the Recipient's Perspective"), for which slightly more data are available. We also consider other arguments against the use of terms like "information" in animal communication (Owings & Morton 1998; Owren & Rendall 1997, 2001).

Goals and Intentionality in Call Production

Animal vocalizations can be elicited by an extraordinary variety of auditory, visual, or olfactory stimuli (reviewed in Bradbury & Vehrencamp 1998). However, one class of stimuli apparently plays no role in eliciting calls from most nonhuman species. Its absence is interesting, because it is probably responsible for eliciting most of the vocalizations used in human conversation.

One function of language is to influence the behavior of others by changing what they know, think, believe, or desire (Grice 1957, Pinker 1994, Jackendoff 1994). When one person talks to another, he imputes mental states such as knowledge, beliefs, and goals to his listener. He assumes that the listener's mental states can be affected by what he hears and that these mental states will, in turn, affect the listener's behavior. Consequently, the speaker assumes providing the listener with information that alters what the listener knows may change the listener's behavior. A theory of mind is called a theory because, aside from introspection, humans have no direct evidence to support these assumptions (Premack & Woodruff 1978).

For humans engaged in conversation, the perception of another individual's mental state is perhaps the most common stimulus eliciting vocalization. By contrast, there is now growing evidence that, while animal vocalizations may have evolved because they can potentially alter the behavior of listeners to the signaler's benefit, such communication is—compared with human language—inadvertent, because signalers are unaware of the means by which vocalizations exert their effects. Male Physalaemus frogs call because calling causes females to approach and other males to move away. Even though females appear to choose among a number of males depending upon the pitch of their call (Ryan 1980, 1985), there is no evidence that a male frog calls because he attributes knowledge or desire to a female, or because he knows that his calls will affect a female's knowledge and that this knowledge will, in turn, affect her behavior.

Several observations and experiments, mostly with nonhuman primates, have attempted to determine whether the perception of another individual's mental state ever serves as an eliciting stimulus for the production of vocalizations. In free-ranging vervet monkeys, infants often give eagle alarm calls to harmless species like pigeons. Typically, nearby adults look up, but rarely give alarm calls of their own. By contrast, when an infant is the first member of its group to give an alarm call to a genuine predator, adults often look up and give alarm calls themselves. In giving or withholding these second alarms, however, adults do not act as if they recognize the infant's ignorance and are attempting to inform the infant that he was correct: Adults give second alarms at similar rates regardless of whether the initial caller was an infant or another adult (Seyfarth & Cheney 1986).

These observations are supported by data on the production of loud calls among chimpanzees, who do not appear to adjust their calling to inform ignorant individuals about their own location or the location of food (Mitani & Nishida 1993, Clark & Wrangham 1994, Mitani 1996). Outside the domain of vocal communication, data on the development of tool use provide a similar picture. Although chimpanzees certainly differ from monkeys in the variety and frequency of tool use (McGrew 1994), there is no evidence that knowledgeable individuals ever actively instruct others (Caro & Hauser 1992) or treat ignorant individuals differently from knowledgeable ones (reviewed in Tomasello & Call 1997).

Both rhesus (*Macaca mulatta*) and Japanese (*M. fuscata*) macaques give alarm calls to predators (or maintenance staff when held in captivity) and coo calls upon finding food (Green 1975, Hauser & Marler 1993). Experiments with captive individuals, however, found no evidence that knowledgeable individuals were more likely to call when they were informed, but their offspring was clearly ignorant, about the nearby presence of a predator or food (Cheney & Seyfarth 1990b).

Free-ranging baboons often give loud "contact" barks when their group is widely dispersed in wooded areas. Because the barks are clumped in time, it often appears that animals are exchanging calls, and that some individuals are calling to inform others of their location. Playback experiments, however, offer no support for this interpretation. When adult female subjects were played an infant's contact bark from a distant loudspeaker, they were significantly more likely to orient toward the speaker if the infant was their own than if it was not. Clearly, females recognized callers individually. Infant identity, however, had no effect on the production of an answering vocalization by the female. Instead, call production depended primarily on the female's own state of separation from the group (Rendall et al. 2000; see also Cheney et al. 1996).

In sum, a variety of results argue that, in marked contrast to humans, nonhuman primates do not produce vocalizations in response to their perception of another individual's ignorance or need for information. This is not to say that calls cannot inform; to the contrary, we discuss below the many ways in which listeners obtain information from a caller who may not, in the human sense, have intended to provide it. Instead, the point to emphasize here is that many vocalizations whose production initially seems goal-directed are not, in fact, as purposeful as they first appear. Like the frog who inadvertently provides information to the bat, adult vervet monkeys inadvertently inform infants about the relation between alarm call type and predator simply by producing alarm calls selectively themselves. Female baboons inform their infants and others within earshot of their own location simply by calling when they themselves risk being lost. At first glance, the frog's communication to the bat seems an inadvertent, evolutionary mistake: hardly a model for how animal communication works. Yet compared with human language, such inadvertent communication in animals may be much more common than previously realized.

COMMUNICATION FROM THE RECIPIENT'S PERSPECTIVE

What (if Anything) Is Communicated?

BACKGROUND   Although the transfer of information from one individual to another is obvious in language, how can we know that it occurs in animals, where we cannot interview subjects and can only assess what an individual may have learned by observing its behavior? Early learning theorists noted that conditioning affects behavior but believed their methods did not allow them to draw conclusions about the intervening mechanisms, which might or might not involve the acquisition of information. Some even thought the notion of information, or knowledge, was irrelevant (Skinner 1974). Applied to the study of animal communication, this view finds parallels in Owren & Rendall's (1997) suggestion that "individual primates use vocalizations to produce affective responses in conspecific receivers" (1997, p. 307) and that "neither referential nor motivational information is necessarily encoded in such signals" (1997, p. 340). Owren (2000, p. 57) further concludes that "the information-based approach has failed to provide significant insight into signaling by both primates and other nonhumans" (see also Owings & Morton 1998).

Other learning theorists, such as Tolman (1932), took a different view, arguing that in any conditioning experiment an animal acquires knowledge, and that the animal's behavior "is only an index that a given cognition has been gained" (Gleitman 1991, p. 124). Modern learning theory examines, among many other questions, whether the outcome of a conditioning experiment (the reward) serves simply to reinforce the association between antecedent events or whether the identity of the reward becomes part of the association itself. For example, if rats are trained that a lever press leads to a food pellet and a chain pull leads to sucrose, does the delivery of these rewards simply strengthen the association between certain events ("when in the experimental chamber, press the lever"), or does the reward become part of the "content of learning" (Rescorla 2000), strengthening the associations between the lever and food and between the chain and water? To test between these views, Colwill & Rescorla (1985) selectively devalued either the food or the water. Devaluing the food diminished lever pressing but not chain pulling, whereas devaluing water had the opposite effect. For rats, learning seemed to have included the acquisition of information about the outcome of different behaviors.

SINGLE PLAYBACK EXPERIMENTS   In their natural habitat, where animals have the opportunity to perform a much wider variety of responses, individuals often react to vocalizations in ways that suggest they have acquired specific information. Vervet monkeys show qualitatively different responses to leopard, eagle, and snake alarm calls (Struhsaker 1967, Seyfarth et al. 1980). Because individuals perform these responses immediately upon hearing a call, without apparently requiring any other supporting information, their behavior strongly suggests that the call has provided them with the information about the presence of a specific predator.

Arguing against this view, Owren & Rendall (2001) draw attention to the fact that vervet alarm calls, like those of many other species, consist of a rapid series of abrupt-onset, broadband pulses with high overall amplitudes: all features de-signed to evoke an individual's attention and induce arousal. Such vocalizations, they argue, have evolved to "induce nervous-system responses in receivers." They conclude that the notion of information has no "value as a conceptual tool" (2001, p. 61).

There is no doubt that animal alarm calls have acoustic features that may make them attention-getting and arousing. Owren & Rendall (2001) are also correct in noting that these basic characteristics have received too little attention in studies of animal communication, and they offer a reasonable explanation of why call types with different functions, such as alarm calls, distress screams, and more re-laxed, within-group vocalizations, take the physical form that they do. The acoustic features of signals are not arbitrary with respect to their function.

Acoustic features alone, however, cannot explain everything. After all, vervet monkeys, suricates, diana monkeys, baboons, and many other species of mammals and birds give acoustically different alarm calls to different classes of predator. All of these alarm call types share many of the same attention-getting, arousing features mentioned above, probably for the reasons that Owren & Rendall (2001) propose. Why, then, are the various alarm calls within each species acoustically so different? Perhaps because, over evolutionary time, natural selection has favored the co-evolution of signalers who warn their kin (Maynard Smith 1965) using different calls for different predators and listeners who recognize the associations between call and referent, thereby acquiring, from each call, the appropriate information.

Upon hearing a vervet monkey's eagle alarm call, nearby animals who are on the ground look up or run into a bush. Animals in a tree look up and/or run down out of the tree and into a bush, and animals already in bushes typically do nothing (Seyfarth et al. 1980, Cheney & Seyfarth 1990a). One could, of course, argue that no information has been acquired and that the eagle alarm call has created in individuals a particular affective state whose effect on behavior differs from one microhabitat to another, thus producing different responses. A more parsimonious explanation, however, posits that calls provide listeners with specific information and that the exact nature of an individual's response to this knowledge varies with his immediate circumstances (Cheney & Seyfarth 1990a).

The reconciliatory grunts of baboons provide another example (Cheney & Seyfarth 1997). Following an aggressive interaction between two female baboons, dominant individuals occasionally grunt to their victims. To test whether such grunts serve a reconciliatory function, we attempted to mimic reconciliation by playing to the subordinate victim of an aggressive interaction her opponent's grunt in the minutes immediately following the fight. As controls, the same victim heard either no grunt at all or the grunt of another, uninvolved dominant female. Playback of her opponent's grunt affected the victim in several ways. After hearing this grunt, the victim was more likely to approach her opponent and to tolerate her opponent's approach than she was after hearing either no grunt or the grunt of an uninvolved female.

As with alarm calls, one could argue that grunts induce in listeners an affective state that makes them more relaxed and receptive to social interactions. In this case, however, the effect is specific to a particular individual. Playback of her opponent's grunt changes the victim's behavior toward her opponent; playback of an uninvolved female's grunt does not. Any change in the victim's affective state, therefore, is specific to her relations with her opponent. It is also manifested in different ways. If the opponent does not subsequently approach the victim, the victim will. If her opponent does approach, the victim is less likely to move away. The variety of changes in the victim's behavior, each contingent on a different set of circumstances, are most simply explained by positing that the victim has acquired information about her opponent's likely intentions.

As a third example, consider the responses shown by baboons to the sound of an aggressive interaction between two members of their group. In an experiment designed to test whether baboons recognize the calls of other group members and also associate signalers with their close genetic relatives, pairs of unrelated females were played sequences of calls that mimicked a fight between their relatives. As controls, the same females heard sequences that involved either only the more dominant female's relative or neither of the females' relatives. When call sequences involved their relatives, subjects looked towards the speaker for a longer duration than when the sequences involved nonkin. When the sequences involved the other female's relative, they also looked towards that female. Subjects did not look towards one another when call sequences involved nonkin (Cheney & Seyfarth 1999). Taken together, these results argue against the view that responses to vocalizations are fixed and invariant (Wallman 1992). They also contradict the hypothesis that calls have been selected solely to induce specific emotional responses in receivers, because the same call, presented in the same context, elicits different responses in different listeners depending in part on which call it is paired with. As with alarm calls and reconciliatory grunts, the simplest explanation is that calls provide listeners with specific information, and each listener acts on this information depending on her particular circumstances.

The hypothesis that calls act directly on a listener's emotions to change the listener's behavior (Owren & Rendall 1997) and the hypothesis that calls achieve their myriad effects because they provide listeners with specific information are not mutually exclusive. More likely, as Owren & Rendall themselves suggest (1997, 2001), both processes are at work, and vocalizations, together with listeners' memories of past interactions, not only change listeners' affect or emotion but also provide them with information about predators, social interactions, changes in social relations, or group movements. Indeed, when we eventually arrive at an understanding of the underlying neurobiology, there may be little difference between "emotional calls" that affect emotions and referential calls that affect mental representations.

A DIFFERENT APPROACH TO THE STUDY OF MEANING   Habituation/dishabituation experiments offer another way to study what is communicated when one animal vocalizes to another. Here the technique (borrowed from research on human infants; see Eimas et al. 1971) is to select two call types from a species' repertoire and collect baseline data on the responses each normally evokes. Then, in habituation/dishabituation trials, a subject hears call type 1 repeatedly until it has habituated, or until the strength of its response has dropped significantly (different variants of the method, adapted to different field conditions, are not discussed here). Then call type 2 is played. If the subject's response is significantly below baseline, it is assumed to have judged call types 1 and 2 as similar, at least in the sense that habituation to call type 1 has presumably caused the subject's weak response to call type 2. By contrast, if the subject's response to call type 2 is strong and not different from baseline, the subject is assumed to treat the two call types as different, at least in the sense that habituation to type 1 has not affected its response to type 2.

Habituation/dishabituation experiments have two advantages over more conventional, single call playback studies. First, they offer an opportunity to study the criteria by which animals compare vocalizations. When subjects treat two calls as similar (in the sense described above), do they do so because the calls have similar acoustic properties and hence sound alike? Or do they use some other criteria? As already noted, habituation/dishabituation studies have shown that diana monkeys treat conspecific leopard alarms and the growl of a leopard as similar to each other but different from both conspecific eagle alarms and the shriek of an eagle (Zuberbuhler et al. 1999a). Similar experiments have shown that vervet monkey listeners treat intergroup "wrrs" and "chutters" given by the same individual as similar but conspecific female leopard and eagle alarms as different (Cheney & Seyfarth 1988); that rhesus monkeys distinguish kin from nonkin and, within the former class, one individual from another (Rendall et al. 1996); that Barbary macaques (*Macaca sylvanus*) distinguish two types of shrill bark (Fischer 1998); that among three of their putative food calls rhesus monkeys treat "warbles" and "harmonic arches" as similar despite their acoustic differences, but both calls as different from grunts (Hauser 1998); and that baboons learn from experience to distinguish "contact" from "alarm" barks if they are acoustically distinct but not if they are acoustically intermediate (Fischer et al. 2000, 2001b).

In many, but not all, of these cases, subjects treated two calls as similar even though the calls are acoustically different. And whereas we cannot be certain that the animals would agree with our own auditory judgments, often the acoustic difference is striking (Zuberbuhler et al. 1999a). In these circumstances results support the view that listeners process calls at two levels, in a manner analogous to the different levels of acoustic and semantic processing found in human language. On the acoustic level their response is initially affected by the call's acoustic features, whereas on the semantic level their response is further determined by the information a call provides.

This is not to say that acoustic processing is unimportant, or that the basic physical properties of sound transmission have not played a major role in structuring animal vocalizations. There are now extensive data supporting Morton's (1977) original view that calls given in aggressive circumstances, for example, tend to be low-frequency and noisy, whereas calls in more friendly circumstances tend to be high-frequency and tonal (e.g., August & Anderson 1987; Hauser 1993; Owren & Rendall 1997, 2001). Given that calls may both induce affective responses in listeners and provide them with information, it is this information component of signals with which habituation/dishabituation experiments are concerned.

But what information, exactly? A second goal of habituation/dishabituation experiments has been to approach the study of meaning from a different perspective, by comparing the information conveyed by one signal with the information conveyed by another. At their most optimistic, investigators envisioned a kind of "semantic space" in which some calls would lie close together and be assumed to have similar meanings (because habituation to one produces habituation to the other), whereas other calls would lie far apart and be assumed to have different meanings (because habituation to one did not produce habituation to the other). Ultimately, it was hoped, it might be possible to build a species' dictionary, in which each call type is defined by its relation (synonym, antonym, or somewhere in between) to the others.

This goal, however, has not proved attainable, primarily because few animal vocalizations have the kind of referential specificity found in predator-specific alarm calls. Consider again, for example, baboon grunts. Because baboons' move grunts are given in a relatively narrow set of circumstances, they have the potential to convey quite specific information. Listeners who have just heard a move grunt have probably learned both the identity of the caller and the fact that the group is about to begin, or has already begun, a move. However, infant grunts are less contextually specific. As a result, it is difficult to say what information they provide to listeners other than the identity of the caller and the occurrence of a nonaggressive social interaction.

Many animal vocalizations are more like the infant grunts of baboons than the alarm calls of suricates or vervet monkeys; they are relatively vague in the information they convey to listeners. Does the inability to specify precisely the meaning of an animal's vocalization represent, as Owren (2000) argues, "a basic failure of the information metaphor"? For several reasons we believe it does not.

In language, where the use of sounds to represent features of the environment is no longer in doubt, the question "What do words mean?" is both fundamental and unresolved. As Wittgenstein (1953), Quine (1960), Putnam (1975), and others have argued, it may never be possible to state precisely what an individual means—and what information a listener acquires—when a speaker uses a particular word. Given the difficulty of specifying the meaning of human words, any attempt to specify the information listeners extract from an animal's vocalization is bound to be even more problematic (Cheney & Seyfarth 1990a, Ch. 5). However, just as the "radical indeterminacy of meaning" (Quine 1960) has not deterred those who study the one-word utterances of children (Fisher & Gleitman 2002) or the confused semantics of neurological patients (Martin 1992) from attempting to determine what a sound means to signaler and recipient, we believe it should not deter those who study the vocalizations of animals from similar research. The inability to specify precisely the information conveyed by a vocalization does not prove that information is entirely absent.

Second, we should not underestimate the rich information that vocalizations can provide to listeners, even when calls are not referentially specific and appear to convey precise information only about the caller's identity. As often noted (e.g., Snowdon 1988), many animal vocalizations are individually distinctive. Beginning with this observation, scientists studying birds, primates, hyenas, and elephants have conducted playback experiments to test hypotheses about individuals' knowledge of their social companions. By using combinations of calls designed to provide listeners with the information that a certain event has taken place (for example, that A and B are involved in a fight, or that D has risen in rank over C), such experiments have shown that birds eavesdrop on singing contests in which they are not themselves involved and subsequently behave differently toward apparent winners and losers (McGregor 2003); that vervets remember which individuals have groomed them in the past and adjust their behavior accordingly (Seyfarth & Cheney 1984); that vervets, rhesus macaques, baboons, hyenas (*Crocuta crocuta*), and elephants (*Loxodonta africana*) recognize the close bonds that exist among matrilineal kin (Cheney & Seyfarth 1980, 1997; Rendall et al. 1996; Holekamp et al. 1999; McComb et al. 2000); and that vervets and baboons recognize others' rank relations (Cheney & Seyfarth 1990a, Cheney et al. 1995b). All of these studies presume that, upon hearing one or a combination of calls, listeners gain at least some information that is extremely precise: information about the identity of the signalers. From this relatively simple starting point animals go on to derive much more complex information about the social events taking place around them, as well as the long-term social relationships these events imply. Contrary to the view that vocalizations have evolved solely to induce affective responses in listeners and that listeners acquire no information from them, these experiments demonstrate that vocalizations do provide nearby "third party" listeners, even predatory bats, with precise information about events. If we grant the acquisition of information to these bystanders, is it logical to deny it to intended recipients?

A third point concerns the future direction of comparative neurobiological research on human and nonhuman species. If we accept the view that information plays little if any role in communication, it follows that the semantic information conveyed by human words is unique, with no parallels in the vocalizations of any nonhuman creatures (Owings & Morton 1998). This conclusion, however, is premature. In fact, we are only beginning to understand the neural mechanisms that allow humans to infer a word's meaning, store it in memory, and compare it with the meaning of other words (e.g., Caplan 1992); the existence of similar mechanisms in animals is an entirely open issue, now being studied with many different methods, including neuroimagery (Martin 1998). Indeed, one purpose of this review is to draw attention to the many cases in which nonhuman primates respond to vocalizations with behavior that suggests they have processed specific sorts of information. Such ethological work may guide neuroscientists in designing those experiments most likely to reveal both similarities and differences between the neural mechanisms that underlie language and those that underlie communication in other species.

INFORMATION THAT LISTENERS DO NOT ACQUIRE   Human listeners routinely treat words and phrases not just as semantic representations of objects and events but also as propositions that express the speaker's disposition to think or behave toward those objects in a particular way (e.g., Pinker 1994). By contrast, although nonhuman listeners acquire an extraordinary variety of information from vocal signals, there is little evidence that they also acquire information about the signaler's mental state. Evidence for a lack of mental state attribution by listeners is typically indirect, and comes in two forms. First, in most animal species no systematic observational data indicate that signalers modify their vocal production depending on the mental state of listeners, nor is there any definitive evidence that animals display mental state attribution in any other domain, such as tool use (see above). We therefore assume it is absent in listeners.

Second, in many cases in which we might be tempted to explain the behavior of listeners in terms of mental state attribution, such explanations are usually less persuasive than simpler competing arguments. Consider, for example, the reconciliatory grunts of baboons. If a dominant female grunts to a subordinate following aggression, this changes the subordinate's behavior (Cheney & Seyfarth 1997; see above). One could conclude that the subordinate has recognized a change in the dominant's attitude toward her; that, for example, the dominant is seeking to make her former victim less anxious or afraid. Equally plausible, however, is the likelihood that the subordinate is responding on the basis of a learned contingency. Through experience and perhaps also by observing the interactions of others, she has learned that grunts are correlated with a reduced probability of attack. She therefore tolerates her opponent's approaches and even approaches her opponent with the expectation that her opponent will not attack her again (Cheney & Seyfarth 1996). Functionally, these two explanations are equivalent. The latter, however, does not require a theory of mind. The listener is able to extract subtle and complex information from her opponent's grunt, but this information does not require her also to attribute intentions, motives, or beliefs to her opponent.

These conclusions may not apply to chimpanzees, for which the results of tests for a theory of mind are mixed. For example, there is some evidence that chimpanzees learn more easily than monkeys to recognize the goals and motives of others. Chimpanzees are better than monkeys, for instance, at assuming another individual's role in a cooperative task and at recognizing intentional gestures such as pointing (Povinelli et al. 1990, 1992a,b). They also seem better at emulating others. When watching a demonstrator use a tool, chimpanzees, unlike monkeys, readily learn the use and function of a tool. However, unlike children, they do not copy the precise motor patterns or methods of the demonstrator (Nagell et al. 1993). As a result, it remains unclear whether the difference in performance between chimpanzees and monkeys stems from chimpanzees' greater capacity to comprehend the goals and intentions of others or from their proficiency in recognizing cause-effect relations (Tomasello et al. 1997, Limongelli et al. 1995, Povinelli & Eddy 1996, Tomasello 1996, Tomasello & Call 1997, Povinelli 2000).

In a far-ranging series of experiments Povinelli (2000) and Povinelli & Eddy (1996) tested whether chimpanzees "appreciate that visual perception subjectively connects organisms to the external world." They argue that to do so the chimpanzees "would have to appreciate that seeing refers to or is 'about' something—in other words, they must interpret seeing as an intentional event" (Povinelli & Eddy 1996, p. 120). Povinelli's evidence argues against such an interpretation. In a typical experiment a chimpanzee was trained to use his natural begging gesture (an outstretched hand) to request food from a human trainer. Then the chimpanzee was given the opportunity to beg from one of two trainers. One trainer was facing the subject and could plainly see him; the other trainer could not because her face was covered (or her eyes were covered, or she was facing in the opposite direction). Given this choice, chimpanzees showed no difference in their preference for one trainer over another. However, 3-year-old children immediately gestured selectively to the person who could see them.

In contrast, other experiments suggest that chimpanzees may have some understanding about the relation between seeing and knowing, even if this understanding is more rudimentary than that of a young child. For example, Tomasello et al. (1998) demonstrated that many nonhuman primates will reliably follow the gaze direction of a human or a member of their own species. Chimpanzees, however, do not simply orient in the appropriate direction and search randomly for something interesting. Instead, they follow gaze direction to a specific geometric location, much as human infants do (Tomasello et al. 1999). More recently, tests by Hare et al. (2000, 2001) suggest that, in at least some situations, chimpanzees know what a conspecific has or has not seen, and from this information may infer what a conspecific does or does not know. Such results do not prove that chimpanzees impute mental states such as ignorance to others or that they recognize that other individuals' visual experiences may be different from their own. They do suggest, however, that some form of a theory of mind may be present in chimpanzees, even if it appears to be absent in other primates.

SUMMARY

In their natural habitat many animals acquire information from the vocalizations of others. Their acquisition of information has some parallels both with human language learning at the one-word stage and with the information acquired by laboratory animals in conditioning experiments. In other respects, however, the acquisition of information by animals is governed by fundamentally different mechanisms from those that underlie language.

Natural selection has favored callers who vocalize in ways that change the behavior of listeners and ultimately return benefit to the caller. Simultaneously, selection has favored listeners who detect the links between specific calls and particular events, thereby extracting whatever information may be relevant to them. In many group-living species, where callers and recipients have overlapping reproductive interests, selection has favored callers who give acoustically different vocalizations in different circumstances, thus allowing listeners to acquire more specific information. This information may include, but is not limited to, information about predators or the urgency of a predator's approach, group movements, intergroup interactions, or the identities of individuals involved in social events. In sum, the co-evolution of caller and recipient has favored signalers who call strategically and listeners who acquire information from vocalizations, using this information to represent their environment.

The inability of animals to recognize the mental states of others places important constraints on their communication and distinguishes animal communication most clearly from human language. With the possible exception of chimpanzees, animals cannot represent the mental state of another. As a result, whereas signalers may vocalize to change a listener's behavior, they do not call with the specific goal of informing others or in response to the perception of ignorance in another. Similarly, whereas listeners extract subtle information from vocalizations, this does not include information about the signaler's knowledge. Listeners acquire information from signalers who do not, in the human sense, intend to provide it.

ACKNOWLEDGMENTS

Much of the research reviewed here was supported by grants from the U.S. National Science Foundation and the National Institutes of Health. We thank Catherine Crockford, Julia Fischer, Tecumseh Fitch, Marc Hauser, Robert Rescorla, and Klaus Zuberbuhler for comments on an earlier draft.

The *Annual Review of Psychology* is online at http://psych.annualreviews.org

LITERATURE CITED

August PV, Anderson JGT. 1987. Mammal sounds and motivation-structural rules: a test of the hypothesis. *J. Mammal.* 68:1–9

Bachorowski JA, Owren MJ. 1995. Vocal expression of emotion: Acoustic properties of speech are associated with emotional intensity and context. *Psychol. Sci.* 6:219–24

Blumstein DT, Armitage KB. 1997. Alarm-calling in yellow-bellied marmots. I. The meaning of situationally variable alarm calls. *Anim. Behav.* 53:143–71

Bradbury JW, Vehrencamp SL. 1998. *Principles of Animal Communication.* Sunderland, MA: Sinauer. 882 pp.

Brogden WJ. 1939. Sensory pre-conditioning. *J. Exp. Psychol.* 25:323–32

Caplan D. 1992. *Language: Structure,*

Processing, and Disorders. Cambridge, MA: MIT Press

Capranica RR. 1977. Auditory processing of vocal signals in anurans. In *Reproductive Biology of Amphibians*, ed. DH Taylor, SI Guttman, pp. 303–17. New York: Plenum

Caro T, Hauser MD. 1992. Is there teaching in nonhuman animals? *Q. Rev. Biol.* 67:151–74

Cheney DL, Seyfarth RM. 1980. Vocal recognition in free-ranging vervet monkeys. *Anim. Behav.* 28:362–67

Cheney DL, Seyfarth RM. 1988. Assessment of meaning and the detection of unreliable signals by vervet monkeys. *Anim. Behav.* 36:477–86

Cheney DL, Seyfarth RM. 1990a. *How Monkeys See the World.* Chicago: Univ. Chicago Press. 377 pp.

Cheney DL, Seyfarth RM. 1990b. Attending to behavior versus attending to knowledge: examining monkeys' attribution of mental states. *Anim. Behav.* 40:742–53

Cheney DL, Seyfarth RM. 1996. Function and intention in the calls of nonhuman primates. *Proc. Br. Acad.* 88:59–76

Cheney DL, Seyfarth RM. 1997. Reconciliatory grunts by dominant female baboons influence victims' behavior. *Anim. Behav.* 54:409–18

Cheney DL, Seyfarth RM. 1998. Why monkeys don't have language. In *The Tanner Lectures on Human Values*, ed. G Petersen, 19:173–210. Salt Lake City: Univ. Utah Press

Cheney DL, Seyfarth RM. 1999. Recognition of other individuals' social relationships by female baboons. *Anim. Behav.* 58:67–75

Cheney DL, Seyfarth RM, Palombit RA. 1996. The function and mechanisms underlying baboon contact barks. *Anim. Behav.* 52:507–18

Cheney DL, Seyfarth RM, Silk JB. 1995a. The role of grunts in reconciling opponents and facilitating interactions among adult female baboons. *Anim. Behav.* 50:249–57

Cheney DL, Seyfarth RM, Silk JB. 1995b. The responses of female baboons (*Papio cynocephalus ursinus*) to anomalous social interactions: evidence for causal reasoning? *J. Comp. Psychol.* 109:134–41

Clark AP, Wrangham RW. 1994. Chimpanzee arrival pant hoots: Do they signify food or status? *Int. J. Primatol.* 15:185–205

Colwill RM, Rescorla RA. 1985. Postconditioning devaluation of a reinforcer affects instrumental responding. *J. Exp. Psychol. Anim. Behav. Proc.* 11:120–32

Dickinson A. 1980. *Contemporary Animal Learning Theory.* Cambridge, UK: Cambridge Univ. Press. 177 pp.

Eimas PD, Siqueland P, Juszyk P, Vigorito J. 1971. Speech perception in infants. *Science* 171:303–6

Enquist M. 1985. Communication during aggressive interactions with particular reference to variation in choice of behaviour. *Anim. Behav.* 33:1152–61

Evans CS. 1997. Referential signals. See Owings et al. 1997, pp. 99–143

Evans CS, Macedonia JM, Marler P. 1993. Effects of apparent size and speed on the response of chickens, *Gallus gallus*, to computer-generated simulations of aerial predators. *Anim. Behav.* 46:1–11

Fischer J. 1998. Barbary macaques categorize shrill barks into two call types. *Anim. Behav.* 55:799–807

Fischer J, Cheney DL, Seyfarth RM. 2000. Development of infant baboons' responses to graded bark variants. *Proc. R. Soc. London Ser. B* 267:2317–21

Fischer J, Hammerschmidt K. 2001. Functional referents and acoustic similarity revisited: the case of Barbary macaque alarm calls. *Anim. Cogn.* 4:29–35

Fischer J, Hammerschmidt K, Cheney DL, Seyfarth RM. 2001a. Acoustic features of female chacma baboon barks. *Ethology* 107:33–54

Fischer J, Hammerschmidt K, Todt D. 1995. Factors affecting acoustic variation in Barbary macaque (*Macaca sylvanus*) disturbance calls. *Ethology* 101:51–66

Fischer J, Metz M, Cheney DL, Seyfarth RM. 2001b. Baboon responses to graded bark variants. *Anim. Behav.* 61:925–31

Fisher C, Gleitman LR. 2002. Language acquisition. In *Stevens Handbook of Experimental Psychology*, Vol. 3. *Learning, Motivation, and Emotion*, ed. CR Gallistel. New York: Wiley. In press

Fitch WT, Hauser MD. 1995. Vocal production in nonhuman primates: acoustics, physiology, and functional constraints on "honest" advertisement. *Am. J. Primatol.* 37:191–220

Fitch WT, Neubauer J, Herzel H. 2002. Calls out of chaos: the adaptive significance of nonlinear phenomena in mammalian vocal production. *Anim. Behav.* 63:407–18

Gautier JP, Gautier A. 1977. Communication in Old World monkeys. In *How Animals Communicate*, ed. T Sebeok, pp. 890–964. Bloomington: Indiana Univ. Press

Gleitman H. 1991. *Psychology*. New York: Norton. 3rd ed.

Green S. 1975. Communication by a graded vocal system in Japanese monkeys. In *Primate Behavior*, ed. LA Rosenblum, 4:1–102. New York: Academic

Grice HP. 1957. Meaning. *Philos. Rev.* 66:377–88

Gyger M, Karakashian SJ, Marler P. 1986. Avian alarm-calling: Is there an audience effect? *Anim. Behav.* 34:1570–72

Hare B, Call J, Agnetta B, Tomasello M. 2000. Chimpanzees know what conspecifics do and do not see. *Anim. Behav.* 59:771–85

Hare B, Call J, Tomasello M. 2001. Do chimpanzees know what conspecifics know? *Anim. Behav.* 61:139–51

Hauser MD. 1993. The evolution of nonhuman primate vocalizations: effects of phylogeny, body weight, and social context. *Am. Nat.* 142:528–42

Hauser MD. 1996. *The Evolution of Communication*. Cambridge, MA: MIT Press. 760 pp.

Hauser MD. 1998. Functional referents and acoustic similarity: field playback experiments with rhesus monkeys. *Anim. Behav.* 55:1647–58

Hauser MD, Marler P. 1993. Food associated calls in rhesus macaques. I. Socioecological factors influencing call production. *Behav. Ecol.* 4:206–12

Heyes CM. 1994. Social cognition in primates. In *Animal Learning and Cognition*, ed. NJ Macintosh, pp. 281–305. New York: Academic

Holekamp KE, Boydston EE, Szykman M, Graham I, Nutt KJ, et al. 1999. Vocal recognition in the spotted hyena and its possible implications regarding the evolution of intelligence. *Anim. Behav.* 58:383–95

Jackendoff R. 1994. *Patterns in the Mind*. New York: Basic Books. 246 pp.

Johnstone R. 1997. The evolution of animal signals. In *Behavioural Ecology: An Evolutionary Approach*, ed. JR Krebs, NB Davies, pp. 155–78. Oxford: Blackwell Sci.

Karakashian SJ, Gyger M, Marler P. 1988. Audience effects on alarm calling in chickens. *J. Comp. Psychol.* 102:129–35

Leger DW, Owings DH, Gelfand DL. 1980. Single note vocalizations of California ground squirrels: graded signals and situation-specificity of predator and socially evoked calls. *Z. Tierpsychol.* 52:227–46

Limongelli L, Boysen ST, Visalberghi E. 1995. Comprehension of cause-effect relations in a tool-using task by chimpanzees (*Pan troglodytes*). *J. Comp. Psychol.* 109:18–26

Macedonia JM, Evans CS. 1993. Variation among mammalian alarm call systems and the problem of meaning in animal signals. *Ethology* 93:177–97

Manser MB. 1998. *The evolution of auditory communication in Suricates, Suricata suricata*. PhD thesis. Univ. Cambridge, Cambridge, UK. 150 pp.

Manser MB. 2001. The acoustic structure of suricates' alarm calls varies with predator type and the level of response urgency. *Proc. R. Soc. London Ser. B* 268:2315–24

Manser MB, Bell MB, Fletcher L. 2001. The information that receivers extract from alarm calls in suricates. *Proc. R. Soc. London Ser. B* 268:2485–91

Manser MB, Seyfarth RM, Cheney DL. 2002. Suricate alarm calls signal predator class and urgency. *Trends Cogn. Sci.* 6:55–57

Marler P. 1961. The logical analysis of animal communication. *J. Theor. Biol.* 1:295–317

Marler P, Evans CS, Hauser MD. 1992. Animal signals: motivational, referential, or both? In

Nonverbal Vocal Communication: Comparative and Developmental Approaches, ed. H Papousek, U Jurgens, M Papousek, pp. 66–86. Cambridge, UK: Cambridge Univ. Press

Marler P, Karakashian SJ, Gyger M. 1990. Do animals have the option of withholding signals when communication is inappropriate? In *Cognitive Ethology: The Minds of Other Animals*, ed. CA Ristau, pp. 187–208. Hillsdale, NJ: Erlbaum

Martin A. 1992. Semantic knowledge in patients with Alzheimer's disease: evidence for degraded representations. In *Memory Functions in Dementia*, ed. L Backman, pp. 119–34. Amsterdam: Elsevier/North Holland

Martin A. 1998. Organization of semantic knowledge and the origin of words in the brain. In *The Origin and Diversification of Language*, ed. NG Jablonski, LC Aiello, pp. 69–88. San Francisco: Calif. Acad. Sci.

Maynard Smith J. 1965. The evolution of alarm calls. *Am. Nat.* 99:59–63

McComb K, Moss C, Sayialel S, Baker L. 2000. Unusually extensive networks of vocal recognition in African elephants. *Anim. Behav.* 59:1103–9

McGregor PK, ed. 2003. *Animal Communication Networks*. Cambridge, UK: Cambridge Univ. Press

McGrew WC. 1994. Tools compared: the material of culture. In *Chimpanzee Cultures*, ed RW Wrangham, WC McGrew, FBM deWaal, PG Heltne, pp. 25–40. Cambridge, MA: Harvard Univ. Press

Mitani J. 1996. Comparative studies of African ape vocal behavior. In *Great Ape Societies*, ed. WC McGrew, LF Marchant, T Nishida, pp. 93–145. Cambridge, UK: Cambridge Univ. Press

Mitani J, Nishida T. 1993. Contexts and social correlates of long-distance calling by male chimpanzees. *Anim. Behav.* 45:735–46

Morton ES. 1977. On the occurrence and significance of motivation-structural rules in some bird and mammal sounds. *Am. Nat.* 111:855–69

Nagell K, Olguin RS, Tomasello M. 1993. Processes of social learning in the tool use of chimpanzees (*Pan troglodytes*) and human children (*Homo sapiens*). *J. Comp. Psychol.* 107:174–86

Owings DH, Beecher MD, Thompson NS, eds. 1997. *Perspectives in Ethology*. New York: Plenum

Owings DH, Hennessy D. 1984. The importance of variation in sciurid visual and vocal communication. In *Biology of Ground-Dwelling Squirrels: Annual Cycles, Behavioral Ecology, and Sociality*, ed. JO Murie, GR Michener, pp. 202–47. Lincoln: Univ. Nebr. Press

Owings DH, Morton ES. 1998. *Animal Vocal Communication: A New Approach*. Cambridge, UK: Cambridge Univ. Press. 284 pp.

Owren MJ. 2000. Standing evolution on its head: the uneasy role of evolutionary theory in comparative cognition and communication. *Rev. Anthropol.* 29:55–69

Owren MJ, Rendall D. 1997. An affect-conditioning model of nonhuman primate vocal signaling. See Owings et al. 1997, pp. 299–346

Owren MJ, Rendall D. 2001. Sound on the rebound: bringing form and function back to the forefront in understanding nonhuman primate vocal signaling. *Evol. Anthropol.* 10:58–71

Owren MJ, Seyfarth RM, Cheney DL. 1997. The acoustic features of vowel-like grunt calls in chacma baboons (*Papio cynocephalus ursinus*): implications for production processes and functions. *J. Acoust. Soc. Am.* 101:2951–63

Pinker S. 1994. *The Language Instinct*. New York: Norton. 494 pp.

Povinelli DJ. 2000. *Folk Physics for Apes*. Oxford: Oxford Univ. Press. 391 pp.

Povinelli DJ, Eddy TJ. 1996. What chimpanzees know about seeing. *Monogr.: Soc. Res. Child Dev.* 61:1–152

Povinelli DJ, Nelson KE, Boysen ST. 1990. Inferences about guessing and knowing by chimpanzees (*Pan troglodytes*). *J. Comp. Psychol.* 104:203–10

Povinelli DJ, Nelson KE, Boysen ST. 1992a. Comprehension of role reversal in chimpanzees: evidence of empathy? *Anim. Behav.* 43:633–40

Povinelli DJ, Parks KA, Novak MA. 1992b. Role reversal by rhesus monkeys but no evidence of empathy. *Anim. Behav.* 44:269–81

Premack D. 1972. Concordant preferences as a precondition for affective but not for symbolic communication (or how to do experimental anthropology). *Cognition* 1:251–64

Premack D, Woodruff G. 1978. Does the chimpanzee have a theory of mind? *Behav. Brain Sci.* 4:515–26

Putnam H. 1975. *Mind, Language, and Reality. Philosophical Papers II.* Cambridge, UK: Cambridge Univ. Press. 457 pp.

Quine WVO. 1960. *Word and Object.* Cambridge, MA: MIT Press. 294 pp.

Rand AS, Ryan MJ. 1981. The adaptive significance of a complex vocal repertoire in a neotropical frog. *Z. Tierpsychol.* 57:209–14

Rendall D. 2003. The affective basis of referential grunt variants in baboons. *J. Acoust. Soc. Am.* In press

Rendall D, Cheney DL, Seyfarth RM. 2000. Proximate factors mediating 'contact' calls in adult female baboons and their infants. *J. Comp. Psychol.* 114:36–46

Rendall D, Rodman PS, Emond RE. 1996. Vocal recognition of individuals and kin in free-ranging rhesus monkeys. *Anim. Behav.* 51:1007–15

Rendall D, Seyfarth RM, Cheney DL, Owren MJ. 1999. The meaning and function of grunt variants in baboons. *Anim. Behav.* 57:583–92

Rescorla RA. 1988. Pavlovian conditioning: It's not what you think it is. *Am. Psychol.* 43:151–60

Rescorla RA. 2000. Multiple mentorship: one example of Henry Gleitman's influence. In *Perception, Cognition, and Language*, ed. B Landau, J Sabini, J Jonides, EL Newport, pp. 39–48. Cambridge, MA: MIT Press

Rizley RC, Rescorla RA. 1972. Associations in second-order conditioning and sensory preconditioning. *J. Comp. Physiol. Psychol.* 81:1–11

Russell JA, Bachorowski J, Fernández-Dols J-M. 2003. Facial and vocal expressions of emotion *Annu. Rev. Psychol.* 54:329–49

Ryan MJ. 1980. Female mate choice in a neotropical frog. *Science* 209:523–25

Ryan MJ. 1985. *The Tungara Frog: A Study in Sexual Selection and Communication.* Chicago: Univ. Chicago Press. 230 pp.

Ryan MJ, Brenowitz E. 1985. The role of body size, phylogeny, and ambient noise in the evolution of bird song. *Am. Nat.* 126:87–100

Ryan MJ, Phelps SM, Rand AS. 2001. How evolutionary history shapes recognition mechanisms. *Trends Cogn. Sci.* 5:143–48

Ryan MJ, Tuttle MD, Rand AS. 1982. Bat predation and sexual advertisement in a neotropical frog. *Am. Nat.* 119:136–39

Scherer KR. 1989. Vocal correlates of emotion. In *Handbook of Psychophysiology: Emotion and Social Behaviour*, ed. H Wagner, A Manstead, pp. 165–97. New York: Wiley

Schon Ybarra M. 1995. A comparative approach to the nonhuman primate vocal tract: implications for sound production. In *Current Topics in Primate Vocal Communication*, ed. E Zimmerman, JD Newman, U Jurgens, pp. 185–98. New York: Plenum

Schusterman RJ, Kastak DA. 1998. Functional equivalence in a California sea lion: relevance to animal social and communicative interactions. *Anim. Behav.* 55:1087–95

Seyfarth RM, Cheney DL. 1984. Grooming, alliances, and reciprocal altruism in vervet monkeys. *Nature* 308:541–43

Seyfarth RM, Cheney DL. 1986. Vocal development in vervet monkeys. *Anim. Behav.* 34:1640–58

Seyfarth RM, Cheney DL. 1997. Behavioral mechanisms underlying vocal communication in nonhuman primates. *Anim. Learn. Behav.* 25:249–67

Seyfarth RM, Cheney DL, Marler P. 1980. Vervet monkey alarm calls: semantic communication in a free-ranging primate. *Anim. Behav.* 28:1070–94

Sherman PW. 1977. Nepotism and the evolution of alarm calls. *Science* 197:1246–53

Sherman PW. 1980. The limits of ground squirrel nepotism. In *Sociobiology: Beyond*

Nature/Nurture, ed. GW Barlow, J Silverberg, pp. 505–44. Boulder, CO: Westview

Sherman PW. 1985. Alarm calls of Belding's ground squirrels to aerial predators: nepotism or self-preservation? *Behav. Ecol. Sociobiol.* 17:313–23

Silk JB, Cheney DL, Seyfarth RM. 1996. The form and function of reconciliation among baboons, *Papio cynocephalus ursinus. Anim. Behav.* 52:259–68

Skinner BF. 1974. *Verbal Behavior.* New York: Appleton-Century-Crofts. 478 pp.

Smith HJ, Newman JD, Symmes D. 1982. Vocal concomitants of affiliative behavior in squirrel monkeys. In *Primate Communication*, ed. CT Snowdon, CH Brown, MR Petersen, pp. 30–49. Cambridge, UK: Cambridge Univ. Press

Snowdon CT. 1988. A comparative approach to vocal communication. In *Nebraska Symposium on Motivation*, Vol. 35. *Comparative Approaches in Modern Psychology*, ed. DW Leger, pp. 145–99. Lincoln: Univ. Nebr. Press

Struhsaker TT. 1967. Auditory communication among vervet monkeys. In *Social Communication Among Primates*, ed. SA Altman, pp. 281–324. Chicago: Univ. Chicago Press

Thompson RKR. 1995. Natural and relational concepts in animals. In *Comparative Approaches to Cognitive Science*, ed. H Roitblat, JA Meyer, pp. 175–224. Cambridge, MA: MIT Press

Tinbergen N. 1951. *The Study of Instinct.* Oxford: Oxford Univ. Press. 228 pp.

Tolman EC. 1932. *Purposive Behavior in Animals and Men.* New York: Appleton-Century-Crofts

Tomasello M. 1996. Chimpanzee social cognition. *Monogr.: Soc. Res. Child Dev.* 61:161–73

Tomasello M, Call J. 1997. *Primate Cognition.* Oxford: Oxford Univ. Press

Tomasello M, Call J, Hare B. 1998. Five primate species follow the visual gaze of conspecifics. *Anim. Behav.* 55:1063–69

Tomasello M, Davis-Dasilva M, Camak L, Bard K. 1997. Observational learning of tool use by young chimpanzees. *Hum. Evol.* 2:175–83

Tomasello M, Hare B, Agnetta B. 1999. Chimpanzees follow gaze direction geometrically. *Anim. Behav.* 58:769–77

Waas JR. 1991. Do little blue penguins signal their intentions during aggressive interactions with strangers? *Anim. Behav.* 41:375–82

Wallman J. 1992. *Aping Language.* Cambridge: Cambridge Univ. Press

Wittgenstein L. 1953. *Philosophical Investigations.* Transl. GEM Anscombe. Oxford: Blackwell Sci.

Zuberbuhler K. 2000. Referential labeling in diana monkeys. *Anim. Behav.* 59:917–27

Zuberbuhler K, Cheney DL, Seyfarth RM. 1999a. Conceptual semantics in a nonhuman primate. *J. Comp. Psychol.* 113:33–42

Zuberbuhler K, Jenny D, Bshary R. 1999b. The predator deterrence function of primate alarm calls. *Ethology* 105:477–90

Zuberbuhler K, Noe R, Seyfarth RM. 1997. Diana monkey long distance calls: messages for conspecifics and predators. *Anim. Behav.* 53:589–604

Annu. Rev. Psychol. 2003. 54:175–203
doi: 10.1146/annurev.psych.54.101601.145118

FIRSTHAND LEARNING
THROUGH INTENT PARTICIPATION

Barbara Rogoff,[1] Ruth Paradise,[2] Rebeca Mejía Arauz,[3]
Maricela Correa-Chávez,[1] and Cathy Angelillo[1]
[1]University of California, 277 Social Sciences 2, Santa Cruz, California 95064;
e-mail: brogoff@cats.ucsc.edu, mcorrea@cats.ucsc.edu, angelill@cats.ucsc.edu
[2]Departamento de Investigaciones Educativas del Centro de Investigación y de Estudios
Avanzados del IPN, Mexico City, Mexico; e-mail: paradise@mx.inter.net
[3]ITESO University, Guadalajara, Mexico; e-mail: rebmejia@iteso.mx

Key Words   age segregation, observation, participation structure, shared endeavors

■ **Abstract**   This article examines how people learn by actively observing and "listening-in" on ongoing activities as they participate in shared endeavors. Keen observation and listening-in are especially valued and used in some cultural communities in which children are part of mature community activities. This intent participation also occurs in some settings (such as early language learning in the family) in communities that routinely segregate children from the full range of adult activities. However, in the past century some industrial societies have relied on a specialized form of instruction that seems to accompany segregation of children from adult settings, in which adults "transmit" information to children. We contrast these two traditions of organizing learning in terms of their participation structure, the roles of more- and less-experienced people, distinctions in motivation and purpose, sources of learning (observation in ongoing activity versus lessons), forms of communication, and the role of assessment.

CONTENTS

0066-4308/03/0203-0175$14.00   **175**

INTRODUCTION

Children everywhere learn by observing and listening-in on activities of adults and other children. Learning through keen observation and listening, in anticipation of participation, seems to be especially valued and emphasized in communities where children have access to learning from informal community involvement. They observe and listen with intent concentration and initiative, and their collaborative participation is expected when they are ready to help in shared endeavors. This tradition, which we refer to as *intent participation*, is prominent in many indigenous American communities and can also be seen in voluntary organizations, interactive museums, and collaborative schools in middle-class U.S. communities.

Intent participation is a powerful form of fostering learning. It contributes to impressive learning such as that accomplished by young children learning their first language and continues in importance throughout life. However, it has received relatively little research attention. It seems often to be taken for granted or overlooked, perhaps because researchers are especially familiar with contrasting instructional approaches used in schooling (based on researchers' own learning history as well as teaching roles).

Our aim is to articulate the multifaceted features of intent participation. To do so, we contrast it with *assembly-line instruction*, which is based on transmission of information from experts, outside the context of productive, purposive activity. This tradition of organizing learning is common in many U.S. schools and middle-class family interactions, perhaps related to historical changes connected with industrialization and child labor laws, which have contributed to compulsory extensive schooling and routine segregation of children from many mature settings.

Our contrast between intent participation and assembly-line instruction is not a dichotomy or a single dimension—there are many other traditions of organizing learning. The contrast is intended to bring features of each of these two systems into relief. The bulk of our paper focuses on examining contrasting features of the two traditions: the roles taken by more- and less-experienced people, the motivation and purposes of activities, the source of learning (observation in ongoing activity or lessons), forms of communication, and the nature of assessment.

First, however, we summarize research indicating that learning through observation and listening-in is pervasive in children's lives and is effective. Although we argue for cultural differences in emphasis on this kind of learning, observation and listening-in are important for all children.

PERVASIVE LEARNING THROUGH OBSERVATION AND LISTENING-IN

Young children are widely known to monitor events around them, learning through observation (Piaget 1962, Trevarthen 1977, Yando et al. 1978, Maccoby & Martin 1983, Uzgiris 1984, Bandura 1986, Meltzoff & Moore 1998, Tomasello 1999). For example, toddlers are often attracted to an object they observe an adult using and engage in similar actions with it (Eckerman et al. 1979, Hay et al. 1985); they evaluate the character of a stranger by observing the reactions of others (Feiring et al. 1983). Children's learning through observation goes far beyond mimicking what they see and hear.

Children's language development is a prime example of the power of learning through keen observation and listening (Akhtar et al. 2001). For example, by monitoring and emulating the language others use, very young children in a number of communities develop an understanding of what language use is appropriate, learning to speak to others with the appropriate respect forms and personal pronouns—usage that requires avoiding forms adults use to address them (Ochs 1988, Oshima-Takane et al. 1996).

Numerous studies in the behaviorist tradition have determined that observation can be very effective for learning (Abravanel & Ferguson 1998). For example, children can learn complex concepts (such as conservation, rules of games, categorization schemes, and rules of syntax) from modeled examples, without explanations (Zimmerman & Rosenthal 1974). Although rewards are sometimes influential (Bandura 1986), often children repeat an observed behavior privately over long periods of time without any reinforcing consequences, after having observed an unrewarded behavior on only a few occasions (Aronfreed 1969). For example, after exposure to models who were reading aloud, preschool children spontaneously picked up books and imitated the adult's reading (Haskett & Lenfestey 1974).

Robust findings indicate that people learn from observing models on television and other media. For example, children are able to learn new vocabulary words after exposure to television stories that contained those words (Huston & Wright 1998). Watching violent television in early childhood predicts later aggressive behavior (Huston & Wright 1998, Bushman & Anderson 2001). Similarly, even short-term exposure to video game violence is associated with higher aggression (Anderson & Bushman 2001). It is clear that highly effective learning takes place through observation of television and other media, as well as with companions.

PROCESSES OF LEARNING THROUGH KEEN OBSERVATION/LISTENING-IN

Some research has compared children's learning from observing with learning from hands-on participation. When U.S. children observed others performing an activity, there were no differences in recall compared with children who participated in the activity directly (Baker-Ward et al. 1990). Learning in European-descent New Zealand children who had participated directly in an event did not differ from learning in those who only observed, when children showed their learning by enacting the event (Murachver et al. 1996).

The distinction between being involved directly and "only" observing may be misleading, however. Observers' attention is likely to be quite different if they expect to be involved than if they observe incidentally. We focus explicitly on *observation as an aspect of participation.* Our term "intent participation" refers to keenly observing and listening in anticipation of or in the process of engaging in an endeavor. (We refer to both watching and listening-in as "observation," because each involves the sort of attentiveness and intentionality that we examine in this paper. What we call "listening-in" has been referred to by other authors as "eavesdropping," which suggests that the people listened to would object, or "overhearing," which suggests passive chancing to hear, rather than active listening.)

The process of learning through observation likely differs dramatically depending on whether the learner is attending to a demonstration designed for their learning, a model provided by persons engaged with them but not for the purpose of instruction, or a model provided by events that are directed to someone else or have no expected audience (which they observe as a third party). However, because there has been little research making such distinctions (Lewis & Feiring 1981), our review does not distinguish between them.

Third-party observation is especially understudied, although the research on language learning and learning from the media makes it clear that it is powerful. Third-party observation appears to be especially important in some cultural communities. For example, learning through eavesdropping was emphasized in an African-American community where toddlers participated in daily community events and spent hours sitting still and listening to adults converse (Ward 1971). Similarly, in Kaluli language learning in Polynesia, little speech is directed to toddlers, but they are surrounded by people talking to each other and commenting on the toddlers' activities within earshot (Schieffelin 1991). Inuit men of Arctic Quebec reported that as boys they learned to hunt from just watching the men and learned vocabulary and many other things by listening to stories that were not intended for them, staying as inconspicuous as possible (Crago 1992). Maori (New Zealand) adults reported that they were "sure that their parents and grandparents deliberately turned a blind eye to them hovering on the fringe of adult conversations as adolescents, allowing them to pick up information" (Metge 1984, p. 10).

In some cultural communities attentiveness may often be more limited when one is not immediately involved, compared with communities that emphasize learning through intent participation. For example, when European-American pairs of 9-year-olds were asked to teach a younger child to play a game, members of the pair often were distracted when not directly involved in the game, whereas Navajo children in the same task remained engaged, observing their partners even when they were not controlling the game moves (Ellis & Gauvain 1992).

We argue that an emphasis on learning through intent participation—though likely present in some settings in all communities—fits especially with the practices of cultural communities that routinely include children in the mature activities that are part of the community's daily life. This integration of children in mature community activities is a key feature of a dynamic constellation of cultural practices related to intent participation.

CULTURAL EMPHASIS
ON LEARNING VIA INTENT PARTICIPATION

Variation in extent of observation by children of different cultural communities has been found in several studies: Young rural Senegalese children observed other people more than twice as often as middle-class European-American children (Bloch 1989). Navajo students quietly observed teachers more than twice as often as Caucasian students in the same classroom (Guilmet 1979). U.S. Mexican-heritage children whose mothers had little experience with school were more likely to observe without requesting further information, compared with both U.S. Mexican-heritage and European-heritage children whose mothers had extensive experience with Western schooling (R. Mejía Arauz, B. Rogoff & R. Paradise, submitted).

Keen observation is often encouraged and taught, for example, in learning through watching in school and Suzuki instruction in Japan (Peak 1986). Likewise, Kenyatta (1953) noted that Gikuyu parents took care to teach children to be good observers. If Rotuman (Polynesian) children ask for instruction, "they are likely to be told to watch a skillful adult in action" (Howard 1970, p. 116).

In many communities, observation skills are emphasized and honed as people attend closely to ongoing events in order to learn the practices of their community. If children are integrated in a wide range of community settings, they are able to observe and listen in on the ongoing activities of their community as *legitimate peripheral participants* (Lave & Wenger 1991). In some communities, young children are included in almost all events. Infants who are routinely carried wherever their caregivers go can attend to their ongoing activities (Désalmand 1983, Whiting & Edwards 1988). For example, Aka parents (in Central Africa) hunt, butcher, and share game while holding their infants (Hewlett 1992).

Mayan toddlers in the Yucatan are permitted to go where they like, so they have opportunities to note the moment-to-moment happenings of their extended family (Gaskins & Lucy 1987, Gaskins 1999). In Kokwet (East Africa) 2- to 4-year-olds spent much of their time watching the activities of family members (Harkness & Super 1992). In a Guatemalan Mayan town, a foraging community in the Democratic Republic of Congo, and a tribal community in India, young children routinely had access to their families' economic activities—weaving, shopkeeping, gathering food, or working in fields or factories (Morelli et al. 2003, Morelli & Tronick 1992, Rogoff et al. 1993).

Children in many communities begin to participate in work and other mature activities from age 3 or 4 (Chamoux 1986, Martini & Kirkpatrick 1992). In a farming community in East Africa, 3- and 4-year-old children spent 25–35% of their time doing chores, whereas middle-class U.S. children of the same ages spent only 0–1% of their time doing chores and 4–5% of their time accompanying others in chores (Harkness & Super 1992).

By 5–7 years of age, children in many communities have substantial responsibilities for child, animal, and household care, participating in most adult activities (Rogoff et al. 1975, Paradise 1987, Whiting & Edwards 1988). When young children are included in the social as well as the economic life of their community, they are participants in the adult world, not "in the way" (Nsamenang 1992).

The opportunities of children in the United States and a number of other nations to participate in a wide range of mature community activities have decreased dramatically over the past century or so. These children are increasingly involved, instead, in specialized child-focused activities—especially schooling—designed to instruct them in skills to be employed in adulthood once they are allowed to be involved in mature activities.

HISTORICAL CHANGES SEGREGATING U.S. CHILDREN FROM MATURE ACTIVITIES

During the twentieth century U.S. children's opportunities to observe and participate in mature activities have been greatly curtailed. In the colonial period the workplace and the home were typically not separated, and young children participated skillfully in family work as well as community social events (Chudacoff 1989, Hareven 1989). In the early 1800s, about 70% of U.S. children shared farm work with their family (Demos & Demos 1969, Hernandez 1994). As industry replaced farming, opportunities declined for children to learn work skills at home.

Children in industrialized communities are now excluded from many mature settings, making it difficult for them to observe the full range of their community's activities (Hentoff 1976). They often stay in settings in which the adults' primary activities are to tend them and the home or school facility and not often to engage in the wider range of work and social activities of their community (Morelli et al. 2003, Whiting & Whiting 1975, Rogoff et al. 1993). [However, U.S. children whose parents work at home are often involved in their parents' work, in a progression from watching, to carrying out simple tasks, to giving regular assistance, to regular work (Beach 1988)].

Over the past century, efforts to protect U.S. children from economic exploitation, to extend their schooling, and to remove them from economic competition with adults have reduced their chances for learning firsthand about adult work and other mature activities (Bremner 1971; Chudacoff 1989). At the beginning of the 1900s child labor laws were introduced in the U.S. to protect children from exploitation in factories. (The primary workforce of the early factories was young children, often ranging in age from 4 to 10 years.)

As industrialization spread, schooling was made compulsory and the amount of time spent in school increased. This further limited U.S. children's opportunities to participate in the mature activities of their families and communities (Chudacoff 1989, Hernandez 1994). Schools began to serve a wider segment of the child population as a specialized child-focused setting that provided exercises to get children ready for later "real world" work, generally without direct contact with actual mature activity (Dewey 1916, Scribner & Cole 1973, Greenfield & Lave 1982, Désalmand 1983).

Limited opportunities to observe and participate in adult activities may restrict U.S. children's understanding of the mature roles of their community (Panel on Youth of the President's Science Advisory Committee 1974, Rogoff 1990). Now, instead of routinely helping adults, children are often involved in specialized child-focused exercises to assemble skills for later entry in mature activities from which they are often excluded in childhood. These specialized child-focused situations— especially schooling, but also pre-school lessons and child-focused conversation in families—often employ instructional practices and a concept of learning that were heavily influenced by the organization of factories, forming a cultural tradition that contrasts with intent participation.

SPECIALIZED CHILD-FOCUSED INSTRUCTION IN SCHOOL, ORGANIZED ON A FACTORY MODEL

In U.S. classrooms children's learning is often assumed to occur primarily by means of the teacher's provision of information, in what has been called a factory model (Callahan 1962). The factory-efficiency approach to learning and teaching is a tradition that became widespread around 1900. It was based on Taylor's time-and-motion studies of steelworkers for industrial efficiency and began to be applied to education to achieve bureaucratic efficiency in the face of enormous growth in student populations. (In 1890 only 4% of U.S. youth graduated from high school. By 1940 half of U.S. youth did.)

Teachers were cast as technical workers who were supposed to insert information into the children, who were seen as receptacles of knowledge or skill. The information itself was broken into bits to be delivered in a specified sequence, like an assembly line. According to the leading educational administration textbook in 1916, written by Stanford's Dean of Education,

> Our schools are, in a sense, factories in which the raw products (children) are to be shaped and fashioned into products to meet the various demands of life . . .. It is the business of the school to build its pupils according to the specifications laid down.

> (Cubberley 1916, p. 338)

In a factory model the teacher strives for efficiency in the delivery of knowledge and applies incentives (or punishments) to induce children to cooperate in the production process. The students cannot speak or help each other without permission from the teacher. The teacher "delivers" the curriculum using specialized forms of discourse, especially quizzing (in which the teacher asks questions to which she knows the answer and evaluates the student's response) to test the receipt of information. Often the teacher directs children's actions without explaining a rationale (see Mehan 1979, Cuban 1984, Gutierrez 1992, Mercer et al. 1988, Hargreaves 1989, Wells 1992, Minick 1993, Rogoff et al. 1996, Matusov & Rogoff 2002).

The idea that learning occurs as a product of "transmission" of knowledge remains a common conceptualization of learning, although U.S. school reform efforts continually attempt to move beyond the transmission model. Some schools do operate according to philosophies related to intent participation (although as specialized child-focused settings, they are distinguishable from family- and community-based traditions in which children are largely integrated in community activities). Nevertheless, analyses of pedagogy in the Third International Mathematics and Science Study noted that U.S. schools still retain a characteristic ideology based on the factory model (Stedman 1997).

Sometimes educational philosophies portray the learner rather than the teacher as the active agent, and then we find the metaphor of acquisition rather than transmission. In both approaches, however, learning is seen as accretion of information or skills, brought across a boundary from the external world to the mind of the learner (Rogoff 1990; Rogoff et al. 1996). This approach to learning has been questioned by sociocultural scholars. Several have proposed instead the idea that learning is a process of transformation of participation in ongoing cultural activities (Rogoff 1990, 2003; Lave & Wenger 1991).

Contrasting with transmission and acquisition models, in intent participation, learners engage collaboratively with others in the social world. Hence, there is no boundary dividing them into sides. There is also no separation of learning into an isolated assembly phase, with exercises for the immature, out of the context of the intended activity.

SPECIALIZED CHILD-FOCUSED INTERACTIONS IN FAMILIES WITH EXTENSIVE SCHOOLING

Within families in communities that emphasize learning in schools, out of the context of shared, productive community endeavors, some features of the factory model can be seen in interactions between young children and their parents. In middle-class European-American families—the primary participants in research on child development—parents often engage with young children in specialized child-focused activities that may help prepare the children for schooling and for their later admission into adult settings. These activities include child-focused conversations that often involve lessons and school-like discourse formats (Blount

1972, Harkness 1977, Heath 1983, Schieffelin & Ochs 1986, Haight 1991, Rogoff et al. 1993).

Middle-class conversational practices may help prepare children for the transmit-and-test formats of school (Beals & Tabors 1995). For example, middle-class caregivers in the United States and Turkey often provided their toddlers with language lessons in a quizzing format like that of factory-model schools. In contrast, Mayan and tribal Indian toddlers were seldom given school-like language quizzing games; they interacted reciprocally with their parents through communication surrounding joint action (Rogoff et al. 1993).

Caucasian families in Hawaii used lesson-style ways of speaking at mealtimes, facilitating success in schools that use the same formats and participation structures (Martini 1995, 1996). Parents asked children to talk about their day and helped them organize their "report" by recasting what children said in conventional forms. Parents protected a child's turn from interruptions, and children sometimes used school ways to get a turn, such as raising their hands.

A study of young children's everyday activities supported the idea that there would be more specialized, child-focused activities accompanying limited access to adult work for 3-year-olds in middle-class families than in two communities where older children routinely contribute to family work (Morelli et al. 2003). In two middle-class European-American communities, 3-year-olds had less opportunity to observe adult productive work and were more often involved in lessons and scholastic play than in an Efe foraging community in the Democratic Republic of Congo and a Mayan town in Guatemala.

In communities in which young children are involved in the mature activities of their family and community, it may be superfluous for adults to organize lessons and specialized conversations to prepare young children with the skills of schooling, to prepare them for the "real" world. Instead of doing exercises out of the context of the productive use of skills and information, young children's integration in family and community activities allows them to become increasingly deeply involved through their intent participation.

TWO MULTIFACETED TRADITIONS
FOR ORGANIZING PARTICIPATION FOR LEARNING

Contrasting processes are involved in *intent participation* as people engage together in a common endeavor and in *assembly-line instruction*, based on transmission of information from experts outside the context of purposeful, productive activity. Although the contrast we present has some resemblance to comparisons of formal and informal learning, we do not see the two traditions as dichotomous. Intent participation and assembly-line instruction are only two of many ways to organize learning. (Other ways would include such traditions as Socratic dialogue, inquiry learning, repetition/reciting, and constructivist discovery, which may share some features and differ in others.)

We see the two traditions as descriptions of *processes*, whereas the informal/formal dichotomy is often applied to *places*. Our distinction is not tied to locales or settings. Although the assembly-line approach may stem from factories and schools, it can occur in many other places, such as family settings. Likewise, intent participation can occur in innovative schools (Dewey 1916, Rogoff et al. 2001).

Any setting may mix these two traditions (and others). For example, in supporting early language development, some families use both assembly-line and intent participation traditions, by quizzing toddlers on vocabulary and by conversing with them to accomplish everyday endeavors together. In schools organized in assembly-line instruction, children often use intent participation to learn to engage in or resist the authority relations and the lesson format of the assembly-line structure itself.

Use of the two traditions is dynamic, not fixed and stable. Mothers from non-industrial communities who have experience in Western schooling more often interact with children in school-like ways—with greater use of praise, language lessons, and assignment of divided tasks—than mothers with little or no schooling (Rabain-Jamin 1989, Richman et al. 1992, Rogoff et al. 1993, Chavajay & Rogoff 2002). Likewise, middle-class parents with experience of helping in a collaborative school are more likely to engage with children in ways that fit with intent participation (Rogoff et al. 2001, Matusov & Rogoff 2002).

The processes of intent participation and assembly-line instruction are not necessarily tied to the type of activities or domain of knowledge (such as practical versus theoretical endeavors or concrete versus abstract information). The distinction is in the form of involvement, not in the subject. For example, either form of participation can be found in the learning of statistics. Learning can occur through intent participation as one learns how to use statistics to carry out ongoing research, or through assembly-line instruction in a class where the material is studied in isolation from its use, without any involvement in research. Likewise, intent participation was very effective for children's learning of both abstract spiritual knowledge and practical skills when Maori (New Zealand) community life was pervasive and strong (Metge 1984).

In the remainder of the article, we contrast different facets of each multifaceted tradition. The facets are not separate, isolated "variables" or a collection of dimensions, but rather are integrated to form each tradition (Rogoff & Angelillo 2002). In Figure 1, we represent the two traditions as multifaceted prisms to emphasize that the different facets describe related aspects of whole traditions. Each tradition undoubtedly has other important facets than the ones on which we focus in this chapter.

PARTICIPATION STRUCTURE

Intent participation involves a collaborative, horizontal participation structure with flexible, complementary roles. This contrasts with assembly-line instruction's hierarchical structure, organized with fixed roles in which someone manages others' participation, acting as a boss.

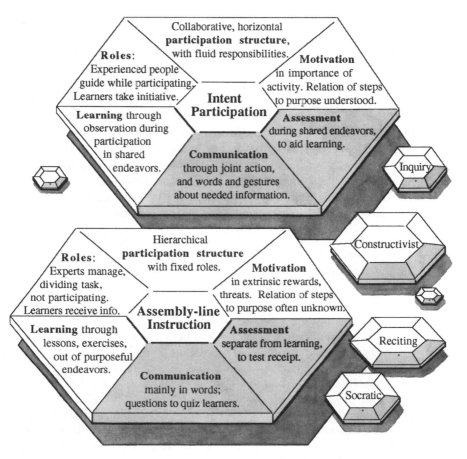

Figure 1   Multifaceted traditions for organizing learning (© B. Rogoff).

The participation structure of intent participation can be illustrated by the social organization of indigenous groups of the Americas, which often involves shared multiparty engagements among several group members, with mutual and fluid negotiation of responsibilities and consensus-based decision making (Lee 1976, Lamphere 1977, Philips 1983, Paradise 1987, Rogoff et al. 1993, Sindell 1997). Pelletier illustrated such horizontal organization of indigenous groups in his description of problem solving among Canadian Manitoulin people, in which everyone pitched in as needed, and no one was in charge.

> If somebody died in the community, nobody ever said: We should dig a grave. The grave was dug, the box was made, everything was set up . . . the one who baked pies baked pies. Everyone did something in that community, and if you tried to find out who organized it, you couldn't.

(Pelletier 1970, pp. 26–27)

Similarly, in traditional Mazahua Mexican leadership, elders protect and guide rather than give orders or dominate (Paradise 1987). Group integration involves each individual following his or her own path in a smoothly functioning coordination with others that is not preplanned or directed.

People may apply their experience with a particular participation structure in new settings. For example, in school, indigenous children often attempt to collaborate with classmates even when teachers discourage them from doing this (Philips 1983, Wolcott 1997). Likewise, some teachers with indigenous background employ the horizontal, collaborative structure of interaction that seems to be common in indigenous communities. For example, Alaskan Native teachers and aides often show a more even distribution of speech and turns at speaking among students and teachers than do European-descent teachers. In addition, they foster speaking as a group rather than calling on individuals in sequence, as in the following observation of an elementary classroom:

> The [European-descent] teacher had arranged the desks of her several students into a large rectangle, and had the students face her and look at her. Her lesson format [was to ask] a question, [wait] for the children to raise their hands to be nominated, and then [call on] a single student to answer . . . . Student responses were brief, in keeping with the focused information requested in the question.
>
> In another corner of the room, a Yup'ik bilingual aide [worked on a story with some students who] were not facing the bilingual aide directly. The aide allowed the students to speak 'out of turn'—that is, without being nominated by herself and without waiting for a student who already had the floor to finish speaking.
>
> [At one point, the teacher walked over.] She told the students to face the aide, straighten their chairs, and pay attention . . . . After the teacher had left and the aide resumed the story lesson, the students were reticent and spoke very little. [The aide later commented that the Yup'ik way of instructing is a conversation in which students] speak to each other freely, helping each other out on a subject . . . . They build on each other.
>
> (Lipka 1994, pp. 64–65)

Although some indigenous teachers working in Western schools organize their classrooms to support horizontal interactions, for others, their acculturation in mainstream pedagogy may result in directive, hierarchical organization (Barnhardt 1981; Erickson & Mohatt 1982; Lipka 1991, 1998).

Hierarchical organization experienced in schools may be extended into participation structures within family life. Indeed, it may replace more collaborative indigenous organization in the family when schooled indigenous individuals become parents. For example, Guatemalan Mayan mothers with 6–9 years of schooling were more likely than Mayan mothers with little or no schooling to attempt to enforce their own agendas with their toddlers—resembling European-American middle-class caregivers (Rogoff et al. 1993). Similarly, in constructing a puzzle with three related children, Mayan mothers with little schooling were usually involved in horizontal shared multiparty collaboration, whereas Mayan mothers with 12 or more years of schooling more commonly engaged in hierarchical division of labor, assigning dyads or individuals separate tasks (Chavajay & Rogoff 2002).

Children of schooled parents may learn the participation structure of assembly-line schooling at home and use it in their relations with others. Triads of U.S. Mexican-heritage children whose mothers had little Western schooling were likely to coordinate together smoothly as they folded paper figures. Triads whose mothers had extensive Western schooling—whether of European or Mexican heritage— were more likely to work solo or in dyads (R. Mejía-Arauz & B. Rogoff, in preparation). This work suggests the importance of considering experience with cultural institutions such as schooling as a key aspect of cultural heritage.

Consistent with the difference in whether the participation structure relies on collaboration or on control by a boss, intent participation and assembly-line learning involve very different roles for both more- and less-experienced people. We address this facet next.

ROLES OF MORE-EXPERIENCED PEOPLE AND OF LEARNERS

In the intent participation tradition, experienced people play a guiding role, facilitating learners' involvement and often participating alongside learners—indeed, often learning themselves. New learners in turn take initiative in learning and contributing to shared endeavors, sometimes offering leadership in the process.

In contrast, in assembly-line instruction, experienced people manage learners' behavior and communication. They subdivide the task, often directing but not actually participating in the activity at hand. They serve as experts, and the learners, in turn, are supposed to cooperate in receiving instruction and information and carrying out assignments.

U.S. classrooms are often organized by teachers transmitting information and managing the students in exercises (Stedman 1997). This hierarchical organization of learning is exemplified by Philips' (1983) observations of a "switchboard participant structure" in which teachers decide which children contribute to class activities, when, and for how long, taking a speaking turn between each child's turn. Children address only the teacher, seldom taking other children's ideas into account in building their own contributions. Often the children are limited to responding briefly to teachers' known-answer quizzing, in the Initiation-Reply-Evaluation format observed in many classrooms (Mehan 1979, Cazden 1988, Hargreaves 1989, McCollum 1989, LaTorra & Renne 2001).

In contrast, Japanese elementary school classrooms often involve conversations in which children build on each other's ideas (Rogoff & Toma 1997, Linn et al. 2000). Indeed, Japanese first-graders take on responsibility, without direct management by an adult, for organizing the class to begin lessons, breaking into small groups to carry out and discuss science experiments, and running class meetings

(Lewis 1995). The teacher encourages the children to solve problems together and reflect on the process. Similarly, children take responsibility for classroom management without direct adult management in several indigenous and rural schools in Mexico (Paradise 1994, Mercado 2001, Bryan & McLaughlin 2002).

Within middle-class families, adults often structure young children's learning by managing children's attention, motivation, and involvement in ways that resemble lessons. For example, middle-class parents in the United States and Turkey were more likely to try to engage toddlers in the parents' own agenda (which often involved a lesson) by means of mock excitement and praise and even by overruling the toddler's own expressed wishes, than were Guatemalan Mayan and rural Indian parents (Rogoff et al. 1993). In another study, U.S. mothers took responsibility for making their toddlers learn; by arousing interest and shaping each step of the toddler's behavior, whereas Gusii (Kenyan) mothers were less managerial; they often modeled the whole performance and appeared to expect the toddler to be able to take responsibility for completing the task as shown (Dixon et al. 1984).

In teaching/learning tasks, Mazahua (indigenous Mexican) parents used a participation structure in which children were treated as responsible contributors to a shared endeavor, coordinating with their parents and sometimes leading the effort (de Haan 2001; see also Chamoux 1986). Children were expected to learn by watching the parent's actions while the children helped; if they did not observe, parents reminded them of their responsibility to watch. They were expected to take on more responsibility as the joint activity proceeded, but were not forced to. In contrast, when Mazahua children worked individually with non-Mazahua teachers, the teacher held the initiative and expected the child individually to perform the task under the teacher's direction. Children's suggestions were evaluated by the teachers as a test of the children's knowledge, not treated as a contribution to a task that needed to be done.

Efforts to transform the structure of formal schooling have encountered challenges related to adults' difficulties in learning to engage in radically different participation structures. For example, in a collaborative school in the United States, parent volunteers often took several years to move beyond the issues of control that characterized their own assembly-line schooling, to develop a collaborative approach with the children (Rogoff et al. 2001, Matusov & Rogoff 2002). Being accustomed to the transmission model, they often found it especially challenging to work with student interest and initiative in shared endeavors.

MOTIVATION AND PURPOSE

In the tradition of intent participation, motivation is generally inherent in the obvious importance and interest of the activity. The purpose of the activity is understood, as is the relation of each step to the overall process. For example, a collaborative U.S. class learned about measurement by designing a habitat for animals when they became concerned about the impact on birds of a loss of trees in the neighborhood. As they designed birdhouses for the habitat, the children could see the purpose of measuring—it served a goal that made sense and was of interest to them (Goodman et al. 2001).

In contrast, in assembly-line instruction the purpose of the activity is often not accessible to the students, and the relation of each step to the overall process often not understood. Assembly-line instruction of disconnected skills and information was observed in classroom research in a report of the Third International Mathematics and Science Study:

> In the U.S., education is based on an "'incremental' assembly line philosophy" that "encourages breaking complex learning down into simpler learning tasks" [quoting Jakwerth 1996]. An ideological faith in mass production, accompanied by a behaviorist push for programmed instruction and objectives, has splintered the U.S. curriculum into many small topical building blocks.
>
> (Stedman 1997, p. 10)

In his classic study of informal education, Fortes pointed out that in schools, knowledge is often of unknown utility. He contrasted this with "real situations" in which the purpose of the activity is usually inherent in the situations in which people learn, and motivation derives from accomplishing real goals:

> A child repeating the multiplication table is participating in the practical activity appropriate to and defined by the school; but measured by the total social reality it is a factitious activity, a training situation constructed for that purpose. The Tallensi [of Ghana] do not make systematic use of training situations. They teach through real situations which children are drawn to participate in because it is expected that they are capable and desirous of mastering the necessary skills.
>
> (Fortes 1970 (1938), pp. 37–38)

In intent participation, the role of an aspect of the activity is understood in the context of the overall process. For example, Vai apprentice tailors have the opportunity to observe the whole process of making a piece of clothing while they contribute to aspects they can manage (Lave & Wenger 1991). Similarly, the children of French marsh-sweepers help process salt by taking responsibility for steps that they can manage, coordinating with their parents in the overall process (Delbos & Jorion 1984). Likewise, in Maori (New Zealand) communities, learners are incorporated into existing working groups with a range of expertise. They are initially given supporting tasks and work close enough to observe the more advanced participants; they move to more complex aspects of the activity as they learn (Metge 1984). This contrasts with the assembly-line approach of breaking a process down into isolated steps and having the learners practice the steps with little or no chance to see how the steps fit together or the overall purpose of the activity.

With the relatively arbitrary nature of information in assembly-line instruction, motivation for learners' involvement is often induced through praise, grades, rewards and threats that are unrelated to the activity. Praising desired behavior may seem second-nature among highly schooled people; however, in some communities it is rare (Metge 1984, Rogoff et al. 1993, Whiting 1996). Indeed, the U.S. school practice of promoting individual competition and recognition through public praise makes some students uncomfortable when it is at odds with their community ethic of collaboration in which individuals contribute their strengths to the group (Deyhle & Swisher 1997). Competitive teacher approval provides both reward and threat to induce children's compliance with assembly-line instruction.

A central topic in teacher training and student-teaching is for new teachers to develop methods to motivate behavioral control of the classroom. They are taught management techniques with rules for the students and consequences for infractions and are encouraged to be strict so the children know they "mean business," so the children will do their part in the participation structure of assembly-line learning (Ball 1980, Seaman 2001).

In the intent participation tradition, children who participate in mature activities see their efforts contribute to the family's food or cash supply. They may not need external markers of the value or correctness of what they do; success or failure of ongoing work is obvious (Whiting & Edwards 1988, Jordan 1989). Adult approval may be communicated by giving more difficult work with less supervision (Whiting & Edwards 1988). However, failure by older children to pay attention or to do a job carefully may result in scoldings or punishment in addition to the direct consequences of failure (Modiano 1973, Metge 1984).

In valued activities in which children make genuine contributions, they may often participate with eagerness, rather than with the resistance that is common in assembly-line schools (Lee 1959, Delbos & Jorion 1984, Lipka 1998, Paradise 1998, de Haan 1999, Gaskins 1999). An indigenous Mexican Mazahua mother responded to an interviewer's question about what happens if a child does not want to learn: "I have never seen anybody having trouble to show a child to get to work. . . . They themselves have interest in doing the things they have to do" (de Haan 1996, p. 8). An example of this kind of interest is provided by a two-year-old helping dig a maize field with her mother, observing and eagerly carrying out a part of the task that aids her mother's efforts.

> The girl starts to remove soil from the bunches of grass her mother has just removed, making the exact same movement she has observed her mother making. Her mother stops digging and watches her. When the mother wants to continue, the girl tells her to stop as she wants to pick up a bunch of grass and remove the soil from it just where the mother wants to start digging. The mother lets her do this and waits. . . . [Soon] the girl has taken over a task from the mother so that the mother can continue digging without having to remove the grass. They work together for about five minutes. . . . When the girl sees

her mother removing the soil from the grass (while the girl was chatting) the girl protests and demands her task back.

(de Haan 1999, pp. 77–78)

In such a tradition for learning, even very young children participate productively in their parents' work activities, frequently on their own initiative, out of recognition of the importance to the family of what they are doing. The attraction of the activity itself provides a self-evident inherent motivation that is supported by parental expectations along with admonitions and direct indications as to what is to be done (Paradise 1985, de Haan 1999, Gaskins 1999). This implies autonomy and keen observation, along with development of skills in organizing and taking responsibility with initiative—which are not encouraged (and are even constrained) in assembly-line instruction.

SOURCES OF LEARNING: OBSERVATION IN ONGOING ACTIVITY OR RECEIVING LESSONS

In intent participation, learning is based on participation in ongoing or anticipated activities, with keen observation and listening. Learners observe to figure out processes they expect to engage in. They seek understanding far beyond that needed for simple mimicry; their roles in shared endeavors often involve coordinating with others, not simple imitation (Delbos & Jorion 1984). Observation is often, but not necessarily, accompanied by pointers from more experienced companions and conversation embedded in the ongoing activity.

Keen attention was apparent in a footloom factory in Guatemala, where novice adults observed a skilled weaver for a period of weeks, asking no questions and receiving no explanations (Nash 1967). The novice might fetch things for the weaver, but did not begin to weave for weeks, until the novice felt competent and began weaving with skill. Similarly,

Navajos do not teach their children, but they incorporate them in every life task, so that children learn themselves, by keen observation. Mothers do not teach their daughters to weave, but one day a girl may say, 'I am ready. Let me weave.'

(Collier 1988, p. 262)

Research in a number of indigenous communities has noted intense observation by young children (Deyhle & Swisher 1997). Guatemalan Mayan toddlers observed their mothers operating novel objects with an intensity that could be seen in the tension in their fingers as they kept themselves from interrupting the action, in order to gain information by observing (B. Rogoff, unpublished data). Among Tseltal and Mazahua people in Mexico, young children and even infants can often be seen holding themselves stock-still while intently watching a person or activity, almost without blinking, completely absorbed (Maurer 1977, Paradise 1987).

Parents in some indigenous American communities structure their children's involvement, beginning with simple aspects of an activity once children show interest and providing well-placed suggestions accompanying their mutual involvement in shared endeavors (Modiano 1973, Ruddle & Chesterfield 1978, de Haan 1999). The structuring of activities in increasingly complex steps is done in the context of being able to see the overall activity in which the steps fit.

Similarly, Kaluli (New Guinea) mothers encourage toddlers to watch events and tell them "Do like that," to indicate key aspects of a task (Schieffelin 1991). Young girls intently observe and facilitate their mothers' work, bringing fire tongs or roasting bananas on the fire. Mothers gradually add new tasks, and daughters work responsibly by age 3–5 years (such as making a small fire to cook themselves a little food).

In communities in which children engage regularly with adults in mature activities, they may seldom be involved in specialized child-focused instruction (Morelli et al. 2003; Rogoff 1990, 2003). For example, Guatemalan Mayan 9-year-olds primarily interacted with adults in the context of joint involvement in household or agricultural work. Their interactions seldom involved explicit instruction—out of 1708 observations, native observers only identified 6 occasions as explicitly involving teaching; shared endeavors provided ample opportunities to learn (Rogoff 1981; see also Gaskins 1999).

Inuit children in the Arctic are expected to take initiative to observe and seek solutions (Briggs 1991). Keen observation requires skill in managing attention, as reflected in this account of a middle-class White child's experience in an Inuit community:

> One day when my eight-year-old daughter was watching some girls her age play a game in the house where we were staying, she turned to the mother who spoke English and said:
> Anna: How do I play this game? Tell me what to do. What are the rules?
> Inuk Mother: (gently) Watch them and you'll see how it goes.
> Anna: I don't know how to learn by watching, can't you tell me?
> Inuk Mother: You'll be able to know by watching.
>
> (Crago 1988, p. 211)

Children who are used to the heavily explanatory, lesson-based approach of schooling may depend more on being told how to do things, even in a situation in which the needed information is available through observation of ongoing events. In the context of a demonstration by an adult, European-heritage and Mexican-heritage children whose mothers had extensive Western schooling often pressed for further information beyond that provided in the demonstration (R. Mejía Arauz, B. Rogoff & R. Paradise, submitted). Indeed, the adult demonstrator reported that it felt like some of the children seemed to try to force her to explain what they were supposed to do (R. Paradise, B. Rogoff & R. Mejía Arauz, in preparation). In contrast, Mexican-heritage children whose mothers had basic schooling more often observed without pressing for more information.

Similarly, Mazahua 9-year-olds showed an ability to notice and infer from their parent's actions what was going to happen or when they needed to dedicate attention. They knew when they could afford to do something else momentarily and when they needed to focus on the parent's activity. "When the parent started a new aspect of the task they would immediately come closer or pay more attention to make sure they would not miss anything" (de Haan 1999, p. 143).

If children are responsible for learning by observing, alertness to multiple ongoing events is crucial. Timesharing of attention allows them to notice nearby events that may be of interest. Guatemalan Mayan 12- to 24-month-olds often skillfully attended to several events simultaneously, with each line of attention maintained without interruption (Rogoff et al. 1993, Chavajay & Rogoff 1999). For example, they often worked an object with their mother and monitored other conversations, maintaining an involvement with the flow of events. Mayan mothers usually attended simultaneously to several events, often articulately communicating with their toddler through gestures, gaze, touch, posture, and timing, while fluently conversing with adults. In contrast, middle-class European-American toddlers and mothers usually attended to one event at a time, either by alternating attention quickly between two events or by focusing only on one. Similar contrasts in the use of simultaneous attention have also been found with U.S. Mexican-heritage and U.S. European-heritage children (M. Correa-Chávez, B. Rogoff & R. Mejía Arauz, in preparation).

Middle-class U.S. parents may scold their children for attending broadly, "Pay attention to what you're doing!" They seem to regard attending broadly as a distraction. However, simultaneous attention to several sources of information is mindful (M. Correa-Chávez, B. Rogoff & R. Mejía Arauz, in preparation). Indeed, Guatemalan Mayan parents expect their children to attend broadly to notice key ongoing events (Chavajay 1993). They urge children to observe ongoing events, and if they give an explanation it is after requesting that the child first attentively observe; if the child does not observe, a parent is likely to scold, "Have you no eyes?" The parents' expectation is that the children take the initiative to observe, not wait for a lesson.

FORMS OF COMMUNICATION

Words are an important aspect of communication in learning by intent participation, accompanying other forms of communication and joint action. However, words have different functions than in assembly-line instruction, where they are used extensively to describe information out of the context of shared endeavors, and known-answer questions are employed to quiz learners.

Participation in lesson formats begins in the first years of life for many children in school-focused communities. For example, middle-class mothers from the United States and Turkey provided toddlers with language lessons by giving running commentary describing events, where their words served no practical function (Rogoff et al. 1993). They asked test questions that requested information they already knew, as did this British mother, commenting on a picture in a book to her 4-year-old:

> And that's a knight. It's a man they called a knight, that used to fight, with a sword. And what's all this he's got on his body? [No answer] He's got armour on.
>
> (Tizard & Hughes 1984, p. 40)

Young Inuit mothers who had attended school were more likely than older Inuit mothers to involve their children in such question-answer routines and labeling of objects, and expected these to be useful in preparing children for school (Crago et al. 1993).

In contrast, communication in intent participation employs words to provide or discuss needed information during (or anticipating) shared endeavors, and questions seek information that is not already known or explore ideas. Adult-child conversation in many communities occurs primarily for the sake of sharing needed information in the context of ongoing activities, rather than serving as lessons to teach children about talk or to provide disconnected bits of knowledge (Ward 1971, Blount 1972, Heath 1983, Ochs & Schieffelin 1984, Crago et al. 1993).

In intent participation, words team with information available from observing ongoing processes, along with articulate nonverbal communication embedded in accomplishing shared endeavors. Explanations are given in the context of the process being learned (Cazden & John 1971, John-Steiner 1984, Kojima 1986). For example, a British 4-year-old commented on something unfamiliar while watching her mother weed, eliciting an explanation:

> Child: There's a dead onion.
> Mother: No, they're not dead onions, they're bulbs.
> Child: Are they dead?
> Mother: No, they'll come up again this year. They store all the food from the old leaves, they all rot down. It stores food, and the next year it comes up again.
>
> (Tizard & Hughes 1984, p. 39)

In addition to comments and explanations embedded in ongoing shared activity, narratives and discussion of hypothetical or potential situations may be extremely important as part of the children's learning in the tradition of intent participation (e.g., Heath 1998).

Learning about important activities—including talk—by watching or listening in as a third party is a preferred way to learn in some communities. For example, in an Athabascan (native Northern Canadian) community,

> the ideal learning situation for a child or young person is to be able to hear the stories of elders . . . speaking to each other as narrator and audience with the child in a third, observational role . . . . Because the child is not directly

required to respond to the narratives, his own autonomy is respected at a time in his life when it is likely to be highly vulnerable. While this three-party narrative situation may not always obtain, those who are able to learn in this way are regarded as very fortunate.

(Scollon & Scollon 1981, pp. 120–21)

The contrast is not whether or not words are used, but the embeddedness or isolation of the words from the endeavors being referred to. In intent participation, talk is used *in the service* of engaging in the activity, augmenting and guiding experiential and observational learning; in an assembly-line lesson, talk is *substituted* for involvement.

ROLE OF ASSESSMENT

Assessment of learning plays a very different role in the two traditions. The difference is crucial in efforts to transform schools and to evaluate formal and informal educational institutions (Shepard 2000). Educational innovations designed to promote participatory learning practices tend to be thwarted and pushed back toward the factory model as a result of the structure of assessments used for accountability. The participation structure of most assessments used for accountability fits with that of assembly-line instruction; hence, most assessment practices inadvertently (or sometimes intentionally) measure the extent to which people have learned to participate in the assembly-line tradition.

Elwood Cubberley, Dean of Education at Stanford, presented the assembly-line model of assessment in his leading educational administration textbook in 1916:

> Every manufacturing establishment that turns out a standard product or series of products of any kind maintains a force of efficiency experts to study methods of procedure and to measure and test the output of its works. . . . [Building pupils demands] continuous measurement of production to see if it is according to specifications [and] the elimination of waste in manufacture." (p. 338)

In assembly-line instruction, assessment has the purpose of inspecting receipt and retention of transmitted information. It focuses on the products that learners are to produce, or on the learners *as* products. Whether a learner spontaneously engages in the activity in question is seldom assessed—in large part because motivation is managed by other people, making both assessment and development of voluntary involvement difficult.

In contrast, in intent participation, assessment includes children's interest and voluntary willingness to be involved as important aspects of learning (Metge 1984, de Haan 1996, Nagai 2001, Rogoff et al. 2001). In many communities that emphasize intent participation, adults expect children to watch and begin to take initiative. If they do not develop interest in pitching in spontaneously, this may be evaluated as problematic. For example, a Mazahua father described his 7-year-old son as lacking interest and the strength to decide for himself to do what needs to be done. The father reported that even when his son sees that he is working and something is missing, his son does not assist without being yelled at. The father criticized, "I am almost forcing him to help me to do it" (de Haan 1999, p. 100). The father contrasted this with the attitude of his 3-year-old son, whom he considered very attentive, reporting that he watches what the parents do and follows suit, perfectly, without needing explanation.

In intent participation, assessment occurs integrally throughout shared endeavors to further learning—not just as an "outcome." The goal is to help children to learn the important skills and ways of their communities. In engaging in a shared endeavor, experienced people, as well as novices themselves, notice the state of understanding and the type of help the novices need. This assessment allows them to determine what to do to support novices' involvement, whether this is in order to advance the novices' learning or to advance the activity itself.

In contrast, assembly-line assessment occurs separately from the learning process, with the purpose of sorting out some people and certifying others for continued application of resources. A goal of many forms of schooling, as bureaucracies, is to select those students who will be allowed to proceed to further opportunities, by ensuring that others fail. Schools, after all, would not be fulfilling their functions of supporting social differentiation and the division of labor if all children were equally successful.

As a tool for sorting, grading on a (normal) curve was introduced by Max Meyer in 1908 in the prestigious journal *Science*, proposing that the top 3% be ranked excellent, next 22% labeled superior, middle 50% judged medium, next 22% inferior, and bottom 3% failing. It caught on a few years later during the era of "scientific efficiency" in which education experts and administrators conscientiously applied industrial models for factory production to schools.

In some settings, the inspection, sorting, accountability, and certification purposes seem to outweigh learning goals, with burgeoning tests monopolizing class time and teachers' instruction. As a Canadian politician pointed out, the push for extensive testing is like telling farmers who are concerned about the growth of their cattle; "weigh the cow, weigh the cow, weigh the cow."

When considering the relative value of different participation structures for organizing learning, it is crucial to consider their varying purposes. In the assembly-line instructional tradition, the learning of some is fostered while the rejection of others as learners is also sought, in line with bureaucratic needs for efficiently sorting individuals and life opportunities. In contrast, in intent participation within families and communities worldwide, the aim may be (although it is not invariably) to support the learning of all members of the community, and learning is organized in ways that allow this aim to be accomplished. Consider the general success and processes of early language learning within families everywhere and of widespread mathematical understanding in Japanese elementary schools, organized in ways fitting the intent participation tradition.

In closing, we return to our point that although people everywhere learn through observation, many communities especially emphasize keen observation in support of participation in ongoing mature activities. We have contrasted two distinct multifaceted traditions for organizing learning, in order to describe and articulate the integrated processes of learning through intent participation. We hope this article encourages heightened recognition and research attention to the process of learning through intent participation, both in communities that use it extensively and in communities where it may currently be overshadowed by other forms of fostering learning.

ACKNOWLEDGMENTS

We are grateful for the comments and challenging discussion of Araceli Valle, Pablo Chavajay, Behnosh Najafi, Fred Erickson, Sally Duensing, Marty Chemers, Trish Stoddart, David Harrington, Kathryn Player, and Rachel Levin. Karrie André provided essential assistance with references. Some of the research reported in this paper was supported by grants from the Spencer Foundation and the National Institutes of Health, and by funding from the UCSC Foundation endowed chair held by the first author.

The *Annual Review of Psychology* is online at http://psych.annualreviews.org

LITERATURE CITED

Abravanel E, Ferguson SA. 1998. Observational learning and the use of retrieval information during the second and third years. *J. Genet. Psychol.* 159(4):455–76

Akhtar N, Jipson J, Callanan MA. 2001. Learning words through overhearing. *Child Dev.* 72(2):416–30

Anderson CA, Bushman BJ. 2001. Effects of violent video games on aggressive behavior, aggressive cognition, aggressive affect, physiological arousal, and prosocial behavior: a meta-analytic review of the scientific literature. *Psychol. Sci.* 12(5):353–59

Aronfreed J. 1969. The concept of internalization. In *Handbook of Socialization: Theory and Research*, ed. DA Goslin, pp. 263–323. Chicago: Rand McNally

Baker-Ward L, Hess TM, Flannagan DA. 1990. The effects of involvement on children's memory for events. *Cogn. Dev.* 5:55–69

Ball SJ. 1980. Initial encounters in the class-room and the process of establishment. In *Pupil Strategies: Explorations in the Sociology of the School,* ed. P Woods, pp. 143–61. London: Croom Helm

Bandura A. 1986. *Social Foundations of Thought and Action: A Social Cognitive Theory.* Englewood Cliffs, NJ: Prentice Hall

Barnhardt C. 1981. Tuning-in: Athabaskan teachers and Athabaskan students. See Spindler 1981, pp. 132–74

Beach BA. 1988. Children at work: the home workplace. *Early Child. Res. Q.* 3:209–21

Beals DE, Tabors PO. 1995. Arboretum, bureaucratic and carbohydrate: preschoolers' exposure to rare vocabulary at home. *First Lang.* 15:57–76

Bloch MN. 1989. Young boys' and girls' play at home and in the community. In *The Ecological Context of Children's Play*, ed. MN Bloch, AD Pellegrini, pp. 120–54. Norwood, NJ: Ablex

Blount BG. 1972. Parental speech and language

acquisition: some Luo and Samoan examples. *Anthropol. Linguist.* 14:119–30

Bremner RH, ed. 1970/1971. *Children and Youth in America. A Documentary History.* Vol. I-II, *1600–1932.* Cambridge, MA: Harvard Univ. Press

Briggs JL. 1991. Expecting the unexpected: Canadian Inuit training for an experimental lifestyle. *Ethos* 19:259–87

Bryan LA, McLaughlin HJ. 2002. *A portrait of autonomy and responsibility in a rural Mexican Escuela Unitaria.* Presented at Meet. Am. Educ. Res. Assoc., New Orleans

Bushman BJ, Anderson CA. 2001. Media violence and the American public: scientific facts versus media misinformation. *Am. Psychol.* 56(6–7):477–89

Callahan RE. 1962. *Education and the Cult of Efficiency.* Chicago: Univ. Chicago Press

Cazden CB. 1988. *Classroom Discourse.* Portsmouth, NH: Heinemann

Cazden CB, John VP. 1971. Learning in American Indian children. In *Anthropological Perspectives on Education*, ed. ML Wax, S Diamond, FO Gearing, pp. 252–72. New York: Basic Books

Chamoux M-N. 1986. Aprrendre autrement: aspects des pédagogies dites informelles chez les Indiéns du Mexique. In *Demain l'artisanat?*, ed. P Rossel, pp. 211–77. Paris: Presses Univ. France

Chavajay P. 1993. Independent analyses of cultural variations and similarities in San Pedro and Salt Lake (Afterword to Rogoff et al. Guided participation in cultural activity by toddlers and caregivers). *Monogr. Soc. Res. Child Dev.* 58(7): Ser. No. 236

Chavajay P, Rogoff B. 1999. Cultural variation in management of attention by children and their caregivers. *Dev. Psychol.* 35:1079–90

Chavajay P, Rogoff B. 2002. Schooling and traditional collaborative social organization of problem solving by Mayan mothers and children. *Dev. Psychol.* 38(1):55–66

Chudacoff HP. 1989. *How Old Are You? Age Consciousness in American Culture.* Princeton, NJ: Princeton Univ. Press

Collier J Jr. 1988. Survival at Rough Rock: a historical overview of Rough Rock Demonstration School. *Anthropol. Educ. Q.* 19:253–69

Crago MB. 1988. *Cultural context in the communicative interaction of young Inuit children.* Doctoral diss., McGill Univ., Montreal

Crago MB. 1992. Communicative interaction and second language acquisition: an Inuit example. *TESOL Q.* 26:487–505

Crago MB, Annahatak B, Ningiuruvik L. 1993. Changing patterns of language socialization in Inuit homes. *Anthropol. Educ. Q.* 24:205–23

Cuban L. 1984. *How Teachers Taught: Constancy and Change in American Classrooms 1890–1980.* New York: Longman

Cubberley EP. 1916. *Public School Administration.* New York: Houghton Mifflin

de Haan M. 1996. *Instruction and cultural meaning; A study of teaching practices of a Native American group, the Mazahuas.* Presented at Conf. Soc. Cult. Res., Geneva

de Haan M. 1999. *Learning as Cultural Practice: How Children Learn in a Mexican Mazahua Community.* Amsterdam: Thela Thesis

de Haan M. 2001. Intersubjectivity in models of learning and teaching: Reflections from a study of teaching and learning in a Mexican Mazahua community. In *The Theory and Practice of Cultural-Historical Psychology*, ed. S Chaiklin, pp. 174–99. Aarhus, Denmark: Aarhus Univ. Press

Delbos G, Jorion P. 1984. *La Transmission des Saviors.* Paris: Masion des Sciences de l'Homme

Demos J, Demos V. 1969. Adolescence in historical perspective. *J. Marriage Fam.* 31: 632–38

Désalmand P. 1983. *Histoire de l'Education en Côte d'Ivoire (History of Education in Ivory Coast). Abidjan, Côte d'Ivoire: CEDA.* Paris: Hatier/Harmattan

Dewey J. 1916. *Democracy and Education.* New York: Macmillan

Deyhle D, Swisher K. 1997. Research in American Indian and Alaska Native education:

from assimilation to self-determination. *Rev. Res. Educ.* 22:113–94

Dixon SD, LeVine RA, Richman A, Brazelton TB. 1984. Mother-child interaction around a teaching task: an African-American comparison. *Child Dev.* 55:1252–64

Eckerman CO, Whatley JL, McGhee LJ. 1979. Approaching and contacting the object another manipulates: a social skill of the one-year-old. *Dev. Psychol.* 15:585–93

Ellis S, Gauvain M. 1992. Social and cultural influences on children's collaborative interactions. In *Children's Development within Social Context*, ed. LT Winegar, J Valsiner, vol. 2, pp. 155–80. Hillsdale, NJ: Erlbaum

Erickson F, Mohatt G. 1982. Cultural organization of participation structures in two classrooms of Indian students. See Spindler 1981, pp. 132–74

Feiring C, Lewis M, Starr MD. 1983. *Indirect effects and infants' reaction to strangers.* Presented at Meet. Soc. Res. Child Dev., Detroit

Fortes M. 1970 (1938). Social and psychological aspects of education in Taleland. In *From Child to Adult*, ed. J Middleton. New York: Natl. Hist. Press

Gaskins S. 1999. Children's daily lives in a Mayan village. In *Children's Engagement in the World*, ed. A Göncü, pp. 25–81. Cambridge: Cambridge Univ. Press

Gaskins S, Lucy JA. 1987. *The role of children in the production of adult culture: a Yucatec case.* Presented at Meet. Am. Ethnol. Soc., San Antonio, TX

Goodman Turkanis C, Bartlett L, Rogoff B. 2001. Never-ending learning. See Rogoff et al. 2001, pp. 225–44

Greenfield PM, Lave J. 1982. Cognitive aspects of informal education. In *Cultural Perspectives on Child Development*, ed. D Wagner, H Stevenson, pp. 181–207. San Francisco: Freeman

Guilmet GM. 1979. Navajo and Caucasian children's verbal and nonverbal-visual behavior in the urban classroom. *Anthropol. Educ. Q.* 9:196–215

Gutierrez KD. 1992. A comparison of instructional contexts in writing process classrooms with Latino children. *Educ. Urb. Soc.* 24:244–62

Haight W. 1991. *Belief systems that frame and inform parental participation in their children's pretend play.* Presented at Meet. Soc. Res. Child Dev., Seattle

Hareven TK. 1989. Historical changes in children's networks in the family and community. In *Children's Social Networks and Social Supports*, ed. D Belle, pp. 15–36. New York: Wiley

Hargreaves A. 1989. *Curriculum and Assessment Reform.* Toronto: OISE Press

Harkness S. 1977. Aspects of social environment and first language acquisition in rural Africa. In *Talking to Children: Language Input and Acquisition*, ed. C Ferguson, C Snow, pp. 309–16. New York: Cambridge Univ. Press

Harkness S, Super CM. 1992. Parental ethnotheories in action. In *Parental Belief Systems*, ed. IE Sigel, AV McGillicuddy-DeLisi, JJ Goodnow, pp. 373–91. Hillsdale, NJ: Erlbaum

Haskett GJ, Lenfestey W. 1974. Reading-related behavior in an open classroom: effects of novelty and modeling on preschoolers. *J. Appl. Behav. Anal.* 7:233–41

Hay DF, Murray P, Cecire S, Nash A. 1985. Social learning of social behavior in early life. *Child Dev.* 56:43–57

Heath SB. 1983. *Ways with Words: Language, Life, and Work in Communities and Classrooms.* Cambridge: Cambridge Univ. Press

Heath SB. 1998. Working through language. In *Kids Talk: Strategic Language Use in Later Childhood*, ed. SM Hoyle, C Temple Adger, pp. 217–40. Oxford: Oxford Univ. Press

Hentoff N. 1976. How does one learn to be an adult? In *Human Development in Today's World*, ed. S White. Boston: Little, Brown & Co.

Hernandez DJ. 1994. Children's changing access to resources: a historical perspective. *Soc. Res. Child Dev. Soc. Policy Rep.* 8:1–23

Hewlett BS, ed. 1992. *Father-Child Relations.* New York: Aldine de Gruyter

Howard A. 1970. *Learning to be Rotuman.* New York: Teachers College Press

Huston AC, Wright JC. 1998. Mass media and children's development. In *The Handbook of Child Psychology*, ed. N Damon, 4:999–1058. New York: Wiley. 5th ed.

John-Steiner V. 1984. Learning styles among Pueblo children. *Q. Newsl. Lab. Comp. Hum. Cogn.* 6:57–62

Jordan B. 1989. Cosmopolitical obstetrics: some insights from the training of traditional midwives. *Soc. Sci. Med.* 28:925–44

Kenyatta J. 1953. *Facing Mount Kenya: The Tribal Life of the Gikuyu.* London: Secker & Warburg

Kojima H. 1986. Child rearing concepts as a belief-value system of the society and the individual. In *Child Development and Education in Japan*, ed. H Stevenson, H Azuma, K Hakuta, pp. 39–54. New York: Freeman

Lamphere L. 1977. *To Run After Them: Cultural and Social Bases of Cooperation in a Navajo Community.* Tucson: Univ. Ariz. Press

LaTorra R, Renne CG. 2001. *Waiting to ask: changing discourse patterns in a community college ESL classroom.* Presented at Meet. Am. Educ. Res. Assoc., Seattle

Lave J, Wenger E. 1991. *Situated Learning: Legitimate Peripheral Participation.* Cambridge: Cambridge Univ. Press

Lee D. 1959. The joy of work as participation. In *Freedom and Culture*, ed. D Lee, pp. 27–38. Prospect Heights, IL: Waveland

Lee D. 1976. *Valuing the Self.* Prospect Heights, IL: Waveland

Lewis CC. 1995. *Educating Hearts and Minds: Reflections on Japanese Preschool and Elementary Education.* Cambridge: Cambridge Univ. Press

Lewis M, Feiring C. 1981. Direct and indirect interactions in social relationships. In *Advances in Infancy Research*, ed. LP Lipsett, I:129-61. Norwood, NJ: Ablex

Linn MC, Lewis C, Tsuchida I, Songer NB. 2000. Beyond fourth-grade science: Why do U.S. and Japanese students diverge? *Educ. Res.* 29:4–14

Lipka J. 1991. Toward a culturally based ped-agogy: a case study of one Yup'ik Eskimo teacher. *Anthropol. Educ. Q.* 22:203–23

Lipka J. 1994. Schools failing minority teachers. *Educ. Found.* 8:57–80

Lipka J. 1998. *Transforming the Culture of Schools: Yup'ik Eskimo Examples.* Mahwah, NJ: Erlbaum

Maccoby EE, Martin J. 1983. Socialization in the context of the family: Parent-child interaction. In *Handbook of Child Psychology.* Vol. 4: *Socialization, Personality, and Social Development*, ser. ed. PH Mussen, vol. ed. EM Hetherington, pp. 1–102. New York: Wiley. 4th ed.

Martini M. 1995. Features of home environments associated with children's school success. *Early Child Dev. Care* 111:49–68

Martini M. 1996. "What's new?" at the dinner table: family dynamics during mealtimes in two cultural groups in Hawaii. *Early Dev. Parent.* 5(1):23–34

Martini M, Kirkpatrick J. 1992. Parenting in Polynesia: a view from the Marquesas. In *Parent-Child Socialization in Diverse Cultures.* Vol. 5: *Annual Advances in Applied Developmental Psychology*, ed. JL Roopnarine, DB Carter, pp. 199–222. Norwood, NJ: Ablex

Matusov E, Rogoff B. 2002. Newcomers and oldtimers: educational philosophies-in-action of parent volunteers in a community of learners school. *Anthropol. Educ. Q.* In press

Maurer E. 1977. ¿Aprender o enseñar?: la educación en Takinwits, poblado Tseltal de Chiapas. *Rev. Centro Estud. Educ.* 7(1):84–103

McCollum P. 1989. Turn-allocation in lessons with North American and Puerto Rican students: a comparative study. *Anthropol. Educ. Q.* 20:133–56

Mehan H. 1979. *Learning Lessons: Social Organization in the Classroom.* Cambridge, MA: Harvard Univ. Press

Meltzoff AN, Moore MK. 1998. Infant intersubjectivity: broadening the dialogue to include imitation, identity and intention. In *Intersubjective Communication and Emotion in Early Ontogeny*, ed. S Braten, pp. 47–62. New York: Cambridge Univ. Press

Mercado R. 2001. *Los saberes docentes como construcción social.* Doctoral thesis. Mexico City: Dep. Invest. Educ. Centro Invest. Estud. Av. IPN

Mercer N, Edwards D, Maybin J. 1988. Putting context into oracy: the construction of shared knowledge through classroom discourse. In *Oracy Matters,* ed. M Maclure, T Phillips, A Wilkinson. Milton Keynes, UK: Open Univ. Press

Metge R. 1984. *Learning and Teaching: He Tikanga Maori.* Wellington: NZ Minist. Educ.

Minick N. 1993. Teacher's directives: the social construction of "literal meanings" and "real words" in classroom discourse. In *Understanding Practice: Perspectives on Activity and Context,* ed. S Chaiklin, J Lave, pp. 343–74. Cambridge, MA: Cambridge Univ. Press

Modiano N. 1973. *Indian Education in the Chiapas Highlands.* New York: Holt, Rinehart & Winston

Morelli GA, Rogoff B, Angelillo C. 2003. Cultural variation in young children's access to work or involvement in specialized child-focused activities. *Int. J. Behav. Dev.* In press

Morelli GA, Tronick EZ. 1992. Efe fathers: one among many? A comparison of forager children's involvement with fathers and other males. *Soc. Dev.* 1:36–54

Murachver T, Pipe ME, Gordon R, Owens JL, Fivush R. 1996. Do, show, and tell: children's event memories acquired through direct experience, observation, and stories. *Child Dev.* 67:3029–44

Nagai Y. 2001. Developing assessment and evaluation strategies for vernacular elementary school classrooms. *Anthropol. Educ. Q.* 32(1):80–103

Nash M. 1967. *Machine Age Maya.* Chicago: Univ. Chicago Press

Nsamenang AB. 1992. *Human Development in Cultural Context.* Newbury Park, CA: Sage

Ochs E. 1988. *Culture and Language Development.* New York: Cambridge Univ. Press

Ochs E, Schieffelin B. 1984. Language acquisition and socialization. In *Culture The-* *ory: Essays on Mind, Self, and Emotion,* ed. RA Shweder, RA LeVine, pp. 276–320. New York: Cambridge Univ. Press

Oshima-Takane Y, Goodz E, Deverensky JL. 1996. Birth order effects on early language development: Do secondborn children learn from overheard speech? *Child Dev.* 67(2): 621–34

Panel on Youth of the President's Science Advisory Committee. 1974. *Youth: Transition to Adulthood.* Chicago: Univ. Chicago Press

Paradise R. 1985. Un análisis psicosocial de la motivación y participación emocional en un caso de aprendizaje individual. *Rev. Latinoam. Estud. Educ.* 15(1):83–93

Paradise R. 1987. *Learning through social interaction: The experience and development of the Mazahua self in the context of the market.* Univ. Penn. Unpubl. diss.

Paradise R. 1994. The autonomous behavior of indigenous students in classroom activities. In *Education as Cultural Construction: Explorations in Socio-Cultural Studies,* ed. A Alvarez, P del Rio, 4:89–95. Madrid: Fund. Infanc. Aprendizaje

Paradise R. 1998. What's different about learning in schools as compared to family and community settings? *Hum. Dev.* 41(4):270–78

Peak L. 1986. Training learning skills and attitudes in Japanese early educational settings. In *Early Experience and the Development of Competence,* ed. W Fowler, pp. 111–23. San Francisco: Jossey-Bass

Pelletier W. 1970. Childhood in an Indian village. In *This Book is About Schools,* ed. S Repo, pp. 18–31. New York: Pantheon

Philips SU. 1983. *The Invisible Culture: Communication in Classroom and Community on the Warm Springs Indian Reservation.* Prospect Heights, IL: Waveland

Piaget J. 1962 (1951). *Play, Dreams and Imitation in Childhood.* New York: Norton. (Original title: *La Formation du Symbole chez l'Enfant: Imitation, Jeu et Rêve Image et Representation.*)

Rabain-Jamin J. 1989. Culture and early social

interactions. The example of mother-infant object play in African and Native French families. *Eur. J. Psychol. Educ.* IV(2):295–305

Richman AL, Miller PM, LeVine RA. 1992. Cultural and educational variations in maternal responsiveness. *Dev. Psychol.* 28(4):614–21

Rogoff B. 1981. Adults and peers as agents of socialization: a highland Guatemalan profile. *Ethos* 9:18–36

Rogoff B. 1990. *Apprenticeship in Thinking: Cognitive Development in Social Context.* New York: Oxford Univ. Press

Rogoff B. 2003. *The Cultural Nature of Human Development.* New York: Oxford Univ. Press. In press

Rogoff B, Angelillo C. 2002. Investigating the coordinated functioning of multifaceted cultural practices in human development. *Hum. Dev.* 45(4):211–25

Rogoff B, Goodman Turkanis C, Bartlett L, eds. 2001. *Learning Together: Children and Adults in a School Community.* New York: Oxford Univ. Press

Rogoff B, Matusov E, White C. 1996. Models of teaching and learning: participation in a community of learners. In *Handbook of Education and Human Development: New Models of Learning, Teaching, and Schooling*, ed. D Olson, N Torrance, pp. 388–414. London: Blackwell

Rogoff B, Mistry J, Göncü A, Mosier C. 1993. Guided participation in cultural activity by toddlers and caregivers. *Monogr. Soc. Res. Child Dev.* 58(7): Ser. No. 236

Rogoff B, Sellers MJ, Pirotta S, Fox N, White SH. 1975. Age of assignment of roles and responsibilities to children: a cross-cultural survey. *Hum. Dev.* 18:353–69

Rogoff B, Toma C. 1997. Shared thinking: community and institutional variations. *Disc. Proc.* 23:471–97

Ruddle K, Chesterfield R. 1978. Traditional skill training and labor in rural societies. *J. Dev. Areas* 12:389–98

Schieffelin BB. 1991. *The Give and Take of Everyday Life: Language Socialization of Kaluli Children.* Cambridge: Cambridge Univ. Press

Schieffelin BB, Ochs E. 1986. Language socialization. *Annu. Rev. Anthropol.* 15:163–91

Scollon R, Scollon S. 1981. *Narrative, Literacy, and Face in Interethnic Communication.* Norwood, NJ: Ablex

Scribner S, Cole M. 1973. Cognitive consequences of formal and informal education. *Science* 182:553–59

Seaman J. 2001. A new teacher learning to share responsibility with children. See Rogoff et al. 2001, pp. 138–41

Shepard LA. 2000. The role of assessment in a learning culture. *Educ. Res.* 29:4–14

Sindell PS. 1997. Some discontinuities in the enculturation of Mistassini Cree children. See Spindler 1997, pp. 383–92

Spindler G, ed. 1981. *Doing the Ethnography of Schooling: Educational Anthropology in Action.* New York: Holt, Rinehart & Winston

Spindler G, ed. 1997. *Education and Cultural Process: Anthropological Approaches.* Prospect Heights, IL: Waveland

Stedman LC. 1997. International achievement differences: an assessment of a new perspective. *Educ. Res.* 26(3):4–15

Tizard B, Hughes M. 1984. *Young Children Learning.* Cambridge, MA: Harvard Univ. Press

Tomasello M. 1999. The human adaptation for culture. *Annu. Rev. Anthropol.* 28:509–29

Trevarthen C. 1977. Descriptive analyses of infant communicative behavior. In *Studies in Mother-Infant Interaction*, ed. HR Schaffer, pp. 227–70. London: Academic

Uzgiris IC. 1984. Imitation in infancy: its interpersonal aspects. In *The Minnesota Symposia on Child Psychology. Vol. 17: Parent-Child Interaction and Parent-Child Relations in Child Development*, ed. M Perlmutter, pp. 1–32. Hillsdale, NJ: Erlbaum

Ward MC. 1971. *Them Children: A Study in Language Learning.* New York: Holt, Rinehart & Winston

Wells G. 1992. *Re-evaluation of the IRF*

sequence. Presented at Conf. Soc. Cult. Res., Madrid

Whiting BB. 1996. The effect of social change on concepts of the good child and good mothering: a study of families in Kenya. *Ethos* 24:3–35

Whiting BB, Edwards CP. 1988. *Children of Different Worlds: The Formation of Social Behavior*. Cambridge, MA: Harvard Univ. Press

Whiting BB, Whiting JWM. 1975. *Children of Six Cultures*. Cambridge, MA: Harvard Univ. Press

Wolcott HF. 1997. Why have minority groups in North America been disadvantaged by their schools? See Spindler 1997, pp. 96–109

Yando R, Seitz V, Zigler E. 1978. *Imitation*. Hillsdale, NJ: Erlbaum

Zimmerman BJ, Rosenthal T. 1974. Observational learning of rule governed behavior by children. *Psychol. Bull.* 81:29–42

Annu. Rev. Psychol. 2003. 54:205–28
doi: 10.1146/annurev.psych.54.101601.145108
First published online as a Review in Advance on August 6, 2002

PSYCHOPATHOLOGY IN THE POSTGENOMIC ERA

Robert Plomin and Peter McGuffin

*Social, Genetic and Developmental Psychiatry Research Centre, Institute of
Psychiatry, King's College London, DeCrespigny Park, London SE5 8AF, UK;
e-mail: r.plomin@iop.kcl.ac.uk, p.mcguffin@iop.kcl.ac.uk*

Key Words DNA, gene, genome, QTL association

■ **Abstract** We are rapidly approaching the postgenomic era in which we will know all of the 3 billion DNA bases in the human genome sequence and all of the variations in the genome sequence that are ultimately responsible for genetic influence on behavior. These ongoing advances and new techniques will make it easier to identify genes associated with psychopathology. Progress in identifying such genes has been slower than some experts expected, probably because many genes are involved for each phenotype, which means the effect of any one gene is small. Nonetheless, replicated linkages and associations are being found, for example, for dementia, reading disability, and hyperactivity. The future of genetic research lies in finding out how genes work (functional genomics). It is important for the future of psychology that pathways between genes and behavior be examined at the top-down psychological level of analysis (behavioral genomics), as well as at the bottom-up molecular biological level of cells or the neuroscience level of the brain. DNA will revolutionize psychological research and treatment during the coming decades.

CONTENTS

0066-4308/03/0203-0205$14.00

INTRODUCTION

Psychopathology is the primary psychological target for molecular genetic attempts to identify genes. Most of what is known about the genetics of psychopathology comes from quantitative genetic research involving family, twin, and adoption studies, not just in demonstrating the ubiquitous influence of genes but also in going beyond heritability to investigate the genetic and environmental etiologies of heterogeneity and comorbidity, to understand the etiological links between the normal and abnormal and to explore the interplay between nature and nurture in development (Plomin et al. 2001a). This review, however, focuses on attempts to identify genes responsible for the heritability of psychopathology. This focus is not meant to denigrate quantitative genetic research, which is even more valuable in the postgenomic era because it charts the course for molecular genetic research (Plomin et al. 2003a), nor is it meant to disparage research on environmental influences, which are as important as genetic influences for most types of psychopathology. For example, an exciting area of research on psychopathology is the developmental interactions and correlations between nature and nurture. Our focus on attempts to identify genes responsible for the heritability of psychopathology in the human species complements the previous *Annual Review of Psychology* chapter on behavioral genetics, which considered single-gene influences on brain and behavior primarily in nonhuman species (Wahlsten 1999), and a recent chapter on human quantitative genetic research on gene-environment interplay (Rutter & Silberg 2002).

THE HUMAN GENOME PROJECT

The twentieth century began with the rediscovery of Mendel's laws of heredity, which had been ignored by mainstream biologists for over 30 years. The word gene was first coined in 1903. Fifty years later the double helix structure of DNA was discovered. The genetic code was cracked in 1966. The crowning glory of genetics in the twentieth century was the culmination of the Human Genome Project, which provided a working draft of the sequence of all 3 billion letters of DNA in the human genome (International Human Genome Sequencing Consortium 2001).

For psychopathology the most important next step is the identification of the DNA sequences that make us different from each other. There is no single human genome sequence—we each have a unique genome. The vast majority of the DNA letters are the same for all human genomes, and many of these are the same for other primates, other mammals, and even insects. Nevertheless, about one in every thousand nucleotide bases of DNA letters differs among people with at least 1% frequency, which means there are at least 3 million DNA variations. Although there are many types of these DNA differences, most involve a substitution of a single nucleotide base pair, called single nucleotide polymorphisms. DNA differences in the coding regions of genes or in the regions that regulate gene expression are responsible for the widespread heritability of psychopathology. That is, when we say that psychopathology is heritable, we mean that variations in DNA exist that increase (or decrease) risk of psychopathology. When all DNA variations are known, especially functional DNA variations that affect transcription and translation of DNA into proteins, the major beneficiary will be research on complex traits such as psychopathology that are influenced by multiple genes.

Progress is being made toward identifying all of the genes in the genome, but much remains to be learned—even about what a gene is. In the traditional sense of the "central dogma" of DNA, a gene is DNA that is transcribed into RNA and then translated into amino acid sequences. Less than 2% of the more than 3 billion bases of DNA in the human genome involves genes in which DNA is transcribed and translated in this way. It is not yet known how many such genes there are in the human genome. It used to be said that there are 100,000 genes, but the 2001 working draft of the human genome suggested far fewer, perhaps as few as 30,000, although estimates of the number of genes have been rising again as the genome becomes better understood. Moreover, some of the other 98% of DNA may be important, for example, DNA that is transcribed into RNA but not translated. For nearly all genes, a complicated process called splicing occurs between transcription and translation. All of the DNA within a gene is transcribed into RNA, but segments of RNA (called introns) are deleted and remain in the nucleus while the other segments (called exons) are spliced back together and exit the nucleus, where they are translated into amino acid sequences. Although in the past introns were thought to be genetic junk that has hitched a ride evolutionarily, it is now known that in some cases introns regulate the transcription of other genes. A recent finding is that many noncoding RNA sequences called microRNA act as genes by producing RNA molecules that regulate gene expression directly, rather than being translated into amino acid sequences (Eddy 2001). Exons are conserved evolutionarily—most of our exons are highly similar to DNA sequences in primates, mammals, and even invertebrates. This implies that the sheer number of such genes is not responsible for the greater complexity of the human species. Subtle variations in DNA rather than the number of genes are responsible for differences between mice and men (Brett et al. 2002). If subtle DNA differences are responsible for the differences between mice and men, even more subtle differences are likely to be responsible for individual differences within the human species. Although many rare and severe disorders caused by a single gene involve mutations in exons, DNA variations in introns and microRNA might be sources of more subtle effects on complex traits such as psychopathology.

THE POSTGENOMIC ERA

Functional Genomics and Behavioral Genomics

As advances from the Human Genome Project continue to be absorbed in DNA research on psychopathology, optimism is warranted about finding genes, the main topic of this review. The future of genetic research will involve a shift from finding genes to finding out how genes work, called functional genomics. Three huge areas of functional genomic research have emerged: gene manipulation, gene expression profiling, and proteomics (Phillips et al. 2002, Plomin & Crabbe 2000).

Gene Manipulation

One way to study how a gene works is to knock it out by breeding mice for which DNA sequences that prevent the gene from being transcribed have been deleted. These are called gene knock-out studies. Genes can also be inserted, or "knocked in." There has been an explosion of research using targeted mutations in mice (Phillips et al. 2002). Newer techniques can produce more subtle changes that alter the gene's regulation and lead to increases or decreases in the frequency with which the gene is transcribed. Techniques are even available to affect particular brain regions and to turn genes on and off at will. The approach is not without problems, however. Currently, there is no way to control the location of gene insertion in the mouse genome or the number of inserted copies of the gene, both of which can affect gene function.

A different approach, using antisense DNA, circumvents some of these problems and does not require breeding. Antisense DNA is a DNA sequence that binds to a specific RNA sequence and thus prevents some of the RNA from being translated, which "knocks down" gene function. Injected in the brain, antisense DNA has the advantage of high temporal and spatial resolution (Ogawa & Pfaff 1996). Antisense DNA knockdowns affect behavioral responses for dozens of drugs (Buck et al. 2000). The principal limitations of antisense technology currently are its unpredictable efficacy and a tendency to produce general toxicity.

Gene Expression Profiling

Genes are transcribed (expressed) as their products are needed. Gene expression can be indexed by the presence of messenger RNA (mRNA), which is transcribed from DNA and then travels outside the nucleus to form a template from which amino acids, the building blocks of proteins, are assembled in sequences in the process called translation. Microarrays are now available that can detect the expression of thousands of genes simultaneously. Unlike DNA studies, in which every cell in the body has the same DNA, gene expression studies depend on the tissue that is sampled. For psychopathology, brain is of course the critical tissue, which will make it difficult to apply this technology to humans. However, gene expression profiling is being used widely in research on animal models to compare brain tissue before and after an event in order to identify genes whose expression is triggered by the event. For example, a gene expression profiling study of more than 7000 genes in 2 strains of mice investigated gene expression in the hippocampus during ethanol withdrawal following chronic ethanol exposure and found that about 100 genes are expressed in the hippocampus during withdrawal (Daniels & Buck 2002). Gene expression profiling is analogous to functional neuroimaging at the level of the gene.

Proteomics

Gene expression profiling assesses gene transcription as indexed by RNA. The next step toward functional genomics is to study the function of the proteins that result from translation of RNA. The term "protein genomics" led to the neologism "proteomics." Proteomics is much more difficult than genomics because, unlike the triplet code of DNA that governs the genome, there is no simple code for understanding the proteome. There are also several complications. First, it has been estimated that about half of all human genes are alternatively spliced into exons and introns and thus translated into different proteins (International Human Genome Sequencing Consortium 2001). Second, after translation proteins are also modified. It has been estimated that for each human gene three different modified proteins with different functions are produced (Banks et al. 2000). Third, although the amino acid sequence of a protein, its primary structure, can be predicted with certainty from the expressed DNA sequence, the mechanism determining secondary and tertiary folding upon which the properties of the protein depend, is currently poorly understood. Fourth, proteins tend to attach themselves to, or form complexes with, other proteins so that understanding protein function ultimately depends on the understanding of protein-protein interactions.

Behavioral Genomics

Gene manipulation, gene expression profiling, and proteomics are examples of bottom-up molecular biological approaches to functional genomics. Nearly all of this research is conducted using animal models because in humans it is not possible to manipulate genes and it is difficult to obtain brain tissue needed for gene expression profiling and proteomics. Although there are mouse models related to psychopathology [e.g., alcoholism (Crabbe 2003), anxiety (Lesch 2003), and dementia (Williams 2002a)], mouse models are obviously more problematic for cognitive disorders such as autism, reading disability, and communication disorders. Nonetheless, as genes are found, even for cognitive disorders, understanding how these genes work in the brain will profit from functional genomic research using animal models (Crusio & Gerlai 1999).

The bottom-up molecular biological approach to functional genomics is not the only level of analysis at which we can investigate how genes contribute to human psychopathology. At the other end of the continuum is a top-down level of analysis that considers the behavior of the whole organism. The term "behavioral genomics" has been suggested to emphasize the potential contribution of a top-down psychological level of analysis toward understanding how genes work

(Plomin & Crabbe 2000). For example, part of understanding how genes work is to understand how genetic effects interact and correlate with experience, how genetic effects on behavior contribute to change and continuity in development, and how genetic effects contribute to comorbidity and heterogeneity between disorders. These are issues central to quantitative genetic analysis, which has gone beyond merely estimating heritability (Plomin et al. 2002c). Behavioral genomic research using DNA will provide sharper scalpels to dissect these issues with greater precision (Plomin et al. 2002b).

Behavioral genomics will make important contributions toward understanding the functions of genes and will open up new horizons for understanding psychopathology. Few psychopathology researchers are likely to join the hunt for genes because it is difficult and expensive, but once genes are found it is relatively easy and inexpensive to make use of them. Although it used to be necessary to collect blood samples, DNA can now be obtained painlessly and inexpensively from cheek swabs. Cheek swabs yield enough DNA to genotype thousands of genes, and the cost of genotyping is surprisingly inexpensive. What has happened in the area of dementia in the elderly will be played out in many other areas of psychopathology. As discussed later, the only known risk factor for late-onset Alzheimer's dementia is the gene APOE. Although the association between APOE and LOAD was reported only a decade ago (Corder et al. 1993), it has already become routine in research on dementia to genotype subjects for APOE to ascertain whether the results differ for individuals with and without this genetic risk factor. For example, the association between APOE and dementia has been found to interact with head injury, smoking, cholesterol level, and estrogen level (Williams 2003). For these reasons, we predict that psychopathology researchers will routinely collect DNA in their research and incorporate identified gene associations in their analyses, which will greatly enrich behavioral genomics.

FINDING GENES

Greater progress by far has been made towards finding genes in the area of psychopathology than in any other area of psychology, although progress has nonetheless been slower than some had originally anticipated. We begin this review with the psychoses (schizophrenia and mood disorders) and then turn to cognitive disorders (dementia, autism, reading disability, communication disorders, mental retardation), and finally consider hyperactivity and alcoholism. Our goal is to provide overviews of recent linkages and associations in these areas, rather than to review quantitative genetic research, provide encyclopedic or historical reviews of molecular genetic research, or discuss the function of the genes (for more detail on these topics, see McGuffin et al. 2002, Plomin et al. 2003b).

A brief description of linkage and association may be useful (Bishop & Sham 2000, Sham 2003). Linkage is a departure from Mendel's law of independent assortment that posits that two genes will be inherited independently. Most of the time independent assortment does take place, but Mendel did not know that genes are on chromosomes. If two DNA polymorphisms (sequences of DNA called DNA markers that differ between individuals)—for example, a DNA marker in a gene for a disorder and another DNA marker—are close together on a chromosome, they will tend to be inherited as a package within families rather than independently as predicted by Mendel. In this way, with a few hundred DNA markers, it is possible to screen the genome for cotransmission between a marker and a single-gene disorder within large family pedigrees. Linkage is most powerful for finding rare single-gene disorders in which a single gene is necessary and sufficient for the emergence of the disorder. For example, the linkage of Huntington's disease with DNA markers was found in a five-generation family of hundreds of individuals when a particular form (allele) of a DNA marker on chromosome 4 was only found in family members who had Huntington's disease (Gusella et al. 1983). Similar linkage studies have identified the chromosomal location of hundreds of single-gene disorders, and the precise DNA fault has been found for many of these disorders. Linkage only points to the neighborhood of a chromosome; a house-to-house search is then needed to find the culprit gene, a process that took 10 years in the case of Huntington's disease (Huntington Disease Collaborative Research Group 1993).

In the 1980s linkage studies of this type were also undertaken for psychopathology even though there was no evidence to suggest that such complex disorders are inherited as single-gene disorders. Early successes were claimed for bipolar depression (Egeland et al. 1987) and for schizophrenia (Sherrington et al. 1988), but neither claim was replicated. It is now clear that this traditional linkage approach can only detect a linkage if the gene has a large effect on the disorder, a situation best exemplified by relatively rare disorders such as Huntington's disease, which has a frequency of about 1 in 20,000 individuals. Common disorders such as psychopathology seldom show any sign of single-gene effects and appear to be caused by multiple genes as well as by multiple environmental factors. Indeed, quantitative genetic research suggests that such common disorders are usually the quantitative extreme of the same genes responsible for variation throughout the distribution (Plomin et al. 1994). Genes in such multiple-gene systems are called quantitative trait loci (QTLs) because they are likely to result in dimensions (quantitative continua) representing liability to disorders (qualitative dichotomies) that only manifest when a certain threshold is exceeded (Falconer 1965). The QTL perspective is the molecular genetic extension of quantitative genetics in which genetic variation tends to be quantitatively and normally distributed.

The goal of QTL research is not to find the gene for a complex trait but rather the multiple genes that make contributions of varying effect sizes to the variance of the trait. Perhaps one gene will be found that accounts for 5% of the trait variance, 5 other genes might each account for 2% of the variance, and 10 other genes might each account for 1% of the variance. If the effects of these QTLs are independent, they would in total account for 25% of the trait's variance. It is unlikely that all of the genes that contribute to the heritability of a complex trait will be identified because some of their effects may be too small to detect or their effects may be nonadditive (called epistasis). The problem is that we do not know the distribution of effect sizes of QTLs for any complex trait in plant, animal, or human species. Not long ago a 10% effect size was thought to be small, at least from the single-gene perspective in which the effect size was essentially 100%. However, for behavioral disorders and dimensions, a 10% effect size may turn out to be a very large effect. If effect sizes are 1% or smaller, this would explain the slow progress to date in identifying genes associated with behavior because research so far has been woefully underpowered to detect and replicate QTLs of such small effect size (Cardon & Bell 2001). There can be no doubt that finding genes for complex disorders will be difficult (Sturt & McGuffin 1985, Weiss & Terwilliger 2000).

Recent research has been more successful in finding QTLs for complex traits because designs have been employed that can detect genes of much smaller effect size. Linkage has been extended to consider QTLs by using many small families (usually pairs of siblings) rather than a few large families. These QTL linkage methods can be used to study the extremes of a quantitative trait or a diagnosed disorder and are able to detect genes that account for about 10% of the variance of the quantitative trait or the assumed liability or susceptibility to the disorder with reasonable sample sizes. The essence of the most popular method, called sib-pair QTL linkage analysis, is to ask whether sharing alleles for a particular DNA marker makes siblings more similar phenotypically. Siblings can share none, one, or two of the alleles they inherit from their parents. Thus, in relation to a particular DNA marker, a pair of siblings can be like adoptive siblings sharing no alleles on average, like dizygotic twins sharing one allele on average, or like monozygotic twins sharing the same two alleles.

Sib-pair QTL linkage analysis assesses the extent to which allele sharing is correlated with sibling phenotypic resemblance. The most popular variant is called the affected sib-pair design, in which both siblings are diagnosed for a disorder (or both are extreme on a quantitative trait). Because the expectation is that siblings share one of their two alleles, linkage for the disorder is indicated if allele sharing is significantly greater than 50% when both siblings are affected.

The second method, called association (or linkage disequilibrium), can detect QTLs that account for much smaller amounts of variance than linkage (Edwards 1965, Risch 2000, Tabor et al. 2002). The fundamental reason for the greater power of association over linkage is that the information content for association is proportional to the QTL heritability (the effect size of the QTL), so that halving the effect size will increase the required sample size fourfold. In contrast, for linkage the information content is proportional to the square of the QTL heritability, so that halving the effect size will increase the required sample size 16-fold (Sham et al. 2000). Association is the correlation between a particular allele and a trait in the population. For example, as discussed below, a gene called apolipoprotein E (APOE) has an allele (called APOE-4), which has a frequency of about 40%

in individuals with late-onset Alzheimer's disease and about 15% in controls. APOE-4 has a large effect, but it is not necessary or sufficient for the development of the disorder—it is a risk factor that increases susceptibility to the disorder. At least a third of individuals with Alzheimer's disease lack the allele, and about half of individuals who have a double dose of this allele survive to age 80 without developing the disease (Williams 2003). It sounds contradictory to refer to a QTL association with a dichotomous disorder such as Alzheimer's disease because diagnosed disorders are present or absent rather than quantitative traits. However, if several genes contribute to the disorder, the genes will produce a continuum of liability to the disorder; only those whose liability exceeds a certain threshold will present as affected.

Most association studies involve case-control comparisons for diagnosed disorders or for extremes of a dimension. One problem with any comparison between two groups such as cases and controls is that inadequate matching between the two groups could jeopardize the conclusion that a particular QTL causes differences in psychopathology between the groups. A check on this possibility is to study associations within families, which controls for demographic differences between cases and controls (Abecasis et al. 2000, Spielman & Ewens 1996). Although such within-family designs have been favored in recent years, there is a strong tendency to use the more powerful and efficient case-control design to find associations and then to use within-family designs and other strategies (Pritchard & Rosenberg 1999) to confirm that associations are not spurious (Cardon 2003, Cardon & Bell 2001).

The following sections review recent linkage and association research on the most active areas of research in psychopathology: schizophrenia, mood disorders, dementia, autism, reading disability, communication disorders, mental retardation, hyperactivity, and alcoholism.

Schizophrenia

Despite large collaborative linkage studies carried out in Europe and North America, identification of the genes involved in schizophrenia remains elusive. Linkages that have received support from international collaborative studies include chromosome 6 (6p24-22), chromosome 8 (8p22-21), and chromosome 22 (22q11-12) (Owen & O'Donovan 2003). Other nominated linkages that have received some replication include chromosomes 1 (1q21-22), 5 (5q21-q31), 10 (10p15-p11), and 13 (13q14.1-q32) (Waterworth et al. 2002). However, in every case there are negative as well as positive findings. For example, a multicenter linkage study of 779 schizophrenic pedigrees excluded linkage on 1q (Levinson et al. 2002). The largest single-center systematic search for linkage, which included 196 affected sib pairs, effectively excluded any gene conferring a relative risk of 3 or more from over 80% of the genome (Williams et al. 1999). In order to detect linkages involving relative risks of 2 with a p of only .05, sample sizes of 800 affected sibling pairs will be needed (Scott et al. 1997).

Interestingly, the linkages on chromosomes 13 and 22 have also been reported to be linked with bipolar disorder (Berrettini 2000). This would be in keeping with the most recent analysis of twin data on schizophrenia and bipolar disorder, which suggests there is considerable genetic overlap (Cardno et al. 2002).

The focus on schizophrenia has turned to association studies that are capable of detecting genes with smaller effect sizes. The most obvious place to begin such studies is with candidate genes involved in the drugs that control schizophrenic symptoms, dopamine and serotonin receptors, although candidate gene studies are also being extended to other gene systems, with hundreds of such reports in recent years (Owen & O'Donovan 2003). Several studies have investigated common polymorphisms in a serotonin receptor gene (5HT2a). A meta-analysis based on more than 3000 subjects supports a small (odds ratios of 1.2 in which 1.0 represents chance) but significant role for the T102C polymorphism of 5HT2a (Williams et al. 1997). Sample sizes of 1000 cases and 1000 controls are required for 80% power to detect an effect of this size ($p < 0.05$). Interest in the dopamine D2 receptor gene faded after initial positive reports were countered by several negative reports from large studies (Owen & O'Donovan 2003). However, the gene that codes for the dopamine D3 receptor has yielded a significant odds ratio of 1.2 in a meta-analysis, although several negative results have been reported (Williams et al. 1998).

Mood Disorders

The story for major depression and bipolar depression is similar to schizophrenia. Large-scale linkage studies of bipolar depression have suggested linkages on chromosomes 12 (12q23-q24) and 21 (21q22) in several but not all studies (Badner & Gershon 2002, Baron 2002, Jones et al. 2002, Kalidindi & McGuffin 2003). Chromosome 18 linkage has also been suggested in several studies but the "hits" have not centered on a single region (Van Broeckhoven & Verheyen 1999). As mentioned in relation to schizophrenia, linkage has also been suggested on chromosomes 13 and 22 (Berrettini 2000). Several other linkage regions have been proposed in at least two studies such as chromosomes 1 (*1q31-32*) and 4 (*4p16*) (Baron 2002) and chromosomes 15 (*15q11*-q13) and 16 (*16p13*) (Kalidindi & McGuffin 2003). For unipolar depression, linkage studies have just begun and findings are unclear (Malhi et al. 2000).

As with schizophrenia, numerous recent studies of mood disorders have attempted to find associations with candidate genes. The gene that codes for serotonin transporter (hSERT) has received the most attention because it is involved in the reuptake of serotonin at brain synapses, which is the target for selective serotonin reuptake inhibitor antidepressants such as Prozac (fluoxetine). A functional repeat polymorphism in the hSERT promoter region (5HTTLPR) was reported to be associated with major depression in a study of 275 cases and 739 controls and with bipolar disorder in a study of 304 bipolar cases and 570 controls (Collier et al. 1996). However, in 8 follow-up studies totaling 719 cases of major depression and 1195 controls, only one study replicated the original finding. For bipolar disorder, of 9 follow-up studies totaling 943 cases and 1164 controls, only two studies replicated the original finding (Lesch 2003). Beginning with a study in 1996 (Lesch et al. 1996), several studies have reported that 5HTTLPR is associated with anxiety-related dimensions in community samples, but 22 studies of more than 5000 subjects do not provide much support for this hypothesis (Lesch 2003). Stronger support for the involvement of 5HTTLPR comes from 8 studies of violent suicidal behavior, of which 5 are positive, and from 8 studies showing an effect on treatment response to selective 5HT transporter inhibitors, of which 6 are positive (Lesch 2003). One study has recently shown an association between 5HTTLPR and postpartum depression (Coyle et al. 2000).

Candidate genes in dopaminergic, noradrenergic, glutaminergic, and GABAergic pathways have also been investigated, but no clear associations have as yet emerged (Jones et al. 2002, Kalidindi & McGuffin 2003). For example, early association research focused on tyrosine hydroxylase, but a meta-analysis of 547 bipolar cases and 522 controls showed no significant effect (Turecki et al. 1997). Three association studies indicate that catechol-o-methyltransferase is associated with rapid cycling in bipolar disorder (Jones et al. 2002).

Candidate gene association studies have also begun to aim at other mood-related disorders such as anxiety and eating disorders, but no promising associations have as yet emerged (Eley et al. 2002). For example, a polymorphism in the promotor region of a serotonin receptor gene (5HT2A) was reported to be related to anorexia nervosa (Collier et al. 1997), but a subsequent meta-analysis showed no statistically significant association (Ziegler et al. 1999).

Dementia

Dementia yielded the first solid QTL finding and it remains the best success story. Research a decade ago focused on a rare (1 in 10,000) type of Alzheimer's disease that appears before 65 years of age and shows autosomal-dominant inheritance. Most of these early-onset cases are due to a gene (presenilin-1) on chromosome 14 (St. George-Hyslop et al. 1992) that was identified in 1995 (Sherrington et al. 1995). As is often the case with single-gene disorders, dozens of different mutations in presenilin-1 have been found, which will make screening difficult (Cruts et al. 1998). A similar gene, presenilin-2, on chromosome 1 and mutations in the amyloid precursor protein gene on chromosome 21 also account for a few early-onset cases (Liddell et al. 2002, Williams 2003).

The three genes that contribute to early onset Alzheimer's disease account for less than 2% of all Alzheimer's cases (Farrer et al. 1997). The great majority of Alzheimer's cases occur after 65 years of age, typically in people in their seventies and eighties. A major advance toward understanding late-onset Alzheimer's disease was the discovery of a strong allelic association with the apolipoprotein E gene (APOE) on chromosome 19 (Corder et al. 1993), the first QTL for psychopathology. This gene has three alleles (confusingly called alleles 2, 3, and 4).

The frequency of allele 4 is about 40% in individuals with Alzheimer's disease and 15% in control samples. This result translates to about a sixfold increased risk for late-onset Alzheimer's disease for individuals who have one or two of these alleles. In a meta-analysis of 40 studies involving 15,000 individuals, elevated frequencies of APOE-4 were found for Alzheimer's patients in each study, although the association was stronger among Caucasians and Japanese and weaker in African-Americans (Farrer et al. 1997). There is some evidence that allele 2, the least common allele, may play a protective role (Corder et al. 1994). Finding QTLs that protect rather than increase risk for a disorder is an important direction for genetic research on psychopathology.

APOE is a QTL in the sense that allele 4, although a risk factor, is neither necessary nor sufficient for developing dementia. For instance, at least a third of late-onset Alzheimer's patients do not have allele 4, and about half of individuals who have a double dose of this allele survive to age 80 without developing the disease (Williams 2003). Because APOE does not account for all the genetic influence on Alzheimer's disease, the search is on for other QTLs. New linkage studies of late-onset Alzheimer's have reported significant linkages on chromosomes 9 and 10 (Liddell et al. 2002, Williams 2003). Finally, more than 40 genes have shown some evidence of association with Alzheimer's disease, but none can be considered confirmed (Schellenberg et al. 2000).

Autism

Just 25 years ago, the origins of autism were thought by many to be entirely environmental, but family and twin studies altered this view, and autism is now one of the major targets for molecular genetic research. In 1998 an international collaborative linkage study reported a strong linkage on chromosome 7 (7q31-33) (International Molecular Genetic Study of Autism Consortium 1998). There have now been seven genome screens for linkage, six of which have found evidence for linkage in the 7q31-33 region (Pericak-Vance 2003). The specific gene in this region has not yet been identified (Bonora et al. 2002). Six of the seven genome screens have also found evidence for linkage on the short arm of chromosome 2, but the specific region differs across the studies. Other linkages have been reported in at least three studies on chromosomes 3, 13, 18, and 19 (Pericak-Vance 2003). A few candidate gene studies have been reported with particular attention on the serotonin transporter gene (Kim et al. 2002) and on genes in linkage regions (Folstein & Rosen-Sheidley 2001).

Reading Disability

One of the first QTLs found to be linked to a human behavioral disorder was a susceptibility gene for reading disability on chromosome 6 (6p21) (Cardon et al. 1994), a finding that has been replicated in three independent linkage studies (Willcutt et al. 2003). The 6p21 linkage has been found for diverse reading measures and also appears to be involved in hyperactivity (Willcutt et al. 2003).

Linkage has also been reported to chromosome 15 (15q21) in three studies (Williams 2002). Association studies are beginning to narrow down the regions on chromosomes 6 and 15 (Morris et al. 2000, Turic et al. 2002). The first genome screen for reading disability found linkage to chromosome 18 (18p11.2) in three samples (Fisher et al. 2002) and also replicated reports of linkage on chromosome 2 (Fagerheim et al. 1999, Petryshen et al. 2000). The linkages appear to be general to reading disability, including diverse processes such as single word reading, phonological and orthographic processing, and phoneme awareness (Fisher et al. 2002). When the specific genes are identified for these linkages, it will be interesting to investigate the extent to which the genes' effects are specific to reading or extend more broadly to language and other cognitive processes (Fisher & Smith 2001).

Communication Disorders

Although molecular genetics has only recently come to communication disorders, several successes have been reported (Fisher 2003). The first gene identified for language impairment involves a unique type of language impairment in a single family known as the KE family. This much-studied family includes 15 linguistically impaired relatives whose speech has low intelligibility and whose deficits involve nearly all aspects of language. In this three-generation family, transmission of the disorder was consistent with a single-gene autosomal dominant pattern of inheritance. A linkage region (SPCH1) was identified on the long arm of chromosome 7 (7q31) (Fisher et al. 1998). The linkage has recently been shown to be due to a single nucleotide substitution in the exon 14 coding region of a gene (FOXP2) in the forkhead/winged-helix (FOX) family of transcription factors (Lai et al. 2001). Despite the authors' caution in noting that the KE family's unusual type of speech and language impairment with a single-gene autosomal inheritance pattern has not been found in any other family, the FOXP2 finding has been hailed in the media as "the language gene." However, a study of 270 low-language children screened from more than 18,000 children showed that not a single child had the FOXP2 mutation (Meaburn et al. 2002). In other words, although the exon 14 FOXP2 mutation appears to be responsible for the unusual speech and language disorder of the KE family, the mutation is not found among children with common language impairment. Other coding-region variants in the FOXP2 gene also show no association with common forms of language impairment (Newbury et al. 2002).

The first genome-wide QTL linkage screen for language impairment has recently been reported (SLI Consortium 2002). The research was a sib-pair QTL linkage study of 252 children from 5 to 19 years old in 98 families in which at least one sibling met selection criteria (at least 1.5 standard deviations below the norms on either expressive or receptive language tests). In addition to expressive and receptive language, phonological short-term memory (nonword repetition) was also assessed. The children were genotyped for 400 markers evenly distributed throughout the genome. The results for all possible sibling pairings suggested linkage on 16q for the nonword repetition test and on 19q for the test of expressive language. Because linkage designs, even QTL linkage designs, can only detect relatively large effects on the order of 10% heritabilities or greater, these findings suggest two genes of large effect, each of which is specific to a single language measure.

Although a QTL linkage of this magnitude has been found for reading disability, a QTL perspective would expect that most genes show a smaller effect size. Moreover, quantitative genetic research suggests that genetic effects on language impairment are general rather than specific to one language process (Dale et al. 2000). Another molecular genetic study of language disability is underway that incorporates several recent trends in QTL research with the goal of identifying language-general QTLs of small effect size (Plomin et al. 2002a). Language-impaired children were identified, not from diagnoses, but from the extreme of a general language factor that emerged from factor analyses of nine diverse tests of language (Colledge et al. 2002). Because large samples and association designs are needed to detect QTLs of small effect size, the study includes 300 language-impaired children and 1000 control subjects in a case-control association design. The design uses a direct association approach in which DNA markers are assessed that can be presumed to be QTLs themselves rather than the much less powerful indirect association approach that uses anonymous DNA markers indirectly associated with the QTL, which is in turn directly associated with the trait. Also, rather than investigating the few available functional DNA markers in candidate genes, a systematic genome scan is being conducted of all DNA markers in coding regions of genes that result in an amino acid substitution. Although such DNA markers are not necessarily functional they are much more likely to be functional than the millions of DNA markers in noncoding regions. Genotyping thousands of DNA markers for such large samples would be daunting, but a technique called DNA pooling is used in which DNA is pooled from the language-impaired group and from the control group (Daniels et al. 1998). The two pools of DNA are genotyped rather than the DNA of all of the individuals in the groups. In order to avoid false positive results, the study includes various replications such as a within-family analysis based on dizygotic twin pairs, which controls for ethnic stratification. This general strategy has been used in the first genome scan for QTL association for cognitive ability (Plomin et al. 2001b), but results have not as yet been reported for the association genome scan of language disability.

Mental Retardation

More than 200 genetic disorders, most extremely rare, include mental retardation among their symptoms (Zechner et al. 2001). For example, phenylketonuria is a single-gene recessive disorder that occurs in about 1 in 10,000 births. Like many other single-gene disorders, the molecular genetics of phenylketonuria is not simple. More than 100 different mutations, some of which cause milder forms of retardation, have been found in the gene (PAH) on chromosome 12 that produces the enzyme phenylalanine hydroxylase (Guldberg et al. 1998).

An important genetic discovery about two decades ago was the association with mental retardation of apparent microscopic breakages, "fragile sites," on the X chromosome. Fragile X syndrome is now known to be the second most common specific cause of mental retardation after Down syndrome (Kaufmann & Reiss 1999). Until the gene for fragile X was identified in 1991, its inheritance was puzzling because its risk increased across generations (Verkerk et al. 1991). The fragile X syndrome is caused by an expanded triplet repeat (CGG) on the X chromosome (Xq27.3). Parents who inherit X chromosomes with a normal number of repeats (6–54) can produce eggs or sperm with an expanded number of repeats (up to 200), called a premutation. This premutation does not cause retardation in their offspring, but it is unstable and often leads to much greater expansions in later generations, especially when it is inherited through the mother. The risk that a premutation will expand to a full mutation increases over four generations from 5 to 50%, although it is not yet possible to predict when a premutation will expand to a full mutation. The full mutation causes fragile X in almost all males but in only half of the females who are mosaics for the X chromosome in the sense that one X chromosome is inactivated. The triplet repeat is adjacent to a gene (FMR1), and a full mutation prevents that gene from being transcribed. Its protein product (FMRP) appears to bind RNA, which means the gene product regulates expression of other genes (Weiler et al. 1997).

Three of the most common single-gene disorders that show effects on IQ but whose primary problem is something other than retardation are Duchenne muscular dystrophy, Lesch-Nyhan syndrome, and neurofibromatosis, caused by genes on Xp21, Xq26, and 17q11.2, respectively. Much more common than such single-gene causes of mental retardation are chromosomal abnormalities that lead to mental retardation. Most common are abnormalities that involve an entire extra chromosome, such as Down syndrome, caused by a trisomy of chromosome 21, which is the single most prevalent cause of mental retardation, occurring in 1 in 1000 births. As the resolution of chromosomal analysis becomes finer, more minor deletions are being found. A study of children with unexplained moderate to severe retardation found that 7% percent of them had subtle chromosomal abnormalities as compared with only 0.5% of children with mild retardation (Knight et al. 1999).

Although severe mental retardation has drastic consequences for the affected individual, mild mental retardation has a larger cumulative effect on society because many more individuals are affected. Despite its importance, there has never been a major twin or adoption study of mild mental retardation, and perhaps as a result there have been no QTL studies. Rather than assuming that mild mental retardation is due to a concatenation of rare single-gene or chromosomal causes, the QTL hypothesis is that mild mental retardation is caused by the same multiple genes that operate throughout the distribution to affect cognitive ability (Plomin 1999).

Hyperactivity

Recent twin study evidence for high heritability of attention-deficit hyperactivity disorder as well as a continuous dimension of hyperactive symptoms has led to a surge in molecular genetic research (Thapar et al. 1999). Although sib-pair linkage studies are underway, most of this research has concentrated on candidate gene association studies. Several groups have reported evidence of associations with the dopamine D4 receptor gene (DRD4), the dopamine transporter gene (DAT1), and the dopamine D5 receptor gene (DRD5) (Thapar 2003). For DRD4, 11 of 15 published studies have found evidence of association comparing cases and controls, and a meta-analysis indicates a significant effect with an odds ratio of $\sim$2 (Faraone et al. 2001). Two of three studies have found a stronger DRD4 association for children who respond well to methylphenidate (Thapar 2003). Meta-analysis of published results for DAT1 found six studies showing significant association and four that did not, with an overall odds ratio of 1.16 (Curran et al. 2001). However, there was significant evidence of heterogeneity between the datasets, and recently a far greater odds ratio of 8 has been reported in a Taiwanese population (Chen et al. 2002). A recent study of 311 pairs of unselected dizygotic twins found significant association between DAT1 and hyperactivity as a quantitative trait both within and between twin pairs (Asherson et al. 2002). DRD5 was also associated with hyperactivity (Daly et al. 1999), and three independent studies have subsequently shown nonsignificant trends in the same direction (Thapar 2003). Finally, two recent reports found evidence for association between a single nucleotide polymorphism in the 5HT1B gene in two large collaborative datasets (Hawi et al. 2002, Quist et al. 2002).

Alcoholism

The most well-known association with alcoholism is a recessive allele (ALDH2*2) that leads to low activity of acetaldehyde dehydrogenase, a key enzyme in the metabolism of alcohol. The buildup of acetaldehyde after alcohol is consumed leads to unpleasant symptoms such as flushing and nausea, thus protecting individuals against development of alcoholism. About half of East Asian individuals are homozygous for ALDH2*2, and hardly any such individuals have been found to be alcoholic. This is the major reason why rates of alcoholism are much lower in Asian than in Caucasian populations (Heath et al. 2003). Moreover, in a Japanese population, individuals with two copies of the ALDH2*2 allele consume ten times less alcohol per month than individuals who do not have the ALDH2*2 allele. Individuals with just one copy of the ALDH2*2 allele drink three times less per month than individuals without the allele (Higuchi et al. 1994). However, because the ALDH2*2 allele is rare in European populations, it contributes only negligibly to alcoholism in European populations (Borras et al. 2000).

Many early studies focused on a common polymorphism close to the dopamine D2 receptor, an association first reported in 1990 (Blum et al. 1990), which led to media reports that "the alcoholism gene" had been found. Subsequent failures to reproduce these results led to an equally uninformed backlash that damaged the credibility of association mapping efforts for all complex traits. A decade later the association remains controversial (Gorwood et al. 2000). A special issue for this dopamine D2 receptor gene polymorphism is that it shows large frequency differences between populations, as does alcoholism, which could create spurious associations if probands and controls are not well matched (Gelernter et al. 1993). Supporting this concern are the negative results that have come from research using within-family designs that control for ethnic stratification (Edenberg et al. 1998).

Of all of the candidate genes examined for association with alcoholism, the most promising are $GABA_A$ receptor genes (on chromosome 5q33-34). Several linkage studies of alcoholism have also been reported (Reich et al. 1999). A large QTL linkage study called the Collaborative Study on the Genetics of Alcoholism (COGA) includes 105 multigenerational families and 1200 families with at least three first-degree relatives including the alcoholic proband (Reich et al. 1998). For the multigenerational families, linkage was suggested on chromosomes 1, 4, and 7. COGA collaborations have led to publication of 68 papers describing diverse analyses of this remarkable dataset (Almasy & Borecki 1999). QTL research has begun to turn to other drugs of abuse, but no clear associations have yet emerged (Ball & Collier 2002, Heath et al. 2003). A promising new area for QTL research is individual differences in response to psychotropic medication (Aitchison & Gill 2003, Masellis et al. 2002).

Although mouse models have been developed for several domains such as depression, anxiety, dementia, and hyperactivity, they have been most widely used for finding QTLs in psychopharmacogenetics, especially for alcohol-related behavior (Craig & McClay 2003). Association studies of mice have definitively mapped at least 24 QTLs for alcohol drinking, alcohol-induced loss of righting reflex, and acute alcohol withdrawal, as well as other drug responses (Crabbe et al. 1999). Current research aims to narrow the chromosomal address of these QTL regions (e.g., Fehr et al. 2002). One study identified 5 QTLs that are associated with the large difference between lines selected for alcohol sensitivity (Markel et al. 1997). Alcohol sensitivity was assessed by sedation or "sleep time" following a dose of alcohol, with the "long-sleep" and "short-sleep" lines differing by 170 minutes. Each of the 5 QTLs conferred a difference in sleep time of about 20 minutes. Thus, if a mouse possessed all 5 short-sleep alleles, its genotype could account for 130 minutes of the total of 170 minutes in sleep-time difference between the long-sleep and short-sleep mice. Finding such sets of QTLs is the goal for human psychopathology. Despite the ability of mouse models to identify QTLs, mouse model QTL research on alcohol has not yet led to the identification of QTLs for human alcoholism. As noted earlier, mouse models are likely to be of greatest benefit for understanding how genes work (functional genomics) rather than for finding human QTLs. The special power of mouse models is the ability to control and manipulate both genotype and environment (Crabbe 2003, Phillips et al. 2002).

CONCLUSIONS

Early molecular genetic work focused on single-gene disorders in which a single gene is necessary and sufficient for a disorder. However, single-gene disorders tend to be severe but rare, whereas less severe but common disorders typical of psychopathology are likely to be influenced by multiple genes. The most recent example is the finding that a mutation in the FOXP2 gene causes language impairment of a severe and unusual sort (Lai et al. 2001). This mutation appears to be unique to the KE family; for example, the mutation was not found in a single child in a sample of 270 low-language children (Meaburn et al. 2002). Similarly, rare single-gene disorders have been found for early-onset dementia and severe mental retardation. It is possible, but seems highly unlikely, that common disorders are a concatenation of such rare single-gene disorders, a hypothesis facetiously called the one-gene-one-disorder (OGOD) hypothesis (Plomin et al. 1994). The field has moved toward a QTL hypothesis, which assumes that multiple genes affect common disorders and result in a quantitative continuum of vulnerability. This QTL perspective suggests that common disorders are the quantitative extreme of the same genetic factors responsible for variation throughout the distribution. The QTL hypothesis is by no means proven, but it is entirely an empirical issue. It predicts that when genes are found that are associated with common psychopathology the genes will be associated with variation throughout the distribution. Thus, phenotypic measurement (Farmer et al. 2002) will continue to be a key issue, but diagnosis of a precise cut-off for psychopathology will be of less concern because cut-offs are arbitrary if disorders are really the extremes of dimensions. For example, a recent book on molecular genetic research on personality views personality traits as endophenotypes of psychiatric disorders (Benjamin et al. 2002).

A major implication of this QTL perspective is that if multiple genes affect common disorders typical of psychopathology, the effect size of a particular gene is likely to be small. However, the distribution of effect sizes of QTLs is not known for any complex trait. From the single-gene perspective, in which the effect size of a gene is 100%, an effect size of 10% seems small. An effect size of 10% is in the range that can be detected by QTL linkage designs with feasible sample sizes. QTL linkages as in the case of the 6p21 linkage for reading disability and the APOE association with late-onset Alzheimer's disease indicate that there are some QTLs of this magnitude. However, the slow progress in identifying replicable associations for complex traits seems most likely to be due to a lack of power to detect QTLs of much smaller effect size (Cardon & Bell 2001). For this reason, it has been recommended that QTL studies aim to break the 1% barrier (Plomin et al. 2003b). Breaking this QTL barrier will require direct association designs using functional polymorphisms and sample sizes much larger than we have seen so far. A gloomier prospect is that if QTL effect sizes are less than 1% or if QTLs interact, it will be difficult to detect them reliably. If that is the case, the solution is to increase the power of research designs even more in order to track down the QTLs responsible for the ubiquitous and substantial heritability of psychopathology. DNA pooling, mentioned above, will be useful in this context because it costs no more to genotype 1000 individuals than 100 individuals.

Although molecular genetic research in psychopathology only began in earnest a decade ago, this is an extremely energetic and exciting area of research. Its future looks bright because complex traits like psychopathology will be the major beneficiaries of postgenomic developments that facilitate the investigation of complex traits influenced by many genes as well as by many environmental factors. This will happen first by finding genes associated with psychopathology and then by understanding the mechanisms by which those genes affect psychopathology at all levels of analysis from the cell to the brain to the whole organism. The most exciting prospect is the integration of quantitative genetics, molecular genetics, and functional genomics for a new focus on behavioral genomics. This integration is more than methodological and technological. Because DNA is the ultimate common denominator, genetic research on psychopathology in the postgenomic era will become increasingly integrated into the life sciences.

The *Annual Review of Psychology* is online at http://psych.annualreviews.org

LITERATURE CITED

Abecasis GR, Cardon LR, Cookson WO. 2000. A general test of association for quantitative traits in nuclear families. *Am. J. Hum. Genet.* 66(1):279–92

Aitchison KJ, Gill M. 2003. Response to psychotropic medication. See Plomin et al. 2003b, pp. 335–61

Almasy L, Borecki IG. 1999. Exploring genetic analysis of complex traits through the paradigm of alcohol dependence: summary of GAW11 contributions. *Genet. Epidemiol.* 17(S1):1–24

Asherson P, Xu X, Mill J, Curran S, Sham P, et al. 2002. The dopamine transporter gene is a quantitative trait locus (QTL) for early hyperactivity. Submitted

Badner JA, Gershon ES. 2002. Regional meta-analysis of published data supports linkage of autism with markers on chromosome 7. *Mol. Psychiatry* 7:56–66

Ball D, Collier DA. 2002. Substance misuse. See McGuffin et al. 2002

Banks RE, Dunn MJ, Hochstrasser DF, Sanchez JC, Blackstock W, et al. 2000. Proteomics: new perspectives, new biomedical opportunities. *Lancet* 356(9243):1749–56

Baron M. 2002. Manic-depression genes and the new millennium: poised for discovery. *Mol. Psychiatry* 7(4):342–58

Benjamin J, Ebstein RP, Belmaker RH. 2002. *Molecular Genetics and the Human Personality*. Washington, DC: Am. Psychiatr. Publ.

Berrettini WH. 2000. Susceptibility loci for bipolar disorder: overlap with inherited vulnerability to schizophrenia. *Biol. Psychiatry* 47:245–51

Bishop T, Sham PC. 2000. *Analysis of Multifactorial Disease*. London: Bios

Blum K, Noble EP, Sheridan PJ, Montgomery A, Ritchie T, et al. 1990. Allelic association of human dopamine D_2 receptor gene in alcoholism. *JAMA* 263:2055–60

Bonora E, Bacchelli E, Levy ER, Blasi F, Marlow A, et al. 2002. Mutation screening and imprinting analysis of four candidate genes for autism in the 7q32 region. *Mol. Psychiatry* 7(3):289–301

Borras E, Coutelle C, Rosell A, Fernandez-Muixi F, Broch M, et al. 2000. Genetic polymorphism of alcohol dehydrogenase in Europeans: the ADH2*2 allele decreases the risk for alcoholism and is associated with ADH3*1. *Hepatology* 31(4):984–89

Brett D, Pospisil H, Valcarcel J, Reich J, Bork P. 2002. Alternative splicing and genome complexity. *Nat. Genet.* 30:29–30

Buck KJ, Crabbe JC, Belknap JK. 2000. Alcohol and other abused drugs. In *Genetic Influences on Neural and Behavioral Functions*, ed. DW Pfaff, WH Berrettini, TH Joh, SC Maxson, pp. 159–83. Boca Raton, FL: CRC Press

Cardno AG, Rijsdijk FV, Sham PC, Murray RM, McGuffin P. 2002. A twin study of genetic relationships between psychotic symptoms. *Am. J. Psychiatry* 159:539–45

Cardon LR. 2003. Practical barrier to identifying complex trait loci. See Plomin et al. 2003b, pp. 59–69

Cardon LR, Bell J. 2001. Association study designs for complex diseases. *Nat. Genet.* 2:91–99

Cardon LR, Smith SD, Fulker DW, Kimberling WJ, Pennington BF, DeFries JC. 1994. Quantitative trait locus for reading disability on chromosome 6. *Science* 266:276–79

Chen CK, Huang YS, Lin SK, Chen SL, Mill J, et al. 2002. Is the size of the genetic risk for ADHD associated with DAT1 underestimated? A study of DAT1 in a Taiwanese ADHD sample. *Mol. Psychiatry.* In press

Colledge E, Bishop DVM, Dale P, Koeppen-Schomerus G, Price TS, et al. 2002. The structure of language abilities at 4 years: a twin study. *Dev. Psychol.* In press

Collier DA, Arranz MJ, Li T, Mupita D, Brown N, Treasure J. 1997. Association between 5-HT2A gene promoter polymorphism and anorexia nervosa. *Lancet* 350:412

Collier DA, Stober G, Li T, Heils A, Catalano M, et al. 1996. A novel functional polymorphism within the promoter of the serotonin transporter gene: possible role in susceptibility to affective disorders. *Mol. Psychiatry* 1:453–60

Corder EH, Saunders AM, Risch NJ, Strittmatter WJ, Schmechel DE, et al. 1994. Protective effect of apolipoprotein E type 2 allele for late onset Alzheimer disease. *Nat. Genet.* 7:180–84

Corder EH, Saunders AM, Strittmatter WJ, Schmechel DE, Gaskell PC, et al. 1993. Gene dose of apolipoprotein E type 4 allele and the risk of Alzheimer's disease in late onset families. *Science* 261(5123):921–23

Coyle N, Jones I, Robertson E, Lendon C, Craddock N. 2000. Variation at the serotonin transporter gene influences susceptibility to bipolar affective puerperal psychosis. *Lancet* 356(9240):1490–91

Crabbe JC. 2003. Finding genes for complex behaviors: progress in mouse models of the addictions. See Plomin et al. 2003b, pp. 291–308

Crabbe JC, Phillips TJ, Buck KJ, Cunningham CL, Belknap JK. 1999. Identifying genes for alcohol and drug sensitivity: recent progress and future directions. *Trends Neurosci.* 22:173–79

Craig I, McClay J. 2003. The role of molecular genetics in the postgenomics era. See Plomin et al. 2003b, pp. 19–40

Crusio WE, Gerlai RT. 1999. *Handbook of Molecular-Genetic Techniques for Brain and Behavior Research*. Amsterdam: Elsevier

Cruts M, van Duijn CM, Backhovens H, van den Broeck M, Wehnert A. 1998. Estimation of the genetic contribution of presenilin-1 and 2 mutations in a population-based study of presenile Alzheimer disease. *Hum. Mol. Genet.* 71:43–51

Curran S, Mill J, Tahir E, Kent L, Richards S, et al. 2001. Association study of a dopamine transporter polymorphism and attention deficit hyperactivity disorder in UK and Turkish samples. *Mol. Psychiatry* 6:425–28

Dale PS, Dionne G, Eley TC, Plomin R. 2000. Lexical and grammatical development: a behavioral genetic perspective. *J. Child Lang.* 27(3):619–42

Daly G, Hawi Z, Fitzgerald M, Gill M. 1999. Mapping susceptibility loci in attention deficit hyperactivity disorder: preferential transmission of parental alleles at DAT1, DBH and DRD5 to affected children. *Mol. Psychiatry* 4:192–96

Daniels GM, Buck KJ. 2002. Expression profiling identifies strain-specific changes associated with ethanol withdrawal in mice. *Genes Brain Behav.* 1:35–45

Daniels J, Holmans P, Plomin R, McGuffin P, Owen MJ. 1998. A simple method for analyzing microsatellite allele image patterns generated from DNA pools and its application to allelic association studies. *Am. J. Hum. Genet.* 62:1189–97

Eddy SR. 2001. Non-coding RNA genes and the modern RNA world. *Nat. Rev. Genet.* 2(12):919–29

Edenberg HJ, Faroud T, Koller DL, Goate A, Rice J, et al. 1998. A family-bases analysis of the association of the dopamine D2 receptor (DRD2) with alcoholism. *Alcohol. Clin. Exp. Res.* 22(2):505–12

Edwards TH. 1965. The meaning of the associations between blood groups and disease. *Ann. Hum. Genet.* 29:77–83

Egeland JA, Gerhard DS, Pauls DL, Sussex JN, Kidd KK, et al. 1987. Bipolar affective disorders linked to DNA markers on chromosome 11. *Nature* 325(26):783–87

Eley TC, Collier DA, McGuffin P. 2002. Anxiety and eating disorders. See McGuffin et al. 2002

Fagerheim T, Raeymaekers P, Tonnessen FE, Pedersen M, Tranebjaerg L, Lubs HA. 1999. A new gene (DYX3) for dyslexia is located on chromosome 2. *J. Med. Genet.* 36:664–69

Falconer DS. 1965. The inheritance of liability to certain diseases estimated from the incidence among relatives. *Ann. Hum. Genet.* 29:51–76

Faraone SV, Doyle AE, Mick E, Biederman J. 2001. Meta-analysis of the association between the 7-repeat allele of the dopamine D(4) receptor gene and attention deficit hyperactivity disorder. *Am. J. Psychiatry* 158(7):1052–57

Farmer A, McGuffin P, Williams J. 2002. *Measuring Psychopathology.* Oxford: Oxford Univ. Press

Farrer LA, Cupples LA, Haines JL, Hyman B, Kukull WA, et al. 1997. Effects of age, sex, and ethnicity on the association between apolipoprotein E genotype and Alzheimer disease. A meta-analysis. APOE and Alzheimer Disease Meta Analysis Consortium. *JAMA* 278(16):1349–56

Fehr C, Belknap JK, Crabbe JC, Buck KJ. 2002. Congenic mapping of alcohol and pentobarbital withdrawal liability quantitative trait loci to a 0.9 cM region of mouse chromosome 4: identification of *Mpdz* as a candidate gene. *J. Neurosci.* 22(9):3730–38

Fisher SE. 2003. Isolation of the genetic factors underlying speech and language disorders. See Plomin et al. 2003b, pp. 205–26

Fisher SE, Francks C, Marlow AJ, MacPhie IL, Newbury DF, et al. 2002. Independent genome-wide scans identify a chromosome 18 quantitative-trait locus influencing dyslexia. *Nat. Genet.* 30(1):86–91

Fisher SE, Smith SD. 2001. *Progress Towards the Identification of Genes Influencing Developmental Dyslexia.* London: Whurr

Fisher SE, Vargha-Khadem F, Watkins KE, Monaco AP, Pembrey ME. 1998. Localisation of a gene implicated in a severe speech and language disorder. *Nat. Genet.* 18:168–70

Folstein SE, Rosen-Sheidley B. 2001. Genetics of autism: complex aetiology for a heterogeneous disorder. *Nat. Rev. Genet.* 2:943–55

Gelernter J, Goldman D, Risch N. 1993. The A1 allele at the D_2 dopamine receptor gene and alcoholism: a reappraisal. *JAMA* 269:1673–77

Gorwood P, Batel P, Gouya L, Courtois F, Feingold J, Ades J. 2000. Reappraisal of the association between the DRD2 gene, alcoholism and addiction. *Eur. Psychiatry* 15(2):90–96

Guldberg P, Rey F, Zschocke J, Romano V, Francois B, et al. 1998. A European multicenter study of phenylalanine hydroxylase deficiency: classification of 105 mutations and a general system for genotype-based prediction of metabolic phenotype. *Am. J. Hum. Genet.* 63:71–79

Gusella JF, Wexler NS, Conneally PM, Naylor SL, Anderson MA, Tanzi RE. 1983. A polymorphic DNA marker genetically linked to Huntington's disease. *Nature* 306:234–38

Hawi Z, Dring M, Kirley A, Foley D, Kent L, et al. 2002. Serotonergic system and attention deficit hyperactivity disorder (ADHD): a potential susceptibility locus at the 5-HT1B receptor gene in a multi-centre sample. *Mol. Psychiatry.* In press

Heath AC, Madden PAF, Bucholz KK, Nelson EC, Todorov A, et al. 2003. Genetic and genotype x environment interaction effects on risk of dependence on alcohol, tobacco, and other drugs: new research. See Plomin et al. 2003b, pp. 309–34

Higuchi S, Matsushita S, Imazeki H, Kinoshita T, Takagi S, Kono H. 1994. Aldehyde dehydrogenase genotypes in Japanese alcoholics. *Lancet* 343:741–42

Hunt. Dis. Collab. Res. Group. 1993. A novel gene containing a trinucleotide repeat that is expanded and unstable on Huntington's disease chromosomes. *Cell* 72:971–83

Int. Hum. Genome Seq. Consort. 2001. Initial sequencing and analysis of the human genome. *Nature* 409:860–921

Int. Mol. Genet. Study Autism Consort. 1998. A full genome screen for autism with evidence for linkage to a region on chromosome 7q. *Hum. Mol. Genet.* 7:571–78

Jones I, Kent L, Craddock N. 2002. Genetics of affective disorders. See McGuffin et al. 2002

Kalidindi S, McGuffin P. 2003. The genetics of affective disorders: current and future. See Plomin et al. 2003b, pp. 481–501

Kaufmann WE, Reiss AL. 1999. Molecular and cellular genetics of fragile X syndrome. *Am. J. Med. Genet.* 88:11–24

Kim S-J, Cox N, Courchesne R, Lord C, Corsello C, et al. 2002. Transmission disequilibrium mapping at the serotonin transporter gene (*SLC6A4*) region in autistic disorder. *Mol. Psychiatry* 7:278–88

Knight SJL, Regan R, Nicod A, Horsley SW, Kearney L, et al. 1999. Subtle chromosomal rearrangements in children with unexplained mental retardation. *Lancet* 354(9191):1676–81

Lai CS, Fisher SE, Hurst JA, Vargha-Khadem F, Monaco AP. 2001. A forkhead-domain gene is mutated in a severe speech and language disorder. *Nature* 413(6855):519–23

Lesch KP, Bengel D, Heils A, Sabol SZ, Greenberg BD, et al. 1996. Association of anxiety-related traits with a polymorphism in the serotonin transporter gene regulatory region. *Science* 274:1527–31

Lesch PK. 2003. Neuroticism and serotonin: a developmental genetic perspective. See Plomin et al. 2003b, pp. 389–423

Levinson DF, Holmans PA, Laurent C, Riley B, Pulver AE, et al. 2002. No major schizophrenia locus detected on chromosome 1q in a large multicenter sample. *Science* 296:739–41

Liddell MB, Williams J, Owen MJ. 2002. The dementias. See McGuffin et al. 2002

Malhi GS, Moore J, McGuffin P. 2000. The genetics of major depression. *Curr. Psychiatry Rep.* 2:165–69

Markel PD, Bennett B, Beeson M, Gordon L, Johnson TE. 1997. Confirmation of quantitative trait loci for ethanol sensitivity in long-sleep and short-sleep mice. *Genome Res.* 7:92–99

Masellis M, Basile VS, Muglia P, Ozdemir V, Macciardi FM, et al. 2002. Psychiatric pharmacogenetics: personalizing psychostimulant therapy in attention-deficit/hyperactivity disorder. *Behav. Brain Res.* 130:85–90

McGuffin P, Gottesman II, Owen MJ. 2002. *The Genetics of Psychiatric Disorders.* Oxford: Oxford Univ. Press. In press

Meaburn E, Dale PS, Craig IW, Plomin R. 2002. Language impaired children. No sign of the FOXP2 mutation. *NeuroReport.* 13(8):1–3

Morris DW, Robinson L, Turic D, Duke M, Webb V, et al. 2000. Family-based association mapping provides evidence for a gene for reading disability on chromosome 15q. *Hum. Mol. Genet.* 9(5):843–48

Newbury DF, Bonora E, Lamb JA, Fisher SE, Lai CSL, et al. 2002. FOXP2 is not a major susceptibility gene for autism or specific language impairment. *Am. J. Hum. Genet.* 70:1318–27

Ogawa S, Pfaff DW. 1996. Application of antisense DNA method for the study of molecular bases of brain function and behavior. *Behav. Genet.* 26:279–92

Owen MJ, O'Donovan MC. 2003. Schizophrenia. See Plomin et al. 2003b, pp. 463–80

Pericak-Vance MA. 2003. The genetics of autistic disorder. See Plomin et al. 2003b, pp. 267–88

Petryshen TL, Kaplan BL, Hughes ML, Field LL. 2000. Evidence for the chromosome 2p15-p16 dyslexia susceptibility locus (DYX3) in a large Canadian data set. *Am. J. Med. Genet.* 96(4):473

Phillips TJ, Belknap JK, Hitzemann RJ, Buck KJ, Cunningham CL, Crabbe JC. 2002. Harnessing the mouse to unravel the genetics of human disease. *Genes Brain Behav.* 1:14–26

Plomin R. 1999. Genetic research on general cognitive ability as a model for mild mental retardation. *Int. Rev. Psychiatry* 11:34–36

Plomin R, Colledge E, Dale PS. 2002a. Genetics and the development of language disabilities and abilities. *Curr. Paediatr.* In press

Plomin R, Crabbe JC. 2000. DNA. *Psychol. Bull.* 126(6):806–28

Plomin R, DeFries JC, Craig IW, McGuffin P. 2003a. Behavior genetics. See Plomin et al. 2003b, pp. 3–15

Plomin R, DeFries JC, Craig IW, McGuffin P. 2003b. *Behavioral Genetics in the Postgenomic Era.* Washington, DC: APA Books

Plomin R, DeFries JC, Craig IW, McGuffin P. 2003c. Behavioral genomics. See Plomin et al. 2003b, pp. 531–40

Plomin R, DeFries JC, McClearn GE, McGuffin P. 2001a. *Behavioral Genetics.* New York: Worth. 4th ed.

Plomin R, Hill L, Craig IW, McGuffin P, Purcell S, et al. 2001b. A genome-wide scan of 1842 DNA markers for allelic associations with general cognitive ability: a five-stage design using DNA pooling. *Behav. Genet.* 31(6):497–509

Plomin R, Owen MJ, McGuffin P. 1994. The genetic basis of complex human behaviors. *Science* 264(5166):1733–39

Pritchard JK, Rosenberg NA. 1999. Use of unlinked genetic markers to detect population stratification in association studies. *Am. J. Hum. Genet.* 65(1):220–28

Quist JF, Barr CL, Schachar R, Roberts W, Malone M, et al. 2002. The serotonin 5-HT1B receptor gene and attention deficit hyperactivity disorder (ADHD). *Mol. Psychiatry.* In press

Reich T, Edenberg HJ, Goate A, Williams J, Rice J, et al. 1998. Genome-wide search for genes affecting the risk for alcohol dependence. *Am. J. Med. Genet.* 81:207–15

Reich T, Hinrichs A, Culverhouse R, Beirut L. 1999. Genetics studies of alcoholism and substance dependence. *Am. J. Hum. Genet.* 65:599–605

Risch NJ. 2000. Searching for genetic determinants in the new millennium. *Nature* 405:847–56

Rutter M, Silberg J. 2002. Gene-environment interplay in relation to emotional and behavioral disturbance. *Annu. Rev. Psychol.* 53:463–90

Schellenberg GD, D'Souza I, Poorkaj P. 2000. The genetics of Alzheimer's disease. *Curr. Psychiatry Rep.* 2:158–64

Scott WK, Pericak-Vance MA, Haines JL. 1997. Genetic analysis of complex diseases. *Science* 275:1327

Sham P. 2003. Recent developments in quantitative trait loci analysis. See Plomin et al. 2003b, pp. 41–53

Sham PC, Cherny SS, Purcell S, Hewitt J. 2000. Power of linkage versus association analysis of quantitative traits, by use of variance-components models, for sibship data. *Am. J. Hum. Genet.* 66:1616–30

Sherrington R, Brynjolfsson J, Petursson H, Potter M, Dudleston K, et al. 1988. Localisation of susceptibility locus for schizophrenia on chromosome 5. *Nature* 336:164–67

Sherrington R, Rogaev EI, Liang Y, Rogaeva EA, Levesque G, et al. 1995. Cloning of a gene bearing mis-sense mutation in early-onset familial Alzheimer's disease. *Nature* 375:754–60

SLI Consortium. 2002. A genome wide scan identifies two novel loci involved in specific language impairment. *Am. J. Hum. Genet.* 70: 384–98

Spielman RS, Ewens WJ. 1996. The TDT and other family-based tests for linkage disequilibrium and association. *Am. J. Hum. Genet.* 59:983–89

St. George-Hyslop P, Haines J, Rogaev E, Mortilla M, Vaula G, et al. 1992. Genetic evidence for a novel familial Alzheimer's disease locus on chromosome 14. *Nat. Genet.* 2:330–34

Sturt E, McGuffin P. 1985. Can linkage and marker association resolve the genetic aetiology of psychiatric disorders? Review and argument. *Psychol. Med.* 15(3):455–62

Tabor HK, Risch NJ, Myers RM. 2002. Candidate-gene approaches for studying complex genetic traits: practical considerations. *Nat. Rev. Genet.* 3(5):391–97

Thapar A. 2003. Attention deficit hyperactivity disorder: new genetic findings, new directions. See Plomin et al. 2003b, pp. 445–62

Thapar A, Holmes J, Poulton K, Harrington R. 1999. Genetic basis of attention deficit and hyperactivity. *Br. J. Psychiatry* 174:105–11

Turecki G, Rouleau GA, Mari J, Joober R, Morgan K. 1997. Lack of association between bipolar disorder and tyrosine hydroxylase: a meta-analysis. *Am. J. Med. Genet.* 74:348–52

Turic D, Robinson L, Duke M, Morris DW, Webb V, et al. 2002. Linkage disequilibrium mapping provides further evidence for a gene for reading disability on chromosome 6p21. *Mol. Psychiatry.* In press

Van Broeckhoven D, Verheyen G. 1999. Report of the chromosome 18 workshop. *Am. J. Med. Genet.* 882:263–70

Verkerk AJMH, Pieretti M, Sutcliffe JS, Fu Y-H, Kuhl DPA, et al. 1991. Identification of a gene (FMR-1) containing a CGG repeat coincident with a breakpoint cluster region exhibiting length variation in fragile X syndrome. *Cell* 65:905–14

Wahlsten D. 1999. Single-gene influences on brain and behavior. *Annu. Rev. Psychol.* 50: 599–624

Waterworth DM, Bassett AS, Brzustowicz

LM. 2002. Recent advances in the genetics of schizophrenia. *Cell. Mol. Life Sci.* 59(2): 331–48

Weiler I, Irwin S, Klinstova AV, Spencer CM, Comery TA, et al. 1997. Fragile X mental retardation protein is translated near synapses in response to neurotransmitter activation. *Proc. Natl. Acad. Sci. USA* 94:5394–400

Weiss KM, Terwilliger JD. 2000. How many diseases does it take to map a gene with SNPs. *Nat. Genet.* 26(2):151–57

Willcutt EG, DeFries JC, Pennington BF, Smith SD, Cardon LR, Olson RK. 2003. Genetic etiology of comorbid reading difficulties and ADHD. See Plomin et al. 2003b, pp. 227–46

Williams J. 2003. Dementia. See Plomin et al. 2003b, pp. 503–27

Williams J. 2002. Language disorders. See McGuffin et al. 2002

Williams J, McGuffin P, Nothen M, Owen MJ, Group EC. 1997. A meta analysis of association between the 5-HT2a receptor T102C polymorphism and schizophrenia. *Lancet* 349:1221

Williams J, Spurlock G, Holmans P, Mant R, Murphy K, et al. 1998. A meta-analysis and transmission disequilibrium study of association between the dopamine D3 receptor gene and schizophrenia. *Mol. Psychiatry* 3:141–49

Williams NM, Rees MI, Holmans P, Norton N, Cardno AG, et al. 1999. A two-stage genome scan of schizophrenia susceptibility genes in 196 affected sibling pairs. *Hum. Mol. Genet.* 8:1729–40

Zechner U, Wilda M, Kehrer-Sawatzki H, Vogel W, Fundele R, Hameister H. 2001. A high density of X-linked genes for general cognitive ability: a runaway process shaping human evolution? *Trends Genet.* 17:697–701

Ziegler A, Hebebrand J, Görg T, Rosenkranz K, Fichter MM, et al. 1999. Further lack of association between the 5-HT2A gene promoter polymorphism and susceptiblity to eating disorders and a meta-analysis pertaining to anorexia nervosa. *Mol. Psychiatry* 4:410–17

Annu. Rev. Psychol. 2003. 54:229–52
doi: 10.1146/annurev.psych.54.101601.145112
First published online as a Review in Advance on August 6, 2002

PROGRESS AND CONTROVERSY IN THE STUDY OF POSTTRAUMATIC STRESS DISORDER

Richard J. McNally

Department of Psychology, Harvard University, 33 Kirkland Street, Cambridge, Massachusetts 02138; e-mail: rjm@wjh.harvard.edu

Key Words PTSD, trauma, memory, childhood sexual abuse, repression, Vietnam veterans

■ **Abstract** Research on posttraumatic stress disorder (PTSD) has been notable for controversy as well as progress. This article concerns the evidence bearing on the most contentious issues in the field of traumatic stress: broadening of the definition of trauma, problems with the dose-response model of PTSD, distortion in the recollection of trauma, concerns about "phony combat vets," psychologically toxic guilt as a traumatic stressor, risk factors for PTSD, possible brain-damaging effects of stress hormones, recovered memories of childhood sexual abuse, and the politics of trauma.

CONTENTS

INTRODUCTION

Research on anxiety disorders has increased dramatically since the early 1980s (Norton et al. 1995). The scientific literature is now vast, defying ready mastery, and even the finest, most ambitious works of scholarship are unavoidably synoptic (e.g., Antony & Swinson 2000, Barlow 2002, Craske 1999). We have learned much about these syndromes, but with progress comes controversy, and the field has had no shortage of either. This has been especially true for posttraumatic stress disorder (PTSD). My purpose is to examine the evidence bearing on the most contentious issues in the field of traumatic stress studies.

THE EMERGENCE OF POSTTRAUMATIC STRESS DISORDER

Military psychiatrists have always recognized that horrific events could trigger acute stress symptoms in previously well-adjusted individuals (Shephard 2001) but most doctors believed these reactions subsided soon after the soldier left the battlefield (Wilson 1994). This conventional wisdom changed in the wake of the Vietnam War. Antiwar psychiatrists, such as Robert Lifton, argued that many veterans continued to suffer severe stress symptoms long after having returned home (Scott 1990). Other veterans, they said, appeared well adjusted upon return to civilian life, only to develop a delayed stress syndrome months or years later. Because there was no place in the existing diagnostic system for either a chronic stress syndrome or a delayed one, these psychiatrists lobbied for inclusion of "post-Vietnam syndrome" in the forthcoming third edition of the *Diagnostic and Statistical Manual of Mental Disorders* (*DSM-III*) (APA 1980, Young 1995). They believed that certain features of this war—such as difficulty telling friend from foe, atrocities, and unclear military goals—made it especially likely that it would produce long-lasting psychiatric illness.

Members of the *DSM-III* task force were reluctant to endorse a diagnosis tied specifically to a historical event. Yet they eventually relented when veterans' advocates persuaded them that the same stress syndrome occurred in survivors of other traumatic events, such as rape, natural disaster, or confinement in a concentration camp. Converging clinical evidence, pointing to a common syndromic consequence of trauma, clinched the inclusion of PTSD in *DSM-III*.

Ironically, historical scholarship has now confirmed that psychiatric casualties seldom occurred in the Vietnam War, relative to other wars: The rate of breakdown was only 12 cases per 1000 men. In contrast, the rate of psychiatric breakdown during the Korean War was 37 per 1000, and during World War II it ranged from 28 to 101 per 1000 (Dean 1997, p. 40). In yet another irony, one prominent sociologist, a former member of Vietnam Veterans Against the War, has argued that advocates for the PTSD diagnosis inappropriately medicalized political dissent when they conceptualized the problems of veterans as a form of mental illness (Lembcke 1998, pp. 101–26).

In any event, the *DSM-III* defined PTSD as a syndrome erupting in response to a "stressor that would evoke significant symptoms of distress in almost everyone" (APA 1980, p. 238). The diagnosis comprised three symptom clusters. The re-experiencing cluster included recurrent intrusive thoughts about the trauma, traumatic nightmares, and "flashbacks." The numbing cluster included feelings of detachment from others, loss of interest in activities, and constricted affect. The third cluster included miscellaneous symptoms such as exaggerated startle, sleep disturbance, and memory impairment or trouble concentrating.

The ratification of PTSD as a formal psychiatric disorder triggered an outpouring of research on trauma and motivated the founding of the International Society for Traumatic Stress Studies and the establishment of scholarly journals devoted to the topic (e.g., *Journal of Traumatic Stress*, launched in 1988). The field has been enriched by the efforts of clinical scientists specializing in trauma, and their findings have placed into sharp relief several contentious issues.

CONCEPTUAL BRACKET CREEP IN THE DEFINITION OF TRAUMA

PTSD is unusual among DSM syndromes in that the diagnostic criteria specify an etiologic event: exposure to a traumatic stressor. Regardless of whatever symptoms may be present, unless a person has been exposed to a qualifying stressor, the diagnosis cannot be made. The architects of *DSM-III* had in mind events such as combat, rape, and earthquakes as the kind of event capable of causing the disorder. However, *DSM-IV* defines traumatic exposure as "the person experienced, witnessed, or was *confronted with* an event or events that involved actual or threatened death or serious injury, or a threat to the physical integrity of self or others," and which evoked "intense fear, helplessness, or horror" (APA 1994, pp. 427–28, emphasis added). Despite references to life threat and injury, *DSM-IV* significantly broadens the definition of a traumatic stressor. For example, a person who merely learns about someone else being threatened with harm qualifies as having been exposed to trauma and is therefore eligible for a PTSD diagnosis (assuming fulfillment of symptomatic criteria).

By broadening the definition of traumatic stressor, *DSM-IV* codifies a kind of conceptual bracket creep. No longer must one be the direct (or even vicarious) recipient of trauma; merely being horrified by what has happened to others now counts as a PTSD-qualifying event. Such secondhand exposure seems qualitatively distinct from being subjected to artillery bombardment for days on end while huddled in a muddy trench. Yet prevailing nosologic practice brackets both kinds of event under the same stressor rubric. With such diverse events deemed causally relevant to PTSD, it will be difficult to identify common psychobiologic mechanisms underlying symptomatic expression.

Noting that a traumatic stressor need not be life-threatening, Avina & O'Donohue (2002) have recently argued that repeatedly overhearing jokes in the workplace may qualify as a stressor that triggers PTSD. PTSD induced by repeated exposure to sexual jokes and, of course, other more serious forms of sexual harassment in the workplace provides the justification for lawsuits to secure "appropriate monetary compensations," argued Avina & O'Donohue (2002, p. 74).

Overhearing obnoxious sexual jokes in the workplace may provide a legal basis for litigation, but it seems unlikely to produce the same psychobiological state of PTSD as violent rape.

Conceptual bracket creep was strikingly evident in the recent national survey conducted by the RAND Corporation on the weekend following the September 11, 2001 terrorist attacks (Schuster et al. 2001). After interviewing a representative sample of 560 adults throughout the United States, Schuster et al. concluded that 44% of Americans "had substantial symptoms of stress" (p. 1507), ominously adding that the psychological effects of terrorism "are unlikely to disappear soon" (p. 1511) and that "clinicians should anticipate that even people far from the attacks will have trauma-related symptoms" (p. 1512). This research team asked respondents whether they had experienced any of five symptoms "since Tuesday" (i.e., September 11, 2001). Respondents were asked to rate each symptom on a five-point scale ranging from one ("not at all") to five ("extremely"). A person qualified as "substantially stressed" if he or she assigned a rating of at least four ("quite a bit") to one of the five symptoms. For example, someone who had "quite a bit" of anger at Osama bin Laden qualified as substantially stressed. As Wakefield & Spitzer (2002) have cogently argued, such surveys medicalize expectable human reactions by failing to discriminate between genuine symptoms of disorder and normal distress reactions.

PROBLEMS WITH THE DOSE-RESPONSE MODEL OF POSTTRAUMATIC STRESS DISORDER

The dose-response model holds that PTSD symptoms worsen as the severity of the stressor increases (March 1993). Many researchers interpret this model in terms of Pavlovian fear conditioning (e.g., Keane et al. 1985b). Hence, traumatic stressors function like unconditioned stimuli that elicit the unconditioned response of terror, establishing neutral cues as conditioned stimuli that elicit the conditioned response of fear. Accordingly, they believe that a laboratory rat's reaction to inescapable electric shock parallels at least some aspects of the human response to overwhelming trauma (Foa et al. 1992, van der Kolk et al. 1985). Just as increasing severity of shock exacerbates a rat's conditioned fear, so should increasing severity of trauma exacerbate a victim's PTSD symptoms.

Some studies are consistent with this prediction. For example, a greater proportion of World War II combat veterans who had been tortured by the Japanese as prisoners of war (POWs) have current PTSD (70%) than do those who had never been captured and tortured (18%) (Sutker et al. 1993). Ex-servicemen wounded in Vietnam are two to three times more likely to have PTSD than are those who returned unharmed (Kulka et al. 1990, p. 54). Proximity to the epicenter of an earthquake predicted severity of PTSD symptoms (Pynoos et al. 1993), and the higher the rate of wounds and fatalities within a combat unit, the higher the rate of psychiatric casualties (Jones & Wessely 2001).

However, many studies fail to support the dose-response model (for reviews, see Bowman 1997, 1999). The relationship between dosage of trauma and resultant psychopathology is far from straightforward. For example, objective measures of accident severity are unrelated to PTSD symptoms among victims of motor vehicle (and other) accidents (Schnyder et al. 2001), and the number of torture episodes is unrelated to PTSD symptom severity among imprisoned Turkish political activists (Başoğlu et al. 1994). Of course, the relationship between dose and response might be nonlinear (Harvey & Yehuda 1999). That is, if PTSD symptoms reach near maximum severity after a certain dosage of exposure, further exposure might not add much to existing levels of psychiatric impairment. For example, a person who is tortured twice may have more symptoms than someone who had never been tortured. Yet a person who has been tortured a dozen times may be no more symptomatic than one who was only tortured twice. Unfortunately, by recasting the dose-response model in nonlinear terms, any pattern between dose and symptoms would be interpretable as confirming the model (except, of course, a linear one).

DISTORTION IN THE RECOLLECTION OF TRAUMA

Data are not the only source of trouble for the dose-response model of traumatic stress. It is plagued by serious measurement difficulties as well. The animal conditioning laboratory provides the conceptual basis for the model, but calibrating stressor magnitude in trauma studies is vastly more complicated than in Pavlovian conditioning experiments. Laboratory stressors are measurable in purely physical terms entirely independent of the animal's behavior (e.g., shock amperage, number of shocks). Yet in the trauma field, researchers usually rely on the retrospective self-reports of the survivors themselves as the sole basis for measuring stressor magnitude. This practice presupposes that psychiatrically distressed individuals can furnish reliable, objective accounts untarnished by clinical state. Scientists have recently shown just how unwarranted this presupposition is.

Several studies show that a survivor's current clinical state affects how he or she remembers the traumatic experience. Longitudinal studies on staff present at a fatal shooting at an elementary school (Schwarz et al. 1993), Gulf War veterans (Southwick et al. 1997), automobile accident survivors (Harvey & Bryant 2000), and former military peacekeepers who had served in Somalia (Roemer et al. 1998) all show that memory of trauma is affected by clinical state. In each of these studies researchers obtained self-reports of traumatic events on two occasions. The more PTSD symptoms a person had at time two, the more severe the person remembered the traumatic experience to have been. For example, Southwick et al. found that 88% of Gulf War veterans remembered their traumatic events differently at time two than how they had originally reported them two years earlier. Seventy-percent recalled a traumatic event at time two that they had not mentioned at time one (one month after the war), whereas 46% failed to mention a traumatic event at time two that they had mentioned at time one. The severity of PTSD symptoms at time two significantly predicted the number of traumatic events mentioned at time two that were not mentioned at time one. Southwick et al. (1997) concluded that veterans with higher PTSD scores "tend to amplify their memory for traumatic events over time" (p. 176).

It is unlikely that the trauma survivors in these studies were lying. Rather, traumatic memories, like all autobiographical memories, are reconstructed from encoded elements distributed throughout the brain (Schacter 1996). The context of retrieval, including clinical state, affects how these recollections occur. Although scientists, who study fear conditioning in rats, once believed that emotional memories are indelible (LeDoux et al. 1989), they have recently discovered that even these memories are subject to alteration (Morrison et al. 2002). What is true for rats is even more true for people. Although people retain traumatic memories very well, even recollections of the most horrific events are not immune to alteration of time (McNally 2003).

THE SPECTER OF THE "PHONY COMBAT VET"

The aforementioned studies concern benign memory distortion, not dishonesty, but two other issues have come to the fore in the trauma field that pose greater problems than mere "normal" memory change. One problem concerns deliberate exaggeration of symptoms in Vietnam veterans seeking to obtain the PTSD diagnosis (Frueh et al. 2000). As many as 94% of veterans with PTSD apply for financial compensation for their illness (McGrath & Frueh 2002), and the incentive to do so is strong, especially for those with limited occupational opportunities (Mossman 1994). A veteran who obtains a service-connected disability rating of 100% for PTSD can earn more than $36,000 per year, tax-free and indexed to inflation, for life (Burkett & Whitley 1998, p. 236). The financial loss is substantial should they ever recover from PTSD. This incentive structure does not mean that most PTSD veterans are malingerers. However, the ease of faking symptoms and the incentives for doing so should worry researchers, who need to ensure that subjects in their studies really do have the disorder. This problem is not confined to Vietnam veterans. The risk of malingered PTSD arises in civil suits following accidents in civilian life as well (e.g., Rosen 1995).

The second problem concerns men who claim to be suffering from combat-related PTSD but who either never saw combat, never served in Vietnam, or never served in the military at all. In their award-winning book, *Stolen Valor*, Vietnam veteran B.G. Burkett and investigative journalist Glenna Whitley thoroughly documented seemingly countless cases of "phony combat vets" (Burkett & Whitley 1998). By obtaining military records, via the Freedom of Information Act, of men whose names had appeared in public (e.g., leaders of veterans' organizations, the actor Brian Dennehy), Burkett & Whitley discovered much fraud. Some alleged combat veterans never saw combat; others never served in Vietnam; and still others were never in the military at all. For example, by obtaining the records of members of the American Ex-POW Association, they discovered that nearly 30% of those claiming to have been held captive by the North Vietnamese were never POWs (Burkett & Whitley 1998, pp. 502–3). The men investigated by Burkett & Whitley are not merely faking symptoms of PTSD; they are faking their history of exposure to trauma itself. Burkett & Whitley estimated that about 75% of those "receiving PTSD compensation are pretenders" (Burkett & Whitley 1998, p. 279).

Given that a vast amount of what we know about PTSD is based on the reports of Vietnam veterans, clinical researchers need to attend to the issues raised by Burkett & Whitley. They recommend obtaining military records directly from the National Personnel Records Center in St. Louis to verify self-reports of combat exposure rather than merely relying on a photocopy of the DD-214 furnished by the veteran himself. The DD-214 is a military transcript, issued to each veteran upon his discharge. It lists his military occupational specialty, receipt of awards (e.g., Combat Infantryman's Badge, Purple Heart), and dates of service. At most, PTSD researchers have usually required only that the veteran furnish a photocopy of his DD-214 as proof of combat exposure, but there are two problems with this procedure. First, one can easily forge combat-related items on the DD-214 by, for example, typing "Purple Heart" on the form. Second, the clerk-typists responsible for completing these forms when a soldier was discharged sometimes failed to include relevant items on the DD-214. Hence, DD-214s may either overestimate or underestimate combat exposure. A veteran's complete military file is much less vulnerable to these validity problems.

It is important to debunk two myths about these military archives. First, contrary to a persistent urban legend in the traumatic stress field, the fire that erupted in the National Personnel Records Center on July 12, 1973 did not destroy the files of Vietnam veterans (Stender & Walker 1974). Not only were the damaged records those of men who served before the Vietnam era, but government archivists were able to reconstruct 94% of them by relying on microfilm and archives stored elsewhere. Second, some veterans claim that the government erased all evidence of their top-secret, covert operations from their record. In reality, details of the covert mission will be redacted, leaving only the dates of the mission and the phrase "Classified Assignment." However, the special training requisite for membership in elite units assigned to covert operations (e.g., the Green Berets) is not redacted (Burkett & Whitley 1998, pp. 285–86).

Burkett & Whitley believe that many studies of combat-related PTSD are contaminated by the inadvertent inclusion of subjects who have lied about their combat trauma. They are especially critical of the National Vietnam Veterans Readjustment Study (NVVRS), an epidemiologic survey that yielded a lifetime PTSD prevalence rate of 30.9% among men who had served in Vietnam (Kulka et al. 1990). This rate of PTSD is astonishingly high, given that only 15% of the men who served in Vietnam were assigned to combat units (Dean 1997, p. 209). To be sure, men with noncombat military occupational specialties (e.g., truck driver) sometimes got in harm's way and developed PTSD. But even after we allow for the ambushed truck drivers and other trauma-exposed noncombatants, explaining the 30.9% PTSD prevalence rate is not easy.

According to Burkett & Whitely (1998), the NVVRS is fatally flawed because the research team failed to verify, via military records, the self-reported traumatic events of the subjects. The NVVRS researchers will likely have an opportunity to correct this oversight: A multimillion-dollar follow-up of the PTSD veterans is in the works. One can only hope that researchers will verify reports of combat exposure this time, thereby addressing Burkett & Whitley's critique empirically.

The most important psychophysiologic study ever done on PTSD also required only that veterans furnish a copy of their DD-214 as evidence of trauma exposure (Keane et al. 1998). Recruiting Vietnam combat veterans from VA hospitals around the country, Keane et al. examined psychophysiologic reactivity to personalized, audiotaped scripts describing actual combat events in 778 veterans with PTSD, 181 veterans with past PTSD, and 369 veterans with no history of PTSD. Relative to combat veterans who never had PTSD, those with the disorder exhibited greater heart rate, skin conductance, electromyographic activity (facial muscle), and diastolic blood pressure during autobiographical combat scripts. Similar findings occurred during a standardized audiovisual combat presentation. Those with past PTSD tended to fall midway between the other groups with regard to physiologic reactivity.

However, approximately one third of the PTSD subjects did not respond physiologically to combat-related stimuli. These data are open to multiple interpretations: (*a*) Psychophysiologic assessment may fail to detect true cases of PTSD, perhaps because a subgroup of patients is biologically nonreactive to traumatic reminders, their self-reports notwithstanding. (*b*) Burkett & Whitley's critique implies that the large group of nonreactive subjects may have contained veterans who either exaggerated their symptoms or fabricated their histories of combat. Without consulting the veteran's military file, it is impossible to rule out any of these possibilities. If Burkett & Whitley are right, then removal of suspicious cases and reanalysis of only corroborated cases of combat-related PTSD would likely result in even stronger psychophysiologic differences between PTSD and non-PTSD groups than Keane et al. had originally reported.

As someone who has done work in this area, I was concerned that phony combat vets might have slipped into my information-processing experiments on PTSD (McNally 1998). Following Burkett & Whitley's suggestion, I obtained military records from the National Personnel Records Center for 34 of my PTSD subjects. The archival data confirmed that all were genuine Vietnam veterans. No subject, for example, who claimed to have fought in Vietnam turned out to have been a cook stationed at Fort Riley, Kansas. Although the richness of the archival record varied across subjects, evidence of combat exposure was clear for most of them. The absence of phony vets in this small pilot study suggests that men who volunteer for research studies are from a different pool than those who have caught the attention of Burkett & Whitley. Indeed, Burkett & Whitley typically investigated men whose public statements and actions seemed suspicious. Nevertheless, the integrity of the PTSD database is at issue here, and researchers should attempt to verify combat experience by consulting military archives whenever possible.

GUILT, SHAME, AND TRAUMA

The conditioning model implies that traumatic stressors cause PTSD by producing toxic levels of fear in victims, but stressors can also traumatize by inciting guilt and shame, not just fear. Among Vietnam veterans, commission of atrocities predicts risk for PTSD beyond that attributable to combat exposure alone (Breslau & Davis 1987). Even among those qualifying for a PTSD diagnosis, commission of atrocities (or at least passive exposure to them) predicts severity of PTSD symptoms beyond that predicted by extent of combat exposure (Beckham et al. 1998, Yehuda et al. 1992).

The fact that guilt about having committed atrocities can produce PTSD not only underscores the moral complexity of trauma, but it exposes another limitation of the animal conditioning model of PTSD. Although some scholars have attempted to conceptualize atrocity involvement as a high-magnitude stressor for the perpetrator (March 1993), this gambit obscures important issues by reversing the roles of victim and victimizer. Unlike fear, which can be experienced by rats, guilt and shame are complex emotions emergent only in animals possessing a sense of self. As Kagan (1998) has observed, one cannot "model" guilt in the rodent conditioning laboratory without distorting the meaning of guilt beyond recognition. Only human beings capable of cognitive self-representation can experience complex self-referent emotions like shame and guilt. Pavlovian animal-conditioning models that reduce trauma to its biological basis cannot capture this uniquely human aspect of trauma.

Of course, committing atrocities can produce PTSD only if these actions violate the person's sense of right and wrong. Brutal acts that are not interpreted as violating one's moral code will not produce PTSD, regardless of how atrocious they appear to others. Osama bin Laden, for example, is unlikely to develop PTSD as a result of his orchestrating the attacks on the World Trade Center.

RISK FACTORS FOR POSTTRAUMATIC STRESS DISORDER

Epidemiologic surveys indicate that a large proportion of the American population has been exposed to traumatic stressors, but only a minority ever develops PTSD. The National Comorbidity Survey revealed that 60.7% of a random sample of American adults had been exposed to traumatic events, but only 8.2% of the men and 20.4% of the women had ever developed the disorder (Kessler et al. 1995). Among the survivors (nearly all injured) of the Oklahoma City terrorist bombing, only 34.3% developed PTSD (North et al. 1999).

Because traumatic stressors produce PTSD in a minority of victims, researchers have endeavored to identify risk factors that predict the emergence of the disorder among those exposed to trauma (Brewin et al. 2000, Yehuda 1999, Yehuda & McFarlane 1995). Risk factor research offends some people, who mistakenly believe that it entails blaming the victim. Yet discovering risk factors is essential for understanding PTSD just as it is for heart disease and other conditions. The alternative to research is ignorance, and ignorance provides an unreliable basis for treatment and prevention of any illness, including PTSD.

Some putative risk factors have been identified among people who already have the disorder. For example, Vietnam veterans with PTSD report lower levels of social support than do those without the disorder (e.g., Keane et al. 1985a). It is difficult to interpret these results. Does a lack of social support slow recovery from the acute stress symptoms? Or do these symptoms alienate possible sources of social support? Or are both processes operative? However, some variables, identified cross-sectionally, are unlikely to be consequences of the illness, and therefore may constitute risk factors. Among these are lower intelligence (McNally & Shin 1995; Vasterling et al. 1997, 2002), neurological soft signs (nonspecific behavioral indicators of central nervous system impairment) (Gurvits et al. 2000), and neuroticism (Breslau et al. 1991, McFarlane 1989). Other apparent risk factors, albeit ascertained via retrospective self-reports, are unstable family during childhood (King et al. 1996), preexisting mood or anxiety disorder (Breslau et al. 1991, Smith et al. 1990), and a family history of anxiety or mood disorder (Breslau et al. 1991, Davidson et al. 1985). Individuals who developed PTSD in response to trauma during adulthood have reported having been sexually (Engel et al. 1993, Nishith et al. 2000) or physically (Bremner et al. 1993) abused during childhood.

Prospective studies designed to identify risk factors for PTSD are scarce. However, researchers have used archival data that predates exposure to trauma as a means of identifying variables that predict PTSD among the trauma-exposed. Schnurr et al. (1993) obtained collegiate Minnesota Multiphasic Personality Inventory scores of Dartmouth College graduates who later served in Vietnam. After controlling for amount of combat exposure, they found that elevations on several scales (i.e., Hypochondriasis, Masculinity-Femininity, Psychopathic Deviate, Paranoia) predicted PTSD symptoms. Using predeployment military testing data, Bramsen et al. (2000) found that negativistic personality traits predicted PTSD symptoms among Dutch peacekeepers who were stationed in the former Yugoslavia.

Macklin et al. (1998) obtained predeployment intelligence test scores for Vietnam combat veterans. The mean predeployment IQ for those who later developed PTSD fell within the normal range (M = 106.3), whereas the mean predeployment IQ for those who did not develop PTSD was well above average (M = 119.0). Lower intelligence predicted current severity of PTSD symptoms, even after Macklin et al. statistically controlled for extent of combat exposure. PTSD symptom severity was unrelated to differences between precombat and current intelligence, thereby indicating that lower intelligence increases risk for PTSD, rather than PTSD lowering current IQ scores. Stated differently, above-average cognitive ability may enhance a soldier's ability to cope with stressors, thereby buffering him against developing PTSD.

Silva et al. (2000) likewise found that IQ was the best predictor of resilience against PTSD among inner city trauma-exposed children and adolescents. These children had been exposed to diverse traumatic events including witnessing robberies, being in fires, and experiencing physical or sexual abuse. Among those with above average intelligence, 67% had neither PTSD nor subthreshold PTSD, whereas among those with below average intelligence only 20% were free of PTSD or PTSD symptoms.

Researchers have also identified peritraumatic (i.e., during the trauma) variables that predict later PTSD. These studies are not truly prospective because measurement occurs after trauma exposure, but they are prospective in the sense that measurement occurs before the person has had time to develop the disorder. Some studies have shown that peritraumatic dissociation predicts PTSD. Time distortion and feelings of unreality did so among trauma-exposed Israeli citizens (Shalev et al. 1996), and time distortion and a sense of bodily distortion predicted PTSD among French citizens exposed to violent crimes (Birmes et al. 2001). Emotional numbing, depersonalization, motor restlessness, and a sense of reliving the trauma predicted PTSD among survivors of automobile accidents in Australia (Harvey & Bryant 1998). Dissociative symptoms—most commonly a sense of time slowing down or speeding up—increased the risk of PTSD by nearly a factor of five among American motor vehicle accident survivors (Ursano et al. 1999). Finally, elevated heart rate among civilian trauma survivors, assessed in the emergency room, predicted subsequent PTSD (Shalev et al. 1998).

DOES TRAUMATIC STRESS DAMAGE THE BRAIN?

Glucocorticoids—cortisol in primates—are released as part of the fight-flight response. Although these stress hormones adaptively facilitate defense in the short term, prolonged glucocorticoid exposure produces hippocampal atrophy, at least in rats and monkeys (for a review, see Sapolsky 2000). Accordingly, some psychiatrists have wondered whether extreme stress might have damaged the hippocampus of trauma survivors. The stress of having chronic PTSD might also wear away at the hippocampus (Bremner 2001).

Consistent with this hypothesis, several magnetic resonance imaging (MRI) studies have shown that the hippocampi of individuals with PTSD are smaller than those of matched control subjects. In one study Vietnam combat veterans with PTSD had significantly smaller (by 8%) right hippocampi than nonveteran control subjects (Bremner et al. 1995), and in another, those with PTSD had significantly smaller left (by 26%) and right (by 22%) hippocampi than a combined group of Vietnam combat veterans and healthy nonveteran control subjects (Gurvits et al. 1996).

Smaller hippocampi are not confined to veterans with combat-related PTSD. Adult PTSD sufferers with histories of childhood physical or sexual abuse have significantly smaller left (by 12%) hippocampi than do nonabused control subjects (Bremner et al. 1997). Women with childhood sexual abuse histories, most qualifying for PTSD, had significantly smaller (4.9%) left hippocampi than nonabused control subjects (Stein et al. 1997).

Although each of the aforementioned studies is consistent with the hypothesis that stress produces hippocampal atrophy in PTSD patients, other facts strongly argue against this interpretation. Rather than being elevated—as the atrophy hypothesis predicts—urinary cortisol levels in people with PTSD are often in the low-normal range (Mason et al. 1986; Yehuda et al. 1990, 1995). The normal range is 20–90 μg/day. In early studies PTSD patients usually had lower values (about 30–40 μg/day) than matched control subjects (about 50–60 μg/day) (Yehuda 1997). However, in a recent, large study on Vietnam veterans, Mason et al. (2001) failed to replicate their original finding of low cortisol in PTSD patients. Ironically, the mean value for these PTSD subjects (61.3 μg/day) was nearly identical to that of the nonpsychiatric control subjects (62.8 μg/day) in one of their original studies reporting low cortisol in PTSD (Yehuda et al. 1990). Thus, cortisol in PTSD is not maintained at high levels for a sufficiently long period of time to produce hippocampal atrophy. Short periods of very high levels of cortisol adaptively mobilize the person for fight or flight; only if such levels are maintained for months or years might damage occur.

For example, because of an adrenal tumor, patients with Cushing's syndrome experience extremely high levels of cortisol that results in explicit memory deficits and hippocampal atrophy (e.g., 508 μg/day) (Starkman et al. 1992). However, not only does surgical correction of the tumor normalize cortisol levels, but it eliminates memory deficits and enables the hippocampus to rebound to its normal size (Starkman et al. 1999).

Recent neuroimaging studies provide additional data against the hypothesis that stress shrinks the hippocampus of trauma survivors. Bonne et al. (2001) used MRI to scan 37 trauma survivors one week following their admission to a hospital emergency room. They rescanned them six months later. By this second assessment, 10 of the 37 subjects had developed PTSD. The PTSD and non-PTSD groups did not differ in hippocampal volume, and PTSD symptom severity was not correlated with hippocampal volume at either scan. Finally, hippocampal volume in the PTSD group remained stable over the course of the 6-month period.

In a landmark study, Gilbertson et al. (2002) may have decisively refuted the atrophy hypothesis. Using MRI, these researchers measured hippocampal volume in a series of monozygotic twin pairs. One cotwin fought in Vietnam and developed PTSD, whereas his brother did not serve in Vietnam and did not have PTSD. If trauma shrinks the hippocampus, then the hippocampi of the PTSD cotwins should be smaller than those of their nontraumatized twin brothers. Although Gilbertson et al. once again found smaller than average hippocampi in subjects with severe PTSD, they also found that the hippocampi of nontraumatized twins were just as small. Not only was PTSD symptom severity negatively correlated with total hippocampal volume in trauma-exposed subjects (r = −0.64), but PTSD symptom severity was just as negatively correlated with the total hippocampal volume of their twin brothers (r = −0.70). The concordance in hippocampal volume between pairs of identical twins—irrespective of the presence of PTSD or trauma history—strongly suggests genetic influence on hippocampal volume. Because the cotwins had not been exposed to traumatic stress, Gilbertson et al. concluded that small hippocampi may constitute a preexisting vulnerability factor for PTSD among the trauma-exposed. These data are consistent with studies showing that PTSD patients report more neurodevelopmental abnormalities than do trauma-exposed people without the disorder (Gurvits et al. 2000). Compromised neurocognitive functioning may impede a person's ability to cope with traumatic stressors.

RECOVERED MEMORIES OF SEXUAL ABUSE

By far the most contentious issue in the field of traumatic stress concerns the accuracy of recovered memories of childhood sexual abuse (McNally 2003). In their award-winning book, Brown et al. (1998) asserted that "approximately a third of sexually abused victims report some period of their lives where they did not remember anything about the abuse and later recovered the memory of the abuse" (p. 196).

Accordingly, because of "massive repression" (Herman & Schatzow 1987, p. 12), Brown et al. (1998) believe that therapists must often apply special techniques to retrieve memories of trauma that presumably lie at the root of diverse symptoms. They assert, "Because some victims of sexual abuse will repress their memories by dissociating them from consciousness, hypnosis can be very valuable in retrieving these memories. Indeed, for some victims, hypnosis may provide the only avenue to the repressed memories" (p. 647).

This claim flies in the face of everything scientists have learned about hypnosis. Not only does hypnosis fail to enhance the accuracy of recollection, but it fosters the production of false memories that are mistakenly experienced as accurate (Kihlstrom 1997, Lynn et al. 1997, Steblay & Bothwell 1994).

The controversy concerning repressed and recovered memories of childhood sexual abuse has been deeply divisive in psychology and psychiatry. Some scholars argue that there is no convincing evidence that people can banish and then recover memories of horrific experiences (e.g., Pope et al. 1998), whereas others proclaim "overwhelming scientific support for the existence of repressed or dissociated memory" (Brown et al. 1998, pp. 538–39). What is most bizarre about this debate is that proponents on both sides appeal to the same scientific studies to support their diametrically opposed positions. How is this possible? Anyone who actually reads the contested studies, however, will immediately realize that the most influential advocates of the traumatic amnesia position misunderstand much of the science they cite. I can only provide illustrative examples of their misreadings here; for further analysis, see McNally (2003) and Piper et al. (2000).

For starters, consider Brown et al.'s (1999) claim that "the burden of proof is on them [skeptics of repressed memories] to show that repressed memories do not exist" (p. 125). They have it exactly backwards: The burden of proof lies on Brown et al. to provide convincing evidence that people can repress and later recover memories of trauma. For logical reasons, the skeptics cannot prove the null hypothesis that repression does not occur.

Many studies have shown that people complain about nonspecific memory impairment following exposure to traumatic events. This is the *DSM-III* symptom of "memory impairment or trouble concentrating" (APA 1980, p. 238). Brown et al. misunderstand what this symptom means, mistakenly believing that it "typically includes both hypermnesia and amnesia" (Brown et al. 1999, p. 27). In reality, it refers to neither; hypermnesia—vivid recollections of the trauma—is, of course, already covered by the diagnostic criterion of recurrent and intrusive recollections of the event. DSM-III memory impairment refers to forgetfulness in everyday life that emerges after exposure to a traumatic event; it does not refer to difficulty remembering the traumatic event itself (i.e., traumatic amnesia).

Brown et al.'s misconstrual is immediately apparent to anyone who reads the studies they cite in support of traumatic amnesia. For example, 88.2% of the witnesses to the catastrophic collapse of the Hyatt Regency Hotel skywalks in Kansas City experienced "repeated recollections" of the disaster, and 27.4% reported "memory difficulties" (Wilkinson 1983). Obviously, these individuals remembered the disaster all too well. Indeed, their preoccupation with vivid, intrusive recollections might have interfered with their ability to concentrate and remember ordinary things in everyday life.

While searching for evidence of traumatic amnesia, Brown et al. sometimes cite findings attributable to direct physical insult to the brain as relevant to psychic trauma. For example, they state that "Dollinger (1985) found that two of the 38 children studied after watching lightning strike and kill a playmate had no memory of the event" (Brown et al. 1998, pp. 609–10). Unfortunately, they fail to mention that both children had themselves been struck by side flashes from the main lightning bolt, knocked unconscious, and nearly killed (Dollinger 1985). Such cases of obvious organic amnesia are irrelevant to psychogenic, traumatic amnesia.

In yet another example, they cite the work of Wagenaar & Groeneweg (1990) as evidence that "amnesia for Nazi Holocaust camp experiences has also been reported" (Brown et al. 1998, p. 156). Wagenaar & Groeneweg studied concentration camp survivors 40 years after their liberation. These investigators compared the memory reports of former inmates with the depositions they had provided about their trauma four decades earlier. After comparing recent recollections with the original reports, Wagenaar & Groeneweg said that inmates exhibited "a remarkable degree of remembering" (p. 80) of their Holocaust experiences, all the more impressive in view of the starvation and head beatings many suffered. "There is no doubt," emphasized Wagenaar & Groeneweg, "that almost all witnesses remember Camp Erika in great detail, even after 40 years" (p. 84). So, why did Brown et al. cite this study as indicating amnesia for Holocaust experiences? As it turns out, several former inmates had forgotten to mention several violent events, plus other minor details (e.g., the name of a sadistic guard), among all the horrific events they had vividly recalled. But with one exception, each camp survivor remembered these temporarily forgotten events after having examined their original depositions. Because autobiographical memory does not operate like a videorecorder, it is not surprising that some of these elderly individuals did not immediately recall every traumatic event that happened in the concentration camp.

Most of the studies adduced by Brown et al. in support of the concept of traumatic amnesia concern sexual abuse, and most suffer from the same fatal flaw. In the modal study (e.g., Briere & Conte 1993) sexual abuse survivors were asked whether there was ever a time when they could not remember their abuse. Nearly 60% said "yes." However, a reported inability to remember one's abuse implies unsuccessful retrieval attempts. If survivors were unaware of their abuse, on what basis would they attempt to recall it in the first place? Obviously, the best way to make sense out of affirmative replies to this question is to assume that survivors interpreted the question as asking, "Has there ever been a time when you did not think about your abuse?" Obviously, not thinking about one's abuse is not the same as being unable to recall it.

In one of the best studies on this topic Williams (1994) and her research team interviewed 129 women who had been medically evaluated for suspected sexual abuse about 17 years earlier when they were children. As part of this general health survey, the interviewers asked questions about childhood sexual experiences and recorded all events mentioned by the subjects. The researchers then judged whether any of the reported events matched the index event recorded in the hospital records. Although 38% (n = 49) of the women did not mention the index event for which they had been taken to the hospital many years earlier, most (n = 33) of them did describe other episodes of sexual abuse. However, 16 subjects denied ever having been sexually abused.

Although Brown et al. interpreted Williams's data as evidence for traumatic amnesia, other explanations are plausible. Some subjects may have been too young either to understand or remember what had happened to them. Several of the nonreporters were under 4 years of age when they were assessed for abuse at the hospital. Hence, ordinary childhood amnesia might have precluded their remembering (or even understanding) what had happened. Also, the 16 nonreporters may have remembered their abuse, but elected not to mention it to the interviewer. It would have been helpful if Williams had done a follow-up clarification interview with subjects who denied ever having been abused to determine whether they had actually forgotten the event or whether they were merely reluctant to report it.

Femina et al. (1990) did such a study with subjects who had documented histories of physical abuse. Those subjects who had mentioned this abuse in an earlier interview but had denied their abuse in a second interview were contacted a third time. During the third interview they were asked to explain the discrepancy between the first and second interviews. Each subject then acknowledged having remembered the abuse during the second interview and admitted to having denied it for various reasons (e.g., dislike of the interviewer). Without such clarification interviews to resolve discrepancies between official records and self-report denial of abuse, it is impossible to distinguish between failure to report abuse and failure to remember it.

The most intriguing evidence for recovered memories of abuse comes from case studies in which the events have been independently corroborated (e.g., Cheit 1998, 1999; Schooler et al. 1997). However, explaining even these cases does not require postulation of any special repression or dissociation mechanism. Consider, for example, a girl who is fondled by a man and who does not think about this frightening (or perhaps confusing) episode for many years. As a young woman, she meets someone who reminds her of the perpetrator, and suddenly remembers the experience. Such a case would constitute a recovered memory of sexual abuse, but not repression or amnesia. That is, during the period when she had not thought about the episode, she might very well had remembered it if someone had asked her whether she had ever had any unwanted sexual experiences. Not only do these cases not involve any special dissociative mechanism, but they not require therapeutic efforts to exhume presumptively repressed memories. Indeed, many people who report recalling memories of abuse after long periods of not thinking about them do not remember these experiences in psychotherapy (Herman & Harvey 1997, McNally et al. 2000a). One does not need a "recovered memory therapist" to be reminded of long forgotten episodes from one's childhood.

Despite all the furor surrounding people who report recovering memories of sexual abuse, research on cognitive functioning in these individuals has scarcely begun. Our group has been conducting studies on four groups of individuals: adults who report remembering abuse after years of not thinking about it ("recovered memory" group); adults who believe they have been abused, but who have no conscious memories of trauma ("repressed memory" group); adults who have always remembered they had been abused (continuous memory group); and adults who deny an abuse history (control group) (McNally 2001). (The terms "recovered memory" and "repressed memory" are in quotes because we were not in a position to determine whether these individuals had, in fact, been abused. The terms, however, describe their phenomenologic experience.)

Some key findings emerging from this research are as follows: Repressed memory subjects report more symptoms of psychological distress (PTSD and depression symptoms) than do continuous memory subjects (who resemble controls), whereas recovered memory subjects fall midway between continuous memory and repressed memory subjects (McNally et al. 2000a). Recovered memory subjects tend to exhibit less imagination inflation than do control subjects following a guided imagery task designed to distort memory (Clancy et al. 1999). Unlike patients with PTSD (McNally 1998), however, including sexually abused children with the disorder (Dubner & Motta 1999), repressed and recovered memory subjects do not exhibit delayed color-naming of trauma words on the emotional Stroop task (McNally et al. 2000b). Repressed and recovered memory subjects do not exhibit a superior ability to forget trauma-related words on a directed forgetting task (McNally et al. 2001), contrary to the hypothesis that they ought to be superior at blocking out memory for material related to abuse. Moreover, childhood sexual abuse survivors with PTSD actually exhibit impaired ability to forget trauma-related material on this task (McNally et al. 1998). Recovered memory subjects are more prone to exhibit false memory effects on the list learning paradigm developed by Deese (1959) and Roediger & McDermott (1995) than are continuous memory subjects (Clancy et al. 2000). Subjects who report having been abducted by space aliens likewise exhibit this false memory effect in the laboratory (Clancy et al. 2002).

THE POLITICS OF TRAUMA

There is never a dull moment in the field of traumatic stress studies. Discoveries are continually intermixed with explosive social controversies. For example, on July 12, 1999, members of the United States Congress unanimously voted to condemn a scientific article on childhood sexual abuse for its alleged moral and methodological flaws. The article contained a meta-analysis of 59 studies that had addressed the long-term psychological correlates of childhood sexual abuse (Rind et al. 1998). Stunning many people, the meta-analysis revealed that subjects who had been sexually abused were nearly as well adjusted as their nonabused counterparts. Less than 1% of the variance in psychological adjustment was attributable to childhood sexual abuse. The meta-analysis indicated that childhood sexual abuse survivors were apparently more resilient than most mental health professionals (who see only the most traumatized cases) had ever suspected. Rind et al. took pains to emphasize that harmfulness must not be confused with wrongfulness: Merely because sexual abuse does not invariably produce long-term psychological damage does not make it morally permissible.

Despite this emphasis, the article incited an uproar among many mental health professionals, talk show hosts, and religious groups. Although scientists had rigorously reviewed the manuscript prior to publication, the critics assumed it must be flawed because it ran counter to prevailing opinion. Hence, they attempted to debunk it on methodological as well as on moral grounds. Politically conservative radio personality "Dr. Laura" railed against Rind and his colleagues and against the American Psychological Association for publishing the article in *Psychological Bulletin*. Condemning it as "junk science at its worst," (quoted in Lilienfeld 2002a, p. 178), she urged Congress to take formal action against the Association. Raymond D. Fowler, Chief Executive Officer of the American Psychological Association, initially defended the scientific quality of Rind et al.'s work and the integrity of peer review (Garrison & Kobor 2002) but when it became clear that Congress was about to condemn the APA itself, as well as Rind et al., Fowler (1999) abruptly reversed himself in a letter written to House Majority Whip, Tom DeLay. Fowler repudiated the article, apologizing to Congress that its policy implications had not been considered during the review process. Fowler also promised that the APA would "seek independent expert evaluation of the scientific quality" of Rind et al.'s article, and would encourage "refutations from researchers and practitioners with expertise in child sexual abuse in an upcoming issue of one of our premier journals."

Fowler's apology did not save Rind and his colleagues from the wrath of Congress. Passing unanimously, House Congressional Resolution 107 stated that "Congress condemns and denounces" Rind et al.'s "severely flawed" article (US House of Representatives 1999). The United States Senate unanimously approved the resolution on July 30, 1999. While political conservatives, religious fundamentalists, and some mental health professionals celebrated the Congressional condemnation, others saw it as a serious threat to scientific freedom. Many psychologists were outraged that the APA had capitulated to political pressure (Lilienfeld 2002a,b).

Keeping his promise to Congress, Fowler asked the American Association for the Advancement of Science (AAAS) to evaluate the scientific merit of Rind et al.'s article. But after an initial evaluation uncovered "no clear evidence of improper application of methodology or other questionable practices on the part of the article's authors," the AAAS committee declined to conduct a full-scale review, noting that it saw no reason to second-guess an article that had already undergone expert peer review (Lerch 1999). In fact, the AAAS sharply rebuked the critics of Rind et al. for misrepresenting the article in the media and for failing to understand the meta-analytic methods they had attacked.

Reverting to the conventional methods of scholarship, some of the critics who had aided Congress in crafting the condemnation published critiques of Rind et al.'s work (Dallam et al. 2001, Ondersma et al. 2001). These were easily rebutted (Rind et al. 2001, Sher & Eisenberg 2002). Ironically, studies on nonclinical populations appearing since the publication of Rind et al.'s meta-analysis have uncovered adverse consequences of childhood sexual abuse (Kendler et al. 2000, Nelson et al. 2002).

In any event, the overriding lesson of this bizarre episode concerns the importance of maintaining a firewall between science and politics (Hunt 1999). This is especially true whenever the topic concerns trauma and its consequences.

ACKNOWLEDGMENTS

Preparation of this chapter was supported in part by NIMH grant MH61268 awarded to R.J. McNally.

The *Annual Review of Psychology* is online at http://psych.annualreviews.org

LITERATURE CITED

Am. Psychiatr. Assoc. 1980. *Diagnostic and Statistical Manual of Mental Disorders (DSM-III)*. Washington, DC: APA

Am. Psychiatr. Assoc. 1994. *Diagnostic and Statistical Manual of Mental Disorders (DSM-IV)*. Washington, DC: APA

Antony MM, Swinson RP. 2000. *Phobic Disorders and Panic in Adults: A Guide to Assessment and Treatment*. Washington, DC: Am. Psychol. Assoc.

Avina C, O'Donohue W. 2002. Sexual harassment and PTSD: Is sexual harassment diagnosable trauma? *J. Trauma. Stress* 15:69–75

Barlow DH. 2002. *Anxiety and its Disorders:* *The Nature and Treatment of Anxiety and Panic*. New York: Guilford. 2nd ed.

Başoğlu M, Paker M, Paker D, Ozmen E, Marks I, et al. 1994. Psychological effects of torture: A comparison of tortured with nontortured political activists in Turkey. *Am. J. Psychiatry* 151:76–81

Beckham JC, Feldman ME, Kirby AC. 1998. Atrocities exposure in Vietnam combat veterans with chronic posttraumatic stress disorder: relationship to combat exposure, symptom severity, guilt, and interpersonal violence. *J. Trauma. Stress* 11:777–85

Birmes P, Carreras D, Charlet J-P, Warner BA,

Lauque D, Schmitt L. 2001. Peritraumatic dissociation and posttraumatic stress disorder in victims of violent assault. *J. Nerv. Mental Dis.* 189:796–98

Bonne O, Brandes D, Gilboa A, Gomori JM, Shenton ME, et al. 2001. Longitudinal MRI study of hippocampal volume in trauma survivors with PTSD. *Am. J. Psychiatry* 158:1248–51

Bowman M. 1997. *Individual Differences in Posttraumatic Response: Problems with the Adversity-Distress Connection.* Mahwah, NJ: Erlbaum

Bowman ML. 1999. Individual differences in posttraumatic distress: problems with the DSM-IV model. *Can. J. Psychiatry* 44:21–33

Bramsen I, Dirkzwager AJE, van der Ploeg HM. 2000. Predeployment personality traits and exposure to trauma as predictors of posttraumatic stress symptoms: a prospective study of former peacekeepers. *Am. J. Psychiatry* 157:1115–19

Bremner JD. 2001. Hypotheses and controversies related to effects of stress on the hippocampus: an argument for stress-induced damage to the hippocampus in patients with posttraumatic stress disorder. *Hippocampus* 11:75–81

Bremner JD, Randall P, Scott TM, Bronen RA, Seibyl JP, et al. 1995. MRI-based measurement of hippocampal volume in patients with combat-related posttraumatic stress disorder. *Am. J. Psychiatry* 152:973–81

Bremner JD, Randall P, Vermetten E, Staib L, Bronen RA, et al. 1997. Magnetic resonance imaging-based measurement of hippocampal volume in posttraumatic stress disorder related to childhood physical and sexual abuse: a preliminary report. *Biol. Psychiatry* 41:23–32

Bremner JD, Southwick SM, Johnson DR, Yehuda R, Charney DS. 1993. Childhood physical abuse and combat-related posttraumatic stress disorder in Vietnam veterans. *Am. J. Psychiatry* 150:235–39

Breslau N, Davis GC. 1987. Posttraumatic stress disorder: the etiologic specificity of wartime stressors. *Am. J. Psychiatry* 144:578–83

Breslau N, Davis GC, Andreski P, Peterson E. 1991. Traumatic events and posttraumatic stress disorder in an urban population of young adults. *Arch. Gen. Psychiatry* 48:216–22

Brewin CR, Andrews B, Valentine JD. 2000. Meta-analysis of risk factors for posttraumatic stress disorder in trauma-exposed adults. *J. Consult. Clin. Psychol.* 68:748–66

Briere J, Conte J. 1993. Self-reported amnesia for abuse in adults molested as children. *J. Trauma. Stress* 6:21–31

Brown D, Scheflin AW, Hammond DC. 1998. *Memory, Trauma Treatment, and the Law.* New York: Norton

Brown D, Scheflin AW, Whitfield CL. 1999. Recovered memories: the current weight of the evidence in science and in the courts. *J. Psychiatry Law* 27:5–156

Burkett BG, Whitley G. 1998. *Stolen Valor: How the Vietnam Generation Was Robbed of its Heroes and its History.* Dallas, TX: Verity

Cheit RE. 1998. Consider this, skeptics of recovered memory. *Ethics Behav.* 8:141–60

Cheit RE. 1999. Junk skepticism and recovered memory: a reply to Piper. *Ethics Behav.* 9:295–318

Clancy SA, McNally RJ, Schacter DL. 1999. Effects of guided imagery on memory distortion in women reporting recovered memories of childhood sexual abuse. *J. Trauma. Stress* 12:559–69

Clancy SA, McNally RJ, Schacter DL, Lenzenweger MF, Pitman RK. 2002. Memory distortion in people reporting abduction by aliens. *J. Abnorm. Psychol.* 111:455–61

Clancy SA, Schacter DL, McNally RJ, Pitman RK. 2000. False recognition in women reporting recovered memories of sexual abuse. *Psychol. Sci.* 11:26–31

Craske MG. 1999. *Anxiety Disorders: Psychological Approaches to Theory and Treatment.* Boulder, CO: Westview

Dallam SJ, Gleaves DH, Cepeda-Benito A, Silberg JL, Kraemer HC, Spiegel D. 2001. The effects of child sexual abuse: comment on

Rind, Tromovitch and Bauserman (1998). *Psychol. Bull.* 127:715–33

Davidson J, Swartz M, Storck M, Krishnan RR, Hammett E. 1985. A diagnostic and family study of posttraumatic stress disorder. *Am. J. Psychiatry* 142:90–93

Dean ET Jr. 1997. *Shook Over Hell: Post-Traumatic Stress, Vietnam, and the Civil War.* Cambridge, MA: Harvard Univ. Press

Deese J. 1959. On the prediction of occurrence of particular verbal intrusions in immediate recall. *J. Exp. Psychol.* 58:17–22

Dollinger SJ. 1985. Lightning-strike disaster among children. *Br. J. Med. Psychol.* 58:375–83

Dubner AE, Motta RW. 1999. Sexually and physically abused foster care children and posttraumatic stress disorder. *J. Consult. Clin. Psychol.* 67:367–73

Engel CC Jr, Engel AL, Campbell SJ, McFall ME, Russo J, Katon W. 1993. Posttraumatic stress disorder symptoms and precombat sexual and physical abuse in Desert Storm veterans. *J. Nerv. Mental Dis.* 181:683–88

Femina DD, Yeager CA, Lewis DO. 1990. Child abuse: adolescent records vs. adult recall. *Child Abuse Neglect* 14:227–31

Foa EB, Zinbarg R, Rothbaum BO. 1992. Uncontrollability and unpredictability in posttraumatic stress disorder: an animal model. *Psychol. Bull.* 112:218–38

Fowler RD. 1999. *APA letter to the Honorable Rep. DeLay (R-Tx).* http://www.apa.org/releases/delay.html

Frueh BC, Hamner MB, Cahill SP, Gold PB, Hamlin K. 2000. Apparent symptom overreporting among combat veterans evaluated for PTSD. *Clin. Psychol. Rev.* 20:853–85

Garrison EG, Kobor PC. 2002. Weathering a political storm: a contextual perspective on a psychological research controversy. *Am. Psychol.* 57:165–75

Gilbertson MW, Shenton ME, Ciszewski A, Kasai K, Lasko NB, et al. 2002. Hippocampal volume as a vulnerability factor for chronic posttraumatic stress disorder: MRI evidence from monozygotic twins discordant for combat exposure. Submitted

Gurvits TV, Gilbertson MW, Lasko NB, Tarhan AS, Simeon D, et al. 2000. Neurologic soft signs in chronic posttraumatic stress disorder. *Arch. Gen. Psychiatry* 57:181–86

Gurvits TV, Shenton ME, Hokama H, Ohta H, Lasko NB, et al. 1996. Magnetic resonance imaging study of hippocampal volume in chronic, combat-related posttraumatic stress disorder. *Biol. Psychiatry* 40:1091–99

Harvey AG, Bryant RA. 1998. The effect of attempted thought suppression in acute stress disorder. *Behav. Res. Ther.* 36:583–90

Harvey AG, Bryant RA. 2000. Memory for acute stress disorder symptoms: a two-year prospective study. *J. Nerv. Mental Dis.* 188:602–7

Harvey PD, Yehuda R. 1999. Strategies to study risk for the development of PTSD. See Yehuda 1999, pp. 1–22

Herman JL, Harvey MR. 1997. Adult memories of childhood trauma: a naturalistic clinical study. *J. Trauma. Stress* 10:557–71

Herman JL, Schatzow E. 1987. Recovery and verification of memories of childhood sexual trauma. *Psychoanal. Psychol.* 4:1–14

Hunt M. 1999. *The New Know-Nothings: The Political Foes of the Scientific Study of Human Nature.* New Brunswick, NJ: Transaction Books

Jones E, Wessely S. 2001. Psychiatric battle casualties: an intra- and interwar comparison. *Br. J. Psychiatry* 178:242–47

Kagan J. 1998. Animal fear and human guilt. *Cerebrum* 1:16–21

Keane TM, Kolb LC, Kaloupek DG, Orr SP, Blanchard EB, et al. 1998. Utility of psychophysiological measurement in the diagnosis of posttraumatic stress disorder: results from a Department of Veterans Affairs Cooperative Study. *J. Consult. Clin. Psychol.* 66:914–23

Keane TM, Scott WO, Chavoya GA, Lamparski DM, Fairbank J. 1985a. Social support in Vietnam veterans with posttraumatic stress disorder: a comparative analysis. *J. Consult. Clin. Psychol.* 53:95–102

Keane TM, Zimering RT, Caddell JT. 1985b. A behavioral formulation of posttraumatic stress disorder in Vietnam veterans. *Behav. Ther.* 8:9–12

Kendler KS, Bulik CM, Silberg J, Hettema JM, Myers J, Prescott CA. 2000. Childhood sexual abuse and adult psychiatric and substance use disorders in women: an epidemiological and cotwin control analysis. *Arch. Gen. Psychiatry* 57:953–59

Kessler RC, Sonnega A, Bromet E, Hughes M, Nelson CB. 1995. Posttraumatic stress disorder in the National Comorbidity Survey. *Arch. Gen. Psychiatry* 52:1048–60

Kihlstrom JF. 1997. Hypnosis, memory and amnesia. *Philos. Trans. R. Soc. Biol. Sci.* 352:1727–32

King DW, King LA, Foy DW, Gudanowski DM. 1996. Prewar factors in combat-related posttraumatic stress disorder: structural equation modeling with a national sample of female and male Vietnam veterans. *J. Consult. Clin. Psychol.* 64:520–31

Kulka RA, Schlenger WE, Fairbank JA, Hough RL, Jordan BK, et al. 1990. *Trauma and the Vietnam War Generation: Report of Findings From the National Vietnam Veterans Readjustment Study.* New York: Brunner/Mazel

LeDoux JE, Romanski L, Xagoraris A. 1989. Indelibility of subcortical emotional memories. *J. Cogn. Neurosci.* 1:238–43

Lembcke J. 1998. *The Spitting Image: Myth, Memory, and the Legacy of Vietnam.* New York: NY Univ. Press

Lerch I. 1999. Letter from the chair of the Am. Assoc. Adv. Sci. Comm. Sci. Freedom Responsib. to Richard McCarty, Exec. Dir. Sci., Am. Psychol. Assoc. (Reprinted in 1999, Nov./Dec.) *Psychol. Sci. Agenda* 12(6):2–3

Lilienfeld SO. 2002a. When worlds collide: social science, politics, and the Rind et al. (1998) child sexual abuse meta-analysis. *Am. Psychol.* 57:176–88

Lilienfeld SO. 2002b. A funny thing happened on the way to my American Psychologist publication. *Am. Psychol.* 57:225–27

Lynn SJ, Lock TG, Myers B, Payne DG. 1997. Recalling the unrecallable: Should hypnosis be used to recover memories in psychotherapy? *Curr. Dir. Psychol. Sci.* 6:79–83

Macklin ML, Metzger LJ, Litz BT, McNally RJ, Lasko NB, et al. 1998. Lower pre-combat intelligence is a risk factor for posttraumatic stress disorder. *J. Consult. Clin. Psychol.* 66: 323–26

March JS. 1993. What constitutes a stressor? The "Criterion A" issue. In *Posttraumatic Stress Disorder: DSM-IV and Beyond,* ed. JRT Davidson, EB Foa, pp. 37–54. Washington, DC: Am. Psychiatr. Press

Mason JW, Giller EL, Kosten TR, Ostroff RB, Podd L. 1986. Urinary free-cortisol levels in posttraumatic stress disorder patients. *J. Nerv. Mental Dis.* 174:145–49

Mason JW, Wang S, Yehuda R, Riney S, Charney DS, Southwick SM. 2001. Psychogenic lowering of urinary cortisol levels linked to increased emotional numbing and a shame-depressive syndrome in combat-related posttraumatic stress disorder. *Psychosom. Med.* 63:387–401

McFarlane AC. 1989. The aetiology of posttraumatic morbidity: predisposing, precipitating and perpetuating factors. *Br. J. Psychiatry* 154:221–28

McGrath JM, Frueh BC. 2002. Fraudulent claims of combat heroics within the VA? *Psychiatr. Serv.* 53:345

McNally RJ. 1998. Experimental approaches to cognitive abnormality in posttraumatic stress disorder. *Clin. Psychol. Rev.* 18:971–82

McNally RJ. 2001. The cognitive psychology of repressed and recovered memories of childhood sexual abuse: clinical implications. *Psychiatr. Ann.* 31:509–14

McNally RJ. 2003. *Remembering Trauma.* Cambridge, MA: Belknap Press/Harvard Univ. Press

McNally RJ, Clancy SA, Schacter DL. 2001. Directed forgetting of trauma cues in adults reporting repressed or recovered memories of childhood sexual abuse. *J. Abnorm. Psychol.* 110:151–56

McNally RJ, Clancy SA, Schacter DL, Pitman RK. 2000a. Personality profiles, dissociation, and absorption in women reporting repressed, recovered, or continuous memories of childhood sexual abuse. *J. Consult. Clin. Psychol.* 68:1033–37

McNally RJ, Clancy SA, Schacter DL, Pitman RK. 2000b. Cognitive processing of trauma cues in adults reporting repressed, recovered, or continuous memories of childhood sexual abuse. *J. Abnorm. Psychol.* 109:355–59

McNally RJ, Metzger LJ, Lasko NB, Clancy SA, Pitman RK. 1998. Directed forgetting of trauma cues in adult survivors of childhood sexual abuse with and without posttraumatic stress disorder. *J. Abnorm. Psychol.* 107:596–601

McNally RJ, Shin LM. 1995. Association of intelligence with severity of posttraumatic stress disorder symptoms in Vietnam combat veterans. *Am. J. Psychiatry* 152:936–38

Morrison PD, Allardyce J, McKane JP. 2002. Fear knot: neurobiological disruption of long-term fear memory. *Br. J. Psychiatry* 180:195–97

Mossman D. 1994. At the VA, it pays to be sick. *Public Interest* 114:35–47

Nelson EC, Heath AC, Madden PAF, Cooper ML, Dinwiddie SH, et al. 2002. Association between self-reported childhood sexual abuse and adverse psychosocial outcomes: results from a twin study. *Arch. Gen. Psychiatry* 59:139–45

Nishith P, Mechanic MB, Resick PA. 2000. Prior interpersonal trauma: the contribution to current PTSD symptoms in female rape victims. *J. Abnorm. Psychol.* 109:20–25

North CS, Nixon SJ, Shariat S, Mallonee S, McMillen JC, et al. 1999. Psychiatric disorders among survivors of the Oklahoma City bombing. *JAMA* 282:755–62

Norton GR, Cox BJ, Asmundson GJG, Maser JD. 1995. The growth of research on anxiety disorders during the 1980s. *J. Anxiety Disord.* 9:75–85

Ondersma SJ, Chaffin M, Berliner L, Cordon I, Goodman GS, Barnett D. 2001. Sex with children is abuse: comment on Rind et al. (1998). *Psychol. Bull.* 127:707–14

Piper A Jr, Pope HG Jr, Borowiecki JJ III. 2000.

Custer's last stand: Brown, Scheflin, and Whitfield's latest attempt to salvage "dissociative amnesia." *J. Psychiatry Law* 28:149–213

Pope HG Jr, Hudson JI, Bodkin JA, Oliva P. 1998. Questionable validity of "dissociative amnesia" in trauma victims. *Br. J. Psychiatry* 172:210–15

Pynoos RS, Goenjian A, Tashjian M, Karakashian M, Manjikian R, et al. 1993. Posttraumatic stress reactions in children after the 1988 Armenian earthquake. *Br. J. Psychiatry* 163:239–47

Rind B, Tromovitch P, Bauserman R. 1998. A meta-analytic examination of assumed properties of child sexual abuse using college samples. *Psychol. Bull.* 124:22–53

Rind B, Tromovitch P, Bauserman R. 2001. The validity and appropriateness of methods, analyses, and conclusions in Rind et al. (1998): a rebuttal of victimological critique from Ondersma et al. (2001) and Dallam et al. (2001). *Psychol. Bull.* 127:734–58

Roediger HL III, McDermott KB. 1995. Creating false memories: remembering words not presented in lists. *J. Exp. Psychol.: Learn. Mem. Cogn.* 21:803–14

Roemer L, Litz BT, Orsillo SM, Ehlich PJ, Friedman MJ. 1998. Increases in retrospective accounts of war-zone exposure over time: the role of PTSD symptom severity. *J. Trauma. Stress* 11:597–605

Rosen GM. 1995. The Aleutian Enterprise sinking and posttraumatic stress disorder: misdiagnosis in clinical and forensic settings. *Prof. Psychol.: Res. Prac.* 26:82–87

Sapolsky RM. 2000. Glucocorticoids and hippocampal atrophy in neuropsychiatric disorders. *Arch. Gen. Psychiatry* 57:925–35

Schacter DL. 1996. *Searching For Memory: The Brain, the Mind, and the Past.* New York: Basic Books

Schnurr PP, Friedman MJ, Rosenberg SD. 1993. Premilitary MMPI scores as predictors of combat-related PTSD symptoms. *Am. J. Psychiatry* 150:479–83

Schnyder U, Moergeli H, Klaghofer R, Buddeberg C. 2001. Incidence and prediction of posttraumatic stress disorder symptoms in severely injured accident victims. *Am. J. Psychiatry* 158:594–99

Schooler JW, Bendiksen M, Ambadar Z. 1997. Taking the middle line: Can we accommodate both fabricated and recovered memories of sexual abuse? In *Recovered Memories and False Memories*, ed. MA Conway, pp. 251–92. Oxford: Oxford Univ. Press

Schuster MA, Stein BD, Jaycox LH, Collins RL, Marshall GN, et al. 2001. A national survey of stress reactions after the September 11, 2001, terrorist attacks. *N. Engl. J. Med.* 345:1507–12

Schwarz ED, Kowalski JM, McNally RJ. 1993. Malignant memories: post-traumatic changes in memory in adults after a school shooting. *J. Trauma. Stress* 6:545–53

Scott WJ. 1990. PTSD in DSM–III: a case in the politics of diagnosis and disease. *Soc. Probl.* 37:294–310

Shalev AY, Peri T, Canetti L, Schreiber S. 1996. Predictors of PTSD in injured trauma survivors: a prospective study. *Am. J. Psychiatry* 153:219–25

Shalev AY, Sahar T, Freedman S, Peri T, Glick N, et al. 1998. A prospective study of heart rate response following trauma and the subsequent development of posttraumatic stress disorder. *Arch. Gen. Psychiatry* 55:553–59

Shephard B. 2001. *A War of Nerves: Soldiers and Psychiatrists in the Twentieth Century*. Cambridge, MA: Harvard Univ. Press

Sher KJ, Eisenberg N. 2002. Publication of Rind et al. (1998): the editors' perspective. *Am. Psychol.* 57:206–10

Silva RR, Alpert M, Munoz DM, Singh S, Matzner F, Dummitt S. 2000. Stress and vulnerability to posttraumatic stress disorder in children and adolescents. *Am. J. Psychiatry* 157:1229–35

Smith EM, North CS, McCool RE, Shea JM. 1990. Acute postdisaster psychiatric disorders: identification of persons at risk. *Am. J. Psychiatry* 147:202–6

Southwick SM, Morgan CA III, Nicolaou AL, Charney DS. 1997. Consistency of memory for combat-related traumatic events in veterans of Operation Desert Storm. *Am. J. Psychiatry* 154:173–77

Starkman MN, Gebarski SS, Berent S, Schteingart DE. 1992. Hippocampal formation volume, memory dysfunction, and cortisol levels in patients with Cushing's Syndrome. *Biol. Psychiatry* 32:756–65

Starkman MN, Giordani B, Gebarski SS, Berent S, Schork MA, Schteingart DE. 1999. Decrease in cortisol reverses human hippocampal atrophy following treatment of Cushing's disease. *Biol. Psychiatry* 46:1595–602

Steblay NM, Bothwell RK. 1994. Evidence for hypnotically refreshed testimony: the view from the laboratory. *Law Hum. Behav.* 18:635–51

Stein MB, Koverola C, Hanna C, Torchia MG, McClarty B. 1997. Hippocampal volume in women victimized by childhood sexual abuse. *Psychol. Med.* 27:951–59

Stender WW, Walker E. 1974. The National Personnel Records Center fire: a study in disaster. *Am. Arch.* 37:521–49

Sutker PB, Allain AN Jr, Winstead DK. 1993. Psychopathology and psychiatric diagnoses of World War II Pacific Theater prisoner of war survivors and combat veterans. *Am. J. Psychiatry* 150:240–45

Ursano RJ, Fullerton CS, Epstein RS, Crowley B, Vance K, et al. 1999. Peritraumatic dissociation and posttraumatic stress disorder following motor vehicle accidents. *Am. J. Psychiatry* 156:1808–10

US House Represent. 1999. July 12. Concurrent Resolution 107 of the 106th Congress

van der Kolk B, Greenberg M, Boyd H, Krystal J. 1985. Inescapable shock, neurotransmitters, and addiction to trauma: toward a psychobiology of post traumatic stress. *Biol. Psychiatry* 20:314–25

Vasterling JJ, Brailey K, Constans JI, Borges A, Sutker PB. 1997. Assessment of intellectual resources in Gulf War veterans: relationship to PTSD. *Assessment* 1:51–59

Vasterling JJ, Duke LM, Brailey K, Constans JI, Allain AN Jr, Sutker PB. 2002. Attention, learning, and memory performances and intellectual resources in Vietnam veterans: PTSD and no disorder comparisons. *Neuropsychology* 16:5–14

Wagenaar WA, Groeneweg J. 1990. The memory of concentration camp survivors. *Appl. Cogn. Psychol.* 4:77–87

Wakefield JC, Spitzer RL. 2002. Lowered estimates—but of what? *Arch. Gen. Psychiatry* 59:129–30

Wilkinson CB. 1983. Aftermath of a disaster: the collapse of the Hyatt Regency Hotel skywalks. *Am. J. Psychiatry* 140:1134–39

Williams LM. 1994. Recall of childhood trauma: a prospective study of women's memories of child sexual abuse. *J. Consult. Clin. Psychol.* 62:1167–76

Wilson JP. 1994. The historical evolution of PTSD diagnostic criteria: from Freud to *DSM-IV. J. Trauma. Stress* 7:681–98

Yehuda R. 1997. Sensitization of the hypothalamic-pituitary-adrenal axis in posttraumatic stress disorder. *Ann. NY Acad. Sci.* 821:57–75

Yehuda R, ed. 1999. *Risk Factors For Posttraumatic Stress Disorder*. Washington, DC: Am. Psychiatr. Press

Yehuda R, Kahana B, Binder-Brynes K, Southwick SM, Mason JW, Giller EL. 1995. Low urinary cortisol excretion in Holocaust survivors with posttraumatic stress disorder. *Am. J. Psychiatry* 152:982–86

Yehuda R, McFarlane AC. 1995. Conflict between current knowledge about posttraumatic stress disorder and its original conceptual basis. *Am. J. Psychiatry* 152:1705–13

Yehuda R, Southwick SM, Giller EL Jr. 1992. Exposure to atrocities and severity of chronic posttraumatic stress disorder in Vietnam combat veterans. *Am. J. Psychiatry* 149:333–36

Yehuda R, Southwick SM, Nussbaum G, Wahby V, Giller EL Jr, Mason JW. 1990. Low urinary cortisol excretion in patients with posttraumatic stress disorder. *J. Nerv. Mental Dis.* 178:366–69

Young A. 1995. *The Harmony of Illusions: Inventing Post-Traumatic Stress Disorder*. Princeton, NJ: Princeton Univ. Press

Annu. Rev. Psychol. 2003. 54:253–76
doi: 10.1146/annurev.psych.54.101601.145105
First published online as a Review in Advance on August 14, 2002

PSYCHOTHERAPY FOR CHILDREN AND ADOLESCENTS

Alan E. Kazdin

Yale University School of Medicine, New Haven, Connecticut 06520-7900

Key Words   child and adolescent therapy research, therapeutic change, child treatment

■ **Abstract**   Child and adolescent therapy has progressed considerably, as reflected in the number of controlled studies, their methodological quality, and identification of evidence-based treatments. Treatments with strong evidence in their behalf are used for several clinical problems. Despite the progress, several key areas have been neglected in research and this has greatly limited what we know about treatment. Prominent among these areas of neglect is research on the mechanisms of change, the moderators of treatment outcome, and the generality of research findings to the conditions of clinical practice. This article highlights progress, characteristics, and limitations of current therapy research. In addition, a research plan is offered to advance research by (*a*) understanding the mechanisms or processes through which therapeutic change occurs, (*b*) drawing on developmental psychopathology research to inform treatment, (*c*) expanding the range of questions that guide treatment research and the range of outcome domains on which treatment conclusions are based, and (*d*) monitoring progress to ensure that critical questions about treatment are addressed.

CONTENTS

The field of child and adolescent psychotherapy has made enormous gains within the past two decades. This progress is especially noteworthy because for many years child therapy research received little attention, in sharp contrast to research on adult psychotherapy. The present article begins with a discussion of the special challenges of psychotherapy with children and adolescents. The empirical basis for current treatments is also discussed, including the current effort to identify evidence-based treatments. Specific techniques are illustrated to convey more concretely the exemplary research that has been completed and the nature of the findings. Also highlighted are the neglect of critical questions about therapy and the very limited progress in understanding how therapy works. A model is offered to direct future research.

TASKS AND CHALLENGES OF PSYCHOTHERAPY FOR CHILDREN AND ADOLESCENTS

Scope of Clinical Problems

The need for interventions stems in part from the wide scope of clinical dysfunctions experienced by children and adolescents.[1] Psychiatric diagnosis is one way of delineating these; diagnoses in general include a few hundred patterns of behaviors that are associated with distress, impairment, and risk of disability (American Psychiatric Association, 1994). Some of these disorders, such as autistic disorder, tics, and attention-deficit/hyperactivity disorder, emerge in infancy, childhood, or adolescence. Many other disorders, such as anxiety, mood, and eating disorders, can arise over the life span. Table 1 describes five categories that represent broad domains of dysfunction. Many diagnosable disorders fall within each of these categories. Of the categories listed in Table 1, externalizing and internalizing disorders constitute the most frequent bases of clinical referrals in children. Clearly, externalizing disorders dominate both therapy research and clinical practice.

Several studies within the United States as well as other studies that span many different countries have yielded rather consistent results on the prevalence of disorders among children and adolescents (4–18 years old). Between 17 and 22%

---

[1]Throughout the chapter I use the term children to represent children and adolescents. The focus is on youth approximately 18 years of age and under. Where the distinction between children and adolescents is pertinent, this will be noted.

TABLE 1   Broad categories of problem domains/disorders

Externalizing disorders: Disruptive behavioral problems that are directed
toward the environment and others. Primary examples include oppositional,
hyperactive, aggressive, and antisocial behaviors.

Internalizing disorders: Emotional problems that are directed toward
inner experience. Primary examples include anxiety, withdrawal, and depression.

Substance-related disorders: Impairment associated with any of a variety
of substances including alcohol, illicit drugs, and tobacco. These disorders, while
important in their own right, are also associated with other psychiatric disorders.

Learning and mental disabilities: A range of problems related to intellectual
and academic functioning including mental retardation and learning disorders. Such
problems are probably underestimated, both in terms of prevalence and impact on
behavior, among children and adolescents referred to treatment because of the
more salient problems that serve as the basis for referral.

Severe and pervasive psychopathology: These problems include disorders that are
recognized to be the more severe forms of psychopathology that have pervasive
influences in the areas of functioning they affect and in their long-term course.
Examples include schizophrenia and autism.

---

suffer significant developmental, emotional, or behavioral problems (see, e.g., US
Congress 1991, WHO 2001). Approximately 70 million children and adolescents
live in the United States. If a prevalence rate of 20% is assumed, then approximately 14 million of our nation's youth have significant impairment caused by an
emotional or behavioral problem. This number underestimates the range of mental
disorders and impairment. Children who remain below the diagnostic thresholds
for severity, number, or duration of symptoms can nonetheless suffer significant
impairment (Boyle et al. 1996, Lewinsohn et al. 2000). Clearly, prevalence rates,
when based on meeting criteria for psychiatric diagnoses, provide a conservative
estimate of child impairment and the need for treatment.

Problems other than psychiatric disorders also warrant intervention. During
adolescence there is an increase in a number of activities referred to as "problem"
or "at-risk" behaviors (see DiClemente et al. 1996, Ketterlinus & Lamb 1994).
Examples include use of illicit substances, truancy, school suspensions, stealing,
vandalism, and precocious and unprotected sex. These are referred to as at-risk
behaviors because they increase the likelihood of a variety of adverse psychological, social, and health outcomes. For example, alcohol abuse is associated
with the three most frequent forms of mortality among adolescents: automobile
accidents, homicides, and suicide (Windle et al. 1996); approximately 90% of automobile accidents among adolescents involve the use of alcohol. The prevalence
rates of problem behaviors are relatively high. For example, in one survey 50.8%
of twelfth-grade students reported some alcohol use in the 30 days prior to the survey; 31.3% reported being drunk at least once; and 4.9% reported using marijuana
daily or almost daily (Johnston 1996). Not all problem behavior may warrant, or

serve as an impetus for, psychotherapy. Those that do are usually associated with impairment or conduct problems, whether or not they meet the threshold for a psychiatric disorder.

Psychotherapy is one of many interventions used to address social, emotional, and behavioral problems of children and adolescents. The number of children in need of services such as psychotherapy and the diversity of the problems to which treatment is applied reflect a major challenge. Psychotherapy is not alone in facing this challenge; other interventions, including treatment (e.g., medication, inpatient hospitalization, day-treatment) and prevention (e.g., early intervention programs, school-based programs), are pertinent as well. In this article I focus on psychotherapy.

Special Features of Treatment

Providing psychotherapy raises special challenges. First, many emotional and behavioral problems that are treated in therapy (e.g., aggression, hyperactivity, anxiety) are often evident in less extreme forms as part of normal development. Psychological treatment may be warranted when the symptoms are extreme, form part of a larger constellation of behaviors, interfere with functioning in everyday life, and do not attenuate with maturation. Deciding whether and when to intervene presents special challenges because many of the seemingly problematic behaviors may represent short-lived problems or perturbations in development rather than signs of lasting clinical impairment.

Second, children, unlike adults, rarely refer themselves for treatment or identify themselves as experiencing stress or symptoms. Problems most commonly referred for treatment are disruptive behaviors, such as aggression and hyperactivity, and are disturbing to others (parents, teachers), who initiate the treatment process. Emotional problems that are less disruptive, such as depression, anxiety, and withdrawal, are more likely to be overlooked by parents and teachers. Whether referred for behavioral or emotional problems, children may not see their symptoms as a problem or in need of treatment. The challenge is to involve the child in treatment and to work toward a change that the child may not view as necessary or even potentially useful.

Third, the dependence of children on adults makes them particularly vulnerable to multiple influences over which they have little control. Parent mental health, marital and family functioning, stress in the home, difficult living circumstances, and socioeconomic disadvantage are a few of the factors that can influence the nature and severity of child impairment and the effectiveness of treatment. Psychotherapy for the child is often only a part of the intervention; significant efforts may be required to address parent and family dysfunction that may contribute to or maintain adjustment problems of the child.

Fourth, in the prototypic image of therapy, a client is seen individually in treatment sessions by a mental-health practitioner. Yet, in child therapy, parents, teachers, siblings, and peers—alone and in various combinations—can play an ancillary, supplementary, supportive, or even primary role in administering treatment. Challenges come from working with others, such as parents, who deliver aspects of treatment to change child behavior. Parent and family problems, such as major depression, substance abuse, or violence in the home, may directly impede delivery of treatment.

Fifth, retaining children and families in treatment is a major challenge. Between 40 and 60% of children, adolescents, and adults who begin treatment drop out early (Wierzbicki & Pekarik 1993). Children are not particularly motivated to come to treatment. In some cases, difficulties in getting the child to treatment (e.g., objections of the child) can contribute directly to dropping out. Parents who stop bringing their child for treatment may simply be choosing a path less strenuous than weekly efforts to persuade the child of the potential value of treatment or to coerce attendance.

Finally, assessing child and adolescent emotional and behavioral problems raises its own set of challenges. Questionnaires and interviews often ask subtle questions about the onset, duration, and intensity of emotional and behavioral problems. Whether young children (e.g., less than six or seven years old) can report on these characteristics is not well established. In most studies, multiple informants (parents, teachers, children) are used to evaluate childrens' emotional and behavioral problems. Measures from different informants often yield different views about the severity and scope of the problems.

CURRENT PROGRESS IN RESEARCH

Overview

Child and adolescent therapy has advanced considerably and the advances are evident in many ways. First, the sheer quantity of controlled-treatment outcome studies is vast. As a conservative estimate, more than 1500 controlled outcome studies of psychotherapy for children and adolescents have been completed (Kazdin 2000b). Second, the quality of studies continues to improve (Durlak et al. 1995). Excellent methodological practices such as evaluating the fidelity of treatment, using treatment manuals, assessing the clinical significance of therapeutic change, and evaluating follow-up have increased in recent years. Third, treatments are now available for many clinical disorders including anxiety, mood disorders, attention-deficit/hyperactivity disorder, oppositional-defiant and conduct disorders, and eating disorders, to mention a few (Mash & Barkley 1998, Morris & Kratochwill 1998).

Fourth and perhaps most significant, firm evidence now shows that therapy for children and adolescents is effective (for reviews, see Weisz et al. 1998, Weisz et al. 1995). Moreover, the magnitude of this effect, when treatment is compared to no treatment, is rather large (effect sizes $\cong$ 0.70).[2] Thus, children who receive

---

[2]These comments are based on recommendations of Cohen (1988) to consider 0.2, 0.5, and 0.8 as small, medium, and large effect size (ES), respectively; ES = (mean of the intervention group minus the mean of the control group) divided by the standard deviation (pooled).

therapy are much better off than are those who do not. This conclusion is critically important when placed in historical context. Basic questions were raised years ago about whether therapy effects surpassed the effects of maturation and recovery processes that often occur without treatment (e.g., Levitt 1957, 1963). Evidence from randomized controlled trials and now multiple reviews of this evidence have redressed this particular concern (Kazdin 2000c).

Evidence-Based Treatments

Research has moved beyond resolving the general query of whether evidence supports the efficacy of therapy. A more recent movement has been toward identifying evidence-based treatments.[3] Independent efforts to identify such treatments within the United States, Canada, and England, to mention three of the countries examined (e.g., Chambless et al. 1998, *Evidence-Based Mental Health* 1998, Nathan & Gorman 2002, Roth & Fonagy 1996), have focused on delineating quite specifically which among the many treatments have evidence in their behalf. Typically, the criteria for delineating treatments include evidence from studies that randomly assign subjects to conditions, carefully specify the client population, utilize treatment manuals, and evaluate treatment outcome with multiple measures. Also, replication of treatment effects beyond an initial study is often required, especially replication by an investigator different from the one who originally demonstrated the effects. Several reviews have identified evidence-based treatments for children and adolescents (see Christophersen & Mortweet 2001, Fonagy et al. 2002, Lonigan & Elbert 1998). The treatments listed in Table 2 are those currently recognized as evidence-based.

Perhaps the most conspicuous feature of the list is its brevity, especially when viewed in the context of the hundreds of child and adolescent therapy techniques that are in use. A conservative count has identified more than 550 different such therapies (Kazdin 2000c). The vast majority of treatments in use have not been evaluated empirically. Clearly, the movement toward identifying those treatments with evidence in their behalf is a significant and welcome advance.

Another conspicuous feature of the treatments listed in Table 2 is the preponderance of cognitive-behavioral treatments. This is no coincidence; approximately 50% of child treatment studies investigate cognitive-behavioral techniques (see Durlak et al. 1995, Kazdin et al. 1990a). Also, studies that count toward establishing a treatment as evidence-based must include several methodological features (e.g., random assignment, use of treatment manuals, replication of effects). These characteristics are much more likely among contemporary studies than studies conducted 20 or 30 years ago, and cognitive-behavioral techniques are more popular in contemporary work. In any case, for several disorders, evidence-based treatments

---

[3]Different terms have been used to delineate evidence-based treatments and include empirically validated treatments, empirically supported treatments, evidence-based practice, and treatments that work (see Kazdin 2000c).

TABLE 2   Treatments for children and adolescents that are evidence-based for key problem domains[a]

Problem domain	Treatment	For reviews, see
Anxiety, fear, phobias	Systematic desensitization Modeling Reinforced practice Cognitive-behavior therapy	Ollendick & King 1998
Depression	Cognitive-behavior therapy "Coping with Depression " course Interpersonal psychotherapy	Asarnow et al. 2001 Cuijpers 1998 Kaslow & Thompson 1998
Oppositional and conduct disorder	Parent management training Problem-solving skills training Multisystemic therapy	Brestan & Eyberg 1998 Kazdin 2002 Sheldrick et al. 2001
Attention-deficit/ hyperactivity	Psychostimulant medication Parent management training Classroom contingency management	Greenhill 1998 Pelham et al. 1998

[a]The techniques noted here draw from different methods of defining and evaluating evidence-based treatments. The techniques are those that would meet criteria for well established or probably efficacious (Lonigan et al. 1998) or those with randomized controlled trials in their behalf (Nathan & Gorman 2002). Evaluation of treatments and identification of those that meet criteria for empirical support are ongoing and hence the above is an illustrative rather than fixed or exhaustive list. Psychostimulant medication is mentioned because this is the standard treatment for attention-deficit/hyperactivity disorder.

have been identified. The compelling evidence that some techniques are clearly the treatment of choice for various child and adolescent problems has entered into clinical practice guidelines (e.g., American Academy of Child and Adolescent Psychiatry 1998).

ILLUSTRATIONS OF TREATMENT RESEARCH

Listing evidence-based treatments does not convey concretely the advances and the high-quality research that has been completed to date. Two treatments are highlighted here to convey the scope of the evidence and progress as well as different foci and models of treatment.

Cognitive-Behavioral Therapy for Child Anxiety

CHARACTERISTICS OF TREATMENT   Cognitive-behavioral treatment (CBT) for anxiety in children focuses on dysfunctional cognitions and their implications for the child's subsequent thinking and behavior (for reviews see Kendall et al. 2000, Kendall & Treadwell 1996). Cognitive distortions are considered to play a central role among children with anxiety. These distortions refer to information processes that are misguided and that lead to misperceptions of oneself or the environment.

Treatment develops new skills, provides new experiences in which the child can test dysfunctional as well as adaptive beliefs, and assists the child in processing new experiences. Strategies used in treatment directly focus on learning new behaviors through modeling and direct reinforcement. In addition, cognitive strategies such as the use of self-statements address processes (information processing style, attributions, and self-talk) considered to mediate anxiety.

The CBT program consists of 16–20 sessions administered individually to the child. Approximately the first half of treatment is devoted to teaching the child steps for coping with anxiety and managing distress. These include recognizing the physiological symptoms of anxiety (e.g., internal signals for anxiety such as sensations of tension); challenging and altering anxiety-provoking cognitions and one's internal dialogue (e.g., generating alternatives to an expectation that bad things will happen); problem solving (e.g., devising a plan to cope with the anxiety, generating alternative courses of action and selecting one); evaluating the coping plan and administering consequences (e.g., self-evaluation and self-reinforcement).

The second half of treatment focuses on applying the newly learned skills by exposing children at first to imaginary and low-anxiety-provoking situations and then later to moderate and more highly anxiety-provoking situations. Exposure is also included as homework assignments in which the child rehearses application of the steps at home and at school. Rewards are earned for completion of these assignments. In the final session of treatment, the child makes a videotaped "commercial" describing the steps and their use in mastering anxiety-provoking situations.

OVERVIEW OF THE EVIDENCE   Treatment has been evaluated with children 9–13 years of age in both randomized controlled trials and single-case experimental studies [please see reviews noted previously (Kendall 1996, 2000)]. Improvements with treatment are evident on multiple child-, parent-, and teacher-report measures of anxiety as well as in other symptom domains, including aggression, social problems, hyperactivity, and depression, and on behavioral observations of child distress. The effects of treatment have been replicated by investigators other than those who have conducted the original treatment trials. Indeed, multiple replications attest to the effects of treatment and maintenance of treatment effects up to 6 years later (e.g., Barrett et al. 2001, Dadds et al. 1999).

The treatment research is exemplary in a number of ways. First, the studies have included children who meet criteria for a diagnosis of anxiety disorders. Second, the impact of treatment has been strong and consistent across studies. Third, many children fall within the normative range of functioning following treatment. Overall, CBT for anxiety disorders is one of the treatments considered to be evidence-based.

Parent Management Training for Oppositional and Aggressive Children

CHARACTERISTICS OF TREATMENT   Parent management training (PMT) refers to procedures in which parents are trained to alter their child's behavior in the home.

Training is based on the general view that oppositional and aggressive behaviors are inadvertently developed and sustained in the home by maladaptive parent-child interactions. Among the many interaction patterns, those involving coercion have received the greatest attention (Patterson 1982, Patterson et al. 1992). Coercion refers to deviant behavior on the part of one person (e.g., the child) that is rewarded by another person (e.g., the parent). Aggressive children are inadvertently rewarded for their aggressive interactions and their escalation of coercive behaviors as part of the discipline practices that sustain aggressive behavior.

The model underlying PMT extends beyond the treatment of antisocial youth or indeed any particular population. PMT draws from basic and applied operant conditioning research. The main focus of operant conditioning is on the contingencies of reinforcement, defined as the relationships between behaviors and the environmental events that influence behavior. Three components are included in a contingency: antecedents (e.g., prompts, setting events); behaviors (e.g., approximations of the desired goal, actions incompatible with those to be decreased); and consequences (e.g., reinforcing prosocial behavior). Enormous progress has been made in understanding how to alter the contingencies of reinforcement to change behavior (see Kazdin 2001, Luiselli & Cameron 1998).

The primary goal of PMT is to alter the pattern of interchanges between parent and child so that prosocial, rather than coercive, behavior is directly reinforced and supported within the family. Treatment is conducted primarily with the parent(s), who implement several procedures at home. The parents meet with a therapist, who teaches them to use specific parenting behaviors, such as establishing the rules for the child to follow, providing positive reinforcement for appropriate behavior, delivering mild forms of punishment to suppress behavior, and negotiating compromises. These parenting behaviors are systematically and progressively developed within the sessions in which the therapist shapes (develops through successive approximations) parenting skills. The treatment sessions provide concrete opportunities for parents to see how the techniques are implemented, to practice and refine use of the techniques (e.g., through extensive role-playing), and to review the behavior-change programs implemented at home. Parent-managed reinforcement programs for child deportment and performance at school, completion of homework, and activities on the playground are routinely included with the assistance of teachers, as available. Over the course of treatment the child may be brought into the sessions to review programs, to learn negotiation skills with the parent, or to help practice how the procedures are implemented in the home. Duration of treatment varies depending on the severity of child dysfunction. Programs for young, mildly oppositional children usually last 4–8 weeks. With clinically referred conduct-disordered children, the programs usually last 12–25 weeks.

OVERVIEW OF THE EVIDENCE   PMT is probably the most well-investigated therapy technique for children and adolescents. Treatment has been evaluated in scores of randomized controlled outcome trials with children and adolescents varying in age (2–17 years) and severity of oppositional and conduct problems (see Brestan & Eyberg 1998, Kazdin 1997). PMT has led to marked improvements in child behavior, as reflected in parent and teacher reports of deviant behavior, direct observational measures of behavior at home and at school, and institutional records (e.g., school truancy, police contacts, arrest rates, institutionalization). The magnitude of change has placed conduct problem behaviors within normative levels of functioning at home and at school. Treatment gains have been maintained in several studies 13 years after treatment; one program reported maintenance of gains 10–14 years later (Long et al. 1994).

In much of the outcome research, PMT has been administered to families individually in clinic settings. Group administration has been facilitated greatly by the development of videotaped materials that present themes, principles, and procedures to the parents. The use of these tapes has been rigorously evaluated and shown to be effective with parents of conduct-problem children (see Webster-Stratton 1996). PMT has been extended to community settings to bring treatment to those persons least likely to come to or remain in treatment (e.g., Cunningham et al. 1995, Thompson et al. 1996) and to early school intervention programs (Webster-Stratton 1998). Apart from direct extensions of PMT to diverse contexts, the evidence in support of this intervention is bolstered by research in related areas. The principles and techniques used in PMT have been used to alter a wide range of clinic and community samples, in diverse settings (home, school, community, institutions), and among virtually all age groups (infants, geriatric patients) (see Kazdin 2001). Thus, the techniques used in PMT have been effectively applied in many different contexts.

ISSUES AND LIMITATIONS OF CURRENT RESEARCH

CBT for anxiety and PMT for oppositional and conduct problems illustrate different clinical problems, orientations (cognitively and noncognitively oriented treatments), and emphases within treatment (focus on child cognitions, parent-child interactions). Other treatments with strong evidence could serve as equally compelling illustrations. For example, among those listed in Table 2, repeated high-quality evaluations of the effectiveness of the "Coping with Depression" course for adolescents (Lewinsohn et al. 1996) and multisystemic therapy for antisocial and delinquent adolescents (Henggeler et al. 1998) also convey exemplary research and progress. Despite the exemplary research that can be readily identified, pervasive problems in child psychotherapy research raise fundamental questions. Two central issues pertain to the relation of research to clinical practice and the limited facets of treatment that are studied.

Departures of Research from Clinical Practice

The ways in which psychotherapy is studied depart considerably from how treatment is implemented in clinical practice. Consequently, the extent to which findings can be applied to work in clinical settings can be challenged. Consider some of the key differences. First, children in most therapy studies are recruited rather than clinically referred. They tend to have less severe, less chronic, and fewer comorbid conditions. Also, recruited children are less likely to have impairment in domains often associated with psychiatric dysfunction (e.g., academic dysfunction, poor peer relations). Second, nonreferred children are more likely to have parents with less psychiatric dysfunction, stress, and impairment; families with less dysfunction and disruption; and environments that are less disadvantaged.

Third, the treatments studied in research depart from treatments used in clinical practice. Many approaches commonly practiced in clinical work (psychodynamic therapy, relationship-based treatment, generic counseling) have very sparse empirical literatures. Indeed, many controlled studies question their efficacy altogether (see Kazdin 2000c). When reviews, such as the present one, note that evidence supports the effects of psychotherapy, it is important to bear in mind that this applies to a minute fraction of the treatments in use and probably not those treatments most commonly used in clinical work.

Fourth, the way in which treatment is administered in research also departs from the way it is administered in practice. In most research, therapy is of a fixed duration (8–10 sessions); it is administered in the schools, to groups of children, and without the direct involvement of the parents (Kazdin et al. 1990a). Moreover the treatments are administered in "pure" form (e.g., one treatment type only, such as cognitive behavior therapy or family therapy) rather than as the eclectic or combined treatments commonly used in clinical practice (Kazdin et al. 1990b). Also, in research, treatments are closely monitored and supervised to ensure they are administered correctly. The use of treatment manuals, observation of treatment sessions, review of sessions with therapists, and ensuring therapist adherence to treatment can, and indeed does, increase effectiveness (e.g., Henggeler et al. 1997; Huey et al. 2000). Such monitoring and quality control of treatment delivery are often absent in clinical practice.

Fifth, the therapists who provide treatment in the context of research are often graduate students or trainees. Providing training, developing mastery of the intervention, and minimizing heterogeneity of delivering treatment may be less difficult in the context of academic settings than in clinical settings. Therapists in clinical practice are usually licensed professionals with years of experience, but these attributes may not translate into mastery of rather specific, manualized treatment. Therapists in clinical practice have fewer opportunities to obtain training and levels of mastery than therapists in the academic environment. The implications of therapist differences and training experiences for generalizing results from research to practice remain to be seen.

The findings from therapy research may pertain to therapy executed in a very special way and have little or no relation to the effects achieved in clinical practice. The extent to which results from research extend to clinical work is very much an open question with sparse evidence on the matter and different conclusions by different reviewers (Shadish et al. 1997, 2000; Weisz et al. 1995).

Restricted Focus of Psychotherapy Research

Research has had a very restricted focus. First, the range of questions evaluated in treatment research is narrow. Most studies focus on questions about the treatment technique (e.g., treatment vs. control or another treatment) without attention to the many conditions (e.g., child, parent, and family characteristics) on which outcomes are likely to depend. Second, studies typically restrict evaluation of treatment outcome to the reduction of symptoms. Symptom change is an important outcome. However, many other domains are likely to be relevant (e.g., impairment, school functioning, peer relations) to current functioning and long-term prognosis.

Third, child therapy research has neglected attempts to understand how treatment works and the processes or characteristics within the child, parent, or family that can be mobilized to foster therapeutic change. If we understood the bases of therapeutic change, we might readily optimize the effectiveness of treatment. Of the hundreds of available treatments, there are likely to be a few common bases or mechanisms of therapeutic change. Perhaps learning through rehearsal and practice, catharsis (alleviation of the symptoms through expression and release), or the mobilization of hope are some of the key or common factors that explain how all or most therapies work. Much more research is needed to explain how and why therapy achieves and induces change.

Overall there are major gaps in knowledge about psychotherapy and its effects. Essentially, we do not understand why treatment works, for whom treatment works, and key conditions that optimize therapeutic change. No detectable movement has been made toward rectifying these gaps. Indeed, third-party payers as well as some research funding agencies emphasize determining whether treatment established in controlled settings can be carried out in practice. Extending treatments to patients is obviously important. The benefits of treatment will be greatly enhanced if the bases of therapeutic change are identified.

DEVELOPING EFFECTIVE TREATMENTS: DIRECTIONS FOR RESEARCH

Steps to Develop Effective Treatments

We need to understand a great deal in order to make treatment effective and to ensure it is applied optimally. Table 3 delineates several steps or areas of research to evaluate different facets of treatment, how treatment relates to what is known about clinical disorders, and how and to whom treatment can be applied to achieve optimal gains (see Kazdin 2000c).

THEORY AND RESEARCH ON THE NATURE OF THE CLINICAL DYSFUNCTION   Treatment ought to be connected with what we know about the onset, maintenance, termination, and recurrence of the clinical problem that is the focus of treatment. Hypotheses about the likely factors leading to the clinical problem or pattern of functioning, about the processes involved, and about how these processes emerge

TABLE 3 Steps for developing treatment

---

1. Theory and research on the nature of the clinical dysfunction
Proposals of key characteristics, processes, and mechanisms that relate to the development, onset, and course of dysfunction. Efforts to empirically test those processes.

2. Theory and research on the change processes or mechanisms of treatment
Proposals of processes and mechanisms through which treatment may achieve its effects and how the procedures relate to these processes. Studies to identify whether the intervention techniques, methods, and procedures within treatment actually affect those processes that are critical to the model.

3. Specification of treatment
Operationalization of the procedures, preferably in manual form, that identify how one changes the key processes. Provision of material to codify the procedures so that treatment integrity can be evaluated and treatment can be replicated in research and practice.

4. Tests of treatment outcome
Direct tests of the impact of treatment drawing on diverse designs (e.g., open studies, single-case designs, full-fledged clinical trials) and types of studies (e.g., dismantling, parametric studies, comparative outcome studies).

5. Tests of moderators
Examination of the child, parent, family, and contextual factors with which treatment interacts. The boundary conditions or limits of application are identified through interactions of treatment × diverse attributes.

6. Tests of generalization and applicability
Examination of the extent to which treatment can be effectively applied to different problems, samples, and settings and of variations of the treatment. The focus is explicitly on seeing if the results obtained in research can be obtained under other circumstances.

---

or operate can contribute directly to treatment research. Many of the approaches to psychotherapy have originated from general models of treatment (e.g., psychoanalytic, family, and cognitive-behavioral) and emphasize processes (e.g., thwarted impulses, maladaptive family processes, distorted cognitions) that have wide applicability across disorders. These processes have often been too general to generate research and to provide testable hypotheses.

Testable hypotheses and then tests of the processes hypothesized to be implicated in the clinical problem are needed. For example, if cognitions are proposed to play a pivotal role in the onset or maintenance of a disorder or pattern of functioning, direct tests of this proposal are needed and ought to be part of the foundation leading toward the development of effective treatment. Research on the nature of the clinical problems is likely to identify subtypes, multiple paths leading to a similar onset, and various risk and protective factors. These characteristics are likely to influence treatment outcome and to serve as a basis for using different treatments with different types of children. Connections of treatment research with psychopathology research could greatly enrich treatment by suggesting possible intervention targets and moderators of therapeutic change.

THEORY AND RESEARCH ON THE CHANGE PROCESSES OR MECHANISMS OF TREATMENT
Conceptual views are needed about what treatment is designed to accomplish and through what processes or mechanisms. Theories of change are distinguishable from theories of onset. The guiding question for therapy research is how does this particular treatment achieve change? The answer may involve basic processes at different levels (e.g., neurotransmitters, stress hormones, memory, learning, information processing, motivation). In turn, these changes may be induced or activated by therapeutic processes such as gaining new insights, practicing new ways of behaving, or habituating to external events.

Theories of change must be followed by empirical tests. Do the intervention techniques, methods, and procedures within treatment sessions actually affect those processes that are considered to be critical to the treatment model? At least three steps are required to conduct the requisite research: specifying the processes or factors responsible for change, developing measures of these processes, and showing that these processes change before therapeutic change occurs. This latter requirement is needed to establish the time line, i.e., processes are changing and are not merely concomitant effects of symptom improvement (see Kazdin 2003). Thus, evidence that the putative process (e.g., parenting practices, cognitions, family interactions) and child symptoms have changed at the end of treatment will not demonstrate that one caused, led to, or mediated the other. In both the child and adult therapy research, it is surprising how little attention has been given to the mechanisms of change, a point to which I return below.

SPECIFICATION OF TREATMENT   Research must specify precisely what is done by the therapist with, for, or to the child (adolescent, parent, or family) during the sessions. Treatments ought to be operationalized, preferably in manual form, so that the integrity of treatment can be evaluated, the material learned from treatment trials can be codified, and the treatment procedures can be replicated in research and clinical practice. Placing treatment into manuals does not rigidly fix treatment or provide a recipe book but rather codifies progress regarding what is essential to include. Much progress has been made on this front and manuals are available for scores of child treatments (see Kazdin 2000c).

The development of manuals is related to research on the mechanisms of therapeutic change. Without knowing how therapy works and what the necessary, sufficient, and facilitative ingredients are, and within what "dose" range they lie, it is difficult to develop meaningful treatment manuals. Treatment manuals may include effective practices, ancillary but important facets that make delivery more palatable, superstitious behavior on the part of those of us who develop manuals, and factors that impede or merely fail to optimize therapeutic change. The difficulty is that without understanding how treatment works, which element in a manual falls into which of these categories is a matter of surmise.

TESTS OF TREATMENT OUTCOME   Outcome studies are central in developing treatment. A wide range of treatment tests (e.g., open studies, single-case experiments, full-fledged randomized clinical trials, qualitative studies, and quasi-experiments) can provide evidence that change is produced and that treatment is responsible for the change (see Kazdin 2003). Though outcome studies are the most common forms of research in child therapy, the types of studies to elaborate treatment outcome are restricted.

For example, the development of effective treatments would be enhanced by qualitative research that rigorously evaluates how clients change, their experience of change over the course of treatment, impediments to change among those who do and who do not improve, and likely factors that may influence responsiveness to treatment. Qualitative research may generate clinically informed theories and hypotheses and fuel quantitative studies that define effectiveness and then test how, why, and for whom treatment is effective.

TESTS OF MODERATORS   Treatment effects may vary as a function of characteristics of the child, parent, family, context, therapist, and other influences. Moderators are characteristics on which outcome depends. Theory, empirical findings, and clinical experience can inform the search for moderators. For example, we know that many sexually abused children are likely to develop cognitions that the world is a dangerous place, that adults cannot be trusted, and that one's own efforts to influence the world are not likely to be effective (Wolfe 1999). Based on this understanding of the problem, one might predict that sexually abused youths with these cognitions would respond less well to treatment than those without such cognitions, if response to treatment were measured by posttreatment prosocial functioning. That is, unless these cognitions are altered in treatment, such children may be more socially restrained than similar children without these cognitions. Perhaps another study using this information would evaluate if the effectiveness of treatment could be enhanced by including a component that focuses on these cognitions.

Multiple child, parent, family, and contextual factors may influence responsiveness to treatment. The sparse evidence suggests that multiple factors contribute to treatment outcome in the way that risk factors accumulate in predicting onset (see Kazdin 2000c). Identifying moderators could greatly influence application of treatment with better triage of patients toward interventions to which they are likely to respond. Understanding how and why moderators exert their influence could have great implications for improving the effectiveness of treatment.

TESTS OF GENERALIZATION AND APPLICABILITY   As a treatment is shown to produce change in a particular context or setting, it is valuable to evaluate the generality of the findings across other dimensions and domains. Tests of generality of a treatment are similar to tests of moderators but they are less conceptually inspired and more application oriented. Can treatment be effective in different ways, for different people, and in different settings? The extension of findings across diverse samples (e.g., clients who vary in age, ethnicity, cultural background) and across disorders also reflects generality and applicability.

Mentioned in the discussion above of the limitations of child therapy research were the many ways in which treatment in research departs from treatment in clinical practice. This disparity has led to an urgent inquiry into whether effects obtained in the research setting can be obtained in clinical settings, an important priority to be sure (National Advisory Mental Health Council 1999, 2001). Such inquiries into the generality of treatments will profit from knowing why and for whom treatment works. In both settings one needs to ensure that the critical components of treatment are included and that a given client with a given characteristic is a good candidate for the intervention.

General Comments

To elaborate and understand a treatment and to be able to optimize its application clinically, the tasks or steps listed in Table 3 ought to be completed, although not necessarily in a fixed order. Typically, a study of treatment focuses first on treatment outcome. If the treatment shows promise, further analyses (steps) are completed. Exploration of each step enables progress over the course of the research.

Few examples in child and adolescent (or adult) therapy research illustrate progression through more than a subset of these steps. Research on parent management training as a means of treating oppositional and aggressive children illustrates several of the steps: conceptualization of conduct problems, research on family processes (inept and harsh discipline practices) that promote the problems, and outcome studies that establish the central role of these practices reflect many of the steps highlighted previously (e.g., Dishion et al. 1992, Forgatch 1991, Patterson et al. 1992). This research not only establishes an effective treatment but provides an empirically supported model of how the problems may develop for many children, how domains of functioning beyond conduct problems are affected, and how to effect therapeutic change.

The steps outlined above emphasize theoretical and empirical development and a progression of research along several fronts. Currently, the accumulation of studies is haphazard. The narrow path through which the research has wandered limits what we can say about therapy. A more proactive stance is one that begins with a model of what we need to know and specifies some of the critical steps to move in that direction.

ACCELERATING PROGRESS IN TREATMENT RESEARCH

Expanding the Focus

QUESTIONS ASKED ABOUT TREATMENT   The steps previously outlined give an overarching framework for the types of knowledge needed to develop therapy. The framework can be translated into concrete questions that can guide individual investigations. Several specific questions need to be answered regarding a particular psychotherapy (see Table 4). Progress can be made by ensuring that for a given

TABLE 4   Range of questions to guide treatment research

1. What is the impact of treatment relative to no treatment?
2. What treatment components contribute to change?
3. What treatments can be added (combined treatments) to optimize change?
4. What parameters can be varied to influence (improve) outcome?
5. How effective is this treatment relative to other treatments for this problem?
6. What child, parent, family, and contextual features influence (moderate) outcome?
7. What processes or mechanisms mediate (cause, influence, are responsible for) therapeutic change?
8. To what extent are treatment effects generalizable across problem areas, settings, and other domains?

treatment and clinical problem these questions, but not necessarily only these questions, are addressed systematically. Some finite number of controlled studies might adequately address these basic questions, after which research could be devoted to the more complex issues (e.g., therapy processes, boundary conditions).

OUTCOMES   The range of outcomes evaluated in research ought to be expanded beyond the exclusive focus on symptom change. Although symptom change is important, it is difficult to find compelling evidence that symptom change, as opposed to reduced impairment or improvements in prosocial functioning, family interaction, or peer relations, is the best predictor of long-term adjustment and functioning. For example, palpable improvements in functioning in everyday life would be very important as an outcome of treatment because impaired functioning contributes significantly to the referral of children for mental health services (Bird et al. 1990, Sanford et al. 1992). Moreover, by focusing almost exclusively on symptom reduction, current therapy research probably underestimates the benefits of child therapy.

Many other outcomes beyond reduction of symptoms are critically important because of their significance to the child, family, and contexts in which the child functions. Table 5 samples some of the key domains that are important to include in outcome research. The relevance of any particular domain may vary by developmental level of the child and clinical disorder (e.g., anxiety, attention deficit disorder) or indeed by subtype of a given disorder. However, for most clinical problems brought to treatment, the benefits of treatment are not captured fully by changes in symptoms. Indeed, the benefits of child treatment are often reflected in decreases in parent psychopathology and stress and improved family relations (Kazdin & Wassell 2000, Szapocznik et al. 1989).

SAMPLES   Sampling of children and adolescents raises multiple issues for research. First, a key concern is that most samples in therapy studies are recruited rather than clinically referred. As part of this recruitment, they are screened in such a way as to make them quite different from the majority of cases seen in clinical work in terms of severity, duration, and scope of dysfunction. These dimensions can

TABLE 5   Range of outcome criteria for evaluating treatment effectiveness

1. Child functioning
   a. Symptoms
   b. Impairment
   c. Prosocial competence
   d. Academic functioning
2. Parent and family functioning
   a. Dysfunction (e.g., symptoms)
   b. Contextual influences (e.g., stress, quality of life)
   c. Conditions that promote adaptation (e.g., family relations and organization)
3. Social impact measures
   a. Consequences on systems (e.g., school activities, attendance, truancy)
   b. Service use (e.g., reductions in special services, hospitalization)

readily affect generality of the findings from research. Clinically referred samples ought to be studied more routinely.

Second, a number of clinical samples are rarely included in therapy research, and greater attention to these samples is important. For example, relatively few outcome studies have evaluated treatments for children of adults who have severe disorders (e.g., depression, alcohol abuse); children with mental retardation, physical handicap, and chronic disease; children exposed to physical or sexual abuse and neglect; juvenile offenders; and homeless youth. Each of these populations has a higher rate of clinical dysfunction than the community at large and represents a high priority for intervention. For example, delinquent youth often have high rates (50–80%) of diagnosable psychiatric disorders (see Kazdin 2000a) but are infrequently included in clinical treatment trials.

Third, more attention is needed to samples of minority and underrepresented groups. An assumption often made is that ethnicity, race, and gender ought to be taken into account in deciding what treatment to provide or whether treatment ought to be adapted in some way. This assumption would be supported if the effects of a well-developed treatment (e.g., evidence-based) were shown to be moderated by one of these variables. I am not suggesting that outcome would or would not be moderated by one of the variables noted above or by other subject and demographic characteristics. However, absence of programmatic research on this issue is a serious deficiency. Evidence that treatment is moderated by one of these key variables would foster the design of new treatments or the adaptation of existing ones. The factors that account for attenuated or improved effects of treatment with one group rather than another are needed as well. Ultimately, understanding the bases for factors that moderate treatment can contribute enormously to treatment and to clinical care.

Systematic Monitoring of Progress

Progress depends not only on a plan for research but also on some effort to evaluate the extent to which gains are being made. Existing methods of reviewing the literature (narrative, meta-analytic) attempt to chart progress. The goal is to encompass as much of the literature as feasible and then to draw conclusions. The problem is that if we, as investigators, have ignored many critical questions about therapy, the conclusions from reviews will be quite limited. Reviews of the literature cannot be expected to bring to light knowledge on critical questions if the constituent studies continue to neglect such questions. For example, the processes through which therapeutic change is achieved (mediators) are rarely studied. Moreover, when the mediators are studied, investigations are not designed to establish the time line between the putative process or mechanism and the observed therapeutic change (Kazdin 2003). In short, the studies are not developed and designed in ways capable of answering this critical question about treatment. Understandably, in this circumstance reviews of research (e.g., Fonagy et al. 2002, Kazdin 2000c, Weersing & Weisz 2002) cannot shed much light on how treatment works.

I recommend a different type of review, one that identifies the progress made on the key questions (Kazdin 2000b). It would be useful to know when progress is made in answering the questions I have listed in Table 4. Such a progress review would consolidate gains in research, identify questions that are not being addressed, and indicate whether more or indeed less research is needed in a particular area. Of course, a review of progress could be proactive, modifying the research agenda and providing, as it were, a midcourse correction.

Continuation of current research, even with improvements in rigor and elegance, will not lead us to the knowledge we need for effective treatment and understanding the change process. It is important not to confuse the accumulation of studies with the accretion of knowledge. In child and adolescent therapy research, the latter depends heavily on a slight shift in the research agenda and more programmatic attention to what we wish to know about treatment. To guide research, three pressing questions immediately come to mind:

What do we wish to know about therapy and its effects?
What of this do we already know?
What needs to be accomplished to fill in the gap between the two prior questions?

It is not safe to assume that the literature will address question number three without some proactive stance about what needs to be accomplished. A plan for therapy research would not rigidly dictate which studies deserve to be completed or published. Rather, it would specify key areas in need of attention and facilitate subsequent evaluation (progress review) of progress.

CONCLUSIONS

Considerable progress has been made in child and adolescent psychotherapy research, as reflected in the quantity and quality of outcome studies and the identification of evidence-based treatments for several clinical problems. Despite the progress, fundamental questions remain about therapy and its effects. As prominent examples, we do not know why or how therapies achieve change, how to optimize therapeutic change, and for whom a particular treatment is well suited.

A great deal of concern in contemporary research focuses on the extent to which treatment effects obtained in research generalize to practice. Because we do not understand why or how most treatments work, we do not know which facets of treatment are particularly important to clinical practice. It is therefore likely that relatively weak or clearly less-than-optimal treatments are being tested in research and proposed for extension to clinical practice.

Much has been learned about child and adolescent psychotherapy, but little of this has been extended to clinical services. Most treatments used in clinical practice have not been evaluated empirically; treatments that have been established as evidence-based are not in widespread use in clinical practice (Kazdin 2000c). One can readily quibble about the research completed to date, noting, for example, that the symptoms of patients recruited in research are not always of the same severity as those seen in clinics; and evidence-based treatments, whether in medicine or psychology, cannot be expected to work in all instances and, for some disorders, even in most instances. Nevertheless, such treatments should represent the first line of attack; they should be used prior to exploratory and non-evidence-based treatments. Further efforts are needed to ensure that treatment research is clinically relevant but also to ensure that clinical practice draws on the remarkable findings already available.

ACKNOWLEDGMENTS

Completion of this article was facilitated by support from the Leon Lowenstein Foundation, the William T. Grant Foundation (98-1872-98), and the National Institute of Mental Health (MH59029). Correspondence concerning this chapter should be directed to: Alan E. Kazdin, Child Study Center, Yale University School of Medicine, 230 South Frontage Road, PO Box 207900, New Haven, CT 06520-7900.

The *Annual Review of Psychology* is online at http://psych.annualreviews.org

LITERATURE CITED

Am. Acad. Child Adolesc. Psychiatry. 1998. Practice parameters. *J. Am. Acad. Child Adolesc. Psychiatry* 37(Suppl.):1–55

Am. Psychiatr. Assoc. 1994. *Diagnostic and Statistical Manual of Mental Disorders.* Washington, DC: Am. Psychiatr. Assoc. 4th ed.

Asarnow JR, Jaycox LH, Tompson MC. 2001. Depression in youth: Psychosocial interventions. *J. Clin. Child Psychol.* 30:33–47

Barrett PM, Duffy AL, Dadds MR, Rapee RM. 2001. Cognitive-behavioral treatment of anxiety disorders in children: Long-term (6-year) follow-up. *J. Consult. Clin. Psychol.* 69:135–41

Bird HR, Yager TJ, Staghezza B, Gould MS, Canino G, Rubio-Stipec M. 1990. Impairment in the epidemiological measurement of psychopathology in the community. *J. Am. Acad. Child Adolesc. Psychiatry* 29:796–803

Boyle MH, Offord D, Racine YA, Szatmari P, Fleming JE, Sanford MN. 1996.

Identifying thresholds for classifying psychiatric disorder: issues and prospects. *J. Am. Acad. Child Adolesc. Psychiatry* 35:1440–48

Brestan EV, Eyberg SM. 1998. Effective psychosocial treatment of conduct-disordered children and adolescents: 29 years, 82 studies, and 5275 kids. *J. Clin. Child Psychol.* 27:180–89

Chambless DL, Baker MJ, Baucom DH, Beutler LE, Calhoun KS, et al. 1998. Update on empirically validated therapies, II. *Clin. Psychol.* 51(1):3–16

Christophersen ER, Mortweet SL. 2001. *Treatments that Work with Children: Empirically Supported Strategies for Managing Childhood Problems.* Washington, DC: Am. Psychol. Assoc.

Cohen J. 1988. *Statistical Power Analysis for the Behavioral Sciences.* Hillsdale, NJ: Erlbaum. 2nd ed.

Cuijpers P. 1998. A psychoeducational approach to the treatment of depression: a meta-analysis of Lewinsohn's "Coping with Depression" course. *Behav. Ther.* 29:521–33

Cunningham CE, Bremner R, Boyle M. 1995. Large group community-based parenting programs for families of preschoolers at risk for disruptive behaviour disorders: Utilization, cost effectiveness, and outcome. *J. Child Psychol. Psychiatry* 36:1141–59

Dadds MR, Holland DE, Laurens KR, Mullins M, Barrett PM, Spence SH. 1999. Early intervention and prevention of anxiety disorders in children: results at 2-year follow-up. *J. Consult. Clin. Psychol.* 67:145–50

DiClemente RJ, Hansen WB, Ponton LE, eds. 1996. *Handbook of Adolescent Health Risk Behavior.* New York: Plenum

Dishion TJ, Patterson GR, Kavanagh KA. 1992. An experimental test of the coercion model: linking theory, measurement, and intervention. In *Preventing Antisocial Behavior,* ed. J McCord, RE Tremblay, pp. 253–82. New York: Guilford

Durlak JA, Wells AM, Cotten JK, Johnson S. 1995. Analysis of selected methodological issues in child psychotherapy research. *J. Clin. Child Psychol.* 24:141–48

Evidence-Based Mental Health. 1998. (A journal devoted to evidence-based treatments and linking research to practice.) *Evid.-Based Ment. Health* 1(1):2–32

Fonagy P, Target M, Cottrell D, Phillips J, Kurtz Z. 2002. *What Works for Whom? A Critical Review of Treatments for Children and Adolescents.* New York: Guilford

Forgatch MS. 1991. The clinical science vortex: a developing theory of antisocial behavior. In *The Development and Treatment of Childhood Aggression,* ed. DJ Pepler, KH Rubin, pp. 291–315. Hillsdale, NJ: Erlbaum

Greenhill LL. 1998. Childhood attention deficit hyperactivity disorder: pharmacological treatments. In *A Guide to Treatments that Work,* ed. PE Nathan, JM Gorman, pp. 42–64. New York: Oxford Univ. Press

Henggeler SW, Melton GB, Brondino MJ, Scherer DG, Hanley JH. 1997. Multisystemic therapy with violent and chronic juvenile offenders and their families: the role of treatment fidelity in successful dissemination. *J. Consult. Clin. Psychol.* 65:821–33

Henggeler SW, Schoenwald SK, Borduin CM, Rowland MD, Cunningham PB. 1998. *Multisystemic Treatment of Antisocial Behavior in Children and Adolescents.* New York: Guilford

Hibbs ED, Jensen P, eds. 1996. *Psychosocial Treatment Research of Child and Adolescent Disorders: Empirically Based Strategies for Clinical Practice.* Washington, DC: Am. Psychol. Assoc.

Huey SJ Jr, Henggeler SW, Brondino MJ, Pickrel SG. 2000. Mechanisms of change in multisystemic therapy: reducing delinquent behavior through therapist adherence and improved family and peer functioning. *J. Consult. Clin. Psychol.* 68:451–67

Johnston LD. 1996. *The Rise of Drug Use among American Teens Continues in 1996: Monitoring the Future Study.* Ann Arbor: Univ. Mich.

Kaslow NJ, Thompson MP. 1998. Applying the criteria for empirically supported treatments to studies of psychosocial interventions for child and adolescent depression. *J. Clin. Child Psychol.* 27:146–55

Kazdin AE. 1997. Parent management training: evidence, outcomes, and issues. *J. Am. Acad. Child Adolesc. Psychiatry* 36:1349–56

Kazdin AE. 2000a. Adolescent development, mental disorders, and decision making of delinquent youths. In *Youth on Trial: A Developmental Perspective on Juvenile Justice*, ed. T Grisso, R Schwartz, pp. 33–84. Chicago: Univ. Chicago Press

Kazdin AE. 2000b. Developing a research agenda for child and adolescent psychotherapy research. *Arch. Gen. Psychiatry* 57:829–35

Kazdin AE. 2000c. *Psychotherapy for Children and Adolescents: Directions for Research and Practice.* New York: Oxford Univ. Press

Kazdin AE. 2001. *Behavior Modification in Applied Settings.* Belmont, CA: Wadsworth. 6th ed.

Kazdin AE. 2002. Psychosocial treatments for conduct disorder in children. See Nathan & Gorman 2002, pp. 57–85

Kazdin AE. 2003. *Research Design in Clinical Psychology.* Needham Heights, MA: Allyn & Bacon. 4th ed.

Kazdin AE, Bass D, Ayers WA, Rodgers A. 1990a. The empirical and clinical focus of child and adolescent psychotherapy research. *J. Consult. Clin. Psychol.* 58:729–40

Kazdin AE, Siegel TC, Bass D. 1990b. Drawing upon clinical practice to inform research on child and adolescent psychotherapy: a survey of practitioners. *Prof. Psychol.: Res. Pract.* 21:189–98

Kazdin AE, Wassell G. 2000. Therapeutic changes in children, parents, and families resulting from treatment of children with conduct problems. *J. Am. Acad. Child Adolesc. Psychiatry* 39:414–20

Kendall PC, Chu BC, Pimentel SS, Choudbury M. 2000. Treating anxiety disorders in youth. In *Child and Adolescent Therapy: Cognitive-Behavioral Procedures*, ed. PC Kendall, pp. 235–87. New York: Guilford. 2nd ed.

Kendall PC, Treadwell KRH. 1996. Cognitive-behavioral group treatment for socially anxious youth. See Hibbs & Jensen 1996, pp. 23–41

Ketterlinus RD, Lamb ME, eds. 1994. *Adolescent Problem Behaviors: Issues and Research.* Hillsdale, NJ: Erlbaum

Levitt EE. 1957. The results of psychotherapy with children: an evaluation. *J. Consult. Psychol.* 21:189–96

Levitt EE. 1963. Psychotherapy with children: a further evaluation. *Behav. Res. Ther.* 60:326–29

Lewinsohn PM, Clarke GN, Rohde P, Hops H, Seeley JR. 1996. A course in coping: a cognitive-behavioral approach to the treatment of adolescent depression. In *Psychosocial Treatment Research of Child and Adolescent Disorders: Empirically Based Strategies for Clinical Practice*, ed. ED Hibbs, P Jensen, pp. 109–35. Washington, DC: Am. Psychol. Assoc.

Lewinsohn PM, Solomon A, Seeley JR, Zeiss A. 2000. Clinical implications of "subthreshold" depressive symptoms. *J. Abnorm. Psychol.* 109:345–51

Long P, Forehand R, Wierson M, Morgan A. 1994. Does parent training with young noncompliant children have long-term effects? *Behav. Res. Ther.* 32:101–7

Lonigan CJ, Elbert JC, eds. 1998. Special issue on empirically supported psychosocial interventions for children. *J. Clin. Child Psychol.* 27(2):138–226

Lonigan CJ, Elbert JC, Johnson SB. 1998. Empirically supported psychosocial interventions for children: an overview. *J. Clin. Child Psychol.* 27:138–45

Luiselli JK, Cameron MJ, eds. 1998. *Antecedent Control: Innovative Approaches to Behavioral Support.* Baltimore: Brookes

Mash EJ, Barkley R, eds. 1998. *Treatment of Childhood Disorders*. New York: Guilford. 2nd ed.

Morris RJ, Kratochwill TR, eds. 1998. *The Practice of Child Therapy*. Needham Heights, MA: Allyn & Bacon. 3rd ed.

Nathan PE, Gorman JM, eds. 2002. *Treatments That Work*. New York: Oxford Univ. Press. 2nd ed.

Natl. Advisory Ment. Health Counc. 1999. *Bridging science and service*. NIH Publ. 99-4353. Washington, DC: NIH

Natl. Advisory Ment. Health Counc. Workgroup Child Adolesc. Ment. Health Interv. Dev. Deployment. 2001. *Blueprint for change: research on child and adolescent mental health*. Washington, DC: NIH

Ollendick TH, King NJ. 1998. Empirically supported treatments for children with phobic and anxiety disorders. *J. Clin. Child Psychol.* 27:156–67

Patterson GR. 1982. *Coercive Family Process*. Eugene, OR: Castalia

Patterson GR, Reid JB, Dishion TJ. 1992. *Antisocial Boys*. Eugene, OR: Castalia

Pelham WE Jr, Wheeler T, Chronis A. 1998. Empirically supported psychosocial treatments for attention deficit hyperactivity disorder. *J. Clin. Child Psychol.* 27:190–205

Roth A, Fonagy P. 1996. *What Works for Whom: A Critical Review of Psychotherapy Research*. New York: Guilford

Sanford MN, Offord DR, Boyle MH, Peace A, Racine YA. 1992. Ontario Child Health Study: social and school impairments in children aged 6–16 years. *J. Am. Child Adolesc. Psychiatry* 31:60–67

Shadish WR, Matt GE, Navarro AM, Siegle G, Cris-Christoph P, et al. 1997. Evidence that therapy works in clinically representative conditions. *J. Consult. Clin. Psychol.* 65:355–65

Shadish WR, Navarro AM, Matt GE, Phillips G. 2000. The effects of psychological therapies under clinically representative conditions: a meta-analysis. *Psychol. Bull.* 126:512–29

Sheldrick RC, Kendall PC, Heimberg RG. 2001. Assessing clinical significance: a comparison of three treatments for conduct disordered children. *Clin. Psychol.: Sci. Pract.* 8:418–30

Szapocznik J, Rio A, Murray E, Cohen R, Scopetta M, et al. 1989. Structural family versus psychodynamic child therapy for problematic Hispanic boys. *J. Consult. Clin. Psychol.* 57:571–78

Thompson RW, Ruma PR, Schuchmann LF, Burke RV. 1996. A cost-effectiveness evaluation of parent training. *J. Child Fam. Stud.* 5:415–29

US Congr. Off. Technol. Assess. 1991. *Adolescent Health* (OTA-H-468). Washington, DC: US GPO

Webster-Stratton C. 1996. Early intervention with videotape modeling: programs for families of children with oppositional defiant disorder or conduct disorder. See Hibbs & Jensen 1996, pp. 435–74

Webster-Stratton C. 1998. Preventing conduct problems in Head Start Children: strengthening parenting competencies. *J. Consult. Clin. Psychol.* 66:715–30

Weersing VR, Weisz JR. 2002. Mechanisms of action in youth psychotherapy. *J. Child Psychol. Psychiatry* 43:3–29

Weisz JR, Donenberg GR, Han SS, Kauneckis D. 1995a. Child and adolescent psychotherapy outcomes in experiments and in clinics: Why the disparity? *J. Abnorm. Child Psychol.* 23:83–106

Weisz JR, Huey SJ, Weersing VR. 1998. Psychotherapy outcome research with children and adolescents. In *Advances in Clinical Child Psychology*, ed. TH Ollendick, RJ Prinz, 20:49–91. New York: Plenum

Weisz JR, Weiss B, Han SS, Granger DA, Morton T. 1995b. Effects of psychotherapy with children and adolescents revisited: a meta-analysis of treatment outcome studies. *Psychol. Bull.* 117:450–68

Wierzbicki M, Pekarik G. 1993. A meta-analysis of psychotherapy dropout. *Prof. Psychol. Res. Pract.* 24:190–95

Windle M, Shope JT, Bukstein O. 1996. Alcohol use. In *Handbook of Adolescent Health Risk Behavior*, ed. RJ DiClemente, WB Hansen, LE Ponton, pp. 115–59. New York: Plenum

Wolfe DA. 1999. *Child Abuse*. Newbury Park, CA: Sage. 2nd ed.

WHO. 2001. *The World Health Report: 2001: Mental Health: New Understanding, New Hope*. Geneva: WHO

Annu. Rev. Psychol. 2003. 54:277–95
doi: 10.1146/annurev.psych.54.101601.145028
First published online as a Review in Advance on August 27, 2002

EYEWITNESS TESTIMONY

Gary L. Wells and Elizabeth A. Olson

Psychology Department, Iowa State University, Ames, Iowa 50011;
e-mail: glwells@iastate.edu; vorndran@iastate.edu

Key Words   witness, testimony, lineup

■ **Abstract**   The criminal justice system relies heavily on eyewitness identification for investigating and prosecuting crimes. Psychology has built the only scientific literature on eyewitness identification and has warned the justice system of problems with eyewitness identification evidence. Recent DNA exoneration cases have corroborated the warnings of eyewitness identification researchers by showing that mistaken eyewitness identification was the largest single factor contributing to the conviction of these innocent people. We review major developments in the experimental literature concerning the way that various factors relate to the accuracy of eyewitness identification. These factors include characteristics of the witness, characteristics of the witnessed event, characteristics of testimony, lineup content, lineup instructions, and methods of testing. Problems with the literature are noted with respect to both the relative paucity of theory and the scarcity of base-rate information from actual cases.

CONTENTS

Eyewitnesses are critical in solving crimes, and sometimes eyewitness testimony is the only evidence available for determining the identity of the culprit. Psychological researchers who began programs in the 1970s, however, have consistently articulated concerns about the accuracy of eyewitness identification. Using various methodologies, such as filmed events and live staged crimes, eyewitness researchers have noted that mistaken identification rates can be surprisingly high and that eyewitnesses often express certainty when they mistakenly select someone from a lineup. Although their findings were quite compelling to the researchers themselves, it was not until the late 1990s that criminal justice personnel began taking the research seriously. This change in attitude about the psychological literature on eyewitness identification arose primarily from the development of forensic DNA tests in the 1990s. More than 100 people who were convicted prior to the advent of forensic DNA have now been exonerated by DNA tests, and more than 75% of these people were victims of mistaken eyewitness identification (Wells et al. 1998, Scheck et al. 2000). The apparent prescience of the psychological literature regarding problems with eyewitness identification has created a rising prominence of eyewitness identification research in the criminal justice system (Wells et al. 2000).

Because most crimes do not include DNA-rich biological traces, reliance on eyewitness identification for solving crimes has not been significantly diminished by the development of forensic DNA tests. Interestingly, research on eyewitness reliability has been done only by psychologists—primarily cognitive and social psychologists—and the psychological literature represents the only source of empirical data on eyewitness identification. The vast criminal justice system itself has never conducted an experiment on eyewitness identification.

COVERAGE OF THIS REVIEW

No review of the eyewitness identification literature has previously appeared in the *Annual Review of Psychology*. Therefore, we include here references to articles from the 1970s and 1980s that we think especially critical to the development of the literature, but we primarily emphasize more recent developments. Also, because the eyewitness identification literature has become so vast, we are necessarily selective in our citations and coverage. Readers should note that this review focuses on eyewitness identification rather than on eyewitness testimony in general. Eyewitnesses commonly testify about many things, such as which hand a gunman used, the color of a car, or recollections of a conversation, but these event memories are outside the scope of this review. The large literature on child eyewitnesses, suggestibility, and recovery of repressed memories is not reviewed here.

BASIC CONCEPTS

The eyewitness identification literature has developed a number of definitions and concepts that require explanation. A *lineup* is a procedure in which a criminal suspect (or a picture of the suspect) is placed among other people (or pictures of other people) and shown to an eyewitness to see if the witness will identify the suspect as the culprit in question. The term suspect should not be confused with the term culprit. A *suspect* might or might not be the *culprit* (a suspect is suspected of being the culprit). *Fillers* are people in the lineup who are not suspects. Fillers, sometimes called *foils* or *distractors*, are known-innocent members of the lineup. Therefore, the identification of a filler would not result in charges being brought against the filler. A *culprit-absent* lineup is one in which an innocent suspect is embedded among fillers and a *culprit-present* lineup is one in which a guilty suspect (culprit) is embedded among fillers. The primary literature sometimes calls these *target-present* and *target-absent* lineups.

A *simultaneous* lineup is one in which all lineup members are presented to the eyewitness at once and is the most common lineup procedure in use by law enforcement. A *sequential* lineup, on the other hand, is one in which the witness is shown only one person at a time but with the expectation that there are several lineup members to be shown.

A lineup's *functional size* is the number of lineup members who are "viable" choices for the eyewitness. For example, if the eyewitness described the culprit as being a tall male with dark hair and the suspect is the only lineup member who is tall with dark hair, then the lineup's functional size would be 1.0 even if there were 10 fillers. Functional size was introduced as a specific measure (Wells et al. 1979), and competing measures have been proposed, such as Malpass's (1981) "effective size." Today functional size is used generically to mean the number of lineup members who fit the eyewitness's description of the culprit.

Mock witnesses are people who did not actually witness the crime but are asked to pick a person from the lineup based on the eyewitness's verbal description of the culprit. Mock witnesses are used to test the functional size of the lineup.

The *diagnosticity* of suspect identification is the ratio of accurate identification rate with a culprit-present lineup to the inaccurate identification rate with a culprit-absent lineup. The *diagnosticity of "not there"* is the ratio of "not there" response rates with culprit-absent lineups to "not there" response rates with culprit-present lineups. The *diagnosticity of filler identifications* is the ratio of filler identification rates with culprit-absent lineups to filler identification rates with culprit-present lineups.

Among variables that affect eyewitness identification accuracy, a *system variable* is one that is (or could be) under control of the criminal justice system, while an *estimator variable* is one that is not. System variables include instructions given to eyewitnesses prior to viewing a lineup and the functional size of a lineup. Estimator variables include lighting conditions at the time of witnessing and whether the witness and culprit are of the same or of different races.

The distinction between estimator and system variables has assumed great significance in the eyewitness identification literature since it was introduced in the late 1970s (Wells 1978). In large part, the prominence of this distinction attests to the applied nature of the eyewitness identification literature. Whereas the development of a literature on estimator variables permits some degree of postdiction that might be useful for assessing the chances of mistaken identification after the fact, the development of a system variable literature permits specification of how eyewitness identification errors might be prevented in the first place.

ESTIMATOR VARIABLES

Estimator variables can be sorted into four broad categories: characteristics of the witness, characteristics of the event, characteristics of the testimony, and abilities of the testimony evaluators to discriminate between accurate and inaccurate witness testimony.

Characteristics of the Witness

Are members of certain groups better eyewitnesses than those of others? The empirical evidence is not overwhelming. For example, there is no clear evidence that males and females differ significantly overall in ability to identify people from lineups. A meta-analysis by Shapiro & Penrod (1986) indicated that females might be slightly more likely to make accurate identifications but also slightly more likely to make mistaken identifications than are males (due to females being more likely to attemp an identification), thereby yielding an overall equivalent diagnosticity for males and females. Although males and females might take an interest in different aspects of a scene and thereby remember somewhat different details (e.g., Powers et al. 1979), overall abilities of males and females in eyewitness identification appear to be largely indistinguishable (but see Brigham & Barkowitz 1978, Shaw & Skolnick 1999).

The age of the eyewitness, on the other hand, has been consistently linked to eyewitness identification performance, with very young children and the elderly performing significantly worse than younger adults. The eyewitness identification errors of young children and the elderly are highly patterned: When the lineup contains the actual culprit, young children and the elderly perform nearly as well as young adults in identifying the culprit, but when the lineup does not contain the culprit the young children and the elderly commit mistaken identifications at a higher rate than do young adults (see the meta-analysis on children versus adults by Pozzulo & Lindsay 1998).

There is little evidence that intelligence is related to eyewitness identification performance. Although an early study by Howells (1938) indicated a significant relation between face recognition accuracy and intelligence, later studies have shown no relation (e.g., Brown et al. 1977). A word of caution is in order here, however, because Howells's sample of witnesses included a much greater range of intelligence at the low end than have later studies. At the low extremes of intelligence, a pattern similar to that found with children seems likely, namely a high rate of mistaken identifications in response to culprit-absent lineups.

The race of the eyewitness has been examined extensively. Although no consistent overall differences attributable to race have emerged, the evidence is now quite clear that people are better able to recognize faces of their own race or ethnic group than faces of another race or ethnic group. A recent meta-analysis by Meissner & Brigham (2001) shows that this effect is robust across more than 25 years of research.

Little published research relates personality characteristics to eyewitness identification accuracy. Hosch et al. (1984) found that high self-monitors (individuals who adapt their behavior to cues regarding what is socially appropriate) are more susceptible to biased lineup procedures than are low self-monitors, and Hosch & Platz (1984) found a relation between self-monitoring and correct identifications. Also, a meta-analysis by Shapiro & Penrod (1986) indicated that individuals high in chronic trait anxiety (a general attitude of apprehension) made fewer mistaken identifications than individuals low in chronic trait anxiety. Their meta-analysis also indicated that field independents (those with a perceptual tendency to differentiate parts of a visual field from the whole) made fewer accurate identifications (but equal mistaken identifications) than did field dependents. However, little research has been directed at the role of personality in eyewitness identification, and no strong theory relating personality to eyewitness identification has emerged.

Characteristics of the Event

A variety of factors affect the ability of an eyewitness to identify the culprit at a later time, including the amount of time the culprit is in view, the lighting conditions, whether the culprit wears a disguise, the distinctiveness of the culprit's appearance, the presence or absence of a weapon, and the timing of knowledge that one is witnessing a crime.

Distinctive faces are much more likely to be accurately recognized than nondistinctive faces (e.g., Light et al. 1979). Faces that are highly attractive or highly unattractive are easier to recognize than are faces that are average in attractiveness (e.g., Fleishman et al. 1976), but what makes a face distinctive is not entirely clear. Because the arithmetic mean (averaged at the pixel level) of several faces (a prototype) is judged to be more attractive than the individual faces that were averaged (see Langois & Roggman 1990), the distinctiveness-recognition relation is probably not due to a simple deviation from the arithmetic mean of individual facial features.

Simple disguises, even those as minor as covering the hair, result in significant impairment of eyewitness identification (Cutler et al. 1987). Sunglasses also impair identification, although the degree of impairment can be reduced by having the targets wear sunglasses at the time of the recognition test (Hockley et al. 1999). Photos of criminal suspects used in police lineups are sometimes several years old. Changes in appearance that occur naturally over time and changes that are made intentionally by suspects can have quite strong effects on recognition. Read et al. (1990) found that photos of the same people taken two years apart were less likely to be recognized as the same people when their appearance had naturally changed (via aging, facial hair) than when their appearance had remained largely the same.

Clearly, at the extreme of low light levels there is a point at which a face cannot be perceived well enough to be recognized later. Surprisingly, however, we know of no experiments that have measured the light levels required for the encoding of faces. We encourage researchers to address this question.

As would be expected, the amount of time a culprit's face is in view affects the chances that the eyewitness can identify the person later (Ellis et al. 1977). However, this relationship depends less critically on the eyewitness's opportunity to view per se and more on the amount and type of attention that the witness directs at the culprit. Given equal exposure time to a face, people are more likely to be able to recognize that face later if they make abstract inferences about it (e.g., is this person honest?) than if they make physical judgments (e.g., does this person have a large or small nose?). Presumably, this effect occurs because the abstract inferences require holistic processing of the face whereas the physical judgments require feature processing (Wells & Hryciw 1984).

In general, the amount of time a culprit's face is in view is not as critical for eyewitness identification accuracy as the type or amount of attention given by the witness. For example, Leippe et al. (1978) exposed unsuspecting people to a staged theft of a package. Some were led to believe that the package contained a valuable item and some were led to believe that the package contained a trivial item. In addition, some learned of the value of the item in the package before the theft and some only learned the value after the thief had fled. Although all had the same opportunity to view the thief, the witnesses who knew the value of the item beforehand were significantly more accurate at identification than the other three groups. Observers often do not realize that they have witnessed a crime until after the culprit has fled. Although they might have had significant opportunity to view the culprit, they might have had little reason to attend closely.

One factor that can signal to eyewitnesses that a crime is occurring is the presence of a weapon. Unfortunately, learning that one is an eyewitness to a crime via the culprit's display of a weapon might not make the person a better eyewitness. A number of studies have been directed at the question of the so-called weapon-focus effect. A meta-analysis of these studies indicates that the presence of a weapon reduces the chances that the eyewitness can identify the holder of the weapon (Steblay 1992). Loftus et al. (1987) monitored eyewitnesses's eye movements and found that weapons draw visual attention away from other things such as the culprit's face. Complicating the issue somewhat is the fact that the presence of weapons or other types of threatening stimuli can cause arousal, fear, and emotional stress. The effects of such stress on memory are still being debated. Some research shows that increased levels of violence in filmed events reduces eyewitness identification accuracy (e.g., Clifford & Hollin 1981) whereas other research has failed to find this effect (e.g., Cutler et al. 1987). Deffenbacher (1983) suggested that the effect is likely to follow the Yerkes-Dodson Law where only very high and very low levels of arousal will impair memory. Christianson's (1992) review of the evidence relating emotional stress to memory suggests that emotional events receive preferential processing; emotional response causes a narrowing of attention (as suggested by Easterbrook 1959) with loss of peripheral details.

Characteristics of Testimony

Considerable interest and research have been directed at the question of whether there are characteristics of an eyewitness's testimony that could be used to postdict whether the witness made an accurate or false identification. The bulk of this research has focused on the certainty (confidence) of the eyewitness. Although early research suggested that the certainty an eyewitness expresses in an identification is largely unrelated to the accuracy of the identification, current analyses suggest a more hopeful but also more complex view of the certainty-accuracy relation. Although any given experiment might show a statistically nonsignificant relation between certainty and accuracy, meta-analyses of the literature show a reliable correlation. Several moderators of the strength of the relation have been identified. One important moderator is the overall accuracy of the eyewitnesses. When accuracy is low (e.g., from poor witnessing conditions), the certainty-accuracy relationship suffers (Bothwell et al. 1987). Later meta-analyses indicate that the certainty-accuracy relation is stronger if the analysis is restricted to those making an identification (choosers only) than if it also includes witnesses who make correct and false rejections (Sporer et al. 1995). In fact, using a weighted average of effect sizes for choosers only, Sporer et al. reported a 0.37 certainty-accuracy correlation across 30 studies. More recent work indicates that directing eyewitnesses to reflect on their encoding and test conditions or asking them to entertain hypotheses regarding why their identification might have been mistaken can improve the relation between accuracy and certainty, especially when this relation is calculated using calibration methods rather than the point-biserial correlation (Brewer et al. 2002).

Although the 0.37 correlation estimate for the certainty-accuracy relation is more optimistic than the early estimates, recent studies suggest the literature might be overestimating the utility of eyewitness certainty in actual cases. In a series of experiments, eyewitness certainty was shown to be highly malleable among eyewitnesses who had made mistaken identifications (Wells & Bradfield 1998, 1999). After making mistaken identifications, some eyewitnesses were given confirming feedback by the lineup administrator ("Good, you identified the suspect") whereas others were given no feedback about their identification. This feedback served to distort the eyewitnesses' recollections of the certainty they had in their identifications. Those given confirming feedback recalled having been very certain in their identification compared to those given no confirming feedback. This certainty-inflation effect is greater for eyewitnesses who make mistaken identifications than it is for those who make accurate identifications, resulting in a significant loss in the certainty-accuracy relation (Bradfield et al. 2002). In actual cases, it is common for lineup administrators (usually the detective in the case) to give confirming feedback to eyewitnesses, thereby inflating the certainty of the eyewitness and confounding the certainty-accuracy relation. Even if the lineup administrator refrains from giving the witness confirming feedback, the witness is likely to make confirming inferences from later events (e.g., an indictment of the identified person). Another real-world factor that can muddle the meaning of eyewitness certainty is repeated testing. Shaw and his colleagues (Shaw 1996, Shaw & McClure 1996) have shown that repeated questioning of eyewitnesses on a matter about which they were inaccurate serves to inflate their certainty that they were accurate. Hence, it is unclear whether the .37 correlation between certainty and accuracy revealed in the Sporer et al. meta-analysis of experiments can be directly applied to actual cases in which there are other influences that inflate the certainty of eyewitnesses.

An even more promising indicator of eyewitness accuracy is the speed with which the eyewitness makes an identification from a lineup. Several studies have now found that witnesses who make accurate identifications from a lineup reach their decision faster than do witnesses who make mistaken identifications (Dunning & Perretta 2002; Dunning & Stern 1994; Robinson et al. 1997; Smith et al. 2000; Sporer 1992, 1993, 1994). In an impressive set of results, Dunning & Perretta found that those who made their decision in less than 10–12 seconds were nearly 90% accurate in their identifications from a lineup whereas those taking longer were approximately 50% correct. The 10–12-second rule was developed post hoc to produce the best separation of accurate and inaccurate witnesses, so some caution is called for with regard to how well the 10–12-second rule works in other situations; but the general relation between accuracy and speed of identification has received support in several studies. In addition, the idea that faster identifications are more likely to be accurate than are slower identifications makes good theoretical sense. It has long been theorized that mistaken identifications result from a deliberated judgment in which witnesses compare one lineup member to another and use inferences and elimination strategies to decide which person must be the culprit whereas accurate identifications result from a more automatic recognition process that does not require comparisons of one lineup member to another (Wells 1984a).

Lay Observers' Judgments of Accuracy

Observers (e.g., jurors) have little ability to make correct discriminations between accurate and inaccurate eyewitness identification testimony. Several methods have been used to assess the adequacy of people's judgments about eyewitness identification accuracy. Surveys, for example, show poor agreement (often less than 50%) between the answers that lay people give about variables affecting eyewitness identification accuracy and the answers researchers score correct based on the empirical literature (e.g., Deffenbacher & Loftus 1982, McConkey & Roche 1989, Noon & Hollin 1987). Another approach has been to use "prediction" studies in which eyewitness identification experiments are described and people are asked to predict the results. The results of these studies show a tendency to overestimate eyewitness identification accuracy and a failure to correctly predict interactions between variables (e.g., Brigham & Bothwell 1983, Wells 1984b).

A third approach is to cross-examine eyewitnesses to staged crimes and to ask subject-jurors to determine whether witnesses made accurate or mistaken identifications. In a series of experiments using this methodology, subject-jurors have shown little or no ability to make such discriminations (Lindsay et al. 1989, Lindsay et al. 1981, Wells et al. 1981, Wells & Leippe 1981, Wells et al. 1979). Because observers' belief rates exceeded eyewitnesses' accuracy rates, these studies are commonly cited as evidence that people are overbelieving of eyewitnesses. However, this pattern of overbelief is restricted primarily to poorer witnessing conditions; when witnessing conditions were good, belief rates and eyewitness identification accuracy rates were more similar. In addition, mock jurors sometimes underbelieved the eyewitnesses who had quite low levels of certainty.

SYSTEM VARIABLES

System variables are those that affect the accuracy of eyewitness identifications and over which the criminal justice system has (or can have) control. In general, these tend to be lineup test factors, such as how witnesses are instructed prior to viewing a lineup or how the lineup is structured. The distinction between system variables and estimator variables is consequential in several respects. Whereas estimator variables can at best increase the probability that the criminal justice system can sort accurate from inaccurate eyewitness identifications, system variables can help prevent inaccurate identifications from occurring in the first place. Consider, for instance, the idea that jurors tend to overbelieve eyewitness identification testimony. Although expert testimony about eyewitness identification might manage to reduce jurors' tendencies to overestimate eyewitnesses' accuracy, the system variable approach might enable eyewitness identification accuracy to match the level of jurors' beliefs (Seelau & Wells 1995).

The procedure used by crime investigators conducting a lineup has been likened to that of researchers conducting an experiment (Wells & Luus 1990). Crime investigators begin with a hypothesis (that the suspect is the culprit), create a design for testing the hypothesis (embed the suspect among fillers), carry out a procedure (e.g., provide pre-lineup instructions and present the group to an eyewitness), observe and record the eyewitness's behavior (witness decision), and then interpret and revise their hypothesis (whether the suspect is the culprit). All the types of things that can go wrong with an experiment to cause misleading results can also go wrong with a lineup. For instance, the instructions might bias the witness, the hypothesis might be prematurely leaked, the design might be flawed, the behavior might be misinterpreted, confirmation biases might be operating, and so on. Indeed, a great deal of the research literature on system variable eyewitness identification could be construed as the extension of sound experimental methodology to the design and procedure of police lineups.

Most system variable research in eyewitness identification can be placed into four categories: instructions, content, presentation method, and behavioral influence. Before reviewing these system variables, however, it is important to understand the role played by the presence versus absence of the culprit in the lineup and the concept of a relative-judgment decision process.

Culprit-present Versus Culprit-absent Lineups

A lineup might or might not include the actual culprit. If police investigators have unknowingly focused on an innocent person as their suspect and place that suspect in the lineup, then the eyewitness(es) will end up viewing a lineup for which the only correct answer is "not there." Research repeatedly shows that culprit-absent lineups present great problems for eyewitnesses. The same eyewitnesses who identified an innocent person from a culprit-absent lineup might otherwise have been able to identify the actual culprit from a culprit-present lineup (Wells 1984a). In one study, for example, 54% of eyewitnesses were able to identify the actual culprit from a 6-person culprit-present lineup and 21% made no identification. When the culprit was removed without replacement (making it a 5-person culprit-absent lineup), however, the rate of no identification rose only to 32%, with the other 68% of the eyewitnesses who saw this lineup mistakenly identifying someone from the 5 remaining members of the lineup (Wells 1993).

A theoretical view that has been used heavily in the eyewitness identification literature is that eyewitnesses tend to use a relative-judgment decision process in making identifications from a lineup (Wells 1984a). The relative-judgment conceptualization states that an eyewitness tends to select a person from a lineup who most resembles the eyewitness's memory of the culprit relative to the other lineup members. Although the relative-judgment decision process permits eyewitnesses to do a reasonable job of identifying the culprit from a culprit-present lineup, when eyewitnesses view a culprit-absent lineup there will likely be one lineup member who looks more like the culprit than the others.

An alternative explanation of the errors witnesses make with culprit-absent lineups is that eyewitnesses tend to have lax criteria of resemblance; under culprit-absent circumstances, innocent lineup members easily meet these undemanding criteria (Ebbesen & Flowe 2002). Experimental data have not yet favored one of these interpretations over the other. Recent mathematical modeling of lineup data by Clark may help to refine our understanding of the roles of both relative judgments and criterion setting (Clark 2002).

Instructions

A variable shown repeatedly to have considerable impact on eyewitness identifications from lineups is the pre-lineup instruction given to eyewitnesses. Malpass & Devine (1981) were the first to demonstrate that the ratio of accurate to inaccurate identifications is strongly affected by whether or not eyewitnesses have been instructed (warned) prior to viewing the lineup that the culprit might or might not be in the lineup. A meta-analysis of the eyewitness identification literature on pre-lineup instructions reveals that the loss of accurate identifications from such instructions is minimal whereas the reduction of mistaken identifications is considerable (Steblay 1997). Steblay's meta-analysis showed that the presence of the "might or might not be present" instruction (compared to no instruction) reduced mistaken identification rates in culprit-absent lineups by 41.6% whereas accurate identification rates in culprit-present lineups were reduced by only 1.9%. Based on this compelling research, the U.S. Department of Justice included this type of instruction in its first set of national guidelines for law enforcement on the collection of eyewitness evidence (Technical Working Group for Eyewitness Evidence 1999).

Lineup Content

When police have a suspect and decide to conduct a lineup, nonsuspect (filler) members of the lineup must be chosen. The importance of the selection of fillers as a system variable was demonstrated early, and it remains one of the primary active issues in the eyewitness identification literature. Ideally, lineup fillers would be chosen so that an innocent suspect is not mistakenly identified merely from "standing out," and so that a culprit does not escape identification merely from blending in. The first experimental demonstration of the importance of filler selection showed what can happen when this idea is not achieved. When fillers did not at all resemble the culprit, eyewitnesses tended to mistakenly identify an innocent suspect who resembled the culprit; when the suspect was the culprit, however, the manipulation of fillers had little effect on the rate of accurate identifications (Lindsay & Wells 1980).

Although the issue of lineup fillers seems simple at first glance, it is in fact complex. In the early demonstrations, researchers used their knowledge of the culprit's identity to select fillers. In actual cases, of course, the identity of the culprit is not known. Using the suspect as a proxy for the culprit will have different effects on rates of accurate and mistaken identification depending on whether the suspect is the culprit or an innocent person. Accordingly, selecting fillers who are highly similar to the suspect can help protect the innocent suspect in a culprit-absent lineup, but can also reduce accurate identifications in a culprit-present lineup (Luus & Wells 1991). Another line of research has shown that using the suspect as the reference point to select fillers can create a "backfire effect" in which an innocent suspect, being the origin or central tendency of the lineup, actually has an increased chance of being identified as the culprit (Clark & Tunnicliff 2001, Navon 1992, Wogalter et al. 1992).

An alternative to the strategy of selecting fillers based on their resemblance to the suspect is to select fillers based on their fit to the verbal description the eyewitness had given of the culprit. This fit-to-description strategy has several practical advantages (see Wells et al. 1994) and has worked well in some experiments (Juslin et al. 1996, Wells et al. 1993). However, biases against the innocent suspect can remain with the fit-to-description method when the description is especially sparse or when the innocent suspect happens to show a high resemblance to the culprit (Clark & Tunnicliff 2001, Lindsay et al. 1994). In actual cases, high resemblance between the innocent suspect and the culprit can occur by chance or it can occur whenever the innocent person became a suspect because she or he resembled a composite or a security video image of the culprit.

Lineup Presentation Method

Many alternatives to the traditional lineup have been proposed and tested, and future research will likely focus on solving the lineup system variable problems. The first proposed alternative to the traditional lineup was the blank lineup control method (Wells 1984a). A blank lineup is one that contains only fillers (no suspect). The eyewitness is first shown the blank lineup under the belief that this is the only lineup to be shown. The identification of someone from a blank lineup is known to be an error (because the lineup members are all fillers), and witnesses who make an identification from a blank lineup can thereby be discarded. Witnesses who do not make an identification from the blank lineup can then be shown the actual lineup (which contains a suspect). Data indicate that eyewitnesses who do not make an identification from the blank lineup are much more reliable on the second (actual) lineup than are those who were not screened with the blank lineup method. In effect, the blank lineup method is analogous to the use of a control condition in a within-subjects design and could be used in actual cases. In general, however, crime investigators have not liked the idea of the blank lineup control method on grounds that it "tricks" the eyewitness and could sever the eyewitness's trust in investigators.

Another proposed alternative to the traditional lineup procedure, and the best known of these alternatives, is the sequential lineup (Lindsay & Wells 1985). Unlike the traditional lineup in which the lineup members are shown to the eyewitness simultaneously, the sequential lineup shows the eyewitness only one lineup member at a time and requires the eyewitness to make a decision ("Is this person the culprit or not?") prior to viewing the next lineup member. The most powerful version of the sequential procedure is one in which the eyewitness does not know how many lineup members are to be viewed. In theory, the sequential lineup procedure prevents eyewitnesses from selecting the person who looks most like the culprit relative to the other lineup members, a process called relative-judgment decision (see above) (Wells 1984a). To the extent that relative judgments are operating, eyewitnesses will have difficulty with culprit-absent lineups because by definition someone in the lineup resembles the culprit more closely than the other lineup members do. Unlike the simultaneous lineup, the sequential lineup prevents eyewitnesses from making a relative-judgment decision because at any point in the sequence a lineup member who has not yet been viewed may turn out to resemble the culprit more than any person viewed thus far. Eyewitnesses must compare each member of the sequential lineup to their memory of the culprit and thus make a more "absolute judgment" about identity. A recent meta-analysis of 25 studies comparing simultaneous and sequential lineups showed that the sequential lineup reduced the chances of mistaken identifications in culprit-absent lineups by nearly one half (Steblay et al. 2001). Unfortunately, the sequential technique was also associated with a reduction in accurate identification rates in culprit-present lineups. Although this reduction was not as great as that in mistaken identifications, it was nevertheless statistically reliable. The pattern of these results has led Ebbesen &

Flowe (2002) to speculate that the sequential lineup raises the criteria for making a positive identification rather than changing the process from relative to absolute judgments.

Another alternative to the traditional lineup is the elimination lineup, a procedure in which the witness's task is to eliminate all but one lineup member and then make a separate decision as to whether that person is the culprit or not (Pozzulo & Lindsay 1999). Although the elimination lineup does not seem to work well with adults, it seems to eliminate some of the problems young children have with lineups.

Behavioral Influence: The Need for Double-Blind Testing

One of the ways that the justice system itself can influence eyewitness identification evidence is through the behaviors of the person who administers the lineup (Wells 1993). Commonly, the person who administers a lineup is the case detective who, of course, knows which member of the lineup is the suspect and which members are fillers. The need for double-blind testing is well established in the behavioral sciences (Rosenthal 1976) but is largely unknown or unheeded in criminal investigation procedures and forensic science (Risinger et al. 2002). Lineup administrators could inadvertently communicate their knowledge about which lineup member is the suspect and which members are merely fillers to the eyewitness through various verbal and nonverbal means. Phillips et al. (1999) manipulated lineup administrators' assumptions about the identity of the culprit and found that this manipulation affected the choices that eyewitnesses made from the lineup, especially when a sequential lineup procedure was used. In addition to influencing eyewitnesses' choice of particular lineup members, the person administering the lineup can cause other problems. Wells & Bradfield (1998, 1999) found that post-identification suggestions to eyewitnesses from lineup administrators led mistaken eyewitnesses to develop high levels of false certainty that they had made an accurate identification. The problem of influence from the lineup administrator is easily fixed by having lineups administered by someone who does not know which lineup member is the suspect and which ones are fillers (Wells et al. 1998).

Base Rates as System Variables

Base rates can be considered system variables in some cases. The important base rate in eyewitness identification is the base rate for the culprit being present versus absent in a lineup. Most mistaken identifications occur when the culprit is not in the lineup. Although the relation between the culprit-absent versus culprit-present base rate and the chances of mistaken identification has been established and modeled mathematically (Wells & Lindsay 1980, Wells & Turtle 1986), the case was only recently made for treating this base rate as a system variable (Wells & Olson 2002). Previously, this base rate was treated as a fixed (albeit largely unknown) variable in actual cases. In fact, however, no laws or rules determine when a suspect is placed in a lineup and, therefore, this base rate varies as a function of the decisions crime investigators make when conducting a lineup. Consider, for instance, two police departments, a lax-criterion department and a strict-criterion department. In the lax-criterion department, investigators will place a suspect in a lineup for the slightest of reasons (e.g., a mere hunch) whereas the strict-criterion department requires certain evidence against a person (e.g., possession of stolen goods) before placing that person in a lineup. These two departments will, over the long run, have different base rates for culprit-present and culprit-absent lineups. Suppose, for example, that over a run of 1000 lineups the lax-criterion department shows 500 culprit-absent lineups and 500 culprit-present lineups whereas the strict-criterion department shows only 100 culprit-absent lineups and 900 culprit-present lineups. Given equivalent eyewitnesses in both of these departments, mistaken identifications of suspects will be nine times as likely in the lax-criterion department than in the strict-criterion department. (These surprising differences in the chances that an identification will be mistaken are simple derivations from Bayes' theorem.) Although the justice system has not yet done so, it could control the culprit-present versus culprit-absent base rate by requiring "probable cause" before placing someone in a lineup (Wells & Olson 2002). The base rate for culprit-present and culprit-absent lineups might be the most powerful system variable affecting the chances of mistaken identification.

PROBLEMS AND PROSPECTS

In spite of the successful application of the eyewitness identification literature, significant work has yet to be done. The eyewitness identification literature has been driven much less by theoretical frameworks than by practical perspectives. Two problems are related to this state of affairs. One is that the premium on application and forensic relevance reduces the interplay and sharing of ideas between eyewitness identification researchers and their counterparts in basic areas of psychology, especially cognitive and social psychology. In addition, the experimental eyewitness identification literature is likely never to be complete enough to cover every possible situation that arises in actual cases; hence, better theory is needed to generalize this body of literature and to fill in gaps regarding what is likely to happen under various conditions.

A second concern is that while laboratory data on eyewitness identification are extensive, some key forms of real-world data are lacking. Certain estimable rates of eyewitness identification behavior and lineup conditions from actual cases could assist the design and interpretation of laboratory work. For instance, there have been no empirical estimates of the base rate for culprit-present versus culprit-absent lineups in actual cases. Although it is difficult to establish the ground truth (actual guilt or innocence) needed for precise estimates of this base rate in actual cases, methods exist for estimating upper limits (see Wells & Olson 2002). In addition, although the identification of a suspect from a lineup usually cannot be definitively classified as an accurate or mistaken identification in an actual case, the identification of a filler is a known error in actual cases and the rate at which these known errors occur can be informative. Two estimates of the filler identification rates in actual cases have been published. Wright & McDaid (1996) reported a rate of about 20% and Behrman & Davey (2001) reported a rate of 24%. One problem in collecting filler identification data from real cases is that police records often do not distinguish between eyewitnesses who make identifications of a filler and those who make no identification, which can result in a serious underestimation of the rate of filler identifications (Tollestrup et al. 1994). Another problem is that filler identification records from actual cases often lack an indication of the level of eyewitness certainty. These problems can be avoided by scripting data collection with police departments.

Actual case data of these types (e.g., base rates, filler identification rates, eyewitness certainty on known errors) can supplement the laboratory literature on eyewitness identification in two important ways. First, actual case data can be compared to laboratory data to see if the general rates of certain behaviors (e.g., nonidentification responses) are similar. Second, the rates for certain conditions in actual cases (e.g., rates of culprit-present versus culprit-absent lineups) are critical for Bayesian estimations of posterior probabilities that cannot themselves be derived from experiments.

Eyewitness identification research is likely to continue to focus on system variables for the foreseeable future because of the way system variables can be mapped onto the problem of improving eyewitness identification accuracy in actual cases. At the same time, estimator variables might be re-emerging with new promise for postdiction for three reasons. First, conditions are being found in which eyewitness certainty might be more closely related to eyewitness identification accuracy than once thought, especially when external influences on eyewitness certainty are minimized. Second, new postdiction variables, such as decision time, are emerging. Third, Bayesian analyses are being used to show that some eyewitness responses to lineups, such as filler identifications, have postdiction value in exonerations. Each of these represent potentially superior estimator variables because they can be more precisely measured in actual cases than can some of the more traditional estimator variables (such as stress or arousal). In any case, there is little evidence that eyewitness identification research is veering away from its applied orientation, especially in the face of recent successes in affecting legal policies and practices (Wells 2001, Wells et al. 2000).

The *Annual Review of Psychology* is online at http://psych.annualreviews.org

LITERATURE CITED

Behrman BW, Davey SL. 2001. Eyewitness identification in actual criminal cases: an archival analysis. *Law Hum. Behav.* 25:475–91

Bothwell RK, Deffenbacher KA, Brigham JC. 1987. Correlation of eyewitness accuracy and confidence: optimality hypothesis revisited. *J. Appl. Psychol.* 72:691–95

Bradfield AL, Wells GL, Olson EA. 2002. The damaging effect of confirming feedback on the relation between eyewitness certainty and identification accuracy. *J. Appl. Psychol.* 87: 112–20

Brewer N, Keast A, Rishworth A. 2002. Improving the confidence-accuracy relation in eyewitness identification: evidence from correlation and calibration. *J. Exp. Psychol.: Appl.* 8:44–56

Brigham JC, Barkowitz P. 1978. Do "They all look alike?" The effect of race, sex, experience, and attitudes on the ability to recognize faces. *J. Appl. Soc. Psychol.* 8:306–18

Brigham JC, Bothwell RK. 1983. The ability of prospective jurors to estimate the accuracy of eyewitness identifications. *Law Hum. Behav.* 7:19–30

Brown E, Deffenbacher K, Sturgill W. 1977. Memory for faces and the circumstances of the encounter. *J. Appl. Psychol.* 62:311–18

Christianson SA. 1992. Emotional stress and eyewitness memory: a critical review. *Psychol. Bull.* 112:284–309

Clark SE. 2002. A memory and decision model for eyewitness identification. *Appl. Cogn. Psychol.* In press

Clark SE, Tunnicliff JL. 2001. Selecting lineup foils in eyewitness identification: experimental control and real-world simulation. *Law Hum. Behav.* 25:199–216

Clifford BR, Hollin CR. 1981. Effects of the type of incident and the number of perpetrators on eyewitness memory. *J. Appl. Psychol.* 66:364–70

Cutler BL, Penrod SD, Martens TK. 1987. The reliability of eyewitness identification: the role of system and estimator variables. *Law Hum. Behav.* 11:233–58

Deffenbacher K. 1983. The influence of arousal on reliability of testimony. In *Evaluating Witness Evidence: Recent Psychological Research and New Perspectives*, ed. SMA Lloyd-Bostock, BR Clifford, pp. 235–51. Chichester, Engl.: Wiley

Deffenbacher K, Loftus EF. 1982. Do jurors share a common understanding concern-ing eyewitness behavior? *Law Hum. Behav.* 6:15–30

Dunning D, Perretta S. 2002. Automaticity and eyewitness accuracy: a 10- to-12 second rule for distinguishing accurate from inaccurate positive identifications. *J. Appl. Psychol.* In press

Dunning D, Stern LB. 1994. Distinguishing accurate from inaccurate identifications via inquiries about decision processes. *J. Pers. Soc. Psychol.* 67:818–35

Easterbrook JA. 1959. The effect of emotion on cue utilization and the organization of behavior. *Psychol. Rev.* 66:183–201

Ebbesen E, Flowe S. 2002. Simultaneous versus sequential lineups: what do we really know? *Law Hum. Behav.* In press

Ellis HD, Davies GM, Shepherd JW. 1977. Experimental studies of face identification. *J. Crim. Def.* 3:219–34

Fleishman JJ, Buckley ML, Klosinsky MJ, Smith N, Tuck B. 1976. Judged attractiveness in recognition memory of women's faces. *Percept. Mot. Skills* 43:709–10

Hockley WE, Hemsworth DH, Consoli A. 1999. Shades of the mirror effect: recognition of faces with and without sunglasses. *Mem. Cogn.* 27(1):128–38

Hosch HM, Leippe MR, Marchioni PM, Cooper DS. 1984. Victimization, self-monitoring, and eyewitness identification. *J. Appl. Psychol.* 69:280–88

Hosch HM, Platz SJ. 1984. Self-monitoring and eyewitness accuracy. *Personal. Soc. Psychol. Bull.* 10:283–89

Howells TH. 1938. A study of ability to recognize faces. *J. Abnorm. Psychol.* 33:124–27

Juslin P, Olson N, Winman A. 1996. Calibration and diagnosticity of confidence in eyewitness identification: comments on what can and cannot be inferred from a low confidence-accuracy correlation. *J. Exp. Psychol. Learn. Mem. Cogn.* 5:1304–16

Langois JH, Roggman LA. 1990. Attractive faces are only average. *Psychol. Sci.* 1:115–21

Leippe MR, Wells GL, Ostrom TM. 1978. Crime seriousness as a determinant of accuracy in eyewitness identification. *J. Appl. Psychol.* 63:345–51

Light LL, Kayra-Stuart F, Hollander S. 1979. Recognition memory for typical and unusual faces. *J. Exp. Psychol.: Hum. Learn.* 5:212–28

Lindsay RCL, Martin R, Webber L. 1994. Default values in eyewitness descriptions: a problem for the match-to-description lineup foil selection strategy. *Law Hum. Behav.* 18:527–41

Lindsay RCL, Wells GL. 1980. What price justice? Exploring the relationship between lineup fairness and identification accuracy. *Law Hum. Behav.* 4:303–14

Lindsay RCL, Wells GL. 1985. Improving eyewitness identification from lineups: simultaneous versus sequential lineup presentations. *J. Appl. Psychol.* 70:556–64

Lindsay RCL, Wells GL, O'Connor F. 1989. Mock juror belief of accurate and inaccurate eyewitnesses: a replication. *Law Hum. Behav.* 13:333–40

Lindsay RCL, Wells GL, Rumpel C. 1981. Can people detect eyewitness identification accuracy within and between situations? *J. Appl. Psychol.* 66:79–89

Loftus EF, Loftus GR, Messo J. 1987. Some facts about "weapon focus." *Law Hum. Behav.* 11:55–62

Luus CAE, Wells GL. 1991. Eyewitness identification and the selection of distracters for lineups. *Law Hum. Behav.* 15:43–57

Malpass RS. 1981. Effective size and defendant bias in eyewitness identification lineups. *Law Hum. Behav.* 5:299–309

Malpass RS, Devine PG. 1981. Eyewitness identification: lineup instructions and the absence of the offender. *J. Appl. Psychol.* 66:482–89

McConkey KM, Roche SM. 1989. Knowledge of eyewitness memory. *Aust. Psychol.* 24:377–84

Meissner C, Brigham JC. 2001. Twenty years of investigating the own-race bias in memory for faces: a meta-analytic review. *Psychol. Public Policy Law* 7:3–35

Navon D. 1992. Selection of foils by similarity to suspect is likely to misfire. *Law Hum. Behav.* 16:575–93

Noon E, Hollin CR. 1987. Lay knowledge of eyewitness behaviour: a British survey. *Appl. Cogn. Psychol.* 1:143–53

Phillips MR, McAuliff BD, Kovera MB, Cutler BL. 1999. Double-blind photoarray administration as a safeguard against investigator bias. *J. Appl. Psychol.* 84:940–51

Powers PA, Andriks JL, Loftus EF. 1979. Eyewitness accounts of males and females. *J. Appl. Psychol.* 64:339–47

Pozzulo JD, Lindsay RCL. 1998. Identification accuracy of children versus adults: a meta-analysis. *Law Hum. Behav.* 22:549–70

Pozzulo JD, Lindsay RCL. 1999. Elimination lineups: an improved identification procedure for child eyewitnesses. *J. Appl. Psychol.* 84:167–76

Read JD, Vokey JR, Hammersley R. 1990. Changing photos of faces: effects of exposure duration and photo similarity on recognition and the accuracy-confidence relationship. *J. Exp. Psychol.: Learn. Mem. Cogn.* 16:870–82

Risinger MD, Saks MJ, Thompson WC, Rosenthal R. 2002. The Daubert/Kumho implications of observer effects in forensic science: hidden problems of expectation and suggestion. *Calif. Law Rev.* 90:1–56

Robinson MD, Johnson JT, Herndon F. 1997. Reaction time and assessments of cognitive effort as predictors of eyewitness memory accuracy and confidence. *J. Appl. Psychol.* 82:416–25

Rosenthal R. 1976. *Experimenter Effects in Behavioral Research.* New York: Irvington

Ross DF, Read JD, Toglia MP, eds. 1994. *Adult Eyewitness Testimony: Current Trends and Developments.* New York: Cambridge Univ. Press

Scheck B, Neufeld P, Dwyer J. 2000. *Actual Innocence.* New York: Random House

Seelau SM, Wells GL. 1995. Applied eyewitness research: the other mission. *Law Hum. Behav.* 19:317–22

Shapiro PN, Penrod SD. 1986. Meta-analysis

of racial identification studies. *Psychol. Bull.* 100:139–56

Shaw JI, Skolnick P. 1999. Weapon focus and gender differences in eyewitness accuracy: arousal versus salience. *J. Appl. Soc. Psychol.* 29:2328–41

Shaw JS III. 1996. Increases in eyewitness confidence resulting from postevent questioning. *J. Exp. Psychol.: Appl.* 2:126–46

Shaw JS III, McClure KA. 1996. Repeated postevent questioning can lead to elevated levels of eyewitness confidence. *Law Hum. Behav.* 20:629–54

Smith SM, Lindsay RCL, Pryke S. 2000. Postdictors of eyewitness errors: Can false identification be diagnosed? *J. Appl. Psychol.* 85:542–50

Sporer SL. 1992. Post-dicting eyewitness accuracy: confidence, decision times and person descriptions of choosers and non-choosers. *Eur. J. Soc. Psychol.* 22:157–80

Sporer SL. 1993. Eyewitness identification accuracy, confidence, and decision times in simultaneous and sequential lineups. *J. Appl. Psychol.* 78:22–33

Sporer SL. 1994. Decision times and eyewitness identification accuracy in simultaneous and sequential lineups. See Ross et al. 1994, pp. 300–27

Sporer SL, Penrod SD, Read JD, Cutler BL. 1995. Choosing, confidence, and accuracy: a meta-analysis of the confidence-accuracy relation in eyewitness identification studies. *Psychol. Bull.* 118:315–27

Steblay NM. 1992. A meta-analytic review of the weapon focus effect. *Law Hum. Behav.* 16:413–24

Steblay NM. 1997. Social influence in eyewitness recall: a meta-analytic review of lineup instruction effects. *Law Hum. Behav.* 21:283–98

Steblay NM, Dysart J, Fulero S, Lindsay RCL. 2001. Eyewitness accuracy rates in sequential and simultaneous lineup presentations: a meta-analytic comparison. *Law Hum. Behav.* 25:459–74

Tech. Work. Group Eyewitness Evidence. 1999. *Eyewitness Evidence: A Guide for Law Enforcement.* Washington, DC: US Dep. Justice, Off. Justice Programs

Tollestrup PA, Turtle JW, Yuille JC. 1994. Actual witnesses to robbery and fraud: an archival analysis. See Ross et al. 1994, pp. 144–62

Wells GL. 1978. Applied eyewitness testimony research: system variables and estimator variables. *J. Pers. Soc. Psychol.* 36:1546–57

Wells GL. 1984a. The psychology of lineup identifications. *J. Appl. Soc. Psychol.* 14:89–103

Wells GL. 1984b. How adequate is human intuition for judging eyewitness testimony? In *Eyewitness Testimony: Psychological Perspectives*, ed. GL Wells, EF Loftus, pp. 256–72. New York: Cambridge Univ. Press

Wells GL. 1993. What do we know about eyewitness identification? *Am. Psychol.* 48:553–71

Wells GL. 2001. Police lineups: data, theory, and policy. *Psychol. Public Policy Law* 7:791–801

Wells GL, Bradfield AL. 1998. "Good, you identified the suspect:" Feedback to eyewitnesses distorts their reports of the witnessing experience. *J. Appl. Psychol.* 83:360–76

Wells GL, Bradfield AL. 1999. Distortions in eyewitnesses' recollections: Can the post-identification feedback effect be moderated? *Psychol. Sci.* 10:138–44

Wells GL, Ferguson TJ, Lindsay RCL. 1981. The tractability of eyewitness confidence and its implication for triers of fact. *J. Appl. Psychol.* 66:688–96

Wells GL, Hryciw B. 1984. Memory for faces: encoding and retrieval operations. *Mem. Cogn.* 12:338–44

Wells GL, Leippe MR. 1981. How do triers of fact infer the accuracy of eyewitness identifications? Memory for peripheral detail can be misleading. *J. Appl. Psychol.* 66:682–87

Wells GL, Leippe MR, Ostrom TM. 1979. Guidelines for empirically assessing the fairness of a lineup. *Law Hum. Behav.* 3:285–93

Wells GL, Lindsay RCL. 1980. On estimating the diagnosticity of eyewitness nonidentifications. *Psychol. Bull.* 88:776–84

Wells GL, Lindsay RCL, Ferguson TJ. 1979. Accuracy, confidence, and juror perceptions in eyewitness identification. *J. Appl. Psychol.* 64:440–48

Wells GL, Luus CAE. 1990. Police lineups as experiments: Social methodology as a framework for properly conducted lineups. *Personal. Soc. Psychol. Bull.* 16:106–17

Wells GL, Malpass RS, Lindsay RCL, Fisher RP, Turtle JW, Fulero S. 2000. From the lab to the police station: A successful application of eyewitness research. *Am. Psychol.* 55:581–98

Wells GL, Olson EA. 2002. Eyewitness identification: Information gain from incriminating and exonerating behaviors. *J. Exp. Psychol.: Appl.* In press

Wells GL, Rydell SM, Seelau EP. 1993. On the selection of distractors for eyewitness lineups. *J. Appl. Psychol.* 78:835–44

Wells GL, Seelau EP, Rydell SM, Luus CAE. 1994. Recommendations for properly conducted lineup identification tasks. See Ross et al. 1994, pp. 223–44

Wells GL, Small M, Penrod SD, Malpass RS, Fulero SM, Brimacombe CAE. 1998. Eyewitness identification procedures: recommendations for lineups and photospreads. *Law Hum. Behav.* 22:603–7

Wells GL, Turtle JW. 1986. Eyewitness identification: the importance of lineup models. *Psychol. Bull.* 99:320–29

Wogalter MS, Marwitz DB, Leonard DC. 1992. Suggestiveness in photospread lineups: Similarity induces distinctiveness. *Appl. Cogn. Psychol.* 6:443–53

Wright DB, McDaid AT. 1996. Comparing system and estimator variables using data from real lineups. *Appl. Cogn. Psychol.* 10:75–84

Annu. Rev. Psychol. 2003. 54:297–327
doi: 10.1146/annurev.psych.54.101601.145225
First published online as a Review in Advance on August 6, 2002

IMPLICIT MEASURES IN SOCIAL COGNITION
RESEARCH: Their Meaning and Use

Russell H. Fazio and Michael A. Olson

*Department of Psychology, Ohio State University, Columbus, Ohio,
43210-1222; e-mail: Fazio@psy.ohio-state.edu*

Key Words   attitude measurement, automatic processing, priming, Implicit
Association Test

■ **Abstract**   Behavioral scientists have long sought measures of important psychological constructs that avoid response biases and other problems associated with direct reports. Recently, a large number of such indirect, or "implicit," measures have
emerged. We review research that has utilized these measures across several domains,
including attitudes, self-esteem, and stereotypes, and discuss their predictive validity, their interrelations, and the mechanisms presumably underlying their operation.
Special attention is devoted to various priming measures and the Implicit Association
Test, largely due to their prevalence in the literature. We also attempt to clarify several
unresolved theoretical and empirical issues concerning implicit measures, including
the nature of the underlying constructs they purport to measure, the conditions under
which they are most likely to relate to explicit measures, the kinds of behavior each
measure is likely to predict, their sensitivity to context, and the construct's potential
for change.

CONTENTS

INTRODUCTION

Over the past few years, there has been a surge of interest in the use of implicit measurement techniques in social psychological research. If this assertion needed any verification, one merely has to call attention to the special issues of four journals recently devoted to the topic: *Journal of Experimental Social Psychology* on "Unconscious Processes in Stereotyping and Prejudice" (Banaji 1997), *Cognition and Emotion* on "Automatic Affective Processing" (De Houwer & Hermans 2001), *Zeitschrift für Experimentelle Psychologie* on "Attitude Measurement Using the Implicit Association Test (IAT)" (Plessner & Banse 2001), and *Journal of Personality and Social Psychology* on "Implicit Prejudice and Stereotyping: How Automatic Are They?" (Devine 2001). The research has involved a variety of domains, including attitudes (e.g., Fazio et al. 1995, Greenwald et al. 1998), stereotypes (e.g., Wittenbrink et al. 1997, Nosek et al. 2002a), self-esteem (Hetts et al. 1999, Bosson et al. 2000, Koole et al. 2001, Rudman et al. 2001b), close relationships (e.g., Banse 1999), and health behavior (e.g., Stacy et al. 1997).

A variety of different implicit measurement techniques have been employed. One such technique involves various priming procedures that have proven useful in the past as a means of assessing what is activated from memory by the presentation of some attitude object (e.g., Gaertner & McLaughlin 1983, Fazio et al. 1986, Greenwald et al. 1989, Perdue et al. 1990). For example, Fazio et al. (1995) examined the consequences of priming participants with photos of black versus white undergraduates. The participants' primary task was to indicate the connotation of an evaluative adjective (e.g., "pleasant" or "awful") as quickly as possible. In the context of a cover story concerning the judgment of word meaning being an automatic skill that should not be disrupted by the participants having to perform an additional task simultaneously, each target adjective was preceded by the brief presentation of a photo. Participants were instructed to attend to these faces so that they would be able to pick them out in a later phase of the experiment. The black and white faces had different consequences for the latency with which participants could indicate the connotation of the subsequently presented target adjective. Relative to what was observed for white faces, black faces facilitated responding to negative adjectives and interfered with responding to positive adjectives. The pattern suggests that, on average, negativity was automatically activated by the black primes.

Probably the most well-known implicit measurement technique is the Implicit Association Test (IAT), developed by Greenwald et al. (1998). This procedure assesses the strength of an association between a target concept and an attribute dimension by considering the latency with which participants can employ two response keys when each has been assigned a dual meaning. The participants' task is to categorize stimuli as they appear on the screen. For example, in the Greenwald et al. (1998) IAT concerning racial attitudes, participants were first asked to categorize names (e.g., "Latonya" or "Betsy") as typical of blacks versus whites. Here, race is the target concept and the keys are labeled "black" and "white." Participants then categorized a variety of clearly valenced words (e.g., "poison" or "gift") as pleasant or unpleasant, which constitutes the attribute dimension. In the critical phase of the experiment these two categorization tasks were combined. Participants performed this combined task twice—once with one response key signifying black/pleasant and the other labeled white/unpleasant, and once with one key meaning black/unpleasant and the other white/pleasant—in counterbalanced order. The question concerns which response mapping participants find easier to use. In the Greenwald et al. (1998) experiment participants were overwhelmingly faster at responding when black was paired with unpleasant than when black was paired with pleasant. On average, then, the participants found it much easier to associate the target concept black with the attribute unpleasant than with the attribute pleasant.

Many additional implicit measurement techniques have been employed: (*a*) Building upon past research that has examined activation by considering how word fragments are completed (e.g., Warrington & Weiskrantz 1968, Tulving et al. 1982, Bassili & Smith 1986, Gilbert & Hixon 1991), a number of researchers have employed some variant of a word-fragment completion task as an implicit measure of self-esteem (e.g., Hetts et al. 1999), racial prejudice (e.g., Dovidio et al. 1997, Son Hing et al. 2002), or stereotypes (Hense et al. 1995, Sinclair & Kunda 1999).

(*b*) On the basis of work that has demonstrated a linguistic intergroup bias (Semin & Fiedler 1988; Maass et al. 1989, 1996), i.e., a tendency to use more abstract language to describe expectancy-consistent behaviors than expectancy-inconsistent ones, the extent to which descriptions of African American targets' positive and negative behaviors include abstract versus concrete language has been employed as an implicit measure of racial prejudice (e.g., von Hippel et al. 1995, 1997).

(*c*) Based on work indicating that social perceivers tend to explain expectancy-inconsistent events more often than expectancy-consistent events (Hastie 1984), von Hippel and his colleagues (von Hippel et al. 1997, Sekaquaptewa et al. 2002) also have developed an implicit measure of racial stereotyping that focuses on whether a participant's completion of a sentence explains the behavior described in the sentence, as opposed to simply continuing the sentence without explaining. Relatively more such explanations in the case of stereotype-incongruent events serve as an indication of stereotype use on this stereotype-explanatory bias measure.

(*d*) Following from the documented tendency of people to prefer the letters that appear in their own names, especially their initials (Nuttin 1985), the name-letter preference effect has been employed as an implicit measure of self-esteem (Koole et al. 2001, Jones et al. 2002, Pelham et al. 2002).

(*e*) De Houwer and his colleagues have introduced an affective variant of the spatial Simon task as an implicit measure of attitudes (De Houwer & Eelen 1998, De Houwer et al. 2001a). Participants are required to make some discrimination of the stimuli (e.g., noun/adjective, man-made/natural) but do so by responding "positive" for one category and "negative" for the other. Given that the stimuli themselves vary in their associated valence, this produces both evaluatively congruent trials, in which the valence of the stimulus and its relevant category signal the same response (e.g., saying "positive" to "flower" because it is a noun), and evaluatively incongruent trials, for which response competition exists (e.g., saying "negative" to "happy" because it is an adjective).

(*f*) Finally, Nosek & Banaji (2001) have introduced the Go/No-Go Association Task (GNAT), a variant of the IAT that does not require the use of a contrast category. In the GNAT participants respond to stimuli that represent the target category and the attribute category "good" but do nothing in response to other stimuli. Response latencies or errors are compared to a block of trials for which the participant must respond to items that represent the target category and "bad."

Various physiological approaches have also been employed as implicit measures of attitudes. Vanman et al. (1997) used facial electromyography (EMG) to examine racial prejudice. Both Phelps et al. (2000) and Hart et al. (2000) examined amygdala activation using functional magnetic resonance imaging (fMRI) procedures as an indicant of racial evaluation. Eyeblink startle response to black versus white faces has also been utilized in this way (Phelps et al. 2000, Amodio et al. 2002). Cardiovascular reactivity measures indicative of challenge versus threat have been employed to examine responses to interaction with blacks and other stigmatized individuals (Blascovich et al. 2001). In addition, Cacioppo and his colleagues have employed event-related brain potentials as an on-line measure of the categorization of stimuli as positive or negative (e.g., Cacioppo et al. 1993, Crites et al. 1995, Ito & Cacioppo 2000).

What these various approaches have in common is that they all seek to provide an estimate of the construct of interest without having to directly ask the participant for a verbal report. Their major appeal is that these indirect estimates are likely to be free of social desirability concerns. Often, though not necessarily true for all of the measures, the participant is unaware that attitudes, stereotypes, etc. are even being assessed. The approaches vary in terms of their attempting to assess what is automatically activated in response to a person or object versus employing a presumed consequence of such activation (e.g., influence upon further information processing, as in the stereotype-explanatory bias) as an indirect estimate.

Most of the research that has been conducted has concerned either various forms of priming or the IAT. Hence, our review focuses on these two implicit measures. The burgeoning nature of this literature makes it very difficult to provide a comprehensive review of all the relevant empirical work. As we compiled relevant articles, we were astounded at how every week was marked by the appearance of new papers. We have made every effort to include recently published and in-press articles. However, to make our task more manageable, we have opted not to include, with very few exceptions, the many relevant conference presentations and unpublished manuscripts that have come to our attention.

Obviously, work on implicit measures relevant to social cognition is in its infancy. The literature, although booming, has not matured to the point at which many firm conclusions can be drawn. When possible, we offer general inferences. More often, however, we offer observations about questions that have arisen as the research has progressed. We hope our structuring the literature into a series of observations or questions that have received, and/or continue to require, attention will prove useful in informing future theory and research.

SOME OPENING OBSERVATIONS

Where's the Theory?

Despite incredible activity, research concerning implicit measures has been surprisingly atheoretical. It largely has been a methodological, empirically driven enterprise. In this review we offer a few observations about issues that have arisen as this area of research has developed. However, readers should be aware that these observations stem from a theoretical perspective that undoubtedly influences how we view and structure this youthful literature. Although it was developed years before this surge of interest in implicit attitude measurement, the MODE model (Fazio 1990, Fazio & Towles-Schwen 1999), we argue, provides a very useful perspective for considering these issues. Moreover, it points to important parallels between the issues that have arisen recently regarding implicit measures and extensively researched questions in classic and current literature regarding attitudes and their influence on judgments and behavior.

The MODE model is one of a class of dual process models (see Chaiken & Trope 1999) that have proven useful in such varied research domains as persuasion, social perception, and attribution. The MODE model's focus on the processes by which attitudes influence judgments and behavior makes it especially relevant to the present concerns. In brief, the model proposes that attitudes can exert influence through relatively spontaneous or more deliberative processes. The former involve judgments of, or behavior toward, an object being influenced by one's construal of the object in the immediate situation—perceptions that themselves can be affected by individuals' attitudes having been automatically activated upon encountering the attitude object. In contrast, deliberative processing involves a more effortful, cost-benefit analysis of the utility of a particular behavior. MODE is an acronym for *m*otivation and *o*pportunity as *de*terminants of whether the attitude-to-behavior process is primarily spontaneous or deliberative in nature. Given the effortful reflection required for deliberative processing, some motivating force is necessary to induce individuals to engage in the processing. The time and the resources to deliberate—what the model refers to as opportunity—also must exist. In addition to delineating two distinct classes of attitude-behavior processes, the MODE model explicitly postulates the possibility of processes that are neither purely spontaneous nor purely deliberative, but instead are "mixed" processes that involve both automatic and controlled components. Any controlled component within a mixed sequence requires, once again, that the individual be both motivated to engage in the necessary cognitive effort and have the opportunity to do so. Such mixed processes are especially relevant to a number of issues that have received attention regarding implicit measures of attitudes.

Where's the Implicit?

We have to express some misgivings about the very terms "implicit" and "explicit" having been imported from cognitive psychology, at least insofar as they are used to refer to implicit versus explicit attitudes, stereotypes, or self-esteem (Greenwald & Banaji 1995). In cognitive psychology, individuals are said to display implicit memory for a prior event when their performance on some task shows evidence of their having been influenced by that prior event, even though they display no explicit memory for the event; i.e., they report no awareness of the event having occurred (see Schacter 1987, Richardson-Klavehn & Bjork 1988, Roediger 1990). For example, after having been briefly presented with a list of words, individuals might show superior performance on a related word fragment completion task, even though they perform only at chance levels on a recognition task in which they indicate the words they had seen earlier.

If this terminology is to have any similar meaning for attitudes (as well as stereotypes, the self, etc.), then it has to imply that implicit attitudes are ones for which individuals lack awareness. Is that the case? Most importantly, how do we know that individuals lack awareness of their attitudes? Nothing about our current implicit measurement procedures, be it a priming method, the IAT, or one of the other techniques mentioned above, guarantees that participants are unaware of their attitudes. Just because an individual shows evidence that a particular evaluation is primed by the presentation of the attitude object does not mean the individual is unaware of the attitude. Likewise, in the IAT just because an individual has more difficulty associating a given attitude object with the category pleasant than with the category unpleasant does not mean the individual is unaware that he or she views the attitude object negatively. Thus, as long as the term "implicit" is to reflect unawareness, we fail to see any justification for labeling these attitudes as implicit. Discordance between scores on an implicit and an explicit measure should not, in and of itself, be taken as evidence that the implicitly measured construct is an unconscious construct. Yet, the implication that the construct is unconscious can exert subtle, and not so subtle, influences on the way in which we approach theorizing about the antecedents and consequences of the construct.

A second troublesome aspect of the implicit-explicit distinction is that it implies preexisting dual attitudes (or whatever the construct of interest might be) in memory. That is, if the terms refer to the constructs themselves, then both an implicit and an explicit attitude presumably exist in memory (see Wilson et al. 2000). However, no current explicit measurement procedure guarantees that an explicit attitude is independently represented in memory. Instead, the response to the explicit measure may be constructed on the spot (see Schwarz & Bohner 2001).

For these reasons, it is more appropriate to view the *measure* as implicit or explicit, *not* the attitude (or whatever other construct). What makes priming or the IAT implicit is that these techniques provide estimates of individuals' attitudes without our having to directly ask them for such information. In this sense, the current techniques do not differ from earlier proposals regarding projective methods (e.g., Proshansky 1943) and other unobtrusive measurement procedures (e.g., Webb et al. 1966). Participants may be unaware that their attitudes are being assessed, but that does not mean they are unaware that they possess those attitudes. We would encourage researchers not to equate an implicitly measured construct with an unconscious one. Although an implicit-explicit dissociation may occur because the implicit measure reflects associations to which the individual lacks introspective access, such a dissociation also may occur because people are reluctant to admit (on the explicit measure) to the tendency that is revealed by the implicit measure (see Greenwald et al. 2002a for a related discussion). This ambiguity alone is reason to be wary of the connotations that the term "implicit" carries regarding unawareness. Logically, reference to an implicit attitude, stereotype, or self-esteem should require evidence of unawareness and not solely the use of an implicit measurement technique.[1]

THE RELATION BETWEEN IMPLICIT AND EXPLICIT MEASURES

The literature has included much discussion of the relation between implicit and explicit measures. Are they correlated with one another or are they discordant? Blair (2001), Dovidio et al. (2001), and Brauer et al. (2000) have provided recent reviews. Within the domain of prejudice and stereotypes, the correlations tend to be quite low (e.g., Fazio et al. 1995, Greenwald et al. 1998, Rudman & Kilianski 2000, Kawakami & Dovidio 2001, Monteith et al. 2001, Ottaway et al. 2001, Rudman & Glick 2001, Devine et al. 2002, Dovidio et al. 2002), although there are occasional reports of significant correlations (e.g., McConnell & Liebold 2001, with respect to the IAT; Lepore & Brown 1997; Kawakami et al. 1998; Wittenbrink et al. 1997, with respect to a priming measure). However, some of the initial research using priming methods or the IAT clearly illustrates a correspondence with

---

[1]Our own preference is for the terms "indirect" and "direct" measures (see Dovidio & Fazio 1992), which are less likely to connote unawareness than are "implicit" and "explicit" (see Richardson-Klavehn & Bjork 1988 for a similar argument). However, the latter terms now appear to be firmly entrenched in the literature.

self-reported attitudes toward mundane, socially noncontroversial objects. When priming techniques were first employed to examine the possibility of automatic attitude activation, attitude objects that participants reported liking or disliking were idiosyncratically selected to serve as the positive and negative primes (Fazio et al. 1986). Similarly, the IAT reveals more positive associations to flowers than to insects, just as people's self-reports indicate (Greenwald et al. 1998). In addition, fairly substantial correlations have been obtained between IAT preference scores and self-reported preferences regarding math versus arts and regarding the 2000 presidential candidates Gore versus Bush (Nosek et al. 2002b).

In our view the variability regarding the correspondence between implicit and explicit measures indicates that discussion of whether a relation exists is not very productive. We already know enough to be able to say that the question has no simple answer. That is, the answer is "it depends." The entire issue is reminiscent of what Zanna & Fazio (1982) referred to as the first generation question regarding the attitude-behavior relation: Is there a relation? Just as in that literature, we need to be asking a "when" question: When, under what conditions, and for what kind of people, are implicit and explicit measures related? The patterns noted above regarding socially sensitive versus nonsensitive issues are consistent with the MODE model (see Dovidio & Fazio 1992, Nosek 2002 for discussions of the role of social sensitivity). The more sensitive the domain, the greater the likelihood that motivational factors will be evoked and exert some influence on overt responses to an explicit measure. The MODE model suggests that the magnitude of the relation between an implicit and an explicit measure will depend on the motivation and opportunity to deliberate. If either motivation or opportunity is relatively low at the time that the explicit response is being considered, then explicit measures should correlate with implicit ones. However, when both motivation and opportunity are relatively high, they are less likely to correlate (see Koole et al. 2001 for evidence on the relevance of opportunity factors to the relation between implicitly and explicitly measured self-esteem).

An unfortunate aspect of this discussion of discordance between implicit and explicit measures is that it appears to have engendered some confusion about the attitude concept. The discussion has raised a conceptual question that we facetiously refer to as "Will the real attitude please stand up?" (e.g., Wilson et al. 2000, Schwarz & Bohner 2001). Is the "real" attitude the one represented by the implicit measure or is it the one reflected in the explicit measure?[2] This question introduces two issues. First, what does "real" mean? There is considerable ambiguity

---

[2]Fazio et al. (1995) have to bear some responsibility for this confusion, largely because they referred to their unobtrusive, priming technique as the "bona fide" pipeline. However, the conceptual ambiguities also stem from the above-noted general lack of theory in the implicit and explicit measures literature. As we indicate, automatically activated attitudes have a very central role in the MODE model, and "bona fide" is simply intended to indicate that any automatic attitude activation occurs farther upstream than the overt response to an explicit measure.

about this, but to the extent that it refers to a measure's predictive validity, it is important to recognize that both implicit and explicit measures can be predictive of judgments and behavior (Fazio et al. 1995, Dovidio et al. 1997). According to the MODE model, which is more predictive depends on motivation and opportunity to deliberate. When motivation and/or opportunity are low, behavior is expected to be largely a function of the automatically activated attitude, and hence, the implicit measure should prove predictive. When motivation and opportunity are high, the explicit measure should be more predictive—presumably because the explicit measure will have been influenced by these same motivational forces.

The second point to note about this question is that any answer is entirely dependent on one's definition of attitude. A response to an explicit measure is often considered an attitude. Such a response meets most definitions of attitude in that it involves favorable or unfavorable evaluation of the object (see Zanna & Rempel 1988, Eagly & Chaiken 1993 for a discussion of such definitions). However, this view fails to recognize that an explicit measure necessarily involves overt expression of one's attitude. Again from the perspective of the MODE model, such expressions are, for want of any better expression, farther "downstream" than automatically activated attitudes. Responding to an explicit measure is itself a verbal behavior that can be affected by motivation and opportunity, as well as whatever is automatically activated. Any motivational factors that might be evoked can influence the overtly expressed judgment, assuming the situation and behavior in question provide the opportunity for deliberative processing.

PREDICTIVE VALIDITY OF IMPLICIT MEASURES

Priming Measures

Numerous reports attesting to the predictive validity of various forms of priming measures have appeared in the literature. Fazio et al. (1995) found estimates of automatically activated racial attitudes to be predictive of a black target's ratings of the quality of her interaction with the respondent; participants for whom negativity had been activated during the priming task behaved in a less friendly manner when they later interacted with the black target. The attitude estimates also correlated with participants' judgments of the extent to which blacks versus whites were deemed responsible for the escalation in tension and riots that ensued following the verdict of not guilty in the trial of the police involved in the beating of Rodney King. Similarly, Dovidio et al. (1997) observed correspondence between attitude estimates based on a priming procedure and nonverbal behaviors exhibited while interacting with a black and a white interviewer. The more negativity toward blacks that the participants revealed during the priming task, the more frequently they blinked their eyes and the less eye contact they maintained while interacting with the black relative to the white interviewer. In a similar investigation, Dovidio et al. (2002) examined white participants' friendliness while engaged in 3-minute conversations with black and white confederates. Their priming measure correlated with relative friendliness toward the black as indicated by the confederates' own ratings, judges' ratings of videotapes of the interactions, and judges' ratings of the participants' nonverbal behavior (i.e., silent videos on which only the participant, and not the confederate, was visible).[3]

Wilson et al. (2000) reported a correlation between a priming measure and the number of times white participants touched a black confederate's hand while exchanging a pen they needed to share repeatedly. Jackson (1997) found participants with more negative implicitly measured racial attitudes to judge less favorably an essay purportedly authored by a black undergraduate. Using a priming measure of racial attitudes, Fazio & Hilden (2001) predicted participants' emotional reactions to a public service ad that evoked a seemingly prejudiced response. In an investigation of attitudes toward fat people, Bessenoff & Sherman (2000) found that a priming measure involving photos of fat and thin women predicted how far participants later placed their own chair from that of a fat woman. Fazio & Dunton (1997) observed a relation between estimates of automatically activated racial attitudes and extent to which categorization by race, as opposed to gender or occupation, served as the basis for judging the similarity of pairs of stimulus photos. Dijksterhuis et al. (2000) employed a subliminal priming measure to assess the extent to which individuals associated the "elderly" with "forgetfulness" and found the measure to predict the degree to which participants themselves displayed memory impairment after activation of the category elderly. Finally, in the domain of implicit self-esteem measures, Spalding & Hardin (1999) found that the extent to which the subliminal priming of "me" and "myself" facilitated responding to positive versus negative words predicted participants' apparent anxiety while they were engaged in an interview regarding their own emotional health, but not if the interview concerned their best friends' health.

More complex patterns of findings also have been observed. In particular, a number of investigations have found the relation between automatically activated racial attitudes, as estimated by a priming measure, and subsequent race-related judgments to be moderated by motivational factors. This research, which has employed Dunton & Fazio's (1997) individual difference measure of motivation to control prejudiced reactions, has uncovered such moderating effects with respect to (*a*) responses to the Modern Racism Scale—an explicit measure of racial attitudes (Fazio et al. 1995, Dunton & Fazio 1997), (*b*) evaluations of the "typical Black male undergraduate" (Dunton & Fazio 1997), (*c*) first impression ratings of black target persons (Olson & Fazio 2002a), and (*d*) anticipated comfort in interacting with a black in various unscripted social situations (Towles-Schwen

---

[3]Interestingly, judges' ratings of the audio channel alone did not relate to the implicit measure but did correlate with an explicit measure, suggesting, as the authors note, that the spoken words stemmed from a more deliberative, motivated process and that the verbal channel provided greater opportunity for exerting such control than did the nonverbal channel. Hence, the data pattern is consistent with the MODE model's predictions regarding the importance of motivation and opportunity (see Fazio & Towles-Schwen 1999).

& Fazio 2002). Consistent with the MODE model, implicitly measured attitudes predicted the various judgments among individuals whose motivation to control prejudiced reactions was relatively low. However, this relation was attenuated as motivation increased. In fact, each of the studies revealed evidence of the relation being reversed among individuals with higher motivation scores. That is, among the highly motivated, those with more negative automatically activated attitudes responded more positively than did those characterized by automatically activated positivity. When the judgmental situation is sufficiently race-related to evoke any motivation to control prejudiced reactions that may characterize individuals, they may respond by overcorrecting for their automatically activated negativity. In terms of Wegener & Petty's (1995) Flexible Correction Model, such individuals possess a naive theory about the biasing effects of their negativity—a theory that overestimates its influence—so they overcompensate. In any case, such findings illustrate the importance of considering motivated processes when examining the predictive validity of an implicit measure. That motivated correction processes can reverse the relation between an implicit measure and overt judgments means that, in situations in which such motivation arises, neglecting to assess motivation to control prejudiced reactions can lead to the erroneous conclusion that the implicit measure is unrelated to the judgment of interest. Instead, the moderating influence of motivational factors may obscure the simple correlation.

In addition to these reports of a priming measure predicting a subsequent judgment or behavior, priming also has proven sensitive when employed as a dependent measure. In an experiment concerning implicit attitude formation via classical conditioning, Olson & Fazio (2002b) had participants undergo a visual task in which one novel stimulus was consistently paired with positively valued stimuli and another with negatively valued stimuli. The names of the two novel stimuli were later presented subliminally as primes during the course of a task in which participants needed to identify the connotation of evaluative adjectives. Responding was faster when the target adjective's valence matched the valence that earlier had been associated with the now subliminally presented prime (see Hermans et al. 2002 for related findings).

Implicit Association Test

A considerable amount of research employing the Implicit Association Test (IAT) has pursued a "known-groups" validity approach, demonstrating that the IAT scores of two groups of individuals differ in the expected way. For example, Japanese-Americans and Korean-Americans have been found to display more positivity toward their respective ingroups (Greenwald et al. 1998), as have East and West Germans (Keuhnen et al. 2001) and Jewish and Christian respondents (Rudman et al. 1999; see Jost et al. 2002 for a system justification perspective on such ingroup bias). IAT effects indicative of ingroup preference have even been found when groups have been created experimentally through a minimal group paradigm (Ashburn-Nardo et al. 2001; see Greenwald et al. 2002b for a related finding and Otten & Wentura 1999 for similar evidence using a priming measure). Similar differences have been obtained with respect to vegetarians and, although less consistently, with cigarette smokers (Swanson et al. 2001). IAT preferences for white over black have been found to be stronger for white than for black respondents, although the (weaker) preference for white does not appear to reverse itself among blacks (Nosek et al. 2002b; but see Livingston 2002). Teachman et al. (2001) found the IAT to discriminate snake and spider phobics, and Banse et al. (2001) found differences between homosexuals and heterosexuals in a sexual orientation IAT. Correspondence has also been observed between IAT scores reflecting the relative favorability of sodas versus juices and self-reported frequency of drinking the two classes of beverages in the past, and between IAT scores concerning high- versus low-calorie foods and self-reports of past eating behavior (Maison et al. 2001). Expected differences have also been revealed in the manner in which men and women associate gender with mathematics (Nosek et al. 2002a). Recently, Greenwald & Nosek (2001) provided a very useful review of such IAT research.

Additional relations of interest involving the IAT have been observed. In an investigation concerning fMRI-assessed activation of the amygdala, Phelps et al. (2000) found the strength of amygdala activation in response to unfamiliar black versus white faces to covary with race preference as assessed by the IAT. Olson & Fazio (2001) found the IAT to be sensitive to the implicit formation of attitudes via classical conditioning. Finally, in a study concerning the strength of association between the target concept "gender" and the attribute categories "career" versus "household," Gawronksi et al. (2002) found IAT scores to relate to memory performance in the "who said what?" paradigm. When unable to retrieve sufficient information from memory, participants with stronger stereotypic associations exhibited a bias toward assigning statements in a stereotype-consistent manner.

In contrast to the numerous investigations concerning known-group differences, less work has been conducted concerning the prediction of behavior from IAT scores. The evidence that does exist is mixed. Disappointingly, Karpinski & Hilton (2001) observed no relation between IAT scores reflecting relative preferences for apples versus candy bars and participants' subsequent choice behavior. However, Greenwald & Farnham (2000) did obtain some evidence suggesting that an IAT-based measure of self-esteem predicted reactions to success versus failure experiences; individuals with higher scores on the implicit self-esteem measure tended to be less affected by the feedback. Similarly, Jordan et al. (2002) reported a positive relation between a self-esteem IAT and a behavioral measure that involved persistence in the face of failure. In addition, Rudman & Glick (2001) found a correlation between an IAT assessment of the association between gender and agency versus communality and judgments of the social skills displayed by a highly agentic female applicant for a job that required social sensitivity. However, no significant correlation was observed when the job description did not necessitate sensitivity to others or with respect to ratings of the hireability of the applicant.

More promising are results from an intriguing and sophisticated investigation conducted by McConnell & Liebold (2001). After a brief interaction with a white experimenter, participants completed a set of questionnaires that included various explicit measures of prejudice, followed by a racial-prejudice IAT. They then interacted with a black experimenter. Both experimenters provided ratings of the interaction, as did judges who examined videotapes of the interactions. Impressively, IAT scores related significantly to the experimenters' and the judges' molar ratings of the interaction with the black versus the white experimenter. In addition, IAT scores indicative of prejudice against blacks were also associated with a variety of micro-behaviors including less speaking time, less smiling, fewer extemporaneous social comments, more speech errors, and more speech hesitations in the interaction with the black (versus white) experimenter.

Although these findings are unquestionably promising, a note of caution is required. As the authors indicated, the confirming results may have been facilitated by the sequence of events. In particular, the interaction with the black experimenter was immediately preceded by the administration of the explicit measures and the IAT, which would have resulted in the conscious activation of racial attitudes. Heightened attitude salience has been shown to increase attitude-behavior consistency (Snyder & Swann 1976, Snyder & Kendzierski 1982). Completion of the IAT also may have encouraged categorization of the second experimenter as "black" instead of as a member of some other applicable social category, which again may have promoted attitudinally consistent behavior.

Such an interpretive issue should not be viewed as calling for administration of the IAT after the behavioral assessment. This order of events merely poses a different set of issues. Instead of illustrating predictive validity, such a relation may be due to an effect of a recently performed and hence salient behavior on the IAT. Researchers interested in the attitude-to-behavior relation in the 1970s and 1980s were very sensitive to this self-perception possibility. This concern remains applicable even when attitudes are measured implicitly instead of explicitly. Indeed, some impressive findings regarding correlations between behavior and the IAT are rendered ambiguous by this possibility. For example, participants in an intriguing study by Lemm (2001) were interviewed about their attitudes toward gay men. Midway through the interview, the interviewer was identified as gay for half the participants. The interviewer rated the participants' apparent comfort level after each of the two interview segments. The change in rated comfort correlated significantly with an IAT involving the target categories gay versus straight. However, the IAT was administered immediately after the interview and, hence, participants' construals of a gay may have been affected by their recent experience. Similarly, a recent study by Asendorpf et al. (2002) involved an interaction with a physically attractive stranger of the opposite sex. After the conversation, participants completed an IAT assessing the strength of the association between "me" and "shy." These IAT scores correlated with coders' global ratings of the shyness exhibited during the interaction, as well as with more micro-ratings of such nonverbal behaviors as body tension. However, as the authors note, it is conceivable that this relation reflects the participants' recent self-observation, and not the IAT's having tapped an enduring and behaviorally predictive trait.

Clearly, more research on the predictive validity of the IAT is needed. Especially informative will be work that administers the IAT prior to the collection of the dependent measure, so as to avoid any possibility that the behavior is influencing the attitude scores, but that also involves some separation in time between IAT administration and the behavior of interest. Indeed, a more optimistic outlook regarding the predictive validity of the IAT is provided by a study by Rudman & Lee (2002), which involved a racial prejudice IAT administered in a separate, earlier session. In the second session participants were exposed to either violent and misogynous rap music or popular music, which served as a priming manipulation of racial stereotypes. A subsequent person-perception task involved the participants evaluating an ambiguously described black or white target. Although the sample was too small for the correlations to differ significantly across conditions, a significant correlation between IAT scores and evaluations of the target was evident only in the condition which involved a black target and prior exposure to rap music.

Some evidence suggests that the ability of the IAT to predict judgments and behavior may sometimes be moderated by motivational factors—just as is true for priming procedures. Florack et al. (2001) observed a moderating influence of need for cognition on the relation between an IAT reflecting favorability toward Turks, relative to Germans, and subsequent judgments of a Turkish juvenile delinquent. The expected relation was most apparent among individuals less inclined to engage in effortful cognitive processing. Hence, future research concerning the predictive validity of the IAT may benefit from the consideration of moderating variables.

Other Measures

Although less widely examined than either priming measures or the IAT, other implicit measures have proven predictive of relevant judgments and behavior. For example, using the linguistic intergroup bias measure mentioned above, von Hippel et al. (1997) found a relation between the implicit measure and the extent to which participants judged a videotaped African-American requesting money from another person as threatening. Similarly, the tendency to engage in the earlier described stereotype-explanatory bias been found to predict the quality of subsequent social interaction (Sekaquaptewa et al. 2002). Spontaneously generating relatively more internal attributions (or fewer external attributions) for a black's stereotype-inconsistent behaviors than stereotype-consistent behaviors was predictive of relatively more positive interactions in a condition involving a black confederate than in one involving a white. Using a word fragment completion task to implicitly measure racial prejudice toward Asians, Son Hing et al. (2002) identified as "aversive racists" those individuals with low-prejudiced scores on an explicit measure but high-prejudiced scores on the implicit measure. Relative to participants who scored low on both the implicit and the explicit measures, these aversive racists exhibited more negative feelings and less discriminatory behavior after having been made to feel hypocritical about the extent to which they lived up to their egalitarian values. Finally, in the self-esteem domain, Hetts et al. (1999) found the positivity of word fragment completions that followed reading an individualistic statement versus a collectivistic statement to relate to the recency of Asian-Americans' immigration to the United States. (Similar findings were obtained in an experiment that involved response latencies to positive and negative target words that had been preceded by the primes "me" versus "us.")

QUESTIONABLE INTERRELATIONS AMONG IMPLICIT MEASURES

One of the most disturbing trends to emerge in the literature on implicit measures is the many reports of disappointingly low correlations among the measures. Bosson et al. (2000) observed null relations among a variety of implicit measures of self-esteem, including the IAT, supraliminal and subliminal priming, and name-letter preference. Brauer et al. (2000) observed a small, albeit significant, correlation of .27 between two versions of a priming measure of attitudes toward women, one based on a lexical-decision task and one based on an adjective-connotation task. Somewhat more promising are the findings obtained by Rudman & Kilianski (2000) in a study that employed as primes schematic drawings of males and females in high and low authority roles. Participants also completed an IAT examining the association between the target concept "gender" and the attribute categories of high- versus low-status occupational roles. IAT scores correlated significantly (ranging from .27 to .38) with a series of contrasts reflecting negativity in response to the high authority female primes relative to various combinations of the other primes. However, no such relations were observed with respect to IATs assessing the association between gender and career versus domestic categories and between gender and agentic versus communal qualities. Additional reports of null relations between IAT and priming measures include the work of Marsh et al. (2001) concerning attitudes toward condom use and Sherman et al. (2002) concerning attitudes toward cigarette smoking. In our own lab we have repeatedly failed to observe correlations between IAT measures and priming measures of racial attitudes ($\underline{r}$'s ranging from $-.13$ to .05 across four studies).

Unquestionably, part of the problem with these disappointing correlations among various implicit measures is their rather low reliability. The problem is certainly not unique to the field of social cognition; it has been noted by cognitive psychologists interested in implicit memory measures as well (e.g., Perruchet & Baveux 1989, Buchner & Wippich 2000). Test-retest reliability for the IAT does tend to reach a respectable level of .6 or higher (Bosson et al. 2000, Greenwald & Nosek 2001), as also is true for the name-letter preference task (Bosson et al. 2000). However, the few reports regarding test-retest reliability for various priming measures have ranged from abysmally low (Bosson et al. 2000) to moderate levels of $\sim$.5 (Kawakami & Dovidio 2001). Such test-retest coefficients are likely to vary considerably as a function of a number of factors. Too few trials are likely to produce inadequate and unstable estimates; we note, for example, that the supraliminal priming measure employed by Bosson et al. included a mere 20 trials, only 4 of which were involved in the calculation of the implicit score. On the other hand, a large number of trials is likely to promote boredom and fatigue, and this problem will grow only more serious the second time the task is performed.

To date, the most sophisticated examination of measurement error and the interrelations among various implicit measures has been provided by Cunningham et al. (2001), who administered each of three implicit measures of racial prejudice on four separate occasions. The measures were (*a*) a response-window version of a supraliminal priming procedure, in which black and white faces served as primes, and participants were required to indicate the valence of a target word before a very brief deadline (a brief response window greatly increases the number of errors made, and changes the focus of the analyses from latencies to error rates) (see Draine & Greenwald 1998); (*b*) a typical race-related IAT involving black and white faces and positive and negative words; and (*c*) a response window version of this same IAT. Although the average test-retest correlation was only .27 and the average intercorrelation only .19, separating measurement error from estimates of stability via a latent variable analysis substantially improved the interrelations. For example, the priming measure now correlated .55 and .53 with the typical and response window versions, respectively, of the IAT.

Measurement error, then, unquestionably plays a role in the low relationships that have been observed among various implicit measures. However, it is not clear that it comprises the full story. The Cunningham et al. (2001) study involved intensive and repeated administration of multiple implicit measures, as well as an explicit measure—all of which should have enhanced participants' awareness that race was the focus of the research. As a result, and as we argue below, responses to the faces presented during the priming task may have been altered from what is typical in a priming measure. Moreover, we have to admit to doubts about what any sophisticated correction for measurement error can accomplish when the interrelation between a priming measure and the IAT are as low as has been reported in some of the work noted above—essentially zero. To better understand any interrelations that might or might not exist, it is important to consider the mechanisms that underlie the various measures.

UNDERLYING MECHANISMS

Careful consideration of the mechanism underlying any given implicit measurement procedure can provide invaluable information about its focus and its similarity to other measures. De Houwer (2002) provided an intriguing structural analysis of a variety of indirect measures of attitude. Here, we focus on a consideration of only the priming and the IAT techniques.

What Drives Priming?

Largely because decades of research in cognitive psychology and, more recently, social psychology have employed priming paradigms, the mechanisms underlying priming measures are fairly well understood. Such implicit measures focus on what is automatically activated by the primed stimulus. Automatic activation of the evaluation associated with a prime produces a processing advantage for evaluatively congruent targets. Both an encoding advantage and a response-competition mechanism have been implicated (see Fazio 2001 for a review). When the task involves word naming, any facilitation produced by the prime is viewed as the result of activation spreading from the prime to the associated evaluation, thus diminishing the amount of additional activation required for the target to reach the threshold necessary for a response (e.g., Bargh et al. 1996, De Houwer et al. 2001b). When the task concerns judging the evaluative connotation of the target, response competition/facilitation is also involved. The evaluation activated by the prime readies the participant to respond when the subsequently presented target is evaluatively congruent, but the response suggested by the prime must be inhibited in order to respond accurately to an evaluatively incongruent target (e.g., Klauer 1998, Wentura 1999, Klinger et al. 2000). In either case, the process is potentiated by the automatic activation of an evaluation associated with the prime, and any consequent effect on the latency of response to positive versus negative targets provides information about the evaluation of the prime.

When priming procedures are employed as an implicit measure, exemplars of the category of interest typically are presented as primes. The average response across the set of exemplars is treated as a measure of attitude toward the group as a whole. For example, photos of blacks and whites might be employed as a means of estimating racial attitudes. Hence, the validity of any priming measure is likely to depend on the representativeness of the stimuli chosen to serve as primes. Indeed, recent findings by Livingston & Brewer (2002) illustrate that different effects can emerge for photos of African-Americans that vary in prototypicality. Whereas the typically observed effects reflecting greater negativity in response to black faces than white faces were replicated when prototypical black faces were employed, this was not true of a set of photos judged to be less prototypical, even though the faces were definitively identifiable as African-American. Once again pointing to parallels with earlier literature concerning attitudes, it is worth noting that considerable evidence exists regarding the role of prototypicality as a moderator of the relation between attitudes toward a general group and behavior toward a specific group exemplar (e.g., Lord et al. 1984; see Lord & Lepper 1999 for a review).

What Drives the Implicit Association Test?

The assumption that forms the basis for the IAT is straightforward: "... if two concepts are highly associated, the IAT's sorting tasks will be easier when the two associated concepts share the same response than when they require different responses" (Greenwald & Nosek 2001, p. 85). Precisely how the IAT works remains unclear, however. What is clear is that an early concern regarding the potential confounding of familiarity with black versus white names in racial IATs, as in Greenwald et al. (1998), is not a serious problem. Since then, researchers have observed IAT effects even after carefully matching stimuli and/or statistically controlling for familiarity (Rudman et al. 1999, Dasgupta et al. 2000, Ottaway et al. 2001).

A number of possible mechanisms for the IAT have received attention recently. Included are (a) the idea that incompatible response mapping produces a *shift in response criteria*, resulting in slower responding to both target and attribute stimuli on such incompatible mapping trials (Brendl et al. 2001); (b) a *figure-ground asymmetry* model that focuses on participants perceiving one response category as figure on the ground of the opposing response category (Rothermund & Wentura 2001); and (c) a *task-set switching* account that focuses on the possibility of respondents neglecting the instruction to switch tasks (assigning stimuli via the attribute categories versus the target categories) during the compatible mapping phase of the IAT, because responding on the basis of the attribute-related information is sufficient to meet the goals of fast and accurate responding (Mierke & Klauer 2001).

Especially informative, in our view, is De Houwer's (2001) consideration of what he refers to as "relevant" and "irrelevant" feature accounts of the IAT. De Houwer noted that the structurally relevant feature of any given target concept stimulus (e.g., "tulip") in the IAT is its membership in one of the target categories ("tulip" is a flower, not an insect). However, one can also maintain that IAT performance is sensitive to what is structurally an irrelevant feature—the valence of individual target stimuli ("tulip" itself is positive). De Houwer (2001) pointed out that the typical IAT perfectly confounds the relevant and irrelevant feature possibilities; all exemplars of the positive target category (e.g., flowers) are themselves positive, and all exemplars of the negative target category (e.g., insects) are themselves negative. To examine whether IAT performance is a function of the valence of the target categories (the relevant feature account) or the exemplars (the irrelevant feature account), he conducted an experiment with British participants that involved the target categories "British" and "foreign" but included both positively valued (e.g., Princess Diana) and negatively valued (e.g., the name of a well-known mass murderer) British names, and positively valued (e.g., Albert Einstein) and negatively valued (e.g., Adolf Hitler) foreign names as the exemplars. Performance was found to be affected only by whether "British" and "positive" were represented by the same or different keys. Contrary to the irrelevant-feature account, whether the individual exemplar was itself positively or negatively valued had no effect. Thus, IAT performance is very much dictated by the task instructions to categorize the target stimuli. The task requires such categorization, encouraging construal of the exemplars in terms of the target categories to such an extent that processing of these stimuli is limited to the relevant task feature—their category membership. This inference is further supported by research conducted by Mitchell et al. (1999), who found different IAT scores for the same stimuli when the names of famous black athletes and white politicians (e.g., Michael Jordan, Jesse Helms) were categorized as black versus white or as athletes versus politicians.[4]

Implications

The importance of these findings is the suggestion that, in contrast to priming measures, the IAT has little to do with what is automatically activated in response to a given stimulus. Although IAT effects are often referred to as "automatic preferences," this use of the term automatic appears to have a very different meaning than it does in the context of priming procedures. In contrast to the latter case, in which the term concerns the spontaneous activation of an evaluation in response to the primed stimulus, for the IAT the emphasis is on controllability: "IAT responses are considered automatic because they are expressed without intention or control, although perceivers may become aware of the attitude under scrutiny during the task" (Dasgupta et al. 2000, p. 317). The distinction is important, and as De Houwer's (2001) findings imply, the IAT seems to assess associations to the category labels, not automatically activated responses to the individual exemplars. Thus, in the context of race, whereas priming procedures provide an estimate of the average evaluation evoked by the black (versus white) faces, the IAT provides an estimate of the strength of association between the category label "black" (versus "white") and negativity.[5] The potential exists for these two estimates to differ, especially in any situation that does not promote categorization of a given person by race.

Its operation at the level of the category also means that the IAT may be influenced by associations other than those involved in a perceiver's own automatically activated response to a given exemplar—ones that are potentially independent of the association between a perceiver's own evaluation and the category in question. Indeed, Karpinski & Hilton (2001) have made exactly this argument. As an explanation for their finding that an IAT revealed an average preference for apples over

---

[4]This is not to say that IAT performance cannot be affected by the specific stimuli that are presented. Indeed, De Houwer (2001, footnote 4) summarized an experiment involving an atypical IAT—one that used evaluatively neutral ("person" and "animal") instead of evaluatively laden target categories. In this case, valence of the individual stimulus items did matter. Moreover, Steffens & Plewe (2001) found that the nature of the items reflecting the attribute dimension can affect IAT scores. Female participants more easily associated "female" with "pleasant" when the pleasant items were more stereotypic of females than males. However, this finding does not speak to whether the valence of the exemplars representing the target categories affects response latencies. The major point we wish to make is not that IATs in which performance is affected by stimulus items cannot be designed, but that the IAT has little to do with the automatic activation of evaluations in response to the target exemplars.

[5]This distinction would not apply for priming measures that involve the subliminal presentation of the words "black" or "white" as primes (e.g., Wittenbrink et al. 1997).

candy bars (a preference that was not apparent on an explicit measure of liking), these researchers noted: "In our society, there are an abundance of positive associations and virtually no negative associations with apples. For candy bars, however, the messages are much more mixed" (p. 783). They suggested that the IAT may be influenced by such environmental associations. To test this idea, Karpinski & Hilton exposed research participants to a large number of word pairings associating the word "youth" with various positive items and the word "elderly" with negative items or vice versa. When the pairings were contrary to greater favorability toward youth, the extent of the preference participants revealed for youth on a subsequent IAT was reduced. In contrast, explicit measures were unaffected.

Such extrapersonal associations may play an important role in IATs that assess racial prejudice. It is possible that even individuals for whom negativity is not automatically activated in response to black exemplars, as assessed by priming, may possess and perceive strong associations between the category "blacks" and negativity; they may recognize, for example, that blacks have been historically portrayed in a negative manner by American society. This knowledge may easily come to mind when the IAT presents them with a black + negative response mapping and may facilitate their responding. This may be why the IAT, relative to priming measures, typically reveals such a higher percentage of a white college student sample to be negative toward blacks. Extrapersonal associations may also bear some responsibility for the finding that black respondents often display negativity toward blacks on the IAT (Nosek et al. 2002b).

However, both Banaji (2001) and Lowery et al. (2001) have persuasively articulated the difficulty of distinguishing cultural associations from personal ones, i.e., of separating the individual from the culture. Where do attitudes originate if not from learning experiences within one's culture? That self and culture are inextricably intertwined is undeniable. However, individual learning experiences certainly can produce an evaluation that differs from what is modal in the culture. An individual with an allergy to peanuts unquestionably develops a strong negative association, one that is easily capable of automatic activation upon reading of their presence in an entree's menu description, yet the individual also possesses the knowledge that most people like peanuts. In a priming assessment of the individual's attitude, photos of peanuts, peanut butter, etc. would probably produce evidence of automatic activation of negativity. Given that the IAT seems to reflect not what is automatically activated when a stimulus is presented but associations to the category response label (in this case, peanuts), it is quite possible that the two measures will produce diverging estimates of our allergy sufferer's attitude. Especially when faced with a response mapping that forces pairing of peanuts and positive, the individual may "recruit" the knowledge of others' generally positive evaluations of peanuts to facilitate the goal of responding quickly. In other words, extrapersonal knowledge may assist the individual in solving the response mapping problem posed by the IAT. If so, the implicit score is affected by knowledge that would not have been automatically activated upon the presentation of peanuts, and hence, some degree of disparity would be observed between the priming and IAT estimates. Moreover, to the extent that this happens more for some peanut-allergy sufferers than others, the two measures may yield different rank orderings of the individuals. Any such disparities, however, should be limited to domains (or individuals) characterized by diverging personal and environmental associations.

In sum, then, consideration of the mechanisms underlying priming and IAT procedures appears to inform issues regarding their predictive validity and inter-relation. Some possibilities arise that, although admittedly speculative, are clearly worthy of future research. The less representative the sample of category exemplars used as primes in the priming procedure, the less valid the estimate of attitude toward the category and also the lower the correspondence with the IAT. In addition, the more variability that exists in evaluative reactions to category exemplars, the less meaningful the average reaction across exemplars becomes and the more likely it is that the mean response will differ from the category evaluation provided by the IAT. For example, for most people, more variability probably exists regarding their evaluation of specific cars than of specific flowers. Moreover, the category "cars" may evoke thoughts of pollution, overcrowded highways, etc. that are not evoked by the presentation of specific cars. Ultimately, the predictive utility of the two methods may depend on the nature of the judgment or behavior one is attempting to predict. Because its focus concerns evaluative associations to the category, the IAT may be superior for predicting behaviors at the category level (e.g., support for a category-related social policy proposal). A priming measure may be superior when predicting behavior toward an exemplar of the category (e.g., judgments of a category member).[6]

EFFECTS OF CONTEXT ON IMPLICIT MEASURES

Explicitly reported evaluations are known to be context dependent. That is, they depend on one's construal of the object in the immediate situation and on the comparison standards employed to make the judgment (e.g., Bruner 1957, Sherif & Hovland 1961, Carlston & Smith 1996, Higgins 1996). Considerable recent research demonstrates that implicit measures also display some sensitivity to context (see Blair 2002 for a detailed review). For example, in a priming procedure, Wittenbrink et al. (2001a) obtained evidence of less automatically activated negativity in response to black faces when those faces were presented within the background context of a church interior as opposed to an urban street corner. Related effects have been observed as a function of individuals' motivational states.

---

[6]IAT scores may predict behavior toward an exemplar to the extent that the situation promotes categorization by race. We note that IAT-behavior correlations were found when the sequence of events made race salient (McConnell & Liebold 2001) and when stereotypically black music, but not other music, preceded trait ratings of a black target (Rudman & Lee 2002).

Sherman et al. (2002) found a priming measure to be sensitive to heavy cigarette smokers' experimentally manipulated level of deprivation; the greater the deprivation, the more positivity these smokers experienced in response to cigarette-related photos. Similarly, Pratto & Shih's (2000) priming measure revealed more evidence of prejudice toward an outgroup on the part of participants characterized by higher social dominance orientation after the status of their ingroup had been threatened. Thus, the evaluations that are automatically activated in response to a given stimulus depend on one's construals of the stimulus in a given context. How a multiply categorizable object or target person is construed in any given situation will determine the attitude that is automatically activated (see Fazio 1986, Smith et al. 1996, Fazio & Dunton 1997 for discussion of such categorization processes).

Similar phenomena have been demonstrated multiple times with respect to the IAT. Essentially, pre-IAT exposure to different kinds of information appears to influence participants' construal of the category labels involved in the IAT. Salient positive information about a given category produces IAT scores indicative of more favorable evaluations of the category. Such manipulations have involved exposure to movie clips that depicted blacks at a harmonious family barbecue versus an argumentative, gang-related scene (Wittenbrink et al. 2001a), presentation of a series of either admired black individuals and disliked whites or disliked blacks and admired whites (Dasgupta & Greenwald 2001), assigning participants to interact with a black partner who occupied a superior or subordinate task role (Richeson & Ambady 2002), exposure to violent and misogynous rap music (Rudman & Lee 2002), and introduction to the IAT (specifically as a procedure for assessing prejudice) by a black versus a white experimenter (Lowery et al. 2001). Finally, in research involving implicit measurement of gender stereotypes, Blair et al. (2001) found that having participants engage in counterstereotypical mental imagery (i.e., imagine a strong woman) reduced the strength of stereotypic associations.[7]

ADDITIONAL QUESTIONS FOR FUTURE RESEARCH

Role of Awareness

We argued above that an implicitly measured attitude should not be assumed to be nonconscious. Our own research regarding the moderating role of motivation to control prejudice would lead us to speculate that people generally are aware

---

[7]These various manipulations of context bear some similarity to the earlier-described manipulation of environmental associations employed by Karpinski & Hilton (2001). We find it puzzling that similar evidence has been interpreted both as problematic for the IAT and as a presumably advantageous sign of the IAT's sensitivity to context. In our view the critical issue to be resolved is whether such contextual manipulations (a) produce an actual change in the relevant mental representation, to which the IAT is sensitive, or (b) simply render momentarily salient positive or negative construals of a given category label, which then assist the participant with the response-mapping problem posed by the IAT.

of their automatically activated racial attitudes. In a variety of studies, the more motivated show evidence of having "corrected" for their automatically activated attitudes. Given that models of correction processes (e.g., Wegener & Petty 1995) require that individuals be aware of a potential bias in order to engage in effortful correction, the implication is that people are aware of their automatically activated racial attitudes. However, such indications of awareness may not arise in other domains, and we do not question that it is possible for people to possess, and be influenced by, attitudes of which they are unaware. In any case, the issue of awareness needs to be addressed more directly.

Stereotype Versus Attitude Activation

Just what associations are activated in response to a given prime: a stereotype and/or an attitude? Wittenbrink et al. (2001b) suggested that it can be either, depending on the nature of priming task; they obtained some evidence suggesting that a priming measure based on a lexical decision is more sensitive to stereotype activation, whereas one based on adjective connotation is more sensitive to attitude activation. Conceptually, however, this suggests an adaptive system that is responsive to what information may prove most functional in terms of meeting the needs of the situation. Hence, stereotypes may be activated only given a relevant processing goal (e.g., Macrae et al. 1997, Livingston & Brewer 2002). Certain decision situations may require some sense of the extent to which a person or object matches some ideal set of attributes, and such a need for attribute information may evoke stereotypes. Other decisions are driven more purely by evaluation and, hence, may be unlikely to evoke associated attribute information, but very likely to evoke associated attitudes.

Changing Automatically Activated Constructs

Literature on the development of automatism points to the importance of consistent and repeated mapping (Schneider & Fisk 1982, Schneider & Shiffrin 1977). Hence, it is thought that such attitudes develop slowly and that any change will be difficult and will require extensive practice. Kawakami et al. (2000) demonstrated that hundreds of trials of overt rejection of the stereotypic association were necessary to produce change in later stereotype activation. Rudman et al. (2001a) observed changes regarding both prejudice (on an IAT) and stereotyping (a priming lexical decision measure) among students enrolled in a semester-long prejudice and conflict seminar. However, other indications in the literature provide a reason for a more optimistic outlook regarding the potential for change that stems, not from negation or heightened sensitivity, but from the creation of new counterstereotypical or counterattitudinal associations. Recall the research presented earlier regarding the malleability of implicit measures. Exposure to counterexemplars reduced the extent of prejudice apparent on the IAT. Moreover, this reduction continued to be observed when participants returned 24 hours later for re-administration of the IAT (Dasgupta & Greenwald 2001). Whether this reflects the learning of a strategy by which participants approached the IAT specifically or an actual change in the associations that might be automatically activated remains to be seen. Whether any such change would persist over extended time and generalize across situations is also unknown. Nevertheless, the various malleability findings imply that appropriate environmental pairings have the potential to counter the associations that have been learned in the past.

FINAL THOUGHTS

Although obviously in its infancy, social cognition research on implicit measures is certainly progressing. One must be impressed by the sheer amount of empirical work that has been conducted in such a short time. As our knowledge base accumulates and our understanding of the mechanisms underlying various implicit measurement techniques increases, the questions that we can ask will become sharper and the contributions to basic theory all the stronger. We are convinced that, when their application, use, and interpretation is guided by relevant theory and past literature, implicit measures have the potential to serve as useful methodological tools for testing hypotheses. Although we have no confidence that all of our speculative commentary will remain applicable as this literature burgeons even further, it is our hope that our efforts here to structure the empirical findings accumulated to date will facilitate such growth and development.

ACKNOWLEDGMENTS

Preparation of this chapter was supported by Senior Scientist Award MH01646 and Grant MH38832 from the National Institute of Mental Health. The authors thank the following individuals for their helpful feedback on an earlier version of the manuscript: Hal Arkes, Marilynn Brewer, Tim Brock, Jan De Houwer, Dick Eiser, Susan Fiske, Tony Greenwald, Kristi Lemm, Brian Nosek, Rich Petty, Laurie Rudman, Jim Sherman, Eric Uhlmann, Bill von Hippel, and Mark Zanna.

The *Annual Review of Psychology* is online at http://psych.annualreviews.org

LITERATURE CITED

Amodio DM, Harmon-Jones E, Devine PG. 2002. Individual differences in the activation and control of affective race bias as assessed by startle eyeblink responses and self-report. *J. Pers. Soc. Psychol.* In press

Asendorpf JB, Banse R, Mücke D. 2002. Double dissociation between implicit and explicit personality self-concept: the case of shy behavior. *J. Pers. Soc. Psychol.* 83:380–93

Ashburn-Nardo L, Voils CI, Monteith MJ. 2001. Implicit associations as the seeds of intergroup bias: How easily do they take root? *J. Pers. Soc. Psychol.* 81:789–99

Banaji MR, ed. 1997. Unconscious processes in stereotyping and prejudice. *J. Exp. Soc. Psychol.* 33:449–560

Banaji MR. 2001. Implicit attitudes can be measured. In *The Nature of Remembering:*

Essays in Honor of Robert G. Crowder, ed. HL Roediger, JS Nairne, pp. 117–50. Washington, DC: Am. Psychol. Assoc.

Banse R. 1999. Automatic evaluation of self and significant others: affective priming in close relationships. *J. Soc. Pers. Relat.* 65:272–81

Banse R, Seise J, Zerbes N. 2001. Implicit attitudes toward homosexuality: reliability, validity, and controllability of the IAT. *Z. Exp. Psychol.* 48:1145–60

Bargh JA, Chaiken S, Raymond P, Hymes C. 1996. The automatic evaluation effect: unconditional automatic attitude activation with a pronunciation task. *J. Pers. Soc. Psychol.* 62:893–912

Bassili JN, Smith MC. 1986. On the spontaneity of trait attribution: converging evidence for the role of cognitive strategy. *J. Pers. Soc. Psychol.* 50:239–45

Bessenoff GR, Sherman JW. 2000. Automatic and controlled components of prejudice toward fat people: evaluation versus stereotype activation. *Soc. Cogn.* 18:329–53

Blair I. 2001. Implicit stereotypes and prejudice. In *Cognitive Social Psychology: The Princeton Symposium on the Legacy and Future of Social Cognition*, ed. GB Moskowitz, pp. 359–74. Mahwah, NJ: Erlbaum

Blair I. 2002. The malleability of automatic stereotypes and prejudice. *Pers. Soc. Psychol. Rev.* 6:242–61

Blair I, Ma J, Lenton A. 2001. Imagining stereotypes away: the moderation of automatic stereotypes through mental imagery. *J. Pers. Soc. Psychol.* 81:828–41

Blascovich J, Mendes WB, Hunter SB, Lickel B, Kowai-Bell N. 2001. Perceiver threat in social interactions with stigmatized others. *J. Pers. Soc. Psychol.* 80:253–67

Bosson JK, Swann W, Pennebaker JW. 2000. Stalking the perfect measure of implicit self-esteem: the blind men and the elephant revisited? *J. Pers. Soc. Psychol.* 79:631–43

Brauer M, Wasel W, Niedenthal P. 2000. Implicit and explicit components of prejudice. *Rev. Gen. Psychol.* 4:79–101

Brendl CM, Markman AB, Messner C. 2001. How do indirect measures of evaluation work? Evaluating the inference of prejudice in the Implicit Association Test. *J. Pers. Soc. Psychol.* 81:760–73

Bruner JS. 1957. On perceptual readiness. *Psychol. Rev.* 64:123–52

Buchner A, Wippich W. 2000. On the reliability of implicit and explicit memory measures. *Cogn. Psychol.* 40:227–59

Cacioppo JT, Crites SL, Berntson GG, Coles MG. 1993. If attitudes affect how stimuli are processed, should they not affect the event-related brain potential? *Psychol. Sci.* 4:108–12

Carlston DE, Smith ER. 1996. Principles of mental representation. See Higgins & Kruglanski 1996, pp. 184–210

Chaiken S, Trope Y, eds. 1999. *Dual Process Theories in Social Psychology*. New York: Guilford

Crites SL, Cacioppo JT, Gardner WL, Bernston GG. 1995. Bioelectrical echoes from evaluative categorization. II. A late positive brain potential that varies as a function of attitude registration rather than attitude report. *J. Pers. Soc. Psychol.* 68:997–1013

Cunningham WA, Preacher KJ, Banaji MR. 2001. Implicit attitude measures: consistency, stability, and convergent validity. *Psychol. Sci.* 12:163–70

Dasgupta N, Greenwald AG. 2001. On the malleability of automatic attitudes: combating automatic prejudice with images of admired and disliked individuals. *J. Pers. Soc. Psychol.* 81:800–14

Dasgupta N, McGhee DE, Greenwald AG, Banaji MR. 2000. Automatic preference for white Americans: eliminating the familiarity explanation. *J. Exp. Soc. Psychol.* 36:316–28

De Houwer J. 2001. A structural and process analysis of the Implicit Association Test. *J. Exp. Soc. Psychol.* 37:443–51

De Houwer J. 2002. A structural analysis of indirect measures of attitudes. See Musch & Klauer 2002. In press

De Houwer J, Crombez G, Baeyens F, Hermans D. 2001a. On the generality of the affective Simon effect. *Cogn. Emot.* 15:189–206

De Houwer J, Eelen P. 1998. An affective

variant of the Simon paradigm. *Cogn. Emot.* 12:45–61

De Houwer J, Hermas D, eds. 2001. Automatic affective processing. *Cogn. Emot.* 15:113–248

De Houwer J, Hermans D, Spruyt A. 2001b. Affective priming of pronunciation responses: effects of target degradation. *J. Exp. Soc. Psychol.* 37:85–91

Devine PG, ed. 2001. Implicit prejudice and stereotyping: how automatic are they? *J. Pers. Soc. Psychol.* 71:757–868

Devine PG, Plant EA, Amodio DM, Harmon-Jones E, Vance SL. 2002. The regulation of explicit and implicit race bias: the role of motivations to respond without prejudice. *J. Pers. Soc. Psychol.* 82:835–48

Dijksterhuis A, Aarts H, Bargh JA, van Knippenberg A. 2000. On the relation between associative strength and automatic behavior. *J. Exp. Soc. Psychol.* 36:531–44

Dovidio JF, Fazio RH. 1992. New technologies for the direct and indirect assessment of attitudes. In *Questions About Questions: Inquiries into the Cognitive Bases of Surveys*, ed. JM Tanur, pp. 204–37. New York: Sage

Dovidio JF, Kawakami K, Beach KR. 2001. Implicit and explicit attitudes: examination of the relationship between measures of intergroup bias. In *Blackwell Handbook of Social Psychology: Intergroup Processes*, ed. R Brown, SL Gaertner, pp 175–97. Malden, MA: Blackwell

Dovidio JF, Kawakami K, Gaertner SL. 2002. Implicit and explicit prejudice and interracial interactions. *J. Pers. Soc. Psychol.* 82:62–68

Dovidio JF, Kawakami K, Johnson C, Johnson B, Howard A. 1997. On the nature of prejudice: automatic and controlled processes. *J. Exp. Soc. Psychol.* 33:510–40

Draine SC, Greenwald AG. 1998. Replicable unconscious semantic priming. *J. Exp. Psychol.: Gen.* 127:286–303

Dunton BC, Fazio RH. 1997. An individual difference measure of motivation to control prejudiced reactions. *Pers. Soc. Psychol. Bull.* 23:316–26

Eagly AH, Chaiken S. 1993. *The Psychology of Attitudes*. Fort Worth, TX: Harcourt Brace Jovanovich

Fazio RH. 1986. How do attitudes guide behavior? In *The Handbook of Motivation and Cognition: Foundations of Social Behavior*, ed. RM Sorrentino, ET Higgins, pp. 204–43. New York: Guilford

Fazio RH. 1990. Multiple processes by which attitudes guide behavior: the MODE model as an integrative framework. See Zanna 1990, 23:75–109

Fazio RH. 2001. On the automatic activation of associated evaluations: an overview. *Cogn. Emot.* 15:115–41

Fazio RH, Dunton BC. 1997. Categorization by race: the impact of automatic and controlled components of racial prejudice. *J. Exp. Soc. Psychol.* 33:451–70

Fazio RH, Hilden LE. 2001. Emotional reactions to a seemingly prejudiced response: the role of automatically-activated racial attitudes and motivation to control prejudiced reactions. *Pers. Soc. Psychol. Bull.* 27:538–49

Fazio RH, Jackson JR, Dunton BC, Williams CJ. 1995. Variability in automatic activation as an unobtrusive measure of racial attitudes: a bona fide pipeline? *J. Pers. Soc. Psychol.* 69:1013–27

Fazio RH, Sanbonmatsu DM, Powell MC, Kardes FR. 1986. On the automatic activation of attitudes. *J. Pers. Soc. Psychol.* 50:229–38

Fazio RH, Towles-Schwen T. 1999. The MODE model of attitude-behavior processes. In *Dual Process Theories in Social Psychology*, ed. S Chaiken, Y Trope, pp. 97–116. New York: Guilford

Florack A, Scarabis M, Bless H. 2001. When do associations matter? The use of implicit associations toward ethnic groups in person judgments. *J. Exp. Soc. Psychol.* 37:518–24

Gaertner SL, McLaughlin JP. 1983. Racial stereotypes: associations and ascriptions of positive and negative characteristics. *Soc. Psychol. Q.* 46:23–30

Gawronksi B, Ehrenberg K, Banse R, Zukova J, Klauer KC. 2002. It's in the mind of the beholder: the impact of stereotypic associations on category-based and individuating impression formation. *J. Exp. Soc. Psychol.* In press

Gilbert DT, Hixon JT. 1991. The trouble with thinking: activation and application of stereotypic beliefs. *J. Pers. Soc. Psychol.* 60:509–17

Greenwald AG, Banaji MR. 1995. Implicit social cognition: attitudes, self-esteem, and stereotypes. *Psychol. Rev.* 102:4–27

Greenwald AG, Banaji MR, Rudman LA, Farnham SD, Nosek BA, et al. 2002a. A unified theory of implicit attitudes, stereotypes, self-esteem, and self-concept. *Psychol. Rev.* 109:3–25

Greenwald AG, Farnham SD. 2000. Using the Implicit Association Test to measure self-esteem and self-concept. *J. Pers. Soc. Psychol.* 79:1022–38

Greenwald AG, Klinger MR, Liu TJ. 1989. Unconscious processing of dichoptically masked words. *Mem. Cogn.* 17:35–47

Greenwald AG, McGhee DE, Schwartz JLK. 1998. Measuring individual differences in implicit cognition: the implicit association test. *J. Pers. Soc. Psychol.* 74:1464–80

Greenwald AG, Nosek BA. 2001. Health of the Implicit Association Test at age 3. *Z. Exp. Psychol.* 48:85–93

Greenwald AG, Pickrell JE, Farnham SD. 2002b. Implicit partisanship: taking sides for no reason. *J. Pers. Soc. Psychol.* 83:367–79

Hart AJ, Whalen PJ, Shin LM, McInerney SC, Fischer H, Rauch SL. 2000. Differential response in the human amygdala to racial outgroup vs ingroup face stimuli. *Neurorep.: Rapid Commun. Neurosci. Res.* 11:2351–55

Hastie R. 1984. Causes and effects of causal attribution. *J. Pers. Soc. Psychol.* 46:44–56

Hense RL, Penner LA, Nelson DL. 1995. Implicit memory for age stereotypes. *Soc. Cogn.* 13:399–415

Hermans D, Baeyens F, Eelen P. 2002. On the acquisition of evaluative information in memory: the study of evaluative learning and affective priming combined. See Musch & Klauer 2002. In press

Hetts JJ, Sakuma M, Pelham BW. 1999. Two roads to positive regard: implicit and explicit self–evaluation and culture. *J. Exp. Soc. Psychol.* 35:512–59

Higgins ET. 1996. Knowledge activation: accessibility, applicability, and salience. See Higgins & Kruglanski 1996, pp. 133–68

Higgins ET, Kruglanski AW, eds. 1996. *Social Psychology: Handbook of Basic Principles.* New York: Guilford

Ito TA, Cacioppo JT. 2000. Electrophysiological evidence of implicit and explicit categorization processes. *J. Exp. Soc. Psychol.* 36:660–76

Jackson JR. 1997. *Automatically activated racial attitudes.* PhD thesis, Indiana Univ.

Jones JT, Pelham BW, Mirenberg MC, Hetts JJ. 2002. Name letter preferences are not merely mere exposure: implicit egotism as self-regulation. *J. Exp. Soc. Psychol.* 38:170–77

Jordan CH, Spencer SJ, Zanna MP. 2002. I love me ... I love me not: implicit self-esteem, explicit self-esteem, and defensiveness. In *Motivated Social Perception: The Ninth Ontario Symposium*, ed. SJ Spencer, S Fein, MP Zanna, JM Olson, pp. 117–45. Mahwah, NJ: Erlbaum

Jost JT, Pelham BW, Carvallo MR. 2002. Non-conscious forms of system justification: implicit and behavioral preferences for higher status groups. *J. Exp. Soc. Psychol.* In press

Karpinski A, Hilton JL. 2001. Attitudes and the Implicit Association Test. *J. Pers. Soc. Psychol.* 81:774–78

Kawakami K, Dion KL, Dovidio JF. 1998. Racial prejudice and stereotype activation. *Pers. Soc. Psychol. Bull.* 24:407–16

Kawakami K, Dovidio JF. 2001. The reliability of implicit stereotyping? Or confronting prejudice: effects of prejudice labeling on stereotype activation. *Pers. Soc. Psychol. Bull.* 27:212–25

Kawakami K, Dovidio JF, Moll J, Hermsen S, Russin A. 2000. Just say no to stereotyping: effects of training in the negation of stereotypic associations on stereotype activation. *J. Pers. Soc. Psychol.* 78:871–88

Keuhnen U, Schiessl M, Bauer M, Paulig N, Poehlmann C, et al. 2001. How robust is the IAT? Measuring and manipulating attitudes of East and West-Germans. *Z. Exp. Psychol.* 48:135–44

Klauer KC. 1998. Affective priming. *Eur. Rev. Soc. Psychol.* 8:63–107

Klinger MR, Burton PC, Pitts GS. 2000. Mechanisms of unconscious priming. I. Response competition, not spreading activation. *J. Exp. Psychol.: Learn. Mem. Cogn.* 26:441–55

Koole SL, Dijksterhuis A, van Knippenberg A. 2001. What's in a name: implicit self-esteem and the automatic self. *J. Pers. Soc. Psychol.* 80:669–85

Lemm KM. 2001. *Personal and social motivation to respond without prejudice: implications for implicit and explicit attitude and behavior.* PhD thesis, Yale Univ.

Lepore L, Brown R. 1997. Category and stereotype activation: Is prejudice inevitable? *J. Pers. Soc. Psychol.* 72:275–87

Livingston RW. 2002. The role of perceived negativity in the moderation of African-Americans' implicit and explicit racial attitudes. *J. Exp. Soc. Psychol.* 38:405–13

Livingston RW, Brewer MB. 2002. What are we really priming? Cue-based versus category-based processing of facial stimuli. *J. Pers. Soc. Psychol.* 82:5–18

Lord CG, Lepper MR. 1999. Attitude representation theory. In *Advances in Experimental Social Psychology*, ed. MP Zanna, 31:265–343. San Diego, CA: Academic

Lord CG, Lepper MR, Mackie D. 1984. Attitude prototypes as determinants of attitude-behavior consistency. *J. Pers. Soc. Psychol.* 46:1254–66

Lowery BS, Hardin CD, Sinclair S. 2001. Social influence effects on automatic racial prejudice. *J. Pers. Soc. Psychol.* 81:842–55

Maass A, Ceccarelli R, Rudin S. 1996. Linguistic intergroup bias: evidence for in-group-protective motivation. *J. Pers. Soc. Psychol.* 71:512–26

Maass A, Salvi L, Arcuri L, Semin GR. 1989. Language use in intergroup contexts: the linguistic intergroup bias. *J. Pers. Soc. Psychol.* 57:981–93

Macrae CN, Bodenhausen GV, Milne AB, Thorn TMJ, Castelli L. 1997. On the activation of social stereotypes: the moderating role of processing objectives. *J. Exp. Soc. Psychol.* 33:471–89

Maison D, Greenwald AG, Bruin R. 2001. The Implicit Association Test as a measure of implicit consumer attitudes. *Polish Psychol. Bull.* 32:61–69

Marsh KL, Johnson BL, Scott-Sheldon LA. 2001. Heart versus reason in condom use: implicit versus explicit attitudinal predictors of sexual behavior. *Z. Exp. Psychol.* 48:161–75

McConnell AR, Liebold JM. 2001. Relations between the Implicit Association Test, explicit racial attitudes, and discriminatory behavior. *J. Exp. Soc. Psychol.* 37:435–42

Mierke J, Klauer KC. 2001. Implicit association measurement with the IAT: evidence of the effects of executive control processes. *Z. Exp. Psychol.* 48:107–22

Mitchell JA, Nosek BA, Banaji MR. 1999. *Dissociated implicit attitudes: examples from race, gender, and profession.* Presented at Annu. Meet. Midwestern Psychol. Assoc., Chicago

Monteith MJ, Voils CI, Ashburn-Nardo L. 2001. Taking a look underground: detecting, interpreting, and reacting to implicit racial bias. *Soc. Cogn.* 19:395–417

Musch J, Klauer KC, eds. 2002. *The Psychology of Evaluation: Affective Processes in Cognition and Emotion.* Mahwah, NJ: Erlbaum. In press

Nosek BA. 2002. *Moderators of the relationship between implicit and explicit attitudes.* PhD thesis, Yale Univ.

Nosek BA, Banaji MR. 2001. The go/no-go association task. *Soc. Cogn.* 19:625–66

Nosek BA, Banaji MR, Greenwald AG. 2002a. Math = Male, Me = Female, therefore Math is not equal to Me. *J. Pers. Soc. Psychol.* 83:44–59

Nosek BA, Banaji MR, Greenwald AG. 2002b.

Harvesting implicit group attitudes and beliefs from a demonstration website. *Group Dynam.* 6:101–15

Nuttin JM. 1985. Narcissism beyond Gestalt and awareness: the name letter effect. *Eur. J. Soc. Psychol.* 15:353–61

Olson MA, Fazio RH. 2001. Implicit attitude formation through classical conditioning. *Psychol. Sci.* 12:413–17

Olson MA, Fazio RH. 2002a. Trait inferences as a function of automatically-activated racial attitudes and motivation to control prejudiced reactions. *Basic Appl. Soc. Psychol.* In press

Olson MA, Fazio RH. 2002b. Implicit acquisition and manifestation of classically conditioned attitudes. *Soc. Cogn.* 20:89–104

Ottaway SA, Hayden DC, Oakes MA. 2001. Implicit attitudes and racism: effects of word familiarity and frequency in the Implicit Association Test. *Soc. Cogn.* 19:97–144

Otten S, Wentura D. 1999. About the impact of automaticity in the minimal group paradigm: evidence from affective priming tasks. *Eur. J. Soc. Psychol.* 29:1049–71

Pelham BW, Mirenberg MC, Jones JK. 2002. Why Susie sells seashells by the seashore: implicit egotism and major life decisions. *J. Pers. Soc. Psychol.* 82:469–87

Perdue CW, Dovidio JF, Gurtman MB, Tyler RB. 1990. Us and them: social categorization and the process of intergroup bias. *J. Pers. Soc. Psychol.* 59:475–86

Perruchet P, Baveux P. 1989. Correlational analyses of explicit and implicit memory performance. *Mem. Cogn.* 17:77–86

Phelps EA, O'Connor KJ, Cunningham WA, Funayama ES, Gatenby JC, et al. 2000. Performance on indirect measures of race evaluation predicts amygdala activation. *J. Cogn. Neurosci.* 12:729–38

Plessner H, Banse R, eds. 2001. Attitude measurement using the Implicit Association Test (IAT). *Z. Exp. Psychol.* 48:82–175

Pratto F, Shih M. 2000. Social dominance orientation and group context in implicit group prejudice. *Psychol. Sci.* 11:515–18

Proshansky HM. 1943. A projective method for the study of attitudes. *J. Appl. Soc. Psychol.* 38:393–95

Richardson-Klavehn A, Bjork RA. 1988. Measures of memory. *Annu. Rev. Psychol.* 39:475–543

Richeson JA, Ambady N. 2002. Effects of situational power on automatic racial prejudice. *J. Exp. Soc. Psychol.* In press

Roediger HL. 1990. Implicit memory: retention without remembering. *Am. Psychol.* 45:1043–56

Rothermund K, Wentura D. 2001. Figure-ground asymmetries in the Implicit Association Test. *Z. Exp. Psychol.* 48:94–106

Rudman LA, Ashmore RD, Gary ML. 2001a. "Unlearning" automatic biases: the malleability of implicit prejudice and stereotypes. *J. Pers. Soc. Psychol.* 81:856–68

Rudman LA, Glick P. 2001. Prescriptive gender stereotypes and backlash toward agentic women. *J. Soc. Issues* 57:743–62

Rudman LA, Greenwald AG, McGhee DE. 2001b. Implicit self-concept and evaluative implicit gender stereotypes: self and ingroup share desirable traits. *Pers. Soc. Psychol. Bull.* 27:1164–78

Rudman LA, Greenwald AG, Mellott DS, Schwartz JLK. 1999. Measuring the automatic components of prejudice: flexibility and generality of the Implicit Association Test. *Soc. Cogn.* 17:437–65

Rudman LA, Kilianski SE. 2000. Implicit and explicit attitudes toward female authority. *Pers. Soc. Psychol. Bull.* 26:1315–28

Rudman LA, Lee MR. 2002. Implicit and explicit consequences of exposure to violent and misogynous rap music. *Group Process. Intergroup Relat.* 5:133–50

Schacter DL. 1987. Implicit memory: history and current status. *J. Exp. Psychol.: Learn. Mem. Cogn.* 13:501–18

Schneider W, Fisk AD. 1982. Degree of consistent training: improvements in search performance and automatic process development. *Percept. Psychophys.* 31:160–68

Schneider W, Shiffrin RM. 1977. Controlled and automatic human information processing. I. Detection, search, and attention. *Psychol. Rev.* 84:1–66

Schwarz N, Bohner G. 2001. The construction of attitudes. In *Blackwell Handbook of Social Psychology: Intraindividual Processes*, ed. A Tesser, N Schwarz, pp. 436–57. Malden, MA: Blackwell

Sekaquaptewa D, Espinoza P, Thompson M, Vargas P, von Hippel W. 2002. Stereotype explanatory bias: implicit stereotyping as a predictor of discrimination. *J. Exp. Soc. Psychol.* In press

Semin GR, Fiedler K. 1988. The cognitive functions of linguistic categories in describing persons: social cognition and language. *J. Pers. Soc. Psychol.* 54:558–68

Sherif M, Hovland CI. 1961. *Social Judgment: Assimilation and Contrast Effects in Communication and Attitude Change.* New Haven, CT: Yale Univ. Press

Sherman SJ, Presson CC, Chassin L, Rose JS, Koch K. 2002. Implicit and explicit attitudes toward cigarette smoking: the effects of context and motivation. *J. Soc. Clin. Psychol.* In press

Sinclair L, Kunda Z. 1999. Reactions to a black professional: motivated inhibition and activation of conflicting stereotypes. *J. Pers. Soc. Psychol.* 77:885–904

Smith ER, Fazio RH, Cejka MA. 1996. Accessible attitudes influence categorization of multiply categorizable objects. *J. Pers. Soc. Psychol.* 71:888–98

Snyder M, Kendzierski D. 1982. Acting on one's attitudes: procedures for linking attitude and behavior. *J. Exp. Soc. Psychol.* 18:165–83

Snyder M, Swann WB. 1976. When actions reflect attitudes: the politics of impression management. *J. Pers. Soc. Psychol.* 34:1034–42

Son Hing LS, Li W, Zanna MP. 2002. Inducing hypocrisy to reduce prejudicial responses among aversive racists. *J. Exp. Soc. Psychol.* 38:71–78

Spalding LR, Hardin CD. 1999. Unconscious unease and self-handicapping: behavioral consequences of individual differences in implicit and explicit self-esteem. *Psychol. Sci.* 10:535–39

Stacy AW, Leigh BC, Weingardt K. 1997. An individual difference perspective applied to word association. *Pers. Soc. Psychol. Bull.* 23:229–37

Steffens MC, Plewe I. 2001. Items' cross-category associations as a confounding factor in the Implicit Association Test. *Z. Exp. Psychol.* 48:123–34

Swanson JE, Rudman LA, Greenwald AG. 2001. Using the Implicit Association Test to investigate attitude-behavior consistency for stigmatized behavior. *Cogn. Emot.* 15:207–30

Teachman BA, Gregg AP, Woody SR. 2001. Implicit associations for fear-relevant stimuli among individuals with snake and spider fears. *J. Abnorm. Psychol.* 110:226–35

Towles-Schwen T, Fazio RH. 2002. Choosing social situations: the relation between automatically-activated racial attitudes and anticipated comfort interacting with African Americans. *Pers. Soc. Psychol. Bull.* In press

Tulving E, Schacter DL, Stark HA. 1982. Priming effects in word-fragment completion are independent of recognition memory. *J. Exp. Psychol.: Learn. Mem. Cogn.* 8:336–42

Vanman EJ, Paul BY, Ito TA, Miller N. 1997. The modern face of prejudice and structural features that moderate the effect of cooperation on affect. *J. Pers. Soc. Psychol.* 73:941–59

von Hippel W, Sekaquaptewa D, Vargas P. 1995. On the role of encoding processes in stereotype maintenance. In *Advances in Experimental Social Psychology*, ed. MP Zanna, 27:174–255. San Diego, CA: Academic

von Hippel W, Sekaquaptewa D, Vargas P. 1997. The linguistic intergroup bias as an implicit indicator of prejudice. *J. Exp. Soc. Psychol.* 33:490–509

Warrington EK, Weiskrantz L. 1968. New method of testing long-term retention with special reference to amnesic patients. *Nature* 217:972–74

Webb EJ, Campbell DT, Schwartz RD, Sechrest L. 1966. *Unobtrusive Measures: Nonreactive*

Research in the Social Sciences. Chicago: Rand McNally

Wegener DT, Petty RE. 1995. Flexible correction processes in social judgment: the role of naive theories in corrections for perceived bias. *J. Pers. Soc. Psychol.* 68:36–51

Wentura D. 1999. Activation and inhibition of affective information: evidence for negative priming in the evaluation task. *Cogn. Emot.* 13:65–91

Wilson TD, Lindsey S, Schooler TY. 2000. A model of dual attitudes. *Psychol. Rev.* 107:101–26

Wittenbrink B, Judd CM, Park B. 1997. Evidence for racial prejudice at the implicit level and its relationship to questionnaire measures. *J. Pers. Soc. Psychol.* 72:262–74

Wittenbrink B, Judd CM, Park B. 2001a. Spontaneous prejudice in context: variability in automatically activated attitudes. *J. Pers. Soc. Psychol.* 81:815–27

Wittenbrink B, Judd CM, Park B. 2001b. Evaluative versus conceptual judgments in automatic stereotyping and prejudice. *J. Exp. Soc. Psychol.* 37:244–52

Zanna MP, Fazio RH. 1982. The attitude-behavior relation: moving toward a third generation of research. In *Consistency in Social Behavior: The Ontario Symposium*, ed. MP Zanna, ET Higgins, CP Herman, 2:283–301. Mahwah, NJ: Erlbaum

Zanna MP, Rempel JK, 1988. Attitudes: a new look at an old concept. In *The Social Psychology of Knowledge*, ed. D Bar-Tal, AW Kruglanski, pp. 315–34. New York: Cambridge Univ. Press

Annu. Rev. Psychol. 2003. 54:329–49
doi: 10.1146/annurev.psych.54.101601.145102
First published online as a Review in Advance on October 4, 2002

FACIAL AND VOCAL EXPRESSIONS OF EMOTION

James A. Russell[1], Jo-Anne Bachorowski[2], and
José-Miguel Fernández-Dols[3]

[1]*Department of Psychology, Boston College, Chestnut Hill, Massachusetts 02467;
e-mail: james.russell@bc.edu*
[2]*Department of Psychology, Vanderbilt University, Nashville, Tennessee 37235;
e-mail: j.a.bachorowski@vanderbilt.edu*
[3]*Departmento de Psicología Social y Metodología, Universidad Autónoma de Madrid;
e-mail: jose.dols@uam.es*

Key Words affect, display rule, perception, nonverbal, communication

■ **Abstract** A flurry of theoretical and empirical work concerning the production of and response to facial and vocal expressions has occurred in the past decade. That emotional expressions express emotions is a tautology but may not be a fact. Debates have centered on universality, the nature of emotion, and the link between emotions and expressions. Modern evolutionary theory is informing more models, emphasizing that expressions are directed at a receiver, that the interests of sender and receiver can conflict, that there are many determinants of sending an expression in addition to emotion, that expressions influence the receiver in a variety of ways, and that the receiver's response is more than simply decoding a message.

CONTENTS

0066-4308/03/0203-0329$14.00 **329**

INTRODUCTION: DEFINITION AND SCOPE

Smiles, chuckles, guffaws, smirks, frowns, and sobs—these and their milder cousins occurring in the fleeting changes in the countenance of a face and in the tone of a voice are essential aspects of human social interaction. Indeed, expressionless faces and voices are considered to be indicators of mental illness, expressive faces and voices to be windows to the soul. The last *Annual Review of Psychology* chapter devoted to this topic (Ekman & Oster 1979) summarized a rich research tradition that was predominant in the study of emotion at that time. Since that chapter, much has changed.

Both scientists and nonscientists traditionally considered smiles, chuckles, and the rest to be "expressions of emotion" (EEs). Ekman & Oster (1979) continued this tradition, but newer work questions the assumptions in both key words: *expression* and *emotion*. *Signals* might be a better term for some cases of EE, although *signal, symptom, symbol, manifestation, display, sign, expression,* and other terms are often used interchangeably, without clear definitions or distinctions. The relation of EEs to emotion (and the nature of emotion) remains unclear. Further, the class of EEs is probably heterogeneous, so any one name will prove misleading. For instance, some EEs are, to use Goffman's (1959) terms, *given* (produced for the purpose of communication) and others are *given off* (side-effects of movements produced for other purposes). The boundaries of the class of emotion expression are not self-evident, leaving us pointing to examples and leaving the category EE conceptually undefined. Indeed, we doubt that it is a scientifically viable unitary category.

History

Traditionally, senders have been thought to "express" or "encode"—that is, emit veridical information about—their internal state, much as a lighthouse broadcasts its visual and auditory warning to any and all who happen to perceive it. In turn, receivers "recognize" or "decode" the message and benefit from it. This image of honest and altruistic broadcasting has deep historical roots. Expressions of emotion were thought of as a God-given and universal language that revealed passions (such as love and hate), virtues (courage), and vices (sloth). These ideas were evident in philosophical, religious, and artistic theories from ancient times to the nineteenth century and continued to appear in later work by anatomists, physiologists, and other scientists (Montagu 1994). Among those scientists was Charles Darwin (1872). Although he relied on traditional assumptions about expression and emotion, Darwin substituted natural selection for God and made important observations about cross-species and cross-cultural similarities in EEs to bolster his argument for that substitution.

The modern era of the study of EEs began in 1962 with a theory proposed by Sylvan Tomkins. Like Darwin, Tomkins and those he inspired (Izard 1971, Ekman et al. 1972) perpetuated many of the traditional assumptions about expression. To these, Tomkins added another ancient idea, that of a small, fixed number of discrete ("basic") emotions. According to Tomkins's theory, each basic emotion can vary in intensity and consists of a single brain process (an "affect program"), whose triggering produces all the various manifestations (components) of the emotion, including its facial and vocal expression, changes in peripheral physiology, subjective experience, and instrumental action. Because they have a single cause, these components tightly cohere in time and are intercorrelated in intensity. Emotions are sharply distinguished from cognitions. The set of theories, methods, and assumptions inspired by Tomkins guided the study of emotion for over a quarter century.

Another assumption found in Darwin and continued by Tomkins—that the same message is encoded and decoded—guided much of the research on EEs: If (except in cases of deliberate, socially induced deception) EEs broadcast veridical information that the receiver recognizes, then researchers can focus on either the encoding or decoding side. Either could establish which of the small number of basic emotions was expressed by a specific facial or vocal pattern. For practical reasons, most research therefore relied on decoding (judgments by observers) to establish just what emotion a specific EE represents. The actual emotional state of the sender was typically neglected.

Some Key Theoretical Advances

Modern evolutionary theory renders obsolete Darwin's specific analysis of EEs, which relied on a Lamarkian inheritance of acquired characteristics, on group selection pressures, and on a characterization of EEs as vestiges. Modern theory instead emphasizes natural selection, the interests of the individual, adaptation, and function (Dawkins & Krebs 1978, Fridlund 1994, Owren & Rendall 2001). A pivotal recognition in modern theories is that EEs, even when given in Goffman's sense, are not broadcast to any and all but are directed at a receiver and evolved to influence that receiver in ways beneficial to the sender. As the interests of sender and receiver only sometimes coincide, it is not always in the sender's interest to provide veridical information. EEs are thus as capable of being deceptive as honest.

A second key recognition was that the receiving side is more than a reflex-like decoding of a message. If EEs evolved to alter the receiver, then a variety of effects can occur. For instance, vocal stimuli can capture the receiver's attention and alter his or her affective state without any emotion being encoded or decoded (Owren et al. 2002). Furthermore, receiving mechanisms were subject to their own course of evolution. The receiver's interest lies not only in detecting cues but also in distinguishing veridical cues from deceptive ones. Receivers also benefit by using cues given off to anticipate the sender's subsequent actions. This last point is underscored by inadvertent communication, such as when a predator uses the prey's EEs to locate it (Seyfarth & Cheney 2003).

The theory of basic emotions has also been cogently criticized (Turner & Ortony 1992), and new conceptions of emotion have emerged (Russell 2003). These conceptions include an emphasis on multicomponent dynamic processes laced with cognition (Scherer 2001, Smith & Kirby 2001), with a looser, more malleable and context-dependent relation among the components (Bradley & Lang 2000b) and with a role for broad primitive affective dimensions such as pleasure-displeasure and activation (Russell & Feldman Barrett 1999, Davidson 2000).

These theoretical advances led us to separate the study of EEs into two topics: (*a*) the receiver's response to an EE (including but not limited to an attribution of emotion to the sender) and (*b*) the sender's production of an EE (there may be a variety of factors influencing the production of a given EE, some of which have little to do with emotion). Evidence for one of these topics cannot be taken as evidence for the other. Evidence of the universality of one cannot be taken as evidence of the universality of the other. Rather than judging emotion attributions as correct or incorrect, we suggest a more descriptive approach to how these two processes work, to what natural selection has bequeathed to the newborn regarding these processes, and to how they develop over the lifetime. Our discussion centers on a psychological analysis of (nonclinical) human adults.

THE RESPONSE OF THE RECEIVER

Recognition of Discrete Emotions

Much research was and still is inspired by the theory that certain EEs signal specific emotions, which receivers decode. Receivers include human infants (Nelson & de Haan 1997) and nonhuman species (Marler & Evans 1997), although Seyfarth & Cheney (2003) observed that, with the possible exception of the chimpanzee, no other species is currently thought to decode EEs in the way that humans are theorized to attribute emotions to the sender. The process of decoding has not been specified but has been characterized as innate (Izard 1994), easy (Ekman 1975), categorical (Calder et al. 1996), and immediate: "The initial translation of an expression into some meaning is likely to be so immediate that we are not aware of the process we go through" (Ekman 1997, p. 334).

In the typical study a facial or vocal EE is presented to a receiver, who then indicates which emotion it signals. The impressive empirical foundation for this theory is the repeated finding that, despite differences in culture, age, or background, receivers agree on the emotion signaled more often than could be achieved by chance (for facial EEs, see reviews by Elfenbein & Ambady 2002 and Russell 1994; for vocal, Johnstone & Scherer 2000). Agreement is typically higher for facial than vocal EEs (Wallbott & Scherer 1986, Hess et al. 1988).

Nevertheless, key problems remain unresolved. One problem concerns the facial or vocal signals chosen for study. The "correct" signal for each specific emotion in these studies was not specified on theoretical grounds, although Darwin's speculations along these lines are sometimes alluded to. Nor was the signal empirically specified by recording the EEs emitted by senders in known emotional states (more on this below). Instead, instances were typically obtained from actors asked to convey emotions through their face or voice. Through an iterative process, those portrayals that achieved highest agreement on the emotion conveyed were selected as the correct signals. One technical question is how to interpret the significance of agreement obtained this way. A deeper theoretical question also arises because this iterative process has not yielded what might have been expected, namely a specific physically characterizable signal for each emotion.

Instead, for each emotion, there is a range of signals that achieve varying degrees of agreement. For example, Ekman & Friesen (1978, Table 11.1) specified 65 different facial patterns they consider to be signals for anger. Comparable difficulties arose in attempts to specify a vocal signature for each basic emotion (Banse & Scherer 1996). No theoretical rationale for this variety has been offered. Further, the sets of "correct signals" resulting from this iterative process have dubious ecological validity—given that we know of no evidence that acted stimuli used in this research correspond to what persons in the specified emotional states produce spontaneously [and some indirect evidence to the contrary (Carroll & Russell 1997)]. Indeed, when spontaneous rather than acted EEs are presented to receivers, the amount of agreement on a specific emotion drops or disappears (Motley & Camden 1988, Yik et al. 1998 for facial; Johnson et al. 1986, Exp. 1, Pakosz 1983 for vocal).

The typical decoding study is also compromised by the task given the receiver. Forcing the receiver to choose one from a short list of emotions can inflate agreement and even produce blatant artifacts (Russell 1994). Providing the receiver with more options lowers agreement (Banse & Scherer 1996). Allowing the receiver to specify any emotion (free labeling) lowers agreement still further (Russell 1994). Some of the artifacts can be eliminated by providing "none of the above" as a response option (Frank & Stennett 2001), and future studies should do so.

A lively discussion centered on the question of universality (Ekman 1994; Izard 1994; Russell 1994, 1995). In an empirical response to that debate, Haidt & Keltner (1999) obtained evidence in the United States and India that was consistent with both proponents and critics. One interesting finding was a "gradient of recognition": Some emotions are more "recognizable" than others, and the gradient is steep enough that the recognizable fades into the unrecognizable. (Because the term "recognition" presupposes that the emotion is present in the stimulus to be recognized, a neutral term such as "attribution" would be preferable.) Attribution depends on the similarity between the sender's and the receiver's language and culture [see Russell (1991, 1994) and Elfenbein & Ambady (2002) for facial EEs, Scherer et al. (2001b) for vocal ones]. Attribution of the specific emotion predicted by Tomkins's (1962) theory also declines as one moves further from a Western cultural background. With participants isolated from Western ways, agreement that smiles indicate something positive is high, but agreement on what emotion to attribute to other facial expressions is low and may or may not exceed chance when method artifacts are eliminated (Russell 1994).

Russell & Fernández-Dols (1997b) summarized the available evidence as consistent with "minimal universality:" (*a*) Facial and vocal changes occur everywhere and are coordinated with the sender's psychological state; (*b*) Most people can infer something of the sender's psychological state from those facial and vocal changes.

The challenge for those who would maintain any stronger version of universality (such as the existence of universal signals for specific emotions) is to find evidence that goes beyond what can be accounted for by minimal universality. The implication is that it is time to pursue other conceptualizations of the receiver's response. (Kappas et al. 1991 and Owren et al. 2002 arrived at similar conclusions, although for different reasons.)

Alternative Views of the Receiver

Receivers do, sometimes, interpret an EE in terms of a specific emotion, but the nature of the interpretive process remains to be determined. There is evidence that attributing a specific emotion to the sender is more complex than the simple, easy, immediate detection of a signal. For example, even when the stimuli are the hypothesized prototypical facial expressions of emotion, the emotion attributed to the expression depends on the context within which it occurs (Carroll & Russell 1996), on the gender of the sender (Widen & Russell 2002), and on the receiver's current affective state (Niedenthal et al. 2000). Hebb (1946) reported that observers learned how to predict the emotions of chimpanzees not by decoding emotion signals from their faces or voices but by learning how the individual chimp's current expressive and other behavior fit into a temporal pattern idiosyncratic to that chimp. Longitudinal studies of clinical samples yielded similar conclusions (Ellgring 1986).

A receiver's typical response might include much more than attribution of an emotion or perhaps no such attribution at all. One well-supported possibility is that the receiver perceives the internal state of the sender in terms of broad bipolar dimensions such as valence (pleasure–displeasure) and activation (sleepy–hyperactivated). Receivers agree with one another in judging EEs along these dimensions. For faces, both dimensions are readily apparent (Russell 1997), even when the receivers are 2-year-olds (Russell & Bullock 1986). For voice, activation dominates (Pittam et al. 1990); valence is weak (Bachorowski 1999, Pereira 2000). Analyses of confusion among emotions inferred from EEs supports this hypothesis (Russell & Bullock 1986 for faces, Pakosz 1983 for voice). Even in Schröder's (2000) promising study of vocal outbursts ("yuck!"), which yield high agreement as to specific emotion, an analysis of confusion among them suggests the presence of valence and activation dimensions.

In addition, faces and voices provide nonemotional information: The receiver notes whether the sender is staring or looking away, laughing with or at someone, shouting because background noise requires it or for another reason. From a facial expression, receivers agree on the sender's situation ["she looks as if she is looking at a small child playing" (Frijda 1969, p. 169)] and likely future action (Frijda & Tcherkassof 1997). Receivers agree that the sender may be conveying a social message such as "back off" or "hello" (Yik & Russell 1999). We anticipate that receivers will agree on aspects of the sender's cognitive state, including attention, uncertainty, puzzlement, determination, anticipated effort, registration of novelty, and sense of control (Smith & Scott 1997).

In short, the receiver probably obtains from an EE information on the sender's valence, activation, quasi-physical actions (such as staring or talking), current situation, future actions, social attitude, and cognitive state. If so, then the receiver might use this information to infer the sender's emotion (Russell 1997). Obviously, the reverse is also possible: Decoding a specific emotion from the EE, the receiver could then infer the other information. Clearly, research is needed on what information the receiver extracts first, easily, automatically, at a younger age, or spontaneously from an EE and what information requires effort, training, or measures that guide or channel the receiver's response into something close to the researcher's a priori hypothesis. The cross-cultural study of such questions is especially needed.

Still Other Effects

EEs produce a variety of effects other than getting the receiver to think "lo, anger" or some other emotion. Laughs elicit laughter; yawns elicit yawns (Provine 1997); and more generally, receivers "mimic" the EEs of senders (Hatfield et al. 1992). A receiver's facial musculature mirrors a face presented nonconsciously (Dimberg et al. 2000). EEs alter the receiver's physiological state (Dimberg & Öhman 1996, Levenson 1996). Vocal EEs alter the receiver's self-reported affect (Bachorowski & Owren 2001)—which is not surprising given that EEs are visual and auditory stimuli, which are known to influence affect along the dimensions of valence and activation (Bradley & Lang 2000b). Indeed, everyday experience shows that sounds alter the hearer's affect, as illustrated by sirens, thunder, and an infant's cry. Receiver's self-reported affect reflects the affective tone of a passage heard (Neumann & Strack 2000) or the affective demeanor of a face seen (Wild et al. 2001), even when the face is presented nonconsciously (Dimberg et al. 2000).

Such evidence is consistent with the theory that EEs function to alter the receiver's state, especially affect. Owren and colleagues (Owren & Rendall 1997, 2001; Owren et al. 2002) questioned the exclusive focus traditionally placed on the receiver's cognitive representation of the message of the EE, suggesting that in addition they alter the receiver's state and thereby serve the larger goal of social influence. Indeed, EEs do alter the course of social interaction. Sender's embarrassment (appeasement) elicits self-reported positive feelings in the receiver (Keltner & Buswell 1997). EEs influence the degree of cooperation, dominance/submission, or antagonism in subsequent interaction (Zivin 1977, Tiedens 2001). Norm violators who smile are treated more leniently than those who do not (LaFrance & Hecht 1995). People whose facial expression is imitated feel that they were better understood and that their interaction was smoother (Chartrand & Bargh 1999). Complementary evidence for the same theme comes from the finding that various EEs are differentially susceptible to serving as a conditional stimulus in a Pavlovian conditioning paradigm (Dimberg & Öhman 1996). In this case, EEs would function to alter long-term interaction.

Owren et al.'s (2002) perspective is nicely illustrated by thinking of EEs as being like infant-directed speech. Infant-directed speech (baby talk) has known acoustic characteristics (Fernald 1991, Katz et al. 1996) and accompanying facial behavior (Chong et al. 2002). It is preferred by infants (Fernald & Kuhl 1987, Cooper & Aslin 1990), elicits their attention, alters their emotional behavior, helps direct their attention to a specific stimulus, and facilitates their learning of associations (Kaplan et al. 1997). Infants deprived of infant-directed speech (e.g., when their caregiver is depressed) show significant learning and developmental deficits (Murray et al. 1996, Kaplan et al. 2002). Perhaps EEs function in a comparable fashion. According to this account, EEs operate on at least two levels. The simple acoustics of the sound elicit attention and alter core affect (valence and activation) directly, but the affect and meaning attributed to the sound also depend on context and prior experience. Thus, hearing laughter is generally a pleasant experience, with voiced more pleasant than unvoiced laughter (Bachorowski & Owren 2001): Sound acoustics have a direct effect. However, the affect-altering effect of EEs also depends on context (J-A Bachorowski, MJ Smoski, AJ Tomarken, & MJ Owren, unpublished manuscript, Vanderbilt Univ.; Kappas et al. 1991; Hess & Kirouac 2000). For instance, hearing a high-pitched shriek might be pleasant during a party but unpleasant when alone in a dark street.

THE SENDER

Surprisingly few studies have tested the basic claim of EEs: Emotions cause them. Perhaps the claim was simply taken as obviously true; perhaps studies of the receiver's decoding of EEs was mistakenly believed to be an adequate test; perhaps practical and ethical concerns hindered research; or perhaps needed measurement techniques were slow in coming and difficult to use. The studies that have been done almost always focused on either facial or vocal changes rather than their combination (Hess et al. 1988 is an excellent counterexample). In this section we therefore review these two literatures separately. We also consider some alternatives.

Emotions as Causes of Facial Expressions

MEASUREMENT   Techniques for facial measurement were slow to develop. Some systems provide not an objective description of facial movement but a description in terms of the emotion (Izard 1979) or affective dimension (AM Kring & D Sloan, unpublished manuscript, Univ. Calif., Berkeley) inferred typically from clusters of physically different movements. An objective but intrusive technique is electromyography, especially useful for brief or small muscular movement (Fridlund & Cacioppo 1986, Tassinary & Cacioppo 1992). Hjortsjö (1969) developed an objective and unobtrusive technique useful for visible movements, based on facial anatomy. Ekman & Friesen (1978) revised this technique and renamed it the Facial Action Coding System (FACS). An updated version of FACS was recently announced (Ekman et al. 2002). H. Oster and D. Rosenstein (unpublished manuscript, Adelphi Univ.) developed a version of FACS for infant faces. Still another system is Katsikitis & Pilowsky's (1988) FACEM, which assesses facial movement in terms of 12 distances between key points on the face.

POSITIVE EMOTIONS   Does happiness produce a smile? There is a clear association between pleasant feelings and zygomatic activity (smiling) (Davidson et al. 1990, Lang et al. 1993, Winkielman & Cacioppo 2001). Yet the relation is far from simple, and happiness is neither necessary nor sufficient for smiling. Kraut & Johnson (1979) found surprisingly few smiling faces among bowlers and hockey fans during happy events—unless they were simultaneously engaged in social interaction (replicated in Spain by Ruiz-Belda et al. 2002). Fernández-Dols & Ruiz-Belda (1995) similarly found smiles limited to social circumstances even for ecstatically happy persons: Olympic gold-medal winners. Even in children, smiling is more associated with the particular social interaction in which they are engaged than with their own happiness (Schneider & Unzner 1992, Soussignan & Schaal 1996): Children smile as much after failure as after success, but smiling is coordinated with eye contact (Schneider & Josephs 1991). Smiling also occurs during humorous films in proportion to self-reported amusement (Ekman et al. 1990), but this same study found little smiling during another pleasant but nonhumorous film.

The proposal that a Duchenne smile (in which zygomatic activity is combined with contraction of the orbicularis oculi) is the index of happiness has yielded mixed results. This distinction has not clarified the causes of smiling or laughter (Keltner & Bonnano 1997, Rosenberg et al. 2001) and does not nullify the general finding of the social nature of smiles. For instance, Duchenne smiles also occur as much after failure as after success (Schneider & Josephs 1991) and may simply be more intense smiles (Schneider & Unzner 1992).

NEGATIVE EMOTIONS   Tomkins's (1962) theory predicts that negative basic emotions—fear, anger, sadness, disgust, and possibly, contempt, shame, and embarrassment—each produce a distinct signal. One interesting examination of this prediction was Camras's (1991) yearlong observational study of her own daughter. Camras found "(1) situations in which we believe an emotion is present yet the facial expression is not seen, and (2) situations in which an expression is observed but does not appear to be best described using the discrete emotion categories of differential emotion theory" (Camras 1991, p. 26). In another study 30 babies were subjected to an arm restraint procedure, to which each baby reacted with distress (Camras et al. 1992). Rather than one common pattern of facial response, however, there were many different patterns, few of which fit the criteria for a discrete emotion signal. Clearly, there is great need for ecological research on what facial activity occurs and under what circumstances.

In the laboratory researchers have tested Tomkins's predictions by using films, slides, and remembered or imagined events to induce emotion, but with similarly weak results (e.g., Fernández-Dols et al. 1997). Rosenberg & Ekman (1994) criticized prior laboratory research but also offered new supporting evidence. While participants viewed four films selected to induce intense negative emotions, their faces were surreptitiously recorded. Participants then watched the films again. This time they reported each emotion they had experienced and pinpointed the time of its occurrence. What was the proportion of hits? Consider all occasions on which participants reported a negative emotion. On what proportion of these occasions did they show the facial expression predicted for that emotion? This figure was not given. Instead, the proportion of hits within a selected subset of these occasions was given, namely, those occasions in which a negative emotion was reported and some facial expression had occurred. For these selected occasions, the proportion of hits was .42 (p > .10) for one film and .50 (p < .05) for another; no figures were given for the remaining two films. Clearly these figures are inflated because the excluded occasions (on which an emotion was reported but no facial expression occurred) were all misses. (Also ignored were occasions on which a facial expression occurred but no emotion was reported.) In addition, it was not clear exactly which facial expressions were considered correct and which incorrect for a given emotion.

A more promising approach capitalized on the fact that some subjects become embarrassed in the laboratory when asked to pose facial expressions (Keltner 1995). In these cases, embarrassment was associated not with a single static configuration (something that could be captured well in a photograph or painting) but with a complex sequence of face and body movements.

SURPRISE   In the most sophisticated set of laboratory studies on this topic to date, Reisenzein (2000) addressed prior technical criticisms and examined the coherence among four components of surprise: cognitive appraisal of the stimulus as unexpected, self report of surprise, reaction time, and facial expression. Reisenzein found that "even with an optimal data analysis design (raw data, within-subjects), the average linear correlations between the different surprise components were— with the important exception of the correlation between [a cognitive appraisal of] unexpectedness and [self-reported] surprise ($r = .78$)—only low to moderate, ranging from .19 ([reaction time]-expression) to .46 (surprise feeling-expression)" (p. 28).

Emotions as Causes of Vocal Expressions

MEASUREMENT   Measurement of vocal acoustics is guided by the source-filter model developed in the 1950s (Stevens & House 1955, Fant 1960, Titze 1994). The "source" refers to the vocal folds, which vibrate in a quasi-periodic fashion during phonation. The rate of vibration directly corresponds to the fundamental frequency (F_0), and is highly correlated with the perception of pitch. Mean F_0 and measures of F_0 variability have been the most commonly studied acoustic cues in research on vocal EEs. More recent advances in digital cue extraction and modeling techniques have made it increasingly feasible to measure these and other sound properties of interest, including minute perturbations in the amplitude and frequency of vocal-fold vibration (Bachorowski & Owren 1995, Protopapas & Lieberman 1997) and glottal airflow characteristics (Cummings & Clements 1995).

The resonance properties of the various cavities and articulators in the supralaryngeal vocal tract contribute to "filter" effects, which are typically indexed by formant frequencies (see Johnson 1997, Lieberman & Blumstein 1988). Recently, emphasis has also been given to the long-term average spectrum (LTAS), which represents the average distribution of energy over the course of continuous speech (Pittam & Scherer 1993). LTAS assessment has the advantage over most other measures of being quick and less susceptible to measurement error. A significant drawback, however, is that LTAS does not directly correspond to sound production at any given moment.

NONLINGUISTIC VOCALIZATIONS   Laughs, cries, sighs, yawns, and other such vocal outbursts seem at first to be good examples of expressions of discrete (although not necessarily basic) emotions: A funny joke elicits amusement, which produces a laugh; a loss elicits sadness, which produces crying; an uninspired lecture elicits boredom, which produces a yawn. Mounting evidence, however, questions whether such vocalizations are each linked to a specific, discrete state.

Infant crying is a good illustration of this conclusion. Different cries were once thought to be associated with different states, such as frustration, fear, hunger, cold, pain, fatigue, or a soiled diaper (Berry 1975). The evidence instead is that the cry more simply indexes the degree of the infant's distress (Barr et al. 2000). The cry's typical acoustic features (abrupt onset, high F_0, high amplitude, and characteristic pulsing) attract the attention of and cause negative affect in the receiver. The marked variability in these acoustic features does not mark different states (frustration, etc.) but lessens the chances of the receiver habituating. The receiver then infers the infant's specific state largely from context (Bachorowski & Owren 2002).

Laughter also illustrates this conclusion. Laughs are produced not only by humor, but also by anger and anxiety (Darwin 1872), attempted self-deprecation (Glenn 1991/1992), being the object of attention (Martin & Gray 1996), appeasement or submission (Deacon 1997, Adams & Kirkevold 1978, Dovidio et al. 1988, Grammer & Eibl-Eibesfeldt 1990) and sexual interest (Grammer 1990, Grammer & Eibl-Eibesfeldt 1990, Dunbar 1996). From this variety, one might be tempted to hypothesize that different types of laughs correspond to different states. We know of no empirical support for this hypothesis. Although laugh acoustics are remarkably variable both within and between laughers (Grammer & Eibl-Eibesfeldt 1990, Bachorowski et al. 2001), they have not been found to vary as a function of self-reported emotion. Instead, laughter varies with social factors such as the sex of and familiarity with one's social partner (J-A Bachorowski et al., unpublished manuscript, Vanderbilt Univ.; Devereaux & Ginsburg 2001). Laughs also provide cues to individuality (Edmonson 1987) and elicit affective responses in listeners (Bachorowski & Owren 2001). The emerging picture is one in which laughter elicits cooperation and a positive relationship with a specific receiver (Owren & Bachorowski 2001).

VOCAL EXPRESSION IN SPEECH   Many studies have examined the vocal characteristics of speech in hopes of defining a vocal signature for each basic emotion. Leinonen et al. (1997) and Johnstone & Scherer (2000) recently provided detailed summaries. So far, the strongest single association found for vocal acoustics has been with the sender's general arousal level (Bachorowski 1999, Cowie 2000, Kappas et al. 1991). The still unanswered question is whether reliable patterns beyond this simple relationship can be established.

A pattern of vocal cues unique to a valence (pleasure) dimension has proven elusive (Tolkmitt & Scherer 1986, Leinonen et al. 1997, Protopapas & Lieberman 1997, Bachorowski 1999, Paeschke & Sendlmeier 2000, Pereira 2000, Trouvain & Barry 2000, Millot & Brand 2001). For example, anger and joy can both produce high F_0 and high amplitude. These basic acoustic effects have been shown for acted portrayals as well as naturally produced speech (Scherer 1989, Johnstone & Scherer 2000) and suggest that the speech acoustics reflect what joy and anger have in common (such as arousal). In a study of speech utterances produced immediately after affectively charged success or failure feedback, changes in three F_0-related measures reflected increases in arousal (Bachorowski & Owren 1995). Effects associated with valence were more ambiguous and depended on interactions with the speaker's sex and trait differences in emotional intensity.

Vocal differences owing to arousal and valence are consistent with a dimensional account of emotion, and therefore a test of predictions from Tomkins's (1962) theory best focuses on negative emotions. An important study by Banse & Scherer (1996) typifies this work. Twelve professional stage actors were asked to read two sentences for each of 28 scenarios (14 emotions × 2 scenarios per emotion). A large number of acoustic features was examined. As expected, the major differentiation was provided by mean F_0, which most reliably indexes arousal. In addition, statistically significant but modest differentiation occurred for separate emotions. Nevertheless, two factors render this result questionable. First, acted portrayals do not necessarily correspond to naturally produced vocal EEs; after all, the actors' job was to convey emotion. Second, tests of differentiated patterning were based not on all 1344 vocal samples obtained but on a subset of 224 judged as the best acted.

Recent studies have attempted to induce emotion in the laboratory rather than to merely simulate it using actors (Bachorowski & Owren 1995, Kappas 1997, Sobin & Alpert 1999, Millot & Brand 2001) or to analyze recordings made outside the laboratory such as in radio and television interviews (Gregory & Webster 1996) or horse-race commentaries (Trouvain & Barry 2000). These studies again confirm the link of vocal expression with sender's general arousal, and, importantly, sometimes show different patterns than those obtained with acted portrayals (Streeter et al. 1983). A vocal signature for each hypothesized basic emotion, however, remains elusive.

Future Directions

Kappas (2002, p. 10) summarized research on emotion and facial movement: "We might be on safer ground than simply insisting, against our better knowledge, that there are fixed links between facial expression and emotions." The theory that a small number of discrete emotions produce a corresponding set of facial signals has yielded at best weak results. Outside Western societies, there is practically no relevant evidence. The evidence on vocal outbursts and vocal characteristics of speech corroborates this trend. This same research, however, has provided some hints of more promising directions.

First, research should not be limited to a small list of emotions or a small set of signals. For example, research in which the face or voice is the dependent variable has found many different patterns. The traditional view of facial expressions focused on static visual configurations (the sort of thing that can be captured in a painting or later in a photograph), one per emotion. Thus much is neglected, such as blushing, paling, and blinking (see, for example, Leary et al. 1992). We suggest a much broader focus on the many possible dynamic patterns in nonverbal facets of action. Although in many respects facial and vocal systems are separate, more study of their joint occurrence (evident in laughter, sobbing, and yelling) is also needed.

In analyzing EEs, it is helpful to move beyond overly simple dichotomies. In response to technical criticisms of research claimed to support Tomkins's theory (Russell 1994) and to the presentation of an alternative to that theory (Fridlund 1994), Rosenberg (1997, p. 88) stated, "implicit in Russell's argument and explicit in Fridlund's is the notion that the face has nothing to do with emotion." Of course, there is some association between EEs and emotion; the question is the nature of that association.

Perhaps facial and vocal changes are more closely tied with what have been thought of as components of the emotion and thus only indirectly with emotion per se. One possible such component is the simple core affect of pleasure and activation (Bradley & Lang 2000b, Russell 2003). Another is the various cognitive steps involved in the processing of the emotion-eliciting stimulus (Smith & Scott 1997, Scherer 2001). Still another is preparation for instrumental action (Frijda & Tcherkassof 1997). Because the components of emotion are at best loosely associated, one can find individual components in the absence of a full emotion and vice versa. The interesting empirical question is what facial and vocal changes occur in these dissociated cases.

Evidence on the social nature of smiles suggests that more scrutiny of social norms and context is warranted for EEs in general. This topic has typically been discussed through an idea introduced by Klineberg (1940) and later named "display rules" (Ekman 1975): that people learn to voluntarily inhibit, produce, or alter their natural EEs. EEs are clearly influenced by culture (Elfenbein & Ambady 2002), gender (LaFrance & Hecht 1995), and group membership (Kirouac & Hess 1999), although whether display rules are the explanation remains largely untested and perhaps untestable (Fridlund 1994).

Owren & Bachorowski's (2001) account of smiling builds on modern evolutionary theory. Two different but related systems underlie the smile (Rinn 1984). Smiles produced by either system manipulate receiver affect. This account is thus consistent with evidence that smiles are highly dependent on the presence of an audience (although that audience can be psychologically rather than physically present) (Fridlund 1994). A phylogenetically older, simpler, reflex-like system produces "spontaneous" smiles as reliable signs of positive feelings toward a specific receiver. Positive affect is therefore necessary but not sufficient for their production. The second system is a more recently evolved version of the first in which "volitional" smiles are produced in a controlled process. In contrast to spontaneous smiles, volitional smiles are emancipated from affect in that they can occur during the experience of any affective state. Sometimes thought of as being "deceptive" or "dishonest," the power of volitional smiles lies in their inherent unreliability as a cue to the sender's state.

Fridlund's (1994) evolutionary account places a similar emphasis on the smile being directed at a receiver but substitutes "friendly intentions" for "positive feelings." Although not denying that emotions and feelings exist or are correlated with EEs, Fridlund argued that the most coherent causal story can be told in more behavior-relevant or functional terms. Fridlund applied the same analysis to other EEs as well, centered on other social intentions, including aggression, appeasement, and help-seeking. Perhaps because this account strays from the traditional assumptions associated with EEs and maintained in previous accounts, it has been frequently misunderstood. For example, "intentional" should not be taken to mean a conscious state, but simply involving a behavioral disposition aimed at a specific receiver. Fridlund's account does not require a simple correlation between the amount of signaling and the degree of sociality of the situation. Nor does Fridlund's account deny that EEs can occur when the sender is alone. Indeed, he offered evidence that EEs produced when alone are directed at an imaginary, implicit, or animistic audience. Like Owren and Bachorowski's (2001), Fridlund's account suggests the power of modern evolutionary theory to overturn long-held assumptions and open the door to fresh perspectives on EEs.

CONCLUSION

The scientific study of emotional expressions has been pursued now for about two centuries (e.g., in 1806 Bell published on the anatomical basis of facial expression). During most of that time the field was in the grip of an ancient set of assumptions, long ago incorporated into common sense and embedded in our language: That emotion expressions express emotions is a tautology, hardly something that seems to require empirical verification. Even the best scientists, including Darwin, implicitly held these presuppositions. Of course, science can progress even with dubious assumptions, but only so far. Emotion expressions may not be expressions and may not be related to emotions in any simple way.

Modern views of evolution are supplanting Darwin's 130-year-old analysis. Rather than broadcast for the benefit of anyone who happens to observe them, at least some EEs are directed at a specific receiver. These shape the affective and behavioral stance of the receiver and likely evolved to do so. Other EEs are simply given off, by-products of actions performed without communicative purpose. Still others likely have other causal histories.

It is unlikely that the receiver simply decodes an emotional message in any simple, reflex-like manner. There are quick, simple, and automatic responses to EEs, but these cannot be assumed to reflect "decoding the emotion." Receivers do sometimes attribute emotion to senders, but doing so is not always quick or simple. Receivers make a variety of interpretations of EEs besides emotional ones.

Of course, most of our conclusions here are tentative and await empirical test. Probably the more important development in the study of EEs in the past decade is a shift in perspective. Old assumptions need to be critically scrutinized and new ideas encouraged and pursued, rather than vice versa. What is exciting is that the hold of the "vice versa" on the field is steadily yielding.

The *Annual Review of Psychology* is online at http://psych.annualreviews.org

LITERATURE CITED

Adams RM, Kirkevold B. 1978. Looking, smiling, laughing, and moving in restaurants: sex and age differences. *Environ. Psychol. Nonverbal Behav.* 3:117–21

Bachorowski J-A. 1999. Vocal expression and perception of emotion. *Curr. Dir. Psychol. Sci.* 8:53–57

Bachorowski J-A, Owren MJ. 1995. Vocal expression of emotion: Acoustic properties of speech are associated with emotional intensity and context. *Psychol. Sci.* 6:219–24

Bachorowski J-A, Owren MJ. 2001. Not all laughs are alike: Voiced but not unvoiced laughter readily elicits positive affect. *Psychol. Sci.* 12:252–57

Bachorowski J-A, Owren MJ. 2002. Vocal acoustics in emotional intelligence. In *The Wisdom in Feeling: Psychological Processes in Emotional Intelligence*, ed. LF Barrett, P Salovey, pp. 11–36. New York: Guilford

Bachorowski J-A, Smoski MJ, Owren MJ. 2001. The acoustic features of human laughter. *J. Acoust. Soc. Am.* 110:1581–97

Banse R, Scherer KR. 1996. Acoustic profiles in vocal emotion expression. *J. Personal. Soc. Psychol.* 70:614–36

Barr RG, Hopkins B, Green JA, eds. 2000. *Crying as a Sign, a Symptom, & a Signal.* New York: Cambridge Univ. Press

Bell C. 1806. *Essays on the Anatomy of Expression in Painting.* London: Longman, Hurst, Rees & Orme

Berry KK. 1975. Developmental study of recognition of antecedents of infant vocalizations. *Percept. Mot. Skills* 41:400–2

Bradley MM, Lang PJ. 2000a. Affective reactions to acoustic stimuli. *Psychophysiology* 37:204–15

Bradley MM, Lang PJ. 2000b. Measuring emotion: behavior, feeling, and physiology. See Lane & Nadel 2000, pp. 242–76

Calder AJ, Young AW, Perrett DI, Etcoff NL, Roland D. 1996. Categorical perception of morphed facial expressions. *Vis. Cogn.* 3:81–117

Camras LA. 1991. A dynamical systems perspective on expressive development. In *International Review of Studies on Emotion,* ed. KT Strongman, pp. 16–28. New York: Wiley

Camras LA, Oster H, Campos JJ, Miyake K, Bradshaw D. 1992. Japanese and American infants' responses to arm restraint. *Dev. Psychol.* 28:578–83

Carroll JM, Russell JA. 1996. Do facial expressions signal specific emotions? Judging the face in context. *J. Personal. Soc. Psychol.* 70: 205–18

Carroll JM, Russell JA. 1997. Facial expressions in Hollywood's portrayal of emotion. *J. Personal. Soc. Psychol.* 72:164–76

Chartrand TL, Bargh JA. 1999. The chameleon effect: the perception-behavior link and social interaction. *J. Personal. Soc. Psychol.* 76: 893–910

Chong SCF, Werker JF, Russell JA, Carroll JM. 2002. Three facial expressions mothers direct to their infants. *Infant Child Dev.* In press

Cooper RP, Aslin RN. 1990. Preference for infant-directed speech in the first month after birth. *Child Dev.* 61:1584–95

Cowie R. 2000. Describing the emotional states expressed in speech. See Cowie et al. 2000, pp. 11–18

Cowie R, Douglas-Cowie E, Schröder M, eds. 2000. *Proceedings of the ISCA Workshop on Speech Emotion, Newcastle, North. Irel.* Belfast: Textflow

Cummings KE, Clements MA. 1995. Analysis of the glottal excitation of emotionally styled and stressed speech. *J. Acoust. Soc. Am.* 98:88–98

Darwin C. 1872. *The Expression of the Emotions in Man and Animals.* London: Murray

Davidson RJ. 2000. The functional neuroanatomy of affective style. See Lane & Nadel 2000, pp. 371–88

Davidson RJ, Ekman P, Saron CD, Senulis JA, Friesen WV. 1990. Approach-withdrawal and cerebral asymmetry: emotional expression and brain physiology I. *J. Personal. Soc. Psychol.* 58:330–41

Dawkins R, Krebs JR. 1978. Animal signals: information or manipulation? In *Behavioral Ecology: An Evolutionary Approach*, ed. JR Krebs, NB Davies, pp. 282–309. London: Blackwell Scientific

Deacon TW. 1997. *The Symbolic Species.* New York: Norton

Devereaux PG, Ginsburg GP. 2001. Sociality effects on the production of laughter. *J. Gen. Psychol.* 128:227–40

Dimberg U, Öhman A. 1996. Behold the wrath: psychophysiological responses to facial stimuli. *Motiv. Emot.* 20:149–82

Dimberg U, Thunberg M, Elmehed K. 2000. Unconscious facial reactions to emotional facial expressions. *Psychol. Sci.* 11:86–89

Dovidio JF, Brown CE, Heltman K, Ellyson SL, Keating CF. 1988. Power displays between women and men in discussions of gender-linked tasks: a multichannel study. *J. Personal. Soc. Psychol.* 55:580–87

Dunbar R. 1996. *Grooming, Gossip, and the Evolution of Language.* Cambridge: Harvard Univ. Press

Edmonson MS. 1987. Notes on laughter. *Anthropol. Linguist.* 29:23–33

Ekman P. 1975. Face muscles talk every language. *Psychol. Today* 9:35–39

Ekman P. 1994. Strong evidence for universals in facial expressions: a reply to Russell's mistaken critique. *Psychol. Bull.* 115:268–87

Ekman P. 1997. Should we call it expression or communication? *Innovation* 10:333–44

Ekman P, Davidson RJ, Friesen WV. 1990. The Duchenne smile: emotional expression and brain physiology II. *J. Personal. Soc. Psychol.* 58:342–53

Ekman P, Friesen WV. 1978. *Facial Action Coding System: A Technique for the Measurement of Facial Movement.* Palo Alto, CA: Consulting Psychologists

Ekman P, Friesen WV, Ellsworth P. 1972. *Emotion in the Human Face.* Elmsford, NY: Pergamon

Ekman P, Friesen WV, Hager JC. 2002. *New Version of the Facial Action Coding System.* http://dataface.nirc.com/Expression/FACS/New_Version/new_version.html

Ekman P, Oster H. 1979. Facial expressions of emotion. *Annu. Rev. Psychol.* 30:527–54

Elfenbein HA, Ambady N. 2002. On the

universality and cultural specificity of emotion recognition: a meta-analysis. *Psychol. Bull.* 128:203–35

Ellgring H. 1986. Nonverbal expression of psychological states in psychiatric patients. *Eur. Arch. Psychiatr. Neurol. Sci.* 236:31–34

Fant G. 1960. *Acoustic Theory of Speech Production*. The Hague: Mouton

Fernald A. 1991. Prosody in speech to children: prelinguistic and linguistic functions. In *Annals of Child Development*, ed. R Vasta, 8:43–80. Philadelphia: Kingsley

Fernald A, Kuhl PK. 1987. Acoustic determinants of infant preference for motherese speech. *Infant Behav. Dev.* 10:279–93

Fernández-Dols JM, Ruiz-Belda MA. 1995. Are smiles a sign of happiness? Gold medal winners at the Olympic Games. *J. Personal. Soc. Psychol.* 69:1113–19

Fernández-Dols JM, Sanchez MA, Carrera P, Ruiz-Belda MA. 1997. Are spontaneous expressions and emotions linked? An experimental test of coherence. *J. Nonverbal Behav.* 21:163–77

Frank MG, Stennett J. 2001. The forced-choice paradigm and the perception of facial expression of emotion. *J. Personal. Soc. Psychol.* 80:75–85

Fridlund AJ. 1994. *Human Facial Expression: An Evolutionary View*. New York: Academic

Fridlund AJ, Cacioppo JT. 1986. Publication guidelines for human electromyographic research. *Psychophysiology* 23:567–89

Frijda NH. 1969. Recognition of emotion. In *Advances in Experimental Social Psychology*, ed. L Berkowitz, 4:167–223. New York: Academic

Frijda NH, Tcherkassof A. 1997. Facial expressions as modes of action readiness. See Russell & Fernández-Dols 1997a, pp. 78–102

Glenn PJ. 1991/1992. Current speaker initiation of two-party shared laughter. *Res. Lang. Soc. Interact.* 25:139–62

Goffman E. 1959. *The Presentation of Self in Everyday Life*. Garden City, NY: Doubleday

Grammer K. 1990. Strangers meet: laughter and nonverbal signs of interest in opposite-sex encounters. *J. Nonverbal Behav.* 14:209–36

Grammer K, Eibl-Eibesfeldt I. 1990. The ritualization of laughter. In *Naturlichkeit der Sprache und der Kultur: acta colloquii*, ed. W Koch, pp. 192–214. Bochum, Ger.: Brockmeyer

Gregory SW, Webster S. 1996. A nonverbal signal in voices of interview partners effectively predicts communication accommodation and social status perception. *J. Personal. Soc. Psychol.* 70:1231–40

Haidt J, Keltner D. 1999. Culture and facial expression: Open-ended methods find more expressions and a gradient of recognition. *Cogn. Emot.* 13:225–66

Hatfield E, Cacioppo JT, Rapson RL. 1992. Primitive emotional contagion. In *Emotion and Social Behavior*, ed. MS Clark, pp. 151–77. London: Sage

Hebb DO. 1946. Emotion in man and animal: an analysis of the intuitive processes of recognition. *Psychol. Rev.* 53:88–106

Hess U, Kirouac G. 2000. Emotion expression in groups. See Lewis & Haviland-Jones 2000, pp. 368–81

Hess U, Scherer KR, Kappas A. 1988. Multichannel communication of emotion: synthetic signal production. In *Facets of Emotion: Recent Research*, ed. KR Scherer, pp. 161–249. Hillsdale, NJ: Erlbaum

Hjortsjö CH. 1969. *Man's Face and Mimic Language*. Lund, Swed.: Studentlitteratur

Izard CE. 1971. *The Face of Emotion*. New York: Appleton-Century-Crofts

Izard CE. 1979. *The Maximally Discriminative Facial Movement Coding System (MAX)*. Newark: Univ. Delaware, Comp. and Netw. Serv., Univ. Media Serv.

Izard CE. 1994. Innate and universal facial expressions: evidence from developmental and cross-cultural research. *Psychol. Bull.* 115:288–99

Johnson K. 1997. *Acoustic and Auditory Phonetics*. Cambridge: Blackwell. 169 pp.

Johnson WF, Emde RN, Scherer KR, Klinnert MD. 1986. Recognition of emotion from vocal cues. *Arch. Gen. Psychiatry* 43:280–83

Johnstone T, Scherer KR. 2000. Vocal communication of emotion. See Lewis & Haviland-Jones 2000, pp. 220–35

Kaplan PS, Bachorowski J-A, Smoski MJ, Hudenko WJ. 2002. Infants of depressed mothers, although competent learners, fail to learn in response to their own mother's infant-directed speech. *Psychol. Sci.* 13:268–71

Kaplan PS, Zarlengo-Strouse P, Kirk LS, Angel CL. 1997. Selective and nonselective associations between speech segments and faces in human infants. *Dev. Psychol.* 33:990–99

Kappas A. 1997. *His master's voice: Acoustic analysis of spontaneous vocalizations in an ongoing active coping task.* Presented at Annu. Meet. Soc. Psychophys. Res., 37th, Cape Cod, MA

Kappas A. 2002. What facial activity can and cannot tell us about emotions. In *The Human Face: Measurement and Meaning*, ed. M Katsikitis, pp. 215–34. Dordrecht: Kluwer

Kappas A, Hess U, Scherer KR. 1991. Voice and emotion. In *Fundamentals of Nonverbal Behavior*, ed. B Rime, R Feldman, pp. 200–38. Cambridge: Cambridge Univ. Press

Katsikitis M, Pilowsky I. 1988. A study of facial expression in Parkinson's disease using a novel microcomputer-based method. *J. Neurol. Neurosurg. Psychiatry* 51:362–66

Katz GS, Cohen JF, Moore CA. 1996. A combination of vocal F_0 dynamic and summary features discriminates between three pragmatic categories of infant-directed speech. *Child Dev.* 67:205–17

Keltner D. 1995. Signs of appeasement: evidence for the distinct displays of embarrassment, amusement, and shame. *J. Personal. Soc. Psychol.* 68:441–54

Keltner D, Bonanno G. 1997. A study of laughter and dissociation: distinct correlates of laughter and smiling during bereavement. *J. Personal. Soc. Psychol.* 73:687–702

Keltner D, Buswell BN. 1997. Embarrassment: its distinct form and appeasement functions. *Psychol. Bull.* 122:250–70

Kirouac G, Hess U. 1999. Group membership and the decoding of nonverbal behavior.

In *The Social Context of Nonverbal Behavior*, ed. P Philippot, RS Feldman, E Coats, pp. 182–210. New York: Cambridge Univ. Press

Klineberg O. 1940. *Social Psychology.* New York: Holt

Kraut RE, Johnston RE. 1979. Social and emotional messages of smiling: an ethological approach. *J. Personal. Soc. Psychol.* 37:1539–53

LaFrance M, Hecht MA. 1995. Why smiles generate leniency. *Personal. Soc. Psychol. Bull.* 21:207–14

Lane RD, Nadel L, eds. 2000. *Cognitive Neuroscience of Emotion.* New York: Oxford Univ. Press

Lang PJ, Greenwald MK, Bradley MM, Hamm AO. 1993. Looking at pictures: affective, facial, visceral, and behavioral reactions. *Psychophysiology* 30:261–73

Leary MR, Britt TW, Cutlip WD, Templeton JL. 1992. Social blushing. *Psychol. Bull.* 11: 446–60

Leinonen L, Hiltunen T, Linnankoski I, Laakso M-L. 1997. Expression of emotional-motivational connotations with a one-word utterance. *J. Acoust. Soc. Am.* 102:1853–63

Levenson RW. 1996. Biological substrates of empathy and facial modulation of emotion: two facets of the scientific legacy of John Lanzetta. *Motiv. Emot.* 20:185–204

Lewis M, Haviland-Jones JM, eds. 2000. *Handbook of Emotions.* New York: Guilford. 2nd ed.

Lieberman P, Blumstein SE. 1988. *Speech Physiology, Speech Perception, and Acoustic Phonetics.* Cambridge: Cambridge Univ. Press

Marler P, Evans C. 1997. Animal sounds and human faces: Do they have anything in common? See Russell & Fernández-Dols 1997a, pp. 133–57

Martin GN, Gray CD. 1996. The effect of audience laughter on men's and women's response to humor. *J. Soc. Psychol.* 136:221–31

Millot J-L, Brand G. 2001. Effects of pleasant and unpleasant ambient odors on human voice pitch. *Neurosci. Lett.* 297:61–63

Montagu J. 1994. *The Expression of the Passions: The Origin and Influence of Charles LeBrun's Conférence sur l'Expression Générale et Particulière.* New Haven, CT: Yale Univ. Press

Motley MT, Camden CT. 1988. Facial expression of emotion: a comparison of posed expressions versus spontaneous expressions in an interpersonal communication setting. *West. J. Speech Commun.* 52:1–22

Murray L, Fiori-Cowley A, Hooper R, Cooper P. 1996. The impact of postnatal depression and associated adversity on early mother-infant interactions and later infant outcomes. *Child Dev.* 67:2512–26

Nelson CA, de Haan M. 1997. A neurobehavioral approach to the recognition of facial expressions in infancy. See Russell & Fernández-Dols 1997a, pp. 176–204

Neumann R, Strack F. 2000. "Mood contagion:" the automatic transfer of mood between persons. *J. Personal. Soc. Psychol.* 79:211–23

Niedenthal PM, Halberstadt JB, Margolin J, Innes-Ker AH. 2000. Emotional state and the detection of change in facial expression of emotion. *Eur. J. Soc. Psychol.* 30:211–22

Owren MJ, Bachorowski J-A. 2001. The evolution of emotional expression: a "selfish-gene" account of smiling and laughter in early hominids and humans. In *Emotions: Current Issues and Future Directions*, ed. TJ Mayne, GA Bonanno, pp. 152–91. New York: Guilford

Owren MJ, Rendall D. 1997. An affect-conditioning model of nonhuman primate signaling. In *Perspectives in Ethology.* Vol. 12: *Communication*, ed. DH Owings, MD Beecher, NS Thompson, pp. 299–346. New York: Plenum

Owren MJ, Rendall D. 2001. Sound on the rebound: bringing form and function back to the forefront in understanding nonhuman primate vocal signaling. *Evol. Anthropol.* 10:58–71

Owren MJ, Rendall D, Bachorowski J-A. 2002. Nonlinguistic vocal communication. In *Primate Psychology: Bridging the Gap Between the Mind and Behavior of Human and Nonhuman Primates*, ed. D Maestripieri. Cambridge: Harvard Univ. Press. In press

Paeschke A, Sendlmeier WF. 2000. Prosodic characteristics of emotional speech: measurements of fundamental frequency movements. See Cowie et al. 2000, pp. 75–80

Pakosz M. 1983. Attitudinal judgments in intonation: some evidence for a theory. *J. Psycholinguist. Res.* 12:311–26

Pereira C. 2000. Dimensions of emotional meaning in speech. See Cowie et al. 2000, pp. 25–28

Pittam J, Gallois C, Callan V. 1990. The long-term spectrum and perceived emotion. *Speech Commun.* 9:177–87

Pittam J, Scherer KR. 1993. Vocal expression and communication of emotion. In *Handbook of Emotions*, ed. M Lewis, JM Haviland, pp. 185–97. New York: Guilford. 1st ed.

Protopapas A, Lieberman P. 1997. Fundamental frequency of phonation and perceived emotional stress. *J. Acoust. Soc. Am.* 101:2267–77

Provine RR. 1997. Yawns, laughs, smiles, tickles, and talking: naturalistic and laboratory studies of facial action and social communication. See Russell & Fernández-Dols 1997a, pp. 158–75

Reisenzein R. 2000. Exploring the strength of association between the components of emotion syndromes: the case of surprise. *Cogn. Emot.* 14:1–38

Rinn WE. 1984. The neuropsychology of facial expression. *Psychol. Bull.* 95:52–77

Rosenberg EL. 1997. Emotions as unified responses. In *What the Face Reveals*, ed. P Ekman, EL Rosenberg, pp. 86–88. New York: Oxford Univ. Press

Rosenberg EL, Ekman P. 1994. Coherence between expressive and experiential systems in emotion. *Cogn. Emot.* 8:201–29

Rosenberg EL, Ekman P, Jiang W, Babyak M, Coleman RE, et al. 2001. Linkages between facial expressions of anger and transient myocardial ischemia in men with coronary disease. *Emotion* 1:107–15

Ruiz-Belda MA, Fernandez-Dols JM, Carrera P, Barchard K. 2002. Spontaneous facial expressions of happy bowlers and soccer fans. *Cogn. Emot.* In press

Russell JA. 1991. Culture and the categorization of emotion. *Psychol. Bull.* 110:426–50

Russell JA. 1994. Is there universal recognition of emotion from facial expressions? A review of cross-cultural studies. *Psychol. Bull.* 115:102–41

Russell JA. 1995. Facial expressions of emotion: What lies beyond minimal universality? *Psychol. Bull.* 118:379–99

Russell JA. 1997. Reading emotions from and into faces: resurrecting a dimensional-contextual perspective. See Russell & Fernández-Dols 1997a, pp. 295–320

Russell JA. 2003. Core affect and the psychological construction of emotion. *Psychol. Rev.* In press

Russell JA, Bullock M. 1986. On the dimensions preschoolers use to interpret facial expressions of emotion. *Dev. Psychol.* 22:97–102

Russell JA, Feldman Barrett L. 1999. Core affect, prototypical emotional episodes, and other things called emotion: dissecting the elephant. *J. Personal. Soc. Psychol.* 76:805–19

Russell JA, Fernández-Dols JM, eds. 1997a. *The Psychology of Facial Expression.* New York: Cambridge Univ. Press

Russell JA, Fernández-Dols JM. 1997b. What does a facial expression mean? See Russell & Fernández-Dols 1997a, pp. 3–30

Scherer KR. 1989. Vocal measurement of emotion. In *Emotion: Theory, Research, and Experience.* Vol. 4: *The Measurement of Emotions*, ed. R Plutchik, H Kellerman, pp. 233–59. New York: Academic

Scherer KR. 2001. Appraisal considered as a process of multilevel sequential checking. See Scherer et al. 2001b, pp. 92–120

Scherer KR, Banse R, Wallbott HG. 2001a. Emotion inferences from vocal expression correlate across languages and cultures. *J. Cross-Cult. Psychol.* 32:76–92

Scherer KR, Schorr A, Johnstone T, eds. 2001b. *Appraisal Processes in Emotion.* New York: Oxford Univ. Press

Schneider K, Josephs I. 1991. The expressive and communicative functions of preschool children's smiles in an achievement-situation. *J. Nonverbal Behav.* 15:185–98

Schneider K, Unzner L. 1992. Preschoolers' attention and emotion in an achievement and an effect game: a longitudinal study. *Cogn. Emot.* 6:37–63

Schröder M. 2000. Experimental study of affect bursts. See Cowie et al. 2000, pp. 132–35

Seyfarth RM, Cheney DL. 2003. Signalers and receivers in animal communication. *Annu. Rev. Psychol.* 54:145–73

Smith CA, Kirby LD. 2001. Toward delivering on the promise of appraisal theory. See Scherer et al. 2001b, pp. 121–38

Smith CA, Scott HS. 1997. A componential approach to the meaning of facial expressions. See Russell & Fernández-Dols 1997a, pp. 229–54

Sobin C, Alpert M. 1999. Emotion in speech: the acoustic attributes of fear, anger, sadness, and joy. *J. Psycholinguist. Res.* 28:347–65

Soussignan R, Schaal B. 1996. Forms and social signal value of smiles associated with pleasant and unpleasant sensory experience. *Ethology* 102:1020–41

Stevens KN, House AS. 1955. Development of a quantitative description of vowel articulation. *J. Acoust. Soc. Am.* 27:484–93

Streeter LA, Macdonald NH, Apple W, Krauss RM, Galotti KM. 1983. Acoustic and perceptual indicators of emotional stress. *J. Acoust. Soc. Am.* 73:1354–60

Tassinary LG, Cacioppo JT. 1992. Unobservable facial actions and emotion. *Psychol. Sci.* 3:28–33

Tiedens L. 2001. Anger and advancement versus sadness and subjugation: the effect of negative emotion expressions on social status conferral. *J. Personal. Soc. Psychol.* 80:86–94

Titze IR. 1994. *Principles of Voice Production.* Englewood Cliffs, NJ: Prentice-Hall

Tolkmitt FJ, Scherer KR. 1986. Effects of

experimentally induced stress on vocal parameters. *J. Exp. Psychol: Hum. Percept. Perform.* 12:302–13

Tomkins SS. 1962. *Affect, Imagery, Consciousness*, Vol. 1. New York: Springer

Trouvain J, Barry WJ. 2000. The prosody of excitement in horse race commentaries. See Cowie et al. 2000, pp. 86–91

Turner TJ, Ortony A. 1992. Basic emotions: Can conflicting criteria converge? *Psychol. Rev.* 99:566–71

Wallbott HG, Scherer KR. 1986. Cues and channels in emotion recognition. *J. Personal. Soc. Psychol.* 51:690–99

Widen SC, Russell JA. 2002. Gender and preschoolers perception of emotion. *Merrill-Palmer Q.* 48:248–62

Wild B, Erb M, Bartels M. 2001. Are emotions contagious? Evoked emotions while viewing emotionally expressive faces: quality, quantity, time course and gender differences. *Psychiatry Res.* 102:109–24

Winkielman P, Cacioppo JT. 2001. Mind at ease puts a smile on the face: psychophysiological evidence that processing facilitation elicits positive affect. *J. Personal. Soc. Psychol.* 81:989–1000

Yik MSM, Meng Z, Russell JA. 1998. Adults' freely produced emotion labels for babies' spontaneous facial expressions. *Cogn. Emot.* 12:723–30

Yik MSM, Russell JA. 1999. Interpretation of faces: a cross-cultural study of a prediction from Fridlund's theory. *Cogn. Emot.* 13:93–104

Zivin G. 1977. Facial gestures predict preschoolers' encounter outcomes. *Soc. Sci. Inf.* 16:715–30

Annu. Rev. Psychol. 2003. 54:351–75
doi: 10.1146/annurev.psych.54.101601.145059
Copyright © 2003 by Annual Reviews. All rights reserved
First published online as a Review in Advance on October 4, 2002

INTERDEPENDENCE, INTERACTION, AND RELATIONSHIPS

Caryl E. Rusbult[1] and Paul A. M. Van Lange[2]

[1]University of North Carolina at Chapel Hill, Chapel Hill,
North Carolina 27599-3270; e-mail: Rusbult@unc.edu
[2]Department of Social Psychology, Free University at Amsterdam,
Van der Boechorsstraat 1, 1081 BT Amsterdam;
e-mail: PAM.van.Lange@psy.vu.nl

Key Words affordance, attribution, communication, interpersonal processes, self-presentation, social motivation, transformation processes

■ **Abstract** Interdependence theory presents a logical analysis of the structure of interpersonal situations, offering a conceptual framework in which interdependence situations can be analyzed in terms of six dimensions. Specific situations present specific problems and opportunities, logically implying the relevance of specific motives and permitting their expression. Via the concept of transformation, the theory explains how interaction is shaped by broader considerations such as long-term goals and concern for a partner's welfare. The theory illuminates our understanding of social-cognitive processes that are of longstanding interest to psychologists such as cognition and affect, attribution, and self-presentation. The theory also explains adaptation to repeatedly encountered interdependence patterns, as well as the embodiment of such adaptations in interpersonal dispositions, relationship-specific motives, and social norms.

CONTENTS

0066-4308/03/0203-0351$14.00 **351**

INTRODUCTION

The essence of a social psychological way of thinking frequently is described in terms of the "power of the situation." Indeed, the familiar equation $B = f$ (P, E) embodies our shared desire to understand the ways in which behavior (B) is shaped not only by properties of the person (P), but also by features of the situation, or social environment (E) (Lewin 1936). Perhaps the essence of a social psychological analysis can be even more fully expressed by construing our goals in terms of the relationships between people. To develop a truly social psychology, we may need to expand our formulation, noting that an interaction (I) between persons A and B can be conceptualized in terms of their needs, thoughts, and motives in relation to one another (A and B) in the context of the specific social situation (S) in which their interaction transpires (Holmes 2002, Kelley et al. 2002). Expressed in an equation, $I = f$ (S, A, B).

To illustrate the utility of an interaction-based analysis, imagine two scenarios for John and Mary, who are deciding where to spend their summer vacation. In one scenario their interests conflict: John wants to go to a beach resort, whereas Mary wants to go to Rome. In this type of situation each person will seek to explain his or her preference ("I need the excitement of Rome") and each will engage in cognitive activity oriented toward understanding the other's needs ("Does John want to relax because he had a stressful year?"). The situation makes it possible for each person to display his or her goals and motives (self-centered vs. prosocial). Communication and information-seeking will center on each person's needs, goals, and motives in relation to those of the partner ("Whose needs are more pressing?" "Will Mary be responsive to my needs?"). The two may rely on fairness norms to resolve their problem ("It's my turn" or "You deserve a break"). Thus, situations involving conflicting interests are interpersonally rich, affording psychological processes such as self-presentation and attributional activity and activating morality- and benevolence-relevant motives and norms.

In a second scenario John's and Mary's interests correspond: Both want to vacation in Rome. Neither is likely to be particularly concerned with information-seeking, self-presentation, or attribution, as there is no problem and "nothing to think about." It is not possible for either person to display benevolent motives because the course of action that would benefit John simultaneously benefits Mary. Interaction is a coordination problem—the two must agree on a date for their vacation, and one person must arrange for travel and lodging. Thus, in comparison to situations with conflicting interests, situations with corresponding interests are relatively simple, in that they are less likely to inspire activities such as information-seeking or self-presentation and are unlikely to present moral dilemmas or questions of benevolence. Instead, they entail coordinating to enjoy the good outcomes that are readily available to the pair ("If we're separated, meet me at the Piazza Navonna").

These scenarios very simply illustrate an important claim: The field of social psychology would benefit from a situation-based understanding of interaction—an analysis that examines each person's needs, cognitions, and motives in relation to one another and in the context of the situation in which the interaction transpires. We suggest that interdependence theory provides a comprehensive account of interaction and relationships by delineating the ways in which social situations shape both intrapersonal and interpersonal processes (Kelley et al. 2002, Kelley & Thibaut 1978, Thibaut & Kelley 1959). Interdependence theory advances a taxonomic model of situations, or a functional analysis of the structure of the social situations interacting people encounter. The theory also relates classes of situations to the particular types of goals and motives that are relevant to dealing with them.

As such, situation structure specifies the interpersonal reality that social cognitive activity is about, in that cognition frequently is oriented toward understanding (*a*) situations, or the unique problems and opportunities inherent a given situation ("Can both persons' needs be met?"), and (*b*) persons, or a given interaction partner's goals and motives ("Will she be responsive to my needs?") (Holmes 2002; Kelley 1984a, 1997). In addition, situation structure specifies the interpersonal reality that social motivation is about, in that (*a*) specific motives are relevant to specific classes of situation and (*b*) from a historic perspective, motives reflect prior adaptation to specific classes of situation (Kelley 1983, Kelley & Holmes 2002, Kelley et al. 2002). Given that cognition and motivation are embedded in the fabric of social situations, the structure and functions of many interpersonal phenomena may be best understood by adopting an interdependence-based analysis. This paper outlines the main principles of interdependence theory, illustrating the utility of this orientation via a review of recent work on interaction and relationships.

INTERDEPENDENCE STRUCTURE AND PROCESSES

Interdependence Structure

MATRICES AND TRANSITION LISTS   The options and outcomes of interaction can be represented using a tool from classic game theory, the outcome matrix (Luce & Raiffa 1957, Von Neumann & Morgenstern 1944). An *outcome matrix* describes interdependence patterns involving two persons (A and B), each of whom can enact either of two behaviors, yielding four combinations representing the consequences of the persons' choices in terms of outcomes for persons A and B (Kelley & Thibaut 1978). Despite their apparent simplicity, matrices are very useful descriptions of social situations, in that matrix patterns describe the intricate ways in which (and degree to which) interaction partners affect their own and one another's well-being. Of course, the matrix is a snapshot of interdependence as it exists at one time. To deal with the sequential and temporal properties of interdependence, a second formal tool was developed. A *transition list* not only represents the behavioral options and outcomes for persons A and B but also specifies the means by which they proceed from one pattern of interdependence to another (Kelley 1984b). Individuals may thus be interdependent not only in affecting one another's immediate outcomes but also in their pursuit of temporally extended goals and in their movement from one situation to another. (Note that matrices and transition lists are theoretical tools and are not intended as literal depictions of lay cognition or motivation.)

NEEDS, PREFERENCES, AND OUTCOMES   What makes specific combinations of behavior on the part of persons A and B pleasurable versus painful? Interdependence theory does not identify an overarching need or drive that fuels interpersonal behavior (e.g., reproduction, security, mastery) (Kelley & Thibaut 1985, Rusbult & Van Lange 1996). Instead, it is assumed that humans have diverse instrumental and social-emotional needs, that some are biologically based whereas others are learned, that needs cover a spectrum from survival to spirituality, and that some needs are pervasive whereas others are unique to specific situations and partners. Many needs are inherently interpersonal and can be gratified only in the context of dyads or groups (e.g., belonging, sexuality, security) (Baumeister & Leary 1995, Drigotas & Rusbult 1992, Hazan & Shaver 1994). Interactions are experienced as pleasurable to the extent that they gratify one or more important needs and are experienced as unpleasant or painful to the extent that they fail to gratify or are antithetical to important needs.

Interaction frequently yields not only concrete outcomes, or direct experiences of pleasure versus displeasure, but also symbolic outcomes, or experiences that rest on the broader implications of interaction (Holmes 1981, Kelley 1979). For example, when John and Mary disagree about where to vacation and John suggests Mary's preferred choice of Rome, Mary enjoys relatively concrete benefits—the disagreement is resolved and Mary enjoys rewards in the form of cultural stimulation, good food and wine, and the pleasure of John's company. At the same time, the fact that John accedes to Mary's preference has symbolic meaning for Mary, yielding positive affect because John has demonstrated that he loves her and is responsive to her needs. The interaction also has symbolic meaning for John, yielding positive affect because he has communicated his love, served as the agent of Mary's pleasure, and confirmed his belief that he is a caring and generous person.

DIMENSIONS OF SITUATION STRUCTURE   Matrices and transition lists provide a means to represent the ways in which interacting peoples' needs are gratified (vs. not gratified) during the course of interaction. That is, these tools allow us to analyze situation structure (Kelley et al. 2002, Kelley & Thibaut 1978). By examining the main effects and interaction of each person's possible behaviors, we can discern the impact on each person's outcomes of the person's own actions (actor control: a main effect of Mary's actions on Mary's outcomes), the partner's actions (partner control: a main effect of John's actions on Mary's outcomes), and the partners' joint actions (joint control: an interaction of John's and Mary's actions on Mary's outcomes). By examining within-cell associations between the partners' outcomes, we can discern the extent to which outcomes for actor and partner are positively correlated (corresponding interests) versus negatively correlated (conflicting interests). These basic components of influence and covariation define four properties of situation structure.

Level of dependence describes the degree to which an individual "relies on" an interaction partner, in that his outcomes are influenced by the partner's actions. Mary's dependence is greater to the degree that John can unilaterally cause her pleasure versus pain, and/or can behave in such a manner as to govern her own behavioral choice. People are independent when situations involve high mutual actor control and are interdependent when situations involve high mutual partner control, joint control, or both. Increasing dependence tends to activate increased situation- and person-relevant attention, cognition, and affect; for example, when John's outcomes are governed by Mary's actions, he is likely to dedicate considerable effort to understanding what the situation is "about" and to developing expectancies about Mary's probable behavior (Arriaga & Rusbult 1998, Fiske 1993). Moreover, because dependence constitutes reliance on a partner for fulfilling important needs, increasing dependence yields persistence in interactions and longevity in relationships (Bui et al. 1996, Drigotas & Rusbult 1992). To reduce the vulnerabilities inherent in such reliance, dependence also yields patterns of cognition and affect that quell feelings of insecurity and promote congenial interaction (e.g., positive illusion, downward comparison) (Murray et al. 1996, Rusbult et al. 2000).

Mutuality of dependence describes the degree to which two people are equally dependent on one another. The concepts of dependence and power are inextricably related, in that to the extent that one person is relatively more dependent, the partner is relatively more powerful. The vulnerability deriving from high dependence (and the power deriving from low dependence) is exacerbated to the extent that dependence is nonmutual. Accordingly, nonmutual dependence affords the expression of exploitation versus benevolence, particularly when partners' interests conflict. We noted above that high dependence reliably activates situation- and person-relevant attention, cognition, and affect, along with adaptations geared toward reducing vulnerability. When dependence is nonmutual, these processes are more pronounced for the dependent partner than for the powerful partner. Mutual dependence yields the sorts of benefits that accrue from balance of power, including more placid and positive emotional experience (less guilt, anxiety), reduced use of threat or coercion, less reliance on norms or contractual agreements, and greater stability and congeniality (Baumeister et al. 1993, Fiske 1993, Drigotas et al. 1999).

Basis of dependence describes the way partners affect one another's outcomes—whether dependence derives from partner control (Mary's outcomes are controlled by John's unilateral actions) or joint control (Mary's outcomes are controlled by the partners' joint actions). Partner control is relatively absolute and externally controlled; that is, the person's outcomes rest in the hands of the partner. Situations involving mutual partner control tend to yield adaptation in the form of exchange (tit-for-tat; "I'll scratch your back if you'll scratch mine"), tend to activate particular patterns of communication (promises, threats), and tend to be governed by morality norms (Axelrod 1984, Clark & Mills 1993, Fiske 1992). Joint control is experienced as relatively more contingent, in that the person's outcomes rest on coordination with the partner's actions. Situations involving joint control tend to yield adaptation in the form of coordination ("Follow my lead"; "You decide"), tend to activate ability-relevant traits and behaviors (problem-solving, taking the initiative), and tend to be governed by rules of conventional behavior rather than morality (Buss & Craik 1980, Fiske 1992, Turiel 1983).

Finally, *covariation of interests* describes the degree to which partners' outcomes correspond, or whether the course of action that benefits John similarly benefits Mary. Covariation varies from perfectly correspondent situations through so-called mixed-motive situations to situations with perfectly conflicting outcomes ("zero-sum"). Covariation is so fundamental to life and so thoroughly defines the possibilities for congenial interaction that humans are predisposed to develop abstract mental representations that help them quickly define whether "What's going on here" is good or bad for them. Situations with conflicting interests activate predictable thoughts and emotions (greed, fear), yield more active and differentiated cognition, information-seeking, and self-presentation ("Can Mary be trusted?"), and afford the expression of specific motives (cooperation vs. competition, trust vs. distrust) (Holmes & Murray 1996, Insko & Schopler 1998, Surra & Longstreth 1990, Van Lange 2000).

TEMPORAL STRUCTURE   Interactions and relationships are dynamic phenomena that typically mutate and evolve. Therefore, interdependence should be understood not only in terms of the immediate outcomes produced by specific combinations of behavior but also in terms of the future behaviors and outcomes that are made available (vs. eliminated) as a consequence of interaction (Kelley 1984b, Kelley et al. 2002). *Extended situations* involve a series of steps prior to reaching a specific goal (e.g., repeated "play" of the Prisoner's Dilemma Game, investment situations). While a person proceeds toward a remote goal, outcomes may change owing to fatigue or satiation, partners may have opportunities to communicate their needs and preferences, and one or both partners may act on the basis of abilities or motives that affect future options (e.g., stamina, self-control). *Situation selection* describes movement from one situation to another, bringing the individual, partner, or dyad to a situation that differs from the previous one in terms of behavioral options, outcomes, or both. Whether to attend a party, visit parents-in-law, or sit close to or far from a colleague are selections that involve entering or avoiding new situations. Situation selections are also revealed in decisions to substantially modify an existing situation, as in changing the topic of conversation.

INFORMATION   The availability of information is the sixth dimension of situation structure. Inadequate information gives rise to ambiguity and misunderstanding, challenging the flow of interaction (Kelley et al. 2002). People may hold incomplete information about (*a*) a partner's outcomes for various combinations of behavior

("How would John feel about going to the beach while I go to Rome?"), (*b*) a partner's goals and motives ("Will John be responsive to my needs?"), and/or (*c*) future interaction possibilities ("If we vacation separately, where will that 'take' our relationship?"). For example, Mary may not fully recognize how much John enjoys her company, thus underestimating the degree to which she can influence his outcomes. And if John initially agrees to vacation in Rome but later finds that he cannot do so owing to a pressing work deadline, Mary may be uncertain about the urgency of his deadline or the benevolence of his motives. Finally, neither John nor Mary may hold precise information about the interaction situations they will face in the upcoming months or more distant future.

COMBINATIONS OF DIMENSIONS   Most social situations are defined by their properties with respect to two or more structural dimensions (Kelley et al. 2002, Kelley & Thibaut 1978). For example, the defining properties of the Prisoner's Dilemma situation are strong partner control and weak actor control, the Hero situation is defined by strong joint control and weak actor control, and the Chicken situation is defined by strong partner control and weak joint control; all three situations involve moderately high mutual dependence and moderately conflicting interests. For example, the Twists of Fate situation involves incomplete information, wherein each person at some point might unexpectedly find himself in a position of extreme unilateral dependence. All possible combinations of the six dimensions define an infinite number of situations. However, a smaller number of "landmarks," or prototypical situations, can be identified (Kelley et al. 2002). Each abstract pattern embodies specific interpersonal problems and opportunities, and each logically implies the relevance of specific goals and motives. Everyday social situations resemble these abstract patterns. For example, the Prisoner's Dilemma is characteristic of interactions involving mutual sacrifice, trading favors, and free-riding; Twists of Fate is characteristic of health crises and other reversals of fortune.

IMPORTANCE OF INTERDEPENDENCE STRUCTURE   Why should we concern ourselves with situation structure? To begin with, situations often exert strong effects on behavior, relatively independently of the partners' personal goals and motives. For example, research on marital communication has identified a "demand-withdraw" pattern of interaction involving repeated demands for change made by wives, met by chronic withdrawal of husbands (Christensen & Heavey 1993, Berns et al. 1999). Arguably, this type of interaction transpires in situations resembling the Threat situation, the key properties of which are that partner A controls reward allocations to both partners, and partner B's only course of action is to deliver a threat that harms them both (Holmes & Murray 1996). Typically, men hold more power in deciding who completes household tasks, with women being dependent on their partners' fairness. If the husband is exploitative, the wife may push to discuss things, perhaps threatening to quit cooking in the meantime. It is in the husband's interests to avoid discussion, because inaction will maintain the status quo. Hoping to bring about change, the wife may voice increasingly strong complaints. Although it might be tempting to explain such behavior in terms of sex differences in abilities, dispositions, or norms, the pattern plausibly results from a specific interdependence situation wherein men act in such a manner to maintain a beneficial status quo. Cultural norms play a role in producing and sustaining the power differential, but contemporary behavior in the situation may simply reflect men's pursuit of self-interest. Thus, interaction sometimes is driven more by situation structure than by the interacting individuals' personal dispositions.

There is a second important reason to concern ourselves with situation structure: Specific situations present specific interpersonal problems and opportunities, and therefore (*a*) logically imply the relevance of specific goals and motives and (*b*) permit the expression of those goals and motives. The term *affordance* describes what a situation makes possible or may activate in interacting individuals (Gibson 1979, Holmes 2002, Kelley et al. 2002). For example, situations wherein partners do not have complete information about one another's preferences afford misunderstanding and information seeking; clearly, situations with complete information do not afford these activities (Erber & Fiske 1984, Ickes & Simpson 1997). For example, situations involving conflicting interests afford the expression of self-centeredness versus concern with collective interests and therefore inspire predictable sorts of cognition and affect (greed, fear) and invite predictable forms of attributional activity and communication ("Does John care about my welfare?"; "Trust me") (Frank et al. 1993, Van Lange & Kuhlman 1994). These sorts of psychological events are irrelevant to situations with corresponding interests. In short, "the mind has the structure it has because the world has the structure it has" (Anderson 1991, p. 428).

Interdependence Processes

TRANSFORMATION PROCESS   As noted above, abstract patterns of interaction outcomes can be formally represented using matrices or transition lists. The phrase *given situation* describes the direct and immediate, "gut level" impact of interacting individuals' combined actions on each person's outcomes. These outcomes are "given" in that they describe immediate effects on the individual, ignoring the partner's interests and ignoring long-term interaction- or relationship-relevant concerns. In a sense, given outcomes represent the "virtual structure" of the situation, or the "S" in the equation $I = f(S, A, B)$.

People sometimes behave in a manner that maximizes direct, given outcomes. This is particularly likely among children, in "simple" situations for which no broader considerations are relevant, among people who lack the inclination or wherewithal to take broader considerations into account, and in situations involving time pressure or other factors that constrain cognitive capacity (Baumeister et al. 1998, Mischel et al. 1996). However, behavioral choices are often based on considerations other than direct, gut level interests. Acting on the basis of broader concerns results from "transformation" of the given situation (see Figure 1). Transformation involves making something of the given situation and essentially frees

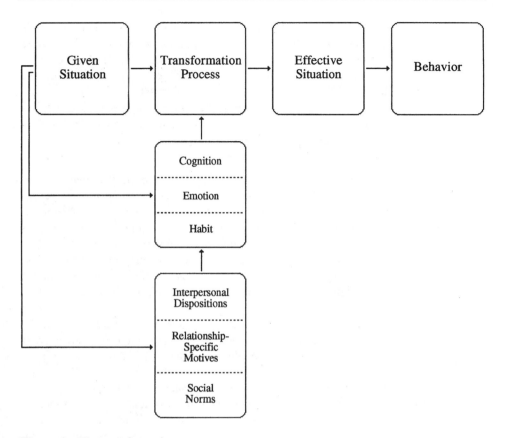

Figure 1   The transformation process.

individuals from control by the given situation, allowing them to be responsive to strategic concerns, long-term goals, or desire to influence a partner's outcomes. For example, John may behave in ways that yield poor direct outcomes because in doing so he can promote Mary's welfare, encourage future reciprocity, or enhance the quality of their relationship. Outcome values resulting from this process constitute the *effective situation*; effective preferences guide behavior. In a sense, transformation can be construed as the point at which the "rubber meets the road," or the person meets the situation, representing the "A" and "B" in the equation $I = f$ (S, A, B) (Kelley 1991).

Transformation constitutes a rule the individual adopts during interaction (Kelley & Holmes 2002, Kelley & Thibaut 1978). Some rules involve sequential or temporal considerations, such as waiting to see how the partner behaves or adopting strategies such as tit-for-tat (Axelrod 1984) or turn-taking. Other rules involve weighting one's own and a partner's outcomes, such as altruism, maximizing the partner's outcomes (MaxOther); cooperation, maximizing the partners' combined outcomes (MaxJoint); equality, minimizing the disparity between one's own and the partner's outcomes (MinDiff); competition, maximizing the relative difference between one's own and the partner's outcomes (MaxRel); and individualism, maximizing one's own outcomes irrespective of the partner's outcomes (MaxOwn) (Kelley & Thibaut 1978, Messick & McClintock 1968). Altruism, cooperation, and equality are prosocial rules; they are oriented toward benefiting another. Individualism and competition are self-interested or antisocial rules; they are oriented toward benefiting the self.

COGNITION, EMOTION, AND HABIT   Given that humans are social animals, human intelligence is highly interpersonal; we are well prepared to construe the world in terms of interdependence (Cosmides & Tooby 1992, Kelley 1997). Cognition and emotion play important roles in stimulating and directing the transformation process, being geared toward: (*a*) discerning what a given situation is "about"—recognizing that it resembles familiar patterns and identifying its key properties; (*b*) evaluating behavioral options in terms of one's own needs and motives; and (*c*) understanding the partner's needs and predicting his or her motives (Kelley 1979, 1984a).

Situation structure helps shape the content of cognition and emotion. For example, situations with the basic structure of the Prisoner's Dilemma are those wherein (*a*) each person could substantially benefit the partner at low cost to self, but (*b*) each may be tempted to benefit the self at substantial cost to the partner. This is the crux of the dilemma when deciding to make a small sacrifice on the partner's behalf or to pitch in and help on a dyadic project rather than loaf and let one's partner do the work. Issues of fear and greed come to mind in such situations ("Will Mary help or hurt me?"; "Shall I try to take a free ride?") (Insko & Schopler 1998). John is likely to exhibit self-centered or antisocial transformation to the extent that he experiences greedy thoughts and desires and to the extent that he predicts or fears that Mary cannot be trusted (Mikulincer 1998, Wieselquist et al. 1999). Thus, the mental events underlying transformation are functionally adapted to situation structure and take forms relevant to that structure.

Cognition and emotion are also colored by distal causes including interpersonal dispositions (e.g., self-control, communal orientation), relationship-specific motives (e.g., commitment, trust), and social norms ("Do unto others as you would have others do unto you") (see Figure 1). For example, competitive individuals interpret a broad range of mixed-motive situations in terms of winning versus losing and therefore attend closely to considerations of "might"—to how competent and powerful interaction partners are and to whether they appear competent and powerful to others (Van Lange 2000, Van Lange & Kuhlman 1994). In contrast, prosocial individuals interpret many situations in terms of collective goals ("Let's develop a congenial arrangement") and attend closely to considerations of fairness and trustworthiness.

Of course, the transformation process does not necessarily rest on extensive mental activity. As a result of adaptation to repeatedly encountered patterns, people develop habitual tendencies to react to specific situations in specific ways, such that transformation comes about with little or no conscious thought (Kelley 1983, Rusbult & Van Lange 1996). Whether the transformation process entails extensive mental activity rests on the degree to which (*a*) the situation is novel, with unknown or complex implications; (*b*) the situation is risky, involving the potential for harm; and (*c*) the partner is unfamiliar, so his motives are not easily predicted (Baumeister et al. 2001, Fincham 2001, Holmes 2002). For example, situations involving high dependence and conflicting interests are likely to yield more extensive analysis, particularly in "high stakes" interactions with strangers (Drigotas et al. 1999, Fiske 1993).

COMMUNICATION, ATTRIBUTION, AND SELF-PRESENTATION   During and following interaction, partners seek to communicate their abilities, motives, and dispositions using both direct and indirect means: verbally and nonverbally, via intimation, direct communication, and action. Although conclusions formed on the basis of communication typically are assumed to be cognitive (i.e., expectations, attributions), such conclusions may also be affective (e.g., person-specific affection or dread). Communication entails two related processes: self-presentation on the part of one person and attribution on the part of the other. The material for self-presentation and attribution resides in the disparity between the given and effective situations, in that deviations from self-centered choice reveal the actor's goals and motives, or "self" (Holmes 1981, Kelley 1979). Thus, possibilities for communicating self-relevant information are limited by given situation structure. For example, it is difficult to convey considerateness (or to discern it) in situations involving highly correspondent interests, in that in such situations, considerate behavior aligns with self-interested behavior.

People engage in *attributional activity* in their attempts to uncover the direct meaning and broader implications of a partner's actions, developing expectations regarding future behavior and seeking to explain prior behavior in terms of underlying dispositions (Fincham 2001, Gilbert 1998, Weiner 1985). Expectations are not particularly accurate in new relationships, as they must be based on probabilistic assumptions about how the average person would react in a given situation; in longer-term relationships, expectations can also be based on knowledge of how the partner has behaved in past situations (Kelley 1991). For example, betrayal may inspire greater distress and more negative inferences in long-term, committed relationships, in part because betrayal by a previously loyal partner constitutes a meaningful departure from well-established expectations of benevolence (Finkel et al. 2002). Of course, the attribution process is not always geared toward forming accurate inferences. Particularly in situations involving high dependence, attributional activity may be geared toward reducing doubt or uncertainty. For example, mutually dependent partners exhibit exceptionally positive interpretations of one another, translating one another's faults into virtues and engaging in downward comparison to place their relationships in a favorable light (Murray et al. 1996, Rusbult et al. 2000, Simpson et al. 2001).

Self-presentation describes individuals' attempts to communicate their abilities, motives, and dispositions to partners. Conveying that one cares for or loves another is most directly (and perhaps most convincingly) communicated by departing from one's interests in order to enhance that person's outcomes (Van Lange et al. 1997b, Wieselquist et al. 1999). Because we do not always hold complete information about our partners' given outcomes, we sometimes mistakenly assume that acts resulting from transformation of a situation reflect the partner's simple preferences. For example, John's acts of loyalty, kindness, or sacrifice may not be visible if Mary fails to recognize the costs he incurred (Drigotas et al. 1995). Indeed, self-presentation may sometimes be geared toward concealing one's true preferences and motives. Individuals may present themselves deceptively so as to invite a particular sort of attribution or to induce a particular form of interaction. For example, John may overstate his desire to vacation at the beach so as to highlight the prosocial motives that underlie his acceding to Mary's wishes. Individuals are particularly inclined to present themselves in a socially desirable light during the early stages of developing relationships (Leary 2001, Tice et al. 1995).

INTERDEPENDENCE AND INTERACTION

Conflicting Interests and Interaction

Situations with conflicting interests involve challenging problems of adaptation ("I want my way!" "Don't you care about my needs?"). This type of situation affords the expression of prosocial motives and yields self-presentation and attributional activity centering on issues of morality and benevolence. Such situations are termed *diagnostic situations*, as they reveal one's own and the partner's transformational tendencies (Holmes & Rempel 1989). For example, Mary can discern John's commitment when she recognizes that he was tempted to be sexually unfaithful but declined to do so.

In one type of diagnostic situation, through no fault of either person, the partners' preferences conflict. Such situations call for sacrifice or willingness to depart from one's immediate interests to promote the partner's interests (Van Lange et al. 1997b). For example, for Mary's sake, John may spend the weekend with his in-laws rather than watching World Cup Soccer. A second type of diagnostic situation is initiated by a partner's "bad behavior," or inconsiderate and irritating acts. Such situations call for accommodation, or inhibiting the impulse to retaliate and instead behaving in a conciliatory manner (Gottman 1998, Rusbult et al. 1991). For example, when John says something rude, Mary may simply pour herself a glass of wine and forget about the incident. A third type of diagnostic situation centers on acts of betrayal, wherein one partner departs from relationship-relevant norms and humiliates or degrades the other partner. Such situations call for forgiveness (Finkel et al. 2002, McCullough et al. 1997).

Situations involving conflicting interests share several properties. To begin with, the impulse toward reciprocity is powerful, particularly for negative reciprocity

(Epstein et al. 1993, Gottman 1998). Given that one's immediate impulse in such situations frequently is self-centered or destructive, prosocial reactions require transformation of the given situation. For example, when people confront accommodative dilemmas and are allowed either limited or plentiful reaction time, those given limited time exhibit more destructive behavior; those given plentiful time for the transformation process are more likely to accommodate (Yovetich & Rusbult 1994). What helps people control the impulse to retaliate and instead exhibit prosocial transformation and behavior? Acts such as accommodation, sacrifice, and forgiveness are promoted by strong commitment, a variable that embodies concern for the interests of the partner and the relationship (Finkel et al. 2002, Rusbult et al. 1991, Van Lange et al. 1997b). Prosocial motives and acts are also more probable among individuals with greater self-control, more secure attachment, greater psychological femininity, and stronger perspective-taking tendencies (Arriaga & Rusbult 1998, Finkel & Campbell 2001, Gaines et al. 1997, McCullough et al. 1997, Rusbult et al. 1991). Moreover, patterns of mutual prosocial behavior appear to represent good adaptation, in that they yield greater couple adjustment and longevity (Carstensen et al. 1995, Van Lange et al. 1997b).

Dependence and Interaction

To understand the implications of dependence, it is helpful to recognize that dependence situations involve "needing" or "relying on" another: Dependence implies vulnerability. When Mary's well-being rests in John's hands, there is no guarantee that he will employ his power in a prosocial manner. The dangers of dependence are enhanced to the extent that dependence is unilateral, involves conflicting interests, or both. [Social psychologists are at least implicitly aware of this situation-defined "hot zone"; many interaction phenomena are examined in situations involving nonmutual dependence (infant behavior in the "strange situation", adult behavior in support-seeking or self-disclosure situations) or conflicting interests (behavior during arguments or following transgressions).]

Dependence situations afford the expression of comfort with (vs. avoidance of) interdependence. When dependence is nonmutual and involves at least moderately conflicting interests, the less dependent partner must decide whether to pursue self-interest or the partner's interests, and the more dependent partner will be particularly oriented toward detecting signs of partner responsiveness. Accordingly, dependence situations are highly diagnostic. For example, John can discern that Mary is trustworthy when she reacts to his dependence in a responsive and prosocial manner, declining to take advantage of her power. Mary can discern that John is dispositionally insecure when he reacts to his dependence with "excessive" anxiety—anxiety that is unwarranted by their history of mutual responsiveness.

Research regarding abusive relationships reveals that people are more likely to remain in such relationships and endure continued abuse to the extent that they are relatively more dependent—when they have high investments (children, shared history) and poor alternatives (low education, little job training) (Johnson 1995,

Rusbult & Martz 1995). Although it might be tempting to explain such behavior in terms of personal dispositions (learned helplessness, low self-esteem), the tendency to persist in a troubled relationship plausibly results from situation-based entrapment—because one has "too much invested" and there is "nowhere to go." Likewise, research regarding the principle of least interest demonstrates that the partner who is less dependent in a relationship tends to "call the shots," exerting control over desired resources; the more dependent partner has less say in decision making, carries the greater burden of interaction costs (is more likely to accommodate, sacrifice), and is more vulnerable to possible abandonment (Attridge et al. 1995, Drigotas et al. 1999, Witcher 1999).

Research regarding attachment processes also illuminates our understanding of dependence situations, in that issues of dependence and security are at the heart of attachment concerns. The adult attachment literature suggests that the intrapersonal and interpersonal adaptations acquired in childhood are carried into adult interactions. For example, securely attached individuals perceive a wide range of dependence situations as safe, experience more positive cognition and affect in such situations, exhibit more trusting expectations about their partners, enact fewer exploitative behaviors, and adopt more constructive strategies in adapting to violations of trust (Baldwin et al. 1996, Mikulincer 1998, Simpson et al. 1996, Tidwell et al. 1996). Insecurely attached individuals exhibit distrustful and destructive cognitive, motivational, and behavioral tendencies not only when they are the more dependent persons in an interaction but also when their partners depend on them. Consistent with the interdependence principle that dependence situations afford attachment-relevant issues, the liabilities of insecure, rejecting, and unresponsive behavior are particularly pronounced when interdependence structure is most problematic—in situations involving nonmutual dependence and conflicting interests (Pietromonaco & Barrett 1997, Simpson et al. 1996): The more problematic the dependence situation, the more attachment concerns arise.

Research regarding rejection sensitivity further enriches our understanding of dependence situations, illuminating the process by which expectancies operate in extended situations (Downey & Feldman 1996, Downey et al. 1998): Women with greater sensitivity to the possibility of rejection develop fearful expectancies regarding partner behavior and exhibit antisocial transformation tendencies: They anxiously expect and readily perceive negativity from their partners and overreact to signs of exploitation, behaving in a provocative and destructive manner during conflicted interaction. Their male partners respond with elevated anger and reciprocal destructiveness, thereby confirming the women's worst fears. As a consequence of such maladaptive interaction, the relationships of rejection-sensitive women exhibit poor adjustment and are more likely to terminate. In contrast, more adaptive patterns of interaction are evident among partners who are less sensitive to the possibility of rejection and who therefore exhibit prosocial expectations and transformations, enacting responsive behaviors and trusting that the partner will reciprocate.

Work on intimacy processes is also relevant to discussions of dependence, in that when individuals disclose self-relevant information, they make themselves vulnerable to possible rejection or exploitation. In such situations, individuals confront a tradeoff between the benefits of disclosure and the risks of exploitation. Individuals display trust when they disclose, placing themselves in a dependent position (Omarzu 2000, Reis & Patrick 1996). When partners exhibit prosocial motives and do not exploit this vulnerability—exhibiting understanding, caring, and acceptance—relationships become more trusting, reciprocal disclosure is elicited, and mutual attraction is enhanced (Collins & Miller 1994, Laurenceau et al. 1998). The vulnerabilities of disclosure are reduced to the extent that dependence is rendered mutual—and, therefore, safe—by reciprocal disclosure (Collins & Miller 1994, Laurenceau et al. 1998). Because of the vulnerabilities inherent in intimacy situations, this sort of dependence is regulated by norms. For example, partners tend to disclose at roughly equal levels of intimacy (it is rude to respond to a tearful confession of drug addition with "nice weather we've been having") and regard it as unacceptable to transmit a close partner's secret to a nonclose third party (Mary can tell John about a colleague's drug addition but should not transmit such information to her masseuse) (Reis & Patrick 1996, Yovetich & Drigotas 1999).

Information and Interaction

Partners engage in considerable information exchange during the early stages of developing relationships. Such exchanges serve a variety of functions, including communicating each person's given outcomes, predicting the partner's goals and motives, and forecasting future interactions. Early information exchange is guided by rules. As noted earlier, reciprocal displays of intimacy are normative, and such exchanges enhance liking (Collins & Miller 1994, Reis & Patrick 1996). Importantly, the impact of intimate exchange on liking extends beyond the impact of information per se, in that effects on liking are more pronounced for the interaction partner than for a third party who obtains parallel information (Insko & Wilson 1977).

In interactions with strangers, people often rely on heuristic, probabilistic assumptions, sometimes in an automatic and unconscious manner. Individuals hold distinct and chronically accessible mental representations of "significant others" and frequently use these representations as templates for interaction with unfamiliar partners (Andersen & Baum 1994, Andersen et al. 1996). When a new partner exhibits traits possessed by a significant other, individuals frequently respond to the person in a manner that mirrors responses to the significant other. A variety of interaction processes—including memory for traits, liking, and facial affect—are influenced by subtle activation of a significant-other representation. Thus, representations of partners with whom one has a history are easily evoked, activated, and applied to new partners: People fill in the informational gaps using their interdependence histories.

Uncertainty regarding a partner's motives is especially pronounced in situations that are prone to misimplementation of action and miscommunication. Misunderstanding is often rooted in *noise*, or discrepancies between the outcomes partner A intends to produce and the outcomes partner B experiences (Axelrod & Dion 1988, Van Lange et al. 2002). For example, in response to Mary's e-mailed request for assistance, John may attempt to offer help that she fails to receive owing to a local network breakdown. The presence of noise—particularly negative noise, when actual outcomes are poorer than intended outcomes—exerts harmful effects on interaction, yielding reduced mutual cooperation. When Mary suffers negative outcomes that she mistakenly attributes to John's lack of responsiveness, she may react with irritation or hostility, which may prompt reciprocal hostility from John, producing a chain of negative reciprocity that harms them both. Such detrimental effects are attenuated when individuals forego strict tit-for-tat and instead give their partners the benefit of the doubt by behaving in a generous manner (i.e., withholding judgment or exhibiting somewhat greater cooperation than the partner).

Situation Selection

Relationships unfold over time via situation selection, which may entail seeking (vs. avoiding) interdependence, locating situations with correspondent (vs. conflicting) interests, or moving toward situations with greater (vs. lesser) information. Individuals may initiate movement into a new situation via behavioral prompts (e.g., a "no strings attached" prosocial act), direct communication (e.g., self-disclosure, proposals regarding interaction), or nonverbal acts (e.g., gaze, tone of voice, smiling).

The seeking of psychological support is an important form of unilateral situation selection. Securely attached individuals are more willing to place themselves in positions of dependence so as to obtain support from their partners, openly discussing their fears and anxieties, inviting physical contact, and exhibiting trusting expectations of partner responsiveness; anxiously attached individuals "pull away" from their partners when stressed (Collins & Feeney 2000, Simpson et al. 1992). In reacting to the support-seeker's anxieties, securely attached partners are highly responsive and readily provide support; anxiously attached partners react with verbal and nonverbal avoidance. This work illustrates the benefits of examining temporally extended situations and demonstrates the importance of examining both "A" and "B" in the equation $I = f(S, A, B)$ (see Introduction): Through the selection of situations and the response to such selections, both partners' tendencies shape the course of extended interaction.

Situation selection is also relevant to the juncture between a relationship and possible alternative relationships. Research on reactions to tempting alternatives reveals that committed individuals deal with tempting junctures by cognitively derogating potential alternative partners ("I bet he has no sense of humor") (Johnson & Rusbult 1989). Moreover, using such defensive cognitive maneuvers to hold temptation at bay appears to be a motivated process, in that the association of commitment with derogation is stronger when temptation is greater—when the alternative is attractive and highly "available." Recent work suggests that committed individuals also forego tempting alternative situations via relatively more automatic perceptual processes—by literally spending less time looking at alternatives (Miller 1997).

STABLE PATTERNS OF ADAPTATION

Individuals initially react to specific situations as unique problems. In a novel situation, John may either systematically analyze the situation or react in an impulsive manner. If his reaction yields poor outcomes, John will behave differently in future situations with parallel structure; if his reaction yields good outcomes, he will react similarly in future, parallel situations. Repeated experience in situations with similar structure gives rise to habitual response patterns, or stable adaptations that on average yield good outcomes (Kelley 1983, Rusbult & Van Lange 1996). Adaptations may reside within persons, relationships, or groups. For example, John may adopt a communal interaction orientation due to interpersonal dispositions that guide his behavior across multiple partners, relationship-specific motives that guide his behavior with Mary, or norms deriving from relevant social sources (Clark & Mills 1993).

Interpersonal Dispositions

Interpersonal dispositions are actor-specific inclinations to respond to particular situations in a specific manner across numerous partners (Kelley 1983). Dispositions emerge because over the course of development, different people experience different interdependence histories, undergoing different experiences with parents and siblings and confronting different problems and opportunities in peer interaction. As a result of adaptation, people acquire dispositions that are reflected in the manner in which they approach specific situations. They develop tendencies to perceive situations in specific ways, to predict specific sorts of motives on the part of interaction partners, and to apply transformations to situations with greater or lesser probability. At least in part, the "interpersonal self" can be construed as the sum of one's adaptations to previous interdependence problems.

For example, children's experiences with parents form the basis for attachment style. Attachment theory focuses on the degree to which caregivers benevolently use their power, offering comfort when the child is in need and serving as a secure base from which the child can explore (Bowlby 1969). Children treated in such a responsive manner develop healthy adaptations, or trusting and secure expectations regarding dependence situations and partners; to the degree that caregiving is unresponsive or exploitative, children develop anxious and fearful expectations regarding dependence, or come to avoid situations in which they need and rely on others (Ainsworth et al. 1978). Later in life secure individuals perceive dependence situations as safe, anticipate prosocial partner motives, and create opportunities for partners to safely seek intimacy; avoidant individuals perceive dependence situations as dangerous and resolve such dilemmas by exploiting their partners or avoiding dependence; anxious-ambivalent individuals experience inconsistent dependence histories and therefore are erratic, alternating between grasping at that which they most desire and cautiously avoiding the risks of dependence (Collins & Feeney 2000, Hazan & Shaver 1994, Simpson et al. 1992).

The functioning of dispositions is also illustrated in work on social value orientations. Given the opportunity to distribute outcomes to themselves and others, some people consistently select options resting on MaxOwn motives (individualism), whereas others are oriented toward distributions of the MaxJoint/MinDiff variety (cooperation) or MaxRel variety (competition). Social value orientations are established and change as a consequence of interdependence experiences. For example, cooperatively oriented individuals are more likely to have had female siblings during childhood, and as individuals grow older, they become more cooperatively oriented (Van Lange et al. 1997a). Social value orientations are associated with distinct patterns of belief regarding others' motives and are reflected in the probability with which transformations are applied to given situations (Messick & McClintock 1968, Van Lange 1999). For example, competitors perceive a wide range of situations as "competitive," believe that others have equally competitive motives, and are unwilling to cooperate even when doing so would maximize their outcomes. As a consequence, they frequently elicit competitive behavior from others, thereby confirming their beliefs about interaction partners ("I'm facing a hostile opponent in a risky situation") and reinforcing their competitive tendencies ("I need to take care of myself").

Relationship-Specific Motives

Relationship-specific motives are inclinations to respond to particular situations in a specific manner with a specific partner (Holmes 1981). For example, commitment emerges as a consequence of dependence on a specific partner and thus is strengthened as a result of high satisfaction, poor alternatives, and high investments (Rusbult et al. 2001). Commitment colors emotional reactions to challenging interaction situations (feeling affection rather than anger when a partner is neglectful) and gives rise to habits of thought that support the decision to persist (use of plural pronouns, positive illusion, derogation of alternatives) (Agnew et al. 1998, Johnson & Rusbult 1989, Rusbult et al. 2000). In turn, benevolent thoughts and feelings promote prosocial transformation, especially in situations of moderate to high correspondence. For example, commitment level predicts prosocial acts such as sacrifice, accommodation, and forgiveness (Finkel et al. 2002, Rusbult et al. 1991, Van Lange et al. 1997b).

In a complementary manner, trust reflects an individual's confidence in the partner's prosocial motives (Holmes & Rempel 1989). Mary develops trust when John behaves prosocially in diagnostic situations, departing from his direct self-interest to promote her interests. His prosocial acts communicate responsiveness to Mary's needs, thereby increasing Mary's trust in his benevolent intentions, increasing her willingness to become dependent, strengthening her commitment, and increasing the odds that she will enact reciprocal prosocial acts (Wieselquist et al. 1999). Thus, behaviors such as accommodation and sacrifice ultimately produce a pattern of mutual cyclical growth, whereby each person's prosocial motives and acts strengthen the other's confidence in the person's trustworthiness, yielding reciprocal prosocial motives and acts.

Social Norms

Social norms are rule-based, socially transmitted inclinations to respond to particular interdependence situations in a specific manner (Thibaut & Kelley 1959). For example, most societies develop rules regarding the expression of anger; such rules help groups avoid the chaos that would ensue if individuals were to freely express hostility. Likewise, rules of civility and etiquette represent efficient solutions to interdependence dilemmas, regulating behavior to yield harmonious interaction.

Long-term partners develop relationship-specific norms to solve interdependence problems. For example, although the temptation to become involved with alternative partners may be acute, the costs of doing so are equally acute. Therefore, most couples comply with existing norms or develop their own norms to govern extra-relationship involvement (Buunk 1987). Similarly, partners adopt rules governing the distribution of resources, adhering to distribution rules such as equity, equality, or need, and experiencing discomfort when these standards are violated (Walster et al. 1978). Many allocation rules are relationship-specific. For example, in parent-child or other communal relationships, the norms guiding behavior are need-based rather than contribution-based (Clark & Mills 1993, Fiske 1992). Thus, normative adaptations, too, regulate interaction by promoting specific sorts of expectation about partners' motives and by prompting specific sorts of motives and behavior in response to specific interdependence patterns.

CONCLUSIONS

Interdependence theory offers a relatively comprehensive analysis of exceptionally complex phenomena: interaction and relationships. Thus, it is not surprising that some aspects of the theory call for further development. We identify two broad areas for future work: First, interdependence theory is an abstract, comprehensive theory. It seeks to illuminate intricate issues and is rooted in and extends complex theories such as game theory, social exchange theory, and social learning theory. As such, the theory may be regarded as a school of thought that provides the concepts, logic, and tools for analyzing, predicting, and explaining interaction and relationships. The theory thus stands as an open invitation to new applications and novel operational definitions.

Second, several new topics have recently been added to the theory (Holmes 2002, Kelley & Holmes 2002, Kelley et al. 2002). For example, contemporary formulations emphasize issues regarding expectancies, information availability, and situation selection. These extensions increase the challenge of understanding cognition, motivation, and the dynamics of interaction and call for further theoretical and empirical attention.

Several strengths of the theory are also noteworthy. One concerns the theory's taxonomic characterization of situations, which provides the field with a much-needed typology of interpersonal situations. To fully understand interaction we must begin by analyzing precisely what a situation affords—the sorts of cognition and affect that are probable, the dispositions, motives, and norms that are activated, and the interpersonal processes that are relevant to interaction. Interdependence theory provides such an analysis.

The transformation concept is a second notable strength, illuminating the significance of departures from direct self-interest. Because interdependence structure in some sense is "real," it exerts meaningful effects on interaction and ultimately makes itself known. Indeed, departures from that which is dictated by given structure forms the basis for attribution and self-presentation. Thus, the transformation concept stands in contrast to prevailing models of rational self-interest, providing a solution to the traditional person-situation problem in psychology.

The theory also serves as one of the few comprehensive analyses of cognition, motivation, and behavior in long-term relationships. Long-term involvements are ideal labs for studying social psychological processes, precisely because they include numerous problematic interactions and are therefore highly diagnostic of human cognition and motivation. The theory thus complements and extends other prominent orientations, including attachment theory and evolutionary theory.

A final strength of the theory lies in its potential for integrating such diverse subfields as close relationships, prosocial behavior, and intergroup behavior. Across subfields researchers employ differing methods, although they frequently examine structurally parallel situations. Interdependence theory eliminates artificial distinctions among subfields via its emphasis on underlying, abstract situation structure, as well as by identifying the intrapersonal and interpersonal processes that reliably emerge from specific patterns of interdependence. As such, interdependence theory stands as an overarching model of social psychological structure and process. We hope that this paper helps convey the comprehensiveness and utility of interdependence theory, as well as its status as a truly social psychological theory of interactions and relationships.

ACKNOWLEDGMENTS

The authors thank Harold Kelley and Susan Fiske for their comments on an earlier draft of this paper.

The *Annual Review of Psychology* is online at http://psych.annualreviews.org

LITERATURE CITED

Agnew CR, Van Lange PAM, Rusbult CE, Langston CA. 1998. Cognitive interdependence: commitment and the mental representation of close relationships. *J. Personal. Soc. Psychol.* 74:939–54

Ainsworth M, Blehar MC, Waters E, Wall S. 1978. *Patterns of Attachment*. Hillsdale, NJ: Erlbaum. 391 pp.

Andersen SM, Baum AB. 1994. Transference in interpersonal relations: inferences and affect based on significant-other representations. *J. Personal.* 62:460–97

Andersen SM, Reznik I, Manzella LM. 1996. Eliciting facial affect, motivation, and expectancies in transference: significant other representations in social relations. *J. Personal. Soc. Psychol.* 71:1108–29

Anderson JR. 1991. The adaptive nature of human categorization. *Psychol. Rev.* 98:409–29

Arriaga XB, Rusbult CE. 1998. Standing in my partner's shoes: Partner perspective-taking and reactions to accommodative dilemmas. *Personal. Soc. Psychol. Bull.* 9:927–48

Attridge M, Berscheid E, Simpson JA. 1995. Predicting relationship stability from both partners versus one. *J. Personal. Soc. Psychol.* 69:254–68

Axelrod R. 1984. *The Evolution of Cooperation*. New York: Basic Books. 241 pp.

Axelrod R, Dion D. 1988. The further evolution of cooperation. *Science* 242:1385–90

Baldwin MW, Keelan JPR, Fehr B, Enns V, Koh-Rangarajoo E. 1996. Social-cognitive conceptualization of attachment working models: availability and accessibility effects. *J. Personal. Soc. Psychol.* 71:94–109

Baumeister RF, Bratslavsky E, Finkenauer C, Vohs KD. 2001. Bad is stronger than good. *Rev. Gen. Psychol.* 5:323–70

Baumeister RF, Bratslavsky E, Muraven M, Tice DM. 1998. Ego depletion: Is the active self a limited resource? *J. Personal. Soc. Psychol.* 74:1252–65

Baumeister RF, Leary MR. 1995. The need to belong: Desire for interpersonal attachments as a fundamental human motivation. *Psychol. Bull.* 117:497–529

Baumeister RF, Wotman SR, Stillwell AM. 1993. Unrequited love: On heartbreak, anger, guilt, scriptlessness, and humiliation. *J. Personal. Soc. Psychol.* 64:377–94

Berns SB, Jacobson NS, Gottman JM. 1999. Demand–withdraw interaction in couples with a violent husband. *J. Consult. Clin. Psychol.* 67:666–74

Bowlby J. 1969. *Attachment and Loss*. New York: Basic Books. 401 pp.

Bui KT, Peplau LA, Hill CT. 1996. Testing the Rusbult model of relationship commitment and stability in a 15–year study of heterosexual couples. *Personal. Soc. Psychol. Bull.* 22:1244–57

Buss DM, Craik KH. 1980. The frequency concept of disposition: dominance and prototypically dominant acts. *J. Personal.* 48:379–92

Buunk B. 1987. Conditions that promote breakups as a consequence of extradyadic involvements. *J. Soc. Clin. Psychol.* 5:271–84

Carstensen LL, Gottman JM, Levenson RW. 1995. Emotional behavior in long-term marriage. *Psychol. Aging* 10:140–49

Christensen A, Heavey CL. 1993. Gender differences in marital conflict: the demand/withdraw interaction pattern. In *Gender Issues in Contemporary Society*, ed. S Oskamp, M Costanzo, pp. 113–41. Newbury Park, CA: Sage. 234 pp.

Clark MS, Mills J. 1993. The difference between communal and exchange relationships: What it is and is not. *Personal. Soc. Psychol. Bull.* 19:684–91

Collins NL, Feeney BC. 2000. A safe haven: an attachment theory perspective on support seeking and caregiving in intimate relationships. *J. Personal. Soc. Psychol.* 78:1053–73

Collins NL, Miller LC. 1994. Self-disclosure and liking: a meta-analytic review. *Psychol. Bull.* 116:457–75

Cosmides L, Tooby J. 1992. Cognitive adaptations for social exchange. In *The Adapted Mind*, ed. JH Barkow, L Cosmides, J Tooby, pp. 163–228. New York: Oxford. 666 pp.

Downey G, Feldman SI. 1996. Implications of rejection sensitivity for intimate relationships. *J. Personal. Soc. Psychol.* 70:1327–43

Downey G, Freitas A, Michaelis B, Khouri H. 1998. The self-fulfilling prophecy in close relationships: rejection sensitivity and rejection by romantic partners. *J. Personal. Soc. Psychol.* 75:545–60

Drigotas SM, Rusbult CE. 1992. Should I stay or should I go?: a dependence model of breakups. *J. Personal. Soc. Psychol.* 62:62–87

Drigotas SM, Rusbult CE, Verette J. 1999. Level of commitment, mutuality of commitment, and couple well-being. *Pers. Relat.* 6:389–409

Drigotas SM, Whitney GA, Rusbult CE. 1995. On the peculiarities of loyalty: a diary study of responses to dissatisfaction in everyday life. *Personal. Soc. Psychol. Bull.* 21:596–609

Epstein N, Baucom DH, Rankin LA. 1993. Treatment of marital conflict: a cognitive-behavioral approach. *Clin. Psychol. Rev.* 13:45–57

Erber R, Fiske ST. 1984. Outcome dependence and attention to inconsistent information. *J. Personal. Soc. Psychol.* 47:709–26

Fincham FD. 2001. Attributions in close relationships: from Balkanization to integration. See Fletcher & Clark 2001, pp. 3–31

Finkel EJ, Campbell WK. 2001. Self-control and accommodation in close relationships: an interdependence analysis. *J. Personal. Soc. Psychol.* 81:263–77

Finkel EJ, Rusbult CE, Kumashiro M, Hannon PA. 2002. Dealing with betrayal in close relationships: Does commitment promote forgiveness? *J. Personal. Soc. Psychol.* 82:956–74

Fiske AP. 1992. The four elementary forms of sociality: framework for a unified theory of social relations. *Psychol. Rev.* 99:689–723

Fiske ST. 1993. Controlling other people: the impact of power on stereotyping. *Am. Psychol.* 48:621–28

Fletcher GJO, Clark MS, eds. 2001. *Blackwell Handbook of Social Psychology*. Oxford: Blackwell. 619 pp.

Frank RH, Gilovich T, Regan DT. 1993. The evolution of one-shot cooperation: an experiment. *Ethol. Sociobiol.* 14:247–56

Gaines SO, Reis HT, Summers S, Rusbult CE, Cox C, et al. 1997. Impact of attachment style on reactions to accommodative dilemmas in close relationships. *Pers. Relat.* 4:93–113

Gibson JJ. 1979. *The Ecological Approach to Visual Perception*. Boston, MA: Houghton Mifflin. 332 pp.

Gilbert DT. 1998. Ordinary personology. In *Handbook of Social Psychology*, ed. DT Gilbert, ST Fiske, G Lindzey, 2:89–150. Boston, MA: McGraw-Hill. 1085 pp.

Gottman JM. 1998. Psychology and the study of marital processes. *Annu. Rev. Psychol.* 49:169–97

Hazan C, Shaver PR. 1994. Attachment as an organizational framework for research on close relationships. *Psychol. Inq.* 5:1–22

Higgins ET, Kruglanski AW, eds. 1996. *Social Psychology: Handbook of Basic Principles*. New York: Guilford. 948 pp.

Holmes JG. 1981. The exchange process in close relationships: microbehavior and macromotives. In *The Justice Motive in Social Behavior*, ed. MJ Lerner, SC Lerner, pp. 261–84. New York: Plenum. 494 pp.

Holmes JG. 2002. Interpersonal expectations as the building blocks of social cognition: an interdependence theory perspective. *Pers. Relat.* 9:1–26

Holmes JG, Murray SL. 1996. Conflict in close relationships. In *Social Psychology: Handbook of Basic Principles*, ed. ET Higgins, AW Kruglanski, pp. 622–54. New York: Guilford. 948 pp.

Holmes JG, Rempel JK. 1989. Trust in close relationships. In *Review of Personality and Social Psychology*, ed. C Hendrick, 10:187–220. London: Sage. 270 pp.

Ickes W, Simpson JA. 1997. Managing empathic accuracy in close relationships. In

Empathic Accuracy, ed. W Ickes, pp. 218–50. New York: Guilford. 352 pp.

Insko CA, Schopler J. 1998. Differential distrust of groups and individuals. In *Intergroup Cognition and Intergroup Behavior*, ed. C Sedikides, J Schopler, CA Insko, pp. 75–107. Hillsdale, NJ: Erlbaum. 468 pp.

Insko CA, Wilson M. 1977. Interpersonal attraction as a function of social interaction. *J. Personal. Soc. Psychol.* 35:903–11

Johnson DJ, Rusbult CE. 1989. Resisting temptation: devaluation of alternative partners as a means of maintaining commitment in close relationships. *J. Personal. Soc. Psychol.* 57:967–80

Johnson MP. 1995. Patriarchal terrorism and common couple violence: two forms of violence against women. *J. Marriage Fam.* 57: 283–94

Kelley HH. 1979. *Personal Relationships*. Hillsdale, NJ: Erlbaum. 183 pp.

Kelley HH. 1983. The situational origins of human tendencies: a further reason for the formal analysis of structures. *Personal. Soc. Psychol. Bull.* 9:8–30

Kelley HH. 1984a. Affect in interpersonal relations. In *Review of Personality and Social Psychology*, ed. P Shaver, 5:89–115. Newbury Park, CA: Sage. 312 pp.

Kelley HH. 1984b. The theoretical description of interdependence by means of transition lists. *J. Personal. Soc. Psychol.* 47:956–82

Kelley HH. 1991. Lewin, situations, and interdependence. *J. Soc. Issues* 47(2):211–33

Kelley HH. 1997. The "stimulus field" for interpersonal phenomena: the source of language and thought about interpersonal events. *Personal. Soc. Psychol. Rev.* 1:140–69

Kelley HH, Holmes JG. 2002. *Interdependence Theory: Situations, Relationships, and Personality*. In preparation

Kelley HH, Holmes JG, Kerr NL, Reis HT, Rusbult CE, Van Lange PAM. 2002. *An Atlas of Interpersonal Situations*. New York: Cambridge Univ. Press. In press

Kelley HH, Thibaut JW. 1978. *Interpersonal Relations*. New York: Wiley. 341 pp.

Kelley HH, Thibaut JW. 1985. Self-interest, science, and cynicism. *J. Soc. Clin. Psychol.* 3: 26–32

Laurenceau JP, Barrett LF, Pietromonaco PR. 1998. Intimacy as an interpersonal process: the importance of self-disclosure, partner disclosure, and perceived partner responsiveness in interpersonal exchanges. *J. Personal. Soc. Psychol.* 74:1238–51

Leary MR. 2001. The self we know and the self we show: self-esteem, self-presentation, and the maintenance of interpersonal relationships. See Fletcher & Clark 2001, pp. 457–77

Lewin K. 1936. *Principles of Topological Psychology*. New York: McGraw-Hill. 231 pp.

Luce RD, Raiffa H. 1957. *Games and Decisions*. New York: Wiley. 509 pp.

McCullough ME, Worthington EL Jr, Rachal KC. 1997. Interpersonal forgiving in close relationships. *J. Personal. Soc. Psychol.* 73: 321–36

Messick DM, McClintock CG. 1968. Motivational basis of choice in experimental games. *J. Exp. Soc. Psychol.* 4:1–25

Mikulincer M. 1998. Attachment working models and the sense of trust: an exploration of interaction goals and affect regulation. *J. Personal. Soc. Psychol.* 74:1209–24

Miller RS. 1997. Inattentive and contented: relationship commitment and attention to alternatives. *J. Personal. Soc. Psychol.* 73:758–66

Mischel W, Cantor N, Feldman S. 1996. Principles of self-regulation: the nature of willpower and self-control. See Higgins & Kruglanski 1996, pp. 329–60

Murray SL, Holmes JG, Griffin DW. 1996. The benefits of positive illusions: idealization and the construction of satisfaction in close relationships. *J. Personal. Soc. Psychol.* 70:79–98

Omarzu J. 2000. A disclosure decision model: determining how and when individuals will self-disclose. *Personal. Soc. Psychol. Rev.* 4:174–85

Pietromonaco PR, Barrett LF. 1997. Working models of attachment and daily social

interactions. *J. Personal. Soc. Psychol.* 73:
1409–23

Reis HT, Patrick BC. 1996. Attachment and intimacy: component processes. See Higgins & Kruglanski 1996, pp. 523–63

Rusbult CE, Martz JM. 1995. Remaining in an abusive relationship: an investment model analysis of nonvoluntary commitment. *Personal. Soc. Psychol. Bull.* 21:558–71

Rusbult CE, Olsen N, Davis JL, Hannon P. 2001. Commitment and relationship maintenance mechanisms. In *Close Romantic Relationships*, ed. JH Harvey, A Wenzel, pp. 87–113. Mahwah, NJ: Erlbaum. 400 pp.

Rusbult CE, Van Lange PAM. 1996. Interdependence processes. See Higgins & Kruglanski 1996, pp. 564–96

Rusbult CE, Van Lange PAM, Wildschut T, Yovetich NA, Verette J. 2000. Perceived superiority in close relationships: why it exists and persists. *J. Personal. Soc. Psychol.* 79:521–45

Rusbult CE, Verette J, Whitney GA, Slovik LF, Lipkus I. 1991. Accommodation processes in close relationships: theory and preliminary empirical evidence. *J. Personal. Soc. Psychol.* 60:53–78

Simpson JA, Fletcher GJO, Campbell L. 2001. The structure and function of ideal standards in close relationships. See Fletcher & Clark 2001, pp. 86–106

Simpson JA, Rholes WS, Nelligan JS. 1992. Support seeking and support giving within couples in an anxiety-provoking situation: the role of attachment styles. *J. Personal. Soc. Psychol.* 62:434–46

Simpson JA, Rholes WS, Phillips D. 1996. Conflict in close relationships: an attachment perspective. *J. Personal. Soc. Psychol.* 71:899–914

Surra CA, Longstreth M. 1990. Similarity of outcomes, interdependence, and conflict in dating relationships. *J. Personal. Soc. Psychol.* 59:501–16

Thibaut JW, Kelley HH. 1959. *The Social Psychology of Groups.* New York: Wiley. 313 pp.

Tice DM, Butler JL, Muraven MB, Stillwell AM. 1995. When modesty prevails: differential favorability of self-presentation to friends and strangers. *J. Personal. Soc. Psychol.* 69:1120–38

Tidwell MCO, Reis HT, Shaver PR. 1996. Attachment, attractiveness, and social interaction: a diary study. *J. Personal. Soc. Psychol.* 71:729–45

Turiel E. 1983. *The Development of Social Knowledge.* Cambridge: Cambridge Univ. Press. 240 pp.

Van Lange PAM. 1999. The pursuit of joint outcomes and equality in outcomes: an integrative model of social value orientation. *J. Personal. Soc. Psychol.* 77:337–49

Van Lange PAM. 2000. Beyond self-interest: a set of propositions relevant to interpersonal orientations. *Eur. Rev. Soc. Psychol.* 11:297–330

Van Lange PAM, Kuhlman DM. 1994. Social value orientations and impressions of a partner's honesty and intelligence: a test of the might versus morality effect. *J. Personal. Soc. Psychol.* 67:126–41

Van Lange PAM, Otten W, DeBruin EMN, Joireman JA. 1997a. Development of prosocial, individualistic, and competitive orientations: theory and preliminary evidence. *J. Personal. Soc. Psychol.* 73:733–46

Van Lange PAM, Ouwerkerk JW, Tazelaar MJA. 2002. How to overcome the detrimental effects of noise in social interaction: the benefits of generosity. *J. Personal. Soc. Psychol.* 82:768–80

Van Lange PAM, Rusbult CE, Drigotas SM, Arriaga XB, Witcher BS, et al. 1997b. Willingness to sacrifice in close relationships. *J. Personal. Soc. Psychol.* 72:1373–95

Von Neumann J, Morgenstern O. 1944. *Theory of Games and Economic Behavior.* Princeton, NJ: Princeton Univ. Press. 625 pp.

Walster E, Walster GW, Berscheid E. 1978. *Equity.* Boston, MA: Allyn & Bacon

Weiner B. 1985. "Spontaneous" causal thinking. *Psychol. Bull.* 97:74–84

Wieselquist J, Rusbult CE, Foster CA, Agnew CR. 1999. Commitment, pro-relationship behavior, and trust in close relationships. *J. Personal. Soc. Psychol.* 77:942–66

Witcher BS. 1999. *The effects of power on relationships and on individuals*. PhD thesis. Univ. NC, Chapel Hill

Yovetich NA, Drigotas SM. 1999. Secret transmission: a relative intimacy hypothesis. *Personal. Soc. Psychol. Bull.* 25:1135–46

Yovetich NA, Rusbult CE. 1994. Accommodative behavior in close relationships: exploring transformation of motivation. *J. Exp. Soc. Psychol.* 30:138–64

Annu. Rev. Psychol. 2003. 54:377–402
doi: 10.1146/annurev.psych.54.101601.145024
First published online as a Review in Advance on August 6, 2002

THE PSYCHOLOGY OF RELIGION

Robert A. Emmons[1] and Raymond F. Paloutzian[2]

[1]Department of Psychology, University of California, Davis, Davis, California 95616;
e-mail: raemmons@ucdavis.edu
[2]Department of Psychology, Westmont College, Santa Barbara, California 93108-1099;
e-mail: paloutz@westmont.edu

Key Words spirituality, religious cognition and emotions, personality, measurement

■ **Abstract** This chapter discusses progress in the psychology of religion by high-lighting its rapid growth during the past 25 years. Recent conceptual and empirical developments are described, with an emphasis on the cognitive and affective basis of religious experience within personality and social psychology. Religion and spirituality as domains of study, as well as being common and important process variables that touch a large portion of human experience, are highlighted. Movement away from the previously dominant measurement paradigm is noted, and particularly promising directions suggestive of an emerging interdisciplinary paradigm are described.

CONTENTS

INTRODUCTION

It has been 15 years since the last (and only) chapter on the psychology of religion appeared in the *Annual Review of Psychology* (Gorsuch 1988). The psychology of religion as an identifiable subfield of psychology has grown rapidly since then. The publication of an increasing number of books on the topic, including several

0066-4308/03/0203-0377$14.00

published by the American Psychological Association (APA), testifies to the vibrancy of the field (Emmons 1999; Hill & Hood 1999; Koenig 1998; Miller 1999; Pargament 1997; Richards & Bergin 1997, 2000; Shafranske 1996). Whereas the more applied areas of psychology such as clinical, counseling, and health have taken the lead in examining links between religion and psychological, physical, and interpersonal functioning, basic subfields are also recognizing that spiritual and religious influences may be profoundly important (e.g., Emmons & McCullough 1999, Paloutzian & Kirkpatrick 1995).

Because of this rapid growth, this chapter cannot provide comprehensive coverage of recent developments for all topics in the psychology of religion. Recent research on religion and spirituality as human phenomena is almost as vast and diverse as religious life itself. A literature search using the PsychInfo database for the period 1988–2001 returned 1198 citations for the term religion and 777 citations for spirituality. This review, therefore, must of necessity be selective rather than exhaustive. Because the clinical psychology of religion has received a great deal of attention, we have chosen to highlight less-well-publicized areas of scholarship in the psychology of religion, particularly in the fields of personality and social psychology, which are new and not already documented by comprehensive summary sources elsewhere. This chapter has several purposes: to document the various trajectories that the psychology of religion has had during the previous century, to explain some of the reasons for the trends that have been observed, to illustrate how all of the topics within the psychology of religion are extensions of and feedback to the overall body of theory and the database from general psychology, and to sketch the newest lines of emerging research that show promise of contributing significantly to psychology during the next few years.

Psychology of Religion Then and Now

In psychology's early days, at a time when all psychological thinking was fresh and new, and when theory, research methods, statistical tools, and subdisciplines within this now immense and rich field were not even dreamed of in their modern form, those who were pioneering this field (Hall 1904, 1917; James 1902; Starbuck 1899; see also Vande Kemp 1992) took it as a serious part of their work to study the psychological aspects of human religiousness. The challenge for the next century of psychologists (i.e., us) is to follow this example and do what they began to do—come to an understanding of the psychological bases of religious belief, experience, and behavior, with the goal of applying this knowledge for human good.

The attention to this topic by the generation of psychologists who came after those early pioneers declined from approximately the mid 1920s until the mid 1960s. Several intradisciplinary reasons for this have been suggested (Paloutzian 1996). These include but are not limited to the establishment of scientific psychology after the model of physics, the separation of psychology departments from their former home in philosophy departments, and the tendency by psychologists to stay away from "taboo" topics that might be considered too philosophical or too theological. However, during this period there were writings by what might be called the "grand theorists" of religion (Freud 1927, Jung 1938; see Wulff 1997 for a complete presentation of these), but these writings did little to advance the psychology of religion in the stricter, data-based sense. That is, these were over-arching theories of human nature that were attempts to explain everything, including religiousness. Although they are rich ideas about what processes may underlie religiousness, they did little to feed the quantitative research that is mushrooming today.

The impressive flowering and maturing of the discipline as we know it today is embedded in the co-occurrence of several factors. Most notably, the re-emergence of the field was partly due to a generation effect. Just as the early work was done by leaders who invested efforts in this topic (Wulff 1998), a new group of psychologists emerged whose concerns included issues of social relevance and whose view of psychology was expansive. The social upheavals of the 1960s made them aware of the need to use their psychological training to study real-life issues such as violence, aggression, prejudice, sexism—to tackle the big problems (Hester 1998). Religion, among the most powerful of all social forces and here as long as there have been human beings [e.g., it has been suggested that humans be thought of as *Homo religiosus* because religion has been present as long as there have been *Homo sapiens* (Albright & Ashbrook 2001)] and showing no sign of going away, is among them. Following the lead of Gordon Allport, in which religiousness was found to be related in important but nonobvious ways to racial prejudice (Allport 1954, Allport & Ross 1967), the dramatic recent growth of the field began.

The Upsurge of the Past Quarter Century

The psychology of religion re-emerged as a full-force, leading-edge research area that contributes new knowledge, data, and professional activity to the rest of psychology. This is apparent upon examination of the recent trends in the publication of textbooks and journal articles, presentations at professional meetings, teaching courses in the psychology of religion, the establishment of new journals, books on clinical and health issues, and the development of psychology of religion research that interfaces the theory and topics of the mainstream discipline. These trends became visible after the establishment of APA Division 36, Psychology of Religion, in 1976.

One of the most obvious evidences of the development of an area of scholarship can be seen by examining the numbers and frequency of books that are published in that area. Textbooks, in particular, are a benchmark source of data because they serve the purpose of summarizing research and they reflect activity in a field. Prior to 1982 one could look far and wide for current books on the psychology of religion and come up empty-handed. No recently published books existed. Things changed quickly during the 1980s, however. Psychology of religion textbooks were published in rapid succession by Batson & Ventis (1982), Paloutzian (1983), Spilka et al. (1985), and Brown (1987), and Wulff's (1991) book was in press before the decade was out. The 1990s saw this trend replicate and expand. Some of the 1980s books came out in second editions, including Batson et al. (1993), Paloutzian (1996), Hood et al. (1996), and Wulff (1997), and other books were added to the list (Beit-Hallahmi & Argyle 1997, Pargament 1997, Spilka & McIntosh 1997). This trend continues as the new century begins (Argyle 2000, Loewenthal 2000). Also, for the first time separate introductory chapters were included in general psychology textbooks (Santrock & Paloutzian 1997, 2000). This flourishing of textbooks feeds the increased teaching of psychology of religion (Hester 2002) and documents the vibrant activity that is a clear sign of the growth of the field.

Textbooks do not make for major contributions to a field on their own, however. They depend on the quality and visibility of the research on which they are based. During the past 25 years psychology of religion material has appeared with increasing frequency in high-end journals. In addition, and added to the already existing psychology of religion journals such as the *Journal for the Scientific Study of Religion* and the *Review of Religious Research*, new journals devoted to this topic have been established. One of them, *The International Journal for the Psychology of Religion* (established in 1990) is published in the United States, and the other, *Mental Health, Religion, and Culture* (established in 1998) is published in the United Kingdom. To complement the function served by journals, the annual series *Research in the Social Scientific Study of Religion* (JAI Press, Inc., established in 1990) and the topic's first *Annual Review* chapter (Gorsuch 1988) appeared, as did a chapter on religion and health (Chatters 2000). Finally, special issues of leading journals are appearing that focus on religious influences on personal and societal well-being (Paloutzian & Kirkpatrick 1995), religion in the psychology of personality (Emmons & McCullough 1999), religion and the family (Parke 2001), religion and adult development (Sinnott 2001), and religion as a meaning system (Silberman 2003). These trends make it clear that individual researchers are including religious dimensions in various aspects of their work and that journals of the highest quality and influence wish to publish it.

Closely related to this is the upsurge in the publication of specialized professional and postgraduate-level books, both those that concern the religious aspects of applied work and those that are handbooks on a specialized topic. For example, in 1996 the APA launched its book series on religious issues in clinical practice and shortly thereafter published a lead article on religion in the *APA Monitor* (Clay 1996). This so far has produced comprehensive handbooks focusing on religion and clinical practice (Shafranske 1996), spiritual strategy for counseling and psychotherapy (Richards & Bergin 1997), psychotherapy with religiously diverse people (Richards & Bergin 2000), and spirituality and treatment (Miller 1999). The same trend is occurring in psychiatry (Bhugra 1996, Boehnlein 2000) and from the perspective of particular theoretical approaches including rational emotive behavior therapy and psychodynamics (Malony & Spilka 1991). Finally, comprehensive handbooks and monographs have appeared on religious experience (Hood 1995) and conversion (Malony & Southard 1992, Rambo 1993), on religion and mental health (Koenig 1998) and physical health (Koenig et al. 2001, Plante & Sherman 2001), cognitive science (Andresen 2001), children's religious cognition (Rosengren et al. 2000), emotion (Corrigan et al. 2000), and spirituality in organizations (Giacalone & Jurkiewicz 2002). This impressive body of material has emerged in less than a decade and documents the increasing attention to spirituality and religion in diverse subfields of psychology.

Progress in Conceptualizing Religion and Spirituality

Our review of developments within substantive areas of the psychology of religion begins with the swelling literature on various meanings that the terms religion and spirituality have taken on. In order for progress to occur in a scientific discipline, there must be a minimum of consensus concerning the meaning of core constructs and their measurement. Agreement on the meaning of spirituality and religion is in short supply, as the religious landscape in the broader culture and in psychology is changing with a new breed of spirituality that is often distinct from traditional conceptions of religion (Hill 1999). Adding to the mayhem, religious and spiritual variables are increasingly being included in experimental and epidemiological studies. Yet how religion and spirituality are conceived and measured vary from study to study.

Over the past decade, there has been arguably more print devoted to conceptualizing religion and spirituality than to any other topic in the psychology of religion. It has become fashionable, both culturally and in the scientific literature, to differentiate between the spiritual and the religious. Psychologists have exerted as much effort as anyone debating the meaning of these terms. The noun "spirit" and the adjective "spiritual" are being used to refer to an ever increasing range of experiences rather than being reserved for those occasions of use that specifically imply the existence of nonmaterial forces or persons. Conceptions of spirituality do not always have a transcendent reference point, a fact that has led to much confusion over its meaning in research contexts. Most contemporary meanings of spirituality do distinguish between religious spirituality, natural spirituality, and humanistic spirituality. Elkins (2001), a vocal proponent of humanistic-oriented spirituality, offers six qualities of spirituality: Spirituality is universal; it is a human phenomenon; its common core is phenomenological; it is our capacity to respond to the numinous; it is characterized by a "mysterious energy" and its ultimate aim is compassion. It is unclear how these qualities would translate into an empirical research program on spirituality, or whether conceptions this broad are even thematically in keeping with the origins of the term. Careful linguistic analyses and precise operational definitions of spirituality need to be emphasized (Moberg 2002).

There has also been no shortage of attempts to define religion. One of the best and simplest definitions to appear in recent years was offered by Dollahite (1998), who defined religion as "a covenant faith community with teachings and narratives that enhance the search for the sacred and encourage morality" (p. 5). Religions are rooted in authoritative spiritual traditions that transcend the person and point to larger realities within which the person is embedded. Spiritualities may be contextualized within faith communities though they need not be. Whereas some have argued that the movement toward spirituality represents a movement away from traditional religion (Elkins 2001), others contend that the increased emphasis on spirituality indicates an increased respect for the inner, contemplative practices of traditional religious systems (Hill et al. 2000, Wuthnow 1998).

Zinnbauer et al. (1999) and Hill et al. (2000) systematically reviewed the evolving meanings of the terms religion and spirituality. Achieving some degree of definitional clarity is desirable, though not necessarily essential for scientific progress and the establishment of a cumulative knowledge base. After all, many disciplines have failed to provide a core consensual definition and have flourished in spite of definitional lacunae. The schism between religion and spirituality is a recent occurrence (Hill et al. 2000) and the two concepts are as much identified with their overlap as with what divides them. Zinnbauer et al. (1999) posited "a search for the sacred" as the common ground between religion and spirituality. They suggest that a dynamic view of spirituality and religion centered on a search process offers considerable potential for understanding the influence of the spiritual and religious realm in everyday life. The sacred core is what is central to both religious and spiritual experience. Building upon this definition, Pargament (1999) has argued that conceiving of spirituality in terms of an ability to imbue everyday experience, goals, roles, and responsibilities with sacredness opens new avenues for empirical exploration. For example, Mahoney et al. (1999) found that when marital partners viewed their relationship as imbued with divine qualities, they reported greater levels of marital satisfaction, more constructive problem solving behaviors, decreased marital conflict, and greater commitment to the relationship, than couples who did not see their marriage in a sacred light. Similarly, Tarakeshwar et al. (2002) found that a strong belief that nature is sacred was associated with greater pro-environmental beliefs and a greater willingness to protect the environment. This finding is notable in that other studies have found conventional measures of religiousness to be negatively associated with pro-environmental attitudes (Kanagy & Willits 1993).

One of the most important papers to appear on the topic is the review by Hill and associates (Hill et al. 2000). On the basis of both historical considerations and a growing empirical literature, the authors caution against viewing spirituality and religiousness as incompatible and suggest that the common tendency to polarize the terms simply as individual versus institutional or "good" versus "bad" is not fruitful for future research. Also cautioning against the use of restrictive, narrow definitions or overly broad definitions that can rob either construct of its distinctive characteristics, the authors propose a set of criteria that recognizes the constructs' conceptual similarities and dissimilarities. Both religion and spirituality include the subjective feelings, thoughts, and behaviors that arise from a search for the sacred. The term "search" refers to attempts to identify, articulate, maintain, or transform. The term "sacred" refers to a divine being, divine object, ultimate reality, or Ultimate Truth as perceived by the individual (p. 68). However, religion may or may not also include the search for nonsacred goals such as social identity or health in the context the search for the sacred, as well as prescribing rituals that facilitate a search of the sacred that are validated and supported by a faith community. Hill et al. (2000) also reviewed a number of recent studies that have empirically examined people's self-descriptions as religious or spiritual (e.g., Zinnbauer et al. 1997). The general findings of these studies is that most people describe themselves as both religious and spiritual, a finding that supports Hill et al.'s claim that the recent emphasis on spirituality represents an expanding conception of religion rather than a postmodern replacement of it.

Progress in Measuring Spiritual and Religious Constructs

Nearly 20 years ago the author of an influential article on the psychology of religion contended that measurement is both the "boon" and "bane" of the psychology of religion (Gorsuch 1984) and argued for a moratorium on new measures of religiousness. Textbooks on psychometric theory state that the major problem in psychology is that of measurement. Measurement is fundamental to scientific progress. Major advances in scientific disciplines are typically preceded by major breakthroughs in measurement methods. The psychology of religion, like other fields of scientific inquiry, will progress neither slower nor faster than allowed by current measurement instruments. The 1980s and 1990s saw an explosion of new inventories in the psychology of religion. With this rapid growth, the need for an authoritative guide to their use has become more important than ever. In recent years private foundations and governmental agencies have commissioned panels of experts to identify the key dimensions of religiousness/spirituality and to recommend instruments for their measurement in basic and applied research. The objective of these efforts, and this chapter, is to make researchers and mental health professionals aware of the existence of pertinent measures as they design their studies and interventions. Only then will needless duplication of scales be avoided, and more importantly, progress will accelerate as cumulative databases are compiled and integrated with theory through programmatic research.

A recently published authoritative reference volume (Hill & Hood 1999) provides detailed information on over 100 standardized measures of religiousness. These are grouped into 17 major clusters including religious beliefs and practices, religious attitudes, religious values, religious development, religious orientation, religious commitment and involvement, spirituality and mysticism, forgiveness, religious coping, and religious fundamentalism. Whereas familiar measures often employed in social scientific research on religion are included (e.g., intrinsic and extrinsic religiosity), so too are less widely accessible scales that tap constructs of interest in and of themselves (e.g., images of God, spiritual maturity, and attitudes toward death), and that may also have a bearing on the well-being and health outcomes being increasingly studied by scientists and health professionals. Work is already well under way on a companion volume focused primarily on measures of spirituality.

Slater et al. (2001) described recent developments in the measurement of spiritual and religious constructs including a review of several new measures of spirituality that do not appear in the Hill & Hood compendium. They advocate research that examines the convergence of multiple measures of spirituality and religiousness in accordance with theoretical frameworks. A good example of this is the article by MacDonald (2000), who examined the latent factor structure among 11 measures of spirituality. He identified 5 dimensions that underlie measurement-based spirituality: cognitive orientation towards spirituality, an experiential/phenomenological dimension, existential well-being, paranormal beliefs, and general religiousness.

RELIGION AND EMOTION: THE AFFECTIVE BASIS OF SPIRITUALITY

The connection between religion and emotion is a long and intimate one. Religion has always been a source of profound emotional experience. Jonathan Edwards described the function of religious emotions in his theological classic *A Treatise Concerning Religious Affections* (1746/1959). Edwards was so struck by the evidentiary force of emotion that he made it a cornerstone of his theology. Love, gratitude, and thankful joy displayed toward God were among the signs of genuine spiritual experience, according to Edwards. A review of his contributions (Hutch 1978) suggests that he can still be read with profit.

Watts (1996), Hill (1999), and Hill & Hood (1999) trace historical developments on the association between religious experience and feeling states. Both Watts and Hill have been vociferous in calling for a greater awareness of the intimate and reciprocal relationships between the psychology of religion and the psychology of emotion and identify several fruitful areas of research that can inform and enrich both fields. An important but rarely cited book on religious ways of knowing (Watts & Williams 1988) devotes an entire chapter to religious approaches to emotion regulation. In a similar vein, Schimmel (1997) historically documents Christian and Jewish teachings on the mastery of envy, anger, pride and other potentially destructive emotions. Averill (1996) suggests that fruitful dialogue might involve a speculation on emotions in an afterlife, an enterprise that might link with social psychological research on affective forecasting (Gilbert et al. 1998).

Watts (1996) distinguishes between two main notions about the role of emotions in religious life: The charismatic movement stresses the cultivation of intense positive emotions and their importance in religious experience and collective religious rituals (see also McCauley 2001), whereas the contemplative tradition stresses a calming of the passions and the development of emotional quietude. In addition to these two approaches to regulating emotions, there is the ascetic view (Allen 1997), which links religion with greater awareness of emotion (possible emotional intelligence, to use a contemporary term) and the creative expression of emotion. Emotional regulation techniques that have their rationales in religious traditions can modulate everyday emotional experience (Schimmel 1997, Watts 1996), providing spiritual rationales and methods for handling problematic emotions such as anger, guilt, and depression. Positive emotional benefits have been reported for Zen meditation (Gillani & Smith 2001) and the cultivation of transpersonal states long associated with spiritual and religious traditions (McCraty et al. 1998). The literature on emotion regulation in adulthood (e.g., Gross 2002) might be mined to see what it offers the psychology of religion; conversely, the field of emotion research might profit from a greater awareness of spiritual and religious influences on felt emotions (Hill 1999). Silberman (2003) suggests three ways in which religion as a meaning system affects emotions. First, religion prescribes appropriate emotions and their level of intensity. Second, beliefs about the nature and attributes of God may affect emotional well-being, and third, religion offers the opportunity to experience a uniquely powerful emotional experience of closeness to the sacred.

A debatable issue continues to be the uniqueness of emotions that are labeled as religious. Are these a separate class of emotions or simply ordinary emotions felt in religious contexts or elicited through religious rituals such as prayer and worship? Advances in philosophy of mind might be helpful here. Murphy (1998) recently argued that religious experience supervenes on ordinary experience, in a top-down, causally efficacious fashion. What makes religious emotion religious are ordinary felt emotions under circumstances that make it apparent to the person that God or a higher power is involved. In d'Aquili & Newberg's (1999) neurotheological approach, experiences of the sacred are partially mediated by the "emotional value operator" function of the mind. Neuroscience research of religious experience has tended to focused on extraordinary spiritual experiences rather than more routine religious experiences (Brown & Mathew 2001), so relatively little is known about the brain's role in everyday religious emotions. Advances in the affective sciences will likely provide new ways of thinking about religious emotions and might eventually impact psychology of religion research.

Unfortunately, empirical work on emotion within a religious or spiritual context has lagged behind theoretical writings of a largely speculative nature. There are only a handful of studies examining emotion and religion/spirituality, and none speak to the thorny issue of distinguishing religious from nonreligious emotions. Samuels & Lester (1985) found that, in a small sample of Catholic nuns and priests, out of 50 emotions, love and gratitude were the most frequently experienced toward God. Another study employed a very different methodology in studying the relationship between emotion and religion. Mayer (1994) classified emotion terms in the books of the Hebrew Bible and examined changes in the frequency of occurrence over the eight-century period during which the books were written. The primary finding was that over time, references to happiness increased; no other emotions were shown to systematically increase or decrease. Although he considers a number of alternative hypotheses, Mayer suggests that this finding can be taken as evidence of the positive psychological benefits of religious culture.

McCullough et al. (2002) found that people who reported high levels of spirituality reported more gratitude in their daily moods, as did people higher in religious interest, general religiousness, and intrinsic religious orientation. Interestingly, however, extrinsic, utilitarian religious orientation and quest-seeking religious orientation were not significantly correlated with the amount of gratitude in daily mood. These findings suggest that people high in conventional forms of religiousness, especially people for whom religion is a fundamental organizing principle (i.e., people high in intrinsic religiousness) and people who report high levels of spiritual transcendence, experience more gratitude in their daily moods than do their less religious/spiritual counterparts. The authors suggest that the presence of gratitude may be a positive affective hallmark of religiously and spiritually engaged people, just as an absence of depressive symptoms is a negative affective hallmark of spiritually and religiously engaged people. This study is one of few attempts to examine the daily emotional lives of spiritual and religious individuals.

The beneficial effects of religiousness on health are well documented. We define religiousness here as a person characteristic, as a belief and meaning system that is stable over time and manifested across diverse situations. Research is just beginning to unravel the complex causal mechanisms responsible for these relationships between religiousness and health endpoints. One particularly promising explanation might involve the experience of religiously engendered emotions such as hope, love, forgiveness, and gratitude (Ellison & Levin 1998). Given that expressions of praise and thanksgiving are key components of religious worship, the physiological effects of gratitude hold promise for understanding religion's impact on health, perhaps even as a mediator of the robust association between religiousness and physical health. George et al. (2000) state that a high priority for future research on spirituality and health is the pursuit of an "epidemiology of spiritual experience" (p. 113) and contend that spiritual experience is the most-ignored dimension of spirituality. Presumably this would include an analysis of the frequency and intensity of religious emotions in daily life. In this vein another promising research program has begun to explore the emotion of "awe" in both its religious and nonreligious contexts (Keltner & Haidt 2002).

The Return to Virtue

The study of virtue is making a comeback in psychology and is at the nexus of the psychology of religion, personality psychology, moral philosophy, and the psychology of emotion (Hill 1999, Snyder & McCullough 2000). The positive psychology movement (Seligman & Csikszentmihalyi 2000) has sought to systematically classify these strengths and human virtues into a comprehensive taxonomy (Peterson & Seligman 2002). Concepts such as forgiveness, love, hope, humility, gratitude, self-control, and wisdom appear as highly prized human dispositions in Jewish, Christian, Muslim, Buddhist, and Hindu thought and are affirmed universal principles in world philosophies and ethical systems. Basic research as well as interventions to cultivate these virtues are well under way and have been yielding fruit. Forgiveness has been an especially vigorous research area, and recent research is reviewed below. A special issue of the *Journal of Social and*

Clinical Psychology (McCullough & Snyder 2000) was devoted to a contemporary appraisal of several virtues (hope, humility, gratitude, self-control, spirituality, forgiveness, wisdom, and love), highlighting their links to physical and psychological well-being. The capstone article by Schimmel (2000) explains how those virtues (and their corresponding vices) were conceptualized historically in classical and religious understandings of human nature.

Sandage & Hill (2001) recently articulated an outline of the construct of virtue by drawing on moral philosophy and recent social science research related to virtue. They suggest six dimensions for the definition of virtue. These include the understanding that virtues: (*a*) integrate ethics and health; (*b*) are embodied traits of character; (*c*) are sources of human strength and resilience; (*d*) are embedded within a cultural context and community; (*e*) contribute to a sense of meaningful life purpose; and (*f*) are grounded in the cognitive capacity for wisdom. Perhaps the most significant point of tension is whether virtues are construed as universal or culturally embedded. These categories are not necessarily mutually exclusive. It seems possible that a particular virtue (e.g., forgiveness) might be universally valued but still locally embedded in specific cultural institutions and rituals. This would mean that forgiveness might be expressed or even defined differently in various cultural contexts and communities. Individualistic models of forgiveness would tend to construe forgiveness as a personal decision or choice, whereas individuals in collectivistic cultures would tend to operate according to strongly proscribed social norms. The overwhelming emphasis in contemporary Western psychological literature is on forgiving others, and there is a relative paucity of literature on repentance (Exline & Baumeister 2000) and seeking forgiveness from others (Sandage et al. 2000).

Research programs have been rapidly developing around several specific virtues. We focus on three that have roots in each the major religions of the world: gratitude, forgiveness, and humility.

GRATITUDE   Gratitude has been defined as "the willingness to recognize the unearned increments of value in one's experience" (Bertocci & Millard 1963, p. 389) and "an estimate of gain coupled with the judgment that someone else is responsible for that gain" (Solomon 1977, p. 316). At its core, gratitude is an emotional response to a gift. It is the appreciation felt after one has been the beneficiary of an altruistic act. Some of the most profound reported experiences of gratitude can be religiously based or associated with reverent wonder toward an acknowledgment of the universe (Goodenough 1998) including the perception that life itself is a gift. In the great monotheistic religions of the world the concept of gratitude permeates texts, prayers, and teachings. Worship with gratitude to God for the many gifts and mercies are common themes, and believers are urged to develop this quality. A religious framework thus provides the backdrop for experiences and expressions of gratitude.

McCullough and colleagues (McCullough et al. 2001) reviewed the classical moral writings on gratitude and synthesized them with contemporary empirical findings. They suggest that the positive emotion of gratitude has three moral functions: It serves as (*a*) a moral barometer (an affective readout that is sensitive to a particular type of change in one's social relationships, the provision of a benefit by another moral agent that enhances one's well-being), (*b*) a moral motivator (prompting grateful people to behave prosocially), and (*c*) a moral reinforcer (which increases the likelihood of future benevolent actions). McCullough et al. (2002) found that measures of gratitude as a disposition were positively correlated with nearly all of the measures of spirituality and religiousness, including spiritual transcendence, self-transcendence, and the single-item religious variables. The grateful disposition was also related to measures of spiritual and religious tendencies. Although these correlations were not large (i.e., few of them exceeded $r = 0.30$), they suggest that spiritually or religiously inclined people have a stronger disposition to experience gratitude than do their less spiritual/religious counterparts. Thus, spiritual and religious inclinations may facilitate gratitude, but it is also conceivable that gratitude facilitates the development of religious and spiritual interests (Allport et al. 1948) or that the association of gratitude and spirituality/religiousness is caused by extraneous variables yet to be identified. The fact that the correlations of gratitude with these affective, prosocial, and spiritual variables were obtained using both self-reports and peer reports of the grateful disposition suggests that these associations are substantive and not simply the product of one-method biases in measurement. This study may be also be useful for explaining why religiously involved people are at a lower risk for depressive symptoms and other mental health difficulties.

FORGIVENESS   The concept of forgiveness has been a topic of philosophical and theological inquiry for thousands of years. Indeed, most religious accounts of optimal human functioning include the capacity to seek forgiveness and grant forgiveness as key elements of the well-functioning human personality. Forgiveness as a contemporary psychological or social science construct has also generated popular and clinical interest and for the most part has been considered apart from the psychology of religion by mainstream psychology (for reviews, see Enright & Fitzgibbons 2000, Fincham 2000, McCullough et al. 2000, Witvliet et al. 2001). The scientific literature on forgiveness is growing rapidly across a number of areas of psychology. Research on forgiveness has focused primarily on four themes: (*a*) developing measures of dispositional forgiveness (Berry et al. 2001, Brown et al. 2001), (*b*) investigating the psychophysiological correlates and health consequences of forgiveness (Berry & Worthington 2001, Farrow et al. 2001, Seybold et al. 2001, Toussaint et al. 2001, Witvliet et al. 2001), (*c*) exploring the dispositional and situational correlates of forgiveness (Maltby et al. 2001, McCullough et al. 1997, Mullet et al. 2002, Sandage et al. 2000), and (*d*) examining the mental health and interpersonal benefits of forgiveness (e.g., Coyle & Enright 1997, Huang & Enright 2000). Few studies have examined links between religion and forgiveness (for exceptions see Edwards et al. 2002, McCullough & Worthington 1999, Wuthnow 2000). An authoritative volume (McCullough et al. 2000) covers theological perspectives, basic psychological processes, and applications in clinical and counseling contexts. The chapter by Rye and associates in the McCullough et al. 2000 volume is a fascinating and enlightening roundtable discussion of forgiveness in Jewish, Christian, Islamic, Buddhist, and Hindu traditions.

There has been limited empirical research on forgiveness published to date that has investigated: (*a*) forgiveness in non-Western contexts (for valuable exceptions, see Huang & Enright 2000, Park & Enright 1997) or (*b*) ethnic or cultural variables related to forgiveness. McCullough et al. (2000) noted the significance of this problem, stating,

> The field [of forgiveness research] still lacks a thorough understanding of the influences of religion, culture, and life situation on people's understandings and experiences of forgiveness. Without addressing religious, cultural, and situational variations, scientific notions of forgiveness are likely to be disconnected from lived experience. (p. 10)

McCullough (2001) makes several recommendations for future research and theory on forgiveness. These include the need for a greater focus on psychological mechanisms that allow dispositionally inclined people to forgive transgressions against them, the need to examine contextualized goals and strivings (Emmons 2000) and appraisals of these goals, and the need for more sophisticated theorizing on the place of forgiveness within broader models of the person. Important clues might be gleaned from the self-regulation literature, particularly with regard to how religious ideologies that emphasize forgiveness can become translated into effective thought-action sequences and then protected from competing intentions (Emmons et al. 1993). With regard to the place of forgiveness in personality, Ashton & Lee (2001) recently posited that forgiveness/nonretaliation is one of three major traits that underlie prosocial tendencies and can account for individual differences in the major dimensions of agreeableness and emotional stability.

HUMILITY   Since medieval times, pride has been one of the deadly sins, and some have argued that pride is the parent of all the vices (Schimmel 1997). Humility, as the antidote to pride, is the realistic appraisal of one's strengths and weaknesses— neither overestimating nor underestimating them. Overall, humility is characterized by an accurate assessment of one's strengths and weaknesses, thinking oneself no better or no worse than others, and being open to new ideas and new information (Tangney 2000). There is little direct research on humility. Researchers who have advocated for the benefits of humble self-appraisals have done so by pointing to the destructive consequences of pride, narcissism, and defensively high self-esteem. In an extensive review of the self-esteem literature Baumeister (1998, Baumeister et al. 1996) found that when people focus directly on enhancing how they see themselves, an artificially heightened and "dark side" of self-esteem emerges. Bushman & Baumeister (1998) found that people who had the highest opinion of themselves were also the most aggressive after being criticized for the poor quality of a written essay. Those with high self-esteem are also more likely to be antagonistic if their view of themselves is threatened, such as being told that one has failed an aptitude test (Heatherton & Vohs 2000). In response to such findings, Baumeister (1998) and Baumeister et al. (1996) concluded that the claims that enhancing self-esteem was the cure to many societal ills was unsupported.

There is an urgent need for tools to measure humility and for studies that examine its real-world consequences. Too much of what is assumed about humility is inferred from research on related constructs. Tangney (2000) described the challenges in developing self-report measures of humility. In a cleverly designed experiment Exline et al. (2000) found that writing about a time in which they felt humble enabled participants to delay defecting in a Prisoner's Dilemma game, relative to both a pride and a control condition. Rowatt et al. (2002) operationalized humility as the difference between individual's evaluations of themselves on positive attributes and their evaluations of others on those same attributes. Evidence was found for a "holier than thou effect": Participants rated themselves to be more adherent to biblical commandments than others, a tendency that was positively correlated with intrinsic religiousness. This general evaluation bias also held for nonreligious attributes, leading the authors to conclude that religious individuals may not necessarily adhere to the dictums of their faith to be humble in comparison to others.

PERSONALITY AND RELIGION

Personality psychology has had a longstanding relationship with the psychology of religion. Kirkpatrick (1999) noted that personality psychology provides a natural home for the study of religion and spirituality in that a concern with the transcendent is an inherent part of what it means to be human. Emmons (1999) argued that personality theory and theology ought to be natural allies; both are concerned, ultimately, with what it means to be a human being. Much progress has been made at the interface of personality psychology and the psychology of religion, as personality researchers from diverse theoretical positions have begun to view religion as a fruitful topic for empirical study. A recent special issue of the *Journal of Personality* (Emmons & McCullough 1999) highlighted diverse ways in which religious and spiritual issues impact personality traits and processes and vice-versa.

Evidence is accruing that spirituality may represent a heretofore unacknowledged sixth major dimension of personality (MacDonald 2000, Piedmont 1999a). Other recent research has similarly noted that spirituality and religiousness are omitted from structural models of personality that are developed around the five factor model (FFM) (Saucier & Goldberg 1998). Piedmont (1999b) demonstrated the value of the FFM for advancing the scientific study of religion. He suggests that the FFM can provide an empirical reference point for evaluating the development of new measures of religiousness and for evaluating the meaning of existing measures. Ozer & Reise (1994) advise that personality researchers routinely correlate their particular measure with the FFM. Given the proliferation of measurement instruments in the psychology of religion, researchers would do well to heed this advice.

RELIGION AND THE FFM   The FFM offers a starting point for exploring the relationship between religiousness and personality functioning. The FFM is an empirically validated and comprehensive taxonomy of individual differences that has been validated cross-culturally (see Digman 1990, McCrae & Costa 1999). There is a growing literature on the Big Five traits and religiousness. MacDonald (2000) found somewhat different patterns of correlations across the Big Five depending upon the domain of spirituality examined. A factor labeled "cognitive orientation toward spirituality" was associated with extraversion, agreeableness, openness, and conscientiousness, whereas an experiential form of spirituality was related to extraversion and openness only. A recent meta-analytic review (Saroglou 2002) reported that religiousness is consistently associated with high agreeableness and conscientiousness and low psychoticism (in Eysenck's model), whereas it is unrelated to the other Big Five traits. One other generalization that appears warranted is that openness tends to be negatively correlated with more fundamentalist measures of religiousness. McCrae & Costa's (1999) model of personality may prove useful for understanding how basic trait tendencies are channeled into characteristic adaptations that include culturally conditioned religious and spiritual goals and attitudes.

New Units of Analysis from Personality Psychology

Personality psychology can introduce new units of analysis for empirically examining religiousness and spirituality in people's lives. Here we describe two recent examples.

SPIRITUAL TRANSCENDENCE   Spiritual transcendence is "the capacity of individuals to stand outside of their immediate sense of time and place and to view life from a larger, more objective perspective. This transcendent perspective is one in which a person sees a fundamental unity underlying the diverse strivings of nature" (Piedmont 1999a, p. 988). In developing the spiritual transcendence scale (STS) a consortium of theological experts from diverse faith traditions including Buddhism, Hinduism, Quakerism, Lutheranism, Catholicism, and Judaism was assembled. This focus group identified aspects of spirituality that were common to all of these faiths. The resulting items were analyzed within the context of the FFM and were shown to constitute an independent individual-differences dimension. The STS manifested a single overall factor comprised of three "facet" scales: *prayer fulfillment*, a feeling of joy and contentment that results from personal encounters with a transcendent reality (e.g., "I find inner strength and/or peace from my prayers or meditations"); *universality*, a belief in the unitive nature of life (e.g., "I feel that on a higher level all of us share a common bond"); and *connectedness*, a belief that one is part of a larger human reality that cuts across generations and across groups (e.g., "I am concerned about those who will come after me in life"). The STS evidenced incremental validity by significantly predicting a number of relevant psychological outcomes (e.g., stress experience, social support, interpersonal style) even after the predictive effects of personality were removed (Piedmont 1999a). For the STS to be shown to capture a universal aspect of spirituality, it would be necessary to evidence that the instrument remains reliable and valid in culturally diverse, religiously heterogeneous samples.

Piedmont & Leach (2002) have already documented the utility of the STS in a sample of Indian Hindus, Muslims, and Christians. Support was found for two of the facet scales and the overall domain (connectedness was not found to be reliable). The STS was presented in English, a second language for these participants. This may have created difficulties in understanding the terminology or the exemplars used, as items lacked relevance in this culture. Nonetheless, these data highlight the value of cross-cultural research on spirituality and show the STS to reflect spiritual qualities relevant across very different religious traditions. However, Moberg (2002) doubts that valid, universal measures of spirituality can be constructed because of differing conceptions of spirituality in different religious traditions. The particularism versus universalism distinction that he identifies is likely to occupy psychologists of religion for some time to come.

ULTIMATE CONCERNS   Yet another way to conceptualize spirituality is in terms of goals or strivings, or what Emmons and colleagues have called "ultimate concerns" (Emmons et al. 1998, Emmons 1999). Emmons (1999), following Tillich (1957) among others, argued that both religion and spirituality deal with people's ultimate concerns and developed a research program to identify ultimate concerns and their role in human personality and subjective well-being. A religious perspective can illuminate the origins of some of the most profound human strivings. Religions, as authoritative faith traditions, are systems of information that provide individuals with knowledge and resources for living a life of purpose and direction. Religion and goals are intertwined in human experience. One of the functions of a religious belief system and a religious world view is to provide "an ultimate vision of what people should be striving for in their lives" (Pargament & Park 1995, p. 15) and the strategies to reach those ends. Religions recommend the ultimate goal of binding with the sacred and prescribe rituals for its realization. Emmons et al. (1998) found that not only is it possible to reliably assess the search for the sacred in personal goals, but that individual differences in sacred goals predicted well-being more strongly than any other category of striving that has been studied, exceeding those for intimacy, power, or generativity goals. Emmons (1999) argues for a more inclusive role of religion and spirituality within personality and motivational psychology.

As our review suggests, researchers have made substantial progress in uncovering some basic facts about the personality contours of religiousness. Missing from much of the empirical exploration of personality correlates of religiousness is an exploration of the underlying mechanisms responsible for the observed associations. We do not yet know whether personality influences the development of religiousness (e.g., the tendency to strive for the sacred, to ask existential questions about one's place in the cosmos), whether religiousness influences personality (as research on personal goals suggests), or whether personality and religiousness share common genetic or environmental causes. Longitudinal data on the relationship between personality and religiousness are sorely needed (McFadden 1999), as are research methodologies for studying the direction of causation between religion and personality. We eventually need to get beyond correlating lists of personality traits with measures of spirituality/religiousness. Waller et al. (1994) sought to identify personality traits that predicted entry into and duration of involvement in an evangelical "disciple-making training course." Disciple makers scored significantly higher on the higher-order factor of constraint (reflecting high harmavoidance, high traditionalism, and high self-control); this factor correlates highly with Big Five conscientiousness. Furthermore, after 24 months, participants with low harmavoidance and low aggression scores were likely to remain in the program, leading the authors to conclude that "personality is a powerful determinant of involvement duration as a disciple-maker" (p. 190). It is especially fascinating that although participants high in harmavoidance initially were attracted to the program, those low in the trait were more likely to remain over time. This dynamic trend would not have been observed by simply examining the correlation between personality and religious activity at a single point in time.

Spiritual Transformation

Another vigorous area of research is that of religious conversion or spiritual transformation. The effects of religious conversion on personality change was one of the first topics studied with empirical research methods when psychology emerged as a science over one hundred years ago (James 1902, Starbuck 1899). The term spiritual transformation is used here to denote what is understood widely in the psychology of religion literature as a "conversion experience." Some researchers have begun to use the term "quantum change" to highlight the profound nature of this religious experience (Miller & C'de Baca 2001). However, it must be noted that one's spiritual transformation can be profound whether it occurs gradually or via a sudden experience. Much of the contemporary scientific psychological research examines the relationship between the self or personality and spiritual transformation. For example, Zinnbauer & Pargament (1998) gave a group of spiritual converts, a group who experienced gradual religious change, and a group of religious adherents who reported no religious change (all subjects were Christian undergraduate students), measures of stress, life events, motivation for change, and sense of self. The authors posited that spiritual conversion should lead to radical personal change. However, they found that self definition changed markedly for both spiritual and gradual converts. In addition, the spiritual converts reported more preconversion stress and perception of personal inadequacy, more improvement in their personal competence, and more spiritual experiences after conversion.

Kirkpatrick (1997, 1998) has published two longitudinal studies of religious conversion. In his 1997 study, 146 women readers of the *Denver Post* were surveyed approximately 4 years apart (times T1 and T2, respectively) about a variety of religious commitments. Of concern was whether different adult attachment styles predicted religious commitment. He found that when religion at time T1 was statistically controlled, those with an insecure-anxious or an insecure-avoidant adult attachment style were more likely than those with a secure attachment style to report finding a new relationship with God by time T2. Insecure-anxious subjects were more likely than those who had secure or ambivalent attachments to report having had a religious experience or a religious conversion during this time period. These results were interpreted as supporting the compensation hypothesis in attachment theory: God serves as a substitute attachment figure for those having difficulty forming human bonds. These findings were replicated and extended in a follow-up study (Kirkpatrick 1998) in which college students were assessed for their attachment styles and religiousness approximately 4 months apart.

Based upon their systematic review of the literature, Paloutzian et al. (1999) argue that spiritual transformation experiences appear to have minimal effect on the "elemental" functions of personality (the Big Five). However, they suggest that spiritually transforming experiences can result in profound life changes at the mid-level functions of personality such as goals, feelings, attitudes, and behaviors. Indeed, these researchers posit that "self-defining" personality functions (such as identity, life meaning) do change dramatically after a spiritual transformation. Few studies published to date are immune from methodological shortcomings such as reliance on cross-sectional, retrospective designs and near total reliance on measures of self-perceived change.

CONCLUSIONS

Although it is clear that the psychology of religion is alive, well, and growing, two questions linger: First, is the rest of psychology embracing its knowledge and data and drawing the relevant connections to its own material as this review would suggest? Second, what is the psychology of religion's current paradigm and what paradigm would have to describe it if its contribution is to unfold to the fullest degree?

The response to the first question depends upon the receptiveness of psychologists in other areas. Emmons (1999) examined this question and put the answer this way:

> ...two recent, comprehensive handbooks of personality (Hogan et al. 1997, Pervin 1990) fail to include religion as a topic of inquiry. A lone reference that appears in one (Megargee 1997) bemoans this very neglect of the topic. Nor does the *Handbook of Social Psychology* (Gilbert et al. 1997) devote any space whatsoever to religion and social behavior. Out of a total of over 3,000 pages in these three presumably comprehensive handbooks, less than 1 page discusses religious influences on personal and social behavior (p. 12).

It appears that although there is research in the psychology of religion that is tied to almost every area of research in general psychology, only a portion of the field, especially that concerned with clinical applications and health psychology, has begun to incorporate the knowledge from the psychology of religion into its own information base and practices.

As to the paradigm issue, Gorsuch (1988) seemingly reluctantly concluded that even as late as the mid 1980s, when other areas of psychology had gone beyond trying to find the purest measure for a concept, the psychology of religion was still in a *measurement paradigm*. Although a definitive compendium of psychology of religion measures has now been published (Hill & Hood 1999) and new measures of important variables continue to appear from time to time [e.g., religious maturity (Leak & Fish 1999), faith development (Leak et al. 1999), spiritual strivings (Emmons 1999)], the evidence indicates that the field has now gone beyond focusing on measurement as its primary concern. The psychology of religion has undergone a paradigm shift. It has emerged as a strong research enterprise whose topics interface almost all areas of psychology, whose scholars produce an impressive body of research, whose research will further develop internationally and cross-culturally, and whose importance is only going to increase.

There is also much to be gained from an increasing dialogue and collaboration between psychologists who specialize in religion and our colleagues in evolutionary biology, neuroscience, philosophy, anthropology, and cognitive science, so that developments in the psychology of religion take into account and build upon advances in these related scientific disciplines. This will need to be accomplished nonreductively, echoing our concerns raised above. A single disciplinary approach is incapable of yielding comprehensive knowledge of phenomena as complex and multifaceted as spirituality. We note with considerable enthusiasm exciting new developments in the cognitive science of religion (Andresen 2001, Barrett 1998, Woolley 2000), the neurobiology of religious experience (Brown et al. 1998, McNamara 2001, Newberg et al. 2001), the evolutionary psychology of religion (Boyer 2001, Kirkpatrick 1999), and behavior genetics (D'Onofrio et al. 1999). With a few exceptions, however, these approaches currently provide promissory notes, and considerably more research is needed before their full contribution can be evaluated. We are sanguine that these developments will ultimately anchor the psychology of religion as strongly in the biological sciences as in the social and clinical sciences and will yield new and scientific ways to talk about the human spirit.

We think, therefore, that the field has changed to such a degree since Gorsuch's (1988) chapter that a new concept is needed to guide it. We call it the *multilevel interdisciplinary paradigm*. This paradigm recognizes the value of data at multiple levels of analysis while making nonreductive assumptions concerning the value of spiritual and religious phenomena. It is the implementation of this paradigm that will carry the day, and this hinges on the interaction between those who study the psychology of religion and their counterparts in the rest of psychology and allied sciences. The field has made great strides in its efforts to say something important to the rest of psychology, and we think what has come before is only a platform and that the field is now poised, ready to begin.

ACKNOWLEDGMENTS

Portions of this chapter were prepared while RFP was Guest Professor, Faculty of Psychology and Educational Sciences, Katholieke Universiteit Leuven, Belgium. The use of the resources of the university is gratefully acknowledged.

The *Annual Review of Psychology* is online at http://psych.annualreviews.org

LITERATURE CITED

Albright CR, Ashbrook JB. 2001. *Where God Lives in the Human Brain*. Naperville, IL: Sourcebooks

Allen D. 1997. Ascetic theology and psychology. In *Limning the Psyche: Explorations in Christian Psychology*, ed. RC Roberts, MR Talbot, pp. 297–316. Grand Rapids, MI: Eerdmans

Allport GW. 1954. *The Nature of Prejudice*. Cambridge, MA: Addison

Allport GW, Gillespie JM, Young J. 1948. The religion of the post-war college student. *J. Psychol.* 25:3–33

Allport GW, Ross JW. 1967. Personal religious orientation and prejudice. *J. Abnorm. Soc. Psychol.* 5:432–43

Andresen J, ed. 2001. *Religion in Mind: Cognitive Perspectives on Religious Belief, Ritual, and Experience*. Cambridge: Cambridge Univ. Press

Argyle M. 2000. *Psychology and Religion: An Introduction*. London: Routledge

Ashton MC, Lee K. 2001. A theoretic basis for the major dimensions of personality. *Eur. J. Personal.* 15:327–53

Averill JR. 1996. Emotions: here and now, then and there. *Int. J. Psychol. Relig.* 6:89–94

Barrett JL. 1998. Cognitive constraints on Hindu concepts of the divine. *J. Sci. Stud. Relig.* 37:608–19

Batson CD, Schoenrade P, Ventis WL. 1993. *Religion and the Individual: A Social-Psychological Perspective*. New York: Oxford Univ. Press

Batson CD, Ventis WL. 1982. *The Religious Experience: A Social-Psychological Perspective*. New York: Oxford Univ. Press

Baumeister RF. 1998. The self. See Gilbert et al. 1998, pp. 680–740

Baumeister RF, Smart L, Boden JM. 1996. Relation of threatened egotism to violence and aggression: the dark side of high self-esteem. *Psychol. Rev.* 103:5–33

Beit-Hallahmi B, Argyle M. 1997. *The Psychology of Religious Behaviour, Belief and Experience*. London: Routledge

Berry JW, Worthington EL Jr. 2001. Forgivingness, relationship quality, stress while imagining relationship events, and physical and mental health. *J. Couns. Psychol.* 48:447–55

Berry JW, Worthington EL Jr, Parrott L III, O'Connor LE, Wade NG. 2001. Dispositional forgivingness: development and construct validity of the Transgression Narrative Test of Forgivingness (TNTF). *Personal. Soc. Psychol. Bull.* 27:1277–90

Bertocci PA, Millard RM. 1963. *Personality and the Good*. Philadelphia: Mckay

Bhugra D, ed. 1996. *Psychiatry and Religion: Context, Consensus and Controversies*. London: Routledge

Boehnlein JK, ed. 2000. *Psychiatry and Religion: The Convergence of Mind and Spirit*. Washington, DC: Am. Psychiatric Press

Boyer P. 2001. *Religion Explained*. New York: Basic Books

Brown LB. 1987. *Psychology of Religious Belief*. London: Academic

Brown SW, Gorsuch R, Rosik CH, Ridley CR. 2001. The development of a scale to measure forgiveness. *J. Psychol. Christ.* 20:40–52

Brown WS, Mathew RJ. 2001. *Neuroscience of Religion and Religious Experiences: Perspective and State of the Research.*

Fuller Theol. Semin., Pasadena, CA. Unpubl. manuscr.

Brown WS, Murphy N, Malony HN. 1998. *Whatever Happened to the Soul?: Scientific and Theological Portraits of Human Nature.* Minneapolis, MN: Fortress

Bushman BJ, Baumeister R. 1998. Threatened egotism, narcissism, self-esteem, and direct and displaced aggression: Does self-love or self-hate lead to violence? *J. Personal. Soc. Psychol.* 75:219–29

Chatters LM. 2000. Religion and health: public health research and practice. *Annu. Rev. Public Health* 21:335–67

Clay RA. 1996. Psychologists' faith in religion begins to grow. *APA Monitor* 27(8):1, 3–5

Corrigan J, Crump E, Kloos J. 2000. *Emotion and Religion: A Critical Assessment and Annotated Bibliography.* Westport, CT: Greenwood

Coyle CT, Enright RD. 1997. Forgiveness intervention with post-abortion men. *J. Consult. Clin. Psychol.* 65:1042–46

d'Aquili E, Newberg AB. 1999. *The Mystical Mind: Probing the Biology of Religious Experience.* Minneapolis, MN: Augsburg Fortress

Digman M. 1990. Personality structure: emergence of the five-factor model. *Annu. Rev. Psychol.* 41:417–40

Dollahite DC. 1998. Fathering, faith, and spirituality. *J. Men's Stud.* 7:3–15

D'Onofrio BM, Eaves LJ, Murrelle L, Maes HH, Spilka B. 1999. Understanding biological and social influences on religious affiliation, attitudes, and behaviors: a behavior genetic perspective. *J. Personal.* 67:953–84

Edwards J. 1959. *Religious Affections.* Ser., Vol. 2, ed. JE Smith. New Haven, CT: Yale Univ. Press

Edwards LM, Lapp-Rincker RH, Magyar-Moe JL, Rehfeldt JD, Ryder JA, et al. 2002. A positive relationship between religious faith and forgiveness: faith in the absence of data? *Pastor. Psychol.* 50:147–52

Elkins DN. 2001. Beyond religion: toward a humanistic spirituality. See Schneider et al. 2001, pp. 201–12

Ellison CG, Levin JS. 1998. The religion-health connection: evidence, theory, and future directions. *Health Educ. Behav.* 25:700–20

Emmons RA. 1999. *The Psychology of Ultimate Concerns: Motivation and Spirituality in Personality.* New York: Guilford

Emmons RA. 2000. Is spirituality an intelligence? Motivation, cognition, and the psychology of ultimate concern. *Int. J. Psychol. Relig.* 10:3–26

Emmons RA, Cheung C, Tehrani K. 1998. Assessing spirituality through personal goals: implications for research on religion and subjective well-being. *Soc. Indic. Res.* 45:391–422

Emmons RA, King LA, Sheldon K. 1993. Goal conflict and the self-regulation of action. In *Handbook of Mental Control*, ed. DM Wegner, JW Pennebaker, pp. 528–51. Englewood Cliffs, NJ: Prentice-Hall

Emmons RA, McCullough ME, eds. 1999. *Religion in the Psychology of Personality. J. Personal.* 67(6):whole issue

Enright RD, Fitzgibbons RP. 2000. *Helping Clients Forgive: An Empirical Guide for Resolving Anger and Restoring Hope.* Washington, DC: Am. Psychol. Assoc.

Exline JJ, Baumeister RF. 2000. Expressing forgiveness and repentance: benefits and barriers. In *Forgiveness: Theory, Research, and Practice*, ed. ME McCullough, KI Pargament, C Thoresen, pp. 133–55. New York: Guilford

Exline JJ, Bushman B, Faber J, Phillips C. 2000. Pride gets in the way: Self-protection works against forgiveness. *Symp. Soc. Personality Soc. Psychol.*, Nashville, TN.

Farrow TFD, Zheng Y, Wilkinson ID, Spence SA, Deakin JFW, et al. 2001. Investigating the functional anatomy of empathy and forgiveness. *NeuroReport* 12:2433–38

Fincham FD. 2000. The kiss of the porcupines: from attributing responsibility to forgiving. *Pers. Relat.* 7:1–23

Freud S. 1927. *The Future of an Illusion.* Transl. J. Strachey, 1961. New York: Norton

George LK, Larson DB, Koenig HK, McCullough ME. 2000. Spirituality and health:

what we know, what we need to know. *J. Soc. Clin. Psychol.* 19:102–16

Giacalone RA, Jurkiewicz CL, eds. 2002. *The Handbook of Workplace Spirituality and Organizational Performance.* Armonk, NY: Sharpe. In press

Gilbert DT, Fiske ST, Lindzey G, eds. 1997. *Handbook of Social Psychology.* Boston: McGraw-Hill. 4th ed.

Gilbert DT, Pinel EC, Wilson TD, Blumberg SJ, Wheatley TP. 1998. Immune neglect: a source of durability bias in affective forecasting. *J. Personal. Soc. Psychol.* 75:617–38

Gillani NB, Smith JC. 2001. Zen meditation and ABC relaxation theory: an exploration of relaxation states, beliefs, dispositions, and motivations. *J. Clin. Psychol.* 57:839–46

Goodenough U. 1998. *The Sacred Depths of Nature.* New York: Oxford Univ. Press

Gorsuch RL. 1984. Measurement: the boon and bane of investigating religion. *Am. Psychol.* 39:228–36

Gorsuch RL. 1988. Psychology of religion. *Annu. Rev. Psychol.* 39:201–21

Gross JJ. 2002. Emotion regulation: affective, cognitive, and social consequences. *Psychophysiology* 39:281–91

Hall GS. 1904. *Adolescence: Its Psychology and Relations to Physiology, Anthropology, Sociology, Sex, Crime, Religion and Education,* 2 Vols. New York: Appleton

Hall GS. 1917. *Jesus, the Christ, in the Light of Psychology,* 2 Vols. New York: Appleton

Heatherton TF, Vohs KD. 2000. Interpersonal evaluations following threats to self: role of self-esteem. *J. Personal. Soc. Psychol.* 78: 725–36

Hester M. 1998. The status of the psychology of religion: an interview with R.F. Paloutzian. *Teach. Psychol.* 25:303–6

Hester M. 2002. Psychology of religion: then and now. In *The Teaching of Psychology: A Tribute to Wilbert McKeachie and Charles Brewer,* ed. S Davis, W Buskist. Mahwah, NJ: Erlbaum

Hill PC. 1999. Giving religion away: what the study of religion offers psychology. *Int. J. Psychol. Relig.* 9:229–49

Hill PC, Hood RW Jr. 1999. *Measures of Religiosity.* Birmingham, AL: Religious Educ. Press

Hill PC, Pargament KI, Wood RW Jr, McCullough ME, Swyers JP, et al. 2000. Conceptualizing religion and spirituality: points of commonality, points of departure. *J. Theory Soc. Behav.* 30:51–77

Hogan R, Johnson J, Briggs S, eds. 1997. *Handbook of Personality Psychology.* San Diego, CA: Academic

Hood RW Jr. 1995. *Handbook of Religious Experience.* Birmingham, AL: Religious Educ. Press

Hood RW Jr, Spilka B, Hunsberger B, Gorsuch RI. 1996. *The Psychology of Religion: An Empirical Approach.* New York: Guilford

Huang ST, Enright RD. 2000. Forgiveness and anger-related emotions in Taiwan: implications for therapy. *Psychotherapy* 37:71–79

Hutch RA. 1978. Jonathan Edwards' analysis of religious experience. *J. Psychol. Theol.* 6: 123–31

James W. 1902. *The Varieties of Religious Experience.* New York: Longmans

Jung CG. 1938. *Psychology and Religion.* New Haven: Yale Univ. Press

Kanagy CL, Willits FK. 1993. A "greening" of religion? Some evidence from a Pennsylvania sample. *Soc. Sci. Q.* 74:674–83

Keltner D, Haidt J. 2002. Approaching awe: a moral, spiritual, and aesthetic emotion. *Cogn. Emot.* In press

Kirkpatrick LA. 1997. A longitudinal study of changes in religious belief and behavior as a function of individual differences in adult attachment style. *J. Sci. Stud. Relig.* 36:207–17

Kirkpatrick LA. 1998. God as a substitute attachment figure: a longitudinal study of adult attachment style and religious change in college students. *Personal. Soc. Psychol. Bull.* 24:961–73

Kirkpatrick LA. 1999. Toward an evolutionary psychology of religion and personality. *J. Pers.* 67:921–52

Koenig HG, ed. 1998. *Handbook of Religion*

and Mental Health. San Diego, CA: Academic

Koenig HG, McCullough ME, Larson DB. 2001. *Handbook of Religion and Health.* New York: Oxford Univ. Press

Leak G, Fish S. 1999. Development and initial validation of a measure of religious maturity. *Int. J. Psychol. Relig.* 9:83–104

Leak GK, Loucks AA, Bowlin P. 1999. Development and initial validation of an objective measure of faith development. *Int. J. Psychol. Relig.* 9:105–24

Loewenthal KN. 2000. *The Psychology of Religion: A Short Introduction.* Oxford: Oneworld

MacDonald DA. 2000. Spirituality: description, measurement, and relation to the five factor model of personality. *J. Pers.* 68:153–97

Mahoney A, Pargament KI, Jewell T, Swank AB, Scott E, et al. 1999. Marriage and the spiritual realm: the role of proximal and distal religious constructs in marital functioning. *J. Fam. Psychol.* 13:321–38

Malony HN, Southard S, eds. 1992. *Handbook of Religious Conversion.* Birmingham, AL: Religious Educ. Press

Malony HN, Spilka B, eds. 1991. *Religion in Psychodynamic Perspective: The Contributions of Paul W. Pruyser.* New York, Oxford Univ. Press

Maltby J, Macaskill A, Day L. 2001. Failure to forgive self and others: a replication and extension of the relationship between forgiveness, personality, social desirability and general health. *Personal. Individ. Differ.* 30: 881–85

Mayer JD. 1994. Emotion over time within a religious culture: a lexical analysis of the Old Testament. *J. Psychohist.* 22:235–48

McCauley RN. 2001. Ritual, memory, and emotion: comparing two cognitive hypotheses See Andresen 2001, pp. 115–40

McCrae RR, Costa PT Jr. 1999. A Five-Factor theory of personality. In *Handbook of Personality: Theory and Research,* ed. LA Pervin, OP John, pp. 139–53. New York: Guilford. 2nd ed.

McCraty R, Barrios-Choplin B, Rozman D,

Atkinson M, Watkins AD. 1998. The impact of a new emotional self-management program on stress, emotions, heart rate variability, DHEA and cortisol. *Integr. Physiol. Behav. Sci.* 33:151–70

McCullough ME. 2001. Forgiveness: Who does it and how do they do it? *Am. Psychol. Soc.* 10:194–97

McCullough ME, Emmons RA, Tsang J. 2002. The grateful disposition: a conceptual and empirical topography. *J. Personal. Soc. Psychol.* 82:112–27

McCullough ME, Kilpatrick SD, Emmons RA, Larson DB. 2001. Is gratitude a moral affect? *Psychol. Bull.* 127:249–66

McCullough ME, Pargament KI, Thoresen CE, eds. 2000. *Forgiveness: Theory, Practice and Research.* New York: Guilford

McCullough ME, Snyder CR. 2000. Classical source of human strength: revisiting an old home and building a new one. *J. Soc. Clin. Psychol.* 19:1–10

McCullough ME, Worthington EL Jr. 1999. Religion and the forgiving personality. *J. Pers.* 67:1141–64

McCullough ME, Worthington EL Jr, Rachal KC. 1997. Interpersonal forgiving in close relationships. *J. Personal. Soc. Psychol.* 73: 321–36

McFadden SH. 1999. Religion, personality and aging: a life span perspective. *J. Pers.* 67: 1081–104

McNamara P. 2001. Religion and the frontal lobes. See Andresen 2001, pp. 237–56

Megargee E. 1997. Internal inhibitions and controls. See Hogan et al. 1997, pp. 581–614

Miller WR, ed. 1999. *Integrating Spirituality into Treatment: Resources for Practitioners.* Washington, DC: Am. Psychol. Assoc.

Miller WR, C'de Baca J. 2001. *Quantum Change: When Epiphanies and Sudden Insights Transform Ordinary Lives.* New York: Guilford

Moberg DO. 2002. Assessing and measuring spirituality: confronting dilemmas of universal and particular evaluative criteria. *J. Adult Dev.* 9:47–60

Mullet E, Barros B, Frongia L, Usai V, Neto F,

Riveiro-Shafighi S. 2002. Religious involvement and the forgiving personality. *J. Pers.* In press

Murphy N. 1998. Nonreductive physicalism: philosophical issues. In *Whatever Happened to the Soul*, ed. WS Brown, N Murphy, N Malony, pp. 127–48. Minneapolis: Fortress

Newberg A, d'Aquili E, Rause V. 2001. *Why God Won't Go Away: Brain Science and the Biology of Belief.* New York: Ballantine

Ozer DJ, Reise SP. 1994. Personality assessment. *Annu. Rev. Psychol.* 45:357–88

Paloutzian RF. 1983. *Invitation to the Psychology of Religion.* Glenview, IL: Scott, Foresman

Paloutzian RF. 1996. *Invitation to the Psychology of Religion.* Needham Heights, MA: Allyn & Bacon. 2nd ed.

Paloutzian RF, Kirkpatrick LA, eds. 1995. Religious influences on personal and societal well-being. *J. Soc. Issues* 51(2):whole issue

Paloutzian RF, Richardson JT, Rambo LR. 1999. Religious conversion and personality change. *J. Pers.* 67:1047–80

Pargament KI. 1997. *The Psychology of Religion and Coping.* New York: Guilford

Pargament KI. 1999. The psychology of religion *and* spirituality? Yes and no. *Int. J. Psychol. Relig.* 9:3–16

Pargament KI, Park CL. 1995. Merely a defense? The variety of religious means and ends. *J. Soc. Issues* 51:13–32

Park YO, Enright RD. 1997. The development of forgiveness in the context of adolescent friendship conflict in Korea. *J. Adolesc.* 20:393–402

Parke RD. 2001. Introduction to the special section on families and religion: a call for a recommitment by researchers, practitioners, and policymakers. *J. Fam. Psychol.* 15:555–58

Pervin LA, ed. 1990. *Handbook of Personality: Theory and Research.* New York: Guilford

Peterson C, Seligman M. 2002. The VIA Taxonomy of Human Strengths and Virtues. Washington, DC: Am. Psychol. Assoc.

Piedmont RL. 1999a. Does spirituality represent the sixth factor of personality? Spiritual transcendence and the five-factor model. *J. Pers.* 67:985–1014

Piedmont RL. 1999b. Strategies for using the five-factor model of personality in religious research. *J. Psychol. Theol.* 27:338–50

Piedmont RL, Leach MM. 2002. Cross-cultural generalizability of the spiritual transcendence scale in India: spirituality as a universal aspect of human experience. *Am. Behav. Sci.* In press

Plante TG, Sherman AC, eds. 2001. *Faith and Health: Psychological Perspectives.* New York: Guilford

Rambo L. 1993. *Understanding Religious Conversion.* New Haven, CT: Yale Univ. Press

Richards PS, Bergin AE. 1997. *A Spiritual Strategy for Counseling and Psychotherapy.* Washington, DC: Am. Psychol. Assoc.

Richards PS, Bergin AE, eds. 2000. *Handbook of Psychotherapy and Religious Diversity.* Washington, DC: Am. Psychol. Assoc.

Rosengren KS, Johnson CN, Harris PL, eds. 2000. *Imagining the Impossible: Magical, Scientific, and Religious Thinking in Children.* New York: Cambridge Univ. Press

Rowatt WC, Ottenbreit A, Nesselroade KP Jr, Cunningham PA. 2002. On being holier-than-thou or humbler-than-thee: a social-psychological perspective on religiousness and humility. *J. Sci. Stud. Relig.* 41:227–37

Rye MS, Pargament KI, Ali MA, Beck GL, Dorff EN, et al. 2000. Religious perspectives on forgiveness. In *Forgiveness: Theory, Practice and Research*, ed. ME McCullough, KI Pargament, CE Thoresen, pp. 17–40. New York: Guilford

Samuels PA, Lester D. 1985. A preliminary investigation of emotions experienced toward God by Catholic nuns and priests. *Psychol. Rep.* 56:706

Sandage SJ, Hill PC. 2001. The virtues of positive psychology: the rapprochement and challenges of an affirmative postmodern perspective. *J. Theory Soc. Behav.* 31:241–60

Sandage SJ, Worthington EL Jr, Hight TL, Berry JW. 2000. Seeking forgiveness: theoretical context and initial empirical study. *J. Psychol. Theol.* 28:21–35

Santrock JW, Paloutzian R. 1997. The psychology of religion. In *Psychology*, ed. JW Santrock. New York: McGraw-Hill. 5th ed.

Santrock JW, Paloutzian R. 2000. The psychology of religion. In *Psychology*, ed. JW Santrock. New York: McGraw-Hill. 6th ed.

Saroglou V. 2002. Religion and the five factors of personality: a meta-analytic review. *Personal. Individ. Differ.* 32:15–25

Saucier G, Goldberg LR. 1998. What is beyond the Big Five? *J. Pers.* 66:495–524

Schimmel S. 1997. *The Seven Deadly Sins: Jewish, Christian, and Classical Reflections on Human Psychology.* New York: Oxford Univ. Press

Schimmel S. 2000. Vices, virtues and sources of human strength in historical perspective. *J. Soc. Clin. Psychol.* 19:137–50

Schneider KJ, Bugental JT, Pierson JF, eds. 2001. *The Handbook of Humanistic Psychology: Leading Edges in Theory, Research,and Practice.* Thousand Oaks, CA: Sage

Seligman MEP, Csikszentmihalyi M. 2000. Positive psychology: an introduction. *Am. Psychol.* 55:5–14

Seybold KS, Hill PC, Neumann JK, Chi DS. 2001. Physiological and psychological correlates of forgiveness. *J. Psychol. Christ.* 20:250–59

Shafranske EP, ed. 1996. *Religion and the Clinical Practice of Psychology.* Washington, DC: Am. Psychol. Assoc.

Silberman I, ed. 2003. Religion as a meaning system. *J. Soc. Issues.* In press

Sinnott JD. 2001. Introduction: special issue on spirituality and adult development, Part I. *J. Adult Dev.* 8(4):whole issue

Slater W, Hall TW, Edwards KJ. 2001. Measuring religion and spirituality: Where are we and where are we going? *J. Psychol. Theol.* 29:4–21

Snyder CR, McCullough ME. 2000. A positive psychology field of dreams: "If you build it, they will come . . . " *J. Soc. Clin. Psychol.* 19:151–60

Solomon RC. 1977. *The Passions.* New York: Anchor

Spilka B, Hood RW Jr. Gorsuch RL. 1985. *Psychology of Religion: An Empirical Approach.* Englewood Cliffs, NJ: Prentice-Hall

Spilka B, McIntosh DN, eds. 1997. *The Psychology of Religion: Theoretical Approaches.* Boulder, CO: Westview/HarperCollins

Starbuck ED. 1899. *Psychology of Religion.* London: Walter Scott

Tangney JP. 2000. Humility: theoretical perspectives, empirical findings and directions for future research. *J. Soc. Clin. Psychol.* 19:70–82

Tarakeshwar N, Swank AB, Pargament KI, Mahoney A. 2002. Theological conservatism and the sanctification of nature: a study of opposing religious correlates of environmentalism. *Rev. Relig. Res.* In press

Tillich P. 1957. *Dynamics of Faith.* New York: Harper & Row

Toussaint LT, Williams DR, Musick MA, Everson SA. 2001. Forgiveness and health: age differences in a U. S. probability sample. *J. Adult Dev.* 8:249–57

Vande Kemp H. 1992. G. Stanley Hall and the Clark school of religious psychology. *Am. Psychol.* 47:290–98

Waller NG, Benet V, Farney DL. 1994. Modeling person-situation correspondence over time: a study of 103 evangelical disciplemakers. *J. Pers.* 62(2):177–97

Watts F, Williams M. 1988. *The Psychology of Religious Knowing.* Cambridge: Cambridge Univ. Press

Watts FN. 1996. Psychological and religious perspectives on emotion. *Int. J. Psychol. Relig.* 6:71–87

Witvliet CV, Ludwig TE, Vander Laan KL. 2001. Granting forgiveness or harboring grudges: implications for emotion, physiology, and health. *Psychol. Sci.* 12:117–23

Woolley JD. 2000. The development of beliefs about direct mental-physical causality in imagination, magic and religion. See Rosengren et al. 2000, pp. 99–129

Wulff D. 1997. *Psychology of Religion: Classical and Contemporary.* New York: Wiley 2nd ed.

Wulff D. 1991. *Psychology of Religion: Classic and Contemporary Views.* New York: Wiley

Wulff DM. 1998. Rethinking the rise and fall of the psychology of religion. In *Religion in the Making: The Emergence of the Sciences of Religion*, ed. AL Molendijk, P Pels, pp. 181–202. Leiden/Boston/Koln: Brill

Wuthnow R. 1998. *After Heaven: Spirituality in America Since the 1950's*. Berkeley: Univ. Calif. Press

Wuthnow R. 2000. How religious groups promote forgiving: a national study. *J. Sci. Stud. Relig.* 39:125–39

Zinnbauer BJ, Pargament KI. 1998. Spiritual conversion: a study of religious change among college students. *J. Sci. Stud. Relig.* 37:161–80

Zinnbauer BJ, Pargament KI, Cole B, Rye MS. 1997. Religion and spirituality: unfuzzying the fuzzy. *J. Sci. Stud. Relig.* 36:549–64

Zinnbauer BJ, Pargament KI, Scott AB. 1999. The emerging meanings of religiousness and spirituality: problems and prospects. *J. Pers.* 67:889–920

Annu. Rev. Psychol. 2003. 54:403–25
doi: 10.1146/annurev.psych.54.101601.145056
Copyright © 2003 by Annual Reviews. All rights reserved
First published online as a Review in Advance on August 6, 2002

PERSONALITY, CULTURE, AND SUBJECTIVE WELL-BEING: Emotional and Cognitive Evaluations of Life

Ed Diener,[1] Shigehiro Oishi,[2] and Richard E. Lucas[3]

[1]Department of Psychology, University of Illinois, Champaign, Illinois 61820;
e-mail: ediener@s.psych.uiuc.edu
[2]Department of Psychology, University of Minnesota, Minneapolis, Minnesota 55455;
e-mail: soishi@tc.umn.edu
[3]Department of Psychology, Michigan State University, East Lansing, Michigan 48824;
e-mail: lucasri@msu.edu

Key Words quality of life, life satisfaction, positive affect

■ **Abstract** Subjective well-being (SWB), people's emotional and cognitive evaluations of their lives, includes what lay people call happiness, peace, fulfillment, and life satisfaction. Personality dispositions such as extraversion, neuroticism, and self-esteem can markedly influence levels of SWB. Although personality can explain a significant amount of the variability in SWB, life circumstances also influence long-term levels. Cultural variables explain differences in mean levels of SWB and appear to be due to objective factors such as wealth, to norms dictating appropriate feelings and how important SWB is considered to be, and to the relative approach versus avoidance tendencies of societies. Culture can also moderate which variables most influence SWB. Although it is challenging to assess SWB across societies, the measures have some degree of cross-cultural validity. Although nations can be evaluated by their levels of SWB, there are still many open questions in this area.

CONTENTS

0066-4308/03/0203-0403$14.00

403

INTRODUCTION

Defining Subjective Well-Being

The field of subjective well-being (SWB) comprises the scientific analysis of how people evaluate their lives—both at the moment and for longer periods such as for the past year. These evaluations include people's emotional reactions to events, their moods, and judgments they form about their life satisfaction, fulfillment, and satisfaction with domains such as marriage and work. Thus, SWB concerns the study of what lay people might call happiness or satisfaction. General reviews of SWB can be found in Argyle (2001), Diener (1984), Diener et al. (1999), and Kahneman et al. (1999).

Everyone's moods, emotions, and self-evaluative judgments fluctuate over time; SWB researchers study these fluctuations but also examine the longer-term mean level differences that exist between individuals and societies. Although each of the components of SWB reflects people's evaluations of what is happening in their lives, the facets of SWB such as positive affect, lack of negative affect, and life satisfaction show some degree of independence (Andrews & Withey 1976, Lucas et al. 1996) and therefore should be measured and studied individually. In many cases, however, researchers continue to measure a single aspect of well-being or ill-being such as depression or life satisfaction, and therefore those are the data that are available for this review.

History of Research on Subjective Well-Being

Several different lines of research come together in the history of the field of SWB. A major influence on the field came from sociologists and quality of life researchers who conduct surveys to determine how demographic factors such as income and marriage influence SWB (e.g., Bradburn 1969, Andrews & Withey 1976, Campbell et al. 1976).

Another influence on the field came from researchers working in the area of mental health, who wanted to extend the idea of mental health beyond the absence of symptoms of depression and distress to also include the presence of happiness and life satisfaction (e.g., Jahoda 1958). Yet another influence was from personality psychologists who studied the personalities of happy and unhappy people (e.g., Wessman & Ricks 1966). Finally, social and cognitive psychologists studied how adaptation and varying standards influence people's feelings of well-being (e.g., Brickman & Campbell 1971, Parducci 1995). These various strands were brought together in integrative reviews by Diener (1984) and Veenhoven (1984). Because of the diverse influences on the field, a variety of methods such as surveys, laboratory experiments, and intensive studies of individuals have all been commonplace.

There are a number of theoretical traditions that have contributed to our understanding of SWB. Humanistic psychology stimulated the interest in positive well-being. A number of factors such as temperament (Lykken & Tellegen 1996), adaptation to conditions (Lucas et al. 2002), and goal striving (Emmons 1986) substantially influence levels of SWB. However, there is currently no single conceptual scheme that unites the field, although attempts at unification have been made (e.g., Diener & Lucas 2000).

SWB is measured in a variety of ways. For the emotional components, for example feelings of joy and contentment, broad survey measures have been used (e.g., "In general how happy are you?"), as well as experience sampling of moods and emotions over time and informant reports from family and friends. The cognitive component of SWB has been assessed with life satisfaction surveys and also with measures of satisfaction and fulfillment in various life domains such as marriage, work, and leisure (see Sandvik et al. 1993 for a description of alternative methods of measurement of SWB).

The Importance of Subjective Well-Being

SWB is one measure of the quality of life of an individual and of societies. Philosophers have debated the nature of the good life for millennia, and one conclusion that has emerged from this debate is that the good life is happy (although philosophers often differ on the definition of happiness). We consider positive SWB to be necessary for the good life and good society, but not sufficient for it. It is hard to imagine that a dissatisfied and depressed culture would be an ideal society, no matter how desirable it is in other respects. A person or society that has high SWB, however, might still be missing an ingredient such as fairness, which people might consider to be essential to a high quality of life. Diener & Suh (1998), working from the philosophical notion of utility, suggested that SWB is one of three major ways to assess the quality of life of societies, along with economic and social indicators. How people feel and think about their own lives is essential to understanding well-being in any society that grants importance not just to the opinions of experts or leaders, but to all people in the society. We therefore maintain that abundant SWB is a necessary, but not sufficient, characteristic of the good society and the good life. As such, the area of SWB is of fundamental importance to the behavioral sciences.

Structure of the Review

In this chapter we focus on two interrelated factors that influence SWB—personality and culture. These two domains are intertwined in that both culture and personality are influenced by social learning, genetics, and their interactions, and both have significant influences on SWB. The parallels between culture and personality are obvious. Both can influence mean levels of SWB, as well as moderate the factors that correlate with people's experiences of well-being. Furthermore, culture can influence personality, and vice-versa. Thus, both levels of analysis are fundamental to our understanding of SWB and are covered in this review.

One aspect of the literature that we do not review concerns the outcomes of SWB—the benefits and costs of the experience of feeling good about one's life. Lyubomirsky et al. (2001) reviewed evidence showing that happiness and high chronic levels of positive affect have benefits in terms of marital quality, income, creativity, sociability, and productivity. However, little is known about how either personality or culture moderates these outcomes. Most of the research has been conducted in western nations, and very little is known about how temperament might alter the benefits of high SWB. Therefore, we eagerly anticipate the time when sufficient empirical work will be available to allow an informative review of this domain. The challenge is to disentangle predictors and consequences of SWB; thus far this has been approached with long-term longitudinal designs and with experimental research in which emotions are manipulated and the results observed.

PERSONALITY AND SUBJECTIVE WELL-BEING

Major Characteristics that Influence Subjective Well-Being

Early SWB researchers focused on identifying the external conditions that lead to satisfying lives. For example, in his influential article entitled "Correlates of Avowed Happiness," Wilson (1967) catalogued the various demographic factors that were related to SWB measures. Yet after decades of research, psychologists came to realize that external factors often have only a modest impact on well-being reports (for a review see Diener et al. 1999). Demographic factors such as health, income, educational background, and marital status account for only a small amount of the variance in well-being measures. Research instead shows that SWB is fairly stable over time, that it rebounds after major life events, and that it is often strongly correlated with stable personality traits. Thus, many researchers have turned their attention towards understanding the relations between personality and SWB.

Although many personality traits have been linked with SWB (see DeNeve & Cooper 1998 for a review), much theoretical and empirical work has focused on the moderate to strong correlations between SWB and the traits of extraversion and neuroticism (Costa & McCrae 1980, Tellegen 1985, Headey & Wearing

1992, Watson & Clark 1992). Lucas & Fujita (2000), for example, conducted a meta-analytic review and found that on average, extraversion correlated .38 with pleasant affect at the zero-order level. Furthermore, when multiple, diverse methods of measurement were used to model the association between extraversion and pleasant affect, the correlation often approached .80. Fujita (1991) found similarly strong correlations when he used structural equation modeling techniques to assess the strength of the correlation between neuroticism and negative affect. Because of the consistency of these findings, many researchers have suggested that extraversion and neuroticism provide the primary links between personality and SWB.

Yet, as DeNeve & Cooper (1998) showed, focusing solely on extraversion and neuroticism may oversimplify the complicated pattern of associations among personality and SWB. There are a number of broad dimensions and narrower traits that have exhibited consistent correlations with SWB constructs. For example, DeNeve & Cooper showed that the Big Five dimensions of agreeableness and conscientiousness correlated approximately .20 with SWB measures, and a number of narrow traits such as repressive defensiveness, trust, locus of control, desire for control, and hardiness all exhibited moderate correlations with SWB. It is clear that these and other traits such as self-esteem and dispositional optimism are related to SWB (Lucas et al. 1996). What is unclear is whether these narrower traits uniquely predict SWB once the shared variance with traits such as extraversion and neuroticism is controlled.

It is also likely that additional nontrait features of personality are related to SWB constructs. Emmons (1986) showed that various features of one's goals (including the existence of important goals, progress towards those goals, and conflict among different goals) can have important implications for emotional and cognitive well-being; other researchers (e.g., Cantor & Sanderson 1999, Higgins et al. 1999, Scheier & Carver 1993) have suggested that the way we approach our goals influences SWB. In addition, researchers have suggested that having a coherent sense of one's personality and acting in accordance with that personality are positively related to well-being (e.g., Donahue et al. 1993, Sheldon et al. 1997), though these findings might not generalize to less individualistic cultures (Suh 1999).

Whether researchers focus on traits or on other nontrait personality factors, they must be careful not to make inferences about causal priority from correlational data. Most studies of personality and well-being are correlational, and although researchers often assume that stable personality traits must influence what they believe to be the more transient feelings of well-being (e.g., Eysenck & Eysenck 1985), there is evidence that the reverse causal direction may be true. For example, Cunningham (1988) and Isen (1987) have shown that inducing pleasant moods can lead to greater feelings of sociability, which is a defining characteristic of the extraversion trait. Thus, it is possible that chronically high levels of positive affect might induce greater sociability. Therefore, researchers must focus attention on determining the causal direction of the observed personality and SWB associations.

This will require developing strong theories about the processes underlying the relations, as well as collecting longitudinal data.

Personality Theories of Subjective Well-Being

Individual differences in both personality and SWB emerge early in life, are stable over time, and have a moderate to strong genetic component (see Diener & Lucas 1999 for a review). These findings have led some to conclude that SWB is primarily determined by our inborn predispositions (e.g., Lykken & Tellegen 1996). Others have argued that the importance of inborn traits may depend on the types of questions we ask about SWB. For example, Lucas et al. (2002a) argued that by looking at SWB within individuals over time, researchers will find that life events and life changes have important implications for well-being beyond the effects of personality. Yet, regardless of the origins of individual differences, personality and SWB researchers must develop precise theories that can explain why certain individuals are chronically happier and more satisfied with their lives. Temperament theories of personality and SWB have been focused primarily on three aspects of individual differences in well-being: (*a*) baseline levels of affective and cognitive well-being, (*b*) emotional reactivity, and (*c*) cognitive processing of emotional information. For example, Headey & Wearing (1992) proposed the Dynamic Equilibrium Model, in which individuals have unique baseline levels of well-being that are determined by their personality. Specifically, they argued that individuals with certain personalities are likely to experience certain types of events—extraverts may be more likely than introverts to get married or to get a high-status job—and these events influence an individual's average level of well-being. Unusual events can move a person above or below this baseline level, but according to Headey & Wearing, the individual will eventually return to baseline as events normalize.

Other researchers have argued that average differences in well-being are due to differences in emotional reactivity. Based on Gray's (1970, 1991) theory of personality, scientists such as Tellegen (1985) and Larsen (e.g., Larsen & Ketelaar 1989, 1991; Rusting & Larsen 1997) argued that extraverts are more reactive to pleasant emotional stimuli than are introverts, and neurotic individuals are more reactive to unpleasant emotional stimuli than are stable individuals. Although there has been some support for individual differences in reactivity in laboratory studies (e.g., Larsen & Ketelaar 1989, 1991; Rusting & Larsen 1997), evidence of real-world reactivity assessed in experience-sampling studies has been mixed (see e.g., Gable et al. 2000, Lucas et al. 2002b), and the small differences in reactivity that have been found do not account for all of the covariance between personality and SWB.

A final temperament variable that might explain the relations between personality and SWB is the way people process emotional information. Rusting (1998) reviewed evidence that the personality traits of extraversion and neuroticism, as well as long-term affective traits and momentary affective states, are related to individual differences in the processing of emotional content. There is evidence that people are more likely to perceive, attend to, and remember emotionally congruent or trait-congruent information better than incongruent information. For example, Derryberry & Reed (1994) found that extraverts were slower than introverts to shift their attention away from rewarding stimuli. Tamir et al. (2002) found that extraverts more quickly related events to their motives when they were in a positive mood, whereas introverts did so more quickly when they were in a negative or neutral mood.

Diener & Lucas (1999) reviewed a number of additional theoretical explanations for individual differences in SWB, including emotion-socialization models and goal models. However, these models are often more useful in explaining the long-term stability and consistency of SWB than the specific links between personality traits and well-being.

Personality-Based Causes of Subjective Well-Being

Most theories explaining the personality–well-being relation have focused on the direct effects of personality on emotional and cognitive well-being. However, it is also likely that there are indirect or interactional effects, such that different events and life circumstances affect well-being differently depending on one's personality. For example, although extraverts are generally happier than introverts, Kette (1991) found that extraverted prisoners were less happy than introverted prisoners. This suggests that the situational features of prison were not congruent with an extraverted disposition. Oishi et al. (2001) illustrated the interaction between personality and situations more directly: They used a daily diary study to show that the experience of physical pleasure was more strongly related to daily satisfaction among high sensation-seekers than among low sensation-seekers. Other researchers have found, however, that extraverts do not react any differently than introverts to social and nonsocial situations and life circumstances (e.g., Diener et al. 1984, Lucas 2001, Pavot et al. 1990).

Moscowitz & Coté (1995; also see Coté & Moscowitz 2000) attempted to resolve the discrepant findings by positing that it is not the congruence between personality and situations that is important for affect, but the congruence between personality and behaviors. They showed that experiencing trait-congruent or trait-incongruent situations was not related to differential levels of affect. For example, extraverts are not necessarily happier in social situations. However, for certain traits (agreeableness, dominance, and quarrelsomeness in one study; agreeableness and neuroticism in another), engaging in trait-congruent behaviors was associated with higher levels of positive affect, and trait-incongruent behaviors were associated with higher levels of negative affect. For example, dominant people are likely to report higher SWB when they are behaving in a dominant manner.

Oishi et al. (1999b) suggested that values play an important interactive role in the associations between personality and well-being. They found that values moderated the relation between specific domain satisfactions and overall life satisfaction and values moderated the effect of daily activities on daily satisfaction. People high in achievement orientation are more likely to take academic success into account than are low sensation seekers when evaluating their satisfaction with their day. Together, these studies suggest that it is necessary to examine units of analysis beyond simple traits and situations to find interactive effects of personality on SWB.

CULTURE AND SUBJECTIVE WELL-BEING

Differences in Mean Levels of Subjective Well-Being Between Nations

Many of the findings on culture and SWB parallel the conclusions on personality and SWB. International surveys of life satisfaction show consistent mean level differences across nations (e.g., Inglehart & Klingemann 2000, Veenhoven 1993). For instance, between the years 1958 and 1987 Japanese life satisfaction fluctuated around 6 on a 10-point scale (Veenhoven 1993). Denmark's national average life satisfaction, on the other hand, fluctuated around a value of 8. Cultural differences parallel to the international differences have been observed within the United States across different ethnic groups. For instance, Oishi (2001a) found that European Americans were significantly more satisfied with their lives than Asian Americans. Similarly, Okazaki (2000) observed that Asian Americans reported higher levels of depression and anxiety than did European Americans. Thus, there are differences between nations, and between ethnic groups within nations.

The Causes of Societal Mean Level Differences in Subjective Well-Being

Many studies are based on the analysis of nations rather than cultures per se because data are collected within each country. However, nations are often aligned with cultures because of their historical development, although obviously there is not a perfect match (e.g., Hermans & Kempen 1998). A comprehensive examination of the effects of culture on well-being can be found in Diener & Suh (2000). A number of factors might explain why societies differ in mean levels of SWB (Diener & Lucas 2000). In the following section we review several variables that appear promising in explaining nation-level differences. In our opinion societal differences in mean SWB are likely to be overdetermined—to be due to several factors, not to any single one.

Wealth and Related Predictors

Diener et al. (1995) found large differences in SWB between nations, which correlated substantially with the average levels of income in those nations. Diener & Biswas-Diener (2002) reviewed a number of studies that report correlations in the neighborhood of .60 to .70 between the wealth of nations and their mean levels of SWB. When we realize that wealthy nations are likely to score higher on human rights, equality, longevity, and democratic governance, the strong relation between wealth and SWB of societies is not surprising. Although attempts have been made to disentangle the effects on SWB of income and the various social indicators that co-occur in wealthier versus poorer nations, these have not been successful because of the high intercorrelation of the predictors and the limited sample size of nations available for such analyses. For example, Diener et al. (1995) concluded that individualism was crucial to the higher happiness levels of wealthy nations, but Schyns (1998) failed to replicate this pattern. Such attempts seem unlikely to achieve a replicable conclusion until we study a larger number of nations and have longitudinal measures of key variables.

Income is most strongly related to SWB at very low levels of money, where small increments in wealth can have a substantial impact. For example, among respondents in the slums of Calcutta, Biswas-Diener & Diener (2001) report a strong correlation of .45 between income and life satisfaction. Diener & Biswas-Diener (2002) report that the correlation between income and SWB is much smaller in economically developed nations. At the between-nation level, Inglehart & Klingemann (2000) report a curvilinear relation similar to that found for individuals (Diener et al. 1993), in which income differences matter most to SWB at low levels of wealth. One explanation for why income matters most at low levels is based on the idea that at low levels of income, increases are likely to be related to inherent human needs, for example obtaining food and shelter, whereas at high levels of income, increases simply lead to the purchase of more luxury items (Veenhoven 1991). The hypothesis is that SWB results from meeting innate and universal human needs and not from meeting desires that are not related to needs. In sum, the explanation for why higher SWB is reported in wealthy nations is unclear, but the finding itself has been replicated many times.

Other Causes of Differences Between Cultures

Social psychological research in North America has demonstrated that self-serving bias occurs in various social judgments ranging from attributions (Zuckerman 1979) to reports of personality (Dunning et al. 1989). Self-serving biases are deviations from reality that put the respondent in a more favorable light than is warranted by the facts. One self-serving bias is self-enhancement, which refers to rating oneself as relatively better compared to how one rates others. Such self-serving biases, however, occur less frequently among East Asians and are weaker when they do occur (e.g., Heine et al. 2000). In contrast, researchers have found self-critical tendencies in self-evaluations and attributions among East Asians (see Heine et al. 1999). Thus, cultural difference in self-enhancement might be one factor causing cultural differences in mean levels of well-being. Oishi & Diener (2001c) found that European Americans overestimated the number of anagram tasks they solved a week earlier, whereas Asian Americans underestimated the number. In a daily diary study, Oishi (2001a) found that European Americans' life satisfaction judgment of the week as a whole was significantly higher than the average of their daily satisfaction during the same seven days, whereas Asian

Americans' life satisfaction of the week as a whole was almost identical to the average of their daily satisfaction.

In a related vein, recent research revealed cultural differences in approach versus avoidance orientation (Lee et al. 2000, Briley & Wyer 2002). For instance, Lee et al. (2000) demonstrated that thinking about one's group membership, which is a chronic collectivist tendency, made people focus on negative consequences (i.e., avoidance or loss focus), whereas thinking about one's self independent of others, which is a chronic individualist tendency, made people focus on positive consequences (i.e., approach or gain focus). In the context of SWB research, Elliot et al. (2001) found that Asian Americans, South Koreans, and Russians pursued more avoidance goals than did European Americans. In sum, cultural factors such as self-enhancement versus self-criticism and approach versus avoidance goals play a role in understanding mean differences in SWB across nations.

Tradeoffs Between Subjective Well-Being and Other Values

An intriguing finding emerging from the field of SWB is that there are tradeoffs that seem inherent in certain societal patterns: cultural strategies that have both costs and benefits. For example, individualistic nations have high mean levels of reported SWB and at the same time also manifest the highest levels of suicide and divorce (Diener 1996). It might be that the very same freedom arising from lowered social restraints on behavior can lead to happiness when things are going well, but can lead to higher levels of pathology such as suicide when things are going poorly. Marginal individuals such as those with mental illness or mental handicaps might have a harder time in individualistic societies than in collectivist ones, whereas people with a large number of strengths and resources might enjoy the individualistic lifestyle more. It is also possible that people who fail to achieve happiness in individualistic nations are more likely to commit suicide because they feel like failures and are less constrained by normative expectations.

Another manifestation of tradeoffs is in the finding that people are sometimes willing to sacrifice immediate happiness for the sake of achieving other goals that are valued in their culture. For example, Asakawa & Csikszentmihalyi (1998) found, using an experience-sampling method, that Asian-American students were more likely to be happy when they were engaging in an activity that was related to important future goals (e.g., academic achievement), whereas Caucasian students were happy when engaging in an activity that was important to them at that moment. Interestingly, Caucasian students tended to be less happy when engaging in an activity that was related to important future goals. Oishi & Diener (2001c) also found that European Americans tended to switch to another task when they did not do one task well, whereas Asian Americans tended to stick with the task that they did not do well on, in order to master it (also see Heine et al. 2001). The decision led to greater future enjoyment of the task of their choice among European Americans than among Asians. This strategy of switching activities when a person does not do well might be a good one in terms of maintaining positive moods.

However, this might not be an ideal strategy in the long run when individuals need to acquire new skills. Similarly, Kim-Prieto (2002) found that Asian-American students were more likely than Caucasian students to choose achievement goals despite the immediate hedonic consequences.

Diener (2000) reported that people in various societies differentially value happiness. Although respondents in all countries said that happiness and life satisfaction are important, those in Latin American countries gave higher importance ratings to SWB than did those in certain other societies, for example those in the Pacific Rim of Asia. These findings are consistent with the idea that people in certain East Asian nations are more likely to sacrifice positive emotions to achieve other goals they deem important, for example achievement. One open question is whether achieving these other goals ultimately leads to higher levels of life satisfaction even though positive moods might be sacrificed in the short run. If people in some cultures are more willing to give up happiness, defined as positive emotions, to obtain valued goals, they might in the long run nevertheless achieve high levels of life satisfaction.

Measurement Validity Across Cultures

Assessing SWB across cultures presents formidable challenges. The existing research suggests that cross-cultural comparisons of SWB have some degree of validity. Scollon et al. (2002a) compared the convergence of several different types of measures of positive affect and negative affect across five cultures. They found that global reports of emotion, experience-sampling-moment reports of mood, and retrospective memories of emotions tended to converge in terms of the relative positions of the cultures. Similarly, Balatsky & Diener (1993) found that memory for good events versus bad events converged with reports of life satisfaction among Russians. Oettingen & Seligman (1990) found that observational coding of smiling led to similar conclusions about the relative depression rates of East Germans versus West Germans, as did ratings of attributions for events found in newspaper articles. Although the multi-method studies to date are encouraging, much more work in this direction is needed.

One concern in cross-cultural research is whether response artifacts such as social desirability or impression management might differentially influence reports of SWB across cultures. Findings to date are somewhat encouraging, but do indicate that for some groups impression management might influence responses more than for other cultural and age groups (Okazaki 2000, Park et al. 1988). Diener et al. (1993) studied differences in responding due to humility, number use (e.g., the desire to use the middle of the scale), and other artifacts, and concluded that these potential contaminants were not necessarily a serious problem in the cross-cultural measurement of SWB. However, Byrne & Campbell (1999) found that different item-response characteristics can influence depression scores across cultures. Because of issues related to cross-cultural measurement, we recommend that investigators continue to use methods that can help assess artifacts and begin using multimethod assessment to guard against various types of measurement error. For example, researchers can use on-line experience sampling (discussed below), recall for good and bad events (e.g., Balatsky & Diener 1993), informant reports, and biological measures such as cortisol. The reader is referred to Sandvik et al. (1993) for a discussion of the convergence of the measurement methods.

One issue is whether measures imported from western nations are valid in nonwestern cultures. Vittersø et al. (2002), for example, found that reports of life satisfaction were less reliable in poorer nations, and therefore the correlation between life satisfaction and the per capita wealth of nations decreased when a correction was made for reliability. In addition, Vittersø et al. found a slightly different structure for the life satisfaction items across cultures. These results indicate that cross-cultural investigators need to examine the factor structure of their scales across cultures, as well as scale reliability. More sophisticated methods of examining participants' responses, such as item-response theory (e.g., Byrne & Campbell 1999) can also be used to carefully examine whether people respond to items in a similar way across cultures.

Scollon et al. (2002b) included indigenous emotion words when they assessed positive and negative affect in five cultures. They found that the indigenous words loaded highly on the emotion factors derived from the western emotion words and in fact sometimes loaded most highly of any emotions on the positive and negative affect factors. This finding suggests that the value of including indigenous emotion words might in part be that they are excellent measures of the underlying emotion factors. It is noteworthy that in all five cultures, Scollon et al. (2001) found a strong two-factor structure for emotions, representing positive and negative affect.

Top-down versus bottom-up influences on SWB (Diener 1984) refer to broad personality and cognitive factors that influence SWB versus events and circumstances that can influence SWB. Leonardi et al. (1999) suggest that different measures may differentially reflect top-down versus bottom-up processes. One example of a top-down factor is positivity, the tendency to view things in a positive light if sufficient leeway is given to do so. An interesting cross-cultural finding suggests that the degree of positivity varies across cultures, is most likely to influence broad, global reports of SWB, and is less likely to influence more specific and concrete reports. Diener et al. (2000) found that when satisfaction with broad domains such as recreation and education was compared to satisfaction with narrower domains such as television and one's professors, the difference predicted life satisfaction. Further, the broad domains were rated as more satisfying than the narrow domains in those nations where life satisfaction was said to be most desirable. The authors interpreted this finding to mean that when satisfaction with specific aspects of life was assessed, the reports depended more on a bottom-up assessment of the rated domain, whereas when satisfaction with broad domains was queried, the reports were driven more by top-down dispositions that vary across cultures. Oishi & Diener (2001a) replicated these findings at the individual level and showed that even controlling for extraversion and neuroticism, individuals high in global life satisfaction evaluated global domains (e.g., social relationships) as more satisfying than those low in life satisfaction, given the same level of satisfaction with the specific, corresponding domains (e.g., friendships and family relationships).

A recent trend in emotion research is to access affect at random moments over time with what is called the "experience-sampling method." These on-line reports of emotion can be averaged to give an indication of people's emotions in their everyday lives. It appears that recalled reports of emotion are influenced by people's expectations and self-concept, not just their on-line experiences of emotion. Wirtz et al. (2001) found that students' memories of their emotions on spring break were predicted by their expectations prior to the vacation, even when the on-line emotional experiences during spring break were controlled. Extending this finding to the cross-cultural context, Scollon et al. (2002a) found that within each of the five cultures they studied, global self-reports of emotional experience predicted recalled emotions over and above on-line measures of emotion. Taken together, these findings suggest that global reports of emotions and life satisfaction, as well as reports of recalled emotions, are likely to reflect not only the on-line experience of emotions but also people's self-concepts and the normative value of the experiences within that culture.

The research to date on cross-cultural measurement of SWB is encouraging. At the same time, researchers need to be alert to the multiple processes that can differentially influence scores across cultures and use multimethod measurement when possible. In addition, much more focused research on the meaning of SWB scores in different cultures is needed.

Different Correlates of Subjective Well-Being Across Cultures

As the evidence for the valid measurement of SWB accumulated, researchers started to examine the processes influencing SWB across cultures. The first question was whether correlates of satisfied people would be the same across cultures. Diener & Diener (1995) examined this question by comparing the size of correlations between various domain satisfactions and global life satisfaction. Although there was no cultural difference in the size of correlation between satisfaction with friends, family, and global life satisfaction, they found a significant cultural difference in the size of correlation between satisfaction with self and global life satisfaction. Whereas satisfaction with the self was strongly correlated with life satisfaction in highly industrialized, individualistic western nations (e.g., Finland, Canada), satisfaction with the self was less correlated with global life satisfaction in less industrialized, collectivist nations such as Cameroon and India, especially for women. Similarly, Oishi et al. (1999a) found that satisfaction with self and one's freedom was a significantly stronger predictor of life satisfaction in nations high in individualism than those low in individualism. This was the case even after controlling for national wealth. In addition, consistent with Maslow's need hierarchy, the correlation between financial satisfaction and global life satisfaction was stronger in poor nations than in wealthier nations. In other words, the picture of satisfied people is similar in one sense (they tend to be satisfied with their family and friendships), but dissimilar in another (satisfied people are not necessarily self-satisfied people or people with a lot of freedom in some cultures).

Suh et al. (1998) showed that the role of internal attributes such as emotions in life satisfaction judgments differs across cultures. In individualistic nations satisfied people are often people who report experiencing a lot of positive emotions. However, this tendency was weaker in collectivist nations such as China and India. Suh et al. theorized that cultural differences exist along the dimension of subjectivism; in most individualist nations it is assumed that listening to oneself gives one answers. On the other hand, in collectivist cultures, in particular East Asian cultures, it is assumed that paying attention to social norms is important and should enter satisfaction judgments. Suh & Diener (2001) in follow-up studies found that perceived acceptance by parents and friends contributed to the life satisfaction of Asian Americans as much as emotions, whereas perceived acceptance by others did not have any additional predictive value over and above emotions in the life satisfaction of European Americans.

Similarly, Oishi & Diener (2001b) found that the type of people who experienced positive changes in well-being differed between Asian Americans and European Americans. European Americans who experienced positive changes in well-being over time achieved the goals they were pursuing for fun and enjoyment (see also Sheldon & Kasser 1998). However, Asian Americans and Japanese who experienced positive changes in well-being achieved the goals that they were pursuing to make others happy. Mesquita & Karasawa (2002) found that Japanese reports of the experience of pleasant emotions were better predicted from relationship concerns than from independent self concerns, whereas European Americans' experience of pleasant emotions was better predicted from self-concerns than from relationship concerns (see also Kitayama et al. 2000). The findings suggest that there are multiple pathways to well-being and they are somewhat different across cultures, depending on internalized cultural values. It is interesting to note that even when there was no cultural difference in explicit goal motivations measured by self-reports, predictors of well-being varied across cultures (Oishi & Diener 2001b). Thus, what makes people happy might be the fulfillment of cultural values, which they do not necessarily endorse at the explicit level (see Heine et al. 2002).

Another important issue is the degree of cross-situational consistency versus situation specificity in SWB. In the U.S. Sheldon and colleagues (Sheldon et al. 1997) found that satisfied people view themselves as consistent across different social roles and situations. For example, Americans who reported being satisfied with their lives viewed themselves as "friendly" to friends, strangers, and coworkers alike. However, Suh (1999) demonstrated that perceived cross-situational consistency of self-concept did not have a strong correlation with life satisfaction in Korea, and consistency was negatively related to likeability and social skills as reported by friends and family members. In addition, Oishi (2001b) found in an experience-sampling study that the well-being of Japanese students is much more context dependent than the well-being of Americans. That is, Japanese emotional experience differed to a greater degree across different situations (e.g., with a romantic partner versus with a stranger) than did the experience of European Americans. These findings again point to cultural variations in SWB due to the varying importance placed on consistency and field independence versus flexibility and context appropriateness (e.g., Nisbett et al. 2001, Heine & Lehman 1997).

Another interesting area of research examines whether across cultures the number of avoidance goals is related to negative well-being. Elliot et al. (2001) found that the number of avoidance goals was not as detrimental to the well-being of Asian Americans, Koreans, and Russians as to the well-being of European Americans. Similarly, Heine & Lehman (1999) found that the discrepancy between ideal and actual self was a stronger predictor of depression among European Canadians than among Japanese. It appears therefore that an avoidance focus has a more detrimental effect on well-being in a culture in which positive thinking is valued than in a culture in which vigilance is valued.

Universal Versus Variable Causes of Subjective Well-Being

A current debate in the field of SWB concerns whether there are human universals for happiness or whether its causes vary according to culture. In the section above we showed that the correlates of SWB vary across society; in this section we report evidence that supports the idea that there are certain variables that correlate with SWB across cultures. Veenhoven (1991) is one proponent of the idea that some societies are more "livable" because they fulfill more universal human needs such as for food, water, shelter, and so forth. In support of the universal livability idea, Veenhoven found that the nations' mean life satisfaction was correlated .84 with their gross national product per capita. Spector et al. (2001) found that locus of control correlated with subjective well-being across all the nations they studied. One challenge, however, is to determine what are the universal human needs.

One universalistic approach derives from humanistic theories of psychology. For example, Ryff (1989) relied on humanism in asserting that there are six universal needs—for autonomy, growth, relationships, purpose in life, environmental mastery, and self-acceptance. Ryff found that the degree to which people reported fulfilling these needs correlated with their reported life satisfaction. Diener et al. (1998), however, suggested that the needs of humanistic psychologists might be weighted toward western values and found that they correlated with life satisfaction more strongly in the United States than in South Korea or China (Sapyta 1997).

An approach to SWB based on inherent and universal human needs is the Self-Determination Theory of Deci & Ryan (2000). This theory posits three basic psychological needs—autonomy, competence, and relatedness—and predicts that fulfillment of these needs is essential for well-being. Deci, Ryan, and their colleagues found that fulfillment of these needs, which they refer to as "intrinsic," such as autonomy, competence, and relatedness, is related to SWB in diverse nations such as the United States, Bulgaria, Germany, South Korea, and Russia

(Chirkov & Ryan 2001, Deci et al. 2002, Ryan et al. 1999, Schmuck et al. 2000, Sheldon et al. 2001). It seems reasonable, of course, to suggest that there are both universal and culture-specific causes of SWB. The empirical challenge is to identify these two types of variables and determine the degree to which universal needs are channeled by the culture.

The question of the universality of the causes of SWB is of immense applied importance. If people can be happy once their universal needs are fulfilled, then the road to high SWB seems clear. If, however, a never-ending spiral of desires and rising standards can influence SWB, then simply fulfilling everyone's basic needs will not be a guarantee of universal happiness. Finally, to the degree that goals and values that are culture specific can influence what leads to SWB, the quest for the "good society" must consider the degree to which specific cultural values are fulfilled.

Studying the Heterogeneity of Cultural Effects

A major critique to existing cross-cultural research is the lack of attention to within-culture variation (Hong et al. 2000, Matsumoto 1999). In typical cross-cultural studies researchers compare a sample from one nation or ethnic group with a sample from another. One fundamental assumption in such research is that members of a cultural group share key experiences that lead to psychological tendencies, albeit in varying degrees, in all or most members of the societies. This assumption is perhaps too strong; for example, there are certainly self-critical Americans and self-promoting Japanese. Furthermore, past studies reveal a surprisingly small difference among cultures in values and self-concept (see Oyserman et al. 2002). Thus, Hong et al. (2000) advocate the dynamic social constructionist approach to cultural psychology, which first assumes the universal presence of lay theories about the self and world and, second, assumes that cultural differences exist in terms of the relative chronic accessibility of each theory. This approach does not require the assumption of within-culture homogeneity and models well the cultural, individual, and situational changes in salient values and self-concept (see Briley & Wyer 2002, Suh & Diener 2001).

Another approach to the problem of within-culture variability is a statistical one. Recently, Eid & Diener (2001) applied multigroup latent class analysis to emotional experiences among Americans, Australians, Chinese, and Taiwanese. Through this analysis they identified the existence of five classes of respondents within each nation (e.g., one class of subjects who reported that positive emotions are very desirable and another class who reported that positive emotions are neither desirable nor undesirable, etc.). Although there was a class of people who reported positive emotions to be very desirable in all four nations, the proportion of the sample belonging in this class varied dramatically across cultures. Multigroup latent class provides an analysis of the homogeneity of the structure of emotions, norms, and other variables across individuals within cultures, as well as revealing how groups of individuals are similar and different across cultures. Thus, it is a promising technique that can reveal elements of universality across cultures, as well as variations within the cultures.

EFFECT SIZES OF PERSONALITY AND CULTURE

How large are personality and cultural effects on SWB? Matsumoto et al. (2001) argue that we should always examine culture effect sizes—and that sometimes they are quite small. Scollon et al. (2002a) found that differences between individuals within cultures accounted for much more variance in affect than did culture. Nevertheless, culture accounted for a significant amount of variance in positive emotions, although not in negative emotions. However, the samples of Scollon et al. were restricted to college students living in urban areas, and therefore their results might not indicate the full range of SWB that might be due to culture. Therefore, we examined the amount of variance in the World Value Survey II (Inglehart et al. 1998) (which consists of national probability samples from 43 nations) that was due to persons within nations versus between-nation differences. Fifteen percent of the variance in life satisfaction, 12% of the variance in satisfaction with health, and 12% of the variance in financial satisfaction was due to between-nation differences. In our International College Sample (see Suh et al. 1998) we also computed the amount of variance owing to nations (N = 39) versus individuals within nations. Twelve percent of the variance in life satisfaction, 18% of the variance in positive emotions, and 11% of the variance in negative emotions was due to between-nation differences. It appears that individual differences within societies produce a large source of variance in SWB but that between-nation differences are far from trivial.

In addition to examining mean-level cultural differences, we can also analyze how cultural change alters average levels of SWB. For example, Inglehart & Klingemann (2000) report very low levels of SWB in the former communist nations of Europe and Asia. The societal dislocations occurring in those countries when their political and economic systems were transformed led to large declines in SWB. The effects of culture change are potentially quite important and deserve much more research.

CONCLUSIONS

There are substantial individual differences in SWB, as well as mean level differences between cultures. We have begun to understand why such differences occur. For example, there are dispositional differences that predispose people to more or less positive affect, and genetics and early rearing seem to contribute to such differences. At the cultural level norms in nations for feeling positive emotions relate to the amount of pleasant emotions reported in those countries.

Are the causes of high SWB universal or are they particular to the culture one lives in? Perhaps both. Some ubiquitous needs such as for temperature control, food, health, environmental control, and social relationships might be necessary for SWB. These needs may be so likely to drive people's desires and goals that they almost inevitably have some impact on SWB. However, there also appear to be differences in goals and values between individuals, and between cultures, that lead to distinct predictors of SWB.

Is there a good culture, and are some cultures bad, as asserted by Edgerton (1992)? It appears that some cultures produce higher levels of SWB than do others. It seems unlikely that the low levels of SWB found in very poor nations and in the former Soviet bloc countries are merely measurement artifacts. At the same time, some differences in SWB between nations appear to be due to the fact that people differentially value SWB. Thus, people may trade some amount of positive emotions in order to obtain other things they value.

Do people want to be happy, or do they want other valued goals more than happiness? Do they want those other goals because they will make them happy? We suggest that people all over the world most want to be happy by achieving the things they value. Proving this assertion represents one research goal of the future.

The *Annual Review of Psychology* is online at http://psych.annualreviews.org

LITERATURE CITED

Andrews FM, Withey SB. 1976. *Social Indicators of Well-Being*. New York: Plenum

Argyle M. 2001. *The Psychology of Happiness*. New York: Taylor & Francis

Asakawa K, Csikszentmihalyi M. 1998. Feelings of connectedness and internalization of values in Asian American adolescents. *J. Youth Adolesc.* 29:121–45

Balatsky G, Diener E. 1993. Subjective well-being among Russian students. *Soc. Indic. Res.* 28:225–43

Biswas-Diener R, Diener E. 2002. Making the best of a bad situation: satisfaction in the slums of Calcutta. *Soc. Indic. Res.* 55:329–52

Bradburn NM. 1969. *The Structure of Psychological Well-Being*. Chicago: Aldine

Brickman P, Campbell DT. 1971. Hedonic relativism and planning the good society. In *Adaptation-Level Theory*, ed. MH Appley, pp. 287–305. New York: Academic

Briley DA, Wyer RS. 2002. *The Effects of Group Membership and Cultural Identity Salience on the Avoidance of Negative Outcomes: Implications for Social and Consumer Decisions*. Hong Kong: Hong Kong Univ. Sci. Technol. Submitted

Byrne BM, Campbell TL. 1999. Cross-cultural comparisons and the presumption of equivalent measurement and theoretical structure: a look beneath the surface. *J. Cross-Cult. Psychol.* 30:555–74

Campbell A, Converse PE, Rodgers WL. 1976. *The Quality of American Life*. New York: Sage Found.

Cantor N, Sanderson CA. 1999. Life task participation and well-being: the importance of taking part in daily life. See Kahneman et al. 1999, pp. 230-43

Chirkov VI, Ryan RM. 2001. Parent and teacher autonomy support in Russia and U.S. adolescents: common effects on well-being and academic motivation. *J. Cross-Cult. Psychol.* 32:618–35

Costa PT, McCrae RR. 1980. Influence of extraversion and neuroticism on subjective well-being: happy and unhappy people. *J. Personal. Soc. Psychol.* 54:296–308

Coté S, Moscowitz DS. 2000. On the dynamic covariation between interpersonal behavior and affect: prediction from neuroticism, extraversion, and agreeableness. *J. Personal. Soc. Psychol.* 75:1032–46

Cunningham MR. 1988. What do you do when you're happy or blue? Mood, expectancies, and behavioral interest. *Motiv. Emot.* 12: 309–31

Deci EL, Ryan RM. 2000. The "what" and "why" of goal pursuits: human needs and the self-determination of behavior. *Psychol. Inq.* 11:227–68

Deci EL, Ryan RM, Gagne M, Leone DR, Usunov J, Kornazheva BP. 2002. Need satisfaction, motivation, and well-being in the work organizations of a former Eastern Bloc country: a cross-cultural study of self-determination. *Personal. Soc. Psychol. Bull.* In press

DeNeve KM, Cooper H. 1998. The happy personality: A meta-analysis of 137 personality traits and subjective well-being. *Psychol. Bull.* 124:197–229

Derryberry D, Reed MA. 1994. Temperament and attention: Orienting toward and away from positive and negative signals. *J. Personal. Soc. Psychol.* 66:1128–39

Diener E. 1984. Subjective well-being. *Psychol. Bull.* 95:542–75

Diener E. 1996. Subjective well-being in cross-cultural perspective. In *Key Issues in Cross-Cultural Psychology*, ed. H Grad, A Blanco, J Georgas, pp. 319–30. Liese, The Netherlands: Swets & Zeitlinger

Diener E. 2000. Subjective well-being: the science of happiness, and a proposal for a national index. *Am. Psychol.* 55:34–43

Diener E, Biswas-Diener R. 2002. Will money increase subjective well-being? A literature review and guide to needed research. *Soc. Indic. Res.* 57:119–69

Diener E, Diener M. 1995. Cross-cultural correlates of life satisfaction and self-esteem . *J. Personal. Soc. Psychol.* 68:653–63

Diener E, Diener M, Diener C. 1995. Factors predicting the subjective well-being of nations. *J. Personal. Soc. Psychol.* 69:851–64

Diener E, Larsen RJ, Emmons RA. 1984. Person × situation interactions: choice of situations and congruence response models. *J. Personal. Soc. Psychol.* 47:580–92

Diener E, Lucas RE. 1999. Personality and subjective well-being. See Kahneman et al. 1999, pp. 213–29

Diener E, Lucas RE. 2000. Explaining differences in societal levels of happiness: relative standards, need fulfillment, culture, and evaluation theory. *J. Happiness Stud.* 1:41–78

Diener E, Sandvik E, Seidlitz L, Diener M. 1993. The relationship between income and subjective well-being: relative or absolute? *Soc. Indic. Res.* 28:195–223

Diener E, Sapyta JJ, Suh EM. 1998. Subjective well-being is essential to well-being. *Psychol. Inq.* 9:33–37

Diener E, Scollon CN, Oishi S, Dzokoto V, Suh M. 2000. Positivity and the construction of life satisfaction judgments: global happiness is not the sum of its parts. *J. Happiness Stud.* 1:159–76

Diener E, Suh EM. 1998. Subjective well-being and age: an international analysis. *Annu. Rev. Gerontol. Geriatr.* 17:304–24

Diener E, Suh EM, eds. 2000. *Culture and Subjective Well-Being.* Cambridge, MA: MIT Press

Diener E, Suh EM, Lucas RE, Smith HE. 1999. Subjective well-being: three decades of progress. *Psychol. Bull.* 125:276–302

Donahue EM, Robins RW, Roberts BW, John OP. 1993. The divided self: concurrent and longitudinal effects of psychological adjustment and social roles on self-concept differentiation. *J. Personal. Soc. Psychol.* 64:834–46

Dunning D, Meyerowitz JA, Holzberg AD. 1989. Ambiguity and self-evaluation: the role of idiosyncratic trait definitions in self-serving assessments of ability. *J. Personal. Soc. Psychol.* 57:1082–90

Edgerton RB. 1992. *Sick Societies.* New York: Free Press

Eid M, Diener E. 2001. Norms for experiencing emotions in different cultures: inter- and intranational differences. *J. Personal. Soc. Psychol.* 81:869–85

Elliot A, Chirkov VI, Kim Y, Sheldon KM. 2001. A cross-cultural analysis of avoidance (relative to approach) personal goals. *Psychol. Sci.* 12:505–10

Emmons RA. 1986. Personal strivings: an approach to personality and subjective well-being. *J. Personal. Soc. Psychol.* 47: 1105–17

Eysenck H, Eysenck MW. 1985. *Personality and Individual Differences.* New York: Plenum

Fujita F. 1991. *An investigation of the relation between extraversion, neuroticism, positive affect, and negative affect.* MS thesis. Univ. Ill., Urbana-Champaign

Gable S, Reis HT, Elliot AJ. 2000. Behavioral activation and inhibition in everyday life . *J. Personal. Soc. Psychol.* 78:1135–49

Gray JA. 1970. The psychophysiological basis of introversion-extraversion. *Behav. Res. Ther.* 8:249–66

Gray JA. 1991. Neural systems, emotion, and personality. In *Neurobiology of Learning, Emotion, and Affect,* ed. J Madden IV, pp. 273–306. New York: Raven

Headey B, Wearing A. 1992. *Understanding Happiness: A Theory of Subjective Well-Being.* Melbourne, Aust.: Longman Cheshire

Heine SJ, Kitayama S, Lehman DR, Takata T, Ide E, et al. 2001. Divergent consequences of success and failure in Japan and North America: an investigation of self-improving motivations and malleable selves. *J. Personal. Soc. Psychol.* 81:599–615

Heine SJ, Lehman DR. 1997. Culture, dissonance, and self-affirmation. *Personal. Soc. Psychol. Bull.* 23:389–400

Heine SJ, Lehman DR. 1999. Culture, self-discrepancies, and self-satisfaction. *Personal. Soc. Psychol. Bull.* 25:915–25

Heine SJ, Lehman DR, Markus HR, Kitayama S. 1999. Is there a universal need for positive self-regard? *Psychol. Rev.* 106:766–94

Heine SJ, Lehman DR, Peng K, Greenholtz J. 2002. What's wrong with cross-cultural comparisons of subjective Likert scales? The reference-group effect. *J. Personal. Soc. Psychol.* 82:903–18

Heine SJ, Takata T, Lehman DR. 2000. Beyond self-presentation: evidence for self-criticism among Japanese. *Personal. Soc. Psychol. Bull.* 26:71–78

Hermans HJ, Kempen HJG. 1998. Moving cultures: the perilous problems of cultural dichotomies in a globalizing society. *Am. Psychol.* 53:1111–20

Higgins ET, Grant H, Shah J. 1999. Self-regulation and quality of life: emotional and non-emotional life experiences. See Kahneman et al. 1999, pp. 244–66

Hong Y-Y, Morris MW, Chiu C-Y, Benet-Martinez V. 2000. Multicultural minds: a dynamic constructivist approach to culture and cognition. *Am. Psychol.* 55:709–20

Inglehart R, Basanez M, Moreno A. 1998. *Human Values and Beliefs: A Cross-Cultural Source Book.* Ann Arbor: Univ. Mich.

Inglehart R, Klingemann H-D. 2000. Genes, culture, democracy, and happiness. See Diener & Suh 2000, pp. 165–84

Isen AM. 1987. Positive affect, cognitive processes, and social behavior. *Adv. Exp. Soc. Psychol.* 20:203–53

Jahoda M. 1958. *Current Concepts of Positive Mental Health.* New York: Basic Books

Kahneman D, Diener E, Schwarz N, eds. 1999. *Well-Being: The Foundations of Hedonic Psychology.* New York: Sage Found.

Kette G. 1991. *Haft: Eine Socialpsychologische Analyse (Prison: A Social Psychological Analysis).* Gottingen, Ger.: Hogrefe

Kim-Prieto C. 2002. *What's a wonderful life? The pursuit of personal pleasure versus ingroup desires.* MS thesis. Univ. Ill. Urbana-Champaign

Kitayama S, Markus HR, Kurosawa M. 2000. Culture, emotion, and well-being: good feelings in Japan and the United States. *Cogn. Emot.* 14:93–124

Larsen RJ, Ketelaar T. 1989. Extraversion, neuroticism, and susceptibility to positive and negative mood induction procedures. *Personal. Individ. Differ.* 10:1221–28

Larsen RJ, Ketelaar T. 1991. Personality and susceptibility to positive and negative emotional states. *J. Personal. Soc. Psychol.* 61:132–40

Lee AY, Aaker JL, Gardner WL. 2000. The pleasures and pains of distinct self-construals: the role of interdependence in regulatory focus. *J. Personal. Soc. Psychol.* 78:1122–34

Leonardi F, Spazzafumo L, Marcellini F, Gagliardi C. 1999. The top-down/bottom-up controversy from a constructionist approach. A method for measuring top-down effects applied to a sample of older people. *Soc. Indic. Res.* 48:187–216

Lucas RE. 2001. Pleasant affect and sociability: towards a comprehensive model of extraverted feelings and behaviors. *Diss. Abstr. Int.* 61(10-B):5610

Lucas RE, Clark A, Georgellis Y, Diener E. 2002. Re-examining adaptation and the setpoint model of happiness: reactions to changes in marital status. *J. Personal. Soc. Psychol.* In press

Lucas RE, Diener E, Eng JS. 2002. *Explaining the extraversion/pleasant affect relation: sociability versus reward-sensitivity.* Work. Pap., Mich. State Univ.

Lucas RE, Diener E, Suh E. 1996. Discriminant validity of well-being measures. *J. Personal. Soc. Psychol.* 71:616–28

Lucas RE, Fujita F. 2000. Factors influencing the relation between extraversion and pleasant affect. *J. Personal. Soc. Psychol.* 79:1039–56

Lykken D, Tellegen A. 1996. Happiness is a stochastic phenomenon. *Psychol. Sci.* 7:186–89

Lyubomirsky S, King L, Diener E. 2001. *Is happiness a good thing? The benefits of chronic positive affect.* Work. Pap., Univ. Calif., Riverside

Matsumoto D. 1999. Culture and self: an empirical assessment of Markus and Kitayama's theory of independent and interdependent self-construal. *Asian J. Soc. Psychol.* 2: 289–310

Matsumoto D, Grissom RJ, Dinnel DL. 2001. Do between-culture differences really mean that people are different? *J. Cross-Cult. Psychol.* 32:478–90

Mesquita B, Karasawa M. 2002. Different emotional lives. *Cogn. Emot.* 16:127–41

Moscowitz DS, Coté S. 1995. Do interpersonal traits predict affect? A comparison of three models. *J. Personal. Soc. Psychol.* 69:915–24

Nisbett RE, Peng K, Choi I, Norenzayan A. 2001. Culture and systems of thought: holistic versus analytic cognition. *Psychol. Rev.* 108:291–310

Oettingen G, Seligman ME. 1990. Pessimism and behavioral signs of depression in East versus West Berlin. *Eur. J. Soc. Psychol.* 20:207–20

Oishi S. 2001a. Culture and memory for emotional experiences: on-line vs. retrospective judgments of subjective well-being. *Diss. Abstr. Int.* 61(10-B):5625

Oishi S. 2001b. *Cross-cultural differences in on-line and retrospective happiness: US vs. Japan.* Symp. Presentation, 13th Annu. Meet. Am. Psychol. Soc., Toronto

Oishi S, Diener E. 2001a. Re-examining the general positivity model of subjective well-being: the discrepancy between specific and global domain satisfaction. *J. Personal.* 69:641–66

Oishi S, Diener E. 2001b. Goals, culture, and subjective well-being. *Personal. Soc. Psychol. Bull.* 27:1674–82

Oishi S, Diener E. 2001c. *Culture and Well-Being: The Cycle of Action, Evaluation, and Decision.* Work. Pap., Dep. Psychol., Univ. Minn. Twin Cities

Oishi S, Diener E, Lucas RE, Suh E. 1999a. Cross-cultural variations in predictors of life satisfaction: perspectives from needs and values. *Personal. Soc. Psychol. Bull.* 25:980–90

Oishi S, Diener E, Suh E, Lucas RE. 1999b. Value as a moderator in subjective well-being. *J. Personal Soc. Psychol.* 67:157–84

Oishi S, Schimmack U, Diener E. 2001. Pleasures and subjective well-being. *Eur. J. Personal.* 15:153–67

Okazaki S. 2000. Asian American and white American differences on affective distress symptoms: Do symptom reports differ across reporting methods? *J. Cross-Cult. Psychol.* 31:603–25

Oyserman D, Coon HM, Kemmelmeier M. 2002. Rethinking individualism and collectivism: evaluation of theoretical assumptions and meta-analyses. *Psychol. Bull.* 128:3–72

Parducci A. 1995. *Happiness, Pleasure and*

Judgment: The Contextual Theory and Its Applications. Mahwah, NJ: Erlbaum

Park KB, Upshaw HS, Koh SD. 1988. East Asian's responses to Western health items. *J. Cross-Cult. Psychol.* 19:51–64

Pavot W, Diener E, Fujita F. 1990. Extraversion and happiness. *Personal. Individ. Differ.* 11:1299–306

Rusting CL. 1998. Personality, mood, and cognitive processing of emotional information: three conceptual frameworks. *Psychol. Bull.* 124:165–96

Rusting CL, Larsen RJ. 1997. Extraversion, neuroticism, and susceptibility to positive and negative affect: a test of two theoretical models. *Personal. Individ. Differ.* 22:607–12

Ryan RM, Chirkov VI, Little TD, Sheldon KM, Timoshina E, Deci EL. 1999. The American Dream in Russia: extrinsic aspirations and well-being in two cultures. *Personal. Soc. Psychol. Bull.* 25:1509–24

Ryff C. 1989. Happiness is everything, or is it? Explorations on the meaning of psychological well-being. *J. Personal. Soc. Psychol.* 57:1069–81

Sandvik E, Diener E, Seidlitz L. 1993. Subjective well-being: the convergence and stability of self-report and non-self-report measures. *J. Personal.* 61:317–42

Sapyta J. 1997. *Conceptions of well-being in independent and interdependent cultures: Shall the twain ever meet?* BS thesis., Univ. Ill., Urbana-Champaign

Scheier MF, Carver CS. 1993. On the power of positive thinking: the benefits of being optimistic. *Curr. Dir. Psychol. Sci.* 2:26–30

Schmuck P, Kasser T, Ryan RM. 2000. Intrinsic and extrinsic goals: their structure and relationship to well-being in German and U.S. college students. *Soc. Indic. Res.* 50:225–41

Schyns P. 1998. Crossnational differences in happiness: economic and cultural factors explored. *Soc. Indic. Res.* 43:2–26

Scollon CN, Diener E, Oishi S. 2001. *An Experience Sampling and Cross-Cultural Investigation of Dialectical Emotional Experiences.* Unpubl. pap., Univ. Ill. Urbana-Champaign

Scollon CN, Diener E, Oishi S, Biswas-Diener R. 2002a. *Culture, Self-Concept, and Memory for One's Emotions.* Work Pap. Univ. Ill. Urbana-Champaign

Scollon CN, Diener E, Oishi S, Biswas-Diener R. 2002b. *Culture and the Experience of Specific Emotions.* Work. Pap., Univ. Ill. Urbana-Champaign

Sheldon KM, Elliot AJ, Kim Y, Kasser T. 2001. What is satisfying about satisfying events? Testing 10 candidate psychological needs. *J. Personal. Soc. Psychol.* 80:325–39

Sheldon KM, Kasser T. 1998. Pursuing personal goals: skills enable progress, but not all goal progress is beneficial. *Personal. Soc. Psychol. Bull.* 24:1319–31

Sheldon KM, Ryan RM, Rawsthorne LJ, Ilardi B. 1997. Trait self and true self: cross-role variation in the Big-Five personality traits and its relations with psychological authenticity and subjective well-being. *J. Personal. Soc. Psychol.* 73:1380–93

Spector PE, Cooper CL, Sanchez JI, O'Driscoll M, Sparks K, et al. 2001. Do national levels of individualism and internal locus of control relate to well-being: an ecological level international study. *J. Organ. Behav.* 22:815–32

Suh EM. 1999. Culture, identity consistency, and subjective well-being. *Diss. Abstr. Int.* 60-09(Sect. B):4950

Suh EM, Diener E. 2001. *The Role of the Self in Life Satisfaction Judgment: Weighing Emotions and Social Information Differently.* Work. Pap., Univ. Calif., Irvine

Suh E, Diener E, Oishi S, Triandis HC. 1998. The shifting basis of life satisfaction judgments across cultures: emotions versus norms. *J. Personal. Soc. Psychol.* 74:482–93

Tamir M, Robinson MD, Clore GL. 2002. The epistemic benefits of trait-consistent mood states: an analysis of extraversion and mood. *J. Personal. Soc. Psychol.* In press

Tellegen A. 1985. Structures of mood and personality and their relevance to assessing anxiety, with an emphasis on self-report. In *Anxiety and the Anxiety Disorders*, ed. AH Tuma, JD Maser, pp. 681–706. Hillsdale, NJ: Erlbaum

Veenhoven R. 1984. *Conditions of Happiness.* Dordrecht, The Netherlands: Reidel

Veenhoven R. 1991. Is happiness relative? *Soc. Indic. Res.* 24:1–34

Veenhoven R. 1993. *Happiness in Nations: Subjective Appreciation of Life in 56 Nations 1946–1992.* Rotterdam, The Netherlands: Erasmus Univ.

Vittersø J, Røysamb E, Diener E. 2002. The concept of life satisfaction across cultures: exploring its diverse meaning and relation to economic wealth. In *Social Indicators Research Book Series: The Universality of Quality of Life Constructs*, ed. E Gullone, R Cummins. Dordrecht: Kluwer Academic. In press

Watson D, Clark LA. 1992. On traits and temperament: general and specific factors of emotional experience and their relation to the five factor model. *J. Personal.* 60:441–76

Wessman AE, Ricks DF. 1966. *Mood and Personality.* New York: Holt, Rinehart & Winston

Wilson W. 1967. Correlates of avowed happiness. *Psychol. Bull.* 67:294–306

Wirtz D, Scollon CN, Kruger J, Diener E. 2001. *What to do on Spring Break? Predicting Future Choice from Online versus Recalled Affect.* Work. Pap., Univ. Ill. Urbana-Champaign

Zuckerman M. 1979. Attribution of success and failure revisited, or: the motivational bias is alive and well in attribution theory. *J. Personal.* 47:245–87

Annu. Rev. Psychol. 2003. 54:427–59
doi: 10.1146/annurev.psych.54.101601.145052
First published online as a Review in Advance on October 4, 2002

COMMUNITY CONTEXTS OF HUMAN WELFARE

Marybeth Shinn and Siobhan M. Toohey

Psychology Department, New York University, New York, New York 10003;
e-mail: beth.shinn@nyu.edu, smt219@nyu.edu

Key Words neighborhood, setting, social ecology, risk

■ **Abstract** This chapter identifies "context minimization error" as the tendency to ignore the impact of enduring neighborhood and community contexts on human behavior. The error has adverse consequences for understanding psychological processes and efforts at social change. The chapter describes a series of theoretical models of how neighborhoods and community settings are associated with various aspects of human welfare and reviews evidence of associations of contexts with health, psychological distress, risky behaviors, psychological attitudes, and child development. It suggests that many psychological processes may play out differently in different contexts and that contextual factors interact with sociocultural characteristics of individuals in predicting outcomes. People, in turn, can shape community contexts. A more sophisticated understanding of the effects of contexts depends on more sophisticated approaches to assessing them.

CONTENTS

0066-4308/03/0203-0427$14.00

INTRODUCTION

The central thesis of this chapter is that psychologists should pay more attention to the community contexts of human behavior. Conditions in neighborhoods and community settings are associated with residents' mental and physical health, opportunities, satisfactions, and commitments. They are associated with children's academic achievement and developmental outcomes, from behavior problems to teenage childbearing. Contexts also moderate other individual or family processes, suggesting that many psychological theories may not hold across the range of environments in which ordinary Americans live their lives. For example, optimal types of parenting may depend on levels of neighborhood risk. Further, as we show below, contextual effects may masquerade as effects of individual characteristics, leading to flawed inferences.

The tendency of observers to underestimate the effects of immediate social situations and overestimate the effects of individual dispositions is sufficiently pervasive that Ross (1977) labeled it the fundamental attribution error. There is a parallel, less readily identified error of ignoring the effects of more enduring contexts, or where situational and personal characteristics are confounded, of attributing all shared variance to individuals. We dub this "undeniable proclivity to attribute causal influences" on individual outcomes "to individual differences in personality, motivation or intellect" (Earls & Buka 2000) as "context minimization error." This error leads to impoverished theory. It also means that social programs and policies that fail to recognize the complex interplay of individuals and social contexts may fail to resolve the social problems they are intended to ameliorate (Caughy et al. 1999).

Ross (1977) suggested that the fundamental attribution error was a shortcoming of the "intuitive psychologist." However, we suggest that lay people may be less susceptible than psychological researchers to context minimization error. Parents who have sufficient resources invest them in arranging contexts they hope will confer advantages on their children, by moving to a good school district and finding the "right" child care arrangements and extracurricular activities. They look for safe neighborhoods and endeavor to prevent their children from falling in with the "wrong crowd." Adolescents are convinced that the "right" elite college will confer life-long advantages. There is much evidence for this lay perspective. High-quality child care is indeed related to language and cognitive development, social competence and adjustment, and better peer relations (Scarr & Eisenberg 1993). Neighborhoods, as we show below, matter for a variety of outcomes. More selective colleges are associated with higher graduation rates, greater attainment of graduate and professional degrees, and substantially higher earnings, controlling for student and family characteristics (Bowen & Bok 1998).

A comprehensive review of research on contextual effects on human welfare is the work of several lifetimes. The more limited goal of this chapter is to use recent research to illustrate associations of neighborhoods and community settings with individual welfare. We begin by describing different but overlapping models of neighborhood influence and suggest that neighborhood contexts may moderate the effects of lower-level processes that take place within them. Next we examine models of settings' influence on welfare. We suggest that influences of contexts depend on sociocultural characteristics of individuals. Transactions between individuals and contexts are not unidirectional, and we illustrate peoples' efforts to modify social contexts. Finally, because sophistication in theory and method go hand in hand, we consider methodological issues. Most important is how confounding of individual and contextual effects may lead to errors of inference.

Studying contexts is not solely the domain of psychology, so we draw in part on the work of sociologists and economists. Within psychology we emphasize the contributions of community psychology, which since its inception, has been concerned with assessing and modifying "the reciprocal relationships between individuals and the social systems with which they interact" (Bennett et al. 1966, p. 7). Community psychologists (Murrell 1973, Rappaport 1977, Seidman 1988) have emphasized multiple levels of context, with higher levels involving multiple individuals, units with internal structure and social organization, and systematic patterns of social interaction (Shinn & Rapkin 2000). Actions at each level can influence or constrain those at other levels (Bronfenbrenner 1979, 1986). Thus, for example, state child care policies can influence staff:child ratios in day care centers, which in turn influence patterns of caregiver-child interaction and quality of care (Phillips et al. 1992).

In this chapter we focus on the immediate social contexts of human welfare in neighborhoods and public community settings such as schools, religious and voluntary associations, and gathering places. Community settings include what Barker (1968) called behavior settings, or standing patterns of behavior bounded in space and time. They also include larger organizations located in communities (e.g., schools) and many face-to-face settings Bronfenbrenner (1979) called microsystems (e.g., bars), but exclude private microsystems (e.g., families). For reasons of space we also exclude the larger social and political forces that may support or undermine communities (e.g., Warren et al. 2001) and features of the physical environment.

NEIGHBORHOODS

Psychologists, sociologists, and economists have paid increasing attention to neighborhood effects on well-being following Wilson's (1987) examination of concentrated poverty and disadvantage experienced by poor urban African Americans. Several theorists have proposed models for how neighborhood characteristics are associated with mental health (Wandersman & Nation 1998), physical health (Caughy et al. 1999), violence (Sampson et al. 1997), and child maltreatment, school failure, delinquency, teen childbearing, and positive youth development (Caughy et al. 1999, Coulton 1996, Furstenberg & Hughes 1997, Jencks & Mayer 1990, Leventhal & Brooks-Gunn 2000). These models overlap, and what some theorists describe as independent models, others consider to be mediating processes. We consider compositional models, in which individuals are influenced by the collective characteristics of their neighbors, and models concerned with social disorganization, social stress, social capital, and closely related constructs.

Compositional Models

In a structural or compositional model, included in all theoretical typologies, individuals are influenced by the aggregate demographic characteristics of their neighbors. Research on compositional characteristics has been spurred in part by the availability of Geographic Information System software that allows researchers to link census or other archival data from defined geographical units, such as census tracts, to individual residents. This has permitted inclusion of information about neighborhoods in studies originally designed for other purposes.

Jencks & Mayer (1990) outlined four ways that neighborhoods could affect children. An epidemic or contagion model emphasizes negative peer influences of poor children. A collective socialization model focuses on the positive influence of affluent adults, who serve as role models and supervise neighborhood children. A relative deprivation model points to possible negative effects of successful neighbors or classmates on self-esteem and motivation. A noncompositional institutional model notes that children in affluent and disadvantaged neighborhoods receive different treatment from teachers, police, and other adults from outside the community who work in local institutions.

Leventhal & Brooks-Gunn (2000) reviewed studies of links between child and adolescent outcomes and neighborhood compositional characteristics, such as income or socio-economic status (SES), racial/ethnic diversity, and residential instability measured at the level of the census tract or block group. Their comprehensive review points to the importance of high SES neighborhoods in predicting academic achievement and low SES neighborhoods and residential instability in predicting behavioral and emotional outcomes including externalizing behaviors, conduct disorder, criminal activity, and substance use. (High and low SES are both contrasted with a middle SES group, so are not perfectly negatively correlated.) Sexuality outcomes, including early, teen, or nonmarital sex and childbearing, were also influenced by levels of employment. Effects were generally modest, defined as less than a third of a standard deviation, and explained about 5% of the variance after controlling for individual or family characteristics. Caughy et al. (1999) additionally noted that poor neighborhoods have been associated with health outcomes such as cardiovascular disease, low birth weight, and premature births, again controlling for individual characteristics.

A long-term experimental study produced far larger effects than those obtained in correlational designs. In the Gautreaux project, low-income minority families from public housing projects in Chicago moved either to more affluent suburbs or to low-income neighborhoods in the city in a "quasi-random fashion" with families assigned to housing units on a first-come, first-served basis. Groups were comparable at the start of the study (Rubinowitz & Rosenbaum 2000, p. 77). Short-term effects on schooling were mixed, with children from the inner city having difficulties in suburban schools, but long-term effects on achievement were striking. Children in families who moved to the suburbs were far more likely than children who moved within the city to graduate from high school (86% vs. 33%), attend college (54% vs. 21%), attend 4-year colleges (27% vs. 4%), be employed full-time if not in college (75% vs. 41%), and receive higher pay and job benefits (Rubinowitz & Rosenbaum 2000, ch. 9).

Results of this study spawned the more extensive Moving to Opportunity experiments ongoing in five cities. Very low-income families who lived in public housing or Section 8 project-based housing in high-poverty areas in central cities were assigned via a random lottery to three groups. One received rental vouchers that could be used only in low-poverty neighborhoods, a second received vouchers that could be used anywhere (the "Section 8" group), and a control group continued to receive their current housing assistance. Short-term results across the five sites showed little impact on families' economic self-sufficiency but greater improvements in reported safety, parents' and children's mental and physical health, and youth delinquency and behavior problems for both experimental groups. Many of the effects were small, but a few were substantial. For example, prevalence of injuries and asthma for children in the Boston low-poverty group fell 74% and 65% relative to controls (Del Conte & Kling 2001). Behavior problems for boys and for younger children in both the low-poverty and the Section 8 conditions in New York fell 30–43% relative to controls (Leventhal & Brooks-Gunn 2002). Results were substantial even though only about 40% of families given the opportunity to move actually did so but analyses compared groups as randomly assigned. Effects are already larger than is typical for correlational studies, and if the Gautreaux pattern is followed, small short-term effects may grow larger over time.

Social Disorganization/Norms/Collective Efficacy

Perhaps the best-developed model for how neighborhoods affect behavior draws on Shaw & McKay's (1942) Chicago-school theory of social disorganization, as articulated more recently by Sampson and colleagues (Sampson & Groves 1989; Sampson et al. 1997, 1999). The theory suggests that ethnic heterogeneity, low socioeconomic status, and residential mobility (all compositional variables) interfere with a community's social organization in terms of local friendship networks and participation in organizations (discussed more below as social capital). Social interaction, participation, and cohesion create a set of shared norms and capacity to control adolescent peer groups who may engage in delinquent or criminal behavior. Collective efficacy is defined as social cohesion among neighbors and willingness to intervene to curb disruptions and obtain resources for the common good. In a study of 343 Chicago neighborhoods (clusters of census tracts), compositional measures of concentrated disadvantage, concentration of immigrants, and low residential stability predicted several indices of violence (perceived violence, victimization, and homicide rates), controlling for individual factors. Collective efficacy mediated a substantial portion of these relationships (Sampson et al. 1997). Later analyses of the same data showed that concentrated affluence and stability were more important than concentrated disadvantage for social exchanges among adults and the extent to which adults interacted with and looked out for neighborhood children (Sampson et al. 1999).

Leventhal & Brooks-Gunn (2000) dubbed this model norms/collective efficacy because of its emphasis on these factors as mediating mechanisms. There is evidence that communities vary with respect to other sorts of norms as well. For example, Caughy et al. (2001) found neighborhood-level differences between descriptive norms for parenting (what adult survey respondents believed mothers and fathers in the neighborhood do) in three neighborhoods (each 6–8 contiguous census tracts). Coulton et al. (1996) found that in Cleveland neighborhoods with high rates of child maltreatment, relative to neighborhoods with low rates, caregivers of young children were more likely to expect retaliation from children or their parents if they intervened to stop child misconduct. Kulik (1998) attributed differences in attitudes toward gender roles and perceptions of gender-typing in occupations among adolescents on a kibbutz and urban adolescents in Israel to the egalitarian orientation of kibbutz culture.

Social Stress, Incivilities

Social stress, including exposure to stressful life events and violence, and incivilities are closely related models of neighborhood influences, whether as independent models (e.g., Coulton 1996) or mediators of compositional effects (Wandersman & Nation 1998). Buka et al. (2001) reviewed evidence that children in cities are exposed to extraordinarily high rates of violence, with about a quarter of urban youth witnessing someone being murdered in their lifetime. Exposure to violence was associated with mental health problems including posttraumatic stress disorder, depression, distress, aggression, and externalizing behavior. Risk for witnessing violence was higher for males and ethnic minorities.

Social stressors extend beyond specific events. Hendryx & Ahern (1997) aggregated perceptions of community problems to the zip code level for over 1800 primarily white residents of 25 zip codes in a northwest urban county. Aggregate perceptions of social problems (domestic violence, homelessness, child abuse, racism, pollution, poverty, unemployment, and other environmental problems) were related to poor mental health, after controlling for individual ratings of these problems.

Griffin et al. (1999) found that neighborhood risk (attitudes about toughness required for survival and perceptions of gang activity and delinquency in the neighborhood) was related to interpersonal aggression in a sample of 452 primarily

African-American sixth-graders at two schools in New York City. Reports of risk-taking behavior significantly mediated the relationship between neighborhood risk and interpersonal aggression. (All measures were collected at the individual level, increasing the possibility of method bias.) Colder et al. (2000) found that perceived neighborhood danger (assessed by parent and child report) was related to aggressive behavior (by child self-report and teacher ratings) in a sample of 732 primarily African-American fifth-graders in ten inner-city and two suburban elementary schools. The relationship was mediated by children's positive beliefs about aggression. Coulton et al. (1996) found that Cleveland neighborhoods with high rates of child maltreatment were also high on mobility, disorder, and threat of victimization.

Cunningham (1999) conducted a longitudinal examination of 384 African-American high school students' perceptions of the resources and constraints in their communities in a Southeastern city. The most common responses to questions about neighborhood conditions that might interfere with reaching life goals were drugs and peer pressure. Perceptions of the seriousness of problems in the neighborhood (including unemployment, gambling, assaults, and poor schools) and the likelihood of a neighborhood teen being the victim of a violent crime increased over 2 years, whereas expectations about getting a stable, well-paying job or completing college decreased.

Social incivilities (e.g., public drunkenness) and physical incivilities (e.g., abandoned buildings, litter) have been linked to fear of crime (Taylor & Covington 1993, Riger 1985) and in turn to anxiety and depression (Wandersman & Nation 1998). Crime and fear have far-reaching consequences for behavior. Furstenberg (1993) and Caughy et al. (1999) drew on qualitative data to describe how parents in dangerous neighborhoods restricted their own and children's ties with the community, monitored children closely, and sought services and social ties outside the community. Danger in the neighborhood even led to restricting positive opportunities such as an after-school program that required returning home after dark (Caughy et al. 1999).

Perkins & Taylor (1996) used three methods to assess disorder for one block in each of 50 neighborhoods in Baltimore. Both residents' perceptions and direct observations of social and physical disorder were aggregated to the block level. Newspaper reports of crime and disorder (e.g., deteriorating housing, racial unrest, prison escapes) were counted for the target neighborhood and adjacent neighborhoods. In hierarchical linear models all three measures of disorder predicted residents' fear of crime (assessed one year after the surveys and observations). Analyses controlled for individuals' perceptions of disorder, the observed disorder of their own homes, and compositional effects of age, race, and gender.

Ross & Jang (2000) found that in a probability sample of 2482 Illinois households, individuals who perceived their neighborhoods as high in physical disorder (e.g., vandalism, graffiti) and social disorder (e.g., crime, drug use) had higher levels of fear and mistrust. Informal social ties to neighbors buffered the negative association of disorder with fear and mistrust, but individuals who perceived their neighborhood as highly disordered had fewer ties with neighbors. Results are consistent with social disorganization theory, but with a starting point of perceived disorder rather than poverty, mobility, and heterogeneity.

Similarly, Caughy et al. (1999) found that crime rates, low levels of neighborhood political organization (voter registration, organizational involvement), and lack of resources (retail and service establishments, health care providers, public agencies) in Baltimore neighborhoods were associated with poor pregnancy outcomes such as low birth weight and preterm delivery. Results controlled for individual risk factors and neighborhood economic conditions. Qualitative interviews showed how crime and resultant fear led to stress, limited freedom of movement, and constrained engagement in behaviors such as exercise that foster health.

Several studies have examined both compositional measures and social stress in studies of adolescents, with complex results. Aneshensel & Sucoff (1996) studied a representative multiethnic sample of 877 12- to 17-year-olds in Los Angeles. They cluster analyzed neighborhoods based on compositional measures of SES and race. Low SES was related to high perceived ambient hazards such as crime, violence, drug use, and graffiti. Hazards, in turn, were related to internalizing (depression, anxiety) and externalizing (conduct, oppositional) symptoms. Residential stability (a compositional variable) and perceived cohesion contributed to lower symptoms. The relation of structural variables to mental health was more complex: conduct symptoms were highest in an "underclass" cluster but oppositional defiant symptoms were highest in middle-class and affluent clusters.

Seidman et al. (1998) studied 754 multiethnic 10- to 17-year-olds sampled from New York schools where most children received free lunches. Two cohorts were drawn from the last year of elementary school and the last year of junior high or middle school. Seidman et al. created a measure of structural neighborhood risk (from multiple indicators of poverty and homicide rates) and cluster analyzed neighborhoods based on a larger sample of participants' reports of hassles (similar to Aneshensel & Sucoff's hazards), cohesion, and involvement in constructive activities. Neighborhood clusters that were high on both hassles and cohesion were associated with highest structural risk, whereas one that was high on cohesion but low on hassles and involvement was associated with lowest risk. Surprisingly, structural risk was inversely associated with antisocial behavior for the older cohort only. Each of the three clusters with high hassles was associated with higher antisocial behavior for the younger or the older cohort but not both.

In one of the few studies of rural neighborhoods, Simons et al. (1996) found that for boys in Iowa a composite measure of community disadvantage was related to lower-quality parenting (judged by ratings of videotaped interactions) and increased affiliation with deviant peers, controlling for family SES. These, in turn, were related to conduct problems and distress. Community disadvantage also had a direct effect on distress. Community disadvantage was not related to outcomes for girls, but the proportion of single-parent households in the community was directly or indirectly related to both conduct problems and distress.

These studies suggest that although neighborhood risk is often associated with poor outcomes, both behavioral problems and exposure to violence are not always highest in neighborhoods with highest risk. At least in some cases, as Jencks & Mayer (1990) suggested, the presence of affluent neighbors may put adolescents at risk. We would have more confidence in the conclusions if the replications across studies were more exact. However, it seems clear that we need to understand multiple aspects of neighborhoods (and families) in concert. Different processes may also operate for adolescents of different ages, and in general, neighborhood effects were stronger for older than for younger children.

Resources, Social Capital, and Sense of Community

Another mediating mechanism proposed by Leventhal & Brooks-Gunn (2000) is availability and quality of resources such as social and recreational activities, child care, schools, medical services, and opportunities for employment. Similarly Coulton (1996) used the term social organization (distinct from social disorganization) to describe the formal and informal networks, institutions, and organizations in the area as an independent model of neighborhood effects. For example, Cleveland neighborhoods with low rates of child maltreatment had more facilities for children (e.g., day care centers, playgrounds or parks) and services (e.g., laundromats, supermarkets, banks) than neighborhoods with high rates of maltreatment (Coulton et al. 1996).

The concept of social organization is similar to that of social capital, defined by Putnam (1995) as "features of social organization such as networks, norms, and social trust that facilitate coordination and cooperation for mutual benefit." Another related concept is sense of community, defined by McMillan & Chavis (1986) as consisting of membership, influence, integration and need satisfaction, and shared emotional connections. Researchers have examined predictors and consequences of sense of community. Both structural features (percentage of owner-occupied homes, per capita income, low proportions of people in the work force, and low population density) and social organization (percentage of registered voters, percentage of residents in neighborhood organizations) predicted psychological sense of community in Baltimore neighborhoods (Brodsky et al. 1999). In a qualitative study of a poor community in Caracas, Garcia et al. (1999) found that sense of community was shaped by the history of the community and its development.

Perkins & Long (2002) described sense of community as one aspect of social capital (along with sense of efficacy of organized collective action, informal neighboring, and organizational participation). Sense of community was strongly related to the other constructs at both the individual and the block level in multilevel analyses for blocks in five neighborhoods in New York City. Sampson (2001) also considered social capital (which we discuss below in the contexts of community settings and efforts at social change) as an important precursor of collective efficacy.

Experiences with social services may also foster social capital. Thompson et al. (1996) examined the experiences of families of homicide victims with the criminal justice system. Family members who were informed about the case's progress and the arrest of a suspect reported more satisfaction with the police. Satisfaction was associated with more positive beliefs (safety, esteem, control, and social support), which were in turn associated with lower psychological distress.

Linkages among systems are also important. Campbell (1998) interviewed a national sample of advocates for rape victims to explore victims' experiences with legal, health, and mental health service systems. Women who had relatively positive outcomes with all three systems (defined as actions that fit their desires with a minimum of advocacy effort) were more likely to live in communities with greater resources and better coordination of services. Campbell & Ahrens (1998) interviewed advocates, directors of rape crisis centers, police officers, prosecutors, doctors, nurses, and rape survivors in 44 communities, half with and half without coordinated community-based services for rape. High-coordination communities were more likely to have integrated service delivery programs, bidirectional interagency training programs, and community reform groups that educated the community and promoted policy reform. Campbell & Aherns concluded that coordinated services led to better outcomes for women by ensuring that service providers understood the multiple contexts of service delivery, the needs of women, and the larger context of violence against women. We consider individual community organizations (rather than service systems) in more detail below under community settings.

Moderating Effects of Neighborhoods

In addition to its direct effects on welfare, neighborhood risk may moderate the effects of family characteristics, peer influences, and social services. In a sample of African-American early adolescents, Gonzales et al. (1996) found interactions between neighborhood risk and maternal restrictive control in the prediction of youths' grade point averages one year later, controlling for earlier grades. Risk, in this case, was assessed as maternal and child reports of risky activities engaged in by youths in the neighborhood. In low-risk neighborhoods low levels of restrictive control were associated with better academic outcomes, as would be expected from the literature on authoritative parenting. The situation was reversed in high-risk neighborhoods, where high levels of restrictive control were associated with better academic outcomes. Not only did neighborhood risk affect parenting, as we saw earlier, but optimal types of parenting varied by neighborhood risk. There was a similar interaction of neighborhood risk for peer support and attachment: The positive effects of peer support held only in low-risk neighborhoods.

Sheidow et al. (2001) found interactions between family and community risk factors in predicting exposure to violence in an unusual sample of African-American and Latino male adolescents living in the inner city in Chicago who were selected to be high in teacher-rated aggression. The authors cluster-analyzed neighborhoods based on both compositional data (including poverty and violent crime) and mothers' and sons' reports of neighborhood social organization and safety. Two clusters had high structural problems but differed on functioning social processes (high social organization and low concern about safety). The third had lower structural problems, low social organization, and low concern about safety. Four family clusters were found based on family relationships and parenting practices. Contrary to previous research, there was no main effect of neighborhood type or family type on exposure to violence in the past year, controlling for earlier exposure to violence, but there was an interaction: The highest increase in exposure to violence occurred for struggling families (poor parenting, structure, cohesion, and beliefs about family) living in inner-city neighborhoods with functioning social processes. Sheidow et al. (2001) suggested that family functioning may be less important in the worst functioning communities, where risk for exposure to violence is widespread, and in communities with a better economic base, where other unmeasured protective practices may be at work.

Caughy et al. (1999) found an interaction between neighborhood risk (low household wealth, high unemployment) and the timing of prenatal care in the prediction of low birth weight. Early prenatal care was indeed protective in low-risk neighborhoods, in accordance with conventional medical wisdom, but not in high-risk neighborhoods. The authors concluded that providing better access to prenatal care to women in poor communities would not ensure improvements in pregnancy outcomes without addressing the other social risks women face.

These studies challenge what we think we know about parenting, peer relationships, and medical care. Seemingly well-established relationships may not be universal. Trickett (1996) points out that a contextualist approach to knowledge means understanding the contexts in which hypotheses hold true. Even hypotheses that have a good deal of support in the psychological literature have often been tested in only limited contexts and may not apply elsewhere.

COMMUNITY SETTINGS

We turn now to the influence of public community settings on human welfare. Indigenous community settings such as churches and local businesses are no doubt influenced by their broader neighborhood contexts. Community-based settings such as libraries, public health clinics, or Head Start centers may also reflect commitment and attention from beyond the immediate neighborhood (Furstenberg & Hughes 1997), are often staffed by people who live elsewhere (Jencks & Mayer 1990), and are sometimes placed in neighborhoods with the explicit goal of countering deprivation. There is also evidence that, especially in resource-poor communities, families seek out and use settings outside their neighborhoods (e.g., Earls & Buka 2000, Furstenberg 1993, Jarrett 1997). For all these reasons, it is important to consider community settings apart from the neighborhoods in which they are located as independent contexts of human welfare.

Community settings are ubiquitous. Barker (1968) catalogued 53,376 occurrences of 884 public behavior settings over the course of a year in a single small town. Community settings include organizations in which people spend substantial portions of time at different life stages: child care centers, schools, colleges, workplaces, retirement homes. They include voluntary organizations, which typically involve less time but may have a major influence such as religious settings, block associations, mutual help groups, and service or recreational clubs. They also include government offices and business locations where consumers or clients go to seek services or goods and often (as in the case of bars, coffee shops, or beauty salons) fellowship.

We consider five models for how community settings influence individual welfare. Unlike neighborhoods, settings are typically created with purposes or instrumental functions that can affect participants' well-being, and they create social roles for participants. Like neighborhoods, settings are sources of social capital, norms, and social stress.

Instrumental Functions

A community setting's purpose may be to provide services or resources that enhance welfare. Doctors' offices provide health care, schools educate, playgrounds offer recreation, shelters give homeless people a place to sleep. Settings with other goals may nonetheless allow individuals to fulfill instrumental needs. The goal of the workplace is to produce widgets, but it allows workers to obtain wages. The simple existence of settings (such as hospitals or businesses that provide jobs) may be important to well-being, and settings that focus on welfare may vary in how well they fulfill their missions. Different types of settings also vary in the dimensions along which they foster individual growth and development. For example, workplaces differ in their emphasis on autonomy, task orientation, and independence; both task-oriented and social groups differ in their focus on independence, learning practical skills, and self-understanding (Moos 2002).

Social Roles

Community settings, like mutual help groups, churches, and volunteer organizations, may also create and shape the roles and sense of identity of individuals. For example, Kingree & Thompson (2000) studied an experimental intervention whereby adult children of alcoholics in treatment for personal substance abuse were assigned to groups for children of alcoholics or substance abuse education classes. Participation in the groups improved self-reported well-being, with improvements mediated by increases in perceived status benefits. The authors concluded that support and discussion in the groups led participants to view their status as an adult child of an alcoholic more adaptively, reducing depression and relapse. The ways members and leaders of Schizophrenia Anonymous groups were viewed, and viewed the referent and expert power of others, depended on the role they played in the groups. These perceptions of power also predicted the perceived helpfulness of the groups (Salem et al. 2000). In small, qualitative studies, Royce-Davis (2001) and Stein & Wemmerus (2001) described the importance of social roles such as productive member of the workforce, student, or wife in helping individuals with mental illness achieve a "normal life."

Settings may create roles for individuals as workers or volunteers. Stewart & Weinstein (1997) examined volunteer participation in three HIV/AIDS organizations: a suburban setting focused on providing individual support, whereas two urban settings focused on information and referral and social change. They found differences in who volunteered, why they volunteered, the roles they undertook, their political and personal efficacy, and how these constructs related to each other and the setting.

Allen et al. (1990) described a Teen Outreach program that involved seventh- to twelfth-grade youths in structured volunteer community-service activities in which they took on meaningful positive roles as help-givers. The program also had a classroom component. In an experimental evaluation at 25 sites nationwide, rates of pregnancy, course failure, and suspension among Teen Outreach participants were about two fifths of that for the control group despite the fact that the program did not address these outcomes directly (Allen et al. 1997). In additional large-scale studies, program success was related to the intensity of the volunteer component (Allen et al. 1990) and to autonomy, relatedness, and the quality of volunteer experiences for middle school students (Allen et al. 1994).

The structure of community settings may provide greater or lesser encouragement to engage in social roles. A particularly salient dimension identified by Barker and his colleagues (e.g., Barker 1968) is the ratio of participants to social roles. Settings with relatively few participants compared with the number of roles are underpopulated. In such settings (e.g., small high schools) individuals feel more pressure to join in activities, take on more responsible roles, and report greater satisfaction relating to their competence and value than in settings with more participants per role.

Social Capital

Social capital is an attribute of community settings as well as neighborhoods. Social capital measured at the building level in 487 distressed inner-city apartment buildings was strongly related to forms of ownership, with highest levels in tenant-owned cooperatives. Social capital was in turn associated with improved building quality, greater security, and lower levels of crime (Saegert & Winkel 1998). Participation in tenant organizations, tenant pro-social norms, and formal participation in building leadership also predicted future crime in the buildings in prospective analyses (Saegert et al. 2002).

Organizational affiliations such as church membership and informal connections to family and friends are central aspects of social capital with important links to human welfare. Both are consistently related to mortality in prospective studies, controlling for earlier health status (see review by House et al. 1988).

In a nationally representative sample with 18,000 respondents, Snowden (2001) found that African Americans, compared with whites of comparable background, were more likely to be involved in churches, clubs, lodges, and other groups. Both organizational affiliation and patterns of informal support, which varied by both race and gender, were related to lower levels of psychological distress.

Effects of organizational membership on welfare may be mediated by social support. Settings vary in the extent to which support is part of their mission. For example, self-help groups are intentional support systems in which members with a common problem both provide and receive support (e.g., Levy 2000). Settings of a particular type may vary in supportiveness. Moos (2002) argued that the quality and interdependence of relationships is a key dimension along which the social climate of settings varies. Maton (1989) characterized churches, mutual help groups, and senior centers as providing high or low levels of support, based on members' responses to questionnaires. In parallel analyses within each type of setting, settings high in support were directly related to well-being or buffered effects of stress on well-being, controlling for individual perceptions of support.

Luke et al. (1991) painstakingly coded behavioral interactions in 510 meetings of 13 groups belonging to a single mutual-help organization. Then they cluster-analyzed groups, based on the frequency of different types of interactions, into four "phenotypes." The phenotypes were reliably related to degree of change experienced by 111 newcomers to the groups (as rated by observers). New members changed most in the groups characterized by relatively high levels of personal questions and self-disclosure and low levels of sharing impersonal information, agreement, small talk, and interpretation. In later research with the same organization, Roberts et al. (1999) found that overall receipt of help was related to adjustment only among individuals who experienced a high degree of group integration. Recent research has examined the nature of postings to on-line mutual-help groups for depression (Salem et al. 1997) and drinking problems (Klaw et al. 2000), although these studies did not relate on-line interactions to individual outcomes. New forms of communication mean that "community" contexts are increasingly divorced from geographic neighborhoods.

Psychological sense of community, which we have discussed as an element of social capital, has often been considered an attribute of community settings as well as geographic locations. Lounsbury & DeNeui (1996) found that among college students, students at smaller schools and those who lived on campus or were members of fraternities or sororities had a greater sense of community. A program that emphasized cooperative learning and a child-centered approach to teaching and classroom management fostered a greater sense of community in three suburban elementary schools, relative to comparison schools (Solomon et al. 1996). Sense of community was related to student outcomes such as liking for school, empathy, and self esteem. Further, it was related to greater acceptance of the different norms and values of the classrooms in the two groups of schools. Sense of community in program classrooms appeared to reflect environments of independence, student influence, fairness, and personal responsibility and in comparison classrooms was related to student acceptance of norms of teacher direction and student compliance.

Hirsch et al. (2000) used qualitative data collected at four Boys and Girls Clubs to show how the clubs fostered a sense of community or sense of "club as home," particularly for early adolescent girls. They noted the importance of attachment to the club, formation of positive peer, adult, and sibling-like ties, and creation of safe spaces for self-expression in promoting girls' self-esteem.

Other consequences of sense of community have included organizational citizenship behavior (Burroughs & Eby 1998) and organizational attachment, job satisfaction, role clarity and lower role strains, psychological distress, and intentions to leave among workers at a research firm (Royal & Rossi 1996). In three high schools students' sense of community was related to less disruptive behavior, less class-cutting and fewer thoughts of dropping out (Royal & Rossi 1996).

A continuing question in this literature is whether sense of community is best thought of as a contextual variable or simply an individual attitude. Interestingly, in the study by Solomon et al. (1996) students' perceptions of sense of community were associated with observational measures of related constructs such as provision for student autonomy and input in the classroom, and classrooms accounted for a substantial portion of the variance in sense of community. Another question concerns the causal direction of relationships.

Setting resources are another aspect of social capital. Kelly et al. (2000) noted that settings often have more resources than members recognize. These may include personal resources such as a school secretary or janitor who connects with children and solves problems. System resources include information, money, influence, and the ability to connect with others outside the system to exchange resources or engage in joint action. Resources also include "traditions, customs, and observances" (Kelly et al. 2000, p. 137) that foster integration and sense of community. Adaptation is the setting's ability to alter its own structures and processes and respond to demands in the external environment. Seidman (1988) described social regularities (social relationships or interdependencies that persist over time) as important characteristics of settings and of links among settings. Kelly et al. (2000) similarly described "processes" of reciprocity, networking, and communication within settings and boundary spanning or establishing relationships with outside systems. The inside-outside distinction is similar to Warren et al.'s (2001) distinction between bonding and bridging forms of social capital. Moos (2002) suggested that dimensions of system maintenance and change, along with relationship dimensions and personal growth dimensions, are key enduring dimensions of environmental systems. These theoretical formulations focus on the complex dynamics of social systems and transactions between people and settings (see also Altman & Rogoff 1987).

Norms

Settings are often characterized by distinct descriptive or injunctive norms (what people do or what they think is acceptable), and both have been related to individual behavior. Allison et al. (1999) collected information on descriptive norms for substance use (both low-level and "hard" drugs) among 283 adolescents at six schools. Norms were defined by self-reported use averaged across all respondents except the target respondent at that school. After controlling for demographic factors, educational placement (e.g., special education), and participants' perceptions of substance use by their parents and peers, school norms were significantly related to participants' own substance use for both classes of substances.

Henry et al. (2000) examined associations of both descriptive and injunctive norms regarding aggression with individual aggressive behavior among 614 ethnically diverse elementary school students in 45 classrooms in 14 economically disadvantaged urban and suburban schools (and later replicated results with students from 21 classrooms in 16 schools). They did not find effects of descriptive norms (aggressive behavior of others in the classroom, as rated by teachers). However, other children's normative beliefs about the appropriateness of aggression were associated with children's behavior both directly and indirectly via associations with children's own beliefs, controlling for both earlier beliefs and earlier aggressive behavior. The authors further assessed the extent to which norms against aggression were made salient by peers (i.e., children's aggression was related to lower peer ratings of popularity and higher peer ratings of rejection) and teachers (i.e., teachers were observed to reprimand aggressive behaviors). Children in classrooms in which both teachers and peers made norms against aggression salient had smaller increases in aggression over a 2-year period than children in classrooms where only teachers or only peers made norms salient.

While norms operate psychologically to affect individual behavior, they also affect human welfare in nonpsychological ways. In a school with norms against aggression, a child is less likely to be victimized. In a gay bar with high norms for condom use, individuals are unlikely to find others willing to engage in unprotected sex, and individuals with poor negotiation skills will have less trouble persuading partners to use condoms. Further, to the extent that condom use reduces the prevalence of HIV infections, even individuals who engage in unsafe practices are less likely to be infected.

Stress

Community settings, like neighborhoods, can be loci for stress. Sandler et al. (2000) described "the ecology of stressful experience" including major life events and cascading experiences that follow from them, more mundane hassles, and chronic stressors. Many of these involve relationships of individuals to settings. Stressful life events include loss of roles, such as employment. Unemployment and job loss have been linked to adverse outcomes such as violence, alcohol abuse, and depression, with effects largely mediated by economic hardship (Price 2000). Seidman et al. (1995) suggest that hassles frequently pertain to particular settings such as neighborhood and school.

Chronic stressors frequently entail hardships, challenges, and conflicts associated with roles in social settings such as school or work (Pearlin 1983) and may fall differentially on different groups. Hughes & Dodge (1997) examined perceptions of interpersonal prejudice at work and institutional discrimination (biased distribution of salaries, benefits, job assignments, and opportunities) for a sample of African-American women. Both forms of race-related job stress were more strongly related to dissatisfaction with the job than were standard measures of work conditions (workload, skill discretion, support from the supervisor). Respondents in lower primary jobs (e.g., clerical or sales) reported more institutional discrimination, and those who worked with fewer other African-Americans reported higher levels of both racial job stressors.

DIVERSE INDIVIDUALS AND DIVERSE CONTEXTS

The study by Hughes & Dodge (1997) highlights the interaction of sociocultural diversity with diversity of ecological contexts (Trickett 1996). Transactions between individuals and contexts depend on characteristics of both. Leventhal & Brooks-Gunn (2000) noted that in their review the benefits of high SES neighborhoods appear to be greater for European-American than for African-American children. They suggested that this may be because African-American children in affluent neighborhoods are likely to be in closer geographic proximity to less affluent neighborhoods (Sampson et al. 1999). Alternatively, affluent neighbors may interact more with European-American children than with African-American children in their neighborhoods, or the professional roles that the affluent neighbors model may seem more attainable to children burdened by poverty, but not racism. Coulton et al. (1996) also found differential associations of neighborhood features with risk for child abuse in African-American and white neighborhoods. For example, block club activities and neighborhood facilities were more strongly associated with low risk in African-American neighborhoods and, having a name for the neighborhood was more positive in white neighborhoods. Perhaps more formal mechanisms for participation are important when informal mechanisms are blocked, or identification of a neighborhood by name has mixed valence where neighborhood boundaries are enforced by segregation.

Diverse groups may feel differentially accepted and supported in the same setting. Waldo (1998) surveyed 1927 students at a university regarding campus climate for gay, lesbian, and bisexual students. Heterosexual students reported experiencing greater acceptance and respect on campus in general and with regard to sexual orientation than lesbian, gay, and bisexual students. Perceived climate for lesbian, gay, and bisexual students also varied by race, gender, religion, fraternity or sorority membership, and undergraduate versus graduate student status. Chesir-Teran (2002) defined heterosexism as the assumption that "heterosexual power and privilege are normal and ideal" along with social regularities or contextual norms that privilege heterosexuality over homosexuality. Drawing on the conceptual framework of Moos & Lemke (1996), he examined four forms in which heterosexism is manifested in high schools. First are physical and architectural features, such as locker rooms that provide privacy between but not within gender, on the assumption that all sexual attraction is heterosexual. Second are policy and program features, such as the existence and enforcement of antidiscrimination and harassment policies, the presence of support groups, such as gay-straight alliances, links with community resources, integration of positive images of homosexuality in the curriculum, and availability of relevant books in school libraries. Third are compositional characteristics such as the numbers of students and faculty who are "out" and aggregate attitudes towards homosexuality. Last are social or behavioral regularities in public expressions of same- and opposite-sex affection, partners who are brought to dances, and use of pejorative language.

Morris et al. (1999) found that 13 police commands (precincts) differed in the extent to which commanders set the tone for integrating diverse police officers, as assessed by officers' ratings of the commander's support and his fairness and sensitivity to diversity. There were differences in ratings by demographic groups of officers (white men, minority men, women) and interactions of groups by command, suggesting that the different groups had systematically different experiences. Further, correlation patterns of these ratings with other variables differed by group. Among women and minority men, perceptions of the commander's sensitivity to diversity were positively related to perceptions of the fairness of rewards in the command; for white men, the correlation was reversed. Aggregate perceptions of the commander (means by subgroup within precinct) were related to individual officers' organizational commitment to the police force, controlling for their own individual perceptions.

Clearly, a single physical setting can be viewed differently and have different associations with outcomes for different individuals. We have focused on sociocultural diversity, but differences in cognitive and developmental status and various personal resources are also important (Moos 2002). Shinn & Rapkin (2000) discussed three forms of person-environment fit. The first form is similarity of the individual to others in the setting on demographic or attitudinal variables. Although there are many advantages to diversity, it can also be a source of strain. Second is match between individual needs and environmental supplies or environmental demands and individual personality or skills. In a classic study, Kelly (1979) showed that high school boys who were "high explorers" (active, involved, assertive) were better adapted than low explorers to a school with a high annual turnover of students and made more friends there; the reverse was true in a school with low turnover. Third is congruence between environmental features and personal preferences. All three forms can be expressed as person-setting interactions, and there is some evidence linking all forms to well-being.

INDIVIDUAL AND COLLECTIVE EFFORTS TO CHANGE COMMUNITIES AND COMMUNITY SETTINGS

Although most of the research we have reviewed emphasizes contextual influences on individuals, community psychologists are also concerned with how individuals and groups can change neighborhoods and community settings to foster human welfare. Past *Annual Review* chapters have been devoted entirely to social and community interventions. Here we highlight only a few recent efforts by community members to change their own communities as well as interventions by social scientists to improve welfare by changing contexts.

A recent book on social capital and poor communities (Saegert et al. 2001) described a number of efforts at social change by community members that both built on and enhanced social capital. African-American women who returned to a southern community with attitudes and skills acquired in the north created organizations that reached out to help others in the community and built external links to bring child care resources to the community (Lopez & Stack 2001). A coalition of Boston ministers brought the police and the community together to combat youth violence, and a similar church-police collaboration developed trust and created zones of safety in Chicago (Sampson 2001). A partnership between community organizations and health provider organizations worked to mobilize community organizations, members, and resources to promote health (James et al. 2001). Congregation-based organizations built on the social capital of religious organizations to develop leaders, social networks, and interorganizational linkages to address social problems (Foley et al. 2001).

Similarly Venkatesh (1999) examined community-based efforts to address gang activity in the Chicago area. A grass-roots agency acknowledged and worked with the leadership of a powerful gang to set up a "community court" where residents could air grievances and address disputes with gang members. The same agency attempted to unite gang members and community residents to work on common concerns such as exploitative grocery store prices, insufficient school funding, and voter registration. In a separate effort, local pastors worked with a female gang to address sexually abusive behaviors by a male gang and increase public safety.

Wandersman & Florin (2000) reviewed the literature on individual and environmental characteristics that promote citizen participation in neighborhood and community development organizations. They also reviewed evidence that such organizations make a difference in reducing physical deterioration and crime, promoting social services, enhancing informal neighboring, and influencing individual attitudes such as trust, confidence, experience of personal and political efficacy, and sense of community. Community organizations influence not only people's psychological sense of empowerment but actual power and decision-making in communities.

Interventions undertaken by social scientists typically have more limited targets. Several researchers have collaborated with community members to reduce underage smoking or drinking. Wagenaar et al. (1999) mobilized communities via education campaigns to monitor alcohol sales and change drinking policies at community events. Biglan et al. (1996) and Jason et al. (1999) worked to enforce bans on sales of tobacco. Teenage testers attempted to purchase the forbidden products from merchants, who faced warnings, fines, or loss of license if they sold the product and rewards if they did not. All three interventions decreased both sales to and use by minors over time or in relation to comparison communities. Lichtenstein et al. (1996) described a consultative intervention that succeeded in changing tobacco control policies in 20 Northwest Indian tribes. This effort was complicated by traditional use of tobacco and the importance of income from tobacco sales for many tribes. Altman & Goodman (2001), Revenson & Schiaffano

(2000), and Reppucci et al. (1999) described additional community-based interventions to improve health.

Intervention efforts may also address specific settings. For example, Miller et al. (1998) used a model developed by Kelly et al. (1991, 1992) based on diffusion of innovation theory to change norms for unsafe sex in three gay hustler bars. Training opinion leaders, identified by bartenders, to disseminate information about condom use led to lower involvement in and frequency of paid unsafe sex by bar patrons. Changes were mediated by frequency of attendance at the bars, suggesting either a dose-response effect or one dependent on degree of attachment to the setting. Black patrons were unaffected, perhaps because the opinion leaders were largely white and Latino. Surprisingly, although behavior changed, descriptive norms (how patrons perceived that "others in the bar" behaved) did not, perhaps because of an overly broad definition of "others," or the use of descriptive rather than injunctive norms.

The studies we have described used rich qualitative data and clever research designs such as multiple baselines, staggered introduction of interventions, and nonequivalent comparison groups to make plausible causal inferences with small numbers of settings that could not always be randomly assigned to conditions. They call attention to the sociocultural diversity of settings, and the importance of working collaboratively with community members of the setting (from religious leaders, to police, to gang leaders, to tribal elders, to natural opinion leaders in bars) in changing community contexts.

Yet another approach to changing contexts is the creation of alternative settings with different structures, goals, and values from existing settings (Sarason 1972). Cherniss & Deegan (2000) reviewed factors associated with success in creating settings and maintaining their alternative vision.

METHODOLOGICAL ISSUES IN ASSESSING COMMUNITY CONTEXTS

In any empirical discipline, theoretical understanding and methodological sophistication go hand in hand. Psychologists have devoted far more time and energy to assessing individual attributes than to assessing the contexts of human behavior or transactions between people and contexts, and lack of appropriate measurement contributes to context minimization error. Thus, we turn to important approaches and challenges in measuring the effects of community contexts. Analysis of contextual and multi-level data is also a critical issue, but beyond the scope of this chapter.

Confusion Between Characteristics of Individuals and Contexts

Characteristics of individuals are naturally correlated with characteristics of social contexts (particularly when contexts are defined in terms of the aggregate characteristics of individuals who reside within them). The confounds, which are known as selection effects (e.g., Tienda 1991), may be due to choice or to constraints:

Immigrants often choose to reside in neighborhoods with other immigrants where language, cultural values, foods, and many other aspects of life are familiar and social networks are available. Poor people tend to live in poor neighborhoods because they cannot afford housing in wealthier communities, and members of minority groups suffer ongoing discrimination and segregation (Massey & Denton 1993). Membership in or attendance at community settings also depends on attraction of individuals to settings, attrition of those who do not find what they are looking for, and often selection among applicants by the settings themselves (Levy 2000, Shinn & Rapkin 2000). Effects of selection, attraction, and attrition often mimic the effects of the settings on behavior. For example, a selective college may both admit more talented students and develop their talents better than a less selective school.

Because of confounding between characteristics of individuals and settings, researchers typically control statistically for individual or family characteristics in estimating the effects of contexts but worry that such controls are insufficient owing to inadequate or incomplete measurement (Duncan et al. 1997). However, to the extent that associations between contextual characteristics and individual behaviors are causal, the attribution of all shared variance to the individual level may over- rather than undercorrect. Similarly, to the extent that neighborhoods influence families or parenting, controlling for family characteristics in studying children's outcomes may overcorrect (Duncan et al. 1997). The possibility of overcorrection is suggested by the larger effect sizes in the Gautreaux and Moving to Opportunity experiments, in which confounds between individuals and neighborhoods were eliminated, than in correlational studies, in which individual characteristics were controlled. Further, in the Gautreaux study neighborhood effects were strongest on educational attainment, employment, and earnings, exactly the types of individual characteristics that are typically controlled. Effects may also be larger in experimental than in correlational studies owing to extreme group designs or poor measures of neighborhood conditions in correlational studies. We return to the latter possibility below. Thus, even well-designed, multilevel correlational studies may fall prey to context minimization error.

Of course, most studies in the psychological literature pay no attention to community contexts but do report associations of individual characteristics, such as race, with outcomes. However, as Wilson (1987) pointed out, poor African-Americans are far more likely to live in neighborhoods of concentrated poverty than are comparably poor white Americans. For example, in a nationally representative sample of 10- to 13- year-old-children, 23.2% of blacks and 0.3% of whites lived in a neighborhood where at least 40% of neighbors were poor (Duncan & Aber 1997). As Leventhal & Brooks-Gunn (2000) showed, neighborhood affluence and poverty are associated with variables such as academic achievement, teen birth rates, and delinquency, even after controlling for family characteristics. Thus, effects of neighborhoods may masquerade as effects of individual characteristics, such as race, with which they are confounded.

Where contexts are not completely ignored, they are often measured in simplistic ways. Simply controlling for neighborhood poverty may underestimate the degree to which the inner-city neighborhoods in which some poor African-Americans reside represent different "ecological niches" for development with respect to education, jobs, marriage opportunities, and opportunities for sustained interaction with mainstream society (Wilson 1987, p. 60). Racial disparities extend beyond the immediate neighborhood, as Sampson et al. (1999) showed in Chicago. Collective efficacy depended not only on characteristics of the immediate neighborhood (defined as clusters of census tracts numbering about 8000 people) but also on collective efficacy in surrounding neighborhoods. Predominantly white neighborhoods were more likely to be high in efficacy than predominantly black neighborhoods. Further, white neighborhoods that were not high in efficacy were far more likely than comparable black neighborhoods to be "spatially advantaged" by being adjacent to neighborhoods with higher efficacy. High-efficacy black neighborhoods were far more likely than comparable white neighborhoods to be "spatially vulnerable" owing to contiguity with low-efficacy neighborhoods. Thus, black youths were doubly disadvantaged by their own neighborhoods and by others nearby.

Even where characteristics of individuals are not confounded with characteristics of contexts, contextual restraints may be confused with individual traits. Examples of this form of context minimization error abound in the case of homelessness, in which the most basic error is to look only at individual causes of homelessness, ignoring information about affordability of housing (Koegel et al. 1996). Characteristics of individuals may also be confused with restrictions of service systems (Shinn & Weitzman 1996). For example, researchers have concluded that homeless families are unusually likely to be headed by single mothers and are nomadic, based on studies in shelters that exclude men and have 30-day limits on stays. They conclude that substance abusers cannot maintain housing based on studies of housing programs that evict anyone found using substances.

Selecting Contexts to Measure

As Bronfenbrenner (1979, 1986) has pointed out, individuals can be influenced indirectly by settings they do not enter. Typically such influences are mediated by more local contextual influences. For example, African-American parents' experience of racism in the workplace influenced the ways they socialized their children to issues of race (Hughes & Chen 1997). Thus, most research focuses on immediate contexts of behavior.

IDENTIFYING BOUNDARIES   One critical issue in assessing contexts is determining their boundaries. In compositional studies neighborhoods are typically defined by census tracts or smaller block groups. This is not a bad starting point. Census boundaries are drawn in consultation with local communities to reflect important physical features and social and ethnic divisions (e.g., Leventhal & Brooks-Gunn 2000). However, people's definitions of their neighborhoods do not necessarily conform to census boundaries. In a small study in one city, Coulton et al. (2001)

found that residents' self-defined neighborhoods were close in size to census tracts but typically included portions of at least two census tracts and three block groups. Further, on average, only 43% of a resident's self-defined neighborhood overlapped with neighborhoods delineated by a majority of other residents of the same block group. Rank order correlations between social indicators calculated for census tracts and for resident-defined neighborhoods were as low as .3.

Even residents' definitions, which may be influenced by neighborhood names or generally acknowledged boundaries, may not reflect the geographic areas that affect them. Areas where residents spend time or through which they travel en route to school, work, shopping, religious services, or recreational activities may be more influential. Thus, family members residing at the same address might have different functional neighborhoods. Smaller areas than census tracts may be important. For example, the area viewed from an apartment window was found important to feelings of safety and adjustment by Kuo et al. (1998). The relevant size of a neighborhood may vary systematically with a person's age, health, or employment status. Tienda (1991) argued that relevant neighborhoods should not be defined in geographic terms at all but in terms of patterns of social interaction. Grannis (1998) showed that linkage of neighborhoods along tertiary streets (small streets designed for pedestrian traffic) was more important than geographic proximity for explaining racial segregation. Given these considerations, it is surprising that neighborhood variables explain as much variance as they do.

Boundaries of community settings may appear easier to define. However, many people who are formally members of churches, mutual-help groups, or fitness centers may never in fact attend. Experience sampling methods can examine people's exposure to settings. For example, Larson et al. (2001) found that European-American children in Chicago suburbs spent more time in school than African-American children in urban Chicago, and both groups spent far less time than middle class youths in Korea and India, because of the length of school days. An important research question is whether weighting environments by the proportion of time people spend in them would enhance their explanatory power, although weighting at the individual level would introduce selection effects.

SAMPLING   Quantitative studies of associations of context with individual outcomes must have a large enough sample of sufficiently variable contexts, and sufficient numbers of individuals within contexts (e.g., Leventhal & Brooks-Gunn 2000). Stratification, for example by race/ethnicity and SES (Sampson et al. 1997), can maximize power to understand effects of potentially confounded variables and purposive samples, such as Coulton et al.'s (1996) sample of neighborhoods high and low in child abuse, can maximize variation on key variables. Contexts change and should be sampled over time to understand processes of change.

Approaches to Measurement

Several theorists have described different approaches to assessment of ecological contexts. Linney (2000) divided these into participant perceptions, more-objective indicators, and measures of social regularities. Livert & Hughes (2002) focused on assessment of contexts and transactions between people and contexts. Shinn & Rapkin (2000) focused on whether the assessment involves aggregating information from or about lower-level units (e.g., people) or takes place at the ecological level of the context itself. Aggregation requires attention to the measurement properties of aggregate measures (Raudenbush & Sampson 1999). We review several approaches to assessing social contexts.

COMPOSITIONAL MEASURES BASED ON ARCHIVAL DATA   Recently, most neighborhood studies have used archival information collected by the census about demographic characteristics of individuals and aggregated them to geographic units such as census tracts. Census data are often employed because they are available and expedient, but the census was not designed to assess aspects of neighborhoods that influence residents, and census variables are relatively distal from behavior (e.g., Earls & Buka 2000). Studies using census data frequently combine multiple variables into indices (Leventhal & Brooks-Gunn 2000) in ways that are inconsistent from one study to the next and are often only loosely linked with theory. Studies rarely correct for systematic biases in the census, such as undercounts of poor and immigrant populations, and census data, which are collected every 10 years, may not represent the current status of changing neighborhoods.

Coulton & Hollister (1998) discussed additional archival data sources to assess other features of communities including housing (e.g., reports of housing code violations), the economy (e.g., unemployment insurance records), safety (e.g., police records, juvenile court filings), education (e.g., public school attendance records), health (e.g., vital records), social services (e.g., public assistance files), and community resources and participation (e.g., community directories). Linney (2000) described the use of archival data to assess social regularities. Archival sources have their own biases and threats to validity (e.g., Coulton & Hollister 1998, Linney 2000, Webb et al. 1981) but could productively be used more widely.

COMPOSITIONAL MEASURES OF PERCEPTIONS   Individual perceptions are frequently used to characterize community settings. Individuals can report on their own attitudes or values, which can be aggregated to create setting-level norms (e.g., Henry et al. 2000), or on characteristics of the setting itself. The social climate scales developed by Moos and colleagues (Moos 1994) assess dimensions of relationships, personal growth, and system maintenance and change in many types of settings. Conceptualizing aggregate perceptions as measures of context may require inter-rater agreement, mean differences among settings, and meaningful relationships of aggregate perceptions with other variables, controlling for individual perceptions (e.g., Shinn & Rapkin 2000). We need to understand how agreement comes about (selection, attraction, attrition, socialization) and understand systematic variation in perceptions.

OBSERVATIONAL INVENTORIES   The conceptual anchors participants use to rate environments are probably shaped by the limited set of comparison environments to which they have been exposed. Trained observers may be better able to evaluate a wide range of environments with a constant metric (e.g., Perkins & Taylor 1996). Inter-rater reliability is crucial but may be easiest to establish for relatively permanent environmental features. Patterns of social interaction are likely to vary by day and time, and for outdoor settings, by weather and season, thereby making sampling of observational periods as important as sampling of locations. Observational measures may miss conditions with high impact, such as drug dealing or violence, which participants have reason to hide or which have low base rates. Linney (2000) described a number of observational inventories for specific settings.

SETTING REGULARITIES   Settings differ in the behaviors they encourage, tolerate, and proscribe. The Multiphasic Environmental Assessment Procedure (Moos & Lemke 1996) systematically assesses program policies in addition to physical and architectural features, collective socio-demographic characteristics of residents and staff, and the social climate of residential facilities such as nursing homes. Multiple instruments measure both stated policies and views of staff who implement them. Both are important and need not match. Linney (2000) called attention to differences between formal policies (such as school desegregation) and social regularities within systems (such as resegregating classes by tracking students).

QUALITATIVE AND DESCRIPTIVE METHODS   Qualitative data can provide rich descriptions of ecological processes that are difficult to capture in other ways (e.g., Caughy et al. 1999, Furstenberg 1993, Plas & Lewis 1996). Potential drawbacks are small samples and questionable reliability and representativeness of findings. Integration of approaches, for example by using quantitative data to select representative contexts for qualitative investigation, is likely to yield greater understanding (e.g., Campbell & Ahrens 1998). The Project on Human Development in Chicago Neighborhoods used stratified random sampling of neighborhoods. Within neighborhoods it employed a variety of assessment techniques including interviews with key informants: Business owners, school administrators, religious leaders, police, and elected officials were systematically sampled from rosters of each of these groups. In addition, people with reputations as leaders were selected by a consensus of nominations from the other groups (Earls & Buka 2000). Qualitative and ethnographic approaches may be particularly useful in understanding social regularities and processes within settings.

CREATIVE APPROACHES   Researchers have used a variety of creative methods for particular purposes. Perkins & Taylor (1996) did a content analysis of newspapers for crime stories in predicting fear of crime. Campbell & Ahrens (1998) analyzed linkages among legal, mental health, and health systems in predicting outcomes for rape victims. Chesir-Teran (2002) proposed a multifaceted analysis of school environments with respect to heterosexism. Crafting measures to capture the theoretically important features of contexts continues to be a challenge.

Ethical Issues

Research in community contexts raises important issues that are not well recognized by the American Psychological Association's code of ethics (e.g., Snow et al. 2000, Trickett 1996, Trickett & Levin 1990). Researchers must take account of differing values, goals, and power held by diverse individuals, groups, organizations, and communities and the complex interactions among them, as well as their own values in undertaking research and interventions (Prilleltensky 2001, Snow et al. 2000). Interventions may have effects, not all of them positive (e.g., Levine & Perkins 1997), that radiate beyond the people and settings that gave consent or participated in planning. Aggregation of information to characterize neighborhoods or settings involves applying information to collectivities, when only individual participants have given consent. Because of these dilemmas, community psychologists frequently call for both community sanction for research and community collaboration in setting a research agenda, designing studies, and determining how information will be used, in the spirit of "nothing about us, without us" (e.g., Nelson et al. 1998). However, identifying appropriate representatives of the community or developing consensus in diverse communities is not always straightforward. Ethical issues, like conceptual and methodological ones, will continue to challenge researchers who attempt to understand the contexts of human welfare.

CONCLUSION

We have argued that community contexts matter for human welfare in ways that psychologists too often ignore. Fruitful conceptual models for understanding links between contexts and behavior include social capital, norms, and social stress. For neighborhoods, compositional effects, mediated by variables such as collective efficacy, are important. For community settings, both instrumental functions and social roles also matter. Context minimization error leads to an impoverished understanding of developmental and other psychological processes, perpetuation of stereotypes, and missed opportunities for intervention. Better psychological theory, more accurate inferences, and successful social change efforts require attention to reciprocal relationships between people and contexts and the ways contextual influences play out for diverse populations.

ACKNOWLEDGMENTS

We thank Tama Leventhal, Douglas Perkins, Ann Rivera, Edward Seidman, and Hiro Yoshikawa for insightful comments on an earlier version of this manuscript.

The *Annual Review of Psychology* is online at http://psych.annualreviews.org

LITERATURE CITED

Allen JP, Kuperminc G, Philliber S, Herre K. 1994. Programmatic prevention of adolescent problem behaviors:the role of autonomy, relatedness and volunteer service in the Teen Outreach Program. *Am. J. Community Psychol.* 22:617–38

Allen JP, Philliber S, Herrling S, Kuperminc GP. 1997. Preventing teen pregnancy and academic failure: experimental evaluation of a developmentally based approach. *Child Dev.* 64:729–42

Allen JP, Philliber S, Hoggson N. 1990. School-based prevention of teen-age pregnancy and school dropout: process evaluation of the national replication of the Teen Outreach Program. *Am. J. Community Psychol.* 18:505–24

Allison KW, Crawford I, Leone PE, Trickett E, Perez-Febles A, et al. 1999. Adolescent substance use: preliminary examinations of school and neighborhood context. *Am. J. Community Psychol.* 27:111–41

Altman DG, Goodman RM. 2001. Community intervention. In *Handbook of Health Psychology*, ed. A Baum, TA Revenson, JE Singer, pp. 591–612. Mahwah, NJ: Erlbaum

Altman I, Rogoff B. 1987. World views in psychology: trait, interactional, organismic, and transactional perspectives. In *Handbook of Environmental Psychology*, ed. D Stokols, I Altman, pp. 7–40. New York: Wiley

Aneshensel C, Sucoff CA. 1996. The neighborhood context of adolescent mental health. *J. Health Soc. Behav.* 37:293–310

Barker RG. 1968. *Ecological Psychology: Concepts and Methods for Studying the Environment of Human Behavior.* Stanford, CA: Stanford Univ. Press

Baumohl J, ed. 1996. *Homelessness in America.* Phoenix, AZ: Oryx

Bennett CC, Anderson LS, Cooper S, Hassol L, Klein DC, et al. 1966. *Community Psychology: A Report of the Boston Conference on the Education of Psychologists for Commu-*

nity Mental Health. Boston: Boston Univ. & South Shore Mental Health Center

Biglan A, Ary D, Koehn V, Levings D, Smith S, et al. 1996. Mobilizing positive reinforcement in communities to reduce youth access to tobacco. *Am. J. Community Psychol.* 24:625–38

Bowen WG, Bok D. 1998. *The Shape of the River: Long-Term Consequences of Considering Race in College and University Admissions.* Princeton, NJ: Princeton Univ. Press

Brodsky AE, O'Campo PJ, Aronson RE. 1999. PSOC in community context: multi-level correlates of a measure of psychological sense of community in low-income, urban neighborhoods. *J. Community Psychol.* 27: 659–79

Bronfenbrenner U. 1979. *The Ecology of Human Development.* Cambridge, MA: Harvard Univ. Press

Bronfenbrenner U. 1986. Ecology of the family as a context for human development: research perspectives. *Dev. Psychol.* 22:723–42

Brooks-Gunn J, Duncan GJ, Aber JL, eds. 1997a. *Neighborhood Poverty.* Vol. 1: *Context and Consequences for Children.* New York: Russell Sage Found.

Brooks-Gunn J, Duncan GJ, Aber JL, eds. 1997b. *Neighborhood Poverty.* Vol. 2: *Policy Implications in Studying Neighborhoods.* New York: Russell Sage Found.

Buka SL, Stichick TL, Birdthistle I, Earls FJ. 2001. Youth exposure to violence: prevalence, risks and consequences. *Am. J. Orthopsychiatry* 71:298–310

Burroughs SM, Eby LT. 1998. Psychological sense of community at work: a measurement system and explanatory framework. *J. Community Psychol.* 26:509–32

Campbell R. 1998. The community response to rape: victims' experiences with the legal, medical, and mental health systems. *Am. J. Community Psychol.* 26:355–79

Campbell R, Ahrens CE. 1998. Innovative

community services for rape victims: an application of multiple case study methodology. *Am. J. Community Psychol.* 26:537–71

Caughy MO, Brodsky AE, O'Campo PJ, Aronson R. 2001. Perceptions of parenting: individual differences and the effects of community. *Am. J. Community Psychol.* 29:679–99

Caughy MO, O'Campo PJ, Brodsky AE. 1999. Neighborhoods, families, and children: implications for policy and practice. *J. Community Psychol.* 27:615–33

Cherniss C, Deegan G. 2000. The creation of alternative settings. See Rappaport & Seidman 2000, pp. 359–77

Chesir-Teran D. 2002. Conceptualizing and assessing heterosexism in high school: a setting-level approach. *Am. J. Community Psychol.* In press

Colder CR, Mott J, Levy S, Flay B. 2000. The relations of perceived neighborhood danger to childhood aggression: a test of mediating mechanisms. *Am. J. Community Psychol.* 28:83–103

Coulton CJ. 1996. Effects of neighborhoods on families and children: implications for services. In *Children and Their Families in Big Cities: Strategies for Service Reform*, ed. AJ Kahn, SB Kamerman, pp. 87–120. New York: Cross-Natl. Stud. Res. Progr., Columbia Univ. Sch. Soc. Work

Coulton CJ, Hollister R. 1998. Measuring comprehensive community initiative outcomes using data available for small areas. In *New Approaches to Evaluating Community Initiatives*, ed. K Fulbright-Anderson, AC Kubisch, JP Connell, pp. 165–220. Queenstown, MD: Aspen Inst.

Coulton CJ, Korbin JE, Chan T, Su M. 2001. Mapping residents' perceptions on neighborhood boundaries: a methodological note. *Am. J. Community Psychol.* 29:371–83

Coulton CJ, Korbin JE, Su M. 1996. Measuring neighborhood context for young children in an urban area. *Am. J. Community Psychol.* 24:5–32

Cunningham M. 1999. African American adolescent males' perceptions of their commu-

nity resources and constraints: a longitudinal analysis. *J. Community Psychol.* 27:569–88

Del Conte A, Kling J. 2001. A synthesis of MTO research on self-sufficiency, safety and health, and behavior and delinquency. *Poverty Res. News* 5(1). http://www.jcpr.org/newsletters/vol5_no1/index.html

Duncan GJ, Aber JL. 1997. Neighborhood models and measures. See Brooks-Gunn et al. 1997a, pp. 62–78

Duncan GJ, Connell JP, Klebanov PK. 1997. Conceptual and methodological issues in estimating causal effects of neighborhoods and family conditions on individual development. See Brooks-Gunn et al. 1997a, pp. 219–50

Earls F, Buka S. 2000. Measurement of community characteristics. In *Handbook of Early Childhood Intervention*, ed. JP Shonkoff, SJ Meisels, pp. 309–24. New York: Cambridge Univ. Press. 2nd ed.

Foley MW, McCarthy JD, Chaves M. 2001. Social capital, religious institutions, and poor communities. See Saegert et al. 2001, pp. 215–45

Furstenberg FF Jr. 1993. How families manage risk and opportunity in dangerous neighborhoods. In *Sociology and the Public Agenda*, ed. WJ Wilson, pp. 231–58. Newbury Park, CA: Sage

Furstenberg FF Jr, Hughes ME. 1997. The influence of neighborhoods on children's development: a theoretical perspective and research agenda. See Brooks-Gunn et al. 1997b, pp. 23–47

Garcia I, Giuliani F, Wiesenfeld E. 1999. Community and sense of community: the case of an urban barrio in Caracas. *J. Community Psychol.* 27:727–40

Gonzales NA, Cauce AM, Friedman RJ, Mason CA. 1996. Family, peer, and neighborhood influences on academic achievement among African-American adolescents. *Am. J. Community Psychol.* 24:365–87

Grannis R. 1998. The importance of trivial streets: residential streets and residential segregation. *Am. J. Sociol.* 103:1530–64

Griffin KW, Scheier LM, Botvin GJ, Diaz T,

Miller N. 1999. Interpersonal aggression in urban minority youth: mediators of perceived neighborhood, peer, and parental influences. *J. Community Psychol.* 27:281–98

Hendryx MS, Ahern MM. 1997. Mental health functioning and community problems. *J. Community Psychol.* 25:147–57

Henry DB, Guerra N, Huesmann LR, Tolan PH, VanAcker R, Eron L. 2000. Normative influences on aggression in urban elementary school classrooms. *Am. J. Community Psychol.* 28:59–81

Hirsch BJ, Roffman JG, Deutsch NL, Flynn CA, Loder TL, Pagano ME. 2000. Inner-city youth development organizations: strengthening programs for adolescent girls. *J. Early Adolesc.* 20:210–30

House JS, Landis KR, Umberson D. 1988. Social relationships and health. *Science* 241: 540–45

Hughes D, Chen L. 1997. When and what parents tell children about race: an examination of race-related socialization among African American families. *Appl. Dev. Sci.* 1:200–14

Hughes D, Dodge MA. 1997. African American women in the workplace: relationship between job conditions, racial bias at work, and perceived job quality. *Am. J. Community Psychol.* 25:581–99

James SA, Schulz AJ, van Olphen J. 2001. Social capital, poverty, and community health: an exploration of linkages. See Saegert et al. 2001, pp. 165–88

Jarrett RL. 1997. Bringing families back in: neighborhoods' effects on child development. See Brooks-Gunn et al. 1997b, pp. 48–64

Jason LA, Berk M, Schnopp-Wyatt DL, Talbot B. 1999. Effects of enforcement of youth access laws on smoking prevalence. *Am. J. Community Psychol.* 27:143–60

Jencks C, Mayer SE. 1990. The social consequences of growing up in a poor neighborhood. In *Inner City Poverty in the United States*, ed. LE Lynn, MFH McGeary, pp. 111–86. Washington, DC: Natl. Acad. Press

Kelly JA, St. Lawrence JS, Diaz YE, Stevenson LY, Hauth AC, et al. 1991. HIV risk behavior reduction following intervention with key opinion leaders of population: an experimental analysis. *Am. J. Public Health* 81:168–71

Kelly JA, St. Lawrence JS, Stevenson LY, Hauth AC, Kalichman SC, et al. 1992. Community AIDS/HIV risk reduction: the effects of endorsements by popular people in three cities. *Am. J. Public Health* 82:1483–89

Kelly JG, ed. 1979. *Adolescent Boys in High School: A Psychological Study of Coping and Adaptation.* Hillsdale, NJ: Erlbaum

Kelly JG, Ryan AM, Altman BE, Stelzner SP. 2000. Understanding and changing social systems: an ecological view. See Rappaport & Seidman 2000, pp. 133–59

Kingree JB, Thompson M. 2000. Mutual help groups, perceived status benefits, and well-being: a test with adult children of alcoholics with personal substance abuse problems. *Am. J. Community Psychol.* 28:325–42

Klaw E, Huebsch PD, Humphreys K. 2000. Community patterns in an on-line mutual help group for problem drinkers. *J. Community Psychol.* 28:535–46

Koegel P, Burnam MA, Baumohl J. 1996. The causes of homelessness. See Baumohl 1996, pp. 24–33

Kulik L. 1998. Effect of gender and social environment on gender role perceptions and identity: comparative study of kibbutz and urban adolescents in Israel. *J. Community Psychol.* 26:533–48

Kuo FE, Sullivan WC, Coley RL, Brunson L. 1998. Fertile ground for community: inner-city neighborhood common spaces. *Am. J. Community Psychol.* 26:823–51

Larson RW, Richards MH, Sims B, Dworkin J. 2001. How urban African American young adolescents spend their time: time budgets for locations, activities, and companionship. *Am. J. Community Psychol.* 29:565–97

Leventhal T, Brooks-Gunn J. 2000. The neighborhoods they live in: the effects of neighborhood residence on child and adolescent outcomes. *Psychol. Bull.* 126:309–37

Leventhal T, Brooks-Gunn J. 2002. The early

impacts of Moving to Opportunity on children and youth in New York City. In *Choosing a Better Life? How Public Housing Tenants Selected a HUD Experiment to Improve Their Lives and Those of Their Children: The Moving to Opportunity Demonstration Program*, ed. J Goering. Washington, DC: Urban Inst. Press. In press

Levine M, Perkins DV. 1997. *Principles of Community Psychology: Perspective and Applications*. New York: Oxford Univ. Press. 2nd ed.

Levy LH. 2000. Self-help groups. See Rappaport & Seidman 2000, pp. 591–613

Lichtenstein E, Lopez K, Glasgow RE, Gilbert-McRae S. 1996. Effectiveness of a consultation intervention to promote tobacco control policies in Northwest Indian tribes. *Am. J. Community Psychol.* 24:639–55

Linney JA. 2000. Assessing ecological constructs and community context. See Rappaport & Seidman 2000, pp. 647–68

Livert D, Hughes D. 2002. The ecological paradigm: persons in settings. In *A Quarter Century of Community Psychology: Readings from the American Journal of Community Psychology*, ed. TA Revenson, AR D'Augelli, SE French, DL Hughes, D Livert, et al. New York: Kluwer Acad./Plenum

Lopez ML, Stack CB. 2001. Social capital and the culture of power: lessons from the field. See Saegert et al. 2001, pp. 31–59

Lounsbury JW, DeNeui D. 1996. Collegiate psychological sense of community in relation to size of college/university and extroversion. *J. Community Psychol.* 24:381–94

Luke DA, Rappaport J, Seidman E. 1991. Setting phenotypes in a mutual help organization: expanding behavior setting theory. *Am. J. Community Psychol.* 19:147–67

Massey DS, Denton NA. 1993. *American Apartheid: Segregation and the Making of the Underclass*. Cambridge, MA: Harvard Univ. Press

Maton KI. 1989. Community settings as buffers of life stress? Highly supportive churches, mutual help groups, and senior centers. *Am. J. Community Psychol.* 17:203–32

McMillan DW, Chavis DM. 1986. Sense of community: a definition and theory. *J. Community Psychol.* 14:6–23

Miller RL, Klotz D, Eckholdt HM. 1998. HIV prevention with male prostitutes and patrons of hustler bars: replication of an HIV preventive intervention. *Am. J. Community Psychol.* 26:97–132

Moos RH. 1994. *The Social Climate Scales: A User's Guide*. Palo Alto, CA: Consulting Psychologists Press. 2nd ed.

Moos RH. 2002. The mystery of human context and coping: an unraveling of clues. *Am. J. Community Psychol.* 30:67–88

Moos RH, Lemke S. 1996. *Evaluating Residential Facilities: The Multiphasic Environmental Assessment Procedure*. Thousand Oaks, CA: Sage

Morris A, Shinn M, Dumont K. 1999. Contextual factors affecting the organizational commitment of diverse police officers: a level of analysis perspective. *Am. J. Community Psychol.* 27:75–105

Murrell SA. 1973. *Community Psychology and Social Systems: A Conceptual Framework and Intervention Guide*. New York: Behavioral

Nelson G, Ochocka J, Griffin K, Lord J. 1998. "Nothing about me, without me": participatory action research with self-help/mutual aid organizations for psychiatric consumer/survivors. *Am. J. Community Psychol.* 26:881–912

Pearlin LI. 1983. Role strains and personal stress. In *Psychological Stress*, ed. HB Kaplan, pp. 3–32. New York: Academic

Perkins DD, Long DA. 2002. Neighborhood sense of community and social capital: a multi-level analysis. In *Psychological Sense of Community: Research, Applications, and Implications*, ed. A Fisher, C Sonn, B Bishop, pp. 291–318. New York: Plenum

Perkins DD, Taylor RB. 1996. Ecological assessments of community disorder: their relationship to fear of crime and theoretical implications. *Am. J. Community Psychol.* 24: 63–108

Phillips DA, Howes C, Whitebook M. 1992.

The social policy context of child care: effects on quality. *Am. J. Community Psychol.* 20:25–52

Plas JM, Lewis SE. 1996. Environmental factors and sense of community in a planned town. *Am. J. Community Psychol.* 24:109–43

Price RH. 2000. Contemporary intersections: unemployment. See Rappaport & Seidman 2000, pp. 961–65

Prilleltensky I. 2001. Value-based praxis in community psychology: moving toward social justice and social action. *Am. J. Community Psychol.* 29:747–78

Putnam RD. 1995. Bowling alone: America's declining social capital. *J. Democr.* 6(1):65–78

Rappaport J. 1977. *Community Psychology: Values, Research, and Action.* New York: Holt, Rinehart & Winston

Rappaport J, Seidman E, eds. 2000. *Handbook of Community Psychology.* New York: Kluwer Acad./Plenum

Raudenbush S, Sampson RJ. 1999. Ecometrics: toward a science of assessing ecological settings, with application to the systematic social observation of neighborhoods. *Sociol. Methodol.* 29:1–41

Reppucci ND, Woolard JL, Fried CS. 1999. Social, community, and preventive interventions. *Annu. Rev. Psychol.* 50:387–418

Revenson TA, Schiaffino KM. 2000. Community-based health interventions. See Rappaport & Seidman 2000, pp. 471–93

Riger S. 1985. Crime as an environmental stressor. *J. Community Psychol.* 13:270–80

Roberts LJ, Salem D, Rappaport J, Toro PA, Luke DA, Seidman E. 1999. Giving and receiving help: interpersonal transactions in mutual-help meetings and psychosocial adjustment of members. *Am. J. Community Psychol.* 27:841–68

Ross CE, Jang SJ. 2000. Neighborhood disorder, fear, and mistrust: the buffering role of social ties with neighbors. *Am. J. Community Psychol.* 28:401–20

Ross L. 1977. The intuitive psychologist and his

shortcomings: distortions in the attribution process. In *Advances in Experimental Social Psychology*, ed. L Berkowitz, 10:173–220. New York: Academic

Royal MA, Rossi RJ. 1996. Individual-level correlates of sense of community: findings from workplace and school. *J. Community Psychol.* 24:395–416

Royce-Davis JC. 2001. "It's the day-to-day living that matters": the meaning and process of community in the lives of a couple with significant psychiatric disabilities. *Am. J. Community Psychol.* 29:807–33

Rubinowitz LS, Rosenbaum JE. 2000. *Crossing the Class and Color Lines: From Public Housing to White Suburbia.* Chicago: Univ. Chicago Press

Saegert S, Thompson JP, Warren MR, eds. 2001. *Social Capital and Poor Communities.* New York: Russell Sage Found.

Saegert S, Winkel G. 1998. Social capital and the revitalization of New York City's distressed inner-city housing. *Hous. Policy Debate* 9:17–60

Saegert S, Winkel G, Swartz C. 2002. Social capital and crime in New York City's low-income housing. *Hous. Policy Debate* 13:189–226

Salem DA, Bogat GA, Reid C. 1997. Mutual help goes on-line. *J. Community Psychol.* 25:189–207

Salem DA, Reischl TM, Gallacher F, Randall KW. 2000. The role of referent and expert power in mutual help. *Am. J. Community Psychol.* 28:303–24

Sampson RJ. 2001. Crime and public safety: insights from community-level perspectives on social capital. See Saegert et al. 2001, pp. 89–114

Sampson RJ, Groves WB. 1989. Community structure and crime: testing social-disorganization theory. *Am. J. Sociol.* 94:774–802

Sampson RJ, Morenoff JD, Earls F. 1999. Spatial dynamics of collective efficacy for children. *Am. Sociol. Rev.* 64:633–60

Sampson RJ, Raudenbush SW, Earls F. 1997. Neighborhoods and violent crime: a multilevel study of collective efficacy. *Science* 277:918–24

Sandler IN, Gensheimer L, Braver S. 2000. Stress: theory, research, and action. See Rappaport & Seidman 2000, pp. 187–213

Sarason SB. 1972. *The Creation of Settings and the Future Societies.* San Francisco, CA: Jossey-Bass

Scarr S, Eisenberg M. 1993. Child care research: issues, perspectives, and results. *Annu. Rev. Psychol.* 44:613–44

Seidman E. 1988. Back to the future, community psychology: unfolding a theory of social intervention. *Am. J. Community Psychol.* 16:3–24

Seidman E, Allen L, Aber JL, Mitchell C, Feinman J, et al. 1995. Development and validation of adolescent-perceived microsystem scales: social support, daily hassles, and involvement. *Am. J. Community Psychol.* 23:355–88

Seidman E, Yoshikawa H, Roberts A, Chesir-Teran D, Allen L, et al. 1998. Structural and experiential neighborhood contexts, developmental stage, and antisocial behavior among urban adolescents in poverty. *Dev. Psychopathol.* 10:259–81

Shaw CR, McKay HD. 1942. *Juvenile Delinquency and Urban Areas.* Chicago: Univ. Chicago Press

Sheidow AJ, Gorman-Smith D, Tolan PH, Henry DB. 2001. Family and community characteristics: risk factors for violence exposure in inner-city youth. *J. Community Psychol.* 29:345–60

Shinn M, Rapkin B. 2000. Cross-level research without cross-ups in community psychology. See Rappaport & Seidman 2000, pp. 669–95

Shinn M, Weitzman BC. 1996. Homeless families are different. See Baumohl 1996, pp. 109–22

Simons RL, Johnson C, Beaman J, Conger RD, Whitbeck LB. 1996. Parents and peer group as mediators of the effect of community structure on adolescent problem behavior. *Am. J. Community Psychol.* 24:145–71

Snow DL, Grady K, Goyetee-Ewing M. 2000. A perspective on ethical issues in community psychology. See Rappaport & Seidman 2000, pp. 897–917

Snowden LR. 2001. Social embeddedness and psychological well-being among African-Americans and Whites. *Am. J. Community Psychol.* 29:519–36

Solomon D, Watson M, Battistich V, Schaps E, Delucchi K. 1996. Creating classrooms that students experience as communities. *Am. J. Community Psychol.* 24:719–48

Stein CH, Wemmerus VA. 2001. Searching for a normal life: personal accounts of adults with schizophrenia, their parents and well-siblings. *Am. J. Community Psychol.* 29:725–46

Stewart E, Weinstein RS. 1997. Volunteer participation in context: motivations and political efficacy within three AIDS organizations. *Am. J. Community Psychol.* 25:809–37

Taylor RB, Covington J. 1993. Community structural change and fear of crime. *Soc. Probl.* 40:374–95

Thompson MP, Norris FH, Ruback RB. 1996. System influences on posthomicide beliefs and distress. *Am. J. Community Psychol.* 24:785–809

Tienda M. 1991. Poor people and poor places: deciphering neighborhood effects on poverty outcomes. In *Macro-Micro Linkages in Sociology*, ed J Huber, pp. 244–62. Newbury Park, CA: Sage

Trickett EJ. 1996. A future for community psychology: the contexts of diversity and the diversity of contexts. *Am. J. Community Psychol.* 24:209–34

Trickett EJ, Levin GB. 1990. Paradigms for prevention: providing a context for confronting ethical issues. In *Ethical Implications of Primary Prevention*, ed. GB Levin, EJ Trickett, RE Hess, pp. 3–21. New York: Haworth

Venkatesh SA. 1999. Community-based interventions into street gang activity. *J. Community Psychol.* 27:551–67

Wagenaar AC, Gehan JP, Jones-Webb R, Toomey TL, Forster JL, et al. 1999. Communities mobilizing for change on alcohol: lessons and results from a 15-community randomized trial. *J. Community Psychol.* 27: 315–26

Waldo CR. 1998. Out on campus: sexual orientation and academic climate in a university context. *Am. J. Community Psychol.* 26:745–74

Wandersman A, Florin P. 2000. Citizen participation and community organizations. See Rappaport & Seidman 2000, pp. 247–72

Wandersman A, Nation M. 1998. Urban neighborhoods and mental health: psychological contributions to understanding toxicity, resilience, and interventions. *Am. Psychol.* 53:647–56

Warren MR, Thompson JP, Saegert S. 2001. The role of social capital in combating poverty. See Saegert et al. 2001, pp. 1–28

Webb EJ, Campbell DT, Schwartz RD, Sechrest L, Grove JB. 1981. *Nonreactive Measures in the Social Sciences.* Boston: Houghton-Mifflin. 2nd ed.

Wilson WJ. 1987. *The Truly Disadvantaged: The Inner City, the Underclass, and Public Policy.* Chicago: Univ. Chicago Press

Annu. Rev. Psychol. 2003. 54:461–90
doi: 10.1146/annurev.psych.54.101601.145221
First published online as a Review in Advance on October 28, 2002

CULTURAL PATHWAYS THROUGH UNIVERSAL DEVELOPMENT

Patricia M. Greenfield[1], Heidi Keller[2],
Andrew Fuligni[3], and Ashley Maynard[4]

[1]Department of Psychology, University of California, Los Angeles, Los Angeles, California 90095; e-mail: greenfield@psych.ucla.edu
[2]Department of Human Sciences, University of Osnabrueck. Osnabrueck, Germany 49069 and Department of Psychology, University of California, Los Angeles, Los Angeles, California 90095; e-mail: hkeller@uos.de
[3]Departments of Psychiatry and Psychology, University of California, Los Angeles, Los Angeles, California 90095; e-mail: afuligni@ucla.edu
[4]Department of Psychology, University of Hawaii, Honolulu, Hawaii 96822; e-mail: amaynard@hawaii.edu

Key Words culture, development, individualism, collectivism, independence, interdependence, socialization

■ **Abstract** We focus our review on three universal tasks of human development: relationship formation, knowledge acquisition, and the balance between autonomy and relatedness at adolescence. We present evidence that each task can be addressed through two deeply different cultural pathways through development: the pathways of independence and interdependence. Whereas core theories in developmental psychology are universalistic in their intentions, they in fact presuppose the independent pathway of development. Because the independent pathway is therefore well-known in psychology, we focus a large part of our review on empirically documenting the alternative, interdependent pathway for each developmental task. We also present three theoretical approaches to culture and development: the ecocultural, the sociohistorical, and the cultural values approach. We argue that an understanding of cultural pathways through human development requires all three approaches. We review evidence linking values (cultural values approach), ecological conditions (ecocultural approach), and socialization practices (sociohistorical approach) to cultural pathways through universal developmental tasks.

CONTENTS

0066-4308/03/0203-0461$14.00

461

INTRODUCTION AND OVERVIEW

An important question is how cultural differentiation and universal phenomena interact in human development. In contrast to earlier *Annual Review* articles focused on cross-cultural issues (Bond & Smith 1996, Cooper & Denner 1998, Kagitçibasi & Berry 1989, Shweder & Sullivan 1993, Triandis & Suh 2002), our review is organized around universal developmental tasks. Each task begins at a particular part of the life cycle; each is a universal component of human ontogeny. However, how these universal developmental tasks are addressed can vary from group to group; they have alternative cultural resolutions. We review evidence showing that the resolutions fit into two contrasting cultural pathways organized around the preferred developmental goals of independence or interdependence. In an important sense, the endpoints of our developmental pathways are the individualistic and collectivistic personality types described by Triandis & Suh (2002) in their *Annual Review of Psychology* article.

The three universal tasks that we discuss are relationship formation, knowledge acquisition, and autonomy/relatedness. Each of these tasks first becomes important (or takes on its greatest importance) at a different period of development: relationship formation at birth, knowledge acquisition in early childhood, and autonomy/relatedness at adolescence. Each of these tasks is conceptualized in core theories within developmental psychology; we will identify these core theoretical approaches and critique them from a cultural perspective.

What is Culture? Its Relationship to Development, History, and Evolution

We view culture as a socially interactive process of construction comprising two main components: shared activity (cultural practices) and shared meaning (cultural interpretation). Both components of cultural processes are cumulative in nature since they occur between, as well as within, generations. Meanings and activities not only accumulate but also transform over both developmental time—across a single life cycle, and historical time—between generations. Cultural processes are based in the biological nature of humans, defining enabling as well as constraining conditions. Contrary to many earlier accounts, however, culture and biology are not opposites, but intrinsically interrelated and complementary (Greenfield 2002, Keller 2002, Fiske 2000).

Cultural processes are founded on an ontogenetic program of development with sensitive periods for different developmental tasks and modes of cultural learning (Greenfield 2000a). These developmental tasks and the modes of cultural learning have evolved in response to selection pressures from the environment. They have evolved both phylogenetically, over evolutionary time, and culturally, over historical time (Cole 1996). Therefore, cultural learning, both process and content, is stimulated by and adapted to a particular ecocultural niche. Cultural learning implies cultural teaching, which itself develops over the life span (Maynard 2002), over historical time (Greenfield 2000a), and over evolutionary time (Greenfield et al. 2000a).

Cultural Pathways Toward Independence and Interdependence: Integrating Three Approaches to Culture and Development

In the past 15 years, a body of evidence has cohered around two developmental trajectories that tie together differences in cultural learning throughout development. Whereas these differences have sometimes been reported as separate, unrelated facts, our model of two cultural pathways places them within a unified developmental theory. This is a model of two idealized developmental pathways, one emphasizing individuation and independence, the other emphasizing group membership and interdependence. Each ideal is part of a larger sociocultural system, the first termed individualistic, the latter, collectivistic or sociocentric. Our conceptualization links to earlier discussions of the "cultural syndromes" of individualism and collectivism (Hofstede 1991, Triandis 1988, 1990; for a critical review see Kagitçibasi 1994, Oyserman et al. 2002, Fiske 2002), as well as to the cultural construction of self as independent and/or interdependent (cf. Kagitçibasi 1990, 1996; Markus & Kitayama 1991). According to this model, adult conceptions of the ideal and actual self also serve as developmental goals that organize socialization experiences in characteristic ways (Kagitçibasi 1990, 1996). These goals, experiences, and the resultant behaviors define pathways across the life span.

This conception of cultural pathways draws on three major types of theory: the ecocultural, sociohistorical, and values approaches. The ecocultural approach emphasizes the causal influence of material conditions in the environment. The values approach, in contrast, emphasizes the causal influence of ideals or meanings inside the psyche. The sociohistorical approach emphasizes the causal influence of social factors: the interactional processes and symbolic tools used in cultural learning, which develop over historical time. Early on, it was recognized that these influences are not mutually exclusive. Whiting & Whiting (1960), for example, noted the persistence of value systems in the face of maladaptive consequences. They recognized that environmental conditions are not always determinative and that psychological ideals can sometimes be stronger.

The values approach is the most central to our model of cultural pathways through universal development.

THE CULTURAL VALUES APPROACH   On the side of social development, the distinction between independent and interdependent pathways of development originates in cross-cultural comparative research identifying altruism and egoism as outcomes of different socialization practices under different environmental conditions (Whiting & Whiting 1973). On the side of cognitive development, the distinction between a more collectivistic and individualistic worldview originates in Greenfield's research in Senegal in which she found greater metacognitive self-awareness—a cognitive separation of self and world—as a result of the Western institution of formal schooling (Greenfield & Bruner 1966). This type of distinction was greatly elaborated by Mundy-Castle (1974) in his contrast between technological intelligence, which is more developed in the independent person characteristic of Europe, and social intelligence, which is more developed in the interdependent person characteristic of Africa. Related explorations of intelligence concepts in different cultures began to appear (Dasen & de Ribeaupierre 1987, Serpell 1994, Sternberg et al. 1981, Wober 1974); all challenged the assumption that technological/scientific intelligence was a universal endpoint of development (Greenfield 1974). They pointed to alternative emphases on social intelligence, a concern with responsible ways of contributing to the social world.

Out of these historical beginnings has grown a conception of alternative pathways of development. In an independent developmental pathway, social obligations are individually negotiated; opportunities to select social relationships (personal choice) and to act freely in those relationships (individual rights) are maximized (Raeff et al. 2000). In an interdependent developmental pathway, in contrast, social obligations and responsibilities are given greater priority, while individual choice is much less important. An independent pathway prioritizes individuation as a developmental goal; an interdependent pathway, by contrast, prioritizes conforming to established social norms as a developmental goal (Nsamenang & Lamb 1994, Weisner 2000, Kitayama 2002).

Culturally relevant developmental goals are represented in the form of implicit ethnotheories of development, i.e., a system of beliefs and ideas concerning the nature of the ideal child and the socialization practices necessary to achieve this ideal (Goodnow 1988, Harkness & Super 1996, McGillicuddy-De Lisi & Sigel 1995). These ethnotheories are shared (and negotiated) among members of cultural communities. These values can be expressed explicitly, as in the study of parental ethnotheories, or implicitly, as in the study of cultural practices, particularly discourse practices (Ochs & Schieffelin 1984, Sigel et al. 1992, Keller et al. 2002b). The growing emphasis on indigenous conceptualizations of parenting goals (Chao 1994, Gutierrez & Sameroff 1990, Yovsi & Keller 2000) has unraveled independence and interdependence as core dimensions, applicable to all developmental domains. Participants from non-Western cultures/immigrants, such as Chinese (Chao 1994), Japanese (Rothbaum et al. 2000), Indians (Saraswathi 1999, Keller et al. 2002b), West Africans [Ogunnnaike & Houser (2002) for Nigeria, Nsamenang (1992) and Yovsi (2001) for Cameroon], and Puerto Ricans (Harwood et al. 1996) subscribe to the cultural ideal of interdependence: their ethnotheories stress decency (responsibility, honesty) and proper demeanor (politeness, respect for elders, loyalty to family) for social and cognitive developmental domains (Harwood 1992).

Participants from Western industrialized cultural communities, such as Germans (Keller et al. 2002a,b), European Americans (Harwood et al. 1996) and Dutch (Harkness et al. 2000b), subscribe to the cultural ideal of independence: their ethnotheories stress self-maximization and independence (creativity, curiosity, assertiveness, self-esteem). High socioeconomic (SES) status and formal education are associated with a more individualistic orientation (Keller et al. 2002b, Palacios & Moreno 1996, Tapia Uribe et al. 1994). Nonetheless, these cultural orientations persist across various socioeconomic and educational backgrounds (Keller et al. 2002b, Harwood et al. 1996). Socialization practices that function to actualize the ethnotheoretical framework within cultural communities begin at birth or even before.

THE ECOCULTURAL APPROACH   The ecocultural approach, also pioneered by anthropologists Beatrice and John Whiting, sees the child's behavioral development and the acquisition of culture as resulting from the interaction between human biological potentialities and environmental conditions (D'Andrade 1994, Whiting & Whiting 1975)[1]. In short, the ecocultural approach emphasizes development as an adaptation to different environmental conditions and constraints (Berry 1976, LeVine 1977, Munroe & Munroe 1994, Super & Harkness 1986, Weisner 1997, Whiting & Whiting 1975, Whiting & Edwards 1988).

For example, Berry (1976) did an extensive cross-cultural study of ecological influences on the socialization and performance of perceptual and cognitive tasks. Berry's definition of ecology includes distal variables of physical environment, economic possibilities, and community size. As another example, Whiting & Edwards (1988) extend their ecological lens to the proximal ecology of maternal behavior; their ecological variables include mothers' workloads, household composition, and support networks. Whiting & Edwards relate maternal behavior, in turn, to children's social development; social behaviors of interest include dependency, obedience, cooperation, and aggression. Of the three approaches, the ecological approach has been the most concerned with stages of development and their ontogenetic links through the life span (Whiting & Edwards 1988, Weisner & Bernheimer 1998).

From the ecocultural perspective, particular economic and environmental conditions create different social structures that favor different developmental pathways (cf Berry 1994). The pathways therefore arise as adaptations to these physical and economic conditions. Thus, the interdependent pathway appears to be an adaptive response to small face-to-face communities and a subsistence economy; these communities value tradition and therefore change slowly. The independent

---

[1]The ecocultural was originally termed the psychocultural and this term is sometimes still used.

pathway, in contrast, appears to be an adaptive response to large, anonymous, urban communities and a commercial economy (Greenfield 2000a, Keller 1997, Keller & Greenfield 2000, Keller et al. 2002b); these communities value innovation and therefore change more rapidly. In slow-changing, subsistence-based ecologies, ethnotheories are transmitted vertically from generation to generation, maximizing historical continuity. In complex and fast-changing societies, on the other hand, parental ideas are negotiated horizontally within generations, relying on public discourse (media) and experts (pediatricians); parental ideas substantially differ between generations (Keller et al. 1984, Hewlett & Lamb 2002).

THE SOCIOHISTORICAL APPROACH   This approach emphasizes processes of social construction, particularly cultural apprenticeship, cultural activities or practices, the use of cultural artifacts, including tools, and the historical dimension of these processes (Cole 1996; Lave & Wenger 1991; Rogoff 1990; Saxe 1991; Scribner 1985; Scribner & Cole 1973, 1981; Vygotsky 1962; Wertsch 1985; Zukow 1989). Social construction is seen as a set of situation-specific activities.

The primary focus of this approach has been on explaining the child's cognitive development. For example, Mistry & Rogoff (1994) demonstrate that memory is context bound and has to be viewed as an activity rather than as a context-free skill. They report studies demonstrating that memory for familiar cultural tools exceeds memory for culturally neutral items. As another example, Japanese abacus experts can recall series of 15 digits forward or backward, whereas their memory span for the Roman alphabet or fruit names matches the usual $7 +/- 2$ units (Hatano 1982).

The sociohistorical perspective is crucial to the model of cultural pathways through universal development. According to this model, each pathway results from a value orientation that generates the construction of socializing practices in particular situations (often called co-construction to reflect the active involvement of the child). These social construction processes include apprenticeship from cultural "experts" in the adult generation, as well as peer interaction (Greenfield & Lave 1982, Maynard 2002). The interactional routines and artifacts that are utilized in cultural learning have a key role in socializing a child to proceed on a particular developmental pathway. (Greenfield 2000a, Rogoff 1990, Mistry & Rogoff 1994, Saxe 1991). Construction processes become particularly salient in bicultural people, where one or the other value system can become prominent in a particular situation (Garcia-Coll et al. 1995).

Criticisms of Independence/Individualism and Interdependence/Collectivism as Basic Cultural Paradigms

One common criticism of these cultural paradigms is that the approach is too simplistic and reductionistic; the dichotomous binary quality of individualism and collectivism is seen as problematical (Killen & Wainryb 2000). This critique refers mainly to cross-cultural questionnaire studies. These studies usually compare national samples of university students to infer cultural differences. Conflicting results (Chan 1994, Fiske 2002, Oyserman et al. 2002, Singelis et al. 1995) are mainly a result of a lack of external validity of the questionnaires, of cultural insensitivity in the assessment, of the failure to consider SES and education as cultural factors, and of an overuse of national labels as a proxy for internal culture. In contrast, we take variables such as education and SES very seriously in this review. Even more important, the developmental research we review relies heavily on the naturalistic observation, ethnography, and culturally adapted techniques that are the heart of cultural psychology and psychological anthropology (Greenfield 1997); it relies not at all on standardized questionnaires administered to various national groups.

Another criticism of the framework involves the notion that independent and interdependent concerns coexist in the same culture (Killen & Wainryb 2000). In response, we note that individual enterprise (independence) and social relationships (interdependence) each have distinctive modes of expression in the two cultural frameworks. For example, freely chosen relationships are valued in the independent framework, while implicit social obligations are a more valued relationship premise in the interdependent framework.

As a closely related response to this criticism, a given behavior may be valued in both types of culture, but its relative priority may be different. For example, sharing with siblings is valued by parents in mainstream U.S. culture, but sharing is considered a matter of personal choice. Among Mexican immigrants to Los Angeles, by contrast, sharing has a much higher priority; it is simply expected (Raeff et al. 2000). Prioritizing one value over another may involve setting boundary conditions for the exercise of the preferred value (Wainryb 1995).

Boundary conditions may also reflect intergroup contact and cultural change processes. For example, the collectivistic Druze community studied by Wainryb (1995) is surrounded by the greater individualism of mainstream Israeli culture. Under these circumstances, the development in Druze children of boundaries on the rightful exercise of authority and the obligation to obey may, among other things, reflect contact with the surrounding national culture. Indeed, the existence of two different systems in bicultural individuals is not evidence against the systems. That they exist as parallel systems, not a random mix of individual traits or proclivities, is demonstrated by the fact that each system can be independently elicited by a culturally relevant prime (Hong et al. 2000; cf. also Kühnen & Oyserman 2002, Kühnen et al. 2001).

The existence of individual differences in the same culture is also seen as a criticism of the independence-interdependence framework. For example, Wainryb and Turiel (1994) found more orientation toward autonomy among males than females in collectivistic Druze culture. However, this criticism treats cultural characteristics as independent (sic!) traits and fails to take into account the systemic nature of cultures. In response to their example, we would see female respect for male authority, a relational feature of collectivistic cultures, as the root of such differential autonomy. Sometimes the between-culture variability among collectivistic cultures or among individualistic cultures is taken as a criticism of the paradigm (Harkness et al. 2000). Qualitative and quantitative variability has been found in both systems (Harkness et al. 2000, Hofstede 1991). The two value systems are merely ideal paradigms that get instantiated in a multiplicity of concrete and historically differentiated cultural contexts.

CULTURAL PATHWAYS THROUGH UNIVERSAL DEVELOPMENTAL TASKS

The conception of developmental pathways implies a coherent and meaningful organization of the developmental tasks over the life span. In principle, the solutions of earlier tasks along the pathway form foundations for later steps along the same pathway. Individual and cross-cultural differences exist in the way each major type of pathway is negotiated. (Note, however, the greater emphasis on individual differences and individuation in the individualistic pathway.) We see each pathway as a kind of developmental canalization of deep cultural meaning. Specific cultural practices then become instantiations of this meaning. Different cultural practices can be used to instantiate the same cultural pathway both across and within cultures (Greenfield 2000b).

We present each developmental issue—relationship formation, knowledge acquisition, and autonomy/relatedness—in the order in which the underlying capacity first matures and becomes a major developmental task. We illustrate cultural continuity across the life span, showing how the results of the earlier tasks prepare, in theory, the way in which later tasks are approached and eventually resolved (Keller 1997). Our plan is to show that each universal developmental issue is subject to a parallel and linked process of cultural differentiation.

Developmental psychology has traditionally assumed the individualistic pathway; recent theory and research in cultural, cross-cultural, and indigenous psychology identifies a set of alternative assumptions (Nsamenang 1999, Nsamenang & Lamb 1994, Saraswathi & Ganapathy 2002). A recent study by D'Andrade indicates that cross-cultural value differences do indeed organize themselves statistically around the single factor of individualism and collectivism (D'Andrade 2002). However, a simple underlying concept does not equate to reductionism, as the discussion of the role of social construction above indicates.

In the remainder of our review, we organize the existing body of knowledge for each of the three developmental domains—relationship formation, knowledge acquisition, and autonomy/relatedness—around these two pathways. For each developmental topic, we try to link variability in environmental conditions over space and time (ecocultural approach), developmental goals (values approach), and socialization practices or interactions (sociohistorical approach), to variability in human development. In the current world of social change and cross-cultural contact, there is often the meeting and even collision of individualistic and collectivistic ideals, as well as endogenous change in response to changing environments. Therefore, examples of colliding and changing pathways also figure into our review.

Close Social Relations from Infancy Through Adulthood

There is agreement across different theoretical approaches that the formation of relationships is the first integrative developmental task that infants and their caregivers have to master (Keller 2002). Because of infants' extreme helplessness (altriciality), they rely on a caregiving environment. In addition to food, shelter, and hygiene, social experiences are crucial for development. In this way, early relationships not only secure survival; they also initiate the infant into the cultural surround and have consequences for mastering the developmental tasks to come.

The core theoretical approach to relationship formation is attachment theory (Bowlby 1969, Ainsworth et al. 1978). Attachment theory stresses the evolutionary basis of attachment relationships as a phylogenetically evolved adaptive system with a core of standard assumptions that are supposed to constitute universals of ontogenetic development. Basically, it assumes that maternal sensitivity, defined as the prompt, adequate and consistent reaction towards infants' cues, is causally linked to attachment security and that this constitutes the normative and healthy developmental pattern across cultures (Grossmann et al. 2002). It further assumes that attachment security is linked to later developmental outcomes in the sense that securely attached children demonstrate more favorable outcomes in a life span perspective than insecurely attached infants (Sroufe et al. 1999). The third core assumption stresses the interrelatedness of the attachment system with the equally evolved exploration system, in that the mother serves as a secure base for infant exploration (Waters et al. 1995).

A closer inspection of these core assumptions, however, indicates that they all assume an independent cultural orientation (Rothbaum et al. 2000). For example, attachment security, as assessed in the strange situation procedure (Ainsworth et al. 1978), evaluates the infant's behavior after separations from the mother in a laboratory environment. Attachment is measured by how well the baby adjusts to separation—his or her ability to enthusiastically reconnect with the mother after she has temporarily abandoned her child to a strange room and/or to an unfamiliar person, as well as the quick return to exploratory play.

However, mothers in different cultures do not treat the baby's desire for proximity in the same way, nor do they take separations as routine (Harwood et al. 1996). Moreover, "strangers" in the United States are less strange and more familiar to babies than they would be in Highland Guatemala, Japan, or other parts of the world (Morelli et al. 1992; Takahashi 1990). Thus, the protocol of the strange situation cannot adequately measure the attachment bond in cultures where the attachment motive is fulfilled by ongoing closeness with no tolerance for separation (Takahashi 1990)[2].

---

[2]Ironically, the "strange situation" was originally developed to measure the culture-specific forms of attachment Ainsworth noticed in the United States, following her 1967 study in Uganda; since, however, it has been carried around the world (LeVine & Miller 1990).

These differences in treatment are far from random. Instead, different practices are based on different developmental goals and different priorities for the development of their children (Greenfield & Suzuki 1998). In cultural communities that value interdependence, the early relational matrix is founded in the ethnotheory of a continuously close mother-child relationship entailing close body contact during day (carrying) and night. One Cameroonian Nso mother said in an ethnographic interview that a baby needs to be bonded to the mother's body (Keller et al. 2002a). Infants in large parts of Africa, Asia, and South America sleep with their mothers, because separation of the infant from the mother is beyond imagination (Morelli et al. 1992, Shweder et al. 1998, Yovsi 2001). Close body contact conveys interactional warmth; such warmth is considered a psychological precursor of interrelatedness and acceptance of norms and values of the parent generation (MacDonald 1992, Radke-Yarrow et al. 1983). An immediate or even anticipatory reaction to infants' distress signals minimizes the self-other distinction, e.g., in Japan (Rothbaum et al. 2000), Cameroon (Yovsi & Keller 2000), India (Saraswathi & Pai 1997), and Mexico (Brazelton et al. 1969).

In cultural communities that value independence, the early relational matrix is founded on an ethnotheory of infants' early independent functioning. The ability of infants to sleep through the night, in a different place or even a different room from the parents, is held in high regard in Germany (Keller et al. 2002a) and the United States (Morelli et al. 1992). An early orientation to the nonsocial world of things and objects further stresses independence from social relationships, e.g., in Germany (Keller et al. 2002b) and in France (Rabain-Jamain & Sabeau-Jouannet 1997). Others' contingent responses to babies' autonomous signals support the development of their independent agency (Keller 2002).

What are the implications of such differences for the development of attachment and what are the developmental consequences for life span development? Differences in socialization styles and practices between Japan and the United States yield one pathway (United States) toward intergenerational tension with emphasis on child and adolescent autonomy (see section on Autonomy and Relatedness, below). Intergenerational tension is resolved by privileging romantic or marital bonds at the expense of intergenerational filial ones (Lebra 1994).

The other pathway (Japan) moves toward close intergenerational harmony across the life span (Lebra 1994, Rothbaum et al. 2000). This pattern is found in other cultural communities, such as Puerto Rico and Mexico. These communities value interdependence more than independence (Harwood et al. 1996, Greenfield & Suzuki 1998, Keller & Greenfield 2000), obedience more than personal choice (Saraswathi 1999), and harmony more than exploration (Rothbaum et al. 2000). The adult cultural ideal of assertiveness and autonomy, highly esteemed in the United States, would be evaluated as immaturity and lack of cultivation in East Asia (Fiske et al. 1998). [We must note, however, that Japan and many other countries have undergone and are undergoing economic development that moves child rearing in an individualistic direction. The results of this change in child rearing can be seen in the babies of working Japanese mothers, whose behaviors are similar to those of the United States (Greenfield & Suzuki 1998).]

In the interdependent model, the child's dependence on the parents comes to be reversed at adulthood when parents become dependent on adult children. That this reversal occurs has been established through the cross-cultural Value of Children Study in countries such as Indonesia, Philippines, Thailand, Taiwan, and Turkey (Kagitçibasi 1996). In individualistic countries such as Germany and the United States, this pattern did not hold. For example, in the United States, some European American parents retain a strong desire to remain independent as they get older; they want their children to spend time with them by choice, not obligation (Suzuki 2000).

Each model is a whole of interrelated parts. A change in one part alone can be dysfunctional. For example, cosleeping is associated with more sleeping problems in the United States, but not in Japan, where it is normative and part of the interdependence cultural complex (Latz et al. 1999). Given the correlational nature of the Latz et al. study, however, the relationship is most likely bidirectional. That is, in some cases in the United States, cosleeping may be a reaction to sleep problems, rather than a cause of them. In any case, sleep problems are less often reported as clinical concerns in Japan than in the United States (Nugent 1994).

CROSS-CULTURAL CONTACT AND CONFLICT   An understanding of the two models of development is particularly important because an independence orientation and an interdependence orientation are on a collision course in multicultural societies. Many immigrants come to individualistic societies from societies that prioritize interdependence over independence (Greenfield & Cocking 1994). This situation can lead to professional recommendations for care, e.g., separate sleeping arrangements, that assume an independence orientation, but conflict with the interdependent orientation of immigrant parents. Observations reveal the same underlying conflict between independence-oriented institutional arrangements and intergenerational interdependence at other parts of the life cycle. For example, some Asian-American adults feel that they ought to take care of their elderly parents, but fear that their parents will end up in a nursing home, an institutional manifestation of independence between the generations.

SUMMARY   In order to better understand the cultural pathways of development, one must study broader cultural values and their instantiation in ethnotheories of development shared by members of different cultural communities. These ethnotheories in turn frame the parenting behaviors that modulate behavioral and ideational development toward the demands of the ecocultural context. We next sample research that indicates how the same cultural pathways apply to the development of knowledge.

Intelligence, Knowledge, and Apprenticeship

THEORIES AND ETHNOTHEORIES OF INTELLIGENCE AND KNOWLEDGE   Clearly, human intelligence and the brain structure that supports it are keys to our adaptation as a species. In developmental psychology, the classical theory of intelligence is that of Piaget. Understanding the basis for Western scientific thought was Piaget's most fundamental theoretical concern (Piaget 1963/1977). Under Inhelder's leadership, Piaget investigated the development of scientific thought (chemistry and physics) in a set of experimental studies (Inhelder & Piaget 1958). This body of theory and research implies the importance of scientific intelligence as a developmental goal. This goal predominates in the same countries that favor the more independent mode of social relations. Conceptually, the goal of scientific intelligence belongs to the individualistic pathway because it emphasizes the person in relation to the world of objects. This goal for the development of intelligence can be seen as compatible with infant caregiving practices that emphasize leaving the infant alone to manipulate technologically appealing toys.

In sharp contrast, social intelligence has been found to be the predominant ideal in Africa and Asia (e.g., Wober 1974, Super 1983, Dasen 1984, Gill & Keats 1980, Serpell 1993, Nsamenang & Lamb 1994, Grigorenko et al. 2001). For example, in Ivory Coast the central feature of the Baoulé concept of intelligence is willingness to help others (Dasen 1984). Competing theories of intelligence may be operative at home and at school, the latter being of European origin (Dasen 1984). Whereas the most comprehensive theory of development in Europe is Piaget's theory of cognitive development, the most comprehensive theory of development in Africa is that of Nsamenang, who outlines stages of development in terms of social roles (Nsamenang 1992). In general, African cultures not only emphasize social intelligence, but also see the role of technical skills as a means to social ends (Dasen 1984). Such conceptions can be seen as collectivistic conceptions of intelligence (Segall et al. 1999). They are, moreover, compatible with infant caregiving practices that emphasize close bodily contact between infant and caregiver, rather than separation and independent manipulation of toys.

Closely related to the individualistic and collectivistic conceptions of intelligence are two different conceptions of knowledge. In a Mayan community in Chiapas, Mexico, the Tzotzil word *na*, meaning "to know," has a more person-centered meaning, compared with the English word *know* (Zambrano 1999). Whereas "to know" in English always involves the mind, *na* often involves the heart and soul. [According to Li (2002), a similar concept of "heart and mind for wanting to learn" is found in China.] Whereas *knowing* connotes factual knowledge, theoretical understanding, or know-how, *na* also connotes knowledge of practice that is habitual and characteristic of a given person; it is very much akin to character (Zambrano 1999). The former type of knowledge is more important in a culture valuing the individual's possession of technical expertise. The latter is more important in a culture placing a greater value on social character.

A similar contrast has been found between Native American and European American conceptions of giftedness (Romero 1994). This research shows that, whereas the dominant U.S. society focuses on identifying and meeting the needs of the "cream of the crop," an individualistic valuing of children who stand out from the group, Keres-speaking Pueblo Indians focus on community and inclusion. In this conception, the special qualities of a "gifted" child are supposed to contribute to the well-being and cohesiveness of the community.

MODES OF APPRENTICESHIP   These two ethnotheories of giftedness are supported by two different sets of apprenticeship practices. By apprenticeship, we simply mean informal teaching and learning, a type of knowledge transmission that has evolved from primitive roots in nonhuman primates (Greenfield et al. 2000a, Boesch 1991, Whiten 1999).

Corresponding to their concept of giftedness, apprenticeship processes that are valued by the Keres include cooperation, mentorship, and intergenerational modeling. "Keen observation, attentiveness, and focused listening are important methods of learning" (Romero 1994, p. 53), while methods valued in the individualistic framework—questioning, skepticism, and curiosity—are not promoted.

Empirical studies of apprenticeship also document two basic models of apprenticeship, one more independent and one more interdependent. The interdependent model is found in traditional weaving apprenticeship in one Mayan community and in modes of guiding children in an experimental puzzle task in another Mayan community (Greenfield 2000a, Chavajay & Rogoff 2002). These modes seem adapted to subsistence economies in which learning takes place in family settings. Indeed, both studies find changes in the model with changes in the ecocultural environment.

Weaving apprenticeship moves toward a more independent mode of learning as subsistence is replaced by commerce (Greenfield 2000a). With formal education, the way in which mothers guide puzzle construction moves from shared multiparty engagement (the whole group focusing on a single aspect of the puzzle) toward division of labor where individuals or dyads work separately on different task components (Chavajay & Rogoff 2002). Both commerce and formal schooling are associated with a more individualistic mode of apprenticeship (Greenfield 2000a, Tapia Uribe et al. 1994).

CROSS-CULTURAL CONTACT AND CONFLICT AT SCHOOL   As in close social relations, research shows the two types of knowledge and intelligence to be on a collision course in a multicultural society. In U.S. schools, teachers focus on independent academic achievement, whereas Latino parents, for example, are often more concerned about social behavior (Greenfield et al. 2000b, Okagaki & Sternberg 1993). These goals are crystallized in a different concept of education, *educación* (Reese et al. 1995). This Spanish word is not an accurate translation of the English word education. Unlike "education," *educación* refers to the inculcation of proper and respectful social behavior; like the Tzotzil *na*, *educación* refers to character. The connotation is that academic learning does not suffice to make a person educated. Similar conflicts occur for families immigrating to the United States from Cambodia, Phillipines, and Vietnam (Okagaki & Sternberg 1993). As another example, two Native American concepts—that one learns by observing rather than by participating and that one learns for the benefit of the group rather than for the self (as discussed above) also lead to mismatches between Native American children and the schools (Suina & Smolkin 1994).

THE DEVELOPMENT OF PERSON KNOWLEDGE: INTENTION, ACTION, AND SOCIAL EF-
FECT   An understanding of self and others is part of our universal evolutionary heritage (Tomasello 1999, Whiten 2002). The mirror neuron system of the
cerebral cortex reveals a common neuromuscular activation for acting oneself and
for understanding the actions of others (Fadiga et al. 1995, Iacoboni et al. 1999).
Because monkeys have a very similar neural system (di Pellegrino et al. 1992,
Rizzolatti et al. 1996), this system for identifying self with others (Favareau 2001)
is likely an ancient component of the human primate heritage.

In ontogeny, the first step in understanding self and others occurs at birth, when
infants discriminate people from things (Trevarthen 1980). Comprehension of
agency as the production of goal-directed action begins in early infancy (Gelman
& Lucariello 2002). An ability to distinguish between self and other as intentional
agents develops at eight or nine months of age (Piaget 1952, Tomasello 1999,
Trevarthen 1980).

At the one-word stage of language development (between one and two years
of age) infants code the intentional action not just of self but of others (Greenfield
& Smith 1976, Greenfield 1980), and this encoding seems to have ancient phylo-
genetic roots (Greenfield & Savage-Rumbaugh 1990). The linguistic encoding of
intentional action becomes more complex with age and the acquisition of language
(Bloom et al. 1975). At the same time, there is very early understanding of the effects of action on other people. Script knowledge, which begins in the second year
of life, involves the understanding of both intentions and effects of human action
(Gelman & Lucariello 2002). It also requires an understanding of the coordination
of action by more than one person.

These two universal capacities—the capacity to encode the intentions of self
and others and the capacity to encode the social effects of one's own and others'
action—provide the groundwork for two distinct cultural emphases in the development of person knowledge. Some cultures emphasize the individual psyche,
individual traits, and the individual intentions behind action (Vinden & Astington
2000); other cultures emphasize the social effects and social context of a person's
action (Duranti 1988, 1993; Shweder & Bourne 1984; Fiske et al. 1998). The
latter also see mind and heart as integrated rather than separate (Lillard 1998,
Zambrano 1999). We see the former as the individualistic emphasis, the latter as
the collectivistic or sociocentric emphasis.

Most literature on theory of mind—the ability to think about other people's
mental states—assumed an emphasis on individual minds (Flavell 1999). We, however, see theory of mind as a special culturally canalized case of person knowledge
(cf. Hobson 1993). We now review the literature indicating the existence of these
two different cultural emphases—individual psyche versus social effects or context—in the development of social understanding or person knowledge. Ideally,
cross-cultural comparison would involve a developmental analysis of tasks tapping
into both of these cultural emphases within the context of universal developments.
A study of social explanation in India and the United States (Miller 1984) did
exactly that: Children in both the United States and India got better at social explanation with age (the universal development). At the same time, children in the

United States increasingly formulated their social explanations of events in terms of an individual's stable traits (emphasis on the individual psyche). Indian children, in contrast, increasingly formulated their social explanations in terms of contextual factors, particularly factors in the social surround (emphasis on social context).

Although it claims universality, we utilize the classical literature on theory of mind to complete the picture of the individualistic pathway to person knowledge. Early steps along this pathway have to do with the acquisition of mentalistic terms; children as young as 22 months first produce mentalistic terms such as know and pretend (Wellman 1990). Later, the child is able to imagine a mental state of affairs in another person different from the information available to oneself (e.g., Perner 1991). Similar trends occur in literate, developed countries, both Western and non-Western (Wellman et al. 2001). The differentiation and individuation of people according to their states of mind is basic to this developmental pathway to social understanding.

However, in the other pathway, mentalistic terms are lacking in the lexicon, are not understood in the same way as the English equivalents, and are not applied to oneself. This phenomenon has been found in a number of subsistence ecologies (Greenfield & Bruner 1966; Vinden 1996, 1999). However, both schooling, with its demand for justifications, and literacy, with its separation of thought (on paper) from thinker, leads to an understanding of the mentalistic term *think* (Greenfield & Bruner 1966). [See Lillard (1998) for a cross-cultural review of the theory-of mind-literature.]

In a nonliterate subsistence ecology in Africa, children between two and four were given a theory-of-mind task that was embedded into a context of social action. In addition, the task utilized the term *heart* rather than *thought* (Avis & Harris 1991). Under these circumstances, Baka children in southeast Cameroon showed the development of social understanding that had been found in the United States and Europe. The results contrasted strongly with another study that (*a*) decontextualized the task, presenting it as a task involving only one actual person, the subject; (*b*) asked about the deceived's thought rather than action in reference to a hidden object; and (*c*) asked about mind rather than heart. Under these conditions, Quechua children between about four and eight performed at chance levels (Vinden 1996). Somewhat more contextualized tasks led to somewhat improved performance in subsistence groups in Cameroon, West Africa (the Mofu), and Papua New Guinea (the Tainae and Tolai) (Vinden 1999). Meta-analysis indicates that, around the world, children from subsistence cultures solve theory-of mind-tasks better when these are presented in context (Wellman et al. 2001). However, Vinden (1999) found a lag in age in all groups relative to children of European-derived cultures; false belief (the understanding that another person has been misled into believing that something is true that is in fact false), assessed using the word "think," was at chance levels at all ages in the two groups most isolated from the outside world of European culture.

Here we interpret a lag as indicating that the skill in question is not valued in a particular culture (LeVine 1997). "With a collectivist or group orientation, personal, mental, and emotional states are relatively unimportant" (Vinden &

Astington 2000, p. 512). In line with the notion that school ecology favors the development of attention to the individual psyche, schooled children performed better on several of the tasks relating to predicting an individual's behavior or emotion in a nonsocial situation (Vinden 1999).

On the other hand, in a culturally important social situation, young children from small, face-to-face societies with subsistence traditions show advanced understanding of the knowledge state and feelings of another person, whose knowledge differs from one's own. In a successful apprenticeship situation, the expert must be aware of how much less the novice knows, in comparison with self. The expert must also be aware of the novice's need for materials and what the novice's motivations are. In a video study of naturalistic interactions, Zinacantec Mayan children ages 3 to 11 taught their 2-year-old siblings everyday tasks in the course of their caregiving interactions (Maynard 2002). Children as young as 4 years old were able to get the necessary materials for tasks and model the tasks for their younger siblings. They were also able to provide useful verbal guidance in teaching, such as narrating a task they were demonstrating and giving commands to the younger child. By the age of 8, children were very adept at simplifying the task for the younger children by giving them parts of tasks, one at a time, and at scaffolding the task by providing complex verbal information. These advanced skills showed an understanding of the knowledge state, material needs, and motivation of the younger children. The social context of sibling caregiving may have played a role in the young children's desire and skill in teaching their younger siblings.

Similar sibling teaching practices were found in another sibling-caregiving culture: the Wolof of Senegal (Rabain-Jamin et al.). Wolof sibling caregivers engage younger siblings in play by guiding them in tasks and by encouraging and reinforcing verbal assertions. Future research is needed to explore the relationship between being a sibling caregiver and the cognitive operations of person knowledge, as assessed in experimental tasks.

In summary, cross-cultural differences in performance on theory-of-mind tasks have been found. The notion of a more contextualized sociocentric pathway, in contrast with a more decontextualized egocentric pathway, each one adapted to different ecological conditions, provides a good fit to the data. In conditions of rapid social change toward Western schooling and commerce, as in Korea and Japan, a more individual-centered person conception seems to develop (Wellman et al. 2001), despite the more sociocentric models of early development described earlier. However, contradiction in Korea and Japan between sociocentric models of early development and socialization (Kim & Choi 1994, Rothbaum et al. 2000) and the development of an individuated notion of false belief (the topic of the Wellman et al. 2001 meta-analysis) could also be considered a challenge to the definition of two coherent pathways of development. Future research in Korea and Japan comparing the development of false belief in rural and urban ecologies and among populations with varying amounts of formal schooling could help address this issue. If the conception of coherent developmental pathways adapted to ecological niches is correct, rural and less-schooled populations should lag in the more individual-centered notions of person such as those that come into play on false belief tasks.

Indeed, it may be culturally significant that person knowledge has been measured so frequently by false belief, the dominant theory-of-mind task. In a false-belief task, the participant must understand that another person has a different perspective (the false belief) from his or her own. It is a task that requires individuation of one's perspective from that of another. Individuation is an important component of the development of the independent self (see section on Autonomy and Relatedness, below). It may be that socialization in interdependent cultures emphasizes *shared* perspectives more than *different* perspectives. Only future research can tell us whether this may be another reason for relatively poor performance on false belief tasks in collectivistic, subsistence cultures.

KNOWLEDGE OF THE PHYSICAL WORLD: THE REPRESENTATION OF SPACE   Lack of space precludes detailed treatment of this domain. We include it in brief in order to show that the concept of two canalized pathways through universal development applies not just to knowledge of the social world, but also to knowledge of the physical world. It is clear that spatial representation develops in participation in cultural activities (Gauvain 1992) and that language-specific patterns of spatial representation affect the ways that children learn to express motion events (Choi & Bowerman 1991).

A universal of spatial representation is that two major kinds of reference systems develop across societies. The egocentric (viewer-centered) system features relative terms such as left and right; the geocentric system features so-called absolute terms such as north and south. From the two-pathways perspective, the interesting point is that geocentric systems utilize reference points shared by the group. In a face-to-face group, north, for example, is in the same direction for everyone. It turns out that more individualistic cultures of European derivation feature egocentric spatial systems, whereas more collectivistic cultures, such as the Maya discussed earlier, feature absolute systems (Levinson 1998, Haviland 1998). In Bali, where geocentric terminology is more important than egocentric terminology for describing space, children as young as 4 or 5 utilize geocentric terminology (Wassman & Dasen 1998). A similar pattern of results was found in rural Polynesia (Troadac & Martinot ND) and in rural India and Nepal (Dasen et al. 2000). In rural Nepal and India, as well as in urban India and Tahiti, the frequency of geocentric encoding increased with age, in line with socialization into the indigenous geocentric system of reference.

Finally, in urban ecologies, the rural traditions of collectivism meet the individualistic ways of the city. Thus, in urban Tahiti and in urban India, both egocentric and geocentric or absolute systems were used by children to solve spatial problems (Dasen et al. 2000, Troadac & Martinot ND). However, in Bali, France, Tahiti, Nepal, and India, it was also clear that the less dominant system could be called into play when task conditions favored it.

SUMMARY   Both the development of person knowledge and the development of spatial knowledge seem to be guided by the same canalized pathways that guide the development of social relations. Within the individualistic pathway, cultures emphasize understanding the individual intentions and traits behind action and the individual psyche more generally (Vinden & Astington 2000). Within the interdependent pathway, cultures give stronger emphasis to the social effects and social context of a person's action (Duranti 1988, 1993; Shweder & Bourne 1984; Fiske et al. 1998). A parallel differentiation takes place within the arena of space. Geocentric spatial systems utilize reference points shared by a face-to-face group (for example, north and south), and these are acquired early by children in collectivistic cultures. In contrast, egocentric (viewer-centered) spatial systems feature relative reference points (left and right) that can vary from person to person (for example, when two people are facing each other), and these spatial systems are acquired early by children in more individualistic urban environments.

Autonomy and Relatedness

Cognitive, physical, and social changes take place as children around the world enter adolescence. These changes create a member of society who is no longer wholly dependent upon other family members for care and survival, and who is becoming able to take on adult-like roles and contribute to the well-being and survival of others. Most families, therefore, inevitably face the question of how to accommodate their increasingly competent and mature children during the years of adolescence. For much of the twentieth century, the position of mainstream psychology in North America and Europe was that adolescence was a period at which children must begin the process of separation from parents. Views of family relationships and autonomy during adolescence were dominated by the psychoanalytic emphasis upon a necessary estrangement between children and parents to avoid the inappropriate application of children's reawakened genital urges to their parents: ". . . nothing helps here except a complete discarding of the love objects of the child, that is, the parents" (Freud 1969).

Empirical research on representative, nonclinical samples of adolescents decisively proved such a belief to be incorrect. Even in independence-oriented societies such as the United States, complete autonomy from parents is antithetical to healthy adolescent development. Rather, a complicated balance between what has been called "autonomy and relatedness" or "individuation and connectedness" appears to be most salutory for adolescent adjustment, in that it provides children the opportunity to develop the ability to think and act independently within the context of supportive relationships with parents (e.g., Grotevant & Cooper 1986). A great deal of research in the past 25 years has been devoted to examining the intricate dance of North American family members as they attempt to develop a healthy sense of independence among adolescents while still retaining supportive relationships with parents.

Yet even though most families in most societies likely undergo a process that includes elements of both autonomy and relatedness, there appear to be variations in the extent to which each dimension is emphasized, expected, and granted during adolescence across different societies, different ethnic groups with the same society, and different socioeconomic conditions, as well as under conditions of social change. In this section, we review studies that document such variations in autonomy and relatedness during adolescence in terms of two general categories: (*a*) behavioral autonomy and parental control, and (*b*) familial duty and obligation.

BEHAVIORAL AUTONOMY AND PARENTAL CONTROL   One frequently studied aspect of autonomy during adolescence has been the ages at which children are allowed to engage in various autonomous behaviors, and research has generally suggested that adolescents from European and Western backgrounds obtain behavioral autonomy at an earlier age than their Asian counterparts. For example, Feldman & Rosenthal (1991) examined ages at which adolescents in Hong Kong, Australia, and the United States expected to be able to go out at night, choose their own clothes, and stay home alone. Overall, the Chinese adolescents had later expectations for autonomy than did their peers in the more Westernized nations. Interestingly, the largest and most consistent differences appeared for behaviors and activities that involved socializing with peers and dating: going to boy-girl parties at night, going out on dates, doing things with friends rather than with family, and going on an overnight trip with friends. There were no differences between youths in Australia and the United States in their autonomy expectations for these activities. Even when they live in a Western society such as the United States, Chinese adolescents still have later expectations for autonomy than do their peers from European backgrounds (Feldman & Quatman 1988, Fuligni 1998).

A great deal of research has examined the extent to which parents from different cultural backgrounds employ control in their parenting during adolescence, although most of the work has been done among various ethnic groups within the United States. Studies have consistently found that European American parents are more likely than other parents to engage in what has been called authoritative parenting, which emphasizes the development of autonomy and self-direction within the context of a warm, supportive relationship (e.g., Steinberg et al. 1991, Dornbusch et al. 1985). Asian American, Latino, and African American parents are more likely than European American parents to employ authoritarian parenting, which focuses on obedience and conformity among children. One reason for the greater emphasis on parental control may be differing cultural values about obedience and the role of parents. For example, Chao (1994) has suggested that the greater frequency of authoritarian parenting among Asian American parents is rooted in a cultural emphasis upon child "training" which focuses on hard work and discipline, rather than intimacy between parents and children.

Greater parental control is also evident among parents with fewer socioeconomic resources, and among families who live in more dangerous and threatening neighborhoods. Steinberg et al. (1991) observed that nonauthoritative parenting was more common among working-class families than among middle-class families, and similar patterns have been noted in other studies (e.g., Dornbusch et al. 1985). One source of the socioeconomic variations may be a greater emphasis upon obedience and conformity among parents from lower socioeconomic backgrounds. An additional source may be the fact that these families are more likely to reside in dangerous neighborhoods, and the greater emphasis upon control reflects a parental desire to protect their adolescents from threat. To that end, Furstenberg et al. (1999) noted how parents in urban areas with low resources tried to keep their teenagers at home and away from the perceived dangers of the neighborhood. Mason et al. (1996) observed that higher levels of parental control were most beneficial for children whose peers engaged in more problem behavior, testifying to the adaptiveness of parental control of their families' immediate environment.

FAMILIAL DUTY AND OBLIGATION   The extent to which families and children emphasize adolescents' responsibility to support, assist, and respect the family has been overlooked in mainstream psychological research. Yet the type of instrumental connection to the family that is implied by family obligation is one that appears to vary across societies, ethnic groups, and even historical periods within the same society. Internationally, the role of children in the maintenance of the household has traditionally been emphasized in Asian, African, and Latin American societies. For example, many Asian cultural traditions, such as Confucianism, have valued family solidarity, respect, and commitment (Ho 1981, Shon & Ja 1982, Uba 1994). Familial loyalty, devotion, and support has also been a socialization goal within many Latin American cultures (Chilman 1993).

Recent studies of immigrant families within the United States have suggested that many Asian and Latin American families continue to emphasize the familial duty and obligation of their adolescents in a new society. Several ethnographies have indicated how such family obligation may even be heightened among immigrants, given parents' limited knowledge of American society and because many adolescents feel indebted to their parents for immigrating to a new society to provide their children with a better life (Gibson & Bhachu 1991, Suárez-Orozco & Suárez-Orozco 1995, Zhou & Bankston 1998).

The emphasis upon familial duty appears to be readily shared by adolescents from Asian and Latin American immigrant families. As one Vietnamese teenager stated to Zhou & Bankston (1998), "To be an American, you may be able to do whatever you want. But to be a Vietnamese, you must think of your family first" (p. 166). Other studies have shown that adolescents from these families emphasize their family obligations more than their peers. For example, Fuligni et al. (1999) found that Asian American and Latino adolescents were more likely than adolescents with European backgrounds to believe that they should help their parents and siblings, both currently and as adults, and were more likely to endorse the importance of making sacrifices for the family. Although immigrants were likely to emphasize some aspects of family obligation more than their peers from American-born families, even adolescents from American-born families with Asian and Latin American roots place more importance upon their family obligation than their European American peers. This pattern suggests that, while some aspects of family obligation may change with time in a new society, Asian American and Latino families continue to emphasize the importance of this instrumental connection to the family across several generations.

A strong emphasis on familial duty during adolescence has also been observed among European immigrants, such as contemporary immigrants from Armenia and early twentieth century Italian immigrants (Lassonde 1991, Phinney et al. 2000). In addition, the role of adolescents in supporting and assisting the family has been heightened in American society during periods of great economic upheaval, such as during the Great Depression and the farm crisis in the Midwest during the end of the twentieth century (Elder 1974, Elder & Conger 2000). Together these findings highlight that while familial duty and obligation certainly have some important cultural roots, this type of connection to the family also can be heightened under conditions of dramatic social and economic change.

SUMMARY   At adolescence, the development of autonomy and relatedness is universal; yet different cultures put differential emphasis on these two components of the human experience. More specifically, behavioral autonomy is highly valued for and by adolescents developing along an independent pathway. In contrast, parental control and familial obligation are relatively more valued for and by adolescents developing along an interdependent pathway. Autonomy and relatedness vary not only across cultures, but across ethnic groups in the same society. Both cultural roots and adaptation to the current ecology play a role in this variability.

CONCLUSIONS AND FUTURE DIRECTIONS

This review has posited the cultural differentiation of two paths of development; one path leads to the independent self, the other to the interdependent self (Markus & Kitayama 1991). Each pathway leads through universal, age-related issues in development: Close relationships, knowledge and intelligence, and autonomy/relatedness were the theoretically central examples that were reviewed. The nature of the issues and their developmental sequencing provide the universals of development.

At the same time, the cultural structuring of each issue leads to contrasting deep-structure outcomes for each domain, one outcome emphasizing independence and individuation, the other outcome emphasizing interdependence and sociocentrism. In this review, we have linked empirical studies on child outcomes to parental values and practices of socialization and apprenticeship. These are the interlinked components of the two cultural pathways through universal development.

This theory of the cultural differentiation of two major developmental paradigms leads, paradoxically, to unifying different developmental domains under one theoretical umbrella. Classical treatments of early relationships, intelligence and knowledge, and autonomy/relatedness are all linked as steps in the developmental path toward independence and individuation. Newer cultural research on these topics is beginning to illuminate parallel steps in the developmental path toward interdependence. Future research must establish outcomes in these different arenas as connected steps on a given cultural path. This will require longitudinal research, as well as cultural research in different regions of the world. Future research will continue to examine the complex processes of development in situations of multi-cultural contact and culture change, both of which are the norm in our postmodern world. All of these lines of research will contribute to the further development of a unified theory of cultural pathways through universal tasks of development.

The *Annual Review of Psychology* is online at http://psych.annualreviews.org

LITERATURE CITED

Ainsworth MDS. 1967. *Infancy in Uganda: Infant Care and the Growth of Love.* Baltimore, MD: Johns Hopkins Press

Ainsworth MDS, Blehar MC, Waters E, Wall S. 1978. *Patterns of Attachment: A Psychological Study of the Strange Situation.* Potomac, MD: Erlbaum

Avis J, Harris PL. 1991. Belief-desire reasoning among Baka children: evidence for a universal conception of mind. *Child Dev.* 62:460–67

Berman J, ed. 1990. *Cross-Cultural Perspectives: The Nebraska Symposium on Motivation, 1989.* Lincoln: Univ. of Nebraska Press

Berry JW. 1976. *Human Ecology and Cognitive Style: Comparative Studies in Cultural and Psychological Adaptation.* New York: Sage

Berry JW. 1994. Ecology of individualism and collectivism. See Kim et al. 1994, pp. 77–84

Berry JW, Poortinga YH, Pandey J, eds. 1997. *Handbook of Cross-Cultural Psychology.* Vol. 1: *Theory and Method.* Boston, MA: Allyn & Bacon

Bloom L, Lightbrown P, Hood L. 1975. Structure and variation in child language. *Monogr. Soc. Res. Child Dev.* 40:–97

Boesch C. 1991. Teaching among wild chimpanzees. *Anim. Behav.* 41(3):530–32

Bond MH, Smith PB. 1996. Cross-cultural social and organizational psychology. *Annu. Rev. Psychol.* 47:205–35

Bowlby J. 1969. *Attachment and Loss.* Vol. 1: *Attachment.* New York: Basic Books

Brazelton TB, Robey JS, Collier G. 1969. Infant development in the Zinacanteco Indians of Southern Mexico. *Pediatrics* 44:274–83

Chan DK-S. 1994. COLINDEX: A refinement of three collectivism measures. See Kim et al. 1994, pp. 200–10

Chao RK. 1994. Beyond parental control and authoritarian parenting style: Understanding Chinese parenting through the cultural notion of training. *Child Dev.* 65(4):1111–19

Chavajay P, Rogoff B. 2002. Schooling and traditional collaborative social organization of problem solving by Mayan mothers and children. *Dev. Psychol.* 38(1):55–66

Chilman CS. 1993. Hispanic families in the United States: research perspective. In *Family Ethnicity: Strength in Diversity*, ed. HP McAdoo, pp. 141–63. Newbury Park, CA: Sage

Choi S, Bowerman M. 1991. Learning to express motion events in English and Korean: the influence of language-specific lexicalization patterns. *Cognition* 41:83–121

Cole M. 1996. *Cultural Psychology: A Once and Future Discipline.* Cambridge, MA: Harvard Univ. Press

Cooper CR, Denner J. 1998. Theories linking culture and psychology: universal and community-specific processes. *Annu. Rev. Psychol.* 49:559–84

D'Andrade R. 2002. *The Three Lives of Values.* Colloq., Dep. Anthropol., Univ. Calif., Los Angeles

D'Andrade R. 1994. Introduction: John Whiting and anthropology. In *Culture and Human Development: The Selected Papers of*

John Whiting, ed. EH Chasdi, pp. 1–13. Cambridge: Cambridge Univ. Press

Dasen PR. 1984. The cross-cultural study of intelligence: Piaget and the Baoulé. *Int. J. Psychol.* 19:407–34

Dasen PR, de Ribeaupierre A. 1987. Neo-Piagetian theories: cross-cultural and differential perspectives. *Int. J. Psychol.* 22:793–832

Dasen PR, Mishra R, Niraula S. 2000. *Ecology, language, and performance on spatial cognitive tasks.* Presented at Congr. Int. Assoc. Cross-Cult. Psychol., 15th, Pulsk, Poland

di Pellegrino G, Fadiga L, Fogassi L, Gallese V, Rizzolatti G. 1992. Understanding motor events: a neurophysiological study. *Exp. Brain Res.* 91:176–80

Dornbusch S, Ritter P, Leiderman H, Roberts D, Fraleigh M. 1985. The relation of parenting style to adolescent school performance. *Child Dev.* 58 (5):1244–57

Duranti A. 1988. Intentions, language and social action in a Samoan context. *J. Pragmat.* 12:13–33

Duranti A. 1993. Intentions, self, and responsibility: an essay in Samoan ethnopragmatics. In *Responsibility and Evidence in Oral Discourse*, ed. JH Hill, JT Irvine, pp. 24–47. Cambridge: Cambridge Univ. Press

Elder GH. 1974. *Children of the Great Depression: Social Change in Life Experience.* Chicago: Univ. Chicago Press

Elder GH, Conger RD. 2000. *Children of the Land: Adversity and Success in Rural America.* Chicago: Univ. Chicago Press

Fadiga L, Fogassi L, Pavesi G, Rizzolatti G. 1995. Motor facilitation during action observation: a magnetic stimulation study. *J. Neurophysiol.* 73:2608–11

Favareau D. 2001. Beyond self and other: on the neurosemiotic emergence of intersubjectivity. *Sign Syst. Stud.* 30(1):57–100

Feldman SS, Quatman T. 1988. Factors influence age expectations for adolescent autonomy: a study of early adolescents and parents. *J. Early Adolesc.* 8(4):325–43

Feldman SS, Rosenthal DA. 1991. Age expectations of behavioural autonomy in Hong Kong, Australian and American youth: the influence of family variables and adolescents' values. *Int. J. Psychol.* 26(1):1–23

Fiske AP. 2000. Complementarity theory: why human social capacity evolved to require cultural complements. *Personal. Soc. Psychol. Rev.* 4:76–94

Fiske AP. 2002. Using individualism and collectivism to compare cultures: a critique of the validity and measurement of the constructs. *Psychol. Bull.* 128(1):78–88

Fiske AP, Kitayama S, Markus H, Nisbett D. 1998. The cultural matrix of social psychology. In *Handbook of Social Psychology*, ed. D Gilbert, S Fiske, G Lindzey, pp. 915–81. New York: McGraw-Hill. 4th ed.

Flavell J. 1999. Cognitive development: children's knowledge about the mind. *Annu. Rev. Psychol.* 50:21–45

Freud A. 1969. Adolescence as a developmental disturbance. In *Adolescence: Psychosocial Perspectives*, ed. G Caplan, S Ledovici, pp. 5–10. Cambridge, MA: Harvard Univ. Press

Fuligni AJ. 1998. Authority, autonomy, and parent-adolescent conflict and cohesion: a study of adolescents from Mexican, Chinese, Filipino, and European backgrounds. *Dev. Psychol.* 34:782–92

Fuligni AJ, Tseng V, Lam M. 1999. Attitudes toward family obligations among American adolescents with Asian, Latin American, and European backgrounds. *Child Dev.* 70:1030–44

Furstenberg F, Cook T, Eccles J, Elder GH, Sameroff AJ. 1999. *Managing to Make It: Urban Families and Adolescent Success.* Chicago: Univ. Chicago Press

Garcia-Coll CT, Meyer E, Brillon L. 1995. Ethnic and minority parenting. In *Handbook of Parenting.* Vol. 2: *Biology and Ecology of Parenting*, ed. MH Bornstein, pp. 189–209. Hillsdale, NJ: Erlbaum

Gauvain M. 1992. Sociocultural influences on the development of spatial thinking. *Child. Environ.* 9:27–36

Gelman R, Lucariello J. 2002. Role of learning in cognitive development. In *Stevens'*

Handbook of Experimental Psychology, vol. 3, *Learning, Motivation, and Emotion*. Series ed. H Pashler, volume ed. CR Gallistel, pp. 395–443. New York: Wiley. 3rd ed.

Gibson MA, Bhachu PK. 1991. The dynamics of educational decision making: A comparative study of Sikhs in Britain and the United States. In *Minority Status and Schooling: A Comparative Study of Immigrant and Involuntary Minorities*, ed. MA Gibson, JU Ogbu, pp. 63–96. New York: Garland

Gill R, Keats DM. 1980. Elements of intellectual competence: judgments by Australian and Malay university students. *J. Cross-Cult. Psychol.* 11(2):233–43

Goodnow JJ. 1988. Parents' ideas, actions, and feelings: models and methods from developmental and social psychology. *Child Dev.* 59(2):286–320

Greenfield PM. 1974. Cross-cultural research and Piagetian theory: paradox and progress. In *The Developing Individual in a Changing World*. Vol. 1: *Historical and Cultural Issues*, ed. KF Riegel, JA Meacham, pp. 322–33. The Hague: Mouton

Greenfield PM. 1980. Towards an operational and logical analysis of intentionality: the use of discourse in early child language. In *The Social Foundations of Language and Thought: Essays in Honor of J. S. Bruner*, ed. DR Olson, pp. 254–79. New York: Norton

Greenfield PM. 1997. Culture as process: empirical methods for cultural psychology. See Berry et al. 1997, pp. 301–46

Greenfield PM. 2000a. Culture and universals: integrating social and cognitive development. In *Culture, Thought, and Development*, ed. LP Nucci, GB Saxe, E Turiel, pp. 231–77. Mahwah, NJ: Erlbaum

Greenfield PM. 2000b. Three approaches to the psychology of culture: Where do they come from? Where can they go? *Asian J. Soc. Psychol.* 3:223–40

Greenfield PM. 2002. The mutual definition of culture and biology in development. See Keller 2002, pp. 57–76

Greenfield PM, Bruner JS. 1966. Culture and cognitive growth. *Int. J. Psychol.* 1:89–107

Greenfield PM, Cocking RR. 1994. *Cross-Cultural Roots of Minority Child Development*. Hillsdale, NJ: Erlbaum

Greenfield PM, Lave J. 1982. Cognitive aspects of informal education. In *Cultural Perspectives on Child Development*, ed. D Wagner, H Stevenson, pp. 181–207. San Francisco: Freeman

Greenfield PM, Maynard AE, Boehm C, Yut E. 2000a. Cultural apprenticeship and cultural change: tool learning and imitation in chimpanzees and humans. In *Biology, Brains, and Behavior*, ed. ST Parker, J Langer, ML McKinney, pp. 237–77. Santa Fe: SAR Press

Greenfield PM, Quiroz B, Raeff C. 2000b. Cross-cultural harmony and conflict in the social construction of the child. See Harkness et al. 2000, pp. 93–108

Greenfield PM, Savage-Rumbaugh ES. 1990. Grammatical combination in *Pan Paniscus*: processes of learning and invention in the evolution and development of language. In *"Language" and Intelligence in Monkeys and Apes: Comparative Developmental Perspectives*, ed. S Parker, K Gibson, pp. 540–78. Cambridge: Cambridge Univ. Press

Greenfield PM, Smith JH. 1976. *The Structure of Communication in Early Language Development*. New York: Academic

Greenfield PM, Suzuki LK. 1998. Culture and human development: implications for parenting, education, pediatrics, and mental health. In *Handbook of Social Psychology*, Vol. 4, *Child Psychology in Practice*, ed. IE Sigel, KA Renninger, pp. 1059–109. New York: Wiley

Grigorenko EL, Geissler PW, Prince R, Okatcha F, Nokes C, et al. 2001. The organisation of Luo conceptions of intelligence: a study of implicit theories in a Kenyan village. *Int. J. Behav. Dev.* 25(4):367–78

Grossmann KE, Keppler A, Grossmann K. 2002. Universalismus und Kultureller Relativismus. Eine bindungstheoretische Analyse (Universalism and cultural relativism. An attachment theoretical analysis). In *Interkulturelle Psychologie. (Intercultural*

Psychology), ed. A Thomas. Goettingen: Hogrefe. In press

Grotevant H, Cooper C. 1986. Individuation in family relationships: a perspective on individual differences in the development of identity and role-taking skill in adolescence. *Hum. Dev.* 29(2): 82–100

Gutierrez J, Sameroff AJ. 1990. Determinants of complexity in Mexican-American and Anglo-American mothers' conceptions of child development. *Child Dev.* 61(2):384–94

Harkness S, Raeff C, Super CM, eds. 2000a. *Variability in the Social Construction of the Child: New Directions in Child and Adolescent Development*, Vol. 87. San Francisco: Jossey-Bass

Harkness S, Super C. 1996. *Parents' Cultural Belief Systems. Their Origins, Expressions and Consequences*. New York: Guilford

Harkness S, Super C, van Tijen N. 2000b. Individualism and the "Western Mind" reconsidered: parents' ethnotheories of the child. See Harkness et al. 2000a, pp. 23–39

Harwood RL. 1992. The influence of culturally derived values on Anglo and Puerto Rican mothers' perceptions of attachment behavior. *Child Dev.* 63(4):822–39

Harwood RL, Schoelmerich A, Ventura-Cook E, Schulze PA, Wilson SP. 1996. Culture and class influences on Anglo and Puerto Rican mothers' beliefs regarding long-term socialization goals and child behavior. *Child Dev.* 67(5):2446–61

Hatano G. 1982. Cognitive consequences of practice in culture specific procedural skills. *Q. Newsl. Lab. Comp. Hum. Cogn.* 4:14–17

Haviland JB. 1998. Guugu Yimithirr cardinal directions. *Ethos* 26:25–47

Hewlett BS, Lamb ME. 2002. Integrating evolution, culture and developmental psychology: explaining caregiver infant proximity and responsiveness in Central Africa and the United States of America. In *Between Culture and Biology*, ed. H Keller, YH Poortinga, A Schoelmerich, pp. 241–69. Cambridge, UK: Cambridge Univ. Press

Ho DYF. 1981. Traditional patterns of socialization in Chinese society. *Acta Psychol. Taiwan* 23:81–95

Hobson RP. 1993. *Autism and the Development of Mind*. Hillsdale, NJ: Erlbaum

Hofstede G. 1991. *Cultures and Organizations: Software of the Mind*. London: McGraw-Hill

Hong Y, Morris MW, Chiu C, Benet-Martinez V. 2000. Multicultural minds: a dynamic constructivist approach to culture and cognition. *Am. Psychol.* 55(7):709–20

Iacoboni M, Woods RP, Brass M, Bekkering H, Mazziotta JC, Rizzolatti G. 1999. Cortical mechanisms of human imitation. *Science* 286:2526–28

Inhelder B, Piaget J. 1958. *The Growth of Logical Thinking from Childhood to Adolescence: An Essay on the Construction of Formal Operational Structures*. New York: Basic Books

Kagitçibasi C. 1990. Family and socialization in cross-cultural perspective: a model of change. See Berman 1990, pp. 135–200

Kagitçibasi C. 1994. A critical appraisal of individualism and collectivism: toward a new formulation. See Kim et al. 1994, pp. 52–65

Kagitçibasi C. 1996. *Family and Human Development Across Cultures: A View from the Other Side*. Hillsdale, NJ: Erlbaum

Kagitçibasi C, Berry JW. 1989. Cross-cultural psychology: current research and trends. *Annu. Rev. Psychol.* 40:493–531

Keller H. 1997. Evolutionary approaches. See Berry et al. 1997, pp. 215–55

Keller H. 2002. The role of development for understanding the biological basis of cultural learning. In *Between Culture and Biology*, ed. H Keller, YH Poortinga, A Schoelmerich, pp. 213–40. Cambridge: Cambridge Univ. Press

Keller H, Greenfield PM. 2000. The history and future of development in cross-cultural psychology. *J. Cross-Cult. Psychol.* 31(1):52–62 (Special issue)

Keller H, Miranda D, Gauda G. 1984. The naive theory of the infant and some maternal attitudes. A two-country study. *J. Cross-Cult. Psychol.* 15(2):165–79

Keller H, Poortinga YH, Schoelmerich A, eds.

2002. *Between Culture and Biology.* Cambridge: Cambridge Univ. Press

Keller H, Voelker S, Yovsi RD. 2002a. Conceptions of parenting in different cultural communities: the case of West African Nso and Northern German women. Submitted

Keller H, Zach U, Abels M. 2002b. The German family—families in Germany. In *Families Across Cultures*, ed. J Roopnarine, U Gielen. Boston, MA: Ally & Bacon

Killen M, Wainryb C. 2000. Independence and interdependence in diverse cultural contexts. See Harkness et al. 2000, pp. 5–21

Kim U, Choi S-H. 1994. Individualism, collectivism, and child development: a Korean perspective. See Greenfield & Cocking 1994, pp. 227–57

Kim U, Triandis HC, Kagitçibasi C, Choi S-C, Yoon G, eds. 1994. *Individualism and Collectivism: Theory, Method, and Applications.* Thousand Oaks, CA: Sage

Kitayama S. 2002. Culture and basic psychological processes—towards a system view of culture: comment on Oyerman et al. (2002). *Psychol. Bull.* 128(1):73–77

Kühnen U, Hannover B, Schubert B. 2001. Procedural consequences of semantic priming: the role of self knowledge for context-bounded versus context-independent modes of thinking. *J. Personal. Soc. Psychol.* 80: 397–409

Kühnen U, Oyserman D. 2002. Thinking about the self influences thinking in general: cognitive consequences of salient self concept. *J. Exp. Soc. Psychol.* 38(5): 492–99

Lassonde S. 2001. Extended schooling, adolescence, and the renegotiation of responsibility among Italian immigrant families in New Haven, Connecticut, 1910–1940. In *Family Obligation and Assistance During Adolescence: Contextual Variations and Developmental Implications*, ed. AJ Fuligni, pp. 43–60. San Francisco, CA: Jossey-Bass

Latz S, Wolf AW, Lozoff B. 1999. Cosleeping in context: sleep practices and problems in young children in Japan and the United States. *Arch. Pediatr. Adolesc. Med.* 153(4):339–46

Lave J, Wenger E. 1991. *Situated Learning: Legitimate Peripheral Participation.* New York: Cambridge Univ. Press

Lebra TS. 1994. Mother and child in Japanese socialization: a Japan-U.S. comparison. See Greenfield & Cocking 1994, pp. 259–74

LeVine RA. 1977. Child rearing as cultural adaptation. In *Culture and Infancy: Variations in the Human Experience*, ed. PH Leiderman, SR Tulkin, A Rosenfeld, pp. 15–27. New York: Academic

LeVine RA. 1997. Mother-infant interaction in cross-cultural perspective. In *Uniting Psychology and Biology: Integrative Perspectives on Human Development*, ed. NL Segall, GE Weisfeld, CC Weisfeld, pp. 339–54. Washington, DC: Am. Psychol. Assoc.

LeVine RA, Miller PM. 1990. Commentary. *Hum. Dev.* 33(1):73–80

Levinson SC. 1998. Studying spatial conceptualization across cultures: anthropology and cognitive science. *Ethos* 26(1):7–24

Li J. 2002. A cultural model of learning: Chinese "heart and mind for wanting to learn." *J. Cross-Cult. Psychol.* 33(3): 248–69

Lillard A. 1998. Ethnopsychologies: cultural variations in theories of mind. *Psychol. Bull.* 123(1):3–32

MacDonald KB. 1992. Warmth as a developmental construct: an evolutionary analysis. *Child Dev.* 63:753–73

Markus HR, Kitayama S. 1991. Culture and the self: implications for cognition, emotion, and motivation. *Psychol. Rev.* 98(2):224–53

Mason CA, Cauce AM, Gonzales N, Hiraga Y. 1996. Neither too sweet nor too sour: problem peers, maternal control, and problem behavior in African American adolescents. *Child Dev.* 67(5):2115–30

Maynard AE. 2002. Cultural teaching: the development of teaching skills in Zinacantec Maya sibling interactions. *Child Dev.* 73(3):969–82

McGillicuddy-De Lisi AV, Sigel IE. 1995. Parental beliefs. In *Handbook of Parenting.* Vol 3: *Status and Social Conditions of Parenting*, ed. MH Bornstein, pp. 333–58. Hillsdale, NJ: Lawrence Erlbaum

Miller JG. 1984. Culture and the development of everyday social explanation. *J. Personal. Soc. Psychol.* 46(5):961–78

Mistry J, Rogoff B. 1994. Remembering in cultural context. In *Psychology and Culture*, ed. WJ Lonner, RS Malpass, pp. 139–44. Boston, MA: Allyn Bacon

Morelli GA, Rogoff B, Oppenheim D, Goldsmith D. 1992. Cultural variation in infants' sleeping arrangements: questions of independence. *Dev. Psychol.* 28(4):604–13

Mundy-Castle AC. 1974. Social and technological intelligence in Western and non-Western cultures. *Universitas* 4:46–52

Munroe RL, Munroe RH. 1994. *Cross-Cultural Human Development*. Prospect Heights, IL: Waveland Press

Nsamenang AB. 1992. *Human Development in Cultural Context. A Third World Perspective*. Newbury Park, CA: Sage

Nsamenang AB. 1999. Eurocentric image of childhood in the context of the world's cultures. *Hum. Dev.* 42:159–68

Nsamenang AB, Lamb ME. 1994. Socialization of Nso children in the Bamenda grassfields of Northwest Cameroon. See Greenfield & Cocking 1994, pp. 133–46

Nugent JK. 1994. Cross-cultural studies of child development: Implications for clinicians. *Zero to Three* 15(2):1, 3–8

Ochs E, Schieffelin B. 1984. Language acquisition and socialization: three developmental stories. See Shweder & LeVine 1984, pp. 276–320

Ogunnaike OA, Houser RF. 2002. Yoruba toddlers' engagement in errands and cognitive performance on the Yoruba Mental Subscales. *Int. J. Behav. Dev.* 26(2):145–53

Okagaki L, Sternberg RJ. 1993. Parental beliefs and children's school performance. *Child Dev.* 64(1):36–56

Oyserman D, Coon HM, Kemmelmeier M. 2002. Rethinking individualism and collectivism: Evaluation of theoretical assumptions and meta-analyses. *Psychol. Bull.* 128(1):3–72

Palacios J, Moreno MC. 1996. Parents' and adolescents' ideas on children: origins and trans-mission of intracultural diversity. In *Parents' Cultural Belief Systems. Their Origins, Expressions and Consequences*, ed. S Harkness, CM Super, pp. 215–53

Perner J. 1991. *Understanding the Representational Mind*. Cambridge, MA: MIT Press

Phinney JS, Ong A, Madden T. 2000. Cultural values and intergenerational value discrepancies in immigrant and non-immigrant families. *Child Dev.* 71(2):528–39

Piaget J. 1952. *The Origins of Intelligence in Children*. New York: Basic Books

Piaget J. 1963/1977. Intellectual operations and their development. Reprinted in *The Essential Piaget: An Interpretive Reference and Guide*, ed. HE Gruber, JJ Vonèche, pp. 342–58. New York: Basic Books

Rabain-Jamin J, Maynard AE, Greenfield PM. 2002. Implications of sibling caregiving for sibling relations and teaching interactions in two cultures. *Ethos*. In press

Rabain-Jamin J, Sabeau-Jouannet E. 1997. Maternal speech to 4-month-old infants in two cultures: Wolof and French. *Int. J. Behav. Dev.* 20(3):425–51

Radke-Yarrow M, Zahn-Waxler C, Chapman M. 1983. Children's prosocial disposition and behavior. In *Handbook of Child Psychology*. Vol. 4: *Socialization, Personality, and Social Development*, ed. EM Hetherington, pp. 469–545. New York: Wiley

Raeff C, Greenfield PM, Quiroz B. 2000. Conceptualizing interpersonal relationships in the cultural contexts of individualism and collectivism. See Harkness et al. 2000, pp. 59–74

Reese L, Balzano S, Gallimore R, Goldenberg C. 1995. The concept of *educacion:* Latino family values and American schooling. *Int. J. Educ. Res.* 23:57–81

Rizzolatti G, Fadiga L, Gallese V, Fogassi L. 1996. Premotor cortex and the recognition of motor actions. *Cogn. Brain Res.* 3:131–41

Rogoff B. 1990. *Apprenticeship in Thinking: Cognitive Development in Social Context*. New York: Oxford

Romero ME. 1994. Identifying giftedness

among Keresan Pueblo Indians: the Keres study. *J. Am. Indian Educ.* 34(1): 35–58

Rothbaum F, Weisz J, Pott M, Miyake K, Morelli G. 2000. Attachment and culture: security in the United States and Japan. *Am. Psychol.* 55(10):1093–104

Saraswathi TS. 1999. *Culture, Socialization, and Human Development: Theory, Research, and Applications in the Indian Setting.* Thousand Oaks: Sage

Saraswathi TS, Ganapathy H. 2002. Indian parents' ethnotheories as reflections of the Hindu scheme of child and human development. See Keller et al. 2002, pp. 79–88

Saraswathi TS, Pai S. 1997. Socialization in the Indian context. In *Asian Perspectives on Psychology*, ed. HSR Kao, D Sinha, pp. 74–92. Thousand Oaks, CA: Sage

Saxe GB. 1991. *Culture and Cognitive Development.* Hillsdale, NJ: Erlbaum

Scribner S. 1985. Vygotsky's uses of history. In *Culture, Communication, and Cognition: Vygotskian Perspectives*, ed. J Wertsch, pp. 119–45. New York: Cambridge

Scribner S, Cole M. 1973. Cognitive consequences of formal and informal education. *Science* 182:553–59

Scribner S, Cole M. 1981. *The Psychology of Literacy.* Cambridge, MA: Harvard Univ. Press

Segall MH, Dasen PR, Berry JW, Poortinga YH. 1999. *Human Behavior in Global Perspective: An Introduction to Cross-cultural Psychology.* Boston, MA: Allyn Bacon. 2nd ed.

Serpell R. 1993. *The Significance of Schooling: Life Journeys in an African Society.* Cambridge: Cambridge Univ. Press

Serpell R. 1994. The cultural construction of intelligence. In *Psychology and Culture*, ed. WL Lonner, RS Malpass, pp. 157–63. Boston, MA: Allyn Bacon

Shon SP, Ja DY. 1982. Asian families. In *Ethnicity and Family Therapy*, ed. M McGoldrisk, JK Pearce, J Giordano, pp. 208–28. New York: Guilford

Shweder RA, Bourne EJ. 1984. Does the concept of the person vary cross-culturally? In *Culture Theory: Essays on Mind, Self, and Emotion*, ed. RA Shweder, RA Levine, pp. 158–99. New York: Cambridge

Shweder RA, Goodnow J, Hatano G, LeVine RA, Markus H, Miller P. 1998. The cultural psychology of development: one mind, many mentalities. In *Handbook of Child Psychology.* Vol. 1: *Theoretical Models of Human Development*, ed. RM Lerner, pp. 865–937. New York: Wiley. 5th ed.

Shweder RA, LeVine RA, eds. 1984. *Culture Theory: Essays on Mind, Self, and Emotion.* New York: Cambridge

Shweder RA, Sullivan MA. 1993. Cultural psychology: Who needs it? *Annu. Rev. Psychol.* 44:497–523

Sigel IE, McGillicuddy-DeLisi AV, Goodnow JJ, eds. 1992. *Parental Belief Systems: The Psychological Consequences for Children.* Hillsdale, NJ: Erlbaum. 2nd ed.

Singelis TM, Triandis HC, Bhawuk DPS, Gelfand M. 1995. Horizontal and vertical dimensions of individualism and collectivism: a theoretical and measurement refinement. *Cross-Cult. Res.* 29(3):240–75

Sroufe LA, Carlson EA, Levy AK, Egeland B. 1999. Implications of attachment theory for developmental psychopathology. *Dev. Psychopathol.* 11(1):1–13

Steinberg L, Mounts NS, Lamborn SD, Dornbusch SM. 1991. Authoritative parenting and adolescent adjustment across varied ecological niches. *J. Res. Adolesc.* 1(1):19–36

Sternberg RJ, Conway BE, Ketron JL, Bernstein M. 1981. People's conceptions of intelligence. *J. Personal. Soc. Psychol.* 4(1):37–55

Suárez-Orozco C, Suárez-Orozco M. 1995. *Transformations: Immigration, Family Life, and Achievement Motivation Among Latino Adolescents.* Stanford, CA: Stanford Univ. Press

Suina J, Smolkin LB. 1994. From natal culture to school culture to dominant society culture: supporting transitions for Pueblo Indian students. See Greenfield & Cocking 1994, pp. 115–30

Super C, Harkness S. 1986. The developmental niche: a conceptualization at the interface of child and culture. *Int. J. Behav. Dev.* 9(4):545–69

Super CM. 1983. Cultural variation in the meaning and uses of children's "intelligence." In *Explorations in Cross-cultural Psychology*, ed. J Deregowski, S Dziurawiec, R Annis, pp. 199–212. Amsterdam: Swets & Zeitlinger

Suzuki LK. 2000. *The development and socialization of filial piety: a comparison of Asian Americans and Euro Americans*. PhD thesis. Univ. Calif., Los Angeles

Takahashi K. 1990. Are the key assumptions of the 'Strange Situation' procedure universal? A view from Japanese research. *Hum. Dev.* 33(1):23–30

Tapia Uribe FM, LeVine RA, LeVine SE. 1994. Maternal behavior in a Mexican community: the changing environments of children. See Greenfield & Cocking 1994, pp. 41–54

Tomasello M. 1999. *The Cultural Origins of Human Cognition.* Cambridge, MA: Harvard Univ. Press

Trevarthen C. 1980. The foundations of intersubjectivity: development of interpersonal and cooperative understanding in infants. In *The Social Foundations of Language and Thought*, ed. D Olson, pp. 316–42. New York: Norton

Triandis HC. 1988. Collectivism and individualism: a conceptualization of a basic concept in cross-cultural social psychology. In *Personality, Cognition, and Values*, ed. C Bagley, GK Verma. London: Macmillan

Triandis HC. 1990. Cross-cultural studies of individualism and collectivism. See Berman 1990, pp. 41–134

Triandis HC, Suh EM. 2002. Cultural influences on personality. *Annu. Rev. Psychol.* 53:133–60

Troadac B, Martinot C. ND. *La representation de l'espace a Tahiti: Variabilite selon les contextes insulaires urbains (Papeete) et ruraux (Moorea).* Work. Pap. Dep. Psych. Dev., Univ. Toulouse-Le Mirail

Uba L. 1994. *Asian Americans: Personality Patterns, Identity, and Mental Health.* New York: Guilford

Vinden P. 1996. Junin Quechua children's understanding of mind. *Child Dev.* 67(4):1701–6

Vinden P. 1999. Children's understanding of mind and emotion: a multi-culture study. *Cogn. Emot.* 13(1):19–48

Vinden P, Astington J. 2000. Culture and understanding other minds. In *Understanding Other Minds: Perspectives from Developmental Cognitive Neuroscience*, ed. S Baron-Cohen, pp. 503–19. Oxford: Oxford Univ. Press

Vygotsky LS. 1962. *Thought and Language.* Cambridge, MA: MIT

Wainryb C. 1995. Reasoning abut social conflicts in different cultures: Druze and Jewish children in Israel. *Child Dev.* 66(2):390–401

Wainryb C, Turiel E. 1994. Dominance, subordination, and concepts of personal entitlements in cultural contexts. *Child Dev.* 65(6):1701–22

Wassman J, Dasen P. 1998. Balinese spatial orientation: some empirical evidence for moderate linguistic relativity. *J. R. Anthropol. Inst., Incorporating Man (N.S.)* 4:689–713

Waters E, Vaughn BE, Posada G, Kondo-Ikemura K. 1995. *Caregiving, Cultural, and Cognitive Perspectives on Secure-base Behavior and Working Models: New Growing Points of Attachment Theory and Research.* Chicago: Monogr. Soc. Res. Child Dev.

Weisner TS. 1997. Support for children and the African family crisis. In *African Families and the Crisis of Social Change*, ed. TS Weisner, C Bradley, PL Kilbride, pp. 20–44. Westport, CT: Greenwood Press/Bergin & Garvey

Weisner TS. 2000. Culture, childhood, and progress in sub-Saharan Africa. In *Culture Matters*, ed. LE Harrison, SP Huntington, pp. 141–57. New York: Basic Books

Weisner TS, Bernheimer LP. 1998. Children of the 1960s at midlife: generational identity and the family adaptive project. In *Welcome to Middle Age! (And Other Cultural Fictions). Studies on Successful Midlife Development*, ed. RA Shweder, pp. 211–57. Chicago: Univ. Chicago Press

Wellman HM. 1990. *The Child's Theory of Mind.* Cambridge, MA: MIT

Wellman HM, Cross D, Watson J. 2001. Meta-analysis of theory-of-mind development: the truth about false belief. *Child Dev.* 72(3): 655–84

Wertsch JV. 1985. *Vygotsky and the Social Formation of Mind.* Cambridge, MA: Harvard Univ. Press

Whiten A. 1999. Parental encouragement in *Gorilla* in comparative perspective: implications for social cognition and the evolution of teaching. In *The Mentalities of Gorillas and Orangutans in Comparative Perspective*, ed. ST Parker, RW Mitchell, HL Miles, pp. 342–66. Cambridge: Cambridge Univ. Press

Whiten A. 2002. Chimpanzee cognition and the question of mental re-representation. In *Metarepresentation*, ed. D Sperber, pp. 139–67. Oxford: Oxford Univ. Press

Whiting BB, Edwards CP. 1988. *Children of Different Worlds: The Formation of Social Behavior.* Cambridge, MA: Harvard Univ. Press

Whiting BB, Whiting JWM. 1975. *Children of Six Cultures: A Psycho-Cultural Analysis.* Cambridge, MA: Harvard Univ. Press

Whiting JWM, Whiting BB. 1960. Contributions of anthropology to the methods of studying child rearing. In *Handbook of Research Methods in Child Development*, ed. P Mussen, pp. 918–44. New York: Wiley

Whiting JWM, Whiting BB. 1973. Altruistic and egoistic behavior in six cultures. In *Cultural Illness and Health: Essays in Human Adaptation*, ed. L Nader, TW Maretzki, pp. 56–66. Washington, DC: Amer. Anthro. Assoc.

Wober JM. 1974. Toward an understanding of the Kiganda concept of intelligence. In *Culture and Cognition*, ed. JW Berry, PR Dasen, pp. 261–80. London: Methuen

Yovsi RD. 2001. *Ethnotheories about breastfeeding and mother-infant interaction. The case of sedentary Nso farmers and nomadic Fulani pastorals with their infants 3–6 months of age in Mbvem subdivision of the Northwest providence of Cameroon, Africa.* PhD thesis. Univ. Osnabrück

Yovsi RD, Keller H. 2000. *Breastfeeding: an adaptive process.* Presented at Conf. Int. Union Anthropol. Ethnolog. Sci. (IUCAES), Agrigento, Italy

Zambrano I. 1999. *From na' to know: power, epistemology and the everyday forms of state formation in Mitontik, Chiapas (Mexico).* Doctoral diss., Harvard Univ.

Zhou M, Bankston C. 1998. *Growing up American: how Vietnamese children adapt to life in the United States.* New York: Russell Sage Found.

Zukow PG. 1989. *Sibling Interactions Across Cultures: Theoretical and Methodological Issues.* New York: Springer-Verlag

Annu. Rev. Psychol. 2003. 54:491–516
doi: 10.1146/annurev.psych.54.101601.145044
First published online as a Review in Advance on August 27, 2002

HUMAN-COMPUTER INTERACTION:
Psychological Aspects of the Human
Use of Computing

Gary M. Olson and Judith S. Olson

School of Information, University of Michigan, 550 East University Avenue, Ann Arbor, Michigan 48109-1092; e-mail: gmo@umich.edu, jsolson@umich.edu

Key Words   groupware, cognitive modeling, ubiquitous computing, usability, social context

■ **Abstract**   Human-computer interaction (HCI) is a multidisciplinary field in which psychology and other social sciences unite with computer science and related technical fields with the goal of making computing systems that are both useful and usable. It is a blend of applied and basic research, both drawing from psychological research and contributing new ideas to it. New technologies continuously challenge HCI researchers with new options, as do the demands of new audiences and uses. A variety of usability methods have been developed that draw upon psychological principles. HCI research has expanded beyond its roots in the cognitive processes of individual users to include social and organizational processes involved in computer usage in real environments as well as the use of computers in collaboration. HCI researchers need to be mindful of the longer-term changes brought about by the use of computing in a variety of venues.

CONTENTS

0066-4308/03/0203-0491$14.00

INTRODUCTION

Human-computer interaction (HCI) is the study of how people interact with computing technology. One major area of work in the field focuses on the design of computer systems. The goal is to produce software and hardware that is useful, usable, and aesthetically pleasing. A closely aligned area is the evaluation of systems in use. This is of course related to design, because to know if a design is useful or usable requires observing it in use. However, this also extends to the study of the larger social consequences of use. Increasingly, evaluation takes place at multiple levels of analysis: the individual, the group, the organization, and the industry or societal sector. The methodological and conceptual issues at these different levels of evaluation are quite different. Psychologists are typically most interested in the smaller levels of aggregation, though Landauer (1995) attempted to provide a largely psychological account of the "productivity paradox," a phenomenon first identified by economists who found a disappointing lack of correlation between the amount of money invested in information technology and changes in industry productivity measures.

This chapter updates and expands the last review of HCI in the *Annual Review of Psychology* (Carroll 1997). There has been steady growth in the field since then, and in our brief chapter we can only highlight some of the most significant changes. We also give explicit attention to the emergence of research at the group and organizational level, often referred to as computer-supported cooperative work or CSCW.

The field of HCI is fundamentally interdisciplinary. The fields of cognitive, social, and organizational psychology are all important to research in the area, but other social sciences such as sociology and anthropology have played key roles, as have such related fields as communication, management, operations research, and ergonomics. Also, a variety of technical specialties from computer science are important. Research in HCI requires literacy in the related fields and often involves multidisciplinary collaboration.

Some think of HCI as a purely applied field. However, being applied does not mean lacking in relevance to basic science. Stokes (1997) argued that the quest for fundamental understanding and considerations of use are two separate dimensions of a 2×2 table rather than opposite ends of a continuum. He used Pasteur as an example of research that sought both fundamental understanding and practical solutions. Whereas some research in HCI is close to purely applied, as we hope to show in this review, much of it falls in Pasteur's quadrant.

THE SCIENCE OF HUMAN COMPUTER INTERACTION

Theoretical advances in HCI are proceeding on a number of different fronts. Modeling of the integration of perceptual-cognitive-motor processes to illuminate the moment-by-moment behavior people exhibit with computers has become more detailed. At the more social level, there is work on distributed cognition, focusing on the interplay of people with their teammates and the artifacts of their interaction. Another class of tasks, that of information retrieval, is receiving attention from HCI researchers. What we do not have yet is a detailed model of social interaction or of some of the larger issues of adoption of innovation. There is significant work to be done to understand what might be unique about the adoption of computation as an innovation, because computational artifacts can be designed in so many different ways.

Cognitive Modeling

One of the longer-running cumulative efforts in HCI is the attempt to understand in detail the involvement of cognitive, perceptual, and motor components in the moment-by-moment interaction a person encounters when working at a computer. This effort stands in contrast to a lot of traditional psychological research in that the goal is to understand how multiple components of behavior interact, not just how one works. This line of work began with the now-classic work by Card et al. (1983) in a book called *The Psychology of Human-Computer Interaction*. In this book they catalogued phenomena from the traditional psychological literature that they believed were at play in HCI tasks: Fitt's Law, Hick's Law, Gestalt principles, the Power law of practice, etc. They built a set of models that separated the knowledge needed to use a particular computer application, called GOMS (an acronym made up of its major components: goals, operators, methods, and selection rules), from the engine that operates on this knowledge to produce behavior, called the model human processor. With this approach, one could determine several important behaviors: the time it takes to do a task (the sum of a number of "cognitive engineering time parameters" including mental and physical acts), which choices people will make when faced with alternative methods, what kinds of errors are likely (e.g., loss of items from short-term memory, a motor slip), and how long it will take for someone to learn a new application.

A number of researchers built on this original work, adding parameters of mental and physical action (e.g., Lerch et al. 1989, Nilsen et al. 1993) and modeling detail about the perceptual processes (Lohse 1991), accommodating overlapping mental processes (John & Newell 1989), and more fully detailing the perceptual-motor interplay (Kieras & Meyer 1997) reviewed in Olson & Olson (1990).

The most significant recent advance is the work in which Kieras & Meyer (1997) determined an overarching architecture of component stores and processes, called EPIC (executive process–interactive control), and modeled a far reaching set of phenomena within it. The components of the architecture are shown in Figure 1. This work is a good example of Pasteur's quadrant, work that is both practically driven and adds to fundamental science. By adhering to the agreed-upon architecture, they forced their explanations of various phenomena to cumulate, to illuminate new aspects of the fundamentals of human behavior. They have focused recently on aspects of eye-hand coordination and the extent to which two hands can be used independently. At the same time, they are driven to explain practical phenomena such as the dual-task performance common in operating a car (interacting with the direction-finder interface while negotiating traffic) or making tactical decisions while following a particular target in a military aircraft. In the style of the SOAR modeling community (Laird 2002), the authors have made their

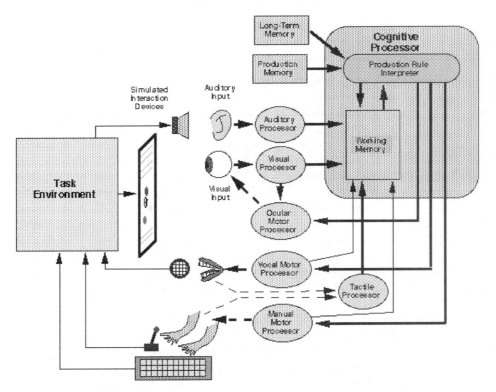

Figure 1   The architectural components included in the EPIC (executive process–interactive control) models of people's behavior with computer applications.

source code available and encourage others to explore both the boundaries of the model and its practical application.

Cognitive modeling has had a number of practical applications. Gray et al. (1993), for example, applied it to the evaluation of two telephone operator keyboards, predicting and confirming empirically that the new keyboard forced a task that required on average 2 seconds longer to enact, an unacceptable performance difference for those considering how many people are needed to staff a large volume of calls. Others have applied cognitive modeling to the design of applications such as a CAD (computer aided design) application and a back-office banking application for deposit slip reconciliation (John 1995). For example, in the back-office banking application the analysis recommended a rearrangement of the visual display so that it required only a single glance to make a comparison rather than multiple glances while also holding information in working memory.

Powerful though this modeling is, it is not universally applicable, nor does it address the full range of questions that appear in the design of computer interfaces. It applies only to skilled users without accounting for how one becomes skilled. Most of the modeling has focused on the more perceptual/motor aspects of tasks (applying it to eye-hand coordination and skilled motor tasks) and less on the more difficult cognitive components (such as those involved in creating a financial model in a spreadsheet application). There are few accounts of individual differences and the role of fatigue and practice in performance. Nor do these models address the larger issues of the fit of the computer system to the goals of work (Olson & Olson 1990).

Distributed Cognition

A second line of theoretical research addresses the more social and contextual aspects of work that the cognitive modeling line does not. This line, called situated cognition or distributed cognition, stems from anthropological and sociological studies of real-world work situations (Olson 1994). It recognizes how people's actions are intimately intertwined with the artifacts of their work; their team member's roles, responsibilities, and actions; and even their cultural and historical setting. This work draws on the methods of ethnography, ethnomethodology, activity theory, and conversational analysis, gathering data from the field instead of the laboratory, generating a number of rich case studies.

The work of Hutchins (1995) is a good example of this work. In his case study he described the ways in which the team in a cockpit engages in the complicated maneuvers involved in landing an aircraft. They collectively prepare their environment so that when the cognitive processing load becomes high in the last moments before landing, they no longer have to make calculations but can merely perceive various settings to trigger actions. For example, they calculate the altitude and speed at which they will have to change the flaps and preset various markers on the cockpit dials. The somewhat complicated calculation is aided by a set of cards that prespecify parameters for various load and weather conditions; the pilot's task is merely to select the appropriate card and post it for others in the cockpit to refer to as they set their parameters and monitor the descent. The close coordination of the individual players' cognitive activities and how they arrange their environment to coordinate actions with others is the key to claiming that the unit of analysis should be the whole system, not the individual. Thus, to understand the behavior of the individuals, one must examine the entire environment in which the activity takes place. "Such factors as the endurance of a representation, the sensory modality via which it is accessed, its vulnerability to disruption, and the competition for modality specific resources may all influence the cognitive properties of such a system" (Hutchins 1995, p. 286).

This line of thinking has inspired a number of design ideas, notably in the design of the work environment. Deep analyses of how people use their desks with its piles of papers and sensitivity to location have led to interfaces that display results of searches in spatial arrangements reflecting some aspect of the material, either its date or content. (Czerwinski et al. 1999). Other analyses of how people work with their whiteboards in both their offices and in meetings led to the development of electronic whiteboards and clever ways to combine electronic and physical artifacts (Moran et al. 1997, Mynatt et al. 1999).

Scope of the Theories

Theories and problems in HCI today parallel some of the theoretical transitions that we witnessed in the 1970s in cognitive science and in the 1960s in verbal learning. The question is, how much of people's behavior can be explained by factors generalizable to all users, regardless of domain expertise or meaning. In the early 1970s in the area of verbal learning, we broke from studying learning of nonsense syllables to learning in richer environments in which meaning was key (Prytulak 1971). In the 1970s there was a lot of work in the spirit of the General Problem Solver (Newell & Simon 1972), attempting to find out the features of people's intellectual processing that were common to everyone, where they relied only on simple general strategies such as hill-climbing and generate-and-test. Soon thereafter, countervailing research focused on the nature of expertise and the specific strategies that experts used rather than generic properties of cognitive processing (e.g., Ericcson & Charness 1994).

In HCI there is a similar transition from understanding generic behavior (Gestalt explanations of the understandability of visual layouts, tradeoffs in using mouse-menu input devices versus learned keystroke combinations) to more knowledge-centered behavior. For example, a recent study of expert/novice searchers of large knowledge sources (such as the World Wide Web) showed that both strategies and successes were highly dependent on domain expertise. The person familiar with medical information sources was much better and faster at confirming the appropriateness of a treatment for a diagnosis than the layman and worse at finding the best price for a consumer product. The search strategies were highly dissimilar and fully dependent on the domain of expertise (Bhavnani et al. 2001).

Human Computer Interaction Work on Information Retrieval

Whereas most of the theory and applications in HCI of the 1980s and early 1990s focused on computationally supported office applications such as word processors and spreadsheets, one of the major theoretical advances of the late 1990s came in an examination of information-retrieval behavior. Spurred by the advent of the World Wide Web and ubiquitous "surfing" behavior, Pirolli & Card (1999) investigated how people decide to continue in a line of searches and when to jump to a different source or search string. To model this behavior they drew on foraging theory from biology. They saw the analogy between the movement of animals from one food source to another (a "patch") and people's movement from one information source to another. They modeled the moment-by-moment decisions people make in their assessment of the value of what they see in search results to predict when they would pop back up to a high level change in a search string or a completely different source such as stopping searching the web and asking a reference librarian. This work also highlighted the importance of the display of the search results in the way it gives clues ("scents") as to whether further selection of an item is likely to be valuable ("to bear fruit"). So, for example, if a Google search returns only headers or urls, it has a less informative "scent" than a display of the sentence fragments that surround the words that match the search string. These bits of information give the user clues as to whether the selection of that item is likely to be useful.

The Card and Pirolli information-foraging work is remarkable not only in its novelty of task and approach, but in the variety of methods they bring to play in their work. They motivate the investigation with some descriptions of real people searching for information—a team of MBAs doing an industry analysis and a consultant writing his monthly report on a topic. From phenomena gleaned from these cases, they worked with mathematical foraging theory, applying various concepts and equations to information rather than food-seeking behavior. Of particular relevance here were calculations on the time a person would spend in a fruitful region of information before moving on to another and the factors that drove the decision to move. They then moved to modeling the moment-by-moment behavior of people conducting their search with an ACT-IF model (the ACT-R model applied to information foraging, IF). The mathematical analyses show aggregate behavioral trends (e.g., average time to linger as a function of richness of the scent), whereas the ACT-IF model allowed them to explore various mechanisms that might account for this behavior. They concluded with an empirical laboratory study of people making such switching decisions in a particular information-retrieval system called the "Scatter/Gather" interface. They made very specific predictions of when someone would stop searching a source (when the average value of a found item dropped below an estimated middle point). They also encouraged designs to give "scent," hints as to the ultimate value of continuing searching on a particular path, such as meaningful labels and revealing search results.

USER INTERFACE DEVELOPMENTS

As computing technology changes, new user interface challenges arise. For instance, in the early days of personal computing screen displays were mostly command lines in green or yellow on a black background. Editing a manuscript included placing explicit formatting characters in the text. With the emergence of graphical user interfaces (GUIs), whole new classes of issues emerged, as well as new opportunities for tapping into key cognitive and perceptual processes. Much of the design of early GUIs was influenced by psychological research (e.g., Johnson et al. 1989). Such systems have been around long enough that they have achieved some level of stability in design, even across different hardware and software platforms.

Now all kinds of new situations are emerging that are challenges to human-computer interaction specialists. We briefly describe some examples of these and indicate the character of some of the psychological issues involved. As applications move from the desktop to more mobile, immersive environments and to a wider set of users, there remain a number of challenges for basic psychology. How do people understand aspects of the digital world as it is embodied in these various devices? How do we capitalize on the strengths of each human, coupling them with assistance from computing, to bring about the most in a productive, satisfying life?

Mobile Devices

In the past decade a wide variety of small mobile devices have appeared. The most common are what are called personal digital assistants or PDAs. These are small handheld devices that have increasingly sophisticated computational capabilities. The user interface challenges are daunting. These devices typically have small screens, and interactions are with a stylus and a small set of buttons. Some models have optional folding keyboards that allow for more traditional interactions. Despite these user interface challenges, such devices have a number of very useful functions and are very popular. Combinations of mobile devices, such as the merging of PDAs and cell phones, are just appearing.

One specialized user interface issue is how to integrate such mobile devices with more traditional computing. For instance, Milewski & Smith (2000) developed a digital address book with location sensors that could be accessed from a regular workstation or from a PDA and that provided information about the availability of others that could be used to coordinate phone calls regardless of where the participants might be. The interface had to be adapted to the capabilities of each device in a way that users found intuitive and natural.

Immersive Environments

Virtual reality environments are artificial 3-D environments created computationally to either mimic a real environment or to create a novel one. These can vary in their immersiveness. The least immersive would be a 3-D environment presented on a computer screen. This could be enhanced by stereo glasses that give a real 3-D experience. Alternatively, the user can wear a head-mounted display for a completely immersive experience. Special rooms such as the CAVE (Cruz-Neira et al. 1992) can surround the user with an immersive experience, with all the surfaces of the room having projected information and with stereo glasses used to create apparent objects that hover in space. Virtual reality environments have been used for a variety of serious as well as playful purposes (see extensive examples in Barfield & Furness 1997).

Collaborative virtual environments are those in which multiple persons interact, either in games or in collaborative activities like data exploration. Because of limitations in computational power, people are usually represented as avatars, simplified, geometric, digital representations of people, who move about in the 3-D space (Singhal 1999). The users in a meeting situation might interact over a digitally represented object, such as a mock-up of a real object (an automobile engine, an airplane hinge, a piece of industrial equipment) or with visualizations of abstract data (e.g., a 3-D visualization of atmospheric data). It has proven difficult to establish mutual awareness or orientation in such spaces, because the small windows do not provide a good sense of where you are (Hindmarsh et al. 1998, Park et al. 2000). There have even been some attempts to merge collaborative virtual environments with real ones, though with limited success so far (Benford et al. 1998).

These virtual environments engage numerous perceptual, cognitive, and social issues. The interface devices for such environments, such as head-mounted displays, wands that allow manipulation and selection of virtual objects, and special data gloves that allow life-like manipulation of virtual objects, all have required extensive human-factors development (Barfield & Furness 1997). A special challenge is integrating such virtual environments with human capabilities to yield enhanced performance and experiences.

Ubiquitous Computing

Weiser (1991) stated, "The most profound technologies are those that disappear. They weave themselves into the fabric of everyday life until they are indistinguishable from it." Through this analysis he forecast what he claimed would be the third wave of computing (after mainframes and personal computers), ubiquitous computing, or as he often called it, ubicomp. This would be when computers would be so small, inexpensive, and ubiquitous that they would disappear. Small computational devices can perform a variety of functions. For example, so-called smart houses have computational devices that can control a variety of functions such as heat, lighting, kitchen appliances, intercoms, entertainment, and telephones. The proliferation of computing devices raises many user interface issues about how to control all of these devices and how to give users adequate flexibility, security, and privacy.

Internet, World Wide Web (WWW)

Although the ubiquity of the Internet and the wealth of information available through it is stunning, the user interface took a giant step backwards from the set of applications people were using before its arrival. There is very little interaction with web sites other than finding and clicking on action buttons that promise continuing good information. Most of the user issues have to do with navigation (how did I get to this site and how do I return to it?), readability of the material presented (font size and color, as well as Gestalt principles of organization), and impatience with long system response times. In order to make sense out of mountains of information in a web site (like the gateway to the University's store of information), designers are borrowing principles from library science, creating a field called information architecture. In information architecture the focus is on the organization, navigation, labeling, and search systems that offer accessibility to the end user (Rosenfeld & Morville 1998). With information architecture coupled with good user interface design principles, there is hope that the users will be better able to realize what information resides in a large web site and then be able to navigate through it to find what they want.

In addition to the design and organization issues are issues of motivation and trust. There are design prescriptions gleaned from empirical studies of web-searching behavior that claim that if in three clicks users do not find information that at least suggests they are on the right track, they will leave the site (Kuegler 2000). This bold prescription harkens to the Card and Pirolli information-foraging theory, making explicit the effort people will expend in an information patch before moving on to another source. Also, when encountering a site for purchasing goods (e.g., Amazon.com) or for getting professional advice (e.g., webMD.com), people need to assess the trustworthiness of the service. Some people are reluctant to enter their credit card information or reveal their illness concerns, whereas others are unconcerned with the potential loss of privacy or even identity theft in these unvetted sites [the *Communications of the Association for Computing Machinery* (CACM) offered a special issue on trust in December 2000]. What is it that makes people trust? How do risk and loss get assessed in the technical world? Do people use the same criteria to assess trust in cyberspace that they do in the physical world?

Extended Populations of Users

Early work on human-computer interaction (HCI) focused little on individual differences. Results were targeted to the educated office worker without disabilities or particular talents. Today there is a healthy interest in interfaces for children and for people with disabilities, including the aging population. Children, for example, have less-well-organized knowledge from which to build metaphorical interfaces, have less-well-developed motor skills, and are interested in new, unsubtle changes in their environment. Design prescriptions follow the recognition of these different capabilities, creating larger and more colorful input devices, heavy use of animation, and explanatory material using speech instead of text (Druin & Soloman 1996).

Interestingly, when conducting usability tests with children, it is impossible to hold their attention span and get them to tell the developer what they do and do not understand. In response to this, knowing that children are very social and interact by talking a lot, usability tests for children are conducted in pairs, allowing them to talk to each other about what ideas they have about how to do things and their guesses about how to get it to work right. Using the natural verbalizations of pairs of children, they achieve what an adult would do under "thinking out loud" instructions.

For people with disabilities there are a number of promising advances. Computers have been outfitted with various input devices that allow people with limited or nonexistent hand motion to enter text. For example, one can speak to a computer that is outfitted with speech recognition devices, and some interfaces show the alphabet one letter at a time, with the user blowing in a tube device when they wish to select that letter. Accompanied with word prediction software tuned to the vocabulary of the user, this device can provide access and "a voice" to people for whom participation with others would be very difficult. There are some interfaces, as well, that are customized to the particular perceptual and motor parameters of the user, in the spirit of GOMS parameters, that then make the interaction maximally efficient for the particular user (Horstman-Koester & Levine 1994).

A number of companies are now also providing "screen readers" to help the visually impaired have access to the very visual web. These are still very unsatisfactory, however, because not enough is understood about how to parse the site to focus on the areas the user wants to attend, not reading the whole screen top down, left to right. By encoding hidden tags in the html, designers can make their sites accessible to the visually impaired through screen readers if they understand the reader's algorithms and the needs of the user to scan and understand the screen. Some web sites provide an automatic evaluation of the visual accessibility of target web sites, giving advice on how to make them more accessible (a portal of these sites is available at http://www.c2t2.ca/landonline/access.html#newtech).

Other advances are making actions and content of applications fit those in non–North American cultures as well. It is simple to think of translating the menu items or the site contents into other languages, but cultural disparities likely require changes more fundamental than simple surface characteristics. For example, icons such as a red cylindrical mailbox, common in the UK, may not be understood by those in other cultures. Also, templates for memos, presentations, etc. would have to be altered to better fit the conversational conventions of the culture (del Galdo & Nielsen 1996).

USABILITY METHODS

The practitioners in the field of HCI, called user-experience engineers (UEEs), use a variety of methods to generate and evaluate applications (details of which appear in Olson & Moran 1996, including extensive references). When they are on the team that generates the functionality of the system, a role sometimes left only to marketing analysts, they employ various methods that closely investigate the setting in which the target users reside, their current activity, and their culture and capabilities. They use contextual design (Beyer & Holtzblatt 1998) and participatory design methods (Muller 1991), which differ only in whether the target users are directly involved in the design or merely consulted about their activity and preferences. Both employ interview and observation techniques, sometimes as deep as ethnography, sometimes not, depending on the time and resources of the project.

In the process of design itself, UEEs employ a number of methods, called formative evaluation. There are very few methods that focus on the design process other than mere lists of design principles. There are a number of methods that help the designer evaluate the prototype design. Among them are the informal use of various checklists, the more formal inspection methods called heuristic evaluation (Nielsen 1993) and cognitive walkthrough (Lewis et al. 1990), and claims analysis (Carroll & Rosson 1992). Each of these inspection techniques goes through the prototype from the user's perspective, attempting to notice those aspects that will cause difficulty for the user, such as having nonobvious words indicate the next action to take, unreadable color combinations, or unexpected locations for next actions. Because these methods do not take a long time and typically involve only two or three expert evaluators, they have received a lot of attention and adoption. When the design is intended to support repetitive tasks with skilled users (e.g., telephone operators or reservations clerks), some employ either the GOMS or keystroke-level analysis to assess various aspects of cognitive load and expected duration of the task (Gray et al. 1993). Such analyses have shown, for example, where a designed task was flawed because it required too much information to be held in working memory for too long, creating a situation ripe for errors.

UEEs who follow recommended practice then evaluate the prototype with a usability test, an activity that is similar to standard psychology experiments. Instead of comparing two or more conditions, the usability test focuses on episodes in task behavior in which the user has difficulty, either pausing longer than expected or making outright errors (Rubin 1994). Some of these usability tests are used to indicate corrections to be made to the application, some are used to assess whether the application is good enough to either implement to real users or to launch in the market.

Early in the 1990s the HCI community engaged in a debate about the cost/benefit of the above listed methods. For example, it is well known that usability tests are expensive in time and expert resources, whereas some of the inspection methods are much less time and resource intense. Similarly, doing a detailed GOMS analysis was thought to require a great deal of expert time and yield no more insights than other more cursory inspection methods. A number of studies then compared the efficacy of various methods on how many and how severe the design issues were that the evaluators could find (e.g. Jeffries et al. 1991, Karat et al. 1992, John & Kieras 1996). Gray & Salzman (1998) criticized these studies for their departure from good experimental design, saying conclusions were unwarranted from the power and control in their designs. The paper sparked a debate among the authors of the original evaluations plus others who have experience with the methods, countering Gray & Salzman's claims that the studies were useless in guiding decisions about which method to use (Olson & Moran 1998). The general consensus, however, is that the inspection methods find a number of design issues, but not all, and are less expensive than running a usability test with real users. The usability tests are good at finding the "show stopper" issues, the points where the user cannot understand the words or paragraphs intended to inform them about what to do. The simple prescription is to do as much evaluation as time and resources allow, and that designs benefit greatly from having at least one real user test the system.

A recent interview study showed there are increasing numbers of UEEs on staff in organizations that build either products for the external market or applications for internal use (Olson 2001). Early usability professionals came to this position with PhDs in psychology or industrial engineering. Today, although those in HCI research have PhDs, there are many UEEs who have masters' degrees in HCI (See http://www.hcibib.org/education/ for a listing of the university programs that offer degrees in HCI). Some larger organizations, understanding the value of usability and functionality in the marketplace, employ a large number of UEEs; IBM, for example, has over 1000. As a community they have a large internal network of expertise and even hold their own internal conference to share their findings and design ideas. Most of the UEEs are heavily involved in both original design and iterative evaluation of applications, some in determining the functionality of the proposed system, and only a few in the decision to launch a system.

The profession is well established and in many organizations enjoys respect for their contribution to making usable products and services and increasing customer satisfaction. There is still a need for better design methods, and perhaps an infusion of usability criteria into the software engineering curriculum. It would be more effective if developers had the sensibilities of user needs and capabilities themselves, rather than having to have usability specialists on a team to work in partnership with the developer.

THE WORKPLACE

As noted in "The Science of Human Computer Interaction" above, much of the early work in HCI focused on productivity tools such as word processing, spreadsheets, databases, calendars, and so forth, but these were mostly studied in isolation from actual work. Issues such as the naming of commands, the layout of screens, the organization of menus, the flow of action sequences, and consistency were examined and behavior was measured on representative but isolated tasks in a laboratory setting. More recently, however, investigators have been interested in the nature of the workplace and in the role of computers in the larger organizational and economic context. In more psychological terms, the shift has been from a perceptual/cognitive perspective to a social/organizational one.

One such line of work has investigated the "productivity paradox." As perhaps described most elegantly by Strassmann (1990), for a long time it has been difficult to show a relationship between investments in computing and measures of productivity. Strassmann presented scatterplots of these two variables that are canonical versions of a zero correlation coefficient. There have been numerous attempts to explain this, but one that is relevant to HCI is Landauer's (1995) argument that the productivity paradox is due primarily to the poor utility and usability of systems. He argued that more widespread use of user-centered development methods could turn this whole situation around. More recent work by Brynjolfsson & Hitt (1998) suggests that computing may at last be producing some measurable gains in productivity and that better-designed systems as well as organizational adjustments may be key.

Some of these changes in the effectiveness of computer tools can be seen with respect to specific tools. In Grudin's (1988, 1994) famous exposé of the early widespread failures of computer-supported cooperative work (CSCW) technologies, he singled out group calendaring as a specific example of poor fit into organizations. These conclusions were based on studies carried out in the early 1980s. In a recent survey of the successful adoption of group calendaring in several organizations, Palen & Grudin (2002) observed that organizational conditions in the 1990s were much more favorable for the adoption of group tools than they were in the 1980s. Individuals found more personal value in being on a calendar, and there was increased social pressure from colleagues after a critical mass of adoption was achieved. Further, the tools themselves had improved in reliability, functionality, and usability.

COMPUTER SUPPORTED COOPERATIVE WORK

One manifestation of the expansion of attention to the group and organizational levels of analysis is the emergence of CSCW as a field. The first conferences on CSCW were held in the United States in 1986 and in Europe in 1989, but the area really flourished in the 1990s. Numerous systems were developed to support human interaction in all combinations of same/different time/place. The human use of such systems involves a wide variety of psychological issues, particularly from social and organizational psychology. We briefly review some representative examples and refer the reader to a more extensive review of this work by Olson & Olson (2002).

E-mail

E-mail has become a universal service just like the telephone (Anderson et al. 1995), often noted as the first successful groupware application (Sproull & Kiesler 1991, Satzinger & Olfman 1992, O'Hara-Devereaux & Johansen 1994, Anderson et al. 1995). With the more recent addition of attachments, people share not only plain text conversation but work objects as well (Garton & Wellman 1995). With this wide adoption have come social consequences. E-mail has widened connectivity to people who previously did not communicate with each other (Sproull & Kiesler 1991). It has given a voice to people who were previously unheard from in discussions (Finholt et al. 1990). Because the speaker does not get feedback from the listener, shy people are more likely to voice their opinions. However, this same lack of social cues has caused people to "flame," to send more extremely emotive messages than they would have done with the immediate social feedback of face-to-face encounters. Although some of this effect is abating with experience, it is still a concern as new users join in the e-mail culture (Hollingshead et al. 1993, Arrow et al. 1996).

The ease of communication and broadcast that e-mail has provided has produced another social consequence, information overload. Some developers have employed techniques from artificial intelligence to block or sort incoming e-mail but have had limited success. It remains difficult to specify the rules of sorting/ blocking in sufficient detail to perfectly sort the wanted from the unwanted (Malone et al. 1988, Winograd 1988). Today, successful handling of the overload involves substantial human intervention (Whittaker & Sidner 1996).

Meeting Support

Shared workspaces are very important in meetings, and a number of shared workspace applications have been created to support meetings. Simple group editors are very effective for free-flowing meetings such as design meetings or brainstorming sessions (Olson et al. 1993). People produced higher-quality work than when using standard whiteboards and paper and pencil but, likely because the technology was new, were less satisfied with the process. They may not yet have learned how to interact with each other and to have their opinions heard or to have decisions come out the way they want them to. The supported meetings also had less verbal discussion, because the growing artifact (e.g., the proposal or report workers were co-constructing) served as a medium of exchange as well as their voice commentary (Clark & Brennan 1991). People reported liking the meetings because work was accomplished in the meeting; the time was not just spent talking about the work.

Some have taken the idea of shared digital objects and displayed them on electronic whiteboards. These whiteboards are large projection surfaces into which people have input by light-pen or through a touch-sensitive screen (Elrod et al. 1992). Several extended case studies of their use give us insight into how people adopt and adapt to their features. Studies at Xerox PARC (Palo Alto Research Center) and at Boeing showed that people value the electronic whiteboards because they could all see and agree to or discuss further proposed changes, even those that require some computation (e.g., a spreadsheet of salary adjustments whose sum cannot exceed a specific fixed amount). Some of these whiteboards were even programmed to handle the implicit structure that appears in the spatial layout of freehand writing. For example, the LiveBoard at Xerox recognized handwritten lists and outlines, allowing easy edits that preserved and used the inherent structure of the display (Moran et al. 1996).

Other meeting support tools take the computational power much further in support of various aspects of meetings. Group-decision support systems embody various brainstorming and voting procedures (Nunamaker et al. 1991). Participants enter their ideas into a central repository in parallel, and evaluate others' ideas in attached comments. Aggregates of individuals' opinions are displayed, triggering additional discussion and refinement. Different voting mechanisms help the decision makers combine their assessments and votes. Evaluation of these systems showed that their use generated more ideas from participants, because they didn't have to wait for one another to stop speaking in order to get a turn. They felt, too, that anonymous voting and rating helped to insure equal participation, not dominated by those in power. However, decisions were not rated as satisfying, and the meetings took longer than normal ones (Kraemer & Pinsonneault 1990, McLeod 1992, Hollingshead et al. 1993).

Supported meetings are slow to penetrate normal organizational life. The literature has shown quite clearly that these meetings produce better outcomes. However, these tools require a new way of working, and people are reluctant to learn new ways of negotiating with each other and getting their ideas heard. As cost of these systems comes down and more people gain experience with them, it will be interesting to see what factors contribute to or detract from easy adoption.

Conferencing Tools: Voice and Video

Those who must coordinate over long distances often use audio- or videoconferencing. Typically special videoconferencing rooms are built linked with high bandwidth connections and compatible camera and projection systems. Some more recent advances in technology have made the capability much cheaper (video over the Internet) and the systems much more interoperable, making the cost reduction sufficient for people to more widely adopt it.

Quality is still an issue, however. When the audio stream is sent with the video, the combined signal is delayed usually on the order of a second, a significant enough delay to disrupt normal conversation. Many experienced videoconference participants know to supplement the video with a standard telephone connection to support immediate voice signals with the additional feature of full-duplex so participants can hear the "backchannel" responses while the speaker speaks (Finn et al. 1997). Also, some technologies that compress and decompress the video stream alter the picture so that people appear to have jerky actions. Because unusual actions are a signal that someone is lying, one can make mistakes in attributing truthfulness merely because of features of the transmission channel (Horn 2001).

These technologies have afforded some good support for remote meetings. In a controlled comparison of meetings with video connectivity and those in which people are collocated, the quality of the work was the same. However, the remote groups were less satisfied with the quality of the discussion, and it took attention to orchestrate their work more than those who were collocated (Olson et al. 1995). Not all groups need video, however. A second study showed that those who know each other well and have a lot of common ground work just as well with audio; strangers or those without common ground benefit most from having video as well as audio (Veinott et al. 1999).

Instant Messaging, Chat, MUDs

With the advent of instant messaging applications like those offered by America Online's AIM, Microsoft's MSN Messenger, and ICQ ("I seek you"), people have the ability to instantly converse with each other through text in real time. When the relay time is short, these interactions can feel like real conversations. Users specify to whom they would like to reveal whether they are on-line through a "buddy list." Symbols next to the list of participants shows who is on-line, who is "away," and who has signed off. This combines awareness of others' activity state as well as access in real time for informal, immediate responses. Although these are very popular among teens, they have also been used effectively in the workplace (Nardi et al. 2000). Babble is a chat system that has been used at IBM for discussions, with a clever graphical display of others' activities for awareness (Erickson et al. 1999).

Some chat systems allow large numbers of participants to converse, with all contributions being shown in one window in chronological order. The question is whether this mixture of conversation threads is difficult for the participants to follow. An evaluation comparing the confusion people have in a chat system with those in face-to-face encounters showed no extra difficulties, even though many more people were participating than normally do in a meeting. People added a few clues to help others keep track of the threads, however, such as reference to names they are responding to and explicit references to the topic in their responses (McDaniel et al. 1996).

A richer form of chat comes in what is called MUDs (derived from Multi-User Dungeons and Dragons, an early multiparty game). MUDs include rapid interchange of conversation interlaced with descriptions of virtual places, objects, and emotions. For example, one can enter a contribution about an action or the state of one's emotion ("Gary enters the room." "Judy smiles.") Also, objects play in the interchange, often having "magical" properties, awarding the recipient with various powers or gifts. There have been examples of MUDs in work settings, such as Waterfall Glen at the Argonne National Lab (Churchill & Bly 1999). Turkle (1995) looked at a number of psychosocial aspects of MUDs, focusing in particular on identity.

Awareness

When people are collocated, they have numerous opportunities to assess whether teammates are available for conversation, what they are working on, etc. Simple glances into people's offices while walking to the printer give a lot of information about their state. People working remotely have no natural source of such information. Various technology solutions have been offered: Video glances into offices (Fish et al. 1993, Bellotti & Dourish 1997) and periodic snapshots instead of full-motion video (Dourish & Bly 1992) were offered at some work settings. However, because many felt these to be more invasive of their privacy than simple walk-bys at the office, these systems have not been widely adopted. The places where these systems succeed are those where the individuals seem to have a reciprocal need to be aware of each other's presence, and they have a sense of cooperation and coordination. Instant messaging systems, on the other hand, seem to be more widely accepted because they allow the users to control what information they are broadcasting to others, and the signal is much less informative about exactly what they are doing. Nardi and her colleagues (2000) found that people liked this aspect of instant messaging. In all of these monitoring applications, awareness and calendaring alike, the issues of trust and privacy loom large (see Godefroid et al. 2000).

Group Calendars

Remote team members work asynchronously with e-mail and attachments and synchronously using chat or video/audio conferencing and shared workspaces. The major technologies to support the transitions from one mode to the other are electronic calendars. In group calendars, participants keep their schedules online in a place that is accessible (for read/write or just read permission) to others they designate. By seeing each other's calendars, it is easier to find times to meet that fit most people's schedules. As such, it is a classic case of misaligned motives: One has to make the effort to enter one's calendar so others may benefit by scheduling one's time (Grudin 1988). Indeed, group calendars were not widely adopted when they first came out. However, with time people have seen how giving to the common good benefits them individually as well, and group calendars are more widely adopted today (Grudin & Palen 1995, Mosier & Tammaro 1997, Palen & Grudin 2002). Apparently such success builds on a culture of sharing and accessibility, something that exists in some organizations and not others (Ehrlich 1987, Lange 1992).

Repositories of Shared Knowledge

In most organizations people share their reports, meeting minutes, customer contacts, etc. in order to coordinate their activities. Modern applications such as Lotus Notes help people to do this in the digital world. People are encouraged to share informal information as well as the more structured formal material, such as new ideas or thoughts, boilerplate for reports, proposal drafts, etc. Unfortunately, these systems are not always successful in gathering shared information. Often, like the case with calendaring, the person who expends the effort to enter information is not always the one that benefits from it. Motivations are misaligned. In fact, in one large consulting firm, the sharing failed outright because the incentive scheme rewarded individual prowess, not group productivity (Orlikowski & Gash 1994).

In organizations in which such a repository has been successful, the incentives were better aligned.

The Web of course provides marvelous infrastructure for the creation and sharing of information repositories. Lotus Notes is now widely used in its Web version, Domino. Environments for sharing such as Worktools (worktools.si.umich.edu) are built on top of Notes. Document management tools such as WebEx (www.webex.com) make it easy to share in a web environment. Systematic research on the use of such improved tools is needed.

Social Filtering

In addition to more-formal sources of information, people use their colleagues for advice and recommendations. One's social network is a rich source of information; the only barrier is finding out who knows what and then asking and receiving an answer. Technological substitutes for this have resulted in "recommender systems." When booksellers such as Amazon recommend books to us, they are using a system that matches one's interests (indicated by previous purchases) with others who have similar purchase profiles. Items the second customer has purchased are then recommended to the first. There is no content analysis here, merely statistical analysis of like people and storage of purchases. A 1997 issue of the *Communications of the Association for Computing Machinery* described and evaluated various systems (Resnick & Varian 1997). The systems that were more acceptable to users were those that explained the choices, not merely listed them (Herlocker et al. 2000). This is an example of the role that trust plays in electronic commerce interactions, a point we discuss next.

Trust of People Via the Technology

It has been said that "trust needs touch" (Handy 1995), and indeed in survey studies, co-workers report that they trust those who are collocated more than those who are remote (Rocco et al. 2000). Those who spend more time discussing nonwork topics with each other, especially on the telephone, trusted their remote colleagues more than those who merely conveyed work-related material by fax and e-mail. However, mere use of the telephone is not the answer. If the only contact people have with each other is over the telephone, they behave in less trusting ways than if they meet face-to-face (Drolet & Morris 2000).

Are there any remedies to this loss of trust over distance? Conventional wisdom says that people should meet face-to-face before conducting work, a result that has been confirmed empirically (Rocco 1998). Zheng et al. (2002) found that it was not necessary to meet beforehand, if instead they communicated about social and personal issues using chat. Exchanging photographs was also effective in increasing trust, whereas merely sharing a resume did not. Bos et al. (2002) reported that richer communication channels such as video and audio facilitated trust formation. Before we get too optimistic about these remedies, however, we should be cautious. Conversation through video is not like "being there." There is no opportunity for the incoming and departure conversations, one has less common ground because the culture and setting of the far location is intrinsically different, and technology can distort how people appear to each other, either too quiet, too tall, or even ill looking (Huang et al. 2002). There is a rich opportunity to study impression formation in these technology-altered settings.

Collaboratories

A collaboratory is a laboratory without walls (Finholt & Olson 1997), and as such is a novel organizational form of considerable interest. From a National Research Council report, a collaboratory is supposed to allow ". . . the nation's researchers [to] perform their research without regard to geographical location—interacting with colleagues, accessing instrumentation, sharing data and computational resources [and] accessing information in digital libraries" (National Research Council 1993, p. 7). Starting in the early 1990s these capabilities have been configured into support packages for a number of specific sciences (see review in Finholt 2002). For example, the Upper Atmospheric Research Collaboratory (Olson et al. 2001) provided space scientists with access to geographically remote instruments as well as each other through a simple chat facility. This allowed scientists from all over the world to participate in collaborative studies using these remote instruments from their home institutions.

A number of companies have also experimented with similar concepts, calling them "virtual collocation." The goal is to support geographically dispersed teams as they carry out product design, software engineering, financial reporting, and almost any business function. In these cases suites of off-the-shelf groupware tools have been particularly important and have been used to support round-the-clock software development among overlapping teams of engineers in time zones around the world (Carmel 1999). There have been a number of such efforts, and it is still unclear as to their success or what features make their success more likely (Olson & Olson 2000).

Collaboratories are of interest to psychologists for two broad classes of reasons. First, as an emerging organizational form, they provide an example of a novel way of organizing in which the usual factors such as communication flows, trust, establishment of common goals, and motivation can be investigated. Second, of course, they provide a new infrastructure for the conduct of psychological research itself. Early collaboratory efforts have been concentrated in the physical and biological sciences, but the concept should be readily used by social scientists as well.

THE LARGER SOCIAL CONTEXT

Computers are rapidly becoming an ordinary aspect of most people's lives. In September of 2001 (U.S. Dep. Commerce 2002), 56.5% of U.S. households had at least one computer, and 50.5% had Internet access. Sixty-seven percent of individuals (as opposed to households) used a computer at home, school, or work. Thus, for at least two-thirds of the U.S. population a computer has become a regular part of their daily lives.

What are the broader psychological effects of computer use? Kraut et al. (1998) reported that greater Internet use, which in their sample was mostly e-mail, led to declines in social interactions with family members and an increase in depression and loneliness. Not surprising, these results triggered widespread discussion and debate, both over the substance of the results and the methods used to obtain them. Recently, Kraut et al. (2002) reported new results that suggest these initial effects may not persist. Interpersonal communication is one of the principal uses of the Internet, and the possible implications of this kind of communication for social life is important to understand. Indeed, Putnam (2000) has wondered whether the Internet can be a source of social cohesiveness. These kinds of questions need to be addressed by additional large-scale studies of the kind carried out by Kraut and his colleagues.

Another concern is the unequal distribution of computing resources. Disaggregating the overall figures on computer and Internet access by income, by ethnic origin, and by presence of disabilities shows clearly that routine computer access is predominantly a characteristic of urban upper-middle-class white families without disabilities. To take just one example, in 2001 Internet use by whites and Asian Americans was around 60%, whereas for blacks it was 40% and for Hispanics 32% (U.S. Dep. Commerce 2002). The growth of access by minorities is encouraging, but they still lag far behind their majority peers. What are the psychological and social costs of this digital divide? We do not yet have clear answers.

SUMMARY AND CONCLUSIONS

As computing technology penetrates our workplaces, homes, schools, community organizations, automobiles, and aircraft, literally every element of our daily lives, having technology that is useful and usable is of paramount importance. Thus, the field of HCI is at the center of the evolution of effective tools to improve the quality of our lives. As the work by Kraut et al. (1998) hints, we should not naively assume that useful and usable technology is going to lead to positive social consequences. As Sproull & Kiesler (1991) pointed out, we tend to design and deploy technology hoping for immediate efficiency gains but ignoring the longer-term, second-order effects that may be more profound and may be undesirable. In the early days of television the optimists talked of civic enlightenment, widespread education, and wholesome entertainment. Few foresaw that it would actually erode social capital, leading to less civic participation, less involvement with family, higher crime rates, and declines in health (Putnam 2000). As psychologists we need to focus on both the immediate issues of design and effectiveness and the longer-term consequences for individual and social behavior.

ACKNOWLEDGMENTS

Preparation of this chapter was facilitated by several grants from the National Science Foundation (ATM-9873025, IIS-9977923, IIS-0085951). Dan Horn made useful comments on an earlier draft.

The *Annual Review of Psychology* is online at http://psych.annualreviews.org

LITERATURE CITED

Anderson RH, Bikson TK, Law SA, Mitchell BM. 1995. *Universal Access to E-mail: Feasibility and Societal Implications.* Santa Monica, CA: Rand

Arrow H, Berdahl JL, Bouas KS, Craig KM, Cummings A, et al. 1996. Time, technology, and groups: an integration. *Comput. Support. Coop. Work* 4:253–61

Barfield W, Furness TA, eds. 1997. *Virtual Environments and Advanced Interface Design.* New York: Oxford Univ. Press

Bellotti V, Dourish P. 1997. Rant and RAVE: experimental and experiential accounts of a media space. In *Video-Mediated Communication*, ed. KE Finn, AJ Sellen, SB Wilbur, pp. 245–72. Mahwah, NJ: Erlbaum

Benford S, Greenhalgh C, Reynard G, Brown C, Koleva B. 1998. Understanding and constructing shared spaces with mixed-reality boundaries. *ACM Trans. Comput.-Hum. Interact.* 5:185–223

Beyer H, Holtzblatt K. 1998. *Contextual Design: Defining Customer-Centered Systems.* San Francisco: Kaufmann

Bhavnani S, Drabenstott K, Radev D. 2001. *Towards a unified framework of IR tasks and strategies.* Presented at 2001 ASIST Annu. Meet., Washington, DC

Bos N, Olson J, Gergle D, Olson G, Wright Z. 2002. Effects of four computer-mediated communications channels on trust development. In *Proc. CHI (Comput. Hum. Interact.) 2002*, pp. 135–40. New York: ACM Press

Brynjolfsson E, Hitt LM. 1998. Beyond the productivity paradox. *Commun. ACM* 41(8):49–55

Card SK, Moran TP, Newell A. 1983. *The Psychology of Human-Computer Interaction.* Hillsdale, NJ: Erlbaum

Carmel E. 1999. *Global Software Teams.* Upper Saddle River, NJ: Prentice-Hall

Carroll JM. 1997. Human-computer interaction: psychology as a science of design. *Annu. Rev. Psychol.* 48:61–83

Carroll JM, Rosson MB. 1992. Getting around the task-artifact cycle: how to make claims and design by scenario. *ACM Trans. Inf. Syst.* 10:181–212

Churchill E, Bly S. 1999. It's all in the words: supporting work activities with lightweight tools. In *Proc. GROUP 1999*, pp. 40–49. New York: ACM Press

Clark HH, Brennan SE. 1991. Grounding in communication. In *Perspectives on Socially Shared Cognition*, ed. L Resnick, JM Levine, SD Teasley, pp 127–49. Washington, DC: APA

Cruz-Neira C, Sandin D, DeFanti T, Kenyon R, Hart J. 1992. The CAVE: audio visual experience automatic virtual environment. *Commun. Assoc. Comput. Mach.* 35(6):65–72

Czerwinski M, Dumais S, Robertson G, Sziadosz S, Tiernan S, van Dantzich M. 1999. Visualizing implicit queries for information management and retrieval. In *Proc. CHI (Comput. Hum. Interact.) 1999*, pp. 560–67. New York: ACM Press

del Galdo E, Nielsen J, eds. 1996. *International User Interfaces.* New York: Wiley

Dourish P, Bly S. 1992. Portholes: supporting awareness in a distributed work group. In *Proc. CHI (Comput. Hum. Interact.) 1992*, pp. 541–47. New York: ACM Press

Drolet AL, Morris MW. 2000. Rapport in conflict resolution: accounting for how nonverbal exchange fosters coordination on mutually beneficial settlements to mixed motive conflicts. *J. Exp. Soc. Psychol.* 36:26–50

Druin A, Solomon C. 1996. *Designing Multimedia Environments for Children.* New York: Wiley

Ehrlich SF. 1987. Strategies for encouraging successful adoption of office communication systems. *ACM Trans. Off. Inf. Syst.* 5:340–57

Elrod S, Bruce R, Gold R, Goldberg D, Halasz F, et al. 1992. LiveBoard: a large interactive display supporting group meetings, presentations, and remote collaboration. In *Proc. CHI*

(Comput. Hum. Interact.) 1992, pp. 599–607. New York: ACM Press

Ericcson KA, Charness N. 1994. Expert performance: its structure and acquisition. *Am. Psychol.* 49:725–47

Erickson T, Smith DN, Kellogg WA, Laff MR, Richards JT, Bradner E. 1999. Socially translucent systems: social proxies, persistent conversation, and the design of 'babble'. In *Proc. CHI (Comput. Hum. Interact.) 1999*, pp. 72–79. New York: ACM Press

Finholt TA. 2002. Collaboratories. In *Annual Review of Information Science and Technology*, ed. B Cronin, 36:73–108. Medford, NJ: Inf. Today, Inc.

Finholt TA, Olson GM. 1997. From laboratories to collaboratories: a new organizational form for scientific collaboration. *Psychol. Sci.* 8:28–36

Finholt T, Sproull L, Kiesler S. 1990. Communication and performance in ad hoc task groups. *Intellectual Teamwork: Social and Technological Foundations of Cooperative Work*, ed. J Galegher, R Kraut, C Egido, pp. 291–325. Hillsdale, NJ: Erlbaum

Finn K, Sellen A, Wilbur S, eds. 1997. *Video-Mediated Communication.* Hillsdale, NJ: Erlbaum

Fish RS, Kraut RE, Root RW, Rice RE. 1993. Video as a technology for informal communication. *Commun. ACM* 36(1):48–61

Garton L, Wellman B. 1995. Social impacts of electronic mail in organizations: a review of the research literature. In *Communication Yearbook*, ed. BR Burleson, 18:434–53 Thousand Oaks, CA: Sage

Godefroid P, Herbsleb JD, Jagadeesan LJ, Li D. 2000. Ensuring privacy in presence awareness systems: an automated verification approach. In *Proc. Comput.-Support. Coop. Work 2000*, pp. 59–68. New York: ACM Press

Gray WD, John BE, Atwood ME. 1993. Project Ernestine: validating a GOMS analysis for predicting and explaining real-world task performance. *Hum.-Comput. Interact.* 8:237–309

Gray WD, Salzman MC. 1998. Damaged merchandise? A review of experiments that compare usability evaluation methods. *Hum.-Comput. Interact.* 13:203–61

Grudin J. 1988. Why CSCW applications fail: problems in the design and evaluation of organizational interfaces. In *Proc. Comput.-Support. Coop. Work 1988*, pp. 85–93. New York: ACM Press

Grudin J. 1994. Groupware and social dynamics: eight challenges for developers. *Commun. ACM* 37(1):92–105

Grudin J, Palen L. 1995. Why groupware succeeds: discretion or mandate? In *Proc. Eur. Conf. Comput. Support. Work '95*, pp. 263–78. Dordrecht, The Netherlands: Kluwer

Handy C. 1995. Trust and the virtual organization. *Harv. Bus. Rev.* 73(3):40–50

Herlocker JL, Konstan JA, Riedl J. 2000. Explaining collaborative filtering recommendations. In *Proc. Comput.-Support. Coop. Work 2000*, pp. 241–50. New York: ACM Press

Hindmarsh J, Fraser M, Heath C, Benford S, Greenhalgh C. 1998. Fragmented interaction: establishing mutual orientation in virtual environments. In *Proc. Comput.-Support. Coop. Work 1998*, pp. 217–26. New York: ACM Press

Hollingshead AB, McGrath JE, O'Connor KM. 1993. Group performance and communication technology: a longitudinal study of computer-mediated versus face-to-face work. *Small Group Res.* 24:307–33

Horn D. 2001. Is seeing believing? Detect deception in technologically mediated communication. In *Proc. CHI (Comput. Hum. Interact.) 2001*, pp. 297–98. New York: ACM Press

Horstman-Koester H, Levine S. 1994. Learning and performance of able-bodied individuals using scanning systems with and without word prediction. *Assist. Technol.* 6:42–53

Huang W, Olson JS, Olson GM. 2002. Proximity and camera angle in video-mediated communication. In *Proc. CHI (Comput. Hum. Interact.) 2002*. New York: ACM Press

Hutchins E. 1995. How a cockpit remembers its speed. *Cogn. Sci.* 19:265–88

Jeffries R, Miller JR, Wharton C, Uyeda KM.

1991. User interface evaluation in the real world: a comparison of four techniques. In *Proc. CHI (Comput. Hum. Interact.) 1991*, pp. 119–24. New York: ACM Press

John BE. 1995. Why GOMS? *Interactions* 11(4):80–89

John BE, Kieras DE. 1996. Using GOMS for user interface design and evaluation: which technique? *ACM Trans. Comput.-Hum. Interact.* 3:320–51

John BE, Newell A. 1989. Cumulating the science of HCI: from S-R compatibility to transcription typing. In *Proc. CHI (Comput. Hum. Interact.) 1989*, pp. 109–14. New York: ACM Press

Johnson J, Roberts TL, Verplank W, Smith DC, Irby CH, et al. 1989. The Xerox Star: a retrospective. *IEEE Comput.* 22(9):11–29

Karat CM, Campbell R, Fiegel T. 1992. Comparison of empirical testing and walkthrough methods in user interface evaluation. In *Proc. ACM CHI (Comput. Hum. Interact.) 1992 Conf. Hum. Factors Comput. Syst.*, pp. 397–404. New York: ACM Press

Kieras DE, Meyer DE. 1997. A computational theory of executive control processes and human multiple-task performance. Part I. Basic mechanisms. *Psychol. Rev.* 104:3–65

Kraemer KL, Pinsonneault A. 1990. Technology and groups: assessments of empirical research. In *Intellectual Teamwork: Social and Technological Foundations of Cooperative Work*, ed. J Galegher, R Kraut, C Egido, pp. 373–405. Hillsdale, NJ: Erlbaum

Kraut R, Kiesler S, Boneva B, Cummings J, Helgeson V, Crawford A. 2002. Internet paradox revisited. *J. Soc. Issues* 58:49–74

Kraut R, Patterson M, Lundmark V, Kiesler S, Mukopadhyay T, Scherlis W. 1998. Internet paradox: a social technology that reduces social involvement and psychological well-being. *Am. Psychol.* 53:1017–31

Kuegler T. 2000. *Make Your Site a Better Information Delivery Tool.* http://www.clickz.com/design/site_design/article.php/822901

Laird J. 2002. *SOAR Home Page.* http://ai.eecs.umich.edu/soar/

Landauer TK. 1995. *The Trouble with Computers: Usefulness, Usability, and Productivity.* Cambridge, MA: MIT Press

Lange BM. 1992. Electronic group calendaring: experiences and expectations. In *Groupware*, ed. D Coleman, pp. 428–32. San Mateo, CA: Kaufmann

Lerch FJ, Mantei M, Olson JR. 1989. Skilled financial planning: the cost of translating ideas into action. In *Proc. CHI (Comput. Hum. Interact.) 1989*, pp. 121–26. New York: ACM Press

Lewis C, Polson PG, Wharton C, Rieman J. 1990. Testing a walkthrough methodology for theory-based design of walk-up-and-use interfaces. In *Proc. CHI (Comput. Hum. Interact.) 1990*, pp. 235–42. New York: ACM Press

Lohse G. 1991. A cognitive model for the perception and understanding of graphs. In *Proc. CHI (Comput. Hum. Interact.) 1991*, pp. 137–44. New York: ACM Press

Malone TW, Grant KR, Lai KY, Rao R, Rosenblitt DA. 1988. The information lens: an intelligent system for information sharing and coordination. In *Technological Support for Work Group Collaboration*, ed. MH Olson, pp. 65–88. Hillsdale, NJ: Erlbaum

McDaniel SE, Olson GM, Magee JS. 1996. Identifying and analyzing multiple threads in computer-mediated and face-to-face conversations. In *Proc. Comput.-Support. Coop. Work 1996*, pp. 39–47. New York: ACM Press

McLeod PL. 1992. An assessment of the experimental literature on electronic support of group work: results of a meta-analysis. *Hum.-Comput. Interact.* 7:257–80

Milewski AE, Smith TM. 2000. Providing presence cues to telephone users. In *Proc. Comput.-Support. Coop. Work 2000*, pp. 89–96. New York: ACM Press

Moran TP, Chiu P, Harrison S, Kurtenbach G, Minneman S, van Melle W. 1996. Evolutionary engagement in an ongoing collaborative work process: a case study. In *Proc. Comput.-Support. Coop. Work 1996*, pp. 150–59. New York: ACM Press

Moran TP, Chiu P, van Melle W. 1997. Pen-based interaction techniques for organizing material on an electronic whiteboard picking and pointing. In *Proc. User Interface Softw. Technol. 1997*, pp. 45–54. New York: ACM Press

Mosier JN, Tammaro SG. 1997. When are group scheduling tools useful? *Comput. Support. Coop. Work* 6:53–70

Muller MJ. 1991. PICTIVE: an exploration in participatory design. In *Proc. CHI 1991*, pp. 225–31. New York: ACM Press

Mynatt ED, Edwards WK, LaMarca A, Igarashi T. 1999. Flatland: new dimensions in office whiteboards: profiles, notes, and surfaces. In *Proc. CHI 1999*, pp. 346–53. New York: ACM Press

Nardi BA, Whittaker S, Bradner E. 2000. Interaction and outeraction: Instant messaging in action. In *Proc. Comput.-Support. Coop. Work 2000*, pp. 79–88. New York: ACM Press

National Research Council. 1993. *National Collaboratories: Applying Information Technology for Scientific Research*. Washington, DC: Natl. Acad. Press

Newell A, Simon HA. 1972. *Human Problem Solving*. Englewood Cliffs, NJ: Prentice Hall

Nielsen J. 1993. *Usability Engineering*. Boston, MA: Academic

Nilsen E, Jong HS, Olson JS, Biolsi K, Rueter H, Mutter S. 1993. The growth of software skill: a longitudinal look at learning and performance. In *Proc. CHI 1993*, pp. 149–56. New York: ACM Press

Nunamaker JF, Dennis AR, Valacich JS, Vogel DR, George JF. 1991. Electronic meeting systems to support group work. *Commun. ACM* 34(7):40–61

O'Hara-Devereaux M, Johansen R. 1994. *Global Work: Bridging Distance, Culture & Time*. San Francisco: Jossey-Bass

Olson GM. 1994. Situated cognition. In *Encyclopedia of Intelligence*, ed. RE Sternberg, pp. 971–73. New York: Macmillan

Olson GM, Atkins D, Clauer R, Weymouth T, Prakash A, et al. 2001. Technology to support distributed team science: the first phase of the Upper Atmospheric Research Collaboratory (UARC). In *Coordination Theory and Collaboration Technology*, ed. GM Olson, T Malone, J Smith, pp. 761–83. Hillsdale, NJ: Erlbaum

Olson GM, Moran T. 1998. Special issue: experimental comparisons of usability evaluation methods. *Hum.-Comput. Interact.* 13(3):whole issue

Olson GM, Olson JS. 2000. Distance matters. *Hum.-Comput. Interact.* 15:139–79

Olson GM, Olson JS. 2002. Groupware and computer supported cooperative work. In *Handbook of Human-Computer Interaction*, ed. JJ Jacko, A Sears. Mahwah, NJ: Erlbaum. In press

Olson JR, Olson GM. 1990. The growth of cognitive modeling in human-computer interaction since GOMS. *Hum.-Comput. Interact.* 5:221–65

Olson JS. 2001. *What's going on out there: what major companies are doing about user experience and why*. Presented at 2001 Meet. Hum. Comput. Interact. Consortium, Winter Park, CO. Univ. Michigan: CREW Tech. Rep.

Olson JS, Moran T. 1996. Mapping the method muddle: guidance in using methods for user interface design. In *Human-Computer Interface Design: Success Cases, Emerging Methods, and Real World Contexts*, ed. M Rudisill, C Lewis, PB Polson, T McKay, pp. 269–302. New York: Kaufman

Olson JS, Olson GM, Meader DK. 1995. What mix of video and audio is useful for remote real-time work? In *Proc. CHI (Comput. Hum. Interact.) 1995*, pp. 362–68. New York: ACM Press

Olson JS, Olson GM, Storrøsten M, Carter M. 1993. Group work close up: a comparison of the group design process with and without a simple group editor. *ACM Trans. Inf. Syst.* 11:321–48

Orlikowski WJ, Gash DC. 1994. Technological frames: making sense of information technology in organizations. *ACM Trans. Inf. Syst.* 12:174–207

Palen L, Grudin J. 2002. Discretionary adoption of group support software. In *Organizational Implementation of Collaboration Technology*, ed. BE Munkvold. In press

Park KS, Kapoor A, Leigh J. 2000 Lessons learned from employing multiple perspective in a collaborative virtual environment for visualizing scientific data. In *Proc. Collab. Virtual Environ. 2000*, pp. 73–82. New York: ACM Press

Pirolli P, Card SK. 1999. Information foraging. *Psychol. Rev.* 106:643–75

Prytulak L. 1971. Natural language mediation. *Cogn. Psychol.* 2:1–56

Putnam RD. 2000. *Bowling Alone: The Collapse and Revival of American Community.* New York: Simon & Schuster

Resnick P, Varian HR, eds. 1997. Special section: recommender systems. *Commun. ACM* 40(3):56–89

Rocco E. 1998. Trust breaks down in electronic contexts but can be repaired by some initial face-to-face contact. In *Proc. CHI (Comput. Hum. Interact.) 1998*, pp. 496–502. New York: ACM Press

Rocco E, Finholt T, Hofer EC, Herbsleb J. 2000. *Designing as if trust mattered. CREW Tech. Rep.*, Univ. Mich., Ann Arbor

Rosenfeld L, Morville P. 1998. *Information Architecture for the World Wide Web.* Sebastopol. CA: O'Reilly

Rubin J. 1994 *Handbook of Usability Testing.* New York: Wiley

Satzinger J, Olfman L. 1992. A research program to assess user perceptions of group work support. In *Proc. CHI (Comput. Hum. Interact.) 1992*, pp. 99–106. New York: ACM Press

Singhal S. 1999. *Networked Virtual Environments: Design and Implementation.* New York: Addison-Wesley

Sproull L, Kiesler S. 1991. *Connections: New Ways of Working in the Networked Organization.* Cambridge, MA: MIT Press

Stokes DE. 1997. *Pasteur's Quadrant: Basic Science and Technological Innovation.* Washington, DC: Brookings Inst. Press

Strassmann PA. 1990. *The Business Value of Computers.* New Canaan, CT: Inf. Econ. Press

Turkle S. 1995. *Life on the Screen: Identity in the Age of the Internet.* New York: Simon & Schuster

US Dep. Commerce. 2002. *A nation online: how Americans are expanding their use of the Internet.* http://www.ntia.doc.gov/ntiahome/dn/anationonline2.pdf

Veinott E, Olson JS, Olson GM, Fu X. 1999. Video helps remote work: speakers who need to negotiate common ground benefit from seeing each other. In *Proc. CHI (Comput. Hum. Interact.) 1999*, pp. 302–9. New York: ACM Press

Weiser M. 1991. The computer for the twenty-first century. *Sci. Am.* 265(3):94–104

Whittaker S, Sidner C. 1996. Email overload: exploring personal information management of email. In *Proc. CHI (Comput. Hum. Interact.) 1996*, pp. 276–83. New York: ACM Press

Winograd T. 1988. A language/action perspective on the design of cooperative work. *Hum.-Comput. Interact.* 3:3–30

Zheng J, Veinott E, Bos N, Olson JS, Olson GM. 2002. Trust without touch: jumpstarting long-distance trust with initial social activities. In *Proc. CHI (Comput. Hum. Interact.) 2002* . New York: ACM Press

Annu. Rev. Psychol. 2003. 54:517–45
doi: 10.1146/annurev.psych.54.111301.145442
Copyright © 2003 by Annual Reviews. All rights reserved
First published online as a Review in Advance on August 27, 2002

THE EARLY EDUCATION OF SOCIOECONOMICALLY DISADVANTAGED CHILDREN

David H. Arnold and Greta L. Doctoroff

*Psychology Department, University of Massachusetts, Amherst, Massachusetts 01003;
e-mail: darnold@psych.umass.edu, greta@psych.umass.edu*

Key Words   education, poverty, preschool, mental health, resiliency

■ **Abstract**   This chapter reviews selected research on the education of low-socioeconomic status (SES) children from birth through the first years of elementary school. Themes include the importance of early academic skills and interest to later achievement; the benefits of integrating knowledge from research on mental health and other areas; the need to utilize and build children's strengths as well as address their weaknesses; and a call to connect research to practice and policy. Relevant research on race and culture is reviewed because ethnic minority low-SES children are at great risk of poverty. Gender is discussed because low-SES boys have poorer general achievement than girls, while very few low-SES girls pursue careers in math- and science-related fields.

CONTENTS

INTRODUCTION

Child poverty has reached epidemic proportions within the United States. Of the 35.6 million people living in poverty in 1997, 14.1 million were children (U.S. Bureau of the Census 1998). One third of American children spend at least one year below the poverty line, and 18% experience extreme poverty (Rank & Hirschl 1999). Younger children are more likely to face poverty (Bronfenbrenner 1996), and its impact may be strongest during children's earliest years (Bradley et al. 2001, Duncan et al. 1998). Among poverty's effects is a devastating negative influence on academic achievement; the relation between socioeconomic status (SES) and underachievement is most dramatic near and below the poverty line (Brooks-Gunn & Duncan 1997, Duncan et al. 1998). Major discrepancies in educational achievement as a function of SES have been well documented since the Coleman report of 1966. For example, only 19% of children from families receiving public assistance have requisite preliteracy skills at kindergarten entry [National Center for Education Statistics (NCES) 2000]. Of fourth-graders eligible for lunch subsidies, only 2% scored as advanced readers and 12% as proficient readers on the National Assessment of Educational Progress (2000) evaluation.

Numerous factors contribute to the relation between SES and educational outcomes, including birth weight, nutrition, housing quality, and access to health care (Bradley & Corwyn 2002). Such factors may, for example, have repercussions on child cognitive functioning or parenting, and in turn, educational achievement [Bolger et al. 1995, Brody et al. 1999, McLoyd 1990, McLoyd 1998, National Research Council (NRC) 2000]. Poor educational attainment is a major cause of poverty, and poverty is a key influence on academic failure. So perhaps it should not be surprising that poverty tends to be chronic, or that poor achievement has massive costs to individuals and society. While children likely require extra educational resources to counteract poverty, schools serving low-SES children receive much lower public funding than schools serving higher-SES children. Only a few states have moved towards funding equity, and even if each state funded schools equally, large between-state discrepancies work against poor children (Grissmer & Flanagan 2002). Thus federal resources and poverty reduction may be necessary to close the SES achievement gap. In addition to more resources, recent strides in knowledge could help improve educational policy.

This chapter reviews selected research on the education of socioeconomically disadvantaged children from birth through the first years of elementary school.

Of course many low-SES children succeed in school, and similar factors are important to the education of all children (NRC 1998). Nonetheless, the high rates of failure among low-SES children warrant specific attention. A major advance in the study of economic disadvantage is increased sophistication in understanding and measuring poverty and SES (Bradley & Corwyn 2002). SES may be a control variable, mediator, moderator, or independent variable, depending on the question of study. SES is fluid and multidimensional; neighborhood SES is relevant as well as individual SES; and the nature, timing, and persistence of poverty matters (Bolger et al. 1995, Brooks-Gunn & Duncan 1997, Duncan et al. 1994). These issues are not the focus of this chapter, but it will be crucial to continue to examine how SES is conceptualized and measured. For simplicity, we use the term SES to refer to the wide range of economic and educational variables, but we recognize the importance of finer distinctions.

Themes of our review include the importance of early academic skills and interest; the benefits of integrating knowledge from mental health and other research disciplines; the need to utilize and build children's strengths as well as address their weaknesses; and a call to connect research to practice and policy. Relevant research on race and culture is included because ethnic minority children are at great risk of poverty. For example, 68% of black children compared to 26% of white children experience poverty (Rank & Hirschl 1999). Gender is also discussed because low-SES boys have poorer general achievement than girls, and on the other hand, very few low-SES girls pursue careers in math- and science-related fields (National Science Foundation 2001).

INTEGRATION OF A POLARIZED FIELD

Basic Skills Versus Meaning-Centered Approaches

One critical recent advance in early education research is reconciliation between two traditionally opposing approaches. Historically, most researchers and educators supported either direct basic skill instruction (e.g., phonics) or meaning-focused instruction (e.g., whole-language). The division between these approaches has cut across education, with the most salient rift in the field of early literacy between those advocating direct phonics instruction and those favoring child-centered or whole-language literacy teaching. However, these approaches are not inconsistent: Directly teaching basic skills within the context of meaningful, interesting experiences is, in fact, essential to educational success.

Basic Skills

In Chall's major review, *Learning to Read: The Great Debate* (1967), she concluded that direct phonics instruction is critical to the development of reading skills. Later, Adams (1990) summarized, with greater methodological rigor, irrefutable research that early core skills influence academic success, and confirmed that direct instruction in phonics facilitates literacy development. Recent reviews from NRC (1998), the National Reading Panel (1999), and others have solidified this conclusion. Results are robust across samples, measures, and research designs (including experiments), providing clear convergent evidence that early deficiencies in core skills impede academic progress. As part of a gradual evolution from nonreader to reader, academically successful children build basic skills prior to formal schooling. The term "emergent literacy" refers to this process of gradually becoming literate, and recent research has provided tremendous clarification of this process (NRC 2001, Senechal et al. 2001, Scarborough et al. 1991, Sulzby & Teale 1991, Whitehurst & Lonigan 1998). The following are among the key early precursors of literacy and academic success: language skills, phonological and syntactic knowledge, letter identification, and conceptual knowledge about print and its conventions and functions. The importance of these early skills can hardly be overstated; for example, Stevenson & Newman (1986) found that the number of letters known at kindergarten entry correlated .52 with reading achievement in high school. The research clearly shows that incidental instruction on basic literacy skills, while surely beneficial, is not sufficient.

Unfortunately, SES differences in these literacy skills emerge very early. Low-SES children enter school, on average, with skills dramatically below their higher-SES peers (Bryant et al. 1994, Stipek & Ryan 1997), and they tend to remain behind. For example, in a recent NCES survey (2000), only 38% of children whose mothers had the least education entered kindergarten able to recognize letters, compared to 86% of children with the most highly educated mothers.

Early education research has focused most prominently on literacy, but the growing early math literature mirrors the literacy field. Poor math trajectories in low-SES children begin very early. Young children's emergent math development appears critical to achievement, and SES differences in these skills can be discerned early (Jordan et al. 1992, Kurdek & Sinclair 2001, Stevenson & Newman 1986). The developing math skills of preschoolers are now better understood, and include informal numerical thinking, quantity comparison, operational addition, and one-to-one correspondence (NRC 2001). Very few low-SES children go on to pursue well-paying careers in math and technology (National Science Foundation 2001), a factor that contributes to chronic poverty. In sum, SES is a powerful predictor of children's academic trajectories, and the influence of SES on children's academic skills begins very early.

Meaning and Interest: Critical for School Success

Children's academic interest is also an important influence on achievement (Eccles & Wigfield 2002, Frijters et al. 2000, Skinner et al. 1990). By "interest," we refer to the cluster of variables that includes interest, motivation, engagement, goals, values, and self-efficacy. These constructs are not identical, and discussing them as a unitary construct does a disservice to the excellent research that has helped untangle their details and mechanisms (Covington 2000, Eccles & Wigfield 2002). Nonetheless, work in these areas converges in demonstrating that interest in all its forms is critical to academic success. The relation between interest and skills begins early in development (Chapman et al. 2000). For example, picture book interest in children as young as 20 months predicts later literacy achievement (Crain-Thoreson & Dale 1992).

Although SES differences in interest emerge at an early age, they are not present as early as skill differences. Before kindergarten, low-SES children show self-confidence and positive school attitudes comparable to higher-SES children (Alexander & Entwisle 1988, Stipek & Ryan 1997), but they are more likely to lose interest within the first years of school (Stipek & Tannatt 1984, Wigfield et al. 1997). Over time, children's competence beliefs and education valuing both decrease and become more stable (Wigfield et al. 1997), indicating the importance of early intervention. Multiple forces work together to decrease interest, including children's increasing recognition that their skills are deficient. Dweck's seminal body of work (e.g., Smiley & Dweck 1994) shows that attitudes about failure and responses to frustration play a key role in sustaining motivation. Although this work has not yet been directly applied to low-SES children, failure experiences seem likely to play an important role in interest trajectories. Other factors likely to exacerbate this problem for low-SES children include teachers' negative stereotypes of children and decreased expectations; parents' attitudes, values, and expectations; and, especially as children get older, peer influences (Ogbu 1978, Steinberg et al. 1992). Furthermore, early motivation is decreased in classrooms that do not incorporate developmentally appropriate practices (Stipek et al. 1995).

Cycles of Failure and Disinterst

Taken together, this research suggests a model of reciprocal influence of skills and interest (Reynolds 1989). For example, reading interest predicts amount of future reading, even controlling for previous reading (Stanovich 1986, Wigfield & Guthrie 1997), and amount of reading predicts future reading skills, even controlling for previous test results (Stanovich & Cunningham 1992). Children who struggle with reading dislike reading (Juel 1988), and children who read less fall further behind. Similar patterns occur in math (Reynolds 1989, Stipek & Ryan 1997). For example, math skills in kindergarten predict math interest in high school (Stevenson & Newman 1986). Teachers may inadvertently exacerbate this cycle by withdrawing their support and involvement when it is most needed (Arnold 1997, Skinner & Belmont 1993). This reciprocal model is directly supported by empirical data; for example, Reynolds (1991) found that academic skills at kindergarten entry influenced grade school academic achievement directly and also indirectly through motivation effects. The relation between interest and achievement appears to start very early, to grow stronger with time (Reynolds 1989, Wigfield et al. 1997), and to be even stronger for low-SES children than their higher-SES peers (Stipek & Ryan 1997). Since both core knowledge and interest are critical for achievement, basic skills must be taught in a way that fosters interest. This integrative approach might appear ambitious, but it should be natural and feasible: Children learn better when interested, and are more interested when they know more. Active learning about interesting topics, which meaning-based approaches advocate, provides an ideal context for skill development. Empirical studies with a focus on both interest and skills have been rare. For example, few intervention studies have explicitly combined meaning-based and skill-based approaches, but those that have show promise (Butynec-Thomas & Woloshyn 1997, Gettinger 1993). Similarly, few outcome studies have included measures of both skills and interest, but those that have are encouraging (Arnold et al. 2002, Morrow & Young 1997, Page-Voth & Graham 1999).

In sum, low-SES children often suffer a negative cycle of failure and disinterest, whereby failure increases disengagement, and disaffection fosters additional failure. Hope arises from the knowledge that equally potent positive cycles are possible, in which academic success could foster interest and vice versa.

UNDERSTANDING AND ADDRESSING THE SES ACHIEVEMENT GAP

Home and School

Many home factors related to SES have been linked to the development of difficulties with achievement and motivation. Particularly impressive is research surrounding early shared reading, which has been linked to emergent literacy and later achievement (Whitehurst & Lonigan 1998). Low-SES children have far fewer books and educational toys and experiences (Bradley et al. 2001, Brooks-Gunn & Duncan 1997). For instance, only half of preschoolers receiving public assistance have alphabet books in their homes, compared to 97% of children with professional parents (McCormick & Mason 1986). Parents' educational attitudes and expectations differ with SES (Battin-Pearson et al. 2000), as do parents' educational behaviors such as early reading and attention to language (NRC 2000). Children from low-SES families may receive, on average, a total of only 25 hours of one-on-one picture book reading by school entry, compared to 1000 to 1700 hours for middle-class children (Adams 1990). From an early age, characteristics of the home environment also influence academic interest, and these home factors differ based on SES (Gottfried et al. 1998). Consistent with this work, low-SES children lose significant ground before school entry and during summers (Alexander & Entwisle 1996), suggesting that early family interventions may be a key aspect of promoting success in school.

In terms of early childcare and school influences, the quality of preschools, kindergartens, and grade schools have all been linked to achievement, and low-SES children tend to have less access to quality education (Phillips et al. 1994, Pianta et al. 2002). These findings have been consistent across wide definitions and measures of quality, including physical classroom characteristics and teacher behaviors (NRC 2001); clearer differentiation of the most important specific factors could guide resource allocation. Studies focusing on teachers have indicated the importance of their role, and teachers have lower expectations and more negative perceptions of low-SES students than their higher-SES peers (Alexander et al. 1987, McLoyd 1998). Further research is needed to understand the causes, mechanisms, and results of these perceptions and expectations.

Early Intervention

Intervention experiments are critical to both science and practice because of their ability to establish causality, demonstrate malleable factors, and guide policy. A strong experimental literature indicates that emergent literacy can be promoted. For example, Whitehurst and others have demonstrated that parent and teacher training to improve preliteracy experiences can foster emergent academic skills in low-SES children (McCormick & Mason 1986, Morrow & Young 1997, Whitehurst et al. 1994). Phonological awareness and processing programs have been similarly successful (Byrne et al. 2000, Foorman et al. 1998). The literature now provides clear guidance for implementing basal reading programs as well (NRC 1998), and individual tutoring has also been shown to promote literacy (Elbaum et al. 2000). Literacy has been fostered with agents ranging from parents to teachers to librarians to volunteers. Much more research is needed on specific early math interventions for preschool children, but preliminary work is encouraging (Arnold et al. 2002, Griffin & Case 1996). With respect to early interest, a laboratory literature has demonstrated that emphasizing learning rather than performance, process rather than outcome, and effort rather than intelligence improves children's motivation and persistence (Elliot & Dweck 1988, Kamins & Dweck 1999, Mueller & Dweck 1998). Although only a small number of applied studies have examined the malleability of young children's interest, these studies suggest early interest can be influenced (Cordova & Lepper 1996, Guthrie et al. 2000, Ortiz et al. 2001).

In terms of broader programs, belief in early intervention is reflected in the massive public investment in the U.S. Department of Health and Human Services' Head Start program. Educational achievement is not the only sensible dimension on which to evaluate Head Start or other programs, which provide innumerable other benefits, from nutritious foods to social experiences (Raver & Zigler 1997, Zigler 1999). Nonetheless, given the size of this investment, it is surprising that more is not known about the effects of such programs on achievement. Early intervention shows consistently impressive short-term effects. With respect to determining longer-term outcomes, some progress has been made recently. For example, the Abecedarian Project (Campbell et al. 2001) shows substantial results of early intervention at age 21, and factors contributing to successful outcomes are being identified (Bryant et al. 1994, Ramey & Ramey 1998, Yoshikawa 1994). In many ways, however, the field remains where it has been for decades, with mixed and controversial conclusions about long-term effects.

The best programs improve performance on achievement testing, lessen grade retention, decrease utilization of special education, and increase graduation rates (Lee et al. 1990, McKey et al. 1985, Reynolds 1991); they can, by these measures, be described as a good financial investment. In a classic example, the Perry Preschool Project (Schweinhart et al. 1993) improved a broad range of adult outcomes and returned taxpayers approximately six dollars for each dollar invested. Not coincidentally, this project integrated core knowledge training and child-centered approaches. However, even children who benefit from these programs continue to lag behind nonpoor children in their academic skills, and the positive effects of most programs diminish over time (Lee et al. 1990). Because fading effects may be the result of experiences following early intervention programs (Lee & Loeb 1995), long-term strategies are essential to promote success, and the specific supports to maintain gains need to be identified. Key program components, mechanisms of effects, individual differences in responses, and influences on replication success have not been addressed adequately in the literature.

Detailed information on early intervention should be forthcoming. Five major current research projects are summarized in the Head Start Advisory Committee report (1999). The Family and Child Experiences Study is examining 3200 children in 40 representative Head Start Programs, with an impressive range of outcome and process variables. The Early Childhood Longitudinal Survey follows children from kindergarten to fifth grade. It includes almost 3000 children who attended Head Start, and examines the effects of daycare quality and the factors influencing parental choice in selecting Head Start. The Early Head Start Research Evaluation Project is investigating the effects of Early Head Start, which serves low-SES pregnant women with young children. The Head Start/Public Schools Early Childhood Transition Demonstration Project examines a transition program designed to support Head Start's interventions. Finally, the Head Start Impact Study offers an impressive, well-conceptualized program for further understanding the effects of Head Start. These latter three studies are particularly important because they include random assignment and offer enough power to explore moderators and mediators of outcomes. In addition to these evaluations, the Department of Education has launched randomized controlled trials of preschool curricula, and several agencies (National Institute of Child Health and Human Development, National Institute of Mental Health, Head Start, and the Department of Education) have funded a collaborative venture for multidisciplinary research on early childhood education. Taken together, the scope, quality, and size of these undertakings are unprecedented, and should shed light on what works best, for whom, under what conditions.

Large-Scale School Reform

For grade-school children, several large-scale school reform initiatives are being used to test the effects of new curricula. For the most part, no evidence of successful outcomes have been produced; rather, the difficulties inherent in implementing and evaluating large-scale reforms are well illustrated (Berends et al. 2002). Some promising results point to potential benefits of schoolwide reforms (Slavin 1996), notably, reading programs based on the research literature can be successfully implemented at the classroom level (Foorman 1997). Improved academic achievement has also been associated with certain after-school programs for children from low-income families (Posner & Vandell 1994). Accountability reforms tying incentives to standardized test results are difficult to evaluate, and currently no clear conclusions can be drawn about their efficacy.

Structural School Factors

A number of structural school factors associated with academic risk have a bearing on children's education in general, and disproportionately affect low-SES children. Class size influences children's achievement, and reducing class size benefits lower-SES children. Convergent evidence comes from careful small-scale experiments, and the notable, if somewhat less rigorous, large-scale studies in Tennessee, North Carolina, and Wisconsin (NRC 2001, Stecher & Bohrnstedt 2000). Teacher ability, education, and pay also have been linked to children's achievement (NRC 2001). Finally, global measures of early childcare quality that include economic resources, student safety, and schools' physical conditions (Bryant et al. 1994, Kontos 1991) have also all been associated with achievement. The policy implications of these findings are direct and obvious.

Computers and Technology

Computers could play a key role in exacerbating or ameliorating the gap in achievement based on SES (Future of Children 2000, Whitehurst & Lonigan 1998). On the one hand, low-SES children currently have less access to computers and technology; only about one in five low-SES children has a computer at home, compared to 91% of high-SES children (Future of Children 2000). On the other hand, as initial research is showing, computers and technology could potentially expose all children to portable well-designed educational programs (Barker & Torgesen 1995). Thus, computer-based instruction as a supplement to traditional teaching is a promising strategy that warrants careful scrutiny.

Race and Culture

Children from ethnic minorities are disproportionately affected by poverty, so it is not surprising that they also experience more academic failure. Approximately 69% of African American students and 64% of Hispanic students show reading skill deficits, whereas only approximately one third of Anglo American children face comparable difficulties (NRC 1998). Few studies have examined differential predictors for low-SES minority compared with Anglo American children. Analyses by Bradley et al. (2001) were particularly notable for their power to compare low- and high-SES populations and to consider Hispanic and African American children separately. Although rough, these groupings nevertheless represent an improvement over those in which all children from ethnic minorities are considered together. Ethnicity moderated a few developmental influences on achievement, although more similarities than differences were found across groups.

SES and racial and ethnic background are strongly related, and thus are difficult to untangle. In addition, such research is challenging because of major differences across and within each ethnic group. SES appears to be the primary force behind academic risk among minority children. Nevertheless, minority status likely adds at least some additional risk of educational underachievement (McLoyd 1998). Given the same individual income, minority families tend to live in poorer neighborhoods with poorer schools than nonminority families (Leventhal & Brooks-Gunn 2000), and community SES predicts achievement beyond family SES (Bryk & Raudenbush 1992, White 1982). In addition, prejudice, discrimination, and limited economic opportunities may increase stress and decrease the limited resources already available to poor families (Garcia Coll et al. 1996, McLoyd 1990), undermine motivation, and impede academic skills (Ogbu 1978). A shortage of minority teachers may have negative repercussions on minority children's achievement, though data about the importance of student-teacher ethnic match are preliminary and mixed (Klein et al. 2001). In addition, acculturation level may play a role in achievement (Nguyen et al. 1999). For nonnative English speakers, navigating two languages provides additional challenges as well as strengths. Education of nonnative English speakers is a complicated and controversial topic, but comprehensive reviews are available (NRC 1997).

Culture may influence learning style, and predominant educational approaches may not be effective for all children (Jacob & Jordan 1987). For example, preliminary studies suggest that African American children tend to learn especially well in cooperative and music-based activities (Allen & Butler 1996, Haynes & Gebreyesus 1992). Culturally accommodated approaches seem to facilitate student participation (Au & Mason 1981) and reduce problem behaviors (Weisner et al. 1988), although a link to achievement has not yet been empirically demonstrated. Overall, this developing area of research suggests potential benefits of adjusting teaching to culture. However, empirical support for this sensible hypothesis remains weak and not yet specific enough to guide implementation.

Finally, most achievement tests were validated primarily with Anglo-American children, and some argue that minority children's poorer performance on achievement measures reflects test bias. However, given the high rates of poverty and academic failure among minority children, they would be expected to perform less well on achievement tests until the SES gap is reduced. In fact, it would be a cause for concern if a test designed to measure or predict educational trajectories did not reflect the disadvantages associated with poverty and minority status. Thus poorer performance by minorities on a test is not necessarily evidence of test bias; rather, differential predictive validity is the primary criterion for achievement test bias (Camilli & Shepard 1994). So far, empirical studies have produced virtually no evidence of cultural bias in predicting achievement (Reynolds 2000). That is, the disadvantages facing minority children likely reside primarily in their opportunities rather than in assessment instruments, and biases largely in society rather than in tests. That said, the psychometric literature on test bias (Camilli & Shepard 1994, Reynolds 2000) must guide assessment validation to uncover and avoid possible bias. Further, given the terrible history of test misuse and misinterpretation, we emphasize that achievement tests do not measure a child's potential, and implore care in creating, describing, and using tests.

Gender

Overall achievement of low-SES boys is poorer than that of girls. This difference is likely due, at least in part, to high rates of externalizing problems, which are discussed below. At the same time, females are generally unlikely to pursue math- and science-related careers, and since low-SES children are also underrepresented in these fields, low-SES girls are doubly at risk. In fact, very few low-SES girls obtain employment in math- and science-related fields, and the statistics for ethnic minority females are especially staggering. In 1997, for example, of 900 recipients of doctorates in computer science there was only one black woman and two Hispanic women (National Science Foundation 2001). Gender differences in math achievement have been analyzed (Royer et al. 1999). For example, girls have lower competence beliefs about math as early as first grade (Eccles et al. 1993). More generally, girls receive less teacher attention from preschool through later years (Fagot & Hagan 1985, Leinhardt et al. 1979). Unfortunately, little beyond demonstrations of general gender differences in attention has been documented in the literature. More information on these differences, their causes, mechanisms, and consequences would be valuable. Further, since most of the early work in this area included only middle-class children, gender trajectories in low-SES children need closer investigation.

Future Research

We highlight four of many lines of research to further understanding of early education. For each of these, and for education research in general, hierarchical linear modeling offers a recently accessible analytic ally (Bradley et al. 2001, Bryk & Raudenbush 1992). A major challenge in educational research is that classrooms are often the appropriate unit of analysis. Since one teacher influences an entire classroom, individual children from the same class often cannot be considered independent cases. Hierarchical linear modeling estimates individual growth curves for each child, and the slopes of these curves become the dependent variable that can be predicted by independent variables at multiple levels, such as children, classrooms, and schools. For example, student and classroom differences in responding to a curriculum could be examined while maximizing statistical power. Hierarchical linear modeling also is ideal for handling missing or erratically spaced data.

First, interest intervention field trials must be conducted both to establish the causal impact of interest on achievement and the mechanisms of its effects, and to provide practical advances. Second, the field is also ready for an experimental approach to foster educational attainment in math and science among girls at younger ages. Though more difficult and costly than correlational work, experiments nonetheless provide the best return on investment. Third, studies need to examine cultural factors in children's education. Stronger correlational and longitudinal studies could then guide experimental tests of incorporating culture into educational programs. This will be a difficult research base to build, not least because of challenges in maintaining statistical power while addressing differences across and within ethnic groups, and an underrepresentation of minority researchers (in part because of factors discussed in this chapter). Fourth, greater focus on the challenges to intervention implementation would be constructive. Program dissemination and fidelity, teacher training, and related topics would be important areas for examination. Dissemination studies in clinical psychology could serve as a partial model for education (Clarke 1995), helping to build bridges from research to practice and policy.

Bridges from Research to Practice and Policy

Although the previous rift between didactic and child-centered approaches has been largely reconciled in theory, this divide remains in much of the applied world. More generally, findings from research are not being implemented. Communication channels between scientists and practitioners have not been established; many empirically validated programs are not portable, user-friendly, or practical in low-SES settings; and incentives to implement empirically validated approaches may be lacking. Models may be unsuitable for the level of teacher support often found in disadvantaged schools, and more and better research is needed on teacher training and its effects. This underutilization of knowledge could and should be studied.

Given the clear connection between early deficits and educational outcomes, programs of early assessment screening should help to identify difficulties before they become entrenched. Existing data suggest that even simple screening tests, such as a basic letter recognition test, can substantively improve predictive validity, albeit with substantial miss rates (NRC 1998). Portable screening procedures should be feasible to validate and could improve resource allocation. In addition, classroom-based assessment (Meisels 1994) and assessment more directly tied to instruction (Shepard et al. 1998) show promise, but remain preliminary.

Finally, not enough is known about monitoring and sustaining children's gains. For example, training programs may need booster sessions or community partners who help to maintain quality. One example includes Head Start's recent decision to create ongoing tracking systems to monitor areas of strength and weakness and to use the information gained to guide program development. More attention must be given to validating and standardizing such processes.

BROADER VIEWS OF ACADEMIC INFLUENCES: BUILDING BETTER BRIDGES

Educational context is much broader even than the multiple factors discussed above. Emotional and behavioral functioning, relationships with adults and peers, and family, school, and community resources are all important influences on children's academic achievement. In each of these areas, low-SES children face increased risks.

Mental Health and School Success

A strong relation has been identified between externalizing problems (e.g., aggression, inattention, impulsivity) and academic underachievement. Comorbidity of these problems is as high as 50%, depending on how they are operationalized (Frick et al. 1991, Hinshaw 1992). The link between behavioral problems and academic development becomes apparent at least as early as preschool (Arnold 1997, Tremblay et al. 1992). These difficulties appear to exert a bidirectional influence on each other, and the prognosis for children with problems in both areas is much worse than for children with problems restricted to one area (Hinshaw 1992). Children with academic problems are likely to experience frustration; decreased interest in learning, and diminished self-esteem; and increased likelihood of becoming disruptive, noncompliant, overactive, and inattentive, thereby exacerbating existing learning problems. During early childhood, attention deficiencies seem to be a key mediator of this process (Finn et al. 1995, Hinshaw 1992). Children with early behavior problems have trouble in paying attention, relating to others, and regulating their emotions, all behaviors related to poor school performance (McLelland et al. 2000). For example, better socioemotional adjustment in kindergarten predicts higher educational attainment (Luster & Pipes McAdoo 1996).

Teachers are likely to inadvertently exacerbate this cycle: Children with externalizing problems tend to misbehave during challenging academic tasks, receive attention from teachers for misbehavior, and escape learning activities (Carr et al. 1991). Furthermore, teachers are likely to avoid children with emotional and behavioral problems (Shores & Wehby 1999). Even as early as preschool, children with behavioral problems receive less academic instruction from teachers (Arnold 1997). Children's negative relationships with kindergarten teachers predict academic difficulties in elementary school (Hamre & Pianta 2001). Moreover, children with learning or behavioral problems are more likely to be rejected and victimized by peers, which further interferes with academic functioning (Wentzel & Asher 1995). Children with delinquent behavior tend to associate with each other and reinforce rule-breaking (Dishion et al. 1996), and so over time, delinquency may become a primary reason for poor school performance (Hawkins et al. 1998). Low-SES children are at greater risk of developing emotional and social problems, such as poor conduct, peer difficulties, and low self-esteem (Attar et al. 1994, Dodge et al. 1994), which increases their risk of academic problems. Risk factors for early delinquency can be identified in the preschool years (Haapasalo & Tremblay 1994, Loeber et al. 1991), underlining the need for early intervention (Guerra et al. 1995).

Externalizing difficulties receive more attention at home and at school than internalizing problems (e.g., anxiety, depression, withdrawal, somatic concerns) because they are highly visible and disruptive. Anxiety or depression often remains untreated because parents and teachers are unaware that children are experiencing such difficulties. Although less is known about the relation between internalizing problems and academic development (Kovacs & Devlin 1998), a growing literature documents the association between children's internalizing symptoms and academic underachievement (Cole 1990, Rapport et al. 2001, Steele et al. 2000). One recent study showed that self-reports of depression by children in first grade predicted their academic functioning at age 14 (Ialongo et al. 2001a), and achievement for children with social withdrawal tends to be especially poor (Ollendick et al. 1992). Internalizing problems are hypothesized to limit achievement through decreased participation, concentration, motivation, and attention from teachers (Rapport et al. 2001). Some studies have reported an increased prevalence of emotional problems for low-SES versus higher-SES children (Roberts & Sobhan 1992), but this social class influence seems to be weaker for internalizing than externalizing difficulties. Given that effective treatments exist for internalizing problems, improved awareness, identification, and implementation of treatment could make a substantial change in children's outcomes (Kendall 1993).

Comorbidity between externalizing and internalizing problems complicates the picture further (Nottelmann & Jensen 1995, Zahn-Waxler et al. 2000) and presents conceptual, practical, and methodological challenges for researchers and educators (Hinshaw 1992). Children with difficulty in one domain are more likely to develop difficulty in the other, and combined problems are associated with a worse prognosis. On the other hand, low-SES children who show good emotional and behavioral adjustment tend to demonstrate better academic performance (Brody et al. 1999, Raver & Zigler 1997). In sum, social, emotional, and behavioral adjustment have traditionally been neglected as components of school success despite their demonstrated relevance (Ramey & Ramey 1998, Raver 2002).

Risk and Resilience: Academic Development in the Context of Families, Schools, and Communities

A host of child, family, school, and community factors place children at increased risk for academic underachievement. For example, perinatal complications, social skills deficits, single-parent status, large family size, parental psychopathology, family conflict, harsh and inconsistent parenting, peer rejection, lack of social support, neighborhood characteristics, and low teacher expectations have all been identified as risk factors (Fortin & Bigras 1997, Grizenko & Fisher 1992, Myers & Taylor 1998). These factors influence each other as well as outcomes in complex ways that are both direct and indirect. The number of risks faced strongly predicts negative outcomes (Brooks-Gunn et al. 1995, Garmezy et al. 1984), and low-SES children are most vulnerable to these risk factors. There has been some progress in uncovering processes, causality, and developmental trends for many of these risks. For example, the influence of teacher practices on parent involvement is moderated by parent background and beliefs (Grolnick et al. 1997).

Fortunately, not all children who face these risks develop negative outcomes. Resiliency refers to children who successfully overcome adverse circumstances (Masten & Coatsworth 1998). Resiliency research, increasingly emphasized in recent years (Luthar & Zigler 1991, Masten & Coatsworth 1995), is important conceptually in recognizing the strengths of children and families, and practically for promoting achievement. Resilience, competence, and related constructs are often defined differently, but consistent protective factors have been identified despite variation in operationalizing constructs: good cognitive functioning, positive temperament, high sociability, close peer friendships, internal locus of control, sense of self-efficacy, high expectations for self, positive sense of self, engagement in activities, close relationship with an adult, effective parenting, access to consistent and warm caregiving, presence of positive adult role models, and strong connections with school (Doll & Lyon 1998).

Resiliency research has increasingly integrated school factors, and suggests that teachers' interpersonal behavior (e.g., support, friendliness), teaching strategies, classroom environment, administrative policies, and student competencies can be a positive influence for at-risk students (Wang & Gordon 1994). Less research has explored the mechanisms of these protective factors, in part because of conceptual and methodological challenges (Luthar et al. 2000). For instance, a particular factor may be protective for one child, a risk factor for another, and neutral for another (Stouthamer-Loeber et al. 2002). Protective factors may reduce problems directly, lower risk factors, or interact with risk factors to diminish their influence; furthermore, children may be successful in some areas but not others, suggesting that thinking of resilience in simple unidimensional terms may not be very useful (Luthar 1993). Nevertheless, the conceptualization of protective factors provides structure for learning about these processes within development and for translating findings to assist in prevention and intervention. This chapter provides examples of selected factors that are likely to be malleable, including effective parenting, positive relationships with adults, and parental involvement in school.

Parenting can protect children from negative educational outcomes. Appropriate and consistent discipline (firm, clear rules; appropriate consequences; and monitoring of behavior), in combination with high parental warmth, is associated with achievement (Masten et al. 1999, Shumow et al. 1998, Werner & Smith 1992). Further, parenting is moderated by SES in that parenting is an even stronger predictor of academic development for low-SES than for higher SES children (Hill 2001).

Positive relationships with family, teachers, and other adults are strong protective factors (Masten 1994) in providing guidance, mentoring, role models, feedback, and resources (Ladd & Burgess 1999). African American children attain higher levels of education when their parents serve as their role models (Luster & Pipes McAdoo 1996), but further research is needed to understand how supportive relationships may operate within different cultural contexts. Feelings of social belonging and community at school have been associated with academic interest and psychological adjustment (Battistich & Hom 1997). Furthermore, children's perception of supportive relationships with teachers are associated with school satisfaction, and children who enjoy school receive more support from teachers, suggesting that positive cycles can form (Baker 1999).

Parent involvement in education is another important factor for building social and academic competence (Booth & Dunn 1996, Reynolds et al. 1992). Examples include contacting teachers, attending school functions, monitoring academic progress, and providing assistance with schoolwork. Increased parent involvement in school reduces the negative effects of poverty on educational achievement and socioemotional adjustment (Marcon 1999, Reynolds 1991, Shumow et al. 1999). Successful early intervention programs increase parent involvement (Miedel & Reynolds 1999), and increased parent involvement has been shown to be a mechanism through which interventions can produce long-term effects on achievement and grade retention (Reynolds 1992). Urban, low-SES children with parents actively involved in their schooling showed less aggression despite exposure to violence than children with parents who are less involved (Richters & Martinez 1993). Parents of low-SES children are likely to have had their own school difficulties, which in turn may decrease their comfort with parent-school interactions. Although studies have demonstrated increased parent involvement within preschool programs such as Head Start, which emphasize involvement, parents tend to be less involved as children enter kindergarten and first grade (Fantuzzo et al. 1998).

Family and demographic factors influence the level of parent involvement; low-SES predicts less involvement, but also appears to make involvement particularly critical (Hill 2001, Raffaele & Knoff 1999). Maternal depression, minority status, and single-parent status are associated with lower parent involvement in school and with SES (Eccles & Harold 1996, Kohl et al. 2000). These risk factors may result in the following barriers to involvement: high levels of stress, lack of support, restrictive work or childcare schedules, discomfort with educational environments, transportation problems, and difficulty communicating in English; however, empirical evidence is scant. More research is urgently needed to understand and promote parent involvement (Raffaele & Knoff 1999).

Despite progress in research on resilience, the mechanisms involved in resilience processes are only partially understood. Factors associated with risk and resilience are not necessarily causal, so theoretically informed research is needed to identify appropriate intervention points. Masten & Coatsworth (1998) highlight the problem with the following example: High self-esteem is associated with resilience, but if self-esteem is a result of competence rather than a cause of it, a self-esteem intervention might have no effect.

Race and Culture

Little research has targeted mental health difficulties among minority children, despite their increased risk for poverty and associated problems. Since mental health and academic difficulties seem to exert a reciprocal influence on each other, children in ethnic minority groups face compounded risks (Brooks-Gunn et al. 1995).

Cultural influences, which appear to be significant, have been inadequately investigated. For instance, studies of depression have identified differences in prevalence and correlates between Caucasian and African American children (Roberts & Sobhan 1992). Furthermore, although a recent study predicted grades in African American children using depressive symptoms, this association was not as strong as in studies of Caucasian children (Steele et al. 2000). Culture may be equally important within resilience research. African American culture has been described as emphasizing strong family bonds, flexible family roles, high achievement orientation, positive self-esteem, and religious beliefs that seem to protect youth against many urban risk factors (Littlejohn-Blake & Darling 1993). The relation between culture and resilience should be explored further. Acculturation may moderate some influences on achievement (Nguyen et al. 1999), but results to date remain preliminary. Within-group as well as between-group differences need to be investigated, and interventions must consider culture. For instance, since extended family members play a critical role in many African American families, integrating family members might be a useful strategy (Jarrett & Burton 1999).

Gender

Externalizing difficulties are more common and more strongly associated with emergent academic development in boys than in girls (Keenan & Shaw 1997, Kellam et al. 1998, Stowe et al. 1999). In contrast, as girls grow older, they are at higher risk of developing internalizing problems. Accompanying academic problems may remain invisible, particularly in early years when less formal evaluation of educational progress occurs. Empirical evidence is consistent with this model; early learning difficulties in girls are underidentified by teachers, despite objective criteria such as standardized tests that diagnose similar numbers of boys and girls with learning problems (NRC 1998, Stowe et al. 1999).

Many mental health interventions are based on research with boys and are more successful for boys than for girls (Farrell & Meyer 1997). Less is known about girls' difficulties, hence interventions tend not to be tailored to their needs. For instance, in the area of aggression, recent research has shown that girls show more relational aggression than boys (Crick et al. 1999), and that this form of aggression is associated with internalizing symptoms, social cognitive processing difficulties, and interpersonal problems (Crick & Grotpeter 1995). Yet no interventions targeting relational aggression have been tested. Better interventions could improve mental health, and in turn, academic achievement, for high-risk girls.

Promising Prevention and Intervention Programs

The positive effects of numerous prevention and intervention programs have been well documented. Weissberg et al. (1991) summarized prevention programs for children's psychosocial problems. Greenberg and his colleagues (2001) reviewed prevention programs that decrease psychopathology and associated factors in children. Miller et al. (1998) examined school-based prevention programs for antisocial behavior based on a resilience framework, and Black & Krishnakumar (1998) provided recommendations to promote strengths through urban interventions. Only a few programs explicitly target both academic growth and mental health, despite their clear connection. We focus on those programs that consider both academic and mental health outcomes for at-risk children.

Early interventions that address both academic and social contexts show the most longstanding gains (Seitz 1991). For example, a prevention program with home- and school-based components for disruptive low-SES kindergarten boys resulted in significantly less grade retention through elementary school in comparison to control children (Tremblay et al. 1995). Early academic intervention programs may help prevent later delinquency (Zigler et al. 1992). One teacher training program produced fewer conduct problems and suspensions from school, and reduced the need for mental health services for intervention children versus control children five years later (Ialongo et al. 2001b). In addition, the Perry Preschool Project, an educationally focused program, provided social gains into adulthood (Schweinhart et al. 1993). Further research is needed, but the programs that have addressed multiple contexts show great promise.

Fast Track is a multicomponent intervention for young children at risk for misconduct. This school-based program utilizes training in social-emotional skills, academic tutoring, parent training, home visits, and teacher education to promote strengths and ameliorate risks beginning in kindergarten. Fast Track shows impressive effects on children's behavior, social-emotional skills, use of special services, parenting, classroom atmosphere, parent involvement in school, and academic skills, compared to programs operating in only one area of child development (Conduct Problems Prevention Research Group 1999a,b).

Henggeler has developed Multisystemic Therapy, a successful program to address behavioral problems in children and adolescents (Henggeler et al. 1998, Schoenwald & Henggeler 1997). This flexible and comprehensive home-based intervention adopts an approach based on a strong theoretical model of delinquency development. This program considers child, family, peer, school, and community contexts. Rigorous outcome studies have demonstrated the positive effects of Multisystemic Therapy on school achievement as well as on behavior and family functioning. The program provides a model for developing, testing, improving, and disseminating an intervention, because outcome studies have enhanced the intervention for different populations and contexts, and careful dissemination models have ensured quality replications. The applicability of this program to younger children has not been tested.

Big Brothers/Big Sisters uses mentors to foster the academic and socioemotional growth of children. In a recent national longitudinal evaluation, researchers reported evidence of improvements in grades, scholastic competence, truancy and substance use rates, and parent and peer relationships in comparison to nonmentored children (Grossman & Tierney 1998). Improved parent-child relationships seem to mediate academic improvements. This program should also be evaluated with younger children.

Such programs help build more inclusive models of achievement as well as guide broader interventions. More research is needed to identify critical aspects of programs. Evaluations of academic programs often only include academic measures, potentially underestimating broad intervention outcomes, since similar risk and protective factors influence both children's academic and mental health and those areas influence each other. Researchers are increasingly exploring resilience within the school context (Doll & Lyon 1998, Pianta & Walsh 1998), and we applaud this trend. Partnerships between schools, communities, and researchers may be more successful than programs that are applied from outside the community, or from within the community without a research basis. Furthermore, despite evidence that child disorders respond well to treatment (Kazdin & Weisz 1998), specific types of treatment, their applicability to specific problems, and factors that influence treatment success and failure require clearer resolution (Greenberg et al. 2001).

Future Research

Any research that ties contextual influences to academic development will further educational research, but four specific research areas are suggested. First, the compelling data that show externalizing problems are a key risk factor in academic failure among boys justify experimental evaluation that will incorporate externalizing treatments more directly into academic programs and settings. A second target for research is mental health influences on academic progress among girls. The utility of addressing anxiety and depression, two of the most treatable problems in clinical psychology, is potentially high. Third, resiliency research has only recently been directly linked to education, and must be extended. We need to understand how educational resilience may operate differently depending on gender, SES, race, and ethnic background. Fourth, closer study of moderating factors associated with cultural differences would facilitate a better match of mental health programs to various cultural needs to promote mental health in minority communities.

Bridges from Research to Practice and Policy

Implementation barriers often prevent the results from clinical and developmental research from being applied successfully to educational settings. Factors influencing participation require explicit research, since families with multiple stressors are the least likely to participate. An understanding of portability, trainability, and the factors influencing implementation choices are essential. Little is known about the supports necessary to move programs successfully from research to applied settings. Given the multiple factors related to academic success, reform has been predictably difficult. On the one hand, research is often misapplied, with a focus on isolated skills or child factors that do not sufficiently consider context and are not broad enough to secure overall success. On the other hand, it is not practical to intervene in all aspects of a child's life, and overly broad attempts may be either overwhelming or too diffuse. Research and theory need to guide the choice of key leverage points and strategies for continued support. An ultimate goal is that careful research can be used to tailor programs to the specific needs of individual children, although with our current knowledge such a matching program is not yet feasible.

SUMMARY

Extensive work remains in understanding and facilitating the educational achievement of low-SES children. At the same time, tremendous progress has been recorded in some areas, and dramatic gains can be anticipated on several fronts. The recent burst of well-planned research funding initiatives leaves us optimistic. Ultimately, the best solution for the educational difficulties of children raised in poverty will be poverty reduction; even ideal educational practices cannot eliminate the devastating impact of inadequate resources. Nevertheless, improved education for low-SES children would promote success, and thereby help reduce poverty and the host of associated disadvantages.

ACKNOWLEDGMENT

We gratefully thank the William T. Grant Foundation for funding that facilitated this work.

The *Annual Review of Psychology* is online at http://psych.annualreviews.org

LITERATURE CITED

Adams MJ. 1990. *Beginning to Read: Thinking and Learning About Print.* Cambridge, MA: MIT Press

Alexander K, Entwisle D. 1988. Achievement in the first two years of school: patterns and processes. *Monogr. Soc. Res. Child Dev.* 53: entire volume

Alexander K, Entwisle D. 1996. Schools and children at risk. See Booth & Dunn 1996, pp. 67–88

Alexander K, Entwisle D, Thompson M. 1987. School performance, status relations, and the structure of sentiment: bringing the teacher back in. *Am. Sociol. Rev.* 52:665–82

Allen BA, Butler L. 1996. The effects of music and movement opportunity on the analogical reasoning performance of African American and White school children. *J. Black Psychol.* 22:316–28

Arnold DH. 1997. Co-occurrence of externalizing behavior problems and emergent academic difficulties in high-risk boys: a preliminary evaluation of patterns and mechanisms. *Appl. Dev. Psychol.* 18:317–30

Arnold DH, Fisher PH, Doctoroff GL, Dobbs J. 2002. Accelerating math development in Head Start classrooms. *J. Educ. Psychol.* In press

Attar BK, Guerra NG, Tolan PH. 1994. Neighborhood disadvantage, stressful life events, and adjustment in urban elementary-school children. *J. Clin. Child Psychol.* 23:391–400

Au K, Mason JM. 1981. Social organizational factors in learning to read: the balance rights hypothesis. *Read. Res. Q.* 17:115–52

Baker JA. 1999. Teacher-student interaction in urban at-risk classrooms: differential behavior, relationship quality, and student satisfaction with school. *Elem. Sch. J.* 100: 57–70

Barker TA, Torgesen JK. 1995. An evaluation of computer-assisted instruction in phonological awareness with below average readers. *J. Educ. Comput. Res.* 13:89–103

Battin-Pearson S, Newcomb MD, Abbott RD, Kill KG, Catalano RF, Hawkins JD. 2000. Predictors of early high-school drop-out: a test of five theories. *J. Educ. Psychol.* 92: 568–82

Battistich V, Hom A. 1997. The relationship between students' sense of their school as a community and their involvement in problem behaviors. *Am. J. Public Health* 87:1997–2000

Berends M, Chun J, Schuyler GL, Stockly S, Briggs RJ. 2002. *Challenges of Conflicting School Reforms: Effects of New American Schools in a High-Poverty District.* Santa Monica, CA: Rand

Black MM, Krishnakumar A. 1998. Children in low-income, urban settings: interventions to promote mental health and well-being. *Am. Psychol.* 53:635–46

Bolger KE, Patterson CJ, Thomson WW, Kupersmidt JB. 1995. Psychosocial adjustment among children experiencing persistent and intermittent family economic hardship. *Child Dev.* 66:1107–29

Booth A, Dunn JF. 1996. *Family-school Links: How Do They Affect Educational Outcomes?* Mahwah, NJ: Erlbaum

Bradley RH, Corwyn RF. 2002. Socioeconomic status and child development. *Annu. Rev. Psychol.* 53:371–99

Bradley RH, Corwyn RF, Burchinal M, Pipes McAdoo H, Garcia Coll C. 2001. The home environments of children in the United States part II: relations with behavioral development through age thirteen. *Child Dev.* 72:1868–86

Brody GH, Flor DL, Gibson NM. 1999. Linking maternal efficacy beliefs, developmental goals, parenting practices, and child competence in rural single-parent African American families. *Child Dev.* 70:1197–208

Bronfenbrenner U. 1996. Ecology of the family as a context for human development: research perspectives. *Dev. Psychol.* 22:723–42

Brooks-Gunn J, Duncan G. 1997. The effects of poverty on children. *Future Child.* 7:55–71

Brooks-Gunn J, Klebanov P, Liaw F, Duncan GJ. 1995. Toward an understanding of the effects of poverty upon children. In *Children of Poverty: Research, Health, and Policy Issues,* ed. HE Fitzgerald, BM Lester, pp. 3–41. New York: Garland

Bryant D, Burchinal M, Lau L, Sparling J. 1994. Family and classroom correlates of Head Start children's developmental outcomes. *Early Child. Res. Q.* 9:289–309

Bryk AS, Raudenbush SW. 1992. *Hierarchical Linear Models: Applications and Data Analysis Methods.* Newbury Park, CA: Sage

Butynec-Thomas J, Woloshyn V. 1997. The effects of explicit-strategy and whole-language instruction on students' spelling ability. *J. Exp. Educ.* 65:291–302

Byrne B, Fielding-Barnsley R, Ashley L. 2000. Effects of preschool phoneme identity training after six years: outcome level distinguished from rate of response. *J. Educ. Psychol.* 92:659–67

Camilli G, Shepard LA. 1994. *Methods for Identifying Biased Test Items.* Thousand Oaks, CA: Sage

Campbell FA, Pungello EP, Miller-Johnson S, Burchinal M, Ramey CT. 2001. The development of cognitive and academic abilities: growth curves from an early childhood educational experiment. *Dev. Psychol.* 37:231–42

Carr EG, Taylor JG, Robinson S. 1991. The effects of severe behavior problems in children on the teaching behavior of adults. *J. Appl. Behav. Anal.* 24:523–35

Chall JS. 1967. *Learning to Read: The Great Debate.* New York: McGraw-Hill

Chapman JW, Tunmer WE, Prochnow JE. 2000. Early reading related skills and performance, reading self-concept, and the development of academic self-concept: a longitudinal study. *J. Educ. Psychol.* 92:703–8

Clarke GN. 1995. Improving the transition from

basic efficacy research to effectiveness studies: methodological issues and procedures. *J. Consult. Clin. Psychol.* 63:718–25

Cole DA. 1990. Relation of social and academic competence to depressive symptoms in childhood. *J. Abnorm. Psychol.* 99:422–29

Coleman J, Campbell EQ, Hobson CJ, McPartland J, Mood AM, et al. 1966. *Equality of Educational Opportunity.* Off. Educ., US Dep. Health, Educ. Welf. Washington, DC: US GPO

Conduct Problems Prev. Res. Group. 1999a. Initial impact of the Fast Track prevention trial for conduct problems: I. The High-Risk Sample. *J. Consult. Clin. Psychol.* 67:631–47

Conduct Problems Prev. Res. Group. 1999b. Initial impact of the Fast Track prevention trial for conduct problems: II. Classroom effects. *J. Consult. Clin. Psychol.* 67:648–57

Cordova DI, Lepper MR. 1996. Intrinsic motivation and the process of learning: beneficial effects of contextualization, personalization, and choice. *J. Educ. Psychol.* 88:715–30

Covington MV. 2000. Goal theory, motivation, and school achievement: an integrative review. *Annu. Rev. Psychol.* 51:171–200

Crain-Thoreson C, Dale PS. 1992. Do early talkers become early readers? Linguistic precocity, preschool language, and emergent literacy. *Dev. Psychol.* 28:421–29

Crick NR, Casas JF, Ku H. 1999. Relational and physical forms of peer victimization in preschool. *Dev. Psychol.* 35:376–85

Crick NR, Grotpeter JK. 1995. Relational aggression, gender, and social-psychological adjustment. *Child Dev.* 66:710–22

Dishion TJ, Spracklen KM, Andrews DW, Patterson GR. 1996. Deviancy training in male adolescents' friendships. *Behav. Ther.* 27: 373–90

Dodge KA, Pettit GS, Bates JE. 1994. Socialization mediators of the relation between socioeconomic status and child conduct problems. *Child Dev.* 65:649–65

Doll B, Lyon MA. 1998. Risk and resilience: implications for the delivery of educational and mental health services in schools. *Sch. Psychol. Rev.* 27:348–63

Duncan GJ, Brooks-Gunn J, Klebanov PK. 1994. Economic deprivation and early child development. *Child Dev.* 65:296–318

Duncan GJ, Yeung WJ, Brooks-Gunn J, Smith JR. 1998. How much does childhood poverty affect the life chances of children? *Am. Sociol. Rev.* 63:406–23

Eccles JS, Harold RD. 1996. Family involvement in children's and adolescents' schooling. See Booth & Dunn 1996, pp. 3–34

Eccles JS, Wigfield A. 2002. Motivational beliefs, values, and goals. *Annu. Rev. Psychol.* 53:109–32

Eccles JS, Wigfield A, Harold R, Blumenfeld P. 1993. Age and gender differences in children's achievement self-perceptions during the elementary school years. *Child Dev.* 64: 830–47

Elbaum B, Vaughn S, Tejero Hughes M, Watson Moody S. 2000. How effective are one-to-one tutoring programs in reading for elementary students at risk for reading failure? A meta-analysis of the intervention research. *J. Educ. Psychol.* 92:605–19

Elliot ES, Dweck CS. 1988. Goals: an approach to motivation and achievement. *J. Personal. Soc. Psychol.* 54:5–12

Fagot BI, Hagan R. 1985. Aggression in toddlers: responses to the assertive acts of boys and girls. *Sex Roles* 12:341–51

Fantuzzo J, Tighe E, Childs S. 1998. Family Involvement Questionnaire: a multivariate assessment of family participation in early childhood education. *J. Educ. Psychol.* 92: 367–76

Farrell AD, Meyer AL. 1997. The effectiveness of a school-based curriculum for reducing violence among urban sixth-grade students. *Am. J. Public Health* 87:979–84

Finn JD, Pannozzo GM, Voelkl KE. 1995. Disruptive and inattentive-withdrawn behavior and achievement among fourth graders. *Elem. Sch. J.* 95:421–34

Foorman BR. 1997. Early interventions for children with reading problems: study designs and preliminary findings. *Learn. Disabil.: A Multidiscip. J.* 8:63–71

Foorman BR, Francis DJ, Fletcher JM,

Schatschneider C, Mehta P. 1998. The role of instruction in learning to read: preventing reading failure in at-risk children. *J. Educ. Psychol.* 90:37–55

Fortin L, Bigras M. 1997. Risk factors exposing young children to behaviour problems. *Emot. Behav. Difficulties* 2:3–14

Frick PJ, Kamphaus RW, Lahey BB, Loeber R, Christ MAG, et al. 1991. Academic underachievement and the disruptive behavior disorders. *J. Consult. Clin. Psychol.* 59:289–94

Frijters JC, Barron RW, Brunello M. 2000. Direct and mediated influences of home literacy and literacy interest on prereaders' oral vocabulary and early written language skill. *J. Educ. Psychol.* 92:466–77

Future Child. 2000. Children and computer technology, executive summary. *Future Child.* 10:2–5

Garcia Coll C, Lamberty G, Jenkins R, McAdoo HP, Crnic K, et al. 1996. An integrative model for the study of developmental competencies in minority children. *Child Dev.* 67:1891–914

Garmezy N, Masten AS, Tellegen A. 1984. The study of stress and competence in children: a building block for developmental psychopathology. *Child Dev.* 55:97–111

Gettinger M. 1993. Effects of invented spelling and direct instruction on spelling performance of second-grade boys. *J. Appl. Behav. Anal.* 26:281–91

Gottfried AE, Fleming JS, Gottfried AW. 1998. Role of cognitively stimulating home environment in children's academic intrinsic motivation: a longitudinal study. *Child Dev.* 69:1448–60

Greenberg MT, Domitrovich C, Bumbarger B. 2001. The prevention of mental disorders in school-aged children: current state of the field. *Prev. Treat.* 4:1–62

Griffin S, Case R. 1996. Evaluating the breadth and depth of training effects when central conceptual structures are taught. *Monog. Soc. Res. Child Dev.* 61:83–102

Grissmer D, Flanagan A. 2002. The role of federal resources in closing the achievement gaps of minority and disadvantaged children. In *Bridging the Achievement Gap*, ed. T Loveless. Washington, DC: Brook. Inst. Press. In press

Grizenko N, Fisher C. 1992. Review of studies of risk and protective factors for psychopathology in children. *Can. J. Psychiatry* 37:711–21

Grolnick WS, Benjet C, Kurowski CO, Apostoleris NH. 1997. Predictors of parent involvement in children's schooling. *J. Educ. Psychol.* 89:538–48

Grossman JB, Tierney JP. 1998. Does mentoring work? An impact study of the Big Brothers Big Sisters program. *Eval. Rev.* 22:403–26

Guerra NG, Huesmann LR, Tolan PH, Van Acker R, Eron LD. 1995. Stressful events and individual beliefs as correlates of economic disadvantage and aggression among urban children. *J. Consult. Clin. Psychol.* 63:518–28

Guthrie JT, Wigfield A, VonSecker C. 2000. Effects of integrated instruction on motivation and strategy use in reading. *J. Educ. Psychol.* 92:331–41

Haapasalo J, Tremblay RE. 1994. Physically aggressive boys from ages 6 to 12: family background, parenting behavior, and prediction of delinquency. *J. Consult. Clin. Psychol.* 62:1044–52

Hamre BK, Pianta RC. 2001. Early teacher-child relationships and the trajectory of children's school outcomes through eighth grade. *Child Dev.* 72:625–38

Hawkins JD, Herrenkohl T, Farrington DP, Brewer D, Catalano RF, Harachi TW. 1998. A review of predictors of youth violence. In *Serious and Violent Juvenile Offenders: Risk Factors and Successful Interventions*, ed. R Loeber, DP Farrington, pp. 106–46. Thousand Oaks, CA: Sage

Haynes NM, Gebreyesus S. 1992. Cooperative learning: a case for African American students. *Sch. Psychol. Rev.* 21:577–85

Head Start Advis. Comm. 1999. *Evaluating Head Start: a Recommended Framework for Studying the Impact of the Head Start*

Program, October 1999 Report. Washington, DC: US Dep. Health Hum. Serv.

Henggeler SW, Schoenwald SK, Boduin CM, Rowland MD, Cunningham PB. 1998. *Multisystemic Treatment of Antisocial Behavior in Children and Adolescents.* New York: Guilford Press. 287 pp.

Hill NE. 2001. Parenting and academic socialization as they relate to school readiness: the roles of ethnicity and family income. *J. Educ. Psychol.* 93:686–97

Hinshaw SP. 1992. Externalizing behavior problems and academic underachievement in childhood and adolescence: causal relationships and underlying mechanisms. *Psychol. Bull.* 111:127–55

Ialongo NS, Edelsohn G, Kellam SG. 2001a. A further look at the prognostic power of young children's reports of depressed mood and feelings. *Child Dev.* 72:736–47

Ialongo NS, Poduska J, Werthamer L, Kellam S. 2001b. The distal impact of two first-grade preventive interventions on conduct problems and disorder in early adolescence. *J. Emot. Behav. Disord.* 9:146–60

Jacob E, Jordan C. 1987. Explaining the school performance of minority students (Theme issue). Afterword: where are we now? *Anthropol. Educ. Q.* 18:365–67

Jarrett RL, Burton LM. 1999. Dynamic dimensions of family structure in low-income African American families: emergent themes in qualitative research. *J. Comp. Fam. Stud.* 30:177–87

Jordan N, Huttenlocher J, Levine S. 1992. Differential calculation abilities in young children from middle- and low-income families. *Dev. Psychol.* 28:644–53

Juel C. 1988. Acquisition of literacy: a longitudinal study of 54 children in first and second grade. *J. Educ. Psychol.* 80:437–47

Kamins ML, Dweck CS. 1999. Person versus process praise and criticism: implications for contingent self-worth and coping. *Dev. Psychol.* 35:835–47

Kazdin AE, Weisz JR. 1998. Identifying and developing empirically supported child and adolescent treatments. *J. Consult. Clin. Psychol.* 66:19–36

Keenan K, Shaw D. 1997. Developmental and social influences on young girls' early problem behavior. *Psychol. Bull.* 121:95–113

Kellam SG, Ling X, Merisca R, Brown CH, Ialongo N. 1998. The effect of the level of aggression in the first grade classroom on the course and malleability of aggressive behavior into middle school. *Dev. Psychopathol.* 10:165–85

Kendall PC. 1993. Cognitive-behavioral therapies with youth: guiding theory, current status, and emerging developments. *J. Consult. Clin. Psychol.* 61:235–47

Klein S, Le V, Hamilton L. 2001. *Does matching student and teacher racial/ethnic group improve math scores?* Presented at Am. Educ. Res. Assoc. Meet., Seattle, WA

Kohl GO, Lengua LL, McMahon RJ. 2000. Parent involvement in school: conceptualizing multiple dimensions and their relations with family and demographic risk factors. *J. Sch. Psychol.* 38:501–23

Kontos S. 1991. Child care quality, family background, and children's development. *Early Child. Res. Q.* 6:249–62

Kovacs M, Devlin B. 1998. Internalizing disorders in childhood. *J. Child Psychol. Psychiatry* 39:47–63

Kurdek LA, Sinclair RJ. 2001. Predicting reading and mathematics achievement in fourth grade children from kindergarten readiness scores. *J. Educ. Psychol.* 93:451–55

Ladd GW, Burgess KB. 1999. Do relational risks and protective factors moderate the linkages between childhood aggression and early psychological and school adjustment? *Child Dev.* 72:1579–601

Lee VE, Brooks-Gunn J, Schnur E, Liaw F. 1990. Are Head Start effects sustained? A longitudinal follow-up comparison of disadvantaged children attending Head Start, no preschool, and other preschool programs. *Child Dev.* 61:495–507

Lee VE, Loeb S. 1995. Where do head start attendees end up? One reason why preschool effects fade out. *Educ. Eval. Policy Anal.* 17: 62–82

Leinhardt G, Seewald AM, Engel M. 1979. Learning what's taught: sex differences in instruction. *J. Educ. Psychol.* 71:432–39

Leventhal T, Brooks-Gunn J. 2000. The neighborhoods they live in: the effect of neighborhood residence on child and adolescence outcomes. *Psychol. Bull.* 126:309–37

Littlejohn-Blake SM, Darling CA. 1993. Understanding the strengths of African American families. *J. Black Stud.* 23:460–71

Loeber R, Stouthamer-Loeber M, Green SM. 1991. Age at onset of problem behaviour in boys, and later disruptive and delinquent behaviours. *Crim. Behav. Ment. Health* 1:229–46

Luster T, Pipes McAdoo H. 1996. Family and child influences on educational attainment: a secondary analysis of the High/Scope Perry Preschool Data. *Dev. Psychol.* 32:26–39

Luthar SS. 1993. Annotation: methodological and conceptual issues in research on childhood resilience. *J. Child Psychol. Psychiatry* 34:441–53

Luthar SS, Cicchetti D, Becker B. 2000. The construct of resilience: a critical evaluation and guidelines for future work. *Child Dev.* 71:543–62

Luthar SS, Zigler EF. 1991. Vulnerability and competence: a review of research on resilience in childhood. *Am. J. Orthopsychiatry* 61:6–22

Marcon RA. 1999. Positive relationships between parent school involvement and public school inner-city preschoolers' development and academic performance. *Sch. Psychol. Rev.* 28:395–412

Masten AS. 1994. Resilience in individual development: successful adaptation despite risk and adversity. In *Educational Resilience in Inner-city America: Challenges and Prospects*, ed. MC Wang, EW Gordon, pp. 3–25. Hillsdale, NJ: Erlbaum

Masten AS, Coatsworth JD. 1995. Competence, resilience, and psychopathology. In *Developmental Psychopathology, 2: Risk, Disorder, and Adaptation. Wiley Ser. on Personality Processes*, ed. D Cicchetti, DJ Cohen, pp. 715–52. New York: Wiley

Masten AS, Coatsworth JD. 1998. The development of competence in favorable and unfavorable environments. *Am. Psychol.* 53:205–20

Masten AS, Hubbard JJ, Gest SD, Tellegen A, Garmezy N, Ramirez M. 1999. Competence in the context of adversity: pathways to resilience and maladaptation from childhood to late adolescence. *Dev. Psychopathol.* 11:143–69

McCormick CE, Mason JM. 1986. Intervention procedures for increasing preschool children's interest in and knowledge about reading. In *Emergent Literacy: Writing and Reading*, ed. WH Teale, E Sulzby, pp. 90–115. Norwood, NJ: Ablex

McKey RH, Condelli L, Ganson H, Barrett BJ, McConkey C, Plantz MC. 1985. *The Impact of Head Start on Children, Families and Communities.* Washington, DC: US GPO

McLelland MM, Morrison FJ, Holmes DL. 2000. Children at risk for early academic problems: the role of learning-related social skills. *Early Child. Res. Q.* 15:307–29

McLoyd VC. 1990. The impact of economic hardship on black families and children: psychological distress, parenting and socioemotional development. *Child Dev.* 61:311–46

McLoyd VC. 1998. Socioeconomic disadvantage and child development. *Am. Psychol.* 53:185–204

Meisels SJ. 1994. Designing meaningful measurements for early childhood. In *Diversity in Early Education: A Call for More Inclusive Theory, Practice, and Policy*, ed. BL Mallory, RS New, pp. 202–22. New York: Teachers College Press

Miedel WT, Reynolds AJ. 1999. Parent involvement in early intervention for disadvantaged children: does it matter? *J. Sch. Psychol.* 37:379–402

Miller GE, Brehm K, Whitehouse S. 1998. Reconceptualizing school-based prevention for antisocial behavior within a resiliency framework. *Sch. Psychol. Rev.* 27:364–79

Morrow LM, Young J. 1997. A family literacy program connecting school and home: effects on attitude, motivation, and literacy achievement. *J. Educ. Psychol.* 89:736–42

Mueller CM, Dweck CS. 1998. Praise for intelligence can undermine children's motivation and performance. *J. Personal. Soc. Psychol.* 75:33–52

Myers HF, Taylor S. 1998. Family contributions to risk and resilience in African American children. *J. Comp. Fam. Stud.* 29:215–30

Natl. Assess. Educ. Prog. 2000. *The Nation's Report Card: Fourth Grade Reading 2000.* Washington, DC: Natl. Cent. Educ. Stat.

Natl Cent. Educ. Stat. 2000. *America's Kindergartners: Findings from the Early Childhood Longitudinal Study, Kindergarten Class of 1998-99, Fall 1998.* Washington, DC: US Dep. Educ.

Natl. Read. Panel. 1999. *Teaching Children to Read.* Natl. Inst. Child Health Hum. Dev. Washington, DC: US GPO

Natl. Res. Counc. 1997. *Improving Schooling for Language-Minority Children: A Research Agenda*, ed. D August, K Hakuta. Committee on Developing a Research Agenda on the Education of Limited English Proficient and Bilingual Students. Comm. Behav. Soc. Sci. Educ. Washington, DC: Natl. Acad. Press

Natl. Res. Counc. 1998. *Preventing Reading Difficulties in Young Children*, ed. CE Snow, MS Burns, P Griffin. Comm. Prevention Reading Difficulties Young Children. Comm. Behav. Soc. Sci. Educ. Washington, DC: Natl. Acad. Press

Natl. Res. Counc. 2000. *From Neurons to Neighborhoods: The Science of Early Child Development.* Comm. Integrating Sci. Early Childhood Dev., ed. JP Shonkoff, DA Phillips. Board Children, Youth, Fam., Comm. Behav. Soc. Sci. Educ. Washington, DC: Natl. Acad. Press

Natl. Res. Counc. 2001. *Eager to Learn: Educating Our Preschoolers*, ed. BT Bowman, MS Donovan, MS Burns. Comm. Early Childhood Pedagogy. Comm. Behav. Soc.

Sci. Educ. Washington, DC: Natl. Acad. Press

Natl. Sci. Found. 2001. *Science and Engineering Degrees, by Race/Ethnicity of Recipients: 1990-1998.* Arlington, VA: Natl. Sci. Found.

Nguyen HH, Messe LA, Stollak GE. 1999. Toward a more complex understanding of acculturation and adjustment: cultural involvements and psychosocial functioning in Vietnamese youth. *J. Cross-Cult. Psychol.* 30:5–31

Nottelmann ED, Jensen PS. 1995. Comorbidity of disorders in children and adolescents: developmental perspectives. *Adv. Clin. Child Psychol.* 17:109–55

Ogbu J. 1978. *Minority Education and Caste.* San Diego, CA: Academic

Ollendick TH, Weist MD, Borden MC, Greene RW. 1992. Sociometric status and academic, behavioral, and psychological adjustment: a five year longitudinal study. *J. Clin. Psychol.* 60:80–87

Ortiz C, Stowe RM, Arnold DH. 2001. Parental influence on child interest in shared picture book reading. *Early Child. Res. Q.* 16:263–81

Page-Voth V, Graham S. 1999. Effects of goal setting and strategy use on the writing performance and self-efficacy parenting, and socioemotional development. *Child Dev.* 61:311–36

Phillips DA, Voran M, Kisker E, Howes C, Whitebook M. 1994. Child care for children in poverty: opportunity or inequity? *Child Dev.* 65:472–92

Pianta RC, La Paro KM, Payne C, Cox MJ, Bradley R. 2002. The relation of kindergarten classroom environment to teacher, family, school, characteristics, and child outcomes. *Elem. Sch. J.* 102:225–39

Pianta RC, Walsh DJ. 1998. Applying the construct of resilience in schools: caution from a developmental systems perspective. *Sch. Psychol. Rev.* 27:407–17

Posner JK, Vandell DL. 1994. Low-income children's after-school care: Are there beneficial effects of after-school programs? *Child Dev.* 65:440–56

Raffaele LM, Knoff HM. 1999. Improving home-school collaboration with disadvantaged families. *Sch. Psychol. Rev.* 28:448–66

Ramey CT, Ramey SL. 1998. Early intervention and early experience. *Am. Psychol.* 53:109–20

Rank MR, Hirschl TA. 1999. The economic risk of childhood in America: estimating the probability of poverty across the formative years. *J. Marriage Fam.* 61:1058–67

Rapport MD, Denney CB, Chung K, Hustace K. 2001. Internalizing behavior problems and scholastic achievement in children: cognitive and behavioral pathways as mediators of outcome. *J. Clin. Child Psychol.* 30:536–51

Raver CC. 2002. Emotions matter: making the case for the role of young children's emotional development for early school readiness. *Soc. Policy Rep.* In press

Raver CC, Zigler EF. 1997. Social competence: an untapped dimension in evaluating Head Start's success. *Early Child. Res. Q.* 12:363–85

Reynolds A. 1989. A structural model of first-grade outcomes for an urban, low socioeconomic status, minority population. *J. Educ. Psychol.* 81:594–603

Reynolds AJ. 1991. Early schooling of children at risk. *Am. Educ. Res. J.* 28:392–422

Reynolds AJ. 1992. Mediated effects of preschool intervention. *Early Educ. Dev.* 3:139–64

Reynolds AJ, Weissberg RP, Kasprow WJ. 1992. Prediction of early social and academic adjustment of children from the inner city. *Am. J. Community Psychol.* 20:599–624

Reynolds CR. 2000. Why is the psychometric research on bias in mental testing so often ignored? *Psychol. Public Policy Law* 6:144–50

Richters JE, Martinez PE. 1993. The NIMH Community Violence Project: I. Children as victims of and witnesses to violence. *Psychiatry* 56:7–21

Roberts RE, Sobhan M. 1992. Symptoms of depression in adolescence: a comparison of Anglo, African, and Hispanic Americans. *J. Youth Adolesc.* 21:639–51

Royer JM, Tronsky LN, Chan Y, Jacson SJ, Marchant H. 1999. Math-fact retrieval and the cognitive mechanism underlying gender differences in math test performance. *Contemp. Educ. Psychol.* 24:181–266

Scarborough HS, Dobrich W, Hager M. 1991. Preschool literacy experience and later reading achievement. *J. Learn. Disabil.* 24:508-11

Schoenwald SK, Henggeler SW. 1997. Combining effective treatment strategies within family preservation models of service delivery. In *Integrated Services for Children and Families: Opportunities for Psychological Practice*, ed. RJ Illback, CT Cobb, HM Joseph, pp. 121–36. Washington, DC: Am. Psychol. Assoc.

Schweinhart LJ, Barnes HV, Weikart DP, Barnett WS, Epstein AS. 1993. *Significant Benefits: The High/Scope Perry Preschool Study Through Age 27*. Ypsilanti, MI: High/Scope Press

Seitz V. 1991. Intervention programs for impoverished children: a comparison of educational and family support models. *Ann. Child Dev.* 7:73–103

Senechal M, LeFevre J, Smith-Chant BL, Colton KV. 2001. On refining theoretical models of emergent literacy: the role of empirical evidence. *J. Sch. Psychol.* 39:439–60

Shepard L, Kagan SL, Wurtz E, eds. 1998. *Principles and Recommendations for Early Childhood Assessments*. Washington, DC: Natl. Educ. Goals Panel

Shores RE, Wehby JH. 1999. Analyzing the classroom social behavior of students with EBD. *J. Emot. Behav. Disord.* 7:194–99

Shumow L, Vandell DL, Posner JK. 1998. Harsh, firm, and permissive parenting in low-income families: relations to children's academic achievement and behavioral adjustment. *J. Fam. Issues* 19:483–507

Shumow L, Vandell DL, Posner J. 1999. Risk and resilience in the urban neighborhood: predictors of academic performance among low-income elementary school children. *Merrill-Palmer Q.* 45:309–31

Skinner EA, Belmont NJ. 1993. Motivation in

the classroom: reciprocal effects of teacher behavior and student engagement across the school year. *J. Educ. Psychol.* 85:571–81

Skinner EA, Wellborn JG, Connell JP. 1990. What it takes to do well in school and whether I've got it: a process model of perceived control and children's engagement and achievements in school. *J. Educ. Psychol.* 82:22–32

Slavin RE. 1996. Research for the future: research on cooperative learning and achievement: what we know, what we need to know. *Contemp. Educ. Psychol.* 21:43–69

Smiley PA, Dweck CS. 1994. Individual differences in achievement goals among young children. *Child Dev.* 65:1723–43

Stanovich KE. 1986. Matthew effects in reading: some consequences of individual differences in the acquisition of literacy. *Read. Res. Q.* 21:360–407

Stanovich KE, Cunningham AE. 1992. Studying the consequences of literacy within a literate society: the cognitive correlates of print exposure. *Mem. Cogn.* 20:51–68

Stecher BM, Bohrnstedt GW. 2000. *Class Size Reduction in California: Summary of the 1998-99 Evaluation Findings.* Palo Alto, CA: Edsource

Steele RG, Armistead L, Forehand R. 2000. Concurrent and longitudinal correlates of depressive symptoms among low-income, urban, African American children. *J. Clin. Child Psychol.* 29:76–85

Steinberg L, Dornbusch SM, Brown BB. 1992. Ethnic differences in adolescent achievement. *Am. Psychol.* 47:723–29

Stevenson HW, Newman RS. 1986. Long-term prediction of achievement and attitudes in mathematics and reading. *Child Dev.* 57:646–59

Stipek JD, Feiler R, Daniels D, Milburn S. 1995. Effects of differential instructional approaches on young children's achievement and motivation. *Child Dev.* 66:209–23

Stipek JD, Ryan RH. 1997. Economically disadvantaged preschoolers: ready to learn but further to go. *Dev. Psychol.* 33:711–23

Stipek JD, Tannatt L. 1984. Children's judge-

ments of their own and their peers' academic competence. *J. Educ. Psychol.* 76:75–84

Stouthamer-Loeber M, Loeber R, Wei E, Farrington DP, Per-Olof H. 2002. Risk and promotive effects in the explanation of serious delinquency in boys. *J. Consult. Clin. Psychol.* 70:111–23

Stowe RM, Arnold DH, Ortiz C. 1999. Gender differences in the relationship of language development to disruptive behavior and peer relationships in preschoolers. *Appl. Dev. Psychol.* 20:521–36

Sulzby E, Teale W. 1991. Emergent literacy. In *Handbook of Reading Research*, ed. R Barr, M Kamil, P Mosenthaw, PD Pearson, 2:727–58. New York: Longman

Tremblay RE, Masse B, Perron D, LeBlanc M, Schwartzman AE, Ledingham JE. 1992. Early disruptive behavior, poor school achievement, delinquent behavior, and delinquent personality: longitudinal analyses. *J. Consult. Clin. Psychol.* 60:64–72

Tremblay RE, Pagani-Kurtz L, Masse LC, Vitaro F, Pihl RO. 1995. A bimodal preventive intervention for disruptive kindergarten boys: its impact through mid-adolescence. *J. Consult. Clin. Psychol.* 63:560–68

US Bur. Census. 1998. *Poverty in the United States: 1997. Curr. Popul. Rep. Ser. P-60, No. 201.* Washington, DC: US GPO

Wang MC, Gordon EW. 1994. *Educational Resilience in Inner-city America: Challenges and Prospects.* Hillsdale, NJ: Erlbaum

Weisner TS, Gallimore R, Jordan C. 1988. Unpackaging cultural effects on classroom learning: Native Hawaiian peer assistance and child-generated activity. *Anthropol. Educ. Q.* 19:327–53

Weissberg RP, Caplan M, Harwood RL. 1991. Promoting competent young people in competence-enhancing environments: a systems-based perspective on primary prevention. *J. Consult. Clin. Psychol.* 59:830–41

Wentzel KR, Asher SR. 1995. The academic lives of neglected, rejected, popular, and controversial children. *Child Dev.* 66:754–63

Werner EE, Smith RS. 1992. *Overcoming the*

Odds: High Risk Children from Birth to Adulthood. Ithaca, NY: Cornell Univ. Press

White KR. 1982. The relation between socioeconomic status and academic achievement. *Psychol. Bull.* 91:461–81

Whitehurst GJ, Epstein JN, Angell AC, Payne AC, Crone DA, Fischel JE. 1994. Outcomes of an emergent literacy intervention in Head Start. *J. Educ. Psychol.* 86:542–55

Whitehurst GJ, Lonigan CJ. 1998. Child development and emergent literacy. *Child Dev.* 69:848–72

Wigfield A, Eccles J, Yoon K, Harold R, Arbreton C, et al. 1997. Change in children's competence beliefs and subjective task values across the elementary school years: a three-year study. *J. Educ. Psychol.* 89:451–69

Wigfield A, Guthrie JT. 1997. Relations of children's motivation for reading to the amount and breadth of their reading. *J. Educ. Psychol.* 89:420–32

Yoshikawa H. 1994. Prevention as cumulative protection: effects of early family support and education on chronic delinquency and its risks. *Psychol. Bull.* 115:28–54

Zahn-Waxler C, Klimes-Dougan B, Slattery MJ. 2000. Internalizing problems of childhood and adolescence: prospects, pitfalls, and progress in understanding the development of anxiety and depression. *Dev. Psychopathol.* 12:443–66

Zigler E. 1999. Head Start is not child care. *Am. Psychol.* 54:142

Zigler E, Taussig C, Black K. 1992. Early childhood intervention: a promising preventative for juvenile delinquency. *Am. Psychol.* 47:997–1006

Annu. Rev. Psychol. 2003. 54:547–77
doi: 10.1146/annurev.psych.54.101601.145041
First published online as a Review in Advance on August 14, 2002

PSYCHOLOGICAL ASPECTS OF NATURAL LANGUAGE USE: Our Words, Our Selves

James W. Pennebaker, Matthias R. Mehl,
and Kate G. Niederhoffer
*Department of Psychology, University of Texas at Austin, Austin, Texas 78712;
e-mail: Pennebaker@psy.utexas.edu, Mehl@psy.utexas.edu*

Key Words   LIWC, text analysis, artificial intelligence, discourse, pronouns, particles

■ **Abstract**   The words people use in their daily lives can reveal important aspects of their social and psychological worlds. With advances in computer technology, text analysis allows researchers to reliably and quickly assess features of what people say as well as subtleties in their linguistic styles. Following a brief review of several text analysis programs, we summarize some of the evidence that links natural word use to personality, social and situational fluctuations, and psychological interventions. Of particular interest are findings that point to the psychological value of studying particles—parts of speech that include pronouns, articles, prepositions, conjunctives, and auxiliary verbs. Particles, which serve as the glue that holds nouns and regular verbs together, can serve as markers of emotional state, social identity, and cognitive styles.

CONTENTS

0066-4308/03/0203-0547$14.00

INTRODUCTION

The ways people use words convey a great deal of information about themselves, their audience, and the situations they are in. Individuals' choice of words can hint at their social status, age, sex, and motives. We sense if the speaker or writer is emotionally close or distant, thoughtful or shallow, and possibly extraverted, neurotic, or open to new experience. Although several *Annual Review* chapters have summarized research on language acquisition, production, comprehension, and its links to brain activity, this is the first to discuss how language and, more specifically, word use is a meaningful marker and occasional mediator of natural social and personality processes.

That the words people use are diagnostic of their mental, social, and even physical state is not a new concept. Freud (1901) provided several compelling examples in his discussion of parapraxes, or slips of the tongue. He pointed out that common errors in speech betray people's deeper motives or fears. Drawing heavily on psychoanalysis, Jacques Lacan (1968) extended these ideas by suggesting that the unconscious asserts itself through language. Indeed, language, in his view, is the bridge to reality. Philosopher Paul Ricoeur (1976) argued that the ways we describe events define the meanings of the events and that these meanings help us keep our grasp on reality. Similar assumptions are implicit in much of the work in sociolinguistics (e.g., Eckert 1999, Tannen 1994), narrative and discourse analyses (Schiffrin 1994), and communication research (Robinson & Giles 2001).

This article explores the methods and recent findings on word use rather than language per se: the styles in which people use words rather than the content of what they say. The distinction between linguistic style and linguistic content can be seen in how two people may make a simple request. "Would it be possible for you to pass me the salt?" and "Pass the salt," both express the speaker's desire for salt and direct the listener's action. However, the two utterances also reveal different features of the interactants' relationship, the speaker's personality, and perhaps the way the speaker understands himself.

Because word use is a relatively unstudied phenomenon, this article focuses on four broad topics. The first deals with ways researchers have tried to study the ways people naturally use words. By "natural," we refer to relatively open-ended responses to questions, natural interactions, and written or spoken text. The most common methodologies include manual word counts and, more recently, computer analyses of language. The second section of this article explores recent findings linking word use to individual differences. The final two sections consider the links between word usage and social or situational differences and how we can use words to mark psychological change.

METHODS OF STUDYING LANGUAGE USE: PSYCHOLOGICAL WORD COUNT APPROACHES

Although many of the assumptions about language as a psychological marker are shared, the methods of studying language and word use have often been a battleground. Most narrative researchers assume that language is, by definition, contextual. Consequently, phrases, sentences, or entire texts must be considered within the context of the goals of the speaker and the relationship between the speaker and the audience. Because of the complexity of communication, this strategy assumes that the investigator must attend to the meaning of the utterances in context. However defined, meaning is believed to be sufficiently multilayered to only be decoded by human judges who then evaluate what is said or written. Qualitative analyses, then, provide the researcher with broad impressions or agreed-upon descriptions of text samples. Very few discourse analyses rely on numbers or statistics (e.g., Schiffrin 1994).

An alternative perspective is that features of language or word use can be counted and statistically analyzed. Quantitative approaches to text analysis have gained increasing popularity over the past half century (for reviews see Popping 2000, Smith 1992, Weber 1994, West 2001). The existing approaches can be categorized into three broad methodologies. *Judge-based thematic content analyses* typically involve judges who identify the presence of critical thematic references in text samples on the basis of empirically developed coding systems (Smith 1992). Thematic content analyses have been widely applied for studying a variety of psychological phenomena such as motive imagery (e.g., Atkinson & McClelland 1948, Heckhausen 1963, Winter 1994), explanatory styles (Peterson 1992), cognitive complexity (Suedfeld et al. 1992), psychiatric syndromes (Gottschalk 1997), goal structures (Stein et al. 1997), arousal patterns associated with cultural shifts (Martindale 1990), and levels of thinking (Pennebaker et al. 1990).

A relatively new approach, *word pattern analysis*, has emerged from the artificial intelligence community. Rather than exploring text "top down" within the context of previously defined psychological content dimensions or word categories, word pattern strategies mathematically detect "bottom-up" how words covary across large samples of text (Foltz 1998, Popping 2000). One particularly promising strategy is latent semantic analysis (LSA) (e.g., Landauer & Dumais

1997), which is akin to a factor analysis of individual words. By establishing the factor structure of word use within a large number of writing samples, it is possible to learn how any new writing samples are similar to one another. Traditionally, this technique has been used to determine the degree to which two texts are similar in terms of their content.

The third general methodology prominent in quantitative text analysis focuses on *word count strategies*. Psychological word count strategies exist for both the analysis of content (what is being said) and style (how it is being said). Whereas they sometimes require rather complex linguistic analysis (e.g., active versus passive voice or metaphoric language use), most current approaches involve simple word counts, such as standard grammatical units (personal pronouns, prepositions) or psychologically derived linguistic dimensions (e.g., emotion words, achievement-related words). Word count strategies are based on the assumption that the words people use convey psychological information over and above their literal meaning and independent of their semantic context. Although some language researchers consider this assumption problematic, others see unique potentials in analyzing word choice because of judges' readiness to "read" content and their inability to monitor word choice (e.g., Hart 2001). With only one exception (Weintraub 1989), the most commonly used approaches presented below are computer based. In this section we briefly review six widely used methods that have evolved from very different theoretical perspectives.

The General Inquirer

Developed by Stone and colleagues in the early 1960s, the General Inquirer (Stone et al. 1966) is generally considered the "mother" of computerized text analysis. The General Inquirer is a compilation of a set of rather complex word count routines. It was designed as a multipurpose text analysis tool that was strongly informed by both need-based and psychoanalytic traditions. Historically, three thematic dictionaries, the *Harvard III Psychosociological Dictionary*, the *Stanford Political Dictionary*, and the *Need-Achievement Dictionary* have been applied the most, with the *Need-Achievement Dictionary* receiving special attention in psychology. The *Need-Achievement Dictionary* was created in an attempt to replace the complex judge-based scoring of achievement imagery in thematic apperception test (TAT) stories by computerized content analysis.

The General Inquirer goes beyond counting words. In a two-step process it first identifies so called homographs (ambiguous words that have different meanings depending on the context). It then applies a series of preprogrammed dis-ambiguation rules aimed at clarifying their meaning in the text. For example, human judges score the statement "He is determined to win" as achievement imagery. The General Inquirer identifies the word "determined" as an ambiguous NEED word and "win" as an ambiguous COMPETE word (because they both can have non-achievement-related meanings) and codes a statement as achievement imagery only if both aspects are present and occur in the NEED-COMPETE order.

The General Inquirer is unique in its flexibility. It can be used to study virtually any topic of interest by creating a user-defined dictionary. Its most critical advantage, the power to perform context-dependent word counts, is also its most serious pragmatic drawback. The construction of a custom dictionary with the specification of disambiguation rules is time consuming and in many cases not worth the extra effort (as compared with simple word counts). Nevertheless, it is not overstated to say that the General Inquirer has given birth to and still continues to shape the scientific field of computerized text analysis.

Analyzing Emotion-Abstraction Patterns: TAS/C

Mergenthaler and his research group realized the need for computer-assisted text analysis when trying to characterize key moments in psychotherapy sessions. Based on Bucci's (1995) referential cycle model, they developed a computer program called TAS/C that focuses exclusively on two language dimensions, emotional tone and abstraction. According to the theory, emotion-abstraction patterns occur periodically in psychotherapy sessions with insight processes (abstraction) following emotional events (emotion) with a time lag (Mergenthaler 1996).

For the analysis of emotional tone, defined as the density (rather than the valence) of emotion words in a given text, a dictionary was developed that contains more than 2000 items. The final restricted list of emotion words captures the three dimensions of pleasure, approval, and attachment which account for roughly 5% of the words of a text (Mergenthaler 1996). Abstraction is defined as the amount of abstract nouns in a given text. Abstract nouns are identified via the use of suffixes such as -ity, -ness, -ment, -ing or -ion. The abstraction dictionary includes 3900 entries and accounts for about 4% of the text. There is no overlap across the two dictionaries.

TAS/C analysis of emotion-abstraction patterns has been successfully applied to verbatim therapy protocols (Mergenthaler 1996) and attachment interviews (Buchheim & Mergenthaler 2000). More recently, TAS/C has been extended to include a measure of referential activity (Bucci 1995). Referential activity refers to the ability to verbalize nonverbal experiences, characterized in speech by concreteness, specificity, clarity, and imagery (Mergenthaler & Bucci 1999). It is captured by counting third person pronouns and prepositions. The TAS/C approach to analyzing language is theory driven and limited to a very narrow spectrum of linguistic styles.

Weintraub's Analysis of Verbal Behavior

At the core of Weintraub's (1981, 1989) explorations into what he calls verbal mannerisms lies the clinical observation that individuals speaking under stress often reveal important information about their degree of psychological adaptation. Drawing on his medical experience, Weintraub argued that psychological defense mechanisms manifest themselves in speech patterns obtained under mildly stressful conditions. For the assessment of these defense mechanisms, he developed a standardized procedure for sampling naturally occurring language. Participants are asked to talk into a microphone for 10 minutes on any topic.

The transcripts are then submitted to a linguistic analysis. Unlike other word count approaches, Weintraub's linguistic analysis is performed by naïve judges who "can score . . . [the transcripts] without extensive knowledge of lexical meaning." (Weintraub 1989, p. 11). The linguistic features he and his colleagues have been interested in are largely intuitively derived and are drawn from clinical experiences of how psychopathology surfaces in patients' language use. Weintraub's most recent work has focused on 15 linguistic dimensions including three pronoun categories (I, we, me), negatives (e.g., not, no, never), qualifiers (kind of, what you might call), expressions of feelings (e.g., I love, we were disgusted), and adverbial intensifiers (really, so).

Weintraub has explored people's verbal behavior in multiple ways. In addition to his main field of interest, the language of psychopathology, he also analyzed the Watergate transcripts, characterized speaking styles of post–World War II U.S. presidents, identified linguistic correlates of intimacy, and related language use to personality. Overall, Weintraub's approach can be considered stylistic. A strong emphasis is put on research that is clinically relevant and can inform psychoanalytically oriented psychotherapy.

Analyzing Verbal Tone with DICTION

Researchers in the area of language use in politics generally tend to focus on the content of political speeches (Winter 1973, Zullow et al. 1988). Roderick Hart (1984) is a communication researcher concerned with the subtle power of word choice. Over the past two decades he has developed and refined a computerized word count program called DICTION (Hart 2001). DICTION is designed to reveal the verbal tone of political statements by characterizing text on five statistically independent master variables: activity, optimism, certainty, realism, and commonality. The rationale behind these master variables is that "if only five questions could be asked of a given passage, these five would provide the most robust understanding." (Hart 2001, p. 45). The five master variables are composed of 35 linguistic subfeatures (e.g., optimism: praise, satisfaction, inspiration, blame, hardship, denial).

DICTION relies on 10,000 search words that are assigned to the categories without overlap. The output is either a profile of absolute values or norm scores based on 20,000 samples of verbal discourse. Special features of DICTION are the ability to "learn," i.e. update its database with every processed text, and a statistical weighting procedure for homographs, words that are spelled the same but have different meanings. DICTION has been used to analyze presidential and campaign speeches, political advertising, public debates, and media coverage. The DICTION approach is style focused and attempts to cover a broad range of linguistic aspects.

Linguistic Inquiry and Word Count

Linguistic Inquiry and Word Count (LIWC) (Pennebaker et al. 2001) was originally developed within the context of Pennebaker's work on emotional writing (Pennebaker & Francis 1996, Pennebaker et al. 1997). It was designed to discover which features of writing about negative life experiences could predict subsequent health improvements. More recently the use of LIWC has been expanded to tracking language use in text sources spanning classical literature, personal narratives, press conferences, and transcripts of everyday conversations (Pennebaker & Graybeal 2001).

LIWC uses a word count strategy whereby it searches for over 2300 words or word stems within any given text file. The search words have previously been categorized by independent judges into over 70 linguistic dimensions. These dimensions include standard language categories (e.g., articles, prepositions, pronouns—including first person singular, first person plural, etc.), psychological processes (e.g., positive and negative emotion categories, cognitive processes such as use of causation words, self-discrepancies), relativity-related words (e.g., time, verb tense, motion, space), and traditional content dimensions (e.g., sex, death, home, occupation). The LIWC dimensions are hierarchically organized. For example, the word "cried" would fall into the categories "sadness," "negative emotion," "overall affect," and "past-tense verb." The program is sufficiently flexible to allow for user-defined categories as well.

Whereas some of the LIWC categories were initially derived from psychological theories (e.g., inhibition words, discrepancy words), most categories try to capture information at a very basic linguistic (e.g., pronouns, articles, prepositions) as well as psychological level (e.g., positive emotions, negative emotions, cognitive words). In its current version LIWC has been most effective in tracking stylistic aspects of language use. However, researchers can use the traditional content categories (e.g., achievement, religion, sexuality) as well as create their own user-defined dimensions.

Biber: Factor Analyzing the English Language

Although Biber's (1988) work on language use was developed as a tool to understand the English language, it has important implications for psychology. Biber, an English professor, undertook an extensive empirical investigation in which he studied which linguistic dimensions emerge when discourse function rather then grammatical function is taken as the organizing principle. The purpose of this inductive approach was to factor analyze language and identify linguistic dimensions that would constitute a useful framework for describing language variations across different text types and genres.

Biber's study comprised two separate steps. The first sampled text from 23 spoken and written genres such as science fiction, humor, and press reports. A total of 481 texts with almost 1,000,000 words were submitted to a broad computerized word count analysis. The linguistic target features were selected without theoretical interest. Among the 67 selected variables were pronouns, adjectives, adverbs, adverbials, tense markers, nominalizations (words with -tion, -ment, -ness, or -ity suffixes), passive voice, and negations.

In the second step Biber submitted these 67 linguistic variables to a factor analysis. Generally words are considered to cluster together according to their grammatical function (e.g., pronouns, articles, prepositions). Biber's factor analytic approach clustered word patterns according to their natural co-occurrence. This provided useful information of a common discourse function behind certain words. Passive voice, for example, tends to statistically co-occur with nominalizations (Biber 1988). This then can help determine the role of words in creating the tone or character of a specific type of text. Biber found 6 general factors: informational versus involved production, narrative versus nonnarrative concerns, explicit versus situation-dependent reference, overt expression of persuasion, abstract versus nonabstract information, and on-line informational elaboration. He later demonstrated that the factors could separate the different linguistic genres of writing. Biber's analyses are groundbreaking in that they restructure the English language according to how it is used in text across different written and spoken genres.

Summary and Evaluation

Word count strategies count words within a given text sample irrespective of the context in which the words occur. They have an undisputed advantage of being able to perform reliably and efficiently with the use of computers. Word count approaches differ among each other in their specificity, i.e., in their attempt to either capture a maximum of words in a given text (e.g., Biber's approach, LIWC) or concentrate on only some linguistic aspects (e.g., TAS/C, need-achievement). In a compelling review of word count approaches, Hart (2001) compares judge-based or discourse approaches with more detached word count strategies by drawing on a metaphor of two people trying to understand a city by driving on the streets or viewing it from a helicopter. Both get quite different—but equally valid— pictures of a city. Whereas the helicopter is likely to miss details at the corner of a specific street, it is able to pick up differential patterns of light. Whereas word count approaches sometimes miss what elementary students could see, they provide linguistic information "from a distance," a distance that normal readers do not have because it is virtually impossible to ignore what is being said and concentrate on how something is said.

WORD USE AS A REFLECTION OF INDIVIDUAL DIFFERENCES

Clearly, there have been a variety of theoretical and methodological approaches to understanding how individuals select their words in natural writing or conversation. A research approach that takes advantage of linguistic styles has not been a staple of most current social, personality, or clinical perspectives. In this section we stand back and summarize psychological features of relatively natural word use. The psychometrics of word use are examined—with particular attention to words that tap linguistic styles. Some of the basic dimensions of word use are then demonstrated to be related to a variety of individual difference variables, such as demographic markers, traditional personality measures, and differences in mental and physical health.

Psychometric Properties of Word Use

The first step in exploring the links between word use and various individual difference markers is to establish the psychometrics of words themselves. That is, do people's word usage patterns fulfill the basic psychometric requirements of stability across time and consistency across context. Several investigators have begun to address this problem.

Gleser et al. (1959) had people talk for 5 minutes about an interesting life experience and obtained a measure of internal consistency by calculating split-half reliabilities. Across 21 language categories (e.g., word count, adjectives, substantives, pronouns, feelings) the average correlation between successive 2-minute intervals was 0.51, providing the first evidence that word choice is stable within a very short time frame. Using the General Inquirer approach, Schnurr et al. (1986) provided further support for the temporal stability of language use by reporting high within-person rank order correlations for the 83 variables of the Harvard III dictionary over a period of one week.

Pennebaker & King (1999) analyzed a large body of text samples taken from diaries, college writing assignments, and journal abstracts written across days and even years and demonstrated good internal consistency (across text type) for 36 language dimensions. The language variables were taken from the LIWC dictionary and comprised standard linguistic dimensions (e.g., articles, prepositions, pronouns) as well as broader psychological concepts (e.g., emotion words, causation words, words indicating social processes). Across several studies, word use in written language emerged as reliable across time, topic, and text source.

In a recent naturalistic field study, Mehl & Pennebaker (2002a) sampled students' everyday conversations twice for two days separated by 4 weeks using a newly developed minimally intrusive recording device called the electronically activated recorder (EAR) (Mehl et al. 2001). Again, the linguistic analyses showed that students' spontaneous word use is stable over time (average test-retest correlation for standard linguistic variables: $r = 0.41$, psychological processes: $r = 0.24$) and consistent across social context (e.g., word use at home versus in public places or in an amusement versus work context). These last two studies provide particularly promising evidence, as they demonstrate reliability based on an extremely large body of text samples (Pennebaker & King 1999) and spontaneous word use sampled from the entire spectrum of participants' everyday real life conversations (Mehl & Pennebaker 2002a).

Taken together, existing studies on the psychometrics of word use suggest that people's word choice is sufficiently stable over time and consistent across topic or context to use language as an individual difference measure. This is true for both basic grammatical categories as well as more psychologically based language dimensions.

Demographic Variables

With language use fulfilling the psychometric properties of an individual difference marker, are there basic differences in word use as a function of age and sex?

AGE   Whereas a fair amount of research exists on discourse and aging (Coupland & Coupland 2001), virtually no studies have addressed how word use changes over the life-span. In two overlapping projects Pennebaker & Stone (2002) explored the links between language use and age. In a cross-sectional analysis, multiple written or spoken text samples from disclosure studies from over 3000 research participants from 45 different studies representing 21 laboratories in 3 countries were subjected to computer text analyses to determine how people change in their use of 60 text dimensions as a function of age. A separate longitudinal project analyzed the collected works of 10 well-known novelists, playwrights, and poets who lived in the past 500 years. The results of the two projects converged in that both studies found pronounced differences in language use over the life-span. Whether famous authors were expressing themselves through their literature, experimental research participants were writing about traumatic experiences, or control participants were writing about their plans for the day, people exhibited remarkably consistent changes in their linguistic styles. With increasing age, individuals used more positive emotion words, fewer negative emotion words, fewer first person singular self-references, more future tense, and fewer past tense verbs. Age was also positively correlated with an increase in cognitive complexity (e.g., causation words, insight words, long words). In addition to challenging some of the cultural stereotypes on aging, these results suggest that language use can serve as a subtle linguistic age marker.

GENDER   In contrast to other demographic variables, the link between word use and gender has been extensively studied. Differences in women's and men's language have received widespread attention within the scientific community as well as in the popular media. Lakoff (1975) published a seminal work relating gender differences in language use to differential access to social power. She argued that women's lack of power in society results in their using a less assertive speech that manifests itself in a higher degree of politeness, less swearing, more frequent tag questions (e.g., "It is …, isn't it?"), more intensifiers (e.g., really, so), and more hedges (e.g., sort of, perhaps, maybe; also known as qualifiers or uncertainty words). Other early literature reviews (Haas 1979, Jay 1980) generally supported these findings. Overall, men were more directive, precise, and also less emotional in their language use.

Recently, Mulac et al. (2001) summarized the findings of more than 30 empirical studies and reported relatively unambiguous gender effects for 16 language features. According to this, typical male language features include references to quantity, judgmental adjectives (e.g., good, dumb), elliptical sentences ("Great picture."), directives ("Write that down."), and "I" references. Typical female language features among others comprise intensive adverbs (e.g., really, so), references to emotions, uncertainty verbs (seems to, maybe), negations (e.g., not, never), and hedges. Contrary to Lakoff (1975), no consistent gender differences were found in tag questions. Also, this review did not find that men and women reliably differed in their use of first person plural or second person pronouns as well as filler words in their natural speech (e.g., you know, like).

In evaluating these results, it is important to consider that, despite the comparatively large number of studies that went into the review, some of the findings are based on only a couple of studies with sometimes rather small language samples and only one text source. The evidence for men using "I," "me," and "my" at a higher rate than women, for example, comes from two studies conducted by Mulac and his colleagues that derived language exclusively from nonpersonal writings such as picture descriptions (Mulac & Lundell 1994) and fourth-grade impromptu essays (Mulac et al. 1990). Gleser et al. (1959)—not listed in Mulac et al.'s (2001) review—reported significantly higher first person singular self-references for women in transcripts of oral narratives about an interesting or dramatic personal life experience. Similarly, Pennebaker & King (1999) also found a higher use of "I," "me," and "my" in female students' stream of consciousness and coming-to-college writings.

Mehl & Pennebaker (2002a) sampled daily conversations of 52 college students in their natural environment using the EAR technology (Mehl et al. 2001). Overall men, compared to women, in their everyday conversations used nearly four times the amount of swear words and considerably more big words (consisting of more than six letters), anger words and articles. Women used more filler words (e.g., like, well), more discrepancy words (would, should, could), and more references to positive emotions, though not more emotion words in general. Again, the transcripts of women's spontaneous everyday speech contained more first person singular references.

Across the various studies women's and men's language differs on a variety of dimensions. Whereas these differences are consistent with a sociological framework of gender differences in access to power, at least some of them are also open to alternative explanations such as women's higher social engagement (e.g., Maccoby 1990). Despite the comparatively large number of studies available on gender differences in language use, no clear picture has yet evolved. Future research must more carefully consider and distinguish among different language sources. Is the data based on written or spoken language? Directed or spontaneous speech? Were same-sex or opposite-sex interactions sampled? Was the language derived from personal or nonpersonal, emotional or neutral material? Also, because language use is an inherently social phenomenon, one has to consider potentially bi-directional effects. In a recent study of e-mail conversations, Thomson et al. (2001) showed, for example, that participants spontaneously accommodate to gender-preferential language used by their conversation partners.

Traditional Personality Measures

As early as 1942, Sanford (1942) argued that verbal behavior was a powerful marker of personality. Several researchers have echoed this observation (e.g., Furnham 1990, Scherer 1979, Weintraub 1989). Although the empirical support is growing, the research linking self-reports of personality and word use is still in its early stages.

THE BIG FIVE   To our knowledge, only one study has attempted to correlate word use to the Big Five personality dimensions (self-reports of extraversion, neuroticism, agreeableness, conscientiousness, and openness to experience). Using multiple writing samples of several hundred college students, Pennebaker & King (1999) found modest but reliable effects of personality on word choice, with correlations ranging between 0.10 and 0.16. Overall, neuroticism was positively correlated with use of negative emotion words and negatively with positive emotion words; extraversion correlated positively with positive emotion words and words indicative of social processes; agreeableness was positively related to positive emotion and negatively to negative emotion words. In addition, neuroticism was characterized by a more frequent use of first person singular, a finding that is consistent with the idea that excessive use of first person pronouns reflects a high degree of self-involvement (e.g., Davis & Brock 1975, Ickes et al. 1986, Scherwitz & Canick 1988, Stirman & Pennebaker 2001, Weintraub 1989).

MOODS AND EMOTIONS   Only a handful of researchers have looked at how other personality variables are linked to unique word choices. Weintraub (1981, 1989) reported that an anxious disposition correlates with the use of first person singular and a high amount of explainers (e.g., because, since, in order to) and negatives (e.g., no, not, never). Self-ratings of anger are associated with an absence of qualifiers and a high use of negatives, rhetorical questions, and direct references to other objects or people. Weintraub (1989) also found that a dominant personality was associated with a high rate of commands, interruptions, and obscenities.

NEED STATES   Pennebaker & King (1999) examined the linguistic correlates of the needs for achievement, power, and affiliation. Whereas the language of achievement motivation assessed with a TAT measure was characterized by a low degree of immediacy (few first person singular pronouns, frequent use of articles, long words, and discrepancy words), an orientation towards the social past (frequent use of past tense and social words, infrequent use of present tense and positive emotions) and a lack of rationalization (infrequent use of insight and causation words, frequent use of negative emotion words), no such pattern was obtained with the Personality Research Form (PRF) measure of achievement orientation. The need for power showed no significant correlations with any of the language factors, either with the TAT or with the PRF measure. Somewhat counter-intuitively, participants high in TAT-based need for affiliation scored low on the social-past language dimension, which suggests that whereas they frequently used positive emotion words and present tense, they did not use many social words and past tense. In the PRF measure the need for affiliation was negatively correlated with making distinctions.

SELF-ESTEEM, SELF-MONITORING, AND MACHIAVELLIANISM   What is the relationship between language and stable aspects of the self? In an attempt to evaluate different measures of implicit self-esteem, Bosson et al. (2000) had participants write for 20 minutes about their deepest thoughts and feelings. Participants' explicit self-esteem assessed with various self-report scales correlated (sometimes marginally) with the use of negative emotion words. Use of self-references, however, were unrelated to both explicit and implicit measures of self-esteem.

Ickes et al. (1986) sought to discriminate between two conceptually related psychological constructs, Machiavellianism and self-monitoring. Coding participants' personal pronoun use in unstructured dyadic interactions, they found that Machiavellianism was related to an increased self-focus as reflected by more frequent use of first person singular pronouns. In contrast, however, self-monitoring was characterized by an increased other-focus as indicated by participants' higher use of second and third person pronouns. The analysis of spontaneous word choice in this study was important in identifying a linguistic marker of focus of attention. This marker helped in clarifying a subtle but critical distinction between two related impression management strategies.

SUMMARY   Although self-reports of personality are often associated with word use, the magnitudes of the relationships are surprisingly small. One explanation is that personality self-reports reflect people's theories of who they are. A self-theory can often be at odds with the ways people present themselves linguistically. Indeed, in at least two studies in which people either wrote about emotional topics (Pennebaker & Francis 1996) or talked about themselves on camera (Berry et al. 1997), judges' ratings of the emotionality of the text samples were more highly correlated with language use than with the writers' or speakers' self-reports of emotionality. This raises the traditional question about the "gold standard" of personality or emotionality: Should we rely on what people say about themselves or what others say about them (e.g., Hofstee 1994)?

Mental Health and Psychopathology

Does language carry diagnostic information about a person's mental health? Is there evidence for distinct psychopathological linguistic styles? The link between language use and clinical disorders has captured researchers' interest for more than 70 years and has resulted in a comparatively large number of clinical case studies as well as empirical investigations (for reviews see Jeanneau 1991, Rieber & Vetter 1995).

GENERAL PSYCHIATRIC DISORDERS   Oxman, Rosenberg, and their colleagues engaged in an extensive enterprise to use the General Inquirer as a diagnostic tool for psychiatric disorders. In a series of studies they showed that computerized linguistic analyses of speech samples are capable of reliably and accurately classifying patients into diagnostic groups, such as schizophrenia, depression, paranoia, or somatization disorder (e.g., Tucker & Rosenberg 1975, Oxman et al. 1982). In a comparison of the computer diagnosis against the diagnosis of professional psychiatrists, the computer diagnosis emerged as superior to clinicians' unstructured reading of the transcripts of patients' speech (Oxman et al. 1988).

DEPRESSION AND SUICIDALITY   In a study of the spontaneous speech of five elderly depressed individuals, Bucci & Freedman (1981) found depression to be related to an elevated use of first person singular pronouns and a lack of second person and third person pronouns. The authors interpret these findings as reflecting a weakness in connecting to others. Similarly, Weintraub (1981) found that when depressed people are asked to talk about any personal topic for 10 minutes, they use "I" at a higher rate than healthy individuals. Rude et al. (2002) confirmed this linguistic self-focus in depression for written language use. In their study, currently depressed students compared with never depressed students used significantly more first person singular pronouns in their personal essays. Interestingly, the effect was exclusively produced by a higher use of the word "I." The use of "me," "my," and "mine" was comparable between the two groups.

Stirman & Pennebaker (2001) sought to learn whether suicidal ideation could be linguistically detected. In an archival study, they compared the language use of 18 suicidal and nonsuicidal poets based on the corpus of their work over their careers. In line with a social disengagement model of suicide, suicidal poets were found to use first person plural pronouns at a lower and first person singular pronouns at a higher rate. They also made fewer references to other people and used more words associated with death. Finally, Lorenz & Cobb (1952) analyzed the language of 10 manic patients and also found that manics use first person singular references at a higher rate. Taken together, the convergent results from studies of depression, suicidal ideation, and mania suggest that affective disorders are characterized by a high degree of self-preoccupation. Attention habitually focused on the self linguistically surfaces in a more frequent use of the first person pronouns such as "I," "me," and "mine" (e.g., Davis & Brock 1975).

SUMMARY   Despite the sometimes conflicting results, language use can be an attractive as well as subtle diagnostic marker. Future clinical studies should be more rigorous in specifying clear clinical inclusion criteria and must rely on well-defined or standardized language samples. Better control conditions are also needed that allow inferences about the uniqueness of word use patterns in clinical versus non-clinical populations. Finally, it is necessary to shift toward a more theoretically fueled approach that helps explain the links between psychopathology and language.

Physical Health and Health Behavior

Can language use inform us about physical health from an individual difference perspective? Can word use distinguish healthy from unhealthy individuals? Studies linking language use to physical health are sparse. However, a small group of studies hints that features of disease- and/or health-related behaviors may be tied to language use.

HEART DISEASE PRONENESS   In a series of studies, Scherwitz (for reviews, see Scherwitz et al. 1985, Scherwitz & Canick 1988) has linked self-involvement to the Type A behavior pattern and coronary heart disease (CHD) outcomes. Self-involvement is operationalized as the frequency and density with which a person uses first person singular pronouns in answering the questions during the structured Type A interview. Results indicate that Type A is positively correlated with the use of first person singular. Of more clinical importance, however, are the findings that first person pronoun use in the structured interview is also related to systolic and diastolic blood pressure, coronary atherosclerosis, and prospectively to CHD incidence and mortality. Interestingly, the relationship between self-involvement and CHD outcomes in most cases remained significant even after statistically controlling for traditional risk factors such as age, cholesterol, cigarette smoking, and Type A behavior (Scherwitz et al. 1985, Scherwitz & Canick 1988).

MORTALITY   Drawing on the growing body of evidence that positive emotional processes can impact health in a salutary way, Danner et al. (2001) analyzed autobiographical sketches from 80 nuns written in their early 20s for emotional content. A strong positive relationship between the number of positive emotion words and life expectancy emerged from the longitudinal data. Although impressive, it again raises the question about which kind of language samples predict which kind of psychological and physical phenomena. Does the fact that nuns used more positive emotion words in a carefully produced one-page essay mean they approach their world in a more positive way in general or is this positivity effect restricted to specific verbal samples only?

Taken together, very few studies have linked word choice, physical health, and health behaviors. The findings, however, are encouraging considering that simply knowing how often an individual uses the words "I," "me," and "my" can provide important information about a risk for future CHD or that simply counting how often a person uses positive emotion words can carry information about that person's life expectancy—information with substantial real-life social importance.

WORD USE AS A REFLECTION OF SITUATIONAL AND SOCIAL PROCESSES

What we say and how we say it changes depending on the situation we are in. Piaget (1926) and other early developmentalists (e.g., McCarthy 1929) noted that young children changed the ways they spoke depending on the context of their interactions. As adults, we know that we use different words when addressing an audience of our peers versus when talking with a close friend. Although research on how language varies as a function of social situations has been systematically addressed in psychology and sociology, very little has relied on word use per se.

Perhaps the first in depth discussion of situational and social variations in language was by Goffman (1959) in his *Presentation of Self in Everyday Life*. Drawing on dramaturgical metaphors, Goffman argued that we all play different roles depending on the situation. In his analyses of groups, for example, Goffman suggested that voice characteristics and other nonverbal and paralinguistic cues shift depending on the formality of the situation, the nature of the audience, and the degree to which the speaker is integrated with or excluded from the other actors. Although he did not focus on the words people used, his work served as an important foundation.

Later research attempted to define which dimensions within social situations are most likely to be associated with language and, eventually, word usage. Hymes (1974), an anthropologist and a founder of sociolinguistics, argued that any speech act must be considered within eight dimensions ranging from the setting of the utterances, who the participants were, the goals of the interaction, etc. Other researchers such as Brown & Fraser (1979) and Forgas (1985) expanded on the idea of developing taxonomic structures of situations to help identify when and how language shifted. Psychological dimensions of situations related to language and communication included the situation's formality, cooperativeness, and involvement. Note that these approaches focused more on the nature of the interactions than on the word usage (Forgas 1985).

Formal Versus Informal Settings

Perhaps the most studied situational variations in the use of language have been between formal and informal situations. In addition to some of the early work on code switching, more recent research on politeness and verbal immediacy mark word shifts as a function of setting.

Code switching refers to changes in language, dialect, accent, or even forms of address that occur—often automatically—among interactants. Among U.S.

Spanish-English bilinguals, for example, it is common for individuals to use Spanish in informal social settings and English in more formal situations. Analyses of bilingual radio programs suggest that speakers may switch to Spanish when talking about emotional topics and English when discussing work, finances, or politics. Parallel findings can be seen in the use of the formal versus informal "you" in Spanish (Usted versus tu), French (vous versus tu), and German (Sie versus Du) (Brown & Gilman 1960, Sebeok 1960, Vaes et al. 2002).

Inherent in formal settings are disparities in power among interactants and an adherence to culturally proscribed norms of behavior. Goffman (1967) suggested that within such status-discrepant situations, individuals engage in "dramaturgic" work to sustain and enhance their public face. Brown & Levinson's (1987) politeness theory takes into account an individual's efforts to preserve the "face(s)" of others with whom one communicates. Whereas politeness theory is comprised of specific linguistic strategies to minimize threat to another's face, most studies are concerned with these tactics at the phrase level. Typically, the corpus of language is independently coded by human judges noting the frequency of each tactic. However, in many of Brown & Levinson's tactics word-level markers of politeness can be parsed out. For example, they propose impersonalizing the speaker and hearer by avoiding the pronouns I and you, using past tense to create distance and time, diminishing the force of speech by using hedge words such as perhaps, using slang to convey ingroup membership, and using inclusive forms (we and let's) to include speaker and hearer.

In an interesting application of the language of politeness in organizational studies, Morand (2000) had participants engage in laboratory role-plays in which they were required to address a hypothetical other of a given high or low status. Morand then independently coded the transcripts for the presence of politeness tactics. At the word level participants used more hedge words, past tense, subjunctive, formal words, honorifics (sir, Mr.), and apologies. Similar word-level findings are embedded in the phrases detected in the majority of politeness studies (Ambady et al. 1996, Brown & Gilman 1989, Brown & Levinson 1987).

A separate group of studies has found support for the centrality of the formal/informal dimension based on inductive analyses of language use. Wiener & Mehrabian (1968) and Mehrabian (1971) posited that a basic dimension to language was verbal immediacy. Individuals who were verbally immediate tend to use the present tense, are more personal in their interaction, and draw on the speaker and audience's shared realities. Markers of verbal immediacy were found to be more common in informal settings than in formal ones. Interestingly, parallel and independent findings have been reported by two other labs. Biber (1988), in his factor analysis of words, considered his first factor to be a marker of formality/informality. Words that loaded on the factor included first person singular and present tense verbs. Indeed, speech samples high on the informality factor tended to be personal conversations or informal writing samples. Using a much larger and homogeneous sample of students' writings, Pennebaker & King (1999) also found that the first and most robust factor was immediacy, which included first person singular, present tense verbs, short words, discrepancy words (would, should, could), and the non-use of articles.

Deception and Honesty

One of the more productive arenas for exploring word use has been in the deception literature. Multiple labs have attempted to discover if people change the ways they talk when being honest versus deceptive. In general, three classes of word categories have been implicated in deception: pronoun use, emotion words, and markers of cognitive complexity. Knapp et al. (1974) found that liars often avoid statements of ownership either to "dissociate" themselves from their words or owing to a lack of personal experience (see also Buller et al. 1996, Dulaney 1982, Knapp & Comadena 1979, Mehrabian 1971). Similarly, Wiener & Mehrabian (1968) reported that liars were more "non-immediate" than truth-tellers, and referred to themselves less often in their stories. In an analysis of five laboratory studies wherein participants were induced either to tell the truth or to lie about their thoughts or behaviors, truth-tellers consistently used a higher rate of first person singular pronouns (Newman et al. 2002).

Other studies have found that when individuals are made to be self-aware they are more "honest" with themselves (e.g., Carver & Scheier 1981, Duval & Wicklund 1972, Vorauer & Ross 1999) and self-references increase (e.g., Davis & Brock 1975). Finally, individuals who respond defensively (i.e., self-deceptively) when discussing personal topics tend to distance themselves from their stories and avoid taking responsibility for their behavior (Feldman Barrett et al. 2002, Schütz & Baumeister 1999, Shapiro 1989). In short, deceptive communications are characterized by fewer first person singular pronouns (I, me, and my).

In addition to pronoun use, the act of deception is generally associated with heightened anxiety and, in some cases, guilt. Several labs have found slight but consistent elevations in the use of negative emotion words during deception compared with telling the truth (e.g., Knapp & Comadena 1979, Knapp et al. 1974, Newman et al. 2002, Vrij 2000).

Finally, some promising results suggest that markers of cognitive complexity are associated with truth-telling. One such word category, referred to as exclusive words, is made up of prepositions and conjunctions such as but, except, without, and exclude. Exclusive words require the speaker to distinguish what is in a category from what is not in a category. In the Newman et al. (2002) studies, truth-tellers used far more exclusive words than did liars. In the act of deception, it is far too complex to invent what was done versus what was not done.

Emotional Upheavals

During periods of stress, trauma, or personal upheavals, people shift in the ways they think and express themselves. The words people use during stressful times change as well. Several studies of both personal and shared traumatic experience suggest that pronouns, emotion words, and other parts of speech subtly change.

PERSONAL UPHEAVALS   Capturing people's word use during times of personal crisis is often difficult and ethically questionable. One strategy is to capture the ongoing speech of public figures during tumultuous and quiescent times. One recent study examined the way Mayor Rudolph Giuliani spoke during his press conferences over his 8 years as mayor of New York City (Pennebaker & Lay 2002). During his first 5 years in office he was generally viewed as hostile, uncompromising, and cold. Indeed, LIWC analyses of his language in 14 press conferences during this time indicated that he used a very low rate of first person singular pronouns, a relatively low rate of positive emotion words, and a high rate of big words. In his sixth year of mayor he was diagnosed with prostate cancer, separated from his wife, and withdrew from the senate race against Hilary Clinton—all within the space of two weeks. In the weeks after these events the press reported that his personality seemed to have changed and that he was becoming a warm person. Analyses of his press conferences during this time found that his use of first person singular almost tripled, his use of positive emotion words increased slightly, and his language became simpler. A year and a half later, in the aftermath of the September 11 attacks, his language switched again. His first person singular pronouns dropped slightly and his use of specific and inclusive first person plural pronouns increased. His use of both positive and negative emotion words increased and his language remained simple but with increasing cognitive complexity (as measured by exclusive words).

SHARED UPHEAVALS   A common observation is that during a shared crisis, people come together. Several studies have demonstrated that immediately after a large-scale trauma individuals drop in their use of the word "I" and increase in their use of "we." In online chat groups immediately after the announcement of the death of Princess Diana, for example, use of first person plural increased by 135% and use of "I" dropped by 12% for approximately a week. By 10 days after the event pronoun use returned to normal levels (Stone & Pennebaker 2002).

More striking was an ongoing study of natural conversations that took place in the weeks surrounding the September 11 attacks. Approximately 15 students wore the electronically activated recorder (EAR) (Mehl et al. 2001) that recorded for 30 seconds every 12.5 minutes for up to two weeks after the attacks. All participants had previously worn the EAR for at least 1–2 days within the weeks prior to the attacks. The language analyses indicated that use of first person plural increased and first person singular decreased for at least 5 days following September 11. Interestingly, the use of "we" words was rarely in reference to the participants' country, ethnic group, or other abstract entity. Rather, the use of "we" generally referred to people in the participants' immediate setting (Mehl & Pennebaker 2002b).

Finally, analyses of the language used in the school newspaper of Texas A&M in the weeks before and after a tragic bonfire accident showed comparable effects. That is, first person plural pronouns doubled, as did the use of negative emotions, and use of big words dropped by over 10% (Gortner & Pennebaker 2002).

Social Interactions

In most cases, when two people interact they use words. Remarkably little research has been conducted on the ways the interactants use words with each other. An exception to this is a study by Cegala (1989), who sought to identify linguistic correlates of conversational engagement and detachment. In the study, 120 participants who did not know each other were asked to engage in a brief casual interaction with a same-sex peer. Participants were preselected on self-reported dispositional involvement in interactions and high-high, low-low, and high-low involvement dyads were created. Contrasts between the couple types showed that highly involved couples used a higher amount of certainty expressions, a higher degree of verbal immediacy, and more relational pronouns (we, us, our).

Beyond word use, numerous studies have pointed to the coordination of communicative behaviors during conversation. Indeed, the development of communication accommodation theory (Giles & Coupland 1991) has explored how individuals adapt to each other's communicative behaviors in order to promote social approval or communication efficiency. According to communication accommodation theory, individuals negotiate the social distance between themselves and their interacting partners, creating, maintaining, or decreasing that distance. This can be done linguistically, paralinguistically, and nonverbally. Specific accommodative strategies may include speech styles, speech rate, pitch, accent convergence, response latency, use of pauses, phonological variations, smiling, or gaze. Most tests of the theory have not focused on word use.

To our knowledge, only one project has explored linguistic accommodation at the word level (Niederhoffer & Pennebaker 2002). In two studies from Internet chat rooms, individuals getting to know one another in dyads exhibited linguistic style matching on both the conversational level as well as on a turn-by-turn level. This coordinated use of language occurs at a remarkably low level and includes word count and use of articles, prepositions, affect words, and cognitive words. These effects appear to hold up across the perceived quality of an interaction, the length of the interaction, whether face-to-face or on an internet-like chat, whether for experimental credit or, in the case of a separate analysis of the Watergate transcripts, to avoid impeachment and imprisonment.

Yet another interesting domain in which to consider communication patterns is within marital interactions. Gottman (1994) created couple typologies on the basis of communication patterns. Similarly, Ellis & Hamilton (1985) proposed that married couples can be distinguished by linguistic themes such as elaboration, complexity, and personal reference (see also Acitelli 1992). However, the majority of research is on a broader level than word use, per se.

One notable exception is the research of Sillars et al. (1997). Using a large sample of married couples, these researchers analyzed the first 40 utterances of discussions about marital problems. They found evidence for linguistic markers of relational characteristics such as increased usage of "we" pronouns in traditional (interdependent), satisfied and older married couples as compared to "I" usage in more autonomous couples. Interestingly, marital relationship subtypes (traditionals, separates, or independents) did not vary in linguistic elaboration (words per utterance, number of nouns and adjectives); however, language use was related to education. More educated participants had longer utterances and used more qualifiers. Similar research suggests that in less traditional couples there is increased usage of uncommon adjectives, nouns, and adverbs (Ellis & Hamilton 1985). Taken together these findings support the idea that surface features of language carry relational meaning. Furthermore, personal pronoun use (I, we) in marital interactions can reflect differences in the degree to which couples frame their relationship as inter- or independent.

WORD USE AS A REFLECTION OF PSYCHOLOGICAL AND HEALTH CHANGE

Since 1986 dozens of studies have demonstrated that writing about emotional upheavals can affect people's psychological and physical health. The typical disclosure studies require participants to write for 3–5 days for 15–30 minutes per day about either emotional or superficial topics. The writing intervention has been found to reduce physician visits for illness (e.g., Pennebaker & Beall 1986, Smyth 1998), improve medical markers of health (e.g., Smyth et al. 1999), bring about higher grades among students (Pennebaker & Francis 1996), and result in higher re-employment rates among adults who have lost their jobs (Spera et al. 1994). These effects have been found for individuals across multiple cultures, age groups, and instructional sets (for a broad review, see Lepore & Smyth 2002).

Why does writing or talking about emotional upheavals affect physical and psychological health? This question, of course, goes beyond the writing paradigm and addresses the broader question of why psychotherapy itself is effective. Several overlapping possibilities exist. One deals with the construction of a narrative. That is, individuals who write about traumas naturally come to a coherent understanding of the event. Further, this understanding is thought to be inherent in the cognitive language of their disclosure. Other possibilities include changes in perspectives when writing that may influence individuals' social orientations.

Use of Cognitive and Emotion Words

One of the primary motivations for developing the LIWC program was to learn if the language individuals use while disclosing emotional topics could predict long-term health changes. Based on the Pennebaker & Francis (1996) pilot study, we found that a particular linguistic "fingerprint" was associated with reductions in physician visits following participation in the disclosive writing. Those who wrote about traumas were more likely to benefit if, over the 3 days of writing, they used a high number of positive emotion words, a moderate number of negative emotion words, and, most important, an increasing number of cognitive (i.e., causal and insight) words from beginning to the last day of writing.

These effects were applied to six writing studies in a more systematic way (see Pennebaker et al. 1997). Again, the same linguistic pattern predicted improved health. The implications of these findings are intriguing. First, use of emotion terms is moderately important. Positive emotion words are linearly related to health, whereas counter to our earlier predictions, negative emotion words are curvilinearly related (an inverse-U function). These findings support current views on the value of optimism (e.g., Scheier & Carver 1985, Peterson et al. 1988). At the same time the negative emotion findings are consistent with the repressive coping literature (Jamner et al. 1988) in that those people who do not use negative emotion words in describing traumatic events are at greater risk for subsequent health problems than those who use at least some negative emotion words.

Most striking, however, are the relative effect sizes for changes in cognitive words. An increasing use of cognitive words accounted for far more variance in health improvement than did emotion words. These data, as noted below, suggest that the construction of a story or narrative concerning an emotional upheaval may be essential to coping. Particularly exciting is that this pattern of effects has now been reported by three independent labs. Keough et al. (KA Keough, J Garcia, CM Steele, unpublished) found that cognitive change over a 2-week diary-writing period was linked to health improvements. In a lab study with medical students, Petrie et al. (1999) discovered that the more individuals' cognitive word counts increased over the 3 days of writing, the greater their lymphocyte counts after each day after writing. Klein & Boals (2001) have reported that an increase in cognitive word use over the days of writing is linked to measures of greater working memory up to 12 weeks after the study.

Use of Word Analyses in Psychotherapy

A small group of psychoanalytically oriented researchers have been interested in the ways clients use language in therapy sessions. Bucci (e.g., 1995) and Mergenthaler (1996) have separately and together (Mergenthaler & Bucci 1999) identified word patterns that predict positive therapeutic outcomes. As noted above, the authors identified three categories of words that are easily captured in computer analyses: emotional tone, abstraction, and referential activity. Using this coding system, the authors argue that successful therapy requires clients to move from highly specific referential activity and high emotional tone to high levels of abstraction. Indeed, analyses of selected psychoanalytic therapy sessions (Mergenthaler 1996) as well as written disclosure essays (Bucci 1995) support these predictions. These patterns of effects are remarkably consistent with the LIWC analyses of Pennebaker et al. (1997).

References to Self and Others: Pronouns and Perspectives

As mentioned above, an alternative computer-based approach to linguistic analysis such as latent semantic analysis (LSA) relies on more inductive ways of establishing the pattern of word use (e.g., Landauer & Dumais 1997). This technique has been used to determine the degree to which two texts are similar in terms of their content. In theory, one might predict that the more similar the content of trauma essays over the 3–4 days of writing, the more the person's health would improve. If one made such a prediction, however, one would be wrong. LSA analyses of three writing studies failed to uncover any relationship between linguistic content and health.

An alternative way to think about writing is to focus on writing style as opposed to writing content. Style is, to a large extent, determined by the most commonly used words, referred to as particles—pronouns, articles, conjunctions, prepositions, and auxiliary verbs. Interestingly, most LSA techniques routinely omit particles because they do not carry the same information as more content-heavy nouns and verbs. Across a series of style-based LSA analyses, we have discovered that particles in general and pronouns in particular have been found to strongly correlate with health improvements. Basically, the more individuals shift in their use of pronouns from day to day in writing, the more their health improves. Across three separate studies, pronoun shifts among trauma writers correlated between 0.3 and 0.5 with changes in physician visits (Campbell & Pennebaker 2002). Closer inspection of these data suggest that healthy writing is associated with a relatively high number of self-references on some days but not others. Alternatively, people who always write in a particular voice—such as first person singular—simply do not improve.

Although the LSA studies are still in the early stages, they suggest that the ability to change perspective in dealing with an emotional upheaval may be critically important. The data also indicate that pronouns may be an overlooked linguistic dimension that could have important meaning for researchers in health and social psychology. After all, pronouns are markers of self-versus group identity (e.g., I versus we) as well as of the degree to which people focus on or relate to others. Pronouns may provide insight into people's level of social integration as well as self-focus.

FUTURE DIRECTIONS IN THE STUDY OF WORD USE

This review is intended to whet researchers' appetite for the power of words in natural language. From a methodological perspective, the analysis of word use is simple, reliable, fast, and relatively inexpensive. In addition, samples of words are readily available from open-ended questionnaire items, the Internet, emails, banks of text corpora, and transcripts of spoken text. Despite the practicality of measuring word use, many of the biggest questions surround their meaning and interpretation. In this final section we point to some intriguing and vexing questions raised by the word use approach.

Which Words Should We be Studying?

Most of this review has focused on words that reflect linguistic style rather than content. Markers of linguistic style are generally associated with relatively common words such as pronouns and articles. Many of the more content-heavy words—nouns, regular verbs, and modifiers—have not yielded many consistent social or psychological effects. This may reflect the fact that linguistic content is heavily dependent on the situation or topic the person is instructed to think or talk about. Three general topics that are ripe for investigation are the analysis of particles, emotions, and traditional content dimensions.

PARTICLES OR FUNCTION WORDS   Particles (which include pronouns, articles, prepositions, conjunctives, and auxiliary words) are remarkable for several reasons. In the English language there are fewer than 200 commonly used particles, yet they account for over half of the words we use. Of particular relevance, research on brain damage to the language areas suggests that particles are processed in different regions and in different ways than content words. For example, damage to Broca's area (a region generally associated with the left frontal lobe) often causes patients to speak hesitantly using nouns and regular verbs but not particles. Damage to Wernicke's area (left temporal lobe) has been reported to cause individuals to speak in a "word salad" wherein they use a high number of particles but with very little content (Miller 1995).

Particles serve as the glue that holds content words together. But particles are more than mere glue. They are referential words that have tremendous social and psychological meaning. To use a pronoun requires the speaker and listener to share a common knowledge of who the referent is. Consider the following: "John went to the store to buy some bread. After getting it, he drove home." The pronouns "it" and "he" are place holders and represent the shared and temporary knowledge that it = bread and he = John. Pronoun use requires a relatively sophisticated awareness of the audience's ability to track who is who. Prepositions are also referential. To know the meaning of over, on, to, etc. demands that the speaker and listener have a rudimentary understanding of the relative, real, or symbolic location of the speaker. Similar arguments can be made about articles (the use of "a" versus "the") and conjunctions (but, which). More informal settings presuppose a shared frame of reference (cf., Brown 1968). Particles, then, can be construed as having tremendous social implications. From a Grice (1975) perspective, the discerning particle user must have some degree of social and cognitive skill.

All particles, of course, are not equally interesting from a social or personality psychology perspective. Of those that have emerged in the word use literature, pronouns are among the most revealing. Use of first person singular, for example, is associated with age, sex, depression, illness, and more broadly, self-focus. First person plural can variously be a marker of group identity and, on occasion, a sign of emotional distancing (Pennebaker & Lay 2002). Second and third person pronouns are, by definition, markers to suggest that the speaker is socially engaged or aware.

Future research must begin exploring the nature of pronouns and other particles in much greater detail. For example, psychological researchers have naively assumed that all first person singular pronouns are comparable. Even William James (1890) argued that there were profound differences between the "active" I and the "passive" me. In fact, factor analyses of individual pronouns often find that all first person singular pronouns do not always load on the same factor (Campbell & Pennebaker 2002). Some very basic psychometric work is needed on pronouns and other particles at the word level to disentangle their mathematical and psychological meaning.

EMOTION WORDS   Virtually every psychologically based text analysis approach has started from the assumption that we can detect peoples' emotional states by studying the emotion words they use. The reality is that in daily speech, emotional writing, and even affect-laden poetry, less than 5% of the words people use can be classified as emotional. In reviewing the various word use studies, it is striking how weakly emotion words predict people's emotional state.

From an evolutionary perspective, language did not emerge as a vehicle to express emotion. In natural speech we generally use intonation, facial expression, or other nonverbal cues to convey how we feel. Emotional tone is also expressed through metaphor and other means not directly related to emotion words. Taken together, it is our sense that emotion researchers should hesitate before embarking on studies that rely exclusively on the natural production of emotion words.

CONTENT WORDS AND THEMES   Although not emphasized in this article, word count strategies are generally based on experimenter-defined word categories. These categories are based on people's beliefs about what words represent. Hence, they are ultimately subjective and culture bound. Content-based dictionaries that are aimed at revealing what people are saying have not yielded particularly impressive results owing in large part to the almost infinite number of topics people may be dealing with. With the rapidly developing field of artificial intelligence, the most promising content or theme-based approaches to text analysis involve word pattern analyses such as LSA. These purely inductive strategies provide a powerful way to decode more technical or obscure linguistic topics. For researchers interested in learning what people say—as opposed to how they say it—we recommend this new analytic approach.

SOME FINAL WORDS: LIMITATIONS AND POSSIBILITIES

The adoption of a word use approach to the analysis of naturally occurring written or spoken language is fraught with problems. Virtually all text analysis programs that rely on word counts are unable to consider context, irony, sarcasm, or even the problem of multiple meanings of words. Many of the traditional problems studied in communication, such as ingroup-outgroup status, formality of settings, and requests, are not easily detected with word counts (cf., Krauss & Fussell 1996). In a discussion of the potential shortcomings of a computer program such as the General Inquirer, Zeldow & McAdams (1993) have questioned whether lower-level word counts can have true psychological meaning. Although this review points to the covariation between word counts and meaning, no one has yet devised a compelling psychological theory of word usage.

The words a person uses clearly have an impact on the listener or reader. Just as the words people choose when talking or writing may betray their thoughts and feelings, those words may be processed at a low or nonconscious level by the listener or reader. Indeed, the speed by which we read or hear words like "the" or "my" in a sentence competes with traditional primes used in experimental or social psychology. The presumed power of the media or of great speakers or writers may ultimately reside as much in how they use words as in what they say (cf., Hogenraad et al. 1995).

Far more topics surrounding word use have been overlooked than covered in this review. We have not discussed differences between English and other languages, the differences between written and spoken language, or the difficulties of second language learning (where most of us make errors in particle use rather than content words). We have not mentioned issues such as intelligence, stereotype communication, language proficiency, or the early development of word knowledge and use.

Despite these shortcomings, the spotty history of word count approaches points to their potential value in psychological research. Most of us are adrift in a sea of words—from the time we awake listening to the radio, to reading the morning paper, to talking with family, colleagues, and friends. And we are spitting out words at almost the same rate at which we are taking them in. Words are a central feature of social, clinical, personality, and cognitive psychology. It is time that we started taking them a bit more seriously and using them as tools in understanding who we are and what we do.

ACKNOWLEDGMENTS

Preparation of this paper was aided by a grant from the National Institutes of Health (MH52391). We are indebted to Sam Gosling and Rod Hart for comments on an earlier draft.

The *Annual Review of Psychology* is online at http://psych.annualreviews.org

LITERATURE CITED

Acitelli L. 1992. You, me, and us: perspectives on relationship awareness. In *Understanding Relationship Processes*, Vol. 1. *Individuals and Relationships*, ed. S Duck, pp. 44–74. Newbury Park, CA: Sage

Ambady N, Koo J, Lee F, Rosenthal R. 1996. More than words: linguistic and nonlinguistic politeness in two cultures. *J. Personal. Soc. Psychol.* 70:996–1011

Atkinson JW, McClelland DC. 1948. The effect

of different intensities of the hunger drive on thematic apperception. *J. Exp. Psychol.* 38:643–58

Berry DS, Pennebaker JW, Mueller JS, Hiller WS. 1997. Linguistic bases of social perception. *Personal. Soc. Psychol. Bull.* 23:526–37

Biber D. 1988. *Variation Across Speech and Writing.* Cambridge: Cambridge Univ. Press

Bosson JK, Swann WB Jr, Pennebaker JW. 2000. Stalking the perfect measure of implicit self-esteem: the blind men and the elephant revisited? *J. Personal. Soc. Psychol.* 79:631–43

Brown P, Fraser C. 1979. Speech as a marker of situation. See Sherer & Giles 1979, pp. 33–62

Brown P, Levinson SC. 1987. *Politeness: Some Universals in Language Usage.* Cambridge: Cambridge Univ. Press

Brown R. 1968. *Words and Things: An Introduction to Language.* New York: Free Press

Brown R, Gilman A. 1960. The pronouns of power and solidarity. See Sebeok 1960, pp. 253–76

Brown R, Gilman A. 1989. Politeness theory in Shakespeare's four major tragedies. *Lang. Soc.* 18:159–212

Bucci W. 1995. The power of the narrative: a multiple code account. In *Emotion, Disclosure, and Health,* ed. JW Pennebaker, pp. 93–122. Washington, DC: Am. Psychol. Assoc.

Bucci W, Freedman N. 1981. The language of depression. *Bull. Menninger Clin.* 45:334–58

Buchheim A, Mergenthaler E. 2000. The relationship among attachment representation, emotion-abstraction patterns, and narrative style: a computer-based text analysis of the Adult Attachment Interview. *Psychother. Res.* 10:390–407

Buller DB, Burgoon JK, Buslig A, Roiger J. 1996. Testing Interpersonal Deception Theory: the language of interpersonal deception. *Commun. Theory* 6:268–89

Campbell RS, Pennebaker JW. 2002. The secret life of pronouns: flexibility in writing style and physical health. *Psychol. Sci.* In press

Carver CS, Scheier MF. 1981. *Attention and Self-Regulation: A Control-Theory Approach*

to *Human Behavior.* New York: Springer-Verlag

Cegala D. 1989. A study of selected linguistic components of involvement in interaction. *West. J. Speech Commun.* 53:311–26

Coupland N, Coupland J. 2001. Language, ageing, and ageism. See Robinson & Giles 2001, pp. 465–86

Danner DD, Snowdon DA, Friesen WV. 2001. Positive emotions in early life and longevity: findings from the Nun Study. *J. Personal. Soc. Psychol.* 80:804–13

Davis D, Brock TC. 1975. Use of first person pronouns as a function of increased objective self-awareness and performance feedback. *J. Exp. Soc. Psychol.* 11:389–400

Dulaney EF. 1982. Changes in language behavior as a function of veracity. *Hum. Commun. Res.* 9:75–82

Duval S, Wicklund RA. 1972. *A Theory of Objective Self-Awareness.* New York: Academic

Eckert P. 1999. *Language Variation as Social Practice: The Linguistic Construction of Identity in Belten High.* New York: Blackwell

Ellis D, Hamilton M. 1985. Syntactic and pragmatic code choice in interpersonal communication. *Commun. Monogr.* 52:264–78

Feldman Barrett L, Williams NL, Fong GT. 2002. Defensive verbal behavior assessment. *Personal. Soc. Psychol. Bull.* 28:776–88

Foltz PW, ed. 1998. Special issue: quantitative approaches to semantic knowledge representation. *Discourse Process.* 25:whole issue

Forgas J, ed. 1985. *Language and Social Situations.* New York: Springer

Freud S. 1901. *Psychopathology of Everyday Life.* New York: Basic Books

Furnham A. 1990. Language and personality. In *Handbook of Language and Social Psychology,* ed. H Giles, WP Robinson, pp. 73–95. New York: Wiley

Giles H, Coupland N. 1991. *Language: Contexts and Consequences.* Pacific Grove, CA: Brooks/Cole

Gleser GC, Gottschalk LA, Watkins J. 1959. The relationship of sex and intelligence to choice of words: a normative study of verbal behavior. *J. Clin. Psychol.* 15:183–91

Goffman E. 1959. *The Presentation of Self in Everyday Life.* Garden City, NY: Doubleday

Goffman E. 1967. *Interaction Ritual: Essays on Face-to-Face Behavior.* Garden City, NY: Anchor & Doubleday

Gortner EM, Pennebaker JW. 2002. The anatomy of a disaster: media coverage and community-wide health effects of the Texas A&M bonfire tragedy. *J. Soc. Clin. Psychol.* In press

Gottman J. 1994. *Why Marriages Succeed or Fail.* New York: Simon & Schuster

Gottschalk LA. 1997. The unobtrusive measurement of psychological states and traits. In *Text Analysis for the Social Sciences: Methods for Drawing Statistical Inferences from Texts and Transcripts*, ed. CW Roberts, pp. 117–29. Mahwah: Erlbaum

Grice HP. 1975. Logic and conversation. In *Syntax and Semantics 3*, ed. P Cole, J Morgan, pp. 41–58. New York: Academic

Haas A. 1979. Male and female spoken language differences: stereotypes and evidence. *Psychol. Bull.* 86:616–26

Hart RP. 1984. *Verbal Style and the Presidency: A Computer-Based Analysis.* New York: Academic

Hart RP. 2001. Redeveloping DICTION: theoretical considerations. See West 2001, pp. 43–60

Heckhausen H. 1963. *Hoffnung und Furcht in der Leistungsmotivation.* Meisenheim, Ger: Hain

Hofstee WKB. 1994. Who should own the definition of personality? *Eur. J. Personal.* 8:149–62

Hogenraad R, McKenzie DP, Morval J, Ducharme FA. 1995. Paper trails of psychology: the words that made applied behavioral sciences. *J. Soc. Behav. Personal.* 10:491–516

Hymes D. 1974. *Foundations of Sociolinguistics: An Ethnographic Approach.* Philadelphia: Univ. Penn. Press

Ickes W, Reidhead S, Patterson M. 1986. Machiavellianism and self-monitoring: as different as "me" and "you." *Soc. Cogn.* 4:58–74

James W. 1890. *The Principles of Psychology.* New York: Holt & Co.

Jamner LD, Schwartz GE, Leigh H. 1988. The relationship between repressive and defensive coping styles and monocyte, eosinophile, and serum glucose levels: support for the opioid peptide hypothesis of repression. *Psychosom. Med.* 50:567–75

Jay TB. 1980. Sex roles and dirty word usage: a review of the literature and a reply to Haas. *Psychol. Bull.* 88:614–21

Jeanneau M. 1991. *Word pattern and psychological structure: empirical studies of words and expressions related to personality organization.* PhD thesis. Dep. Applied Psychol., Umeå Univ., Sweden

Klein K, Boals A. 2001. Expressive writing can increase working memory capacity. *J. Exp. Psychol.: Gen.* 130:520–33

Knapp ML, Comadena MA. 1979. Telling it like it isn't: a review of theory and research on deceptive communications. *Hum. Commun. Res.* 5:270–85

Knapp ML, Hart RP, Dennis HS. 1974. An exploration of deception as a communication construct. *Hum. Commun. Res.* 1:15–29

Krauss RM, Fussell SR. 1996. Social psychological models of interpersonal communication. In *Social Psychology: Handbook of Basic Principles*, ed. ET Higgins, AW Kruglanski, pp. 655–701. New York: Guilford

Lacan J. 1968. *The Language of the Self: The Function of Language in Psychoanalysis.* Baltimore: Johns Hopkins Press

Lakoff RT. 1975. *Language and Woman's Place.* New York: Harper & Row

Landauer TK, Dumais ST. 1997. A solution to Plato's problem: the latent semantic analysis theory of the acquisition, induction, and representation of knowledge. *Psychol. Rev.* 104:211–40

Lepore SJ, Smyth J. 2002. *The Writing Cure.* Washington, DC: Am. Psychol. Assoc.

Lorenz M, Cobb S. 1952. Language behavior in manic patients. *Arch. Neur. Psych.* 67:763–70

Maccoby EE. 1990. Gender and relationships:

a developmental account. *Am. Psychol.* 45: 513–20

Martindale C. 1990. A *Clockwork Muse: The Predictability of Artistic Change.* New York: Basic

McCarthy D. 1929. A comparison of children's language in different situations and its relation to personality traits. *J. Genet. Psychol.* 36:583–91

Mehl MR, Pennebaker JW. 2002a. *The Sounds of Social Life: A Psychometric Analysis of Students' Daily Social Environments and Natural Conversations.* Submitted

Mehl MR, Pennebaker JW. 2002b. *The Social Dynamics of a Cultural Upheaval: Everyday Social Life in the Aftermath of the September 11 Attack on America.* In preparation

Mehl MR, Pennebaker JW, Crow MD, Dabbs J, Price JH. 2001. The electronically activated recorder (EAR): a device for sampling naturalistic daily activities and conversations. *Behav. Res. Methods Instrum. Comput.* 33:517–23

Mehrabian A. 1971. Nonverbal betrayal of feeling. *J. Exp. Res. Personal.* 5:64–73

Mendoza NA, Hosch HM, Ponder BJ, Carrillo V. 2000. Well . . . ah . . . hesitations and hedges as an influence on jurors' decisions. *J. Appl. Soc. Psychol.* 30:2610–21

Mergenthaler E. 1996. Emotion-abstraction patterns in verbatim protocols: a new way of describing psychotherapeutic processes. *J. Consult. Clin. Psychol.* 64:1306–15

Mergenthaler E, Bucci W. 1999. Linking verbal and non-verbal representations: computer-analysis of referential activity. *Br. J. Med. Psychol.* 72:339–54

Miller G. 1995. *The Science of Words.* New York: Sci. Am. Library

Morand DA. 2000. Language and power: an empirical analysis of linguistic strategies used in superior-subordinate communication. *J. Organ. Behav.* 21:235–48

Mulac A, Bradac JJ, Gibbons P. 2001. Empirical support for the gender-as-culture hypothesis: an intercultural analysis of male/female language differences. *Hum. Commun. Res.* 27:121–52

Mulac A, Lundell TL. 1994. Effects of gender-linked language differences in adult's written discourse: multivariate tests of language effects. *Lang. Commun.* 14:299–309

Mulac A, Studley LB, Blau S. 1990. The gender-linked language effect in primary and secondary students' impromptu essays. *Sex Roles* 23:439–69

Newman ML, Pennebaker JW, Berry DS, Richards JM. 2002. Lying words: predicting deception from linguistic styles. *Personal. Soc. Psychol. Bull.* In press

Niederhoffer KG, Pennebaker JW. 2002. Linguistic synchrony in social interaction. *J. Lang. Soc. Psychol.* In press

Oxman TE, Rosenberg SD, Schnurr PP, Tucker GJ. 1988. Diagnostic classification through content analysis of patients' speech. *Am. J. Psychiatry* 145:464–68

Oxman TE, Rosenberg SD, Tucker GJ. 1982. The language of paranoia. *Am. J. Psychiatry* 139:275–82

Pennebaker JW, Beall SK. 1986. Confronting a traumatic event: toward an understanding of inhibition and disease. *J. Abnorm. Psychol.* 95:274–81

Pennebaker JW, Czajka JA, Cropanzano R, Richards BC, Brumbelow S, et al. 1990. Levels of thinking. *Personal. Soc. Psychol. Bull.* 16:743–57

Pennebaker JW, Francis ME. 1996. Cognitive, emotional, and language processes in disclosure. *Cogn. Emot.* 10:601–26

Pennebaker JW, Francis ME, Booth RJ. 2001. *Linguistic Inquiry and Word Count (LIWC): LIWC 2001.* Mahwah, NJ: Erlbaum

Pennebaker JW, Graybeal A. 2001. Patterns of natural language use: disclosure, personality, and social integration. *Curr. Dir. Psychol. Sci.* 10:90–93

Pennebaker JW, King LA. 1999. Linguistic styles: language use as an individual difference. *J. Personal. Soc. Psychol.* 77:1296–312

Pennebaker JW, Lay TC. 2002. Language use and personality during crisis: analyses of Mayor Rudolph Giuliani's press conferences. *J. Res. Personal.* 36:271–82

Pennebaker JW, Mayne TJ, Francis ME.

1997. Linguistic predictors of adaptive bereavement. *J. Personal. Soc. Psychol.* 72:863–71

Pennebaker JW, Stone LD. 2002. *Words of Wisdom: Language Use Across the Lifespan.* Submitted

Peterson C. 1992. Explanatory style. See Smith 1992, pp. 376–82

Peterson C, Seligman MEP, Vaillant GE. 1988. Pessimistic explanatory style is a risk factor for physical illness: a thirty-five-year longitudinal study. *J. Personal. Soc. Psychol.* 55:23–27

Petrie KP, Booth RJ, Pennebaker JW. 1999. The immunological effects of thought suppression. *J. Personal. Soc. Psychol.* 75:1264–72

Piaget J. 1926. *The Language and Thought of the Child.* New York: Harcourt, Brace, Jovanovich

Popping R. 2000. *Computer-Assisted Text Analysis.* London: Sage

Ricoeur P. 1976. *Interpretation Theory: Discourse and the Surplus of Meaning.* Fort Worth, TX: Texas Christian Univ. Press

Rieber RW, Vetter HJ. 1995. *The Psychopathology of Language and Cognition.* New York: Plenum

Robinson WP, Giles H, eds. 2001. *The New Handbook of Language and Social Psychology.* Chichester, UK: Wiley

Rude SS, Gortner EM, Pennebaker JW. 2002. *Language Use of Depressed and Depression-Vulnerable College Students.* Submitted

Sanford FH. 1942. Speech and personality. *Psychol. Bull.* 39:811–45

Scheier MF, Carver CS. 1985. Optimism, coping, and health: assessment and implications of generalized outcome expectancies. *Health Psychol.* 4:219–47

Scherer K. 1979. Personality markers in speech. See Sherer & Giles 1979, pp. 147–209

Scherwitz L, Canick J. 1988. Self reference and coronary heart disease risk. In *Type A Behavior Pattern: Research, Theory, and Intervention*, ed. K Houston, CR Snyder, pp. 146–67. New York: Wiley

Scherwitz L, Graham LE, Ornish D. 1985. Self-

involvement and the risk factor for coronary heart disease. *Advances* 2:6–18

Schiffrin D. 1994. *Approaches to Discourse.* Cambridge, MA: Blackwell

Schnurr PP, Rosenberg SD, Oxman TE, Tucker GJ. 1986. A methodological note on content analysis: estimates of reliability. *J. Personal. Assess.* 50:601–9

Schütz A, Baumeister RF. 1999. The language of defense: linguistic patterns in narratives of transgression. *J. Lang. Soc. Psychol.* 18:269–86

Sebeok TA. 1960. *Style and Language.* Cambridge: MIT Press

Shapiro D. 1989. *Psychotherapy of Neurotic Character.* New York: Basic Books

Sherer KR, Giles H, eds. 1979. *Social Markers in Speech.* Cambridge: Cambridge Univ. Press

Sillars A, Shellen W, McIntosh A, Pomegranate M. 1997. Relational characteristics of language: elaboration and differentiation in marital conversations. *West. J. Commun.* 61:403–22

Smith CP, ed. 1992. *Motivation and Personality: Handbook of Thematic Content Analysis.* Cambridge, MA: Cambridge Univ. Press

Smyth JM. 1998. Written emotional expression: effect sizes, outcome types, and moderating variables. *J. Consult. Clin. Psychol.* 66:174–84

Smyth JM, Stone AA, Hurewitz A, Kaell A. 1999. Effects of writing about stressful experiences on symptom reduction in patients with asthma or rheumatoid arthritis. *JAMA* 281:1304–9

Spera SP, Buhrfeind ED, Pennebaker JW. 1994. Expressive writing and coping with job loss. *Acad. Manag. J.* 37:722–33

Stein NL, Folkman S, Trabasso T, Richards TA. 1997. Appraisal and goal processes as predictors of psychological well-being in bereaved caregivers. *J. Personal. Soc. Psychol.* 72:872–84

Stirman SW, Pennebaker JW. 2001. Word use in the poetry of suicidal and nonsuicidal poets. *Psychosom. Med.* 63:517–22

Stone LD, Pennebaker JW. 2002. Trauma in real time: Talking and avoiding online conversations about the death of Princess Diana. *Basic Appl. Soc. Psychol.* 24:172–82

Stone PJ, Dunphy DC, Smith MS, Ogilvie DM. 1966. *The General Inquirer: A Computer Approach to Content Analysis.* Cambridge, MA: MIT Press

Suedfeld P, Tetlock PE, Streufert S. 1992. Conceptual/integrative complexity. See Smith 1992, pp. 393–400

Tannen D. 1994. *Gender Discourse.* New York: Oxford Univ. Press

Thomson R, Murachver T, Green J. 2001. Where is the gender in gendered language? *Psychol. Sci.* 121:171–75

Tucker GJ, Rosenberg SD. 1975. Computer content analysis of schizophrenic speech: a preliminary report. *Am. J. Psychiatry* 132:611–16

Vaes J, Paladino M-P, Leyens J-P. 2002. The lost e-mail: prosocial reactions induced by uniquely human emotions. *Br. J. Soc. Psychol.* In press

Vorauer JD, Ross M. 1999. Self-awareness and feeling transparent: failing to suppress one's self. *J. Exp. Soc. Psychol.* 35:415–40

Vrij A. 2000. *Detecting Lies and Deceit: The Psychology of Lying and the Implications for Professional Practice.* Chichester, UK: Wiley

Weber RP. 1994. *Basic Content Analysis.* Newbury Park, CA: Sage

Weintraub W. 1981. *Verbal Behavior: Adaptation and Psychopathology.* New York: Springer

Weintraub W. 1989. *Verbal Behavior in Everyday Life.* New York: Springer

West MD, ed. 2001. *Theory, Method, and Practice in Computer Content Analysis.* New York: Ablex

Wiener M, Mehrabian A. 1968. *Language Within Language: Immediacy, a Channel in Verbal Communication.* New York: Appleton-Century-Crofts

Winter DG. 1973. *The Power Motive.* New York: Free Press

Winter DG. 1994. *Manual for Scoring Motive Imagery in Running Text.* Univ. Mich. 4th ed. Unpublished manuscript

Zeldow PB, McAdams DP. 1993. On the comparison of TAT and free speech techniques in personality assessment. *J. Personal. Assess.* 60:181–85

Zullow H, Oettingen G, Peterson C, Seligman MEP. 1988. Explanatory style and pessimism in the historical record: CAVing LBJ, presidential candidates, and East versus West Berlin. *Am. Psychol.* 43:673–82

Annu. Rev. Psychol. 2003. 54:579–616
doi: 10.1146/annurev.psych.54.101601.145030
First published online as a Review in Advance on November 18, 2002

DIARY METHODS: Capturing Life as it is Lived

Niall Bolger, Angelina Davis, and Eshkol Rafaeli

*Psychology Department, New York University, New York, New York 10003;
e-mail: niall.bolger@nyu.edu, aed232@nyu.edu, erm5@nyu.edu*

Key Words experience sampling method, longitudinal designs, electronic data
collection, self-report measures, multilevel models

■ **Abstract** In diary studies, people provide frequent reports on the events and experiences of their daily lives. These reports capture the particulars of experience in
a way that is not possible using traditional designs. We review the types of research
questions that diary methods are best equipped to answer, the main designs that can
be used, current technology for obtaining diary reports, and appropriate data analysis
strategies. Major recent developments include the use of electronic forms of data collection and multilevel models in data analysis. We identify several areas of research
opportunities: 1. in technology, combining electronic diary reports with collateral measures such as ambulatory heart rate; 2. in measurement, switching from measures based
on between-person differences to those based on within-person changes; and 3. in research questions, using diaries to (*a*) explain why people differ in variability rather
than mean level, (*b*) study change processes during major events and transitions, and
(*c*) study interpersonal processes using dyadic and group diary methods.

CONTENTS

INTRODUCTION

Gordon Allport, writing in 1942, pointed out that an acquaintance with the "particulars of life" is the beginning of all psychological knowledge—scientific or otherwise. "Psychology needs to concern itself with life as it is lived, with significant total-processes of the sort revealed in consecutive and complete life documents" (Allport 1942, p. 56). This chapter reviews the state of the art in research answering Allport's call, broadly defined today as diary methods. Methods for documenting the particulars of life have improved considerably over the years. Diaries, self-report instruments used repeatedly to examine ongoing experiences, offer the opportunity to investigate social, psychological, and physiological processes, within everyday situations. Simultaneously, they recognize the importance of the contexts in which these processes unfold. Thus, diaries are designed to capture the "little experiences of everyday life that fill most of our working time and occupy the vast majority of our conscious attention" (Wheeler & Reis 1991, p. 340).

A fundamental benefit of diary methods is that they permit the examination of reported events and experiences in their natural, spontaneous context, providing information complementary to that obtainable by more traditional designs (Reis 1994). Another is the dramatic reduction in the likelihood of retrospection, achieved by minimizing the amount of time elapsed between an experience and the account of this experience. Diaries provide the field of psychology with a powerful set of methods for studying various human phenomena, including personality processes (e.g., Bolger & Zuckerman 1995, Fabes & Eisenberg 1997, Rhodewalt et al. 1998), marital and family interaction (e.g., Almeida et al. 1999, Downey et al. 1999, Repetti & Wood 1997), physical symptoms (e.g., Suls et al. 1994), and mental health (e.g., Alloy et al. 1997). Wheeler & Reis (1991), and more recently Reis & Gable (2000), have provided comprehensive reviews of multiple domains in which diary methods have been used. Edited volumes, summarizing diary research in particular domains [e.g., psychopathology (deVries 1992)] have begun appearing. Recently, Stone & Shiffman (2002) proposed a set of guidelines for the reporting of diary studies. Rather than overlaps with these authors, we provide an overview of the current and potential uses of diaries, and we call attention to some of the limitations of this method. We do so in three major sections.

The design section reviews the types of questions appropriately addressed using diary methods, presents an overview of the main designs, and draws attention to the limitations of such designs. The technology section reviews the evolution of measurement and instrumentation in diary research and discusses the benefits and costs of each successive innovation. Finally, the analysis section presents the basic analytic concepts that should be considered by a researcher before conducting diary research. Throughout the chapter, we provide examples of research questions from the field of adult relationships. These examples are designed to illustrate the breadth of information that can become available when diary methods are used to study a particular domain.

DIARY STUDY DESIGN

A Typology of Research Questions

The effectiveness of diary study designs depends on careful consideration of the question(s) one seeks to answer. A poorly designed diary study can involve considerable effort but may yield little useful information. Three broad types of research goals can be achieved using diary designs: (*a*) obtaining reliable person-level information; (*b*) obtaining estimates of within-person change over time, as well as individual differences in such change; and (*c*) conducting a causal analysis of within-person changes and individual differences in these changes.

AGGREGATING OVER TIME: WHAT IS THE TYPICAL PERSON LIKE, AND HOW MUCH DO PEOPLE DIFFER FROM EACH OTHER?   It is common in psychological research to ask participants to retrospect over weeks and months and provide summary accounts of their psychological states and experiences. Depression symptom scales ask for retrospection over 14 days (e.g., the Center for Epidemiologic Studies Depression Scale; Radloff 1977). Life event inventories ask for retrospection over six months to a year (Dohrenwend et al. 1978). The perils of retrospection have been reviewed elsewhere (e.g., Nisbett & Wilson 1977, Ross 1989, Tourangeau et al. 2000). Diary data can be used to generate summary accounts without the biases introduced by retrospection over relatively long periods. In addition to yielding estimates of within-person central tendency, the diary approach can show how much people vary over time in variables of interest. The value of diary methods for such descriptive purposes has been emphasized by several prominent researchers (e.g., Affleck et al. 1999, Tennen et al. 1991).

We begin our discussion with a hypothetical study that uses aggregation. A researcher is interested in investigating women's perceptions of intimacy in their romantic relationships in everyday life. The researcher wishes to assess (*a*) the degree of intimacy the typical woman in a committed relationship feels on average, (*b*) the extent to which the typical woman's feelings of intimacy vary over time, and (*c*) whether women differ from one another in their average feelings of intimacy and in the variability of their feelings of intimacy over time (see Table 1). The first step is to determine an appropriate diary design.

Even when diaries are used solely to obtain aggregate measures, researchers must determine the frequency and duration of assessments that are appropriate for the phenomenon under study. If the researcher believes intimacy could vary from

TABLE 1 Examples of research questions, design, technology, and statistical analysis for time-based diary studies

I. Aggregating over time (Intervention Study; see Figure 1)

Abstract research questions	What is the typical person's (a) average level of Y? (b) variability in Y?	What are the between-person differences in (a) average level of Y? (b) variability in Y?	What are the sources of between-person differences in (a) average level of Y? (b) variability in Y?
Concrete research questions: intimacy examples	What is the typical woman's (a) average level of intimacy? (b) variability in intimacy?	How much do women differ in their (a) average level of intimacy? (b) variability in intimacy?	How much do women in the intervention group differ from those in the control group in their (a) average level of intimacy? (b) variability in intimacy?
Design	Time-based diary completed weekly for 16 weeks	Time-based diary completed weekly for 16 weeks	Time-based diary completed weekly for 16 weeks
Technology	PDA or paper and pencil	PDA or paper and pencil	PDA or paper and pencil
Statistical model (multilevel)			
Name	One-Way Random Effects ANOVA[a]	One-Way Random Effects ANOVA	Means-As-Outcomes Model
Specification	Level 1: intercept Level 2: intercept	Level 1: intercept Level 2: intercept Variance of L-1	Level 1: intercept Level 2: intercept, group Group differences in L-1
Relevant parameters	Average L-1 (a) intercepts (b) error variance[b]	(a) intercepts (b) error variances	(a) intercepts (b) error variances
Abstract research questions	What is the typical person's (a1) starting level of Y? (a2) rate of change in Y?[c] (b) residual variability in Y?	What are the between-person differences in (a1) starting level of Y? (a2) rate of change in Y? (b) residual variability in Y?	What are the sources of between-person differences in (a1) starting level of Y? (a2) rate of change in Y? (b) residual variability in Y?

II. Modeling time (Intervention Study; see Figure 1)

Concrete research questions: intimacy examples	What is the typical woman's (a1) starting level of intimacy? (a2) rate of change in intimacy? (b) residual variability in intimacy?	How much do women differ in their (a1) starting level of intimacy? (a2) rate of change in intimacy? (b) residual variability in intimacy?	Do women in the intervention group differ from those in the control group in their (a1) starting level of intimacy? (a2) rate of change in intimacy? (b) residual variability in intimacy?
Design	Time-based diary completed weekly for 16 weeks	Time-based diary completed weekly for 16 weeks	Time-based diary completed weekly for 16 weeks
Technology	PDA or paper and pencil	PDA or paper and pencil	PDA or paper and pencil
Statistical model (multilevel) Name	Linear Growth Model	Linear Growth Model	Linear Growth Model with Level-2 Predictor
Specification	Level-1: intercept, time Level-2: intercept	Level-1: intercept, time Level-2: intercept	Level-1: intercept, time Level-2: intercept, group
Relevant parameters	Average L-1 (a1) intercept (a2) time slope (b) error variance	Variance of L-1 (a1) intercept (a2) time slopes (b) error variances	Group differences in L-1 (a1) intercept (a2) time slopes (b) error variances

III. Modeling within-person process[d] (Daily Conflicts Study; see Figure 2)

Abstract research questions	What is the typical person's (a1) level of Y when X does not occur (is 0)?[e] (a2) change in Y when X occurs (when X differs by one unit)? (b) residual variability in Y?	What are the between-person differences in (a1) level of Y when X does not occur? (a2) change in Y when X occurs? (b) residual variability in Y?	What are the sources of between-person differences in (a1) level of Y when X does not occur? (a2) change in Y when X occurs? (b) residual variability in Y?

(Continued)

TABLE 1 (*Continued*)

Concrete research questions: intimacy examples	What is the typical woman's (*a1*) level of intimacy on days when no conflicts occur? (*a2*) difference in intimacy between conflict and no-conflict days? (*b*) residual variability in intimacy?	How much do women differ in their (*a1*) level of intimacy on days when no conflicts occur? (*a2*) difference in intimacy between conflict and no-conflict days? (*b*) residual variability in intimacy?	Do women low in Relationship Quality (RQ) differ from those high in RQ in their (*a1*) level of intimacy on days when no conflicts occur? (*a2*) difference in intimacy between conflict and no-conflict days? (*b*) residual variability in intimacy?
Design	Time-based diary completed daily for 28 days	Time-based diary completed daily for 28 days	Time-based diary completed daily for 28 days
Technology	PDA or paper and pencil	PDA or paper and pencil	PDA or paper and pencil
Statistical model (multilevel)			
Name	Random-Coefficients Regression Model	Random-Coefficients Regression Model	Intercepts-and-Slopes-as-Outcomes Model
Specification	Level 1: intercept, conflict day; Level 2: intercept	Level 1: intercept, conflict day; Level 2: intercept	Level 1: intercept, conflict day; Level 2: intercept, RQ RQ differences in L-1
Relevant parameters	Average L-1 (*a1*) intercept (*a2*) conflict day slope (*b*) error variance	Variance of L-1 (*a1*) intercepts (*a2*) conflict day slopes (*b*) error variances	(*a1*) intercepts (*a2*) conflict day slopes (*b*) error variances

aNames of statistical models are taken from Raudenbush & Bryk (2002); bResearch questions about level-1 variances require models that allow for heterogeneous error variances; cFor simplicity, we assume linear rates of change with time; dAlthough not shown here, process models should include controls for any time trends; eFor simplicity, we describe a cross-sectional analysis. For details on a longitudinal analysis, see text.

day to day, but can be recalled quite well over the span of a day, he or she may choose a fixed assessment schedule in which participants provide reports at fixed times (e.g., daily for four weeks). Obtaining sufficient diary entries will enable the researcher to address questions not only about between-person differences in feelings of intimacy but also about between-person differences in the variability of feelings of intimacy. Between-person differences in variability is an important but neglected topic in psychological research [but see the work of Kernis and colleagues for a notable exception (e.g., Greenier et al. 1999)].

The traditional alternative to using aggregated diary data has been the use of single reports in which participants attempt to recall their experience. Such retrospection is often plagued by biases. Participants' limited ability to recall often results in retrospective "aggregate" responses that reflect faulty reconstruction of the phenomena of interest. Retrospection is susceptible to state-congruent recall: The current state cues similar or similarly valenced instances, leading to a biased report (e.g., Bower 1981). A related finding is that respondants, at least when reflecting on pain, tend to rely on a "peak-end" rule, giving more weight to the peak levels and to the most recent levels of experience rather than equally weighting each instance (Redelmeier & Kahneman 1996) or day (Stone et al. 2000). Shiffman et al. (1997) demonstrated that subjective aggregates have a poorer fit to actual (diary-reported) experiences, than do empirical aggregates based on these responses. Thus, one advantage of diary-based data, even for such simple questions, lies in the reduction in systematic and random sources of measurement error, and with it the increase in validity and reliability.

Still, a researcher uninterested in modeling time or other within-person factors may question the need for a diary study. Indeed, it is unlikely that a diary design will be used solely in a study of this kind. However, seemingly simple questions such as these can be posed and answered within more elaborate diary designs, and they should be examined before moving on to more complex ones (detailed below). For example, if within-person variability in a measure is small, there is little point in pursuing within-subject research questions. Also, in such cases it is more likely that retrospective accounts will be accurate.

MODELING THE TIME COURSE: HOW DOES A TYPICAL PERSON CHANGE OVER TIME, AND HOW DO PEOPLE DIFFER IN CHANGE OVER TIME?   In addition to their utility in answering questions that do not directly involve time as a factor, diary designs are excellent for studying temporal dynamics. By having participants report their experiences over hours, days, weeks, and sometimes months, researchers can ask questions such as: Does the variable of interest fluctuate from morning to night, behave differently on weekends and weekdays, or have a certain growth visible over weeks or months? Do individuals differ in these changes over time? If so, what explains these varying time courses? Traditional longitudinal designs can also address these questions, but because they typically involve only a small number of repeated measurements taken at long intervals, they cannot capture changes with the same fidelity. Of course, diary designs place a greater burden on participants, and as we will argue later, such designs are best implemented at times when change is likely to occur.

Consider examples of how incorporating time can augment our understanding of intimacy, its average, and its variability. Intimacy is defined as an individual's feelings of being understood, validated, and cared for by another individual (Reis & Shaver 1988). A researcher may be interested in whether intimacy levels are stable or variable during a person's typical day. The diary design discussed earlier obtained intimacy ratings only once per day. For the present purpose, multiple intimacy ratings will be necessary within each day, using a fixed assessment schedule (e.g., every three waking hours, or every eight hours to represent morning, afternoon, and evening) for a period lasting two or three weeks.

Consider a different research example. An investigator is interested in temporal patterns in a young mother's intimacy with her spouse following the birth of their first child. Existing longitudinal research (e.g., Hackel & Ruble 1992) shows that levels of marital satisfaction often decline after the birth of the first child. Using weekly diaries over several months, it would be possible to determine when and to what extent the decline occurs for the average mother. Moreover, individual differences in this pattern (i.e., in both the level of intimacy reported shortly after giving birth and the effect of elapsed time on intimacy reported in the subsequent months) can also be assessed. These individual differences may be accounted for by person- or couple-level characteristics such as prenatal relationship satisfaction or length of the relationship with the spouse.

At times, researchers may be interested in cyclical, rather than linear, changes over time. Diary data have been used to examine circadian or diurnal rhythms (e.g., Clark et al. 1989, Dermer & Berscheid 1972, Rafaeli & Revelle 2002), weekly cycles (e.g., Larsen & Kasimatis 1990), as well as longer time-units [e.g., menstrual cycles (cf. van Goozen et al. 1997), and seasons (Reardon et al. 2001)]. The cyclical nature of such data can be modeled using sine/cosine curves; procedures such as spectral analysis (Larsen 1990) are used to obtain the various parameters of these curves (length, amplitude, phase, and fit to the data).

Within-person variability can be modeled with various predictors besides time. We chose, however, to specifically highlight the importance of time as a factor because of the surprising frequency with which it has been overlooked in diary research. One of the greatest strengths of diary designs is their ability to characterize temporal dynamics, such as diurnal cycles, weekday versus weekend effects, seasonal variation, or the effect of time to, or since, an event. We urge researchers to use diary designs for this purpose and to investigate temporal effects in existing diary data.

MODELING WITHIN-PERSON PROCESSES: WHAT IS THE WITHIN-PERSON PROCESS FOR THE TYPICAL PERSON, AND HOW DO PEOPLE DIFFER IN THESE PROCESSES? The most challenging questions that can be studied using diary designs are those that address the processes that underlie within-person variability. Diaries can help determine the antecedents, correlates, and consequences of daily experiences. They can also be used to evaluate whether individuals differ in these processes, and if so, determine the sources of these individual differences.

Many diary studies have focused on questions of this sort, characterizing within-person processes and individual differences. For example, Almeida et al. (2001) investigated influences on the quality of father-child interactions. Mendoza-Denton et al. (2002) investigated the effects of race-based rejection experiences on adjustment to college. Along the same lines, a possible question in our ongoing example would be the identification of factors affecting intimacy on a moment-by-moment basis. Consider an investigation of the influence of social support and social hindrance on feelings of intimacy among married women (cf. Vinokur et al. 1996). The researcher may request participants to complete diary entries following instances of perceiving support or hindrance from their partner. The relevant instances could be of any duration and may be appropriate for self-report so long as they fit the investigator's preestablished definition. Diary data have been used in a similar application to examine the link between perceived partner responsiveness and intimacy across a range of social interactions (Laurenceau et al. 1998).

In such a study, the researcher must also decide on the rate and timing of self-reports. If these are high-frequency events, he or she may wish to ask participants to report only on some instances or on a certain number of instances each day [cf. work done with the Rochester Interaction Record (RIR) (e.g., Wheeler & Nezlek 1977, Tidwell et al. 1996)]. Allowing this choice runs the risk of introducing each participant's bias in selecting some instances and overlooking others. This risk can be minimized with appropriate subject training (such as that conducted in RIR studies).

The researcher must also choose whether to have participants report on the relevant events immediately after their occurrence or to allow participants to postpone responding at inopportune moments (recognizing that the latter concession may work against the recall accuracy, or reliability, of the reports). The researcher may request completion of entries at the conclusion of appropriate events, with the stipulation that they may be postponed under specified circumstances.

Diary studies of within-person processes are mostly nonexperimental, allowing putative causes and consequences to occur naturally. Like all nonexperimental designs, they at best allow weak inferences about cause and effect. However, as we will discuss in more detail below, diary designs are superior to traditional designs in examining processes because they allow investigators to examine the temporal sequencing of events and to control for third variables by using participants as their own controls. To do so, diaries are commonly analyzed using methods of longitudinal data analysis. For example, in a study of the effects of receiving support on participants' mood, Bolger et al. (2000) controlled for participants' previous day's mood. Kennedy et al. (2002) examined conflict and anger at the end of the day while adjusting for anger reported upon waking that morning.

Finally, few diary studies have capitalized on major events and transitions to study psychological change and to model the processes underlying it. Examples are school and family transitions, and scheduled health and occupational events.

Such studies are powerful because they target periods when people and their environments are in flux, and they yield fine-grained data on mediating variables during such periods. For recent examples, see Bolger et al. (2000) and Mendoza et al. (2002).

SUMMARY   Diary research is most effective when the design and the research question are complementary in form. As the previous three sections illustrate, well-designed diary studies can answer questions regarding aggregates of experiences over time, temporal patterns of experiences, and the factors affecting changes in these experiences. For each type of question, diary studies can provide information about the average person, between-person variability, and predictors and determinants of this variability. Table 1 provides examples of such questions.

Types of Diary Designs

After identifying the questions that guide an investigation, researchers are faced with concrete decisions regarding design, technology, and data analysis. Diary studies have often been classified into the three categories of interval-, signal-, and event-contingent protocols (e.g., Wheeler & Reis 1991). The interval-contingent design, the oldest method of daily event recording, requires participants to report on their experiences at regular, predetermined intervals. Signal-contingent designs rely on some signaling device to prompt participants to provide diary reports at fixed, random, or a combination of fixed and random intervals. Event-contingent studies, arguably the most distinct design strategy, require participants to provide a self-report each time the event in question occurs. This design enables the assessment of rare or specialized occurrences that would not necessarily be captured by fixed or random interval assessments.

As we see it, diary studies serve one of two major purposes: the investigation of phenomena as they unfold over time, or the focused examination of specific, and often rare, phenomena. It appears to us that the three-way classification blends this conceptual distinction with the technological issue of signaling. Instead, we incorporate interval- and signal-contingent designs into a single category, which we call time-based designs.

TIME-BASED DESIGNS   Most diary studies, particularly those focused on within-person processes, involve time-based designs. Examples of these include single-day units [e.g., exploring end-of-day intimacy in relationships (e.g., Laurenceau et al. 2002) and daily levels of stress and mood (e.g., Bolger et al. 1989)] and hourly variations in specific processes or experiences [e.g., examining time-of-day effects on felt-intimacy levels, or within-day fluctuations of moods (e.g., Rafaeli & Revelle 2002)]. Additionally, questions about the aggregate levels of a variable (for example, mean levels of intimacy) are often most appropriately studied using time-based designs, which can be used to systematically sample participants' responses within a day, week, or year. Research with time-based design is often concerned with ongoing experiences that can be assessed within the course of a typical period. Rare or highly specified experiences are difficult to assess using a time-based design and should be investigated using the event-based design, discussed next.

Investigators designing time-based studies must decide on the most suitable interval for assessment. Assessment times can follow fixed, random, or a combination of intervals. In fixed-schedule designs, researchers choose schedules that include either specific times of the day (e.g., 10 AM, 4 PM, 9 PM) or specific time intervals (e.g., every three waking hours, every evening). Variable schedules involve the assessment of experiences according to a random pattern that is undisclosed to the participants. Users of variable schedules are often concerned with momentary experiences such as psychological states, as in the case of the classic work on adolescent self-esteem by Larson & Csikszentmihalyi (1978).

The selection of schedules and intervals should be theoretically and/or empirically guided. Some phenomena show considerable regularity and can be studied using fixed schedules. For example, a researcher interested in dietary habits may find a fixed-time schedule of morning, afternoon, and evening reports to be most appropriate because it captures individuals' traditional eating behaviors. Phenomena such as intimacy, mood, or other ongoing experiences may also be best addressed with a fixed-interval schedule (e.g., every three waking hours, once per day). A variable schedule may be most appropriate for other phenomena, particularly those sensitive to reactivity or expectation.

Fixed schedules   When using a fixed-time schedule, the spacing of intervals is an important consideration. Too long an interval may obscure natural cycles (e.g., diurnal rhythms) or exclude important intervening events and processes. Lengthy intervals may also contribute to the risk of biased retrospection which diary research explicitly seeks to minimize. More distant events are less likely to be recalled accurately; they are also more likely to be influenced by retrospection and by current psychological states (cf. Shiffman et al. 1997).

Retrospection bias may be a more pronounced problem for some phenomena than for others. Concrete, objective events (e.g., number of caffeinated beverages consumed) may be less susceptible to recall bias than are transient subjective feelings such as pain or mood. For example, retrospective reports of pain experiences may be highly influenced by the general level of pain experienced, making it difficult to accurately report the absolute level of the pain experienced each day (Redelmeier & Kahneman 1996).

Intervals that are too short may also be problematic. One possible problem is an unfavorable signal-to-noise ratio. Specifically, researchers may miss slower-acting processes (e.g., day-to-day, week-to-week changes) if data are collected and analyzed at intervals that are much shorter than what is needed to capture the change process (e.g., hourly). Another possible problem is the considerable (and perhaps unnecessary) burden placed on participants by frequent reporting.

Many areas of psychology have yet to develop theories that specify the appropriate time lag for a given phenomenon (see Gollob & Reichardt 1987). Nonetheless, when diary researchers elect to use fixed-interval response schedules, they need to decide at the outset what interval is most appropriate. Two questions are paramount: What time lag is acceptable between the experience and the description, and what time frame is likely to reveal dynamic processes that are of interest? As a rule, it is better to err on the side of shorter intervals, because the data can then be analyzed with lags of different lengths.

Finally, while a fixed time interval has the benefit of being well suited for longitudinal data analysis, we caution researchers against selecting this (or any other) design feature solely on the basis of data analytic concerns. Such choices carry the risk of producing findings that do not meet the particular operational circumstances and theoretical goals of the research. As we discuss in the section on Diary Data Analysis, below, we believe analysis and design decisions should be considered together.

Variable schedules   For certain purposes, researchers may choose variable- or combination-(variable plus fixed) schedule designs. The major benefit of these is their ability to randomly sample moments in a participant's day. Take, for example, a research project investigating the frequency of stress experiences among students approaching an exam. Assessing the participants at random, and inquiring about the present moment, may reduce the potential for biased reports. In contrast, a fixed schedule may sensitize participants to stress because of the routine anticipation of reporting times.

A potential limitation of the random as opposed to fixed schedule is participant burden. Diaries become intrusive when participants are required to complete entries immediately following randomly timed signals. With fixed schedules, the burden is smaller because the timing of diary entries is predictable and can (to some extent at least) be accommodated into a participant's schedule. To ease the intrusiveness of randomly timed signals, researchers may allow participants to postpone responding at inopportune moments. However, allowing delays in the completion of an entry may introduce bias, whereby participants select the times on which they want to report.

Both fixed and random time-based designs allow (and at times require) the use of signaling or notification. Participants can describe their current activity when signals are delivered; alternatively, a researcher may decide to direct participants in advance to follow a certain response schedule. We discuss some practical considerations of signaling in the section on Technology, below.

EVENT-BASED DESIGNS   Event-based designs require participants to provide reports at every instance that meets the researcher's preestablished definition. An event-based design is usually most appropriate for diary studies of specific classes of phenomena or processes, especially those that are isolated and/or rare. For example, Jensen-Campbell & Graziano (2000) reported on an event-based study of interpersonal conflict using the RIR in early adolescence; similarly, Laurenceau et al. (1998) used this design in examining the link among disclosures, responsiveness, and intimacy. In our running example, a study of the association of feelings of intimacy with occurrences of support and hindrance illustrates a typical use of event-based diaries.

The event-based design requires a clear definition of the triggering event(s). Any ambiguity as to which events fall within that definition may lead participants to omit relevant exemplars. To reduce ambiguity, those designing an event-based diary study should consider identifying a single class of events as focal (e.g., Laurenceau et al. 1998). Examining multiple classes of events greatly increases the possibility of confusion as to whether a given event should be reported, as well as the risk of participant burden. Both these risks may lead to a decrease in the number of episodes reported and a weakening of the study's usefulness.

The focus of event-based studies on selected events is both their strength and their drawback. This selection carries at least two risks. The first risk is that participants may not reliably identify each relevant event. The second risk lies in overgeneralizing from the event-based responses to the person's general experience. This risk may exist even when all relevant events are comprehensively reported; for example, the hypothetical researcher examining feelings of intimacy in response to support and hindrance situations may mistakenly draw conclusions about average or typical intimacy levels, when in fact the reports about intimacy were all generated at atypical times.

Time- and event-based designs are not mutually exclusive. Mixed or combination schedules can markedly strengthen a study design. For example, Mohr et al. (2001) combined time- and event-based methods to investigate interpersonal experiences and alcohol consumption in different contexts. Interpersonal events were recalled at end of day with time-based (i.e., daily) diaries, whereas drinking behaviors were monitored with event-based diaries completed throughout the day. In another possible combination design, the occurrence of a particular event (e.g., an argument, a stressful event) triggers a series of subsequent diary reports that trace the temporal sequelae of the event (e.g., Stone et al. 1998).

SUMMARY   Diary studies typically focus either on unfolding dynamic phenomena or on specific (and often rare) events. The appropriate design for a study follows directly from its focus, and each design has some benefits and some liabilities.

Limitations in the Use of Diaries

Although diary methods offer many benefits, especially when compared to traditional survey designs, it is important to consider what is known about their problems and limitations. One practical concern is that diary studies often require detailed training sessions to ensure that participants fully understand the protocol (Reis & Gable 2000). Moreover, in order to obtain reliable and valid data, diary studies must achieve a level of participant commitment and dedication rarely required in other types of research studies. The burden of repeated queries and responses places substantial demands on the participant. To address this, investigators usually design diary instruments that are short and take several minutes to complete. Doing so can limit diary studies to less in-depth reporting of a phenomenon at each time of measurement.

Little is known about the effect of diary completion itself on participants' experience or responses. Several effects, including reactance, habituation, increased complexity, and gradual entrainment, are possible, particularly in more socially reactive behaviors. Reactance refers to a change in participants' experience or behavior as a result of participation in the study. At present, there is little evidence that reactance poses a threat to diaries' validity. For example, Litt et al. (1998) reported that although their participants noted being more aware of the monitored behavior, the behavior itself was not reactive. In several diary studies, Gleason et al. (2001) have documented negative mood elevation in the initial days; in each, the initial spike in negative affect was short-lived, and it dissipated within two to three days. These authors argue that diaries may lead to less reactivity than other forms of data collection because of a habituation process. On the other hand, habituation, and more specifically the development of a habitual response style when making diary entries, may have some deleterious effects. For example, participants may develop a tendency to skim over sections of a diary questionnaire that rarely applies to their experience and may omit responses even at relevant times.

With repeated exposure to a diary questionnaire, participants' understanding of a particular construct may change in at least three possible ways. First, a more complex understanding of the surveyed domain may develop, as may enhanced encoding or retrieval of domain-relevant information. No study has directly tested this, but Thomas & Diener (1990) provide some indirect evidence against this possibility, at least with mood: Accuracy in recalling moods did not differ following an intensive diary period. Second, while participants may not develop a more elaborate or complex knowledge of the monitored domain, the experience of the diary study may entrain their conceptualization of the domain to fit with those measured in the diary. For example, a study of daily intimacy inquiring about three types of intimacy indicators may steer participants to become conscious of these indicators and to be less sensitized to others. Third, research by Pennebaker and colleagues (e.g., Suedfeld & Pennebaker 1997) has documented therapeutic outcomes to a certain kind of self-reflective recollection process. These outcomes, however, have not been found in simple quantitative ratings such as are typical in most diary studies.

Finally, not enough is known about personality (e.g., conscientiousness) or symptom [e.g., alcohol consumption (cf. Litt et al. 1998)] effects on response compliance or styles. Additionally, individual differences in various dimensions (e.g., learning disabilities) may lead to selective biases in the ability to respond to diary questionnaires. We concur with Reis & Gable (2000), who suggest that these and other potential effects of diary methods should be investigated both for methodological and theoretical reasons.

Design Section Summary

We urge (*a*) care in selecting a design that captures the temporal patterns (if a time-based design is called for) or typical base rate (if an event-based design is called for) of the phenomenon under investigation; (*b*) minimization of the limitations inherent in diary design, such as participant burden and response bias, by understanding their origin; and (*c*) recognition of the variety of questions that can be asked about the phenomenon (examples are detailed in Table 1).

DIARY STUDY TECHNOLOGY

This section describes the evolution of diary research technology. After close to 40 years of relying on simple paper and pencil methods, two major waves of change in diary research occurred in the last two decades: the augmentation of paper diaries with signaling devices and the emergence of electronic means of data collection. The most recent technologies promise to increase the ease of providing diary reports and to integrate these reports with physiological and other collateral measures.

Paper and Pencil Diaries

Paper and pencil (P&P) diaries were the earliest and are still the most commonly used approach in diary research. Studies using this approach began appearing in the 1940s (e.g., Stonborough 1942; cf. Allport 1942). Both the technology and the benefits of simple P&P studies are clear. Participants are equipped with folders, booklets, or packets of questionnaires, one for each diary entry. In a pretesting session, they are instructed on how to complete and return the diaries; in some studies, they complete the first diary entry in the laboratory. The process of setting up P&P studies does not differ from most other questionnaire studies. Additionally, because P&P forms or questionnaires are familiar to participants, P&P is the easiest technology for participants to use. Diary studies using simple P&P techniques have several prominent limitations, however, most of which have been highlighted elsewhere (e.g., Feldman Barrett & Barrett 2001, Shiffman & Stone 1998). The simplest one is the risk of honest forgetfulness, where participants fail to remember the scheduled response times (in time-contingent protocols) or fail to have the diaries at hand (in both time- and event-contingent protocols). This is compounded by the risk of retrospection error, where participants rely on (benign) reconstruction or (deliberate) fabrication to complete missed entries, potentially defeating the main benefit of diaries, namely, their ability to obtain accurate, real-time information.

Both honest forgetfulness and retrospection error are related to a third problem, uncertain compliance. Compliance needs to be considered in terms of both the number of entries and their validity. The former is easy to estimate; the latter, unfortunately, is not. Several researchers have used debriefing interviews to obtain self-reported compliance indices, with mixed results (cf. Feldman Barrett & Barrett 2001). Others have attempted to use verification information; for example, Rafaeli & Revelle (2002) asked participants to report the time of response, while simultaneously obtaining collateral information from a separate computerized task, thus identifying those who are prone to inaccuracy. Though useful, neither of these techniques fully guarantees compliance.

Uncertain compliance is likely to be more problematic in some areas than in others. For example, studies of temporal patterns of responses or of fleeting subjective experiences (such as pain or mood) might be more adversely affected by uncertain compliance. The same is true for studies of phenomena that require detailed encoding of particular episodes (cf. Shiffman 2000).

An additional limitation in P&P diaries is the absence of response-time information, which may be quite valuable. Researchers who are interested not only in the actual response, but also in questions of automaticity, salience, or certainty of response, may find this limiting.

Several of the shortcomings of P&P methods are not specific to diaries and occur in any questionnaire study. However, in the context of some diary studies, these problems may be compounded because of the enormous quantity of data amassed. One of these is human error, either in the response or in the entry stages. For example, it is not uncommon for participants to skip whole sections of a P&P questionnaire; in a multiday diary study, this behavior often goes undetected until the end of the data collection, when it is too late to correct.

Another shortcoming that exists with other self-report methods but increases in scale in diary studies is that of burden of data entry and handling. Even in relatively small diary studies, the data records number in the thousands. To minimize data entry errors it is necessary to double-enter at least a sample of these data.

Finally, because of the risk that prior days' responses in P&P diaries may be viewed by others in their environment, participants may hesitate to be completely truthful in their responses about interpersonal events and emotions. This concern can be mitigated, however, by asking participants to seal the pages of completed diaries (e.g., Bolger et al. 1989, Laurenceau et al. 2002).

We have found the following suggestions useful in implementing P&P diary studies. First, make the diaries easily portable: Arrange the diaries as pocket-sized booklets, stapled or bound, thus allowing participants to carry them around in one piece. Second, reduce the possibility of participant error: In fixed-schedule studies, for example, preprint the dates and times of expected responses onto the diary sheets in order to keep participants on track. Reduce demand characteristics by clarifying the importance of accurate over numerous responses. Asking participants to note whether the entry was completed "on time" (in a way that recognizes that at times it will not be) can also be helpful; so too can collection of responses at several interim points during the length of the study.

Third, pilot test your diary on participants from the population to be studied. Diary forms that seem straightforward to researchers may pose unforeseen difficulties for participants. Finally, maintain ongoing contact with participants, in a personal yet nonintrusive manner. Diary studies are time-consuming, and this personal contact retains participants more than do monetary incentives or dependence upon goodwill towards science. This last suggestion applies to diary studies of all methods, paper-and-pencil or otherwise.

Augmented Paper Diaries

Over the past three decades, researchers have developed methods that begin to address the limitations of simple P&P diaries. Historically, these methods have been identified with the experience-sampling method (ESM) (Csikszentmihalyi & Larson 1992) and the ecological momentary assessment (EMA) method [(Stone & Shiffman 1994); note that EMA studies are not restricted to those using signals]. Participants' responses are still collected using P&P questionnaires, but these are augmented with signaling devices, such as pagers (e.g., Dabbs et al. 1997, Larson & Csikszentmihalyi 1978), preprogrammed wristwatches (e.g., Litt et al. 1998), or phone calls (e.g., Morrison et al. 1999).

These augmentations offer a remedy to the first problem of P&P protocols (honest forgetfulness) and some relief for the next two (retrospection and uncertain compliance). Rather than relying on a participant's timeliness or individually devised methods of self-reminder, ancillary devices can be preprogrammed to signal randomly or at fixed intervals, prompting research participants' responses and relieving them of the need to keep track of the appropriate occasions for response. Such methods offer an improvement over simple P&P for time-based protocols but are of limited utility for event-based studies. It may be possible to randomly signal participants and obtain sufficient responses for some high-frequency or prolonged events [e.g., being alone (Larson & Csikszentmihalyi 1978)]. However, time-based signals (whether random or fixed in schedule) are likely to miss many discrete events, even those that occur numerous times each day (e.g., smoking).

The augmented approach keeps the benefits of simpler P&P protocols, particularly from the participant's perspective. The ease of making P&P responses is identical, while the signaling device eliminates the burden of remembering to complete diary entries. At the same time, some of the limitations of simpler P&P designs (retrospection error, uncertain compliance, cumbersome data entry and data management) remain.

From the researcher's perspective, several other factors may reduce the appeal of these methods. First, setup is somewhat more involved and costly. Signaling devices need to be purchased, programmed, and maintained, and participants need to be trained in their usage. Additionally, these methods magnify the problem of disruptiveness. Being beeped to complete a smoking-cessation or relationship-quality diary entry in the middle of a job interview or a first date may be an unacceptable disruption. Potential participants may anticipate this and decline participation or adopt behaviors that defeat the purpose of the studies (e.g., not carrying the signaling device).

To address these problems, researchers need to be aware of their participants' schedules and must choose and program the signals in a way that is minimally disruptive of the participants' routines (e.g., sleep, classes, meetings, etc.). Though feasible, this often requires added attention, such as tailoring the signaling schedule individually for each participant.

Handheld and Electronic Data Collection

Electronic data collection methods of various forms began appearing over the last decade (Feldman Barrett & Barrett 2001; Shiffman 2000). Typically, these studies use handheld computers (i.e., palmtop computers, personal digital assistants) equipped with custom-designed questionnaire programs.

Several such programs have been developed. Perrez & Reicherts (1996) describe one of the earliest programs, COMRES, which has been used fruitfully, especially in Europe. The first to be used extensively was the Electronic Diary (see Stone et al. 1998), which has been applied to various health and social psychology questions for over a decade now (e.g., Paty et al. 1992). Several researchers have developed their own diary programs [e.g., PMC-diary for Palm Pilots (Rafaeli & Revelle 1999); ISIS for pocket PC (Raffety 2001)]. A major contribution to the field was made by Barrett & Feldman-Barrett (2000), who used a National Science Foundation grant to develop a freeware diary program for handheld devices (Experience Sampling Program, or ESP).

The benefits of such programs are immediately visible. First, they allow for signaling. Second, they provide time-stamps (and date-stamps) for responses. When taken together with appropriately designed questions, such as ones that focus on the present moment, these features obviate the problems of forgetfulness and uncertain compliance. In fact, time-stamping provides a direct measure of compliance. By examining the times of the responses, researchers can immediately identify diary entries that were completed on time, within a reasonable delay period after a signal, or at unacceptable times. Additionally, researchers are often interested in ensuring that entries were completed in their entirety within a certain time. Electronic diaries can document or even enforce this. For example, ESP allows researchers to determine the maximal acceptable length of time for each answer, or for the entire questionnaire, in time-contingent protocols; PMC allows researchers to do so in event-based protocols as well. Both programs have defined times (typically, immediately after the completion of one entry) during which further diary entries are disallowed.

A third benefit available in some of the programs is flexibility in the presentation of questions. Some programs allow randomization (e.g., ISIS, ESP) and/or hypertextuality [i.e., the ability to present different questions based on responses (ISIS)] of the presentation of items. These features allow the diaries to be less cumbersome and repetitive. More exciting still is the possibility of the assessment paradigm adapting dynamically to the provided responses. For example, Shiffman et al. (1997) report on a study of smoking behavior in which the content and timing of questions changed in response to the pattern of earlier responses.

Fourth, electronic diaries offer major advantages in terms of data entry, management, and accuracy. Since participants enter their responses directly into the electronic diaries, the processes of transcribing and double-checking the data, which are costly and error prone, are bypassed. Additionally, the programs typi-cally prevent responses that are out of range, and they minimize the risk of skipped questions (since the items are typically presented in sequence, ending only when the whole entry has been completed).

Fifth, to varying degrees, these programs simplify the process of taking into ac-count the participant's schedule. For example, ESP allows the researcher to set both start and end times for each participant at the beginning of the diary period. These could be obtained by inquiring about each participant's typical schedule. Some-what more flexibly, PMC allows participants to put the diary to sleep, scheduling it to wake at a personally convenient time; it also allows "snoozing" the diary for variable lengths of time. As Shiffman (2000) notes, the ability to constrain the diary signals to appropriate times allows a more comprehensive sampling of those times.

In selecting or developing an electronic diary program, researchers may find specific capabilities to be particularly important. Two features relate to flexibility in the presentation of questions: an ability to randomize item presentation (both within blocks and in whole blocks) and an ability to display several different response formats (e.g., Likert scales, check boxes, etc.). These features are particularly useful when the diary questions are of different sorts and when researchers want to avoid response sets.

Several features address the usability of diary programs. Does the program allow participants to review and change their answers (i.e., to back up in the diary)? In ongoing research, we have found that participants strongly favor the ability to retrace one or several steps. Does the program "take over" the electronic device, disallowing access to any other program? Often this is useful in constraining the use of a device (e.g., conserving battery power, reducing the risk of participant access to stored answers). However, as the use of handheld devices becomes more prevalent, researchers may wish to allow their programs to run in the background of participants' proprietary devices. In that case, a diary program that takes over the device would be a liability. Another feature to consider is whether a program allows event-based responses, time-based responses, or both within the same study.

Finally, several features can make diary entries quick or slow to complete. One is the number of questions presented on each screen. Most programs, including ESP (but not ISIS), have the mixed blessing of presenting only one question at a time. This may improve the processing of each question, but it may also lengthen the total time needed to complete the diary and therefore increase the burden. In some programs, tapping or pressing the answer advances the diary. In others, particularly ones where multiple questions appear at once, participants are required to tap a special key (e.g., "NEXT") after each completed page. In lengthy diaries, this extra keystroke adds noticeably to diary completion times.

Although handheld devices are the most popular means of electronic data col-lection, they are not the only ones. Some researchers have turned to Web-based questionnaires or to phone-in protocols (Searles et al. 2000). One benefit of these methods is their ability to secure the responses immediately while maintaining many of the advantages of handheld data collection. Their main drawback is inconvenience for participants, who complete a diary entry on a phone or a computer connected to the Internet. As mobile Web access for handheld computers becomes common and affordable, the functional differences among handheld, phone, and Web-based programs will likely disappear.

Promising though they are, electronic diary collection methods do have some limitations. The first is the development cost of the appropriate program. At the time the first electronic diary studies were published, these costs were prohibitive for many researchers. However, recent advances have brought electronic data collection within reach for many researchers. Some find it best to develop a new program tailored to their specific needs (e.g., Perrez et al. 2000, Rafaeli & Revelle 1999, Raffety 2001). Others have adapted existing programs (e.g., Mohr et al. 2001). Finally, the arrival of a federally funded freeware program, ESP (Barrett & Feldman Barrett 2000), means that all researchers have access to a basic program suitable for many purposes.

Costs do accrue at other stages of electronic data collection. Electronic devices require maintenance and may break or need replacement. Nonetheless, development and operation costs can be offset, in part or in full, by savings on data entry, management, and storage, as well as by increased data integrity (which can translate into greater reliability, greater power, and lower sample sizes).

Currently, affordable handheld devices leave much to be desired in technical terms. Font size tends to be small, visual contrast is not very sharp, and the battery power of the devices does not always suffice for longer studies. Additionally, these devices are best suited for handling simple, close-ended responses. The incorporation of open-ended responses remains difficult at present. However, given the speed of innovation in the design of handheld devices, these technical limitations can be expected to lessen greatly in coming years.

Other limitations of electronic data collection methods are likely to be more enduring. Key among these are the cost and resources needed to train participants in the use of such devices. Typically, researchers have found it necessary to devote at least 30 minutes, and often more, to acquainting participants with the use of an electronic diary. This training is usually carried out individually and in person. Thus, for large samples, and for studies where many participants never meet face-to-face with the researchers (e.g., Bolger et al. 2000), the use of electronic devices can be problematic.

Additionally, a concern for the field as a whole is the possible risk of perpetuating a "digital divide," i.e., differential access of individuals of various groups to participation in research. For example, researchers may hesitate to use high-cost devices in studies of poverty. Such hesitation could subtly steer research towards more convenient or accessible populations and away from economically disadvantaged participants. Similarly, computer literacy may affect participants' willingness to enroll in electronic diary studies. Clearly we need more published studies on the feasibility of using electronic diary studies in a broader range of special populations.

Emerging Opportunities

We and others (e.g., Shiffman 2000, Feldman Barrett & Barrett 2001, Feldman Barrett & Jamner 2000) see several avenues of opportunity in the technology of diary studies. These can be divided broadly into two types: continued improvement in self-report diary technology, and integration of collateral information collection into research protocols.

IMPROVING SELF-REPORT TECHNOLOGY   At least two types of advances in self-report methodology are in progress. First, improved mobile communication allows online, duplex (i.e., interactive) contact with participants. For example, researchers can now send questions to, and receive responses from, participants in real time. This allows a dynamic tailoring of questions for specific participants; at the very least, it offers an additional method for increasing compliance by maintaining contact with participants (e.g., Jamison et al. 2001).

Second, advances in voice recording and recognition as well as in linguistic analysis technology allow the inclusion of verbal reports into diary research. Rather than relying only on close-ended questions, researchers are now able to request open-ended responses, or to sample speech naturalistically, examining these responses within the context of daily functioning (e.g., Pennebaker & Graybeal 2001).

INTEGRATION OF COLLATERAL INFORMATION   The inclusion of information that goes beyond self-reports offers much promise for a more comprehensively ecological psychology. The technology allowing such integration is already available and in use, particularly in the field of behavioral medicine. For example, Jamner et al. (1998) describe research examining the concordance of heart rate, blood pressure, and subjective mood that incorporated ambulatory monitors of the physiological indices. Shapiro & Goldstein (1998) used similar physiological indices along with an objective monitor of movement, the wrist actigraph, which allows accurate tracking of physical movement during both wakefulness and sleep. Multichannel recorders are now capable of jointly tracking indices of heart rate, blood pressure, respiration, and physical activity; it is only a question of time before unified devices allow an integration of these indices with self-reported written or spoken responses. (For a review of several ambulatory monitoring techniques in psychophysiology and psychology, see Fahrenberg & Myrtek 1996.)

Technology Section Summary

Innovations in diary research technology are rapidly occurring. Various researchers are working to improve our technical ability to conduct ecologically valid research that would be minimally intrusive and maximally reflective of individuals' ongoing feelings, thoughts, goals, behaviors, and circumstances.

DIARY DATA ANALYSIS

Data analyses of diaries address the three types of research questions discussed earlier: What is an individual's typical or average experience, and how do people differ in these averages; what is the time course of a person's experiences, and how do people differ in their time courses; and what processes underlie changes in a person's experiences, and how do people differ in these processes? We discuss general statistical approaches to each type of question; where necessary, we also discuss special data-analytic issues that arise in certain types of diary studies (e.g., estimating measurement models, analyzing dyadic diary data).

Statistical methods for diary data analysis must address several key issues that make these data unique. First, the data involve repeated measurements, and thus the within-person data points cannot be assumed to be independent. Second, the dependence of the observations is often serial, in that diary reports adjacent in time are more similar than those more distant in time. Third, the number of diary reports is often large and varies from person to person, making usual repeated-measures analyses infeasible. Finally, temporal patterns and cycles are often present in the data, and thus flexible classes of mathematical models need to be considered. A consensus is emerging among diary researchers that multilevel models (also called hierarchical linear models, general mixed models, and random regression models), modified to handle repeated-measures data, are appropriate for diary data analysis. Although these models are complex, we believe they are in important respects easier to intuit than other complex, widely used models such as structural equation modeling (SEM) or meta-analysis.

Those wishing instruction on multilevel models can consult major textbooks geared toward social scientists (Hox 2002, Raudenbush & Bryk 2002, Snijders & Bosker 1999). A brief introduction to multilevel models is provided by Kenny et al. (1998). Reis & Gable (2000) also discuss the benefits of multilevel analysis in their review of diary work in personality and social psychology. Also useful are two edited volumes on longitudinal data analysis (Moskowitz & Hershberger 2002, Sayer & Collins 2001).

A number of sound and flexible multilevel modeling programs are currently available. The most commonly used in diary research are two freestanding programs [HLM (Bryk et al. 1996) and MLWin (Prosser et al. 1996)] and one module of the SAS statistical software system called PROC MIXED (SAS Institute 1999). For readers interested in working with PROC MIXED, Singer provides an especially useful introduction to basic analysis issues for estimating time-course models with longitudinal data (Singer 1998, 2002). Finally, note that specific multilevel models [i.e., for growth curve analysis (Willett & Sayer 1994)] can be estimated within an SEM framework and that more general multilevel capabilities are beginning to be available in multivariate software systems such as LISREL (Jöreskog & Sörbon 1996), EQS (Bentler 1995), and Mplus (Muthén & Muthén 2002).

Aggregating Over Time: What is the Typical Person Like, and How Much Do People Differ from Each Other?

The first approach uses only averaged, summary data on the repeated measurements obtained from the diary. Although diary designs by necessity obtain repeated measurements on participants, researchers may not necessarily be interested in temporal or within-subject patterns in the data. Rather, the researcher may choose simply to summarize each person's within-person data in the form of averages (e.g., means) and variability (e.g., variances) and to examine between-person averages and variability in these summary measures.

An example of this approach is a study where a researcher uses a time-based weekly diary design to document intimacy levels in married women over a 16-week period. We can expect such a design to result in a more valid picture of daily intimacy over that period than would be obtained from a retrospective report summarizing the entire four months.

THE TYPICAL PERSON'S AVERAGE AND VARIABILITY   Figure 1 shows a graph of hypothetical data for a sample of four women over the 16 weeks. Since the first set of research questions ignores the patterning over time, we begin by examining the small bell-shaped curves along the Y axis of the graph. These are summary distributions of weekly intimacy scores for each of the four women. Taking participant

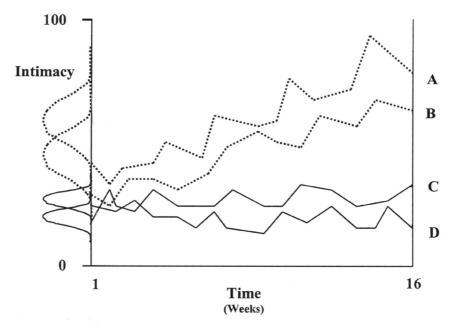

Figure 1   Hypothetical data of four participants in Intervention Study (16-week weekly diary study of intimacy following brief intervention or control).

C as an example, we can see (*a*) how intimate she felt with her partner on a typical week over the 16-week period (about 35 units on a 0–100 scale); and (*b*) to what extent her level of intimacy varied over time (the participant's standard deviation is about 3 units).

In this example, there are visible differences between women in their typical levels of intimacy and in their variability in intimacy, with those with lower levels of intimacy showing less variability. Nonetheless, we may be interested in characterizing the mean and variance of an average person in the sample. To do so we can calculate (*a*) the average level of intimacy for the average person (about 40 units) and (*b*) the variability of intimacy for the average person (about 4 standard deviation units).

Estimates of the mean and standard deviation of intimacy for the typical woman can be obtained in two main ways. The first is simply to calculate a mean and standard deviation separately for each participant and obtain arithmetic averages of these to estimate the mean and standard deviation for the typical participant. This approach will suffice if each participant provides many repeated measurements (Kenny et al. 1998). However, a better approach, and one that will pay particular dividends when research questions become more complex, is to use a multilevel analysis.

The multilevel analysis has us specify a statistical model with two levels: level 1, a within-person level, and level 2, a between-person level. The within-person level specifies that each woman's intimacy score is composed of her average intimacy plus that score's deviation from her average. Similarly, the between-person model specifies that a woman's mean intimacy score is composed of the overall mean score across all women and that particular woman's deviation from the overall mean. For more statistical detail on this model, see Raudenbush & Bryk (2002, ch. 2), where it is called a One-Way ANOVA with Random Effects. Using this multilevel model, one can obtain a summary measure of variability for the typical person: the level-1 error variance.

As noted earlier, for the data illustrated along the Y axis in Figure 1, the average woman had an average intimacy of approximately 40 units, and the variability around her average was approximately 4 units. One must be careful when calculating these averages, however. Although in many diary studies the notion of an average person is useful, in our particular example it is misleading because there are two distinct subgroups.

ASSUMPTIONS ABOUT WITHIN-PERSON VARIATION   Diary data are longitudinal. Even if the investigator has no direct interest in time as a factor, the data are ordered in time and this ordering may be relevant to one's analyses. In this respect, diary data are often different from other nested data. For example, when the nesting involves persons within groups, the ordering is often inconsequential. In contrast, with the intimacy data in our example it is plausible that adjacent diary reports are more similar than reports farther apart. This will occur if time bears any systematic relation to scores on intimacy (e.g., if there is growth or decline in intimacy over time). It can also occur even in the absence of a systematic effect of time, in cases where unmeasured influences on intimacy (e.g., child-care problems) have some stability from day to day, thereby leading the daily reports to be dependent due to this common influence. When adjacent data have stronger dependence on one another than nonadjacent data, a pattern of autocorrelation will be observed (West & Hepworth 1991).

Because the correlation between adjacent data points is typically positive (when it exists), autocorrelation generally leads to estimates of within-person variability that are smaller than they would be if the reports were independent of one another. This produces a downward bias in standard errors and overly liberal tests of significance. Available multilevel software such as HLM and PROC MIXED in SAS allow one to model autocorrelation in within-person error terms and correct for this biasing influence. As we will see, though, autocorrelated errors in simple models such as the one we have discussed may disappear when these models are expanded to include omitted variables, such as the child-care problems cited in the example above (Singer 2002). Introductory discussions of autocorrelation in multilevel models can be found in Hox (2002) and Snijders & Bosker (1999). Advanced treatments can be found in Diggle & Liang (2001), McCulloch & Searle (2001), and Verbeke & Molenberghs (2000).

BETWEEN-PERSON DIFFERENCES IN AGGREGATED DATA   The extent to which there are between-person differences in a level-1 variable (intimacy in our example) must be determined in models of between-person differences. As drawn in Figure 1, the summary distributions clearly indicate that women differ in their average intimacy over time. With actual diary data there is often a large degree of overlap in individuals' distributions, and appropriate statistical tests are needed to determine if these distributions differ from one another. Further emphasizing the need for appropriate statistics, it is known that distributions of sample means such as these will show more variability than would true means (Raudenbush & Bryk 2002). This is because the observed mean of each woman's intimacy will be an imperfect estimate of her true mean due to sampling error (and possibly measurement error). Not surprisingly, the uncertainty in the estimate of between-person variability is greatest when within-person sample sizes are small.

Fortunately, a multilevel analysis, specifically the One-Way ANOVA with Random Effects described earlier, will produce unbiased estimates of the between-person variability. Recall that level 1 of this model specifies that each woman's intimacy score is composed of her mean intimacy plus that score's deviation from the mean. Similarly, the level-2 model specifies that a woman's mean intimacy score is composed of the overall mean score across all women, and that particular woman's deviation from the overall mean.

All multilevel modeling software can handle models of this kind and all provide (*a*) a significance test of whether the data show between-person variability in means and (*b*) an estimate of the size of that variability (as a variance or standard deviation). Likewise, these programs can allow for (and provide tests of) individual differences in the within-person variability, which, of course, are a feature of the example data. For more detail on this specific model, see Raudenbush & Bryk (2002).

EXPLAINING BETWEEN-PERSON DIFFERENCES   To the extent that people do differ from one another, the notion of a "typical person" is less useful in describing the data and suggests the need to investigate sources of between-person variability. In nonexperimental diary studies these can involve relatively stable characteristics of participants (e.g., personality) or of their environment (e.g., the quality of the neighborhood they live in). In experimental work (e.g., when testing an intervention program), one may be interested in comparing the levels of the outcome in an experimental group and in a control group. Assume that the data presented along the Y axis of the graph in Figure 1 are the result of an intervention to boost intimacy in a sample of women from distressed couples. Further assume that the two women with the highest mean intimacy score (A and B, represented by dashed distributions) are from the intervention group and the remaining two (C and D, represented by solid distributions) are from the control group.

The effect of the intervention on average intimacy can be analyzed using a means-as-outcomes model (Raudenbush & Bryk 2002). Level 1, the within-person level of the model, as before, specifies that each woman's intimacy score on a given week is the sum of her average across all weeks plus that week's deviation from her average. Level 2, the between-person level of the model, now specifies that each woman's average intimacy is the sum of the mean intimacy for women in her intervention group (experimental versus control) plus her deviation from that mean. Because Figure 1 shows that the within-person variability differs by condition, the multilevel analysis would need to allow for this to obtain optimal tests of significance. A test of autocorrelation in the within-person errors is also advisable, and if present, the autocorrelation should be modeled, thereby obtaining unbiased estimates of within-person variances.

Modeling the Time Course: How Does a Typical Person Change Over Time, and How Do People Differ in Change Over Time?

In addition to the aggregate analyses described in the previous section, time-based diaries allow investigators to examine changes in levels of variables over time. Using our intimacy example, researchers might be interested in following the women over time to examine changes in intimacy. When considering the time course of intimacy for the average woman, two basic questions can be asked: (*a*) What was an average woman's intimacy level at the beginning of the diary study, and (*b*) what was the average woman's time course in intimacy?

THE TYPICAL PERSON'S TIME COURSE   The data shown in the body of Figure 1 reveal the time course of intimacy for the four women. We see that the four women's intimacy levels are very similar at time 1, that there is a divergence over time, and that the growth process for each woman is approximately linear. Even though in this example women differ in their time courses, we can still average over these differences and characterize the intimacy of someone who is average in terms of starting values and rates of change.

An appropriate modeling approach here would be a linear growth model. We specify at level 1 or the within-person level that a woman's intimacy score on a given week is the sum of (*a*) her starting level; (*b*) her rate of change per week, multiplied by the number of elapsed weeks; and (*c*) a residual term, her actual score's deviation from her predicted value for that week. At level 2 or the between-person level, we specify that each woman's starting value (or rate of change) is the sum of the mean starting point (or mean rate of change) plus her deviations from those averages. From this model, the starting value, rate of change, and residual variance for the typical person can be obtained.

BETWEEN-PERSON DIFFERENCES IN CHANGE   In addition to estimates for the typical person, the multilevel model just described will provide estimates (and tests of significance) of between-person variability of the starting values and rates of change in intimacy. Note again that the observed variability in starting values and rates of change, if these were obtained from separate regression analyses instead of a multilevel model, would be biased upwards. In the case of slopes based on small numbers of observations, this bias can be severe (Raudenbush & Bryk 2002).

Figure 1 was constructed so that after allowing for individual differences in starting values and rates of change, the residual variances of the growth model at level 1 would not differ across women (whereas the within-person residual variances around the simple mean in the previous section did differ). Other things being equal, large individual differences in slopes will result in individual differences in residual variances in Y at level 1 unless the cause of these differences is accounted for in the model. Also, allowing for individual differences in growth can eliminate autocorrelation in within-subject errors, as demonstrated by Singer (1998, 2002).

EXPLAINING BETWEEN-PERSON DIFFERENCES IN CHANGE   The data in Figure 1 were drawn to illustrate the time courses of intimacy for women in an intervention study. In the example, random assignment was effective: The two groups did not differ in their initial levels of intimacy. The control group shows essentially no change over time whereas the treatment group shows an increase, on average. The multilevel model that can be used to explain between-person differences is a modification of the one used in the previous section. In this case, the level-1 model remains the same, but the level-2 or between-person model provides estimates of a mean intercept and a mean slope for each condition. Within each condition, individual women are allowed to show deviations from the average for their condition. For example, although the experimental group shows increases in intimacy over time, one woman (A) in the group has a slightly higher rate than the other (B).

Modeling Within-Person Processes: What is the Within-Person Process for the Typical Person, and How Do People Differ in These Processes?

The third and most complete approach to understanding diary data involves developing an explanatory model of the factors affecting within-person variability in the data. Such models may evolve from an initial model of the time course in the dependent variable (e.g., Bolger & Eckenrode 1991) or from an interest in explanatory variables that are not necessarily related to elapsed time in the study (e.g., Swim et al. 2001). Whether or not temporal changes are of interest in one's study, based on our experience it is wise to include in process models parameters for elapsed time in the study and for cyclical effects such as time of day or day of week. Some factors of interest (e.g., social support) may show considerable temporal variability, such as weekday versus weekend differences, and any attempt to estimate support effects should hold constant day of the week, as it is a plausible third variable in the relationship between support and distress.

To illustrate a process model, we continue with a focus on intimacy as a dependent variable but change the example to one of a daily diary study of women in a cohabiting relationship over the course of a typical month. If one wishes to understand the processes underlying day-to-day variability in intimacy, one needs to examine daily events in the relationship that can bring partners together or push them apart. For illustrative purposes, we have chosen to focus on daily conflicts. Daily conflicts have been shown in previous work to be more powerful than any other daily stressor in affecting mood (Bolger et al. 1989).

Figure 2 presents four panels of fictitious data for four women (E, F, G, and H), showing daily changes in intimacy (again on a 100-point scale) over 28 days.

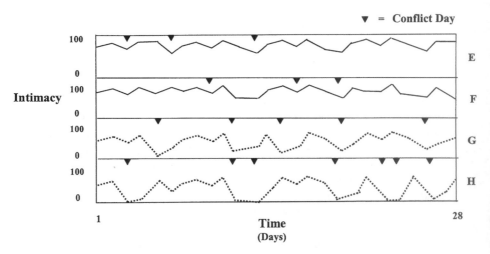

Figure 2   Hypothetical data of four participants in Daily Conflicts Study (28-day diary study of intimacy and daily conflicts).

The downward pointing triangles at the top of each panel indicate days on which a conflictual or hindering interchange occurred between the woman and her partner. Several features of the data are noteworthy. First, unlike the previous example, there are no time trends; for all women gross levels of intimacy do not change over the course of the study. Second, the women show differences in exposure to daily conflicts, with participants E and F showing the greatest exposure and participants G and H showing the least. Third, the women show differences in average levels of intimacy, with participants E and F showing high levels and participants G and H showing moderate to low levels. Fourth, the latter two participants show greater variability in daily intimacy than the former two. Finally, there are marked differences in the extent to which conflicts are associated with declines in intimacy. Participants E and F show small declines whereas participants G and H—particularly H—show much larger declines and ones that last more than a single day.

WITHIN-PERSON PROCESS MODEL FOR THE AVERAGE PERSON AND BETWEEN-PERSON DIFFERENCES IN PROCESS   Process models that characterize both the average person and between-person differences present no major new problems in terms of analysis. The main issue to be dealt with is whether, and if so, how, to use the longitudinal nature of the diary design to study lagged effects as a means of addressing the possibility of bidirectional processes. For example, the relation between conflict and intimacy is likely to be bidirectional (low intimacy makes conflict more likely, and conflict leads to decreased intimacy), and it would seem important to demonstrate that earlier conflict predicts later declines in intimacy, controlling for earlier intimacy. This approach is the same as is used in traditional panel analyses, but with a diary design the lagged analysis is within—rather than between—subjects and is therefore less vulnerable to rival hypotheses.

For the example data, a possible approach would be to create two new variables—one-day lagged versions of conflicts and of intimacy—and examine whether, controlling for lagged intimacy, lagged conflict predicts current intimacy. The example data show that such effects are present for participants G and H and absent for participants E and F. One could begin an analysis by estimating separate level-1 regressions for each woman, where the main coefficient of interest would be the one for lagged conflicts. These coefficients could then be averaged to arrive at a between-person average. We have already discussed how the variability in these coefficients would be inflated due to sampling error (and possibly measurement error), but the average coefficient would give an unbiased estimate of the population value.

A more appropriate multilevel modeling approach is what Raudenbush & Bryk (2002) call a Random-Coefficients Regression Model. This model provides appropriate estimates and tests of the average of the level-1 slopes for conflict, and of the variance of these slopes. Such an analysis would show evidence of an average effect of conflict but would also show evidence of between-person differences in this effect. It would likely not show any between-person differences in level-1 residuals. Once the effect of conflict is taken into account, the remaining variability does not differ across persons (but note that if one carried out a simpler analysis, aggregating the data over repeated measurements, one would find that participants G and H have greater within-person variability than participants E and F).

To keep the exposition simple, Table 1, part III describes a random-coefficients model in which only contemporaneous (cross-sectional) relations between conflicts and intimacy are examined. By replacing contemporaneous conflict with lagged conflict and lagged intimacy, however, a longitudinal analysis can be performed, as discussed above. Level 1 of the model specifies that a given woman's intimacy score on a given day is the sum of (a) her average intimacy score on days when no conflicts occur, (b) the additional decrement in intimacy associated with conflict days, and (c) a residual score, her actual intimacy score's deviation from her predicted value for that day. At level 2 or the between-person level, we specify that each woman's level-1 coefficient is the sum of that coefficient for the average woman, plus her deviation from that average. This model can be used to produce the estimates and tests described earlier: the coefficients for the average woman, between-person differences in these coefficients, and between-person differences in level-1 errors.

EXPLAINING BETWEEN-PERSON DIFFERENCES IN WITHIN-PERSON PROCESSES   The example has been constructed to show between-person differences in within-person processes. Assume that participants E and F are women who report high baseline levels of relationship quality (RQ), whereas G and H are those who report low RQ. To investigate the relation between baseline RQ and conflict processes, we now use what Raudenbush & Bryk (2002) call an Intercepts-and-Slopes-as-Outcomes Model. The level-1 model is unchanged, but the level-2 model specifies that between-person differences in intercepts and slopes are a function of RQ. Such an analysis would show that, compared to low-RQ women, high-RQ women have higher intimacy scores on days when no conflicts occur, and show smaller decrements in intimacy when conflict days occur.

Other Data Analysis Issues

MEASUREMENT MODELS FOR WITHIN-PERSON DATA   We have just described how theoretical models of causal processes can be estimated using time-based diary data. Readers will have noted that our first and primary concern was to specify the factors that affect within-person variability, how people differ from themselves. An unstated assumption of this approach, however, is that the concepts we wish to model are adequately measured within subjects. With diary data it is rarely clear that this is so. Most validation studies of psychological measures involve between-subject designs, and there is no guarantee that these measures are reliable and valid for assessing within-person variability (Borsboom et al. 2002). Thus diary researchers who adapt well-validated between-subject measures should consider whether the items they propose using have a similar factor structure within subjects similar to that known to obtain between subjects. Furthermore, the possibility needs to be considered that within-person measurement models differ across people (Molenaar 1999).

To date, there is little published empirical work on measurement models using diary data. Given the importance of this topic, we see it as an area deserving much more research activity. Some notable exceptions include work on the within-subject structure of affective experience (Feldman 1995), and on an integrated measurement and structural model for diary data [using SEM (Kenny & Zautra 1995, 2001)]. A groundbreaking measurement approach that has to date been neglected by diary researchers involves dynamic factor analysis models such as those developed by Molenaar (1985), McArdle & Epstein (1987), and Nesselroade et al. (2002). Future diary work should draw on these and related models when developing and validating measures. One possible reason why measurement issues have been neglected thus far is that measurement models have not yet been incorporated into popular multilevel modeling software. As noted earlier, however, this situation is changing, with programs such as LISREL, EQS, and MPlus incorporating multilevel capabilities. Until technical advances allow measurement models to be routinely included in multilevel models, we recommend that researchers at least confirm the adequacy of measures using within-subject data that are pooled after centering around each subject's mean. This approach will demonstrate that measurement models are sound at the level of the average person for data collected over time. To do so, researchers need to fit a factor model to the pooled within-person data set. An example of such an analysis on 2300 person-days of data on 9 emotion items can be found in Thompson & Bolger (1999).

DATA ANALYSIS OF DIARY DATA ON DYADS, FAMILIES, AND OTHER GROUPS   We have argued that diary data can provide a useful window on the processes affecting change in a person over time. Because social interactions are likely to be important determinants of how people change, and because of the importance of close relationships to such interactions, some diary researchers have attempted to study change processes by collecting diary data on dyads, families, and other important social groups (e.g., Almeida & Kessler 1998, Bolger et al. 1989, Larson & Richards 1994, Perrez et al. 2000, 2001, Roberts & Levenson 2001).

Although analysis issues become more complicated when diary data on dyads and groups are involved, the statistical models required need not change: Multilevel models can be used effectively for this purpose. Dyadic and group-based diary data can be analyzed in two main ways. The first treats the persons within the larger social group as the main focus and takes account of nonindependence between persons due to their common group membership. In the case of married couples, this involves obtaining separate estimates of within-person parameters for husbands and wives while adjusting for possible correlation in the residual of the model attributable to the couple level of analysis. An important example of this approach can be seen in work by Raudenbush et al. on the relationship between work and family events in married couples (Barnett et al. 1993, Raudenbush et al. 1995). A modification of this approach that incorporates additional sources of nonindependence—one due to omitted transient couple-level influences (i.e., concurrent within-couple residual correlation), and the other due to omitted transient person-level influences (i.e., day-to-day within-person residual correlation)—can be found in Kennedy et al. (2002).

The second major approach explicitly decomposes the relation between diary measures X and Y into components that reflect covariation operating at the between-group level, between-person within-group level, and within-person level (Kashy & Kenny 2000). This approach is akin to Kenny & la Voie's (1985) work on separating individual and group effects, and to Gonzalez & Griffin's (1999) work on decomposing correlations on data from dyads into dyadic and individual components. A model exposition of this approach can be found in Wilhelm (2001), with analyses from the Fribourg Family Project in Switzerland. The data set consisted of six reports per day for seven days from mothers, fathers, and adolescent children from 96 families. Wilhelm describes a multilevel analysis that decomposes influences on emotional states into between-family, within-family, within-person, and within-day components.

Analysis Section Summary

We have presented an overview of three major approaches to diary data analysis. Often, a single study calls for the use of all three approaches. The classification scheme can be used by researchers to systematically consider the questions they might ask in a diary study, and to determine which ones are interesting given their particular substantive problem. Thus, a researcher may begin by asking, "Do I have any prediction regarding the average (aggregate) level of my variable? What about its variance? Do I expect the average or the variance to vary between people?" and so on, thereby arriving at a data analysis plan.

CONCLUSIONS

Diary research offers a unique window on human phenomenology. As diary researchers, we are clearly enthusiastic about the multiple benefits of using such designs in the study of temporal dynamics, within-person process, and other questions. We hope this enthusiasm proves contagious. At the same time, we have tried to offer a candid look at the dilemmas, irritations, and problems of using diaries to investigate psychological processes. To use diary methods effectively, these problems need to be acknowledged and addressed, but they should not deter researchers from setting out on important studies of the particulars of everyday life.

ACKNOWLEDGMENTS

We are grateful to James Cranford, Lisa Feldman Barrett, Geraldine Downey, Susan Fiske, Marci Gleason, Jean-Phillippe Laurenceau, Meinrad Perrez, Harry Reis, Saul Shiffman, Patrick Shrout, Arthur Stone, Howard Tennen, and members of NYU's Couples Research Lab for their suggestions during the preparation of this chapter. Work on this paper was supported in part through NIMH grant R01-MH60366 awarded to the senior author.

The *Annual Review of Psychology* is online at http://psych.annualreviews.org

LITERATURE CITED

Affleck G, Zautra A, Tennen H, Armeli S. 1999. Multilevel daily process designs for consulting and clinical psychology: a preface for the perplexed. *J. Consult. Clin. Psychol.* 67:746–54

Alloy LB, Just N, Panzarella C. 1997. Attributional style, daily life events, and hopelessness depression: subtype validation by prospective variability and specificity of symptoms. *Cogn. Ther. Res.* 21:321–44

Allport GW. 1942. *The Use of Personal Documents in Psychological Science.* New York: Soc. Sci. Res. Counc.

Almeida DM, Kessler RC. 1998. Everyday stressors and gender differences in daily distress. *J. Personal. Soc. Psychol.* 75:670–80

Almeida DM, Wethington E, Chandler AL. 1999. Daily transmission of tensions between marital dyads and parent-child dyads. *J. Marriage Fam.* 61:49–61

Almeida DM, Wethington E, McDonald DA. 2001. Daily variation in paternal engagement and negative mood: implications for emotionally supportive and conflictual interactions. *J. Marriage Fam.* 63:417–29

Barnett RC, Marshall NL, Raudenbush SW, Brennan RT. 1993. Gender and the relationship between job experiences and psychological distress: a study of dual-earner couples. *J. Personal. Soc. Psychol.* 64:794–806

Barrett DJ, Feldman Barrett L. 2000. *The Experience-Sampling Program (ESP).* http://www2.bc.edu/~barretli/esp/

Bentler PM 1995. *EQS Structural Equations Program Manual.* Encino, CA: Multivariate Software

Bolger N, DeLongis A, Kessler R, Schilling E. 1989. Effects of daily stress on negative mood. *J. Personal. Soc. Psychol.* 57:808–18

Bolger N, Eckenrode J. 1991. Social relationships, personality, and anxiety during a major stressful event. *J. Personal. Soc. Psychol.* 61:440–49

Bolger N, Zuckerman A. 1995. A framework for studying personality in the stress process. *J. Personal. Soc. Psychol.* 69:890–902

Bolger N, Zuckerman A, Kessler RC. 2000. Invisible support and adjustment to stress. *J. Personal. Soc. Psychol.* 79:953–61

Borsboom D, Mellenbergh GJ, van Heerden J. 2002. The theoretical status of latent variables. *Psychol. Rev.* In press

Bower GH. 1981. Mood and memory. *Am. Psychol.* 36:129–48

Bryk AS, Raudenbush SW, Congdon RT. 1996. *HLM: Hierarchical Linear and Nonlinear Modeling with the HLM/2L and HLM/3L Programs.* Chicago: Scientific Software Int.

Clark LA, Watson D, Leeka J. 1989. Diurnal variation in the positive affects. *Motiv. Emot.* 13:205–34

Csikszentmihalyi M, Larson R. 1992. Validity and reliability of the Experience Sampling Method. See deVries 1992, pp. 43–57

Dabbs JM Jr, Strong R, Milun R. 1997. Exploring the mind of testosterone: a beeper study. *J. Res. Personal.* 31:577–87

Dermer M, Berscheid E. 1972. Self-report of arousal as an indicant of activation level. *Behav. Sci.* 17:420–29

deVries MW, ed. 1992. *The Experience of Psychopathology: Investigating Mental Disorders in Their Natural Settings.* New York: Cambridge Univ. Press

Diggle P, Liang KY. 2001. *Analyses of Longitudinal Data.* New York: Oxford Univ. Press

Dohrenwend BS, Krasnoff L, Askenasy AR, Dohrenwend BP. 1978. Exemplification of a method for scaling life events: the PERI Life Events Scale. *J. Health Soc. Behav.* 19:205–29

Downey G, Purdie V, Schaffer-Neitz R. 1999. Anger transmission from mother to child: a comparison of mothers in chronic pain and well mothers. *J. Marriage Fam.* 61:62–73

Fabes RA, Eisenberg N. 1997. Regulatory control and adults' stress-related responses to daily life events. *J. Personal. Soc. Psychol.* 73:1107–17

Fahrenberg J, Myrtek M, eds. 1996. *Ambulatory Assessment: Computer Assisted Psychological and Psychophysiological Methods in Monitoring and Field Studies.* Seattle, WA: Hogrefe & Huber

Feldman LA. 1995. Valence focus and arousal focus: individual differences in the structure of affective experience. *J. Personal. Soc. Psychol.* 69:153–66

Feldman Barrett L, Barrett DJ. 2001. An introduction to computerized experience sampling in psychology. *Soc. Sci. Comput. Rev.* 19:175–85

Feldman Barrett L, Jamner LD. 2000. *Capturing the vicissitudes of life: electronic experience sampling.* Workshop presented at Annu. Meet. Soc. Personal. Soc. Psychol., 1st, Nashville, TN

Gleason MEJ, Bolger N, Shrout P. 2001. *The effects of research design on reports of mood: comparing daily diary, panel, and cross-sectional designs.* Presented at Annu. Meet. Soc. Personal. Soc. Psychol., 2nd, San Antonio, TX

Gollob HF, Reichardt CS. 1987. Taking account of time lags in causal models. *Child Dev.* 58:80–92

Gonzalez R, Griffin D. 1999. The correlation analysis of dyad-level data in the distinguishable case. *Pers. Relat.* 6:449–69

Greenier KD, Kernis MH, McNamara CW, Waschull SB, Berry AJ, et al. 1999. Individual differences in reactivity to daily events: examining the roles of stability and level of self-esteem. *J. Personal.* 67:185–208

Hackel LS, Ruble DN. 1992. Changes in the marital relationship after the first baby is born: predicting the impact of expectancy disconfirmation. *J. Personal. Soc. Psychol.* 62:944–57

Hox J. 2002. *Multilevel Analyses: Techniques and Applications.* Mahwah, NJ: Erlbaum

Jamison RN, Raymond SA, Levine JG, Slawsby EA, Nedeljkovic SS, et al. 2001. Electronic diaries for monitoring chronic pain: 1-year validation study. *Pain* 91:277–85

Jamner LD, Shapiro D, Alberts J. 1998. Mood, blood pressure, and heart rate: strategies for developing a more effective ambulatory mood diary. In *Technology and Methods in Behavioral Medicine*, ed. DS Krantz, A Baum, pp. 195–220. Mahwah, NJ: Erlbaum

Jensen-Campbell LA, Graziano WG. 2000. Beyond the school yard: relationships as moderators of daily interpersonal conflict. *Personal. Soc. Psychol. Bull.* 26:923–35

Jöreskog KG, Sörbom D. 1996. *LISREL 8 User's Reference Guide.* Chicago: Scientific Software Int.

Kashy DA, Kenny DA. 2000. The analysis of data from dyads and groups. In *Handbook of Research Methods in Social Psychology,* ed. HT Reis, CM Judd, pp. 451–77. New York: Cambridge Univ. Press

Kennedy JK, Bolger N, Shrout PE. 2002. Witnessing interparental psychological aggression in childhood: implications for daily conflict in adult intimate relationships. *J. Personal.* In press

Kenny D, Kashy D, Bolger N. 1998. Data analysis in social psychology. In *Handbook of Social Psychology*, ed. D Gilbert, S Fiske, G Lindzey, pp. 233–65. New York: McGraw-Hill

Kenny DA, la Voie L. 1985. Separating individual and group effects. *J. Personal. Soc. Psychol.* 48:339–48

Kenny DA, Zautra A. 2001. Trait-state models for longitudinal data. In *New Methods for the Analysis of Change*, ed. A Sayer, LM Collins, pp. 243–63. Washington, DC: Am. Psychol. Assoc.

Kenny DA, Zautra A. 1995. The trait-state-error

model for multiwave data. *J. Consult. Clin. Psychol.* 63:52–59

Larsen RJ. 1990. Spectral analysis of longitudinal data. In *Statistical Methods in Longitudinal Research: Time Series and Categorical Longitudinal Data. Vol. 2: Statistical Modeling and Decision Science*, ed. A von Eye, pp. 319–50. San Diego, CA: Academic

Larsen RJ, Kasimatis M. 1990. Individual differences in entrainment of mood to the weekly calendar. *J. Personal. Soc. Psychol.* 58:164–71

Larson R, Csikszentmihalyi M. 1978. Experiential correlates of time alone in adolescence. *J. Personal.* 46:677–93

Larson R, Richards M. 1994. *Divergent Realities: The Emotional Lives of Mothers, Fathers, and Adolescents.* New York: Basic Books

Laurenceau JP, Feldman Barrett L, Pietromonaco PR. 1998. Intimacy as an interpersonal process: the importance of self-disclosure, partner disclosure, and perceived partner responsiveness in interpersonal exchanges. *J. Personal. Soc. Psychol.* 74:1238–51

Laurenceau JP, Feldman Barrett LA, Rovine MJ. 2002. Intimacy in marriage: a daily-diary and multilevel modeling approach. Submitted

Litt MD, Cooney NL, Morse P. 1998. Ecological momentary assessment (EMA) with treated alcoholics: methodological problems and potential solutions. *Health Psychol.* 17: 48–52

McArdle JJ, Epstein D. 1987. Latent growth curves within developmental structural equation models. *Child Dev.* 58:110–33

McCulloch CE, Searle SR. 2001. *Generalized, Linear, and Mixed Models.* New York: Wiley

Mendoza-Denton R, Downey G, Purdie V, Davis A, Pietrzak J. 2002. Sensitivity to status-based rejection: implications for African-American college students' college experience. *J. Personal. Soc. Psychol.* In press

Mohr CD, Armeli S, Tennen H, Carney MA, Affleck G, et al. 2001. Daily interpersonal experiences, context, and alcohol consumption: crying in your beer and toasting good times. *J. Personal. Soc. Psychol.* 80:489–500

Molenaar PCM. 1985. A dynamic factor model for the analysis of multivariate time series. *Psychometrika* 50:181–202

Molenaar PCM. 1999. Longitudinal analysis. In *Research Methodology in Social, Life, and Behavioural Sciences*, ed. HJ Ader, GJ Mellenbergh, pp. 143–67. Thousand Oaks, CA: Sage

Morrison DM, Leigh BC, Gillmore MR. 1999. Daily data collection: a comparison of three methods. *J. Sex Res.* 36:76–81

Moskowitz DS, Hershberger SL, eds. 2002. *Modeling Intraindividual Variability with Repeated Measures Data: Methods and Applications.* Mahwah, NJ: Erlbaum

Muthén B, Muthén L. 2002. *Mplus Version 2 User's Guide.* Los Angeles, CA: Muthén & Muthén

Nesselroade JR, McArdle JJ, Aggen SH, Meyers JM. 2002. Dynamic factor analysis models for representing process in multivariate time-series. See Moskowitz& Hershberger 2002, pp. 235–65

Nisbett RE, Wilson TD. 1977. Telling more than we can know: verbal reports on mental processes. *Psychol. Rev.* 84:231–59

Paty JA, Kassel JD, Shiffman S. 1992. The importance of assessing base rates for clinical studies: an example of stimulus control of smoking. See deVries 1992, pp. 347–52

Pennebaker JW, Graybeal A. 2001. Patterns of natural language use: disclosure, personality, and social integration. *Curr. Dir. Psychol. Sci.* 10:90–93

Perrez M, Reicherts M. 1996. A computer-assisted self-monitoring procedure for assessing stress-related behavior under real life conditions. See Fahrenberg & Myrtek 1996, pp. 51–67

Perrez M, Schöbi D, Wilhelm P. 2000. How to assess social regulation of stress and emotions in daily family life? A computer-assisted family self-monitoring system

(FASEM-C). *Clin. Psychol. Psychother.* 7: 326–39

Perrez M, Wilhelm P, Schoebi D, Horner M. 2001. Simultaneous computer assisted assessment of causal attribution and social coping in families. See Fahrenberg & Myrtek 2001, pp. 25–43

Prosser R, Rasbash J, Goldstein H. 1996. *MLn User's Guide.* London: Inst. Educ.

Radloff LS. 1977. The CES-D Scale: A self-report depression scale for research in the general population. *Appl. Psychol. Meas.* 1: 385–401

Rafaeli E, Revelle W. 1999. *Personality, Motivation, and Cognition (PMC) Diary Program.* http://personality-project.org/pmc/diary.html

Rafaeli E, Revelle W. 2002. Affective synchrony: individual differences in mixed emotions. Submitted

Raffety BD. 2001. *Interactive Software Interview System (ISIS).* Email raffety@ccplex.com

Raudenbush SW, Brennan RT, Barnett RC. 1995. A multivariate hierarchical model for studying psychological change within married couples. *J. Fam. Psychol.* 9:161–74

Raudenbush SW, Bryk AS. 2002. *Hierarchical Linear Models: Applications and Data Analysis Methods.* Thousand Oaks, CA: Sage. 2nd ed.

Reardon A, Young MA, Blodgett C. 2001. *Patterns of symptom remission in seasonal affective disorder.* Poster presented at Annu. Meet. Soc. Res. Psychopathol., Madison, WI

Redelmeier DA, Kahneman D. 1996. Patients' memories of painful medical treatments: real-time and retrospective evaluations of two minimally invasive procedures. *Pain* 66: 3–8

Reis HT. 1994. Domains of experience: investigating relationship processes from three perspectives. In *Theoretical Frameworks in Personal Relationships*, ed. R Erber, R Gilmore, pp. 87–110. Mahwah, NJ: Erlbaum

Reis HT, Gable SL. 2000. Event-sampling and other methods for studying everyday experience. In *Handbook of Research Methods in Social and Personality Psychology*, ed. TH Reis, MC Judd, pp. 190–222. New York: Cambridge Univ. Press

Reis HT, Shaver P. 1988. Intimacy as an interpersonal process. In *Handbook of Relationships*, ed. SW Duck, pp. 367–389. Chichester, UK: Wiley

Repetti RL, Wood J. 1997. Effects of daily stress at work on mothers' interactions with preschoolers. *J. Fam. Psychol.* 11:90–108

Rhodewalt F, Madrian JC, Cheney S. 1998. Narcissism, self-knowledge organization, and emotional reactivity: the effect of daily experiences on self-esteem and affect. *Personal. Soc. Psychol. Bull.* 24:75–87

Roberts NA, Levenson RW. 2001. The remains of the workday: impact of job stress and exhaustion on marital interaction in police couples. *J. Marriage Fam.* 63:1052–67

Ross M. 1989. Relation of implicit theories to the construction of personal histories. *Psychol. Rev.* 96:341–57

SAS Inst. 1999. *SAS/STAT User's Guide, Version 7.* Cary, NC: SAS Inst.

Sayer AG, Collins LM, eds. 2001. *New Methods for the Analysis of Change.* Washington, DC: Am. Psychol. Assoc.

Searles JS, Helzer JE, Walter DE. 2000. Comparison of drinking patterns measured by daily reports and timeline follow back. *Psychol. Addict. Behav.* 14:277–86

Shapiro D, Goldstein IB. 1998. Wrist actigraph measures of physical activity level and ambulatory blood pressure in healthy elderly persons. *Psychophysiology* 35:305–12

Shiffman S. 2000. Real-time self-report of momentary states in the natural environment: computerized ecological momentary assessment. In *The Science of Self-reports: Implications for Research and Practice*, ed. AA Stone, JS Turkkan, CA Bachrach, JB Jobe, HS Kurtzman, VS Cain, pp. 277–96. Mahwah, NJ: Erlbaum

Shiffman S, Hufford M, Hickcox M, Paty JA, Gnys M, et al. 1997. Remember that? A comparison of real-time versus retrospective recall of smoking lapses. *J. Consult. Clin. Psychol.* 65:292–300

Shiffman S, Stone AA. 1998. Ecological momentary assessment: a new tool for behavioral medicine research. In *Technology and Methods in Behavioral Medicine*, ed. DS Krantz, A Baum, pp. 117–31. Mahwah, NJ: Erlbaum

Singer JD. 1998. Using SAS PROC MIXED to fit multilevel models, hierarchical models, and individual growth models. *J. Educ. Behav. Stat.* 23:323–55

Singer JD. 2002. Fitting individual growth models using SAS PROC MIXED. See Moskowitz & Hershberger 2002, pp. 135–70

Snijders TAB, Bosker RJ. 1999. *Multilevel Analysis: An Introduction to Basic and Advanced Multilevel Modeling.* Thousand Oaks, CA: Sage

Stonborough THW. 1942. The continuous consumer panel: a new sampling device in consumer research. *Appl. Anthropol.* 2:37–41

Stone AA, Broderick JE, Kaell AT, DelesPaul PAEG, Porter LE. 2000. Does the peak-end phenomenon observed in laboratory pain studies apply to real-world pain in rheumatoid arthritics? *J. Pain* 1:212–17

Stone AA, Schwartz JE, Neale JM, Shiffman S, Marco CA, et al. 1998. A comparison of coping assessed by ecological momentary assessment and retrospective recall. *J. Personal. Soc. Psychol.* 74:1670–80

Stone AA, Shiffman S. 1994. Ecological momentary assessment (EMA) in behavioral medicine. *Ann. Behav. Med.* 16:199–202

Stone AA, Shiffman S. 2002. Capturing momentary, self-report data: a proposal for reporting guidelines. *Ann. Behav. Med.* 24:236–43

Suedfeld P, Pennebaker JW. 1997. Health outcomes and cognitive aspects of recalled negative life events. *Psychosom. Med.* 59:172–77

Suls J, Wan CK, Blanchard EB. 1994. A multilevel data-analytic approach to evaluation of relationships between daily life stressors and symptomatology: patients with irritable

bowel syndrome. *Health Psychol.* 13:103–13

Swim JK, Hyers LL, Cohen LL, Ferguson MJ. 2001. Everyday sexism: evidence for its incidence, nature, and psychological impact from three daily diary studies. *J. Soc. Issues* 57:31–53

Tennen H, Suls J, Affleck G. 1991. Personality and daily experience: the promise and the challenge. *J. Personal.* 59:313–38

Thomas DL, Diener E. 1990. Memory accuracy in the recall of emotions. *J. Personal. Soc. Psychol.* 59:291–97

Thompson A, Bolger N. 1999. Emotional transmission in couples under stress. *J. Marriage Fam.* 61:38–48

Tidwell MCO, Reis HT, Shaver PR. 1996. Attachment, attractiveness, and social interaction: a diary study. *J. Personal. Soc. Psychol.* 71:729–45

Tourangeau R, Rips LJ, Rasinski K. 2000. *The Psychology of Survey Response.* New York: Cambridge Univ. Press

van Goozen SHM, Wiegant VM, Endert E, Helmond FA, et al. 1997. Psychoendocrinological assessment of the menstrual cycle: the relationship between hormones, sexuality, and mood. *Arch. Sex. Behav.* 26:359–82

Verbeke G, Molenberghs G. 2000. *Linear Mixed Models for Longitudinal Data.* New York: Springer

Vinokur AD, Price RH, Caplan RD. 1996. Hard times and hurtful partners: how financial strain affects depression and relationship satisfaction of unemployed persons and their spouses. *J. Personal. Soc. Psychol.* 71:166–79

West SG, Hepworth JT. 1991. Statistical issues in the study of temporal data: daily experiences. *J. Personal.* 59:609–62

Wheeler L, Nezlek J. 1977. Sex differences in social participation. *J. Personal. Soc. Psychol.* 35:742–54

Wheeler L, Reis HT. 1991. Self-recording of everyday life events: origins, types, and uses. *J. Personal.* 59:339–54

Wilhelm P. 2001. A multi-level approach to

analyze ambulatory assessment data: an examination of family members' emotional states in daily life. In *Progress in Ambulatory Assessment: Computer-assisted Psychological and Psychophysiological Methods in Monitoring and Field Studies*, ed. J Fahrenberg, M Myrtek, pp. 173–89. Kirkland, WA: Hogrefe & Huber

Willett JB, Sayer AG. 1994. Using covariance structure analysis to detect correlates and predictors of individual change over time. *Psychol. Bull.* 116:363–81

Annu. Rev. Psychol. 2003. 54:617–40
doi: 10.1146/annurev.psych.54.101601.145034
First published online as a Review in Advance on August 6, 2002

QUALITATIVE AND QUANTITATIVE ANALYSES OF HISTORICAL DATA

Dean Keith Simonton

*Department of Psychology, University of California, Davis, One Shields Avenue,
Davis, California 95616-8686; e-mail: dksimonton@ucdavis.edu*

Key Words   historiometry, psychobiography, psychohistory, history

■ **Abstract**   Although the typical study in psychology involves the quantitative analysis of contemporary research participants, occasionally psychologists will study historical persons or events. Moreover, these historical data may be analyzed using either qualitative or quantitative techniques. After giving examples from the subdisciplines of cognitive, developmental, differential, abnormal, and social psychology, the distinctive methodological features of this approach are outlined. These include both data collection (sampling, unit definition, etc.) and data analysis (both qualitative and quantitative). The discussion then turns to the advantages and disadvantages of this research method. The article closes by presenting the reasons why (*a*) psychologists will probably continue to use historical data and (*b*) quantitative analyses may eventually replace qualitative analyses in such applications.

CONTENTS

0066-4308/03/0203-0617$14.00

INTRODUCTION

Imagine the typical empirical study published in a mainstream psychology journal. Or examine the sample investigations used to illustrate the official APA style in the *Publication Manual of the American Psychological Association* (2001). All of these studies tend to share certain features, two of which I wish to emphasize here.

1. The data collected are inherently quantitative in nature. This attribute holds for both laboratory experiments (e.g., reaction time, error counts, behavior frequencies, and similarity judgments) and correlational studies (e.g., Likert-type ratings on personality inventories or attitude questionnaires). Even when qualitative assessments are included, they are most often secondary to the quantitative assessments. An example is the use of protocol analysis in cognitive psychology (Ericsson & Simon 1984). Moreover, with recent advances in computerized administration of experiments and tests, the data can often be collected so that the participant's response is directly converted into quantitative scores in the investigator's database, all set for subsequent statistical analyses. In a sense, the investigator only knows his or her participants via the numbers they provide for those later statistics.

2. The data collected seldom if ever have any intrinsic importance. The data would not even exist if the researcher had not bothered to design the investigation in the first place. Although occasionally other investigators might ask for copies of the data, such requests are rare and usually reflect the desire to reanalyze the data using some other technique. The data have so little intrinsic value that researchers have to be specifically advised to retain them. "Authors of manuscripts accepted for publication in APA journals are required to have available their raw data throughout the editorial review process and for at least 5 years after the date of publication" (*Publication Manual of the American Psychological Association* 2001, p. 137). It is not surprising that APA authors have to be so admonished. After all, the participants were most likely anonymous animals, children, undergraduates, survey respondents, or other individuals in which the investigator takes no personal interest. Both the participants and the data they provide are merely the means to an end: the testing of nomothetic hypotheses about human thought, affect, or behavior.

In contrast, imagine a totally different type of psychological inquiry. To begin with, the researcher did not actually collect the data, but rather others already carried out the compilation. Even more oddly, these "others" were almost never scientists but rather historians, biographers, or archivists. As a consequence, the data collection was not designed to address some scientific question, but because the information was inherently interesting or valuable. In particular, the data represented what the collectors considered to be worthy of the "historical record." That is, the data concerned events or persons deemed sufficiently significant to deserve preservation in the various annals that define the "memory" of human civilization. Not only are the data to be preserved in perpetuity rather than just for 5 years, but the data would still exist even if psychology had never emerged as a scientific discipline.

Just as critically, these historical data are almost entirely qualitative in nature. This emphasis is immediately apparent upon reading the history of any major event or the biography of any famous person. Except for a few dates and other numbers scattered here and there, the archival record tends to consist of words: descriptions, narratives, speculations, interpretations, and the like. To be sure, sometimes the historical record may include substantial quantitative information, as is evident in the many and varied compilations of sports statistics (e.g., *The Baseball Encyclopedia* 1996). Even so, historical data seldom come "ready-made" in quantitative form. Consequently, if psychologists want to use this information in a scientific inquiry, they usually have only two somewhat contrasting options: (*a*) The recorded information can be retained in its original form and then subjected to a qualitative interpretation or (*b*) the information can be quantified by some objective coding scheme and then subjected to a statistical analysis like the typical data set in psychology.

My goal here is to discuss the qualitative and quantitative analysis of historical data in psychological science. In particular, I (*a*) give some representative examples of the ways that psychologists have adopted this research strategy, (*b*) describe the methods unique to these applications, (*c*) outline the advantages and disadvantages of the general methodology, and (*d*) speculate on the future utility of the approach in the discipline.

EXAMPLES

Psychologists have often included informal references to historical events and personalities to illustrate a principle or make an argument (e.g., James 1880). Even so, the first genuine qualitative analyses that were governed by a specified set of methodological rules did not appear until the advent of psychobiography and psychohistory—a development strongly associated with the psychoanalytic movement. In fact, the landmark work of this type was Freud's (1910/1964) psychoanalytic interpretation of the life and work of Leonardo da Vinci (Elms 1988). Surprisingly, the first quantitative analyses of historical data appeared long before this classic effort. Indeed, such quantitative analyses likely predate any other quantitative methodology in the behavioral sciences. The Belgian mathematician Adolphe Quételet—best known for his introduction of the normal curve and for coining the word "statistics"—published the first bona fide scientific application in 1835. In particular, Quételet took data on the dramas written by eminent French and English playwrights to conduct a quantitative analysis of the relation between age and achievement. Another pioneering inquiry was Francis Galton's (1869) *Hereditary Genius*, which used biographical data to assess the heritability of intellectual ability via the family pedigree method. To put these dates in perspective, Quételet's (1968) work appeared a quarter century before Fechner's classic experimental studies in psychophysics, and Galton's (1869) book was published almost a decade before Wilhelm Wundt founded the first laboratory for conducting original research in experimental psychology. Galton's *Hereditary Genius* also appeared five years before he himself introduced questionnaire methods (Galton 1874). Moreover, by the early twentieth century quantitative analyses of historical data had already acquired a special name, historiometry (Woods 1909, 1911; see also Cox 1926; Simonton 1990b).

Since the time of Quételet, Galton, and Freud, psychological analyses of historical data, whether qualitative or quantitative, have attracted psychologists from many subdisciplines. The result is a significant contribution to psychology's store of cumulative knowledge. Below I highlight some of the representative findings in five subdisciplines: cognitive, developmental, differential, abnormal, and social (see also Simonton 1998c, 1999).

Cognitive Psychology

It is sometimes claimed that cognitive psychologists tend to concentrate on the generic human mind completely divorced from its biographical and historical context (Gardner 1987). Yet that focus has not prevented them from exploiting historical data in their research. For instance, Neisser (1981) directly compared conversations recorded on the White House "Watergate" tapes with John Dean's Senate testimony regarding those conversations in order to learn how memory functions in a naturalistic setting (see also Hirst & Gluck 1999). Another example comes from the extensive literature on problem solving, especially that devoted to the process of scientific discovery. Sometimes the results of laboratory experiments and computer simulations are directly applied to the interpretation of the laboratory notebooks of famous scientists (e.g., Kulkarni & Simon 1988, Tweney 1989). Other times notable scientific discoveries will be replicated in experimental or computer simulations using the same data that inspired the original finding (Bradshaw et al. 1983, Langley et al. 1987).

Finally, I must mention the vast literature on conceptual (or integrative) complexity. Measures used in more conventional investigations (Schroder et al. 1967) were first converted into content-analytical coding schemes that could be applied to almost any historical document (Suedfeld et al. 1992). This enabled researchers to determine how the performance and decision making of historic leaders was determined by their information-processing complexity. The leaders studied have included US presidents (Tetlock 1981b), Canadian prime ministers (Ballard 1983), US senators (Tetlock 1981a, 1983; Tetlock et al. 1984), British parliamentarians (Tetlock 1984), Soviet politicians (Tetlock & Boettger 1989), US Supreme Court Justices (Tetlock et al. 1985), the leaders of various revolutions (Suedfeld & Rank 1976), and even presidents of the American Psychological Association (e.g., Suedfeld 1985).

Developmental Psychology

As already pointed out, the first historiometric analysis concerned the relation between age and achievement (Quételet 1968). Since then a great many other investigators have pursued the same research topic (Raskin 1936, Lehman 1953, Dennis 1966, Schulz & Curnow 1988, Ohlsson 1992). As a result, there has now accumulated an imposing corpus of empirical findings (Simonton 1988a) and theoretical models (Simonton 1997a). Moreover, this research tradition has expanded to cover the entire human life span, from birth to death. Thus, at one end of the spectrum, many psychologists have used historical data to study the impact of genetic endowment (Bramwell 1948, Galton 1869, Simonton 1983) as well as the repercussions of specific types of childhood and adolescent experiences, such as birth order (Bliss 1970, Zweigenhaft 1975, Stewart 1991), parental loss (Eisenstadt 1978), role models and mentors (Boring & Boring 1948; Simonton 1977a, 1988b), and education and expertise acquisition (Hayes 1989; Simonton 1991b, 2000a). At the other end are studies that examine the psychological changes that occur in the final years of life (e.g., Suedfeld & Piedrahita 1984, Simonton 1989b, Lindauer 1993). Some even look at the factors that might influence a person's life span (Davis 1986, Coren & Halpern 1991, Kaun 1991, Cassandro 1998, McCann 2001, Schulz & Bazerman 1980). These studies highlight one of the distinct assets of this data source: the ability to examine the human being over the entire life span, from the moment of conception to death.

As the foregoing examples suggest, developmental psychologists have favored quantitative rather than qualitative analyses. Even so, noteworthy exceptions do occur from time to time. For instance, some psychologists have used such methods to study the creative careers of single individuals (Gruber 1974, Wallace & Gruber 1989) or to conduct comparative studies of several creative lives (Gardner 1993).

Differential Psychology

Ever since Galton's (1869) classic study, quantitative psychologists have often analyzed historical data to examine individual differences in intellectual ability (Woods 1906, Thorndike 1936). Among the most innovative of these inquiries was Terman's (1917) estimation of an IQ score for Francis Galton himself, a calculation that was based on Galton's early childhood achievements. This method was then extended and elaborated by Cox (1926) to produce IQ estimates for 301 geniuses, these scores then being correlated with the achieved eminence that the individuals attained (cf. Simonton 1976a, Walberg et al. 1978). Cox's ambitious investigation was also notable for introducing techniques for assessing the personality traits of historical figures. She was then able to determine the personality profiles that influenced both achievement and career choice. Since then many other psychologists have attempted to gauge the personality characteristics of eminent creators, leaders, and other celebrities (Thorndike 1950, Cattell 1963, Simonton 1986b, McCrae 1987). Although these measurements were all based on biographical data, other psychologists have pursued a different approach, applying content analytical methods to historical documents or products (Smith 1992). Especially provocative are the many investigations that have assessed political leaders, such as US presidents, on such motives as power, achievement, and affiliation (e.g., Winter 1987b, Spangler & House 1991).

Psychologists with a more qualitative orientation have tended to approach historical data very differently. In line with traditional psychobiography, the goal is often to explain the idiosyncratic behaviors or beliefs of eminent individuals, such as Adolf Hitler, Richard Nixon, King George III, Vincent Van Gogh, and Leonardo da Vinci (Runyan 1988b, Elms 1994). For instance, a large number of psychobiographers have attempted to decipher why Van Gogh cut off his ear (Runyan 1981). Nevertheless, sometimes qualitative analyses will be applied to multiple cases with the aim of teasing out nomothetic conclusions. A well-known example is Abraham Maslow's (1970) attempt to determine the characteristics of the self-actualizing personality though the analysis of exemplars such as Abraham Lincoln, Eleanor Roosevelt, Harriet Tubman, Albert Einstein, Martin Buber, Walt Whitman, Pierre Renoir, and Pablo Casals.

Abnormal Psychology

One of the oldest debates in psychology is the relation between exceptional achievement and psychopathology—the "mad-genius" controversy. Qualitative analyses tend to address this issue by conducting single-case studies based on the biographies of creators or leaders with obvious disorders (e.g., Hershman & Lieb 1998). Historiometric analyses, in contrast, have approached this question in three different ways. The first approach is to assess the types and levels of psychopathology displayed by historical personalities in various domains of achievements (Juda 1949; Ludwig 1992, 1995; Post 1994, 1996; Kaufman 2001). The second is to investigate the genetics of psychopathology and achievement, especially using the family pedigree method (Myerson & Boyle 1941, Juda 1949, Karlson 1970, Jamison 1993). The third and last line of attack is to identify the environmental factors that underlie the occurrence of various psychopathological disorders (Masserman 1983, Pennebaker 1990, Simonton 1998d).

Most often these quantitative analyses use large samples, but single-case studies do appear from time to time. Examples include studies of the relation between manic-depression and creativity in Robert Schumann (Weisberg 1994), the relation between stressful events and mental breakdowns in King George III (Simonton 1998d), and the relations among fame, self-consciousness, and substance abuse in Kurt Cobain, Cole Porter, and John Cheever (Schaller 1997). These single-case studies, in combination with the multiple-case investigations, have notably advanced our appreciation for the causal intricacies connecting psychopathology and creative achievement.

Social Psychology

Social psychologists have been using historical data for a very long time (Simonton 1998c). In fact, what is often credited as the first laboratory experiment in the field can also be considered the first quantitative analysis of historical data (e.g., Triplett

1898). Not only is the usage very old, but very extensive besides. A large number of central substantive issues have been investigated using this methodological approach. Indeed, because historical data inherently embed individual behavior in a social context, applications of this approach may be more useful in social psychology than in another subdiscipline within psychological science. In any case, the following four sets of applications can be considered representative:

1. Research on attitudes and attitude change has always had a prominent place in social psychology. Hence, it is fitting that social psychologists have sometimes used historical data to gauge the real-world relevance of experimental results regarding attitudes and attitude change. For instance, political elections, such as US presidential primaries, have been used to test repeated-exposure effects (Grush et al. 1978, Grush 1980). A different kind of example comes from the literature on the authoritarian personality. Although the initial inquiries were based on interviews, questionnaires, and inventories using contemporary research participants (Adorno et al. 1950), historical data was eventually used to demonstrate how authoritarianism emerges as a response to conditions of external threat (Sales 1972, 1973; Padgett & Jorgenson 1982; Doty et al. 1991; McCann 1999). One specific behavioral manifestation of this response is the relation between economic downturns and the lynching of blacks in the southern United States (Hovland & Sears 1940, Hepworth & West 1988; but see Green et al. 1998, Mintz 1946).

2. Because the studies just cited were actually dedicated to testing the frustration-aggression hypothesis (Dollard et al. 1939), they could also be used to illustrate how social psychologists have used historical data to study aggression and violence, an important topic in the field. Another instance is the research on whether homicides are a partial consequence of violence displayed in the mass media (Phillips 1986). A considerable literature on the extent to which mass violence and personal aggression are increased by high ambient temperatures has also developed (Baron & Ransberger 1978; Carlsmith & Anderson 1979; Anderson 1987, 1989; Anderson & Anderson 1996). One inquiry on this subject took advantage of sport statistics (Reifman et al. 1991), a form of historical data that has been used to examine other determinants of aggression as well (Frank & Gilovich 1988, Miller et al. 1991).

3. The first social psychological study to exploit historical data also used sports statistics, but this time to assess social facilitation effects (Triplett 1898). Other investigators have used such data to investigate other group processes, such as the home-field effects (Baumeister & Steinhilber 1984, Courneya & Carron 1992, Baumeister 1995). Social psychologists have used many other kinds of historical data to study group phenomena. For instance, data on the differential success of the songs written by the Beatles have been used to assess social-loafing (Jackson & Padgett 1982). Political history has been an especially rich source of raw information. One classic application is Janis's

(1982) research on groupthink, which was based on the decision-making processes used during crises of international importance. This investigation is also distinctive in that it represents one of the rare examples in social psychology of a qualitative rather than quantitative analysis. Even so, subsequent inquiries have subjected historical data on groupthink phenomena to quantitative analyses (Tetlock 1979; Herek et al. 1987, 1989).

4. Leadership has perhaps attracted more historical data analyses than any other topic in social psychology. The bulk of this research has concentrated on political and military leaders such as monarchs (Winter 1993), presidents (Simonton 1988c, Zullow & Seligman 1990), Canadian prime ministers (Ballard 1983), Soviet Politburo members (Hermann 1980), army generals (Simonton 1980a, Suedfeld et al. 1986), and revolutionaries (Suedfeld & Rank 1976). Several researchers have scrutinized the elusive phenomenon of leader charisma (Simonton 1988c; House et al. 1991; O'Connor et al. 1995; Deluga 1997, 1998). Other investigators have tried to determine the relative influence of individual and situational factors, a contemporary manifestation of the classic Great Person versus Zeitgeist controversy (Simonton 1984b, Ballard & Suedfeld 1988). Some of these latter inquiries have even tested individual $\times$ situation interaction effects to detect whether effective leadership demands "the right person at the right place and right time" (e.g., Simonton 1987, Winter 1987b). The research findings have potential practical value insofar as they provide an inventory of variables that can predict leadership in real-world settings.

The foregoing examples do not come close to exhausting all the ways in which social psychologists have taken advantage of the wealth of information available in the historical record (for additional examples see Simonton 1998c).

METHODS

It should now be evident that historical data have been successfully applied to a great variety of substantive areas in psychology. Because these applications required methodologies that are distinct to this class of data, it is necessary to provide at least an overview of such methods. I begin with data collection and then turn to data analysis.

Data Collection

The first decision that must be made in almost any psychological study is sampling. When psychologists turn to historical data, the answer to this question is often self-evident (Simonton 1999). The sample for psychobiographers, for example, consists of the historical figures whose lives need some kind of psychological interpretation (Elms 1994). The sampling decision becomes a little more complicated in multiple-case investigations, such as those favored in historiometric analyses

(Simonton 1990b). In the simplest instances the samples are self-defining, because the number of relevant cases is finite and manageable. Examples include presidents of the American Psychological Association (Suedfeld 1985), the first ladies of US presidents (Simonton 1996), Nobel laureates (Manniche & Falk 1957), and Olympic athletes (Schulz & Curnow 1988, Fernandez-Dols & Ruiz-Belda 1995). When the potential samples are more open ended and ill defined, a commonplace sampling strategy is to apply the eminence criterion (Simonton 1999). The most eminent individuals in a domain are not only the most representative of the phenomenon of interest, but information about such subjects is likely to be more extensive and reliable (Cox 1926, Simonton 1976a).

In one crucial respect analyses of historical data must address an issue that seldom has a counterpart in more conventional research methodologies: the question of unit definition. In other words, when a study consists of a sample of size N, what is being counted when determining N? What is the unit on which the variables are to be assessed? With the exception of neuroscientists who focus on single neurons and a few other distinctive instances, most psychological research is based on the individual, human or nonhuman. Although most analyses of historical data also use the individual as the unit of analysis, the exceptions are more numerous and diverse. For instance, some researchers will define "micro-units" consisting of creative products (Arnheim 1962, Simonton 1998b, Zickar & Slaughter 1999), leader actions or decisions (Simonton 1980a, Janis 1982, Suedfeld & Bluck 1988), or some other cross-sectional unit smaller than a single human being. Alternatively, psychologists may use "macro-units" such as whole nations (Charness & Gerchak 1996). When investigators turn to longitudinal research, the potential choices proliferate. Thus, a psychologist may study music or literature across consecutive themes or sections (Martindale 1990, Simonton 1990a), creators or leaders across consecutive age periods (Lehman 1953; Simonton 1977a, 1998d; Porter & Suedfeld 1981), US presidents across consecutive congresses (Simonton 1987), and nations or civilizations across consecutive years (Cattell & Adelson 1951, Cattell 1953, Tetlock 1985), generations (deCharms & Moeller 1962; Simonton 1975b, 1976b, 1988c, 1997b), or even larger time units (Cattell 1903, McClelland 1961, McGuire 1976). Complicating matters all the more, the units can sometimes be combined in distinctive combinations, such as individual-generational analysis (Simonton 1976c, 1977b, 1980c, 1984a). Historical data thus offer enormous flexibility in the types of cases that enter into the analysis.

Once the researcher has decided on the most appropriate sample and unit definition, the next step is to find the necessary sources of raw data. In general, there are two types of historical data, primary and secondary (Simonton 1990b). The most commonly used primary source is the written document. Some of these documents may be public, such as campaign speeches, inaugural addresses, diplomatic communiqués, court decisions, poems, short stories, publication titles, and journal abstracts (e.g., Tetlock 1981a,b; Tetlock et al. 1985; Martindale & Martindale 1988; Simonton 1992b), whereas others may be private, such as correspondence and diaries (e.g., Porter & Suedfeld 1981, Schaller 1997, Suedfeld & Bluck 1993).

Nonverbal materials provide another useful primary source, including artworks, musical compositions, architectural monuments, and various cultural artifacts (e.g., McClelland 1961, Simonton 1980b, Hasenfus et al. 1983, Devlin & Nasar 1989, Lindauer 1993). Secondary sources, in contrast, provide information compiled by historians and other scholars. The most common sources are biographies, histories, encyclopedias, biographical dictionaries, bibliographies, and obituaries (Dennis 1954, Deluga 1997, Harrison et al. 1988, Simonton 1998a). These works may be either general (e.g., the *Encyclopaedia Britannica* 1994) or specific (e.g., Zusne 1984). It should be pointed out that often the selection of a data source comes before the sample is determined. That happens when the sampling criterion is whether an individual has an entry in one or more reference works (Galton 1869; Cattell 1903; Simonton 1991a,b).

Data Analysis

Although data collection procedures are often very similar across diverse applications, the subsequent data analyses differ dramatically depending on whether the study is qualitative or quantitative.

QUALITATIVE ANALYSES   Some psychologists adopt a comparative method, comparing and contrasting two or more individuals or events to tease out common components or attributes (McCurdy 1960, Gardner 1993). In such investigations the methodology differs very little from the comparisons and contrasts seen in traditional historiography (e.g., Plutarch's *Lives*). Psychobiographers, on the other hand, have developed techniques that depart significantly from historiographic practice. From the very beginning, the psychobiography was treated as a special form of clinical case study; that is, the investigator would interpret the historical information as if it came from an actual session with a client (Freud 1910/1964; Erikson 1958, 1969). The only genuine difference arises from the fact that the psychobiographer is engaged in classical assessment "at a distance"—necessarily so when the subject is a deceased historical celebrity. Eventually, however, researchers began to realize that there are certain methodological pitfalls inherent to psychobiographical analyses. As a consequence, recent psychobiographers have attempted to devise more sophisticated methods to help ensure that these pitfalls can be successfully avoided (Runyan 1982, 1988a; Alexander 1988, 1990; Elms 1994). For instance, great care must be exercised to avoid such problems as negative or positive transference, circular reasoning, psychological reductionism, and the overinterpretation of biographical particulars.

QUANTITATIVE ANALYSES   Psychologists conducting historiometric studies have a special advantage over those doing qualitative studies: The discipline has already accumulated a diverse and powerful repertoire of techniques. Obvious examples are the measurement methods found in psychometrics and psychological assessment. Although these analytical methods were designed for use with contemporary research participants, they often can be applied directly to historical data with minor or even minimal modifications (Simonton 1990b, 1999). Thus, by adapting already established psychometric measures, historical figures have been assessed on characteristics as diverse as intelligence, cognitive style, personality, motivation, psychopathology, interests, beliefs, and values (McClelland 1961, McCrae 1987, Winter 1987a, Zullow et al. 1988, Tetlock et al. 1994). Admittedly, it is not uncommon for psychologists to devise special measurement strategies unique to historical data. For instance, computerized content analytical schemes have been created to investigate music compositions (Paisley 1964, Simonton 1980c, Cerulo 1989). Even so, the majority of measurements seen in the psychological analysis of historical data have manifest counterparts in more mainstream research.

The latter statement requires even greater emphasis when it comes to statistical analysis. Once historical data has been quantified in the form of concrete variables, those variables can be subjected to the same analytical tools seen in standard correlational studies. These tools include factor analysis (Cattell & Adelson 1951, Cattell 1953, Knapp 1962, Simonton 2000c), cluster analysis (Simonton 1986b, 1988c), multidimensional scaling (Hasenfus et al. 1983), multiple regression (McCann 1992, Cassandro 1998), path analysis (Simonton 1977b), structural equation models (Simonton 1991c, 1996), and mathematical models (Simonton 1979, 1997a). The only departure is the somewhat more prominent place of time-series analysis, a technique otherwise not very conspicuous in most psychological research (Rotton & Frey 1985; Tetlock 1985; Hepworth & West 1988; Simonton 1992a). The relative prominence of time-series analysis stems from the fact that historical data lend themselves quite readily to longitudinal designs, such as studying individuals or civilizations across time. In contrast, the majority of psychological inquiries collect only cross-sectional data in which there is no time dimension, whether historical or biographical.

Despite the fact that quantitative analyses of historical data can proceed in pretty much the same manner as analyses using more conventional data sources, there is one statistical issue that has yet to be resolved. The "significance test controversy," which has been a recurrent problem in mainstream research (Morrison & Henkel 1970, Harlow et al. 1997), becomes even more problematic in many historiometric inquiries (Simonton 1999). The difficulties arise because such studies often sample the entire population of interest. Under such circumstances, it is not clear what inferential statistics are most appropriate, nor even whether inferential statistics are required. If an inquiry samples all Nobel laureates or all US presidents or all Olympic medalists, to what larger population are the results to be generalized?

EVALUATION

Like any method in psychology, analyses of historical data have both advantages and disadvantages. The following evaluation begins by treating the disadvantages, because they probably represent the main reasons why most psychologists do not adopt this approach. The evaluation concludes with a discussion of the advantages that provide the rationale for some psychologists departing from the investigative norms (for further discussion, see Simonton 1990b, 1998c, 1999; Elms 1994).

Disadvantages

Naturally, the drawbacks of historical data are not the same for both qualitative and quantitative analyses, and so they should be examined separately. In the case of qualitative studies, the main disadvantage is the very fact that they are qualitative rather than quantitative. Many psychologists believe that quantitative analyses are far more scientific—more objective and rigorous—than qualitative analyses. Moreover, this belief enjoys some support in the empirical (quantitative) research on human information-processing capacities (Meehl 1954, Faust 1984). The human mind is not very adept at drawing valid qualitative inferences from data as complex as those found in the historical record. Indeed, sometimes conclusions drawn from qualitative studies are disconfirmed when the same historical data are subjected to quantitative analysis (e.g., Tetlock 1979, Simonton 1998d).

Although quantitative methods permit more rigorous and precise inferences from the historical record, other disadvantages remain. The following three problems are perhaps the most pervasive:

1. Quantitative analyses of historical data are invariably correlational and thus can be considered weak according to the criterion of internal validity (Campbell & Stanley 1966). That is, the investigator can only draw causal inferences with extreme care. Unlike the laboratory experiment in which the independent variable can be directly manipulated, correlational studies must always be concerned with the possible intrusion of spurious relations (Simonton 1990b). Quasi-experimental designs, such as time-series analysis, cannot completely obliterate this drawback.

2. Historical data are not always as reliable as those found in more conventional data sources. Sometimes the record contains informational gaps or errors that can contaminate any analysis, whether qualitative or quantitative. For instance, Cox's (1926) study of 301 geniuses could not include William Shakespeare simply because so little was known about his early life. Even when she thought the data was sufficiently reliable for a particular historical figure, the resulting IQ estimate would sometimes have an extremely low reliability coefficient.

3. Perhaps the most obvious drawback is that historical data have limited theoretical or substantive applicability. Notwithstanding the tremendous diversity of topics already addressed using these methods, there are probably a great many more issues for which the annals of history can provide no resolution. For example, historical data rarely have any scientific utility for comparative and physiological psychologists (but see Coren & Porac 1977, Macmillan 2000).

Despite all these disadvantages, psychologists who have chosen to exploit this data source usually had excellent reasons for doing so, as will become apparent next.

Advantages

Probably the single most important reason for analyzing historical data is that such analyses permit the investigation of research topics that cannot be addressed any other way. This rationale is most conspicuous in the case of psychobiography. Psychologists who want to comprehend historic figures have no other option but to resort to the analysis of historical materials (e.g., McCurdy 1953, Rosenberg 1989, Fancher 1998). Yet a psychologist does not have to be a psychobiographer to believe that history might provide useful data for either qualitative or quantitative analysis. Consider the following four potential justifications for such usage:

1. Although correlational studies can be easily criticized for their inferior internal validity, they often compensate by possessing superior external validity (Campbell & Stanley 1966). Laboratory experiments sometimes may have questionable external validity because (*a*) they introduce artificial situations and manipulations that evoke unrepresentative responses, such as "guinea pig" effects, expectancy effects, and demand characteristics (e.g., Rosenthal 1976) or (*b*) they sample unrepresentative research participants, especially college students taking introductory psychology courses (e.g., Sears 1986). Historical data are necessarily "unobtrusive" and "nonreactive," and thus cannot be contaminated with experimenter effects (Webb et al. 1981). Moreover, because historical data come from the "real world," there can be no doubt that the results are applicable to the world beyond the research laboratory.

2. Even if experimental results seem prima facie applicable to the world outside the laboratory, there persists a profound gap between merely extrapolating those findings to the outside world and actually demonstrating that those findings can be so generalized. An outright empirical demonstration removes the intrinsically speculative nature of the extrapolation. Hence, historical data cannot only support research with inherent external validity, but also provide the means to establish the generality of results obtained from more conventional research methods (Sales 1972; Martindale 1973, 1990; Simonton 1980c, 1986a; Jackson & Padgett 1982; Triplett 1898).

3. The historical record contains information about events and personalities of great practical importance. As a result, these data have tremendous value for those researchers wishing to deal with significant issues and problems in the real world. Probably the most dramatic examples concern human violence. Besides studying the factors underlying homicide and other forms of personal aggression (Anderson & Anderson 1984, Phillips & Hensley 1984, Miller et al. 1991), psychologists have made major strides in understanding the psychological roots of war and other forms of collective violence

(Winter 1987a, 1993; Suedfeld & Bluck 1988). This understanding includes increased knowledge about international crises (Raphael 1982, Suedfeld et al. 1993, Guttieri et al. 1995) and what it takes to make adaptive responses to those crises (Suedfeld & Tetlock 1977, Suedfeld et al. 1977). Needless to say, conventional research methodologies can only tackle such problems indirectly and with much less convincing results. Indeed, any attempt to address these issues via laboratory methodology would probably raise severe ethical objections that would terminate the effort.

4. Psychology aspires to produce scientific knowledge that is truly universal. In other words, psychological theories and findings should apply to all human beings, not just to that subset of *Homo sapiens* who happen to live in the same time and place as the researcher. Yet most of the human research conducted in psychology uses participants who are both contemporaries and compatriots. In contrast, the historical record constitutes a rich repository of information about human behavior in a great diversity of cultures and historical periods. This feature enables the investigator to determine whether certain findings can claim the status of cross-cultural and even transhistorical universals. Indeed, by combining data from several times and places into a single analysis, it is possible to conduct direct statistical tests for the cross-cultural and transhistorical invariance of any observed correlations. For example, key findings concerning the relation between age and achievement have been replicated across both space and time (Lehman 1953; Simonton 1975a, 1988a, 1997a).

Because each method in psychology has its distinctive strengths and weaknesses, the optimum strategy is always to adopt methodological pluralism whenever possible. Accordingly, research using historical data can often be fruitfully combined with laboratory experiments and other standard approaches. Triplett (1898) was the first to show that results obtained by conventional methods could be corroborated by analyses of the historical record, and others have followed suit (Martindale 1973, 1990; Simonton 1986a,b).

CONCLUSION: THE PROSPECTS

Since 1835, when Quételet published his pioneering analysis of the age-creativity relation, historical data have attracted some of the key figures in psychological science. To name names, this rich data source has been used by such notables as Galton (1869, 1883), Ellis (1926), J.M. Cattell (1903), Freud (1910/1964), Thorndike (1936, 1950), Terman (1917), Hovland (Hovland & Sears 1940), Murray (1981), Erikson (1958, 1969), Skinner (1939, 1942), R.B. Cattell (1953, 1963), Maslow (1970), Sears (Sears et al. 1978), Simon (Kulkarni & Simon 1988), McClelland (1961), Janis (1982), McGuire (1976), Neisser (1981), and Seligman (Satterfield & Seligman 1994). Moreover, studies dealing with historical data have appeared in numerous journals, both general and specialized (see references below). Given that these researchers and journals represent several subdisciplines and theoretical orientations, it seems likely that this usage will continue well into the future.

In fact, I would argue that several trends encourage such continued applications. First, there have occurred many methodological advances that should render the historical record a far more useful source of scientific data. Among these advances are latent variable models, time-series analysis, and hierarchical linear models (Simonton 1991c, 1998d; Zickar & Slaughter 1999). In addition, the advent of the positive psychology movement has made the discipline more receptive to investigators who wish to examine the best exemplars of positive human traits (Snyder & Lopez 2002). Among these exemplars are those who made a name for themselves for their display of creativity, leadership, talent, wisdom, or spirituality (Gardner 1993, 1997; Simonton 2000b). Another movement that is more open to the analysis of historical data is the recent resurgence of the psychology of science (Feist & Gorman 1998). This field of inquiry encompasses not only the scientific study of eminent scientists, but also the study of great psychologists (Coan 1973, Over 1982, Simonton 2002).

Finally, there are two related trends taking place in the larger society beyond psychology. The first concerns the accelerating richness of the potential historical database. History in antiquity was the luxury of a handful of civilizations, and even then the record was confined largely to the elite classes of society. Now the annals take in the entire human population, and do so in a far more egalitarian fashion. This richness is coupled with the second trend, namely the enhanced availability of this wealth of information. Increasingly more of the historical record is assuming electronic form, especially with the advent of the World Wide Web. Each day it becomes ever more possible to download the raw historical data directly from the internet—such primary sources as speeches, poems, music, film clips, and art prints and such secondary sources as biographical entries and historical chronologies. To illustrate, the Internet Movie Database at http://us.imdb.com/ offers a wealth of information on over 200,000 motion pictures. The data is rendered all the more accessible by the inclusion of a powerful search engine.

Besides predicting that historical data will continue to have a place in psychology, I also will risk another prediction: The proportion of quantitative analysis should increase relative to qualitative analysis. This forecast is partly founded on the advances in statistical analysis already mentioned, as well as various improvements in the precision and power of computerized content analysis (Martindale 1990; Simonton 1990a, 1992b). Furthermore, several recent investigations have shown how historiometric methods could be fruitfully applied to problems that were traditionally the province of qualitative psychobiography (Swede & Tetlock 1986; Winter & Carlson 1988; Rosenberg 1989; Simonton 1989a, 1998d). Hence, future analyses of historical data may eventually become almost exclusively quantitative. This result would have the added benefit of rendering historical data analyses more compatible with the core research methods used in psychology.

The *Annual Review of Psychology* is online at http://psych.annualreviews.org

LITERATURE CITED

Adorno TW, Frenkel-Brunswik E, Levinson DJ, Sanford RN, eds. 1950. *The Authoritarian Personality*. New York: Harper. 990 pp.

Alexander IE. 1988. Personality, psychological assessment, and psychobiography. *J. Pers.* 56:265–94

Alexander IE. 1990. *Personology: Method and Content in Personality Assessment and Psychobiography*. Durham, NC: Duke Univ. Press. 280 pp.

Anderson CA. 1987. Temperature and aggression: effects on quarterly, yearly, and city rates of violent and nonviolent crime. *J. Pers. Soc. Psychol.* 52:1161–73

Anderson CA. 1989. Temperature and aggression: ubiquitous effects of heat on occurrence of human violence. *Psychol. Bull.* 106:74–96

Anderson CA, Anderson DC. 1984. Ambient temperature and violent crime: Tests of the linear and curvilinear hypotheses. *J. Pers. Soc. Psychol.* 46:91–97

Anderson CA, Anderson KB. 1996. Violent crime rate studies in philosophical context: a destructive testing approach to heat and southern culture of violence effects. *J. Pers. Soc. Psychol.* 70:740–56

Arnheim R. 1962. *Picasso's Guernica: The Genesis of a Painting*. Berkeley: Univ. Calif. Press. 139 pp.

Ballard EJ. 1983. Canadian prime ministers: complexity in political crises. *Can. Psychol.* 24:125–29

Ballard EJ, Suedfeld P. 1988. Performance ratings of Canadian prime ministers: individual and situational factors. *Polit. Psychol.* 9:291–302

Baron RA, Ransberger VM. 1978. Ambient temperature and the occurrence of collective violence: the "long, hot summer" revisited. *J. Pers. Soc. Psychol.* 36:351–60

Baumeister RF. 1995. Disputing the effects of championship pressures and home audiences. *J. Pers. Soc. Psychol.* 68:644–48

Baumeister RF, Steinhilber A. 1984. Paradoxical effects of supportive audiences on performance under pressure: the home field disadvantage in sports championships. *J. Pers. Soc. Psychol.* 47:85–93

Bliss WD. 1970. Birth order of creative writers. *J. Individ. Psychol.* 26:200–2

Boring MD, Boring EG. 1948. Masters and pupils among the American psychologists. *Am. J. Psychol.* 61:527–34

Bradshaw GF, Langley PW, Simon HA. 1983. Studying scientific discovery by computer simulation. *Science* 222:971–75

Bramwell BS. 1948. Galton's "Hereditary" and the three following generations since 1869. *Eugen. Rev.* 39:146–53

Campbell DT, Stanley JC. 1966. *Experimental and Quasi-Experimental Designs for Research*. Chicago: McNally. 84 pp.

Carlsmith JM, Anderson CA. 1979. Ambient temperature and the occurrence of collective violence: a new analysis. *J. Pers. Soc. Psychol.* 37:337–44

Cassandro VJ. 1998. Explaining premature mortality across fields of creative endeavor. *J. Pers.* 66:805–33

Cattell JM. 1903. A statistical study of eminent men. *Pop. Sci. Mon.* 62:359–77

Cattell RB. 1953. A quantitative analysis of the changes in the culture pattern of Great Britain 1837–1937, by p-technique. *Acta Psychol.* 9:99–121

Cattell RB. 1963. The personality and motivation of the researcher from measurements of contemporaries and from biography. In *Scientific Creativity: Its Recognition and Development*, ed. CW Taylor, F Barron, pp. 119–31. New York: Wiley

Cattell RB, Adelson M. 1951. The dimensions of social change in the U. S. A. as determined by the P-technique. *Soc. Forces* 30:190–201

Cerulo KA. 1989. Variations in musical syntax: patterns of measurement. *Commun. Res.* 16:204–35

Charness N, Gerchak Y. 1996. Participation

rates and maximal performance: a log-linear explanation for group differences, such as Russian and male dominance in chess. *Psychol. Sci.* 7:46–51

Coan RW. 1973. Toward a psychological interpretation of psychology. *J. Hist. Behav. Sci.* 9:313–27

Coren S, Halpern DF. 1991. Left-handedness: a marker for decreased survival fitness. *Psychol. Bull.* 109:90–106

Coren S, Porac C. 1977. Fifty centuries of right handedness: the historical record. *Science* 198:631–32

Courneya KS, Carron AV. 1992. The home advantage in sport competitions: a literature review. *J. Sport Exerc. Psychol.* 14:13–27

Cox C. 1926. *The Early Mental Traits of Three Hundred Geniuses.* Stanford, CA: Stanford Univ. Press. 842 pp.

Davis WM. 1986. Premature mortality among prominent American authors noted for alcohol abuse. *Drug Alcohol Depend.* 18:133–38

deCharms R, Moeller GH. 1962. Values expressed in American children's readers: 1800–1950. *J. Abnorm. Soc. Psychol.* 64: 136–42

Deluga RJ. 1997. Relationship among American presidential charismatic leadership, narcissism, and related performance. *Leadership Q.* 8:51–65

Deluga RJ. 1998. American presidential proactivity, charismatic leadership, and rated performance. *Leadership Q.* 9:265–91

Dennis W. 1954. Productivity among American psychologists. *Am. Psychol.* 9:191–94

Dennis W. 1966. Creative productivity between the ages of 20 and 80 years. *J. Gerontol.* 21:1–8

Devlin K, Nasar JL. 1989. The beauty and the beast: some preliminary comparisons of "high" versus "popular" residential architecture and public versus architect judgments of same. *J. Environ. Psychol.* 9:333–44

Dollard J, Doob L, Miller NE, Mowrer OH, Sears RR. 1939. *Frustration and Aggression.* New Haven, CT: Yale Univ. Press. 209 pp.

Doty RM, Peterson BE, Winter DG. 1991.

Threat and authoritarianism in the United States, 1978–1987. *J. Pers. Soc. Psychol.* 61: 629–40

Eisenstadt JM. 1978. Parental loss and genius. *Am. Psychol.* 33:211–23

Ellis H. 1926. *A Study of British Genius.* Boston: Houghton Mifflin. 396 pp. Rev. ed.

Elms AC. 1988. Freud as Leonardo: why the first psychobiography went wrong. *J. Pers.* 56:19–40

Elms AC. 1994. *Uncovering Lives: The Uneasy Alliance of Biography and Psychology.* New York: Oxford Univ. Press. 315 pp.

Encyclopaedia Britannica. 1994. Chicago: Encyclopaedia Britannica. 32 vols., 15th ed.

Ericsson KA, Simon HA. 1984. *Protocol Analysis: Verbal Reports as Data.* Cambridge, MA: MIT. 426 pp.

Erikson EH. 1958. *Young Man Luther: A Study in Psychoanalysis and History.* New York: Norton. 288 pp.

Erikson EH. 1969. *Gandhi's Truth: On the Origins of Militant Nonviolence.* New York: Norton. 426 pp.

Fancher RE. 1998. Biography and psychodynamic theory: some lessons from the life of Francis Galton. *Hist. Psychol.* 1:99–115

Faust D. 1984. *Limits of Scientific Reasoning.* Minneapolis: Univ. Minn. Press. 198 pp.

Feist GJ, Gorman ME. 1998. The psychology of science: review and integration of a nascent discipline. *Rev. Gen. Psychol.* 2:3–47

Fernandez-Dols J-M, Ruiz-Belda M-A. 1995. Are smiles a sign of happiness? Gold medal winners at the Olympic Games. *J. Pers. Soc. Psychol.* 69:1113–19

Frank MG, Gilovich T. 1988. The dark side of self- and social perception: black uniforms and aggression in professional sports. *J. Pers. Soc. Psychol.* 54:74–85

Freud S. 1964. *Leonardo Da Vinci and a Memory of His Childhood.* Transl. A Tyson. New York: Norton. 101 pp. (Original published 1910)

Galton F. 1869. *Hereditary Genius: An Inquiry into Its Laws and Consequences.* London: Macmillan. 390 pp.

Galton F. 1874. *English Men of Science: Their*

Nature and Nurture. London: Macmillan. 270 pp.

Galton F. 1883. *Inquiries into Human Faculty and Its Development*. London: Macmillan. 387 pp.

Gardner H. 1987. *The Mind's New Science: A History of the Cognitive Revolution*. New York: Basic Books. 423 pp.

Gardner H. 1993. *Creating Minds: An Anatomy of Creativity Seen Through the Lives of Freud, Einstein, Picasso, Stravinsky, Eliot, Graham, and Gandhi*. New York: Basic Books. 464 pp.

Gardner H. 1997. *Extraordinary Minds: Portraits of Exceptional Individuals and an Examination of Our Extraordinariness*. New York: Basic Books. 178 pp.

Green DP, Glaser J, Rich A. 1998. From lynching to gay bashing: the elusive connection between economic conditions and hate crime. *J. Pers. Soc. Psychol.* 75:82–92

Gruber HE. 1974. *Darwin on Man: A Psychological Study of Scientific Creativity*. New York: Dutton. 495 pp.

Grush JE. 1980. Impact of candidate expenditures, regionality, and prior outcomes on the 1976 Democratic presidential primaries. *J. Pers. Soc. Psychol.* 38:337–47

Grush JE, McKeough KL, Ahlering RF. 1978. Extrapolating laboratory exposure research to actual political elections. *J. Pers. Soc. Psychol.* 36:257–70

Guttieri K, Wallace MD, Suedfeld P. 1995. The integrative complexity of American decision makers in the Cuban missile crisis. *J. Confl. Resolut.* 39:595–621

Harlow LL, Mulaik SA, Steiger JH, eds. 1997. *What If There Were No Significance Tests?* Mahwah, NJ: Erlbaum. 446 pp.

Harrison AA, Struthers NJ, Moore M. 1988. On the conjunction of national holidays and reported birthdates: one more path to reflected glory? *Soc. Psychol. Q.* 51:365–70

Hasenfus N, Martindale C, Birnbaum D. 1983. Psychological reality of cross-media artistic styles. *J. Exp. Psychol. Hum. Percept. Perform.* 9:841–63

Hayes JR. 1989. *The Complete Problem Solver*. Hillsdale, NJ: Erlbaum. 357 pp. 2nd ed.

Hepworth JT, West SG. 1988. Lynchings and the economy: a time-series reanalysis of Hovland and Sears 1940. *J. Pers. Soc. Psychol.* 55:239–47

Herek GM, Janis IL, Huth P. 1987. Decision making during international crises: Is quality of process related to outcome? *J. Confl. Resolut.* 31:203–26

Herek GM, Janis IL, Huth P. 1989. Quality of U.S. decision making during the Cuban missile crisis. *J. Confl. Resolut.* 33:446–59

Hermann MG. 1980. Assessing the personalities of Soviet Politburo members. *Pers. Soc. Psychol. Bull.* 6:332–52

Hershman DJ, Lieb J. 1998. *Manic Depression and Creativity*. Amherst, MA: Prometheus. 230 pp.

Hirst W, Gluck D. 1999. Revisiting John Dean's memory. In *Ecological Approaches to Cognition: Essays in Honor of Ulric Neisser*, ed. E Winograd, R Fivush, W Hirst, pp. 253–81. Mahwah, NJ: Erlbaum

House RJ, Spangler WD, Woycke J. 1991. Personality and charisma in the U.S. presidency: a psychological theory of leader effectiveness. *Admin. Sci. Q.* 36:364–96

Hovland CI, Sears RR. 1940. Minor studies in aggression. 6. correlation of lynchings with economic indices. *J. Psychol.* 9:301–10

Jackson JM, Padgett VR. 1982. With a little help from my friend: social loafing and the Lennon-McCartney songs. *Pers. Soc. Psychol. Bull.* 8:672–77

James W. 1880. Great men, great thoughts, and the environment. *Atl. Mon.* 46:441–59

Jamison KR. 1993. *Touched with Fire: Manic-Depressive Illness and the Artistic Temperament*. New York: Free Press

Janis IL. 1982. *Groupthink: Psychological Studies of Policy Decisions and Fiascoes*. Boston: Houghton Mifflin. 349 pp. 2nd ed.

Juda A. 1949. The relationship between highest mental capacity and psychic abnormalities. *Am. J. Psychiatry* 106:296–307

Karlson JI. 1970. Genetic association of

giftedness and creativity with schizophrenia. *Hereditas* 66:177–82

Kaufman JC. 2001. The Sylvia Plath effect: mental illness in eminent creative writers. *J. Creat. Behav.* 35:37–50

Kaun DE. 1991. Writers die young: the impact of work and leisure on longevity. *J. Econ. Psychol.* 12:381–99

Knapp RH. 1962. A factor analysis of Thorndike's ratings of eminent men. *J. Soc. Psychol.* 56:67–71

Kulkarni D, Simon HA. 1988. The process of scientific discovery: the strategy of experimentation. *Cogn. Sci.* 12:139–75

Langley P, Simon HA, Bradshaw GL, Zytkow JM. 1987. *Scientific Discovery: Computational Explorations of the Creative Processes.* Cambridge, MA: MIT Press. 357 pp.

Lehman HC. 1953. *Age and Achievement.* Princeton, NJ: Princeton Univ. Press. 359 pp.

Lindauer MS. 1993. The old-age style and its artists. *Emp. Stud. Arts* 11:135–46

Ludwig AM. 1992. Creative achievement and psychopathology: comparison among professions. *Am. J. Psychother.* 46:330–56

Ludwig AM. 1995. *The Price of Greatness: Resolving the Creativity and Madness Controversy.* New York: Guilford. 310 pp.

Macmillan M. 2000. *An Odd Kind of Fame: Stories of Phineas Gage.* Cambridge, MA: MIT Press. 562 pp.

Manniche E, Falk G. 1957. Age and the Nobel prize. *Behav. Sci.* 2:301–7

Martindale AE, Martindale C. 1988. Metaphorical equivalence of elements and temperaments: empirical studies of Bachelard's theory of imagination. *J. Pers. Soc. Psychol.* 55:836–48

Martindale C. 1973. An experimental simulation of literary change. *J. Pers. Soc. Psychol.* 25:319–26

Martindale C. 1990. *The Clockwork Muse: The Predictability of Artistic Styles.* New York: Basic Books. 411 pp.

Maslow AH. 1970. *Motivation and Personality.* New York: Harper & Row. 369 pp. 2nd ed.

Masserman IM. 1983. Political business cycles, presidential elections, and suicide and mortality patterns. *Am. Sociol. Rev.* 48:711–20

McCann SJH. 1992. Alternative formulas to predict the greatness of U.S. presidents: personological, situational, and zeitgeist factors. *J. Pers. Soc. Psychol.* 62:469–79

McCann SJH. 1999. Threatening times and fluctuations in American church memberships. *Pers. Soc. Psychol. Bull.* 25:325–36

McCann SJH. 2001. The precocity-longevity hypothesis: earlier peaks in career achievement predict shorter lives. *Pers. Soc. Psychol. Bull.* 27:1429–39

McClelland DC. 1961. *The Achieving Society.* New York: Van Nostrand. 512 pp.

McCrae RR. 1987. Creativity, divergent thinking, and openness to experience. *J. Pers. Soc. Psychol.* 52:1258–65

McCurdy HG. 1953. *The Personality of Shakespeare.* New Haven, CT: Yale Univ. Press. 243 pp.

McCurdy HG. 1960. The childhood pattern of genius. *Horizon* 2:33–38

McGuire WJ. 1976. Historical comparisons: testing psychological hypotheses with cross-era data. *Intern. J. Psychol.* 11:161–83

Meehl P. 1954. *Clinical versus Statistical Prediction: A Theoretical Analysis and a Review of the Evidence.* Minneapolis: Univ. Minn. Press. 149 pp.

Miller TQ, Heath L, Moican JR, Dugoni BL. 1991. Imitative violence in the real world: a reanalysis of homicide rates following championship prize fights. *Aggress. Behav.* 17:121–34

Mintz A. 1946. A re-examination of correlations between lynchings and economic indices. *J. Abnorm. Soc. Psychol.* 41:154–60

Morrison DE, Henkel RE, eds. 1970. *The Significance Test Controversy: A Reader.* Chicago: Aldine. 333 pp.

Murray H. 1981. Introduction to *Pierre.* In *Endeavors in Psychology: Selections from the Personology of Henry A. Murray,* ed. ES Shneidman, pp. 413–81. New York: Harper & Row

Myerson A, Boyle RD. 1941. The incidence of manic-depression psychosis in certain socially important families: preliminary report. *Am. J. Psychiatry* 98:11–21

Neisser U. 1981. John Dean's memory: a case study. *Cognition* 9:1–22

O'Connor J, Mumford MD, Clifton TC, Gessner TL, Connelly MS. 1995. Charismatic leaders and destructiveness: an historiometric study. *Leadership Q.* 6:529–55

Ohlsson S. 1992. The learning curve for writing books: evidence from Professor Asimov. *Psychol. Sci.* 3:380–82

Over R. 1982. The durability of scientific reputation. *J. Hist. Behav. Sci.* 18:53–61

Padgett V, Jorgenson DO. 1982. Superstition and economic threat: Germany 1918–1940. *Pers. Soc. Psychol. Bull.* 8:736–41

Paisley WJ. 1964. Identifying the unknown communicator in painting, literature and music: the significance of minor encoding habits. *J. Commun.* 14:219–37

Pennebaker JW. 1990. *Opening Up: The Healing Power of Confiding in Others*. New York: Morrow. 251 pp.

Phillips DP. 1986. Natural experiments on the effects of mass media violence on fatal aggression: strength and weakness of a new approach. In *Advances in Experimental Social Psychology*, ed. L Berkowitz, 19:207–50. New York: Academic

Phillips DP, Hensley JE. 1984. When violence is rewarded or punished: the impact of mass media stories on homicide. *J. Commun.* 343:101–16

Porter CA, Suedfeld P. 1981. Integrative complexity in the correspondence of literary figures: effects of personal and societal stress. *J. Pers. Soc. Psychol.* 40:321–30

Post F. 1994. Creativity and psychopathology: a study of 291 world-famous men. *Br. J. Psychiatry* 165:22–34

Post F. 1996. Verbal creativity, depression and alcoholism: an investigation of one hundred American and British writers. *Br. J. Psychiatry* 168:545–55

Publ. Manual Am. Psychol. Assoc. 2001. Washington, DC: Am. Psychol. Assoc. 439 pp. 5th ed.

Quételet A. 1968. *A Treatise on Man and the Development of His Faculties*. New York: Franklin. Reprint of 1842 Edinburgh transl. of 1835 French original. 126 pp.

Raphael TD. 1982. Integrative complexity theory and forecasting international crises: Berlin 1946–1962. *J. Confl. Resolut.* 26:423–50

Raskin EA. 1936. Comparison of scientific and literary ability: a biographical study of eminent scientists and men of letters of the nineteenth century. *J. Abnorm. Soc. Psychol.* 31:20–35

Reifman AS, Larrick RP, Fein S. 1991. Temper and temperature on the diamond: the heat-aggression relationship in major league baseball. *Pers. Soc. Psychol. Bull.* 17:580–85

Rosenberg S. 1989. A study of personality in literary autobiography: an analysis of Thomas Wolfe's *Look Homeward, Angel. J. Pers. Soc. Psychol.* 56:416–30

Rosenthal R. 1976. *Experimenter Effects in Behavioral Research*. New York: Irvington. Enlarged ed. 500 pp.

Rotton J, Frey J. 1985. Air pollution, weather, and violent crime: concomitant time-series analysis of archival data. *J. Pers. Soc. Psychol.* 49:1207–20

Runyan WM. 1981. Why did Van Gogh cut off his ear? The problem of alternative explanations in psychobiography. *J. Pers. Soc. Psychol.* 40:1070–77

Runyan WM. 1982. *Life Histories and Psychobiography*. New York: Oxford Univ. Press. 288 pp.

Runyan WM. 1988a. Progress in psychobiography. *J. Pers.* 56:295–326

Runyan WM, ed. 1988b. *Psychology and Historical Interpretation*. New York: Oxford Univ. Press. 306 pp.

Sales SM. 1972. Economic threat as a determinant of conversion rates in authoritarian and non-authoritarian churches. *J. Pers. Soc. Psychol.* 23:420–28

Sales SM. 1973. Threat as a factor in authoritarianism: an analysis of archival data. *J. Pers. Soc. Psychol.* 28:44–57

Satterfield JM, Seligman MEP. 1994. Military

aggression and risk predicted by explanatory style. *Psychol. Sci.* 5:77–82

Schaller M. 1997. The psychological consequences of fame: three tests of the self-consciousness hypothesis. *J. Pers.* 65:291–309

Schroder HM, Driver MJ, Streufert S. 1967. *Human Information Processing: Individuals and Groups Functioning in Complex Social Situations.* New York: Holt, Rinehart & Winston. 224 pp.

Schulz R, Bazerman M. 1980. Ceremonial occasions and mortality: a second look. *Am. Psychol.* 35:253–61

Schulz R, Curnow C. 1988. Peak performance and age among super athletes: track and field, swimming, baseball, tennis, and golf. *J. Gerontol.* 43:113–20

Sears DO. 1986. College sophomores in the laboratory: influences of a narrow data base on social psychology's view of human nature. *J. Pers. Soc. Psychol.* 51:515–30

Sears RR, Lapidus D, Cozzens C. 1978. Content analysis of Mark Twain's novels and letters as a biographical method. *Poetics* 7:155–75

Simonton DK. 1975a. Age and literary creativity: a cross-cultural and transhistorical survey. *J. Cross-Cult. Psychol.* 6:259–77

Simonton DK. 1975b. Sociocultural context of individual creativity: a transhistorical time-series analysis. *J. Pers. Soc. Psychol.* 32:1119–33

Simonton DK. 1976a. Biographical determinants of achieved eminence: a multivariate approach to the Cox data. *J. Pers. Soc. Psychol.* 33:218–26

Simonton DK. 1976b. Do Sorokin's data support his theory?: a study of generational fluctuations in philosophical beliefs. *J. Sci. Study Relig.* 15:187–98

Simonton DK. 1976c. Philosophical eminence, beliefs, and zeitgeist: an individual-generational analysis. *J. Pers. Soc. Psychol.* 34:630–40

Simonton DK. 1977a. Creative productivity, age, and stress: a biographical time-series analysis of 10 classical composers. *J. Pers. Soc. Psychol.* 35:791–804

Simonton DK. 1977b. Eminence, creativity, and geographic marginality: a recursive structural equation model. *J. Pers. Soc. Psychol.* 35:805–16

Simonton DK. 1979. Multiple discovery and invention: zeitgeist, genius, or chance? *J. Pers. Soc. Psychol.* 37:1603–16

Simonton DK. 1980a. Land battles, generals, and armies: individual and situational determinants of victory and casualties. *J. Pers. Soc. Psychol.* 38:110–19

Simonton DK. 1980b. Thematic fame and melodic originality in classical music: a multivariate computer-content analysis. *J. Pers.* 48:206–19

Simonton DK. 1980c. Thematic fame, melodic originality, and musical zeitgeist: a biographical and transhistorical content analysis. *J. Pers. Soc. Psychol.* 38:972–83

Simonton DK. 1983. Intergenerational transfer of individual differences in hereditary monarchs: genes, role-modeling, cohort, or sociocultural effects? *J. Pers. Soc. Psychol.* 44:354–64

Simonton DK. 1984a. Artistic creativity and interpersonal relationships across and within generations. *J. Pers. Soc. Psychol.* 46:1273–86

Simonton DK. 1984b. Leaders as eponyms: individual and situational determinants of monarchal eminence. *J. Pers.* 52:1–21

Simonton DK. 1986a. Dispositional attributions of presidential leadership: an experimental simulation of historiometric results. *J. Exp. Soc. Psychol.* 22:389–418

Simonton DK. 1986b. Presidential personality: biographical use of the Gough Adjective Check List. *J. Pers. Soc. Psychol.* 51:149–60

Simonton DK. 1987. Presidential inflexibility and veto behavior: two individual-situational interactions. *J. Pers.* 55:1–18

Simonton DK. 1988a. Age and outstanding achievement: What do we know after a century of research? *Psychol. Bull.* 104:251–67

Simonton DK. 1988b. Galtonian genius, Kroeberian configurations, and emulation: a generational time-series analysis of Chinese civilization. *J. Pers. Soc. Psychol.* 55:230–38

Simonton DK. 1988c. Presidential style: personality, biography, and performance. *J. Pers. Soc. Psychol.* 55:928–36

Simonton DK. 1989a. Shakespeare's sonnets: a case of and for single-case historiometry. *J. Pers.* 57:695–721

Simonton DK. 1989b. The swan-song phenomenon: last-works effects for 172 classical composers. *Psychol. Aging* 4:42–47

Simonton DK. 1990a. Lexical choices and aesthetic success: a computer content analysis of 154 Shakespeare sonnets. *Comput. Humanit.* 24:251–64

Simonton DK. 1990b. *Psychology, Science, and History: An Introduction to Historiometry.* New Haven, CT: Yale Univ. Press. 291 pp.

Simonton DK. 1991a. Career landmarks in science: individual differences and interdisciplinary contrasts. *Dev. Psychol.* 27:119–30

Simonton DK. 1991b. Emergence and realization of genius: the lives and works of 120 classical composers. *J. Pers. Soc. Psychol.* 61:829–40

Simonton DK. 1991c. Latent-variable models of posthumous reputation: a quest for Galton's *G. J. Pers. Soc. Psychol.* 60:607–19

Simonton DK. 1992a. Gender and genius in Japan: feminine eminence in masculine culture. *Sex Roles* 27:101–19

Simonton DK. 1992b. Leaders of American psychology, 1879–1967: career development, creative output, and professional achievement. *J. Pers. Soc. Psychol.* 62:5–17

Simonton DK. 1996. Presidents' wives and first ladies: on achieving eminence within a traditional gender role. *Sex Roles* 35:309–36

Simonton DK. 1997a. Creative productivity: a predictive and explanatory model of career trajectories and landmarks. *Psychol. Rev.* 104:66–89

Simonton DK. 1997b. Foreign influence and national achievement: the impact of open milieus on Japanese civilization. *J. Pers. Soc. Psychol.* 72:86–94

Simonton DK. 1998a. Achieved eminence in minority and majority cultures: convergence versus divergence in the assessments of 294 African Americans. *J. Pers. Soc. Psychol.* 74:804–17

Simonton DK. 1998b. Fickle fashion versus immortal fame: transhistorical assessments of creative products in the opera house. *J. Pers. Soc. Psychol.* 75:198–210

Simonton DK. 1998c. Historiometric methods in social psychology. *Eur. Rev. Soc. Psychol.* 9:267–93

Simonton DK. 1998d. Mad King George: the impact of personal and political stress on mental and physical health. *J. Pers.* 66:443–66

Simonton DK. 1999. Significant samples: the psychological study of eminent individuals. *Psychol. Methods* 4:425–51

Simonton DK. 2000a. Creative development as acquired expertise: theoretical issues and an empirical test. *Dev. Rev.* 20:283–318

Simonton DK. 2000b. Creativity: cognitive, developmental, personal, and social aspects. *Am. Psychol.* 55:151–58

Simonton DK. 2000c. Methodological and theoretical orientation and the long-term disciplinary impact of 54 eminent psychologists. *Rev. Gen. Psychol.* 4:1–13

Simonton DK. 2002. *Great Psychologists and Their Times: Scientific Insights into Psychology's History.* Washington, DC: Am. Psychol. Assoc.

Skinner BF. 1939. The alliteration in Shakespeare's sonnets: a study in literary behavior. *Psychol. Rec.* 3:186–92

Skinner BF. 1942. A quantitative estimate of certain types of sound-patterning in poetry. *Am. J. Psychol.* 30:64–79

Smith CP, ed. 1992. *Motivation and Personality: Handbook of Thematic Content Analysis.* Cambridge: Cambridge Univ. Press. 708 pp.

Snyder CR, Lopez SJ, eds. 2002. *The Handbook of Positive Psychology.* New York: Oxford Univ. Press

Spangler WD, House RJ. 1991. Presidential effectiveness and the leadership motive profile. *J. Pers. Soc. Psychol.* 60:439–55

Stewart LH. 1991. The world cycle of leadership. *J. Anal. Psychol.* 36:449–59

Suedfeld P. 1985. APA presidential addresses:

the relation of integrative complexity to historical, professional, and personal factors. *J. Pers. Soc. Psychol.* 47:848–52

Suedfeld P, Bluck S. 1988. Changes in integrative complexity prior to surprise attacks. *J. Confl. Resolut.* 32:626–35

Suedfeld P, Bluck S. 1993. Changes in integrative complexity accompanying significant life events: historical evidence. *J. Pers. Soc. Psychol.* 64:124–30

Suedfeld P, Corteen RS, McCormick C. 1986. The role of integrative complexity in military leadership: Robert E. Lee and his opponents. *J. Appl. Soc. Psychol.* 16:498–507

Suedfeld P, Piedrahita LE. 1984. Intimations of mortality: integrative simplification as a predictor of death. *J. Pers. Soc. Psychol.* 47:848–52

Suedfeld P, Rank AD. 1976. Revolutionary leaders: long-term success as a function of changes in conceptual complexity. *J. Pers. Soc. Psychol.* 34:169–78

Suedfeld P, Tetlock P. 1977. Integrative complexity of communications in international crises. *J. Conf. Resolut.* 21:169–84

Suedfeld P, Tetlock PE, Ramirez C. 1977. War, peace, and integrative complexity. *J. Confl. Resolut.* 21:427–42

Suedfeld P, Tetlock PE, Streufert S. 1992. Conceptual/integrative complexity. See Smith 1992, pp. 393–400

Suedfeld P, Wallace MD, Thachuk KL. 1993. Changes in integrative complexity among Middle East leaders during the Persian Gulf crisis. *J. Soc. Issues* 49:183–99

Swede SW, Tetlock PE. 1986. Henry Kissinger's implicit theory of personality: a quantitative case study. *J. Pers.* 54:617–46

Terman LM. 1917. The intelligence quotient of Francis Galton in childhood. *Am. J. Psychol.* 28:209–15

Tetlock PE. 1979. Identifying victims of groupthink from public statements of decision makers. *J. Pers. Soc. Psychol.* 37:1314–24

Tetlock PE. 1981a. Personality and isolationism: content analysis of senatorial speeches. *J. Pers. Soc. Psychol.* 41:737–43

Tetlock PE. 1981b. Pre- to postelection shifts

in presidential rhetoric: impression management or cognitive adjustment. *J. Pers. Soc. Psychol.* 41:207–12

Tetlock PE. 1983. Cognitive style and political ideology. *J. Pers. Soc. Psychol.* 45:118–26

Tetlock PE. 1984. Cognitive style and political belief systems in the British House of Commons. *J. Pers. Soc. Psychol.* 46:365–75

Tetlock PE. 1985. Integrative complexity of American and Soviet foreign policy rhetoric: a time-series analysis. *J. Pers. Soc. Psychol.* 49:1565–85

Tetlock PE, Armor D, Peterson RS. 1994. The slavery debate in antebellum America: cognitive style, value conflict, and the limits of compromise. *J. Pers. Soc. Psychol.* 66:115–26

Tetlock PE, Bernzweig J, Gallant JL. 1985. Supreme Court decision making: cognitive style as a predictor of ideological consistency of voting. *J. Pers. Soc. Psychol.* 48:1227–39

Tetlock PE, Boettger R. 1989. Cognitive and rhetorical styles of traditionalist and reformist Soviet politicians: a content analysis study. *Polit. Psychol.* 10:209–32

Tetlock PE, Hannum KA, Micheletti PM. 1984. Stability and change in the complexity of senatorial debate: testing the cognitive versus rhetorical style hypothesis. *J. Pers. Soc. Psychol.* 46:979–90

Thorndike EL. 1936. The relation between intellect and morality in rulers. *Am. J. Sociol.* 42:321–34

Thorndike EL. 1950. Traits of personality and their intercorrelations as shown in biography. *J. Educ. Psychol.* 41:193–216

Triplett N. 1898. The dynamogenic factors in pacemaking and competition. *Am. J. Psychol.* 9:507–33

Tweney RD. 1989. A framework for the cognitive psychology of science. In *The Psychology of Science: Contributions to Metascience*, ed. B Gholson, WR Shadish Jr, RA Neimeyer, AC Houts, pp. 342–66. Cambridge: Cambridge Univ. Press

Walberg HJ, Rasher SP, Hase K. 1978. IQ correlates with high eminence. *Gifted Child Q.* 22:196–200

Wallace DB, Gruber HE, eds. 1989. *Creative People at Work: Twelve Cognitive Case Studies.* New York: Oxford Univ. Press. 302 pp.

Webb EJ, Campbell DT, Schwartz RD, Sechrest L, Grove JB. 1981. *Nonreactive Measures in the Social Sciences.* Boston: Houghton Mifflin. 220 pp. 2nd ed.

Weisberg RW. 1994. Genius and madness? A quasi-experimental test of the hypothesis that manic-depression increases creativity. *Psychol. Sci.* 5:361–67

Winter DG. 1987a. Enhancement of an enemy's power motivation as a dynamic of conflict escalation. *J. Pers. Soc. Psychol.* 52:41–46

Winter DG. 1987b. Leader appeal, leader performance, and the motive profiles of leaders and followers: a study of American presidents and elections. *J. Pers. Soc. Psychol.* 52:196–202

Winter DG. 1993. Power, affiliation, and war: three tests of a motivational model. *J. Pers. Soc. Psychol.* 65:532–45

Winter DG, Carlson DG. 1988. Using motive scores in the psychobiographical study of an individual: the case of Richard Nixon. *J. Pers.* 56:75–103

Woods FA. 1906. *Mental and Moral Heredity in Royalty.* New York: Holt. 312 pp.

Woods FA. 1909. A new name for a new science. *Science* 30:703–4

Woods FA. 1911. Historiometry as an exact science. *Science* 33:568–74

Zickar MJ, Slaughter JE. 1999. Examining creative performance over time using hierarchical linear modeling: an illustration using film directors. *Hum. Perform.* 12:211–30

Zullow HM, Oettingen G, Peterson C, Seligman MEP. 1988. Pessimistic explanatory style in the historical record: CAVing LBJ, presidential candidates, and East versus West Berlin. *Am. Psychol.* 43:673–82

Zullow HM, Seligman MEP. 1990. Pessimistic rumination predicts defeat of presidential candidates, 1900 to 1984. *Psychol. Inq.* 1:52–61

Zusne L. 1984. *Biographical Dictionary of Psychology.* Westport, CT: Greenwood. 563 pp.

Zweigenhaft RL. 1975. Birth order, approval-seeking, and membership in Congress. *J. Individ. Psychol.* 31:205–10

AUTHOR INDEX

Subject Index

A

Aberrant learning
  addiction and, 31–36
Abnormal psychology
  historical data and, 617,
  622
Abstraction
  psychological aspects of
  natural language use, 551
Accuracy
  eyewitness testimony and,
  284–85
Achievement gap
  early education and
  low-socioeconomic status
  children, 522–36
Action
  cultural pathways through
  universal development
  and, 474–77
Adaptation
  interaction, independence,
  and relationships,
  367–69
Addiction
  aberrant learning, 31–36
  context, 39–41
  decision-making, 44–46
  dedication, 47
  drug reward pursuit, 41
  explicit learning, 32–33
  implicit learning, 33–36
  incentive sensitization,
  36–44
  introduction, 26–27
  learning, 39–41
  loss of inhibitory control,
  44–46
  miscellaneous addictions,
  46
  neurobiology, 38–41

opponent process theory,
  27–31
  pleasure, 27–31
  psychomotor sensitization,
  37–38
  S-R habit learning, 33–35
  S-S habit learning, 34–36
  summary, 46–47
  withdrawal, 27–31
Adjusting-delay procedures
  operant conditioning and,
  138
Adolescents
  biology, context, and
  developmental inquiry,
  12–14
  child and adolescent
  psychotherapy research,
  253–72
  cultural pathways through
  universal development
  and, 461–82
Affect
  facial and vocal
  expressions of emotion,
  329–43
  psychology of religion and,
  377, 384
  subjective well-being and,
  403–20
Affective communication
  signalers and receivers in
  animal communication,
  153–56
Affordance
  interaction, independence,
  and relationships, 351–70
Age
  psychological aspects of
  natural language use,
  556–58

Age segregation
  firsthand learning through
  intent participation,
  175–97
Aggregating over time
  diary methods and, 581,
  586, 602–5
Aggressive behavior
  child and adolescent
  psychotherapy research,
  260–62
Agrammaticism
  language processing and,
  56–58, 74, 79
Alarm calls
  signalers and receivers in
  animal communication,
  148–53, 155–57, 161, 163
Alcoholism
  psychopathology in the
  postgenomic era and,
  220–21
Alzheimer's disease
  language processing and,
  69
  psychopathology in the
  postgenomic era and,
  215–16, 222
Ambiguity of measure
  biology, context, and
  developmental inquiry,
  10–11
Ambulatory heart rate
  diary methods and, 579
American Sign Language
  (ASL)
  neuroimaging studies of
  language production and
  comprehension, 100, 107
Amnesia
  posttraumatic stress

677

animal communication,
145–68
Language processing
common lexical
phonological
representations, 65–66
conclusions, 80–81
dissociations among
syntactic abilities, 69–70
grammatical
representations of words,
67–69
independence of semantic
and syntactic
representations, 70
independent lexical
phonological
representations, 65–66
introduction, 57–58
lesion studies, 72, 79
morphological processing,
68–69
neuroanatomy, 72–74,
79–80
neuroimaging studies,
61–63, 72–74, 79–80
neuropsychological
studies, 59–61, 63–66
patterns of sentence
production deficits in
aphasia, 74–80
semantic representations of
words, 66–68
sentence comprehension,
69–74
sentence processing, 69–74
sentence production, 74–80
sentence-production
disorders, 75–80
spoken word production,
63–65
spoken word recognition,
59–63
word-class effects, 67–68
word processing, 58–69
working memory, 71,
78–79

Large-scale school reform
early education and
low-socioeconomic status
children, 524–25
Latency
operant conditioning and,
117
Latent semantic analysis
psychological aspects of
natural language use, 569,
571
Lateral extrusiate regions
neuroimaging studies of
language production and
comprehension, 108
Lax-criterion department
eyewitness testimony and,
290
Lay observers
eyewitness testimony and,
284–85
Learning
addiction and, 25–47
early education and
low-socioeconomic status
children, 517–36
firsthand learning through
intent participation,
175–97
Lesion studies
language processing and,
72
Lexical phonological
representations
language processing and,
65–66
Life satisfaction
subjective well-being and,
403–20
Linear waiting
operant conditioning and,
125–26
Lineup
eyewitness testimony and,
277–91
Linguistic inquiry and word
count (LIWC)

psychological aspects of
natural language use, 547,
553–68
Listeners
signalers and receivers in
animal communication,
145–68
Listening-in
firsthand learning through
intent participation,
175–97
Longitudinal designs
diary methods and,
579–611
Love
psychology of religion and,
385–86
Low-level linguistic
processing
neuroimaging studies of
language production and
comprehension, 93–96
Loxodonta africana
signalers and receivers in
animal communication,
165
Lutheranism
psychology of religion and,
391

M
Macaca spp.
signalers and receivers in
animal communication,
159, 163
Machiavellianism
psychological aspects of
natural language use, 559
Magnetic resonance imaging
(MRI)
neuroimaging studies of
language production and
comprehension, 92, 100,
109
posttraumatic stress
disorder and, 240
Magnetoencephalography

CUMULATIVE INDEXES

CONTRIBUTING AUTHORS, VOLUMES 44–54

CHAPTER TITLES, VOLUMES 44–54

Community Psychology

Education and Counseling

Educational Psychology

Emotion

Personnel Development and Training

Personnel Psychology

HUMAN FACTORS

Psycholinguistics

Psychology and Culture

Sensation and Perception

Sensory Processes

Sleep

See BIOLOGICAL PSYCHOLOGY

Social Psychology

Social Psychology: Attitude Structure

Social Psychology: Collective Social

Special Topics

Special Topics in Psychopathology: Language and Communication

Timely Topics

Vision

See SENSORY PROCESSES